Memoirs *of a* Millennium

by

Ted Pocock

Grosvenor House
Publishing Limited

The right of Ted Pocock to be identified as the author of this
work has been asserted by him in accordance with Section 78
of the Copyright, Designs and Patents Act 1988

The book cover picture is copyright to Ted Pocock

This book is published by
Grosvenor House Publishing Ltd
28-30 High Street, Guildford, Surrey, GU1 3EL.
www.grosvenorhousepublishing.co.uk

A CIP record for this book
is available from the British Library

ISBN 978-1-78148-455-5

For my dearest Meg,
who doubled the enjoyment of meandering,

and for our children Tig and Emily,
whose company and curiosity have enlivened it since the last
quarter of the twentieth century,

and in the new century, their partners also,
Minda Lowry and Paul Christensen,
and now the new joys of our days, their children
Theo and Finley Lowry Pocock,
and Sophie and Toby Pocock Christensen;

and my gratitude to them all,
for being loving, interesting, interested, and tolerant,

and to those teachers, colleagues and friends
who encouraged searching, from the outset.

Know then thyself, presume not God to scan;
The proper study of Mankind is Man...
A Being darkly wise, and rudely great:
With too much knowledge for the Sceptic side,
With too much weakness for the Stoic's pride,
He hangs between: in doubt to act, or rest;
In doubt to deem himself a God, or Beast;
In doubt his Mind or Body to prefer;
Born but to die, and reas'ning but to err;
Alike in ignorance, his reason such,
Whether he thinks too little, or too much:
Chaos of Thought and Passion, all confus'd;
Still by himself abus'd, or disabus'd;
Created half to rise, and half to fall;
Great lord of all things, yet a prey to all;
Sole judge of Truth, in endless Error hurl'd:
The glory, jest, and riddle of the world!

Alexander Pope: *An Essay on Man* (1733)

TABLE OF CONTENTS

FOREWORD

Ted Pocock and I met in 1956 in search of the unknowable – the logic behind the Soviet economic system. The Oxford lecture hall was empty of both students and lecturer so Ted and I went off to a pub and shared complaints about supercilious Brits. Thus began a friendship so close that half a century later he shared with me an early draft of his Memoirs of a Millennium. I carried it with me on my lap top for a further decade, during which time I tirelessly pressed him to publish. The story was that he was preoccupied with writing simpler stories for his grandchildren. I always suspected, however, that he could not come to terms with the final stage of creation – release into the hands of those who thought they could improve it.

Now my Goddaughter Emily has taken that step – polishing and preparing a work of unparalleled scholarship and personal insight for a wider audience. Thank you, Emily. Ted would agree.

In his own introduction Ted described his career and his memoir as meandering. As one who followed him through countless museums and monasteries from Bruges to Trebizond, I can testify that he did not meander. He dug in, and you must too as you follow him from the dawn of the second millennium to its end. The stories he tells are monumental. But he adds a personal perspective which brings them alive.

As a one time student of Russian and Byzantine history, I found Ted's description of the beginnings of Kievan Rus in the 10th century impeccably sourced and brilliantly described. But he also tells the story from the standpoint of one who was in Moscow during Gorbachev's effort to alter the course of Russia. By adopting Christianity from Byzantium, Vladimir formed the ideological underpinnings of what eventually claimed to be the third Rome. Gorbachev found these underpinnings all too hard to uproot. Today, Putin cites the ideology of Vladimir's time as the basis for Russian exceptionalism and moral certainty.

A hallmark of Ted's time in Moscow was his support for dissidents – those who rebelled against official doctrine. His chapter on Vladimir underlines Orthodoxy's emphasis on ritual and dogma over theology and inquiry, a problem which Gorbachev faced in his efforts to introduce perestroika.

Other issues from the Viking past persisted as well. As Vladimir shopped around for a state religion, Islam was an instant non-starter because of the prohibition on intoxicating drink. Ted describes the tale of Vladimir's celebrants downing an immense cup of wine in a single gulp. To Ted, this seemed "a typical Russian party". Gorbachev found this cultural heritage resistant to change as well.

What makes Ted's account of the dawn of Rus particularly appealing is the picture he draws of the atmosphere and architecture as he saw it in person. The display of the remains of the early Russian saints in the Monastery of the Caves in Kiev may seem too like Lenin's mausoleum in Moscow. But his description of the skyline of Vladimir on a cold still winter's day brings to mind the city's Kievan roots.

Ted's chapter on "Tamburlaine of Samarkand" follows logically if not chronologically from the history of early Russia. Set in the contrasting "slow warmth of Central Asia" this account draws heavily on the work of Shakespeare's contemporary Christopher Marlowe as well as contemporary accounts by Arab and Western witnesses. While grasping for conquests beyond those of Genghis Khan, Darius of Persia and Alexander of Macedonia, Tamburlaine was also seeking to dominate the Silk Road and the commerce which linked China and Europe. In the process he destroyed the Knights Hospitaler in the Levant, the Ottoman Empire of Bayezeth, the Golden Hordes of Genghis Khan's descendants, the Delhi Sultanate of India. Saved as they believed by the icon of the Virgin of the Virgin of Vladimir the Russians cowered in their Kremlins while Tamburlaine's short attention span drew him elsewhere. Finally death overtook him on the verge of the conquest of Ming dynasty in China.

Tamburlaine was certainly a destroyer. Ted recalls Vereshchagin's Apotheosis of War, a painting in Moscow's Russian Museum showing a pyramid of skulls in the midst of a sunbaked plain. He razed Delhi, but then he took its artisans hostage and marched them to his capital Samarkand which he made into an ornament of the world. Ted describes how to look out over the Registan complex in Samarkand and see it as Tamburlaine did. His heirs then reversed the flow by bringing the Moghul architecture and Persian gardens which are the glory of north India still.

Tamburlaine lives through literature and music as well as history and architecture, as Ted reminds us. In addition to dozens of plays and epic poems, there was a flowering of 18th century operas culminating with Hayden's Tamerlano in 1719.

Of course there are many more adventures during Ted's personal millennium. Fans of British history will be intrigued by the chapter on Devorguilla of Galloway, a key player in the Great Cause of Scottish independence which is an issue again today. She was also the wife of John de Balliol, nominal and perhaps illiterate founder of Balliol College. Then there is John Ledyard of Connecticut, a graduate of my alma mater Dartmouth College in New Hampshire, who made a name for himself as an explorer, mercenary and key figure behind Jefferson's Louisiana purchase. To conclude the millennium Ted resurrects Yuan Shikai of Beijing, an ineffectual general caught up in the birth struggles of modern China, a fitting bookend to Vladimir's role in the formation of Russia.

I will never regret that my pursuit of the unknowable led me to that Oxford lecture hall in 1956. Now the reader can appreciate some of what I gained through a half century of friendship.

Robert Barry

ENCOUNTERS AND EXCURSIONS

One of history's uses is to remind us
how unlikely things can be.

Jonathan Spence

When I retired from the Australian diplomatic service I embarked on writing a history of our era's second Millennium, which was just concluding. I decided to look at just a few aspects of the Millennium through the lives and times of ten disparate people – roughly a century apart – in ten different countries – whom I had encountered during its last half-century. It is, to some degree, "memoir" as well as history, but only in the sense that the people and places are those that I encountered and became interested in over the course of my life.

I became interested in them while studying history, politics and international affairs at Adelaide, Oxford and Princeton universities, or while on the diplomatic postings I then had the good fortune to experience: at Cairo, in a Middle East stirred by Nasser's Arab nationalism; at a Cold War-dominated United Nations, during the dismantling of the old European colonial empires; at Phnom Penh and Saigon, during the controversial second Vietnam War; at Seoul, with the two Koreas, Japan and China still mired in mutual suspicion following almost a century of wars; in Moscow, at the end of the Cold War, just before Russia ended the Soviet Union itself; and at Paris and Brussels, as Western Europe was being transformed into the European Union. The posting in Moscow included of course the Central Asian "Republics" of the then Union of Soviet Socialist Republics, and Mongolia; a second posting in Paris involved dual accreditation to Morocco; and between Paris and Brussels there was a brief assignment in Islamabad, shortly before the Taliban takeover in Afghanistan. These experiences, meandering geographically and by pre-occupation, are reflected – but not by any means paralleled – in the book.

Most of the ten people I decided to write about were involved, in one way or another, with some of the powerful and often pernicious obsessions of the Millennium: religious, ideological and racial fanaticism, imperialism, nationalism and great power relations, political and diplomatic manoeuvering, the uses and abuses of most varieties of power – all still around in some form during that last half-century. But the book is not a history of that Millennium. It is a memoir in the narrower sense of where and how I became interested in these ten people through my encounters with surviving aspects of their political, intellectual or cultural legacies. In addition to these professional origins, my personal interest was also captivated by the excursions on which they took me into their own times, and – not least – to their visible remains: the superb buildings, haunting ruins, great art for which they were responsible, or the fascinating towns or beguiling landscapes with which they were closely associated – places and treasures some of which are famous, some off the beaten track.

In all this there is the occasional person, event or place that sparked the exploration of irresistible byways. But if chapters meander away from their main subject there is usually a reason – or at least a reasonable excuse. I take refuge with Laurence Sterne, the 18th century Irish novelist, who wonderfully justified such byways in *The Life and Opinions of Tristram Shandy*,

> "Digressions, incontestably, are the sunshine; – they are the life, the soul of reading; – take them out of this book for instance, – you might as well take the book along with them".

In writing the stories of the ten people I was particularly interested in their reactions to others who were, in whatever ways, different, and in finding accounts of them and places and events by outsiders: travellers, scholars, soldiers, missionaries, merchants – and, yes, ambassadors. As a result, the outcome is something of a kaleidoscope of cross-cultural perceptions and responses: fascination, prejudice, misapprehension or sheer bafflement, principally between, but at times also within, the West, the Middle East and Central Asia, and East Asia. Someone called it "the conversation of cultures" – and might have added, "and deafness".

It seems to me that no nation or religion or race has had a monopoly, or even a consistently good track record, when it has come to understanding, tolerance or just plain good behaviour. However, many of my characters, sometimes in very small ways, sometimes in most unexpected ones, showed an attractive gift for intellectual curiosity, which was part of their appeal, whatever else they were up to. They also raise in varying degrees the question whether individuals really make a difference. I think the common-sense answer is that they can and do, though not always in the way they intend or may claim to be doing. Amongst these ten there are only three who could be claimed to have made such a difference: Vladimir, Tamburlaine, Hideyoshi. Of the lot, not all were successful, certainly not admirable. There are only two women: it was a millennium in which men had the far greater chance of being successful – and not admirable. Here is a brief outline of who the ten people are, and of what they were involved in. How I encountered them is in the individual chapters that follow.

Vladimir of Kiev (956-1015): Russia

Viking-origin Vladimir, whose capture of Kiev began Russia's history, was said by the chroniclers to have decided that the traditional tribal idols were inadequate to his new princedom, and that he considered Judaism, Islam and Catholicism before the riches of Byzantium led him to decide on Orthodox Christianity. The forcible conversion of his people initiated Russians into toeing the party line, and the close relationship between Church and State has remained a pernicious influence in Russian, even at times Soviet, politics and society. It was also a major factor in much of the glory of Russia's subsequent art and architecture.

Godfrey of Bouillon (1060 – 1100): Palestine

From what is now southern Belgium, Godfrey became a leader of Christian Europe's First Crusade to everybody's Holy Land, and the capture of Jerusalem from its new Turkish overlords. It was not the first clash between the West and Islam – let alone the West and Asia – but Godefroy's weakness contributed disastrously to its becoming a bitter marker in relations right up to the present, even though subsequent Crusades were themselves ultimately failures.

Jayavarman VII of Angkor (ca.1125/35 – ca.1220): Cambodia

No "gentle Buddhist", as it became fashionable to regard him, and Cambodians generally, until the brutal reign of his admirer Pol Pot, but a megalomaniac nationalist who prosecuted a ruthless first Indochina War. He built, next to Angkor Wat, the magnificent and mysterious Bayon, at exactly the same time as Chartres Cathedral was also being built according to theological principles, curiously, with Cambodian parallels. A fascinating picture of the country by a Chinese trader shows some enduring features of Khmer society.

Devorguilla of Galloway (1209-1290): Scotland

A devout noblewoman who helped establish a College in Oxford's fledgling University, though it was then an institution solely for men in clerical orders. She had married into the Balliol family whose members were embroiled in trying to secure Scotland's independence against England's early attempts to begin the Empire at home. But her son King Edward Balliol was undermined by the treachery of a fellow Scot, and it was the College, not her family, which played a role during later British history.

Tamburlaine of Samarkand (1336-1404): Central Asia

Tamburlaine swept out of Transoxiana, in the middle of Eurasia, to engulf Persia, Russia, Syria, India and Turkey in what Shakespeare's contemporary, Christopher Marlowe, would have us believe was an indiscriminate sea of Sunni, Shiite, Orthodox Christian and Hindu blood. But while his conquests were often barbarous, and extended beyond those of Darius of Persia, Alexander the Great and his own ancestor Genghis Khan, Tamburlaine's primary aim was probably control over the fabled Silk Road between Europe and China, to finance the glorious architectural and other extravagances of his capital at Samarkand, and to underwrite his last major ambition, the conquest of China itself.

Marcantonio Raimondi of Bologna (1480-1534): Italy

A little-known Italian print-maker who worked for the great Raphael, and the famous German artist, Albrecht Dürer, share –

and sell – the Renaissance. Raimondi is the first of our ten characters of whom we have an authentic portrait – painted, life-size, by Raphael himself, in one of the most important rooms in the Vatican. This is a midway rest from politics, religions and armies: well, until European politics, religion and an army catch up with poor Raimondi as well.

Toyotomi Hideyoshi of Osaka (1536-1599): Japan

Hideyoshi was the first to unify Japan under a central government – himself. But his ambitions were wider, and his attempts to establish the first greater East Asia co-prosperity sphere, by way of invading his neighbours, are still a lively memory in Korea, also a major victim in modern times of Japan's second such venture. Extraordinarily, our knowledge of Hideyoshi owes a great deal to Portuguese Jesuit missionaries who came to know him intimately, just before his rival and successor closed Japan to all outside contacts for what turned out to be two and a half centuries.

Sophie Charlotte of Prussia (1668-1705): Germany

Sister of King George I of England, married to the first King of Prussia – the only Prussian leader from his father to Hermann Goering to be more interested in architecture than armies – Sophie was a genuine daughter of the Enlightenment, mentored by her friend the great polymath Leibniz at a time when the latter was trying to interest the Courts of Europe in intellectual and commercial exchanges with China: just as direct contacts were being made, also through the Jesuits. But her son re-launched the long progression of German militarism into our time.

John Ledyard of Connecticut (1751-1789): The USA

Having sailed to Alaska with Captain Cook on his last, fatal, voyage, Ledyard tried to persuade Thomas Jefferson of the prospects for a great trade in furs from the Pacific Northwest to China, and Jefferson sent him to explore them – via Siberia. Catherine the Great made sure he didn't succeed, but Ledyard's advocacy may have helped influence President Jefferson's Louisiana Purchase and the foundations of the United States' Pacific destiny. His record of his encounters, in Alaska, the Pacific, and Russia, show a man of acute curiosity in and sympathy for people of other cultures.

Yuan Shikai of Beijing (1859-1916) : China

Throughout the Nineteenth Century, China looked – especially from Beijing – like becoming the East Asian version of Africa, carved up between the European colonial powers and Japan, with the United States, despite protestations to the contrary, increasingly involved through an enormously widespread missionary presence. Yuan Shikai, an ineffectual general, found himself trying to protect China's interests against Japanese and Russian interference in Korea, getting caught up in the Boxer Rebellion and its aftermath of further foreign intervention, undermining the tottering Ching Dynasty, then hi-jacking the new republican constitution, and eventually failing in a bizarre attempt to establish himself as Emperor. Much of his floundering efforts was recorded by his Australian ex-journalist political adviser.

Starting Point

There is a view amongst historians that people should be judged only by the standards of their times, and that people who write now should not "project themselves into the past...with their own feelings, ideas, intellectual and moral prejudices".* I can not agree, which is why I set out my own prejudices here.

Of course it is necessary to understand the way in which people's actions in the past were informed by different motivations and circumstances from our own, but there is no good reason for us not to say so when we find those actions unacceptable. At the beginning of the disastrous 20th century the English writer G.K. Chesterton censoriously observed that "when people cease to believe in something they do not believe in nothing – they believe in anything". So be it. This is no reason for imposing an ideological or theological or any other strait-jacket. It is the unique viewpoint – the One True Message that can explain, and therefore excuse, everything – that has been and is still our most dangerous and grievous belief. This is true whether it is religious, based on belief in prescriptions from a Higher Being; or ideological, based on

---

* The French historian and *Résistant* Marc Bloch

belief in privileged access to some Ultimate Truth; or racial, based on belief in a distorted evolutionary hierarchy of species. The presumption of moral superiority not merely allows but in due course often compels at least the conversion, and, if that is unsuccessful or insufficient, the marginalisation, and then, if required, the elimination, of those not favoured with its possession through the workings of an ineffable providence, a more expert knowledge, or a superior genetic stock. We can see something of all these lethal pretensions, in many parts of the world, through the centuries that have created us as we are. And regrettably they are still around, which I shall revert to in the Epilogue.

Church of Intercession upon Nerl (1165),
Bogolyubovo, Russia. Wikimedia/Alexei Troshin

RUSSIA

VLADIMIR OF KIEV: UNORTHODOX PURSUITS

"Hard as it is for the head
to be without shoulders
bad is it for the body
to be without head."

The Song of
Igor's Campaign, ca 1186 CE[1]

When people think of Vikings, they tend to think of bearded marauders in winged helmets who descended from the North Sea on the coasts of northern France and the British Isles, and of their daring sea-faring cousins who reached the coasts of North America five hundred years before Christopher Columbus. But those who were to have the greatest impact on world history were other cousins who came to be known as Rus, and later as Russians: bands of river-farers who descended Russia's forest-dark waterways to carve out a foothold in a new country, a country which was to become a principality, a kingdom, an empire, a superpower – and now, another country...but still not like others.

We were posted in the Soviet Union between 1984 and 1987 – first the year of Chernenko, which turned out to be the last of the *ancien* Russian Communist *régime*, then what turned out to be most of the first half of Gorbachev's short and extraordinary reign. After the gloom of the mercifully short-lived Chernenko reaction, the Gorbachev changes were exciting, if still somewhat un-nerving: however optimistic anyone might

---

1   Tr. Vladimir Nabokov (New York 1960)

have been about them, however percipient in hindsight, no-one then *knew* – or, given Gorbachev's entirely orthodox *nomenklatura* background, had any right to expect – that the changes would be pursued, let alone succeed, in moving the Soviet Communist Party away from its domination of the Soviet and East European people, or its hostility to the West.

During this period, one of the pillars of the orthodox Soviet propaganda machine was the Russian Orthodox Church. There was something grotesque, after the persecutions of the Lenin and earlier Stalin years, in the extent to which the Church hierarchy had not only accepted (understandably) Stalin's 1943 olive branch to get it on-side in the darkest days of the struggle against Nazi Germany, but had gone back to the comfortable role it had traditionally played under the Tsars as the hand-maiden of the state and the prop of Slavophilism – "the messianism of backwardness", as Trotsky called it. During the Cold War it lent itself enthusiastically to the Kremlin's campaigns for "peace" and disarmament...of the West. Even in our time, when we accompanied visitors to the Patriarchal monastery of Zagorsk (now Sergiev Posad), self-righteous prelates were still unctuously peddling *"mir y druzhba"* ["peace and friendship"] as they sat down to great feasts that would have fed dozens of the little old women in black skirts and scarves who filled their parish churches when not queuing endlessly for a small ration of pork fat – if there was any. Since the fall of the Soviet Union the Church has continued to align itself with the chauvinist reactionaries, of far left and far right.

Russian Orthodoxy began, just before the end of the first millennium, under Vladimir of Kiev, Saint Vladimir the Great, an extraordinary leap for a barbarian only three (or perhaps four) generations from his marauding Viking forebears, and for his country, which was mostly where the Ukraine now is. Vladimir converted following the development by the Rus of a relationship, partly through marauding but especially through trading, with Orthodox Byzantium, the successor to the Roman Empire and at that time one of the world's greatest cities, a great emporium at the junction of the Silk Trade routes between Europe and Asia.

From earlier times there had also been trade with the Abbasid Caliphate in Baghdad, and contacts with Christian Germany and the little-known temporarily-Jewish kingdom of Khazars on the Volga River; and this whole surprising range of connections was claimed by the ancient Russian chronicler to have played a role in Vladimir's decision to choose a new religion for himself and the Rus. Very soon, the Russian

Orthodox Church developed its own independent identity – and a magnificent architecture, some of which can still be seen in Kiev, Novgorod and Vladimir; and the internal and external framework it created for the Russian state and society is also still discernible. While our main knowledge of Vladimir and his new state comes from the Russian Chronicle, there are also surviving glimpses of Kievan Rus from Byzantines and Arabs – and, soon, marriage alliances all over Europe.

The principal people in this chapter are as follows:

- Olga (c.890-969) – mother of Svyatoslav, for whom she acted as regent from 945-c.963, grandmother of Vladimir. Christian convert.

- Svyatoslav (c.942-972) – leader of the Rus from 945-972. Vladimir's father.

- Yarolpolk (c.958-960) – eldest son of Svyatoslav

- Oleg (unknown-977) – second son of Svyatoslav

- **Vladimir** (c.958-1015) – youngest son of Svyatoslav. Grand Prince of Kiev and ruler of Kievan Rus from 980-1015.

- John I Tzimisces (925-976) – Emperor of Byzantium from 969-976. Defeated Svyatoslav 972.

- Leo the Deacon (c.950-unknown) – Byzantine historian and chronicler.

But within a century and a half of Vladimir's momentous reign his country would be virtually obliterated, and its remains enslaved, by the greatest terror ever to sweep across the Silk Road from the East: the Mongols of Genghis Khan. Russian power would shift and grow in the north, around Moscow, in a symbiotic relationship with the invaders. And that also left its mark on Russian history.

These traditions, after the brief muddled attempts at democratic change in the Yeltsin years, are still around. State and church again give each other mutual support: a leader once again autocratically decides what is best for the people, the church once again lulls them into believing that acquiescence is their duty.

The same Norse stock exploded out of Scandinavia over the last two centuries of the first millennium CE across half a hemisphere, driven by a combination of domestic pressures and the lust – and talent – for adventure and dominion. Eastwards, those, mostly from Sweden, who became known to the native Slavs as Varangians, came to rule over and then merge with the Slavs of Novgorod in northern Russian, then move down the lakes and rivers to Kiev (now Kyyiv, the capital of Ukraine), far to the south. Southwards, down the North Sea, those known as Northmen, mostly from Denmark, became the Normans of Normandy in France, and early in the new millennium overran Calabria and Sicily as well. Westwards, those known as Vikings, mostly from Norway but also Denmark, pushed further and further across the north Atlantic, into England, Ireland, Iceland, Greenland, and, finally but only briefly, America.

All this diaspora became Christian – mostly before their homelands did. In places – and as was repeatedly to occur in Russia down the centuries – this radical change was decreed and then enforced by the ruler; in others, the process was a more gradual recognition that that way lay promise...and preferment. As it happened, around the same time as Vladimir converted and was forcibly converting the Slavicised Rus in the east, this other conversion was going on far to the west. In 999 the Viking Greenlander Leif Ericsson, "Leif the Lucky", visited Norway, where he too was converted to Christianity. He was then bidden by King Olaf I Tryggvason – who, as an exile with his mother, had grown up at Vladimir's pre–Christian court in Novgorod – to convert the Greenland colony, founded thirteen years before by Icelandic Vikings under the leadership of Leif's own father. The next year, in the year 1000, Leif set out from Greenland to explore a new land to the west which had earlier been spotted from the sea by the Icelander Bjarni Herjolfsson; and in that same year Leif the Lucky became the first known European to set foot in the American continent.[2]

Over the course of this past millennium Kievan Rus became Russia, which eventually stretched imperially eastwards until it reached the Pacific Ocean in 1639; later, it was the largest part of the USSR, one of the two superpowers of the second half of our recent

---

2 This link - at one remove, through Olaf Tryggvason - between America and the beginnings of Russia, is paralleled in the life of the protagonist of the 1800 chapter, John Ledyard of Connecticut, who seems to have been the first citizen of the United States to meet a Russian.

century. Vladimir's conversion produced a Church which became the support and the instrument of Russian autocracy and nationalism throughout the 736 years of his Varangian Dynasty, the 304 years of its Romanov successors, and the last 48 years of the Communist regime's 74–year existence. Leif's expedition to America, on the other hand, only produced a three–year Viking settlement – probably in Newfoundland – which was then wiped out by a group of native hunter–gatherers, leaving the continent to itself until the next waves of Europeans, following Columbus five centuries later, wiped out a large part of all the native groups in the Americas in the course of creating European societies there, of which one, the United States, came in our day to be the other superpower.

While this chapter is primarily about Vladimir's apparently crucial role in the sudden and unlikely conversion of Russia to Christianity, understanding that decision requires us to go back to beginnings. The histories of other societies – Mesopotamia, Egypt, China, India, Greece and Rome and the European and Middle Eastern areas they colonised, controlled or abutted – evolved gradually from the mists of time; Kievan Rus's – Russia's – history began pretty much from a standing start under Vladimir's alien dynasty. What we know now of that beginning was created retrospectively by an elite which had not existed at the time, but which had an oral tradition and undoubtedly some (though only church) documents on which to base it. Our focus is thus also on the beginnings of *recording* history.

There are two main strands. There is this virtual eruption of Rus as an entity, out of the dark forests and lakes of the borderlands between Europe and Asia, then its conversion, only a hundred and twenty years later, to become a state ruled jointly – though not equally – by dynasty and church. And there is Kievan Rus's relationship with Byzantium, the diminished but still splendid and powerful remains of the Roman Empire to its south, out of which that conversion grew. That relationship was always at the forefront of the new country's concerns, for dynastic, strategic, political and commercial reasons. And above all, it raised the issue of Russia's conception of its own status by comparison with the rest of the world, an obsession which has never left it to this day.

The sources of history

"These are the narratives of bygone years regarding the origin of the land of Rus, the first princes of Kiev, and from what source the land of Rus had its beginning.

Let us accordingly begin this narrative. After the Flood, the sons of Noah divided the earth among them. To the lot of Shem fell the Orient…To the lot of Ham fell the southern region…To the lot of Japheth fell the northern and western sections…[The] following nations…are a part of the race of Japheth: the Varangians…[The] Slavic race is [also] derived from the line of Japheth…"

This is the beginning of the written history of Russia. The pagan state of Kievan Rus was still illiterate during its first hundred or more years; with the arrival of Christianity churchmen began making some records, but whether of legend or history is uncertain, and how much was written down before the Mongols razed Kiev to the ground is not known. The main and almost the only survival, the oldest source now remaining of those semi–fabled times, is the *Povest' vremennykh let*, "the Tale of Bygone Years", known usually as the *Primary Russian Chronicle*.[3] There were two foundations under the *Chronicle*, both of equal importance: one was the requirement of Vladimir's dynasty to confirm its legitimacy as the head of the Russian state; the other was the necessity, in a Christian state, to present that legitimacy as founded on the dynasty's relationship to the Church. This symbiotic relationship between State and Church – between power and belief – was to prove a permanent feature of Russian society.

It is now generally agreed that the *Primary Chronicle* as now known was transcribed and collated during the second decade of the 12th century from one or more earlier Russian chronicles, several Byzantine sources and, for the previous half century, from living memory. The compilation was long believed to have been made by a monk called Nestor at Kiev's Monastery of the Caves, the *Pecherskaya Lavra*, and it was accordingly known as the *Chronicle of Nestor*. Scholarly opinion accepts that some of the earlier underlying chronicles were probably Nestor's work, but the extant text, known from a copy made two centuries later, in 1337, is now attributed to an unknown scribe–author working, also at the Monastery of the Caves, between 1113 and 1117. One can envisage his painstaking labour from a vivid note in the margin of a manuscript written in Western Europe about the same time:

---

3   The only English–language edition is by S.H.Cross and O.P.Sherbowitz–Wetzor (Cambridge MA 1930;1973), from which all quotations throughout the chapter are taken unless otherwise identified – including at the head of the above and other sections. It will be referred to as the *Primary Chronicle* or just the *Chronicle*, the author as Cross, who was the original translator–editor.

"Careful with your fingers! Don't touch writing! You don't know what it is to write. It's a crushing task; it bends your spine, blurs your eyesight, creases your stomach, and cracks your ribs".[4]

There is somewhat less agreement, despite a couple of centuries of argument, about where the transitions lie between legend, early (probably oral) history, and actual memory – all seen through a thick veil of piety.

Of course, at the time the *Chronicle* was composed the only people capable of writing were monks or priests. The result was history seen entirely in religious terms. The origins of Russia accordingly derived from holy scripture – to the cleric the Bible was *factual* history, as it was six hundred years later to the great Isaac Newton, who still accepted the Biblical origins of the world whose physical attributes he so scientifically measured, and as it still is today, despite all the intervening evidence to the contrary, to Christian fundamentalists. In later times there were those who accepted even the non–Biblical parts of the *Chronicle* as gospel – or at least the bits that suited this or that historicist or (usually) chauvinist scheme. The study of sources from Kievan Rus's neighbours and contacts – Byzantine, Arabic–Persian, Armenian, Khazar, German, Italian – have confirmed and contradicted passages, and adjusted some of the chronology, sometimes significantly as we shall see. It is interesting to see these comparative readings of the historical record; it is also fun to try to investigate what motives underlay the *Primary Chronicle*'s version – and the actions attributed to its protagonists, especially those of Vladimir himself.

Within around a century of the labours of our unknown Kievan monk, extraordinary national literature was being set down across the West, much of it, like the *Primary Chronicle*, designed to record – or romanticise – the origins of, or crucial episodes in, each society's history. But there are interesting differences. The Chronicle is itself marked by a number of Biblical episodes, starting with Russia's origin under the sons of Noah, and other passages, which may be historical or not, from the Christian Church's hagiographical tradition. But there are no wizards, dragons or other supernatural creatures; there are no poetic flights by historical characters such as those that burst forth in the Icelandic Sagas; the *Chronicle* does not include mythical tales of national origins, such as the violent paganism of Germany's *Nibelungenlied*, or the romanticised

---

4   Quoted by Jacques Barzun in *From Dawn to Decadence*.

chivalry of the Anglo–French Arthurian cycle; and it is not a poetic idealisation like the *Chanson de Roland* or the *Poema del Cid*, which gave France and Spain their national epics.

In the comparative spareness of the *Primary Chronicle* it is as if that early Russian chronicler was trying hard to set down what he believed were the simple facts of Russia's origins, from whatever source, without myth and magic. Even ecclesiastical tradition could be infiltrated by the actual world, as demonstrated in a wonderful episode just after the Slavs and others had emerged as separate peoples. At that time St Andrew, the first of the twelve Apostles, is described as having ascended the River Dnieper and then observed to his companions:

> '"See ye these hills? So shall the favour of God shine upon them that on this spot a great city shall arise, and God shall erect many churches therein'...After offering his prayer to God, he descended from the hill on which Kiev was subsequently built, and continued his journey up the Dnieper.
>
> He then reached the Slavs at the point where Novgorod is now situated...He went thence among the Varangians and came to Rome, where he recounted what he had learned and observed. 'Wondrous to relate,' said he, 'I saw the land of the Slavs, and while I was among them, I noticed their wooden bathhouses. They warm them to extreme heat, then undress, and after anointing themselves with an acid liquid, they take young branches and lash their bodies. They actually lash themselves so violently that they barely escape alive. Then they drench themselves with cold water, and thus are revived. They think nothing of doing this every day, and though tormented by none, they actually inflict such voluntary torture on themselves. Indeed, they make of the act not a mere washing but a veritable torment' ".

Designed to confer apostolic predestination on Kiev's greatness, St Andrew's wholly unauthenticated visit to Russia becomes instead an excuse to give a vivid, astonished description of the sauna – suggesting that the writer of this section of the *Chronicle* was a Byzantine Greek monk unfamiliar with everyday northern practices.

Andrew was later to be made patron saint of Orthodox Christian Russia, a not so subtle bid to rival Rome's claims to primacy based on its appropriation of his younger brother Peter, who was only the second Apostle. It is an honour St Andrew shared with Greece, where he is traditionally held to have evangelised; with Burgundy, because of the belief that the Burgundians had originated in Russian Scythia, in which the late medieval *Golden Legend* said he began his evangelising; and with Scotland, where there was a similar and even more geographically unlikely tale of origins.[5]

The arrival of the Varangians

"The Varangians from beyond the sea imposed tribute upon the Chuds, the Slavs, the Merians, the Ves, and the Krivichians...The tributaries of the Varangians drove them back beyond the sea and, refusing further tribute, set out to govern themselves. There was no law among them, but tribe rose against tribe. Discord thus ensued among them, and they began to war one against another...They accordingly went overseas to the Varangian Russes...[and said:] 'Our land is great and rich, but there is no order in it. Come to rule and reign over us'. They thus selected three brothers, with all their kinsfolk, who took with them all the Russes and migrated".[6]

Calculating from the birth of Adam, the chronicler dated the invitation to the Varangians and the arrival in Novgorod of Rurik (also spelled Riurik or Ryurik) and his two brothers, "with their kinsfolk", to between the years 6368 and 6370 – which, thanks to the inclusion of Byzantine rulers for the last 542 years, put the dates at 860 to 862 in our own era.[7] Here, with the arrival of these easternmost of the Vikings, the

---

5   The *Golden Legend* (tr. W.G.Ryan, Princeton NJ 1993) is a compilation of the lives of the Saints made about 1260 by an Italian Dominican priest, Jacobus de Voraigne. It rapidly became second only to the Bible in popularity, such that there still exist over a thousand manuscript copies made before the advent of printing two centuries later, when it was translated and published in hundreds of editions in every Western European language. On St Andrew and Scotland, see 1300 chapter: Devorguilla of Galloway.

6   The Chuds, etc, were other Eastern Slav tribes. The Rus (sometimes accented as Rus'), which gave Russes and Russia itself is of very obscure origin; less direct variations in various tongues were Rukh, Rhos, Rotsi, Rugi and Ruotsi, the latter being an early Finnish word now held to be the most likely sponsor of the term the Slavs applied to the Varangians.

7   The Romanovs, settling on 862 as the date of Rurik's arrival, celebrated its millennium in 1862; the intensely Russophile Balakirev marked it by composing an overture on Russian themes, called *1000 Years*, though he revised it twenty years later as simply *Rus*.

Primary Chronicle accounts for their subjugation of the Slavs by recording both legend and early folk–tales handed down orally – precursors of the *byliny*, literally "what happened in the past", that became so popular from the 11ᵗʰ to the 19ᵗʰ centuries. But the important point the chronicler is making is of course that the northerners' attempt at conquest had been repulsed; their eventual presence was the result purely of a Slav invitation. It is interesting that Russian history was already being air–brushed before it was even history.

For there is no question that, for at least half a century, the Varangians had already been moving in, establishing trading posts and forts, beginning near Novgorod (which they called Holmgard) in the north, then taking control of and intermarrying with the Slav tribes. But trade was from the beginning an important objective; and the fact that Arab conquest of the Middle East, North Africa, Sicily and Spain (635–732) had disrupted the Mediterranean trade routes between northern Europe and Byzantium no doubt encouraged Varangian enterprise.

Developments in Russia were soon noticed both in Byzantium, mostly when they impinged on it, and in the equally sophisticated Arab–Persian world, where a series of remarkable geographer–historians were putting together reports and eye–witness accounts of the entire world as they knew it. One of the earliest was the Persian Ibn Khurradadhbih, who had the splendid position of Director–General of the Department of Posts and Intelligence at the court of the Abbassid Caliph Ahmed al–Mutamid in Baghdad at the end of the 9ᵗʰ century. He wrote in his work *The Book of Itineraries and Kingdoms* (c888) that the Varangian Rus had by then developed three trade routes to the south: down the Volga to the Caspian Sea and thence to Khorasan and Baghdad; and down both the Dnieper and the Don to Byzantium.[8] But it was the nearer riches of Byzantium, the Norses' *Micklegarth*, "the Great City", that made the Dnieper the favoured route.

It is still hard even at this stage of Varangian intervention to tell what is legend and what history. Rurik sounds like a figure of legend, but some historians have identified him with the Norse pirate Roric of Jutland (peninsular Denmark, now called Jylland), which he held as a vassal of

---

8 Ibn Khurradadhbih, who became a personal friend of the Caliph's, was also the author (according to a later Arab writer) of works on the appreciation of singing and musical instruments, of cooking, of drinking, and of "boon companions and fellow revellers" – and still had time to run the Caliphate's postal and spy systems!

Charlemagne's grandson, the Emperor Lothair, and used as a base for marauding as far afield as England, France and Germany. He can well be envisaged at the other end of the Baltic as well; but argument then revolves around whether Roric–Rurik simply seized the Novgorod area, or whether – reflecting the *Primary Chronicle*'s version – he and his troops were in fact invited as mercenaries to protect one Slav group against another, and then turned on their employers.

There is even more fun to be had in this foundational fog: chauvinist 18th–19th century Russian historians selectively rejected the *Primary Chronicle* version, and insisted that before the Varangians arrived the eastern Slavs had already developed a state as sophisticated as Charlemagne's Carolingian Empire. The Communists, who were supposed to do away with the nation state (their own as well as everyone else's), would have none of it either: the 1960 *Outline History of the USSR* attributed the "unscientific theory" of any Varangian role to malicious German historians:

"The existence of Varangian mercenaries in the service of Russian Princes had no very great effect on the social structure and culture of Ancient Rus as their numbers were insignificant and their social and economic development was at a lower level than that of Rus".

But, on mature reflection, even Soviet historians became revisionists: the 1970 third (and last) edition of the *Great Soviet Encyclopedia* choked off the argument with the elucidation that

"the formation of Kievan Rus was preceded by a period (sixth–eighth century) during which the preconditions of feudal relations ripened in the depths of a military democracy".

One ingenious writer, to avoid both the chauvinist/Soviet sin of flatly contradicting the *Primary Chronicle* and the equally unpopular error of conceding that Russia was partly a foreign invention, turned the Varangians into north Russian partners in some sort of a joint trading company improbably based in the middle of France at Rodez – from which, with a further effort, came "Rus". Those of us who come from countries where we all, even the indigenous inhabitants, ultimately came from somewhere else, might find these propositions comical, but extraordinary things did happen: half a millennium before Rurik, bands of Alans, one of the Sarmatian groups originally from Iran, made their way from the northern Caucasus (where their descendants still live in Ossetia) right across Europe into France and even Spain and Portugal; others moved closer by, and became the Croats and Serbs.

The Russian and Soviet chauvinists did point up one thing: it is indeed curious that a people who became so nationalistic accepted, to meet the requirements of the ruling dynasty, a birth story in the *Primary Chronicle* attributing the state's origins to foreigners; and it is not surprising that it should have caused historiographic uproar. On the other hand, and not unexpectedly, it had a certain snob value in some circles: it is said that every Russian who came to call himself "prince" over the next nine hundred years, until the Bolshevik Revolution, claimed to be descended from Rurik, who may have been Roric, or one of his brothers, who have never been identified as anyone at all.

Svyatoslav: Vladimir's father

One hundred years after the arrival of the Varangians, we find a dynasty bent on establishing a presence among neighbours not known for their tolerance. It's not surprising, then, to discover that Vladimir's father Svyatoslav, leader of the Rus, was above all a warrior:

> "Stepping light as a leopard, he undertook many campaigns. Upon his expeditions he carried with him neither wagons nor kettles, and boiled no meat, but cut off strips of horseflesh, game, or beef, and ate it after roasting it on the coals. Nor did he have a tent, but he spread out a horse–blanket under him, and set his saddle under his head; and all his retinue did likewise".

This was the official picture: the simple leader of simple soldiers. But perhaps one of the few to be mounted: a later Persian writer, Sharaf al–Zaman Tahir Marvazi, physician at the court of the Seljuk Sultan Malik Shah of Roum (Anatolia), wrote that the Russians'

> "valour and courage are well known, so that any one of them is equal to a number of any other nation. If they had horses and were riders, they would be a great scourge to mankind".

The other side of the picture was expressed, probably during Svyatoslav's actual lifetime, by another Persian, the compiler of the *Hudud al–Alam,* "The Regions of the World": the Rus were "evil–tempered, intractable, arrogant–looking, quarrelsome, and warlike". [9]

Svyatoslav's campaigns began with one that was to prove expensive to Kievan Rus. In 965 in order to expand the tribute base to tribes on the Volga who were under the suzerainty of the Khazars, an antagonistic neighbour to the southeast, he attacked and crushingly defeated the Khazar state itself, from the Don to the Caspian Sea.

It is surprising to find that Judaism had been the state religion of the Khazars, an apparently unique occurrence of Judaic state power between then and the foundation of Israel in the middle of the 20th century. A certain amount is known about the Khazars from the documents of their Byzantine and Arab opponents – though not from the still–unlettered Rus – but unfortunately not a single line of the Khazar language has remained to us.[10]

Jewish Khazars were initially a very long–term reflection of the Diaspora of the Jews following the destruction of the Temple in Jerusalem in 70 CE by the Roman Titus, son and eventual successor to the Emperor Vespasian. According to a letter – called the *Genizah Letter* – written by a subject of the King of the Khazars in the mid–10th century, Jews had come to Khazaria from Armenia, where they had been for an unknown length of time, "fleeing before idol–worshippers" – Greek Orthodox Christians – "whose yoke they were unable to bear". In 628 Byzantium had captured Armenia, which at that time extended westwards into present–day Turkey and eastwards as far as northwestern Iran; and it was the subsequent decree by the Byzantine Emperor Heraclius that all Jews in the Empire must convert to Christianity – the first of such a kind – that sent the Armenian Jews fleeing northwards in the early 630s. The Khazars received them well, and, intermarrying, the *Letter* said, they "became one people".

---

9   Marvazi: *China, the Turks and India*; tr. V.Minorsky (London 1942). The *Hudud al–Alam* – also tr. V.Minorsky (London 1937;1970) – was completed in 982 by an unknown Persian geographer in the then prosperous province of Guzganan, now the barren Jozjan region southwest of Balkh in northern Afghanistan.

10   There has been speculation that some at least of the later East European Jews were descended from the Khazars; but this has not been established, and – given the strong traditions of scholarship in Judaism – the disappearance of the language is a strong factor in questioning it.

Writing just before al–Masudi, in the early 930s, al–Istakhri, a Persian geographer, said matter–of–factly in his *Book of the Ways and Realms*:

> "The Khazars are Moslems, Christians and Jews, and among them are a number of idolaters. The smallest group is the Jews, most of them being Moslems and Christians, though the king and his court are Jews…The king has seven judges from the Jews, Christians, Moslems and idolators. When the people have a law–suit it is they who judge it…[The king] transmits his orders to them, which they carry out".[11]

It sounds a remarkable society, but sadly one that couldn't withstand Svyatoslav's onslaught.

Ibn Hawqal, another Arab contemporary, described the fate of one of the main Khazar cities, in what is now Russia's Dagestan, on the west coast of the Caspian:

> "There were in Samandar many gardens, and it is said that it used to contain forty thousand vineyards. I asked about it…of a man who had recently been there. He said: 'There is not an alms for the poor in any vineyard or garden, if there remains a leaf on the bough. For the Russians descended upon it, and not a grape nor a raisin remained in the place' ".[12]

The timing made it a Pyrrhic victory: the stable Khazar state had protected Rus's east–southeast flank towards the Caucasian steppe. Now Rus was open to the onslaught of the Pechenegs (sometimes spelled Patzinaks), the next after the Magyars in the succession of barbarians to pour out of Central Asia, who were right then pushing westwards. They were described in the next century, still very much on the scene, by the

---

11 Quoted by Dunlop. Al–Istakhri was from Fars, in southwest Persia; he was also a traveller in the Arab Middle east, and probably ended up writing in Baghdad.

12 Ibn Hawkal was an inveterate traveller: born in scholarly Nisibis (now Turkish Nusaybin, on the border with Syria), he has been traced between 943 and 973 on visits to North Africa, Spain, the southern edge of the Sahara, Egypt, Armenia, Azerbaijan, Iraq, Persia, Khiva and Transoxiana, and finally Sicily, where his trace was lost.

Byzantine court official Michael Psellus in his history of his times, the *Chronographia*,[13]

> "They are more difficult to fight and harder to subdue than any other people...They wear no breastplates, greaves or helmets, and carry no shields or swords. Their only weapons and sole means of defence is the spear...In one dense mass, encouraged by sheer desperation, they shout their thunderous war–cries and hurl themselves pell–mell upon their adversaries and push them back, pressing against them in solid blocks, like towers, then pursuing them and slaying them without mercy".

However Svyatoslav, the *Chronicle* implies, was determined on empire. After the Khazar campaign he immediately struck southwestwards, where he

> "overcame the Bulgarians, and captured eighty towns along the Danube. He took up his residence there, and ruled in Pereyaslavets [near Varna in the Danube delta, in present–day Romania], receiving tribute from the Greeks".

The account is disingenuous: in fact the Byzantine Emperor Nicephorus II Phocas paid Svyatoslav *in advance* a huge bribe in gold to subdue the Bulgars on his behalf while he was engaged against the Arabs. It was a decision he came to regret when he realised just how capable and ambitious the Kievan Prince was.

Svyatoslav was still on the Danube when the Pechenegs invested Kiev itself, trapping his mother, Olga, and his three sons: Yaropolk (also spelled Iaropolk), Oleg and Vladimir. The first two were the children of Svyatoslav's wife, about whom all that seems to be known is that she was *not* a Hungarian princess – a good indication of the status of women in monastic scriptoria. Vladimir, the youngest, was the child of Malusha, one of Olga's attendants (lady–in–waiting, stewardess, housekeeper have variously been suggested); she was also the sister of Dobrynya, one of Svyatoslav's chief military lieutenants. If they were Slavs, as is believed, Vladimir was the first in the Rurikid line to have both Varangian and Slav blood. It was perhaps for this very reason that, as one story has it,

---

13   Tr. E.R.A. Sewter (London 1953)

on her return from Constantinople Olga had exiled the pregnant Malusha in outrage, though given her status Malusha's condition seems unlikely to have been her own decision; but it has helped date Vladimir's birth at about 960.

The rescue of the royal family owed nothing to Svyatoslav, and perhaps something, still, to legend – the rescue being effected, according to the *Primary Chronicle*, through the heroism of a boy who swam the Dnieper under arrow–fire to raise help, which was then successful primarily through making sufficient noise to convince the Pechenegs to flee because they thought Svyatoslav was back. It does not match Psellus's image of the invincible barbarians. Svyatoslav, reproached by the people that "you neglect your own country", eventually did return,

> "collected an army, and drove the Pechenegs out into the steppes. Thus there was peace".

But he had another shock in stall for the Kievans.

Svyatoslav: wider ambitions

> "I do not care to remain in Kiev, but should prefer to live in Pereyaslavets on the Danube, since that is the centre of my realm, where all riches are concentrated; gold, silks, wine, and various fruits from Greece, silver and horses from Hungary and Bohemia, and from Rus furs, wax, honey, and slaves."

Svyatoslav's announcement to his mother and boyars, which the *Primary Chronicle* says he made in 969, showed that his focus had in fact permanently shifted. Perhaps it was this that proved too much for Olga: she died three days later. Svyatoslav allowed her the Christian burial she requested. "Olga was the precursor of the Christian land", the *Chronicle* memorialised in hindsight; but she did not pass on her belief before her death to her son or any of her grandsons. In fact there is no claim that she converted anyone else at all.

Before he left, Svyatoslav appointed his eldest son Yaropolk to administer Kiev in his absence, the next, Oleg, to Dereva. The *Chronicle* says Novgorod asked for their own Prince, and when both the other young men refused the responsibility, Vladimir's uncle, Dobrynya, suggested the nine–year–old–boy – a neat solution which secured the effective control of the north for Dobrynya himself. It proved to be wise for Vladimir too.

Svyatoslav's attachment to his new fief was not just sybaritic: the Danube was obviously better placed than Kiev for trade, which, with Otto I's defeat of the Magyars, could now reach across westwards with Central Europe as well as southwards with Byzantium. However Pereyaslavets was not yet in fact the centre of Svyatoslav's realm: on his return to Bulgaria he first had to take the hostile city by storm. Thereafter he mixed the gloved hand with the iron fist in strengthening his authority: he suborned some of the Bulgarians by confirming their king in his capital with all the trappings of royalty; the plebs were less fortunate: twenty thousand were impaled at Philippopolis (now Plovdiv) to encourage the rest to surrender. He was now master of Byzantium's chief European neighbour.

But by 970 Svyatoslav had much grander plans. According to the Byzantine historian Leo Diaconus (Leo the Deacon), writing in his *Historia* some fifty years later, he threatened Nicephorus's assassin and brand new successor, the Emperor John I Tzimisces, with breathtaking assurance:

> "If you reject my proposals you will have no choice, you and your subjects, but to leave Europe for ever, where you have scarcely any territory left to call your own and where you have no right to dwell. Retire then to Asia, and leave Constantinople to us. Only then can you hope to achieve a genuine peace between the Russian nation and yourselves".

His predecessors had discovered that Constantinople's seawards defences were far too strong for any assault by longboats; Svyatoslav determined to attack by land from the west. Not the least of his threat was that he had persuaded large numbers of Hungarians and Pechenegs to join his campaign. The Byzantines claimed there were over 300,000 men on the Russian side against their own 12,000; the *Primary Chronicle* contended there were 100,000 Byzantines facing Svyatoslav's 10,000 – everyone always tried to present themselves as facing overwhelming odds: it excused defeat and glorified victory. Historians think the Byzantine figure for their own forces was probably right, while the Russians understated their 50,000 nomad–reinforced alliance.

The outcome was in any case indecisive: the Russians were routed in a battle well inside present–day European Turkey, forcing Svyatoslav to retreat to the Danube, but a revolt by Nicephorus's nephew prevented John Tzimisces from following up his victory. The *Primary Chronicle*, on the contrary, has it that Svyatoslav won, and then was bought off – just as his father was supposed to have been – by a terrified Emperor, with lavish gifts and a peace treaty. The chronicler's final resolution of Svyatoslav's life thus replicated the inventions previously made for Oleg and Igor: this man, who had stubbornly set his head against the Christian entreaties of his sainted mother, even risked her and his children's lives in the pursuit of his ambition, had nevertheless once again, in daring mightily, outfaced the Emperor of Byzantium.

Leo the Deacon's account of what happened was rather less flattering to Russian self–esteem, but by no means a piece of Byzantine triumphalism. He recorded that when John Tzimisces finally made his move in 971 he seized an advantage by first destroying the Bulgarians' capital; but he was then forced into a three–month siege of Svyatoslav at the port of Dristra on the Danube (now Silistra, on the Bulgarian–Romanian border). At one point John offered in frustration – or desperation – to settle the issue by single combat with his Russian opponent. Svyatoslav refused, and his eventual attempt to break out almost succeeded. But when it failed he finally sued for peace, asking simply for safe conduct to retreat across the Danube. John Tzimisces agreed with such relief that he even confirmed Russian trading rights in Constantinople.

There then followed the first summit meeting involving a Russian head of state – at Svyatoslav's request, according to the Byzantines: the *Primary Chronicle* makes no mention of it. The description by Leo Diaconus focussed primarily however on this first sight of a leader of this aggressive power thrusting at Byzantium:

"The Emperor arrived at the bank of the Danube on horseback, wearing golden armour, accompanied by a large retinue of horsemen in brilliant attire. Svyatoslav crossed the river in a kind of Scythian boat; he handled the oar in the same way as his men. His appearance was as follows: he was of medium height – neither too tall, nor too short. He had bushy brows, blue eyes, and was snub–nosed; he shaved his beard but wore a long and bushy moustache. His head was shaven except for a lock of hair on one side as a sign of the nobility of his clan. His neck was thick, his shoulders broad, and his whole stature pretty fine. He seemed gloomy and savage. On one of his ears hung a golden ear–ring adorned with two pearls and a ruby set between them.

His white garment was not distinguishable from those of his men except for cleanness".

The two leaders did no convivial handshaking at this summit: Leo noted that Svyatoslav did not come ashore or even stand – he remained seated in the boat while talking with John Tzimisces. The Byzantines were very much aware that even in defeat this man saw himself as the equal of their Emperor.

But his downfall came as he moved up the Dnieper on his way back to Kiev. The *Primary Chronicle* has a lapidary account:

"When spring came, [in 972,] Svyatoslav approached the cataracts, where Kurya, Prince of the Pechenegs, attacked him; and Svyatoslav was killed. The nomads took his head, and made a cup out of his skull, overlaying it with gold, and they drank from it".

The first dream of a Russian empire died with him. It would flicker again when his grandson made the next – and last – Kievan Rus attack on Byzantium. Then the dream of empire would not be resurrected for more than four hundred years – and this time not from Kiev but from Moscow.

Vladimir Prince of Kiev[14]

"Alas, the evil treachery of men!"

Svyatoslav's eldest son Yaropolk succeeded him; Oleg remained in Dereva and Vladimir in Novgorod. There are signs that Yaropolk may have had some degree of interest in Christianity – but Roman, not the

---

14   There is only one biography available in English: Vladimir Volkoff's *Vladimir the Russian Viking*. Written more as an historical novel, it treats rather uncritically both Vladimir ("shine on, truly *great* Prince") and the *Primary Chronicle*. One can be understanding of but somewhat unnerved from an historical viewpoint by finding in the Foreword the statement that Vladimir's

"memory has inspired the author to cope with more than one ordeal in his personal life; he would like to offer this modest work in the spirit of an ex–voto".

I have found Franklin and Shepard, Vernadsky, and others more useful; but I have drawn on some of Volkoff's interesting quotations from early Russian literary sources, which are marked [V].

Orthodoxy of his grandmother. A German chronicler recorded Rus envoys appearing at the court of the Emperor Otto I in Quedlinburg in March 973, a year after Svyatoslav's death, eleven since Adalbert of Trier's aborted visit to Kiev following Olga's approach to the Emperor. Unfortunately we do not know more. Given Svyatoslav's attitude to Christianity, the assumption must be that this new mission to the Emperor of the West was sent by Yaropolk.

Perhaps the Roman influence in Kiev had made some ground with him during Svyatoslav's almost continuous absence during the eight years since 965; perhaps, contrariwise, the young Yaropolk was interested in a closer Western connection as a useful counterbalance to whatever inroads Byzantine influence may have achieved since his grandmother's conversion to Orthodoxy. At all events, there was a sequel: in 977 he received in Kiev the Legates of Pope Benedict VII, the creation and creature of Otto's son and successor, the Emperor Otto II, whose anti–Byzantine policies the Pope assisted where he could. Was Yaropolk really interested? Or was the Pope anxiously following up on the earlier talks in Quedlinburg? Or did Benedict simply see Rus as a potential ally against Byzantium? Again, we do not know.

Meanwhile another project had taken Yaropolk's attention. In 976 he had moved against his brother Oleg in Dereva. Fleeing with his followers before the attack, Oleg fell, the *Primary Chronicle* says, from a bridge over a moat. The next day Yaropolk's men

"dragged bodies from the moat from morning till noon, and found Oleg under the other corpses".

Seeing the writing on the wall, Vladimir "fled abroad", and Yaropolk became "the sole ruler of Rus".

The *Chronicle* says no more about where Vladimir went during his two years or so in exile, other than that he returned with "Varangian allies". The Norse Sagas relating to Olaf Tryggvason[15] – who as King of Norway would be responsible for Leif Ericsson's travel across the North Atlantic – give a few hints about his relations with Vladimir, but not about those particular years. It may be recalled that Olaf and his mother had been given refuge at Vladimir's court at Novgorod about 970; the

---

15 N. de Baumgarten: "Olaf Tryggwison Roi de Norvège et ses relations avec Saint Vladimir de Russie", in *Orientalia Christiana*, Vol. XXIV – I (Rome 1931).

two boys were then of a similar age – Vladimir about ten, Olaf about two years older – and they spent four years together. By the time Vladimir had to flee several years after Olaf's departure, the latter had been battle–hardened, starting at the age of about sixteen in the Battle of Dannewirk against the Emperor Otto II in 974. Some stories had Vladimir joining Olaf in raids on the coasts of Western Europe; Olaf would indeed raid England a little over a decade later, and defeat King Ethelred the Unready, whose consequent alliance with the Normans would lead to a more permanent invasion in 1066.

But Vladimir may have remained in the eastern Baltic raising his "Varangian allies" – who, Baumgarten has concluded from the Sagas, may well have included Olaf, who seems to have returned to Russia about the same time. Vladimir apparently retook Novgorod with ease, perhaps a sign that his – or at least his uncle–guardian Dobrynya's – rule had been more acceptable to the citizens than that of Yaropolk's lieutenants; or perhaps because his Varangian allies made it the prudent thing to do. Without delay he seems to have set out southwards to deal with Yaropolk.

Once again it is trickery which delivers Kiev to Vladimir, as it had originally to Oleg, and again to secure it for Olga following Igor's death. This time, Vladimir suborned one of Yaropolk's chief retainers, Blud, into betraying Yaropolk. Blud began by lulling him into a false sense of security: "Can a tomtit challenge an eagle?" Then when the tomtit turned out to be Vladimir, Blud falsely persuaded the manipulable Yaropolk to seek terms in person.

> "Yaropolk came accordingly before Vladimir, and when he entered the door, two Varangians stabbed him in the breast with their swords, while Blud shut the doors and would not allow his men to follow him".

It is curious that Kiev, "the mother of Russian cities", could only be taken by deceit. Was cunning more admirable than heroism, or even merely better military tactics? Someone suggested it was simply a metaphor for success by diplomacy, a point which the dead and even some diplomats might contest. But wait: Oleg was never a Christian; Olga's bloodthirsty trickery of the Derevlians, and Vladimir's brutal deception of his half–brother, both occurred *before* they became Christians. This move from pagan horror to Christian virtue is about to be underlined even further.

But first, the *Chronicle* indicates that Vladimir had to face one more problem before he could truly call himself master of Kiev: his Varangians – presumably the allies he had raised for his liberation of Kievan Rus – contended that

"This city belongs to us, and we took it; hence we desire tribute from it…".

So in due course Vladimir manoeuvred those he did not want into moving on to Byzantium – the first occasion on which Russia acted according to earlier undertakings to supply men; but he thoughtfully (and prudently) forewarned the Emperor before their arrival:

"Varangians are on their way to your country. Do not keep many of them in your city, or else they will cause you such harm as they have done here. Scatter them therefore in various localities, and do not let a single one return this way".

Thus

"Vladimir then began to reign alone in Kiev",

and became, in 980, at around twenty, unchallenged Prince of Kievan Rus.

Vladimir the pagan

"For at this time the Russes were ignorant pagans. The devil rejoiced thereat, for he did not know that his ruin was approaching."

The *Primary Chronicle* launches straight into painting the picture of Vladimir's paganism. As the chronicler warms to the theme, the worse Vladimir gets. First it is his beliefs:

"He set up idols on the hills outside the castle…: one of Perun, made of wood with a head of silver and a moustache of gold, and others…The people sacrificed to them, calling them gods, and brought their sons and their daughters to sacrifice them to these devils. They desecrated the earth with their offerings, and the land of Rus and this hill were defiled with blood".

Dobrynya, appointed governor of Novgorod, likewise set up an idol there.

After the sins of the spirit, the sins of the flesh. While still in the north Vladimir took as his first wife one Rogneda, whose Norse father had relatively recently established himself as Prince of Polotsk. Took, literally: Rogneda, the *Primary Chronicle* asserts, had responded to the half–Slav Vladimir's first overture that

> "I will not draw off the boots of a slave's son, but I want Yaropolk instead";

so Vladimir attacked Polotsk, killed her father, and carried her off as he moved south. After the fall of Kiev he "had intercourse" with Yaropolk's wife, a Greek nun who had been brought back by Svyatoslav as one of the spoils of the latter's first Bulgarian campaign; the result was his first known child, Svyatopolk – "from a sinful root evil fruit". Now, as Prince,

> "Vladimir was overcome by lust for women...He was insatiable in vice. He even seduced married women and violated young girls, for he was a libertine like Solomon...The charm of woman is an evil thing".

The *Chronicle* spells out his conquests: his lawful wife Rogneda, the Greek nun aforementioned, a Czech, another Czech, and a Bulgarian, by all of whom he had children; then there were three hundred concubines at Vyshgorod, three hundred at Belgorod, two hundred at Berestovo, and another account adds a further three hundred at Rodnya. If no–one bothered to record the name of a reigning princess, it is not surprising that other women did not count for much – a *bylina*, one of the epic Russian folk–tales whose origins go back to Kievan Rus, described a division of the spoils after a campaign:

> "What at the sharing was dear?
> What at the sharing was cheap?
> Good horses went for seven roubles,
> Sharp sabres went for five roubles,
> Steel maces went for three roubles,
> But the females, they went for nothing:
> Old women for half a coin,

Young women for two halves,
A fair maiden for a whole coin." [V]

Not that Vladimir would have had to pay.

In addition to women, sacrificing children and driving nails through enemies' brains, there must have been plain wassail. Another of those *byliny* described a princely gathering:

"They have filled a cup of green wine,
They have filled a cup of strong beer,
They have filled a cup of strong mead,
They have poured all three cups into one cup.
Now the cup holds a pail and a half,
Now the cup weighs sixty pounds" [V]

– and the hero grips it in one hand and drinks it in one swallow. It sounds, actually, like a fairly typical Russian party; and for all the efforts to portray Vladimir before his conversion in as bad a light as possible, it is worthy of note that the *Primary Chronicle* at no stage accuses him – or his predecessors or successors for that matter – of drunkenness.

The truth of Vladimir's beliefs and behaviour is hard to judge: eight – or eleven – hundred concubines does perhaps sound hyperbolic, though the Saxon chronicler Thietmar of Merseburg described Vladimir as *fornicator immensus et crudelis* on the basis of reports that had come back to Germany. That he worshipped pagan idols would be in keeping with similar practices elsewhere in Viking territories; moreover, as the illegitimate son of a concubine, who had been absent from Kiev since he was ten, he might have seen the cultivation of local gods as conducive to his acceptance; and the fact that he had Dobrynya emulate his actions in Novgorod as well suggests he might have been trying to promote a "national" cult to reinforce his own authority.

The question may also be asked as to what the *Primary Chronicle*'s sources are by now. The beginning of Vladimir's reign was only a hundred and thirty or so years from the time of the *Chronicle*'s compilation, and one may wonder to what extent oral history – as distinct from legend and traditional folk–tales – could now have been making a contribution. Historians have been rightly concerned to document their reconstructions of times past, including trying to document documents like the *Primary Chronicle*; but recent attention in a number of places to the experience of indigenous peoples has suggested that some oral traditions also require credence. Chain–of–evidence plays a role. While medieval lifespans were generally notoriously shorter than ours, we have already noted in Kievan Rus the longevity of a number of the rulers, and might assume that others in the lay and clerical governing elite could have shared their good fortune. By 980 the sources of the *Primary Chronicle* may thus be reinforced by memory at only one or two removes.[16]

All the same, the *Chronicle*'s emphasis on Vladimir's paganism in both his beliefs and behaviour have suggested to many that there was a deliberate attempt by the chronicler to paint his early life in the blackest possible terms so that his subsequent conversion to a life of Christian virtue would be made all the more striking. And the prelude to that conversion comes up right after Vladimir's blackest deed, when the choice by lot of a youth or maiden to be sacrificed to Perun fell on the son of a Christian Varangian who had been converted in Byzantium, and who gave a final ringing condemnation of Vladimir's gods before his and the boy's inevitable doom:

> "These are not gods, but only idols of wood. Today it is, and tomorrow it will rot away...The God whom the Greeks serve and worship...made heaven and earth, the stars, the moon, the sun, and mankind...But what have these gods created? They are themselves manufactured. I will not give up my son to devils".

But the story of Vladimir's conversion to Christianity, beginning three years later in 986, is striking enough without any need for souped–up contrasts.

Vladimir the convertible

> "[In 987] Vladimir summoned together his boyars and the city– elders, and said to them, 'Behold, the Bulgars came before me

---

16   A very small personal example: my elderly maternal grandmother told me that, as a young girl, she had been told by her husband's aged grandmother (my great–great–grandmother) of the bonfires she remembered seeing on the hills of southern England in 1815 for the Duke of Wellington's victory at Waterloo. It is an unimportant event: but it came to me from nearly two centuries ago through only one intermediary. How much more is observation of a ruler likely to be remembered and passed on over a much shorter timespan?

urging me to accept their religion. Then came the Germans and praised their own faith; and after them came the Jews. Finally the Greeks appeared, criticising all other faiths but commending their own...What is your opinion on this subject, and what do you answer?' The boyars and the elders replied, 'You know, oh Prince, that no man condemns his own possessions, but praises them instead. If you desire to make certain, you have servants at your disposal. Send them to inquire about the ritual of each and how he worships God'."

Vladimir's choosing of a new religion was thus presented in the *Primary Chronicle* as having been a two–phase process: first, as it was only proper to expect, the four religions' emissaries came to him, as supplicants; then, as he was still unconvinced, his emissaries visited them, as judges. In considering them we shall treat the two phases together by religion – the religions of Rus's neighbours or near–neighbours.

The Rus had no easy access to the great east–west Silk Routes that linked China with India, Persia and the Levant. Kiev would thus probably have had little knowledge of the nonrevealed and polytheistic religions of China and India, or – probably just as important for Vladimir's purposes – of the countries themselves. For most of the tenth century China had in fact been going through the tortuous turmoils that kept it unstable and helplessly divided between the fall of the Tang Dynasty and the rise of the Northern Sung; India at the time was described by a Chinese Buddhist pilgrim as fragmented into seventy kingdoms, an Indian text mocking that the kings themselves were "but foam upon the waves". As will be apparent, Vladimir, the centraliser, would not have found such customs attractive.

But why did the Prince of Rus have any interest in *any* new religion? And could there be any truth, in any case, in the story of his deciding to adopt one on a comparative basis? And, if there was, one might sceptically ask was it, rather, on a *competitive* basis?

The answer to the first question could have a number of strands – though not, as the *Great Soviet Encyclopedia* held, that Vladimir was "spurred by the need to replace the old ideology of the clan and tribal system by the ideology of nascent feudalism", as if he foresaw the path that Leninism would require him to take. The most obvious influences would have been those of the two branches of Christianity, in particular that coming from his own grandmother's conversion, and the likely continued presence in Kiev – however uncomfortably – of Orthodox

Christians as the result of her patronage. Vladimir also had the example of Bulgaria's conversion to Orthodoxy almost a century before, though his father's varied fortunes may have devalued it.

There may also have been a residual presence of Roman Church adherents from Yaropolk's brief reign, as suggested earlier. It is no doubt a measure of the difficulties in travelling from west to east in those times – when long–distance travel was difficult other than by boat and portage, and in the absence of significant east–west rivers between the Dvina, too far to the north, and the Danube, too far to the south – that while Roman missionaries converted both the Poles and the Hungarians, Kievan Rus's two western neighbours, they achieved so little independent penetration further east. But Vladimir may well have known of these recent conversions, of King Mieszko I of Poland (963) and Duke Geza of Hungary (985), as well as of those of King Harold Bluetooth of Denmark (974) and his old friend Olaf Tryggvason (late 970s?) – though not all succeeded in converting at once their entire fiefdoms as well. There is no mention of any of these in the *Primary Chronicle*; but given the enquiring mind as well as the ambition which it attributes to Vladimir, he must have wondered what advantage his contemporaries saw in this Roman Christianity.

What about comparing his four neighbouring religions before making a choice? When this is not simply taken at face value it tends to be regarded as entirely mythical. The truth of what exactly occurred matters less to us than the politics and prejudices revealed in the telling of the stories.

The first possibility: Islam

> "Vladimir was visited by Bulgars of Mohammedan faith, who said, 'Though you are a wise and prudent prince, you have no religion. Adopt our faith, and revere Mahomet.' "

These were not the Bulgarian Bulgars, but the Volga Bulgars. The original Turkic Bulgars were another of those nomadic hordes who had poured westwards out of Central Asia in the early centuries of the first millennium CE, about the same time as the Huns first appeared on the eastern fringes of Western Europe, settling north of the Black Sea around the Sea of Azov. In the middle of the 7th century they split up under pressure from the Khazars, and one group went five hundred kilometres southwestwards to the Balkans to become the ancestors of the Bulgarian Bulgars.

The other Bulgar group moved from the Sea of Azov a thousand kilometres northeast to the middle Volga, around present–day Kazan, not far south of where the Trans–Siberian Railway crosses the great river; and there they established a state which lasted some six hundred years – longer than Europeans have so far been in the Americas. Early in the 10th century these Volga Bulgars became Moslem, and it was they who were proposing Islam to Vladimir in 986. It was a generous gesture, given that the year before, according to the *Primary Chronicle*, Vladimir had attacked and "conquered" them – by longboats up the Volga, a good old–fashioned Viking raid – but then had backed off:

> "May peace prevail between us", the Bulgars declared, "till stone floats and straw sinks".

When Vladimir asked the Bulgar envoys what was the nature of their religion,

> "they replied that they believed in God, and that Mahomet instructed them to practice circumcision, to eat no pork, to drink no wine, and, after death, promised them complete fulfilment of their carnal desires...They also spoke other false things which out of modesty may not be written down. Vladimir listened to them, for he was fond of women and indulgence, regarding which he heard with pleasure. But circumcision and abstinence from pork and wine were disagreeable to him. 'Drinking', he said, 'is the joy of the Russes. We cannot exist without that pleasure' ".

The Moslems' response to Vladimir was about behaviour, not theology. And a life of carnal bliss in the next world obviously appealed to a man who had at least six wives/mistresses, and eight or perhaps eleven hundred concubines. But the accounts agree on one thing: Vladimir's sticking point was the Moslem requirement for total abstinence; then they diverge again, the politically correct one being that this was incompatible with surviving in a cold climate, the other, Vladimir's irresistibly convincing exclamation: "We cannot exist without that pleasure!" A thousand years later Mikhail Gorbachev was the first to try to reverse Vladimir's judgement; but it was Vladimir who was proved still right.

It would be rash to say that vodka was not Vladimir's real reason for rejecting Islam, but there was another in the *Primary Chronicle*: ritual.

When Vladimir's emissaries – "good and wise men to the number of ten" – went, first, among the Bulgars, they

> "beheld the disgraceful actions of the Bulgars and their worship... We beheld how they worship in their temple, called a mosque, while they stand ungirt. The Bulgar bows, sits down, looks hither and thither like one possessed, and there is no happiness among them, but only sorrow and a dreadful stench. Their religion is not good".

The *Chronicle* is not yet finished with blackening Islam: later, when finally the fourth envoy arrives, a "scholar" from Orthodox Byzantium, he immediately bursts out to Vladimir:

> "We have heard that the Bulgarians came and urged you to adopt their faith, which pollutes heaven and earth. They are accursed above all men, like Sodom and Gomorrah...The day of destruction likewise awaits these men...who do evil and abomination. For they moisten their excrement, and pour the water into their mouths, and anoint their beards with it, remembering Mahomet. The women also perform this same abomination, and even worse ones".

The reason for this additional attack on Islam is not apparent in Russian terms: it was presumably a Byzantine interpolation, prompted by some event in the long and inexorable destruction of the Orthodox Empire by its Moslem foes.

There is an interesting additional reference to Russian – specifically Vladimir's – interest in Islam in the later account by the Persian Marvazi, the writer who was grateful the Russians were not horsemen. Marvazi has it all wrong, but in an instructive way: he says the Rus became Christians early in the 10th century, but

> "the faith blunted their swords, the door of their livelihood was closed to them, they returned to hardship and poverty, and their livelihood shrank. Then they desired to become Muslims, that it might be lawful for them to make raids and holy war, and so make a living by returning to some of their former practices. They therefore sent messengers to the ruler of Khwarazm [or Khorezm, now in Turkmenistan–Uzbekistan], four kinsmen of their king...

called Vladimir...The Khwarazm–shah was delighted and...sent someone to them to teach them the religious laws of Islam. So they were converted".

Of course they were not; but Marvazi's story is taken by some to be a muddled reference to the emissaries the *Primary Chronicle* says Vladimir sent to the Moslem Volga Bulgars – who themselves sought religious instruction from Khwarazm.

From the standpoint of the Russians the additional factor that needs to be taken into account is the political and social context of contemporary Islam. Notwithstanding Vladimir's raid, the Islamic Volga Bulgar state was a viable one, and remained so for another three hundred years, resurrecting itself after the Mongol invasion in 1237, and only finally succumbing to Tamburlaine in 1361. But it was small, militarily uninteresting as an ally, and remote from the trade routes of major interest to Kievan Rus – factors which might have induced the Bulgars to seek closer ties with their increasingly powerful western neighbour, but calculated to cause their rejection by the latter.

If Vladimir knew of the confusion then reigning throughout the Islamic world he would have been even further disinclined to join it. Indeed, over the past half century it had been splitting up, as the Abbasid Caliphate in Baghdad, which for the previous two centuries had had temporal and spiritual authority over the entire Moslem world, slipped into what was to be irreversible decline. First, in 920, Fatimids in North Africa, doctrinal opponents of the Abbasids, proclaimed for the first time a separate independent Caliphate, in Tunisia. Eight years later the Ummayads, Caliphs in Damascus for the first Islamic century before being overthrown and massacred by the Abbasids, proclaimed yet another Caliphate, in Spain, to which one member of the family had managed to flee. The Abbasids' number was up: in 945 Baghdad itself was overrun by Iranian usurpers, though they paid lip–service to the Caliph's continued spiritual authority. Then in the 970s the Byzantine Emperor John I Tzimisces, after reconquering most of Mesopotamia, made a spectacularly successful campaign against the Arabs in the Levant, recovering most of Syria, the Lebanon, and Palestine.

What would Vladimir have made of this picture of Islam? It would not have looked like a winner at this stage of its history; and judging by what is known of Vladimir, he clearly preferred winners. There is another aspect of Islam that one suspects would not have appealed to Vladimir even if it had not at that time been seriously divided, or had he judged it likely to recover its unity: the institution of the Caliphate. Originally the Caliph had held both spiritual and temporal power; the Abbasid Caliphs laid considerable emphasis on their being the protector of the religion of Islam, a role which at least partially survived, as noted earlier, after the dynasty's temporal overthrow. Vladimir would not have liked the supervision of an alien theocrat.

The second possibility: Roman Christianity

> "Then came the Germans, asserting that they were come as emissaries of the Pope. They added, 'Thus says the Pope: Your country is like our country, but your faith is not as ours. For our faith is the light. We worship God, who has made heaven and earth, the stars, the moon, and every creature, while your gods are only wood'."

The distinct echo here of the defiant speech made in Kiev by the Greek Christian against Vladimir's intention to sacrifice his son to Perun is enough to arouse suspicion about this supposed consideration of Roman Christianity. For it was not a separate faith at the time of Vladimir's conversion: there was only the one Holy Catholic and Apostolic Church, with differing Orthodox Greek and Roman Latin rites. The Patriarch of Constantinople still accepted the Church Council's decision in 381 that he should rank second to the Patriarch Bishop of Rome; after his conversion to Orthodoxy Vladimir still entertained perfectly normal relations with Rome. But the situation rankled, especially when the Pope started creating Holy Roman Emperors in the West: the Emperor in Constantinople regarded himself as the only legitimate successor, in an unbroken line, to the Emperors of the Romans.

As the Eastern and Western parts of the Church drifted away from each other, the close combination of Church and State in Byzantium came to stand in ever sharper contrast to the unruly West and the pretensions and humiliations of its Popes. By the time of Vladimir's choice they were only sixty–five years away from the bitter final break, the Great Schism, in 1054, when the Pope of Rome and the Patriarch of Constantinople mutually excommunicated each other and each other's Church. The schism of course endures to this day – longer, now, than the one Holy Catholic and Apostolic Church did.

Cross, the *Primary Chronicle*'s translator, accordingly believed that the entire episode of Vladimir's consideration of the Roman Church was inserted under the influence of Byzantine polemical attacks against it. Nevertheless, with the Papacy's close ties to the Holy Roman Emperors, rulers not only of Germany but often of much of Italy, including Rome itself, it is worth considering what Vladimir would have made of an approach seeking his conversion to the Western Church. As far as the *Chronicle* is concerned it was perfunctorily handled and got short shrift. When the German missionaries made their initial approach, and Vladimir enquired what their teaching was, their response was scarcely up to the highest exegetical standards:

> "'Fasting according to one's strength. But whatever one eats or drinks is all to the glory of God, as our teacher Paul has said.' Then Vladimir answered, 'Depart hence; our fathers accepted no such principle'."

As with the Moslems, the Germans' presentation is said to be about behaviour, not theology; and once again Vladimir's envoys' concern, when they report back, is with ritual – and of course dismissive:

> "We went among the Germans, and saw them performing many ceremonies in their temples; but we beheld no glory there".

And that is all those ten good and wise men had to say about the Roman Church.

The *Primary Chronicle* however is not prepared to leave its anti–Roman polemics at that. Once again there is an addition by the Orthodox scholar – after his outburst to Vladimir on Moslems – on the Roman faith:

> "It differs but little from ours, for they commune with wafers... which God did not give them, for he ordained that we should commune with bread...They do not so act, for they have modified the faith".

The focus on the details of ritual is reinforced yet again, much later, when Vladimir's decision has been made and he is receiving instruction in the Orthodox faith:

> "Do not accept the teachings of the Latins, whose instruction is vicious. For when they enter the church, they do not kneel before

the images, but they stand upright before kneeling, and when they have knelt, they trace a cross upon the ground and then kiss it, but they stand upon it when they arise...Such is not the tradition of the Apostles. For the Apostles prescribed the kissing of an upright cross",

and so on. Finally, however, a point of substance:

"Avoid their doctrine; for they absolve sins against money payments, which is the worst abuse of all".

In just over five hundred years Martin Luther would agree.

While it would not be surprising if an initial approach had been made by German missionaries – they had after all been active, successfully as we saw, in many places in Eastern Europe – it is more curious that Vladimir's emissaries supposedly then also visited "Germany" (no doubt the Ottonian Court) rather than Rome itself. While Vladimir's rebuff is therefore said by some to have been rejection of subservience to the Pope, others, perhaps with more recent experience in mind, have seen it primarily as rejection of any German overlordship.

Vladimir is certainly unlikely to have contemplated subservience to the Emperor; but preoccupied as the Germans were with Italy, it could have occurred to *them* to look for an ally. Already masters of Lombardy and, most of the time, Rome, they had their eyes on the south, which had been in turmoil since raids by the Arabs, who controlled North Africa and still held Sicily, had disrupted weakening Byzantine control over the previous century. The Byzantine Emperor John I Tzimisces and his nephew and successor, Vladimir's contemporary the Emperor Basil II, were themselves keenly interested in recovering Byzantium's Italian provinces. It would have been helpful to the Ottonians to have Kievan pressure on Constantinople from the north – or at least (if they had known about it) to have stopped Vladimir from propping up Basil with six thousand fully–equipped Varangians, as he was shortly to do.

But, as we shall then see, Vladimir had a quite different perspective on Byzantium. In any case Otto II suffered a disastrous defeat by the Arabs in Calabria in 982, a year before he was killed trying to take Venice, and his three–year–old son and heir was in no position to take up the cause. Southern Italy remained in chaos until, forty years later, young adventurers from the Varangians' cousins transplanted in

Normandy began creating a new kingdom – even before they conquered another one in England – in southern Italy and Sicily. This glittering Viking outpost was the only West European society of which I am aware where racial and religious toleration matched that in Khazaria: the Norman Hauteville rulers' officials were Arabs, Greeks and Jews as well as their own countrymen, and they administered their own law codes in their own languages as had their Khazar co–religionists. But French envy and rapacity ensured that it would only last two centuries. The Holy Roman Empire on the other hand would recover and somehow survive for eight, until another conqueror, Napoleon, abolished it in 1806.

Quite apart from the fact that the Germans frequently had the Popes in their hands, the latter were often in those of others even less suitable. Even Vladimir at his pagan best might have found 10th century Rome unedifying in the field of spiritual leadership. Earlier in the century Pope John X had been strangled by the daughter of his lover, the ex–prostitute Marozia, to make way (after two fill–ins) for *her* son by Pope Sergius III (who had murdered his predecessor) to become, at eighteen, Pope John XII:

> "We read with some surprise", Gibbon wrote, not really surprised at all, "that the worthy grandson of Marozia lived in public adultery with the matrons of Rome; that the Lateran palace was turned into a school for prostitution, and that his rapes of virgins and widows had deterred the female pilgrims from visiting the tomb of St Peter, lest, in the devout act they should be violated by his successor";

he died of a stroke at twenty–eight, in bed with a married woman.[17] The Pope who would have sent German missionaries to see Vladimir was John XIV, not elected but selected and installed by the Emperor Otto II, on whose death the Pope's many enemies had him arrested, deposed, beaten, imprisoned, and in four months starved to death. His successor, John XV, also active in the Empire's interest, who would have received

---

17 *The History of the Decline and Fall of the Roman Empire*, Chapter XLIX. Gibbon added the splendidly pungent judgement:

"The protestants have dwelt with malicious pleasure on these characters of antichrist; but to a philosophic eye, the vices of the clergy are far les dangerous than their virtues".

Vladimir's emissaries had they gone to Rome, was merely avaricious and nepotistic. It is hard to imagine this navel–gazing institution focussing on the conversion of the Slavs.

The great struggles between powerful Popes and powerful Emperors were not yet upon poor Italy, but the seeds had long since been laid in a way which, assuming Vladimir could have known of it, would have discouraged him from looking towards Rome. This was the notorious "Donation of Constantine". Constantine the Great was claimed, in a compilation made by a French cleric about 842, to have given his contemporary Pope Sylvester I, and all his successors in the Holy See, full temporal as well as spiritual authority over all Catholic empires, kingdoms and principalities; and for six hundred years this was vigorously called upon by successive Popes in their efforts to bend the secular powers of Europe to the Papal will and the benefit of the Papacy's own territorial States of the Church. Until 1440, when Lorenzo Valla, a Renaissance humanist, conclusively proved that this and the whole compilation were forgeries. But in Vladimir's time the "Donation" was still there for the assertion, with all the authority of Constantine if not of the Popes of the day; and Vladimir would no more have accepted the supervision of an alien Catholic theocrat than that of an alien Islamic one.

The third possibility: Judaism

> "The Jewish Khazars heard of these missions [to Vladimir], and came themselves saying, 'We have learned that Bulgars and Christians came hither to instruct you in their faiths. The Christians believe in him whom we crucified, but we believe in the one God of Abraham, Isaac, and Jacob."

As with the two previous groups, Vladimir asked the Jews what their religion was; and as had the others, they responded with its behavioural requirements:

> "its tenets included circumcision, not eating pork or hare, and observing the Sabbath".

We then come to the first variation: Vladimir asks what is on the face of it a curious follow–up question: where is their "native land?" – and the answer is not Khazaria.

"They replied that it was in Jerusalem. When Vladimir demanded where that was, they made answer, 'God was angry at our forefathers, and scattered us among the gentiles on account of our sins. Our land was then given to the Christians'. The Prince then demanded, 'How can you hope to teach others while you yourselves are cast out and scattered abroad by the hand of God? If God loved you and your faith, you would not be thus dispersed in foreign lands. Do you expect us to accept that fate also?' "

While there is no anti–Semitism involved, this is a cooked–up disposal of Judaism by the *Chronicle*. Vladimir may well have known more about it, through the long–standing presence of Khazars in Kiev, than he did about either of the Christian contenders, whose presence there was small and tenuous at best, or about the Islam of the Volga Bulgars, which probably had none. But there is no reference to the previously key element of ritual, or, of course – as with the other two – to any investigation of theology. And there can be no question of despatching emissaries to Khazaria: it no longer existed, thanks to his father's destructive campaign, and even before then had begun turning towards Islam to secure Khiva's support against invading Turks on its east.

In these circumstances the Diaspora becomes the main issue – which is reinforced later by the Orthodox scholar, who sees it, as was conventional in both Orthodox and Roman theology, as punishment for the Jews' crucifixion of Christ. It is thus central to Vladimir's perceptions, and he takes it to mean that Judaism would be completely at odds with his ambition to enhance his power through religious unity. By the time the *Primary Chronicle* was compiled, centralised political authority, supported unquestioningly by the one true religion, was already the only acceptable view (if not always the practice) of the Russian state.

Towards the decision: Orthodoxy

"Vladimir then inquired [of the Orthodox scholar] why God should have descended to earth and should have endured such pain. The scholar then answered and said, 'If you are desirous of hearing the story, I shall tell you from the beginning why God descended to earth'. Vladimir replied, 'Gladly would I hear it'."

There follow in the *Primary Chronicle* eleven pages – almost a tenth of its entire length – with the scholar's summarisation of the Old and New Testaments. At the end,

> "he exhibited to Vladimir a canvas on which was depicted the Judgement Day of the Lord, and showed him, on the right, the righteous going to their bliss in Paradise, and on the left, the sinners on their way to torment. Then Vladimir sighed and said, 'Happy are they upon the right, but woe to those upon the left!' The scholar replied, 'If you desire to take your place upon the right with the just, then accept baptism!' Vladimir took this counsel to heart, saying, 'I shall wait yet a little longer', for he wished to inquire about all the faiths."

Despite that long exegesis, we are left in suspense! Is this just an effective narrative device? Or does it reflect a real search by Vladimir, still not decided, now about to send forth his emissaries?

In any event, as soon as they reach Constantinople there is a whole new approach: the outcome is suddenly inevitable –

> "On the morrow, the Emperor sent a message to the patriarch to inform him that a Russian delegation had arrived to examine the Greek faith, and directed him to prepare the church and the clergy, and to array himself in his sacerdotal robes, so that the Russes might behold the glory of the God of the Greeks. When the Patriarch received these commands, he bade the clergy assemble, and they performed the customary rites. They burned incense, and the choirs sang hymns. The Emperor accompanied the Russes to the church, and placed them in a wide space, calling their attention to the beauty of the edifice, the chanting, and the pontifical services and the ministry of the deacons, while he explained to them the worship of God. The Russes were astonished...".

The report of his ten good and wise men underlined the impact:

> "The Greeks led us to the edifices where they worship their God, and we knew not whether we were in heaven or on earth. For on earth there is no such splendour or such beauty, and we are at a loss how to describe it. We only know that God dwells there among men, and their service is fairer than the ceremonies of other

nations. For we cannot forget that beauty. Every man, after tasting something sweet, is afterward unwilling to accept that which is bitter, and therefore we cannot dwell longer here".

Well they might have been astonished. The great cathedral (mosque, since 1453) of Hagia Sophia in Istanbul, even empty as it is today, overwhelms any visitor. It is not surprising that visitors from Kiev, where structures were still only in wood, would be stunned by its magnificence. It was already a venerable four hundred and fifty years old; the vast interior surmounted by its huge dome, without any internal pillars; splendidly decorated screens and silken hangings, on walls completely covered with polychrome marbles; brilliant patterned mosaics, in places with Christ and the Virgin, Saints and Emperors, rising above into the vast dome, all against gold backgrounds making a great glinting golden shell; the clergy and the Court in the richest vestments, like those still seen in the mosaics, processing with ostentatiously–encased holy relics (some now in the Treasury of St Mark's Basilica in Venice), following a highly–elaborated centuries–old ritual adorned by rich choral singing; the whole scene lit by thousands of lamps and tapers.

Of course the celebration of Divine Service in Hagia Sophia would far surpass anything, anywhere else at the time, in meeting the Kievan boyars' and elders' advice to Vladimir: to have his emissaries visit the four faiths, and specifically to

"Send them to inquire about the ritual of each and how he worships God".

The impact of Byzantine ritual – on "right praising", the Russian translation of "orthodox" – turned out to be overwhelming, not only at the time of Vladimir but thereafter as well. Byzantine Orthodoxy as a whole was adopted uncritically, but, as Billington observed, without assimilating Byzantine culture's classical foundations or philosophic traditions. Once adopted, *nothing* could be changed.

The focus on ritual and the outward manifestation of God's glory, rather than on intellectual debate – the beauty and comfort of the service, rather than the exhortation and challenge of the sermon – was to become the permanent characteristic of the Russian Church. In a volume on the Church in 1982 the Metropolitan (Archbishop) Pitirim of Volokolamsk, representing the Patriarchate of Moscow, wrote succinctly, in comparing Roman Catholicism and Russian Orthodoxy, of the "contrast between the culture of 'intelligence' in the West, and that of the 'heart' in the East".

The story of Vladimir's ecclesiastical investigations lay at its foundation.

In case beauty were not enough, the Kievan boyars came up with an argument they might have thought of putting to Vladimir a whole lot earlier:

> "If the Greek faith were evil, it would not have been adopted by your grandmother Olga who was wiser than all other men".

The tough frontiersman, the well–known fornicator, the idolatrous maker of uncountable human sacrifices, the belated searcher after enlightenment, is finally persuaded by his sainted grandmother's example that had always been before him:

> "Vladimir then inquired where they should all accept baptism, and they replied that the decision rested with him".

But for Vladimir the question was not only where, but when.

Towards the decision: diplomacy

> "After a year had passed...Vladimir proceeded with an armed force against Kherson, a Greek city...and he sent messages to the Emperors Basil and Constantine, saying, 'Behold, I have captured your glorious city. I have also heard that you have an unwedded sister. Unless you give her to me to wife, I shall deal with your own city as I have with Kherson'. When the Emperors heard this message they were troubled, and replied, 'It is not meet for Christians to give in marriage to pagans. If you are baptised, you shall have her to wife."[18]

---

18   The two Emperors were brothers who had become the Co–Emperors Basil II and Constantine VIII, at the ages of six and three, on the death of their father Romanus II in 963. In fact Nicephorus II Phocas, as another Co–Emperor from 963 to 969, and John I Tzimisces from 969 to 976, actually ruled during these periods; miraculously Basil and Constantine survived, with Basil then being pre–eminent from 976 until 1025 – an extraordinarily long rule of just on fifty years, and reign of sixty–two – followed by Constantine from 1025 to 1028.

While Vladimir's conversion may not have come out of the theological blue, it most certainly did not take place in a political vacuum. Despite its focus on the religious issue, even the *Primary Chronicle* concedes there were dynastic considerations. But it gets the chronology wrong, and omits mentioning that there were also other matters of state: strategic issues, military questions, trade. When Vladimir looked to Byzantium there was more than truth and beauty in the eyes of the beholder.

For despite the inroads of the Arab and Turkic Moslems over almost four centuries, Byzantium was still the greatest state in the region of Europe and western Asia, still fully recognisable as the heir to one of the world's greatest empires. Its territory still included a toehold in southern Italy, all of Greece and most of the Balkans south of the Danube, stretched right across Anatolia as far as Lake Van on the edge of the Caucasus, and it had recently reincorporated the Levant down to Palestine. Constantinople, the Great City, was a vast opulent metropolis of palaces and cathedrals, souks and monasteries. There was no city remotely like it in Western Europe. Not so much later, a Byzantine diplomat sent abroad lamented:

> "Oh, land of Byzantium, oh thrice–happy city, eye of the universe, ornament of the world, star shining afar, beacon of this lower world, would that I were within you, enjoying you to the full! Do not part me from your maternal bosom!"

With a million cosmopolitan inhabitants it was bigger than most neighbouring countries, a major centre of money and processing, and of trade routes linked to the Baghdad Caliphate and the further Orient, to the developing courts and towns of Western Europe, to the Caliphates of North Africa and Spain. It was Constantinople that had lured the Varangian traders and freebooters southwards down the Russian river systems in the first place; and Kievan merchants had for a century been pursuing their own standing in this great marketplace. Vladimir himself, though he had not visited – and never would – must also have been allured by such manifest testament to success. Increasing trade with this glittering emporium was the obvious policy for Vladimir to adopt; attacking Kherson, Byzantium's major trading centre and last settlement on the north shore of the Black Sea, does not seem to be the obvious tactic for implementing it.

If Vladimir was interested in a new religion as a means for strengthening Rus unity, the pre–eminence of Byzantium made Orthodoxy the obvious choice. By the time of the *Primary Chronicle*, of course, the Islamic Seljuk Turks, surging in their turn out of Central Asia, had long since defeated Byzantium and captured its Emperor Romanus IV Ducas in the Battle of Manzikert, and swept on to overrun Asia Minor, Baghdad and Jerusalem – a series of disasters that contributed to the launching of the First Crusade in 1095.[19] This would probably not have changed Vladimir's view of Islam – but it is interesting to wonder if it would have changed his view of Byzantium.

However it was not in fact Vladimir who first looked to Byzantium: it was the other way round. Basil also was confronted by complex questions. Not least, right at this time, as fate would have it a leading general, Bardas Phocas, nephew of Nicephorus II Phocas, escaped from prison in the east of the Empire, where he had been confined for rebelling against Nicephorus's successor John Tzimisces, raised armed revolt again, and made his way unopposed across the whole of Anatolia, raising supporters as he approached the Bosphorus. With Moslem enemies on his southern and eastern frontiers, Arabs and Germans in the Italian rump, and resurgent Bulgars in the northwest, there was only one direction in which Basil could realistically turn to save Constantinople: to Kiev. The Arab historian Yahya ibn Sa'id al–Antaki, a Christian Egyptian writing his *History* in the great Byzantine city of Antioch a few decades later, recorded that under the pressure of the rebellion, Basil

> "was obliged to ask for the help of the king of the Russians, who were his enemies. The [Russian] agreed to do so; after which they made an alliance of kinship, and the king of the Russians married the sister of the Emperor Basil on the condition that he would be baptised with all the people of his country".

The known facts confirm this version, and it gives a rather different slant from the *Primary Chronicle*'s chronology: all this was agreed *before* there was any attack on Kherson, and as a consequence of an approach by *Basil*. The negotiations are thought to have taken place over the winter of 987–988. The Byzantines claimed that Vladimir regarded himself bound by his father Svyatoslav's undertaking to the Emperor John II Tzimisces to assist if "any foe" attacked him, which seems unlikely even supposing the offer was ever made; but in any case in 988

---

19 See 1100 chapter: Godefroy de Bouillon

Vladimir despatched to Constantinople six thousand fully–equipped Varangians.

They would surely not have gone had Vladimir not received a significant *quid pro quo*: and this was undoubtedly the promise of marriage to the Emperors' sister Anna, on condition of conversion to Christianity. Although there is no indication in the *Primary Chronicle* of domestic discontents at this stage, still only eight years after Vladimir's seizure of power, he would have been well aware that marriage with Anna would significantly strengthen his legitimacy. At the same time such a match would uphold the view that had been evident in the actions of – or rationalisations about – his predecessors: that Russia was most certainly now the equal of anyone.

Though, as far as a marriage alliance was concerned, who in fact proposed what to whom? The *Chronicle* of course says it was Vladimir who asked for Anna. But is it possible that Basil already knew Vladimir was interested in a new religion for himself and his people, and that in his own hour of desperation, uncertain what Vladimir's response would be to his plea for help, he threw in his sister as a sweetener right at the beginning? – on condition, of course, of his actual conversion. It might account for one tradition that Vladimir was baptised in Kiev *before* he attacked Kherson.

The *Primary Chronicle* account of course has Vladimir doing the asking (though after Kherson instead of before). Then, it says, when Basil and Constantine ruled out any marriage contract with a pagan, Vladimir immediately responded that he was willing to accept baptism from the Greeks, "having already given some study to their religion"; and when the Emperors heard this they persuaded their sister Anna to consent to the match. However there was still a bit of jockeying:

> "They then requested Vladimir to submit to baptism before they should send their sister to him, but Vladimir desired that the Princess should herself bring priests to baptise him".

This *Chronicle* version undermines of course the idea of Vladimir's having previously decided for religious reasons to convert to Orthodoxy: it implies he did so only for the mercenary reason that it was the condition for marrying Anna.

If it was indeed Vladimir who requested Anna's hand the sequel would surely not have been as calm as the *Chronicle* makes out: it would in fact have caused uproar in Constantinople. Anna was a *Porphyrogenita*, a Princess born like her two brothers "in the Purple" to a reigning

Emperor, Romanus, and his wife Theophano.[20] Twenty years before, Liudprand of Cremona's second mission to Constantinople, for the Holy Roman Emperor Otto I, had been to ask the Emperor Nicephorus II Phocas for the then five–year–old Anna as wife for the future Otto II, and the reply had been succinct:

> "It is unheard of that a daughter born in the purple of an emperor born in the purple should contract a foreign marriage. Still, great as is your demand, you shall have what you want if you give what is proper: Ravenna, namely, and Rome with all the adjoining territories from thence to our possessions".

Indeed, the outrageous pretension of the Western Emperor resulted in his envoy's being personally treated most undiplomatically: uncomfortably housed, badly fed (the food "fairly foul and disgusting"), insultingly received, his master pointedly abused. In consequence, in his report on his mission, *Relatio de legatione constantinopolitana*, "The Embassy to Constantinople", Liudprand's description of Nicephorus Phocas is the most hilariously malicious hatchet–job ever penned by an ambassador:

> "a monstrosity of a man, a dwarf, fat–headed and with tiny mole's eyes; disfigured by a short, broad, thick beard half going gray; disgraced by a neck scarcely an inch long; piglike by reason of the big close bristles on his head; in colour an Ethiopian and, as the poet says, 'you would not like to meet him in the dark'; a big belly, a lean posterior...; foul smelling, and discoloured by age";

and he described an imperial procession into Saint Sophia like that which was to overwhelm Vladimir's emissaries twenty–five years later, but with a different perspective:

> "As Nicephorus, like some crawling monster, walked along, the singers began to cry out in adulation: 'Behold the morning

---

20 Romanus was as "purple" as any Emperor of Byzantium ever was: he was not only the son of an Emperor, both his maternal and paternal grandfathers were Emperors, as was the latter's father also, the founder of the Macedonian Dynasty; an uncle plus a grand–uncle as well were among his predecessor Emperors. The Empress Theophano, an ambitious, unscrupulous, amoral, breath–taking beauty, was the daughter of a Pelopponesian innkeeper.

star approaches: the day star rises: in his eyes the sun's rays are reflected: Nicephorus our prince, the pale death of the Saracens'. And then they cried again: 'Long life, long life to our prince Nicephorus. Adore him, ye nations, worship him, bow the neck to his greatness'. How much more truly might they have sung:– 'Come, you miserable burnt–out coal; old woman in your walk, wood–devil in your look; clodhopper, haunter of byres, goat-footed, horned, double limbed; bristly, wild, rough, barbarian, harsh, hairy, a rebel, a Cappadocian!"

Nicephorus, Liudprand summed up with his most damning invective, was

"a liar, a cheat, a pitiless and arrogant man as cunning as a fox, full of hypocritical humility, avaricious, covetous, an eater of garlic, onions, and leeks, and a water drinker".[21]

Vladimir was no Holy Roman Emperor: he was not even a mere foreigner but a barbarian, a pagan sacrificer of humans, with multiple wives or partners already and hundreds of concubines. And six thousand Varangians, even well–armed, sound somewhat less of a bargain for an Imperial princess than Ravenna and Rome. Was there anything else? – perhaps a promise of additional troops if these were not enough? In fact they were: they arrived in plenty of time, "a fine body of men" the Byzantine historian Michael Psellus tells us; and Basil

"had these men trained in a separate corps, combined with them another mercenary force, divided by companies, and sent them out to fight the rebels".

They carried out a cross–Bosphorus massacre of Bardas's forward camp early in 989, and then were instrumental in the final rout of the usurper two months later. Extraordinarily, Bardas Phocas died during his opening

---

21   The *Embassy* is also in Wright: *Op. cit.* Despite his appearance, manners and eating habits, Nicephorus Phocas was in fact a highly successful military commander and Emperor, known to the Arabs, whom he pushed back beyond the Euphrates, as "Hammer of the Saracens". His sarcophagus bore the inscription: "You conquered all but a woman" – in reference to his wife Theophano's participation in his assassination by John Tzimisces, his successor as Emperor...and as Theophano's husband.

charge in this second battle – a lucky javelin shot? a stomach disorder? poison provided by Basil to Bardas' cupbearer?

> "For my own part", Psellus says, "I prefer to express no opinion on the subject and ascribe all the glory to the Mother of the World".

Bardas's troops fled; but that did not stop the Varangians from massacring them anyway.

It is clear that the agreement was made: Vladimir would marry the *Porphyrogenita* Anna, whether she was offered or had to be asked for. But by mid–989 the Emperors had not yet produced her; and it was then that an angry Vladimir attacked Kherson – and captured it, once again, by treachery! – to force them to carry out their side of the bargain. And he threatened another attack on Constantinople itself, with what degree of credibility no one knew; but after all the ups and downs of Kievan Rus's relations with – and designs on – Byzantium, and the recent danger from Bardas, perhaps Basil and Constantine felt they had no choice but to constrain Vladimir from following his grandfather's longboats or his father's footsteps. And now, moreover, his six thousand giant Varangians were right there in Constantinople with their gigantic battle–axes, a powerful additional encouragement to uncooperative Emperors. They blinked: taking Anna's courage in their own hands, they

> "sent forth their sister, accompanied by some dignitaries and priests. Anna, however, departed with reluctance. 'It is as if I were setting out into captivity', she lamented; 'better were it for me to die at home'. But her brothers protested, 'Through your agency God turns the land of Rus to repentance, and you will relieve Greece from the danger of grievous war. Do you not see how much harm the Russes have already brought upon the Greeks? If you do not set out, they may bring on us the same misfortunes'. It was thus that they overcame her hesitation only with great difficulty".

So Anna was shipped off to Kherson to meet the waiting Vladimir. It is hard to imagine what that young woman, brought up in the absolute heights of privilege and luxury, must have felt.

Then, according to the *Chronicle*,

> "Vladimir was baptised in the Church of St Basil, which stands at Kherson upon a square in the centre of the city, where the

Khersonians trade...After his baptism, Vladimir took the Princess in marriage. Those who do not know the truth say he was baptised in Kiev...As a wedding present for the Princess, he gave Kherson over to the Greeks again...".

This old Kherson – not to be confused with present–day Ukrainian Kherson, on the Dnieper just above its delta – was originally the ancient Chersonesus, founded as a Greek colony about the 5th century BCE. It was on the coastal outskirts of Sebastopol (and was therefore closed "for security reasons" during our time in the Soviet Union). There are still some Byzantine ruins there, though in his fascinating book *Black Sea* Neal Ascherson records that "the site has been devastated by fortress–building and bombardment and above all by early Russian archeologists, ploughing down through the substrata to find 'evidence' of the baptism of Vladimir of Kiev...".

And so Vladimir the Christian took his Christian wife to Kiev, along with her train of ecclesiastics and various holy relics. The *Primary Chronicle* says he also

"appropriated...four bronze horses, which now stand behind the Church of the Holy Virgin, and which the ignorant think are made of marble."

The Emperor Basil II continued his remarkable reign for another thirty–five years. The Varangians remained in Byzantium, and became the Emperor's famed personal Varangian Guard, known for their blond–headed tallness and their huge battle–axes. For a century the Guard was composed primarily of Norse mercenaries recruited via Russia; but as time went on it increasingly had Danes, and then Englishmen who had left in anger after the Norman conquest, and who particularly relished the opportunity, when it came, to fight against the new Norman state in southern Italy. They were as unsuccessful there as their fathers had been against William the Conqueror. The final irony lay in the demise of this largely Western Catholic Varangian Guard: slaughtered in 1204 defending Constantinople against the Fourth Crusade – Western Catholics, led by Venice.[22] The Guard was never revived.

---

22 The Venetians, incidentally, themselves "appropriated" another four bronze horses which had dominated the Constantinople Hippodrome (now the Beyazit Meydani) in the centre of the city since the reign of Constantine the Great, and

The conversion of Rus

> "When the Prince arrived at his capital, he directed that the idols should be overthrown...Thereafter Vladimir sent heralds throughout the whole city to proclaim that if any inhabitants, rich or poor, did not betake himself to the river [for baptism], he would risk the prince's displeasure. When the people heard these words, they wept for joy, and exclaimed in their enthusiasm, 'If this were not good, the Prince and his boyars would not have accepted it'."

(Thus the Russian people wept for the next thousand years, and for the same reasons, but not for joy.)

Some of the idols at Kiev were cut to pieces, others were burned; in a final acknowledgement of the chief god Perun, Vladimir

> "appointed twelve men to beat the idol with sticks, not because he thought the wood was sensitive, but to affront the demon who had deceived man in this guise".

The idols were cast into the Dnieper, in a rather nice symmetry with the succeeding conversion of the people, in "a countless multitude", in the same river. This mass baptism was voluntary, the *Primary Chronicle* insists, and even took place in the winter; which, given the climate, has a distinct echo of something else: the "spontaneous" enthusiasm of the unfranchised masses for later Tsars and Commissars.

What happened, though, to all those now–excess wives? Presumably Anna made sure they were removed from the scene – to a convent became the practice of future tsars – but the *Primary Chronicle* is silent: until the year 1000, when it records only that in this year "Rogned died, Yaroslav's mother". And all those concubines? – there were not enough convents.

Vladimir next

> "ordained that wooden churches should be built and established where pagan idols had previously stood...He began to found

---

hauled them off – with a lot more loot – to adorn St Mark's Basilica. But no longer: twenty–odd years ago they were moved inside for protection from pollution; copies now dominate the Piazza. The Kiev horses were never heard of again.

churches and to assign priests throughout the cities, and to invite the people to accept baptism in all the cities and towns".

So, over the course of the following twenty–five years of Vladimir's reign, Russia became Christian. The completeness of the conversion is underlined in the language: the word for "peasant" and "Christian" is the same.

But even the *Primary Chronicle* in due course admits that the relics of paganism required constant vigilance for some time. Novgorodians, perhaps, as northerners, better pagans in the first place, seem to have remained susceptible: almost a century later, in 1071, a magician appeared in Novgorod, and

> "harangued the people, and by representing himself as a god he deceived many of them; in fact, he humbugged almost the entire city. For he claimed to know all things, and he blasphemed against the Christian faith...There was finally an uprising in the city, and all believed in him so implicitly that they went so far as to desire to murder the bishop...Then Gleb [Prince of Novgorod, Vladimir's great–grandson] hid an axe under his garments, approached the magician, and enquired of him whether he knew what was to happen on the morrow or might even occur before evening. The magician replied that he was omniscient. Then Gleb enquired whether he even knew what was about to occur that very day. The magician answered that he himself would perform great miracles. But Gleb drew forth the axe and smote him, so that he fell dead".

Thus Russian rulers would resolve philosophical arguments with their critics.

Did Vladimir, in creating a new Christian nation, consciously have in mind Constantine the Great?

> "He is the new Constantine of mighty Rome", the *Primary Chronicle* intoned, "who baptized himself and his subjects; for the Prince of Rus imitated the acts of Constantine himself".[23]

But the parallels were by no means exact: Constantine claimed to have been converted in 312 after seeing a flaming cross before one of his

---

23 So did Peter the Great: in his wars seven hundred years later his standards bore Constantine's cross.

major victories; he issued an edict of toleration for Christians the following year, but it was only eleven years later that Christianity became a state religion, though paganism was still not persecuted; and he was only baptized himself when he was dying thirteen years after that, in 337. In the *Primary Chronicle*'s record – or reconstruction – of Vladimir's shift from pagan chieftain to Christian Prince he showed neither such caution nor such tolerance. On his conversion he immediately set about ensuring the conversion of everyone else as well, constructing churches and monasteries in his capital and wherever he went, laying the foundations for a state which would rule with the Church but not be ruled by it.

It was a calculated and highly autarchic political step, including in its religious aspect: there is no hint anywhere of a revelation by God, no vision, such as Constantine's, from Christ or the Holy Spirit or the Virgin, only a visit from a solitary scholar–missionary with a Bible and a picture of the Last Judgement – though Baumgarten believes the influence of Vladimir's old friend, the now–Christian Olaf Tryggvison, was instrumental, during a stay of undetermined length at Kiev immediately before Vladimir's decision. A half century later Bishop Hilarion, the first Russian to become Metropolitan of Kiev, discounted both Divine intervention and the Orthodox scholar–missionary in accounting for Vladimir's conversion – it was solely due to Vladimir himself:

"How didst thou believe?...Thou hadst not seen Christ, hadst not followed in his footsteps...hadst read neither law nor prophets... Not having seen an apostle come into thy land and by his poverty and nakedness and hunger and thirst incline thy heart to humility...; not having seen devils being cast out by the name of Christ, the sick in good health, fire transformed into cold, the dead rising, not having seen all these things, how didst thou then believe? O amazing miracle!...[Thou], O blessed one, without any of these didst run to Christ, only through good thinking and intelligence". [V]

A secular interpretation would be that it was Vladimir, the Russian, who alone would be the arbiter of the nation's destiny, not an alien Trinity.

After he had accepted conversion himself, he undoubtedly felt quite sincerely that all his countrymen should believe also, for the benefit of their souls – and equally sincerely that such a regimen would enhance the power of the Rurikid state. By enforcing conversion on all the Rus through the agencies of the State and the Church he thereby elevated these to the same status in the Russian context as that traditionally enjoyed elsewhere only by more exalted Givers of Revelation. It was integral to the canon, already alluded to, that was carefully crafted to justify Vladimir's successors – descended from a Prince of extraordinary judiciousness, indeed a true Saint – in holding supreme power over their subjects, supported by a Church that had been favoured by a quite extraordinary Grace. And the canon provided equally a set of ready-made, mutually reinforcing religious and political beliefs emphasising Russians' sense of difference from others through the uniqueness of their temporal and spiritual leaders.

This canon had a long and successful life. Kiev was, before very long, the Second Jerusalem; Moscow became the Third Rome under the Romanovs; the Communist Party of the Soviet Union was the vanguard of the proletariat of the entire world; Stalin, in his day, *beyond* worldly:

"O'er the earth the rising sun sheds a warmer light,
Since it looked on Stalin's face it has grown more bright".[24]

Vladimir's Russia

"Vladimir was fond of his followers, and consulted them concerning matters of administration, wars, and government. He lived at peace with the neighbouring Princes, Boleslav of Poland, Stephen of Hungary, and Udalrich of Bohemia, and there was amity and friendship among them."

These somewhat uncharacteristic attributes for a Russian leader are part of the *Primary Chronicle*'s recital of the benefits the reformed Vladimir bestowed on his people as the result of his conversion. The first mentioned was education: he

"took the children of the best families, and sent them for instruction in book–learning".

---

24   The words were written by Sergei Prokofiev, for his cantata *Hail to Stalin*, composed in 1939 near the end of the Great Purges in which Stalin had some 18 million people arrested and 7 million shot, including virtually all the top Communist Party leadership and Red Army High Command. The cantata is a measure of the prostitution of the intellectuals in the Soviet state.

Some have seen in this the beginnings of Russian modernization; it might also be seen as the beginnings of the *nomenklatura*. There was also a social services program: Vladimir

> "invited each beggar and poor man to come to the Prince's palace and receive whatever he needed, both food and drink, and marten–skins from the treasury. With the thought that the weak and the sick could not easily reach his palace, he arranged that wagons should be brought in, and after having them loaded with bread, meat, fish, various fruits, mead in casks, and kvass, he ordered them driven through the city. The drivers were under instructions to call out, 'Where is there a poor man or a beggar who cannot walk?' To such they distributed according to their necessities"

– thus pre–empting Bakunin by nine centuries. Note the inclusion of alcohol: "We cannot live without that pleasure", as Vladimir had told the Moslem Bulgars.

On the law and order front, we are told, the too–fierce pagan was now the too–soft Christian: bandits increased to such an extent through Vladimir's "fear of the sin entailed" in punishing them, that the bishops had to remind him that

> "he was appointed of God for the chastisement of malefaction...,
> but only after due process of law".

It is easy to be too sceptical about some of this. Apart from their hagiographic purpose in attributing them all to Vladimir personally, these benefactions clearly symbolised changes that really did begin to be made in Kievan Rus with the advent of Christianity. Indeed, one might imagine that most were due as much to the efforts of the Church itself; and it was certainly the Church that sustained them.

The list of other princes with whom Vladimir shared good relations is interesting. All three of those western neighbours (the third being in fact Boleslav II of Bohemia, nephew of Good King Wenceslas) were themselves also Christians, though of the Roman rite. More striking of course is the *absence* of any further mention whatsoever of the Emperor Basil II of Byzantium, Vladimir's brother–in–law, or of the relations between Kievan Rus and the Empire over the last quarter–century of

Vladimir's rule.[25] Perhaps this was the ultimate assertion of equality: so solidly founded in the Imperial relationship and their common Christianity that it did not need to be mentioned. Somehow it does not sound like Vladimir, or any of his successors either. Sovereign equality *always* had to be reiterated – unless an assertion of superiority was required, Russian, Orthodox, Imperial, Soviet.

It was in fact a continuous issue, precisely *because* of Vladimir's conversion. Because Byzantine Emperors claimed (even if not always successfully) authority over the Patriarch of Constantinople, the Patriarchate's claim to authority over a daughter church like the Russian was thereby accompanied by Byzantium's claim to political suzerainty over the state as well. This was a constant cause of contention, because it meant that the Emperor as well as the Patriarch would oppose efforts by daughter churches to achieve autocephalous status – ecclesiastical autonomy. Indeed, two years after the conversion of Tsar Boris I of Bulgaria, in 860, he had withdrawn his allegiance from the Patriarch of Constantinople when his demand for an autonomous Bulgarian church was denied, and asked Pope (later Saint) Nicholas I to send him a bishop and priests. The sequel was more farcical than philosophical: the assertive Nicholas responded with alacrity, but gave his legates secret instructions to ensure Bulgarian subjection to Rome; a disillusioned Boris turned again to Constantinople, more hopefully because a palace revolution had replaced both Emperor and Patriarch – only to have the Patriarch's authority reasserted in the same terms as before. It was to be another sixty years before Constantinople recognised a separate Bulgarian Patriarchate.

The Russians were no doubt aware of Bulgaria's ecclesiastical travails. Indeed, Vernadsky has contended that Olga went to Constantinople in the 950s primarily to secure autonomy for a Russian Church; that it was when this was refused that she asked the Holy Roman Emperor for a bishop; and that the short shrift given to Adalbert of Trier in Kiev in 962 was in fact the rejection of Otto's similar

---

25   It is of interest that within ten years of Vladimir's marriage to Anna there was another move by the Ottonians to marry into Basil's family: Otto II, who had been so contemptuously rejected when Liudprand of Cremona presented his suit, now sought his niece Zoe, Constantine's daughter, for his son. This time the proposal was met with enthusiasm, but the young Otto III died before she reached Rome to become Empress of the West. Instead she went on to her scandalous series of Byzantine husbands and to reign over the East.

expectation of both political and ecclesiastical subservience. Whether or not Russian nationalism can be projected that far back, it is clear that avoiding political subservience to Byzantium through the ecclesiastical back door was a constant for Kievan Rus's rulers after they converted to the Orthodox Church; and with the exchange of mutual excommunications between the Byzantine and Roman Churches in 1054, which established what became a permanent division between Orthodoxy and Catholicism, Constantinople's perspective on its Russian offspring required even more vigilance.

However, despite the Russian Church's dependence, especially in the early days, on the Greeks' theological, liturgical, clerical and linguistic assistance, and despite the fact that all but two of its Metropolitans continued to be appointed and consecrated by the Patriarch of Constantinople, Kiev was in the main successful in maintaining its distance in this quiet, sometimes arcane, but always very real standoff. Subservient as the Metropolitans of the Russian Church were to the Grand Dukes of Kiev, even Greek incumbents mostly behaved independently of Constantinople.[26]

An approving 20th century ecclesiastical writer observed that both Greek and Russian Metropolitans were "duly conscious of their rights and obligations". And so were all their successors: Patriarchs, the Holy Synod installed by Peter the Great as a state organ specifically to run the Church for the Tsars, which it did until the Bolshevik Revolution, and the reinstalled post–1943 Patriarchs. The tradition meant that Russia never experienced the conflicts between the ecclesiastical and secular powers that beset the West, to the cost of both and frequently of every one else within shot – but also to the benefit of vigorous theological and political debate, and the eventual separation of Church and State.

The Mongol invasion aided autonomy, as it largely cut off Russia from Byzantium. Further, an extraordinary contribution was made by

---

26 Ironically, the tension between Russian and Greek only exploded centuries later, in the 1660s, when the Russian Church itself sought to introduce reforms to bring it back more closely into line with surviving Greek Orthodox practice. It was the only reformation movement the Russian Church experienced: not surprisingly it was focussed on ritual – centrally, on whether the sign of the cross should be made by two (Russian) or three (Greek) fingers. The Moscow Patriarchate won with the latter, and it produced a permanent split between the main body of the Church and the impenitent Old Believers, who were brutally persecuted by both Romanovs and Church. But they survived them – and their Communist successors.

the Mongols themselves: whether pagan as at first or Islamic after 1313, they not only tolerated the Russian Church but actually exempted its considerable lands from taxation and the men working on them from military conscription. This considerably encouraged the Russian Church's strength as well as independence of Byzantium – though at the price, which Church leaders were almost always prepared to pay, of compromising themselves with their current secular overlords. Formal Church independence of Constantinople only came in 1448 – five years before the Great City's fall to the Ottoman Turks, twenty–four before the Grand Duke Ivan III of Moscow married Sophia Paleologus, niece of the last Emperor of Byzantium, and thirty–two before he repudiated allegiance to the Mongols.

A common religion was no guarantee, then or ever, of peaceful relations. The Emperor Basil II spent fifteen of Vladimir's last years fighting Bulgaria, which he annexed to the Empire in 1018, earning his title of *Bulgaroctonus* – "the Bulgar–slayer" – by blinding thousands of prisoners after his final victory and sending them back to their last Tsar in groups of a hundred, each led by a man left with one eye. There is no suggestion that Vladimir was ever asked for – or offered – additional military support to Basil's long, grinding series of campaigns, beyond the original six thousand Varangians.

Nor is there any sign of any cooperation between the brothers–in–law against the Pechenegs, by now thoroughly entrenched across the steppes north of the Black Sea, though at times during his campaigns Basil tried to employ or buy off these marauders, and for much of the 990s Vladimir was himself fighting them: "He directed an all–Russian struggle against the Pechenegs", the *Great Soviet Encyclopedia* choked out, "in which all strata and classes had an interest". All the Primary Chronicle conceded, even for its hero, was that he "often" overcame them. Most striking was a series of perhaps a hundred protective forts and five hundred kilometres of ramparts that he built against them. As a *bylina* boasted:

> "Not a rider will ride through,
> Not a footsoldier will march through,
> Not a beast will run through,
> Not a bird will fly through,
> And, if it does, not without losing a feather". [V]

Vladimir's authority and legitimacy were confirmed by the minting of coins, in gold and silver, the first ever in Russia. Their roughness has led to the conclusion that, with typical chauvinism, he had them made by Russian rather than Byzantine craftsmen; but they still display him crowned with a Byzantine–style Imperial diadem. There is no mistaking the origin of the blunt inscription:

HERE IS VLADIMIR ON HIS THRONE. AND THIS IS HIS GOLD.

And the portrait of Vladimir – the long gloomy face, bushy eyebrows, large staring eyes, huge drooping moustache – immediately brings to mind Leo Diaconus's description of his father Svyatopolk, come to meet the Emperor John Tzimisces on the banks of the Danube all those years ago.[27]

Vladimir himself died in 1015, four years after Anna. The year before, his second oldest surviving son, Yaroslav, governor in Novgorod, had suddenly refused to pay the annual tax to Kiev. "Repair roads and build bridges", Vladimir exclaimed, intending to attack him, but he died first, at his summer residence at Berestovo, now near the Monastery of the Caves but then outside Kiev.

> "But his death was kept secret, for Svyatopolk [his eldest son] was in Kiev. But at night his companions took up the flooring between two rooms, and after wrapping the body in a rug, they let it down to the earth with ropes. After they had placed it on a sledge, they took it away and laid it in the Church of the Virgin that Vladimir himself had built. When the people heard of this, they assembled in multitude and mourned him, the boyars as the defender of their country, the poor as their protector and benefactor. They placed him in a marble coffin, and buried the body of the sainted Prince amid their mourning".

Vladimir's ignominious initial conveyance was presumably a reflection of concern about the intentions of the illegitimate Svyatopolk, the son of the Greek nun – "from a sinful root evil fruit is produced", the *Chronicle* thundered at his birth; "filled with lawlessness", "impious and evil". And it was no doubt this fear that led the chronicler to lament that

> "If we had been zealous for [Vladimir], and had offered our prayers to God in his behalf upon the day of his death, then God, beholding our zeal, would have glorified him".

---

27   Volkoff reproduces three coins from the Hermitage Museum, St Petersburg.

It seems a fitting footnote to a history so full of gaps that the date of Vladimir's canonization has not been preserved. While some think it occurred about the middle of the 11th century, the earliest written reference to him as a Saint and *Isapostolos*, "Equal of the Apostles", did not come until 1254, fourteen years after the fall of Kiev to the Mongols.

The great days of Kievan Rus

The great days of Kievan Rus, after Vladimir's death, were marked – despite the difficulties posed by the vast distances – by a rapid interplay with Europe that Russia has never seen to the same extent since. His effective successor was his son Yaroslav the Wise (reigned 1019–1054), the sixth of Vladimir's twelve sons. He first had to overcome his older surviving brother, Svyatopolk the Accursed, ruling in Kiev, who had by then eliminated three other brothers, giving rise in this familial bloodletting to the creation of the two who went most meekly, Boris and Gleb, as the first home–grown and home–slain Saints of the new Russian Church, even before their founder father had been elevated to this heavenly company. None of this brawling brood was the offspring of the fastidious *Porphyrogenita* Anna.

The quiet that descended on Kievan Rus's relations with Byzantium was broken only once, in 1043, when Yaroslav the Wise sent a fleet against the scandalous and profligate Empress Zoe and her Co–Empress sister, Theodora – nieces of Vladimir's Anna – and the third of Zoe's three Emperor husbands, Constantine IX Monomachus. Why Yaroslav did so is very unclear: possibly he was responding to some Byzantine slight or pretension, perhaps even a theological one; possibly he thought, unwisely, that with Byzantium's Court lost in luxury, and most of the borders under attack, he could make some gains, though to what end is hard even to guess at. But, in a curious echo of Romanus Lecapenus's response to the Russian attack a hundred years before in 941, Michael Psellus says his employer the Emperor Constantine IX had to "gather together some hulks of the old fleet" to resist the Russians; and then their fleet was again destroyed by storm and Greek Fire. A few men managed to get to shore, and

> "a great massacre of barbarians took place and a veritable stream of blood reddened the sea: one might well believe it came down the rivers off the mainland".

Until the Mongols invaded a century later, Russia and Byzantium did not fight again; by the time Russia was finally independent of the Mongols,

Byzantium no longer existed. Thereafter its successor Ottoman Empire and Russia fought all the time, periodically troubling all Europe right up to the beginning of last century.

Yaroslav was a builder: of Kiev, notably, as we shall see later, but also of alliances. There remained a strong Norse connection: he himself married a daughter of Olaf Sköttkonung, the first King of Sweden, who had converted to Christianity in 995. But he cast his net much wider. Making political advantage from his Christian credentials Yaroslav married his sister to Casimir I of Poland, two of his three daughters to Henry I of France (who, being illiterate, used his Russian wife as his secretary) and to Andrew I of Hungary, and sons to three German princesses and one Byzantine, from the Monomachus family of Zoe's Constantine. Billington has noted in *The Icon and the Axe* that these promising openings to Western Europe were never made secure: instead, Russia was continually drawn eastwards "into a debilitating struggle for control of the Eurasian steppe". Even before the Mongols arrived the number of Western marriages was declining; afterwards it would take until the 18th century before the reintroduction of a notable and eventually fateful line of German princesses into the Romanov family.

Yaroslav also gave refuge at his court to King Olaf II Haraldson of Norway, who, less lucky or tough than Vladimir, was kicked out when he tried to forcibly convert his own stubborn countrymen, apparently less easily pushed into rivers than Russians. Olaf went on to become a Catholic Saint; but Norwegian politics being what they were, Yaroslav ended up giving asylum as well to Olaf's two successors, his son Magnus the Good, and his half–brother Harald Hardrada the Ruthless – who married Yaroslav's third daughter.

Harald was called the "Thunderbolt from the North" by the German chronicler Adam of Bremen: he had fought in Olaf's losing battle as a fifteen–year–old; then for Yaroslav the Wise, against Poland; and then, already a legendary warrior, with the Varangian Guard for Byzantium, in the Greek islands, Asia Minor, the Caucasus, Bulgaria and Palestine, where he apparently made a pilgrimage to Jerusalem. In a precursor to the Crusades, he and the Guard also fought against the Moslems in Sicily, in the Bronte area on the western foothills of Mount Etna, bestowed in 1799 by a much later King of Sicily on Lord Nelson after his victory in the Battle of the Nile. The scandalous Empress Zoe wanted to marry Harald, in between her other three husbands, but Harald had unfinished business in Scandinavia. By 1047 he had gained the whole of Norway, but still not content, fought for the next seventeen years for a piece of Denmark. The Thunderbolt of the North had only one battle left, and this time he lost: he was killed, trying to invade England with his Norwegian Vikings in 1066, by Harold of England, at Stamford Bridge in the north, only nineteen days before Harold himself was killed at Hastings in the south in William the Conqueror's successful Norman Viking invasion.[28]

Harold of England's family fled to Denmark after Hastings; and his grand–daughter Princess Gytha married the last great leader of Kievan Rus, Vladimir II, known as Monomakh after his Byzantine mother, the niece of Zoe's third husband Constantine Monomachus. It was during this Vladimir's reign between 1113 and 1125 that the *Primary Chronicle* was given the form we have been following. One wonders what Gytha made of its sole reference to her ancestral country, included right near the beginning among Japheth's lot:

> "In Britain, many men sleep with one woman, and likewise many women have intercourse with one man. The people carry on without jealousy or restraint the vicious customs of their ancestors".

There was one last flirtation with Rome. Yaroslav the Wise was succeeded in 1054 by his eldest surviving son, Izyaslav; but Rurikid stability now came under challenge again when first, a distant cousin, and then his next younger brother, Svyatoslav, usurped the throne. In 1075, shortly after his second deposition, Izyaslav turned up in Mainz, on the Rhine, at the court of the Holy Roman Emperor Henry IV, seeking support. It was the first visit to Western Europe by a Russian leader, and the only one asking for rescue. But it was not successful,

---

28   There is a curious connexion between Harald Hardrada's successor as King of Norway, his son Olaf III, "Olaf Kyrre the Peaceful", and the Viking intrusion into North America that took place just after Leif Ericsson's voyage there during Vladimir of Kiev's reign. Following Leif's discovery, a Greenlander settlement was established in "Vinland" about 1008, but it only lasted three years, and exploration efforts only a further ten; then all was silence. The search for the site of the settlement lasted far longer; but eventually, in 1960, the remains of a Viking village which could match what is known of Vinland was found at a place called (with delightful Canadian bilingualism) L'Anse–aux–Meadows, near the shore at the tip of Newfoundland's Northern Peninsula. Until now, despite innumerable searches, only one other piece of Viking remains has been discovered in North America: a coin, found at an American Indian site in Maine, from the reign, between 1066 and 1093, of Olaf Kyrre the Peaceful.

either because Henry was preoccupied with Western struggles which led him the following year to declare the new Pope Gregory VII deposed, or because brother Svyatoslav bribed him, according to the chronicler Lambert of Hersfeld, with

> "more gold and silver and fine garments than anybody could remember ever having been brought into the German kingdom at one time".

The throne of Kievan Rus was obviously worth hanging onto.

Izyaslav then sent a son to Rome to seek the support of the Pope himself, a startling move only twenty–one years after the Great Schism between Rome and Constantinople: the Abbot of the Monastery of the Caves, the future Saint Theodosius, had personally instructed Izyaslav

> "not to join the Latin faith; not to adopt their customs; to avoid their communion; to avoid all their teachings; to despise their traditions...If they ask food or drink from us in God's name, give them some but in their bowls; if they have no bowls, give them some in our bowls, but then wash and pray, for they do not believe rightly and their habits are unclean: they eat with dogs and cats... They eat lions and wild horses and asses and strangled animals and carrion and bears and beavers and beavers' tails, and during Lent they eat meat after dipping it in water...When they sin, they do not ask forgiveness from God, it is their priests who forgive them for a consideration ...they go to war and they serve wafers..." [V],

and so on. Things must have been desperate to risk one's son to such a diet.

It is not surprising there was later speculation that Izyaslav had been expelled from Kiev in the first place because of pro–Roman inclinations. Gregory, who was later canonized, was an ambitiously zealous and powerful reformer; he shaped the entire future of the Catholic Church through his assertion of universal jurisdiction over all religious and lay members of the Church, and not least over temporal rulers, whom he claimed the Papacy was able to excommunicate – and thereby deprive of their rights as well as their thrones – at will. The Austrian Catholic historian Friedrich Heer asserts that Gregory

> "planned to build up a European league of peoples in the form of one great European system of vassalage, in which individual states would be bound to St Peter by legal–political ties";

and it was in this context that the Pope responded to Izyaslav's approach by offering the "protective relationship" of the Papacy.[29] But nothing came of this either, perhaps because Izyaslav regained Kiev, though only briefly before being killed in battle with a nephew; or perhaps his interest in Rome was only ever mercenary.

It was about this time that the German monk Adam of Bremen, in the "description of the islands of the north" in his *History of the Archbishops of Hamburg–Bremen*, described the city of Kiev as "the rival of Constantinople's realm" – and made the earliest known reference to Leif Ericsson's Vinland. Within fifty years, having withstood the menace of the Pechenegs, Kiev was cut off from Byzantium and its markets by – still they come! – the next barbarian wave, the Turkic Kipchaks, known also as Cumans, but by the Russians as Polovtsi. It was their defeat of Prince Igor of Novgorod that gave birth to the epic poem *The Song of Igor's Campaign*:

> "...Kiev groaned in sorrow,
> and so did Chernigov in adversity;
> anguish spread flowing
> over the Russian land;
> abundant woe made its way
> midst the Russian land,
> while the princes forged discord
> against their own selves,
> while the pagans, with victories
> prowling over the Russian land,
> took tribute...
> from every homestead".[30]

It was the first great work of Russian literature and the only one known from before the Mongol invasion. It is known in the West mostly through having inspired Borodin's richly musical, sprawling, great opera *Prince Igor*, source of the concert–hall "Polovtsian Dances" that have made the name of Igor's victors even better known than his.

---

29 Heer adds the interesting observation that "the last pope to entertain this vision of the nations combining under papal leadership was Pius XII", when, as Cardinal Secretary attending a World Eucharistic Congress in Budapest in 1938, he proposed, with a reference to Gregory VII, a crusade directed primarily against...Soviet Russia.

30 Tr. Nabokov: *Op. cit.*

As Rus disintegrated into rival principalities through Rurikid family rivalries like those that preceded the rise to power of both the first Vladimir and then his son Yaroslav the Wise, and that next undermined the latter's son Izyaslav, Kiev's position inexorably declined. Both state and Church power in due course shifted northeast, first to Vladimir–Suzdal, and then, during the Mongol occupation, to Moscow. It was claimed that by the end of Kievan Rus there were ten thousand churches and two hundred monasteries; and it was the Church that was more responsible than the princes for sustaining Russian identity through the centuries of darkness. In a later proverb Moscow was proclaimed the heart of Russia, which it has remained ever since; half a millennium later again, Tsar Peter's St Petersburg, opening on to the Baltic and Western Europe, became, for two hundred and seventeen years – and is still, in the view of its inhabitants – the head. It was Moscow which forged the unified Russian state, St Petersburg which created the Russian Empire that stretched to Central Asia and the Pacific, Vladimir's Church which cemented and upheld their prerogative.

Ritual
The Church's fixation on ritual, however, deprived Russians of theological argument, the idea of questioning dogma, the experience of debate about received opinion and challenges to it. This rigidity extended into the fields of government and administration, producing political conformity as well, as the consequence of the Church's role as the handmaid and instrument of the rulers of the state – a role Vladimir had intended it for, and from which it resiled for only the brief period of (severe) persecution between the Bolshevik Revolution and Stalin's call in 1943 to resume it, to which it responded with alacrity and which it then maintained until the death of the Soviet Union.

The result was a pernicious symbiosis: it was not simply that authority – Church, Romanov dynasty, Communist Party – did not need to adapt itself to critical review; it was also that few people – 17th century Old Believers, 19th century Westernizers and Anarchists, 20th century Bolsheviks and Soviet dissidents – developed the capacity to criticize the bases of authority. The Communists' repeated doctrinal squabbles were not an exception to this: as their deadly outcomes revealed, they were the disguise for unremitting power plays. As authority ossified, oppression accumulated.

There has often been a view that the Russians have been somehow predisposed to acceptance of dictatorship, the result of the long Mongol occupation which induced a supposedly "Asiatic" cast of mind, or simply the inevitable result of their long subjection to autocratic Tsar and shorter–term Commissar. Military centralization was certainly essential to resist and eventually expel the Mongols; political centralization was ruthlessly maintained by Romanovs and Communists because they preferred it. But I simply do not believe the Russian people are innately subservient or servile. Obviously, when orthodoxy was enforced by persecution, fear was a powerful disincentive to criticism and change. But even when persecution and fear are removed, as has been happening since the fall of the Soviet Union a mere twenty years ago, the development of a more open society and government requires those skills that the long reign of authoritarian ritual–centred Church and Party prevented the people from learning: questioning received wisdom and challenging authority based on it, pushing authority itself to encourage debate. And finding the courage to use those skills in the face of the ecclesiastical and secular ideologues who continue to try to stop them.

Under the Soviet system the Church suffered brutal persecution, like every other vestige of the old regime; but, like other churches in the face of tyrants throughout history, it attached supreme importance to survival. In his last testament in 1925, the Patriarch Tikhon, who had been installed after the abolition of Peter the Great's Holy Synod following the downfall of the Tsar, and was known as anti–Soviet, nevertheless abjured the faithful:

"Without sinning against our faith or against our Church, refusing any concession, any compromise in the sphere of faith, it is advisable, as citizens, to be loyal to Soviet authority, and to work for the common good".

The period of repression matched the Church to its long hesychast tradition: unknown ascetics saving the world by prayer.

Then, in the darkest days of World War II, Stalin called on old–fashioned Great Russian patriotism in the desperate resistance to the Nazi invasion; and this included a reconciliation with the Church, with useful resonance not only nationalistically, but also with Russia's Western Allies. The Church, which was allowed in 1943 to install a new Patriarch, responded enthusiastically, even to the point, Alexander Werth reported, of saying special prayers for Stalin, one Metropolitan referring to him as "our common Father". There was more than an element of farce when Stalin himself told the British Ambassador that "in his own way, he also believed in God". The Church remained useful to the Soviet State throughout the Cold War. In the middle of it, Alexander Sozhenitsyn wrote on 17 March 1972, in a letter to the Patriarch of Moscow:

> "Do not allow us to suppose, do not force us to think that for the bishops of the Russian church, earthly authority is higher than heavenly authority, earthly responsibility more terrifying than responsibility to God."

At a time when the trapdoor to the West was kept slammed shut in the postwar Stalinist period, then under Khrushchev and Brezhnev, the only Russians allowed through it were Church leaders, and others, promoting the Peace Movement, designed to encourage the disarmament of the Western, though not the Soviet, Alliance. It was not until Gorbachev's policy of *perestroika*, in the late 1980s, that this one-way mirror began to be turned into a two–way door for the Russian people.

There can be no doubt that during their terrible decades of suffering and degredation, cynically inflicted in the supposed cause of a glorious future, the dead manufactured in almost equal numbers by repeated Soviet brutality and sudden German savagery, many Russians found considerable comfort in the Church's long and abiding emphasis on the consolations of prayer. But not, as can be seen from the despairing cry by the deeply devout Solzhenitsyn, from the Church. Christianity failed in the face of Communism as it did in the face of Fascism and Nazism.

The role of ritual in the Church had the effect of encouraging acquiescence – even contentment – through the comforting or numbing repetitive observation of familiar outward forms. The Soviet Communists knew this very well, and cleverly adapted some of those forms to their own doctrines. First, adoration of the godlike leader – one of his earliest collaborators remarked on "an aura of 'chosenness' about Lenin". It was reinforced after his death by the incorruptible body in its marble reliquary in Red Square, just like that of St Sergius in its silver sarcophagus (presented by Ivan the Terrible) at the Patriarchal seat in Sergeiev–Zalesky (Soviet Zagorsk). Lenin became tsar–patriarch of Soviet Russia; by the end of the Soviet period he was also the new Christ, especially after Stalin, tsar–patriarch for nearly thirty years, who had ruthlessly purged almost everyone as apostates, was found to have been the antichrist.

It was a transfer of the cult of personality from someone who had turned out to be, after all, only a man, to one who was living Man.

There was the profusion of sculptured images and photographic icons, the badges of "Baby Lenin", the paintings of Lenin suffering the little children to come unto him, and on and on, with a Stalin interlude. Christ–like, Lenin also transcended death: we have a retrospective collection of devotional poems, published in 1986 while we were living in Moscow, entitled *Ever Among the Living*. Liturgically, the Communist Party used the repeated invocation of the key texts and precepts from a body of sacred literature containing revealed truth, from kindergarten – in front of altar–like "Lenin corners" – through the Komsomol youth movement, to incessant Party and workplace meetings, and on a calendar of Soviet feast days. And there was the confessional, individual and en masse, before the most powerful, pervasive and predatory inquisition the world has ever known, from which there was never absolution.

Late in the Soviet era the writer Alexander Zinoviev cried, in *The Yawning Heights*, "But when will all this end?"; and answered despairingly: "Not before people stop queuing at the tomb of the Teacher". The queues are no longer as long, no longer compulsory; but the embalmed body still lies in the second Holy Sepulchre in Red Square, up against the Kremlin wall, appropriately, inevitably, by the *Spasskaia Bashnya* – the Saviour Gate.

In the new Russia there is no orthodoxy, but a fetid scramble of the new and some of the old re–presented as new, the honest, the crooked, the opportunist, all seeking salvation – or profits or power. Some see the new Russia as a normal country, as in some ways it is, even with all this, and they want a normal place in the world. Some want a return to old values – but whose? – and still see a unique destiny – but what? The Russian Church has allied itself with the Slavophile nationalists, old chauvinists become new xenophobes. It is more part of the problem than of the solution.

Epitaph for Kievan Rus

"On February 11 of this year, there was a portent in the Crypt Monastery [in Kiev]. A fiery pillar appeared which reached from earth to heaven; lightnings illuminated the whole countryside, and thunder was heard in the sky at the first hour of the night. The whole populace beheld the miracle. The pillar first stood over the stone refectory, so that its cross could not be seen. Then it moved a little, reached the church, and halted over the tomb of Theodosius. Then it rose, as if facing to the eastward, and forthwith became invisible. This portent was not an actual pillar of fire, but an angelic manifestation...For an angel appears wherever there are blessed abodes and houses of prayer..."

The year was 1110, and this was the last entry in the *Primary Chronicle*. But the pillar of fire was a portent of something else for Kievan Rus. Yaroslav the Wise's far–flung dynastic ties contributed to the fortunes of Kiev as the major trading centre between Scandinavia and Byzantium, but it was brought low by the continued squabbles of his descendants. As we have noted, power drifted northwards, fragmenting into a whole collection of small Russian principalities. In 1099 the capture of the Holy Land by the First Crusade[31] reopened the Mediterranean trade route from Western Europe, side–lining the route through Russia. Then the defeat of Byzantium in 1204 by the West European Christians supposedly on their Fourth Crusade against the Saracens seriously undermined what remained of Kiev's trading position.

The Mongols first appeared on the eastern horizon in 1223: a few of the divided princes combined with the Polovtsi to attack them, after executing envoys offering a deal, and success in a minor skirmish led to an imprudent dash which came up against the main Mongol army. The result was total disaster, but after pursuing the fleeing Rus back towards the Dnieper the Mongols were called back east: Genghis Khan had learned what he wanted to know. Their sudden arrival and sudden disappearance unsettled the Russians: a chronicler wrote

"We do not know where these evil Tartars came from and whither they went; only God knows".

Then the fury of the Mongol invasion in 1240 ended everything. Six years later, the Italian missionary Fra Giovanni da Pian del Carpino, on his way to the Khan's headquarters on the Don before his own epic pre–Marco Polo voyage to China, passed by Yaroslav's great city of six hundred churches and described what had happened. As first published in English in 1598–1600 by the historical geographer Richard Hakluyt, somewhat quixotically in his *"The Principal Navigations Voyages Traffiques and Discoveries of the English Nation Made by Sea or Over-land to the Remote and Farthest Distant Quarters of the Earth at any*

---

31   See 1100 chapter: Godefroy de Bouillon

time within the compasse of these 1600 Yeeres"[32], Fra Giovanni said that the Tartars

> "set forward against Russia, and made foule havocke there, destroying cities and castles and murthering the people. They layd siege a long while unto Kiow the chiefe citie of Russia, and at length they tooke it and slue the citizens. Whereupon, traveiling through that countrey, wee found an innumerable multitude of dead mens skulles and bones lying upon the earth. For it was a very large and populous citie, but it is nowe in a maner brought to nothing: for there doe scarce remaine 200 houses, the inhabitants whereof are kept in extreme bondage".

The land of Kievan Rus around Kiev itself was Mongol for a century. After that it became Lithuanian, then Polish, Cossack, Russian, Polish/Russian, Russian/Austro–Hungarian, tossed from one oppressor to the next, carved up, divided, rearranged. Somehow it developed a Ukrainian identity that provided it with a brief independence after the fall of the Romanovs; but it was then overrun by Germans and Austrians until the end of World War I, became independent again but fought over by Whites and Reds and Poles, then engulfed by the Soviet Union. Consciously or unconsciously echoing the *Primary Chronicle*'s pillar of fire over Kiev, in 1924 Mikhail Bulgakov concluded *The White Guard*, his book on his beloved city during those last convulsions, like this:

> "Above the bank of the Dnieper the midnight cross of St Vladimir thrust itself above the sinful, bloodstained, snowbound earth toward the grim, black sky. From far away it looked as if the cross–piece had vanished, had merged with the upright, turning the cross into a sharp and menacing sword.
>
> But the sword is not fearful. Everything passes away – suffering, pain, blood, hunger and pestilence. The sword will pass away too, but the stars will still remain when the shadows of our presence and our deeds have vanished from the earth. There is no man who does not know that. Why, then, will we not turn our eyes toward the stars? Why?"

---

32 Reprinted by the Hakluyt Society: Vol.1 (Glasgow 1903)

Well, we did not. Less than ten years later the Ukraine was devastated by Stalin's agricultural sovietization, seventeen years later by Nazi invasion and the fearful campaigns to win it back for the Soviet Union. Not everything has passed away; but Kiev has survived. And in 1991, happily without a shot being fired, Ukraine became independent again – happily or not remains to be seen. But whether the capital of the Ukraine is still the mother of Russian cities seems moot: perhaps more, now, a widowed aunt.

The remains of Kievan Rus: a short journey

Kiev

The places we think of as quintessentially Russian are in Moscow: the Kremlin and its cathedrals, St Basil's in Red Square. But Kiev and Novgorod were already three hundred years old before Moscow was founded in the mid–12th century. The Moscow Kremlin was not begun for another three hundred years after that, after the fall of Constantinople and Russia's liberation from the Mongols – and it is interesting to note that the earliest and largest of the Kremlin cathedrals, the *Uspensky Sobor*, the Cathedral of the Assumption, was built for Ivan the Terrible's father in the late 1470s by an *Italian* architect, Alberti Fioraventi, imported from Bologna (and nicknamed "Aristotle" by his admiring Russian colleagues). St Basil's came a hundred years later again, about the time the dome of St Peter's in Rome was completed and Breughel was immortalising life in Flanders. St Petersburg was of course still another century and a half away, built by Peter the Great in the first years of the 18th century, just as Yale College was being founded and Buckingham Palace was begun.

You can still find glimpses of Kievan Rus in Kiev; but they are also in Novgorod, 180 kilometres south of St Petersburg; and in Vladimir, about the same distance to the east of Moscow. They do not show how the people lived at that time: all that has long since disappeared – except, perhaps as could still be seen in the 1980s, in remote villages in the forests, where small wooden houses, *izbas*, huddle beside muddy or frozen tracks, wood stacked beside them for cooking and heating, small fields are still prepared for spring planting with horse–drawn ploughs, and drab–clad people are small and defeated–looking from the ungrateful daily grind. The glimpses of ancient Kievan Rus are mostly of how magnificently the rulers and their entourages and probably some of the townspeople worshipped; and they are all well worth the excursion.

Almost all that remains of Vladimir's Kiev from around 1000 is the site: the long, heavily wooded northern bank of the River Dnieper, looking out across the vast lowland steppe spreading away to the south; and the hilltop near the 18th century blue and white and gold Baroque confection of St Andrew's Cathedral (designed by Rastrelli, another Italian), where Vladimir established the original fortress of Kiev, which his son Yaroslav the Wise expanded southwest along the plateau to where he built the St Sophia Cathedral.

In fact the site is not quite all that remains: on the highest part of the plateau, the flat hilltop just to the south of St Andrew's, you can see the excavated outline of the foundations of the Church of the Tithe, the very first structure in Russia to have been built of stone, bricks and mortar. It was known as the *Desiatinnaya*, "the Tenth", because Vladimir endowed it with a tenth of his income when he built it between 989 and 996. It is a simple plan, showing a basically square–sided church whose internal aisles formed a cross, the centre of which, symbolising the centre of the universe, was undoubtedly surmounted as in Byzantium by a dome whose interior was painted with the image of Christ *Pantocrator*, the Saviour. It was to be the pattern of all Russia's churches; so that Vladimir's visual legacy, so small in stone, survives in so many places in spirit.

Yaroslav the Wise was the great builder of Kievan Rus, using the visual grandeur of architecture and fresco to strengthen the people's bonds to the Church. He began the construction in stone and brick of Russia's oldest buildings, the two Cathedrals of St Sophia: that in Kiev between 1037–1049, consciously designed to compete with Constantinople's Hagia Sophia; that in Novgorod between 1045–1050. It was more than a century before the foundation stone of Notre Dame in Paris was laid by Pope Alexander III, the first lawyer to become Pope. By the end of Yaroslav's reign there were said to be six hundred churches in Kiev, though many were undoubtedly only of wood, and the figure may be closer to piety than reality.

The Cathedral of St Sophia, the *Sofisky Sobor*,[33] now a bit lost in the 19th and 20th century structures of the Upper Town, is Yaroslav's great masterpiece, the first testimony to the Russian Church's manifestation of theology in art and architecture. The design was an elaboration on the Tithe Church, appropriate for this Russian successor to its magnificent

---

33 Known, when we were there in Soviet times, as the "St Sophia Museum Complex of History and Architecture".

namesake in Constantinople. The exterior now has bits and pieces that were added to it over the centuries: the thirteen domes – the central one for Christ, the others for his twelve Disciples – increased to nineteen, their cupolas converted to helmet shapes, a new front, the whole plastered and whitewashed like so many Russian churches, except for patches on the apse walls which have been cleared back to their original stone and flat red brick construction inherited from Byzantium.

It is in the interior that the 11th century comes alive, the dark aisles vanquished by the brilliance of the crossing under the high dome; the end of the nave, the whole Cathedral, dominated by the great six–metre–high mosaic, on the vault of the central apse behind and above the iconostasis, of the *Virgin Orans*, a brilliant, blue–robed figure in its gleaming, golden archway, praying for this people down through the centuries. The walls were once covered in fresco – "painted without human hands", it was said, "by artists whose brushes were guided only by God".

In St Sophia they were also guided by God's local representative: they included portraits painted during their lifetime of Yaroslav the Wise and his Swedish wife Ingigerd, together with their children. Not surprisingly they have fared less well than the mosaics: the wall with Yaroslav and Ingigerd was removed as recently as the 18th century – official vandalism is by no means an invention of the 20th. Only five royal children are left in fresco now; one wonders how long any of these young innocents survived the fratricidal war that followed Yaroslav's death, like the one from which he had himself emerged the victor after Vladimir died.

In the stair–towers there are, surprisingly, purely secular frescoes: some of Imperial Constantinople, but others of everyday court life with musicians and dancing buffoons, and scenes of royal hunts. The latter – such as "The Bear Hunt", and "Attack of an Enraged Animal" – must have reflected Yaroslav's interests, and they find a striking echo in a passage of the *Testament* of his grandson Vladimir Monomakh[34]:

"I have made a practice of hunting a hundred times a year with all my strength, and without harm...Two bisons tossed me and my horse on their horns, a stag once gored me, one elk stamped upon me, while another gored me, a boar once tore my sword from my thigh, a bear on one occasion bit my kneecap, and another wild

---

34 Published with Cross's *Primary Chronicle*

beast jumped on my flank and threw my horse with me. But God preserved me unharmed.

I often fell from my horse, fractured my skull twice, and in my youth injured my arms and legs when I did not reck of my life or spare my head. In war and at the hunt, by night and day, in heat and cold, I did whatever my servant had to do, and gave myself no rest".
These Rurikids did not easily lose their Viking character.

Kiev's other great remnant of the 11th century is the *Pecherskaya Lavra*, the Monastery of the Caves (also known as the Crypt Monastery)[35], scattered among the trees along the great wooded bank sloping down to the Dnieper a little to the south of the Old City, near the summer residence where Vladimir died. The earliest parts are essentially the caves after which the monastery is named, where the founder monks took up residence shortly before the end of Yaroslav's reign; only the ruins remain of the first building, the Cathedral of the Assumption, consecrated in 1089: it was blown up by the Germans on 3 November 1941. The other churches, the refectory, the dormitories, the Metropolitan's palace, were built over later centuries, from the twelfth to the nineteenth.

But the sanctity of the Monastery derives primarily from the occupants of the two labyrinths of caves, the Near Caves towards the top of the hillside, the Far Caves below, each with three twelfth–century underground churches. These catacombs are by no means as extensive as those of the early Christian martyrs in Rome; and they are not like the charnel houses at St Catherine's Monastery in Sinai, with their fastidious stacks of carefully sorted skulls and femurs and so on; because of the physical properties of the Kievan caves, the bodies buried there are "incorruptible". The Near Caves of St Anthony contain the bodies of seventy–three saints, dressed in costly vestments, lying in open coffins, like mummies. Amongst them is the Monk Nestor, the precursor to whom the *Primary Chronicle* was for so long attributed.

Novgorod
The only city in Russia to avoid the scourge of the Mongols' first invasion and subsequent two centuries of their hegemony was Novgorod,

---

35 The Monastery was also turned into a museum by the Soviets, but in 1988 Gorbachev handed it back to the Church at the time of the commemoration of the latter's millennium. The Patriarch of Constantinople was invited to the celebrations, but declined to attend; the Pope was not invited.

known reverentially and almost anthropomorphically as Lord Novgorod the Great. Originally, as we have seen, under the same Rurikid rule as the rest of Kievan Rus, in the 12th century it asserted its independence from Kiev under a ruler elected initially by a popular assembly, which was in due course supplanted by an oligarchy of its highly successful merchants. Early in 1238, when Batu Khan's great campaign swept up from southern Russia, destroying in succession Riazan, insignificant Moscow and rich Vladimir, it headed northwest towards Novgorod; but the Mongol attempts to drive on the city were foiled by the weather: not the snow and ice that so hampered Napoleon and Hitler, but the spring thaw, which turned the surrounding countryside into a huge boggy marsh. The Mongols turned back a hundred kilometres short of their objective. They did not return – until the Muscovites brought them more than two centuries later – turning instead to the total destruction of Kiev, and to marauding even further westwards, across Lithuania, Poland, Hungary, Austria, and northern Italy: it was recorded that Batu's campfires could be seen from the Campanile of San Marco in Venice, and it was not then as high as it is now.

New threats now came from the north and west: at the same time as Kiev was being overrun Novgorod's then reigning prince, Alexander Nevsky, defeated a Swedish invasion at the River Neva, which earned him his sobriquet; two years later he turned back an attack by the Teutonic Knights in the Battle on the Ice, celebrated by Sergei Eisenstein in his 1938 movie "Alexander Nevsky".[36] Nevertheless within ten years Nevsky was obliged to submit to the Mongols' suzerainty; but Novgorod itself was never occupied by them.

It was thus spared the depredation and ruin wrought on Rus's other ancient cities, and you can still gain a very good sense of the balance it developed between prince and merchants. The centre is still no bigger than it was centuries ago. Like most ancient towns it is on a river, but unlike many it was built from the start on both sides, so there are two old areas facing each other across the swift flood or the ice. On the west bank of the River Volkhov is the *Detinets*, the Novgorod Kremlin: its

---

36 In making the film about this early Russian hero Eisenstein clearly had in mind pleasing Stalin, then at the height of his Great Purges. Amusingly, in 1942, to boost old–fashioned un–Soviet Russian patriotism in the face of the German invasion, Stalin re–established the "Order of Alexander Nevsky" originally established by Peter the Great's widow and successor, the Empress Catherine I, but abolished in 1917 by Lenin.

huge brick walls replaced the original Varangian walls between the early 14th and late 15th centuries, surrounding the Cathedral of St Sophia – begun in 1045 before its namesake in Kiev was finished – and the ecclesiastical quarter.[37] Directly opposite, on the lower eastern shore, is the *Torgovaya*, literally the trade side, from which the self–governing Novgorod merchants did business all across the Baltic and as far as England.

From the Torgovaya side the great brick circuit of the *Detinets* appears to be floating above the river, with above it again the massive white bulk of St Sophia's, crowned by its golden central dome stretching upwards as the Novgorodians liked their churches to do. From the Kremlin side, four 12th century churches, tall and white and silver–domed, rise in the Torgovaya between the river and the lake beyond, above the long white arcade of the *Gostinny Dvor*, an 18th century marker of the ancient marketplace. Upstream, other monasteries and small churches dot the placid banks of the Volkhov towards Lake Ilmen, near where in 1471 Ivan III, perfidiously using the Mongols as allies, made the first of Moscow's attempts to destroy Novgorod's independence. He eventually succeeded, and compounded Novgorod's disaster by purging its cosmopolitan elite and enforcing the mass deportation of the majority of its citizens to Moscow – two firsts in what were to become two long and bloody Russian serials.

Vladimir

Vladimir, to the north–east of Moscow, owed its origin to a fortress built in 1108 by Vladimir Monomakh, Yaroslav's grandson. By then Rus was well and truly split between the Rurikids. His son (by the Anglo–Saxon Gytha) and eventual successor, Yuri, only held Kiev for two years. He achieved fame, however, as Yuri Dolgoruki, "Long–Arm", for founding distant Moscow in 1147, also with a fortress, where the Kremlin now stands. But the decisive shift was made by Yuri's son, Andrei Bogolyubsky, "the God–loving", who, convinced that Kiev was no longer viable, moved the capital to Vladimir in the 1150s as a better–located base for re–establishing central control of Rus.

---

37 In one of the great thick–walled brick towers of the Novgorod Kremlin, in the late Soviet period, when it was hard to find anything really edible in Russia's few restaurants, there was, wildly improbable as it seemed, a charming and excellent little restaurant. It has gone, along with the bureaucratic machine that no doubt, somehow, authorised it.

He was not to succeed: it would only be the Grand Duke Ivan IV, the Terrible, of Moscow who would eventually become Tsar of All the Russias in 1547 – a century after the Metropolitan of Moscow had declared the independence of the Russian Church from the Greek. However Andrei had underlined the significance of the permanent eclipse of Kiev by bearing northwards Russia's protector, the *Vladimir Mother of God* icon, which was eventually, like everything else, to be taken by Moscow.[38]

In the late afternoon of a clear winter's day, the temperature perhaps minus twenty degrees but the air absolutely still, there is a magical view of old Vladimir from the high ridge to the south of the River Klyasma: smoke from the gingerbread–decorated wooden houses in the valley mingling with a rising mist from the river; above, the snow–covered northern bank rising up to the high plateau of the old citadel; and surmounting that again, the lofty forms of the Uspensky and Dmitrievsky Cathedrals, their white stone a pale shade of gold in the weak last rays of the sun; and the five gilded cupolas of the first and the single one of the second still glinting brightly against the blank, faded, almost lilac, white of the enormous sky. In the absolute stillness there arises from among the almost invisible houses, below the smoky mist, the bark of a dog, the voice of a mother calling children inside. Vladimir could have been like this in the four decades between the completion of the Cathedrals, right at the end of Kievan Rus, and the arrival of the Mongol hordes. Now, since the end of the Soviet period, there are also church bells again, as in the olden time.

---

38   Believed by many of the faithful to be an actual portrait of the Virgin by St Luke, it was in fact a 12th century Byzantine work whose veneration increased unlike that of any other. In 1395 it was moved again from Vladimir to Moscow to protect that city from Tamburlaine (1400 Chapter); later it became known also as *Our Lady of Kazan*, for assuring Ivan the Terrible's final victory over the Tartars at that city in 1552; and it was credited with further miracles at the time of other troubles and attacks right up to Napoleon's. Finally, in the 1920s, it was removed from the Assumption Cathedral in the Kremlin by the Soviets, and put in a museum; which prompted an Old Believer (cited by Billington in *The Icon and the Axe*) to proclaim:

"The Queen of Heaven, divesting herself of her regal robes, issued forth from he Church to preach Christianity in the streets".

But in fact the streets were filled with icons of Lenin and Stalin and various Soviet saints for a long, long time. The icon is now in the Tretyakov Museum, its miracles now needed for internal rather than external reasons.

The older Cathedral of the Assumption, the *Uspensky Sobor*, was built in his new capital by Andrei Bogolyubsky, in the incredibly short period between 1158 and 1160. It was designed by the best architects the Grand Duke could obtain: it is said that some were even sent by the Holy Roman Emperor, Frederick I Barbarossa. The result was an unprecedented lightness and elegance – notwithstanding the vicissitudes of subsequent fire, pillage, and "improvement" (including the four corner domes, added in 1189). It is especially stunning from the Dmitrievsky Cathedral to the east, looking towards the beautifully rounded forms of the three apses and their high friezes of blind arcades, a motive repeated around the five cupola drums above. The influence of Western European Romanesque, rare in Russian buildings, is unmistakable. Although the exterior was originally highly coloured, the walls frescoed, the arcading gilded, it now has the simplicity of the beautiful white Vladimir limestone, a transition from colour to purity to which we have become accustomed in Western Romanesque architecture also.

The nearby Dmitrievsky (St Demetrius) Cathedral, built at the very end of the twelfth century by Andrei Bogolyubsky's brother and successor Vsevelod, known as "Big Nest" for his vast brood of offspring. It is in striking contrast to the simplicity of the Assumption Cathedral, not merely for its single dome: the upper half of all its facades, and the elegant arcading beneath, are richly decorated with a great profusion – a fine brocade – of stone bas–relief. Near the top various kingly heroes appear, not only holy ones like Solomon and David, but also classical ones like Hercules and Alexander the Great, all presumably intended to indicate the stamp of the builder. They are surrounded by other figures and by all manner of creatures: griffins, peacocks, leopards, lions, doves, eagles, pheasants, deer, centaurs, panthers, interspersed amongst a decorative forest of magical trees. But this exquisite sculpture was not to be repeated: the third dimension was held by the Orthodox Church to interfere unacceptably with true spiritual understanding.

Bogolyubova

If there is such a thing it can surely be found nearby. About ten or so kilometres to the east, off the main road to Nizhny Novgorod, just before the churches of Bogolyubova town and across the little River Nerl, is the most exquisite remaining example of the architecture of Kievan Rus: the Church of the Intercession–of–the–Virgin–on–the–Nerl. It also was built by Prince Andrei Bogolyubsky, in 1165, in memory of his son Izyaslav, killed in a campaign against the Volga Bulgars.

It is at the far end of the architectural spectrum from Kiev's St Sophia, its isolation in stark contrast to the cities that have pressed in on all that remains in Kiev, Novgorod and Vladimir. And it has survived Batu Khan, eluded Tamburlaine, Napoleon and Hitler, and outlasted Lenin and Stalin.

You approach it from a long distance, along a huge meadow lined on the river bank by old elms; the field is blanketed in winter with knee-deep snow, the tree branches black against a bleached sky, and in summer with a vivid mass of knee-deep grasses and wildflowers under a brilliant blue. There is no sound on a clear day, except perhaps the rustling of the grasses by summer zephyrs – but in winter, nothing. It is like a great open processional way, with, far off, raised on a small (entirely man-made) hill above the crisp white or green, the gleaming little white church, seemingly carved from a single block of marble, the dark grey dome raised on an exceptionally high, slender drum – a tall cathedral in miniature, waiting serenely in the vast silence for the homage that is its due. Close-up, across the frozen pond, or reflected in its bright blue summer water, the church reveals its carvings, prefiguring by thirty years the intricate stone brocade of the Dmitrievsky Cathedral in Vladimir: the wonderfully various heads on the consoles supporting the blind arcading around the lower part of the walls, the figures and animals on the upper walls above. And the crowned King David at the top of each of the three central bays makes clear that this, too, is a statement of regal authority.

But it is from across the wide meadow that the Intercession-on-the-Nerl stays most vividly in the memory – pure, absolutely alone, in that huge Russian landscape under the vast Russian sky. This is, still, Kievan Rus.

Godfrey of Bouillon statue, Brussels, Belgium. Wikimedia/Witia

PALESTINE

GODFREY OF BOUILLON: WHERE ANGELS FEAR TO TREAD

The polytheists have swelled in a torrent of terrifying extent.
How long will this continue?
Armies like mountains, coming again and again, have ranged
Forth from the lands of the Franks...
They push violently into the mire those who venture forth.
And those who would fight they make them forget with money...

The heads of the polytheists have already ripened,
So do not neglect them as a vintage and a harvest!

Ibn al–Khayyat, ca. 1100 CE, on Palestine

Let me raise my voice in lament, weep and mourn for the calamity
that has befallen,
How dear they were to me! My entrails are seared for Your dear
ones, O God!...

Let not Your foes triumph!...
Cast down their triumph and pour out the lifeblood of the enemy,
May it be dashed against a purple garment.
Array their defeat, 'crush the winepress', with Your outstretched arm!

Rabbi Elizier bar Nathan, ca. 1150 CE, on the Rhineland

(Moslem and Jew both lamenting Christian massacres
during the First Crusade.)

My first diplomatic posting was in Cairo in 1962-1963. The Embassy
had not long since re-opened after the debacle of the Anglo-French
attempt to invade the Suez Canal Zone, which Gamal Abdul Nasser had

nationalised in 1956 – just as the PO passenger liner *Himalaya*, on which I was sailing to study at Oxford, was about to enter the Canal from the Red Sea. We had an exciting transit, buzzed by Egyptian Air Force jets and tracked all the way through the Canal by the Egyptian Army's artillery, as though they feared invasion by a few hundred Australian travellers. (Given their experience of bored Australian troops billeted near Cairo during the First World War, they may have felt such prudence was wise.) As the Anglo-French fiasco unfolded later in the year I felt that, had we been equally misguided as to try to do so, we tourists might not have mounted a much more incompetent invasion. Australia atavistically and misguidedly gave its support to the British view that Egypt could not be trusted to run both efficiently and fairly such an important international asset as the Canal. Before I left Canberra for the Embassy five and a half years later I was asked to report on how in fact the Egyptians were managing it – which was, in brief, much better than it had been managed before.

I respected Nasser's successes, when he had them: as an Australian impatient with my country's archaic Imperial ties with Britain I had developed anti-colonial attitudes of my own when studying the post-war struggles for independence in the British, Dutch and French colonies in Southeast Asia. But the Middle East turned out to be much more complex and volatile. Anti-colonialism was followed, as for a time in Southeast Asia, by the cross-currents of nationalism and distrust, later to become a long bitter war following the advent of a fundamentalist Shiite theocracy in Iran; as everywhere, there were the conflicting pressures of the Cold War superpowers seeking security or advantage; but the United States' unfortunate propensity to settle for propping up reactionary rulers (and not only where oil was at stake) had the added dimension of cutting right across efforts to overcome Arab hostility (encouraged by the Soviets) to Israel.

Even with the Soviet Union no longer part of the equation, the other cross-currents have continued to bedevil the region. Despite more moderate European efforts, and those of Middle East states prepared to negotiate with Israel, it has still not proved possible to overcome the uncompromising ideologues on either side and to develop ways of communicating clearly, let alone of establishing more enduring connections. In fact at the start of this new millennium, Islamic fundamentalists' terrorist attacks on the West and the Western responses in Afghanistan and Iraq have seen a deterioration in relations that threatens a disruption of connection itself.

The principal people in this chapter are as follows:

- **Godfrey of Bouillon** (c.1060-1100) – one of the leaders of the First Crusade, and first Crusader ruler of Jerusalem, styled "Protector of huge Holy Sepulchre"

- Baldwin of Boulogne (c.1058-1118) – brother of Godfrey and successor as ruler of Jerusalem after his brother's death, taking the title "King of Jerusalem" in 1100

- Eustache of Boulogne (unknown-c.1125) – older brother of Godfrey and one of the leaders of the First Crusade

- Bohemond of Taranto (c.1058-1111) – one of the leaders of the First Crusade, became Prince of Antioch

- Tancred de Hauteville (1075-1112) – one of the leaders of the First Crusade and nephew of Bohemond of Taranto

- Raymond of Saint-Gilles (c.1041-1105) – one of the leaders of the First Crusade

- Stephen of Blois (c.1045-1102) – one of the leaders of the First Crusade

- Emperor Alexius Comnenus (1056-1118) – Emperor of Byzantium

- Anna Comnena (1083-1153) – daughter of Emperor Alexius and author of the Alexiad, an account of her father's reign

- Pope Urban II (c.1042-1099) – Pope from 1088-1099. Delivered a speech in Clermont in November 1095 that launched the First Crusade

- Henry IV (1050-1106) – Holy Roman Emperor from 1084-1105

- Fulcher of Chartres (c.1059-unknown) – eye-witness chronicler of the First Crusade. Accompanied Stephen of Blois on Crusade, later chaplain to Baldwin "King of Jerusalem"

Some say the long history of Western-Moslem distrust began with the Christian Crusades against Islam at the end of the 11th century, though retroactive blame could go much further back to the Moslem conquest of Catholic Spain and Sicily and the beginning of the Turks' relentless dismantlement of Orthodox Byzantium – eventually to be obliterated completely. I have a vivid memory of a spectacular Egyptian movie idolising Saladin (played by a youthful and still unknown Omar Sharif), who had indeed been a paragon of chivalry in victory over England's Richard the Lionheart in the Third Crusade. Memories do last – or are re-created: there is an 1860 statue of a defeated but heroic Richard outside the British Houses of Parliament; and as recently as 1992 the late Syrian dictator Hafiz Assad erected a statue of Saladin, abjectly attended by two defeated Crusaders, in Damascus. Given the desperate situation of contemporary Kurds in Turkey, Iraq, Iran and Syria, there is a bitter irony in the Arab world's adulation of this greatest of anti-Crusader leaders, for Saladin was a Kurd. It is not so much the actual history as this disinterred imagination of that history that informs and distorts current connections.

Years after my Cairo posting, my interest in the link between the Crusades and the modern Middle East was revived by visits to two castles: the great Crusader castle of Krak des Chevaliers in Syria, and (during our last posting, in Belgium) the castle of Bouillon, deep in the southern Ardennes, not far from the sites of the bloody battles in late 1944 that followed Nazi Germany's last effort to break out of the tightening Allied ring. It was the home of Godfrey of Bouillon, one of the leaders of the First Crusade, whose original motives of assisting Byzantium and recovering the Christian holy places in Palestine were essentially of the same kind as those impelling its Moslem opponents; but, as in all wars, there were also more concrete rewards in mind. Venice, the main European anchor of trade routes to Asia, still trading comfortably with Egypt and carefully with Central Asia through Seljuk territories, was reluctant to participate until the Crusades clearly offered prospects for making money out of their successes...or failures. They were probably the only ones, on either side, to come out ahead in the whole two-century calamity.

Then as now, religious intolerance was hopelessly mixed on all sides with territorial ambitions, between Catholic and Orthodox Christians almost as much as, and in the disastrous episode of the Fourth Crusade, more than between them and their Moslem supposed enemy. Despite the claimed resonance of the Crusades in the contemporary Middle East, there was apparently surprisingly little about them in Arabic literature until the 20th century; there was more from the Jews of Germany, who were terrorised and massacred in a different prefiguration of modern times as the First Crusade began its journey down the Rhine. But most of our information about Godfrey of Bouillon and his Crusade comes from near-contemporary Christian sources; and despite their hagiography, they reveal a man who made his own mixed contribution to issues still confounding Western relations with the Middle East, but who in some ways was not the worst representative of an impulse that is these days simultaneously hard to understand and scarily resurgent.

The road to Jerusalem
Our road to Jerusalem begins in the middle of the Place Royale in Brussels. In front of the uninteresting eighteenth century Church of Saint Jacques–sur–Coudenberg (on the site of a chapel of the Dukes of Burgundy), there is a monument; it looks down the hill over the roofs of the old city and its famous Grand'Place – seen between the great Museums of Fine Arts on the left, and the new Museum of Musical Instruments in the splendid Art Nouveau former home of an "Old England" chain store on the right. It is a somewhat nondescript equestrian statue, a nineteenth century conception of a medieval knight mounted on his charger. Its inscription, in French and Flemish, like many inscriptions in language–riven Belgium, reads thus:

Godfrey of Bouillon
First King of Jerusalem
Born at Baisy in Brabant
Died in Palestine 17 July 1100
...
Unveiled on 24 August 1848 during the reign of Leopold I

Belgium had only been Belgium for eighteen years at that time, and it was searching for authentic heroes for a geographical construction that had been ruled by almost everyone in Europe *except* Belgians since Julius Caesar had conquered the Gallo–Celtic *Belgae* tribes between 57 and 50 BCE. However there were decidedly mixed strands behind national pride in Godfrey, line by line of that inscription – not to mention errors in two of them.

Godfrey was the earliest of these new Belgian heroes, and he was indeed Godfrey of Bouillon, Duke of Lower Lotharingia – or Lorraine – in the Holy Roman Empire, who became known as "the Great Crusader". But in fact he had had to pawn his county of Bouillon, including its great castle stronghold, to a Bishop with whom he had spent the previous five years feuding, in order to finance his participation in the First Crusade.

The inscription had to omit his birth date, because it is not known closer than "*circa* 1060"; and the claim for his birthplace at Baisy (now Baisy–Thy), thirteen kilometres south of Waterloo on the road of conquest – or defeat – between Brussels and Paris, was hotly contested by some nineteenth century French historians. The latter, equally determined to see Godfrey as an ornament to their nation, have claimed he was born at Boulogne – merely because that is where his mother, St Ida, Countess of Boulogne, lived with his father the Count. Across the Rhine, a German historian, ignoring Belgium entirely, said Godfrey was "essentially" not French but one of "our *Volk*". Across the Channel, an English historian regretfully but at least accurately noted that Godfrey did not have "English blood in his veins". The Great Crusader was a hot property in the nationalistic nineteenth century.

Godfrey did indeed die in July 1100, though all the contemporary chroniclers gave the date as the 18th, not the 17th. It is even more curious in the circumstances – of mid–nineteenth century Belgium – that the inscription merely called the place "Palestine" rather than "the Holy Land", the "liberation" of which had been the objective of the Crusade in the first place.

And while Godfrey was certainly the first Crusader ruler of Jerusalem, he was never "King": out of piety, it was said, he refused to accept a royal crown in the city where Christ had received the Crown of Thorns, and became *Advocatus Sancti Sepulchri*, "Protector of the Holy Sepulchre". Piety or cunning: the leading French Crusader had been the first to turn down the crown, for the same pious reason – but he omitted to think up the clever alternative. Godfrey perhaps was genuinely devout, strongly influenced by his mother; at the same time he was a tough fighter, including against the Church where his own interests so required, and a participant, in common with all his colleagues, in the massacre and looting that followed the Crusaders' capture of Jerusalem. He was a startling symbol, right at the beginning of the Crusading movement, of the contradiction between hunger for peace of mind and hunger for a piece of earthly reward.

The inscription's final irony lies in the inaugurator of Godfrey's statue, Leopold I. The first King of the Belgians was not Belgian, but German, son of the insignificant Duke of Saxe–Coburg–Saalfeld: a former page of Napoleon's; later a general in the army of Tsar Alexander I of Russia, fighting his former employer; uncle of Queen Victoria of England, widower of her cousin the daughter of the Prince Regent; married to a daughter of Louis–Philippe, the new "King of the French". Not long after Belgium had become a country, in 1831, Leopold had become King of the Belgians when he was selected for the job by their new political leaders; like Godfrey, he was the second choice, after the Franco–American hero Lafayette had turned down the offer of the throne – and after consideration had been given to the Duke of Leuchtenberg, son of Napoleon's step–son Eugène de Beauharnais; the Duc de Nemours, Louis–Philippe's second son; the Archduke Charles of Austria, younger brother of the Emperor Francis II; Prince Adam Czartoryski, hero of the 1830 Polish revolution against Russia; and the most improbable candidate of all, Count Stanislaw Rzewuski, whose only qualification was that he had made some important friends in Belgium when he had been a tourist there several years before.

The Great Powers had been shopping Leopold around for a year or so: he had already, the year before he parachuted into Belgium, turned down the throne of recently–independent Greece. But the Belgians increasingly accepted him as their new king while at the same time their French neighbours were becoming increasingly dissatisfied with theirs. By 1848 the Citizen King Louis–Philippe had been ousted from France by his citizens and revolution was spreading across the whole of Europe. How could son–in–law Leopold be celebrating an ancient Belgian hero in the middle of all this?

Godfrey to his contemporaries

Hero? It depended on the point of view.

Within a few years of Godfrey's death, his tomb in the Church of the Holy Sepulchre in Jerusalem described him simply, but already inaccurately, as

> "The illustrious Godfrey of Bouillon, who conquered all this country for the Christian religion"

About the same time, one of the earliest chroniclers, the anonymous author of the *Gesta Francorum et aliorum Hierosolimitanorum*, "The Deeds of the Franks and other Jerusalemites", was already adding to Godfrey's lustre, also in Latin and still inaccurately, as

> "Terror of Egypt, disperser of the Arabs, panicker of the Persians… image of the warrior, strength of the people, anchor of the Church".

Within a century, when the Jerusalem–born Archbishop William of Tyre wrote the first comprehensive history of the First Crusade, based largely on the accounts of earlier chroniclers, Godfrey had taken on an even more unreal allure:

> "He was a man of integrity, generous, pious and God–fearing, upright, enemy of everything evil, serious and resolute in speech. He despised the glories of this world, which, in these times and particularly in the profession of arms, is rare. He was assiduous in prayer and pious works, well–known for generosity, enormously affable, benevolent and compassionate, exemplary in all his actions and beloved of God... The general view was that his practice of the profession of arms and his valour in combat were without equal".

In the West it was only the beginning.
The chronicles recording Godfrey's life in Lorraine, before the First Crusade converted him into this paragon, apparently all attest to his fairly vigorous military activity, either in support of his liege lord the Holy Roman Emperor or of his own direct territorial interests; but there is very little on his character, which was to become so exemplary. However there is one report of the time he set out on the Crusade, included in a Hebrew chronicle attributed to Solomon bar Simson, a Jew from Speyer in the Rhineland:

> "It was at this time that Duke Godfrey, may his bones be ground to dust, arose in the hardness of his spirit, driven by a spirit of wantonness to go with those journeying to the profane shrine, vowing to go on this journey only after avenging the blood of the crucified one by shedding Jewish blood and completely eradicating any trace of those bearing the name 'Jew', thus assuaging his own burning wrath".

The atrocities committed in the last century have deep historical roots. Solomon bar Simson recorded that a Rabbi of Mainz sent a messenger with this news to "King" [the Holy Roman Emperor] Henry IV, then in Italy; and he continued:

> "The king was enraged and dispatched letters to all the ministers, bishops, and governors of all the provinces of his realm, as well as to Duke Godfrey, containing words of greeting and commanding them to do no bodily harm to the Jews and to provide them

with help and refuge. The evil duke then swore that he had never intended to do them harm. The Jews of Cologne nevertheless bribed him with five hundred *zekukim* [six thousand ounces] of silver, as did the Jews of Mainz. The duke assured them of his support and promised them peace".

Godfrey was the *only* great crusading lord who acted against the Jews. And although this is the only report of his involvement in their mistreatment, and Solomon bar Simson does not accuse him of having participated in actual massacres, this blot on his character – which was either ignored or condoned by the Christian chroniclers – can not be expunged.

Halfway to Jerusalem, the first Crusaders had a notable series of encounters in Constantinople with the *Basileus*, the Emperor Alexius Comnenus of Byzantium. They were by no means all friendly; but Alexius's adoring biographer, his daughter Anna Comnena, who rarely minced words in her *Alexiad*, let Godfrey off rather lightly: she noted, not altogether accurately, that

"He was a very rich man, extremely proud of his noble birth, his own courage and the glory of his family. (Every Celt [she added] desires to surpass his fellows.)";

but she clearly distinguished him from

"the more villainous characters (in particular Bohemond [of Taranto] and his like) [who] had an ulterior purpose, for they hoped on their journey to seize the capital itself, looking upon its capture as a natural consequence of the expedition".

Then, about Godfrey in the very few contemporary Moslem sources on the First Crusade's bloody progress through Turkey, Syria, Lebanon and so to the bloodiest battle of all, the capture of Jerusalem – nothing. "The sack of Jerusalem", the modern Lebanese historian Amin Maalouf has written, "aroused no immediate sensation" in the Moslem world. Godfrey, according to most of the Christian chroniclers, the first to breach the walls of the Holy City, no doubt condoned, and perhaps participated in the subsequent frenzied massacre of every Moslem and Jew in it. A week later he was created by his squabbling colleagues *Advocatus Sancti Sepulchri*; but his role was reflected, in one of the oldest Moslem chronicles of the Crusade, that of the Syrian al–Azimi, about 1160 CE, only by the lapidary remark

"Then they [the Franks] turned to Jerusalem and conquered it from the hands of the Egyptians. Godfrey took it".

No mention of the terrible massacre. No mention of Godfrey's great sacrilege of taking as his personal residence, when he became *Advocatus*, the Aqsa Mosque on the Moslem Haram – the Jewish Moriah, the Christian Holy Mount.

The paucity of records was partly the result of the disunity amongst the Moslems as well, which contributed so heavily to their successive defeats by the Europeans, all the way from western Turkey to Jerusalem; and partly it was a reflection of Moslem lack of interest in the Crusaders as individuals. In her massive new study of the Moslem sources, *The Crusades – Islamic Perspectives*, Carole Hillenbrand concluded that the evidence – in relation to the entire Crusading period – demonstrates

"all too clearly that medieval Muslim chroniclers were not interested in the wellsprings of the Franks' behaviour. As far as they were concerned, an inscrutable – and malign – destiny had foisted these foreigners on them, and it was their duty as pious Muslims to defend the Dar al–Islam [the Islamic community] and send them packing. They were not concerned to probe the religious or for that matter the economic motivation of their foes".

It was only with Godfrey's death – by three different means, two of them incorrect – that he reappeared, for the last time, in the twelfth century Syrian chronicles. It is the supreme irony that, already by the time of William of Tyre, the Great Crusader, first ruler of Europe's first overseas colony, had barely entered and by then had all but disappeared from the Moslem view.

Godfrey's Lotharingia

That Godfrey of Bouillon became, when he was about twenty–seven, Duke of Lower Lotharingia or Lorraine, was partly due to his illustrious ancestors, partly to his own exertions, and partly to quirks in both. But by the time of his elevation Lotharingia was not all that much to be Duke of. It had originally been created by Louis the Pious, the feckless son of the great Charlemagne. The latter spent a lifetime subduing and uniting the principalities and lordships of much of western Europe; in 800 CE he was able to be crowned by the Pope as Holy Roman Emperor, ruler of a western successor to the Roman Empire that was the first more–or–less united Europe.

However Louis, unable to grasp his father's ambition, proceeded along the old lines to divide the Empire among his sons: the Franks' *Francia* on the west, the Teutons' *Germania* on the east, and, in between, a curious hodge–podge strip running from Flanders up the Rhine and through Switzerland and Lombardy as far as Rome itself: Lotharingia. None of the three kingdoms was anything like the centralised nation–states that Francia and Germania eventually became: each was a patchwork of princedoms, duchies, margravates, counties and lordships, overlaid by a different patchwork of bishoprics, abbeys, monasteries and convents which were in many cases substantial landholders in their own right. Not all the former owed allegiance to the same king or emperor, and bishops and abbots played a fierce game of secular politics while bearing allegiance to the Pope – or not, depending on the current balance between their spiritual and temporal concerns.

The result was a constant struggle for loyalties and advantage, usually backed up, or led up front, by military force. Neighbour often fought neighbour, to the general misery of their populations – except when Emperor, King or Pope gathered all their subjects together to fight each other, which caused general misery for everyone. Notwithstanding established feudal duties claimed and acknowledged, in practice interweaving obligations, undermining bribes, and over-weaning ambitions could play havoc with the theoretical scheme of medieval life. Godfrey of Bouillon was to suffer from this at home; on the Crusade, everyone was to suffer from it.

From the beginning Francia and Germania fought, not least to gain possession of a completely unviable Lotharingia – indeed, the last time the lands in the Rhineland area changed hands between them was in 1945, for the fifth time in seventy–five years. Although Lothair, the first ruler of Lotharingia, was also Emperor, his son lost both the Imperial title and Italy, and more was to go. Within a century the Empire itself became settled firmly on the German–speaking principalities and bishoprics of central Europe, where it remained until dismantled by Napoleon in 1804. The days of even the rump of independent Lotharingia were numbered: before the end of the tenth century it had, through the failure of French covetousness and the force of German arms, come entirely under the control of the latter. It had also been divided into the two Dukedoms of Upper and Lower Lotharingia. The former was to the south, an extended version of modern Lorraine, stretching from Trier on the Mosel (the historic birthplace, about 274 CE, of Constantine the Great, founder of the Byzantine Empire) to Metz, Nancy and Verdun in north–eastern France. Godfrey's Lower Lotharingia, to the north [i.e. further down the Rhine], spread between the bishoprics of Cambrai in north–western France, Utrecht in southern Holland and Cologne on the German Rhine, while that of Liège, where Bouillon was situated, occupied the central position both geographically and politically. Neither Duchy was coterminous with the bishoprics which indicated its outline; both were totally artificial constructs, based on family connections, the outcomes of dynastic squabbles, and the accidents of aristocratic acquisitiveness. These mosaic–states would have meant little to the poor farmers and small tradesmen who comprised most of the populations, other than as another layer of demands and depredations – perhaps, occasionally, protection.

Godfrey's ancestry

It was certainly a help to Godfrey to be descended from the great Charlemagne, through both his father and mother even though on both sides the descent was partly through daughters, never as good for ancestry as sons. And as Godfrey, in his own generation, was only the second son, he might well never have appeared in history at all.

His father's family came from a string of royals with inauspicious sobriquets: Louis the Pious's youngest son Charles the Bald through Louis the Stammerer, Charles the Simple (who gave up Normandy to the Viking Norsemen) and Louis the Foreigner – the last three Kings of France – then four generations later to Ida of Bouillon, who married his father, Count Eustace II of Boulogne. Eustace had first married Goda, sister of King Edward the Confessor of England; she was dead, and Eustace already married to Godfrey's mother, when he switched sides and fought with William of Normandy in the conquest of England. Near the end of the Battle of Hastings in the Bayeux Tapestry, he is there, carrying a Papal banner and pointing back at William at the very moment the Conqueror, having had three horses hacked down from under him, is lifting the visor of his helmet to shout at his Normans (according to a contemporary chronicle):

"Look at me, I am alive, and, by God's help, I shall win".

His mother's family was less royal but more closely tied to Lorraine. It was descended from Louis the Pious' son Lothair, who got Lotharingia and first go of the Holy Roman Empire; both in due course went elsewhere, but early in the eleventh century, after six generations during which daughters had married into a variety of French noble families, the Holy Roman Emperor Henry II granted to a descendant what was by then Lower Lotharingia. His nephew the third Duke, Godfrey the Bearded, was our Godfrey's maternal grandfather.

In 1057 Godfrey the Bearded's brother, Frederick of Lorraine, Cardinal–Abbot of Monte Cassino, was elected Pope as Stephen X.[39] Perhaps this was why his nephew–in–law Eustace was carrying a Papal banner at Hastings? This close connection to Rome should have stood the Dukes of Lower Lorraine in good stead; but for several reasons it did not, not the least being Stephen's death just short of eight months into his pontificate.

Stephen had also been chosen without reference to the Imperial Court in Germany, the Cardinals probably taking advantage of the fact that the new Emperor Henry IV was only seven, to elect a prelate sympathetic to the reformist party. This ecclesiastical faction was seeking to break this traditional tie with the Empire, and to make the Church, including the investiture of its bishops, totally independent of secular control by the Emperor (and the other emerging national monarchies). It was soon to triumph when one of Stephen's closest advisers, the reformer Cardinal Hildebrand, was elected Pope Gregory VII. Gregory was responsible for what the twentieth century French Dominican theologian Cardinal Yves Congar called

> "the greatest turning point" in the entire theological history of the Church, "making the Church itself into a legal institution...[with] the affirmation of papal power as the basis of everything".

This mildly named "Investiture Controversy" was to pit Pope and Emperor against each other, tear Western Europe apart, and end up with Henry IV – with Godfrey at his side – chasing Gregory out of Rome. It left a legacy of hostility and warfare between Romans and Germans until the Reformation.

---

39 Stephen was re–numbered IX in 1961, along with all the other Pope Stephens, following the disbarment of the original Stephen II who had had a stroke – in 752 – before his consecration.

And there was to be one other drawback for Godfrey in his Papal connection. Pope Stephen, while still a Cardinal, and his other close adviser, Humbert of Mourmoutiers, Cardinal–Bishop of Silva Candida, had already played a fateful role in relations between Rome and Byzantium. Both were bigoted and stiff–necked, but – or perhaps therefore – they had been chosen by Stephen's predecessor but one, Pope Leo IX, to go to Constantinople to try to sort out both theological and political differences standing in the way of a joint Catholic–Orthodox front against the aggressive new state founded by Norman freebooters in Sicily and southern Italy. The Byzantine Emperor Constantine IX Monomachus seemed well disposed, but the Orthodox Patriarch was as hostile to Rome as the two Cardinals were to Constantinople. In the event the latter lost their temper; and on 16 July 1054 they marched, in full canonicals, into Santa Sophia, in the middle of Mass, deposited on the high altar a Bull of Excommunication of the entire Eastern Church, marched out again, and went back to Rome. The Great Schism has never been healed. And one wonders to what extent the difficulties Godfrey of Bouillon experienced with the Byzantine Emperor forty years later reflected the sour memory in Constantinople of his great–uncle Cardinal Frederick of Lorraine.

Godfrey's grandfather, Frederick's elder brother Duke Godfrey the Bearded, was the family rebel, who at one stage or another managed to offend everybody. He was once excommunicated by the Pope and twice deprived of Upper Lorraine by the Emperor, though these falls from grace resulted from his turbulent personal ambitions rather than any interest in the gathering storm over the roles of Pope and Emperor. On his deathbed, reformed and devout, he endowed the family Abbey of St Hubert with substantial landholdings...belonging to his knightly vassals.

His elder child, Ida, Godfrey of Bouillon's mother, could not, as a woman, inherit. Lower Lorraine thus went to her brother, Godfrey the Hunchback, a tough fighter despite his infirmity, who unqualifiedly supported the Emperor, militarily and politically, just as Pope Gregory VII and Henry IV were establishing their battle stands. This Godfrey was the only Duke to join Henry's bishops in abusively declaring Gregory deposed; the Pope counter–attacked by excommunicating Henry and declaring Godfrey his "personal enemy". However Godfrey the Hunchback left a longer–lived and much more implacable enemy than the Pope: his wife, the Countess Matilda of Tuscany. She had deserted him within two years of their marriage and returned to Italy, to become a powerful and skilful supporter of the Papacy against the Emperor and his supporters until her death, at a great age, in 1115.

Godfrey the Emperor's man

One of the many whom Matilda targetted was her nephew–in–law Godfrey of Bouillon, unexpectedly propelled into her sights. For, as her hated husband the Hunchback lay dying in 1076 – having, during a quarrel with a vassal, "been stabbed [as the chronicler matter–of–factly put it] with a sharp weapon between the buttocks while on the privy" – he named fifteen year–old Godfrey as his heir. This came totally out of the blue. Godfrey, as only the second son of Count Eustace of Boulogne and Countess Ida, had no standing in the feudal scheme of things; and perhaps it was for this very reason that Godfrey the Hunchback felt his young nephew would be able to focus his attention on his beloved Lorraine for which he had fought so boisterously.

In fact, Godfrey was said to have received an education – well, at least some Latin – such as was more consonant with an intended career in the Church. This was a normal path for second sons, particularly those of especially devout mothers; and it possibly explains why the young heir immediately placed himself under the tutelage of the Bishop of Liège, rather than returning to his father Eustace II, who was still at Boulogne when he was not overseeing his vast estates in Norman England (the largest, according to the Doomsday Book, after those of William the Conqueror and his brother Robert of Mortain).

It is curious that there seems in fact to be no reference to Godfrey's relationship with his father, either before his inheritance from Godfrey the Hunchback in 1076, or during the next twelve or eighteen years (depending on the source) of Count Eustace's life – only with his mother, who remained a strong influence right up to Godfrey's departure for Palestine. The other curiosity in Godfrey's personal life is the fact that he never married, something which in those days was normally regarded as absolutely essential for the preservation of lands and other property within the immediate family. But there is apparently no hint of any form of liaison in the chronicles, nor any as to the reason why, and it is pointless to speculate.

In fact, however, although the Dukedom of Lower Lorraine had by now been in the family through five title–holders over three generations, it was not hereditary by right: as with virtually all medieval dukedoms, its investiture was still within the prerogative of the monarch. And Henry IV promptly bestowed Lower Lorraine on his own two year–old son Conrad – that is, kept it under his own control. It was not, apparently, out of any hostility to Godfrey of Bouillon, whom he consoled with the Margravate of Antwerp, but perhaps because of doubts that the youth had the force of character and the backing of his vassals to be able adequately to support the Imperial cause. So Godfrey had not only to prove himself, he had to struggle to protect the rest of his domains now that the umbrella of the Dukedom had gone.

It was now that Godfrey centred his life and activities on Bouillon. Since as far back as the eighth century the Château de Bouillon has been set on the same high rocky outcrop, the security of its fortifications enhanced by its being almost surrounded by one of the extraordinary series of more than twenty U–shaped bends cut by the River Semois as it snakes its way – like an Andy Goldsworthy serpentine – through the heavily–wooded, sparsely–populated hills across the south of Belgium's Luxembourg Province. (It is just across the border with France from Sedan, where the Emperor Napoleon II's defeat by Bismarck's Prussia in 1870 resulted in one of Lotharingia's latter–day carve–ups, the German seizure of Lorraine and Alsace; Louis Napoleon, captured by the Prussians, was imprisoned in Bouillon village's Hôtel de la Poste the night after his capitulation.) The core of the massive castle stronghold that one sees today was there in Godfrey's time, but it was extended in the sixteenth and seventeenth centuries. There are magnificent views of the Château from the hills which overlook it on all sides; and from these perspectives its huge walls and great bastions give it a decidedly medieval appearance.

Godfrey was probably bitter at Henry's decision not to confirm him in the Dukedom, though as this came only a month after his uncle's totally unexpected death–bed decision to name him his heir, he had not had long to develop much sense of loss. In any case, his mother, the saintly Ida, is said to have "exerted a calming influence"; and he could not in any case afford to indulge any resentment of the Emperor in the face of the immediate efforts by the rancorous Matilda of Tuscany, supported by Pope Gregory, to claim most of her late husband's lands and to encourage other claimants to go after the rest.

Godfrey's struggle against these predators was complicated by the fact that, as Margrave of Antwerp, he was also obliged to answer Henry's calls for aid in his own campaigns against his enemies. Godfrey is thus said to have acquitted himself heroically in the fight against rebellious Saxony; and then, committing himself not only for the Emperor but equally clearly against the Pope, Godfrey accompanied

Henry on his invasion of Italy, which led to the expulsion of Gregory VII from Rome in 1084 and the creation of the antipope Clement III, who crowned Henry Holy Roman Emperor in St Peter's. Forty years later, the English chronicler William of Malmesbury was to write that in fact it was Godfrey who was the first to break through the walls of Rome after a two–year siege by the Imperial forces. He was also, the chroniclers claimed, the first to break through the walls of Jerusalem eleven years later. There is a distinct suspicion that Godfrey's subsequent fame retroactively increased his prowess.

Godfrey the Duke

It is nevertheless clear that his loyal and perhaps effective military service through these years did impress the Emperor; for three years later, in 1087, when Henry made his son Conrad King of Rome (as the heir to the Empire was known), he rewarded Godfrey with the Dukedom of Lower Lorraine that had eluded his grasp on the death of his uncle eleven years before. Through these years, despite his absences on Imperial service, Godfrey had fought off the depredations on his other possessions, including a very determined effort by the Bishop of Verdun and his allies to take Bouillon itself. This struggle, in which he was finally successful, was purely territorial: it had nothing to do with the continuing Investiture slugging match between Godfrey's Emperor and the Bishop's Pope.

However the last of the local campaigns in which Godfrey was involved (at least that we know of) was indeed a reflection of that match – and, this time, Godfrey was on the other side.

When his old guardian, Bishop Henri of Liège died in 1091, the Emperor – still exercising his claimed right of investiture – appointed a vigorous supporter of his Imperial cause, one Otbert. Bishop Otbert immediately began throwing his weight around, and right away was opposed by Godfrey, particularly when he deposed the Abbots of two monasteries, including that of St Hubert, for being inadequately supportive of the Emperor. The *Chronicle of St Hubert* said that in Godfrey's efforts to force Otbert to reinstate the Abbots, the decisive moment came with an appeal he made to a number of his fellow lords in 1095:

"What help, companions", Godfrey reportedly cried, "can we hope from God, we who, while His churches are perishing, not only do not come to their defence, but do not even interpose any word of objection? Certainly the most benign plan of the Creator has deserved this much of us, having constituted us administrators of His realm, that each of us individually deny Otbert our service, we whom Providence has chosen for the protection of His right in this our time".

Otbert was obliged to give in.

The remarks attributed to Godfrey are a rare instance where his own voice is suggested in the chronicles. They may have contributed to his reputation for great piety – or may have reflected his subsequent hagiography. But they have two other interesting aspects. One is the repeated emphasis, in such short compass, on Godfrey's (and his companions') rule over Lorraine as being ordained by God as distinct from being conferred by the Emperor. The other is his alleged solicitude for the Church. The latter may represent no more than his loyalty to important Abbeys in his domains; but even if so, it was an attitude at variance with his previous fierce loyalty to the Emperor, to the extent of having joined the first sack of Rome and the attempted overthrow of Pope Gregory VII.

One might wonder whether he had become less comfortable with Henry IV's continuing intransigence in the face of the more moderate stand of the new Pope, Urban II, a Frenchman, former Abbot of the great reforming Benedictine Abbey of Cluny – Godfrey had not joined the Emperor in his second sack of Rome and the expulsion of Urban II in 1090. Or perhaps he was leaving a sinking ship, as had his predecessor as Duke of Lorraine, Henry's own son Conrad, King of the Romans, who had deserted his father and been crowned King of Italy with the support of the implacable Matilda of Tuscany. It was after this blow that Henry's position began what was to become an irreversible decline.

By this time Godfrey had spent most of twenty years fighting, either for the Emperor or himself. He was said to have been brave, though as we noted earlier this may of course have been inflated by subsequent legend. He was said to have been pious, but this might have been to some extent a reflection of his mother's devoutness and benefactions. Godfrey himself seems to have battled against bishops and abbeys as though they were just other competing land-holders – as in some respects they were – but he apparently behaved better towards them when St Ida was present.

The *Chronicle of St Hubert* rather pointedly said that with the death of Godfrey's uncle, Godfrey the Hunchback, "justice and peace, which he had maintained in a memorable way, departed with him".

This judgement leaves a distinct question mark over the character and ability of Godfrey of Bouillon. But, by virtue of his rank, he was about to become one of the commanders of a great military expedition.

The launching of a Crusade

Earlier in 1095 – six months before Godfrey's final showdown with Bishop Otbert – the Byzantine Emperor Alexius IX Comnenus had sent envoys to a Catholic Church Synod in Piacenza, seeking help. While he claimed that the tide had been turned against his Seljuk Turk enemies since the disasters of 1071 – when they had captured and murdered his predecessor the Emperor Romanus IV Ducas, and seized Jerusalem and Palestine from the Arabs – he now sought Western reinforcements so as to break their power completely. Pope Urban responded sympathetically, no doubt seeing an opening for bringing Constantinople back under Rome's control. Both were to be disappointed; Alexius was to be horrified.

Later in 1095 Urban announced that he was travelling to France "out of concern for the misfortunes of the Eastern Church". The culmination of his efforts came with the Council of Clermont [now Clermont–Ferrand, in the Auvergne in central France], where, in addition to his cardinals, thirteen archbishops, two hundred and twenty–five bishops, hundreds of "lords and knights" and probably at least as many priests, and "thousands of others" – presumably townspeople and yeomen from neighbouring regions – all gathered for the decisive sermon Urban preached on 27 November. The chroniclers' reports vary in some details: it is not certain that any was actually present, though they are believed to have relied on – perhaps sometimes even reliable – eyewitness accounts.

Fulcher of Chartres (who set out on the Crusade with Stephen of Blois, brother–in–law of Robert, Duke of Normandy, the Conqueror's son, and later became chaplain to Godfrey's brother, and successor in Jerusalem, Baldwin) wrote his *Historia Hierosolymitana*, which appeared in 1105, as though he was present. The Pope, he said, insisted on an end to the sort of civil discord and unruliness that Godfrey had spent the previous twenty years engaged in, and demanded the fulfilment of

> "a certain further duty, God's concern and your own. For you must hasten to carry aid to your brethren dwelling in the East, who need your help, which they have often asked. For the Turks, a Persian people, have attacked them, as many of you already know, and have advanced as far into Roman territory as that

part of the Mediterranean which is called the Arm of St George [fronting Constantinople/Istanbul]; and by seizing more and more of the lands of the Christians, they have often already conquered them in battle, have killed and captured many, have destroyed the churches, and have devastated the kingdom of God. If you allow them to continue much longer, they will subjugate God's faithful yet more widely.

Wherefore, I exhort with earnest prayer – not I, but God – that, as heralds of Christ, you urge men by frequent exhortation, men of all ranks, knights as well as foot–soldiers, rich as well as poor, to hasten to exterminate this vile race from the lands of your brethren, and to aid the Christians in time".

Though the term "Crusade" – from Spanish "marked with the Cross" – did not come into use for several more centuries (and the English word not until the 1750s), Urban quite specifically saw the Christian expedition for which he called as a means for diverting domestic aggression abroad; and he was not choosy:

> "I speak to those present; I proclaim it to the absent...Let those who have been accustomed to make private war against the faithful carry on to a successful issue a war against infidels, which ought to have been begun ere now. Let those who for a long time have been robbers now become soldiers of Christ. Let those who once fought against brothers and relatives now fight against barbarians, as they ought. Let those who have been wearing themselves out to the detriment of body and soul now labour for a double glory".

For this was the clinching enticement in Urban's message:

> "If those who set out thither should lose their lives on the way by land, or in crossing the sea, or in fighting the pagans, their sins shall be remitted. This I grant to all who go, through the power vested in me by God".

Fulcher, for unknown reasons, makes it sound as if the Pope only had in mind aiding Byzantium. But others made clear that the "liberation" of Jerusalem from the Seljuk Turks was to be an equally or even more important objective. Robert the Monk (also known as Robert of Rheims), who claimed to have been present in Clermont, asserted that Urban wanted to be sure his audience understood who Seljuk Turks were:

> "They destroy the altars, after having defiled them with their uncleanness. They circumcise the Christians, and the blood of the circumcision they either spread upon the altars or pour into the vases of the baptismal font. When they wish to torture people by a base death, they perforate their navels, and, dragging forth the end of the intestines, bind it to a stake; then with flogging they lead the victim around until his viscera have gushed forth, and he falls prostrate upon the ground. Others they bind to a post and pierce with arrows. Others they compel to extend their necks, and then, attacking them with naked swords, they attempt to cut through the neck with a single blow. What shall I say of the abominable rape of the women? To speak of it is worse than to be silent".

Supposing that this is not merely Robert's embroidery, it would have sounded absolutely realistic to the Pope's listeners: these horrors were no different from those visited upon the unfortunate losers in Western Europe's own endless internecine aggression that Urban wanted to divert onto the Turks.

And Robert the Monk insisted that the Pope had placed Jerusalem at the heart of his call:

> "Jerusalem is the navel of the world; the land is fruitful above others, like another paradise of delights. This the Redeemer of the human race has made illustrious by His advent, has beautified by His presence, has consecrated by suffering, has redeemed by death, has glorified by burial. This royal city, therefore, situated at the centre of the world, is now held captive by His enemies, and is in subjection to those who do not know God, to the worship of the heathen. Therefore, she seeks and desires to be liberated and does not cease to implore you to come to her aid. From you, especially, she asks succour, because, as we have already said, God has conferred upon you, above all nations, great glory in arms".

Pope Urban was, after all, a Frenchman.

The French responded – immediately, with the cry *Deus le volt*, "God wills it"; soon thereafter, with the development of a wildly enthusiastic movement to descend, by the thousands, on Constantinople and the

Holy Land. The Emperor Alexius, when he heard, was appalled: instead of the mercenaries whom he had asked for, to serve as he saw fit, it soon became clear that he would be faced by several uncoordinated – and, it soon became even clearer – undisciplined armies of the combative trouble–makers whom Pope Urban was trying to get rid of from the West.

The first was the rag–tag "People's Crusade" roused by the preaching of Peter the Hermit, a French monk whose graphic tales of horrors perpetrated on Christians in Jerusalem, where he claimed to have been on pilgrimage, helped raise an "army" of some twenty thousand, bands of soldiers, riffraff, women and camp–followers, mostly from northern France and the Low Countries. They began by massacring Jewish communities in the Rhineland, brawled their way across Germany and Hungary, reacted violently against Alexius's concern at their chances against the Turks, and, when the remnants insisted on crossing the Bosphorus anyway, were duly decimated by the latter at Nicaea in western Anatolia.

The other armies of the First Crusade had much greater numbers of experienced soldiers and were led by great nobles; they could accordingly have posed a far greater threat to Byzantium, but their leaders' own jealousies and ambitions soon enabled Alexius to play them off against each other. Unlike in the later Crusades, there were no monarchs. The German, the Holy Roman Emperor Henry IV, was still under interdict of excommunication, and too preoccupied anyway with challenges at home to his failing grip on power. King William II Rufus of England, the Conqueror's son, was likewise involved in domestic struggle against rebellious nobles. King Philip I of France had different domestic difficulties: married to Queen Berthe for twenty years, he had seduced Bertrade de Montfort, "the fat Fleming", wife of his cousin the Duke of Anjou, then married her and locked up the Queen in a royal castle. Not surprisingly, he, too, had been excommunicated.

The Crusaders were overwhelmingly French – which is why they came to be called, generally, Franks. The main force was mostly Provençal, led by the Pope's Legate, Bishop Adhemar of Le Puy, and Raymond of Saint–Gilles, Count of Toulouse; the second, from the west and north, was led by Prince Hugh of Vermandois (brother of the King of France), Duke Robert of Normandy (brother of the King of England), and Stephen of Blois (Robert's brother in–law); and the third, mostly Lorrainers from the north, was under Godfrey of Bouillon and his younger brother Baldwin. His older brother, Count Eustace III of

Boulogne, marched with the Normans, another indication of the gap between Bouillon and Boulogne. The last army, the most dangerous of the lot, was that of Bohemond of Taranto, scion of the Norman free–booting Hauteville family which had conquered Apulia and Sicily over the previous fifty years; with his ambitions there blocked by his half–brother, he had already twice attacked the Byzantine Empire in Greece, the second time getting as far as capturing Macedonia and Thessaly before Alexius out–manouvred him. But he was to prove even more difficult for his Crusader colleagues than for the Emperor of Byzantium.

How many were there altogether? Fulcher of Chartres said that by the time the four armies had united – or perhaps come together would be a better description – before the battle of Nicaea, after crossing the Bosphorus, there were six hundred thousand; Albert of Aix, with the benefit of more sources, said three hundred thousand. Medieval writers were notoriously poor mathematicians – as well as determined to make the best possible impression. The latest study, by John France, suggests a figure of perhaps sixty thousand at Nicaea, of whom about seven thousand were mounted lords and knights. But allowing for losses up to that point, including Peter the Hermit's twenty thousand, he estimates that a hundred thousand must have originally set out from their homes, the equivalent of one and a half million from present–day France, Germany, England and Italy. Pope Urban's call had had an extraordinary impact. In 1788 Gibbon wrote:

> "A new spirit had arisen of religious chivalry and Papal dominion: a nerve was touched of exquisite feeling; and the sensation vibrated to the heart of Europe".

Holy war, unholy demagoguery

In fact the nerve was one of ideological zeal, religious fanaticism: "Holy War". St Augustine had argued that, in times of danger to the faith, Christians could take to arms "by command of God and by lawful authority". Pope Gregory VII had ensured that only the Pope could interpret the command of God to the Church, which was the only lawful authority. From here it was a short step to Urban's call for this Holy War against the heathen, and a shorter step for the Crusaders therefore to feel justified in any action, trickery, slaughter, looting, land–grabs, against anyone who got in their way, infidel Turks and Arabs, Orthodox Greek Christians, Jews who merely happened to be on the spot. In 1751 the philosopher and historian David Hume, in his *History of England*, had been sharper than Gibbon, his younger and eventually more famous contemporary:

> "When all the particular [ecclesiastical] superstitions, therefore, were here united in one great object, the ardour for military enterprises took the same direction; and Europe, impelled by its two ruling passions, was loosened, as it were, from its foundations";

and he excoriated

> "the tumult of the crusades, which now engrossed the attention of Europe, and have ever since engaged the curiosity of mankind, as the most signal and most durable monument of human folly that has yet appeared in any age or nation".

But of course we had not then had the twentieth century.

How, why, did such a huge host of disparate people come to be motivated to commit themselves to the Crusade? – from dukes and princes and lords to those catalogued, in quintessentially English terms, by the English chronicler William of Malmesbury, writing just after the Crusade:

> "Then the Welshman left his forests and neglected his hunting. The Scotsman deserted his fleas with which he is most familiar. The Dane abandoned his drink and was temporarily sober. And the man of Norway turned his back on raw fish".

Had Hume been looking back from our post–twentieth century vantage point, perhaps he might have seen a certain parallel with our times here: it can not be pushed too far, but the coming together of this huge movement bore some similarities with the huge popular success of the Nazis in Germany before Hitler's takeover at the beginning of 1933.

Both took place in similar economic, social and emotional climates: economic conditions were difficult, in towns, especially, aggravated by severe food shortages; young men at loose ends found employment in brawling, dressed up in the eleventh century by the sons of the landed with notions of "chivalry", in Germany by the need to save Europe from Communism; the venial, unreformed medieval Church, and the handicapped and increasingly beset Weimar Republic in the 1920s, had not delivered the salvation expected of them by people bitter with their lot and with no apparent means of improving it.

Into this ripe situation came the clarion calls of Urban and Hitler. The Pope offered the chance of sharing in the rescue of Christendom through an exalting Holy War against the Infidel; it carried the prospect of exciting activity ennobled by self–sacrifice for the common good, the possibility of personal betterment through loot, and the certainty of spiritual salvation through the benefit of plenary indulgences for all previous sins. Hitler offered the chance of sharing in the rescue of Germany through an exalting campaign against domestic communists and socialists, a necessary war for "living–room" against Slavic "sub–humans", and a ruthless campaign against an "international Jewish conspiracy" (though the latter was played down somewhat in the crucial years leading to power); he offered the prospect of personal betterment through full employment in return for self–sacrifice for the common good, and the certainty of spiritual salvation through participation in Germany's national renewal and sacred destiny.

There were of course differences. The Pope's call was mainly aimed at and mainly responded to by the people of the territories that became France, with all their capacity for unruly individualism, Hitler's at the German people with their capacity for dangerous acceptance of discipline. And while both saw the need for war to achieve their aims, Urban might have discouraged massacres, though he does not seem to have commented on those of the Rhineland Jews, Antioch or Maarat an–Numan (he died fourteen days after the capture of Jerusalem, before news could have reached Rome); whereas Hitler had already proclaimed in *Mein Kampf* and innumerable speeches his intention to eliminate "racial pollution" – to eradicate homosexuals and gypsies, to "root out" the Jews, to subjugate the subhuman Slavs.

The equivalent, in twentieth century terms, of one and a half million people enthusiastically joined the First Crusade. In 1932, in the last two elections before Hitler became Chancellor, first 13.7 then 11.7 million Germans freely voted for the Nazis. How many Franks would have still marched in the First Crusade if they had thought that "liberating" the Holy Sepulchre would mean massacring the entire population of Jerusalem? How many Germans would have still voted for Hitler if they had thought that "root out" the Jews would mean trying to annihilate them?

What in fact *did* all these people think they were doing?

Godfrey the Crusader

Godfrey the Lorrainer was the only one of the Holy Roman Emperor's nobles to join the Crusade. There was probably a mixture of opportunity and motive not open to or shared by Henry's German princes: a degree of alienation from the Emperor, as noted earlier, after the Otbert affair; a new attitude not only to a Pope who was more moderate in his attitude to the Imperial bishops, but one who had opened up a vast new panorama of Holy War, with its prospect of combining piety (which would please mother) and adventure under the auspices of the Church. Some speculate that Godfrey was stirred by the enthusiasm of the northern French nobles; but he might have already been stirred much more directly by the Pope's reference at Clermont to his own family – indeed to Godfrey himself, in effect – when, according to Robert the Monk, Urban exhorted:

> "Let the deeds of your ancestors move you and incite your minds to manly achievements; likewise, the glory and greatness of King Charles the Great, and his son Louis [the Pious], and of your other kings, who have destroyed the kingdoms of the pagans, and have extended in these lands the territory of the Holy Church...Oh most valiant soldiers and descendants of invincible ancestors, be not degenerate, but recall the valour of your forefathers".

In any case, Godfrey, now about thirty–five, had secured his own domains; the Emperor Henry's cause was distinctly failing. Perhaps Godfrey was becoming bored.

The decision to go crusading once taken, Godfrey had to raise the considerable funds required, and to persuade his noble and yeoman followers to join him. The latter was apparently not difficult. As elsewhere, a wave of enthusiasm swept over the Duchy of Lower Lorraine; Godfrey was joined by the holders of lordships whose names are still spread across the region: Hainaut, Stavelot, Esch, Toul, Dixmude, Bruges, Audenarde, Nivelles, Fleurus, Mons, Tournai, Ypres [Ieper], Brussels, Namur, Courtrai, and, apparently at a very late stage, his younger brother, Baldwin of Boulogne, and there were others from Luxembourg and the Mosel. In this context Godfrey had one specific virtue: he was able, the chronicler Otto of Freising said, to mediate

> "between the French and the German Franks – who enjoyed taunting each other with bitter and hateful jokes – because he

had grown up on the border of the two peoples and spoke both languages. In this way he contributed much to their getting along peacefully".

It was a lesson the Belgian army forgot: in the First World War unknown numbers of Flemish–speaking troops were lost because their more aristocratic Francophone officers could not communicate with them.

Godfrey's total force was estimated by Anna Comnena, by the time it had reached Constantinople, as consisting of ten thousand knights and seventy thousand foot–soldiers, which was a wild exaggeration: it was probably of the order of ten, perhaps even fifteen, thousand, with up to a tenth being lords, knights and other mounted cavalry. Some must have had some experience in the Emperor's wars; many had probably experienced no more than the local lawlessness endemic in Lorraine.

Anna Comnena's other comment on Godfrey was also wrong: he was not "a very rich man". It took him a great deal of effort to raise funds for the new adventure, unlike his co–Crusader, Duke Robert of Normandy, who pawned his entire duchy to his brother, King William Rufus of England, for the literally princely sum of ten thousand marks of silver – though the ruthless collection of such a huge amount cost William even further popularity. Godfrey had no alternative but to adopt the same method, and it was his most valuable personal property, the County and Château of Bouillon, that he had to pawn – ironically, to Bishop Otbert of Liège, from whose covetous grasp Godfrey had spent the preceding years protecting them. The sum raised was around one thousand five hundred marks of silver; like the King in England, the Bishop had to resort to ruthless measures to raise such a sum, with the result that the abbeys of his diocese were stripped. The sale of other castles, mills and lands raised in addition "many pounds of gold and silver".

However Bouillon was not sold to Bishop Otbert, an important pointer to Godfrey's intentions. Bouillon was mortgaged with the option for Godfrey to redeem it on his return from the Holy Land, or for his brother Baldwin to do so if he did not. This arrangement suggests that at this stage at least Godfrey had no intention of carving out for himself a new principality in the Middle East, at the expense (as was to happen with others – including Baldwin) of the Emperor of Byzantium, whose rights the Crusaders were supposedly going to help recover. At the same time Godfrey's arrangement to redeem Bouillon undermines the later romantic legend that Godfrey had sworn to devote the rest of his days to the protection of the Holy Places. The evidence suggests a reasonably practical and careful Godfrey.

So, in August of 1096, Godfrey and his army set out to march through Imperial territory, up the Rhine and down the Danube, then to cross Catholic Hungary and pass into the Byzantine Empire at Nish [in what is now south–eastern Serbia, not far from the Bulgarian border]. Right at the beginning came Godfrey's extortions from the Jews of Cologne and, a little further up the Rhine, those of Mainz.

The Rhineland: crusade against the Jews

Or, rather, from the remnants of those communities: they, and other Jewish communities in the Rhineland, had already been assaulted far more brutally by some of the bands associated with Peter the Hermit's People's Crusade. There are three early Hebrew chronicles of these events; all start by saying of the Crusaders, in the words of Solomon bar Simson – who also said it specifically of Godfrey – that

> "as they passed through the towns where Jews dwelled, they said to one another: 'Look now, we are going a long way to seek out the profane shrine [the Holy Sepulchre] and to avenge ourselves on the Ishmaelites [the Moslems], when here, in our very midst, are the Jews – they whose forefathers murdered and crucified him for no reason. Let us first avenge ourselves on them and exterminate them from among the nations so that the name of Israel will no longer be remembered, or let them adopt our faith and acknowledge the offspring of promiscuity' ".

This was not simply Jewish propaganda. The chronicle of the German monk Ekkehard of Aura, who was to accompany the second wave of Crusaders in 1101, confirmed that the leader of one of the largest bands in Peter the Hermit's "army", Count Emich of Leiningen,

> "a man long of very ill repute on account of his tyrannical mode of life...usurped to himself the command of almost twelve thousand cross bearers. As they were led through the cities of the Rhine and the Main and also the Danube, they either destroyed the execrable race of the Jews wherever they found them (being even in this matter zealously devoted to the Christian religion) or forced them into the bosom of the Church...[they] slaughtered the exiled Jews through greed of money, rather than for the sake of God's

justice, although the Jews were opposed to Christ. The Lord is a just judge and orders no one unwillingly, or under compulsion, to come under the yoke of the Catholic faith".

The chronicles contain searing accounts of the massacres by Emich's band: the brutalities against men, women and children alike, the resistance of a few, the resignation of most in the face of overwhelming force. They are all the more poignant in our own age, which has seen even greater pogroms against Jews in Europe, including in that same Rhineland.

Christianity and Judaism had begun developing doctrinal differences by the time of the martyrdom in Jerusalem – by the Jewish authorities – of the Apostle James "the Less" (who some identified as the brother of Jesus) in Jerusalem in CE 62, shortly before the great Jewish diaspora following the failure of their revolt against the Romans in Palestine. Both official persecution and unauthorised pogroms spread in their wake after the Roman Empire was converted to Christianity by the Emperor Constantine at the beginning of the fourth century. However over the post–Roman centuries in Western Europe a delicately–balanced toleration developed. The secular authorities recognised the economic value of the mostly small Jewish communities, some of which flourished; the ecclesiastical authorities were critical of the Jews for allegedly knowing the truth about Jesus from their own contemporary witnesses but who still rejected it and refused to convert to Christianity. Along with their separate religious practices and social exclusiveness, this marked the Jews off as quite different, perhaps not quite wholly human; still this mostly did not result in persecution, though it was certainly held to justify legal disqualification and social discrimination.

The surge of religious enthusiasm that accompanied the First Crusade was sufficient to dislocate this lengthy balance of a sort: in the first instance, into the outbreaks of violence against Jews, mostly in the restricted area of the German Rhineland. Over time, with additional theological argument and growing popular prejudice – accusations of the ritual murder of Christian children, of the profanation of the Sacrament – the Jews became subjected to Europe–wide intolerance, persecution and exclusion. Their choice was often conversion or death, or, if lucky, exile.

With the earliest preaching of the Crusade in northern France, there had been a riot against the Jews in Rouen, and a letter from there to the Rhineland communities warned of the impending threat to them also.

Peter the Hermit or his followers may have been behind these developments as he recruited across the area; certainly by the time he reached Trier in April 1096 he terrified the Jewish community there, and in May his army tried to force the community in Regensburg to undergo baptism. But the worst offenders were from Swabia (roughly Baden and Wurttemberg) and the Rhineland itself: beginning in May and continuing through June and early July the troops commanded by Emich of Leiningen attacked the Jewish community at Speyer, then moved on to Worms and Mainz; some then spread out to Cologne and a whole series of towns from there to Dortmund, others to Trier and even Metz, massacring their Jews as they went.

As in more recent times, the Jews themselves did nothing to provoke these first pogroms in Europe: it would surely have been recorded most prominently in the Christian chronicles if they had – but there is nothing. As in Nazi Europe, it was their mere existence that was provocative of wholesale murder. Curiously, it is only in the Hebrew chronicle of Solomon bar Simson that there appears an example of Jewish offensiveness towards Christianity as such: he says that in Mainz, as many of the Jewish community began to commit suicide rather than accept forcible conversion to Christianity by Emich, they cried out:

> "Look and behold, O Lord, what we are doing to sanctify Thy Great Name, in order not to exchange You for a crucified scion who was despised, abominated, and held in contempt in his own generation, a bastard son conceived by a menstruating and wanton mother".

It would seem that such reverse prejudice was not widely prevalent amongst the Jews; nor could it have been widely known amongst Christians, or we would have had understandably enraged reactions, certainly not, as in some places, the support of the bishop, nor the edict from the Emperor Henry IV, provoked by Godfrey's threats, commanding that the Jews be protected. Indeed in 1097 Henry went further, and authorised the return to Judaism of those who had been forced to accept "conversion" to Christianity.

Nor at this stage was hostility to Jewish money–lending a significant factor: it was in the next century, after the Catholic Church began enforcing the Christian ban on taking interest from other Christians, that Jewish communities became extensively involved in usury, and consequently widely hated by those who could not or did not want to repay their loans. Over virtually the entire route of all the Crusading armies there was extortion and looting – as with undisciplined armies all over the world at all times – as they sought to sustain themselves on the march. But the Rhineland Jewish communities had the double misfortune of being amongst the more prosperous European Jewish settlements, as well as on the direct path of the most undisciplined of all the Crusaders. They had been actively and peacefully engaged, perhaps for a century or more, in business and trade, though the community in Speyer had in fact been established there only twelve years earlier, on the invitation of the Bishop, who had seen it as contributing to the economic development of the city. Thus these Jewish communities' economic standing made them targets for lawless fund–raising; even only two months after the depredations of the People's Crusade, those in Cologne and Mainz still had sufficient money as to expose them to Godfrey's further blackmail when he and his army passed through.

But the targeting of the Jews was not just financial: it was clearly based on religious prejudice, especially that of Crusaders from the regions neighbouring the Meuse and the Rhine – some from Godfrey's duchy, and probably including Godfrey himself. Already, since the middle of the century, there had been images in illuminated manuscripts, made between Liège and southern Germany, in which those scourging, mocking and crucifying Christ were depicted as Jews of their time. There was thus anti–Semitism in the monastic establishments and elsewhere in the Church where these aids to worship were made and used (there were to be far more, including more visible frescoes and stained–glass windows, in the next two centuries). Godfrey was a child of this Church.

However, the Jewish writers each acknowledged that some of the bishops in the Rhineland made some effort to protect various Jewish communities, though there were variations, ambivalence, cowardice, perhaps treachery. The anonymous Mainz author of the *Narrative of the Old Persecutions* described two contrasting examples, first in Speyer:

> "On the Sabbath, the measure of justice began to fall upon us. The errant ones [Emich's Crusaders] and the burghers first plotted against the holy men, the saints of the Most High, in Speyer, and they planned to seize all of them together in the synagogue. Told of this, the saints arose on Sabbath morning, prayed quickly, and departed from the synagogue. When the enemy saw that their plot to take them all captive together had been frustrated, they rose up

against them and slew eleven of them. This was the beginning of the persecution...

When Bishop John heard of this, he came with a large army and wholeheartedly aided the community, taking them indoors and rescuing them from the enemy. The bishop then took some of the burghers and cut off their hands, for he was a righteous man among the Gentiles, and the Omnipresent One used him as a means for our benefit and rescue... Bishop John saved them, for the Lord had moved him to keep them alive without taking a bribe – for it was the Lord's doing to grant us a vestige and a remnant by the bishop's hand".

But at Mainz the story was different:

"When the saints, the Pious ones of the Most High, the holy community of Mainz, heard that some of the community of Speyer had been slain and that the community of Worms had been attacked a second time, their spirits failed and their hearts melted and became as water...All the Jewish community leaders assembled and came before the bishop with his officers and servants, and said to them: 'What shall we do about the news we have received regarding the slaughter of our brethren in Speyer and Worms?' They replied: 'Heed our advice and bring all your money into our treasury and into the treasury of the bishop. And you, your wives, sons, and all your belongings shall come into the courtyard of the bishop. Thus will you be saved from the errant ones'. Actually, they gave this advice so as to herd us together and hold us like fish that are caught in an evil net and then turn us over to the enemy. The bishop assembled his ministers, servants, and great noblemen in order to rescue us from the errant ones, for at first it had been his desire to save us, but in the end he turned against us".

Contrasting it with God's actions at Speyer, his inaction in Worms and elsewhere caused Simon bar Simson to cry out:

"God, the maker of peace, turned aside and averted His eyes from His people, and consigned them to the sword. No prophet, seer, or man of wise heart was able to comprehend how the sin of the people infinite in number was deemed so great as to cause the destruction of so many lives in the various Jewish communities. The martyrs endured the extreme penalty normally inflicted only upon one guilty of murder. Yet, it must be stated with certainty that God is a righteous god, and we are to blame".

This is an anguish that is painfully familiar to the twentieth century.

From the Rhine to Constantinople

Although the German nobles generally had not shown any interest in the Crusade, as Godfrey's army moved on further across southern Germany it collected additional adherents.

The German chronicler Ekkehard of Aura gave a picture of its passage:

"The West Franks [that is, the French] could easily be induced to leave their lands, since for several years Gaul had suffered, now from civil war, now from famine, and again from excessive mortality; and, finally, that disease ['St Antony's Fire' as it was then called, or erysipelas] which had its origin in the vicinity of the church of St Gertrude of Nivelles[40] alarmed them to such an extent that they feared for their lives...

But for the East Franks, the Saxons, the Thuringians, the Bavarians, and the Alemanni this trumpet call [to the Crusade] sounded only faintly, particularly because of the schism between the empire and the papacy...And so it came to pass that almost all the Teutonic race, at first ignorant of the reason for this setting out, laughed to scorn the many legions of knights passing through their land, the many companies of foot soldiers, and the crowds of country people, women, and little ones. They regarded them as crazed with unspeakable folly, inasmuch as they were striving after uncertainties in place of certainties and were leaving for naught the land of their birth, to seek with certain danger the uncertain land of promise; and, while giving up their own possessions, they were yearning after those of strangers. But although our people are more perverse than other races, yet in consideration of the promise of divine pity, the enthusiasm of the Teutons was at last turned to this same proclamation, for they were taught, forsooth, what the thing really meant by the crowds passing through their lands".

---

40 Nivelles was actually in Godfrey's domains; his mother had sold the abbey her lands at Baisy to help finance his crusading.

Others also needed convincing of this new crowd's bona fides. Such had been the damage inflicted on life and property by the passage of Peter the Hermit's unruly mob that when Godfrey's army arrived at the Hungarian border the Catholic King Coloman demanded hostages before it could proceed. Godfrey decided on prudence, and also (without consulting him) on sending his brother Baldwin, plus wife and family, as the hostages; but Albert of Aix recorded that he also announced to the army that,

> "under sentence of death, they should neither touch nor take by force anything in the Kingdom of Hungary, and should stir up no quarrel, but that everything should be exchanged for a just price".

It worked:

> "And so, day by day, in quiet and peace, with full measure and just sale, the Duke and his people crossed the Kingdom of Hungary",

and were rejoined by Baldwin and family on the other side. Godfrey crossed into Byzantium in what is now eastern Yugoslavia, and the situation continued the same, even without hostages: the Emperor appealed for an orderly passage and promised abundant supplies; in return, Godfrey

> "proclaimed to all that thereafter they should touch nothing with undue violence, except food for their horses",

and all proceeded smoothly as far as Philppopolis [present day Plovdiv, in southern Bulgaria] – notwithstanding the qualifications.

From then on everything went awry. Godfrey received a message that one of the leaders of the crusading army from northern France, Hugh of Vermandois, the French King's brother, had arrived at Constantinople ahead of his companions and was being held "in chains and in prison". A messenger was sent demanding Hugh's release; and, Albert of Aix said, when he returned with a negative response,

> "the Duke [Godfrey] and all his company burned with wrath; and they refused any longer to keep faith and treaty of peace with [the Emperor]. Immediately, by a command of the Duke, all that land

was given over in plunder to the alien pilgrims and knights, who, delaying there for eight days, laid waste the whole region".

The fact that the information about Hugh of Vermandois was wrong, and Godfrey's reaction was so violent, were indicative of the deep suspicions the Catholic Westerners had of the Orthodox Greeks of Byzantium.

As the Catholic armies congregated at Constantinople this suspicion was fully reciprocated by the Byzantines: Anna Comnena wrote of the Celts (as she called the Franks),

> "They were all of one mind and in order to fulfil their dream of taking Constantinople they had adopted a common policy...To all appearances they were on pilgrimage to Jerusalem; in reality they planned to dethrone Alexius and seize the capital. Unfortunately for them, he was aware of their perfidy from long experience".

But Alexius, as she wrote further on,

> "had an uncanny prevision and knew how to seize a point of vantage before his rivals".

He needed to, with this lot.

He had two main objectives: first, to protect Constantinople itself by limiting the Westerners' access to what Fulcher of Chartres called "the excellent and beautiful city"; second, to protect the Empire by having the Western leaders formally accept him as their overlord, in case they tried to set up their own principalities in lands they won back from the Turks. This would be as close as he could get to turning these dangerous Western Catholic armies that Urban II had aroused into the subservient mercenaries he had asked the Pope for in the first place. To achieve this he was prepared to shower them with gifts and subsidies; and the strategy quickly succeeded, as, ironically, so far from being a prisoner, the vain and pompous Hugh of Vermandois had already sworn his fealty before Godfrey's angry arrival in December 1096. For the next five months stubbornness and hostility followed each other on both sides, as Alexius sought to ensure Godfrey's good faith before the other Crusade leaders arrived, and Godfrey tried to keep his freedom of action until then.

The stand–off had its comical moments: Anna Comnena says Alexius did meet some of Godfrey's counts, whom he urged to persuade Godfrey to take the oath;

"The Latins, however, wasted time with their usual verbosity and love of long speeches, so that a false rumour reached the Franks that their counts had been arrested by Alexius".

Godfrey not only declined to take an oath to the Eastern Emperor, perhaps because he had already sworn allegiance to the Western one, but twice refused even to visit Alexius, presumably fearing treachery; twice, in anger, Alexius retaliated by cutting off Godfrey's supplies; twice Godfrey's men attacked and looted the outskirts of the city in reprisal, the second time on Easter Eve, in April 1097. Alexius's piety turned out to be keener than Godfrey's: he was genuinely shocked, and told the Westerners,

"If you must fight, we too shall be ready, but after the day of the Saviour's Resurrection".

He was in fact unable to wait so long. According to the *Alexiad*, Hugh of Vermandois then tried to persuade Godfrey to desist from his menaces and to

"yield to the Emperor's wish, unless he wanted to learn a second time how experienced a general Alexius was...But Godfrey rebuked him sternly. 'You left your own country as a king,' he said [he was the King's brother], 'with all that wealth and a strong army; now from the heights you've brought yourself to the level of a slave. And then, as if you had won some great success, you come here and tell me to do the same.' 'We ought to have stayed in our own countries and kept our hands off other peoples' [countries]', replied Hugh. 'But since we've come thus far and need the Emperor's protection, no good will come of it unless we obey his orders.' "

When, next, Godfrey's men attacked new envoys sent by Alexius, the Emperor's piety – and patience – ran out: a sharp attack by the Imperial troops routed Godfrey's men, or as Anna Comnena put it, with uncharacteristic modesty,

"As the Romans showed greater spirit the Latins gave way. Thus Godfrey not long after submitted...",

and on Easter Sunday, along with his brother Baldwin and the other Lorraine lords, swore his acknowledgement of the Emperor as overlord of any lands they might conquer, and to hand over to him any of his lands they might reconquer. After receiving "generous largesse" and being entertained at a great banquet, Godfrey and his men were shipped with great relief across the Bosphorus to Asia Minor.

Now, with Godfrey's taking of the oath, the process went amazingly smoothly: Alexius seduced the Crusader leaders one by one as they turned up. Stephen of Blois, William the Conqueror's son–in–law, who should have known better, has left, in a letter to his wife, an example of how the Crusaders naively swallowed Alexius's line:

> "Truly, the Emperor received me with dignity and honour and with the greatest affection, as if I were his own son, and he loaded me with most bountiful and precious gifts. In the whole of our army of God there is neither duke nor count nor other noble person whom he trusts or favours more than myself".

One by one, dressed in full fig – "robes woven in purple and gold, bordered in ermine, sable, squirrel and vair" – in a desperate attempt to impress this luxurious Court, the Crusaders swore Godfrey's oath, though "deceitful, treacherous...disagreeable, ill–natured" Bohemond of Taranto, as Anna Comnena characterised him, had absolutely no intention of honouring it; and army by army they were shipped across the Bosphorus.

All but Raymond of Saint–Gilles, Count of Toulouse, who resolutely refused to swear the same oath as the others, who all begged him to do so to avoid further trouble with the Emperor. A great aristocrat with royal connections, he probably feared having to serve under the unaristocratic and untrustworthy Bohemond, who had ingratiated himself with Alexius in the hope of getting command of all the Christian forces – though in fact there was no way the Emperor would ever trust Bohemond with anything. Raymond felt that *he* should have the supreme command because of the special relationship he claimed with Pope Urban II, who had actually discussed his plans for the Crusade with him, but who had in fact refused him the leadership in favour of Bishop Adhemar of Le Puy. Eventually he swore a modified oath, which the Emperor accepted, apparently because, as Anna Comnena said, her father had for Raymond

> "a deep affection, for several reasons: the count's superior intellect, his untarnished reputation, the purity of his life. He knew

moreover how greatly Raymond valued the truth: whatever the circumstances, he honoured truth above all else. In fact, Saint–Gilles outshone all Latins in every quality, as the sun is brighter than the stars".

It is a touching tribute across a deep divide, though it proved to be excessive.

Helping the Emperor of the East to secure an oath of allegiance from virtually all the Western leaders seems to have been about the only occasion during the entire Crusade that Godfrey played anything like a leadership role, if such a turnaround could be so described. It is a pity there is no record of the reaction of the Emperor of the West, Godfrey's former liege lord, Henry IV; perhaps he would have been amused – after all, Alexius was no great friend of Rome. Had Godfrey been more skilful and awaited the arrival of all the armies, the outcome, for Constantinople and Byzantium and perhaps for a good deal more, might have been different. But Godfrey, as arrogant as any of the Western Crusaders, was contemptuous as much of the Greeks' diplomacy as of their military skills. By running rings around him, provoking him into a series of blusters that, alone, he had no way of winning, Alexius carefully undermined the threat the First Crusade posed to both the City and the Empire.

All it cost Alexius was the bribes and the subsidies he handed out to the avaricious Westerners; and whether they were aware of it or not, Albert of Aix noted with irony:

"A surprising thing, everything the Duke shared with his soldiers that came from the Emperor promptly returned to the Imperial Treasury to pay for food and all the other supplies. Nothing surprising about that: the Emperor had for the entire Empire the monopoly for the sale of wine, oil, wheat, barley and all foodstuffs. As the result, the Imperial Treasury is always full, and no handout manages to exhaust it".

Alexius never lost sight of his main game: his own situation. All he had ever wanted was some mercenaries to help him fight the Turks; now he could not even do that.

"He would have liked", his daughter said, "to share in the expedition against the barbarians, too, but he feared the enormous numbers of the Celts".

There was no way he would now leave the vicinity of Constantinople. And the First Crusade was on its own.

Constantinople to Antioch

The Crusader armies were now all together for the first time.

"Who ever heard such a mixture of languages in one army?", marvelled Fulcher of Chartres; "There were Franks, Flemish, Frisians, Gauls, Allobroges, Lotharingians, Alemanni, Bavarians, Normans, Angles, Scots, Aquitanians, Italians, Dacians, Apulians, Iberians, Bretons, Greeks, and Armenians".

They first captured Nicaea [present–day Iznik], capital of Kilij Arslan, the Turkish Sultan of Roum, in June 1097, though only after a five–week siege and with the eventual support of Alexius's ships on the lake side of the city. Stephen of Blois wrote home again:

"God has triumphed and the very large city of Nicaea was surrendered...We read that the Holy Fathers of the primitive Church held a synod at Nicaea [the first Church Council, in 325 CE]...[and] were led by the teaching of the Holy Spirit to confirm there the faith of the Blessed Trinity. And this city, which because of its sins later became a mistress of error, now by the mercy of God has been made, through His unworthy servants, a disciple of truth. I tell you, my beloved, five weeks after leaving Nicaea we will be in Jerusalem, unless Antioch resists us".

They would not be in Jerusalem until one day short of two years later, and not only because Antioch resisted.

At Nicaea the Crusaders adopted tactics which drew the scorn of Anna Comnena:

"The heads of many Turks they stuck on the ends of spears and came back carrying these like standards, so that the barbarians, recognising afar off what had happened and being frightened by this defeat at their first encounter, might not be so eager for battle in future. So much for the ideas and actions of the Latins".

And so much for the tactics as well: only two weeks afterwards they nearly came to grief at Dorylaeum [Eskishehir, halfway to Ankara], where Bohemond's forces were attacked while those of Godfrey, Raymond and Hugh were taking a separate route; by quick reactions and good luck they managed to come together and destroy the army of Kilij Arslan. Fulcher of Chartres had sharp words for the decision of Godfrey and his companions to separate the army, "for what reason I do not know". But he surely knew perfectly well: the leaders were already squabbling, and were soon to split their forces even more seriously.

In the meantime they had to make their way across the vast expanse of Anatolia through the height of summer; and although the Turks here were no longer up to standing and fighting, they were sufficiently organised to implement a pretty effective scorched earth policy. The author of the *Gesta Francorum* described the horrors of that three–month slog:

> "We went on pursuing the most iniquitous Turks, who daily fled before us...[They] burned and devastated everything that was convenient or useful...Accordingly, we were following them through deserts, and dry and uninhabitable land, from which we scarcely escaped and came out alive. Hunger and thirst pinched us on all sides, and there was absolutely nothing for us to eat, unless, by chance, tearing and grinding grain with our hands, we continued to exist on such food as wretchedly as possible. There most of our cavalry ceased to exist...For want of horses, our men used oxen in place of cavalry horses, and because of the very great need, goats, sheep, and dogs served as beasts of burden".

Many were lost as the armies wound their way through Antioch–in–Pisidia [Yalvach] and Iconium [Konya] to Heraclea [Eregli] on the northern edge of the Taurus Mountains.

There, the Crusader force divided, and would never be fully reunited; rather, it would continue to suffer further splits before Jerusalem was reached – and after. It is no surprise that the first breakaway was Bohemond's nephew Tancred, one of this Crusade's two great–grandsons, along with five grandsons, of the old Tancred de Hauteville whose six sons had founded Norman Sicily and Apulia. With the intention of carving out a separate principality for himself, young Tancred slipped away south from Heraclea to the Turkish–controlled Greek–Armenian city of Tarsus, birthplace of St Paul, near the Cilician coast – only to be beaten to it by Godfrey's young brother Baldwin. Some considered that Godfrey had despatched Baldwin to head off Tancred's bid, because he feared it would strengthen Bohemond's already evident ambition to control Antioch. That may have been so; Albert of Aix said that rivalry broke into the open when Tarsus seemed to favour Bohemond, of whom they knew, over Godfrey, of whom they didn't, leading Baldwin to rage:

> "Bohemond and this Tancred, whom you regard highly and before whom you tremble, are by no means the greatest and mightiest leaders of the Christian host; not comparable are they at all to my brother Godfrey, a duke and leader of the whole army of the Franks, nor indeed to any of his family. For my brother Godfrey is a prince, and duke of a great dominion, the foremost in the realm of the august Emperor of the Romans, which he holds by the right of inheritance from his noble ancestors. He is revered by the whole army, and great and small willingly obey his voice and counsel, for he has been chosen and constituted head and lord by all. Bear in mind, too, that you and all your possessions, even this town, will be consumed and destroyed with sword and fire by this duke; and no Bohemond, nor this Tancred, will be able to champion or defend you".

The assertion of the aristocratic Carolingian Godfrey's superiority over the upstart Norman Bohemond is no surprise; the claim of Godfrey's being chosen as leader of the entire army is. It is not supported by anyone else – let alone by the continuing fractiousness of the Crusade's leaders.

Godfrey's claim to any sort of leadership was in any case promptly undermined by his boastful brother: leaving a garrison in Tarsus, Baldwin himself struck out on his own, past the head of the Gulf of Iskenderun, across the Euphrates, to the small county of Edessa [now Urfa, in south–east Turkey near the Syrian border]. Edessa was an Armenian city subject to Byzantium; threatened by the Turks, its ruler and people welcomed Baldwin and his Lotharingians as saviours, but in two weeks the former was dead and Baldwin was Count of Edessa. It was only the beginning: the chronicler Raymond of Aguilers, travelling with Raymond of Saint–Gilles, commented that "Everyone wished to make his own fortune; no–one thought of the common good". It was exactly as Alexius had feared.

Antioch
Until Christmas Day 1100, Baldwin was to play no further role in the First Crusade, other than to furnish supplies from the comfortable

distance of his prosperous new fief. Tancred, beaten at his own game, rejoined the Crusade; his principality would have to wait. The bulk of the Crusaders took a circuitous route into Syria, north–east to Caesarea [Kayseri] in Cappadocia, south again over the difficult Anti–Taurus to Marash, and thence to Antioch [Antakya]. There, Stephen of Blois' fear was realised: Antioch resisted. In fact the great walled city of Antioch resisted the Crusaders' siege for nearly eight months, from October 1097 until June 1098.

Antioch was a turning point: in due course it destroyed Turkish resistance to the Crusade; but it also destroyed any semblance of Crusader unity, and at the same time as it brought division it brought deprivation and death. The Crusaders' strength had already been diminished by the departure of Baldwin; there were more losses from the repeated sorties by the Turks, from starvation during the bitter winter, from Turkish forces coming to the relief of the starving city, from plague at the beginning of summer.

Near the end, Stephen of Blois deserted with some four thousand men and sailed for western Anatolia, where he met up with the Emperor and a Byzantine army on the way to the support of the hard–pressed Westerners at Antioch; and on top of his desertion, Stephen told Alexius that the Turks had already annihilated the Crusader army. At that news Alexius turned back to protect Constantinople from the expected further advance of the Turks. It was an honest and reasonable decision on the basis of Stephen's intelligence, but Alexius was never forgiven by the Western Christians for this "Greek betrayal". Stephen returned to France to his beloved wife, the Conqueror's daughter, who was so furious and ashamed that she forced him to go right back East with the second group of Crusaders in 1101; he was killed in battle at Ramleh, near Jaffa, the next year, trying vainly to recover his honour.

The city of Antioch, though still not the citadel, fell at the beginning of June 1098 only because it was betrayed by the commander of one of the towers, who was suborned by Bohemond – though it was appropriate enough, as the Turks had themselves captured it by treachery from the Byzantines only thirteen years before. Raymond of Aguilers summed up the outcome:

> "When the enemy saw our men on the mountain above them, some fled through the gates, others threw themselves headlong from the walls…A joyous spectacle appeared to us, with those who had withstood us for so many months now completely trapped.

Our joy over the defeated enemy was great, but we grieved for the more than thirty horses that had their necks broken in the streets".

There were rich spoils for the Crusaders in the city, but no food.

But almost immediately a huge Turkish army under Kerbogha, Atabeg of Mosul, which had been fruitlessly besieging Edessa, arrived at Antioch, too late to save it but completely turning the tables. As Raymond of Aguilers recounted:

> "While our men were busy counting their spoils...We were watching the pagan dancing girls and feasting in splendour, not at all mindful of God who had blessed us, when suddenly, on the third day, we ourselves were under siege. And this was more dangerous for us because the upper citadel was still in enemy hands".

The besieged besiegers were now reduced to eating horse's head without the tongue, goat entrails, stewed leaves and withered plants, "the blood of their own chargers".

Collapsed Crusader morale was now revived by the sudden "discovery" in the Church of St Andrew, as the result of a vision by a Provençal peasant, one Peter Bartholomew, of the "Holy Lance", the one that had pierced Christ's side on the Cross. No matter that there was already a Holy Lance among the Imperial treasures in Constantinople, discovered eight centuries earlier by St Helena, the Emperor Constantine's mother – even the initially sceptical Bishop Adhemar of Le Puy went along with this spiritual boost. After three days' fasting and processing from church to church, with Adhemar carrying the Lance, the Crusaders launched what in the circumstances must have been close to a suicidal attack on Kerbogha's forces. The Turks were caught completely by surprise, and totally routed:

> "The enemy abandoned their camp", the anonymous author of the *Gesta Francorum* exulted, "leaving their pavilions, with gold and silver and rich furnishings, as well a sheep, oxen, horses, mules, camels, asses, and also corn, wine, flour, and many other things that we badly needed...We returned to the city with great rejoicing, praising and blessing God who had given victory to his people".

However it was Bohemond's generalship that deserved the credit for this annihilation of the Moslem threat, as it had been his cunning that had opened the city to the invaders three weeks before. The road to Jerusalem was now open, but the Crusade leaders immediately decided to postpone taking it for five months. There was certainly a need to recover after the traumas of Antioch; but delay also resulted from deepening rivalries among the leadership, made worse by the death of the Papal Legate, Bishop Adhemar, and above all over Bohemond's claim to Antioch, which he steadily made good on the ground.

It was in putting together the history of the siege of Antioch that William of Tyre came up with one of the best parts of Godfrey's legend: in the midst of one of the many skirmishes, he struck a mounted Turk with such a powerful sword–blow that Godfrey sliced him – armour included – in two, at the level of the waist,

> "through the navel, so cleanly that the top half crashed to the ground, and the other half remained sitting on the horse, which went back into the town with the other [Saracens]".

In fact Godfrey seems to have lost ground at Antioch: from what the chroniclers say, he had not played any kind of outstanding role during the siege, the counter–siege, or their endings. Afterwards, he seems to have spent a large part of the time in the more congenial surrounds of brother Baldwin's Edessa, and in establishing his own hold on several cities in and near the Euphrates valley which Baldwin had bestowed on him. It looked suspiciously like the beginnings of a land–grab such as his admirers subsequently protested had never crossed his mind.

Bohemond was justifying his claim to Antioch, notwithstanding his oath to the Emperor Alexius, on the grounds of Alexius's failure to come to the Crusaders' support. The other leaders pretended to be scandalised by this sophistry, but, where they could, quietly availed themselves of its cover for their own greed. Count Raymond of Saint–Gilles, ambitious himself rather than concerned about the proprieties of the claim, increasingly took the lead in resisting Bohemond's ambitions.

In their paralysis, the Crusaders were descending further and further into barbarism. From his Edessan bases Godfrey captured a number of other fortified towns, but he was not even concerned that they be infidel: one unfortunate place was ruled by an Armenian who displeased Godfrey; he burned it to the ground, and had twenty of its defenders blinded. Count Raymond, refusing to budge so as not to leave Antioch to Bohemond, and developing territorial ambitions of his own, undertook an attack against the Turkish town of Maarat an–Numan, to the south–east of Antioch; Bohemond, suspicious – rightly – of Raymond's intentions, insisted on joining the expedition; and it was as if they then felt they had to compete in horror. A siege–tower was built to breach the walls,

> "and behind the siege–tower stood the priests and clerics in their vestments, praying God to defend his people, to exalt Christendom and cast down idolatry…When the Saracens saw that our men had undermined the wall, they panicked and fled into the city…
>
> Then Bohemond sent interpreters to the Saracens, promising safety to those who would take wives and children and goods into a palace that lay above the gate. Our men all entered the city and seized whatever loot they could find, and when it was dawn they killed everyone they met, man or woman. There were Saracen corpses in every corner of the city, and we could not go through the streets without treading on dead bodies.
>
> Then Bohemond went into the palace where the enemy, at his invitation, had taken refuge, and he stripped them of all their wealth and belongings. Some of them he had killed and others taken to Antioch to be sold as slaves".

It was at this point that Raymond of Saint–Gilles tried to bribe the other commanders to accept his leadership – against Bohemond rather than specifically to lead on to Jerusalem. He had plentiful funds: too ill to participate in the final attack against Kerbogha, he had been well enough to get most of the booty from the latter's camp, before his companions had returned from the battlefield. Dukes Godfrey and Robert of Normandy, the Count of Flanders, even Bohemond's nephew Tancred, were offered substantial amounts. Only Tancred accepted, perhaps not so much out of greed or even need but because Bohemond wanted him to keep an eye on his competitor. Still none of the leaders focussed on the critical issue, the terrible decline in the condition of the armies.

The last stretch

Again, Godfrey does not seem to have played any significant role in the decision, finally, in January 1099, to march on to the Crusade's supposed goal, Jerusalem. Neither, for that matter, did any of the other leaders: it was the rank and file who forced the decision on them.

"The people cried out", Raymond of Aguilers recorded, " 'First quarrels about Antioch, now quarrels about Maarat! Will the Princes squabble over every place that God shall give us, while the army of the Lord suffers?'...These men were desperate, for the army was so hungry that we greedily ate the already fetid bodies of the Saracens thrown into the swamp two or more weeks before. These events frightened us, as well as others, and many of our people wandered away, despairing of help".

In these circumstances, the massacre at Maarat an–Numan might perhaps be seen from a new perspective: as the monstrous behaviour of men whose leaders' neglect had made them monsters, the product not so much of *their* religious fanaticism as of their leaders' – though such distinctions would not of course have registered with the slaughtered. Raymond of Aguilers, the priest–chronicler, implicitly distinguished between the unacceptable cannibalism of the men – "to whom life was not very dear, and for whom long fasting had led to contempt for self" – and the understandable massacres unleashed by their leaders.

But the common soldiers came up with their own solution to the Crusade's terrible impasse:

" 'Since the Princes are unwilling to lead us to Jerusalem, let us choose some brave knight whom we can serve loyally and safely, and he will take us to Jerusalem...Let those who want the Emperor's gold keep it, and likewise those who covet the wealth of Antioch. But let us take up our march with Christ as leader, for whose sake we have come this far' ".

In the face of rebellion by his men – rather than their piety, let alone their starvation – Count Raymond, "invoking the compassion of God and the protection of the Saints", led his army out of Maarat an–Numan, not aiming so much at Jerusalem as at somewhere where they could find supplies. But he went barefoot..."as a devout Christian pilgrim".

Duke Robert of Normandy, with Tancred, at once set out from Antioch to join him. It took several more weeks, and continuing defections of their troops to Raymond, for Godfrey and Count Robert of Flanders to decide they would follow – but only a month after that. The suspicion remains that Godfrey was reluctant to be torn away from establishing a principality of his own in northern Syria adjacent to his brother's; but in due course he too marched southwards. To start with, the two groups which did set out followed two different routes: Count Raymond, Duke Robert and Tancred marched by the inland route direct from Maarat an–Numan through Masyaf; Duke Godfrey, Count Robert and, initially, Bohemond, took the coast road south through Latakia. There Bohemond broke his vow and turned back to finish taking control of Antioch. Baldwin stayed in Edessa. For these two, Jerusalem was no longer even a fig–leaf for their personal ambitions. Another leader missing more definitively was Hugh of Vermandois: delegated some time before to, in effect, challenge the Emperor Alexius to come and formally take possession of Antioch, he had simply deserted.

Krak des Chevaliers

Before the two marching columns met up near what is now the border between Syria and Lebanon, just to the north–east of Tripoli, Raymond's forces captured the fortress of Hosn al–Akrad, "the Castle of the Kurds", where the great Krak des Chevaliers now stands.

T.E.Lawrence – Lawrence of Arabia – called the Krak "perhaps the best preserved and most wholly admirable castle in the world". Even more emphatically, the twentieth century English historian T.S.R.Boase wrote:

> "As the Parthenon is to Greek temples and Chartres to Gothic cathedrals, so is the Krak des Chevaliers to medieval castles, the supreme example, one of the great buildings of all times".

He was right.

Like the Château de Bouillon – though on a far greater scale – the Krak was repaired, rebuilt, extended and strongly re–fortified after the First Crusade. The substantial Arab castle captured by Raymond of Saint–Gilles formed the core; in the twelfth century the major work was undertaken by the later Crusaders of the military–religious Order of the Knights Hospitallers; and there are various Arab overlays of the next century, after what had come to be called "the key of Christendom" fell to the Moslems in CE 1271, when the last Crusader foothold in the whole of Palestine had only twenty years left.

This is the castle seen today, riding the long rock spur of a hill above the tiny village of al–Husn, fifty kilometres west of Homs: a vast complex of defences within defences, walls and bastions in two great rings, the inner one, entered through an enormous vaulted ramp, enclosing chapel, great hall, towers and keep around courtyards at different levels built over a maze of underground chambers. The entire structure is massive, and its parts are massive – the *inner* enclosure, above the enormous exterior fortifications, is bound on the south and west sides by a huge wall, twenty–five metres thick at its base and twenty–five high: the Arabs called it simply "The Mountain". From the hot, dry Syrian plain to the east, or from further up the ridge to the south, the Krak des Chevaliers not so much sits on, as rides its vast rocky base, a huge masonry battleship bristling with fortifications, forever becalmed.

The castle still stands virtually complete, in part a powerful symbol of the first Western attempt to impose its dominance on the Middle East, in part a superb monument to a period when, as it eventually turned out, Occident and Orient were more closely balanced in power than at any time since. There was something of this balance already in the Castle of the Kurds' first encounter with the Crusaders. Because the local inhabitants had taken refuge in it with all their herds, Raymond decided to attack it for provisions rather than strategic requirements at that stage. The defenders, well aware of the Westerners' needs and habits, let out the animals, and, as anticipated, the Crusaders immediately scrambled after them, including Raymond's bodyguard, so that he was almost captured when the Turkish defenders suddenly attacked. After this stupidity a serious attack was mounted the following day – but the wily defenders had slipped away from the castle during the night. The honours were even.

When the Mameluke Sultan Baibars of Egypt eventually captured the Krak des Chevaliers from the Knights Hospitallers in 1271, it was also not so much by his successful breaching of the outer walls as by a psychological campaign that induced the last defenders to surrender the virtually impregnable inner fortress. The Krak was never again besieged. Baibars, Lawrence of Arabia wrote, "was frequently generous enough to extend his aegis over the works of his predecessors, by cutting in his own inscriptions"; and, as at the Krak, by making his own additions where those enemy predecessors had built so superbly.

There was further irony in the Krak's uneventful subsequent history. After some time the great castle was no longer useful militarily to the Mamelukes or their Ottoman successors, and it was occupied by Moslem villagers who lived in it for centuries, until they were cleared out in 1934 by...the French. Following the First World War defeat of the Ottoman Empire, Syria and Lebanon had been made a French mandated territory under the League of Nations: the Franks were back! The Krak was within the Lebanon administrative region, and, this time around, the

Krak was occupied by more gentle crusaders: the French antiquities authorities – although, in an ultimate outbreak of nationalist Crusader nostalgia, they did declare the castle a "Monument of France". The final gesture of the modern Franks came with the independence of Lebanon and Syria in 1945, when, as compensation for a farewell colonial bombardment of Damascus, the French "gave" the Krak des Chevaliers back to Syria. What would old Baibars of Egypt have made of all this latter–day Frankish meddling?

Jerusalem at last

As far as the orthodox Sunni Moslems at the time of the First Crusade were concerned, the meddling of Baibars' heretical Shi'ite Fatimid predecessors in Egypt were part of the problem faced by Islam as the Crusaders advanced. Ibn al–Athir recorded:

> "Some say that when the Fatimid rulers of Egypt saw the conquests [by the Crusaders] of the Seljuk Turks, they took fright and asked the Franks to march into Syria, to make a zone of safety between the Fatimids and these Turks. Allah alone knows the truth".

From Cairo, the boy–Caliph's Vizier al–Afdal had already made overtures to the Byzantine Emperor; he got shrewd interest but not substantive assistance. Before the fall of Antioch, he had also suggested to the Crusaders that Syria and Palestine be partitioned between them and Egypt, but he completely mis–read the Christians: he offered them Beirut and Syria, and would keep Palestine and Jerusalem for the Fatimids. But, for the Crusaders, possession of Jerusalem was non-negotiable; there was no deal. Thrashing around after the fall of Antioch to the Crusaders, with Kerbogha's Turkish army routed, the Fatimids then attacked Jerusalem, of all places, themselves, allowing the Turkish garrison to retreat to Damascus but damaging the city walls and the last shreds of Moslem solidarity. From then on, virtually all the way to Jerusalem, local Moslem leaders betrayed each other to make deals with the Westerners.

Little therefore now stood in the way of the Crusaders. Would they *now* press on to Jerusalem? No. Instead, Raymond of Saint–Gilles laid siege to the totally unimportant town of Arqa, just to the south of the Krak des Chevaliers, in the hope of extorting "as much gold and silver as [he] could desire" from its overlord, the rich Emir of Tripoli, as a first step to carving out his own principality there. The pointless siege dragged on unsuccessfully for three months, embroiling Godfrey and his column of Crusaders whom Raymond summoned to his assistance on the basis of a false rumour that he was under threat. Bitter divisions among the leaders poisoned all relationships:

> "So many and such great disputes arose between the leaders of our army", Raymond of Aguilers recalled, "that almost the whole army was divided".

A prominent victim was the "discoverer" of the Holy Lance, Peter Bartholomew. To assuage revived doubts about its authenticity, Peter was pressured to undergo trial by ordeal to establish his truthfulness. Guibert of Nogent described Peter's run through ten metres of narrow path between burning olive branches – with "the crowd, eager for any novelty, heap[ing] more stuff upon the fire" – and back again:

> "When he came out of the fire...he was welcomed by an infinite crowd of people. And seeing that he had emerged little hurt, they wished to keep something of him for relics, either from his clothes or from his body, so they clutched at him and pulled him about and hacked him, trampling and dragging him here and there, till the poor helpless fellow gave up the ghost".

So, being dead, he had obviously been guilty. But the price was the loss of the talisman of the Holy Lance.

As it turned out, however, the Emir of Tripoli blinked first, and ended the nuisance siege of Arqa by buying off Raymond with gold and silver, and "fifteen very valuable horses". He was still concerned, rightly, about the security of Tripoli itself, for which he was prepared to see Jerusalem in the hands of these infidels rather than those of the heretic Fatimids. The *Gesta Francorum* claimed that

> "the treaty we made with him also said that if we could defeat the Emir of Cairo, and take Jerusalem, then the Emir of Tripoli would be christened and hold his land from our leaders".

In any event, the Emir's guides led the Crusaders southwards.

During the siege of Arqa a message had come from the Emperor Alexius saying he was now ready again to set out to join the Crusade and lead it to Jerusalem – if the Crusaders would wait a few months for him.

Raymond of Saint–Gilles, who seemed to find any number of excuses for not pressing on to Jerusalem, wanted to wait; he no doubt saw advantage for himself from the Emperor's further favouritism. But no–one else wanted to be subject to Byzantium, oaths notwithstanding, and they prevailed. Probably correctly, from their viewpoint: it is almost certain that Alexius had no intention of joining the Crusaders. He was still in close touch with the Fatimids in Cairo throughout this period; and he was quick to assure them, in response to their urgent appeals as the Westerners entered their territory, that he had no control over the Crusaders – he was certainly not supporting them, and his only interest in Palestine was in the protection of Orthodox Christians there. This double–dealing outraged the Crusaders when they learned of it in due course; their own double–dealing was of course for a sacred purpose.

Past Beirut, Sidon [Saïda], Tyre, Acre [Akko] and Caesarea to Ramleh [Ramla] the Crusade processed, neither molesting these cities on their way nor being resisted by their fearful inhabitants, with the sole exception of a sortie by the garrison of Sidon, which earned the inhabitants the destruction of their crops outside the walls. By Ramleh, the sixty thousand who had conquered Nicaea two years before were down to twenty thousand. More quarrels broke out among the leaders, some wanting to attack at once, taking advantage of the absence of Fatimid resistance so far, others fearing a siege during summer, others wanting to march against the "real enemy", Egypt. In the event, order broke down again and the greed of their followers made the decision for them: Raymond of Aguilers says that on 6 June 1099

> "because of a habit customary to us, to occupy forts and estates on the way by placing a personal standard there, many rose at midnight and galloped off without companions, to gain the villas and farms that are in the meadows of the Jordan. A few, however, to whom the command of God was more precious, walked with naked feet and sighed heavily for the contempt of the divine word".

On the road at Emmaus representatives of the entirely Christian population of Bethlehem met the Crusaders' column to beg for liberation from their Turk overlords; Tancred (and Godfrey's cousin Baldwin of Le Bourg) rode off to the rescue. His subsequent claim to the lordship of the town was the basis for future squabbles with the other leaders, who argued that Bethlehem, as the site of the Nativity, was sacred – unlike the towns *they* had grabbed.

By the afternoon of 7 June the First Crusade was camped outside the walls of Jerusalem.

The fall

The siege was difficult, but nothing like Antioch. Two factors would force an urgent attempt on the city: first, it was soon learned that the Vizier al–Afdal was on the march from Egypt with a huge relieving army; second, thirst. From now on, events would proceed at a rate not previously seen on the Crusade, partly because (Bethlehem notwithstanding) there was far less wrangling amongst the leaders so close to their original goal.

On 13 June a first, hasty attack, more pious than professional, egged on by an aged hermit on the Mount of Olives, failed. And the water situation became worse. Some water was available from the Pool of Siloam, "which bubbles straight up out of the earth"; but

> "the frantic and violent push to drink the water caused men to throw themselves into the pool and many beasts of burden and cattle to perish there in the scramble. The strong in a deadly fashion pushed and shoved through the pool, choked with dead animals and filled with struggling humanity, to the rocky mouth of the flow, while the weaker had to be content with the dirtier water... In the fields, horses, mules, cattle, sheep, indeed most of the beasts, had no strength to move. They died of thirst and rotted where they fell, making a most sickening stench throughout the camp...And as if this was not bad enough, the sun and the dust and the hot summer wind left men gasping" [Raymond of Aguilers].

The only alternative to the Pool of Siloam raised problems of a different kind:

> "We suffered so badly from thirst that we had to take our horses and other animals six miles to water, going in fear and apprehension all the way...We sewed skins of oxen and buffaloes, and used them to carry water these six miles. We drank the water from these leather sacks, though it stank, and what with this foul water and coarse barley bread we were distressed and afflicted every day. Saracens used to lie in wait for our men by every spring and pool, surprising us and cutting us to pieces. Then they would carry off our beasts to their caves and secret places" [*Gesta Francorum*].

The chronicles say the Crusaders were rescued by the arrival on 17 June of supplies – bread, wine and fish – at the nearby port of Jaffa, brought by English and Genoese ships which had run the Egyptian naval blockade. The siege will endure for another month yet, but we hear no more of the water problem.

The relief fleet was soon overrun by the Egyptians due to carelessness, but the besiegers of Jerusalem were able to salvage "ropes, hammers, nails, axes, mattocks and hatchets" from the ships, so that finally it became possible to construct wooden siege–towers, though the timber had to be brought from some distance away – Raymond of Saint–Gilles forcing

> "the Saracens from captured castles and towns to work as serfs. You could see fifty or sixty of them carrying on their shoulders a building beam too heavy for four pairs of oxen to drag. Collectively, we pressed the work, we laboured, built and cooperated, and neither sloth nor unwillingness retarded our work".

This new spirit of cooperation was matched, according to Raymond of Aguilers, by a renewed sense of devotion as well; and he describes a procession like that which Joshua had led two thousand years before to bring down the walls of Jericho. Yet again there was a three–day fast: then

> "Clergymen with crosses and the relics of Saints [led] the procession with knights and able–bodied men following, blowing trumpets, brandishing arms, and marching barefooted. We gladly followed the orders of God and the Princes...God was now on our side because our bad luck now turned to good and all went well".

The walls of Jerusalem did not fall down; but the Moslems unwittingly helped Crusader morale at this juncture:

> "Despite the omissions of many events," Raymond added in his account, "I cannot overlook this one: During the noisy march around Jerusalem, the Saracens and Turks walked along the top of their walls poking fun at us, and they blasphemed with blows and vulgar acts (against) crosses placed on yoked gibbets along the walkways. We, in turn, confident of the nearness of God's

compassion, because of these very abuses pressed forward by day and night the final assault preparations".

The assault was set for the night of 13–14 July. It says something about religious fervour that starving Crusaders could time and again launch an assault after three days of fasting.

The main strikes were to be by Raymond of Saint–Gilles from the south, near the Mount Sion Gate; Godfrey of Bouillon (with his older brother Count Eustace of Boulogne), due to attack from the north, seized an advantage by moving his position during the night to the extreme east of the northern wall between the Gate of Herod [Bab es Sahireh; also known as the Gate of Flowers] and the Storks' Tower [Borj Laqlaq] at the corner with the east wall. [The Palestine Archeological Museum, also known as the Rockefeller Museum after its founder, is on the site of Godfrey's camp.]

Through 14 July the Crusaders made little headway and suffered considerable losses from stones and Greek fire in trying to advance the siege–towers up to the inner walls.

> "With the coming of night", Raymond of Aguilers wrote, "fear settled down on both camps...Alertness, labour, and sleepless anxiety prevailed in both camps...The Christians besieged the city willingly for the Lord, and the pagans resisted reluctantly for Mohammed's laws. Incredible activity went on in both camps during the night".

With their knowledge of previous Crusader behaviour at Antioch and Maarat an–Numan, the Moslem defenders were in fact a good deal less reluctant than Raymond in hindsight allowed; and he himself admitted that, by mid–day on 15 July,

> "we were in a state of confusion, a phase of fatigue and hopelessness brought on by the stubborn resistance of many remaining defenders, the lofty and seemingly impregnable walls, and the overwhelming defensive skill of the Saracens...[A] council debated the wisdom of withdrawing our machines since many were burned or badly shattered...".

It was now that Godfrey of Bouillon, not a trail–blazer since the affair of the oaths to Emperor Alexius in Byzantium two years before, seized the day. The crucial moment was described by Raymond of Aguilers:

> "A youth shot arrows ablaze with cotton pads against the ramparts of the Saracens which defended against the wooden tower of Godfrey and the two counts [of Normandy and Flanders]. Soon mounting flames drove the defenders from the ramparts. Hurriedly Godfrey lowered the drawbridge which had defended the tower, and as it swung from the middle of the tower it bridged [to] the wall, and the Crusaders, unafraid and undaunted, poured into the city".

Two Flemish knights, Litold and Gilbert of Tournai, raced across, followed by Godfrey and his Lotharingians; Godfrey immediately sent men to open the Gate of the Column [now the Damascus Gate] in the centre of the west wall; Tancred and his men tore into the streets, the Moslems fleeing before them to the Haram es–Sherif, the Temple Mount. Raymond of Saint–Gilles, meanwhile, was still meeting stiff resistance on the southern city wall, under the defence of Iftitqar ad–Daula, the Fatimid governor; but by mid–afternoon he realised that Jerusalem had been lost in his rear, and he and his body–guard took refuge in the Tower of David.

"This day", Raymond wrote,

> "shall be celebrated to the praise and glory of the name of God, who, answering the prayers of His Church, gave in trust and benediction to His children the city and fatherland which He had promised to the [Church] Fathers".

The massacres
One of the earliest extant accounts of the fall of Jerusalem is, surprisingly, Jewish – and the unknown author of the letter, writing from Egypt in early 1100, made abundantly clear whom he would choose between the Christian Crusaders and the Moslem Fatimids:

> "You may remember, my Lord, that many years ago I left our country to seek God's mercy and help in my poverty, to behold Jerusalem and return...The Sultan [either the new Caliph al–Musta'li, or conceivably his Vizier, al–Afdal] – may God bestow glory upon his victories – ...caused justice to abound...in a manner

unprecedented in the history of any king in the world...Thus I had come to hope that because of his justice and strength God would give [Palestine] into his hands, and I should therefore go to Jerusalem in safety and tranquility...

When, however, God had given Jerusalem, the blessed, into his hands this state of affairs continued for too short a time to allow for making a journey there. The Franks arrived and killed everybody in the city, whether of *Ishmael or of Israel*; and the few who survived the slaughter were made prisoners. Some of these have been ransomed since, while others are still in captivity in all parts of the world.

Now, all of us had anticipated that our Sultan – may God bestow glory upon his victories – would set out against [the Franks] with his troops and chase them away. But time after time our hope failed".

The earliest extant Moslem account of the fall of Jerusalem suggests less than outrage at the loss of the heretical Fatimid city:

"Then they [the Crusaders] turned to Jerusalem," Al–Azimi of Aleppo wrote laconically about sixty years later, "and conquered it from the hands of the Egyptians. Godfrey took it. They burned the Church of the Jews".

Not even a mention of the massacre of the Moslem inhabitants, who were certainly not all Shiites. Writing about the same time, Ibn al–Qalinisi of Damascus, another Sunni, said

"A number of people fled to the sanctuary and a great host were killed. The Jews assembled in the synagogue, and the Franks burned it over their heads".

It almost seems that, at this early stage, the massacre of the Jews had registered more vividly.

By 1200 the massacre of the Moslems is clearly marked – as well as exaggerated in number – but Ibn al–Jawzi of Baghdad was more interested in material losses:

"Among the events in this year [*sic*] was the taking of Jerusalem by the Franks...They killed more than 70,000 Moslems there.

They took forty–odd silver candelabra from the Dome of the Rock, each one worth 360,000 *dirhams*. They took a silver lamp weighing forty Syrian *ratls*.[41] They took twenty–odd gold lamps, innumerable items of clothing and other things".

Thirty years later, Ibn al–Athir of Mosul again cites seventy thousand killed in the Aqsa Mosque, and adds that

"among them [was] a large group of Moslem imams, religious scholars, devout men and ascetics from amongst those who had left their homelands and lived in the vicinity of that Holy place".

Before the end of the fifteenth century the Mameluke historian Ibn Taghribidi, from an Egypt once again orthodox Sunni, was writing that 100,000 Moslems had been killed, including the old and the sick, in both the Dome of the Rock and the Aqsa Mosque. But this was just another medieval figure.

Judging by the earliest histories, there was not much in the way of contemporary Moslem accounts of the fall of Jerusalem for the Moslem historian to draw upon. Then, clearly, as time went on, the massacres got worse. But what might look at first sight like propaganda probably reflects instead the gradual use of the *Christian* chronicles. For the Christians not only admitted to the massacres, right from the beginning, but were positively boastful of them. Just as the Rhineland Jews had to be "exterminated from among the nations", so God's vengeance was called down on the Moslems, "a race absolutely alien to God" as Guibert of Nogent put it.

Raymond of Aguilers, who was present in Jerusalem as Chaplain to Raymond of Saint–Gilles, Count of Toulouse, was in the forefront. Having noted that

"Among those who entered first were Tancred and the Duke of Lorraine, and the amount of blood that they shed on that day is incredible",

---

41   In fact, Tancred had looted *eight* huge silver lamps from the Dome of the Rock.

Raymond went on:

"Now that our men had possession of the walls and towers, wonderful sights were to be seen. Some of our men (and this was more merciful) cut off the heads of their enemies; others shot them with arrows, so that they fell from the towers; others tortured them longer by casting them into the flames. Piles of heads, hands, and feet were to be seen in the streets of the city. It was necessary to pick one's way over the bodies of men and horses. But these were small matters compared to what happened at the Temple of Solomon [the Haram], a place where religious services are ordinarily chanted. What happened there? If I tell the truth, it will exceed your powers of belief. So let it suffice to say this much, at least, that in the Temple and porch of Solomon, men rode in blood up to their knees and bridle reins. *Indeed, it was a just and splendid judgement of God that this place should be filled with the blood of the unbelievers, since it had suffered so long from their blasphemies*".

This grotesque exultation in such cold–blooded inhumanity scarcely requires my added emphasis. Seventy years later William of Tyre would say "it was impossible to look upon the vast numbers of the slain without horror". Only the Governor and his body–guard were spared, by Raymond of Saint–Gilles, and allowed to leave. Unlike the early Moslem historians, Raymond of Aguilers, the chronicler–priest, did not mention the massacre of the Jewish inhabitants.

Although "the city was filled with corpses and blood" (or because of it, in the eyes of the Crusader chroniclers), for Raymond of Aguilers it was a great Christian victory:

"Now that the city was taken, it was well worth all our previous labours and hardships to see the devotion of the pilgrims [i.e. the Crusaders] at [the Church of] the Holy Sepulchre. How they rejoiced and exulted and sang a new song to the Lord!...This day, I say, will be famous in all future ages...; this day, I say, marks the justification of Christianity, the humiliation of paganism, and the renewal of our faith".

The soldier–follower of Tancred, who was also present and who subsequently wrote the *Gesta Francorum*, appended to his account a guide for the future pilgrim who, "coming from the western lands, wishes to go to Jerusalem". It is hard to see the author's little walking-tour in the context of the horrors of the sack of the Holy City, for it conveys something of the naive faith which had inspired some of the ordinary Crusaders in the first place. It begins:

> "In Jerusalem is a little cell, roofed with stone, where Solomon wrote the Book of Wisdom. And there, between the temple and the altar, on the marble pavement before the holy place, the blood of Zechariah was shed. Not far off is a stone, to which the Jews come every year, and they anoint it and make lamentation, and so go away wailing. There is the house of Hezekiah king of Judah, to whose span of life God added fifteen years. Next to it is the house of Caiaphas, and the pillar to which Christ was bound when he was scourged. At the Nablus gate is Pilate's judgement-seat, where Christ was judged by the chief priests. Not far off is Golgotha, that is 'The place of the skull', where Christ the Son of God was crucified, and where the first Adam was buried, and where Abraham offered his sacrifice to God. From thence, a stone's throw to the west, is the place where Joseph of Arimathea buried the body of the Lord Jesus, and on this site is a church, beautifully built by Constantine the King. From Mount Calvary the navel of the world lies thirteen feet to the west...";

and so on, for three more delightful pages.

The legacy

The Lebanese historian Amin Maalouf, writing in 1984 in *The Crusades Through Arab Eyes*, one of the few books on the Crusades from a Moslem standpoint, saw the sack of Jerusalem as "the starting point of a millennial hostility between Islam and the West". That the ferocity of the massacres left, in due course, a bitter legacy is undoubted; that the Crusades were responsible for the entire future course of Islamic–Western relations seems a large claim.

There has been offensive and counter–offensive between Islam and Christianity for fourteen hundred years. It began from Mecca with the extraordinary Arab invasions following the death of Mohammed in 632 CE, at the expense principally of Christians and Persians. A substantial part of Orthodox Byzantium was conquered between 634 and 644 CE, with Jerusalem itself falling in 638, and the first siege of Constantinople beginning as early as 673. Catholic Spain was overrun in the breathtakingly short period between 711 and 721, the Moslem advance into France only being stopped near Poitiers in 732. Sicily was occupied by 827, though lost again by mid–eleventh century; Rome itself was pillaged in 846.

The Crusades can be seen as the first Christian counter–offensive. The Crusader states which began in Palestine two hundred years later with the capture of Jerusalem in 1099 lasted for two hundred years. Jerusalem itself was recaptured by Saladin in 1187 (though held again by the Holy Roman Emperor Frederick II, by treaty with the Sultan of Egypt, between 1229 and 1244); the last Crusader foothold was eliminated with the capture of Acre by Sultan Baibars in 1291, a tremendous Moslem victory.

The continued counter–counter–offensive shifted from the Arabs to the Ottoman Turks: with their capture of Constantinople in 1453 the thousand year–old Byzantine Empire, the eastern heir to the Roman Empire, ceased to exist; Europe itself continued to be threatened: Vienna was besieged in 1529 and again in 1683. From the Catholic side, the last of the crusader counter–offensive, the *Reconquista* of Spain, was completed in 1492 as Columbus was discovering the Americas; but none of the projects mooted during the 14th– 15th centuries by popes and European kings for the re–conquest of the Holy Land itself came to fruition.

The European counter–counter–counter–offensive began with the Portuguese Vasco da Gama's opening, six years after Columbus's feat, of a sea route to India and the spice trade with Asia, by–passing the ancient eastern Mediterranean and Middle East trade routes that the Moslems had come to dominate. Dutch and British penetration of Moslem Malaya and the East Indies [Indonesia] followed in the 16th–17th centuries, and British conquest of Moghul India in the 18th–19th. By the end of the latter century, European imperialism was carrying the British, French, Dutch and eventually the Germans back into the Middle East from which they had been routed in 1291, as well as into North Africa. Between 1798 and 1801 Napoleon tried to grab Egypt, but failed; in 1882 Britain succeeded, after six years' dual control with France. The 18th–19th centuries saw the gradual expansion of Russia, Byzantium's Orthodox successor, into the Moslem Caucasus and Central Asia, as well as pressure on the Ottoman Balkans.

The Islamic counter–counter–counter–counter–offensive was begun by Ottoman Turk pan–Islamic ideas at the end of the 19th century, was in due course taken up by the Arabs, particularly after the collapse of the Ottoman Empire in 1922, and is in many ways – and places – still continuing, or, some would say, struggling. The Versailles system at the end of the First World War saw what was in some degree a limited European acceptance of this last reversal with the introduction of the League of Nations' Mandates, which gave Britain and France only temporary jurisdiction over the arbitrarily divided Middle Eastern areas of the former Ottoman Empire. Anticolonialism developed its own momentum, though it was only after the Second World War that these territories and European colonies in Africa and Asia began getting – or wrenching from their colonial masters – their complete independence, a process which only reached the Soviet Union's Caucasian and Central Asian "Republics" with the USSR's collapse in 1991.

This independence movement has in some cases been interrupted or interfered with, though rarely significantly threatened, by Western (increasingly United States) intervention, as with the ousting of the Mossadeq Government in Iran in 1953 and the Anglo–French Suez Canal intervention in 1956; the major oil companies were often an incitement to, or an arm of, Western meddling; the Cold War saw competitive interference by Nato and Warsaw Pact countries. But while the whole independence process now appears pretty much irreversible, the uses made of that independence have not been uniformly successful. The Arab Spring uprisings showed the level of discontent with the mainly military dictatorships that had been ruling for decades, and the continuing three-way tension between strong-arm nationalists, democrats and Islamic fundamentalists remains evident.

Since 1947, in the Middle East the blame for the breakdown in East-West relations has largely been placed on the creation by the Western powers – with initial Soviet support – of the State of Israel in Palestine, unfortunately at the expense of the Palestinians. At the same time, faced with this development, Islamic solidarity has had to compete with Arab nationalism; and it has rarely been successful.

Into the political gaps left behind by nationalist failures, pan-Islamic extremist groups have taken their anti-Western grudges into their own hands and launched a series of terrorist attacks on what they perceive as western imperialism, the most significant being the attacks in New York in September 2001. The Western response, the invasion of Afghanistan and then Iraq, is just the latest in this thousand-year-old conflict.

It seems impossible – and in any event, unprofitable – to try to draw up a balance sheet of blame and damages from this long and unhappy series of actions and reactions. But it is striking the extent to which Amin Maalouf sheeted so much home to the Crusades:

"In the Orient these holy wars led to long centuries of decadence and obscurantism. Assaulted from all quarters, the Muslim world turned in on itself. It became over–sensitive, defensive, intolerant, sterile – attitudes that grew steadily worse as world–wide evolution, a process from which the Muslim world felt excluded, continued".

There is of course a jump here, from the specific responsibility of the "holy wars" for decadence and obscurantism during the ensuing centuries, which may be debated, to Arab *perceptions* in recent times.

From her careful review of the Islamic sources, Carole Hillenbrand notes in her study, *The Crusades: Islamic Perspectives*, that

"the Islamic world was slow to draw lessons from the Crusades, their first experience of European interventionism...The Muslims showed little interest in the Crusades as a discrete entity, as a phenomenon of world history...The first work on the Crusading phenomenon by a Muslim, [was] written in 1899...".

It was only with the expansion of European imperialism through the Middle East – and, perhaps it could be added, Moslem areas elsewhere – in the second half of the 19th century that

"the idea of parallels between European policies past and present crystallised in the Muslim consciousness".

It is somewhat amusing that it was 19th century *European* eulogising of Saladin, Sultan of Egypt and Syria, long admired in the West as Richard the Lionheart of England's chivalrous – and more successful – opponent in the Third Crusade of 1189–1192, that turned him, when it spread to the Middle East, into what Hillenbrand describes as "the prototypical religio–political fighter against foreign oppression", a status he still holds. It is not surprising – witness the utterly contemporary ring of his message to Richard the Lionheart in 1192:

"Jerusalem is as holy to us as it is to you; it is even more important for us, because it was there that our Prophet made his miraculous nocturnal journey, and it is there that our community will be reunited on Judgement Day. It is therefore out of the question for us to abandon it. The Moslems would never accept it. As for territory, this land has always been ours, and your occupation is only transitory. You were able to settle in it because of the weakness of the Moslems who then peopled it, but so long as there is war, we will not allow you to enjoy your possessions."

Even as the Moslem, and particularly the Arab, world developed the sometimes incompatible ideas of pan–Islamic cooperation and national independence, another complication confounded the equation. Maalouf's own analysis led him to a conclusion that many have shared:

"Modernism became alien. Should cultural and religious identity be affirmed by rejecting this modernism, which the West symbolised? Or, on the contrary, should the road to modernisation be embarked upon with resolution, thus risking loss of identity? Neither Iran, nor Turkey, nor the Arab world has ever succeeded in resolving this dilemma. Even today we can observe a lurching alternation between phases of forced Westernisation and phases of extremist, strongly xenophobic traditionalism".

And Maalouf kept coming back to the Crusades:

"The Arab world – simultaneously fascinated and terrified by these Franj [Franks], whom they encountered as barbarians and defeated, but who subsequently managed to dominate the earth – cannot bring itself to consider the Crusades a mere episode in the bygone past…Today, on the eve of the third millennium, the political and religious leaders of the Arab world constantly refer to Saladin, to the fall of Jerusalem and its recapture. Israel is regarded as a new Crusader state".

In a very real sense, facts are unimportant: everything is in the perception.

"It seems clear", Maalouf concluded, "that the Arab East still sees the West as a natural enemy. Against that enemy, any hostile act – be it political, military, or based on oil – is considered no more than legitimate vengeance. And there can be no doubt that the schism between these two worlds dates from the Crusades, deeply felt by the Arabs, even today, as an act of rape".

For the Westerner, for whom, say, the outrage of Pearl Harbour sixty years ago is no impediment today to a healthy relationship with Japan, such a fixation on events seven to nine centuries ago is difficult to comprehend. But it is Maalouf's perception that has to be dealt with.

Advocatus Sancti Sepulchri

On 17 July 1099, two days after the capture of Jerusalem, the leaders met to consider the government of their conquest. Right from the beginning the clergy insisted that a "spiritual vicar" be appointed first, and he would preside over the election of "a ruler to preside over secular matters". This might have worked if the Papal Legate, Bishop Adhemar of Le Puy, had still been alive; as it was, with no senior clergyman still present, the leaders simply went into cabals and intrigues to select a leader, something they had been incapable of throughout the entire duration of the Crusade. As usual, there were sharp divisions, but now there were fewer candidates.

Only six of the leaders were in Jerusalem; two – Duke Robert of Normandy and Count Robert of Flanders – wished to return to Europe; two were not in the running – Count Eustace of Boulogne, who had always been overshadowed by his brother Godfrey of Bouillon, and Tancred, who was impetuous and had the disadvantage of being Bohemond's relative. That left Raymond of Saint–Gilles, Count of Toulouse, and Godfrey, and it was to the former that the others first offered the crown, as the close associate of the late Legate – and the wealthiest of the Crusaders.

As related at the beginning of this chapter, Raymond coined the famous line that he would not be king in the city where Christ had worn a Crown of Thorns. His motive was almost certainly not pure piety. There is no indication that he favoured the establishment of an ecclesiastical state. Some said his own soldiers opposed his acceptance, as they wished to return to Provence, but he could undoubtedly have bought their continued support. The other leaders were a different question: he knew well enough that his previous effort at buying "leadership" – after Antioch – had failed utterly. Did he think that no-one else would be able to accept the crown after he rejected it, and they would all therefore *have* to accept him this time? Or was he trying to wangle the selection of one of the lesser nobles whom he thought he could control? It would seem that he either did not expect the crown to be offered to Godfrey, or that Godfrey would not accept it if it were. He certainly reacted that way.

Whatever Raymond's scheme, it did not come off. The crown was offered to Godfrey, and he did accept. Or, rather, he refused the crown, but, as we know, promptly chose to become "Defender of the Holy Sepulchre". The chroniclers and subsequent writers have mostly accepted this as a sincere indication of Godfrey's devoutness. Indeed, William of Tyre, adding another element to the legend, contended that only a single reservation was expressed about Godfrey's character when the claims of the different leaders were examined: his closest companions said

> "he had one extremely annoying habit that, when he was in a church where he had heard Mass and Our Lord's service, he was unable to leave. He willingly listened to many stories and lives of the Saints; in fact he listened to too many, to such an extent that many times he displeased his companions, and the food was spoiled many times because he spent too long in the monasteries".

But all leaders of the Crusade were experienced, if in varying degrees, in ruling their European domains; probably all of them, certainly including Godfrey, had maintained or advanced their position by the usual political devices of persuasion, cunning and deceit; careful and clever scheming was not outside either the skills or the principles of this lot. A little scepticism seems overdue in this matter of the foundation of the Crusader Kingdom of Jerusalem.

How else to explain how Raymond was so comprehensively wrong-footed? Had it been indicated to him that Godfrey, like him, would not accept the crown? Of course Godfrey would not accept "The Crown", and may have been as sincere as Raymond in his reason; but he certainly accepted the *position*. The early chroniclers are unclear as to how soon Godfrey's acceptance came about; they said he accepted reluctantly, but that would be consonant with their determination to emphasise his piety; to all appearances his reluctance was speedily overcome. It is known that both the Duke of Normandy and the Count of Flanders favoured Godfrey's election; so the suspicion naturally arises that, while making what they considered to be an unavoidable gesture to Raymond, this group had colluded to produce the outcome they favoured, supported by other lords – and clergy – who preferred the low-key and independent Godfrey to Raymond, arrogant and autocratic, and who truckled to the hated Emperor Alexius to boot.

For want of anyone better, Arnulf, chaplain to the Duke of Normandy, was made Patriarch. Arnulf saw it as his immediate duty to torture a group of Syrian Orthodox priests who were believed to have hidden a relic of the True Cross. All non–Catholic Christians were expelled from the Church of the Holy Sepulchre, where the Moslem Arabs – but not the Turks or their Fatimid successors – had allowed all the sects to worship. The Crusade did not see itself as an ecumenical movement.

Raymond, trying to be tricky, now felt tricked, and reacted angrily and petulantly towards Godfrey and indeed the new state itself. Although he participated in the crushing victory over the Egyptian Vizier Al–Afdal at Ascalon [Ashquelon, just north of Gaza] a month after the capture of Jerusalem, which assured both Godfrey's and the Kingdom's position, he then tried to secure the area for himself, but he was thwarted by a surprisingly determined Godfrey. Raymond then essentially took himself and his followers off. But he had vowed to stay in Palestine, and he spent the years before his death in 1105 carving out the County of Tripoli which he had eyed so covetously at the time he besieged stubborn Arqa during the march to Jerusalem. However he never did succeed in capturing Tripoli itself, which only fell in 1109, to Tancred, who had become Regent of Antioch when his uncle Bohemond had returned to Europe in 1104 – to cook up with the Pope, Paschal II, a campaign against the Emperor Alexius. Robert of Normandy and Robert of Flanders had set off for Europe, as planned, after Ascalon.

Godfrey was left with only three hundred knights and two thousand foot–soldiers. Yet, by early 1100, he had carefully used this modest force, with valuable help from a Pisan fleet, to expand the territory of the Kingdom of Jerusalem over the maritime Palestine hinterland, as well as eastwards to the River Jordan and even beyond. Tancred had already, in 1099, established himself as Prince of Galilee in a lightning campaign, though while the principality was nominally part of the Kingdom of Jerusalem, Tancred tended to act independently. This fifth lordship was an important step for the defence of Jerusalem and towards the establishment of an almost continuous line of Crusader states from the Kingdom of Jerusalem in the south of Palestine through Raymond's Tripoli to Bohemond's Antioch and Baldwin's Edessa in northern Syria. With the defeat of the Egyptian Fatimids various local Moslem sheikhs – in the cities on the Palestine coast, and inland to the east and north – recognised that the Crusaders were there for the long haul, sought their own accommodations with the Europeans, and accepted Godfrey's suzerainty. In May 1100 a joint punitive expedition by Godfrey and Tancred against the troublesome Emir of Damascus, known as "the Fat Peasant", resulted in the latter's submission and agreement to pay tribute to Godfrey "for the sake of commerce".

By mid–1100 Godfrey was ruler of what was becoming a more coherent state, neighboured by a number of subdued Moslem emirates, and with the port at Jaffa becoming a useful trading centre. His main problem was now internal. The previous Christmas a new Papal Legate, Archbishop Daimbert of Pisa, had arrived in Jerusalem and immediately insisted on being consecrated Patriarch in place of the learned but low-ranking cleric (Arnulf, the Duke of Normandy's chaplain) whom the Crusaders had chosen from those available at the time of the capture of the city. Daimbert made clear he intended to assert the ecclesiastical superiority that the Crusaders had rejected at that time, not just nominally but in practice; and the fact that it was Daimbert who had brought the very useful Pisan fleet with him made it difficult for Godfrey to stand up to him. In April 1100 Daimbert wrote to the Bishops of Germany, asking for aid for the infant Kingdom, without so much as mentioning Godfrey.

But it was not to matter. In mid–June, as he was returning along the coast from the expedition against Damascus, Godfrey was taken ill. He had that day been honoured by the Emir of Caesarea with a sumptuous banquet, so it was not surprising that the rumour developed that he had been poisoned. But that was not the case: Godfrey had typhoid. Back in Jerusalem his condition continued to deteriorate until his heart gave out on 18 July 1100. He was probably no more than forty years old, and had been ruler in the Holy Land for almost exactly one year.

He was a man who was as brave as but no braver than most of his contemporary lords; whose piety, while apparently pronounced, was that of a Christianity which could readily encompass the persecution and murder of non–Christians, a piety that never got in the way of his capacity to scheme for his own ends; and who could manage a dukedom, an army, a new state well enough, but who did not always have the force of personality to ensure his leadership over the competing pretensions of others. It was not so much to his outstanding qualities, but more to the fact that he had no egregious deficiencies of prowess, devotion or character, and was not so forceful as to have made enemies of his compatriots, that he owed his elevation to sovereignty over Jerusalem and his subsequent adulation by those chronicling these dramatic times. Godfrey raised none of the partisan passions that go with the reckless hero or the demanding saint: his most remarkable qualities were mostly posthumous.

After lying in state for five days Godfrey was buried in the Church of the Holy Sepulchre of which he had been titular defender; his tomb was put at the entrance to the Chapel of Adam (so called because from the 3rd century it was believed that Adam had been buried there and that it was his skull which had given Golgotha, "the Place of the Skull", its name), itself at the entrance to Golgotha, the site of the Crucifixion. The tomb was still there when the French Romantic *littérateur* Chateaubriand received the Order of the Holy Sepulchre in the Church in 1806, and it survived the fire that engulfed the Church two years later; but it did not survive the restoration by a Greek architect, one Comninos, who removed it because it "compromised the architecture" – or perhaps because Godfrey had broken his oath to the Emperor of Byzantium seven hundred years before.

The question of the succession soon began to look ugly. Some say that on his death–bed Godfrey had bequeathed Jerusalem to his brother Baldwin, Count of Edessa, others that it had been to the Patriarch Daimbert. But the latter was not there at the time and Godfrey's Lotharingian followers were; they seized the Citadel and called for Baldwin. Daimbert appealed to Bohemond for assistance – on the understanding that the Prince of Antioch would be subject to the Patriarch of course – but the letter never reached him: before he heard of Godfrey's death Bohemond had set out to assist the town of Melitene [Malatya] in eastern Cappadocia, but he was ambushed and spent the next three years as the prisoner of the Turks. The way was thus open for Baldwin.

Here was a man of a different mettle: on first receiving the news, Fulcher of Chartres said,

"he mourned the death of his brother a little, but rejoiced a good deal more in his inheritance".

Baldwin promptly marched south, entering Jerusalem on 9 November, to the joy of the populace according to the ever–flattering chroniclers; and – less pious or less needing to be devious than his older brother – he was crowned King of Jerusalem by the thwarted Patriarch Daimbert in a splendid ceremony on Christmas Day 1100.

Godfrey the hero
It was King Baldwin I who was to become, over the eighteen years of his strong reign, the real founder of the Kingdom of Jerusalem. But it was Godfrey, the first European to rule in the Holy City, who became famous. Although, as noted earlier, he largely disappeared from the Moslem histories, in Europe he remained well in view. The chroniclers' works went through numerous editions and translations, from 1101 when Raymond of Aguilers' account was first taken back to France. In English, the first account was *Godeffroye of Boloyne or the Siege and Conqueste*

of Jerusalem, William Caxton's own translation of the French version of William of Tyre's *L'Estoire d'Eracles, Empereur, et la Conqueste de la Terre d'Outremer*, which he printed in 1481, only five years after he had established the first printing press in London.

But Godfrey was not merely the subject of histories: in due course poets, dramatists, authors, composers would all mine his vein. Much of this began at Ferrara, late in the Italian Renaissance, when the poet Torquato Tasso wrote his epic *Il Goffredo*, "Godfrey", more famously known by its 1575 published title *Gerusalemme Liberata*, "Jerusalem Delivered". As early as 1600 there appeared in London *Godfrey of Boulogne or the Recoverie of Jerusalem done into English by Edward Fairfax Gent*, a complete translation of Tasso's poem dedicated to Queen Elizabeth I, and beginning:

> "The sacred armies and the godly knight
> That the great sepulchre of Christ did free
> I sing; much wrought his valour and foresight,
> And in that glorious war much suffer'd he:
> In vain 'gainst him did hell oppose her might,
> In vain the Turks and Morians armed be;
> His soldiers wild, to brawls and mutines prest,
> Reduced he to peace; so heaven him blest".

While Tasso's fear that the poem would incur the wrath of the Counter-Reformation unhinged his mind, it had instant success throughout Western Europe; it would influence writers as various as Spenser and Voltaire. But it is by no means all Godfrey: most of *Gerusalemme Liberata* is about chivalric romance – and the triumph of Christian virtue – between a bevy of Oriental enchantresses, though most notably the Damascene Armida, and nice young Christian knights, such as a wholly imaginary Tancred the Norman and Rinaldo of Este; and these characters proved irresistible to opera composers from Monteverdi (*Il Combattimento di Tancredi e Clorinda*, 1624), through Lully (*Armide*, 1686), Handel (*Rinaldo*, 1711), Gluck (*Armide*, 1777), Haydn (*Armida*, 1784) and, after several lesser lights, Rossini (*Tancredi*, 1813, and *Armida*, 1817).

Godfrey himself nevertheless retained his own chivalric aura. In 1751 David Hume, in his *History of England*, had excoriated the Crusades, as we saw earlier, as "the most signal and most durable monument of human folly that has yet appeared in any age or nation". His younger contemporary Edward Gibbon was likewise no great admirer of the

Crusades; but, in the fifth and final volume (1788) of his magisterial *The Decline and Fall of the Roman Empire*, Gibbon wrote:

> "The first rank both in war and council is justly due to Godfrey of Bouillon; and happy would it have been for the crusaders, if they had trusted themselves to the sole conduct of that accomplished hero, a worthy representative of Charlemagne...His valour was matured by prudence and moderation; and, in the tumult of a camp, he practised the real and fictitious virtues of a convent. Superior to the private factions of the chiefs, he reserved his enmity for the enemies of Christ; and though he gained a kingdom by the attempt, his pure and disinterested zeal was acknowledged by his rivals".

In the nineteenth century, just as the Tasso–based operas were sputtering out, Sir Walter Scott gave the Crusades their greatest boost since Tasso himself with *Ivanhoe* (1819), *The Talisman* and *The Betrothed*, published together as *Tales of the Crusaders* (1825), and *Count Robert of Paris* (1831), the last being set in the Emperor Alexius's Constantinople at the time of the arrival of Godfrey of Bouillon and the First Crusade. Directly or indirectly, these inspired more operas: Meyerbeer's "melodrama eroico" *Il Crociato in Egitto* appeared in 1824, followed by Rossini's *Ivanhoe* in 1826; and a combination of Tasso and Scott gave rise in the latter year to another Italian epic poem, *I Lombardi alla Prima Crociata* ["The Lombards in the First Crusade"], by Tomasso Grossi, which Verdi used for his fourth opera, with the same title, in 1843 at La Scala, Milan – the chorus featuring more Lombards than participated in the First Crusade. But that was not the end of this particular affair: four years later, invited to write for the Paris Opera and lacking time and inclination to start from scratch, Verdi produced a re–worked version of *I Lombardi* in French, called *Jérusalem*, which was first performed in Paris on November 1847 and then before King Louis–Philippe in the Tuileries Palace; it was not particularly successful, but that did not stop it from being translated into *Italian* for performance in Venice (where it was a flop) and – of all places – Moslem Constantinople.

When he saw it in Paris Louis–Philippe had only three months left as King of the French before the latter rose up against him and drove him into exile in the first of the wave of revolutions that swept across Europe in 1848. But in the last years before his overthrow he had been responsible for the most extensive and most outrageous piece of crusadolatry ever: the *Salles des Croisades* at Versailles, part of the

Museum of the History of France that Louis–Philippe dedicated to "All the Glories of France". The rooms, executed by the architect Frédéric Nepveu, had to be designed around the door of the Hospital of St John of Jerusalem from Rhodes, which had been presented to Louis–Philippe by the Ottoman Sultan Mahmud II – one wonders if he ever knew what his French counterpart intended it for. The Gothic–style panelling was designed for the insertion of twenty–odd paintings illustrating chronologically the history of all the Crusades of the 11th–13th centuries; and along the tops of the walls and on the surfaces of square columns that march down both sides of the rooms were placed escutcheons intended to receive the arms of the families which had won fame in the Crusades. The latter project was a wild success: the pretentious bribed genealogists and historians to lay claim to being Crusader heirs; one gentleman did a nice business in selling totally phony family trees before he was unmasked. Nepveu recorded that

> "To preserve some margin and to satisfy the demands of families which might later make claims in the event of involuntary omissions, His Majesty has decided to have escutcheons rather than simple crosses placed in the majority of the coffers of the four new ceilings".

As for the paintings, Louis–Philippe was not too fussy: his main aim was to ensure an overall chronological and narrative sequence. The artists thus ranged from minor Academists to the great Delacroix – though it is said that the man in charge, the Director of the Royal Museums, instructed the latter to do a painting which "isn't like a Delacroix". He did anyway, and his contribution, "The Capture of Constantinople by the Crusaders" (the shameful Fourth Crusade of 1204, in which the Catholics turned against Byzantium), was regarded as so important that it was transferred to the Louvre in 1885 and replaced by a copy. Louis–Philippe got his narrative, but his idea of chronology collapsed when the canvasses were fixed in place according to size, with the largest in the place of honour, the Grand Gallery. The paintings are in the full grand nineteenth century romantic–pompous style – robes flying, banners waving, devout Crusader eyes raised heavenward, infidels dying or dead, all set in romantic landscapes dominated by castles that have just fallen to the glorious French, or are just about to.

The *Salles des Croisades* are a riot of Orientalist fantasy about the romance and heroism of French Crusaders. They are enormous fun, but they are nothing like the Crusades.

Godfrey in Brussels

When Louis–Philippe fled from the citizens of Paris on 24 February 1848, a certain nervousness was aroused in Brussels that was not entirely assuaged by the announcement on 1 March by Lamartine, Beaumarchais' successor as France's leading romantic poet, now Foreign Minister of the new Second Republic, that the latter had no desire to interfere with its neighbours. King Leopold was sanguine about the state of Belgian opinion:

"Here, thank God", he wrote about this time, "I do not quite see what more could be desired. We are to such an extent *Liberalised* [a play on the first Liberal Government in Belgium, elected the previous June] that, with the exception of universal suffrage, I do not quite see what could be done in the way of novelty".

But he added that he had written to the Prime Minister

"to beg him to keep an eye on the agents of trouble who might be sent us from Paris".

Leopold proved to be right on both counts: Belgium did indeed stay calm, and there was a threat from Paris. It proved to be one of the most hilarious episodes in Belgian history. The story is told by an historian called Demetrius C. Boulger in the second volume, published in 1909, of his *History of Belgium*:

"Notwithstanding the pacific assurances and honourable intentions of the Provisional French Government...it was well that military precautions were not neglected, and that a close watch was kept on the French frontier. Whatever the French Minister might say about the desire of himself and his colleagues to respect Belgian independence, this did not prevent the extreme Republicans from wishing to extend the alleged benefits of their political system to their neighbours, and especially to Belgium [as in 1795]. The Belgian colony in Paris was also large, and it necessarily included some elements not greatly attached to the cause of law and order. The Parisian extremists and the Belgian exiles conceived that it would be a fine thing to put an end to the Monarchy in Belgium, as had been done in France, and to treat King Leopold in the same way as his father–in–law. And about the middle of March they resolved to make their first move.

The leaders of the plot decided to make use of the railway, and they engaged a special train ostensibly for a holiday trip for some hundreds of Belgians to visit Brussels. Trains were not then as fast as they have since become, and it was arranged that the party should receive provisions *en route*. Still more important, they were to be supplied with muskets and ammunition at Valenciennes. The arrangements were good, but they broke down. Provisions were not forthcoming, and warning reached the Belgian authorities at Mons, who prepared a prettily devised ruse for the reception of the invader. The train, with its 800 warriors on board, reached Valenciennes in safety. They were still enthusiastic if hungry, and on the train stopping in the station they waited for their arms with admirable patience. While thus expectant the French engine was removed, and a powerful Belgian engine attached in its place. The train at once moved off at a good pace, and dragged the band of invaders towards Belgium. Even then the occupants did not seem to realise what was taking place. The first station on crossing the frontier at this point is Quievran, where the train was turned into a siding, and promptly surrounded by troops held in readiness. The invaders jumped out of the carriages in panic, but, being surprised and unarmed, had no choice save surrender. The only wounded were those who injured themselves by jumping too heedlessly out of the carriages...

Such was the fate of the advanced guard of the Republican army of invasion".

Subsequent trains stopped before the border and the French went home.

"A certain number, however, of the Belgians, who had seen in the adventure a good way of getting home without paying for their railway ticket, quietly crossed into Belgium as loyal and devoted citizens".

And so, as revolution shook Berlin, Vienna, Venice, Rome, Milan, Naples, Prague and Budapest, in a calm and loyal Brussels King Leopold of the Belgians was able to devote his time to the inauguration of a statue of Godfroy de Bouillon the Belgian, proudly but incorrectly called the First King of Jerusalem.

Bayon temple, Angkor Thom, Cambodia. Wikimedia/Hans Stieglitz

CAMBODIA

JAYAVARMAN VII:
MERIT AND DEMERIT

Sometimes people have merit, high status, possessions, more than anyone else, for sure, and on other occasions people are small and low, their lineage and descendants insignificant, like poor orphans altogether. This is destiny; suffering comes as a result of what we have done; merit and demerit are all mixed up together.

Document Concerned with the Annals of King Ang Chan, 1856

The perception of modern Cambodia is largely the result of French colonialist attitudes: the Cambodians' ineptness in modern times in the face of their more vigorous – and aggressive – Vietnamese and Thai neighbours gave rise to the myth of their being "gentle Buddhists". It was the justification for France's taking Cambodia under its "protection" in the 19th century; and it was used contrariwise by Norodom Sihanouk in the 1960s, to obscure his duplicitous and reckless involvement of "neutral" Cambodia in North Vietnam's strategy in the last Indochina war. Then, in 1975, there began the vast massacres carried out by the Pol Pot regime. Which particular gentle Buddhists did one suppose carried out the killings? This was not genocide, as it is often called, one race seeking to annihilate another: it was fratricide – and sororicide, parricide, matricide, infanticide. It is not being callous to say that I was not really surprised.

I first visited the ancient temples of Angkor in 1962, on the way to my first posting, in Cairo, during a brief visit to a Foreign Service classmate who had already been posted to our Embassy in Phnom Penh – little expecting that I would be assigned there myself six years later. That first visit was a harum-scarum one, vividly marked in my memory by my colleague's hair-raising driving over the narrow road between Phnom Penh and Angkor, in between (just) its astounding collection of bullock-carts, hand-wagons, playing children, wobbling old men, women husking grain spread on mats, who all travelled – who inhabited – the highway; together with, on the way back, at night, thousands of large frogs that came down all over it with a drenching monsoon downpour. We were not the only ones to experience frogs: in 1297 Zhou Daguan (Chou Ta-kuan), a Chinese official who has left the only account of life at Angkor during (or at least just after) the days of its glory, had noted that

"the natives do not eat the frogs, though these swarm over the roads at night".

Visits to Angkor from Phnom Penh during my two years there in the later sixties were more relaxing, but had to come second to focussing on the tense situations in Cambodia itself and in Indochina more generally during those dark days of the Vietnam War. By the time my wife and I visited Cambodia at the beginning of 1972 from Saigon, where we spent two years during the last-but-one stage of the Indochina War, we could not visit Angkor at all: the communist insurgency which had begun in neighbouring Battambang province around the time of my posting had cut the ancient temples off from the outside world. It was only three years until Pol Pot.

We have been back since, for an extended stay of visits to virtually all the temples in the Angkor complex, and multiple visits to some at different times of the day – and even an excursion to the remote and rarely visited temple at Banteay Chhmar, close to the Thai border. Despite the increase in the number of tourists, the temples – even Angkor Wat itself, the best known – are deserted, apart from the occasional saffron-clad bonze, or white cow, in the early morning before the tour buses disgorge their progeny and again after they have consumed them and departed in the evening. The monuments are better protected than ever; the roads, and the unsprung *cyclo* passengers, still suffer.

The hostility that existed between Cambodia and its neighbours during the 1960s was reminiscent of the situation during the greatest days of the ancient Khmer Empire at the end of the 12th century. The builder of that Empire was Jayavarman VII, mythologized as the supreme "gentle Buddhist" by his French successors, but a ruthless conqueror who was regarded by Pol Pot as the only worthy figure in all previous Cambodian history. Half a century after his father's cousin built the more famous Angkor Wat, Jayavarman built the more mysterious

Bayon temple-mausoleum, the greatest of the monuments to his megalomania. We shall attempt to discover him mainly through 20th century French archeological and epigraphical interpretations; but we have Zhou Daguan's eyes to give us a description of life at Angkor just after Jayavarman, before Thai pressures forced its abandonment to the jungle in which a whole series of Westerners "discovered" it between the 16th and 19th centuries.

The principal people in this chapter are as follows:

- Suryavarman II (birthdate unknown) – Khmer ruler from 1113-1150. Cousin of Jayavarman VII's father. Builder of Angkor Wat.

- Yasovarman II (birthdate unknown) – Khmer ruler from 1160-1165/6. Possibly the older brother of Jayavarman VII.

- **Jayavarman VII** (c.1125-c.1220) – Khmer ruler from 1181-1220. Builder of Angkor Thom, the Bayon, Ta Prohm, Preah Khan, the Elephant Terrace and the Leper King Terrace.

- Indravarman III (birthdate unknown) – Khmer ruler from 1295-1308, during the time of Zhou Daguan's visit. Related by marriage to Jayavarman VII's grandson.

- Zhou Daguan (1266-1346) – Minor Chinese official. Author of Notes on the Customs of Cambodia.

Zhou, travelling with an ambassador from Kublai Khan's successor as Emperor of China, received some cultural shocks – and titillation – from his thorough canvassing of a kingdom China regarded as a tributary, like all its neighbouring states. Several centuries earlier, Indian merchants had introduced Indian religion and kingship into Cambodia and other Southeast Asian states; while Cambodia was not now on a major trade route, Chinese traders had long been sailing around the Indochinese and Malaysian coasts as far as India, and Zhou would report on goods of commercial interest to China. Arab merchants were also just beginning to expand into Southeast Asia around the time Zhou was in Angkor. This was not long before Marco Polo, on his way home from Cathay, said he met "Saracen" merchants in Sumatra, where they had "converted the natives to the Law of Mahomet"; but, curiously, Islam would leave Indochina largely untouched.

As I was writing this chapter I found a curious and completely unexpected Angkorian parallel with French architecture – at Chartres; and it was not simply because of the coincidence that the Bayon was constructed over exactly the same three decades as the first great campaign in the construction of the Cathedral. During our first posting in Paris in the mid-1970s my wife's visiting parents thoughtfully rented a place in the country where small grandchildren could do God-given Australian things like play on grass, in those days strictly forbidden in Paris's parks and strictly policed by whistle-blowing humourless neo-storm-trooper *gardiens*. (Not far from our apartment was a small park, with a few swings, free in Australian parks but here charged by the minute, and, what was worse, entirely gravelled. I complained to a Quai d'Orsay wife, when conversation at a diplomatic dinner was avoiding our then nuclear-testing-strained relationship, that gravel was terrible on small hands and knees. "But Monsieur", she said reprovingly, "Marcel Proust played there.") Our getaway was the little converted *Orangerie* in the forested park of the 19th century Château de Mémillon, a tiny cottage with huge sun-facing arched windows opening out onto an unforbidden lawn surrounded by ancient trees, high on a bank overlooking the little Loir River, a tributary of the famous Loire.

We were only thirty kilometres south of Chartres, and the great Cathedral, one of the first Gothic monuments of the Age of Faith, became our parish church – at least for organ recitals. We investigated its stained glass, its sculpture, its iconography, its ecclesiastical, historical and architectural roles; with the aid of the remarkable work of an Australian architect, we were able to examine its very foundations. So when, thirty years later, I discovered an investigation by an American on the conceptual foundations of Angkor Wat, with which the Bayon shares similar philosophical origins, I was struck by the differing but comparable cosmological, astronomical and numerological principles involved in the alignment, layout and construction of both masterpieces, curious parallels on opposite sides of the world at a time when neither city even knew the other existed. There are obvious limits to comparing Angkor and Chartres; but it was a coincidence I could not resist in this look at the time of Angkor's greatness.

Faces in the forest

A century ago Pierre Loti, a French naval officer as well as a writer, was one of the first ordinary tourists to visit still largely unknown Angkor, the vast and mysterious temple complex in remote north–western

Cambodia, which French explorers, archeologists and vandals had only "discovered" some forty years before. Aside from the heat, about which he complained constantly, Loti's overwhelming impression on 28 November 1901 when he first arrived at the sprawling temple–city of Angkor Thom, constructed by King Jayavarman VII at the turn of the 12th–13th centuries, was of the enveloping jungle; and he wrote, in a vivid passage of *Un Pèlerin d'Angkor* (which went through forty–two editions in its first year):

> "It is the 'fig tree of the ruins' that reigns today as master over Angkor. Above the palaces, above the temples which it has patiently prized apart, everywhere it triumphantly spreads its pale smooth branches, spotted like snakes, and its vast dome of leaves. At the beginning it was no more than a tiny seed, sown by the wind on a frieze or the summit of a tower. But, as soon as it could germinate, its roots, like slender threads, insinuated themselves between the stones to go down, down, guided by a sure instinct, towards the earth, and, when at last they reached it, they rapidly swelled with nourishing sap, until they became enormous, disconnecting, unbalancing everything, splitting open the thick walls from top to bottom; then, inevitably, the structure was lost.
>
> The forest, always the forest, and always its shade, its intense oppression. It feels hostile, murderous, smouldering with fever and death".

It was also Loti who gave the first atmospheric description of the great four–faced towers that are the most visible and striking aspect of the Bayon, Jayavarman's great temple–mausoleum at the centre of Angkor Thom:

> "In the midst of the dripping brambles and lianas, it is necessary to wield a stick to force a path to the temple. The forest grips it tightly everywhere, smothers it and crushes it; enormous 'fig trees of the ruins', completing its destruction, grow everywhere right up to the summits of its towers...
>
> I raised my head towards these towers overhanging me, drowning in greenery, – and I suddenly shivered with an unknown fear on seeing a huge fixed smile coming down at me from above,...and then yet another smile, over there on another section of wall,...and then three, then five, then ten; they are everywhere,

and I was observed from all directions... They are of such super–
human proportions, these masks sculptured in the air, that it takes
a moment to comprehend them; they smile under their great flat
noses and keep their eyelids half closed, with an unknowable mute
femininity; one could say discreetly mocking old ladies...".

Jayavarman would not have been pleased – for the faces were (probably)
his.[42] The huge four–faced towers are overwhelmingly the most
distinctive aspect of the Bayon, and appear also on the gate–towers into
the surrounding Angkor Thom. They are also on Jayavarman's earlier
small Angkor temples of Banteay Kdei and Ta Prohm and in the
enormous but rarely–visited temple of Banteay Chhmar, 160 kms to
the northwest. But despite the extraordinary sculpture–architecture
of the face–towers, they – like Angkor itself – had often disappeared
from the curiously unobservant view.

The discoveries of Angkor

The man usually credited over the past century with having been the first
to "discover" Angkor – the first European, at least – was Henri Mouhot,
a Frenchman who had moved to England, where he married a daughter
(or niece) of the explorer Mungo Park.[43] His journey of exploration in
Siam, Cambodia and Laos in 1860–61 was primarily as a naturalist, but
his report on Angkor – published in England in 1864 from his letters
and journals, after his death in Laos – was the first in any detail. Mouhot
enquired into everything and was in many ways extraordinarily
thorough during his brief exploration; the second volume of his papers
included, for example, an appendix containing, amongst other things, a

---

42 Or not – this is by no means agreed by the experts: see below. I should
acknowledge here and now that Cambodia's political and artistic history has
long been, and is still, not so much a field of study as a minefield, reflecting
scholars' efforts to interpret and re–interpret very limited evidence in the interests
of greater accuracy – or, it sometimes seems, cleverness – not always in the most
cooperative way. I will indicate the main areas a scholarly friend has described
as "dangerous turf"; but, not a scholar, I can only hope the mines I have
undoubtedly blundered onto have not proved fatal. (Incidentally, we encounter
Loti again in the 1900 chapter: Yuan Shikai.)

43 Mungo Park was a protégé of Sir Joseph Banks, who sent him to explore
the River Niger in West Africa six years after John Ledyard (1800 chapter) had
died on the way to carry out a similar commission. Park also died there, on a
second expedition.

"Cambodian Vocabulary", covering thirty–two pages of a variety of words, then the names of the numbers, cardinal points, seasons, days, months and years, then a guide to pronunciation, and then...the Lord's Prayer in Khmer.

It was probably Angkor Wat that Mouhot saw as a temple "rival to that of Solomon and erected by some ancient Michelangelo". He was the first European to record seeing a face–tower, on one of the gateways into Angkor Thom, further spraying artistic references around by remarking on its "four immense heads in the Egyptian style" – a reference, presumably, to the columns of the 1st century BCE Temple of Hathor at Denderah, on the Nile below Luxor, each topped by four faces of the goddess. The connection he made has a certain irony: the first European to "discover" Denderah, the Anglo–Irish Reverend (later Bishop) Richard Pococke, thought, on seeing it late in December 1737, that Hathor's faces "must have been executed by one of the best Greek sculptors". Mouhot penetrated further to see the Bayon's own faces, on thirty–two overgrown towers by his count, but referred to them rather curiously as "roofs...embellished, at about two–thirds of their height, with four gigantic sculptured heads" – without speculation as to whom they might represent. But at least Mouhot *saw* them; and as far as I have been able to determine, he was, after their long history, apparently the first ever to refer to them in print.

Ten years later Mouhot's role as the "discoverer" of Angkor – which he himself, poor chap, never pretended to – was blasted by a fellow Frenchman, the missionary Father Charles–Émile Bouillevaux, who had visited Angkor in 1850, ten years before Mouhot, but had not made much of it in his first report. However, in his revised memoirs, by which time the long dead Mouhot had made Angkor famous, he loosed a most unchristian broadside:

"Before continuing, we wish to protest against certain examples of exaggeration and charlatanism. There are people who claim to have made important discoveries in Cambodia and elsewhere, but the majority of these fine discoveries have been known about for a very long time. Thus, for example, the pagoda of Angcor and the ruins of Angcor–Thôm were not found, as is said, by Mouhot, for the very good reason that they had never been either forgotten or lost. Previous missionaries knew them, and refer to them briefly. The Portuguese travellers of the 16th century visited them, and finally, certain 13th century Chinese chroniclers mention them in

their accounts, in a more or less clear fashion. Mouhot saw Angcor
after several others, and in particular
after I did...".

In his first version Boiullevaux did not notice, or at least did not bother
to mention, the Bayon face–towers; in the second he did refer to
"immense heads of the Buddha" – and called them "placid and stupid".
He now also found the Bayon "somewhat reminiscent of the Egyptian
style" – an idea lifted straight from Mouhot!

Father Bouillevaux was right, though, about one thing: Angkor had
only been "lost" to Europeans because of national divisions and short
memories. Among those earlier missionaries he referred to would have
been Father Henri Langenois, who, just over a hundred years before had
actually visited Angkor, and who had written in 1783 not much more
than that it was "the Indians' Babel, a centre of superstition". A hundred
years before that yet another French missionary, Father Chevreuil, had
written, in 1668, that

> "there is a very old and famous temple about eight days' journey
> from this tribe [where he was living]...This temple is renowned
> among all the Gentiles [heathens] of five or six great Kingdoms, as
> Rome is among Christians;...It is called Onco".

Still no mention of the face–towers in these accounts. And neither
Langenois nor Chevreuil seems to have been aware of any previous
reports.

In fact Angkor had been lost in Portugal and Spain over the eighty
years before Chevreuil's brief reference to it. In the late 16th century an
abortive Spanish interest in adding Cambodia to the empire Spain was
just beginning to acquire in the Philippines, largely promoted by a pair
of incompetent free–booters, had attracted the "travellers" to whom
Bouillevaux referred – mostly missionaries from Spanish Manila or
Portuguese Malacca. In his *Angkor and Cambodia in the XVIth Century
According to Portuguese and Spanish Sources*, Bernard–Philippe Groslier
identified five reports based on these missionaries' accounts that were
published between 1601 and 1609. Not all refer to Angkor or the Bayon,
none to the latter's face–towers.

It is amusing though to see how these reports, all derived from the
period since the mid–1500s and some from obviously the same sources,
attribute the temples to an amazing array of wildly different origins: one

(thinking along the same lines as would Bishop Pococke) said the "ancient city" was built by Alexander the Great, or the Romans; another that "there are many Jews in the Kingdom of China; it was they who built in Camboxa the city of Angor";[44] a third that "an eminent man in the field of letters supposes that [the constructions] are the works of Trajan", the 2nd century CE Roman Emperor, but he added, delightfully, that "although the latter had extended the Empire more than his predecessors, I have not read that he had reached as far as Camboxa".

These attributions reflected the belief, prevalent until the early 20th century, that the original Khmers had totally disappeared. The year before Mouhot's famous visit, a paper, compiled from notes by an English traveller called E.F.J. Forrest and an American missionary called S.R. House, which was read to the Royal Geographic Society in London but which remained largely un-noticed, expressed that view succinctly: Angkor Wat, it said,

> "stands like a mighty sphinx frowning contemptuously on the infantine and barbaric state of the arts and science of the people who are now the denizens of the forests and plains in its vicinity...".

No-one could believe that the post-Angkor Cambodians could possibly have built such masterpieces. Not even some post-Angkor Cambodians themselves: they told Henri Mouhot variously that Angkor Wat was built by the King of the Angels, or by giants, or – in uttermost self-abnegation – that "It made itself".

Zhou Daguan, the Chinese reporter

So, we arrive back at 1296–1297 and the most famous of all accounts of Angkor, the only one known to have been made during the period when it was still the capital of Cambodia: *Notes on the Customs of Cambodia* by the minor Chinese official Zhou Daguan (Chou Ta-kuan).[45] If the

---

44 By an odd coincidence, at almost exactly the same time, in 1605, the Jesuit missionary Matteo Ricci was meeting Jews in Peking who claimed to have been in China for five centuries. They did not, however, claim to have built Angkor.

45 Zhou Daguan's *Notes* on his stay in Cambodia were incorporated in a Yuan (Mongol) Dynasty compilation of documents in the fourteenth century. They were first translated into a Western language by a French scholar, Abel Rémusat, in 1819, at a time when Europe had long forgotten – to the extent that it had ever known of – the 18th and 17th century French missionaries' reports

city – Angkor Thom – was no longer the capital of the vast and powerful kingdom that it had been under Jayavarman VII in the last two decades of his reign between 1181 and 1219, the Cambodians were nevertheless still significant enough to attract the early attention of the new Emperor of China, Cheng Zong (Ch'eng–tsung), born Timur, the grandson and successor of the great Kublai Khan (Marco Polo's emperor), and a fervent Buddhist. In the Preface to his *Notes on the Customs of Cambodia*, Zhou Daguan tells us that in mid–1295, in only the second year of his reign,

> "the holy Son of Heaven sent an ambassador to recall these people to their sense of duty and designated me as his travelling companion";

and the delegation stayed in Angkor for a year, from August 1296 until July 1297.

> "Certain it is", Zhou tells us, "that in so short a time the customs and peculiarities of this country could not have been revealed to us in all their details; however, we were at least in a position to outline its principal characteristics".

The result is a most engaging mixture of fascination, understanding description, shrewd comment, startling credulity, uncomprehending prejudice – characteristic, it could be said, of most foreigners' observations, of anywhere, at any time.

The land Zhou Daguan saw has scarcely changed:

> "After crossing the frontier...one sees everywhere close–grown thickets of scrub forest; the great estuaries of the Mekong cover hundreds of miles; the heavy shade of old trees and trailing rattan

---

and those of the Portuguese and Spanish from the century before that. After Angkor's modern "discovery", the *Notes* were re–translated, in 1902, by the French Sinologist Paul Pelliot (who two years earlier had won the *Légion d'honneur* during the Boxers' siege of the Peking Legations and who went on to a career discovering - and appropriating - ancient Buddhist treasures on the Silk Road in China). My quotations are taken from a 1967 translation by J.G.d'A. Paul of Pelliot's version, published in Bangkok, where I purchased it during my own stay in Cambodia. A new edition, translated by M. Smithies, was published in Bangkok in 2001.

vines forms a luxuriant covert…Half–way on one's journey the country opens up suddenly, without a sign of trees. As far as the eye can see there is nothing but an abundance of wild millet"

– now, cultivated rice. And so is the heat recognisable:

"Cambodia is an excessively hot country and it is impossible to get through the day without bathing several times…the water is always as hot as though on a stove: not until the fifth watch does it cool off a bit before the rising sun brings back the heat".

It was to be the common complaint of all subsequent visitors.

There is a further source for some aspects at least of the every–day life of the people, in Jayavarman's time and indeed earlier in his century: vignettes squeezed into the bottom of the great bas–reliefs in the Bayon; and other aspects of ordinary life are detectable, by way of ingenious interpretation as we shall see, in the earlier Angkor Wat. Many of the little scenes showing Cambodians at work and at leisure would have been seen by Zhou Daguan in real life a century later – just as some are still there to be seen in real life today. The Bayon bas–reliefs mainly illustrate Jayavarman VII's military activities; most of his biography – and, indeed, the history of Angkor – has been deduced during the twentieth century by a series of eminent French scholars who, as one of the greatest of them, Georges Coedès – whose publications covered the extraordinary span from 1906 to 1962 – said, have "meticulously translated inscriptions on stelae, and minutely studied the evolution of artistic forms".[46] Angkor in fact became something of a French academic industry during the 20th century: Rose Macaulay remarked of its ruins that

"All is now desolate, fantastic, and ambushed with ghosts; the erroneous opinions of archeologists twitter among them like bats".

In due course, long before Pol Pot sowed Angkor with mines, the archeologists and the epigraphers and the historians and mere visitors sowed the interpretative minefield that now has to be tip–toed through:

---

46   Quotations from inscriptions – mostly originally in Sanskrit, indicative of the long duration of Indian influence on Khmer culture – are from the works by Coedès, Stern and Briggs cited in the Bibliography.

not only whether or not those Bayon faces are Jayarvarman's, but also whether or not they are smiling, and whether the eyes are open, or half–open, or closed. And so on. But, between the variety of sources available, we can perhaps discern a ghostly portrait of the living Jayavarman; and, in any case, Zhou Daguan's *Notes* provide an invaluable as well as entertaining framework for envisioning the circumstances in which, and the people over whom, he ruled.

The (brief) background of Jayavarman's Cambodia: Indianisation

Cambodia, like the predecessor states of the countries that now form the rest of the region, emerged over the first half of the first millennium CE in a peninsular and island Southeast Asia that was gradually "Indianised" – in ways that, in the beginning, were not so dissimilar from those that were to be followed in this same region by the French, British and Dutch from the middle of the second millennium. Indian traders began setting up outposts, partly for local trade, partly as stopping–off places on the way to and from southern China – which was not only important in the area but also the source of much of our information about it. They were followed, like their European successors, by an educated elite, members of administrative and priestly castes, who carried Indian religion, political organisation, architecture and sculpture with them.

Why Indian systems and values appealed to the peoples of Southeast Asia has been puzzled over, but several factors are regarded as having had a combined influence: a similarity between Indian values and those already in existence in Southeast Asia (while conversely the strength of the latter could account also for the failure of the caste system to be transferred); beyond this, the belief that the more advanced organisation and technology that Indians were able to offer proceeded precisely from the worship of their particular deities; and, founded on these but perhaps not least, Indian emphasis on a hierarchical social order that appealed strongly to the local ruling elites and jelled to a significant extent with traditional systems.

After the opening phases of the spread of India and of Europe, Indians and Europeans diverged between what they did and what they did not do. In the former respect, the Indians gradually became closely involved and in places intermarried with the local ruling groups, resulting, directly or indirectly, in rule becoming based on the cult of an Indian deity identified with the ruler. In the latter respect, India did not follow up this Indianisation with the despatch of armies, administrators or colonists who would take control on behalf of their parent state, frequently at the expense of the colonised. (On the other hand it can be said in the Europeans' favour that, eventually, they also sent archeologists to help rescue a glorious past that had in some places fallen into local neglect.)

Occasional emigration into Southeast Asia from India continued after major political and social turmoil in the latter; but the link lay more in an interchange of visits by priests and of course traders, and presumably artists as well.[47] The continuing contacts helped reinforce the hold of Hinduism and Buddhism on the rulers and eventually the people of the region; but, politically, unlike the later European colonies, the Indianised states of Indochina, Malaysia and Indonesia developed quite autonomously from their great Indian parent – or, more accurately, parents, India being by no means unified. Unfortunately, like the parents, the offspring states added the internecine warfare that was endemic in the Subcontinent to their own quarrelsome tradition.

Religion was to play a crucial role both in the establishment of Indianisation and in the subsequent structure and functioning of the state. Of the various forms of Indian religion carried to Southeast Asia, in Cambodia the cult of the king, identified with Shiva as the guardian of the state, was for long the most popular. But after three centuries the cult of Vishnu, the thousand–named, was favoured for the same purpose by Suryavarman II, the builder of Angkor Wat.

Buddhism, with its missionary zeal and lack of caste and racial prejudice, was present from the beginning, but for centuries it was uninfluential. Then, following Suryavarman, Cambodia would observe both its main forms, which had already been present: Mahayana, more commonly associated with North Asia; subsequently, after a Hindu reaction, Theravada in its Singhalese form, following its penetration through Burma and Thailand.

---

47   In fact I can't help wondering whether the uncharacteristic naturalism of the movement and drapery of a pre–Angkor statue of Krishna Govardhana (in the National Museum of Cambodia, Phnom Penh; illustrated in Jessup Zephir, p.161) might even indicate a Khmer sculptor's contact with far–off Ghandaran art, the reflection of Alexander the Great's 4th century BCE invasion of the northwest of the Indian Subcontinent, and where (and in the other Kushan capital in Mathura, in northern India) the representation of the Buddha first began in the 1st century CE. During the previous five centuries he had been represented by symbols (such as the stupa, sacred tree, pair of footprints, etc), just as, though for only about half that length of time, Christ was also (by a cross or fish); in due course worshippers wanted to know "what they looked like".

No ruler was ever indifferent to religion and its observances: they were the essence of their status, and (as Bentley noted in *Old World Encounters* in relation to China) rulers did not give either Hindus or Buddhists free reign, but "ensured they properly supported the dynasty". At the same time, unlike in Europe, religious intolerance was rare: kings at times showed zealotry for one cult but tolerance for others continued; there could be parallel observances; syncretism of various kinds between the cults was frequent. Jayavarman VII, the first king to make Angkor Buddhist, invoked the Mahayana vehicle, but made no effort to "convert" the Hindu temples of his predecessors, and aspects of Hindu teachings and mythology still appeared in his own.

By the end of our first millennium the map of Indochina was still pre–modern: the Cambodians, as they had long been, in the centre; Burmese to the west, but the Thai now descending the valley of the Menam River between them and the Cambodians; Laotians to the north, above the Dangrek Range; Cham to the east, between Cambodians and the South China Sea. These were the Indianised states, but they never stopped fighting each other, even when all of them in due course became Buddhist. Vietnamese, pushed from southern China and never Indianised, were beginning to force their way down the east coast of Indochina from the north. Over the second millennium Cambodia would be continually squeezed: from the west by the Thai, from the 13th century on; from the east, for the first half of the millennium by the Cham,[48] then for the entire second half by the Vietnamese. This might recall Poland, but Cambodia was never partitioned in the same way, it was simply occupied: Angkor, for long periods, by the Thai; the whole country, for nearly a century following its "discovery", by the French; most recently, by the Vietnamese, for over a decade.

Angkor the capital

During the three centuries after the founding of the Angkor monarchy, Cambodia's kings were preoccupied principally with getting and trying to hold their thrones. It is a scene of seemingly endless revolts, usurpations and civil wars, lit by an inscription that one of them "cut off

---

48   Some time before or after the fall of Champa to the Vietnamese, in 1471, numbers of Cham were converted to Islam, presumably by traders from Malaya or Indonesia; some fled to Cambodia where their descendants, now eighty thousand or so and still Moslem, have lived a largely separate but generally tolerated life.

the heads of a crowd of kings". Before the 12th century only Jayavarman VII's maternal great–grandfather Suryavarman I, himself a usurper, seemed to stand out. He showed his determination in an oath he had over five hundred of his supporters take, and which he engraved – with their names – on the main gateway to his palace (later covered, and thus preserved, by one of the terraces of Jayavarman VII's own palace):

"All of us offer our life and our unfailing devotion, to our Lord Shri Suryavarman...
   If any of us should break this oath, we ask that future sovereigns inflict on them all manner of royal torture. If there should be any traitors amongst us who do not abide fully by this oath, may they be reborn in the thirty–two hells, for as long as the Sun and the Moon shall last...".

He reigned throughout the first half of the 11th century, and seems to have been the only king to have significantly expanded the kingdom during the 9th–11th centuries – mainly northwards into Laos.

But through the 10th and 11th centuries, despite all the domestic strife, Angkor itself was steadily expanded: laced with comprehensive water-works, sprinkled with temples and temple–cities. The reservoirs were enormous: the East Baray reservoir (7x2 kms), built by Yasovarman I, the founder of Yasodharapura, at the turn of the 9th–10th centuries, and now rice fields; and the biggest of the Barays, the West (8x2 kms), the only one still (almost) filled with water, begun by Suryavarman I just over a century later. The building of temples was prodigious.[49] Then in the first half of the 12th century we arrive at the vast magisterial symbol by which Angkor is best known, the almost intact temple–mountain of Angkor Wat, built by Suryavarman II in the southeast corner of Yasodharapura.

The earlier Roluos temples and many of the later ones at Angkor itself were dedicated to Shiva. But there were blips, in the manner of Khmer royal theological eclecticism: Yasovarman I, who built the Shaivite Bakheng as the foundation royal temple of Yasodharapura, also

---

49   In the 10th century, the East Mebon and Pre Rup, and everyone's favourite, the exquisite and exquisitely carved rose–coloured "Citadel of the Women", Banteay Srei, 25kms to the northeast; in the 11th century, Ta Keo, the Phimeanakas (the "Gold Tower" in the Yasodharapura Royal Palace, and the site of one of Zhou Daguan's more sensational – and significant – stories), the Baphuon, and the West Mebon.

built a Buddhist temple and, on Phnom Krom, a mountain south of Angkor near the Tonle Sap lake, one dedicated to the Hindu trinity – Brahma, Shiva, Vishnu; a temple dedicated to Vishnu was built under his son; a century later Suryavarman I's elder son built both the Shaivite Baphuon and the Vishnuite West Mebon; then, a century after that, Suryavarman II dedicated Angkor Wat and his other temples to Vishnu – with, as so often, extra cover, the little Shaivite complex of Preah Pithu. Indeed, frequently supplementary or alternative gods appear in temples dedicated to someone else: eclecticism and ecumenicalism were more typical than not.

Throughout the first three centuries of the Angkorian monarchy, Hinduism, or, more precisely, Shaivism, was clearly favoured over Buddhism. Why, towards the end, there was a noticeable shift from Shiva to Vishnu is unclear. Perhaps Suryavarman II, the first real breakaway from Shaivism, was influenced by a contemporary revival of Vishnuism in India; perhaps he fell under the spell of a particularly persuasive Brahman teacher – or a particularly persuasive wife. From this distance it is hard to tell whether, ultimately, the choice between the Hindu cults was more than a matter of theological taste – or the desire to placate more than the one divinity. The worship of Shiva and Vishnu is in the same canon; but Cambodia never experienced anything like the wars, persecutions and bloodshed that shifts within the same canon have caused and are still causing in Europe and the Middle East.

The King

After Suryavarman, who ruled between 1113 and 1150, we come to Jayavarman VII. There is a view that he was probably born in 1125, and another – this being Cambodiology – that he could not possibly have been ninety–five when he died in 1220 – if indeed he lived until 1220. But it seems likely that the young Prince grew at least to early manhood under the great warrior–builder Suryavarman II, his father's cousin; and although the inscriptions on the stelae are silent about his early years, we have the liberty that the professional historians do not to see if we can plausibly fill some of the gaps. And it seems to me that such an overlap with Suryavarman could have been crucial in developing the younger man's character, skills and tastes.

Zhou Daguan wrote of his time in Angkor:

"I have heard it said that in previous reigns the marks of the King's chariot wheels were never seen outside the palace gates – a precaution against unforeseen violence. The present ruler...caused a splinter of sacred iron to be grafted into his own body, so that any thrust of knife or spear could do him no harm. Once this was brought about, the new King ventured forth. During my stay of over a year in the country I saw him emerge four or five times...".

However he was by no means invisible the rest of the time:

"Every day the King holds two audiences for consideration of affairs of state. No list of agenda is provided. Functionaries and ordinary people who wish to see the Sovereign seat themselves on the ground to await his arrival...[After arriving in "only one" golden palanquin, to the sound of "blasts on conch shells",] Two girls of the palace lift up the curtain with their slender fingers" [note those "slender fingers"; we shall hear more of this] "and the King, sword in hand, appears standing in the golden window. All present – ministers and commoners – join their hands and touch the earth with their foreheads, lifting up their heads only when the sound of conchs has ceased...When the affairs of state have been dealt with the king turns back to the palace, the two girls let fall the curtain, and everyone rises. From all this it is plain to see that these people, though barbarians, know what is due to a Prince".

This King, Indravarman III, was the third after Jayavarman VII, the son–in–law and usurping successor of Jayavarman's grandson, who had succeeded one of Jayavarman's sons. Court protocol had undoubtedly been well fixed over a long period. There is a Chinese account from about mid–13th century in very much the same terms, by Ma Tuan-lin. Ma, who has been called "China's Pliny", made a compilation of reports around 1273, some twenty years before Zhou Daguan's voyage, on China's "barbarian" neighbours and (in particular) their relations with the Celestial Kingdom.[50] Ma's histories and descriptions of at least the

---

50 Ma's compilation is similar to that which characterises Marco Polo's later celebrated *Travels*, according to some recent research: indeed, some of Marco Polo's paragraphs appear to have been lifted from Ma Tuan–lin. Like both Pliny and Marco Polo, Ma also had a somewhat vacuum–cleaner approach to his sources. There is a tantalising, but unfortunately undocumented, suggestion in Sir Henry Yule's amazingly detailed annotations of his translation of the *Travels*

identifiable countries were no doubt based primarily on the records made at the times they sent embassies to the imperial capital, in the case of Cambodia from at least the 5th century CE, and from Champa somewhat earlier, up to the early 13th century, not long before he compiled them. Like Zhou Daguan, Ma, in his chapter on what the Chinese called "Chin–la", remarked on the deep obeisances of even the most elevated of the Cambodian king's subjects – a practice which still existed in only slightly modified form when I last met with an exiled King Norodom Sihanouk in the early 1990s.

Protocol had probably not changed by Zhou's time, but Khmer kingship had, drastically. Indravarman was a wimp by comparison with his great–grandfather–in–law. For Jayavarman VII is now regarded as having been the greatest Cambodian King, for liberating the nation, for conquering the neighbours, for building more than all his predecessors combined, and, withal, for exceptional, caring devoutness. We shall look at these as we go along: Jayavarman's military prowess, his architecture, his beliefs and their effect on his governing, beginning with their development under Suryavarman II.

The Buddhist
However it is not to Suryavarman's influence that we have to look for help with Jayavarman's religious profession, on which he broke with Suryavarman's state cult of Vishnu. The main suggestion seems to be that he was influenced by Buddhist monks from the Nalanda monastery in Bihar, in northeast India, a major teaching centre closely associated with the Buddha himself; and that they had fled before the third Moslem onslaught on India, by Mohammed Ghuri from Afghanistan. Nalanda bonzes were particularly devoted to the Mahayana form of Buddhism, so their arrival in Cambodia could certainly help explain Jayavarman's attachment to that Vehicle. However the Ghuris only reached as far as Bihar in the early 1190s; and Jayavarman had already dedicated his first major Buddhist temple, Ta Prohm, in 1186, when Mohammed Ghur was only beginning his invasion of north India. It therefore seems we need to look elsewhere for the beginnings of Jayavarman's Buddhism, and there are aspects of his genealogy that are suggestive here.

---

that Zhou Daguan "may have personally known Marco Polo". (In the present book, in the 1300 chapter: Devorguilla of Galloway, we come to the question whether Marco actually went to China.)

Jayavarman was descended on both sides from kings of Cambodia – in fact, on both sides from usurping kings, his father's uncle having stolen the throne from his mother's father, himself the son of a usurper.[51] As might be expected, there was a strong Shaivite connection throughout the extended royal family; but in both lines there were also those inexplicable switches between cults that we have previously noted as characteristic of Cambodia.

On Jayavarman's paternal side, neither his usurping great–uncle nor the latter's sibling successor completed any buildings, but they were said to be "traditionalists" – so presumably Shaivite. They were followed by their sister's grandson, Suryavarman II, because (according to an inscription),

> "still quite young at the end of his studies, [he] proved to be the answer to the desires of the royal honour of his family...".

In fact the desires were all his: he seized the throne from the second great–uncle, after what one inscription circumspectly described as a "one–day battle". Another did not prevaricate about the obvious extent of Suryavarman's preparations:

> "Releasing the ocean of his armies on the field of combat, [Suryavarman] gave terrible battle; leaping on the head of the elephant of the enemy king, he slew him, just as Garuda swooping down from the top of a mountain kills a snake".

As we have previously noted, Suryavarman dedicated Angkor Wat, his main construction and temple–mausoleum, to Vishnu – some believe to himself as Vishnu. His successor, Dharanindravarman II, his cousin on his mother's side, Jayavarman VII's father, was Buddhist. This shift from Hinduism to Buddhism amounted to more than a switch between the Hindu divinities Shiva and Vishnu, but why Dharanindravarman in particular made it we do not know. *Another* particularly convincing cleric – this time a monk?

Jayavarman's wife's lineage suggests another intriguing possibility. His usurping maternal great–grandfather, Suryavarman I, built temples

---

51 I have tried to simplify genealogical explanations and to avoid citing *every* name: they are confusingly cognate, overly repetitive, and often not necessarily relelevant.

dedicated to Shiva. *His* elder son, as we saw, dedicated one to Shiva, then one to Vishnu; but, unusually, he was said to be hostile to Buddhism, which was not a trait ascribed to previous Khmer kings. Perhaps it was because he distrusted his younger brother and heir apparent who seems likely to have been Buddhist. This younger brother, Jayavarman's maternal grandfather, who eventually succeeded his older sibling, also left no temples. He was said to be "peace–loving", which was a possible though in Cambodia not a necessary characteristic of a Buddhist; but he was also said to have retired to a "monastery", which certainly suggests Buddhism. How did *he* become Buddhist? Was Cambodia filled with irresistible proselytisers of all persuasions?

If he had been Buddhist, his daughter, Jayarajachudamani, Jayavarman's mother, could well then have led her husband, and, in due course, son, to Buddhism. No doubt her marriage to Jayavarman's father was based on considerations of state policy, in particular the resolution of the dynastic conflict between the two usurping lines; but it seems likely that the resentful ex–royal family would have wanted someone with some character to become the link to the family that had usurped their throne. We do not know exactly what influence his mother played in Jayavarman's life; but there was often a strong matrilineal element in Cambodian royalty; and it is interesting that Jayavarman himself set some store on claiming descent, through his mother, from the pre–Angkorian kings of Cambodia.

For Jayavarman, Buddhism was not a religion of withdrawal, of otherworldly meditation: it was just as much the state religion as Hinduism had been for most of his predecessors. Coedès believed that, from the beginning of Angkor, images were made with the names and appearance of actual humans, but as the *devaraja*, the god–king, with the attributes of that member of the Hindu or Buddhist pantheons with which the person was to be identified in death, and perhaps had been in life. As those predecessors identified themselves with Shiva or Vishnu as the guardian of the state, so Jayavarman derived his identity from Buddha, an identification that was at the core of his building program, the very essence of his cult of himself, as we shall see later. There are those who believe this identification was not just of himself as Buddhist: it was of Jayavarman as an apotheosis of Buddha, claimed by an inscription at Ta Prohm, the temple dedicated to his mother, as the *Jayabuddhamahanatha*, "the great saviour Jayavarman the Buddha" (as Coedès interpreted it). Others, rejecting this reading and the idea that Jayavarman saw himself as any kind of deity, have seen him rather as seeking to fix in stone his humility before Buddha – though that view tempts the thought, given his constructions, that he must have been monumentally humble.

It will be three more centuries before we find the next portrait from life of the subjects of these chapters. But for Jayavarman we have a number of portraits in the Bayon bas–reliefs, and not just one but five accessible individual portraits: five splendid sandstone sculptures – two with the full figure seated cross–legged, three just the head (undoubtedly the remains of full figures).[52] The two sculpted figures show a stocky, solidly–built man, a little overweight and beginning to expand at the waistline. The heads of both, and the individual heads, are all recognisably of the same man, though the features of H3 look to be those of an older Jayavarman, more jowly. All have the eyes cast down and closed; and all but one (a grimmer H2) have the celebrated "sourire d'Angkor", the smile of Angkor, a description bestowed by the French archeologists originally on the *apsaras*, the heavenly females in the bas–reliefs of Angkor Wat and elsewhere: veritable chorus lines in various dance poses and various hair–dos, but identically simpering – never sombre, never laughing, depiction of the teeth being regarded in Asian art (and, in some places, life) as unseemly.

From a physical viewpoint it is reasonable, on the basis of the stocky figures, to describe Jayavarman's physique as powerful, notwithstanding his chubbiness. But drawing conclusions about the *character* of the person from these portraits is where the mischief begins.

Jayavarman was undoubtedly portrayed *as he wanted to be perceived as being like*. The Buddhist pose of "compassion and humility", the downcast, closed eyes often characteristic of representations of the Buddha, were intended to convey that Jayavarman embodied the master's humility and piety, leaving his modern admirers to argue whether that went as far as identifying himself with Buddha or merely

---

52 A full figure (S1), seated cross–legged but without arms, and a head (H1) are in the National Museum of Cambodia, Phnom Penh; the second full figure statue (S2), similar in form and condition to the other, was found at Phimai (now in Thailand), and is in the National Museum, Bangkok; the other two heads (H2 and H3) are both in France, at the Musée Guimet, Paris. I have numbered them for ease of reference in the text. All are illustrated (in black white) in Stern, Figs 194–200; S1, H1 and H3 are illustrated (in colour) in Jessup Zephir, pp 300–303. The portraits of Jayavarman in the bas–reliefs of the Bayon are much smaller and more stylized, but experts have claimed to recognize the sculptures from those more historically–identifiable versions.

closely approximating Buddha's virtues. But we are familiar throughout history, to the present day, with official portraits representing our leaders as looking more regal, more beautiful, more honest than we have known them to be (and in Stalin's case the obverse, airbrushed out of all earthly existence). It is thus an unwarranted step to conflate convention with reality, to contend that, because of Jayavarman's appearance in his portrait sculpture, he actually possessed or approximated Buddha's virtues, that he was actually humble and pious in real life. A King who built himself one of the greatest temple–mausoleums of all time, and styled himself King of Kings (*Rajadhiraja*) and Universal Monarch (*Cakravartin* – a monarch who uses force to defend the Buddhist faith), who had portraits made of himself as actually or ambiguously close to divine. Pious, who knows; but humble?

It is conventional to follow the French archeologists in using the sculptures to deduce Jayavarman's *character* as one of benevolent superiority – an application, it seems to me, very close to the discredited "science" of physiognomy that was popular in their day to demonstrate the opposite in non–European races. The argument is circular in any case: the representational conclusions are projected onto certain of Jayavarman's actions in order to confirm those very conclusions. These heads can thus be looked at as conveying whatever you want them to convey – aided, as with those in the face–towers, by the angle of the viewpoint and by the lighting falling upon them: anything from a self–absorbed, sweet resignation to a self–obsessed, steely resolve.

A judgement of the character of the god–king or even the mere king of kings has to be based on a critical appraisal of what we know of his attitudes and activities. We can accept that these elegant sculptures show us pretty much what Jayavarman *looked* like. Now we can look at his life and works and try to figure out what he actually *was* like.

The warrior
While not in religion, in other things Jayavarman was close to Suryavarman II's model; and it is likely that the military arts came first. It would have been normal in those times, as it was in Europe, for a young Prince of the Royal House to be trained in arms and command, often beginning as young as fifteen. Given his later skills as a tactician and strategist, Jayavarman must have had substantial training, and by the best available teachers; and Suryavarman and his staff fitted that bill perfectly.

War would have been prominent in the young prince's life. After the domestic focus during most of the previous centuries, on civil war and building temples and irrigation works, Suryavarman was a warrior who pushed out Cambodia's boundaries to their greatest extent up to that time; an inscription stated:

> "He saw the kings of the other countries that he desired to subjugate coming to bring tribute. He himself went into the countries of his enemies and eclipsed the glory of the victorious Raghu"

– an apposite tribute, Raghu being an ancestor of Vishnu's incarnation as Rama, the hero of the *Ramayana*. Most notably, after raids against Champa, he attacked Vietnamese Annam in 1128 when Cham forces recoiling from his invasion took refuge there, then again annually for several years, and yet again in 1138; in 1145 he launched an invasion against Champa, took the capital Vijaya (now Binh–dinh), and occupied the country. He only held it for four years, but the war he had launched would last off and on until the end of the century, and end up engulfing both states. In 1150 there were renewed attacks on Annam and fighting to the west in what was to become Thailand.

At the time of Suryavarman's invasion of Champa Jayavarman could well have already had a subordinate command in that successful campaign. The campaigns in 1150 however seem to have been unsuccessful in both the east and the west; but they could have been an equally valuable lesson for an up–and–coming young officer. So far we have been making reasonable assumptions. When we now come to the evidence of an inscription, we are unfortunately left hanging: Jayavarman is recorded as having left Angkor to go to Champa, but not when.

Suryavarman died around 1150, and was succeeded by his cousin, Jayavarman's father, Dharindravarman II, whose Buddhist fervour was recorded but apparently nothing else of his reign. On his death around 1160, he was succeeded by Yasovarman II, perhaps a son, perhaps a nephew. Jayavarman seems immediately to have left for Champa, where he was to stay until about 1165. It has often been assumed that he had expected to succeed his father, and that he therefore fled in fear of his life, or (to meet the expectations presumed of a Buddhist) simply voluntarily, in renunciation, to avoid civil war. In either case, the choice of Champa as refuge would seem a bit odd after Suryavarman's relentless campaigns, in which Jayavarman had in all likelihood participated himself.

Perhaps he had wanted the throne – we do not know; but even if he was disappointed at not getting the succession, Yasovarman does not seem to have been his enemy; indeed, one of Jayavarman's young sons was recorded as having risked his own life to put down a revolt against Yasovarman. But, most important, Jayavarman trusted the new king enough to leave his beloved wife, Jayarajadevi, in Angkor: an affecting inscription recorded that,

> "Taught by her older sister, Indradevi [who, as we shall see, was to have the last word], considering Buddha and the well–loved object of her aspirations, she followed in the serene path of the sage, who walked between the fire of torments and the sea of sorrows".[53]

In the light of these factors, it seems possible that Jayavarman could have gone – voluntarily indeed – to Champa *on behalf of* Yasovarman: as a hostage, a pledge against renewal of war between the two countries, at a time when Cambodia was preoccupied with the aftermath of Suryavarman's long reign and Champa with continuing Vietnamese pressure. It is relevant that the Chinese chronicler Ma Tuan–lin, recorded that, prior to the 1170s,

> "For a long time Cambodia had friendly relations with Champa, to which it was paying every year a fixed tribute in gold".

The hypothesis fits the sequel. When in about 1165 a usurper, Tribhuvanadityavarman, "a servant ambitious to arrive at the royal power", overthrew Yasovarman, Jayavarman was able to leave the Cham capital, and

> "returned in great haste to aid King Yasovarman. But Yasovarman had been stripped of throne and life by the usurper...".

The inscription on the loving Jayarajadevi recorded her husband's return, noting her

---

53 The Musée Guimet in Paris also has a ravishing full–figure sculpture believed to be of Jayarajadevi, kneeling, naked above the waist, but like Jayavarman's full–figure sculptures, without arms. It too is illustrated (in colour) in Jessup Zephir, p.305.

"asceticism, her virtuous conduct, her tears, her likeness to Sita [Rama's beautiful wife], found by her husband and then separated from him, her body thinned by observances, her religion, her devotion to him, her joy at this ultimate return".

But her prayers were not yet wholly answered:

"Having, by her exertions recovered her husband...she desired to see (freed) the land plunged into a sea of misfortunes...";

Jayavarman, however, merely

"remained in Cambodia waiting for the propitious moment to save the land heavy with crimes".

Here was another mystery in his life: where did he wait? And why? The propitious moment he was waiting for came only when the usurper king Tribhuvanadityavarman was slain during a horrendous Cham invasion twelve years later, in 1177. What, then, was Jayavarman doing during those twelve intervening years? That he did not take up armed resistance when he returned in 1165 may have again been out of concern – as was posited about his behaviour at Yasovarman's succession – to avoid civil war. But it may equally have been because the usurper so rapidly secured his position that any challenge would have been suicidal. Or it might have been that Jayavarman accepted the new regime because, from 1167, Angkor was faced with a new and by far the most dangerous threat from Champa in over three centuries.

Invasion
After a renewed attack in 1170, Champa thought it had come upon a secret weapon: Ma Tuan–lin recorded that in 1171

"a mandarin from the [Chinese] province of Fukien, called Ki–yang–kiun, who, going for a sail, was carried by the wind to the coast of Champa. This kingdom was at war with that of Cambodia; on both sides elephants were used in combat, without great advantage to either. Ki–yang–kiun advised the King of Champa to use horsemen armed with bows and crossbows, to whom he would teach the art of shooting arrows while riding. The King...charged Ki–yang–kiun with securing horses. Ki–yang–kiun bought a few dozen. The success of this innovation was enormous; victory declared itself for Champa".

This was Chinese hyperbole: with only a few dozen horses, this could have been no more than a border clash, though perhaps successful in capturing a number (though scarcely an enormous number) of slaves. The following year, when the Cham King sent "a great number" of men to Hainan to obtain horses, they were not made welcome and retaliated by sacking the place and carrying off the inhabitants; and there followed an imbroglio with the Chinese over the next couple of years, not least because there turned out be an Imperial ban on the sale of horses anyway.

The decisive outcome of Cham hostility followed, but in only the most lapidary manner in Ma Tuan–li's account: in 1177

"the King of Champa suddenly assailed the capital of Cambodia with a powerful fleet [by way of the Mekong–Tonle Sap river system], pillaged it and put the king [Tribhuvanadityavarman] to death, without listening to any proposal of peace".

The capital, Yasodharapura, was totally sacked, the wooden palaces burned, even some of the temples desecrated – it is said that there are some stones in structures built just afterwards that still show the evidence of the viciousness of the Cham destruction.

We do not know what role, if any, Jayavarman played in this disaster. Did he join the fight against the invaders? Or, while apparently not seeking to undermine Tribhuvanadityavarman through twelve long years, had he held himself aloof and simply watched the disaster happen – and his own chances suddenly open up? There were no doubt inscriptions which are now lost; but, on the whole, the silence on such a crucial event suggests that Jayavarman did not play a role in it, or at least not one that could be presented as glorious.

But there is an inscription which says that, the usurper gone, his wife Jayarajadevi was again pushing Jayavarman to act: the land was

"heavy with crimes", and she wanted him to "draw the earth out of this sea of misfortune into which it was plunged".

Ma Tuan–lin also recorded that now, at last, Jayavarman, zealous Buddhist though he was, was filled with a "great hatred", and "swore that he would wreak on [the King of Champa] a devastating revenge, which he succeeded in carrying out after eighteen years of patient dissembling".

This, too, was Chinese hyperbole: it took Jayavarman eighteen years to bring Champa to total submission; but he did not dissemble for quite that long.

Recovery

First, however, he had to expel the Cham from Cambodia itself, then he had to reunify a country thrown into turmoil by their invasion; but there are more absences from the records of Jayavarman's life: how and precisely when he did so are not known. Before he could do either he obviously would have had two major tasks: re–assemble or even re–create and re–train an army, and establish a new administration to ensure its support. That the first was achieved, and the Cham expelled within four years, is testimony to the martial and strategic skills which Jayavarman must have mastered in his younger days. How exactly he did so is recorded only laconically: according to one inscription, he conquered the Cham king "whose warriors were as an ocean without limits"; according to another, Jayavarman,

"founding himself in the law, killed in combat the enemy chief with a hundred million arrows to protect the [country]".

Hyperbole was not a Chinese preserve.

One of the finest bas–reliefs in the outer gallery of the Bayon shows a naval battle with the Cham, presumably at this time, against their invasion fleet still on the Tonle Sap. In the 35m long by 3m high series of scenes, the Khmer, bare–headed with round shields, arrive at the scene from the west; the Cham, identifiable by their funny upside–down magnolia–flower helmets and strangely elongated, hooked axe–head shields, arrive from the east, ship after ship, each with long rows of rowers' heads and long rows of warriors behind, spears or bows at the ready; and, beneath and above and around them all, huge shoals of great fat fish, and a lot of crocodiles. At one point three Cambodians swimming amongst the fish look for all the world like frogmen attacking the on–rushing Cham galleys.

There is of course much more to the Bayon bas–reliefs. The larger outer gallery shows further episodes from Jayavarman's battles with the

Cham, with troops of soldiers marching, marching, marching (like miniature versions of Darius's legions of Medes and Persians at Persepolis), accompanied by huge numbers of commanders mounted on elephant–back – in one scene, everyone, it seems, from corporal on up: there are eight mounted officers to fifty–six foot–soldiers. The sheer mass of detail, the variety of activity and incident, are staggering.

The inner gallery bas–reliefs, by contrast, usually in two, sometimes in three registers, almost all depict scenes from *Hindu* mythology, many relating to Vishnu – the dedicatee of Suryavarman's Angkor Wat – but also scenes from the *Mahabharata*, part formal, part life–like, with its hero Krishna, the avatar of Vishnu, and other scenes with Shiva as well, so no–one is left out. Whether these scenes – which also portrayed battles – symbolised aspects of the historical world in the outer reliefs is not clear; but all this in a temple dedicated to Buddha is a fine example of the religious inclusiveness noted earlier.

The second task, re–establishing the royal administration, was probably the more difficult. Apart from his own sons, who were apparently active, the ranks of possible ministers may have been thin: there may have been a few of his father's senior officials still alive, but it was now twenty years since the latter's death; and while Yasovarman, as a close relation, was probably also Buddhist, along with appropriate officials, he too had been dead for fifteen years; and it seems doubtful that Jayavarman would have wanted to make use of the usurper's surviving ministers. But, again, the fact that the state was functioning by 1181 suggests that Jayavarman had also picked up administrative skills along the way, perhaps during his youthful time at Suryavarman's court, perhaps even during those five years of exile, probably at the Court, in Champa. In any event, it was in 1181 that Jayavarman finally felt sufficiently in control of the country to have himself anointed king.

Still he was prevented from revenge on Champa by further domestic dissension: within a year or two he was faced by a revolt in southern Battambang province, not far southwest of Angkor itself (the area where the communist Khmer Rouge revolt against Sihanouk began in the 1960s). A Cham inscription recorded that it was put down by a young Cham prince, Vindyanandana, to whom Jayavarman had taught "all the sciences and military skills" and to whom he entrusted the command "seeing that the prince was well versed in military skills". While Vindyanandana's role reflected a division within the Cham ruling elite, as was about to become clearer, it evokes again Jayavarman's previous curiously ambivalent relations with Champa.

Now, indeed, Jayavarman did pass a number of years apparently dissembling as far as Champa was concerned. They would have been far from idle years: presumably he was repairing the irrigation system on which Cambodia's economy depended – any interruption of maintenance work resulted in dangerous silting; reconstructing the more or less coterminous state and religious structure, as we saw earlier; and, increasingly, developing Cambodian military strength even further so as to be able to wreak his revenge on Champa.

And also – and not least – he began his stupendous building program at Angkor: Ta Prohm as his mother's funerary temple, dedicated in 1186, and Preah Khan (supposedly on the site of his land victory over the Cham occupiers) as his father's, dedicated in 1191. Both are substantial, their outer walls measuring 700x1000m and 700x800m respectively, and we shall come back to them later. The timing of this work suggests that the economy must have been well on the way to recovery by about 1183, to allow this building activity to begin, given the cost and number of workmen and artisans that would have been involved. Some high pressure training must have been required, first, in this area also: it was by now forty years since the last building program under Suryavarman II, and nothing had been built during the intervening period.

Revenge

Jayavarman is said to have waited, as well, for a further Cham provocation. It came in 1190, but as it was *after* he had ensured Annamese neutrality earlier that year, perhaps it was itself provoked, indicating that it was only now that he was ready to attack. While it is fairly clear what the outcome was, it is not altogether clear who did what. A Cham inscription says that Jayavarman sent his Cham protégé, Prince Vindyanandana,

> "at the head of the troops of Cambodia to take Vijaya [Binh–dinh, the Cham capital] and defeat the king. He captured the king and had him conducted to Cambodia by the Cambodian troops. He proclaimed...[the] brother–in–law of the King of Cambodia as king of the city of Vijaya".

Ma Tuan–lin, however, places Jayavarman himself at the centre of a more thoroughgoing revenge:

> "The king of Cambodia swept down on the capital of Champa at the head of a huge army, wiped out the inhabitants, seized

in his palace the king on whom he was meting out vengeance, took him into captivity, after having had his counsellors and ministers killed, and put on the throne of Champa in his place a Cambodian officer".

This "officer", Jayavarman's brother–in–law, was in fact king of only the north; in the south Prince Vidyanandana decided to rule himself, though still under Jayavarman's suzerainty.

The sequel, however, was something else again: within a year a rebellion overthrew Jayavarman's brother–in–law, and Vidyanandana shed his allegiance, conquered the northern half of the country, and by 1192 was king of a reunited Champa. Outraged at this treachery by his former pupil and trusted general, Jayavarman tried to invade Champa in 1193 and again, with a larger army, in 1194, but was pushed back both times by Vidyanandana. Clearly, Jayavarman had trained him too well. All the same, these defeats so soon after the great victory of 1190 suggest that Jayavarman's attention and interest was already being focussed elsewhere: and, indeed, the years when he left Champa alone must have coincided with those when he began construction of the new capital at Angkor, the city of Angkor Thom, and its central temple–mountain, the Bayon.

It was perhaps a further distraction that, at some point during this period, Queen Jayarajadevi died, noted for her numerous pious works after Jayavarman had become king:

"[She] filled the earth with a shower of magnificent gifts [of precious objects and Chinese cloth, and also sponsored pious dance performances]...She erected piously her three *gurus* [her father, mother and husband] in gold set with jewels, like incandescent suns...[She] erected everywhere her father, brother, friends, relatives and members of he family, known to her or of whom she had heard talk".

These Buddhist portrait–apotheoses were also made by Jayavarman of his family: at Ta Prohm, two hundred and sixty small images once surrounded the central apotheosis of his mother, at Preah Khan, five hundred and fifteen that of his father. Altogether, he was responsible for setting up 20,400 of these divinities, "in gold, in silver, in bronze, in stone".

Jayavarman assuaged his grief by marrying Jayarajadevi's older sister, Indradevi. She it was who authored her sister's encomiums; but she did not hesitate to promote herself as well:

"Surpassing by her charm those who are endowed with beauty, and by her knowledge the intelligence of the philosophers...in the Buddhist temple of Nagendratunga, the leader in the world in holy knowledge; and appointed by the King head professor in that of Tilokattara, she was always arranging teaching for masses of women...Intelligent by nature, wise, very pure, devoted to King Jayavarman, having composed this panegyric and turned aside from all [her] other talents, she shines with brilliance".

That ominous first phrase may suggest why the youthful Jayavarman had not married such a paragon in the first place. It was of course Indradevi who had recorded her predecessor's repeated but ineffectual efforts to get Jayavarman to rescue Cambodia from its "sea of misfortune". So it was perhaps she who now steeled him to keep his promise of revenge on Champa for having caused it.

In 1199 Vindyanandana requested, and received, investiture as King of Champa by the Emperor of China. This possibly still held Jayavarman back from tackling Champa; Ma Tuan–lin's record suggests that there had been no contact between Angkor and the Chinese capital since 1147, but now, in 1201, Jayavarman himself contacted the Song Court, perhaps to ensure that his designs would not risk undoing from that quarter. The Song dynasty recorded that

"He sent an embassy to present a letter to the Emperor and to carry in tribute some products of the country and two trained elephants...Then, on account of the aloofness [distance] due to the maritime way, he did not renew the tribute".

Such nugatory offerings may have been calculated to persuade the Chinese that Angkor was not worth their attention, much as Tamburlaine's "tribute" of 15 horses and 2 camels seems to have been intended almost two centuries later.

But now Jayavarman was ready to strike again at Champa. This time, however, instead of trying yet another frontal assault, somehow he managed to suborn one of Vindyanandana's uncles, and somehow, though not until 1203, the latter managed at long last to overthrow the treacherous Cham King. For the rest of Jayavarman's life, until about 1220, Champa was securely a province of Cambodia. There had also been some Cambodian expansion in the mid–90s: the extent of direct control is unclear, but it extended as far north as Vientiane in Laos; and it is thought that to the west, where defensive/offensive military activities against the Burmese kingdom of Pagan had continued intermittently since he took power, the latter may have at least for a time become a tributary state.[54] Cambodia was now at the widest extent it ever had been, and that it ever would be.

Seventy years later, in Zhou Daguan's time, all these accretions had gone. In 1285, ten years before Zhou's visit, Jayavarman's grandson had offered tribute to Kublai Khan as the latter's Mongol legions penetrated deep into Indochina, possibly even into Cambodia itself. Cambodia's military strength had by now entirely dissipated; as for the army, Zhou observed that

"Soldiers move about unclothed and barefoot. In the right hand is carried a lance, in the left a shield. They have no bows, no slings, no missiles, no breastplates, no helmets...".

In the Bayon reliefs their forebears not only had bows but also ballistas for firing projectiles, some mounted on elephants, some on a hand–cart. Zhou concluded dismissively:

"Generally speaking, these people have neither discipline nor strategy".

It has remained true, by and large, with the exception of the Pol Pot period, for the whole of Cambodian history since Jayavarman VII.

The builder

Today, Jayavarman's fame rests mainly on his buildings, and that is perhaps what he intended anyway. They are the only masterpieces of Khmer architecture after Angkor Wat, and their varying states of preservation or restoration convey vividly a sense both of the apogee of Cambodia and of its inexorable subsequent decline at the hands of nature and man. Other than through sheer megalomania, Jayavarman's vast building program has never been satisfactorily explained – it has been estimated that more stone was cut, moved and shaped in

---

54 The Thai, Angkor's nemesis just over two centuries later, were at this stage still pressing their way down the Menam River from their origins in southern China; they would only come up against the Khmer after Kublai Khan's crushing of Pagan at the end of the 13th century.

Jayavarman's reign than under all his predecessors combined.[55] Perhaps that is all there ever was, dressed as piety.

Once again we can turn back to Suryavarman II for influence on the young Jayavarman. Suryavarman is believed to have begun the building of Angkor Wat soon after he became king in 1113, and it was largely finished by the time of his death in 1150. Throughout Jayavarman's childhood, youth and possibly up to young manhood he would thus have seen the extraordinary temple–mausoleum, far larger than anything ever built at Angkor before, being constructed for himself by his second cousin who identified himself with Vishnu. The scale and the lavishness of the decoration of Suryavarman's masterpiece must have seized not only his imagination but also his ambition.

That this stayed with him, and that he had already developed ideas by the time he became king, is suggested by the scale and complexity of his building plan, and the speed with which it was put into effect and completed. In the thirty years of his reign Jayavarman is credited with the Bayon, three more major temples and two other significant ones, the stone terraces and other structures associated with the long–gone royal palace, and the huge walls of the new city of Angkor Thom. These measured twelve kilometres around, enclosing 150 hectares, and were surrounded on all four sides by a moat 100 metres wide connected with the city's irrigation system. A century and a half later the new walls of Florence, then the greatest city in Italy, measured eight kilometres around.

It took the French experts a while to decide all this was in fact Jayavarman's work. For several decades he was believed to have been an insignificant ruler, with no major works to his credit; and it was only as the result of the meticulous study of artistic styles, and the discovery and transcription of extra inscriptions, that Coedès was able to conclude, in 1929, that Angkor Thom and the Bayon belonged to the 12th and not the 9th century. The Bayon's identification with Buddhism had only

---

55   There is something unconvincing in the contention by the prolific French scholar Jean Boisselier (in Jessup Zephir) that Jayavarman is "wrongly taxed with megalomania; in fact, he was simply following the example of Aśoka [Ashoka], the model for all Buddhist builders". The main construction program of Ashoka, the 3rd century BCE Mauryan Emperor of northern India whose conversion to Buddhism was instrumental in its dissemination, was the erection of *eighty–four thousand* stupas, but they were to house what he believed were the eighty–four thousand atoms of Buddha's mortal remains; he built no vast temple–mausoleum to his own glory – or humility.

been made by Louis Finot, another epigrapher, five years before. These attributions made, the impression was staggering: it was as if Jayavarman had been driven by some special compulsion to build and go on building – on a far greater scale than that of any of his predecessors – duplicating and triplicating his shrines, seeking to match or outdo Suryavarman in the city of Angkor Thom and its Bayon, built to the glory of the Buddha, and equally his own.

Coedès argued that, within the overall program, there was an elaborate plan of construction designed to ensure that Jayavarman's own status as *Buddharaja*, the Buddhist version of the traditional god–king, was well and truly stamped on the map of his capital and the consciousness of his subjects. This was by linking, in Buddhist doctrinal terms, the two parental tomb–temples we have previously noticed, Ta Prohm and Preah Khan, with his own temple–mausoleum, the Bayon, at the centre of his city of Angkor Thom, to enshrine the Buddhist trinity. Ta Prohm enshrined his mother in the likeness of Prajnaparamita, "the Perfection of Wisdom", mother of all the Buddhas, and sometimes represented as a goddess personifying the Word of Buddha. Preah Khan enshrined his father in the likeness of Lokeshvara [= Avalokiteshvara], "the Compassionate Lord of the World", one of the greatest Boddhisattvas; and, in accordance with religious tradition, in the middle, at the Bayon, Buddha himself, with the features of Jayavarman. Coedès summed up the imagery of the three temples by saying

"Thus they created on a kilometric scale, appropriate to a great king, this triad which heretofore had only been produced in small sculpture".

The denial of Jayavarman's pretension to the status of *Buddharaja* leaves hanging the deified status of his mother and father, as represented in Ta Prohm and Preah Khan, which does not seem to be challenged. There is thus a cogency in Coedès's presentation that remains even when subsequent interpretations are taken into account. If he erred, it was perhaps more in his underemphasising various aspects of the non–Buddhist elements which informed Jayavarman's ecumenical scheme of things, particularly in his temple–mausoleum, the Bayon.

Now the magnitude and majesty of Jayavarman's (and others') works can be easily seen: some of the immediately surrounding jungle has gone, so they can mostly be seen in their entirety; the French archeologists have cleared almost all the temples themselves; some have been put back together in places, others have been restored integrally by the process of anastylosis, pioneered by the Dutch at Borobudur, in which the entire temple is recorded, the parts still standing deconstructed, and the whole rebuilt with the original materials, with only the most discreet use of new ones. Ta Prohm, however, has been left as nature had enveloped it with giant figs and kapok trees, apart from the clearing of an access pathway through the temple, with the expressly romantic purpose of giving visitors an impression of what the first European "discoverers" had found at Angkor. The result has produced as much purple prose as the rest of Angkor combined: even a Briton could write

"The strange, haunted charm of the place entwines itself about you as you go, as inescapably as the roots have wound themselves about the walls and towers...Everywhere around you, you see Nature in this dual role of destroyer and consoler; strangling on the one hand, and healing on the other; no sooner splitting the carved stones asunder than she dresses their wounds with cool, velvety mosses, and binds them with her most delicate tendrils; a conflit of moods so delicate and feminine...".

The French poet Paul Claudel pithily remarked, "An atmosphere of fever and decay"; but he was talking about the temple, not about effusions from across the Channel.[56]

Angkor Thom and the Bayon
It was the great walls of Angkor Thom that struck Zhou Daguan first and foremost in the whole of Angkor; and his description was pretty accurate:

"The wall of the city is some five miles in circumference [8kms, too short by a third]. It has five gates, each with double portals... Outside the wall stretches a great moat, across which access to the city is given by massive causeways. Flanking the causeways on each side are fifty–four divinities resembling warlords in stone, huge and terrifying...Above each gate are grouped five gigantic heads of Buddha, four of them facing the four cardinal points of

---

56   The first comment, by Winifred Ponder (1936) is cited in D.F. Rooney: *Angkor Observed* (Bangkok 2001); Claudel's, from his *Journal* (1921), is cited by Dagens.

the compass, the fifth head, brilliant with gold, holds a central position. [Here he erred again, perhaps bedazzled by gilding at the top of the towers: there was no fifth head.] On each side of the gates are elephants, carved in stone [in fact, the three–headed elephants of Indra].

The walls, about twelve feet [4m] in height, are built entirely of cut stone blocks, set close and firm, with no crevices for weeds to grow in...The inner side of the wall resembles a glacis, more than sixty feet [20m] wide, at the top of which are huge gates, closed at night and swung open in the morning. Dogs are forbidden entrance, as are criminals whose toes have been cut off".

Zhou Daguan then went on to the Bayon, starting with a key phrase:

"At the magical centre of the Kingdom rises a Golden Tower flanked by more than twenty lesser towers and several hundred stone chambers. On the eastern side is a golden bridge guarded by two lions of gold, one on each side, with eight golden Buddhas spaced along the stone chambers...".

It is very odd that he makes no mention of all the faces – unless his mention of only twenty–odd towers (out of fifty–four) indicates that, as a layman, a foreigner and a non–Buddhist, he was never allowed to get close enough to the Bayon to be able to see them. He then refers to two other towers to the north, the Baphuon and another tower of gold (the Phimeanakas) in the royal palace, and concludes:

"These are the monuments which have caused merchants from overseas to speak so often of 'Cambodia the rich and noble' ".

The gold, and all it represented, has long since gone, but much of the stonework remains.

Zhou Daguan's placing of the Bayon at "the magical centre of the Kingdom" was a precise characterisation of Jayavarman's intention – and it is the most striking indication of the inextricable layering of Buddhist and Hindu symbolism. Angkor Thom as a whole, "the Great City", was in the form of a *mandala*, a microcosm both of the whole Angkorian kingdom and of the universal macrocosm beyond, derived from Hindu mythology – in particular, the description of the capital of

Indra, the king of the gods in the pre–historic *Veda*, the original source of Brahmanism and hence Hinduism.

Jayavarman did place the Bayon at the city's exact centre, the temple–mountain representing Mt Meru, the abode of the earliest Vedic gods, the axis of the universe, linking the heavens and the earth and the underworld, surrounded by the four continents, and the source of the life–giving waters for each. The outer wall of the city represents the ring of mountains around the Earth; the moat around the wall represents the Ocean of Infinity beyond. In due course Buddhists also adopted Mt Meru as the centre of an identically arranged universe, though of course with different attributions and attributes.[57] Virtually all the temple–mountains built at Angkor, and back to Borobudur, the Bayon's great Buddhist predecessor, were also based on this same cosmology, notwithstanding some variations in execution, and the fact that some were peopled by Hindu deities, others by Bodhisattvas, and in Jayavarman's buildings, both. It is interesting to note that it was not a French archeologist, but an Englishman, the traveller John Thomson, the first photographer to visit Angkor, who first identified this symbolism in the architecture of Angkor, and compared it with Borobudur.[58]

---

57 In the ancient literature Mt Meru's height is expressed in impossibly extravagant measurements. But long ago it became identified by Hindu (and later, Buddhist) pilgrims with Tibet's Kangrinpoche, known in English as Mt Kailas, in the western Himalayas north of the Nepal border where it meets the sector of the India/China border that is in dispute (loosely referred to as the Aksai Chin). It is still the site of an important Buddhist pilgrimage, a 52km circuit around the mountain and its neighbouring sacred lakes. Kailas, though (in photographs) an isolated, striking ice–pyramid atop a monumental stratified plinth, is not the obvious choice for the role: at 6,714m it is a thousand metres lower than the mountain now known as Gurla Mandhata, within sight of it but seventy kilometres closer to India, and two thousand lower than Everest, seven hundred kilometres to the east; and more extraordinarily, it is also, in the words of the main work on it, "highly inaccessible for any wishing to approach it from the plains of India" (J.Snelling: *The Secret Mountain*; London 1990) – though Australian travel agencies now offer the occasional four–wheel–drive tour. The reason Mt Kailas had the legend of Mt Meru attached to it is not known: but the best (indeed the only) guess seems to be that it is, or is at least close to, the source of four rivers, as in the traditional cosmology – the four great rivers of northern India: the Indus, the Sutlej, the Karnali/Ghaghara/Ganga (Ganges) and the Tsangpo/Brahmaputra.

58 In his *The Straits of Malacca, Indo–China and China*, published in London in 1875.

Jayavarman built the Bayon as a Buddhist, and it was dedicated to Buddha. Boisselier, however, in "The meaning of Angkor Thom" (in Jessup Zephir), was convinced that Jayavarman identified himself with Indra, not only the king of the gods but also the most warlike. This would have been a useful attribution for a ruler determined to dominate not only his own country but also those around it, but it does not enhance his reputation for humility. But it is rather a clear example of the striking contrast between the monotheistic religions which originated in the Middle East and those which originated in India, where devotees could worship various deities simultaneously and the gods themselves could have multitudinous attributes and manifestations which invited such pluralism – including interpretative variation and, dare I say, confusion.

The structural symbolism was in fact spelled out in sensuous language in an inscription found in one of the corner pavilions of Angkor Thom's outer walls (in which Jayavarman's city, though new, was referred to by its predecessor's name, perhaps to underline its legitimacy):

"The city of Yasodharapura – like a young girl of good family, who is well matched to her fiancé, and burning with desire – adorned with a palace of precious stones and bedecked with ramparts, was married by the King, during a magnificent celebration, for the propagation of the people's welfare ...[The city's walls are like] the chain of mountains which encloses the Universe and the city's moat like the Ocean which surrounds it: the one scrapes the blazing sky with its summit; the other in its unfathomable depths touches the world of the snakes: this mountain of victory and this ocean of victory built by this King imitate the range of his immense glory".

While imitating its prototypes in concept, the Bayon was unique in three repects, and all three give us insights into Jayavarman's purposes. The first is that, whereas the outer walls and moats of all previous Cambodian temple–mountains simply surrounded the temple itself (and perhaps subsidiary buildings such as libraries), the Bayon's outer wall and moat surround the entire capital city – thereby enclosing not merely a variety of other earlier and contemporary temples, shrines and structures, but, in particular, the royal palace as well. Thus was the earthly abode of the godlike or god–king encompassed, along with his divine abode, within the same sacred precinct.

The Bayon's second unique symbolism was as a microcosm of the kingdom as a whole. The structure of its massive central tower has been judged, by its tight fit within the surrounding structure, as having emerged from a revision of the original, traditional, totally right–angled plan of the rest of the temple: it is round, apparently designed to give equal value to the eight (later increased to sixteen) shrines around the central one, built to house images of the divinities associated with particular provinces, and encircling the image of Buddha/Jayavarman within the central sanctuary itself in a representation of his protective embrace of the entire country. From a distance the central tower stands out, but the four corner towers of the temple's upper level, representing the four principal mountain peaks surrounding Mt Meru, absolutely clear in Angkor Wat, are almost overwhelmed by the profusion of towers on the lower levels. But closer up the tapering and reducing number of staircase steps on each side, and the shortening of each successive higher section, visually accentuate the sense of height and restore the mountain–effect.

But there was more. For the third unique aspect of the Bayon is of course its most striking feature: the four great faces that proliferate on the towers, layer upon layer, from the first level of the temple, in increased numbers through the second level, and on up to the third level and the massive heads, now gone, that undoubtedly marked the four sides of the central sanctuary's lofty peak. There has been as much trouble with counting the heads as there has been with noticing them: Zhou Daguan, as we saw, mentioned the central "Golden Tower flanked by more than twenty lesser towers", but did not place here also the "gigantic heads of Buddha" that he had observed on the gates into Angkor Thom. One of the earlier 19th century French visitors, Doudart de Lagrée, mentioned forty–two faces, Loti fifty; but they both saw the Bayon when it was totally overgrown by the jungle. They would no doubt have been astounded to find that there are almost a hundred and fifty – the state of parts of the ruins seeming to preclude a more precise count. Coedès's colleague Paul Mus thought that for complete symmetry there should have been fifty–four towers, but it has since been established that there were in fact originally forty–nine, of which now only thirty-seven are still standing.

With the problems of seeing and counting the heads has gone the even more fraught problem of identifying them. At various times they have been identified by the European experts, for cogent reasons, as the heads of Brahma (the four–headed), or Shiva, or the Bodhisattva Lokeshvara, or of course Buddha himself – as Zhou Daguan did, with the Angkor Thom heads anyway. It was researches in the 1920s–1930s by Finot, Coedès and Mus which confirmed that the Bayon had been built by Jayavarman as a foundation dedicated to Buddha, and they were the first to suggest that the faces were those of the Bodhisattva Lokeshvara (in the form of Samantamukha, "who has faces in all directions") with the features of Jayavarman himself. As to the proliferation of faces, Mus suggested that each tower, like the innermost circle of chapels, might have corresponded to a province or a provincial religious centre, and that the faces therefore represented Jayavarman's

"administrative and religious power extending to each corner of Cambodian territory by means of this unique sign".

Thus Jayavarman's fixed smile symbolized not only his authoritarian benevolence but also the comprehensive reach of his strong political grip.

In the most recent determination, described by Jessup in 1997 (in Jessup Zephir) as "at the moment the most convincing" – an indication of the impermanence of Cambodiology – Boisselier decided that the faces are those of the first of those mentioned above, the ancient Hindu creator–god Brahma (in his variously–named "ever young" form), which reflects his focus on Jayavarman's identification with Indra from the same pantheon. It is probably impertinent to have the feeling that this shift sideways allows the warlike and destructive Indra to be converted into the constructive Brahma, the all–inclusive balancer of opposites – just in case the features *are* Jayavarman's.

The amateur traveller Paul Loti put his finger on the essential before the archeologists really got going:

"From on high the four faces on each of these towers face the four cardinal points, looking out in every direction from beneath lowered eyelids. Each face has the same ironic expression of pity, the same smile. They proclaim and repeat in a haunting way the omnipresence of the god of Angkor".

The royal power blessing the four corners of the kingdom could still be that of any of the candidates who have been proposed, all of whom have all–seeing or all–directional powers. Any one of them could have the features of Jayavarman. And it would be characteristic of his eclecticism if he had envisaged the faces as incorporating all the key aspects of his own character as he wished it to be projected: Indra the warlike, achieving power over his whole people and their enemies; Brahma the balancer, ruling wisely and fairly; Buddha the compassionate, the source of merit for the entire kingdom.

The Bayon is as much sculpture as architecture – talking in terms of its unique structure, its hundreds of square metres of bas–reliefs aside. It is not as well preserved as Angkor Wat, not as expansive, not as serene; but it has a forcefulness that makes it a more intensely personal reflection of the person and purpose of Jayavarman VII than Angkor Wat is of Suryavarman II.

Jayavarman's people

So far we have seen Cambodia only from the top down; now we shall see what we can from the bottom up, assuming, as we can, that most of the characteristics of Jayavarman's people that Zhou Daguan observed had been still pretty much the same seventy years before – and indeed there are some that changed little right into the 20th century.

The people of Cambodia set Zhou Daguan in top Middle Kingdom form:

> "The customs common to all the southern barbarians are found throughout Cambodia, whose inhabitants are a coarse people, ugly and deeply sunburned. This is true not only of those living in the remote fastnesses of the sea islands but of the dwellers in centres of population. It applies equally to the ladies of the court and the womenfolk of the noble houses…".

In many respects Zhou showed a lively understanding of his host country's inhabitants. In a later comment he even managed a little rueful, if somewhat back–handed, respect:

> "Generally speaking, the people of Cambodia are very simple. On seeing a Chinese they show him timid respect and call him 'Buddha', throwing themselves on the ground before him and bowing low. An increasing number, however, are learning to outwit the Chinese and doing harm to a great many of our countrymen who have visited there".

One cannot help wondering whether Zhou was writing from uncomfortable experience.

There were three social classes in Angkorian Cambodia, described by Zhou in very much the same terms as by Brother Gaspar da Cruz nearly four centuries later. Above them, at the top of the heap, was of course the royal family. As we heard earlier, Zhou saw the king occasionally abroad, more often in the palace audience hall; but he saw no more of the royal way of life:

"I have heard it said that within the palace are many marvellous sights, but these are so strictly guarded that I had no chance to see them".

The next group of citizens consisted of those who, in addition to the most senior priesthood, were involved in running the country: "a hierarchy of ministers, generals, astronomers" – who "can calculate the eclipses of the sun and of the moon", and who were probably astrologers as well, as in Europe until well after Newton – "and other functionaries...For the most part princes are selected as office–holders; if not of princely rank they offer their daughters as royal concubines". Their dress, and their parasols and transport when they go out, Zhou noted, were all minutely graded – exactly as were the accoutrements and privileges allowed at Versailles in its grandest days.

Next came the priesthood, amongst whom he identified three groups: (Hindu) Brahman "men of learning", the bonzes, or Buddhist monks , and "Taoists", from their description Shaivite Hindus, who, Zhou said, have monasteries smaller than the Buddhist temples "for Taoists do not attain the prosperity of the Buddhist sectarians" – indicating that Buddhism had made a comeback from its post–Jayavarman persecution.

But the Buddhist establishment was by Zhou's time no longer of the version of the Mahayana vehicle that Jayavarman had patronised, a cult of the crown and the court, involved not just in building but also in adorning, servicing and maintaining a state religious structure that any Renaissance Pope would have envied. Within a generation of Jayavarman's death this overbearing royal burden had been swept away, forever as it turned out, by the populist appeal of a Theravada vehicle, stricter through its engagement of lay–people in monastic service but with a simpler doctrine no longer peopled by so many extraneous deities from an increasingly forgotten Hinduism. This was an un–establishment cult appealing directly to the people, and eventually enfolding them as the Church did in pre–Renaissance Europe; and its spread was undoubtedly helped by the fact that it did not require the population's expenditure of the vast amounts of labour and tribute required to meet the huge costs of the construction and upkeep of its predecessor. The new monks are still recognisable today from Zhou's description:

> "The Buddhist monks shave the head, wear yellow robes, bare the right shoulder, knot a strip of yellow cloth round the waist and go bare–foot...Their temples, which are often roofed with tile, contain only one statue...".

These temples were built of wood, like ordinary houses, and the one statue was of Buddha. Since Jayavarman VII there had been no more temple–tombs built for god–kings at Angkor, nor would there be in its remaining hundred and forty years.

Finally, there were all the rest, who made Jayavarman's glory possible: the army, the tax–collectors, the craftsmen, the traders, the workmen in the quarries, the irrigation system and the fields. At the bottom of this heap, beneath all others, were those about whose correct designation there has also been learned debate: first called "slaves" by Zhou Daguan and as da Cruz also saw them, then "serfs", later "servants", most recently "assigned workers", which sounds suspiciously as unfree as the first. Zhou said

> "Savages [from the mountains] are purchased to serve as slaves... [Some people] have more than a hundred...; only the very poor have none at all...If the slaves flee and are caught, they are tattooed on the face, or else an iron collar is placed around their neck...[or] carry these shackles on their arms and legs".

But there could be worse: an inscription refers to the punishment of a worker who had fled the estate where he was born (was he *not* a "savage"?) – his eyes were gouged out and his nose chopped off.

Then there were two small groups who provoked Zhou Daguan's disdain:

> "sorcerers who practice their arts on the Cambodians. How utterly absurd!";

and those his translator called catemites,

> "in the market place...every day, making efforts to catch the attention of the Chinese in the hope of rich presents. A revolting, unworthy custom this!"

Apart from royal bodyguards, maidservants and musicians, and the dismal soldiery, there are only a few occupations that Zhou notices, not so much through observing the actual occupations as through their products: the wood and thatch houses of the commoners, "not one of whom would dare place the smallest bit of tile on his roof"; various agricultural items, gathered as much as planted; chariots and palanquins, boats and oars. This might not be just Chinese superiority to the details of ordinary life: elsewhere he shows acute powers of observation, and it would not be surprising if many of the skills that had been so heavily used by Jayavarman no longer existed.

However some of the Bayon bas–reliefs show (usually in the bottom register) a wider range of everyday life, often in vivid and animated detail: men fishing, playing chess (including in a boat), wrestling, betting on a cock–fight; women de–lousing, playing with children, giving birth, blowing the coals under a cooking pot – numerous activities that are still familiar sights in modern Cambodia. One is not: a cassowary, a native of Australia and New Guinea, introduced by some mysterious route into the king's menagerie.

Traders

The route was no doubt part of the network of traders in small ships, sailing from port to port along the coasts of South, Southeast and East Asia, a small-scale maritime Silk Road that ferried many of the same goods as were being carried from oasis to oasis, far to the north, by huge caravans of camels, ships of the Central Asian deserts. The network connected Cambodia with its neighbourhood: still with India, whose travelling merchants had "Indianised" Southeast Asia in the first place, as we have seen; with island Southeast Asia, whose Javan and Sumatran kingdoms had also had long connections with the Indochinese peninsula, as we also saw; and with China, whose traders sailed as far afield as India,[59] but whose attitude to the Khmer kingdom is amply demonstrated by Zhou Daguan's statement of the purpose of the mission which he was accompanying there: "to recall these people to their sense of duty" – to pay tribute to the Son of Heaven.

---

59 A result of the influence of Chinese traders in India, introduced in the time of Kublai Khan and thus exactly contemporary with Zhou Daguan, is the arched bamboo fishing net, with a light attached to the centre to attract fish, that is still used at Kochi (Cochin) in the southwest state of Kerala.

Zhou's extensive observations on Cambodian products of interest to China, particularly those "of value", suggest that he may have had a role in identifying not just trade possibilities but what tribute the mission would graciously deign to receive from these particular barbarians: the distinction between trade and tribute was sometimes rather fine (as we shall see in two centuries' time in Tamburlaine's relations with the Chinese court). However his references to numbers of Chinese coming to the country, sailors and others, confirm that there was also a fairly lively trade being carried on by the coastal shipping, which could access Angkor directly via the Mekong and Tonle Sap during the wet season.

Zhou may indeed have had a more personal interest in trade matters. In a study of Song embassies – contemporary with Jayavarman – Herbert Franke noted that Beijing court officials repeatedly complained about the size of embassies to neighbouring mainland tributary states, the result largely of people wishing to be included for the prestige and opportunity for official advancement involved. Embassies to overseas destinations like Angkor would have undoubtedly been smaller because of costs and, not least, the deterrence of the unknown; but Franke adds that "travel in the retinue of an envoy...could be profitable, not only because of the customary presents received in the host country, but also because of the chance to conduct private trade with foreigners". On the other hand, Franke says later, involvement in private trade was strictly forbidden by law and punishable by two years' hard labour, the missions' superiors and their deputies being subject to the same penalty if they failed to prevent such activity. Some sort of "arrangement" with private Chinese traders, based on official contacts and introductions, could no doubt have been profitable if mission members were willing to risk it – or superiors connived. But, not surprisingly, Zhou gives no hint whatever of any interest in private trade, and there is none of receiving gifts either.[60]

---

60   H.Franke: "Sung Embassies: Some General Observations", in M.Rossabi, ed: *China Among Equals: the Middle Kingdom and its Neighbours 10th - 14th centuries*. Franke cites from China's records its embassies' reports of countless official "flowery" banquets of strange food, countless dance and theatrical performances accompanied by strange music, problems of protocol, of lodging, of dress, sometimes of hardship, sometimes of safety - all very familiar in varying degrees still. Exchanges of gifts are still made, and are still a touchy issue of appropriateness and equivalence; illicit trade is not unknown - a colleague of mine visiting a foreign capital was invited to the home of his former counterpart

However trade items certainly attracted Zhou's lively attention. In his report he identified first what he called Cambodian "products of value" – to China: rare kingfisher feathers (for ornamenting court dress jewellery), elephant tusks (for intricately carved ornaments), "pale veined" rhinoceros horns (for what is still called, in East Asia, "stamina"), and beeswax (for votive candles). He adds, as "among the ordinary products", eagle-wood (calambac, for incense), cardamom, gamboge (a yellow pigment, the name derived from the country), raw lacquer, chaulmoogra oil (used in the treatment of leprosy before antibiotics) and pepper, and approximates this second group to the first by describing the qualities and collection processes of both. Additional Chinese imports from Cambodia, identified in Chinese sources,[61] were a red insect dye for silk, orpiment (yellow arsenic pigment), unidentified "aromatic substances" – and slaves.

The Chinese goods "most appreciated' in Cambodia Zhou lists as gold and silver, "light mottled double-threaded silks", tin goods, lacquered trays, green porcelain (no doubt celadon, at its artistic peak under the Song Dynasty which had recently been brought down by Kublai Khan's Mongols), mercury, vermilion, paper, sulphur, saltpetre, sandalwood, angelica root, musk, lengths of hemp, umbrellas, iron cooking pots, copper trays, fresh-water pearls, tung oil, bamboo traps and baskets, wooden combs, needles and rush mats (and another Chinese list includes also leather drums, wine and sugar). It is an impressive list; but Zhou adds:

"What the people most desire to obtain, beans and wheat, are forbidden exports from China",

which suggests that – aside from insufficient production in China itself – Cambodian agricultural production was already suffering from less competent water-management, and perhaps also from the developing Thai pressures that would drive the Angkorian Dynasty from Angkor in a century and a half. The only mention Zhou makes of the commercial opposition is the observation that, though some (very poor) fabrics were woven in Cambodia itself, and some came from Siam and Champa,

---

in Moscow from that country, and expressed (yes, envious) surprise at the large collection of Russian icons, whose export was strictly forbidden: "Didn't you have a diplomatic bag?" - not subject to foreign inspection - was the laconic reply.

61   Referred to in Boulnois: *Silk Road*

"the most esteemed are in general those which come from India, for their fine and delicate texture"

- no doubt, along with Chinese double-threaded silks, among the "very rich and sheer" robes he saw being worn at the Court.

Many of these Chinese goods – gold and silver, silks, porcelain, mercury, vermilion, sulphur, saltpetre, sandalwood, musk, pearls, even the iron pots and copper trays – must have been traded to the Court, the monasteries and the army, in return for the Cambodian "products of value" that were undoubtedly mostly under their officials' control: especially as, he says, in payments "for really big transactions, gold and silver are used". It is hard to see that there is much among the imported goods which the ordinary town dweller or peasant could afford, which might explain Zhou's reference to their prostrating themselves before Chinese in "respectful awe". But elsewhere he says that

"In petty trading, one pays in rice, grain, or Chinese goods; after that come textiles; and for really big transactions, gold and silver are used",

so the Chinese coastal traders must have been successfully selling some small items.

The main impression he gives of local petty trading is close to that found in the bas-reliefs, where you can find a woman squatting under a canopy selling fish:

"In Cambodia it is the women who take charge of trade...There are no shops in which the merchants live; instead they display their goods on matting spread upon the ground. Each has her allotted place. I have heard it said that the authorities collect rental for each space".

Women are still traders in the villages today, after seven or eight more centuries, still squatting on woven bamboo mats, lucky if they have a spare piece of cloth overhead to give shade. And, slyly, Zhou noted that, because traders at that end of the market were women,

"a Chinese, arriving in the country, loses no time in getting himself a mate, for he will find her commercial instincts a great asset".

Women

Zhou Daguan has been described as having been obsessed by Angkor's splendour – or at least as much as any Chinese could be by barbarian pretension. But what he was really obsessed by was Angkor's women: remember the delightful but otherwise inessential detail of the two girls' "slender fingers" raising the curtain for the King's audience. As well as in trade, he observed them in his twenty pages in many aspects, some with a culturally superior disdain or disgust, some with a prurient curiosity. There is a judicious use of "it is said" that sometimes carries hints of more first–hand experience than Zhou is prepared to admit to. But there is also an engaging acknowledgement: at a palace audience, he tells us,

> "the ladies of the Court were drawn up on both sides of the veranda below the window, changing places now and then to get a better look at us, and thus giving me a good chance to see them"; and he explains that "when a beautiful girl is born into a family, no time is lost in sending her to the palace...".

On their appearance:

> "Generally speaking, the women, like the men, wear only a strip of cloth, bound round the waist, showing bare breasts of milky whiteness. Their hair is fastened up in a knot, and they go bare–foot, even the wives of the King...
>
> Women of the people...[wear on their arms] gold bracelets and rings of gold on their fingers: the palace women and the court ladies also observe this fashion...
>
> The Cambodian women age very rapidly, doubtless because of too early marriage and motherhood. When twenty or thirty years old they resemble Chinese women of forty or fifty...".

On their customs:

> "Some of the women make water standing up – an utterly ridiculous procedure...
>
> [Cambodian] women are entirely ignorant of sewing, dress–making and mending. They are barely able to weave fabrics with the produce of the cotton tree, nor do they know how to spin with a wheel...Looms are unknown to them...

When a daughter is born to a Cambodian family, it is customary for the parents to express for her the wish: 'May the future bring thee a hundred, a thousand husbands!'

Daughters of rich parents, from seven to nine years of age (or eleven, in the case of poor people) are handed over to a Buddhist or Taoist priest for deflowering...I have been told that at a given moment the priest enters the maiden's pavilion and deflowers her with his hand, dropping the first–fruits into a vessel of wine. It is said that the father and mother, the relations and neighbours, stain their foreheads with this wine, or even taste it. Some also say that the priest has intercourse with the girl; others deny this..."

On sexual activity:

"Once a Cambodian woman's child is born, she immediately makes a poultice of hot rice and salt and applies it to her private parts. This is taken off in twenty–four hours, thus preventing any untoward after–effects and causing an astringency which seems to renew the young mother's virginity...[62]

Everyone with whom I talked said that the Cambodian women are highly sexed. One or two days after giving birth to a child they are ready for intercourse: if a husband is not responsive he will be discarded. When a husband is called away on matters of business, they endure his absence for a while; but if he is gone as much as ten days, the wife is apt to say, 'I am no ghost; how can I be expected to sleep alone?'. Though their sexual impulses are very strong, it is said some of them remain faithful...

When it comes to weddings it is the custom to make presents of textiles; this obligation is lightly assumed, however, as bride and groom have often had pre–nuptial intercourse. In this there is seen no cause for shame, or even surprise...

Male and female slaves have intercourse, but it would be unheard of for the master of a house to have sexual relations with them."

---

62 Jessup has noted that "recent studies are exploring the custom (still observed in some regions) of isolating the woman who has given birth and placing her [for a time, and at a safe distance] over non–stop burning fires".

On the temptation of the Chinese:

> "If by chance" [note that "by chance"] "a Chinese, arriving in the country after long abstinence, should assuage his appetite with one of the woman slaves, and the fact became known to her owner, the latter would refuse to be seated in the presence of a man who had defiled himself with a savage...
>
> Every few days the women of the town, in groups of three or five, stroll down to the river to bathe. Here, at the water's edge, they drop the strip of cotton that clothes them, joining thousands of other women in the river. Even the women of noble birth mingle in these baths and think nothing of it, although they show themselves from head to foot to any bystanders who may appear. Not a day passes without this happening. On days of leisure the Chinese often treat themselves to the spectacle. In fact, I have heard it said that many of them enter the water to take advantage of whatever opportunity offers...".

Zhou Daguan's last word on women also involved those scallywag Chinese:

> "Chinese sailors coming to the country note with pleasure that it is not necessary to wear clothes, and, since rice is easily had, women easily persuaded, houses easily run, furniture easily come by, and trade easily carried on, a great many sailors desert to take up permanent residence".

Not quite the done thing, of course, but still...a hint of envy?

Criminals

Criminals formed another category of citizen that Zhou Daguan mentioned, or at least their punishments:

> "Lesser crimes are dealt with by cutting off feet or hands, or by amputation of the nose...In dealing with cases of great seriousness, recourse is not had to strangulation or beheading [as in China]; outside the West Gate, however, a ditch is dug into which the

criminal is placed, earth and stones are thrown back and heaped high, and all is over".[63]

A broader picture of unacceptable behaviour is provided in the bas–reliefs at Angkor Wat. Eleanor Mannikka, in her survey of the temple's symbolism, noticed that the inscriptions for the scenes of the thirty–two hells tell a larger and in some cases different story from Zhou's. Theft was the most common cause for consignment to the hells, twelve of them being for those who stole land, houses, elephants, horses, carts, shoes, sandals, parasols, rice, strong liquor, the possessions of priests and the poor, flowers – a vivid catalogue of what was regarded as valuable in Angkorian society. Another hell was for those who burned villages and towns, another for the murder of women and children; as now, military action was presumably not included in either. There were hells for denigrating the gods or religious leaders, parents or friends; for urinating or defecating on sacred ground; for eating unconsecrated food; for being insane or avaricious, a glutton, debtor, charlatan or liar, or abusing something said in confidence; or (pre–empting future thought-police) for desiring someone's death or misfortune.

Mannikka remarks that, as in many places and times, these punishments would be more likely to fall on those at the bottom of the social scale than on those above them. The realism of these hells exactly matches the way in which the tortures of the damned in contemporary European depictions of *The Last Judgement* – by Giotto, for example – often mirrored the actual treatment of offenders at that time; the main difference being that European painters – like Jan van Eyck, for instance – included bishops, kings and even popes among the damned.[64]

Wives were chattels; sleeping with someone else's was thus theft, and warranted the illicit lover's consignment to one or other of three hells. But, a century and a half after Angkor Wat, Zhou Daguan reported that

"no punishment is prescribed for adultery or gambling. If the husband of an adulterous woman is informed of what is going on,

---

63 I heard of a modern version of this in the late 1960s: captured Red Khmer rebels were buried in the ground, but only up to their necks, and were then decapitated by bulldozer.

64 Giotto: Scrovegni Chapel, Padua; van Eyck: Metropolitan Museum of Art, New York

he has the lover's feet squeezed between two splints of wood till the pain is unendurable and he surrenders all his property as the price for liberation"

– no doubt a nice basis for the odd scam. Over time, adultery had thus become less frowned upon (as in other times and places); but unlike in Christian and Islamic societies the wives, who were obviously still chattels, were still not punished. Perhaps that contributed to the freedom Zhou observed in women's behaviour.

Jayavarman's builders

By the end of the thirteenth century there were no great building projects that might have attracted Zhou's attention to the armies of men who would have been involved. No one that I am aware of has managed to estimate the number Jayavarman must have been using during the twenty or thirty years of his huge campaign of building and adorning temples. The vast majority of the population lived extremely simply: they built their own dwellings, poles supporting straw thatch roofs, bamboo mats as walls; ate rice and limited amounts of vegetables and fish obtained from family members, or occasionally purchased in the markets; dressed minimally in *sampots*, simple wrap–around lengths of woven cotton – very much as still happens today.

But behind the huge numbers directly involved in Jayavarman's vast projects there had to be large numbers of other people providing essential support: an agricultural work–force capable (as we shall see later) of producing double its own requirements; procurers of salt, from the mountains or seacoast according to Zhou Daguan; boat–makers for the fisheries on the Tonle Sap, working, Zhou says, entirely with axes and chisels to hollow out logs or make planks, and "incurring thus a great waste of wood and labour"; and, notwithstanding Zhou's dim view of Cambodian women's domestic skills, spinners, loom–makers and weavers to produce cloth for bonzes and masses.

For the temples, the labour required was far more complex and required considerable skills in a great variety of trades. For the preparations, there were "doctrinal architects" (whom we shall come back to), designers, surveyors; miners, foundrymen and refiners, metal–workers and blacksmiths to make and keep sharp implements: for digging and farming, saws, levers and chisels for quarrying and shaping stone, axes for cutting bamboo and timber; cart–makers and bullock–breeders to haul materials; road–workers to hack out tracks through the jungle and maintain them in usable condition; hydrologists and huge numbers of workmen to dam rivers or streams and dig additional water channels, construct dykes to enclose, and in part dig out, the vast moats or reservoirs associated with some of them; and diggers and soil–carters to build up on the mostly flat Angkor plain the earthen interiors of some of the temple–mountains and the dams, dykes and reservoir walls. For the materials, stonemasons to mark measurements and quarrymen to cut the sandstone or laterite blocks; handlers for the elephants which had to move the blocks from the quarries, some forty kilometres away, to the river, then later from the connected city waterways and moats to the building sites; boat or raft–builders and rope–makers, then raftsmen and oarsmen for the water journey to move the stones between the two; woodcutters to cut bamboo and timber.

For the actual construction, there were scaffold–builders, and carpenters for occasional structural woodwork; more specialized stone–cutters to dress and abrade the stones so accurately and so smoothly that they could be set "with no crevices for weeds to grow in", as Zhou Daguan observed; work gangs for laying the stones; crane–builders, pulley–makers and operators for raising them. For the decoration, draftsmen and template–makers to depict the form of the ornamented blocks, and sculptors to carve them, usually after the stones were erected into place; designers, experts in the Buddhist scriptures, and even more specialized sculptors to carve the elaborately detailed bas–reliefs, with their eleven thousand figures; more sculptors and painters, goldsmiths, silversmiths and jewellers to make and decorate the images to be placed in the temples.

Every stage would have also required supervisors; many processes would have required considerable training, and thus instructors; every individual required food. There is a bas–relief in the Bayon that shows a couple of the processes involved, though, curiously or perhaps characteristically, it shows construction of a Vishnuite temple. One is the movement of small blocks suspended from each end of a long pole across a man's shoulders, still a familiar manner of carrying in Cambodia, and similar to the movement of larger blocks suspended from a pole carried over the shoulders of four men depicted in a 1968 photograph of restoration work at Angkor under the French.[65] The bas–relief also shows blocks being fitted together, one suspended over another so that it

---

65 Dagens, p.116

can be moved back and forth to abrade the two surfaces to a crevice–less fit. And that is about all. For the quantity of Jayavarman's building works, his bas–relief designers and carvers – unlike their Romanesque and Gothic contemporaries in Europe – gave very little credit to their legions of fellow–workers.

Angkor and Chartres: symbolism in stone

There were, of course, no direct links between Angkor and Chartres at this period. The initial idea for this comparison was purely as a self-indulgent exploration of two edifices built in the same era that we have explored and enjoyed over the years. But as I began to look into the details, it became more interesting; the differences, though obvious and expected, demonstrated some of the fundamental political and cultural differences between the two societies. But it was the unforeseen similarities that emerged between these two buildings thousands of miles apart that were most intriguing.

It has been estimated that Angkor Wat took about thirty–five years to build, between about 1115 and 1150. Angkor Thom and the Bayon possibly took somewhat fewer, from 1195 until 1220. Chartres Cathedral, begun in the same year as the Bayon, was mostly finished by the late 1230s, though the spire on the north tower was not put up for another three centuries.[66] How long things took in Europe depended mostly on the availability of funds to buy materials and pay for enough qualified builders who could handle the equally extraordinary technological demands of the new Gothic style developing at that time: pushing, with buttressing and breath–taking hubris, the vaulting of cathedral naves (with interlocking keystone arches) higher and higher – the sin of reaching for the heavens condemned by St Bernard of Clairvaux – and opening up their walls to larger and larger expanses of stained glass.

When the new cathedral at Chartres was begun, in what is now France there were already five major cathedrals which had recently begun construction; during the forty years until Chartres' virtual completion a further eleven were begun. But in fact the projects demanding skilled craftsmen extended across the Channel as well at

---

66   The main source used for the construction of Chartres is John James's exhilarating *Chartres: The Masons who built a Legend.*

that time: and in England there were four cathedrals already under construction and another seven started before Chartres' completion.[67]

There was no central monarchy to enforce labour service, exact contributions of money or food, or to capture the requisite number of slaves. Each cathedral was the undertaking of an ambitious local bishop, who had to enthuse his own faithful with the fervour necessary to produce the finance, materials and workers combined. In 1200 Paris was one of the largest cities in Europe with a population around 100,000; London around 20,000; the town of Chartres had only 9,000, though the cathedral had the advantage as a major pilgrimage centre of receiving external royal and noble financial contributions as well as the pittances of the poor, and for that reason was built to hold ten thousand of the faithful, fifteen when crowded. During the main period of the construction of Chartres, the average number working on site at any one time – stone–cutters, masons, carpenters, sanders, smiths, glass-makers, roofers, labourers – fluctuated somewhere between 100 and 300 men; most of the labourers were local, most of the more skilled were itinerants, going from cathedral to cathedral in the various bishoprics in France and England following the availability of money.

At Angkor the rate of construction seems to have been more a question of the availability of labour. Claude Jacques estimated the population of Angkor three hundred years earlier, at the time of the construction of the Eastern Baray, as about 40,000; about 6,000 (including an unknown number of slaves) worked on the reservoir, taking something like 6 million working days to build (including excavating the soil for) its 17.6 km embankment. The job involved the movement of as much earth as is nowadays required to construct about 100 kms of motorway, and took upwards of three years. The 12km circumference of Angkor Thom, with its 8m high stone wall, backed by a 25m wide earth embankment, and surrounded by its 100m-wide moat, is unlikely to have taken many fewer working days.

---

67   For interest, and to give a better sense of the press of construction, the cathedrals already begun, and the commencement dates of those begun in the three and a half decades after Chartres was, are as follows. France: still under construction in 1195 – Paris (Notre Dame), Laon, Vézelay, Sens, Le Mans; commenced after Chartres – 1200 Bourges, Soissons, 1201 Rouen, 1211 Rheims, 1215 Auxerre, 1220 Metz, 1225 Beauvais, 1230 Strasbourg, Bayeux. England: still under construction – Canterbury, Lincoln, Peterborough, York; commenced after Chartres – 1200 Lichfield, 1208 Southwark, 1215 Rochester, Lincoln, 1220 Salisbury, Wells, 1224 Worcester.

There is a great dearth of estimates of Angkor's population under Jayavarman VII. But even if it had doubled over the three centuries, as China's is estimated to have done under the Tang and Sung dynasties during the same period,[68] it seems unlikely to have been sufficient for this and all the other projects underway during Jayavarman's reign; so again, slaves, possibly in large numbers, were also used. Zhou Daguan refers to the domestic slaves in the city in his day as being "wild men from the hills"; but those who slaved for Jayavarman's ambition were more likely to have been Cham, Lao and others captured in his numerous invasions and border wars.

The turreted silhouette of the Bayon is totally different from that of Chartres' high nave and two mis–matched spires. The Bayon is still scarcely visible from only a short distance into the surrounding jungle. Chartres close–up is equally enveloped by the urban jungle of a modern city; but its two pinnacles can be seen from a great distance, especially on the little ridge–road from Maintenon, across a great sweep of the grain–fields of the Beauce, a view the same today as that when the north spire was completed in the first decade of the 16th century. There are the odd similarities between the two great contemporary structures: the square Bayon is some 150m a side, the central face–tower originally about 50m high; Chartres is 130m long, the nave roof 51m high. The main axes of both are directed towards the rising sun, their main entrances on the west.

But their differences are of course much greater than their similarities: the almost solid mountain versus the vaulted space, the huge square flat footprint versus the deep cruciform foundations, the dry–stacking of vast quantities of huge stones, like children's building blocks, versus the flying buttresses supporting curtain walls opened for great expanses of stained glass. Yet – apart from the elephants – in the construction much of the sheer hard work of the labourers and some of the craftsmen must have been very similar: for the quarrymen and stone–cutters, those who manipulated crowbars, cranes, ropes and pulleys, loading rafts or carts and lifting the great blocks into place at dizzying heights, the stone–dressers and stone–carvers (though at Chartres the stones were carved on the ground, before rather than after they were set into place).

The main difference, of course, was between the nature of the mountain–temple and the cathedral. Though both were regarded as

---

68   See McEvedy Jones: *Atlas of World Population History* (Bibliography, General).

the earthly abode of divinity, the former was also inseparably linked to its builder's conception of himself, not only in relation to divinity but also in relation to his earthly role. So, as we have seen, it contained a series of small shrines around the central one, symbolising the royal power over and protection of the entire kingdom, and only the priests were permitted to go into the inner sanctums where they ministered to the images representing the king in both his roles, as well as all the attendant gods. The cathedral, however, although also the earthly house of an unearthly living God, was essentially a hollow vessel for all his people to worship him congregationally and commune (literally) with his flesh and blood; so the priests were charged as much with instructing the people in the west–end nave as with adoring the deity whom they preserved in the east–end chancel.

Visibly, the structure of the Angkorian temple and European cathedral paralleled each other as allegories, reflecting their respective belief systems. Structurally, the temple–mountain of Angkor Wat, like the Bayon, represents Mt Meru as the axis of the universe, linking the heavens to the four–sided earth of the inner temple–levels, and surrounded by the mountains of the outermost wall and its moat–ocean. Its Hindu mandala plan symbolises the totality of inner and outer existence, with deities allocated in its various parts to convey further meaning or prompt reflection.[69]

Chartres' cruciform cathedral, for its part, symbolises Christ's sacrifice on the cross, its layout representing man's journey: from the mundane, outside the west entrance, through the great façade (the only part of the old cathedral to have survived the terrible fire of 1194), with its trinities of splendid sculpted portals and stained–glass windows – "painted with light", it has been said – programmed together to depict Christ's birth, life and death, and then on through the nave, to redemption, at the high altar, through Christ's resurrection. The Christian trinity of God the Father, the Son and the Holy Ghost is represented again with three major apses wrapping around the altar.

In fact the temple–mountain as well as the cathedral both physically represent the passage from the outer world to the divine; but whereas the four direct routes to the central sanctuary in the former suggest a variety

---

69 A schematic illustration by Groslier (in *Inscriptions du Bayon*) of the mandala of the Bayon looks startlingly but delightfully like an elegant, doubled Tudor rose (rather than the lotus one might expect), each petal identified with one or, often, triple tutelary divinities.

of ways to get there, the cathedral, like all Christian churches, allows only the one. The respective theologies are even more clear to any visitor in the magnificent stone carving at each place, though there is one striking similarity: at Chartres, the sculpture and stained–glass in the portals and nave, showing the lives of the Virgin and Christ, were made to instruct and inspire a mostly illiterate people in obedience to the Church; and the bas–reliefs in the outer gallery of the Bayon, showing Jayavarman's conquest of the Cham and consecration as king, strongly suggest that they too were intended to instruct and inspire an illiterate people to revere and obey their lord.

However, at Angkor, it is in the inner, non–public, gallery that the traditional beliefs are rendered visible in the images of Shiva, Vishnu and Buddha; in the nine–headed Khmer *naga,* the water–guardian serpent, and its enemy, Vishnu's mount, the *garuda,* with its human body and bird's wings, beak and claws; and in the innumerable representations of the various incarnations of the deities, as well as the teeming characters (human and animal) from the centuries–old favourites, the *Ramayana* and the *Mahabharata.* At Chartres, on the other hand, the images and scenes of traditional belief are all in public view in sculpture and glass: in the first place those of the Virgin Mary, to whom the cathedral was dedicated, and Christ her son; of the latter's apostles, myriads of Old Testament kings and prophets and multitudes of Christian saints; and of the saved, the damned, the devils, the hobgoblins and weird creatures (human and animal) from the all–time favourite *Revelations of St John the Divine.* I must add, too, that, as at the Bayon, there are little genre scenes at Chartres also, especially in the stained–glass windows: farming, hunting, wine–making, writing, playing music – even, *pace* one of Zhou Daguan's comments on Khmer women, a (later) sculpture of the Virgin herself...sewing.

Angkor and Chartres: meaning in measurement

We now come to an underlying parallel, unexpected and certainly not readily visible: in the use of cosmology, astronomy and astrology, mathematics and numerology in the design and proportions of both the Cambodian and European structures – not in matching plans or identical measurements (though this did occur twice), but in "the transformation of space into time and divinity". In neither case can it be asserted that this remarkable application of arcane knowledge and calculation, beyond the awareness of any but the initiated, was more important than the outward and visible forms and symbolism; but in both cases it appears that there were underlying schemas that were intended to reinforce those external signs.

An ingenious detailed analysis of measurements and composition, and of their numerical, calendrical and cosmological significance, has been made for Chartres by the Australian architect John James, in *The Masons who built a Legend* (1982); and it has been done by an American scholar, Eleanor Mannikka, in an article (1977, when she was still Eleanor Morón), doctoral thesis (1985) and finally a book, *Angkor Wat* (1996), on the latter temple. Unfortunately there does not yet seem to be an examination of the Bayon itself from this perspective;[70] but despite its and Angkor Wat's different dedications, dimensions and structures, both contain references which, against the shared general cultural background and assumptions of Angkor's kings, will, I believe, allow the concepts, if not always the detail, to be considered in both contexts. But the idea that these investigations offer uncanny parallels between Angkor and Chartres is entirely mine.[71]

Mannikka and James themselves wrote in near–parallel terms of their conclusions. Mannikka observed that the architects were "able to provide all of the chambers, axes, and galleries of Angkor Wat with measurements that were cosmologically or calendrically significant" – and also, she noted in her searches, the measurements of circumferences, access bridge and causeway, courtyards, columns, doors, windows, stairways, towers. At Chartres James likewise found that "walls, piers, shafts, chapels, every last detail of the plan" evolved from one or other or a combination of similar intellectual techniques involving the symbolism of numbers and geometry: as he summed up, "nothing in the plan is irrelevant or accidental".

Mannikka first established a metric value (to five decimal points!) for the Cambodian unit of measurement used at Angkor Wat, the *cubit*, which she noted was traditionally based on the distance from the elbow to the finger–tips – almost certainly the elbow and finger–tips of Suryavarman himself. The king's body, as well as his heavenly attributes, were thus part of the physical nature of his temple–mountain. Using this

---

70   However Mannikka is apparently currently working on the Bayon.

71   I find the exercise curiously fascinating and in fact good fun, if at times a bit overwhelming in meaningfulness. The responsibility for the following abbreviated summaries – of what are extensive, detailed and complex arguments by the authors – is of course mine; but I hope, even if inaccuracies have appeared, that they convey something of the flavour of the results of their investigations.

unit, Mannikka found measurements in the geometry and numerology of Angkor Wat clearly related to its cosmological and astronomical context, providing it with a symbolism far more complex than is apparent at first sight.

Chartres was, of course, totally different – yet strangely like. The cathedral was built in the developing new Gothic style, and indeed had the first unified Gothic interior; and it has come down to us virtually intact from the time it was built, the blessing of being away from most invasion routes, an absence of jungle, and perhaps the awe of all later architects. James's investigation of the origins of Chartres reads almost like a detective story as it tracks down the master builders who were responsible for the cathedral's construction – identified, in the absence of any surviving documentation, by their distinctive mason's marks and design elements, and by the lengths of the different values of the "foot" that they used. Through the consequent ability to visualise "the order in which everything had been cut and placed", James's examination of the concepts underlying the plan and structural details discovered that the cathedral was built up (like Angkor) on the basis of elements – separately, overlapping, in combination – based on numbers, geometry and the calendar.

Early in the 5th century St Augustine had written:

"God made the world in measure, number and weight: and ignorance of number prevents us from understanding things that are set down in the Scripture in a figurative and mystical way"

– of which Mannikka cites an intriguing cross–cultural echo in Ramachandra Kaulachara's treatise six centuries later:

"He, the Creator (Vishvakarman, the "All Accomplishing")...lays out the plan of the universe according to measure and number".

There is another parallel to note between Angkor Wat and Chartres: if these complex schemas do not merely reflect the ingenuity of modern authors, but are close to their builders' intentions – which, given, the remarkable closeness of the respective correspondences, seems highly likely – then the builders of both must surely have been guided by "doctrinal architects" – people at both places who knew what numbers were significant for that building, and in what context and in what combinations they needed to be used. At both places they are likely to have been people with double attributes: at Angkor, they seem to have been the most elevated priests, though they must have had advisers who ensured they well understood what was architecturally possible; at Chartres, where James thinks they were the master–builders themselves, the Chapter priests must have ensured they clearly understood what was theologically necessary. Ramachandra Kaulachara, our Orissan architect, wrote that the Creator

> "is the prototype and model of the temple builder, who also unites in his single person, the architect, the priest, the sculptor".

Did the Bishop, in his person? Did Jayavarman?

And, finally, both authors came out parallel in assessing the significance of their conclusions. In Mannikka's view, "The measurements themselves filled the temple with auspicious, protective, beneficial numbers...It was the number that mattered, not knowledge of the number". While all could grasp the temple's layout as leading to the mountain of the gods, and the cathedral's plan as a pathway to redemption, there could have been no expectation that the uninitiated who used them would ever understand all the other meanings so deeply embedded in their every proportion and aspect. But it was sufficient that they should know that each had been built in such a way that would make, as James put it, "every step a devotion". It is in these two sets of conclusions that the parallels between the architects' approaches at Angkor and Chartres are, I think, remarkable.

James also identified a curious 30cm displacement in the west end of Chartres' central axis as having been deliberately made by the master–builder then in charge, apparently, James believes, on the basis of a tradition separate from traditional Christian theology – perhaps a reflection of the "mysteries" of their trade which masons so jealously guarded, for arcane or simply proprietorial reasons. And, interestingly, he cites another unexpected Indian parallel: an early Buddhist treatise instructing the architect of a temple always to displace the *linga* symbol of Shiva off–centre, a recognition of the gap between the Actual and the Ideal.

This little link raises a final thought. Numerology, belief in the supposedly mystical properties of numbers, existed in ancient Mesopotamia, as another, equally legitimate, aspect of mathematics, just as astrology was of astronomy. It (and other aspects of these disciplines) passed on to classical Greece, where in the 6th century BCE Pythagoras developed it; Pythagoreanism then passed it on to Western Europe, probably via the Islamic scholars who rescued the Greek classics after the fall of Rome, and it had some influence in medieval Christian monastic tradition . Numerology seems also to have entered aspects of Indian thought by the early centuries CE, perhaps a direct transfer eastwards from Mesopotamia, like aspects of astronomy and astrology, perhaps from Pythagoras by way of Alexander the Great's impact on the Subcontinent, from which it was passed on to Southeast Asia. There are obviously many gaps in these apparent links; but it is intriguing to wonder whether somewhere, at some time in the distant past, the obsessions of the builders of Angkor and Chartres in the 12th century had a common origin. That would be the neatest parallel of all.

Agriculture and irrigation

The actual construction of Jayavarman VII's temples was just the beginning. We do not have details for Angkor Thom or the Bayon, but the requirements for the service of his smaller temples of Ta Prohm and Preah Khan are staggering enough.[72] The Ta Prohm stele says it was serviced by 79,365 people, who included 18 high priests, 2,740 officiants, 2,232 assistants, and 615 dancers, and was provisioned by 3,140 villages. Its property included 40,620 pearls, thousands of precious stones, and gold dishes weighing more than 500 kilograms; it required 40,095 sets of clothing annually. Preah Khan, in its stele, prayed to future kings, on its own behalf and that of its associated foundations,

> "that in these foundations, the men and women...numbering 306,372, the villages numbering 13,500, that all, whether made of stone or wood, which serves the divine ritual, that all that shall be preserved absolutely intact".

The annual consumption of rice was 38,000 tons. And the organisation of the vast provisioning requirements must have involved yet another army of rice carters, fishermen, vegetable growers, for the most basic diet.

The head begins to spin at the quantities of people, processes, products and provisions required by the totality of Jayavarman's building megalomania. Military activity, to the west, to the north, and especially

---

72   This refers to the temples themselves; the outer enclosures are very large: Ta Prohm's 700m x 1000m, Preah Khan's 700m x 800m. The Bayon has no similar temple–specific outer enclosure, just the 3km x 3km Angkor Thom walls.

to the east to subjugate Champa, must also have cost a good deal for men and elephants, weapons and supplies. One would guess that there were some good and many bad consequences for the people. The pressures on the rice farmers in particular – or their womenfolk – must have been enormous with such a drain of manpower away from the land, into the army or the building program, at times both: and, as noted earlier, the final subjugation of Champa coincided with the construction of Angkor Thom and the Bayon. It has been estimated that the surplus needed for Jayavarman's projects required production of *double* the output sufficient to meet the farmers' own requirements for food and seed. And over and above all the rest, food had to be provided to the considerable population of temple bonzes who produced absolutely nothing – except merit.

The requisition of their produce must have left those who remained on the land on a perpetual treadmill, and probably on the breadline, even though rice–growing was still, after Jayavarman's time, apparently a remarkable success story. Seventy years later, Zhou Daguan observed this, with as much admiration as he was able to sum up:

"Generally speaking, three or four crops a year can be counted on...In this country it rains half the year; the other half has no rain at all. From the fourth to the ninth moon [May to October] there is rain every afternoon, and the level of the Great Lake may rise seven to eight fathoms [about 15 metres – a figure a bit on the high side]. Large trees go under water, with only the tops still showing...However from the tenth moon to the third moon of the following year [November to April] not a drop of rain falls; the Great Lake is navigable only for the smallest craft, and the depth of the water is only three to five feet [1–2m]...Farmers who have noted when the rice is ripe and the height to which the water then rises in flood, time their sowing according to these findings".

Such productive agriculture was long attributed to a vast irrigation system, in which monsoonal rainfall and the small rivers running down from the hills to the north had been harnessed by the Cambodian kings to fill the gigantic reservoirs – the *barays* – and temple moats they had created around the central Angkor region, in order to distribute water throughout the dry season via an elaborate system of canals. Zhou Daguan mentioned some of the major water features: the "great moat" around Angkor Wat (5.5 kms in length x 200m wide), though not the one around Angkor Thom (12kms x 100m); the West Baray (8 x 2.2 kms, about 1,680 hectares, which he mistakenly called "the eastern lake"), but not the actual East Baray (7.5 x 1.8kms); and "the northern lake" (the Preah Khan Baray, 3.5kms x 900m), with "a square golden tower" in the middle – Jayavarman's now–high–and–dry exquisite little temple of Neak Pean.

That Zhou made no reference whatsoever to the barays' being part of a huge irrigation system was long dismissed as immaterial, just like Marco Polo's failure to mention the Great Wall of China, notwithstanding the eighteen years he claimed to have been within a hundred kilometres of it. But just as Marco Polo's lacuna is now explained by the view that there was no "Great Wall" at the time he claimed to have been in China, so it is now argued that there was no "huge irrigation system" for Zhou Daguan to see at Angkor either.

Some experts have now suggested (or categorically stated, as Cambodiologists tend to do) that there was no omission in Zhou's account because recent aerial photography shows no connection between the reservoirs and the numerous canals in the growing areas. So what water supply was there? It is another piece of Angkor's dangerous turf; but the exciting novelty of the aerial survey's discovery led to the new baby throwing out all the baray water.[73]

The result, in summary, is the series of theories that have come to progressively minimalise the scale of the Ankgor irrigation system. The traditional view, already referred to, was that there was a vast integrated system of rivers, barays, moats and canals, to control and when necessary supplement the natural water supply from the monsoonal rains and the annual flooding of the Tonle sap. The middle position seems to have derived partly from the aerial surveys' apparent elimination of the involvement of the barays, partly from the calculation that the barays did not hold enough water to irrigate rice for the entire population (something of a strawman argument, as the barays were previously only

---

73   For the arguments relating to Angkor I have drawn on Higham: *The Civilization of Angkor* (2001), though not in the form or sequence in which I have summarized them, and on Dumarçay: "Khmer Hydraulics", in Jessup Zephir (1997). The argument relating to Marco Polo is in A. Waldron: *The Great Wall of China* (Cambridge 1992), who concludes that by his time in China the series of walls built by ancient Chinese dynasties had disappeared; the Great Wall we know today is almost entirely a post–Marco Ming Dynasty construction. (See also 1300 chapter: Devorguilla of Galloway.)

ever seen as part of a connected system, never as sufficient in themselves). In any event, with the barays eliminated, the extensive system of canals still needed explaining; and the conclusion was that they were used to control water supply for rice cultivation through the rise and fall of the annual flooding of the Tonle Sap (the back–flow from the Mekong during the rainy monsoon season), as well as the small but usually permanent rivers coming down from the Kulen plateau. In addition, Zhou Daguan noticed that the Cambodians grew a special kind of rice adapted to the Tonle Sap water system:

> "There is, moreover, a certain kind of land where the rice grows naturally, without sowing. When the water is up one fathom, the rice keeps pace in its growth. This, I think, must be a special variety".

It is: floating rice, still cultivated, and capable of growing to a stem–height of *six* metres – three times Zhou's estimate. How much of the crop it constituted is another question. The minimalist theory eliminates not only the barays but the Tonle Sap as well: it holds that the rainfall was itself sufficient for rice cultivation, supplemented during particularly–dry dry seasons by small dams in various temples and many small tanks dug to below the water table on individual land–holdings.

There are two consequential issues: what could have been the main purpose of such huge public works as the barays if they were not part of the immigration system? And how were the various schemes organised? The responses have matched the theories in being progressively minimalist in both cases.

The barays were not only vast: even judging only by the massive amount of work they involved, they were obviously vitally important for something. The work was not just a matter of their development, from damned streams to retain water above ground level behind elevated dikes: there is also evidence of a constantly maintained battle against silting, requiring re–diversion of rivers, re–excavation, and at times raising the level of kilometres of dikes. It was probably primarily for this reason that the traditional theory was adopted. In the view of those who favour the middle theory, the barays were maintained to supply drinking water to the city's inhabitants. However, in *Civilization of Angkor*, Higham has made the hydraulically–minimalist suggestion that they were intended solely for the same symbolic purpose as the moats around the temples, which were of course part of the cosmographic plan: representing the ocean that surrounds the temple representing the earth, with the Mt Meru–sanctuary at the centre linking earth to heaven. In Higham's view,

"it would be hard to conceive of a better way of projecting power and majesty than to construct such monuments [as the barays] to create heaven and earth".

But a question remains. Even if gratifying the king's majesty *was* the main purpose of the barays, would it not seem odd if their usable volumes of water, stored and kept with great labour beneath their reflecting surfaces, could not also be applied to practical purposes – perhaps only for drinking, but perhaps even for supplementing the water for cultivation during bad dry seasons?

It is believed the cultivation of rice at Angkor reached its peak during the reign of Jayavarman VII, but there is one curious fact about related construction and control: no Jayavarman inscription has been found that refers to irrigation. Which raises the obvious question: surely such a ruler as Jayavarman VII would have boasted of bringing water to the rice fields if he had done so? The minimalists have accordingly concluded there was *no* central control over the individual landholders whose rice was cultivated by farmers (owners, indentured, slaves) using, as mentioned earlier, simply rainfall supplemented by the tanks they individually sank as they deemed necessary.

But this argument seems to ignore Jayavarman's character and policies, the nature of his government and the scale of his requirements. Such an authoritarian, who had struggled mightily – and successfully – to bring the state administrative, religious and provincial instrumentalities under his control, seems highly unlikely to have left to the uncertainties of the rainfall and the well–digging initiative of private landholders such a crucial aspect of his power as the assurance of the water supply required not only to feed the population but also to support major military campaigns and simultaneously build colossal temples and other public works. With only a small level of trade, all the economy could provide the king was labour and foodstuffs, supplemented from time to time by slaves and tribute from the neighbours.

In an earlier work[74] Higham himself pointed out that there were so many references to "cadastral surveys, assessments of land capability and fixing of tribute in kind" as to "indicate a central concern for this

---

74   *The Archeology of Mainland Southeast Asia* (1989)

crucial matter". There is a strong implication here that the collection of the crop and its distribution were centrally managed, and it is hard to imagine its being otherwise. Even with the middle theory, it is hard to see how the water supply could have been treated differently: the considerable manpower and expense involved in re–routing river flows and in maintaining the canal network would seem to imply state involvement and probably control. The mere allocation of manpower between army, building and agriculture clearly required a firm and central hand, with or without inscriptions.

The absence of inscriptions *is* odd. The absence of any regular propitiation of the gods by the monarch to ensure the regular supply of water from the rain and the rivers and the flooding of the Tonle Sap would be odd. But there was indeed a close connection between the kings of Angkor and water, and Zhou Daguan picked this up himself during his visit. The king, he reported, ascended nightly to sleep at the top of the "golden tower", the Phimeanakas, that he had observed rising out of the palace:

"It is common belief that in the tower dwells a genie, formed like a serpent with nine heads [the *naga*, symbol of water], which is Lord of the entire kingdom. Every night this genie appears in the shape of a woman, with whom the sovereign couples...At the second watch the King comes forth and is then free to sleep with his wives and his concubines. Should the genie fail to appear for a single night, it is a sign that the King's death is at hand. If, on the other hand, the King should fail to keep his tryst, disaster is sure to follow".

Trust Zhou to pick up another sex story. The legend carries echoes of other rulers' ceremonies for ensuring a state's good fortune: the precisely timed, though in his case less frequent, propitiation by the Chinese emperor of the gods at the Temple of Heaven; the Doge of Venice's annual, though in his case chaste, marriage to the sea; and the one–off, though in his case totally secret, ceremony undertaken by a new Japanese Emperor with the state's founding Sun Goddess.

In fact Zhou's story is an echo of the Khmer kings' foundation myth, according to which their ancestry began with the union between an itinerant priestly Indian Brahman, named Kaudinya, and Soma, the Cambodian daughter of the King of the *Nagas*. The myth thus not only united the Indian and Khmer bases of Cambodia's cultural identity – Hindu tradition with local animism and ancestor worship – but it also underlined a key aspect of the country's very existence: the central role of water in the kings' heritage. Indeed, there was a legend that Jayavarman built the Bayon itself at the suggestion of a *naga*; and, whether at the top of the palace tower or on the ground, he was undoubtedly instrumental in trying to ensure that there was an adequate supply of the water the *naga* symbolised and on which the state depended.

Jayavarman as social progressive

Apart from whatever Jayavarman did or was credited with doing to ensure the people's sustenance, and apart from its essential value to his military and building programs, there are three areas where he has been identified as socially progressive: the construction of chains of rest houses and of hospitals outside Angkor, and of usable roads where these amenities were located. These have often been characterised as further expressions of his benevolent concern for the welfare of his people, the assumption being that they were all intended for the benefit of pilgrims making their way to various shrines – a view, I suspect, more than a little connected with those images of Jayavarman as or like the compassionate Buddha.

And again, perhaps so. The devout making their way to some place of devotion or consolation would certainly have appreciated having a way cleared through the jungle, raised above flooded ground, bridged over the more significant rivers. But whether your ordinary widow, say, could make use of the rest houses and be succoured in the hospitals seems somewhat less certain: it could well have depended on who else was making use of them.

Which was most likely, and perhaps most often, the army. The major roads, either built or improved by Jayavarman, ran from the capital 225 kms northwest to the important Khmer outpost at Phimai (northeast of Nakhon Ratchasima in present–day Thailand), 750 kms due east to Binh–dinh, the capital of Champa, and formed a 580 km circuit around the centre of the country between Angkor and the far side of the Tonle Sap. This pattern looks military more than anything else: means for the rapid movement of men, fighting elephants and supply trains to wherever they were required.

Phimai was certainly a significant Buddhist pilgrimage centre; but it had also been one of Suryavarman II's military headquarters, and would still have been a key location under Jayavarman against the increasing pressure from the Thai pushing down the Menam valley. The road straight to the heart of the subject (and former enemy) state of Champa would have been Jayavarman's chief military highway, though, again, it would no doubt have been used as a pilgrimage route also as far as Suryavarman's important sanctuary at Beng Mealea, located near it in its Cambodian sector. The same logistical consideration seems likely for the internal circuit road also: together with some shorter roads out of Angkor to other population centres, it conveys the impression of a means for maintaining internal control – and, of course, for the requisition and delivery of labour and food to a capital which was forever hungry for both.

Zhou Daguan, noting that every village had a "temple, or at least a pagoda", together with a "local mandarin" (representing the central authorities), added that

"Along the highways there are resting places like our post halts".

Despite the village context, this has generally been taken to refer to the 121 state rest houses that Jayavarman had constructed, referred to in the stele of Preah Khan as "houses with fire". They were long halls about 15m x 5m, built of stone, some with a small chapel attached, and about 12 to 15 kms apart, and it has mostly been assumed that they were stopping places for religious pilgrims. But, again, their location, as described in an inscription, raises suspicions that their purpose was purely sacred: 57 were on the military highway to Champa, between Angkor Thom and Binh–dinh, 44 were on the internal circuit, 17 between Angkor and Phimai – 118 out of the total 121. And that description "houses with fire": could that refer to signal fires, rather than a cosy hearth in a steaming tropical climate? As with most things Cambodian, there is a counter–argument: that, in the whole of Khmer history, stone was never used for secular structures, even royal palaces, other than for their foundations. Our devout widow could no doubt use those rest houses on the way to a holy place; but the strong suspicion emerges that she might frequently have had to squeeze in with high officials and couriers and senior commanders on their way to the borders or around the interior. Because there is no record of any alternative accommodation for them.[75]

---

75 Cf. a modern summary description of the Chinese system with which Zhou Daguan compared the Cambodian, which I came across after writing the above:

"Post stations organised the movement of official mail and tribute, offered hospitality to travelling dignitaries, served as military outposts with warning

Another major inscription on the stele of Ta Prohm describes 102 hospitals in the Cambodian kingdom, dedicated to the Buddhist god of healing. Curiously, while giving many details, it does not say who had them built, but foundation steles found at a number of their sites say it was Jayavarman VII. The latter steles state that an establishment housed thirty–two people, including two doctors, six medicine–grinders, twenty–two assorted helpers, and two persons to tend the Buddha image; in addition, sixty–six people – also workers, but unspecified – could be housed at their own expense. The list of provisions supplied from the royal warehouses included, Coedès says, exact quantities of rice (with a priority allocation for offerings to the divinities), honey, sugar, camphor, sesame, spices, black mustard, cumin, nutmeg, coriander, fennel, cardamon, ginger, cubeb, vetiver, cinnamon, myrobalan and jujube vinegar – presumably for their medicinal rather than culinary value. In fact there seems to have been no indication of the number of patients who could be dealt with at any one time. The first inscription referred to says that, together, the hospitals annually used provisions (including for their ten thousand staff members) comprising 11,192 tons of rice, 2,124 kg of sesame, 3,402 nutmegs, 1,960 boxes of salve for haemorrhoids, and so on in exquisite detail.

The location of about a third of the hospitals has been identified; but as the sick could not be housed, doctrinally, in permanent structures, all that has remained are the stone foundations of the usual enclosing wall, with, again, a small chapel within it. They are scattered widely from near Vientiane (Laos) in the north to near the (present) border with Vietnam in the south; most of those identified were to the west of Angkor, including in what is now Thai territory, but whether this indicates a deliberate pattern or just the accidents of survival and discovery is not known. There was one near each of the gates of Angkor Thom; the most accessible nowadays is the small ruined chapel of Ta Prohm Kel in the forset near Angkor Wat's west entrance causeway.

Jayavarman's scattering of clinics inevitably reminds me of Sihanouk's; and of the little diplomatic corps in late–1960s Cambodia (with one exception, an appalling lot), whom it amused Sihanouk to use as mobile flower–pots to decorate functions at which he was officiating, standing in sticky discomfort in the saturated heat, waiting for, indeed actively seeking, the ineffable blessing of the modern god–king's

---

beacons to alert at times of threat, and also served as inns for ordinary travellers". (Wood: *The Silk Road* – see Bibliography, General)

attention; amongst numerous other occasions, this was especially acute in the less formal circumstances which attended his opening of yet another provincial dispensary. And I remember also being told by an insider that, after everyone's departure, the boxes of pharmaceuticals were all packed up and taken off to grace the next dispensary that Monseigneur was to inaugurate. (Though judging by Angkorian times, the modern diplomatic corps was lucky: Zhou Daguan relates thirteen occasions when "foreign ambassadors were invited by the King to enjoy the spectacle", at the New Year festivities which lasted a fortnight, and at another twelve festivals associated with the months, each of which lasted ten days.)

Whether the hospitals and their provisioning amounted to a national health service for all our poor widows is not altogether certain. The sceptic might once again suppose that the strategically placed centres – especially those on the far northern, western and southern frontiers of Jayavarman's expanded state – would have been invaluable for the support of an army almost perpetually involved in cross–border skirmishing if not larger engagements.

Jayavarman himself was of course earning merit, in the Buddhist scheme of things, by establishing or maintaining the hospitals; that first inscription said

> "He suffered from the maladies of his subjects more than from his own; for it is the public grief which makes the grief of kings, and not their own grief",

and also that

> "Full of deep sympathy for the good of the world, the King expresses this wish: all the souls who are plunged in the ocean of existence, may I be able to rescue them by virtue of this good work".

These seem noble sentiments – even if somewhat impaired by the somewhat less self–effacing connotation of the conclusion:

> "May all the Kings of Cambodia, devoted to the right, carry on my foundation, and attain for themselves and their descendants, their wives, their officials their friends, a holiday of deliverance in which there will never be any sickness".

In any case, the sentiments are conventional expressions of the conception of the king as the embodiment of his people; although they may be, they are not necessarily a literal characterisation of Jayavarman's personal beliefs.

Jayavarman's legacy

Jayavarman VII is thought to have died in 1219, perhaps in 1220; whenever exactly he was born, by then he would have been at least in his eighties, an extraordinary life–span at the time and in the circumstances.

> "The rulers are buried in the stupas," Zhou Daguan wrote, "but I do not know whether their bodies, or only their bones, are so bestowed".

Those bones have never been found. Coedès identified as sarcophagi a dozen "stone tubs", found scattered about Angkor; but none was found at the Bayon, none identified as Jayavarman's.

However in 1933 French archeologists uncovered, at a depth of 14m in the pit beneath the central tower of the Bayon – at the bottom of the axis of the Universe – a 3.6m high sandstone statue of what Coedès called the *Buddharaja*, and which he described as

> "not only a Buddhist substitute for the Sivaite Devaraja [god–king] but also a statue of apotheosis of the founder king",

Jayavarman – and "undoubtedly" with his features. It was in pieces, probably smashed by his anti–Buddhist grandson; but since 1935 it has sat, reconstructed, in lonely isolation in the forest of Angkor Thom, not far from the triumphal way leading from the Victory Gate to the entry in the centre of the Elephant Terrace to what was Jayavarman's palace.

A simple but dignified enclosure has been made, surrounded by a low wall, leading from its eastern entrance to the three ascending platforms at the far end, each guarded by fierce–looking stone lions – which (as you would by now expect) some say are welcoming visitors; they are now gently mottled by brown and green lichens. The *Buddharaja* is on the uppermost level. The hexagonal drum–like base is built up of eighteen wide–and–narrow bands of stone; and the figure, this time whole, is seated cross–legged, the hands folded in the lap, above the drum on top of three huge coils of the *Mucilinda–naga*, the great snake which protected Buddha from the raging flood–waters,[76] and whose great seven–headed cobra–fan rears up protectively behind the upper body and head of the Buddha–with–the–features–of–Jayavarman.

The image invokes both Cambodia's foundation–myth of the marriage between the Brahman and the daughter of the *naga*–king, and the protection–myth recounted by Zhou Daguan of the king's nightly renewal of his kingdom through intercourse with the *naga*–princess at the top of the Phimeanakas. Over his left shoulder someone has draped the brilliant orange robe of a bonze: the Buddha, perhaps even the king, is still real here in his great city of Angkor Thom. But as we approach there are no other visitors to be guarded against or welcomed; only an old woman is whisking to another place the carpet of leaves fallen from the great fig and kapok trees overshadowing the entire enclosure. Our widow, perhaps.

There has often been a view that Jayavarman himself had been one of the sick – with leprosy. This has been based not so much on the mis–named "Leper King" statue (now a copy) on one of the sumptuously carved terraces of what was the Angkor Thom palace – a name deriving from the appearance given by lichen growths on the figure – as from the fact that the very last scene in the Bayon's inner gallery of bas–reliefs depicts a king being given leprosy by a spitting snake. No–one is really sure that the king is Jayavarman: the inner gallery, while also containing depictions of everyday life, is based primarily on ancient Hindu literary myths, unlike the outer one which relates to the historical Jayavarman.

Once again, Zhou Daguan has something about the subject:

> "By some it is said that leprosy is the outcome of climatic conditions. Even one of the sovereigns fell victim to the disease, and so the people do not look upon it as a disgrace. It is my humble opinion that as a rule the illness results if one takes a bath immediately after sexual intercourse – a practice which, I am told, is very prevalent here",

– a diagnosis which, after all else we have heard from Zhou, should come as no surprise. But unfortunately we can still not be certain that the

---

76 Of the placid, sacred Lake Manasarovar, at the foot of Mount Kailas; on the occasion when the incident occurred Buddha is said to have climbed Kailas in three giant strides, and preached to eight million gods from a golden throne on the summit. The lake was not only venerated by Buddhists: some of Mahatma Gandhi's ashes were scattered there by some of his followers after his assassination in 1948.

leper king was Jayavarman. He could have been one of the three since Jayavarman, or even one of his predecessors. Or it is possible that Zhou's remark was based on that scene in the Bayon, though he never specifically mentions the bas–reliefs, and it is difficult to identify any other apparent reference to them, probably because he was never permitted to enter what was then Angkor's most sacred precinct. Alternatively, the statue on Jayavarman's palace terrace may have already been nick–named Leper King by the time of Zhou's visit, of which he heard gossip, as it is unlikely that he was permitted to penetrate there either.

But it is conceivable that the bas–relief was not literal but metaphoric: in this sense, the symbolism of the king being spat on by a snake, representing the Khmer kings' founding *naga*, amounts, in Cambodian terms, to the startling implication that he had lost his royal mandate. Could this have been the case? There is no reference to any domestic rebellion or revolt in Champa after Jayavarman's final reduction of it by 1203; he thus does not seem to have allowed his dominating power to slip away. We know, however, that his death had two consequences: the loss of empire and the removal of Mahayana Buddhism as the state cult. Both may well have been reactions against the burdens that Jayavarman had placed on the people through them: the need to maintain a huge army for the control of Champa and the other borders extended beyond ethnic Cambodia to the very limits of submissive populations; and the huge burdens of the extravagant megalomania of his building program and its associated servicing. The absence of Jayavarman's iron fist could well have rendered the requirements of priestly administrators and army commanders too exhausting to obtain – and their own domestic interests more possible, and congenial, to pursue.

First, the empire began to disintegrate: Champa defected almost immediately, and tributaries around the north end of the Malay peninsula were lost within a decade; by mid–century, the extension of Mongol control into southern China and through Yunnan against Burma was resulting in pressure on the Thai to move south against the Khmers. Louis Finot commented:

"There is no evidence that these [Khmer] people resisted the aggression with vigour. Perhaps they even looked on it as a deliverance....".

Thai expansion was destined to be lethal to the Angkorian kingdom: already in 1295 Zhou Daguan mentioned that "only recently, during the war with Siam, whole villages have been laid waste". Raids continued during the 14th century, with the capture and sack of Angkor itself in 1353 and again in 1394; and forty years later the capital was moved to Phnom Penh because Angkor was no longer able to be defended. The truth was that, after the collapse of Jayavarman's powerful Khmer Empire, a weak and ineffectual Khmer monarchy could never avert the temptation that a permanently shrunken Cambodia offered to the capable and assertive states which soon came to bracket it. It was, on a shorter time–scale, comparable with Pharaonic Egypt's fortunes: the decline of a civilisation as a consequence of its own successes and excesses.

From Jayavarman on – except, after 1864, for the ninety–year colonial "protectorate" during which France swallowed the whole country – Cambodia survived not so much by playing off its rapacious Thai and Vietnamese neighbours against each other, as by each of their ambitions offsetting the other's. It involved Cambodia's acknowledging the suzerainty of either Thailand (including its control of Angkor and its neighbouring provinces between 1594 – after a disastrous Khmer attack on the Thai capital – and 1907) or Vietnam, or at times a degree of both; but real disaster only came with the collapse of Sihanouk's policy of hostility to Thailand and appeasement of Vietnam, a misreading of the latter's intentions which led to its invasion and occupation of the entire country in the 1980s.

Of the military and political leaders who are the subjects of some of these chapters, Jayavarman is the only one to have had so little impact on the world beyond his own state – and that, a negative one. His main impact was in the crushing of Champa, from which it never really recovered even after it had thrown off Cambodia's yoke, and which led on in two centuries to the virtual destruction of the Cham as a people by the more aggressive Vietnamese; and Cambodia has paid for that crushing through Vietnamese aggressiveness ever since. The destruction of Champa's distinct artistic genius is also a loss, judging by the relatively little Cham sculpture that still exists, which shows a subtler human–ness than is suggested by the more formal and ritualistic sculpture of Angkor. Undoubtedly, however, the Khmers were by far the more consummate architects, builders and craftsmen; and the Khmers' art was absorbed by their Thai conquerors, though the latter were also influenced by their Burmese neighbours to the west. Beyond that, Angkor's influence disappeared forever under the thick layer of the enveloping jungle.

The departure of the court from Angkor left its great monuments at the mercy of their two worst enemies: that jungle – and thieves. The

Thai were the first human predators: after 1431, according to a late Cambodian chronicle, a Thai king

> "removed the august statues of the Buddha made of gold, silver, bronze and precious stones, as well as a number of statues of the August Bull [Nandin, Shiva's mount] and of other animals".

This was not just loot: at least some of the images symbolised, as we saw earlier, the authority of the Khmer king, which would now pass to his Thai counterpart. In the mid–16th century the Burmese did the same to the Thai, and for the same symbolic reason, when they sacked the latter's then capital at Ayuthaya and removed some of the Angkorian images; in 1734 these followed the court to Mandalay, where they are still.

The next robbers were the French, dressed up of course in high moral tone. In the 1870s, before the establishment of the *École Française d'Extrême Orient* to study and preserve the monuments, Louis Delaporte, supposed to be leading an exploratory mission from Saigon via the Mekong to Hanoi, went instead to Angkor and subsequently returned to France with "some seventy pieces of sculpture and architecture", not for symbolic but for cultural reasons, to go in the Louvre; they are now among the glories of Paris's Musée Guimet. Then, in 1923, the still-unpublished young André Malraux hacked off five pieces of Banteay Srei, not for symbolic or cultural reasons, but to make money to pay his debts. He was caught, tried and found guilty of cultural theft – and let off in response to the outrage of the French self–proclaimed progressive literary establishment, who (variously) protested that the "audacity" of "this marvellous boy" in carrying off "two or three stone dancing–girls from an unknown temple in the vicinity of Angkor" should not prevent him "from accomplishing what all have had a right to expect of him" – that last a small monument of French literary gobbledegook all in itself. Forty years later Malraux was de Gaulle's Minister for Culture, and author of an act to protect cultural property...in France, of course.

Most recently, notwithstanding what they did to their fellow–countrymen, the soldiers of the opposing Cambodian factions in the long civil war mostly avoided actually fighting in Angkor itself, though they stopped all conservation work for the best part of two decades. But the turmoil in the 1970s and 1980s resulted in considerable outright theft, by them or others, of pieces which then sold on the Bangkok and international markets. The traffic was a far cry from what Henri Mouhot had noted a hundred and twenty years before: he crossed, he wrote, from Angkor into Thailand proper "near a small piece of water, where some customs officers are stationed – three poor wretches – whose duty it is to arrest the depredators who lie in wait for the buffaloes and elephants coming down here from the lake and neighbouring districts".

Contemporary smuggling of highly marketable pieces of the temples has probably not yet been brought under complete control; little has been recovered.

Jayavarman's spiritual legacy disintegrated even faster than the temples. The Mahayana Buddhism that he used as the foundation of his power was also almost immediately under siege. As we have seen, Jayavarman's, and for that matter, his father's, devout Buddhism had not resulted in the destruction of the Hindu images of their predecessors; but Jayavarman had no such luck with his own offspring. For unknown reasons there are few records of the reigns of the son and grandson who succeeded him; however both seem to have reacted sharply against Jayavarman's religious cult, the former trying to reinstate Shaivism, though apparently unsuccessfully; the latter, after 1243, installing a syncretic cult of Shiva and Vishnu identified as the deity *Hari–Hara*, whose image was installed in place of Jayavarman's Buddha at the centre of the Bayon, while other Buddhas were destroyed or re–carved *in situ* as Hindu images – some can still be seen at Preah Khan. Thereafter, as Finot put it,

"The [Thai] conqueror…offered the vanquished a precious compensation; he offered them a gentle religion [the Theravada form of Buddhism] whose doctrine of resignation suited this tired and discouraged people most appealingly…We can understand why the Khmer people accepted it without repugnance and happily put aside the burden of their former glory".

As we saw earlier, by the time of Zhou Daguan's visit seventy–five years after Jayavarman's death, Theravada Buddhism had already become embedded in a Cambodian people exhausted by its preceding cults.

The Leper King bas–relief is believed to have been carved under Jayavarman VII's grandson, Jayavarman VIII, who piously took his name, and who, though he displaced the Bayon's Buddhas when he restored Hinduism, still left untouched the entire outer gallery of the Bayon with its vivid record of his grandfather's heroic leadership in delivering the nation and wreaking vegeance on its enemies. It thus seems possible that that bas–relief depicting the Leper King was Jayavarman VII after all – not the portrait of a king dying of a terrible disease, but the symbol of a man whose over–weening pride had forfeited him the unalloyed respect of his successors.

Jayavarman the man

Perhaps we can now venture the overall assessment of Jayavarman VII's character for which the mere contemplation of the devout smiles carved in stone was simply inadequate.

There was a frequent Western assumption before 1975 that, from Jayavarman to Sihanouk – who, during my time in Cambodia, skilfully flannelled many journalists and most diplomats to this effect – Cambodian Buddhists are "gentle" people, incapable of the violence of which they have only ever been the victims. True, they at least did not wage war for religious reasons, like most of the Christian and Islamic persuasions. But already, in 1860, in the early days of French penetration, Henri Mouhot, not seduced by ideological inclinations, said robustly that "Corruption and barbarity are general in Cambodia". There was and is no contradiction between Cambodians and killing: that sentimental myth should have been definitively dismissed with the arrival of Pol Pot and his Khmer Rouge, though even then there were still those who clung to it, insisting these butchers were merely revolutionaries justifiably opposing imperialism. But even before, the myth should have been destroyed, whether by Sihanouk, even if on a relatively small scale, clandestinely removing critics and opponents; or Jayavarman "wiping out the inhabitants" of Champa's capital and elsewhere.

We have now followed Jayavarman through his career. We have seen what he did, examined why he did it, judged him for what he was not. But what, finally, was he like?

That he was officially devoted to the Mahayana form of Buddhism as it existed in his time is clearly beyond question: his building program attests to that. But quite apart from the pious exigencies of official inscriptions, even if he was actually deeply religious it was not a matter of his being ruthless or pious – it was ruthlessness *and* piety. Some writers have conceded the terrible burden of his buildings and their servicing, fewer mention the added burden of his military campaigns, most generally manage to imply that his supposedly charitable works offset all this for his humblest subjects. One, one of the most famous, rhapsodised about the typical one of these:

"Frugal and with no great needs; respectful of the gods; submissive to the law; satisfying his hunger without difficulty, yes, the Khmer was happy".

What *I* find – heretically – is someone like a proto–Mussolini: totally controlling the machinery of state; seeking self–glorification through territorial expansion abroad, and, at home, the construction of grandiose symbols of personal power; dispensing efficiency and public works allegedly in the interests of the common man, but only as those interests were defined by the ruler himself and only insofar as they promoted *his* own interests. Jayavarman as Buddha, Mussolini as Caesar Augustus. Even portrait sculptures in both cases – though Mussolini, always on or over the edge of the ludicrous, intended to have himself represented as… Hercules, I have not been able to find out whether dressed or undressed, as tall as the top of St Peter's dome.

The sequels to their deaths were equally alike: the disavowal of their personal ideologies, the disbandment of their armies, the disappearance of their empires, the disintegration of much of their political structures. Mussolini has not yet been "lost" for half a millennium, though he will be, as Westerners thought Jayavarman was. But the latter has still not been forgotten in Cambodia: he was the one person in Cambodian history whom the Pol Pot regime unashamedly admired. And he was Sihanouk's favourite too.

Of the two despots, though, in fact of all those who have cast their bloody or impotent shadows across this benighted and hapless country, it is Jayavarman who has the last laugh – or smile. Cambodia has never again seen the shadow of his achievements, however we evaluate them. Many would finish, as we started, with the words of Pierre Loti looking again at those faces on the Bayon:

"In broad daylight, how much they had lost their alarming power. This morning they seem to say to me: 'We are truly dead, you see, and completely harmless; it is not with irony that we smile with our closed eyes; no, it is because we now have peace without dreams…' ".

I think it is time, rather, to recall the usual human condition – merit and demerit all mixed up together. And time to question whether that is a smile at all.

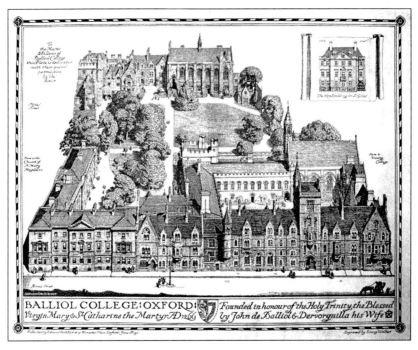

Balliol College, Oxford, England. Author's own engraving.
Photo courtesy Tim MacDonald.

SCOTLAND

DEVORGUILLA OF GALLOWAY: SAVING HEARTS AND MINDS

"See stern Oppression's iron grip,
Or mad Ambition's gory hand,
Sending, like blood–hounds from the slip,
Woe, Want, and Murder, o'er the land!"

Robert Burns: *The Winter Night*

I was not entirely happy when I first arrived at Oxford as a Rhodes Scholar at the end of 1955, shocked mainly by how different England turned out to be from my expectations of somewhere rather like Australia, but with more water and grandeur. Like most of the Colonials (as we were called), I found it wasn't like that at all: there was only one shower and it was often, unfathomably, locked; and the food and the weather were both appalling. But the dazzling range of intellects was soon utterly seductive: here was the real grandeur.

Thanks to a kind word from Hugh Stretton, the Australian historian and man-about-town-planning, I had been admitted into his old College, venerable and distinguished Balliol – for which, the politician/biographer Roy Jenkins cautioned fellow old boys, "enthusiasm is all right provided you do not inhale". Even the un-plumbed Dreaming Spires themselves turned out to be a cultivable taste, though Balliol itself is no architectural marvel: "*C'est magnifique*", someone punned on the French General Bosquet's remark on the Charge of the Light Brigade, "*mais ce n'est pas la gare*". In due course the atmosphere of learning and, yes, privilege, took away the odour in Hall of the weekly kippered herrings; besides, we found a cheap Indian restaurant, which we patronized for three years except during its temporary closures by the health authorities for currying cat.

In the Balliol College Bidding Prayer those who went to chapel still expressed

> "most humble and hearty Thanks...[for] the Liberality of JOHN BALLIOL and DEVORGUILLA his Wife, Founders of this College,...and others our Pious Benefactors";

and, with a reduced likelihood of being heard, besought the

> "Grace so to use them, as may make most for our Furtherance in Virtue, and Increase in Learning, for the Comfort and Salvation of our own Souls, and the Benefit and Edification of our Brethren".

I was surprised to find that a woman had played such a role in those days, for we are talking of a religious foundation for men in the middle of the 13th century, about when the plumbing was designed; by the mid-16th century the governing Fellows were still forbidding even laundresses past the gate, and Balliol was still exclusively for men in the 1950s. But what role had Devorguilla played? And why? Many years after Balliol, my wife and I discovered the exquisite Abbey of Dulce Cor, "Sweetheart Abbey", near Dumfries in southern Scotland, which Devorguilla of Galloway also founded, in memory of her husband – and to house his sweet heart.

Not long after Devorguilla herself died in 1290, their son, also John Balliol, became King of Scotland; and though aided by William Wallace, the romanticised "Braveheart", he played a hapless role in the tangled and bloody contest launched by England's King Edward I, starting the British Empire right at home, as he followed up his conquest of Wales with a sustained attempt to add Scotland to his trophies. For John, resistance was an anticolonial struggle *ante nominem*, at the very dawn of European nationalisms; but he was undermined by a fellow Scot who, as the winner, is much more famous now.

Edward had the troops and funds to invade Scotland because he had welshed on an undertaking to the Pope to resume Crusading against the Moslems: territorial greed was by no means just directed against the Infidels. This failure, and that of his French counterpart, led the first Franciscan Pope, Nicholas IV, to try an even more startling campaign much further east, despatching a fellow Franciscan friar to convert Kublai Khan at the far end of the Silk Road along which Marco Polo had (perhaps) just travelled. Twenty years earlier, in 1272, when Edward

The principal people in this chapter are as follows:

- **Devorguilla of Galloway** (c.1210-1290) – founder of Balliol College, Oxford, and Sweetheart Abbey, Dumfries, Scotland. Wife of Old John de Balliol and mother of King John Balliol of Scotland.

- **John de Balliol** (unknown-1268) – founder with Devorguilla of Balliol College, Oxford. Husband of Devorguilla and father of King John Balliol of Scotland. Referred to in this chapter as Old John de Balliol.

- **King John Balliol** (c.1249-1315) – Candidate in the Great Cause and King of Scotland from 1292-1296. Son of Old John Balliol and Devorguilla.

- **King Edward I** (1239-1307) – King of England from 1272-1307. Known as Edward Longshanks and the Hammer of the Scots. Participated in the eighth Crusade.

- **Robert Bruce** (c.1210-1295) – candidate for King of Scotland during the Great Cause, in opposition to John Balliol. Grandfather of King Robert the Bruce.

- **William Wallace** (unknown-1305) – one of the leaders during the Wars of Scottish Independence.

- **Tedaldo Visconti** (c.1210-1276) – Archdeacon of Liege and senior Vatican representative in the Crusader States during the eighth Crusade. Later Pope Gregory X from 1271-1276.

- **Rusticello of Pisa** (dates unknown) – Genoan romance writer and co-author of The Travels of Marco Polo. Accompanied Lord Edward (later King Edward I) on the eighth Crusade.

- **Giovanni da Montecorvino** (1247-1328) – Italian Franciscan missionary and Archbishop of Cathay. Founder of the earliest Catholic missions in India and China.

himself had actually gone Crusading, before he became king, he might just have met Marco in Acre, the Crusaders' last foothold in Palestine – where Edward was accompanied by the Genoan romanticist Rusticello, who was later to write down what Marco said was the story of his travels to Cathay. Another of Edward's companions, an Italian diplomat who was elected Pope while they were in Acre, provided the Polos, returning to China, with the response to Kublai Khan's request for a hundred learned men: two Dominicans, who chickened out after a couple of weeks. Which perhaps accounted for Nicholas's later choice of a Franciscan emissary to go to the fabled east, charged with converting "the Lord Chaan" (Khan); in due course Fra Giovanni da Montecorvino was elevated to "Archbishop of Cathay", but found the Emperor, while tolerant, "too far gone in idolatry".

Devorguilla herself, who would have known of Crusaders and Infidels – and perhaps even of Marco Polo? – from her brother-in-law and one of her two sons who had been in Palestine with Edward (the other died there), also shared the gentler teachings of the new Franciscan Order, founded about the time of her own first birthday. Her very different sensibilities and pursuits won my heart; and while this chapter ranges across these wider connections of her family and her faith, it is governed by the slim but engaging story of Devorguilla's quiet strength.

In August 1300 King Edward I of England, having been rampaging against the Scots in their southwestern province of Galloway on his third campaign to subdue Scotland in four years, came to a halt for the winter in a great red sandstone abbey a few kilometres to the south of Dumfries. It had been a bloodless swing through a country laid waste and ransacked for provisions; Edward's only loss had been the capture of his cook. There were other abbeys and castles in the neighbourhood where Edward could as easily have gone, but here he could make a rest and a political point at the same time: Sweetheart Abbey had been founded by Devorguilla, the last heiress of Galloway and mother of his opponent, the King of Scotland, John Balliol. The Abbey is the first in the story of hearts that unexpectedly marks this bitter end of a century.

Eight years earlier Edward had in fact supported John Balliol for the throne when the old line of Scottish monarchs died out; but he had then invaded Scotland and deposed his own choice when John had asserted Scotland's independence. This use of Devorguilla's Abbey was a small point in Edward's quest to conquer Scotland, as he had previously conquered Wales; but nothing was too small an insult, or too solemn an oath, in the pursuit of what had become the obsession of his last years. For this implacable imperialist, "Hammer of the Scots" – *Scottorum malleus*, as is painted on his tomb in Westminster Abbey – the wogs began at Berwick.

It is interesting to look – briefly – at Scotland as Edward's Vietnam: an effort to control a foreign country, sometimes in association with frequently unreliable indigenous allies, sometimes directly, using large–scale traditionally–organised armed forces, which were continually undermined and eventually defeated by guerrilla campaigns which came together as a national resistance movement. It would be silly to push the analogy any further – though it is irresistible to note that the man who initially withdrew England from the Scottish adventure, Edward's son and successor King Edward II, came to an even stickier end than the man who disengaged the United States from Vietnam, President Richard Nixon – the younger Edward had his insides burned out by a red–hot poker inserted in his anus, but pushed through a horn so no exterior marks would show. But enough – Scotland's independence movement was largely provoked, and sustained, by Edward I's ruthless and sustained ambition; and its echo is still provocative today in a decentralising Great Britain.

It was to Sweetheart Abbey that the English King's home-grown ecclesiastical opponent, Robert of Winchelsey, Archbishop of Canterbury brought Pope Boniface VIII's blunt criticism of Edward's efforts to conquer Scotland:

> "We in no wise doubt it to be contained in the book of your memory how from ancient times the Kingdom of Scotland pertained by full right...to the foresaid Roman Church and that, as we have understood, it was not feudally subject to your ancestors...nor is it to you".

Boniface was not simply responding to his Scots petitioners or, even their more important French backers, but was already headed full speed for the position he was to outline three years later in his extraordinary Bull *Unam Sanctam*:

> "...temporal authority should be subject to spiritual...it is altogether necessary to salvation for every human creature to be subject to the Roman Pontiff".[77]

---

77 We have a portrait of Boniface: in the only surviving fragment of a fresco painted by Giotto in 1300, in the Basilica of St John Lateran in Rome, showing the Pope proclaiming the Church Jubilee that year.

Edward (like most crowned heads) was outraged: his response to the Pope was totally unrepentant. And it cited, on the authority of all the lawyers and churchmen who knew what was best for them, an English claim to Scotland dating back, biblically, to Eli and the Prophet Samuel, and, classically, to the landing in uninhabited Britain of Brutus, great–grandson of Virgil's Aeneas, the last of the Trojans, who had then given England to his eldest son Locrinus, Scotland to the second, Albanactus, and Wales and Ireland to others – the younger ones all – surprise! – subject to Locrinus of England. At the same time, he may well have felt obliged to try to beat the Scots playing their own genealogical game: Alexander III, the last King of Scotland before John Balliol, had traced his ancestry back to the Princess Scota, the unlikely–sounding daughter of an unidentifiable Egyptian Pharaoh; her descendants, having arrived in Scotland by way of Scythia, in southern Russia, were converted there by St Andrew, the first Apostle called by Christ, in person. (By an odd coincidence not known to either party at the time, the Russians were also claiming that they had been converted by busy Andrew.) But it was all really no matter to Edward: by myth or by massacre he was determined to have Scotland.

John de Balliol and Devorguilla his wife

The Balliols had originally been imperialists themselves: the family, from Bailleul–en–Vimeu, near Abbeville in Picardy, in northern France, had been part of William the Conqueror's invasion of England, and had been rewarded with extensive lands, particularly near Durham on the northern frontiers of Norman England. Here they built, at the end of the eleventh century, the great Castle Barnard, which a century and a half later was still in the possession of John de Balliol, the father of the future king (whom we shall refer to, to lessen confusion, as Old John).

Old John married a great Scottish heiress, Devorguilla of Galloway. She was descended from three Kings of Scotland: Duncan I, creator of the kingdom in 1034, murdered by Macbeth six years later; and his son Malcolm III, who overthrew Macbeth in 1057; and she was the great–great–granddaughter of David I, who had consolidated the kingdom during the first half of the following century. She was thus herself in line of succession to the throne of Scotland. Devorguilla was also a great English land–holder in her own right, as the descendant of the Norman invaders: from Adeliza, Countess of Huntingdon, William the Conqueror's sister; and from the Earls of Chester, from whom she inherited the estate of Fotheringhay, near Peterborough, which had originally belonged to the brother of Harold, the last Anglo–Saxon King of England – the same Fotheringhay whose castle was to be the last prison of Mary Queen of Scots, where she was executed (somewhat incongruously, in the banqueting hall) in 1587, exactly three hundred years after Devorguilla's last visit there. As the current heir to both lines, Devorguilla herself bore the arms of both Huntingdon and Chester

Devorguilla's father, Alan of Galloway, had been one of the barons at Runnymede to whom bad King John had been forced to grant the Magna Carta in 1215. Old John de Balliol, however, was a King's man, supporting John's son Henry III against Simon de Montfort, the architect of Parliament, and the barons. He had also been made a Regent of Scotland during the minority of the ill–fated Alexander III: an indication not merely of John's standing in the two kingdoms but also of the ambiguity in the relations between them.

It is not known how John and Devorguilla met, but it can undoubtedly be assumed that his father, the Lord of Barnard Castle, and hers, the last Prince of Galloway, saw political advantage and greater security in this union of two great families of northern England and southern Scotland, on either side of that contested border, and of their extensive landholdings in both countries, as well as (still, almost two hundred years after the Conquest) in northern France. But, however it began, it is evident that this also was (or became) a great love–match, lasting with apparently undiminished intensity for thirty-five years of married life, and sustained by Devorguilla's vivid remembrance of her "sweet, silent companion" throughout the further twenty-two years of her widowhood. Such lengthy fidelity is remarkable in any age, but all the more for a time when the alliances of great families were subject to the whims and strategies of kings and churchmen, and when, besides, lifetimes were considerably shorter than they are now. This was a late medieval high romance, against a suitable background of great causes, fierce loyalties, effortless betrayals, noble deeds and, even, piety.

Scholarly foundation

Old John died in 1268 as the Lord Edward, as Henry III of England's heir was known, was making his preparations to join St Louis IX of France on his ill–fated second Crusade, which was supposed to free Jerusalem but ended up failing to conquer Tunisia. John had not played a particularly prominent role in either the political or military affairs of England during his fairly long life, though he was captured, along with King Henry and the Lord Edward himself, at the disastrous battle of

Lewes in 1264 during the Barons' War, and he played a part in the settlement after Simon de Montfort's defeat the following year. Henry recognised Old John's contribution by having his arms carved in stone with those of his other supporters in the northern choir aisle of Westminster Abbey (the seventeenth shield from the east end). Before these excitements of his last years he seems to have been active mostly in the administration of his large estates scattered through seventeen English counties, but particularly concentrated in the North in the region of his great stronghold of Barnard Castle. It was here that occurred the events which led him to co–found what became the first of the colleges of what was then the rudimentary University of Oxford, an unlikely step for a man who was possibly not even literate. One may indeed wonder whether it was entirely his own.

The chronicles relate that, in the late 1250s, boundary disputes between Balliol and his powerful neighbour Walter de Chirkham, the Bishop–Palatine of Durham, had led the latter to use his unfair ecclesiastical advantage of being able to excommunicate a number of Balliol's men, who had, the Bishop charged, "unjustly vexed and enormously damnified" land he claimed as his own. Old John reacted in a way that might have stood his youngest son in good stead when he became King of Scotland: he laid an ambush for the Bishop, and in H.W.C. Davis's words,

"subjected him when captured to some indignities, and carried off a part of his retinue. The Bishop laid his complaint before the King [Henry III], and obtained a writ condemning the outrage in the strongest language and demanding instant reparation. From loyalty or calculation the offender submitted, and the men of Durham were edified by the spectacle of this haughty baron prostrating himself in penitential garb before the doors of their Cathedral, while the Bishop applied the scourge with no gentle hand".

Davis adds, though, that

"the humiliation was no doubt endured with the better grace as Balliol retained possession, in part at least, of the disputed lands; in 1297 the claims of the See of Durham were still unsatisfied".

The scene underlines the power of the clergy: at the time John was not only a great land–holder in his own right but also one of the Regents of

Scotland and, in England, King Henry's appointee as Governor of the Castle of Carlisle, Keeper of the Castle of Nottingham, and Sheriff of the Counties of Cumberland, Derby and Nottingham. There is another curious little cross–reference here: not all that long before, one of Old John's predecessors as Sheriff of Nottingham had of course been "vexed and damnified" himself, it was said, deservedly, by that enduring champion of the common people, Robin Hood; and *they* said merry Robin was a dispossessed Earl...of Huntingdon.

The public whipping was only part of Old John's punishment: the Bishop imposed the additional penance of a substantial act of charity. And it was thus that, in 1263, Old John hired a house in Oxford to accommodate sixteen poor Scholars, with an allowance of eight pence a week each. So began Old Balliol Hall, which became Balliol College, in the outlying Horsemonger Street, which became the central present–day Broad Street. But why a benefaction for students? And why Oxford? The Bishop must have had a considerable influence, if not a wholly decisive voice, over the choice of charity, but it is surprising that he did not favour one closer to home – though there was no university to endow at Durham for more than another six hundred years.

Was the project Devorguilla's? She was a person of some culture, having been brought up at the English court of her grandfather, David Earl of Huntingdon, the younger brother of Kings Malcolm IV and William the Lion. She clearly had a very close relationship with her husband, and her cooler head may have helped compensate for his rashness. And, significantly, Devorguilla, noted for her piety, also had close connections with the Franciscans – and the Franciscans were already prominent at Oxford.

The two orders of preachers, St Dominic's Dominicans – the *Domini Cani* – and St Francis's newer Franciscans – the *Fratres Minores*, already outbidding their elder brethren in humility – had reached England in the first quarter of the century, during the lifetimes of their founders, even quicker than the Black Death was to do in the reign of Edward's and Devorguilla's grandson. The Dominicans' rule was recognised by the old and frail but long–lasting Pope Honorius III in 1216, the Franciscans' in 1223; and the Dominican Blackfriars were in England by 1220, a year before St Dominic's death, the Franciscan Greyfriars by 1224, two years before St Francis's. The Dominicans were established at Oxford within a year of their arrival in England, the Franciscans within a year of theirs, a recognition perhaps of Oxford's importance already as an intellectual centre, or at least a centre of clerical education, as well probably a further competitive step for the hearts and minds of the English. (They did not always succeed: in the next century an English chronicler, Henry Knighton, of the Augustinian or Austin Cannons, a preaching Order pre–dating the Dominicans and Franciscans, and, in Henry's view, holier than they, wrote that when the Black Death swept through Marseilles "not one of the hundred and fifty Franciscans survived to tell the tale. And", he added, "a good thing too".)[78]

The Franciscans made a particular effort to court the friendship of the North of England and of Scotland, and we know that in our present context they had succeeded: already in 1262, perhaps even before Old John de Balliol's imposed act of charity in Oxford, he and Devorguilla had founded, near the Old Burgh of Dumfries, looking across the River Nith towards "the purple hills of Galloway", a Greyfriars Priory (with its Chapel where the third and most famous Robert the Bruce was to murder Devorguilla's other grandson, Comyn the Red, forty–four years later). Nothing remains of the Priory, but the Nith is still spanned in Dumfries town by six of the original nine massive arches of Devorguilla's Bridge, built at the same time, by the same master–mason it is said, with the same red sandstone that was to be used in the Abbey of Sweet Heart many years afterwards.

It could thus have been through Devorguilla's and Old John's Franciscan connections that the decision was arrived at to meet the Bishop of Durham's penance by paying for an establishment of poor Scholars at Oxford, under the tutelage of the Franciscans. At first, Balliol Hall was simply a place of residence; the Scholars received their eight pence each week from Balliol's agents, but they went elsewhere in the University for their studies. Balliol intended the institution to become permanent: on his death in 1268, his will assigned money for the purchase of land that would provide a continuing income, and his eldest son, Hugh, who died on the Lord Edward's Crusade, made the purchases before leaving for Palestine. By 1276 Peter de Cossington had bequeathed the young foundation a copy of Boethius's *De Musica*, which is still in the College Library. The possession of a book was not an inconsiderable matter: on his death thirty years later King Edward I's royal library contained three.

In 1274, eleven year after Balliol's foundation, Merton was the first Oxford College to be founded with a charter as well as an endowment.

---

78   Recounted in Norman Davies: *Europe*

The next charter was Balliol's: in 1282 Devorguilla took her husband's foundation in hand and gave it its first statutes, making it self–governing, followed by further grants of land and buildings over the next two years. The first seal of the College dates to just before this, about 1280; it shows Devorguilla, holding a shield of arms with the lion of Galloway, and Old John, holding his with the simple border (*orle*) of the Balliols, together supporting a College building looking improbably like a Greek temple, and with the Virgin and Child on the roof under a Gothic canopy, flanked by Devorguilla's hereditary arms of Chester and Huntingdon. This raises an interesting thought: as we have noted and will see further, Devorguilla was devoted to her husband's memory; but of the four arms on the shield of the College they founded, three are Devorguilla's.

Of course by this time Devorguilla was long since alone in supporting the foundation; and on the seal she fixed to her Statutes in 1282 she *is* alone: an elegant full–length figure, though the face is indistinct, no doubt very fashionable in a long mantle falling in folds, her head draped in a wimple also with folds falling from its sides. In her hands she holds up the shields of both Balliol and Galloway – with those of Chester and Huntingdon again on either side. But this time, on the reverse, are the Galloway and Balliol arms together, half–and–half (*paled*) on the same shield, as in the present College arms: evidence then and reminder now of John and Devorguilla's enduring love–match.

In making her provisions for the College, Devorguilla was guided by an old friend, and possibly her father–confessor, the Franciscan Friar Richard of Slikeburne, himself a native of Durham; and, until new statutes were issued in 1507, one of the two Visitors who oversaw the welfare of the College was always a Franciscan. As a further sign of Devorguilla's closeness to the new College, the first principal elected under her statutes was Walter of Fotheringhay, from the great estate she had inherited from the Anglo–Norman Earls of Chester. So began the College's long and sometimes distinguished career. When, today, its members propose the toast *Floreat Domus de Balliolo*, it is in honour of both "John Balliol and Devorguilla his Wife, Founders of the College".

The last English Crusader

Only a few years after Devorguilla's statutes, King Edward of England began to come under Papal pressure to mount a new crusade to save what was left of the Crusader states in Palestine.

By then there was not much: Jerusalem had definitively fallen in 1244, Caesarea in 1265, Jaffa and Antioch in 1268, the great castle of Krak des Chevaliers in 1271. Thereafter Acre, the last stronghold, was under threat from the Moslem Baibars, the powerful new Mameluke ruler of Egypt. Nicholas, the one hundred and eighty–ninth Pope, the first Franciscan friar to be elected, and the first Pope to be elected unanimously, was acting largely under the unlikely prompting of a non–Christian Mongol ruler, the Ilkhan Arghun of Persia, great–nephew of Kublai Khan, Emperor of China and Grand Khan of the Mongol Empire. Arghun was, he said, anxious to join with the Christians to defeat the Mamelukes.

This was not something entirely new – at least in Christian imaginations. The legend of Prester John began spreading through Europe from unknown origins in the late 12th century. He was said to have a vast empire somewhere in the Orient, far to the east of the Crusader territories then in the Holy Land, beyond the Saracens who were pressing them so sorely.[79] And, it was believed, this Prester John was not only wealthy and powerful, but Christian.

It was not solely a matter of the wish being father to the thought: the growth of the legend coincided with the awesome explosion of the Mongols out of the Gobi steppelands; and there were garbled, but partly accurate, reports of Mongol tolerance of, and even intermarriage with, Nestorians. Nestorianism was a branch of Christianity which the Roman and Byzantine Churches, still united, had branded as heretical at the Council of Ephesus in 431 and driven eastwards across the Middle East and the steppes of Central Asia, where the Nestorians established small outposts from Persia to China. From what was a standing start at the very beginning of the 13th century, when the Mongol tribes were unified by Genghis Khan, these supposedly potentially Christian Mongol hordes were overrunning northern China by 1215, Persia by 1220, Russia by 1237. Kiev, where this book began, was sacked in 1240.

By this stage the Vatican decided it was worth approaching the Khans, for two reasons: for peace, to try to fend off the terrible northern Mongol threat to Europe itself; and for war, to persuade the southern Mongols to join with the Crusaders in a pincer movement against the

---

79 Though by the time by the time the 20th century Scottish politician and adventure story writer John Buchan got hold of him, Prester had become resident in Africa.

Moslems of Baghdad; and no–one seemed to find any great inconsistency in these objectives. The 13th century thus saw European clerics begin trekking eastwards to court the Great Khan in Karakorum (in western present–day Mongolia), before Kublai Khan established himself in China as Emperor, before any West Europeans became involved in the long history of direct trade with China, and half a century before Marco Polo. The first recorded visit to the Far East was in 1246 by an Italian friar, Giovanni di Pian di Carpini, a disciple of St Francis of Assisi himself and already sixty–five, an enormously fat man who had to ride a very sturdy donkey rather than a horse the six thousand kilometres across Central Asia to seek the Mongols' support – after visiting Russia to propose (not for the last time) that the Orthodox Church accept Papal supremacy, but on this occasion to oppose...the Mongols.

Neither Giovanni di Pian di Carpini, sent by Pope Innocent IV while he was in Lyon under the "protection" of St Louis IX, nor William of Rubruck, a French Franciscan sent in 1253 by Louis himself for similar reasons, ever reached China itself: both visited Kublai Khan's predecessors at Karakorum. In about 1262, the two elder Polos, Marco's father Niccolò and uncle Maffeo, saw Kublai there on the first of the expeditions described in the *Travels*. (Coleridge's Xanadu was taken from the Xamdu described in Samuel Purchas's 1626 world survey *Purchas his Pilgrimage*; it was actually Shang–tu, way to the east of Karakorum in present–day Chinese Inner Mongolia, where Kublai Khan had decreed his stately pleasure dome, which was marvelled at in the story of the second Polo voyage. Its remains are apparently still – if barely – visible.)

Neither of these Papal embassies having produced the desired results, suddenly, just over twenty years later, came the message from the Ilkhan Arghun in the reverse direction. It was immediately given enthusiastic credence, partly because of the long–standing belief in Prester John, and partly, notwithstanding that Arghun was reputedly "something of a Buddhist", because he was the son of and was married to Nestorian Christians. Following his accession to the Ilkhanate in 1284, and supported by his (Mongol) Nestorian Patriarch Mar Yaballaha III, Arghun sent letters and embassies to Rome and to Philip IV of France and Edward of England urging over and over a new joint crusade against the Moslems – in 1285, in 1287, in 1289, and yet again in 1290. And sensing the advantages gained by flattery at the Holy See, in 1289 he also had his second son, the future Ilkhan Oljaitu, christened Nicholas in honour of the Pope. It worked with Nicholas, but Oljaitu converted in due course to Islam.

Through all this sustained campaign Arghun never concealed that his main objective was the destruction of the Mamelukes, to complete the Mongol conquest of Asia:

> "As the land of the Saracens will lie between yourselves and us, together we will surround and strangle it...We will drive out the Saracens with the help of God, the Pope, and the Grand Khan".

But, presumably recognising that this might not have been enough to tempt the Christian kings, who had still not responded to the first three letters, he added in the last one what he must have thought was the ultimate temptation:

> "If you on your part will send troops at the time fixed, we will recapture Jerusalem and give it to you. But," he added prudently, "it will be useless for our troops to march if you fail at the rendezvous".

Arghun had surely pressed all the right buttons, and Pope Nicholas backed him every step of the way. But it was of course Louis and Edward who had the bigger battalions – and Louis was still too busy trying to regain the throne of Sicily for his own family, after his insufferable brother Charles of Anjou had been driven out, years before, by the popular uprising known as the Sicilian Vespers. In 1290 Edward finally promised Nicholas to undertake a new Crusade in 1293, and in 1290–1291 a general exhortation to take the Cross was preached throughout England, at the same time as Nicholas's appeal was broadcast in all of Europe as far as Finland and Iceland, and perhaps even to the disappearing remains of Viking Greenland. In England it simply amounted to milking the faithful: Edward had already become obsessed by Scotland. Acre itself fell in 1291: Christian Palestine was gone forever.

When making his repeated efforts over the preceding years Arghun must have thought Edward was his best bet, because Edward had himself been a crusader, on the eighth Crusade, led by Philip of France's father, Louis IX, in 1270. It was Louis' second Crusade, and even more disastrous than his first, on which, twenty years earlier, Louis had got himself captured at Damietta in Egypt; this time he got a fatal dysentery at Carthage in Tunisia. He was canonised in 1297, not just because he built the Sainte Chapelle in Paris, though that surely should have been reason enough. Louis was supposed to be leading his second Crusade back to Egypt again; Tunis was a diversion, on what turned out to be the wholly mistaken presumption that the Bey was ready to convert to Christianity – a story invented, some alleged, by Louis' villainous brother Charles in his pursuit of a Mediterranean kingdom for himself. This example of the continuous habit of wishful thinking about would–be Christians cost Louis his life; Charles, on the other hand, made a mint when the Bey bought him off.

The Lord Edward arrived just after, with his small band from England, Scotland, and the Low Countries. For all his cynicism, he seems to have been genuinely shocked by Charles's mercenary deal with the infidel and his subsequent defection, with the French crusaders, back to Europe:

> "By the blood of God", he announced in Carthage, "though all my fellow soldiers and countrymen desert me, I will enter Acre with Forvin, the groom of my palfrey, and I will keep my word and my oath to the death".

For once he did: he was in Acre by May 1271, just thirty–one days after the Crusaders had lost the great fortress of Krak des Chevaliers in Syria, and stayed, ineffectually, for only sixteen months. This was nothing like his great–uncle Richard the Lionheart's swashbuckling role in the Third Crusade eighty years before, even though that had been equally unsuccessful. Many English nobles had promised to come on this Crusade with Edward, but most reneged; only a thousand men had followed him.

So what has all this to do with Devorguilla? Accompanying Edward on this Crusade were her two eldest sons, Hugh and Alexander, and her Hunband's brother Eustace de Balliol. Although there is much we do not know about Devorguilla, it is safe to assume that she had a close interest in this Crusade.

Edward hoped in vain for support from the Crusader Kingdom of Cyprus; instead he found the Venetians were selling timber and iron to the Moslems to make arms, and the Genoese were running the Egyptian slave–trade. With his little army Edward made a few excursions against the surrounding Mamelukes, but achieved nothing. During that year Hugh de Balliol, the eldest son of Old John and Devorguilla, died in the Holy Land, of combat or contagion. Alexander, however, survived, to die back at Castle Barnard in 1278 – leaving young John as unexpected heir, as it turned out, to…Scotland.

God's little Acre

Edward and the Balliols' most interesting companion in Acre in 1271 was Tedaldo Visconti, Archdeacon of Liège, who had known the prince since a Vatican diplomatic mission to England in 1265, and had accompanied him in command of a band of Netherlanders – presumably to fight, as Tedaldo was not yet a priest, notwithstanding his elevated position as administrative head of the semi–independent Prince–Bishopric of Liège, then part of the Holy Roman Empire, now part of Belgium. It seems highly likely that, through Tedaldo, Edward also met Marco Polo, in Acre at that time with his two uncles, on their way back to the court of Kublai Khan. The senior Polos had already met the Grand Khan in the mid–1260s at Ghengis Khan's old capital of Karakorum, on the steppes southwest of Ulaanbaatar in present–day Mongolia; and the Khan had, according to the account in Marco's *Travels*, given the brothers a letter asking the Pope to

> "send up to a hundred men learned in the Christian religion, well versed in the seven arts,[80] and skilled to argue and demonstrate plainly to idolators and those of other persuasions that their religion is utterly mistaken...Furthermore the Grand Khan directed the brothers to bring oil from the lamp that burns above the sepulchre of God in Jerusalem".

No wonder Western wishful thinking about the conversion of the heathen kept being refreshed.

After their first voyage the Polos had waited two years in Venice for the election of a new Pope who could provide them with their hundred learned men, but in vain: the College of Cardinals was still deadlocked after the death of the last Pope in 1268. So they decided to move on to Acre, where Tedaldo, as senior Vatican representative in the Crusader States, gave them a message for Kublai Khan – but no learned men. The Polos set off anyway, but had only reached Lesser Armenia (in southeast Turkey at the corner of the Mediterranean) when they were called back to Acre with the news that Tedaldo Visconti had been elected Pope, as Gregory X. After a three year gap, the Cardinals, who had been meeting yet again, had finally been locked in the Papal Palace in Viterbo by the

---

80   The basic subjects of Medieval learning, derived from Rome: the Trivium of Grammar, Logic, Rhetoric; the more advanced Quadrivium of Geometry, Arithmetic, Astronomy, Music.

local authorities, who then, at the urging of the Minister–General of the Franciscan Order, Bonaventure, later made a Saint for other reasons, had proceeded to remove the palace roof and started cutting rations to – successfully – force an outcome.

Tedaldo was not able to be much more helpful to the Polos as Pope than he had been a few weeks before as Legate: all he could provide in addition, save a Papal letter, was two Dominicans, Brother Nicholas of Vicenza and Brother William of Tripoli [in the Crusader State of that name in modern Syria]. They were such poor specimens that one almost suspects the intrusion of rival Franciscan historiography: on the road to the Grand Khan the little party only got back as far as Lesser Armenia again, when a sudden irruption by Egyptian forces made the Dominicans "scared at the prospect of going farther", and they promptly deserted the Polo expedition. And these two were the beginning and end of any talk of a hundred learned men. The impression is inescapable that, for all their protestations about trying to convert the Orient, the Popes preferred to focus on trying to control the West.

The Lord Edward and the Balliols had another very interesting companion at Acre: one Rusticello of Pisa, another piece in the jigsaw who is frequently omitted from the histories. According to Frances Wood, Rusticello seems to have gone to Palestine in Edward's employ as a writer. Two of his "romances" survived, both based on King Arthur and the Knights of the Round Table, and both in French, Edward's native tongue and the language, for another hundred years still, of the Plantagenet English court. What exactly Rusticello was doing with Edward on a Crusade is unclear: maybe he wanted the experience, so as to be able to describe battles and deeds of derring–do with greater accuracy, or at least gusto; maybe he was required to write entertainments for when Edward hosted other princely Crusaders, or to while away the long days and nights of tedium between battles and feasts; or maybe Edward took him along to record his feats of arms and his displays of piety. This thought is suggested by Rusticello's next appearance in history: chronicling the feats of...Marco Polo.

After Edward left Sicily in 1272, having just succeeded to the throne while still on the way home from his Crusade, Rusticello disappears from view until, according to the Prologue of Marco's *Travels*,

"in the year of the Nativity of Our Lord Jesus Christ 1298, while he [Marco Polo] was in prison in Genoa, wishing to occupy his leisure as well as to afford entertainment to readers, he caused all these things to be recorded by Messer Rustichello of Pisa, who was in the same prison".

Rusticello had apparently been languishing in Genoese captivity since 1284, when he had been captured in a sea battle between his captors and the Pisans – like Marco himself, captured by the Genoese in a sea battle with the Venetians in 1296. Finding a novelist and a merchant in their states' navies is unexpected – until one learns from John Julius Norwich that, in preparation for the war with Genoa that Venice launched at the end of 1294, all able–bodied male citizens between the ages of seventeen and sixty had been registered and warned to be ready for instant conscription; and all the more need for conscription in little Pisa. Posterity was fortunate that Marco Polo should have come across a familiar ghost–writer just when he had time to spin his tales.

If they were indeed his, that is. Scholars have pointed out that the opening of Marco Polo's *Travels* – "Emperors and kings, dukes and marquises, counts, knights and townsfolk..." – comes from one of Rusticello's romances; that the account of Marco's welcome by the Great Khan closely follows Rusticello's description of the arrival of Tristan at King Arthur's court at Camelot; and that there are numerous other parallels as well. Rusticello noted in the Prologue that "what Marco told was only what little he was able to remember"; even some of that has been found to be more in the realm of romance than of reality, at least as far as Marco was concerned.

Frances Wood's careful conclusion, from her analysis of the text, is that while the description of Marco's father's and uncle's earlier visit to the court of the Great Khan at Karakorum is credible, and while there was also much valuable information on China and the Middle East in *The Travels*, it was second–hand: there was no second voyage, and Marco, for his part, never went to China, "probably never travelled much further than the family's trading posts on the Black Sea and in Constantinople" – and, she adds, more provocatively, "was not responsible for Italian ice–cream or Chinese dumplings". As Rusticello wrote in the Prologue, "What more shall I say?" But what we can say is that in one sense it doesn't matter what Marco himself did or didn't see: his *Travels* inspired curiosity for centuries, and, in due course, even accuracy.

It is entertaining to think of the three Polos, Rusticello, the Legate Tedaldi, and, who knows? even the young Lord Edward and the Balliols, sitting around some time in 1271, between May (when Edward arrived) and September (when Tedaldo left as Pope), all together in some corner of Acre, which was virtually all that was left of the Crusader states – in Edward's "great chamber", where, on 16 June the following year, a member of the fanatical Moslem Order of Assassins, hired by the Egyptian Mameluke Sultan Baibars, stabbed him with a poisoned dagger; or in the Legate's noble lodgings, probably, given Venice's 13th century suzerainty over his native Piacenza, in the Venetian Quarter next to the harbour; perhaps the awe–struck seventeen year old Marco meeting the glib literateur–cum–entertainer Rusticello in some coffee shop or *brasserie d'Outremer*.

They were all interested in "the East", but for varying reasons and in varying dimensions. Rusticello was a soaker–up of tales; some of the Middle Eastern legends which turned up all those years later in *The Travels of Marco Polo* could well have come originally from Acre's cafes and bars. That the elder Polos themselves were fully focussed on the east, the Far East, goes without saying: they had actually been there, and they were still, and continued for another thirty years to be, intensely interested and involved in the commercial possibilities whether or not they in fact undertook a second voyage to the lands of the Great Khan of China. The Legate's military responsibilities in Edward's Crusade kept him focussed – including throughout his pontificate – more on the vain attempt to re–liberate the holy places. It was to this end, rather than out of any sense of contrition or theological healing, that he took steps to overcome the breach that earlier Crusaders had created with Byzantium; but all he could raise to convert the whole of Cathay were those two timorous Dominicans. This was an eastern policy of a sort, but one might say not very far–seeing.

How far eastwards Edward's own interest extended is unclear, but it certainly went as far as the Mongol kingdom of Persia. Shortly after his arrival in Acre he had sent an embassy of three Englishmen to the Ilkhan Abaga, seeking his support against the Moslem Mamelukes. In due course it came, was insufficient and withdrew, and was highly profitable in loot for Abaga, but not militarily for the rump Crusader state, which now had only twenty years to go. All Edward could do for it, before he left, was to arrange with Baibars a truce of ten years, ten months, ten days and ten hours, and go off to organise more allies and a bigger Crusade. But of course he didn't, not then, not fifteen years later when Pope Nicholas began pressuring him.

With the failure of the Christian kings to support a new Crusade, Nicholas turned in a totally unexpected direction. He persuaded himself that the Ilkhan Arghun's willingness to fight with them against the common Mameluke enemy warranted an entirely different mission by the Church: the conversion to the One True Faith of the Mongols themselves, and especially of Argun's great–uncle the Great Khan himself, Kublai Khan. And so, in 1289, just after Arghun's death as it happened, Nicholas chose the fourty–four year old Franciscan friar Giovanni da Montecorvino to go, with one assistant (who died on the way), to Khanbalik – Peking – where Kublai Khan had moved his capital in 1264. And off he headed into the distant and still unknown East, with his simple instruction: convert the Mongol Khan – and all the Mongols. Nicholas would never see him again; his colleagues must have wondered if any of them ever would. They didn't.

Scotland: the marriage ploy

When he abandoned his own Crusade in 1272 the Lord Edward set off on a leisurely return to England, stopping in Rome to see his former companion–in–arms Pope Gregory and to participate in a hair–raisingly risky all–in chivalric tournament in Châlons – even though he had already become King. Once King, whatever he might promise Popes about Crusades – or anything else – his preoccupations were to be entirely at home: first with Wales, which he conquered in a series of brutal campaigns between 1277 and 1284; then with his French possessions in Gascony between 1286 and 1289; and finally with Scotland, which he first tried to obtain by marriage and then, for the rest of his days, by war.

Though there was one curious and picturesque interlude in this relentless pursuit of power: in 1278, as it was getting under way, the hard–headed Edward had the presumed bodies of King Arthur and Queen Guinevere exhumed and reburied more splendidly in the Abbey of Glastonbury, where Joseph of Arimathea was said to have buried the Holy Grail, and where he, St Helena the mother of Constantine the Great, St Patrick of Ireland and St David of Wales, among numerous others, were said to have been laid to rest. Rusticello, if he was listening, must have been tickled pink.

As fas as Scotland was concerned, the marriage Edward had in mind was his own son's. The pharaonically–descended King Alexander III died in 1286, leaving as his direct descendant only his three year old grand–daughter Margaret Maid of Norway, the child of his daughter and King Erik II of Norway. Edward, seeing his chance, paid one shilling and five pence for prayers for Alexander's soul, and proposed to Erik the betrothal of the little Queen of Scotland to his own two year old son and heir, who later went on to become Christopher Marlowe's unsuitable King Edward II.

In 1290, as Acre was entering its last year as a Christian city, Margaret set sail for England and little Edward, and the union, under their eventual heir, of the two kingdoms. But this would turn out to take another three hundred and thirteen years: by the time the ship had reached the Orkneys the little girl had succumbed to the rigours of North Sea travel. It was the end of the House of Dunkeld, which had united Scotland over the course of two and a half centuries. But it had not united the Scots.

The Jews of England

1290 can not be let go without taking note of another act done by Edward the Crusader in the name of Christian piety – and possibly to raise money against military contingencies that might already have been forming in his head. It was the year he expelled the entire Jewish community from England, not the first and certainly not the last European ruler to attempt a "final solution" of "the Jewish problem".

When the first Jews had arrived in Britain is not known: probably under the Romans; they were certainly there prominently following the Norman Conquest. As elsewhere in Europe, they were associated with commerce and money–lending, and subjected to the financial resentment of avidly indebted kings and nobility, the casuistic theological hostility of the Church, and the murderous ignorant bigotry of the people – largely because of the Christian invention of child–murder stories.

All three factors contributed to Edward's decision, but why he chose such a drastic course as the complete expulsion of the entire Jewish community – by then shrunk to about two thousand five hundred people, half its earlier size – is not clear. Only about eighteen families controlled most of the wealth, an easy enough target, one would have thought, for one so adept as Edward at squeezing what he wanted out of his subjects – or others, as the Scots found. Some historians have suggested that it was indeed precisely Edward's success in having squeezed the wealthy Jews that led to their expulsion: there was nothing more to extract from them, and their place as his financiers was already being taken by the new Florentine international bankers. He certainly did not raise much from their final expropriation: about £9,000, it was recorded, not even double the claim by the monks of Sweetheart Abbey for the damage Edward and his troops did there ten years later.

The rest of the Jewish community appears to have lived in abject poverty, perhaps – as in other places and other times – seen as a threat by others who were battling for crusts at the same economic level. The mob, with prejudices fanned by the Church, periodically burst out with murderous pogroms; in the disordered state of the kingdom during Henry III's troubles with the barons, the Jews were all but eliminated in London, Canterbury, Northampton, Winchester, Worcester, Lincoln and Cambridge. But the mob's views seem hardly likely to have influenced Edward unless he had wished them to. It was said that his mother, the unpopular Eleanor of Provence, Queen of Henry III, was the decisive influence; the sources of her apparently virulent antisemitism are unrecorded, but Christian piety seems, as so often, to have been the motive. Paul Johnson notes there are grounds for the suspicion that the Franciscans, who had been behind a royal decree preventing Jews from buying urban land, "may have been an element in securing their expulsion".

Whatever Edward's own motives, he was not inventing a policy: expulsion had been tried as a "solution" to "the Jewish problem" in the Rhineland in 1012, in France in 1182 and again in 1254 – on this occasion by the future St Louis, between Crusades against the Moslems, who ordered that the layman,

> "when he hears any [Jew] speak ill of the Christian faith, should defend it not with words but with the sword, which he should thrust into the other's belly as far as it will go"

– and in Upper Bavaria in 1276.

After Edward's expulsion of Jews from Gascony in 1289 and from England in 1290, Philip IV expelled them from Normandy in 1296 and from the whole of France, yet again, in 1306, though this time more thoroughly. Many moved to Spain, where Jewish intellectuals played an important role in the royal administration and the universities, until there, too, Christianity finally caught up with them in the form of the brutalities of the Inquisition and their final expulsion in 1492, just as the Moors were finally expelled from the Iberian peninsula and Columbus discovered the New World.

Many began the drift eastwards across Europe to new lands on the borders of Lithuania–Poland and Russia, where in due course Catherine the Great would sequester them in the Polish–Ukrainian Pale. Nineteenth century policies of "Russianisation" institutionalised the pogrom and drove survivors out; until, to stem the rising radical discontent with the moribund autocracy, the Tsar's new Minister of the Interior in 1902 proposed the solution of "drowning the revolution in Jewish blood". From this it was not long – or far – to Germans providing the Final Solution for almost all Europe's Jews who were left.

In England Edward I's measure stood for three and a half centuries, until Oliver Cromwell allowed the return of Jews in 1655. The distinguished English historian George Macaulay Trevelyan sought to make the best of it in his 1926 *History of England*:

"When the Jews returned to England in the Stuart and Hanoverian era, they found the English in control of their own money–market and of the other intellectual professions. And by that time the new Bible–reading culture of the English had diminished the religious hatred against the Chosen People. For these reasons the relation of the Jews to the English was renewed under happier auspices than even now prevail in lands where the natives have not had the wit or the opportunity to contract the habit of managing their own affairs".

The Great Cause
With the death of the unmarried Margaret of Norway the throne of Scotland was vacant. There were soon thirteen candidates, and for some unfathomable reason the Scots decided to appeal to Edward to resolve the succession. True, when Queen Margaret was to marry the little Prince Edward, the King had undertaken by treaty that Scotland should be "separate and divided from England according to its rightful boundaries, free in itself and without subjection"; but the voracious appetite he had already demonstrated in swallowing Wales might have given the Scots pause. However it did not, and so began what was called the Great Cause, and after that the Scottish Wars of Independence that would pit the Scots, under John Balliol, William Wallace, Robert the Bruce and John's son Edward Balliol against three successive Edwards of England and, from time to time, one another.

"Separate and divided...free in itself and without subjection" Scotland might, for the moment, be, but all thirteen candidates had to recognise Edward I as their feudal superior before the adjudication of the Great Cause would even begin. This was a bitter pill, but with the Scots hopelessly divided, as so often, amongst themselves, it had to be swallowed. It was then followed, after a year's manoeuvring, by the deliberations of no fewer than one hundred and four "auditors", all distinguished and learned persons of Scotland and England, forty chosen by each of the two main candidates, twenty–four appointed by Edward. And there were as well consultations with clerical jurisprudents in various continental European universities.

The only two serious candidates were both, ironically, from the Anglo–Scots baronage established in the border regions following the Norman Conquest: Old John and Devorguilla's surviving son, young John Balliol; and Robert Bruce, grandfather of the man known in the history books as Robert the Bruce, whose family name, like the Balliols', came from their place of origin in France, Brix, in the Cotentin of William the Conqueror's Normandy. Three others were also descended in varying degrees of (greater) distance from the Scottish royal family; while seven were illegitimate offspring of various parts thereof; and the thirteenth was an unrealistic ambit bid by the child–Queen's father, Eric II of Norway.

Of the two main candidates, young John Balliol's claim was slightly the better, being through the eldest daughter of David Earl of Huntingdon, brother of King Malcom IV and King William the Lion, who had adopted the lion rampant as Scotland's coat of arms – for heraldic rather than heroic reasons. Robert Bruce's claim was through a younger daughter, but one generation less distant from the throne. However it seems hard to believe that anyone could have expected an outcome based on anything other than King Edward's calculation of England's interest. Presumably the candidates saw it that way too; so they must surely have made suitable promises to their feudal overlord, notwithstanding the efforts of their future apologists to portray them as nothing but patriots born and bred.

King John Balliol's short and unhappy reign

On 17 November 1292 Edward announced his – and the auditors', naturally – choice of John Balliol: "saving our right and that of our heirs when we shall wish to speak thereupon", another ominous note. But John had not been bred to this at all. He was already about twenty in 1271 when his brothers went off with Edward on Crusade, three years after the death of their father, suggesting that his mother Devorguilla put her foot down about her baby's going to war. There are in fact suggestions in the chronicles that young John had a scholarly education, undoubtedly the only son to do so; and as he was the youngest brother, he was probably intended for the Church. He had only had to take on family responsibilities when his second oldest brother Alexander died in 1278; but this apparently meant little in the way of practical experience, no doubt because his mother, who would live for another twelve years still, almost to the beginning of the Great Cause, was clearly a formidable business manager in her own right. At all events, the new King John was rapidly to demonstrate that he had not been trained in either politics or war.

But, in the light of subsequent events in Scotland, three other factors that were to bedevil the Scottish cause also came into play. While Devorguilla's saintly reputation undoubtedly stood John in good stead, he still suffered, particularly among the ordinary Scots, from the disadvantage of being only half a Celt: his father, Old John de Balliol, had been a wholly post–Conquest Englishman, part of the Anglo–Norman establishment. With the Scottish nobles, John's second problem was that, although Devorguilla's mother was the niece of a King of Scotland (whence came his claim to the throne), the Balliols, while very considerable landholders in England, had never been ennobled; and John's standing was therefore held inferior by the persistently narrow–minded and self–interested earls and nobles of Scotland. Third, John was not simply not a leader: more important, he was ultimately not the victor. It was his bitterest opponent, Robert the Bruce, who eventually won, and whose supporters and apologists therefore got to write the history. John thus suffered the same posthumous fate as England's Richard III and Russia's Boris Godunov

The most curious behaviour after the resolution of the Great Cause was, however, Edward's. He immediately made apparent that "though he had submitted to be bound by certain promises, made for a time, and while the throne of Scotland was vacant, now that a king had been appointed, he did not intend to be hampered by those promises for the future". Almost immediately, he treated his own choice as King with contempt: John was summoned to Westminster to answer, like a common felon, to charges involving land claims and even an unpaid wine bill of the long–dead King Alexander. He maintained a shred of dignity by refusing to answer and fleeing secretly back to Scotland, but had undermined his authority with the Scots by having gone to London in the first place.

Edward gave every appearance of goading John Balliol into rebellion as an excuse to invade Scotland, though the terms on which he had appointed John could have led him to control the country without the bloodshed. Edward would clearly not be satisfied simply with the security of England's northern border; nor with the pacification of Scotland, nor even with indirect control over it through King John Balliol. He had decided that Scotland had to be once again an integral part of the kingdom that Brutus, like an early Charlemagne, had so foolishly partitioned, below the fifty–sixth parallel, between his sons.

King John did rebel, in 1295, pushed from behind by some of the Scottish magnates. Edward's demand for troops to fight with him in France was rejected out of hand by the Scottish Parliament; and then the final break was made: the signature of a treaty that year with Edward's enemy, King Philip IV of France. The alliance was to be cemented by the marriage of King John's newly princely son, Edward Balliol, to one of Philip's nieces. Thus began what came to be called the "Auld Alliance". The *Collins Encyclopedia of Scotland* noted how relations between the two countries developed: "The traffic in brides and embassies encouraged a French appreciation of things Scottish, especially soldiers, and a Scottish appreciation of things French, especially claret; a considerable trade in both resulted". The Alliance would bedevil relations between England, Scotland and France for almost five hundred years, until the defeat of Bonnie Prince Charlie's rebellion in 1745.

Edward forgot his French war and reacted to the treaty, promptly invading Scotland from northeast England. He besieged Berwick, the first town in Scotland across the Tweed, and, after leading the successful attack in person and allowing the castle garrison honourable surrender terms, ordered the execution of all the remaining ordinary townsmen, eight thousand of them, some said eleven. Edward's outrage promptly precipitated equally ferocious Scots retaliation in the west. It is extraordinary how quickly attitudes on both sides became a hatred that would endure for centuries: within a couple of years an Englishman was versifying propaganda, even before the trade in claret had begun,

"For Scottes
Telle I for sottes
And wrecches unwar".

The "ignorant wretches" had already jeered at "Edward Longshanks".

This first campaign was humiliatingly short: within twenty–one weeks Edward had taken Edinburgh and Stirling, the two main cities; at Perth, John submitted and Edward deposed him, outrageously further humiliating him personally by having his tabard, emblazoned with his – and Scotland's – armorial bearings, ripped off him publicly, like some medieval Dreyfus, and sent him to the Tower of London. The Scottish nobles and clergy – including Abbot John of Devorguilla's Sweetheart Abbey – had to render homage to the English King. And, to underline Edward's view of Scotland's place in his scheme of things, he had the sacred Stone of Scone, on which the head of the dying St Columba, the founder of Iona, had rested, and on which Scottish Kings had been crowned for centuries, removed to Westminster Abbey. There it remained until Prime Minister John Major tried, unsuccessfully, to prevent a Scottish National Party landslide by returning the Stone of Destiny before the British general elections in 1997. Causes are not always great.

In his four years as King, John had summoned four Parliaments in Scotland, a respectable frequency, and established new sheriffdoms; and, through his defiance of Edward, he led – even if pushed – the first round of the Scottish Wars of Independence. But he never established himself in Scottish hearts. However, notwithstanding some Bruce versions of history, his status as the crowned King of Scots was to continue to be upheld by one of the greatest Scottish patriots of all time, William Wallace, nowadays likely to be known as "Braveheart"[81] – another of the hearts we encounter in this sketch.

John owed his eventual freedom to Wallace: the latter's intercession in 1299 with Pope Boniface VIII, who the following year was to so sharply reprove Edward's treatment of Scotland, secured John's release from the Tower into Papal custody in France. In 1301 he was released from Papal jurisdiction, a free man, but only as long as he remained in exile. There were rumours of French moves to restore him to his throne, but they seem never to have been anything more than that. And King John Balliol died in obscurity in 1315, still in France, probably back in his ancestral lands at Bailleul–en–Vimeu.

Braveheart
Edward did not enjoy his cruel victory over John for long. Wallace's guerrilla uprising began almost as soon as he had returned to England,

---

81   Enquiries of various learned societies in Scotland failed to elicit the origin of this nickname; and I eventually found it in a book, *Mel Gibson and His Movies*, by Brian Pendroigh (London 1997). It came from an American, Randall Wallace, described as a "professional writer" but no relation of William, who invented it for a film–script he wrote in 1993 which he called "Braveheart", and which was eventually made into the movie starring Gibson. "It was", Randall Wallace was quoted as saying, "about courage and heart".

leaving behind, as he thought, his problems with his French possessions in Gascony, south of Bordeaux, and his French pretensions against Philip IV. But in Scotland Edward's first problem came from the other side of the Scottish imbroglio. Candidate Robert Bruce's son had supported Edward against his father's successful rival John Balliol, an indication of the bitterness amongst the Scots parties; and it is therefore not surprising that he then pressed Edward for the crown after John's rout in 1296. It is said that this second Robert Bruce had been with the Lord Edward on his Crusade; but King Edward now dismissed him with the withering exclamation: "Have we nothing else to do but win kingdoms for you?" Edward never allowed either loyalty or sentiment to interfere with his objectives.

Wallace's story is a great romance, and some is indeed no more than that, recorded from spoken legends and embellished two hundred years later by Henry the Minstrel, better known as Blind Harry (though scholars now doubt that he was): six thousand rhyming couplets which he had committed to memory and said or sung on his wanderings, including, for a time, at the court of King James IV, Mary Stuart's grandfather. But there can be no questioning of the bloody nose Wallace gave Edward at a time when Scotland's fortunes were at one of their lowest ebbs, or of the encouragement his feats gave his countrymen at that time – or, as so often in Scottish history, some of them – and a good many more since.

It has often been noted that Wallace was neither of the great landed baronage nor of the oppressed peasantry, which might be thought to have given him an advantage: he came from the middle, the small landholding gentry, no threat to either the position of the great or the existence of the lowly. What really distinguished him, however, was that he was pure Celt, which set him off from the frequently Anglo–infiltrated noble families but endeared him *prima facie* to the ordinary Scots. He had been born about the time of King Edward's return to England after his accession to the throne in Sicily on his way back from his Crusade. He was thus only in his early twenties when he began his guerrilla activities in the Scottish lowlands in 1297, very soon after John Balliol's defeat. They were extraordinarily successful, in extremely difficult conditions. The region was extensively farmed, so it was perhaps the support of the country people that provided his bands with concealment from the English, rather than the deep forests and mountainous terrain usually associated with guerrilla movements; and there has been speculation that the wandering friars may have supplied him with the intelligence he needed for his daring moves – both to strike and to escape.

And escape he did, time and again, causing the English occupation forces more anger at his elusiveness than damage from his attacks. Though attack he could, and did: with thirty men he overran Lanark, halfway between Glasgow and Edinburgh but further south, and killed the English sheriff. Blind Harry said the English retaliated by burning his house and killing his wife, and this is still part of the Braveheart legend; but dreary modern historians say he did not have a home or a wife. One wonders if the legend was around during his lifetime, passed from mouth to mouth amongst the ordinary people to help them explain to themselves this elusive, political warrior, with his towering zeal to fight the English.

Soon enough, with success, some of the great nobles came to fight with him. But that was all – in the fragmented society of Scotland the leading nobles, each being in absolute power over his own men, would not accept a single command: they would fight *with* Wallace – as and when *they* so chose – but not *for* him. Edward, indulging in a campaign against the French in Flanders in a prelude to the Hundred Years War, demanded that his commanders carry more decisively into Scotland the fight against this man whom he had come to call "the King's enemy". The Scottish lords rapidly went down to defeat before this repeat invasion because they could not agree on the order of precedence in which they should go into battle.

But young Wallace pressed on with his guerrilla campaign, and, in one episode, chased Anthony Bek, Bishop of Durham, out of Glasgow and back across the border. There was a nice symbolism in this: Bek, a successor of Old John of Balliol's nemesis, had considerable standing in England as Bishop of the County–Palatine of Durham, an historical leftover giving him a jurisdiction elsewhere enjoyed by the sovereign alone; he had been instrumental in the marriage negotiations with Norway; and as Edward's man he had enthroned John Balliol as Edward's King of Scotland at Scone. But, on John's rebellion, fall and exile, Bek had also obtained John's great estates in the north of England, including the family seat of Barnard Castle. Wallace's little escapade looks very much like a payback.

Edward's cross–channel distractions resulted in a very desultory follow–up to his forces' initial rout of the Scottish nobles, and in this interval Wallace gathered together an army of commoners, perhaps forty thousand, and almost two hundred mounted troops; and, with no previous military experience other than his hit and run raids, opposed a new English army at the river bridge to Stirling Castle, north of Glasgow, in September 1297. The English commander, John de Warenne, Earl of Surrey, by bizarre coincidence of the family inter–relationships of the time, the uncle of John Balliol's wife, did not have the heart for battle, perhaps because of this connexion, and sent peace emissaries to Wallace. "Carry back this answer", Wallace said: "We have not come for peace but to fight to liberate our country". And de Warenne was egged on to fight by the Treasurer of England, Hugh de Cressingham, "handsome but too fat" as a chronicler described him, distrusted by the English and hated by the Scots. Wallace's tactics worked brilliantly: the English were slaughtered, five thousand in as many minutes, as they tried to cross the bridge to attack the Scots. The rest of the invaders fled. Not Cressingham: his body was found after the battle and the angry Scots skinned it. It was later said that Wallace wore a belt made from the skin of Treasurer Cressingham. It would have been a popular symbol.

Wallace followed up this stunning victory as decisively as he had managed the battle itself. Within a few weeks all of Scotland was swept clear of the English, and raids were pushed across the border to give the English some of their own medicine. Suddenly the Scottish nobles were in on the chase, even James the Steward of Scotland, whose family was to become the ruling House of Stuart in two generations' time, who had been dealing with de Warenne right up to Stirling Bridge. The chronicles are again incomplete, but following his great victory Wallace was made – or declared himself? – Guardian of the Kingdom. The title is instructive: as noted earlier, throughout his war of independence against the English, Wallace made clear that he was fighting for his legitimate king, John Balliol. This undoubtedly cost him the support of those opposed to the exiled king; but this was only part of the problem: as another chronicler said, Wallace himself continued in any case to be "deemed base–born by the earls and the nobles".

Edward hammers the Scots
In 1298 Edward, now sixty, began his second invasion of Scotland, and, once again, soon defeated the Scottish army, at Falkirk, just to the south of Stirling Bridge. Scotland was again under English rule. That it was not yet entirely under English control is evident from the fact that Edward was back there again two years later, and at Sweetheart Abbey late in 1300 on his third pacification, manifesting his superiority over the Balliols and receiving the chastisement of Pope Boniface for his continued

efforts to subdue the Scots. That there was still support abroad for the Balliols, even though it was now four years since King John's defeat and deposition, is suggested by the fact that Edward had spent the campaign season that year on a sweep through Galloway, Devorguilla's province, which John had of course inherited, rather than in the areas of Ayr and Lothian where Wallace had been active much more recently.

What was left of Wallace's short life had some curious parallels with what John Balliol was just then experiencing. Details are few, but it is known that Wallace was in France in 1300, appealing to Philip IV for support under the Franco–Scottish mutual security treaty of 1295. Did he meet John Balliol there? Was this the source of those rumours of French interest in restoring John to his throne? Was John himself interested? – it does not seem to have been rumoured that John sought to return to his kingdom during the nine months while Wallace was its Guardian. There was a curious political ballet at this point: Philip initially imprisoned Wallace and offered to hand him over to Edward; Edward thanked him but asked him to hang on to Wallace; then Philip changed his mind and let Wallace go free. Food for rumours certainly, especially as, on Wallace's return to Scotland in 1303, Edward ordered his immediate elimination: Costain notes that "the records mention many instances of grants paid to cover the cost of raids undertaken for the sole purpose of his capture". Why hadn't Edward taken Wallace when Philip offered him? What was Philip's price, that it was too great or too difficult for Edward to pay?

It is the more intriguing because by then Edward had the brother–in–law of his enemy Philip. In 1299 a truce had been patched up between the two, and, as part of the bargain, Edward thought he was getting the beautiful Blanche, the elder of Philip's two sisters, in return for handing over Gascony. It seems an extraordinary price for such an acquisitive Plantagenet to pay for a second wife when he already had an heir: could he have been thinking of siring an alternative to the young Prince Edward, already extravagantly involved with a young man called Piers Gaveston? As it turned out, an extremely stubborn Blanche would have none of an old king: she had determined to wed the heir to the Holy Roman Emperor, to become a young empress (though, in the event, she became neither queen nor empress). An apparently genuinely embarrassed Philip then offered his younger sister Marguerite as a replacement, but it took the forceful intervention of Pope Boniface to persuade Edward to accept second best, and Philip had to give Gascony back. It turned into a love match, on both sides; and after the king's death in 1307, far away, in sight of Scotland, Marguerite wrote that "When Edward died, all men died for me".

Ten thousand Scots had been killed at Falkirk, which contributed to the difficulties the English continued to experience in trying to establish direct rule over Scotland during the ensuing six or seven years. Resistance, after Wallace's defeat, might be down, but resentment was up; the nobles who had been too proud to fight under him now vilified him for having failed, but his personal nobility had engraved itself in the hearts and minds of the people. He kept the passion of resistance alive until it was picked up by the unlikely next leader, Robert the Bruce, at this time still a supporter of the English.

Edward's measures to control Scotland seem very different from those he had used to dominate Wales twenty years earlier. In Scotland a cash-strapped Edward built not one castle: as if in unavoidable affirmation of its separateness, English military governors had to rule the resentful land from captured Scottish castles. In Wales, however, Edward had reorganised the government by incorporating it into England, and above all had built a series of nine virtually impregnable castles, not only as absolutely safe havens for the English garrisons, but also as demonstrations to the natives of the permanence of English domination.

There is an interesting footnote: it has been observed that one of the greatest of Edward's Welsh castles, Caernarvon, built in 1283–84 on the site of a Norman fortress, bears a striking resemblance to the walls of Constantinople, with its striped bands of brick and stone and its polygonal towers at intervals around the outer perimeter. There was an old legend that Caernarvon was the birthplace of the Emperor Constantine (in fact, it was present–day Niš, in southern Serbia not far from Bulgaria), and, sure enough, not long after construction began, the builders found the body of Constantine's father, called Magnus Maximus (in fact, he was Constantius Chlorus, a brilliant and successful Roman general), which Edward had re–buried in the castle's new chapel with appropriate ceremony. There is of course an echo here of Edward the Romantic's 1278 re–interment of the presumed King Arthur and Queen Guinivere at Glastonbury. Can we hear Rusticello again, just before he is captured by the Genoans: "Emperors and kings, dukes and marquises, counts, knights, and townsfolk..."?

After his return to Scotland from France, Wallace continued his elusiveness rather than his guerrilla war, but sooner or later it was bound to happen: in 1305 he was betrayed to the English by fellow Scots. He was taken immediately to London, the next day to the travesty of a trial in Westminster Hall, was not allowed to speak in his own defence, and was of course found guilty, and then hanged, drawn and quartered within an hour of sentence. Four parts of his body were sent for public display throughout the two kingdoms: the right arm to Newcastle, the left to Berwick, the left leg to Stirling , the right to Perth. It was uncharacteristically restrained of Edward not to send the head on a tour of Scotland; it was stuck instead on a spear on London Bridge.[82] It was usual in this form of execution to burn both the remainder of the body and the gallows used for the hanging; so the brave heart became ashes somewhere in a rejoicing London.

Robert the Turncoat

At long last it was the turn of the Bruces, grandfather having been passed over in the Great Cause, and father knocked back by a king with other things to do than find him a kingdom. Young Robert the third Bruce had certainly not given up trying: by the time of Wallace's execution, he had changed sides between the Scots and the English no fewer than five times. It was fortunate for the Scots that, at this particular time, he was back on theirs, for he turned out to be a particularly successful leader. But notwithstanding the heroic stature he subsequently achieved, the youngest Bruce does not come down the ages as a man of valour and integrity like Wallace. There is his obvious opportunism up to his final "conversion" in 1306; even then, one gets the feeling he opposed Edward I as much out of spiteful resentment as for any other reason; and, at the end, he still seemed as much interested in his own right to the throne as in English recognition of Scotland's independence.

Robert the Bruce was precipitately converted to the Scottish nationalist cause early in 1306 when he murdered the man he hated as his chief rival. With John Balliol's son in exile in France, this was John's nephew, Comyn the Red of Badenoch; and the murder took place in the Franciscan Priory that Devorguilla had endowed at Dumfries. Why Comyn met him there was never discovered, nor whether the murder was planned or in hot blood. At all events, with Wallace and the leader

---

82   Such a custom lasted a long time; writing of the Turkish occupation of Bosnia, Ivo Andric' said about the bridge in his *Bridge Over the Drina*: "there too, right up to 1878 [when Austria took over from the Turks], hung or were exposed on stakes the heads of all those who for whatever reason had been executed, and executions in that frontier town, especially in years of unrest, were frequent and in some years...almost of daily occurrence".

of the Balliol claim both dead, Bruce's way was now clear to assert his claim to the throne, in succession to those of his grandfather and father.

It was a measure as much of Bruce's higher social standing as of rage against the English occupation that saw him immediately joined by an imposing array of clerics and nobles, including some for whom at Falkirk Scotland had been less important than their own social superiority to Wallace. Within two months Bruce was crowned at Scone, and the Scottish standard of rebellion against England was raised for the third time in ten years.

Edward was taken by surprise: after six years of what he had been assured by his intelligence experts was an increasingly pacified Scotland, he could see light at the end of the tunnel. In fact he was in the process of establishing an English–style administrative machinery, to replace the military governors, when news of this new rebel offensive reached him. Already ailing, Edward appointed his feckless son to lead an army against Bruce; but the latter recklessly threw his small army against an advance English force and was beaten so badly that he had to flee to the western isles. Prince Edward pushed ahead ruthlessly: every one of the Scots who came into English hands was executed on his orders, some brutally and after hideous torture; one, the feisty Countess of Buchan, was imprisoned in an open cage in an exposed turret of Berwick Castle, where she was kept for four years. But within the year Scotland was again in turmoil, and again led by Robert the Bruce, still on the side of the independence movement.

When the next English vanguard lost a skirmish, the declining king decided that he must lead the army himself, on his fourth invasion of Scotland, if he was ever to overcome this upstart "Kynge Hobbe", as he called Robert the Bruce – "hobbe" being a corruption of Robert that had come to mean a rustic, a clown. He misjudged the man Bruce had become, and he missed his personal appointment with him: carried northward in a horse–litter when he could no longer ride, Edward rapidly faded, and died in 1307 on Solway Firth, in sight of Scotland on the far shore, forever beyond his grasp. He had two last commands for his son: to carry his dead body at the front of the army so he could lead it to victory over the Scots; and afterwards to have one hundred knights go on Crusade, taking his heart for burial at the church of the Holy Sepulchre in Jerusalem.

Costain cites an inventory made ten days later of the possessions King Edward had had with him for the invasion of Scotland, mostly holy relics: "a purse containing a thorn from the Crown of Christ, a sliver of wood from the Holy Cross, one of the nails from the Cross, a bone from the arm of St Osith [an obscure Anglo–Saxon princess, mother of Charlemagne's contemporary Offa, the first king to call himself *Rex Anglorum*], one from the head of St Lawrence, a fragment of the sponge which was lifted to Christ on the Cross – more than a hundred relics in all". Were they a measure of Edward's devotion? Or of a passion, perhaps dating back to the bazaars of Acre, to collect sacred objects much as he would seek to collect secular kingdoms?

The new King Edward II did not carry out either of his father's wishes. Nor did he do anything further against the Scots: Christopher Marlowe recorded that his interest was elsewhere –

> "My heart is an anvil unto sorrow,
> Which beats upon it like the Cyclops' hammers,
> And with the noise turns up my giddy brain,
> And makes me frantic for my Gaveston".

Young Edward was soon back in London, where his Gaveston awaited him, anxious to

> "...have wanton poets, pleasant wits,
> Musicians, that with touching of a string
> May draw the pliant King which way I please".

The third heart in this story never did get back to Scotland, and no closer to Jerusalem than its resting place in Westminster Abbey.

The Archbishop of Cathay

At this stage, suddenly, sixteen years after he had disappeared into the mysterious and still unknown Orient, there is news of Giovanni da Montecorvino, Pope Nicholas's substitute for King Edward's Crusade. Letters written from Khanbalik arrived in Rome; extraordinarily, two still survive.[83] Although Giovanni was the first Christian missionary ever to get to Peking, he is less famous than the Polos, less well known even than Carpini and Rubruck, because he never returned to the West to recount his adventures; yet in his own way he was as remarkable as any of them.

---

83   They were republished by Christopher Dawson in 1980, translated from Giovanni's Latin, in *Mission to Asia*.

It is clear that the first of the two letters, dated 8 January 1305, in his twelfth year there, was the first report Giovanni had written since his arrival in China, perhaps because previously there had been no traveller who seemed likely to be able to get it back to Rome. Typically, there is no mention of such a courier in the letter itself, but we learn from the second that, at least as far as the Crimea, it was the "Lord Cothay Chaan" – probably meaning Tokhtai (or his representative), Khan of the Golden Horde, who at that time dominated most of Russia including the Crimea (which was to remain Mongol until 1783), and who had married a daughter of the Byzantine Emperor Andronicus II Paleologus. The implication seems to be that Giovanni was unable to use the Mongols' own amazing courier system, but had to wait until there was someone sympathetic to carry his mail.

The second letter, in 1306, may not have been the last; but Giovanni's isolation seems to have discouraged him from correspondence. He was obviously not a wordy person in any case: the letters are tantalisingly brief, and mix the vaguest generality about the context in which he found himself with the minutest detail about his particular likes and dislikes.

His first letter begins with the last, recording his tribulations with the Nestorians,

"who call themselves Christians, but behave in a very unchristian manner";

and he goes on to describe them in all too recognisable terms when he writes that

"they did not allow any Christian of another rite to have any place of worship, however small, nor to preach any doctrine but their own".

But with Giovanni the Nestorians went further:

"both directly and by the bribery of others [they] have brought most grievous persecutions upon me, declaring that I was not sent by the Lord Pope, but that I was a spy, a magician and a deceiver of men..And this intrigue lasted above five years, so that I was often brought to judgment, and in danger of a shameful death. But at last, by God's ordering, the Emperor came to know my innocence...".

And so Giovanni's mission could begin:

> "I have built a church in the city of Khanbalik, where the chief residence of the king is, and this I completed six years ago [in 1299] and I also made a tower and put three bells in it. Moreover I have baptised about 6,000 persons there up to the present, according to my reckoning. And if it had not been for the aforesaid slanders [by the Nestorians] I might have baptised 30,000 more, for I am constantly baptising".

One suspects Giovanni is not above inflating his soul–count a little, to convince his superiors back home of his success in saving Tartar hearts and minds. At the same time he dangles the supreme bait to back up his call for reinforcements:

> "If I had even two or three fellow coadjutors, perhaps the Emperor the Chan might have been baptised. I beg for some brethren to come, if any are willing to do so, so being as they are such as are anxious to offer themselves as an example and not to gain notoriety...I ask the brethren who shall receive this letter that they should do their best to bring its contents to the notice of the Lord Pope and Cardinals and the Procurator of our [Franciscan] Order in the Curia".

Giovanni had already done what most missionaries saw as their first requirement:

> "I have an adequate knowledge of the Tartar language and script... and now I have translated into that language and script the whole of the New Testament and the Psalter and have had it written in beautiful characters".

And there was one aspect of his achievement that obviously afforded him particular satisfaction, for he details it at length – his choirboys:

> "Also I have purchased by degrees forty boys of the sons of the pagans, between seven and eleven years old, who as yet knew no religion. Here I baptised them and taught them Latin and our rite, and I wrote for them about thirty psalters and hymnaries and two breviaries by which eleven boys now know the office...And the

Lord Emperor takes much delight in their singing. And I ring the bells for all the Hours and sing the divine office with a choir of 'sucklings and infants'. But we sing by rote because we have no books with the notes...".

Nevertheless, for all his satisfaction with his achievements, Giovanni cannot resist a note of personal weariness:

"...for twelve years I have not received news of the Roman Curia, and of our Order and of the state of the West...I have already grown old, and my hair is white from labours and tribulations rather than years, for I am fifty–eight years old".

Giovanni's other letter is dated thirteen months after the first, 10 February 1306. This time he sounds less bouncy, and begins with the bitter complaint that

"never until this year have I received letters or good wishes from any Brother or friend, so that it seemed to me that no one remembered me...and now I find from reliable men who have come to the Lord Chaan [Khan] of Cathay with the envoys of the aforesaid Lord Cothay that my letter has reached you".

He had nevertheless soldiered on, and we discover he had *not* been entirely alone:

"...I have begun a new house before the gate of the Lord Chaan, and the distance between his court and our house is only a stone's throw...Master Peter of Lucalongo, a faithful Christian and a great merchant, who was my companion from Tauris [Tabriz, in Persia], bought the land for the house...I received the site at the beginning of August and with the aid of my benefactors and helpers it was completed by the feast of St Francis, with a surrounding wall and buildings and simple offices and a chapel which can hold two hundred people...I assure you it seems a marvel to all who come from the city and elsewhere, when they see the place newly made and a red cross set aloft above it...The Lord Chaan can hear our voices from his chamber, and this is told as a wonder far and wide among the nations, and will count for much according to the disposition and fulfilment of God's mercy";

and he adds:

> "And I have divided the boys and placed some in the first church and some in the second and they sing office by themselves. But I celebrate Mass in each in alternate weeks as the chaplain, for the boys are not priests".

He has also continued his proselytising:

> "I have had six pictures made of the Old and the New Testaments for the instruction of the ignorant, and they have inscriptions in Latin, Turkish and Persian, so that all tongues may be able to read them".

The implication seems to be that these languages have been added to the "Tartar language", Mongol or Uighur, referred to in the first letter. It is interesting – and was to prove fatal to the long term success of the mission – that there was no Chinese.

Giovanni is still trying to convey the extent of his success while at the same time tempt Rome into reinforcing his mission:

> "…I have a place in [the Khan's] court and the right of access to it as legate of the Lord Pope, and he honours me above the other prelates, whatever their titles. And although the Lord Chaan has heard much of the Roman Curia and the state of the Latins, yet he greatly desires to see envoys come from those parts. In this country there are many sects of idolators who have different beliefs, and there are many kinds of monks with different habits, and they are much more austere and strict in their observance than are the Latin religious".

It is amusing to see Giovanni marshalling arguments that, allowing for the difference of context, might still be used today by an ambassador in foreign parts to persuade his government to send a Ministerial trade mission to counter the more vigorous efforts of the competitors.

And as is often still the case, Giovanni got a cheaper alternative. When his message finally got through to the Vatican, in 1307, Pope Clement V, the French puppet who moved the Papacy to Avignon and supported the French King's ruthless suppression of the Crusader Knights Templar, issued a Bull in return:

"Taking...into very careful consideration your conspicuous diligence in this holy work, we choose you...to be Archbishop in the great and honourable city of Khanbalig, in the realm of the magnificent prince the great king of the Tartars...committing to you the full charge of all the souls"

– then numbering somewhere around sixty million.

To help Giovanni cover this parish Clement also sent – at long last, the new Archbishop must have felt – seven bishops, though only three reached Peking. By 1318, when we hear from one of them, Peregrine of Castello, one of these is dead, but the survivors have been joined by four friars, at least; Archbishop Giovanni is still alive, and Bishop Peregrine tells us "his outward life is good and hard and difficult". We hear of him once more, in 1326: he is still going! – but the reference is only in passing, in a letter from the last of the three original bishops, the self-centred and self-satisfied Andrew of Perugia. In fact Giovanni lived another two years, dying at eighty–one, still in Peking, in the thirty-seventh year of his mission to Cathay.

The main mission he had set himself, the conversion of the Great Khan, from which all else would follow, was not achieved. Already in his first letter, he announced crisply that, on his arrival

"I summoned the Emperor himself to receive the Catholic faith with the letters of the Lord Pope, but he was too far gone in idolatry".

Despite being a lone figure in that vast and complex social and religious landscape, here was the essence of the supremely self–confident imperialism that would in due course follow the Cross all over the world. There is nothing however in Giovanni's letters that even faintly suggests he went the further mile that was to mark later imperialism of asserting the racial superiority of the Christians over the lesser breeds without the Law.

It is remarkable, in fact, that neither of Giovanni da Montecorvino's letters – nor, for that matter, the later ones from Peregrine and Andrew – says anything about Yuan China itself, the Mongol overlords, the masses of the Chinese people. All Giovanni said in his first letter was

"Now from what I have seen and heard, I believe that there is no king or prince in the world who can equal the Lord Chan in the extent of his land, and the greatness of the population and wealth".

He added nothing in the second. Peregrine said

"If I were to write an account of the state of this mighty empire – the greatness of its power, the size of its armies, the extent of its territory, the amount of its revenue and its expenditure of charitable relief – it would not be believed";

and Andrew, perhaps too idle to say anything original, virtually repeated Peregrine's remarks – it looks as though he had a copy.

Were they all just overwhelmed by it all? Carpini and Rubruck had not been, even if they did only get to the Great Khan's headquarters in the vast empty spaces of the Mongolian steppe; and Marco Polo was so notorious for his tales of the prodigious wonders of Cathay (whether he had been there in person or not) that he was already known as *Il Milione*, "Marco Millions". It is hard to avoid the conclusion that Giovanni da Montecorvino and his little band of Franciscans were really not very interested in Cathay. It may have been because of the intense focus of their devotion to the propagation of their faith in a very small compass; it may have been a lack of imagination; but they would not have been the last for whom it may have been a veiled, even unconscious, contempt. In later times much Christian missionary effort in China (and elsewhere, for that matter) became inextricably bound up with – it might be said compromised by – European military and economic imperialism; but it is rather hard to see the lone expedition of Giovanni da Montecorvino in those terms.

How soon the Peking mission would disappear, Giovanni would have been devastated to learn. Within the next few decades the crumbling Yuan Dynasty finally collapsed, and in 1368, exactly forty years after his death, the Chinese Ming began their three centuries of power. The Franciscan mission did not outlive the change, suggesting that the converts, bought and otherwise, had themselves – as indicated by the language clue – all been foreigners, presumably mostly the ruling Mongols, now chased out by the new rulers. And Giovanni's extraordinary little group of people, forerunners of the largest religious missionary efforts ever undertaken, or likely to be, was forgotten. When the great Jesuit missionary Matteo Ricci arrived in Peking in 1600, in the last decades of the Ming Dynasty, there was no memory whatever, either in Rome or in Peking, that he had had any predecessors in the Chinese capital. The effort to convert China began all over again, with the same extravagant hopes that had marked Pope Nicholas's decision and Pope Clement's Bull.

The last Balliol and the last Bruce

There was a dismal symmetry in the lives of the last Balliol and the last Bruce. With the victor writing – or rewriting – the history, there appeared the seamless progression of Robert the Bruce's spiderweb, an heroic success here, a judicious conciliation there, inexorably, inevitably, leading to his triumphant securing of Scotland's independence. Certainly, after his previous zigzags in and out of Edward's camp, the going was now easier:

> "I am more afraid", Bruce said, "of the bones of the father dead, than of the living son; it was more difficult to get half a foot of land from the old king than a whole kingdom from the son".

Nevertheless it still took time to overcome not only English opponents but also Scottish rivals; cross–border raids, which laid waste the whole region, continued for the rest of his twenty–year reign, notwithstanding his stunning victory against a considerably superior English army in 1314 at Bannockburn, near Stirling, by then the last Scottish castle in English hands.

At least his domestic rivals were now overcome, and a united Scotland stood behind the famously eloquent *Declaration of Arbroath* in which, in 1320, Bruce's Chancellor Bernard de Linton appealed to Pope John XXII:

> "For so long as a hundred of us remain alive, we will never in any way be bowed beneath the yoke of English domination; for it is not for glory, riches or honour that we fight, but for freedom alone, that which no man of worth yields up, save with his life".

But although the incompetent Edward II had abandoned his father's Scottish ambitions, it was not until 1328, after he had been imprisoned and murdered by his outraged Queen and her ambitious lover, that the sixteen year old Edward III signed the Treaty of Northampton recognising Scotland as "free, quit and entire, without any kind of feudal subjection". And even with the Papacy at Avignon in the "Babylonian captivity" of France, Scotland's ally, it was only now that Pope John finally lifted the sentence of excommunication that had been placed on Bruce after Comyn the Red's murder in 1306; and only the following year that the Pope recognised Bruce's own sovereignty and the independence of Scotland. But by then King Robert was dead.

It is interesting that he echoed one of King Edward I's last wishes, whether unconsciously, because it was in the air in those times, or deliberately, to show he was of equal measure: he commanded that his heart be carried by Scottish Crusaders for burial in the Church of the Holy Sepulchre in Jerusalem. This fourth of our hearts got further than King Edward's, but on the way to the Holy Land its bearers stopped in Spain, and joined a new crusade just being launched against the Moors; and James Douglas, with the heart around his neck in a silver casket, was ambushed and killed. But somehow, the chroniclers said, the heart was rescued, taken back to Scotland, and buried in Melrose Abbey. There, excavations in the 1920s uncovered "a mummified heart enclosed in a cone–shaped container of lead". However by then the cult of relics had passed – except, paradoxically, in the Soviet Union: at this very time, as the Bolsheviks broke open the reliquaries of the saints to show they contained only ordinary bones, word spread that God had deliberately turned the holy relics into old bones so they would not fall into the hands of the godless Communists.[84]

The new King Edward soon picked up where his grandfather had left off: the "perpetual peace" of 1328 only lasted four years. While it is unclear whose idea it was, the third Edward was soon supporting – and manipulating – the claim to the Scottish throne of Edward Balliol, King John's son, returned from exile. In 1332 he was crowned at Scone, but lost all credibility by having to swear fealty to the English king. Less than three months later he also lost a small skirmish, and fled back to England, on an unsaddled horse it was said, to underline the ignominy; and there he stayed, Edward III's pensioner until he died, childless, in 1364. So ended the Balliol family – though not, thanks to his grandparents, the family name.

Robert the Bruce had been succeeded by his five year old son David I, already married for a year to Edward III's little sister Joan of the

---

84   Related by Serge Schmemann in *Echoes of a Native Land* (London, 1997)

Tower, to seal the Treaty of Northampton. His career turned out as sorry as Edward Balliol's, and curiously parallel. After the latter's victory David fled to the refuge of Château Gaillard, the great fortress built in one year by Richard the Lionheart, where King John Balliol had been held for a time; he returned to Scotland in 1341, long after Edward Balliol had been chased back to England, but was himself captured by Edward III five years later when he imprudently tried to invade England; and he spent the next eleven years as the latter's prisoner in the Tower of London, where his wife had been born. His nephew Robert the Steward made no attempt to ransom him, perhaps because he was also David's heir: these Bruces never seemed to differentiate between the interests of the state and their personal ambition.

But after Edward III had captured the King of France in his great victory at Poitiers in 1356, and had had King Edward Balliol renounce the Scottish crown in his own favour, the Scots realised they were alone and must sue for peace; and to secure it King David Bruce, like King Edward Balliol before him, had to swear fealty to the English King. By then the Black Death had devastated both countries, and the Scots suffered in addition from the huge ransom Edward III required for David's release, which was still being paid twenty years later, long after his death, childless, like King Edward Balliol. With his successor Robert the Steward came the Stuart dynasty that would reign in Scotland until it peacefully took over the English throne as well, when Elizabeth I died, childless, in 1603.

The last part of Scotland to be in English hands, Berwick, which had been so brutally bloodied right at the beginning of Edward I's first invasion, was recaptured in 1461, but lost again, permanently, in 1482. And that was all the English gained from a hundred and eighty–six years of imperialist ambition against what the *Declaration of Arbroath* called

> "us Scots dwelling in this little Scotland, beyond which there is no human abode, and desiring nothing but our own"

– Berwick, and a Scottish nationalism that now has to be negotiated through the ballot box.

Devorguilla and her "sweet silent companion"

The death of the last Balliol brings us back to that of the first in this chapter, and to the first of the hearts we have encountered. It appears in the story of Devorguilla as told in the metrical *Orygynale Cronykil of*

Scotland, written a hundred and twenty years after her death by Andrew of Wyntoun[85]:

> When the Balliol that was her Lord,
> Who married her, as they record,
> Had sent his soul to his Creator,
> Before he was laid in sepulchre
> His body she had opened quickly
> And had his heart removed completely.
>
> And that same heart, as men said,
> She embalmed and had it laid
> Inside a coffer of ivory
> Which she had had made purposely,
> Enamellèd and perfectly wrought,
> Locked, and bound with silver bright,
> With spices having all good scents
> Coming all from well-known plants.
>
> And always when she went to meat
> That coffer she had by her seat
> Just as if her Lord were present,
> And to it she was reverent.
>
> And there she had set every day,
> As before was her Lord's way,
> All his courses, covered well
> In purest silver-made vessel,
> Brought from the kitchen and there set;
> And when she made her rise from meat,
> All those courses she had then
> Taken and given among poor men,
> All those courses, great and good,
> She had them given for their life's food.
>
> And this thing she never ceased to see
> While living in this world was she.

---

85   I have taken the text from those in Wentworth Huyshe's *Devorgilla, Lady of Galloway* and John Jones's *Balliol College*, but have rewritten it somewhat freely in modernish language – in the interests of understanding, but at the expense, I fear, of its orygynall charm.

Thus she lived with her "sweet silent companion", and honoured his memory with charity to the poor. But Catholic belief also required the saying of prayers for the souls of the dear departed, and on 10 April 1273 Devorguilla signed a charter establishing a new Cistercian Abbey near the River Nith, downstream from Dumfries close to the Solway Firth, on whose other shore Edward I of England, creator and destroyer of Devorguilla's son King John, would die thirty-four years and many battles later. The isolated site was perfect for the ascetic Cistercian rule, founded in France early in the twelfth century by St Bernard of Clairvaux: it was on broad fertile ground, to provide work and food for the monks; near water, for the transport of building materials, for drinking, crops, sheep and fishponds, and for powering cornmills; and, above all, secluded from the world, for the obligation and consolation of contemplation. Thus Andrew of Wyntoun again:

> She founded then in Galloway
> Of Cistew's Order one Abbay.
> *Dulce Cor* she had them all –
> That is, Sweet Heart – that Abbay call.
> And now the men of Galloway
> Call that place the New Abbay.

– the Old Abbey being its mother–house of Dundrennan, further west in Galloway near Kirkcudbright, where Mary Queen of Scots spent her last night on Scotland's soil before making the fatally ill–advised move of seeking the protection of Elizabeth of England.

It was logical that Devorguilla should have decided on a Cistercian house: many of the greatest abbeys of England were Cistercian – Fountains, Tintern, Rievaulx; and, most important, it was David I, King of Scots, grandfather of Devorguilla's grandfather David Earl of Huntingdon, who had first invited the Cistercians of Rievaulx into his kingdom, still in St Bernard's lifetime, and (in the words of Huyshe) "gave them the lovely glen on the south side of the Tweed [well above Berwick] wherein to build Melrose", in the heart of what became Sir Walter Scott country. As it turned out, Devorguilla's would be the last Cistercian foundation in Scotland. The Cistercian abbeys are now all ruins, victims of the Reformation, the Scottish abbeys victims previously of the cross–border raids of the English. Already in 1300 "the poor monks, the Abbot and Convent of Our Lady of Sweet Heart" were petitioning Edward I for £5,000 for damage to their property burned and destroyed during the wars – certainly an ambit claim, for this was a huge amount, enough to recruit six thousand foot–soldiers, about the size (not including the cavalry) of Robert the Bruce's whole army at Bannockburn.

The ruins of Sweetheart Abbey make a striking impression, especially after the great grey sandstone remains of the northern Abbeys at Fountains and Rievaulx. On a sunny day the bright red sandstone walls stand out sharply against the brilliant green of the carefully manicured grass, extending right down the still–standing but roofless nave, its sturdy but elegant arches marching towards the finely–detailed hollow tracery of the great east window above where the high altar once stood at the end of the choir. And in front of the altar once lay the tomb containing the mortal remains of Devorguilla, holding – but let Andrew of Wyntoun continue:

> She ordained in her will, duly,
> And bade them honour it truly,
> That heart they should then rest
> And lay between her two breasts
> When they should make her sepulchre;
> To her Lord she did this honour.

And so they did, as Devorguilla willed, though she actually died in England – fittingly, on the Feast of St Agnes, patron saint of the betrothed – in her manor house of Kempston, near the nunnery at Elstow, in Bedfordshire, which had been founded by her ancestor Judith Countess of Huntingdon, William the Conqueror's niece, "to salve her conscience", it was said, for engineering her husband's death to marry someone else. Elstow is now better known as the home of John Bunyan; Devorguilla's manor has long gone, and the nunnery likewise, though there are still the remains of the cloister and the fishponds beyond the later Norman village church. Early in the 20th century, Huyse reported, the villagers believed the nunnery precincts were still haunted by a lady in white,

> "Muttering her prayer
> To the midnight air
> And her Mass for the days that are gone".

But whose ghost it was no–one was certain.

Devorguilla's original monument in Sweetheart Abbey was destroyed during the Reformation, along with the cloister and the monastic buildings grouped as always on the southern side of the Abbey church, and further afterwards when the ruins were used as a quarry; but in 1932 fragments of a later tomb were recovered and re–assembled in the south transept. They are there still. What remains of the inscription reads:

VILLA . FUDATRIX . HUI .
MON[ ]ASTII . QUE . OBIIT . S M CCLXXIIII
Devorgilla fundatrix huius monasterii quae obiit 1284
(Devorguilla, foundress of this monastery, who died in 1284)

– which is the wrong date. Devorguilla did not die until 1290, that fateful year in which Margaret the Maid of Norway died at sea on her way back to Scotland, catapulting Devorguilla's son into the line of succession to its crown; in which Edward I cleansed England of its Jews as he considered how to take advantage of the sudden vacancy on the Scottish throne; and when the redoubtable Giovanni da Montecorvino was wending his slow way to a destiny which would have amazed Devorguilla but which she would have understood implicitly. She was in her eighty–first year, an extraordinarily great age for those times.

Devorguilla left a further legacy of £100 to "the Principal and Scholars" of Balliol College. The Principal himself was one of the executors of her estate, but extracting the money from the Balliol family was another matter. It remained unpaid by Devorguilla's heir, young John, even though the College sued him in the King's Chancery. Perhaps he was too busy running for King of Scotland over the next two years; when he won the crown he might have paid up promptly, but he didn't, and almost immediately became entangled in any case in Edward I's vicious web that brought him down four years later. Then he was a prisoner in the Tower of London for the next seven years, and finally in obscure exile in France for his last fourteen. What estates he might still have had there is not known, but funds were undoubtedly short and uncertain, and his mother's legacy to the College was not to be forthcoming. His son, Devorguilla's grandson, Edward Balliol the younger, continued in exile throughout the unhappy reign of King Edward II of England; but as we saw earlier, *his* son, the teenage King Edward III (there are too many Edwards here), who began his fifty–year reign in 1327, began manipulating young Edward Balliol towards a puppet Scottish throne. This scheme did not achieve its soon–to–be–aborted goal until 1332; but it seems that the new King was already suborning and subsidising young Balliol before then, for in 1330 he paid Balliol College his grandmother's £100.

By then the College had received another major endowment, the direct consequence of that other brutal policy of Edward I: the expulsion of the Jews. Oxford had a large Jewish community, with its own synagogue and a ghetto in what is now the very centre, stretching along the west side of St Aldate's from Carfax to Christ Church. Like all Jewish property it became the King's, and he bestowed the synagogue and nine adjacent houses on William Burnel, Archdeacon of Wells, the brother of one of his Ministers. They intended to found a college themselves, but when the brother died the scheme lapsed, and in 1305 William bequeathed the whole property to Balliol College – though what his connexion was is not known. The Crown then tried to seize the property back, arguing that it was not inheritable; but the litigious College, having earlier sued the King of Scotland, now went to court against the King of England – and won, though it took until 1314, nine years, a protracted adjudication even by modern standards. The Burnel bequest was then confirmed, while her son was in the North, by Edward I's widow, the Dowager Queen Margaret, sister of King Philip IV of France, who all those years ago had joined her husband in ignoring Pope Nicholas's and the Ilkhan Arghun's desperate pleas for a new Crusade. Out of the misfortune of England's Jews the Principal and Scholars of Devorguilla's College would continue to be lodged and fed.

Above Devorguilla's epitaph in Sweetheart Abbey lie the remains of her effigy – vigorously carved with no great finesse, the head and feet now missing, the folds in her robe deep stylised slashes. But that is not what seizes the attention: it is the hands, joined together over her breast, gracefully, peacefully, holding between them the effigy of the silver-bound coffer containing her "sweet silent companion", Old John's heart, that was buried with her beneath these vaults all those centuries ago. Her love for that man is palpable in this image, on the green grass, surrounded by the great red roofless arches, in this place, surrounded by the silence of its remoteness:

> A better Lady than she was none
> In all the Isle of Great Britain.
> She was most pleasing in beauty,
> But men should love her for her bounty.

Map of Central Asia from 1562 (Russia, Muscovy and Tartary),
by Anthony Jenkinson showing Samarkand (Shamarcandia).
Author's own map. Photo courtesy Tim MacDonald.

Central Asia

Tamburlaine of Samarkand: The Scourge of Man

The Worldly Hope men set their Hearts upon
Turns Ashes – or it prospers; and anon,
Like Snow upon the Desert's dusty Face
Lighting a little Hour or two – is gone.

Fitzgerald's *Rubaiyat of Omar Khayyam*

Tamburlaine[86] also comes from our time in the Soviet Union, more correctly the Union of Soviet Socialist Republics. There were fifteen of these "republics": Russia itself; the three Baltic states of Latvia, Lithuania and Estonia; the two additional phoney (at that time) United Nations members Byelorussia and Ukraine; isolated Moldavia; the three distinctive and prickly Caucasian republics of Georgia, Armenia and Azerbaijan; and the five Russian-controlled Moslem Central

---

86   We have a problem with orthography: Tamburlaine's name in Mongol was Timur (though some have it as Timour, or Temür, said to be closer to the original Turkic form), but he has been variously known, in English, also as Tamberlane or Tamerlane or Tamerlin or Timur the Lame, all corruptions of Timur–i–Leng, Timur–i lang, Timur Lenk, or (heaven help us) Timur *lenk*, which derive from the abusive epithet applied by his enemies to a man who was larger than life but lame in one leg. The version used here, except where variants occur in citations, is from the most widely–known English language version of the name, the play *Tamburlaine the Great*, written two hundred years afterwards by Christopher Marlowe, Shakespeare's contemporary and possibly occasional co–author. The only full–length biography in English of which I am aware (and on which I have drawn, especially for quotations from otherwise inaccessible sources) uses the same version: *Tamburlaine the Conqueror* by Hilda Hookham. Other names also vary, depending on idiosyncracies of transliteration or authorial preference.

Asian republics of Turkmenistan, Uzbekistan, Tajikistan, Kirghizia and Khazakstan. Ambassadors and official visitors were encouraged to see the benefits that "Soviet power" had brought to these "equal partners" of the overwhelmingly dominant Russian "Federation"; and there was always the marginal hope that a visit might reveal a trade opportunity that was not visible from the centre of the Soviet web in Moscow – even though the only means of pursuing any would be with the centrally-located spider itself.

Republican "equality" was like all other Soviet egalitarianism: controlled by those who were more equal. The President, Communist Party First Secretary, Prime Minister, Mayor, Dog-Catcher of the republics was always a local; but each one's deputy was almost always a Russian. And this deputy held the real power. The whole system, especially in the Central Asian Republics, virtually replicated the British Raj in India, and, on occasional visits with imperial emissaries, one was treated to the comical anachronism of the three tiers behaving exactly as under the Raj: Moscow officials openly looking down on the republic-based Russians as tedious colonial hicks; both looking down on the "natives" as politically untrustworthy and socially unspeakable, on whom a firm hand would prevent undesirable misunderstandings; and the natives, deprived of any self-government and most religious freedom, resentful of both sets of masters.

With the collapse of the Soviet Union, its Central Asian "republics" became independent states, though some are still ruled dicatorially by the same Communist *apparatchiks* who in our time were carrying out Moscow's heavy-handed bidding. Islam, playing a greater role in the wider region, has injected some of these mostly-mismanaged fledgling states into the new Great Game in the Eurasian heartland, replacing the two old ones between Imperial Russian and British Empires, and subsequently Soviet and American superpowers, with today's ideological (and in places military) conflict between American and Islamic fundamentalisms.

There is, though – just as travellers to India had long found – a timeless charm in the slow warmth of Central Asia, with old men whiling away their days over aromatic pipes and sweet green tea in the shaded *chaikhanas*, in the shadow (in Uzbekistan) of the staggeringly beautiful remains of the great mosques and tombs in Bokhara and Samarkand, the latter built by Tamburlaine, the successor to the great Mongol empire-builder Genghis Khan, inspirations for the Moghul treasures of India built by their descendants. But the old men we saw lounging in the shade were Uzbeks, and their ancestors had not even arrived in Samarkand and Bokhara when Tamburlaine swept out of Transoxiana to engulf Persia, Russia, Syria, India and Turkey in an indiscriminate sea of Sunni, Shiite, Orthodox, Hindu and Catholic blood.

The principal people in this chapter are as follows:

- Tamburlaine (1336-1405) – conqueror of large parts of west, south and central Asia. Founder of Samarkand.

- Toqtamysh (c.1380-1406) – Khan of the Golden Horde and challenger to Tamburlaine. Descendent of Ghengis Khan.

- Sultan Bajazeth I (1354-1403) – Sultan of the Ottoman Empire from 1389-1402.

- Johanns Schiltberger (c.1381-c.1440) – Bavarian prisoner of and soldier for Sultan Bajazeth I and subsequently Tamburlaine. Author, after his escape, of an eye-witness account of a number of Tamburlaine's battles and of life in Samarkand under Tamburlaine.

- Ibn Arabshah (c.1390-1450) – writer and traveller held captive in Tamburlaine's Samarkand. Author of The Wonders of Destiny in the History of Timur.

- Ruy Gonzales de Clavijo (unknown-1412) – sent by King Henry III of Castile as ambassador to the court of Tamburlaine in Samarkand from 1403-1405. Author of an account of his embassy.

While his primary objective in every case seems to have been power, in some cases an aspect, perhaps a primary aspect, of that aim was gaining control over the entire central Silk Road: by securing Persia, destroying the alternative route through the Russian steppes, adding the route from India, and then pushing his control out to the Mediterranean and the very gates of Constantinople, he could add trade profits and taxes to the loot that kept his armies loyal and financed the glorious extravagances of his capital at Samarkand. His greatest ambition, eastwards to conquer China, was played out in a game of intelligence gathering and deception along the eastern Silk Road – but too late, for he died on it as he set out, bogged down in a deeply frozen landscape, still in Central Asia.

Not surprisingly, he has subsequently had a fairly uniformly bad press, though this was not entirely the case with his contemporary chroniclers, an interesting collection from Spain, Germany, North Africa and Syria. All these outsiders agreed on his military genius; for the rest, the Christian Europeans seemed more impressed than judgemental, and the two Moslems were bitterly divided. Even Christopher Marlowe, Shakespeare's contemporary, who wrote two plays about Tamburlaine, was awed by the ambiguity of his ambition. From the perspective of our own recent devastating century, this man – or monster – seems familiar. Like the reactions to him.

In 1400 Tamburlaine besieged Damascus, and Johanns Schiltberger, "a Native of Bavaria", one of a number of contemporaries (though only two Europeans) who knew him and his court, provided an account of the city's fall. Schiltberger, from near Munich, was only thirteen when, in 1394, he accompanied "a lord named Leinhart Richartingen" in response to the appeal of King Sigismund of Hungary for assistance against the invading Ottoman forces of the Sultan Bajazeth I (whom we shall meet later in this chapter), and only fifteen when captured by the Turks in the crushing defeat of the Christian forces at the disastrous battle of Nicopolis (now Nikopol, on the Danube in northern Bulgaria). (One of the few other prisoners not decapitated on the spot was the French contingent's commander, Marshal Boucicault, who had a penchant for the losing side: fifteen years after being ransomed from the Turks he was captured by the English at Agincourt, this time dying in captivity.) Schiltberger kept his head but was pressed into the Turkish army, and was then captured a second time, at Ankara in 1402, when Bajazeth was himself defeated by Tamburlaine; and he then served under Tamburlaine, his son Shahrukh and grandson Ulugh Beg, until escaping and returning to Munich in 1427.

While Schiltberger himself was not present at Damascus, he had plenty of opportunity, starting two years later, to listen to those who were; and in his subsequent recollections, *The Bondage and Travels of Johann Schiltberger, a Native of Bavaria, in Europe, Asia, and Africa*, he wrote:

"Then Tämerlin stormed the city and took it by assault. And now, soon after he had taken the city, came to him the Geit, that is as much as to say a bishop, and fell at his feet, and begged mercy for himself and his priests. Tämerlin ordered that he should go with his priests into the temple [the great Ummayad Mosque]; so the priests took their wives, their children and many others, into the temple for protection, until there were thirty thousand young and old. Now Tämerlin gave orders that when the temple was full, the people should be shut up in it. This was done.

[*We catch our breath: we know where this is going. We have been here, in Europe, in our own times.*]

Then wood was placed around the temple, and he ordered it to be ignited, and they all perished in the temple. Then he ordered that each one of his [soldiers] should bring to him the head of a man. This was done, and it took three days; then with these heads were constructed three towers, and the city was pillaged".

If we have lost the capacity to be shocked, we still have enough to be horrified. Genocide, "the annihilation of a race", is a word that only came into the English language in 1944, to describe Hitler Germany's strenuous and almost successful effort to annihilate the Jews of Europe. It is a word that has come to be applied more variously since, in some cases with the accurate sense of its origin, as in Rwanda, in others to denote any large–scale killing, for ethnic or religious reasons, or political as in the slaughter of their fellow–countrymen by the Pol Pot regime in Cambodia. It is interesting, though, that Stalin's similar ideological slaughter of five times that number of *his* fellow–countrymen is not referred to as genocide. As someone has remarked, these definitions only matter to the living, not the dead.

Tamburlaine was not guilty of genocide in the sense of trying to eradicate an entire race: he simply killed whoever got in his way. As he conquered on a vast scale, there was a correspondingly vast number of victims, but there seems to be no evidence that race or creed made any difference. Tamburlaine was a Turkicised Mongol and a Moslem, but he slaughtered his co–religionist Turkoman, Persian, Arab, Indian, Mongol, Turkish and Egyptian Moslems as well as Manichaeans, Zoroastrians, Jews, Hindus, and Orthodox, Armenian, Georgian, Nestorian and Catholic Christians, members of the whole variety of races and creeds that lay between the Mediterranean and China, the Russian heartland and the Indian Ocean. It is hard to get round the conclusion that Tamburlaine was prepared to use whatever force was needed to achieve his ambitions for conquest and plunder, he saw terror as a useful means for those purposes, and his methods had no regard for the race or religion of their objects.

However the Damascus story has been questioned, on the grounds that Tamburlaine's contemporary the Catholic Archbishop Jean of Sultaniyeh (in northern Iran)[87] said he later burned a temple full of Jews in Bursa, in western Anatolian Turkey, and a 1416 biography of Tamburlaine by an Italian, B. de Mignanelli, said that later still, in Aleppo, he had the temple filled with Jews slaughtered by the sword: the argument, by Michael Shterensis in *Tamerlane and the Jews*, being that, as the three stories are suspiciously similar, they are therefore probably apocryphal, deriving from hostile Christian propaganda. His conclusion, from admittedly limited contemporary Jewish sources, is that "Timur never oppressed the Jews for being Jews". Which is not to say that Jews did not suffer when caught, like anyone else, in Tamburlaine's path. It is thus possible that there were three such appalling events; but it is indeed odd that none is referred to in the Arabic accounts – even by Tamburlaine's bitterest critic, though both he and others excoriated him for the appalling massacres he did carry out at both Aleppo and Damascus, and elsewhere.

It has been pointed out, rightly, that the Christian Crusaders at times massacred whole cities, the First Crusade's decimation of the Moslem and Jewish population of newly "liberated" Jerusalem being the most notorious;[88] but while establishing a certain kind of immoral equivalence, it can not exculpate Tamburlaine – it simply incriminates his Christian predecessors. And it has also been argued, in a different kind of exculpation, that Tamburlaine frequently tried to negotiate the surrender of states or provinces or cities, and only committed massacres when their rulers resisted his demands. Voltaire – who had an opinion on everything and everyone – had long since elevated this contention to a higher morality:

"There is one circumstance which may give us an advantageous idea of Tamerlane's character, which is, that we find him, through

---

87   The Archbishopric of Sultaniyeh had been established by Pope John XXII, in 1318, in the Ilkhan Oljaitu's capital, which had been founded by his father, Hulagu's grandson Arghun. It was a major city then and in Tamburlaine's time; now the shell of Oljaitu's tomb, still with its vast dome, is about all that remains. The archbishopric seems to have died out after 1425.

88   See 1100 chapter: Godfrey of Bouillon

the whole course of this war, strictly observant of the laws of nations".

But it was almost always Tamburlaine and not the states and provinces and cities that chose who should observe these "laws" of surrender–or–else; and over time there were thousands of ordinary people – tens of thousands – hundreds of thousands – who did not seek to be his opponents. Voltaire's "laws" made them just as dead as if Tamburlaine had not bothered to observe them at all.

What impels such a man as this? Christopher Marlowe was in no doubt:

> "Villains, these terrors, and these tyrannies
> (If tyrannies war's justice ye repute),
> I execute, enjoin'd me from above,
> To scourge the pride of such as Heaven abhors;
> Nor am I made arch–monarch of the world,
> Crown'd and invested by the hand of Jove,
> For deeds of bounty or nobility;
> But, since I exercise a greater name,
> The scourge of God and terror of the world,
> I must apply myself to fit those terms,
> In war, in blood, in death, in cruelty,
> And plague such peasants as resist in me
> The power of Heaven's eternal majesty".[89]

It was not just the grand sweep of destiny: Marlowe made Tamburlaine's monstrousness entirely personal as well – as in his outburst against the captured Kings of Jerusalem, Trebizond and Soria (Syria):

> "Well, bark, ye dogs: I'll bridle all your tongues,
> And bind them close with bits of burnish'd steel,
> Down to the channels of your hateful throats;

---

89 All The Archbishopric of Sultaniyeh had been established by Pope John XXII, in 1318, in the Ilkhan Oljaitu's capital, which had been founded by his father, Hulagu's grandson Arghun. It was a major city then and in Tamburlaine's time; now the shell of Oljaitu's tomb, still with its vast dome, is about all that remains. The archbishopric seems to have died out after 1425. from *Tamburlaine the Great* (Parts I and II) are from the Everyman's Library edition.

And, with the pains my rigour shall inflict,
I'll make ye roar, that earth may echo forth
The far–resounding torments ye sustain".

Marlowe, you might think, as a twenty–three–year–old poet, was taking licence, pouring forth in 1587 the first heady rush of Elizabethan dramatic verse that Shakespeare was soon to seize and make his own, exploding onto the stage in 1592 with *Henry VI*, *Richard III* and *The Comedy of Errors* – all in a year. The play's full title was

> "Tamburlaine the Great. Who, from a Scythian Shephearde by his rare and wonderfull Conquests, became a most puissant and mightye Monarque. And (for his tyranny and terrour in Warre) was tearmed, The Scourge of God";

and it was a great success, resulting in the sequel, later in 1587 or in 1588:

> "The Second Part of the bloody Conquests of mighty Tamburlaine. With his impassionate fury for the death of his Lady and loue faire Zenocrate: his fourme of exhortacion and discipline to his three sons, with the manner of his own death".[90]

Marlowe the Christian's descriptions of Tamburlaine's bloodthirstiness was in fact quite mild by comparison with those of another of

---

90   The success lasted until the Puritans closed down the theatres in mid–17th century England, and it was not performed again in London until 1953. A modern critic has written that the story of Tamburlaine

> "may be found in as many as one hundred Renaissance sources, told from varying points of view, and it is now impossible to know how many or how few of these sources Marlowe read".

However the weight of opinion seems to favour the origins of his play being mainly in the Spaniard Pedro Mexía's *Silva de Varia Lección*, published in Seville in 1540, for the first part, and in the Italian Petrus Peridinus's *Magni Tamerlanis Scytharum Imperatoris Vita* – itself partly based on Mexía – published in Florence in 1553, for the second, with suggestions of numerous other influences in both. And it seems likely that Mexía's own work derived from the only other European eyewitness account of Tamburlaine: by another Spaniard, whom we shall meet when he arrives in Samarkand in 1403.

Tamburlaine's contemporaries, the Syrian Moslem known, fortunately, in short, as Ibn Arabshah. Ahmed ibn Muhammed ibn 'Abd Allah ibn Ibrahim Shihab al–Din Abu 'l–'Abbas al–Dimashki al–Hanafi al–Adjami ibn Arabshah, to give him his full name, was captured at the age of eight in Damascus in that year of 1400; he was taken off to grow up in Tamburlaine's capital at Samarkand, and stayed – or was kept – there until 1411, seven years after Tamburlaine's death, learning, according to the *Encyclopedia of Islam*, Persian, Turkic and, interestingly, Mongol to add to his native Arabic. After subsequent studies in various Mongol and Central Asian Islamic centres, he became the confidant between about 1415 and 1424 of the Ottoman Sultan Mohammed I, son of Sultan Bajazeth I, Schiltberger's first captor, at his temporary capital of Erdine, in European Turkey, virtually all that remained of the Byzantine Empire twenty–nine years before its fall. He subsequently returned to Syria as a scholar and writer, then moved to Cairo for his last decade, dying there in 1450.

Describing the aftermath of Tamburlaine's defeat of Bajazeth, two years after his own capture, Ibn Arabshah wrote in *The Wonders of Destiny in the History of Timur* that on Tamburlaine's orders his men

"shaved heads, amputated necks, crushed arms, cut off shoulder-blades, burnt livers, scorched faces, gouged out eyes, split open bellies, blinded the sight, made tongues mute, blocked the hearing, crushed noses to the earth and brought low the lofty noses, lacerated mouths, shattered chests, crushed backs, pounded the ribs, split navels, melted hearts, severed sinews, shed blood, injured private parts, did violence to souls, destroyed men, poured out bodies like molten images, destroyed lives…".

Like a great litany of curses, Ibn Arabshah's successive calumniations of Tamburlaine roll out in *The Wonders of Destiny* –

that Deceitful one
that villain
that demon
this viper
that faithless despot
this bastard
that treacherous imposter
that flood

that covetous one
that deceiver
that wicked one
that traitor
that Exceeding Disaster
that tyrant
that obstinate one
that owl
that cunning deceiver
that lame one
that hunter
that punishment
that vainglorious one
that cloud
that profane man...

Ibn Arabshah's bitterness resulted from being kept a hostage; but it was also religious. He was a Sunni Moslem, as was Tamburlaine; but whereas Ibn Arabshah was highly orthodox, Tamburlaine was everything but. The Mongols could be extraordinarily tolerant in their racial and religious attitudes: Kublai Khan, for example, employed foreigners of all descriptions, Buddhists, Christians (both Nestorian and, if one believes Marco Polo as distinct from the Chinese official annals, Catholic), Indians, Moslems, Nepalese, Persians, variously as administrators, artists, engineers, soldiers – partly, though, because the Mongols did not trust their Chinese subjects. Tamburlaine seems to have been less catholic; but his religious approach still, or at least periodically, reflected the traditional shamanist Mongol toleration of all religions, based on the hope that spiritual good might come from any, and the conviction that political support could come from all, if they were treated correctly. A Persian writer pinpointed the difference with the story that when the Mongols first invaded Persia in the 13th century, in the city of Ray the jurists of the Islamic Shafite school of law went out to greet them and encouraged them to slaughter the other half of the city which was subject to the Hanafite school; the Mongols did so, but saying to themselves "What good can be expected of men who plot to have their own countrymen's blood shed?" they killed the Shafites too – a very Mongol solution to a very rational question.

The Mongols also allowed women a public role and an independence that shocked Ibn Arabshah: Tamburlaine's wives accompanied him on many campaigns; and they and his daughters–in–law held their own parties – mixed parties, where they amused themselves by making the men drunk, not a difficult task among the Mongols. This attitude to alcohol is another indication of the lightness with which Tamburlaine's court wore its Islam. In religion Tamburlaine's own tolerance even extended, at least at an intellectual level, to Shi'ism – the form of Islam which gradually diverged from the mainstream until a breakaway Shi'ite Caliphate was established by the Fatimid Dynasty in Egypt in the 10th century – to the extent that, in a debate with theologians in captured Aleppo in 1400, he confused everyone by accusing the Sunni Syrians of following false doctrine, and, said Ibn Arabshah,

"the Moslems were in perplexity and their heads were being cut off".

Tamburlaine's knowledge of Shi'ism must have resulted from discussions with theologians, not from immediate experience, as it was not until Persia's conversion to Shi'ism in the 16th century that it gained supremacy (which it still has today) in the region of his home base.

Barthold, the great Russian scholar of Tamburlaine's age, observed in *Four Studies on the History of Central Asia* that

"More often than not religion was for Timur a means for attaining some political aim, rather than a cause determining his actions... No wonder that Muslim doctors of law always feared some snare in their conversations with Timur".

Many of Tamburlaine's campaigns were launched in the name of fighting idolators and infidels, but that was no barrier to fighting the faithful as well whenever his imperial ambitions required. On numerous occasions, when his emirs, uncertain or exhausted, doubted a course of action he proposed, he also made use of forecasts by Sufis or astrologers, which always conveniently supported doing what he proposed. Gibbon skewered this too:

"his sound understanding may tempt us to believe that a superstitious reverence for omens and prophecies, for saints and astrologers, was only affected as an instrument of policy".

But there was another element also: while he made use of prophets and clerics, Tamburlaine had no need of them as intermediaries – he believed he had his own revelation. He let it be known that he had "visions of angels, and that he did not do anything, and did not wish to, unless by the special commandment of God";

and as his official history, the *Zafer–name*, expressed it:

"When God wills something, He furnishes the causes by which it may be brought about according to His providence. To Tamburlaine and his posterity, He had destined the empire of Asia".[91]

However much he was brought to admire Tamburlaine's military genius, the rigidly orthodox Ibn Arabshah could not bring himself to forgive what seemed a combination of hypocrisy and sacrilege.

Schiltberger and Ibn Arabshah were writing some time after the Syrian campaign, by hearsay from Tamburlaine's associates. Schiltberger was not at Damascus; Ibn Arabshah was there but, as previously noted, was only eight at the time. But a remarkable sixty–eight–year–old North African scholar and traveller, known, also fortunately, in short, as Ibn Khaldun, was not only there but was an unexpected participant in events, as he subsequently recounted in his *Universal History*. Wali al–Din 'Abd al–Rahman ibn Muhammad ibn Muhammad ibn Abi Bakr Muhammad ibn al–Hasan ibn Khaldun was born and educated in Tunis in 1332, losing his parents to the Black Death in 1349. Interspersed with periods of study, teaching and prison, he participated in numerous plots and counterplots in the Sultanates of Fez and Granada and elsewhere in the Maghreb, usually managing to end up on the winning team. He finally moved definitively to Cairo in 1382, and lost his family in a shipwreck as they followed him shortly afterwards. Appointments twice as chief *kadi* (civil judge) by the Mameluke Sultans Baruk and Faraj were terminated by local chauvinists, and he spent fourteen years as an increasingly celebrated teacher.

In 1400 he was obliged to accompany Sultan Faraj on an expedition to Damascus to stop Tamburlaine's depredations; but the Sultan secretly escaped back to Cairo as soon as Damascus was surrounded, leaving his troops, the Damascenes and Ibn Khaldun to the mercies of Tamburlaine's siege. At this stage Tamburlaine gave Ibn Khaldun the opportunity to switch sides yet again; but in fact he returned to Cairo – being stripped and robbed by brigands en route – where he was again appointed and

---

91 The *Zafer–name* appears to have been published only in Persian; quotations have been taken from secondary sources.

dismissed as *kadi* four times, dying in 1406 shortly after his sixth appointment. The *Encyclopedia of Islam* says he has been severely criticized for his ambition and frequent changes of loyalty – but was always re–employed. His *Universal History*, on which he worked up to his death, was the first systematic survey of the Islamic world, but included nowhere else. He said only that he had heard that

> "the philosophic sciences were thriving in Europe. But God knows what goes on in those parts".

What is extraordinary is that it was Tamburlaine who asked to see Ibn Khaldun, who had to be let down by ropes from the city wall and escorted through the Mongol armies, thirty–five times in all, in January and February 1401. How Tamburlaine knew of the scholar's presence in the city is a mystery, but he often talked with *ulema* and scholars, even though all about them might be being massacred: even Ibn Arabshah conceded that

> "Timur loved learned men...; he gave the highest honour to the learned and doctors and preferred them to all others and received each of them according to his rank and granted them honour and respect; he used towards them familiarity and an abatement of his majesty; in his arguments with them he mingled moderation with splendour, clemency with rigour and covered his severity with kindness...; by nature he spurned actors and poets";

and, he added, Tamburlaine

> "was not deceived by intricate fallacy nor did hidden flattery pass him; he discerned keenly between truth and fiction, and caught the sincere counsellor and the pretender by the skill of his cunning".

Tamburlaine was keen to quiz Ibn Khaldun on his native Maghreb, but said

> "I am not satisfied. I desire that you write for me the whole country of the Maghrib – its distant as well as its nearby parts, its mountains and its rivers, its villages and its cities – in such a manner that I might seem actually to see it".

Such questioning, with Tamburlaine, makes one suspicious; but if a thought of conquest stirred in his mind, he was never to pursue it, though no–one was ever confident about that until he was dead. He also wanted Ibn Khaldun's views on historical topics, including, notably, on heroes in history, a topic Marlowe saw as close to Tamburlaine's heart:

> "Is it not passing brave to be a king,
> And ride in triumph through Persepolis?
> ...A god is not so glorious as a king:
> ...To ask and have, command and be obey'd;
> When looks breed love, with looks to gain the prize".[92]

Ibn Khaldun, clearly highly flattered by all this attention from the man whom he reciprocated by addressing as "the Sultan of the Universe and Ruler of the World", later summed up his impressions of Tamburlaine:

> "It is simply that he is highly intelligent and very perspicacious, addicted to debate and argumentation about what he knows and about what he does not know".

He openly enjoyed his times with the conqueror, feasting, in the sly words of Ibn Arabshah, while others were too nervous to eat,

> "like one who if he lives will be praised by his people, but if he dies, will come to Allah with a full belly".

But he also gave a straightforward, factual account of Tamburlaine's despoliation of Damascus: the extortion of money by trickery and torture, the confiscation of all property and animals, the torching of the city and the destruction of the Great Mosque. Ibn Khaldun does not refer to incineration of people within the latter, but he does talk of

---

92 Persepolis, near Shiraz in southern Iran, was the magnificent capital of the first great Persian Empire, of the Achaemenian Dynasty; it – and Persia – was captured in 330 BCE by Alexander the Great in perhaps his greatest triumph; but within weeks he was responsible for the destruction by fire of Xerxes' vast palace, some said in a drunken acceptance of a Greek courtesan's demand for retribution for Xerxes' pillage of her native Athens. The ruins, twenty–three centuries later, are still magnificent.

"the acts of barbarous torture, outrage, rapine, and murder, perpetrated on men, women, and children and the unsurpassed and unheard of acts of violence against the whole population".

None of this, unfortunately, incompatible with high intelligence.

The conquest of the heartland: Central Asia

By 1400 Tamburlaine was about sixty–five. He was born near Samarkand into a minor Turkicized Mongol tribe, his great–great–grandfather having been a commander in the army of Chagatei, one of the sons of Genghis Khan, that conquered Transoxiana, the area between the two great rivers of Central Asia – the Oxus (now called the Amu Darya) and the Jaxartes (the Syr Darya) in present–day Uzbekistan.[93] Ibn Arabshah said he had seen

"the genealogy of Timur traced without a break to Jenghizkhan through females, snares of Satan".

But in fact Tamburlaine himself claimed a connection with the first great Mongol conqueror only by descent from a rather remote common

---

93   The areas around Samarkand had a variety of names over the centuries, depending on the movements of tribes and invaders and the rise and fall of dynasties. Tamburlaine's heartland between the two rivers is sometimes referred to as Sogdiana, after the satrapy of the ancient Persian Empire that Alexander the Great conquered in the 4th century BCE and long since disappeared. Transoxiana, a convenient term for this area which I have used, coincided fairly much with present–day Uzbekistan. It included Tamburlaine's earliest conquests: Mawarannahr, around Samarkand and Bokhara, a term not used at all by some historians or encyclopaedias; and Khwarazm (Khwarizm or Khorezm; Gibbon's Carizme) to the north, sometimes starting from around Bokhara, sometimes only from Khiva northwards to Urgench, the remains of a kingdom that included Transoxiana as well as most of Persia before the first Mongol invasion. His next conquests also became part of his heartland: Khorasan (or Khurasan), to the south of the Oxus between Mashad in present–day northeast Persia and Herat in northwest Afghanistan; and Bactria to its east, around Balkh, now in northern Afghanistan. The entire area from the Caspian to Samarkand became known in the 19th century as Russian Turkestan (present–day Xinjiang being Chinese Turkestan), though sometimes as Transcaspia; the western part is now Turkmenistan. What area all these covered varied with circumstances, and maps purporting to show them (when they are shown at all) seem to vary likewise: the essential is thus the major city dominating the different regions. And there may be even more varieties in place names in quotations, as they depend, like people's names, on authorial idiosyncrasy.

ancestor. The only title Tamburlaine ever assumed was *Gurgan*, "Son–in–law", in 1370, after he took as the chief of his numerous wives Saray–Mulk–khanum, one of the wives of the Emir of Balkh whom he had just defeated in his first major military victory: as the daughter of a Khan who *was* descended from Genghis Khan, Saray–Mulk–khanum gave Tamburlaine the title used on all formal occasions, on his coins, and in the Friday prayers in the mosques.

The point was curiously important to him: he always saw himself as re–creating, recovering, Genghis Khan's vast empire; but even at the height of his own vast successes he was meticulous in abjuring any royal title for himself, always insisting that he ruled solely in the name of the legitimate Chagatei Khan. He regularly ensured there was one – but they were merely a series of faceless puppets: Ibn Arabshah said

"he appointed a deputy in his own name...of the seed of Chingiz–khan...to repel the calumnies of detractors and cut off the piercing point of every tongue...and the Khan was in his bondage like a centipede in mud".

With a startlingly modern image, his contemporary, the ruler of Kashgaria (now part of China's far western Sinkiang province), confirmed this when he wrote:

"In my day, Khans are treated in Samarkand like political prisoners".

Ironically, the only exception was the last of Tamburlaine's Khans, Sultan Mahmud, an able general who led the pursuit at the battle of Ankara in 1402 which resulted in the capture of the Ottoman Sultan Bajazeth.[94] But he died shortly afterwards, and Tamburlaine this time named no replacement.

Despite his hostility, Ibn Arabshah drew a vivid pen–portrait of Tamburlaine:

"tall and of lofty stature..., big in brow and head, mighty in strength and courage, wonderful in nature, white in colour, mixed with red, but not dark, stout of limb, with broad shoulders, thick

---

94   This is Marlowe's spelling; sometimes it is Bajazet, Bayezit or Bayazid.

fingers, long legs, perfect build, long beard, dry hands, lame on the right side, with eyes like candles, without brilliance, powerful in voice;...firm in mind, strong and robust in body, brave and fearless, like a hard rock".

It is a remarkable picture of a seventy–year–old man. He was also intellectually alert, not only with a passion for conversation with learned *ulemas*, as already noted, but with keen secular interests also. Ibn Arabshah noted particularly that he was

"greatly given to reading and hearing histories...He was constant in reading annals and histories of the prophets of blessed memory and the exploits of kings and accounts of those things which had formerly happened to men abroad and at home and all this in the Persian tongue. And when readings were repeated before him and those accounts filled his ears, he seized hold of that matter and so possessed it that it turned to habit, so that if a reader slipped, he would correct his error, for [Ibn Arabshah could not resist needling] repetition makes even an ass wise. But he was illiterate, reading, writing, and understanding nothing in the Arab tongue".

It was during one of Tamburlaine's earliest martial exploits in Transoxiana, a sheep–stealing raid against another local tribe, that he was damaged in the right knee by an arrow, whence his name;

"So mutilation was added to his poverty and a blemish to his wickedness and fury",

Ibn Arabshah observed with satisfaction. Ibn Khaldun saw forty years after the incident that Tamburlaine

"dragged [the right leg] when he went on short walks, but when he went long distances men carried him on their hands".

But of course, like any Mongol, he was totally at home in the saddle – as it turned out, from Izmir to Delhi. With advances and retreats, trickery and tactical brilliance, by 1370 Tamburlaine, at the age of thirty–five, was undisputed ruler of the whole of Transoxiana, Khorasan and Bactria as far south as the Hindu Kush. On the last of this group of campaigns, on his way to terminate the Emirate – and Emir – of Balkh,

Tamburlaine met and was impressed by a Moslem divine, Sayyid Baraka,[95] who was to stay with him for the rest of his days – and afterwards: the Sayyid was buried in the tomb Tamburlaine built in Samarkand, and when he died he himself was buried alongside his spiritual mentor, facing him. However the Sayyid's presence did not help Balkh: the *Zafer–name* said

> "blood flowed in rivers and heads rolled like balls in a game of polo".

Samarkand, the city on which Tamburlaine was to lavish his extraordinarily cultivated attention, was the secure base to which he always returned after each of his expeditions – except the last one. He was so constantly on the road of conquest that he really spent little time there; but from the beginning he had cultivated the clergy, the merchants, the agricultural producers, and the still largely nomadic Chagatei aristocracy who formed his officer corps, and the loyalty of all four groups was constantly replenished with the plunder from palaces and provinces seized in expedition after expedition.

In addition, Samarkand, and indeed all the major cities of Transoxiana, was an important staging point on the Silk Road, the great web of caravan routes that had continued to stretch (notwithstanding interruptions) between the Mediterranean and China and India since Roman and Han and Ashokan times – though it only received its now–famous sobriquet from the German geologist–geographer Baron Ferdinand von Richthofen late in the 19th century. The taxes generated for Tamburlaine by the great transit markets at Samarkand and Bokhara were undoubtedly a factor in his inexorable drive to extend his control over the entire central nexus of the Silk Road trade.

After securing Transoxiana his attention turned to the neighbouring emirates, which he overcame one after the other, though sometimes only after repeated campaigns: Moghulistan (sometimes known as Semirechiye) to the east, from the the Issyk Kul lake in Kyrgyzstan as far as Urumqi and Turpan in northwest China, and still under the rule of legitimate Chagatei heirs – campaigns in 1370, 1374, 1376, 1383, 1389, 1390; Khwarazm to the north – in 1372, 1373, 1379, 1388); Khorasan to the

---

95 Sayyid was a title given to a descendant of the Prophet Mohammed through the fourth Caliph ("successor"), Ali, his cousin and son–in–law, recognized by Shi'ites as the true interpreter of the Prophet's teachings.

southwest – in 1381, 1382. Sistan, further southeast around Kandahar in southern Afghanistan, was added in 1383:

> "Whatever was in that country", the *Zafer–name* said, "from potsherds to royal pearls, from the finest fabrics to the very nails in the doors and walls, was swept away by the winds of spoliation").

The necessity for repeated campaigns reflected the looseness of Tamburlaine's imperial structure: based on tribute from the subject regions rather than administration from the centre – which was wherever Tamburlaine himself happened to be – it required repeated reminders, at least in these early stages, to ensure that homage and taxes continued to be paid. Nevertheless, by the mid–1380s he had virtually re–created the khanate of Chagatei.

As for the laws of war, the historian of Central Asia René Grousset described Tamburlaine's capture of Kabul, for example, as

> "a rare comedy of Oriental hypocrisy, complete with protestations of friendship, conciliatory embraces, and pious maxims from the Koran ejaculated at every turn, followed by betrayals, surprise attacks, and summary executions *à la turque*".

Notwithstanding the deployment of every trick in the trade, throughout his campaigns Tamburlaine set perhaps the greatest store on intelligence. However reluctantly, Ibn Arabshah gave him considerable credit for a system which, like the KGB of a later empire, gathered up *everything*:

> "He had placed through his realm his informers and in other kingdoms had appointed his spies; and these were emirs like Atilmish, one of his allies, or learned fakirs, like Masaud Kahajani, his chief minister, or traders seeking a living by some craft, ill–minded wrestlers, criminal athletes, labourers, craftsmen, soothsayers, physicians, wandering hermits, chatterers, strolling vagabonds, sailors, wanderers by land, elegant drunkards, witty singers, aged procuresses and crafty old women, like the deceiver Dalla, and men who had won much experience and journeyed through east and west…They brought to him events and news from the furthest borders, described to him what things were excellent there and were remarkable, made known to him the weights received there and the prices of things, marked their [staging] posts and cities,

mapped their roads...set forth their leaders, emirs, magnates, excellent men, nobles, rich and poor, the name, surname, title and family of everyone and craft which they practised and tools which they used. And in this way he marked those things with his attention and by his prudence had all kingdoms in his power... how great was his cunning, deceit, and dissimulation".

The *Zafer-name*'s perspective was of course different: God had destined to Tamburlaine and his posterity

"the empire of Asia, foreseeing the mildness of his rule, which would bring happiness to his subjects"

– those who survived the execution of his destiny. Even Voltaire asked

"which would be preferable, being Tamerlane's dog or his subject? It is evident that the condition of his dog would be by far the better one".

The great conquests: Persia

By the early 1380s Tamburlaine was invading Persia, the former Mongol Ilkhanate of Genghis Khan's grandson Hulagu, which had disintegrated after two generations, partly because of Hulagu's grandson Ghazan's conversion to Islam against the wishes of his more conservative lieutenants. By the middle of the decade Tamburlaine was far to the west of modern-day Tehran, overran Azerbaijan for the first of five times, and then Georgia – the first of his *eight* invasions of that hapless but feisty Christian country.[96]

Part of Tamburlaine's intentions for this westward extension was undoubtedly to try to bring more of the southern tier of the Silk Road under his control, just as the southwards extension of his power into Khorasan and Sistan provided not only security in that direction but also control over the Silk Road spur linking Central Asia and India. A Spanish ambassador whom we shall meet properly later reported on his way through northern Persia in 1403 that in "the great city of Tabreez... even now there are more than two hundred thousand inhabited houses",

---

96 Bukharin, a close collaborator of Lenin's, and a member of Stalin's Politburo until 1929, came to the view that the frequent bloody raids into the Caucasus by Genghis Khan and Tamburlaine "left their traces" on Stalin's character. He was executed in 1938 following Stalin's last public purge "trial".

and that the city of Sultaniyeh, whose ruins are about halfway between Tabriz and Tehran (which did not yet exist then), "is not so large as Tabreez, though it possesses more trade". The Sultaniyeh market was what particularly impressed him:

"Every year, especially in the months of June, July, and August, very large caravans of camels arrive, with great quantities of merchandise…This city has a great traffic, and yields a large revenue to the lord [at that time Tamburlaine's son Miranshah]. Every year many merchants come here from India, with spices, such as cloves, nutmegs, cinnamon, manna, mace, and other precious articles… merchants come here for silk, even Venetians and Genoese… From Cathay vessels come within sixty days journey of this city [to the then island–port of Hormuz, in the Persian Gulf near present–day Bandar–Abbas]…These ships bring many pearls, and some of them bring rubies, (which are very fine in Cathay), and much spice…All the merchants who come from the land of the Christians, from Caffa [or Kaffa, in the Crimea] and Trebizond [Trabzon, on the Black Sea coast of eastern Turkey], and the merchants of Turkey and Syria, come every year, at this time, to the city of Sultanieh, to make their purchases".

It is a good pocket–size description of Silk Road trade, though with two notable omissions: what the Western merchants brought to sell, and the silk from China, still probably the major item traded from east to west until the British began importing tea in vast quantities in the 18th century. There is one other point of interest: originally, the traffic in pearls (as in the highly–valued coral) was in the opposite direction, from the Mediterranean to Central Asia and China.

From the foothills of the Caucasus, Tamburlaine swooped down on the Fars region, to master Isfahan and (passing by Persepolis) Shiraz before the end of the decade, though he would have to re–conquer them six years later, in 1393, after the puppets he installed there began pulling their own strings.[97] Here his new subjects began to feel the "mildness of his rule": in Sabzevar

---

97 The *Zafer–name* recorded that on that second expedition into Fars Tamburlaine stopped at Dezful, west of Isfahan near the Iraq border, to admire the bridge, used by his army, which had been built by Roman prisoners after the defeat of the Emperor Valerian by the Persian Sassanid King Shapur I in 260 CE.

"nearly two thousand prisoners were piled alive, one on top of the other, and cemented with mud and brick, to form towers";

in another city, the *Zafer–name*, recorded,

"our soldiers made a mountain of dead bodies, and built towers with their heads".

In Isfahan, the *Zafer–name* speaks of seventy thousand heads

"which were piled in heaps outside the walls…and of which towers were then built in various parts of the town".

But there were survivors, and here in these gracious cities of perfumes, wines and fine carpets Tamburlaine expanded the program he had begun in Herat of sending – before the massacres – learned clerics and scientists back to Samarkand, as well as skilled craftsmen of all kinds, together with their portable tools and their families. Gradually he would build up – at the expense of everywhere else – a concentration in his capital of knowledge and craftsmanship which he would in due course put to work there in spectacular fashion.

Hookham recounts the delightful story that in Shiraz Tamburlaine met the celebrated Persian poet Shams ed–Din Mohammed, known by his pseudonym Hafiz, and by his contemporaries as "Sugar–lip" for the sweetness of his poetry. In one of his verses Hafiz had written:

"If that unkindly Shiraz Turk would take my heart within her hand,

I'd give Bukhara for the mole upon her cheek, or Samarkand".
Tamburlaine is said to have summoned Hafiz and declaimed:

There is another such bridge, with some dozen arches still standing but not in use, on the road from Shiraz south towards Bishapur, where, in a gorge, two of the magnificent Sassanid cliff bas–reliefs show Valerian's defeat and submission to Shapur. It was obviously worth celebrating: the submission is repeated again on a huge bas–relief at Naqsh–i Rustam, near Persepolis. It is said that this was not the Romans' furthest east: in about 104 BCE a Han Chinese army had clashed with and defeated a force (perhaps Huns), partly composed of captive Roman soldiers, in Transoxiana – Tamburlaine's own heartland.

"With the blows of my lustrous sword have I subjugated most of the habitable globe, and laid waste thousands of towns and counties to embellish Samarkand and Bukhara, my native towns and seats of my government; and you, miserable wretch that you are, would sell them both for the black mole of a Turkic woman of Shiraz!"

Hafiz replied:

"Sire, it is through such prodigality that I have fallen on such evil days",

and the delighted Tamburlaine rewarded him handsomely.[98] Tamburlaine's return expedition in 1393 was not poetic: he had the entire Muzaffarid dynasty, the rulers of Fars, either killed or blinded, to discourage any others' temptation by disloyalty.

Sooner or later, everyone reported the towers of skulls; but surprisingly, for such a vivid image, they seemed to disappear from view – there is no mention of them in Marlowe – until they reappeared a half–millennium later in St Petersburg, in the 1870s. The painter Vasily Vereshchagin, one of the new realist school of Russian painters, exhibited *The Apotheosis of War*, inscribed by the artist on the frame: "Dedicated to all great conquerors of the past, present and future".[99] The 1871 painting shows, in a brilliantly sunny but devastated Central Asian landscape, a pyramid of grinning skulls, about twenty–five rows high, pecked clean by a flight of black crows.[100]

Vereshchagin undoubtedly had Tamburlaine in mind – around the same time he had also painted the gates of his tomb and other views of Samarkand. But the artist was a pacifist, a most unusual stand in the Russia in those (indeed most) days, and the painting, three years after the capture of Samarkand by General Konstantin Petrovich von Kaufmann,

---

98   When Hafiz died two years later he was buried at Shiraz in a mausoleum (now reconstructed, but in a delicious garden) still visited by pilgrims to the wordsmith who out–duelled the great conqueror.

99   In the Tretyakov Gallery, Moscow.

100   There was a more recent, industrial–age, sardonic evocation of these grisly structures: the French sculptor Arman's 1982 work *Long Term Parking*, at Jouy–en–Josas outside Paris – a stack of fifty–nine cars embedded in a twenty–metre–high tower of concrete.

was also a challenge to the campaigns still underway to extend the Russian Empire into the remaining Central Asian Tartar emirates, the last independent relics of Tamburlaine's heartlands. *The Apotheosis of War* caused a scandal, and the Tsar, Alexander II, demanded its withdrawal from exhibition. The atmosphere in Russia at the time of this imperial expansion was exemplified by its first notable explorer of Central Asia, Nikolai Przhevalsky, who wrote in 1877, after his first, four–year, expedition:

> "Our military conquests in Asia bring glory not only to Russia; they are also victories for the good of mankind. Carbine bullets and rifled cannon bear those elements of civilization which would otherwise be very long in coming to the petrified realms of the Inner Asian khans".

Vereshchagin, however, nothing daunted, then painted in 1878, the year the Tsar himself joined the army in a victorious war against the dying Ottoman Empire, an equally extraordinary anti–war picture, of an Orthodox priest, accompanied by an army officer, saying the Office of the Dead over a vast plain covered with thousands of naked *Russian* corpses: *The Vanquished*.[101] Vereshchagin anticipated the real world, though they were not to be Russian corpses: in 1881, when the Russians stormed the town of Gëok Tepe (now Gekdepe, in southern Turkmenistan), they killed twenty thousand inhabitants, pursuing panic–stricken men, women and children for seventeen kilometres with horse, foot and cannon;

> "they lay", an eye–witness said, "in rows like freshly mown hay, as they had been swept down by the *mitrailleuses* and cannon".

The future Viceroy of India and British Foreign Secretary, George Nathaniel Curzon, already a Member of Parliament, visited Gëok Tepe eight years later, and noted in his book *Russia in Central Asia in 1889* that the more than four kilometre walls had been

> "stripped of their upper half immediately after the capture in order to cover the bodies of the thousands of slain".

---

101   Also in the Tretyakov.

The victorious commander was General Mikhail Skobolev, a hero of the recent Turkish war; Curzon said

> "it was written of him that 'he rode to battle clad in white, decked with orders, scented and curled, like a bridegroom to a wedding, his eyes gleaming with wild delight, his voice tremulous with joyous excitement'...The Turkomans called him *Guenz Kanli*, or Bloody Eyes".[102]

Just after the battle Dostoevsky wrote triumphantly in his diary:

> "Let the conviction grow among all these millions of people [in Central Asia], to the very orders of India, and even within India, if you like, of the invincibility of the white tsar and the omnipotence of his sword".[103]

Skobolev himself said

> "I hold it as a principle that in Asia the duration of peace is in direct proportion to the slaughter you inflict upon the

---

102 Curzon was to become increasingly obsessed about Russia's penetration of Central Asia and the threat he continued to believe, as Viceroy, that it posed to British India (see 1900 chapter: Yuan Shikai). In the present context he added the sweeping judgement:

> "I have narrated or revived these incidents, because, repellent though they be to nineteenth–century notions, and discreditable to the Russian character, they do not stand alone in the history of Russian Conquest in Central Asia, but are profoundly characteristic of the methods of warfare by which that race has consistently and successfully set about the subjugation of Oriental peoples".

A greater contrast, he said, "can scarcely be imagined to the British method, which is to strike gingerly a series of taps, rather than a downright blow". Fifteen years later, in an engagement during the "diplomatic mission" to Tibet on which Curzon himself sent Colonel Francis Younghusband with an armed escort of a couple of dozen British and over a thousand Ghurka and Sikh troops of Britain's Indian Army, a Tibetan position resisting the invasion was overrun, and some Sikhs, led by a "handful" of British soldiers, rode, according to a contemporary newspaper report, "for twelve miles on the flanks of these wretched Thibetans shooting them down from the saddle". (French: *Younghusband* – Bibliography, 1900)

103 *A Writer's Diary*, vol.2, tr. K.Lantz (Evanston Ill 1994).

enemy. The harder you hit them, the longer they will stay quiet afterwards".

Which was exactly Tamburlaine's view.

The great conquests: northwards to Russia

It was after these campaigns against Persia, Azerbaijan and Georgia that Tamburlaine finally came to deal with the Golden Horde – and in so doing, to save Russia, as it turned out, though that was certainly not what he intended, nor what the Russians themselves anticipated at the time. The Golden Horde was the khanate bestowed on Jochi, another of Genghis Khan's sons, when the Mongol Empire broke up following the latter's death in 1227. Under Jochi's son Batu Khan the territory of the Golden Horde was extended from the River Yenisei in central Siberia westwards north of the Aral and Caspian seas, and across what is now southern Russia, conquering the capital at Kiev (when Moscow was still a mere village), and for a time penetrating as far as Poland and the Adriatic Sea.[104]

By the end of the 1380s Tamburlaine dominated two of the other three successor states of Genghis Khan's empire, the Chagatei Khanate of Central Asia and the Ilkhanate of Persia. (The fourth, Kublai Khan's China, under the Yuan Dynasty, had been overthrown a decade earlier by the Chinese Ming Dynasty.) The Golden Horde's territory, known as Kipchak, was centred on the great city founded by Batu Khan at Sarai, some hundred kilometres up the Volga above Astrakhan, on its tributary the Akhtuba; and Tamburlaine's opponent was its mercurial and still largely nomadic ruler, Toqtamysh, a descendant of Genghis Khan's first son's first son. It was a genealogy which counted for much with Tamburlaine, despite Toqtamysh's behaviour.

Ironically, Toqtamysh owed his position to Tamburlaine. About the time the latter began his run to take control of Transoxiana, Toqtamysh was beginning his to take control of the White Horde, the eastern faction of the Golden Horde. In the early 1370s he sought Tamburlaine's help in this campaign, got it, was driven out, got it again, and was driven out of the White Horde's area for the second time. This time Tamburlaine, though still preoccupied with his own campaigns to extend his realm in Central Asia, himself marched northwards into the steppe, in 1377, and

---

104   See 1000 chapter: Vladimir of Kiev. The Mongol invaders were known to the Russians as Tartars; the two terms are used here interchangeably.

inflicted a serious defeat on the eastern Horde – but still not serious enough to secure his client Toqtamysh's supremacy. Eventually, the following year, and again with Tamburlaine's support, Toqtamysh finally made it.

The ambitions of the new Khan of the White Horde now turned to Kipchak, the land of the Golden Horde itself. The Golden Horde, conqueror of Kievan Rus, was no longer what it had been: earlier in the century, the Black Death, originating in the Mongol lands further east, had decimated its ranks. The factionalism which followed amongst the Horde's leaders was mirrored by that between the Russian princedoms of Chernigov, Tver, Vladimir and Moscow which had emerged following the destruction of Kiev, and which had accordingly continued to be obliged to pay tribute to the Golden Horde.

In 1380 the Khan of the Horde was threatened on the one side by the newly successful Toqtamysh, just as, to his north, Grand Duke Dmitri of Moscow, with the support of other Russian princes, felt himself strong enough to stop paying the regular tribute. Mamai Khan made the mistake of thinking he could quickly put an end to this totally unprecedented impudence and then use Russia's resources to deal with Toqtamysh. But in the battle of Kulikovo Pole, "the Field of Curlews", the tables were turned: near the Don River sixty kilometres southeast of Tula, the Grand Duke became Moscow's first national hero – Dmitri Donskoi, "Dmitri of the Don" – for winning the first ever Russian victory over the hated Mongol overlords.[105]

Toqtamysh seized his chance: within a year he too defeated Mamai and became Khan of the Golden Horde at Sarai, reigning over the entire steppe from the Aral Sea west to the Dniester River

---

105   In 1908, in his poem "On Kulikov Field", the young Russian poet Alexander Blok (1880–1921) wrote of the impermanence of victory:

"We only dream of calm. The battle's never done.
Through dust and blood,
Eternally the steppeland mare flies on,
Trampling the sod...

The sunset and the heart astream with blood.
No calm, not anywhere.
Weep, heart! Weep loud! Past field, past wood
Gallops the steppeland mare."

It was prophetic of Blok's own failure to find calm, a decade later, in the disillusioned aftermath of the Revolution he initially welcomed.

(near present–day Odessa). Such a lord naturally expected the resumption of the long–standing tribute of the Russian princedoms; and when they refused, carried away by the narrow victory at Kulikovo, Toqtamysh ruthlessly invaded, sacking Vladimir and Suzdal, and in 1382 razing Moscow to the ground. It would take the Grand Dukes of Muscovy another century to finally shake off the Tartar yoke, two to remove them from all European Russia (bar the Crimea).

With his restoration of the power of Kipchak, Toqtamysh saw himself not only as the legitimate successor to Batu, but as entitled to restore the empire of Genghis Khan himself; so he unhesitatingly turned against his mentor and frequent saviour, the mere upstart Tamburlaine, and demanded his submission. He misjudged his man; but it would still take Tamburlaine the best part of ten years to deal with him. Toqtamysh's first strike came in 1385, when he descended through the Caucasus to besiege Tabriz, at the westernmost end of Tamburlaine's sway; the city, according to the *Zafer–name*, struggled for a week

"like a half–dead hen doing an unwilling act",

then surrendered to pillage and slaughter before Toqtamysh withdrew. Two years later the latter made an even more brazen foray down the same route while Tamburlaine was nearby in the Karabakh (the area in present–day Azerbaijan disputed by Armenia), his favourite wintering base when away from Samarkand. He lost the engagement, but interestingly Tamburlaine, with his curious respect for the legitimate Mongol line, did not react with his usual savagery: instead of slaughtering his prisoners, he sent them back to Toqtamysh with food and equipment, reproaching his "son", according to the *Zafer–name*, in affectionate grief rather than anger at the disloyalty of his protégé.

Toqtamysh was unimpressed. Within months he descended down the east of the Caspian, forcing Tamburlaine to race sixteen hundred kilometres from Shiraz back across Persia to protect Transoxiana and Samarkand itself. Toqtamysh did not wait for him and withdrew; but later in 1388 he returned, with an army that included troops from Moscow according to the *Zafer–name*, this time circling round through present–day Kyrgyzstan, but again avoiding battle. After a campaign eastwards against Moghulistan, Tamburlaine, in 1391, deciding enough was enough, led a huge army in pursuit of what proved to be an extremely elusive Toqtamysh – for four long, dry months, a thousand kilometres across the vast western desert of Kazakhstan as far as the headwaters of the River Tobol (almost to Kurgan on the Trans–Siberian Railway). There he found the first clue to Toqtamysh's whereabouts, and finally caught up with him another seven hundred kilometres to the west, across the Ural Mountains, near Samara – and defeated him! Here, beside the Volga, the *Zafer–name* recorded,

> "the seat of the empire of Jochi, the great Genghis Khan's son,... Tamburlaine had the satisfaction of ascending [the] throne. The most beautiful ladies of his seraglio were beside him, and each lord had his own lady and each person held a goblet in his hand. The whole army took part in the entertainments...For twenty–six days they enjoyed all the pleasures...".

But again, Tamburlaine allowed Toqtamysh to escape, and left Kipchak – once more that curious deference to the imperial line? – to imperial Mongol pretenders. Toqtamysh took no time to recover his throne, and his strength, and in 1395 again attacked down west of the Caspian Sea, through the passes of Dagestan into Azerbaijan.

Finally, Tamburlaine's wrath was aroused, and he led an army back through Persia to the Caucasus. Toqtamysh recognised the changed mood, but Tamburlaine rejected his attempt at excuses and pressed on to attack his army on the banks of the River Terek at Tartartoub, a hundred–odd kilometres west of Grozny, capital of modern–day Chechnya, the region of bitter battles by Caucasian Moslems against the Russians in the 19th century, and now again since the end of the twentieth.[106] Ibn Arabshah gives a vivid picture – in a single sentence! – of the frenzy of the battle:

> "Then both armies, when they came in sight one of the other, were kindled, and mingling with each other became hot with the fire of war and they joined battle and necks were extended for sword–blows and throats outstretched for spear thrusts and faces were drawn with sternness and fouled with lust, the wolves of war set their teeth and fierce leopards mingled and charged and the lions of the armies rushed upon each other and men's skins bristled,

---

106 Tartartoub itself was in fact the site of a clash in 1846 between Imperial Russian troops and the guerrilla forces of the extraordinary Moslem Imam Shamyl of Daghestan, who led a successful guerrilla resistance against Russian efforts to control the Caucasus from 1831 until his defeat in 1857–59.

clad with the feathers of arrows and the brows of the leaders drooped and the heads of the captains bent in the devotion of war and fell forward and the dust was thickened and stood black and the leaders and common soldiers alike plunged into seas of blood and arrows became in the darkness of black dust like stars placed to destroy the Princes of Satan, while swords glittering like fulminating stars in clouds of dust rushed on kings and sultans nor did the hoses of death cease to pass through and revolve and race against the squadrons which charged straight ahead or the dust of hooves to be borne into the air or the blood of swords to flow over the plain, until the earth was rent and the heavens like the eight seas; and this struggle and conflict lasted above three days; then dust appeared from the stricken army of Toqtamysh...".

It was a near–run thing: Tamburlaine, fighting like an ordinary soldier,

"his arrows all spent, his spear broken, but his sword still brandished",

nearly went down; but in the end Toqtamysh was beaten.

This time, Tamburlaine sent his troops in pursuit until Toqtamysh vanished into the vast forests around Kazan. And, according to the *Zafer–name*, as they went the troops looted all the country of its treasures:

"There were gold, silver, furs, rubies, and pearls, there were young boys, and there were girls of great beauty".

Russian responses to Tamburlaine

Tamburlaine and the Russian princedoms did not actually fight directly, and it is no doubt for this reason that we probably have a better view of his influence on them from the receiving side than we do of the responses of his actual conquests, who were so crushed or at least cowed that their versions of the experience has scarcely survived. But, even without actual conflict, Tamburlaine's campaigns in one way and another had a significant impact on the nascent Russian state and society.

It is curious that, during the long struggles against Toqtamysh, Tamburlaine apparently made no effort to seek Russian support against the common enemy, as his Persian Ilkhan predecessors had appealed for Christian Europe's support against the Egyptian Mameluke rulers of

Syria during the Crusades,[107] or as Tamburlaine himself did later, before and during his campaigns against the Ottoman Turks, when he made approaches not only to the Byzantine rumps (both Constantinople and Trebizond, independent of the former since the Catholic invasion of 1204) but also to Genoa and Venice for support in the Turks' rear – though all these efforts were unsuccessful.[108]

Interestingly, in 1394, Toqtamysh himself had offered an alliance to the Mameluke Sultan Barquq of Egypt against Tamburlaine. Why did Tamburlaine not try to encircle Toqtamysh? One can only speculate about possible factors: mainly, perhaps, his apparent continual expectation, almost to the end, that Toqtamysh would eventually see his duty to his former benefactor and return to the fold; or perhaps he felt that, notwithstanding Dmitri Donskoi's victory over Khan Mamai, after Toqtamysh's crushing defeat of the Muscovites a mere two years later the Russian princedoms had little to offer him – they were in fact obliged to continue paying tribute to Toqtamysh's weak successor.

Nor, for their part, did the Russians appeal to Tamburlaine for support against Toqtamysh – with their traumatic experience of Mongol conquest and rule since 1240 such an idea was probably never even considered. In any case, in 1395 events rapidly developed precisely contrary to such a thought: after the pursuit of Toqtamysh beyond the Volga Tamburlaine lunged westwards across southern Russia from the Volga to the Dnieper, destroying everything in his path as he went, including the Genoese–Venetian trading port of Tana, on the Sea of Azov; then he swooped back round and headed northwards up the Don – directly towards Moscow.

The Grand Duke Basil I, better forewarned or better prepared than his father Dmitri Donskoi had been against Toqtamysh, moved his army a hundred kilometres south of Moscow to a defensive position on the River Oka. At the same time the terrified city had the most holy icon of Russia, the *Vladimir Mother of God*, a Byzantine icon of the Virgin

---

107   See 1300 chapter: Devorguilla of Galloway.

108   Trebizond, now Trabzon, on the Black Sea coast of Turkey not far from the border with Georgia, survived the Ottomans' capture of Constantinople in 1453 by another eight years. Two years after surrendering to Sultan Mahomet II, the last Emperor and his children were executed in (now) Istanbul, and their bodies thrown to the dogs outside the ancient Byzantine walls. Tamburlaine would have approved: David Comnenus, a descendant of Byzantium's 12th century ruling dynasty, had resisted valiantly.

Mary which many Russians believed had been painted from life by St Luke,[109] expressly brought from Vladimir to inspire the defence. The icon was perhaps of more value to the Muscovites than the army on the Oka: at Yelets, still three hundred and fifty kilometres from Moscow, Tamburlaine wheeled again, southwards to the mouth of the Don, then eastwards to Astrakhan across the Don and Kuban steppes, where the local Circassian tribes burned the grass before the invaders, a precursor to Russia's scorched earth policy in front of Napoleon's invasion four centuries later.

What was the purpose of this lunging around the western fringe of Toqtamysh's former territory? Why did Tamburlaine not head straight for Moscow? Did he in fact ever really intend to attack Moscow? Why, with a reputation for ferocity worth half a dozen divisions, did he suddenly turn back after getting so close? The only answers to these questions are other questions: Was his army too wearied after fighting and pursuing Toqtamysh? Did he receive reports that the Muscovite army was stronger than he had anticipated? Or was he simply warning Moscow of the acceptable limit of its territory? – Yelets was after all not far from its previous reach to Kulikova Pole. The argument that he turned back because destroying Kipchak was more important to him seems convincing only if it is assumed he feared defeat by the Russians: otherwise he might have expected to prevail against them and then deal with Kipchak at leisure.

But there is no doubt that what really saved Moscow in the longer term, and helped it immeasurably on the course Dmitri Donskoi had already set of assuming the leadership of the squabbling Russian princedoms, was Tamburlaine's utter destruction of Kipchak. Unlike his almost respectful withdrawal following victory over Toqtamysh at Samara four years before, this time he looted, destroyed and killed systematically through the Golden Horde's heartland, concluding with the total razing of the great capital city and Silk Road trading centre of Sarai, not far down the Volga River from Stalingrad (now Volgograd) – destroyed by another terrible conqueror, from the West, in the middle of our own past century. Sarai's extent was such, said Ibn Arabshah, that

"they say that a slave of one of the magnates of this city fled and fixed his abode in a place by the side of the road and opened a shop where he supported himself by trade; and that base fellow

---

109   See 1000 chapter: Vladimir of Kiev.

remained for about ten years – but his master never met him or found him or saw him, because of the size of the city and the multitude of its people".

Tamburlaine changed all that: the *Zafer–name* recorded that while their city burned, the survivors of Sarai were "driven before the army like sheep", in bitter cold; what a modern writer described as "the twenty square miles of bright water, tall mosques, workshops, palaces and winding streets" disappeared forever. Though, not long ago, a Russian archeologist found, amongst what little remains, skeletons – the heads, hands and feet all cut off.

It has long been said that Dmitri Donskoi's victory at Kulikova Pole in 1380 shattered the legend of the Tartars' invincibility; it might be added that the defeat of Toqtamysh and destruction of Sarai in 1395 shattered the Tartars. The destruction of the Horde's trading base meant the disappearance of the attendant manufacturing crafts and agricultural support on which it depended; and the consequent transfer of the northern Silk Road southwards removed the revenues which the once–valuable trade route had provided to the Horde – and added to Tamburlaine's control over and profit from the trade between East and West.

A decade or more later Ibn Arabshah wrote that

"the cultivated part of Dasht [Kipchak] became a desert and a waste, the inhabitants scattered, dispersed, routed and destroyed, so that if anyone went through it without a guide and scout, he would certainly perish losing the way, even in summer; since winds, lifting and scattering sands, hide the way, passing over it, and wipe it out. But in winter, since snow falling there collects on the road and covers it,...its stages and watering places are fearful wastes and the roads utterly deadly and difficult".

The overlordship exercised by Toqtamysh over the Mongols confronting Russia never really recovered. Within half a century internal bickering led to the establishment of three separate Khanates, which were separately a nuisance from time to time but never united to become a major threat again.[110]

---

110 They nevertheless lingered for some time: Kazan on the middle Volga, blocking access to Siberia, until 1552, and Astrakhan, downriver in the old

The only Russian city not to be conquered by the Mongols was Novgorod, though three years after Tamburlaine's final great campaign against the Golden Horde there was talk of a threat involving, of all people...Toqtamysh. In reality, the main threat to Novgorod at this time was from a strong and expanding Lithuania, the most powerful state in Eastern Europe, stretching from near Warsaw and Pskov in the north almost to the Black Sea across most of what are now Belarus and Ukraine. After Tamburlaine's withdrawal from Russia, Toqtamysh, bouncing back from defeat – yet again – for another try at power, tried to seize control of the remnants of the Horde whom Tamburlaine had confided to a reliable ally, the Amir Edigey; when he failed he fled again – Toqtamysh did a lot of fleeing in his career – this time to Lithuania.

There, once again, his plausibility persuaded the Lithuanian Grand Duke to agree to restore him to the khanate of the Golden Horde in return for Toqtamysh's ceding his suzerainty rights over Russia to Lithuania – which, given the element of fantasy in such rights, one would have thought was a rather lop–sided bargain. Toqtamysh must have been even more persuasive than that: for instead of the Grand Duke's following up his recent conquest of Smolensk with an attack on Novgorod, as would have been logical, he switched targets and supported Toqtamysh's Tartar rump against Edigey in the far south. There, near Dnepropetrovsk, the Amir defeated the invaders. Toqtamysh was put to flight yet again (though this was still not to be the last heard of him) and the threat to Lord Novgorod the Great's independence shifted from the alien west to fraternal Moscow – fatally.

In the meantime, during the decades when Tamburlaine was aiding, pursuing and finally overwhelming Toqtamysh and destroying Sarai, prosperous Novgorod was enjoying the continuation of the artistic flowering which had begun in Kievan times.[111] Merchants from the city, the eastern–most participant in the great trading Hanseatic League, maintained close connections with Constantinople, which also of course remained a focus for the Orthodox clergy between the fall of Kiev and the rise of an independent Russian church following the fall, in turn, of Byzantium. And it was probably these connections that resulted in the

---

heartland between Sarai and the Caspian, and hence the weakest, until 1556, both conquered by Tsar Ivan IV; the Khanate of the Crimea, which blocked Russian access to the Black Sea and a warm–water port, not taken from its Ottoman overlords, by Catherine the Great, until 1783.

111   See 1000 chapter: Vladimir of Kiev.

arrival in Novgorod in the 1370s, about the time Toqtamysh finally succeeded in becoming Khan of the White Horde, of one of the greatest fresco painters of all time, a migrant from Byzantium known as Theophanes the Greek.

Little is known about Theophanes' earlier life, though one tradition has it that he had painted in Constantinople itself and then in Kaffa (now Feodosia), the Genoese trading base on the southeastern shore of the Crimea.[112] We do not know why he went to Novgorod: some believe he may have been invited there by merchants who traded with the south. It must have been a difficult and dangerous journey, as much of the way was still in the hands of the Mongols of the Golden Horde, already coming under pressure from Toqtamysh – perhaps the early impact of this on Kaffa contributed to Theophanes' move.

During his early years in Novgorod Theophanes painted his wonderful frescoes in the Church of Our Saviour of the Transfiguration–in–Elijah–Street, a delightful name deriving not from a transcendental event at that location, but from the Russian practice of hyphenating place names (which they probably got from the French who do the same with streets). The church itself, a miniature masterpiece of Russian architecture built only a few years before, stands out by the elegant decoration of its surfaces: elongated windows in trinities, a multitude of variegated appliquéd crosses, and in contrast, the strict symmetry of the brick fret-working of the tall drum beneath the cupola, seemingly pointing to the unified perfection of heaven.

The Transfiguration Church's frescoes have a forcefulness unlike any others. Its masterpiece, the *Old Testament Trinity*, is breathtakingly expressionistic, the huge sweep of the central angel's wings arcing

---

112 Feodosia was originally the ancient Greek colony called Theodosia, but it had been reduced to a village after being overrun by the Huns in the 4th century CE. In the 13th century, after the Greek Empire had been disrupted by the Catholic Fourth Crusade's treacherous seizure of Constantinople, it was re-founded by the Genoese as Kaffa (or Caffa). It became the capital of their trading possessions in the Black Sea, and by the following century is said to have had a population of a hundred thousand. But, just after this, in 1347, it was in Kaffa that the Black Death first arrived among Europeans from its birthplace somewhere far to the east across the Mongol Silk Route; its fleeing sailors and merchants took it on to Constantinople, which it decimated, then westwards, and within twenty years it had killed more than a third of the population of the whole of Europe. Nevertheless Kaffa survived as a major trading centre for another century, until it was captured in 1475 by the Crimean Tartar Khanate.

majestically down the slightly asymmetrical apse of the church's Trinity Chapel, completely enfolding its two companions seated either side of an angular, almost Picasso–like, chalice. But the three faces are absolutely alike, stern but handsome, rather pretty even, strikingly different from the nearby aged prophets – young people, each with a mop of dark curls tied with white ribbons trailing away in elegant arabesques.

It is tempting to imagine that Theophanes could have come into contact in Kaffa with Italian painting introduced via Genoa, which for the preceding century had been amassing great wealth from the Crusades. The wealthy Catholic merchants in Kaffa had undoubtedly built churches, alongside the Byzantine churches where Theophanes worked; and their altar–pieces (perhaps even frescoes?) might well have been influenced by the new style transforming the face of Italy through the works earlier in the century by Giotto, Simone Martini and the Lorenzettis. We do not know what was there, or what Theophanes might have seen; but it is a nice thought that, though he was steeped in Byzantium's great traditions, the freedom from its rigidity in his Novgorod painting was just possibly influenced by a firsthand cross–cultural contact in Genoese Kaffa with some of the early fruits of the Renaissance in Italy.

Theophanes painted with broad brushstrokes: the figures in a burnt red on a black ground overpainted in white; faces, robes, angels' wings modelled in sweeping black strokes and dashes of white highlights; prophets and hermits with enormously long streaks of white beard on faces of pure anguish. The elongated figures inevitably bring to mind the work of his fellow–countryman Domenico Theotocopoulos working in Spain exactly two centuries later – El Greco. Theophanes' almost explosive human passion stands in marked contrast to the highly formal art of Byzantium: this is the painting of uncertainty – Theophanes' old home Constantinople under threat of imminent destruction by the Ottoman Turks, his adopted home Novgorod under threat from Lithuania on one side and Moscow on the other, all Russia apprehensively watching the long duel between the equally dangerous threats of the Golden Horde and Tamburlaine.

A wonderful description of Theophanes at work has miraculously come down to us in a fragment of a letter from Epiphanius, the biographer of Russia's greatest saint, Theophanes' contemporary, Sergius of Radonezh, a rare documentation of a painter at such an early date:

"...no one ever saw him looking at models as some of our painters do who, being filled with doubt, constantly [peer at] them casting their eyes hither and thither, and instead of painting with colours they gaze at the models as often as they need to. He, however, seemed to be painting with his hands, while his feet moved without rest, his tongue conversed with visitors, his mind dwelled on something lofty and wise, and his rational eyes contemplated that beauty which is rational".

The *Old Testament Trinity*, has just such a magnificent dash, as if Theophanes' feet and hands had to race to keep up with the holy wind of inspiration.[113]

Early in the new century Theophanes was in Moscow painting, together with his younger associate and, some say, pupil, Andrei Rublev, icons for the iconostasis – the great gilded icon–screen – of the Moscow Kremlin's Cathedral of the Annunciation, after which he disappears from our view.

Rublev himself came to be more extensively associated with Vladimir, whose two cathedrals were described at the end of the 1000 chapter on Vladimir of Kiev. The interior of the older Cathedral of the Assumption, the *Uspensky Sobor*, was completely covered by frescoes; some, though sadly faded, remain, including in particular a cycle of *The Last Judgement*, painted by Rublev in 1408 following the sacking of the city in 1382 by Toqtamysh and again in 1405 by the Amir Edigey. Parts have long since disappeared – with the result that there is virtually nothing left of Hell, while Paradise largely survives. It is as if – unlike in the great West European Last Judgements in Torcello, Padua, Orvieto and Rome – Rublev did not care to dwell on the punishment of the

---

113 The *Old Testament Trinity* came from the early Christian tradition of interpreting the Old Testament as prefiguring the New: three angels, the three men who appeared to Abraham to announce that his aged wife would bear a son, Isaac (Genesis, chapter 18), represent the Holy Trinity of the New Testament, and foreshadow the Incarnation; the chalice before them recalls Abraham's willingness to sacrifice Isaac, presaging God's sacrifice of Christ on the Cross. The earliest known such Old Testament Trinity is in fact in Rome (a fifth century mosaic in Santa Maria Maggiore); but Theophanes, together with Andrei Rublev – who painted for St Sergius's monastery the most famous icon of the *Old Testament Trinity* (now in the Tretyakov) – made the anticipatory, symbolic Trinity peculiarly Orthodox Russia's own, at a time when Western European painting was fixing on the representation of the New Testament Trinity of the Father, Son and dove of the Holy Spirit.

damned: as if, by the time he was painting the cycle, the people of Vladimir had already suffered enough punishment here on earth.

Indeed, the memory of Batu Khan's initial Mongol onslaught a hundred and sixty years before was still very much alive in long–suffering Vladimir. On the north side of the other Cathedral, St Demetrius's, a touching portrayal of its builder, Grand Duke "Big Nest" Vsevelod, with his five sons, the littlest sitting on his knee, had been sculpted when the Cathedral was built at the very end of the 12th century, only a few decades before Batu's Golden Horde appeared from the unknown east. Then, during thirty–one years, according to the old Russian chronicle of the first Mongol invasion,

> "the Tartars battered the town with their wall–battering instruments; they released arrows without number. Prince Vsevelod [another Vsevelod, son of one of those five boys on the Cathedral wall] saw that the battle waxed yet more fierce, took fright because of his youth, and went forth from the town with his small company, carrying with him many gifts and hoping to receive his life. Batu, like a wild beast, did not spare his youth, but ordered that he be slaughtered before him, and he slew all the town. When the bishop, with the princess and her children, fled to the church [the nearby Uspensky Sobor], the godless one commanded it to be set on fire. Thus they surrendered their souls to God".

And thus was Vladimir's repeated Hell that Rublev painted in his lost fresco, just after the death of Tamburlaine, who had created other Hells elsewhere.[114]

---

114 Rublev returned to Moscow, and died there at the Andronikov Monastery in 1430. In his last years he frescoed the walls of the Monastery's Cathedral of the Saviour, said to have been built on a mass grave of Muscovite soldiers who fell at the Battle of Kulikovo Field in 1380, though three hundred kilometres seems a considerable distance for the creation of a sort of medieval Arlington Cemetery. No respecters of anyone else's history, Napoleon's soldiery burned the Cathedral, and Rublev's frescoes with it, when they sacked Moscow in 1812 in their frustration over the then Russian army's scorched–earth elusiveness. (Napoleon also stole the golden framework of the iconostasis from the Kremlin's Cathedral of the Annunciation, but the middle rows of icons by Theophanes and Rublev survived, to be put back in place in the new screen where they managed to survive Lenin and Stalin also.) The Soviet Union

The great conquests: southwards to India

India had not been part of the Genghis Khan empire that Tamburlaine seemed to be re–creating, but it had been the scene of raids by the latter's Central Asian predecessors, notably in 1303, when a Mongol army besieged Delhi for two months. These successive earlier raids were essentially plundering expeditions; Tamburlaine would dignify his own with high religious purpose. According to the *Zafer–name*, his aim was solely to make war on the enemies of Islam:

> "The Koran emphasizes that the highest dignity to which man may attain is to wage war in person on the enemies of the Faith. This is why the great Tamburlaine was always concerned to exterminate the infidels, as much as to acquire merit as from love of glory".

No matter that the Sultanate of Delhi *was* Moslem: Tamburlaine considered the Sultans had been too lenient with their pagan Hindu subjects. But it was their internecine feuds following the death in 1388 of the last great Tughluk Sultan, Feroz Shah, on which Tamburlaine was better informed: over the intervening ten years, five of Feroz Shah's sons and grandsons had grabbed and lost his throne. Anarchic Delhi was clearly ripe for the picking.

In *The Decline and Fall of the Roman Empire* Gibbon records that when Tamburlaine first proposed to his princes and emirs the invasion of India

> "he was answered by a murmur of discontent: 'The rivers! and the mountains and deserts! and the soldiers clad in armour! And the elephants, the destroyers of men!' "

– presumably the memory was still alive of the twenty elephants that had helped the then Khwarazmshah Sultan defend Samarkand (though unsuccessfully) against Genghis Khan.[115] But, Gibbon adds,

---

established the Andrei Rublev Museum of Ancient Russian Culture and Art at the Andronikov Monastery, to house icons removed from closed or destroyed churches; but with impenetrable Soviet logic, none of Rublev's icons was put there.

115   Elephants had been an Indian weapon for a long time. In the mid–7th century the Chinese Buddhist monk Xuanzang was on pilgrimage in northern India at the time of the brief but splendid reign of King Harsha–Vardhana, a

"the displeasure of the emperor was more dreadful than all these terrors".

So the army set out early in 1398, four hundred thousand strong, according to Schiltberger, "ninety–two squadrons of a thousand horse" alone, plus foot–soldiers, according to Gibbon, who said Tamburlaine observed "with pleasure" that that number

"most fortunately corresponds with the ninety–two names or epithets of the prophet Mahomet".

Ibn Khaldun (who was not one of Gibbons' sources) had likewise said of Tamburlaine's army at Damascus,

"if you estimate it at one million it would not be too much, nor can you say it is less".

But this business of the numbers in the armies is bedevilled by the amplification factor of Tamburlaine's reputation: his admirers attribute him with vast forces because of his overwhelming victories, his opponents attribute him with the same multitudes because of their overwhelming defeats. His armies were by no means all Mongols and Turkmen of his heartland domains; these formed the core of his forces, but as he swept to and fro across Central and West Asia, the Caucasus and Persia, he accumulated a heterogeneous collection of others, either directly or through the new adherence of emirs and princelings bringing, before they had no choice in the matter, their followers to join his legions.

---

convert to Buddhism with whom the monk spent some time, and who eventually ruled from the Ganges delta to the border of Kashmir and westwards to Gujarat and the Arabian Sea. In the context of debate about the inflatability of military numbers in Tamburlaine's time, it is interesting to note that Xuanzang's report to the Chinese Emperor on his travels, which is generally regarded as remarkably accurate, recorded that Harsha's army included an elephant corps of *sixty thousand*, as well as one hundred thousand cavalry. And he noted a practice not mentioned in the Arab sources on Tamburlaine's Indian campaign, so perhaps discontinued: it was the custom to feed the elephants huge quantities of wine before battle, presumably to give them drunken courage and ferocity. (S.H.Wriggins: *The Silk Road Journey with Xuanzang* (Boulder, CO 2004))

Eventually they included some of everyone, as the jaundiced Ibn Arabshah recorded of the army at Damascus in a splendidly zoomorphic incantation:

"There were men of Turan, warriors of Iran, leopards of Turkistan, tigers of Balkhshan, hawks of Dasht and Khata, Mongol vultures, Jata eagles, vipers of Khajend, basilisks of Andakan, reptiles of Khwarizm, wild beasts of Jurjan, eagles of Zaghanian and hounds of Hisar Shadman, horsemen of Fars, lions of Khorasan, and hyenas of Jil, lions of Mazanderan, wild beasts of the mountains, crocodiles of Rustamdar and Talqan, asps of the tribes of Khuz and Kerman, wolves of Ispahan, wearing shawls, wolves of Rei and Ghazni and Hamadan, elephants of Hind and Sind and Multan, rams of the provinces of Lur, bulls of the high mountains of Ghor, scorpions of Shahrizor and serpents of Askar Makram and Jandisabur...To these were added hyena–cubs of slaves and whelps of Turkomans and rabble and followers and ravening dogs of base Arabs, and gnats of Persians, and crowds of idolators and profane Magi; people [he concluded, finally out of breath] whom no list could cover and no roll include".

In the light of modern debate on gender roles, a more sober observation by Ibn Arabshah is also of interest:

"There were also in his army many women who mingled in the mêlée of battle and in fierce conflicts and strove with men and fought with brave warriors and overcame mighty heroes in combat with the thrust of the spear, the blow of the sword and shooting of arrows; when one of them was heavy with child and birthpangs seized her, while they were on the march, she turned from the way and withdrawing apart and descending from her beast, gave birth to the child and wrapping it in bandages, soon mounted her beast and taking the child with her, followed her company".

As the vast army set off for India it still did not yet of course include those recruits from Hind and Sind and Multan, but it soon would:

"he marched with such vigour", Ibn Arabshah conceded, "that he almost overtook the birds".

First, they had to pass between the five–thousand–metre peaks of the Hindu Kush (in Afghanistan), fighting off bandits entrenched in the massive range, at times having to use pulley and tackle to negotiate deep ravines: the *Zafer–name* said Tamburlaine had to be lowered on a litter three hundred metres, from ledge to ledge, down a precipice. His Chief Queen and his grandson Ulugh Beg participated in this strenuous journey – as they did on many of his campaigns – but were sent back to Samarkand from Kabul to avoid the Indian climate.

By the time he approached the Indus, Tamburlaine was marching in the footsteps of Alexander the Great, who was heading, in his case, into the totally unknown, in 326 BCE, one thousand seven hundred and twenty–four years before. And near Attock, in almost exactly the same place as his Macedonian predecessor, Tamburlaine crossed the great river in the same manner, on a bridge of boats.[116] Across the Indus, Tamburlaine's forces still had to cross two of its major tributaries, the Chenab at Multan, and the Sutlej further east; from there they marched straight across the top of the Cholistan desert towards Delhi. Tamburlaine had got further east than Alexander, and perhaps he even knew it: the trace of the ancient conqueror Iskander had been preserved – as it still is – in local folk tales almost everywhere he had been.

Before reaching the final showdown at Delhi, Tamburlaine killed off the hundred thousand prisoners he had accumulated so they would not hamper his progress – just like that; they were, after all, only pagan Hindus. Hookham notes that it was said Tamburlaine objected to the inclusion of the number of prisoners slain in the record of the campaign: a cook should be judged by the success of the dish, he argued, not by

---

116 During the Raj the British built road and railway bridges at Attock, and several other road bridges lower down the Indus; but between Mithankot on the west bank and Chachran on the east, about six hundred kilometres south of Attock and a similar distance north of Karachi, there was still in 1992 a bridge of boats, pretty much like those of Alexander and Tamburlaine. It spanned all four channels of the Indus at that point, the plank roadway over the main channel being constructed across thirty–four of the sturdy flat–bottomed wooden boats, three to four metres apart, each about fourteen metres in length and about four across at four–wheel–drive road–bearing level. I do not know how frequently the bridge and the boats are replaced, but that year there was one with the date "1941" carved deep into an end–post. As we watched, a camel train made its way across, some of the beasts laden with brushwood fuel and some with great woven rattan paniers of grain, much as the trains of Alexander's and Tamburlaine's armies must have included.

the blood on his hands during the preparation. Probably because of this great slaughter the Indians resisted more heroically than he had anticipated. The dreaded elephants were placed to the fore of the Indian defence; and, Ibn Arabshah reported,

> "they built on all the elephants towers armed with shields and filled each tower with soldiers proved in desperate enterprises and bold, after strengthening the towers with strong coverings, and they hung from them bells and fearsome gongs, which might call to flight the fiercest foe, and fastened to their trunks the finest swords, which are called swords of Hind".

But in the decisive battle at Panipat outside Delhi on 17 December 1398 Tamburlaine deployed two stratagems against them: as Ibn Arabshah had grudgingly to admit,

> "he used cunning to unravel the net [of the Indian army] and stew them in their juice thicker than broth".

In the first, an early version of James Bond's dirty tricks, Tamburlaine

> "used keen thought in fashioning spikes of iron, with three extremities of new design, recalling by their horrid shape the dogma of the Trinity or the triangle of the geometricians; and they made for him many thousands of them; and he marking the places where the elephants would stand in lines scattered the spikes by night and so prepared for them and the men with them slaughter and lamentation".

But that was not all: in addition,

> "Timur ordered that five hundred swift camels [Schiltberger, not surprisingly, said twenty thousand!] should be got and their saddles and carts stuffed with dried reeds and cotton soaked with oil and that they be driven in front of the cavalry, until the two armies came in sight of each other and when they were drawn up for battle, and nothing remained but slaughter, those bundles and loads should be set on fire and they should be driven against the frightened elephants, and when the camels felt the heat of the fires, then they cried out and leapt and rushed against the elephants...

And when the elephants saw the fires and heard the cry of the camels and saw their form and presence, while they groaned and leapt and thudded with the strokes of their hooves, in fear they turned against their drivers and trampled on them and against their riders and mutilated them and trod down the cavalry and broke the infantry".

And so it was. "Soon", the *Zafer–name* said,

"one saw the ground strewn with elephants' trunks mingled with the bodies and heads of the dead".

The Sultan took refuge in Gujerat; Tamburlaine made a triumphal entry into his conquered capital. During his fifteen days there he was enthroned on the throne of the Sultans, and was greeted there by one hundred and twenty ceremonial elephants:

"These well–trained elephants", the *Zafer–name* recorded, "bowed their heads and knelt before him in obeisance, and all trumpeted at the same moment, as if rendering homage".

Unusually, Tamburlaine agreed to the mullahs' request that he spare the citizens – though for a high price, of course – and he retired to his headquarters outside the city, the fifth Delhi, established by Feroz Shah (and stretching from Old Delhi beyond the Diplomatic Enclave in present–day southern New Delhi). But within the city things soon got out of hand: the citizens resisted when authorized "requisition" became pillage. Some say that what followed was one of the rare occasions, perhaps the only occasion, on which Tamburlaine lost control of his troops, others that he gave the order himself in outrage: at all events his troops looted, burned the city to the ground, and massacred or enslaved the entire population. Tamburlaine allegedly made the best of it:

"Although I was desirous of sparing them, I could not succeed, for it was the will of God that this calamity should befall the city".

Once again, "minarets" were made with the heads of the slaughtered. When Tamburlaine left, loaded with loot, his pious duty completed by flaying Hindus alive on the way, he left behind, as at Sarai, nothing. It was said that for two months nothing in Delhi moved, not even a bird.

By the time Alexander the Great had penetrated into India east of the present–day region of Lahore and Amritsar he heard of another great Indian kingdom to conquer, yet further east on the sacred Ganges River. But, for the first time in his career, he faced revolt, because it had also been reported that the ruler of Magadha had a whole army of – elephants. Not tens or hundreds, but thousands upon thousands. Alexander flew into a rage at his recalcitrant officers, then a sulk; he told his Macedonians they were free to go home and "tell their friends they had deserted their king in the middle of their enemy". Nothing worked, and a conveniently unfavourable priestly reading of a special sacrifice enabled Alexander to follow the wishes of the gods and turn his relieved army down the Indus on the way back to Persia.

But when Tamburlaine left the ruins of Delhi he did not turn straight back to Samarkand: he headed northeast for the Ganges, and actually crossed it, according to Gibbons' sources, seventy odd kilometres south of Dehra Dun. Perhaps he found the dusty plains as did his descendant Babur, the first of the Moghul Emperors:

"Hindustan is a country that has few pleasures to recommend it. The people are not handsome; they have no idea of the charms of friendly society…no good horses…no grapes or musk melon…no ice in cold water, no good food or bread in their bazaars".

The move was not for any particular military reason that now seems apparent – but it *was* where Alexander had never trod. The thought comes again, irresistibly: Tamburlaine was consciously emulating, and surpassing, his Macedonian predecessor. Two years later, outside besieged Damascus, Alexander was one of the heroes of history – along with Caesar, Chosroes (descendant of the Persian Sassanid King Shapur) and Nebuchadnezzar – of whom Ibn Khaldun and Tamburlaine would talk.[117]

---

117 Alexander's 2nd century CE biographer Arrian, a Greek officer in the Roman army, recalled that the Macedonian general Nearchus, the great conqueror's boyhood friend who accompanied him on the Indian expedition, had recorded a legend that Cyrus the Great, the 6th century BCE founder of the Achaemenid Dynasty that Alexander had terminated just before his destruction of Persepolis, had crossed the Baluchistan desert, but, reaching the Indus with only seven survivors, was unable to go any further. And, Arrian said, when "Alexander heard these old stories they inspired him to go one better".

It is said that it was on the banks of the Ganges that Tamburlaine, now sixty-three, received the news of the ambitions of the Ottoman Turk Emperor Bajazeth, far off to the west beyond newly restive Azerbaijan and Georgia, that caused him to return to Samarkand to prepare for a new campaign to deal with all three, leaving only a minor and, as it turned out, very impermanent local Moslem prince as his viceroy in India. It highlights the curious nature of Tamburlaine's empire, as a vast circle of principalities, surrounding his Central Asian heartland, which he would raid and raid again but never establish a subordinate imperial administration in any of them. If they rose in revolt, as they frequently did, it simply presented another opportunity for looting them.

It would no doubt have been difficult, in any case, to establish an administration in the wake of the depopulation and devastation that Tamburlaine's conquests invariably caused; and it was no doubt difficult to avoid the sacking of conquered cities and the seizure of agricultural crops en route when there was no alternative way for the army – whether it was forty thousand or four hundred thousand – to be fed and paid. It was the intelligence system we have already noted, throughout the length and breadth of central and west Asia, and into Russia, India, Persia, Egypt and Turkey, which enabled him to react to events with a rapidity that constantly caught his opponents off-balance. But Tamburlaine never returned to India.

Golden Samarkand

Tamburlaine was interested everywhere he went in

> "what things excelled there and were remarkable...the craft which [everyone] practised and tools which they used".

The interest was far from being only military, as we have seen with his despatch, from a series of cities, of savants and craftsmen to Samarkand: his soldiers were forbidden to massacre and loot a defeated city until a choice had been made, Ibn Arabshah said, of an

> "infinite multitude of lawyers, theologians, men who knew the Koran from memory, and learned man, craftsmen, workmen, slaves, women, boys and girls".

Before leaving Delhi, before even the massacre of the hundred thousand prisoners, Tamburlaine, the destroyer of cities, had again separated out the skilled craftsmen from the populace, to send back to work on the beautification of his own capital. And, along with them, went the elephants, to be used on his construction projects.

> "Timur", Ibn Arabshah reported, "gathered from all sides and collected at Samarkand the fruits of everything; and that place accordingly had in every wonderful craft and rare art someone who excelled in wonderful skill and was famous beyond his rivals in his craft".

They included

> "goldsmiths...polishers of gems...many painters...planters of trees...innumerable sculptors of glass, bronze and other things"

– with stonemasons, sculptors and stucco–workers from Isfahan, Azerbaijan and Delhi, mosaic–workers from Shiraz.

> "Then shall my native city Samarcanda,
> And crystal waves of fresh Jaertis' stream,
> The pride and beauty of her princely seat,
> Be famous through the furthest continents;
> And there my palace royal shall be plac'd,
> Whose shining turrets shall dismay the heavens,
> And cast the fame of Ilion's tower to hell:
> Through the streets, with troops of conquer'd kings,
> I'll ride in golden armour like the sun;
> And in my helm a triple plume shall spring,
> Spangled with diamonds, dancing in the air,
> To note me emperor of the three–fold world".

Marlowe was writing from his vivid imagination. But in fact we have the second European eyewitness to Tamburlaine's court at Samarkand – and his breathless descriptions of Tamburlaine's splendour easily match Marlowe's. He was a Spaniard, Don Ruy Gonzalez de Clavijo, and his account, *Narrative of the Embassy of Ruy Gonzales de Clavijo to the Court of Timour, at Samarkand, AD 1403–6*, seems likely to have been the origin of the work by the 16th century Spaniard Mexía which Marlowe used for his play. Clavijo was sent by King Henry III of Castile as ambassador to Tamburlaine in a repeat of the fallacy that had lured

European monarchs to court Genghis Khan two centuries before: that the enemy of my enemy must be my friend. By the time of his voyage in 1403–1405 Europe knew of Tamburlaine's defeat of the Ottomans, the greatest threat to Byzantium and, beyond it, to Austria and Hungary, and was again alive with rumours of the Mongols' supposed Christian sympathies. Clavijo was received with great courtesy, but he was to find no interest in the problems of Europe – Tamburlaine's mind was already turned east.[118]

Clavijo's lengthiest descriptions, quite fascinating in their detail, are of what fascinated him most: the splendours of the court of Timour Beg, as he called Tamburlaine, the settings and protocol of his audiences with the latter; the elaborate marquees, with multicoloured silk hangings, crimson carpets, in various gardens outside the city; the entertainments and feasts given in them, with bowls and drinking vessels and even tables of gold and silver, but (as in many times and places) not necessarily attuned to a foreign ambassador's palate:

"meat boiled, roasted, and dressed in other ways...the most honourable piece was the haunch of the horse...pieces of the tripes of the horses [served in] entire sheep's heads".

He attended the weddings of six of Tamburlaine's grandsons, including his successor Ulugh Beg, where the wine, notwithstanding Mohammed's adjuration, always flowed copiously –

---

118   Alexander the Great had been to Samarkand, too – in 328 BCE, two years before his invasion of India – when, as Maracanda, it was renowned as the capital of the Persian province of Sogdiana: "Everything I have heard about the beauty of Maracanda is true", he said, "except that it is more beautiful than I could imagine". And it was at Samarkand that, in a fit of drunken rage, Alexander murdered one of his senior commanders and closest friends, Cleitus, who, also drunk, had unwisely criticized his generalship. Alexander's extremes of remorse may well have further contributed to undermining his authority which was to be so stunningly challenged two years later in India. He did not leave any other mark in Samarkand, but also turned east, founding one of his many Alexandrias, *Alexandria Eschate*, Alexandria–the–Furthest, two hundred kilometres away on the Jaxartes River, the Syr Darya, on the very frontier of the Persian Empire. The city was later to be re–named Antioch, then Khojend by Tajik invaders, then, when in the USSR, "as other names became splendid" (as Robin Lane Fox put it), Stalinabad, then when he was unmasked, Leninabad. Now, in a Tajikistan independent since 1991, it is Khojend again. Thus do conquerors come and go.

"no feast, we were informed, was regarded as a real festival unless the guests drank themselves silly".

Even Ibn Arabshah, that implacable one, conceded the "charm and beauty" of these extravagances:

> "'Tis Paradise! The full moon shines.
> In Eden what could rival this
> Eternal spring? All joy combines –
> Our only care to drink and kiss!"

But, pulling himself together, the old sermonizer added that Tamburlaine then

> "slept away his drunkenness and presently returned to his own vomit".

Afterwards, Clavijo reported, the great conqueror was anxious to see the progress of his buildings in the city: and, ordering his horse to be saddled for him, Tamburlaine "entered Samarkand as the soul enters the body". Clavijo essayed, unsatisfactorily, a description of Samarkand itself:

> "The city of Samarcand is situated in a plain, and surrounded by an earthen wall. It is a little larger than the city of Seville, but, outside the city, there are a great number of houses, joined together in many parts, so as to form suburbs. The city is surrounded on all sides by many gardens and vineyards...Amongst these gardens...there are great and noble houses, and here the lord has several palaces... Many streams of water flow through the city, and through these gardens...there are many cotton plantations, and melon grounds, and the melons of this ground are good and plentiful...a wonderful quantity of melons and grapes".

And he went on at some length about the melons. Clavijo clearly saw a good deal more of the palaces and gardens outside than of the city itself, which was not surprizing as that was where the court usually resided, moving about quite frequently from one to another when Tamburlaine was at home, as the great and lesser princes of Europe would do between their numerous chateaux in a later age.

But he did visit the citadel within the city, where a thousand armourers were said to be kept at work unceasingly making bows, arrows, armour and helmets. And he also saw what a great entrepôt Samarkand was, at the centre of the Silk Road now that, by the time he was there, Tamburlaine had forced it into the bounds of his domains:

> "Russia and Tartary send linen and skins; China sends silks, which are the best in the world, (more especially the satins), and musk, which is found in no other part of the world, rubies and diamonds, pearls and rhubarb, and many other things. The merchandise which comes from China is the best and most precious which comes to this city...From India come spices, such as nutmeg, cloves, mace, cinnamon, ginger, and many other things".

Like Ibn Arabshah, he also noted Tamburlaine's habit of collecting craftsmen,

> "especially all those who were skilful in any art. From Damascus he brought weavers of silk, and men who made bows, glass, and earthenware...From Turkey he brought archers, masons, and silversmiths. He also brought men skilled in making engines of war: and he sowed hemp and flax, which had never before been seen in the land. There was so great a number of people brought to this city, from all parts, both men and women, that they are said to have amounted to one hundred and fifty thousand persons, of many nations, Turks, Arabs, and Moors, Christian Armenians, Greek Catholics, and Jacobites, and those who baptise with fire in the face, who are Christians with peculiar opinions".[119]

---

119 These last were possibly survivors of Manichaeism, followers of the 3rd century CE Parthian prophet Mani (sometimes Manes), who founded a missionary religion based on Zoroastrianism, Christianity and Buddhism, whose very inclusiveness guaranteed the hostility of its constituents. It thrived for half a millennium from North Africa (St Augustine was a Manichean before his conversion) right across the Silk Road trading centres into China (where the remains of a Manichean temple have been found as far south as Quanzhou, Marco Polo's "Zayton"), and was adopted by the Uighur Khanate in the 8th century; but it gradually faded away in the face of Zoroastrian and then Moslem persecution on the western end of the Silk Road and isolation on the eastern end in China. Much of what is known about Manichaeism comes from the finds made in 1904 at Karakhoja (now Gaochang), near Turpan in China's

Craftsmen were housed by trade, not by ethnicity; but, Clavijo said, all
was harmonious:

> "Good order is maintained in Samarqand with utmost strictness
> and none dare fight with another or oppress his neighbours by
> force. Indeed as to fighting, that Timur makes them do enough,
> but abroad".

But there is very little in the way of description of the fabled mosques
and mausoleums with which Tamburlaine was beautifying his capital, or
of the fifteen or so elaborate gardens with their palaces – including one
in the Chinese style: the first Chinoiserie? – surrounding the city in the
rich valley of the Zerafshan River. Clavijo's audiences and feastings were
in vast tented pavilions, with cloth of gold and silk hangings set with
pearls and emeralds and turquoises and rubies, and fountains with
apples floating in them. Of the palaces themselves he notes, on a couple
of occasions, that they were there in the background,

> "very finely built of brick ornamented with tiles wrought variously
> in gold and blue".

Tamburlaine himself, the heir to nomads, obviously preferred the tents
to the palaces during the brief intervals during which he was actually in
Samarkand.

It is the blues of the tiles of Tamburlaine's Samarkand that make
the most vivid impression today. There is not a great deal of his creation
left in the unedifying concrete of the modern Soviet city, and the most
recognizable of its ancient monuments, the three great mosques
and *medresseh* (schools) around the Registan plaza, are the work of
Tamburlaine's grandson Ulugh Beg and later potentates. But there are
three great reminders: Tamburlaine's own tomb, the *Gur Emir*, the so–
called Mausoleum of *Bibi Khanum*, and the necropolis of *Shakhi–Zinda*
on the edge of the old city. They are all stunningly beautiful in their
different ways and degrees of incompleteness: whether seen glowing
red–bricked in the shimmering furnace of mid–summer; or with the

---

western Xinjiang province, by the German archeologist Albert von Le Coq;
amongst other treasures, he removed the only known frescoed portrait of
Mani to Berlin, where it was destroyed by Allied bombing during the Second
World War.

turquoise domes capped by snow in mid–winter, when – indeed – the last rays of the setting sun can turn the frost golden against the pale blue of the sky, making the monuments look "wrought variously in gold and blue".

The Shakhi–Zinda, "the Shrine of the Living King", is in fact like a long, narrow street, its series of steps and rising pathway closely lined by three sets of small, domed mausoleums and mosques stretching up beyond the great entrance portal erected by Ulugh Beg (where, on baking mid–summer days, peddlers wait in the cool of the deep shade with bowls of refreshing, slightly bitter, green tea). It is best seen as a whole from across the rumpled open ground, dotted with grave stones, to the west, from where the solid brick bases of the buildings and their elaborately tiled drums and multi–formed domes – some brilliant blue, some fluted white, one magnificently patterned – slope gently down in a long disorderly procession to Ulugh Beg's gate.

The complex takes its name from Kasim ibn Abbas, a Moslem saint and cousin of the Prophet Mohammed, who is said to have brought Islam to Samarkand in the 7th century and to be still living because, when beheaded for this, he grabbed his head – like St Denis, the first Bishop of Paris – and leaped into a nearby well. In the nineteenth century the hopeful legend grew up that he would reappear to defeat the Russians; the Soviets said nonsense, the place was originally the site of an ancient cult worshipping the ruler of an imaginary underground kingdom, which "the Moslem clergy camouflaged with the name of Kasim". But now the Russians are gone. Kasim's shrine is near the far end of the Shakhi Zinda, and the four–tiered grave–marker (for the absent body?), covered with elaborate tiles and gilt, is not only pre–Tamburlaine but probably pre–Genghis Khan. Its neighbouring mausoleums, and those in the central group, were built in the earlier part of Tamburlaine's reign for various close relations, and a later one for one of his wives.

Everything in Shakhi–Zinda, walls, doorways, domes, is covered with a profusion of tiles in patterns of dark blue and turquoise: some in wonderful geometries, others – everywhere – with quotations from the Koran in one or other or both of the blues, or picked out in white, in a multitude of the scripts in which Arabic is written by the greatest calligraphers. The doorway to the tomb of Shadi–Mulk, Tamburlaine's niece, is framed on each side of its slim entrance columns – themselves covered in the finest elaborately carved tilework – by *forty–one* different vertical bands of tiles, six in floral patterns, two with Koranic inscriptions, one of these in a tightly rectangular calligraphy decorated with little knotted finials, the other in elegantly flowing, looping white arabesques over rich blue leaves. The impression in the azured and shadowed Shakhi–Zinda is not one of mourning but of the utmost exhilaration – "bringing to later generations", a Soviet guidebook remarked with typical Great Russian condescension, "the greatness of a people that has not been subjugated either by rulers or by religion".

Nearer the centre of Samarkand, the Bibi Khanum Mosque is only a ruined shell, though enough remains – a vast, cracked arch, flying above the high entrance façade glazed with rigidly rectangular patterns of an infinity of exclamations of the greatness of Allah, half of the great dome – to reveal the measure of its original greatness. An unknown Arab chronicler wrote,

"Its dome would have been unique had it not been for the Heavens, and unique would have been its portal had it not been for the Milky Way".

In 1875, the first known American to see it, the young St Petersburg–based diplomat Eugene Schuyler, one of the first Western visitors after the Russian conquest, it had been

"converted into a market for cotton, and is full of mules and horses (which are stabled there), and of carts placed there for safe–keeping".

To see the mosque's remains in silence now, cleared out and cleaned up by Soviet restorers, is to be reminded rather of the great Cistercian abbey ruins, like Fountains in Yorkshire or Jumièges in Normandy (though they are three hundred and fifty years older): the great pointed arch, the crumbled masonry amongst the old trees, the simple grass (patchy in Samarkand) where congregations of the faithful once stood.

Ibn Arabshah wrote that Tamburlaine

"had seen in India a mosque pleasant to the sight and sweet to the eye; its vault was beautifully built and adorned with white marble and the pavement likewise; and being greatly pleased with its beauty, he wished that one like it should be built for him at Samarkand".

The mosque in India was that built by Sultan Feroz Shah in the 1350s in the north of his (the fifth) Delhi, where Tamburlaine had stopped for prayer as he began his march out of the captured city into northern Hindustan.[120] The Bibi Khanum was begun during his absence on the India campaign, but as it was still incomplete on his return its continuation was influenced by Feroz Shah's mosque. The famous elephants were used to haul blocks of stone as Tamburlaine tried to hurry his mosque to completion.[121]

The mosque's size, almost that of Milan Cathedral, was its doom: the materials could not endure the load–bearing strain, even less, therefore, withstand earthquakes; and it is said to have begun to collapse shortly after it was built. The eponymous Bibi Khanum may or may not have been Tamburlaine's wife, and may or may not have been a daughter of the Chinese Emperor, but it seems likely that this was the mosque which Clavijo described as "the most respected in the city"; and the one that,

> "When it was finished [Tamburlaine] thought the entrance was too low, so he ordered the building to be pulled down;

---

120   Only the rear – western – wall of the mosque still stands in Feroz Shah Kotla ("Citadel"), an attractive garden a short way to the south of Shah Jahan's Red Fort in Old Delhi. The garden's main treasure today is the carved pillar that Feroz Shah had removed from Meerut (thirty kilometres to the north) and installed here, in what were then his palace grounds, because he thought the inscription was a magic charm. It might not have survived the mullahs – or Tamburlaine, for that matter – had they known what it really was: it was only in 1837 that an Englishman, James Princep, deciphered it as the ancient Brahmi script of the edicts promoting Buddhism issued by the great 3rd century BCE Indian Emperor Ashoka (whose exiled grandfather, incidentally, had met Alexander the Great, in the great religious centre of Taxila, just after the latter had crossed the Indus).

121   There were only fourteen elephants left by the time of Clavijo's visit – he thought twelve years after Tamburlaine had turned the tide against them at Panipat, though in fact it was only six. He was seeing the animal for the first time in his life, and left a very creditable page–long description for his fellow Spaniards; he saw them "run, and perform tricks", but, ever practical, observed

> "from what I then saw, that one elephant is worth a thousand men in a battle; for when they are amongst men, they rush about more wildly, and fight better";

and he noted an innovation, something that had not been reported as an Indian practice:

> "When they make them fight, they bind their trunks with spikes of iron, and fasten swords upon them...as the tusks are too high up for them to wound with them".

and that it might be sooner rebuilt, he took charge of one part himself".

There is an engaging story of Tamburlaine trying to speed up the rebuilding by squatting by the foundations as they were being dug, and throwing cooked meat and coins down to the workers to encourage them, "as though one should cast bones to dogs in a pit" – an early version of the Soviets' Stakhanovite shock–brigades. This impatient whipping on of his masons was of a piece with his failure to pause long enough to establish an imperial administration in the rush to go off on further conquests.

Tamburlaine's personal intervention may account for the existence of the great archway – and perhaps for the inexpert engineering. The ever–vitriolic Ibn Arabshah quoted a contemporary, "a wise man, clever and of keen judgement", who, after stones fell from the roof on those at prayer, sending them all fleeing, said

"this mosque should be called Haram [forbidden by the Sacred Law] and prayer in it the prayer of fear";

and added, for good measure, a suggested inscription for its porch:

"I hear that thou buildest a mosque out of rapine
But, praise be to Allah! thou pleasest not;
Like him who maintains orphans by harlotry,
Woe to thee! mayest thou not enjoy love or gain alms".

Clavijo also reports on Tamburlaine's ruthless development of a downtown shopping mall: as there was, he says,

"not a place for the orderly and regular display of the merchandize for sale, the lord ordered that a street should be made in the city, with shops for the sale of merchandize. This street was commenced at one end of the city, and went through to the other...[The builders] began to work, pulling down such houses as stood in the line by which the lord desired the street to run, and as the houses came down, their masters fled with their clothes and all they had: then, as the houses came down in front, the work went on behind. They made the street very broad, and covered it with a vaulted roof, having windows at intervals to let in the light.

As soon as the shops were finished, people were made to occupy them, and sell their goods; and at intervals in the street there were fountains. A great number of workmen came into the city, and those who worked in the daytime, were relieved by others who worked all night. Some pulled down houses, others levelled the ground, and others built the street; and day and night they made such a noise, that they seemed to be like so many devils. This great work was finished in twenty days, which was very wonderful".

There was a modern real estate sequel as well:

"the owners of the houses which were pulled down went to certain...friends of the lord; and one day, when they were playing at chess with the lord, they said that, as he had caused those houses to be destroyed, he ought to make some amends to the owners. Upon this he got into a rage, and said, "This city is mine, and I bought it with my money...".

The other gem of Tamburlaine's Samarkand is his own tomb, the *Gur Emir*, "the grave of the king". In fact Tamburlaine had it built to bury his favourite grandson, Mohammed Sultan, who died in 1403 on the return march from the Aegean Sea, but his own body was also interred there after his death in 1405, facing, as we noted earlier, his long–time spiritual adviser Sayyid Baraka. It was possibly to the celebration of the completion of this monument that Clavijo and his fellow ambassadors were invited, "since even the minnows have their place in the sea" – an eloquent piece of insincere ambassadorial self–deprecation.

For those less inclined to indulge in the pleasure of ruins, the Gur Emir is a refreshing change, as it is still virtually as Tamburlaine had it built (its now disappeared *medressah* having been built by the young Mohammed Sultan himself). Its most striking feature is its gorgeous dome, a unique melon shape, standing clear above the high entrance portal, its flutes so deeply incised as to be almost round, and covered in tiles of an astonishing blueness inset with thousands of stylised flowerets in, as usual, a darker cobalt blue. The tiles themselves are in large part replacements over the centuries; but the form and the colour are Tamburlaine's own. The great drum of the dome is patterned with gigantic white Koranic citations outlined in dark blue, large enough for the faithful to read them from two kilometres away; the entrance portal is a riot of floral patterns in brilliant blues, gold and white; the interior vault, all gilded and carved stucco, like a series of intricately patterned Persian carpets. This is the art not only of supreme confidence but also of absolute certainty, of the infinite number of ways of praising the true God.

Visiting the Gur Emir thirteen years after Schuyler, George Nathaniel Curzon wrote:

> "I do not pretend to understand the impulse that drives pilgrims in shoals to the graves of the departed great, yet there is something inspiring, even if it be a melancholy inspiration, in standing above the dust of one who was both a king among statesmen and a statesman among kings, whose deeds even at this distance of time alike astonish and appall, and whose monumental handiwork, still surviving around, a later and more civilised age has never attempted to equal".

Tamburlaine's tomb is simply a large plain block of cool dark green jade, said to be the largest in the world, from Chinese Turkestan: "Only a stone, and my name upon it", he is supposed to have breathed as he lay dying.

The Arabic inscription goes further, tracing his and Genghis Khan's origins to Buzanchar, the common ancestor who was all Tamburlaine ever claimed, the offspring, the Mongols had long since believed – in an interesting parallel with the Christians, perhaps a well–spring of the latter's endless wish to find Christendom among the Mongols – of a maiden, Alankuva, who had conceived from a heavenly light.[122]

---

122   Actually, according to *The Secret History of the Mongols*, things were a little more complex. Buzanchar was the third of three boys born to Alankuva, after she had had two by a Mongol father; and the *History* said that

> "One day in spring, as she was cooking dried mutton, she sat the five boys down in order, [and saying to these older two that] their suspicions about the origin of the other three were reasonable, [she explained that] 'Each night, a brightly shining golden man, entering by the top opening of the tent or by the light over the top of the door, rubbed my stomach and his brilliant light embedded itself in my belly; when it came out, it came crawling out like a golden dog, in the rays of the sun or the moon. What use is it to reply to you in words? For those who understand, the sign is obvious that these three sons must be the sons of Heaven' ".

Of course not only the Mongols had trouble with the siblings of virgin–births. The *New Testament* refers to James, Joseph, Simon and Jude as "brothers of the Lord"; theologians, bothered by the original assumption that they were sons of

Tamburlaine's actual grave, covered by an even plainer marble slab, is in the crypt directly below. Here, you stand on a level with the great conqueror – no nonsense like having to bow your head to look humbly down on the last lying–place of that other great despot, Napoleon Bonaparte.

Nevertheless, while we do not know the full scale of Samarkand's original construction, there was clearly in Tamburlaine, in his urgent construction of great temples and tombs, the piercing of streets through the city from one end to the other, that megalomania which leads tyrants to try to leave their mark in domineering architectural triumphs. And there is another modern sequel: with Adolf Hitler, who ordered his architect Albert Speer to re–plan and re–build the centre of Berlin with a grand avenue five kilometres long linking a huge triumphal arch to a domed assembly hall for one hundred and eighty thousand people – on a scale "comparable only to ancient Egypt, Babylon and Rome". But with this bizarre difference: for Berlin, Hitler and Speer *planned* its ruins, deciding to use special materials in order, Speer said,

> "to build structures which even in a state of decay, after hundreds or (such were our reckonings) thousands of years, would more or less resemble Roman models".

The impatient Tamburlaine had no time to design Samarkand's ruins; but, in the way of all conquerors, his works became ruins anyway.

The great conquests: west to Ottoman Turkey

Tamburlaine's next campaign after his return from India was against the Egyptian Mamelukes in 1400, during the course of which he destroyed their province of Syria – Aleppo, Hama, Homs, Baalbek and, as we have seen, Damascus. It was at Aleppo that he first used his elephants in western Asia, which spread instant panic and contributed to the immediate surrender of the city. The citadel took four more days. Then, while the garrison was massacred, towers made of severed heads, and the city pillaged, Tamburlaine indulged in his periodic pastime of learned discourse with the local *ulema*, the Moslem theologians:

Mary and Joseph born after the virgin birth of Christ, have argued – following St Jerome's insistence on Mary's perpetual virginity – that they were Joseph's sons by a former marriage, or sons of his brother's marriage with a different Mary, or by someone else's sons by the Virgin Mary's sister ...Mary.

"I am not a man of blood", he said to them – while, Gibbon tells us, "the streets of Aleppo streamed with blood, and re–echoed with the cries of mothers and children, with the shrieks of violated virgins" – "and God is my witness, that in all my wars I have never been the aggressor, and that my enemies have always been the authors of their own calamity".

He sounds distinctly modern.

Only one great power now survived in the whole of Asia west of Samarkand: the Ottoman Empire of Bajazeth I, the great–grandson of the founder of the dynasty that would rule Turkey, the Balkans and much of the Middle East until 1922. Bajazeth had been proclaimed Sultan on the battlefield of Kosovo Polje, "the Field of Blackbirds", in 1389 – a fateful battle still much in the propaganda of hatred during the ripping up of Yugoslavia in the 1990s – when the Turkish army crushed their Orthodox Balkan opponents under Prince Lazar of Serbia, putting his country under Moslem domination until 1878; but Bajazeth's father, Murad I, was killed, stabbed by a Serb posing as a deserter. Seven years later, at Nicopolis, Bajazeth crushed the largest and last European crusade against Islam – the battle in which the fifteen–year–old Johanns Schiltberger was captured, and assigned to Bajazeth himself.

"In the pride of victory", Gibbon wrote, "Bajazet threatened that he would besiege Buda; that he would subdue the adjacent countries of Germany and Italy; and that he would feed his horses with a bushel of oats on the altar of St. Peter at Rome. His progress was checked, not by the miraculous interposition of the apostle; not by a crusade of the Christian powers, but by a long and painful fit of the gout…[An] acrimonious humour falling on a single fibre of one man, may prevent or suspend the misery of nations."

Bajazeth Yildirim, "Bajazeth the Thunderbolt", was in any case now master of a powerful empire: in European Rumelia he held Thrace, Macedonia, Serbia and Bulgaria – though still not quite besieged Constantinople, a tiny island in a Moslem sea; and he held Asian Anatolia as far east as Tamburlaine's Azerbaijan borderlands. For Tamburlaine the target must have been irresistible, though it was Bajazeth, whose main target was Constantinople, who opened the hostilities by attacking one of Tamburlaine's eastern Anatolian vassals in what seems like a fit of inad-vertance – especially as Tamburlaine, responding to the reports he had received far away on the banks of the Ganges, was right next door, putting down disturbances in Azerbaijan and Georgia (which was "destroyed utterly"[123]). His first reaction was to taunt Bajazeth:

"Dost thou not know [Gibbon quotes his epistle] that the greatest part of Asia is subject to our arms and our laws? that our invincible forces extend from one sea to the other? that the potentates of the earth form a line at our gate? and that we have compelled fortune herself to watch over the prosperity of our empire? What is the foundation of thy insolence and folly?...Thou art no more than a pismire; why wilt thou seek to provoke the elephants?"

And in mid–1400 Tamburlaine besieged Bajazeth's fortified city of Sivas in central Turkey. It surrendered on condition that Tamburlaine would not shed the garrison's blood; Tamburlaine agreed, and kept his promise – all three (some say four, Schiltberger said five) thousand were thrown, alive, into wells.[124] Schiltberger said Tamburlaine also "took nine thousand virgins to his own country" from the city, which may, perhaps, be doubted on a number of grounds.

However Tamburlaine said he had "intended only to twist Sultan Bajazeth's ears": it was to be another two years before he invaded the Ottoman Empire. Perhaps he was reluctant to attack Bajazeth while the latter was hard–pressing what little remained of the Byzantine Empire at Constantinople, which Bajazeth had had under siege since 1397. While any such reluctance proved temporary – and the interval was in any case occupied by dealing with the Egyptian Mamelukes in the invasion of Syria and the re–capture of Baghdad – there was a stab at the kind of diplomatic dealings with "the enemy of my enemy" that, as we saw,

---

123 This was Tamburlaine's fifth invasion of Georgia. Each time its capital Tbilisi suffered further destruction: in fact, in the course of some forty invasions over the twelve hundred years between 600 and 1800, by Mongols, Persians and Turks, its 6th–7th century Zion Cathedral, known to the Georgians as Sioni, was repeatedly destroyed, including on this occasion, and had to be rebuilt. This may account for the weariness apparent in a later reconstruction: a 1981 (Soviet) guidebook to Tbilisi says that after further destruction by the Persian Shah Aga Mohammed Khan Qajar in 1795, the bell tower was restored...in 1939.

124 I have come across this promise–keeping elsewhere, in a different context: when I lived in Phnom Penh over thirty years ago there was a pit on the northern outskirts where pious Buddhists threw their dogs so as not to be guilty of taking their lives. So the dogs took one another's.

neither he nor the Russians had tried when they were both dealing with Toqtamysh. It came from Byzantium.

During this two year interval the Emperor of besieged Byzantium, Manuel II Paleologus, was making humiliatingly unsuccessful visits to Milan, Paris and London to raise a new crusade, or at least funds, for the defence of Constantinople against the Ottomans. He was well received but not well recompensed: France's King Charles VI offered a measly twelve hundred men for one year, led by Marshal Boucicault, recently ransomed from Bajazeth after his capture at Nicopolis; England's new King Henry IV handed over £4,000 said to have been raised in church collection boxes – but this was only to replace the £2,000 donated the previous year by Richard II (his cousin and predecessor whom he had had murdered to gain the throne), which had been entirely embezzled by a Genoese money–broker; and the Pope in Rome and the anti–Pope in Avignon were more preoccupied with opposing each other than more distant Turks.

In Manuel's absence from Constantinople, the Regent, his nephew and predecessor (there was a history there) John VII Paleologus, seems to have tried to do a deal with everyone – perhaps simultaneously: neither the sequence nor the substance is entirely clear. In the sense of "enemy of my enemy" dealings, he sent messages through Dominican monks to Tamburlaine urging him to take the field against Bajazeth, and offering to support him with men and galleys. But this may have been an insurance measure rather than his main aim, because some say he had previously offered to surrender Byzantium to Bajazeth if the latter beat Tamburlaine, others that he was bargaining with Bajazeth over what he would get out of it; and in case neither worked, still others say, he offered the Byzantine throne to the King of France in return for a well–financed exile there. Tamburlaine responded to John with a demand for twenty galleys (plus twenty more from the Genoese trading colony at Pera, across the Golden Horn from Constantinople), and warning against trying to do a deal with Bajazeth.

Surprisingly, Charles VI apparently also made an approach to Tamburlaine at this stage, in 1401 or early 1402 – or at least his officials did: called by the French "Charles le Bien–Aimé", the Beloved, he was known to the English as "Charles the Foolish" because he was insane for the last thirty of his thirty–four years' reign. But what was the French objective? No–one knows, as our only knowledge of its existence is from the letter in reply that Tamburlaine sent, via the Catholic Archbishop Jean of Sultaniyeh, just before he set out in pursuit of Bajazeth. Although, after Nicopolis, the French had every reason to want revenge on Bajazeth, it seems unlikely – given their response to the Emperor Manuel, who was still in Paris at the time – that they had made any proposals to Tamburlaine for military cooperation, though it is hard to fathom what else could have prompted the contact at that particular time. In any event Tamburlaine himself made no reference to any proposal for an alliance in his letter, nor did he himself propose one: instead, his only request was that Charles "treat with benevolence Tartar merchants who came to France" – apparently one of a "round robin" to the rulers of Europe for the protection of trade.[125] And so it seems that Tamburlaine was not tempted to have his enemy's European enemies become his friends.

By the time Tamburlaine returned to Karabakh after Baghdad, both the Byzantines and the Pera Genoans confirmed their readiness to provide assistance. But what? His concern was to have their fleets cut Bajazeth off from reinforcements from his Rumelian provinces in Europe; and his last known letter to John VII, sent in May 1402, asked only for twenty galleys to be sent to Trebizond, as though he thought he already had assurances for the blockade of the Bosphorus. If so, he was to be rudely disabused: neither John nor the Genoans made the slightest effort to prevent the – obviously welcome – withdrawal of Bajazeth's forces from their neighbourhood in European Turkey. Tamburlaine's enemy's Byzantine enemy was by no means his friend.

One wonders indeed whether Tamburlaine ever set any store by his exchanges with John. Right up to this return to the Karabakh he had in fact kept at Bajazeth to avoid a shameful conflict between fellow Moslems, while demanding the return of this and that disloyal local chieftain – "the enemies of Allah" – who had been given sanctuary by the Ottoman ruler. This unyielding exchange continued right up to Tamburlaine's move into Turkey: Bajazeth's envoys met him then for the last time, with a provocative message – "O ravening dog named Timur" – in which Bajazeth resorted to inexcusable insult:

---

125 This is the conclusion of a French scholar, based on the letter discovered in the French Archives in the early 1820s – H. Moranvillé: *Mémoire sur Tamerlan et sa Cour par un Dominicain, en 1403*, in *Bibliothèque de l'École des Chartes*, Vol. 55 (Paris 1894). Tamburlaine's emissary – perhaps, Moranvillé thought, self–appointed – was a French or Italian Dominican Bishop of Nakchivan (now in Azerbaijan) who had been created "Archbishop of the East and Ethiopia" in Persian Sultaniyeh – Europe still struggling with geography.

"If thou hast not courage to meet me in the field, mayest thou again receive thy wives after they have thrice endured the embraces of a stranger".

But the die was already cast, and in thirteen days of forced marches Tamburlaine's army of two hundred thousand men covered the nearly four hundred kilometres from Sivas to Ankara, outflanking Bajazeth, who had to turn back west to meet it.

Then on 28 July 1402 – on the plain near Ankara where the great Roman general Pompey had secured Asia Minor for Rome by defeating King Mithradates VI of Pontus in 66 BCE – the two sides fought a day-long battle. Estimates of the numbers involved varied from as few as forty thousand to nearly a million and a half men according to the overwhelmed Schiltberger, who was there somewhere amongst Bajazeth's troops, though Archbishop Jean of Sultaniyeh, who was with Tamburlaine and his army two weeks before the battle, said he had

"X hundred thousand men and at least VIII hundred thousand horses; and as for camels and other beasts, they are without number. He has also XL fighting elephants".

The most convincing estimate seems to be that Bajazeth's army was about the same size as Tamburlaine's – giving still a colossal encounter involving some four hundred thousand men, one of the largest battles before the First World War.[126] Bajazeth's numbers included, it is interesting to note, the Orthodox King Stephen of Serbia and Serbian troops; but Gibbon said the elephants – which he contended were now down to thirty–two – were "the trophies rather than the instruments of victory". Victory was nevertheless Tamburlaine's, and with it the mighty Bajazeth himself, who fell from his horse in his effort to escape from the pursuing Khan of Chagatei.

Also captured, for the second time in his short life, was Schiltberger, now twenty–two; and he was to remain in Tamburlaine's train for the latter's remaining three years and with his son and grandson for twenty–two more. By curious coincidence, the Battle of Ankara was also at the origins of Ruiz de Clavijo's embassy to Tamburlaine, and thus the only

---

126   Cf. Waterloo: Napoleon with 125,000, Wellington 93,000 plus Blücher arriving late in the day with 120,000; and Gettysburg: Union 85,000, Confederacy 65,000.

other contemporary European report on him. According to Markham, in his introduction to Clavijo, two Spanish knights, who had been sent earlier by the latter's master Henry III of Castile to report on the Ottomans, happened to be present at the battle; afterwards, they were well received by the victorious Tamburlaine, who sent them back to Spain with an envoy of his own, a gracious letter to Henry, and "rich presents of jewels and maidens" – including two Christian women, one of whom, Angelina, niece of King Sigismond of Hungary, had been captured (along with Schiltberger) by Bajazeth when he defeated Sigismond's European army at Nicopolis in 1396, and had now been "rescued by Timour from the harem of the brutal Turk". Tamburlaine's courtesy led Henry – like an earlier succession of Popes and kings of France and Spain (see 1300 chapter) – to hope that the Christians' enemy's enemy would become their ally; and he sent Clavijo off immediately, in the company of Tamburlaine's returning envoy.

Tamburlaine followed up the victory at Ankara with a race to the Aegean. In describing the capture of Sinope (now Sinop, on central Turkey's Black Sea coast) Ibn Arabshah revealed that he was not entirely immune to the charms of the "snares of Satan":

> "It has a mountain more beautiful than the buttocks of the houris
> of Paradise, and adjoining it is a pass more graceful than the
> slenderest loin".

Bursa, the Ottoman capital, was overrun and put to the sack; Tamburlaine's grandson Abu Bakr galloped as far as Nicaea (Iznik), "slaying and looting everywhere" the *Zafer-name* recorded with relish. Any understanding he may have thought he had with John VII in Constantinople and his Genoan allies was utterly confounded: instead of cutting off the fleeing Ottomans' retreat, their galleys did a nice business ferrying them across the Bosphorus at extortionate prices, though the Genoese were said to have kept some for slaves.

At a more leisurely pace Tamburlaine himself proceeded southwards to besiege the Crusader Knights Hospitalers' stronghold at Smyrna (Izmir) on the coast, taking in fourteen days the fortress that had successfully withstood Bajazeth's own siege for seven years. However that was not the chief ground for satisfaction: the elimination of this handful of Christians, the last remaining European foothold in Asia, was *ex post facto* justification for crippling the Moslem Ottoman Empire – despite appearances, Tamburlaine had now won a Holy War:

"The Muslims entered the city praising Allah, to whom they offered the heads of their enemies in thanksgiving".[127]

In some places, among assorted Christians, Tamburlaine's great conquest of Turkey created a sort of schizophrenia. On the one hand there were the usual extravagant hopes amongst West Europeans terrified of the Ottomans but unable, or unwilling, to bestir themselves out of a Munich–like paralysis: the old myth that the Moslem Mongols harboured crypto–Christians soon cropped up again. It may have been this which prompted King Henry III of Castile to send Ruy Gonzales de Clavijo, in 1403, to Samarkand, though the reply of Charles VI of France to Tamburlaine's letter sounds curiously flat: in agreeing to offer protection to "Tartar merchants", he simply asked for reciprocity for French traders and more generally for Christians. Manuel gave up his begging with relief when news reached Paris that Tamburlaine had defeated and captured the Turkish Sultan, and we hear no more of diplomatic minuets between the Byzantines and Tamburlaine. But it was a false dawn for Christendom in any case: all Tamburlaine did was save Constantinople for another half century – it took one of Bajazeth's sons only ten years to recover the empire that Tamburlaine divided up among a raft of princes and emirs, and then only until 1453 for his great–grandson Mahomet II to finally capture the rump of what had been the great Byzantine Empire.

---

127   Smyrna, reputedly the birthplace of Homer, was the site of another human disaster six centuries later. During that time it had retained a substantial Greek population, and when the British and French were manouvring to carve up the collapsing Ottoman Empire at the end of the First World War, in which it had chosen the losing side, Greece was encouraged by British Prime Minister David Lloyd George to occupy Smyrna and its region, a move which prompted the revolt led by the Ottoman General Mustapha Kemal in mid–1919 that would eventually lead to modern Turkey's independence in 1922. Then in 1920, with further British encouragement, the Greek army launched an attack across western Anatolia towards Ankara, and it was only in September the following year that the revivified Turkish army under Kemal was able to halt and then reverse the Greeks' advance. Their retreat rapidly became a rout, and the mass evacuation from Turkey of a million and a half Greeks was begun in mid–1922. But racial hatred exploded in Smyrna as Turkish forces invested the city: fire in the Armenian quarter spread to the Greek city to accompany the killings – and an American correspondent wrote that "The problem of the minorities here is solved for all time". (See D. Fromkin: *A Peace to End All Peace*; London 1989)

On the other hand there were also terrifying rumours that Tamburlaine intended next to deliver a final blow to the Egyptian Mamelukes, sweep on across the squabbling emirates that had succeeded the Almohads in North Africa and Granada, then roll up Western Europe eastwards through Spain, France, Italy and Germany, returning to Samarkand via another swipe at Russia. Marlowe echoed these rumours, but put them at sea: on his capture, Bajazeth still blusters to Tamburlaine that

> "...though the glory of this day be lost,
> Afric and Greece have garrisons enough
> To make me sovereign of the earth again";

which causes a triumphalist outburst from Tamburlaine himself:

> "Those walled garrisons will I subdue,
> And write myself great lord of Africa:
> So from the East unto the furthest West
> Shall Tamburlaine extend his puissant arm.
> The galleys and those pilling brigandines,
> That yearly sail to the Venetian gulf,
> And hover in the Straits for Christians' wreck,
> Shall lie at anchor in the Isle Asant,
> Until the Persian fleet and men–of–war,
> Sailing along the oriental sea,
> Have fetch'd about the Indian continent,
> Even from Persepolis to Mexico,
> And thence unto the Straits of Jubalter;
> Where they shall meet and join their force in one,
> Keeping in awe the Bay of Portingale,
> And all the ocean by the British shore;
> And by this means I'll win the world at last".

That Tamburlaine had unfinished business with the Mamelukes was true; and his careful quizzing of Ibn Khaldun about the Maghreb, just two years earlier, would – in the unlikely event anyone by then had heard of it – have lent some credence to a North African campaign. But the spectre of the invasion of the whole of Europe was purely fanciful, more indicative of the terror inspired since the time of Batu Khan by the name "Mongols" than of anything Tamburlaine is ever likely to have considered. A more likely threat would have been a continuation of his campaign against the defeated Ottomans into their European provinces – which could have led on into Central Europe via shattered Hungary: like his Mongol predecessor in 1241 and Bajazeth's Ottoman descendants in 1529 and 1683, Tamburlaine might easily have got to the gates of Vienna. But there is no evidence that Tamburlaine ever considered that either. The Anglo-American historian Bernard Lewis remarked that

> "For the mediaeval Muslim from Andalusia to Persia, Christian Europe was still an outer darkness of barbarism and unbelief, from which the sunlit world of Islam had little to fear and less to learn".

Instead, Tamburlaine stopped at the Sea of Marmora, then he turned for home. Archbishop Jean of Sultaniyeh said that, in addition to his train of khans and emirs,

> " he also had with him the Grand Turk, whom he treated very honourably. And, when he tried to escape, he had him tied up with chains of gold".

The Archbishop heard about Tamburlaine's victory at Ankara and the subsequent capture of Bajazeth after he had left the former's camp, probably by the time he reached Trebizond, where he seems most likely to have gone to seek a ship down the Black Sea on his way to Paris;[128] and for the benefit of the King of France he inserted these developments into his translation of Tamburlaine's letter. However it seems a bit surprising that Tamburlaine's most valued captive ever would have been so loosely guarded, so soon after his apprehension, that he could even try to escape at that early stage; or that Tamburlaine would use his gold on manacles. Perhaps the wily Archbishop, anxious to promote relations between his Sire and his See, was simply putting the glossiest possible construction on Tamburlaine's behaviour. Because in due course a much less gallant story emerged.

When *The First Part of Tamburlaine the Great* was performed in London in 1587 it immediately made Marlowe's name as a great dramatic poet. But, as is the way of public taste, his popular fame – and Tamburlaine's notoriety – derived from the sensational theatrical effects

---

128 Two years later the Castilian Ambassador Clavijo travelled by sea between Constantinople and Trebizond on his way to Samarkand.

in the second scene of Act IV, whose stage direction and first line tell it all:

"*Enter* Tamburlaine, Techelles, Theridimas, Usumcasane,
Zenocrate, Anippe, *two* Moors *drawing* Bajazeth *in a cage*...

Tamb. Bring out my footstool.
[*They take Bajazeth out of the cage.*"

As the scene proceeds, Tamburlaine rubs in his vindictiveness:

"But villain...
Fall prostrate on the low disdainful earth,
And be the footstool of great Tamburlaine,
That I may rise into my royal throne...
Now clear the triple region of the air,
And let the Majesty of Heaven behold
Their scourge and terror tread on emperors...

Put him in again.   [*They put him into the cage*...

There, while he lives, shall Bajazeth be kept;
And, where I go, be thus in triumph drawn;
And thou, his wife, shall feed him with the scraps
My servitors shall bring thee from my board...
Not all the kings and emperors of the earth,
If they would lay their crowns before my feet,
Shall ransome him, or take him from his cage...*"

The image of the Ottoman Emperor, the victor of Nicopolis, where he destroyed the last chivalry of Europe, being dragged in a cage from Ankara to Samarkand, has fascinated popular curiosity and divided historians ever since. Gibbon devoted three entire pages of *The History of the Decline and Fall of the Roman Empire* to a learned discussion of the "vulgar credulity" of the iron cage, drawing on an astonishing variety of sources in his search for the truth: Voltaire, the *Zafer–name*, Khondemir, Ebn Schoumah, Barthélemy d'Herbelot, Ibn Arabshah, Marshal Boucicaut, Lodovico Muratori, Gian Francesco Poggio, Lefant, Fabricius, Andrea de Redusiis de Quero, James de Delayo, Busbequius, Cantemir, George Phranza, Hanckius, Nikolaos Chalcondyles, Michael

348

Ducas, Edward Pocock[129], Leunclavius, names of 15th to 18th century writers known and unknown from all over Europe and the Middle East. Gibbon decided that in "the first ostentatious interview" between the victor and his prisoner Tamburlaine "affected the character of generosity", as Archbishop Jean had reported. But, accepting also that an escape attempt by Bajazeth

"provoked the Mogul [sic] emperor to impose a harsher restraint",

Gibbon eventually concurred with Marlow that

"in his perpetual marches, an iron cage on a wagon might be invented, not as a wanton insult, but as a rigorous precaution".[130]

Ibn Arabshah describes the menacingly inexorable courtesy with which Tamburlaine imposed his other great humiliation on Bajazeth:

"Then [Tamburlaine] one day held a public banquet and when the wing of hilarity was loosened for gentle and simple, he rolled up the carpet of prohibition and command and unrolled the carpet of wine and music and when the place was full of men he ordered that [Bajazeth] should be brought in; and he came with trembling heart and hampered by his fetters, but he ordered him to be of good courage and put aside his fear and seating him comfortably and treating him with courtesy, he removed his sadness. Then he ordered the circles of merrymaking to be formed and they were formed; and he ordered that the sun of wine should move from the east of the goblet to the west of the lips and it was done: but as soon as the clouds of veils were scattered from the sun of the

---

129 An earlier one than the present author, the first Professor of Arabic at Oxford (1636) and subsequently Professor of Hebrew; his name is spelled Pocock by Gibbon, but more commonly Pococke, including on his elegant memorial in Oxford Cathedral.

130 Gibbon says that, according to a Byzantine writer, Tamburlaine had read "in some fabulous history a similar treatment of one of his predecessors, a [Sassanid] king of Persia", who in some sort of wishful revenge for Valerian's defeat by Shapur I had been captured by a Roman emperor and "enclosed in the figure of a cow's hide" – a fable, Gibbon sniffs again, which "will teach us to appreciate the knowledge of the orientals of the ages which preceded the Hegira".

cupbearers and stars were circling in the sky of society, rising quickly at the command of Timur like new moons, [Bajazeth] saw that the cupbearers were his consorts and that all of them were his wives and concubines"

– shamefully naked, in the presence of the entire court. Gibbon saw this as retaliation for Bajazeth's insult, in the exchange of letters years earlier, to Tamburlaine's own wives. Some said it was this that caused Bajazeth to beat his own brains out against the walls of his iron cage.

After the great success of *The First Part of Tamburlaine the Great* Marlowe rushed out *The Second Part of Tamburlaine the Great* to cash in on his sudden popularity. But the sequel required another crowd-pleaser to match Bajazeth in his cage, and Marlowe unerringly found it – the third scene of Act IV, by which point the plebs in the pit must have been as anxious as a soccer crowd waiting for a home–team goal, begins:

> "*Enter* Tamburlaine, *drawn in his chariot by the*
> Kings of Trebizon *and* Soria, *with bits in their mouths,*
> *reins in his left hand, and in his right hand a whip*
> *with which he scourgeth them...; Orcanes king of*
> Natolia, *and the* King of Jerusalem, *led by five or six*
> *common soldiers...*
>
> *Tamb.* Holla, ye pamper'd jades of Asia!
> What, can ye draw but twenty miles a–day,
> And have so proud a chariot at your heels,
> And such a coachman as great Tamburlaine...
> You shall be fed with flesh as raw as blood,
> And drink in pails the strongest muscadel:
> If you can live with it, then live, and draw
> My chariot swifter than the racking clouds;
> If not, then die like beasts, and fit for naught
> But perches for the black and fatal ravens".

"The Kings of Natolia and Jerusalem" are of course harnessed in their turn when "the Kings of Trebizon and Soria" fade:

> "These jades are broken winded and half–tir'd...
> So; now their best is done to honour me,
> Take them and hang them both up presently."

This time, it was pure invention. But Marlowe's imagination could still not match the horrors which Tamburlaine actually inflicted on his victims – though, admittedly, it would be difficult to reproduce on stage, for example, the twenty–eight towers, each consisting of some fifteen hundred heads, counted by the reliable Persian historian Hafiz–i Abru as he walked *half–way* around the periphery of Isfahan after Tamburlaine's visitation in 1388.

The great conquests: eastwards to China

Tamburlaine was not only a forward planner but a long–distance one as well: on the banks of the Ganges, as we saw, he began planning the invasion of Ottoman Turkey; on the shores of the Bosphorus, so far from plotting invasions of Europe via the Maghreb or the Balkans, he began planning the invasion of Ming China. Or so it was said; but in fact he had had China in his mind, if not yet exactly in his sights, long since. His Central Asian heartland had been surrounded by a ring of great powers, and successively he had humiliated them: Persia, Kipchak, India, Egypt, Turkey. But Tamburlaine was not simply setting out to add the east to the conquests he had already made in the north, the south and the west: his relationship with the Chinese Empire was more complicated than that of equalling or excelling, as he had in Western Asia, the conquests of his Mongol predecessors. It was, in fact, another example of the difficulties and complications – and temptations – that for centuries have beset neighbouring counties in their relations with a China whose self–absorption has manifested itself fitfully in timorousness, bluster, aggression or disdain.

As we have seen, an important element in all of Tamburlaine's conquests had been the establishment of his control over the riches of the various western filaments of the Silk Road, either by direct conquest in Transoxiana and Persia or destruction of the alternative route through Russia, though, because of other commitments or temptations, he did not maintain his control westwards across Turkey beyond a tributary Trebizond, or southwards to India beyond Afghanistan. The idea of controlling as well the great eastern filament of the Silk Road to China itself, passing either side of the Taklamakan Desert from his province of Ferghana, was thus undoubtedly prominent in his thoughts about this next campaign to the east.

However there was another factor involved which must have figured equally prominently in this ambition. In China, Kublai Khan's great Mongol Yuan Dynasty had been replaced by the native Chinese

Ming Dynasty in 1368, just as Tamburlaine, in his early thirties, was graduating from local sheep–stealing to securing his hold over Samarkand. Twelve years later, as he was completing his conquest of the former Chagatei Khanate, the first sector of the empire established by Genghis Khan to be brought under his control, a Ming foray north of the Gobi desert into the old Mongol heartland destroyed forever Karakorum, Genghis Khan's capital, leaving only the giant marble tortoise still there today.

Tamburlaine's reaction when he heard of this does not seem to have been recorded; but it equally does not seem too great a stretch of the imagination to see this as giving rise to his first thought of recovering, eventually, this crucial part of the Mongol succession to Genghis Khan – quite apart from the added attraction of the fabled wealth of China and the Silk Road thither. And having carefully, over the last two decades of the 14th century, gained control – if not permanent government – of the other major constituents of that empire which had been established by Batu Khan of the Golden Horde and the Ilkhans of Persia, and seen off any threat from his only other powerful neighbours – India, Egypt, Turkey – the time for dealing with China was at last come.

There had already been preparations, though there are amusing differences of interpretation between scholars who have focussed on Tamburlaine and those who have focussed on the Chinese Emperors at the other end of the developments.[131] Part of the problem seems to arise from different records or traditions at either end; part arises from what look like deliberate distortions – not by the scholars, be it hastily said, but by the original writers responsible for official histories. There is an added dimension of indubitable mutual miscomprehension by each side of the other's motives: in the inevitable exchanges of gifts whenever emissaries visited, Tamburlaine assumed he was receiving the Emperor of China's acknowledgement of him as an equal at the very least, while Hongwu, like all Chinese rulers, assumed he was receiving the submission from Tamburlaine to which he believed himself entitled from all "barbarians". There were ample grounds for confusion.

It begins, for us, with the French historian René Grousset saying that when the first Ming Emperor, Hongwu, sent ambassadors into Central

---

131   The main sources in this context are Lo and Rossabi, but Grousset, Hookham and Levathes also deal with these issues. It is not always easy to be certain that they are talking about the same event, especially in relation to the exchanges of emissaries between the two empires.

Asia in 1385 to obtain homage from the local khans they were successful in Xinjiang with the descendants there of Genghis Khan's son Chagatei, the first Khan of Turkestan. But when they went further west to Samarkand the ambassadors were arrested by Tamburlaine, and had difficulty securing their release. However the very existence of such a mission has been challenged because it has not been found in the Chinese dynastic history. This was usually a detailed record, but not always an entirely accurate one as we shall see: the bureaucrats compiling it, naturally conscious of their own necks, were more solicitous of the glory of the Son of Heaven than of the inclusion of anything which might reflect on it. So one is led to wonder whether a mission could have been sent to Tamburlaine in 1385, but not recorded by officials who thought an ignominious failure might appear demeaning to posterity.

This is a possible explanation for Tamburlaine's then sending a mission in 1387 – in return – to Beijing; it was recorded in the latter as bearing "tribute", though as this consisted only of 15 horses and 2 camels it is somewhat surprising that it was not recorded as an insult rather than a submission. A further offering from Tamburlaine was recorded as arriving in Beijing in 1388, this time with 300 horses – and 2 more camels, and another in 1389 with 205 horses, and again in 1392, 64 horses, 6 camels, plus "velvet, swords and armour": both were described as "embassies" with "tribute".

It is however inconceivable that Tamburlaine was in fact sending tokens of submission to the infidel usurper of the Mongol throne of China. Rossabi says

> "it seems likely that these [embassies] consisted not of official emissaries but merely of Central Asian merchants who represented themselves as Timur's envoys in order to gain access to China. These traders knew they could only enter China as official envoys, not as private citizens".

The Chinese coveted Central Asian horses, especially those from the Ferghana valley, along the present–day Kyrgyzstan–Uzbekistan border. They were known as Heavenly Horses because they were said to be descended from those that carried the legendary Emperor Muh Wang to the Mountains of the Immortals; some Western records claimed that, on the contrary, they were descended from Bucephalas, Alexander the Great's horse that carried him from Macedon until its death in his eastern–most battle, on the banks of the Jhelum (Gr. Hydaspes) River (now in northeast Pakistan).[132] The Tang Emperors had imported tens of thousands when its sway extended as far as the borders of Ferghana itself (for a few months in 750–751 it even occupied Tashkent); it is thus an interesting contrast that by the end of the 14th century, before Ming China had recovered Gansu and the territories further west lost with the disintegration of Mongol power, Tamburlaine's marginal offerings were recorded in Beijing – with a straight face – as formal tribute, and horse traders as official embassies.

This approach could of course have been designed to elevate the scope of the Dragon Throne's dominion; but it also suggests that the Chinese Court, in formally accepting 574 horses and 10 camels over the course of five years as the satisfactory offerings of a tributary, may have had a very limited idea of the scope of Tamburlaine's dominion. On the other hand, it also makes one wonder just how private all those horse traders were: in the discussions of these expeditions there seems to be a neglect of Tamburlaine's obsession with intelligence – the multitude and variety of all those agents he employed and deployed everywhere of interest to him, who

> "brought to him events and news from the furthest borders, described to him what things were excellent there and were remarkable, made known to him the weights received there and the prices of things, marked their [staging] posts and cities, mapped their roads…".

It is inconceivable that, having spied so efficiently and effectively everywhere else, Tamburlaine would not have sought to do the same in China as he began thinking about his last great campaign, culminating his re–creation of the Genghizid empire. And who better than horse traders, if he knew – and he surely did – how passionate the Chinese were about the horses of his Ferghana valley. Though the numbers of horses offered for free were strictly limited – there was no point in extravagance if the Chinese were foolish enough to be happy with the odd hundred plus a camel or two. And besides, there was every point in

---

132   Part of the mystique of the Ferghana horses related to the belief that they sweated blood, an appearance in fact caused by harmless parasites under the skin that dyed their sweat. One can imagine their appearance, perhaps, from the *Sancai/San–ts'ai* (three–colour) glaze frequently used on Tang ceramic horses, with their brownish streaks running down the yellowish bodies and legs.

keeping the Chinese ignorant as to just how many horses – and everything else – Tamburlaine had.

However they had glossed the "embassies" and their "tribute" hitherto, the Beijing bureaucrats now graduated to what some have seen as outright forgery: another embassy, they recorded in the official history, arrived in 1394 with another 200 horses – and a letter from Tamburlaine himself addressed to the Son of Heaven:

> "The splendour of your reign is bright like the heavenly mirror, and lights up the kingdoms, the adjoining as well as the far...Your Majesty has graciously allowed the merchants of distant countries to come to China to carry on trade. Foreign envoys have had a chance of admiring the wealth of your cities and the strength of your power...Owing to your solicitude there have been established post–stations to facilitate the intercourse of foreigners with China, and all the nations of distant countries are allowed to profit by this convenience".

It has been protested that there is no way Tamburlaine "could have written such a fawning self–deprecatory missive". It certainly seems unlikely that Tamburlaine simply intended to flatter the infidel Hongwu as an equal to an equal: the Timurid documents frequently referred to the Chinese Emperor by the particularly insulting sobriquet (amongst Moslems) as Tonguz Khan – "Pig Emperor". But there are two grounds – the mirror image of each other – for speculating that Tamburlaine could indeed have written in such terms.

The first derives from his obsession with intelligence, in which the traders along the Silk Road played an invaluable role. Half a millennium later, the British explorer and official Francis Younghusband, during a prolonged stay in Kashgar in 1890, observed after talking for intelligence purposes with traders from Kashmir, China, Afghanistan, Bokhara, Ferghana and Constantinople that

> "They discussed politics constantly as their trade depended so much on the political situation".

During the course of the 7th to 9th centuries, the great wealth of the Tang Dynasty, and its expansion westwards beyond present–day Xinjiang almost to Tashkent, had resulted in considerable activity on the Silk Road between central China and the equally wealthy Abasssid Caliphate centred on Baghdad.[133] The extension of Mongol power from China right across Central Asia in the 13th and 14th centuries provided the security for another expansion in the Silk Road trade.

The goods exchanged at the major trading centres, all set out in separate sections, were extraordinarily various, and a great deal broader than those that Ambassador Ruiz de Clavijo had remarked at Sultaniyeh in 1403: from Tamburlaine's heartland, carpets, harness equipment, armour and enamel work; from the Russians, furs, linen, leather goods and wax; from the west Siberian Kipchaks, sheep, cattle and horses; from the Chinese, silks, drugs, musk, rhubarb, pearls, coral, jade, precious stones and porcelain; from the Indians (or originally from Southeast Asia), pepper, nutmeg, ginger, cinnamon, cloves, muslins, indigo and other dyes; from the Mediterranean Moslems, damasks, cotton goods, glass, swords, armour and other metal–ware; from Europeans, much less, woollen goods, silver and copper, but not yet what was to become Europe's most abiding export – guns; gold and silver wares and jewellery from all directions; fruits, wines, grains, salt and other local goods in shorter stages. Much of the trade is said to have been conducted in "kebeki" dinars, named after Kebek, the last effective Chagatei Khan (ruled 1318–1326); and the term is said to be the origin of "kopek", the Russian cent.

The Central Asian merchants had begun settling in the Chinese Silk Road provinces during the Tang period of expanded trade, but the Moslem communities in China increased substantially during the Mongol Yuan Dynasty, both in numbers and also in influence: Hookham points out that the Mongols' religious tolerance was matched by their unwillingness to rely on Chinese officials alone, with the result that

---

133 The 9th century Persian geographer Ibn Khurradadhbih (who, as noted in the 1000 chapter, had the splendid position of Director–General of the Department of Posts and Intelligence at the court of the Abbassid Caliph Ahmed al–Mutamid) described in his work *The Book of Itineraries and Kingdoms* (ca 888) the complex of trade routes that then existed across Persia and through Bokhara and Turkestan to China, as well as the less–used and often–longer sea route via the Persian Gulf, the Indian Ocean and the South China Sea. This was the period which saw the beginning of the importation into China of the Persian cobalt which would produce the brilliant underglaze blues of Ming blue and white ceramics – an enormous quantity of which was made specifically for the Islamic countries of western Asia, with some of the vessels' shapes and the decoration based on Islamic metalware prototypes (see Medley: *The Chinese Potter*). It is thus not surprising that the Ottoman Sultans' former Topkapi Palace in Istanbul should have the largest collection of Chinese porcelain outside China itself.

individual Moslems, mostly from Central Asia, were employed as administrators, bankers and tax collectors. Ibn Battutah, the remarkable Tangiers–born Arab traveller who visited every Moslem society from Spain to Sumatra, said in his lively account, *A Gift to Those Who Contemplate the Wonders of Cities and the Marvels of Travelling*, that in the 1340s he found that

> "In every city of China there is a quarter where the Muslims live separately and have mosques for their Friday prayers and other assemblies. They are highly regarded and treated with respect... There is a Shaikh al–Islam [religious leader] to whom all the affairs of the Muslims are referred. There is also a qadi [Islamic jurist] who gives judgements among them".[134]

This isolation of groups of Moslems was in part the result of official policy under Chinese dynasties of insulating barbarians from the local population; but it was mutually convenient, as it usually also reflected Moslem opposition to assimilation. The difference with the attitude of Central Asian Uighurs (with their Manichaean background) was neatly encapsulated by the remark of one of the latter:

> "We are not like the pelicans which roost on the beams and just happen to wet their wings".

Members of the Moslem community resident in China were thus in a position to play an invaluable role in gathering and passing information to visiting traders; and the successive traders' "embassies" during Tamburlaine's preparations for the invasion of China would have been well placed to contact them and convey the intelligence back to Samarkand.

Four decades later, in the 1380s, when several hundred Samarkand merchants were captured during a Chinese campaign against northern Mongols, Hongwu ordered their release to go home. If this at first appeared a generous gesture, within a few years it could have been interpreted otherwise: in 1392 the Governor of Gansu Province was ordered to expel the Moslem merchants there – the largest concentration

---

134   *The Travels of Ibn Battutah*, abr. T.Mackintosh–Smith (London 2003). The great traveller's full name was even longer than the title of his book: Shams al–Din Abu Abdallah Muhammad ibn Abdallah ibn Muhammad ibn Ibrahim Ibn Battutah al–Lawati al–Tanji al–Maliki al–Maghribi.

in China – and more than twelve hundred accompanied the so–called embassy to China that year on its return journey to Samarkand.

The "release" of the captured merchants now would have seemed more like the beginning of a Ming reaction against the Moslem Central Asian presence in China; and it must have raised the question in Samarkand as to whether it was simply a chauvinistic measure designed to give greater Chinese control over the Silk Road trade, or whether Beijing suspected the resident Moslem merchants were not to be trusted. In any case it must have been a serious blow to intelligence–gathering, and could help account for Tamburlaine's "fawning" letter of 1395, obviously sent directly after the return to Samarkand of the expelled traders: to restore access to information on China and the way thither, there was an urgent need to allay any suspicions that Samarkand's interests were anything other than commercial, and (for trade reasons also) to secure the restoration of its merchants' free access.

A development in Chinese foreign policy at this time, that older historians had been puzzled by, has been linked by the Chinese historian Jung–pang Lo to concern in Beijing about Tamburlaine's intentions. Apart from the timing – why now? – there was nothing new in the promulgation in 1395 of an imperial edict, the *Ancestral Instructions*, in which Hongwu laid down some basic principles for China's foreign policy based on speeches he had made to the entire top ranks of officials as long ago as 1371 and 1372:

"We should chastise the barbarian states beyond our frontiers which threaten China but we should not take arms against those which do not threaten us…As for the little barbarian states beyond our frontiers, over the mountains and across the sea, located in far corners [of the world], it is my view that if they do not menace China we should not invade them. But the nomadic barbarians (Hu and Jung) of the west and the north have for generations been a danger to China; we have no alternative but to be on guard against them. You ministers should bear these words in mind and know my desire…

The eastern barbarians [the Japanese] are not, like the northerners, a danger to our hearts and stomach. They are no more than mosquitoes and scorpions…

[I enjoin my] descendants of later generations not to rely on the wealth and power of China to seek the temporary glory of war or to wage wars without good cause".

In singling out the danger from northern nomads Hongwu was doing no more than recalling the whole of China's history, from the earliest times to the Mongol takeover which had begun nearly two hundred years before – and which would be repeated by the Manchu when they overthrew the Ming three hundred years after him. But there was no reference to Tamburlaine: admittedly he was not of the "Hu and Jung", but he certainly qualified as a "barbarian of the west" against whom China would need to be on guard. However a new element, not derived from the Emperor's speeches two decades before, was a list appended to the edict of fifteen small states which Hongwu now said China would *not* invade: Korea, Japan, the then states of Indochina, Thailand, Java, Brunei, and other small principalities which have long since been swallowed up by the states of Southeast Asia.

The purpose of this curious exclusionary announcement, long a puzzle to historians, was suggested by Jung–pang Lo as being part of preparations in Beijing for dealing with Tamburlaine. Hongwu, he believed, was specifically seeking the goodwill of these fifteen states so China would be safe on the east and south while it braced for an expected attack from the west. Hongwu, Lo thought, would have known that Tamburlaine was clearly working to re–create the Mongol Empire of Genghis Khan and his descendants. Genghis's grandson Kublai Khan, still imbued with the traditional Mongol tolerance of all religions that supported the ruler, had been converted by the Chinese Confucian ethic, the Yuan Dynasty hiccup thus fitting relatively seamlessly into the flow of Chinese history; but Tamburlaine on an Islamic *jihad* would constitute an altogether different kind of threat to traditional China.

It is an ingenious argument for explaining the purpose of that curious appendix, but perhaps too ingenious as it relates to Tamburlaine. The absence of any reference to the latter may simply have reflected Beijing's lack of intelligence at this stage about his intentions – after all, it was still another two years until Tamburlaine would begin the physical preparation of the route his army would take to China. The Ming might have become suspicious of the activities of Central Asian merchants resident in China, as suggested earlier, but there is a strong possibility that that was about all they knew at this stage, and that their knowledge of Tamburlaine's power and conquests was a great deal less. And Tamburlaine's 1395 letter to Hongwu may well have been designed to keep things that way as he contemplated his future course of action.

So as well as being designed to restore his intelligence assets in China, the flowery insincerity in which the letter was expressed – not altogether unknown in modern diplomatic discourse – could have been intended by Tamburlaine, contrariwise, as disinformation also, to reinforce the impression, conveyed by the "tribute" of a few horses and camels, of his insignificance, at a time when not only his preparations for moving against China were still far from complete, but he was still preoccupied with dealing with both Tokhtamysh of the Golden Horde and Sultan Barquq of Egypt – in alliance since early 1394. The possibility that this may have been the case is reinforced by his subsequent action.

The Chinese, recording the receipt of the letter, said the Ming Emperor "approved of its style", and ordered that Tamburlaine's emissaries be accompanied back to Samarkand by four of his own senior officials – the Senior Secretaries Fu An and Kuo Chi, the Censor Yao Ch'en, and the Eunuch Liu Wei. (They were said to have had an escort of fifteen hundred men, though perhaps not all the way to Samarkand, as they were not referred to at the Timurid end.) Rossabi says this was Hongwu's first "major" embassy to Tamburlaine (leaving open the question of Grousset's "minor" 1385 mission?), and it backfired badly from the Chinese viewpoint. Whatever Tamburlaine had intended to achieve with his letter, it was not the Emperor's lofty assumption, in his response, that he was a mere vassal, and he demanded that the Chinese ambassadors perform the same ritual obeisances to him as did his own subjects, which not surprisingly they refused to do.[135] But there was surely more than this behind Tamburlaine's insistence on extending the ambassadors' welcome beyond your usual round of formal calls, banquets, receptions and other diplomatic niceties: he had them escorted

---

135 This problem of ambassadors who represent proud sovereigns being required to show what was considered excessive reverence towards overweening heads of state is one that has been around in diplomacy for a very long time. The first Arab ambassador sent to China, by the early 8th century Umayyad Caliph Walid I, refused to bow to anyone but Allah, and only just escaped with his head. But perhaps the most famous episode was that of the lavishly–equipped first British embassy to China, four hundred years after Tamburlaine, when in 1793 the Earl of Macartney, after weeks of standoff over the nine–fold head–to–the–ground–prostration of the kowtow, finally secured agreement that he would do no more than go down on one knee and bow his head when he presented King George III's valuable gifts to the Ching Emperor Qianlong; but that was insufficient to allow of any substantive discussions, and the embassy was politely escorted back to its ships with not a thing to show for the effort or the expense. (See also 1900 chapter: Yuan Shikai)

around some of the cities he had captured – Herat, Tabriz, Isfahan, Shiraz – on a tour that lasted *six* years!

It is usually said that Tamburlaine was anxious to demonstrate his power through showing his conquests, but this is not borne out by the fact that the ambassadors were still detained in Samarkand on their return – Hookham says the principal envoy (it is not clear which of the four is meant) did not arrive back in Beijing until 1407, two years after Tamburlaine's death, though of course having failed so dismally in his mission he may not have been unduly diligent about turning up back at the foreign department with only his poems on *Curious Things Seen on a Journey to the West*. Meanwhile, in 1397, when Hongwu sent another embassy – led by Surveillance Commissioner Ch'en Te–wen – to discover the fate of the first, it too was detained by Tamburlaine.

It is hard to escape the conclusion that so far from wanting to demonstrate his power to the Chinese, he was intent on exactly the opposite: determined to *prevent* knowledge of his capacities from being conveyed back to Beijing. This may not have just been a matter of concealing his own intentions, still at the planning stage; perhaps, in the light of Hongwu's swoop on Karakorum, Tamburlaine had some concern that Hongwu could strike at him also, especially if the Ming were to become too keenly aware of his own unfinished business with India, Egypt and Turkey.

Two years later, parallel with intelligence–gathering – and those possible countermeasures – Tamburlaine began giving more substance to any specific Chinese fears by putting other aspects of his plan into action. The first was diplomatic: the arrangement, in 1397, of his own marriage (his sixth or seventh) to a daughter of the Khan of Moghulistan (roughly southern present–day Kazakhstan), a member of the royal family of Chagatei and ruler of a strategic sector of the route towards China from his Transoxianian heartland. He also began to develop the more northerly route, to "move the frontier further east" (as Barthold put it), in two ways: he instructed his eldest grandson and designated heir, Muhammed–Sultan, already ruler of Ferghana, to establish forts and supplies along the route used by the diplomatic missions, around the north of the Tien Shan mountains past Lake Issyk Kul; and the young man was also to conscript workers to develop agriculture along the same axis – a curious charge from a nomad, but essential to a commander needing provisions for large forces he was intending to lead that way.

It was at about this time that messengers from Mongol pretenders to the Chinese throne came to seek support from Tamburlaine, and he gave sanctuary to several Yuan Dynasty notables who had been dispossessed by the Ming, a fairly sure sign of an intention to meddle in someone else's affairs. Then in 1399 a set–back: a joint preparatory campaign by Muhammed–Sultan and his younger half–brother Iskander into Chinese Turkestan, south of the Tien Shan, went awry when the latter raced ahead, losing potential allies by pillaging as far as Kashgar and Aksu to the north of the Taklamakan Desert and Khotan to the south – the furthest east by Moslems since Arab armies had crossed the Tien Shan during the reign of the Caliph Walid I, less than a century after Mahomet. The fifteen–year–old Iskander boastfully sent trophies, including "nine fine girls", to grandfather Tamburlaine, who was not amused, and he was hauled back. (Muhammed–Shah put him under arrest, and it was not until 1403, after the Turkish campaign, that he was forgiven.)

The most encouraging news, however, came from China itself at the end of 1399: Hongwu had died the previous year, and his sons were disputing the succession. There was consequently a hiatus in Chinese attempts to recover their lost ambassadors. But although the new Ming Empire was considerably weakened during the five years before the fourth son came out on top as the Yongle Emperor, the development of the route east to cope with a huge army of invasion was still not far enough advanced for Tamburlaine to contemplate any immediate action; and in any case he still had other objectives. The first during this period, the conquest of Delhi, can be seen in the nature of a vanity project – outdoing Alexander? – rather than a strategic necessity; but the next two, against first the Egyptian Mamelukes and then the Ottoman Turks, certainly were – it would have been suicidal for Tamburlaine to move against China without having first removed the threat that these two posed to his control of the Caucasus, Persia, and indeed Transoxiana itself.

After the campaigns in Syria and Iraq, in 1401–1402, the senior Emir Allahdad was sent to the eastern marches with trains of captives to speed up the production of crops and food supplies for the route to China; military forces as well as more captives began to be transferred east directly from Anatolia after the campaign against Bajazeth and the Ottoman Turks. Many were Black Sheep Turcomans but there were also Christian Armenians, and, some said, Georgian volunteers (as in the old army custom: "I want volunteers: you, you, you..."?). According to Ibn Arabshah, Tamburlaine ordered that

"Every man should give his whole care to sowing the fields and if anyone were compelled by necessity, he should rather omit his regular prayers than tillage

– a scandal to the orthodox Arabshah, which is no doubt why he reported it. Allahdad was also instructed to establish, as far as China,

> "the situation of those realms and show the nature of the way through them and the paths...their cities and their villages, valleys and mountains, castles and forts, the nearer parts and the remote, the deserts and hills, landmarks and towers, waters and rivers, tribes and families, passes and broad roads, places marked and those without signs of the way, dwelling places and houses for travellers, explaining the distances between all the stages...".

Clavijo said Tamburlaine received the Emir's report,

> "bound and reduced to a square shape, showing everything according to his command, to right and left, villages and mountains, earth and sky",

before he had even returned to Samarkand.

Such dispatch suggests that a good deal of the information was ready to hand; but later, when envoys arrived from Yongle in the middle of 1404, Clavijo discovered that Tamburlaine sought from

> "certain men who had travelled from Khanbaliq with those ambassadors, as from those who had come in charge of the caravan of camels, exact information concerning the many strange peculiarities in the country over which the Emperor was lord, with details of the great wealth and number of the Chinese people".

There was never enough intelligence.

By 1404 virtually all Tamburlaine's preparations had been accomplished. His focus was now fully on China. By this stage he would presumably have known from his network of spies that Yongle had used alliances with, or, if more convenient, campaigns against Mongol khanates bordering China in his ruthless rebellion to seize the throne from his nephew Hui–ti, Hongwu's designated successor. He would thus have been aware that, while for a time China had been weakened by brutal civil war, the new Emperor was potentially far more dangerous than his predecessor.

There has also been speculation that Yongle was more alert to the potential threat posed by Tamburlaine than was Hongwu. Jung–pang Lo cites the suggestion of another Chinese historian, Hsü Yü–hu, that it was knowledge of Tamburlaine's steadily mounting preparations that led Yongle, soon after his accession in 1403, to order the preparation of the first of the extraordinary sea voyages by Admiral Zheng He (Cheng Ho) throughout Southeast Asia, South Asia, as far as the Arabian Peninsula and the east coast of Africa. The later determined expunging of Zheng He's achievements from the official records has meant that the precise purpose of these voyages has always been something of a mystery; but Hsü believed the timing of the first great voyage, which got underway in 1405, was intended, by combining naval power with diplomacy, to induce the maritime nations of Southeast Asia, the Indian Ocean and the Persian Gulf to befriend China at a time of great danger from Tamburlaine.

However Rossabi has questioned this theory: his own researches in the Chinese histories produced no evidence, he says, of

> "any unusual preparations to counter the threat of the most powerful military figure of that era".

The only relevant reference he found in the Ming chronicles was an entry dated 25 March 1405 – thirty–five days, in fact, after Tamburlaine's death – stating that

> "the Emperor, learning of an imminent attack on China by a Muslim from Samarkand, ordered Sung Sheng, his military commander in Gansu, to make adequate preparations. One fails", Rossabi added, "to detect any urgency in these instructions, and there is no hint of an effort to strengthen the defenses in that border region. It appears unlikely that the emperor knew the size and military capability of the force that faced him in Central Asia".

Given what else we know about him, Yongle, newly arrived in power after an extraordinarily determined campaign, does not seem likely to have been unduly smug or lazy: it would seem rather that Tamburlaine's measures of deception had been outstandingly successful.

Tamburlaine's last direct contact with the Chinese came in 1404. Clavijo reported that, immediately before his arrival, new envoys, and a caravan of

> "as many as eight hundred camels, laden with merchandise, came from Cambalu to this city of Samarcand, in the month of June",

and that Tamburlaine

> "forthwith had ordered the whole of this caravan, men and goods, to be taken into custody, and that none should return to China".

It was far too close to invasion–time to allow any word to get back to Beijing.

Schiltberger also recorded the new Chinese embassy arriving in Samarkand that year, on Tamburlaine's return from Turkey with this remarkably survivable Bavarian now in his train:

> "At about this time, the great Chan, king of Chetey [Cathay], sent an ambassador with four hundred horsemen, to demand of [Tamburlaine] the tribute which he had forgotten, and kept for five years. Tämerlin took the ambassador with him, until he came to his above–named capital, and sent him from there to tell his lord, that he would neither pay tribute nor be subject to him, and that he should himself pay *him* a visit".

And Clavijo likewise reported Yongle's demand

> "of the tribute...which Timur year by year had formerly paid".[136]

Of course, as far as we know, there had not only been no offerings or messages of any kind from Samarkand – whether from Tamburlaine himself or his pseudo–ambassadorial merchants – for ten years, since the occasion of Tamburlaine's famous letter of 1394, but he was also *still* detaining the two sets of ambassadors sent by Yongle's father in 1395 and 1397.

Clavijo confirms Tamburlaine's reaction to this first approach by the new Emperor in describing a small diplomatic minuet that would have

---

136   This is the only occasion on which both Clavijo and Schiltberger record eyewitness accounts of the same event. One wonders whether they ever met. The self–important aristocratic Castilian ambassador would not have been inclined to seek out the youthful Bavarian ex–squire even if he had heard of his presence in Samarkand; in any case, Schiltberger, still only twenty–three, was an infidel prisoner, so probably not playing any very visible role in Tamburlaine's court, though he seems likely to have had the boldness to make himself known to Clavijo if they had come in contact. But neither mentions the other.

left the Chinese ambassador in no doubt about the ruler's view. Feeling very much the Castilian Ambassador, he wrote that, at a welcoming feast of roast horse–meat, the unwitting or incompetent Chief of Protocol

> "began placing us in a seat below that of one who it appeared was the ambassador of Chays Khan, the Emperor of Cathay...His Highness at this moment noticed that we, the Spanish ambassador, were being given a seat below that of this envoy from the Chinese Emperor, whereupon he sent word...to inform this Chinaman that the ambassadors of the King of Spain, the good friend of Timur and his son, must indeed take place above him who was the envoy of a thief and a bad man, the enemy of Timur, and that he his envoy must sit below us: and if only God were willing, he Timur would before long see to and dispose matters so that never again would any Chinaman dare come with such an embassy as this man had brought".

While the Spanish ambassador's mission, designed to encourage Tamburlaine to favour Christian Europe against the Ottoman menace, would seem to have been better served by peaceful relations between Tamburlaine and the Chinese Emperor, leaving the former's eastern flank secure, Clavijo could nevertheless not resist enjoying "this Chinaman's" discomfort, nor forebear to add that

> "This Emperor of China is called Chays Khan or Emperor of the Nine Empires, but the Tartars [Tamburlaine's court] call him Tanguz, a name given in mockery, signifying Pig Emperor".

The title had been transferred to Yongle from his father.

There is one pleasing little symmetry between Tamburlaine and Yongle. As well as the famous elephants – or at least those still left over from their military service – Clavijo also saw in one of the gardens surrounding Samarkand a giraffe, which had been presented to Tamburlaine by the Mameluke Sultan of Egypt, for some unsuccessful purpose. Just ten years later, on 20 September 1414, Yongle was also presented with a giraffe, brought back after his fifth voyage by Admiral Zheng He from the city–state of Malindi in Africa (north of Mombassa on the Kenyan coast). Like Clavijo's omission of the elephant's trunk, a Chinese poet's description of this auspicious creature, which was taken to be a real–life version of a heavenly unicorn (*qilin*), managed to omit its long neck; but there is a delightful painting of it [in the National Palace Museum, Taipei], complete.

It is be hoped that Clavijo was not misled (as many of his successors have been in such circumstances) into thinking Tamburlaine's blunt putdown of his Chinese colleague indicated any particular regard for himself: the Court chronicles, referring to the presence of the European ambassadors at a royal feast, observed that "even chaff finds its way to the sea". Shortly afterwards, he and the rest of the chaff (Mobile Flowerpots, in our day) were present with Tamburlaine at the dedication of the Gur Emir in Samarkand, the great mausoleum the great conqueror had had erected for his favourite grandson, Muhammad–Sultan, and which was also to be his own. It was to be Clavijo's last royal occasion.

We have now followed the apparent sequence in Tamburlaine's planning for dealing with China: first, gathering intelligence through pseudo–"tribute" missions and traders, starting in the 1380s; second, contrariwise, keeping information from the Ming as much as possible; third, alliance with the Khan of Moghulistan; fourth, military and agricultural preparation of the route further east; fifth, disposal of any threat from Egypt and Turkey. There was only one step left: to convince his emirs and military commanders to follow him on the most audacious and challenging campaign ever, to complete the compass of his ambition by adding the East – and its spoils – to North, South and West:

"Almighty God has subjugated the world to our dominion and the will of the Creator has entrusted the countries of the earth to our power".

The Ming were usurpers who had seized the Mongol Yuan Dynasty's Chinese Empire; this was a wrong to be righted. We do not know whether Tamburlaine thought Yongle's traditional claim of overlordship might foreshadow an actual effort to assert it; at a minimum, from the viewpoint of encouraging his forces to take up this newest and greatest crusade, the timing of its intolerable presumption was perfect.

And it was indeed to be a crusade. We noted earlier Hongwu's expulsions of Moslem traders from Chinese territory in the mid–1390s. Then some reports of the turmoil following his death in 1398 had made the (unsubstantiated) claim that a hundred thousand Moslems had been massacred in China. Aggression against his neighbours had almost always been presented by Tamburlaine as the punishment of heresy, even though most of them were fellow Moslems. Now, said the *Zafer–name*, he decided "out of the generosity of his heart" to bring the One True Word to genuine infidels and persecutors of Moslems – by the sword as more expeditious than by example.

There was a sad irony involved in this intolerance: within a couple of years the Emperor Yongle was to issue an edict describing the followers of Islam as "sincere, good and loyal subjects", ordering that all mosques be protected, and decreeing that

> "Official, military and civilian [households] and other categories of people shall not maltreat, insult, cheat or bully [Moslems]; and whosoever dares to knowingly disobey Our command...shall be punished according to the crime".

It was about the time the extraordinary Indian Ocean voyages were being undertaken for the Emperor by his great admiral, the Grand Eunuch Zheng He – a Moslem. But then, as we have seen, religion was more often the rationalisation than the substance of Tamburlaine's ambitions.

So Tamburlaine summoned a great *quriltai*, the traditional consultative assembly of all his subordinate emirs and military commanders, to consider his proposal to invade China. And they responded as he would have expected:

> "If the Emperor unfurls his standard", the *Zafer–name* recorded them as saying, "we are his slaves. We will follow him; if need be, we will die for him".

And many of them did. Though they need not have: Tamburlaine, now around seventy, was failing physically, and, knowing it, was determined to push ahead at once, dismissing his generals' urging that the campaign be put off until the spring. So the troops and the armaments and the provisions, five hundred specially iron–plated wagons and the surviving elephants, thousands and thousands of horses and camels, were gathered together at Samarkand, and on 27 November 1404 Tamburlaine led the force of two hundred thousand – Schiltberger said "eighteen hundred thousand"! – towards the east.

> "Never had there been seen – never, perhaps, would there be seen again – so mighty an army".

On this point, of course, Clavijo was wrong: in 1812 Napoleon led six hundred and eighty thousand men, mostly to their doom, against Russia; and in 1941 Hitler, from the safety of his bunkers, sent over three and a half million troops, mostly to *their* doom, against the Soviet Union. But in fact Clavijo was not there to see Tamburlaine's army go. On 21 November he had left Samarkand, believing his embassy was being hastened away because, as they had heard from "trustworthy and well–informed" sources, Tamburlaine was lying on his deathbed.[137] Tamburlaine's preparations for the gigantic expedition had been concealed from Clavijo too.

But on a second point, Clavijo was right:

> "The thoughtful reflected upon the Arab proverb which proclaims that when prosperity has reached its peak it approaches a decline. Many people, when they saw the dazzling beauty of this innumerable host and the endless supply of arms and equipment that had been collected together so quickly in the imperial camp, frankly admitted that Tamerlane's glory could rise no higher; they feared, and with reason, that the tide of his fortune was about to turn, that some disaster would overtake him".

And the cause of the disaster was the same as that which was to overtake Napoleon and Hitler in their turn: General Winter.

Tamburlaine stubbornly pushed forward, straight across the bitter wastes of the Kyzylkum Desert and over the frozen Jaxartes. But, says Ibn Arabshah in a wonderful passage,

> "Winter poured round them with its violent storms and scattered against them its whirlwinds sprinkling hail and roused above them the lamentations of its tempests and discharged against them with full force the storms of its cold and descended with its herald, proclaiming to Timur, 'If you are one of the infernal spirits, I am the other; we are both old and have grown weak while destroying

---

137   Hookham notes that Tamburlaine sent no message back to the King of Castile, but the Ambassador of Sultan Faraj of Egypt was sent back to Cairo at the same time with a letter "of exquisite calligraphy and sentiment" that was more than forty *metres* long and one and a half wide, though admittedly making demands of Faraj – for the Sultan of Baghdad, gagged and bound, but just the head of one of Bajazeth's ex–allies.

countries and men...; if you have slain souls and frozen men's breath, truly the breaths of my frost are far colder than yours...by Allah! the heat of piled coals shall not defend you from the frost of death nor shall fire blazing in the brazier'. Then he measured over him from his store of snow what could split breastplates and dissolve the joints of iron rings and sent down upon him and his army from the sky of frost some mountains of hail and in their wake discharged typhoons of his searing winds, which filled their ears and the corners of their eyes and drove hail into their nostrils and thus drew out their breath to their gullets...; and on all sides the whole earth became [one] with the snow that fell from above, like the plain of the Last Judgement or a sea which God forged out of silver. When the sun rose and the frost glittered, the sight was wonderful, the sky of Turkish gems and the earth of crystal, specks of gold filling the space between".

Tamburlaine's men were in no condition to appreciate this glittering steppe landscape:

"Therefore many perished of his army, noble and base alike and winter destroyed great and small among them and their noses and ears fell off scorched by cold and their order was confounded... Yet Timur cared not for the dying and grieved not for those that perished".

Tamburlaine the mortal

By mid–January 1405, Tamburlaine himself was now near death, and the army had to halt, four hundred kilometres from Samarkand, at the then major Silk Road town of Otrar, on the Syr Darya about fifty kilometres south of where the little Arys River runs into it (which the very first Christian envoy to the Mongol Khans, the Franciscan Giovanni di Piano Carpini, had passed through in the early summer of 1246). There was a rich historical irony in the end of the last great Mongol coming in this place. In 1218, when the first great Mongol Genghis Khan had secured control over all the Mongol and other Central Asian tribes, he found himself faced on the west by the then significant empire of Khwarazm; and whether or not he already had any longer–term intentions, he initiated relations by sending to Otrar a caravan of 450 merchants and even more camels to begin trading. However the governor of the town, for reasons still only speculated on, siezed all the goods and massacred every trader and camel driver – save one of the latter who escaped back to Genghis. It was inevitable that he would retaliate, though doing so all the way to the gates of Damascus, Vienna and Moscow must nevertheless have owed something to more than the Governor of Otrar's brutal stupidity.

Extraordinarily, at Otrar, in these last days, envoys arrived from Toqtamysh, still wandering in the steppes, offering to Tamburlaine, as before, that

> "If I am forgiven, then my head will never move from the yoke of submission, nor my foot from the path of obedience".

And, as before, Tamburlaine believed him, and promised his help when he returned from China: his respect for the line of Genghis Khan never really died. This time, however, Toqtamysh was too late.

Marlowe gives Tamburlaine a moving death scene – but at Babylon – with his sons and grandsons, an undying vision of his ambition:

> "Give me a map; then let me see how much
> Is left for me to conquer all the world.
> That these, my boys, may finish all my wants.
> > [One brings a map.
> Here I began to march towards Persia,
> Along Armenia and the Caspian Sea,
> And thence unto Bithynia, where I took
> The Turk and his great empress prisoners.
> Then march'd I into Egypt and Arabia;
> And here, not far from Alexandria,
> Whereas the Terrene and the Red Sea meet,
> Being distant less than a full hundred leagues,
> I meant to cut a channel to them both,
> That men might quickly sail to India...
> I came at last to Græcia, and from thence
> To Asia, where I stay against my will;
> Which is from Scythia, where I first began,
> Backward and forwards near five thousand leagues.
> Look here, my boys; see, what a world of ground
> Lies westward from the midst of Cancer's line
> Unto the rising of this earthly globe,
> Whereas the sun, declining from our sight,

Begins the day with our Antipodes!
And shall I die, and this unconquered?
Lo, here, my sons, are all the golden mines,
Inestimable drugs and precious stones,
More worth than Asia and the world beside;
And from th'Antarctic Pole eastward behold
As much more land, which never was descried,
Wherein are rocks of pearl that shine as bright
As all the lamps that beautify the sky!
And shall I die, and this unconquered?"[138]

Tamburlaine – Marlowe – makes no mention of the last great campaign against the Emperor of Cathay.[139] As you would anticipate, Ibn Arabshah describes Tamburlaine's miserable end in frozen Otrar differently – in gleeful detail:

---

138 Marlowe based his remarkable geography on the *Theatrum Orbis Terrarum*, the first atlas, first published in Antwerp in 1570 by Abraham Ortelius. I can't resist contrasting Marlowe's spacious geography scene between Tamburlaine and his sons and grandsons, with the anguished map scene between Boris Godunov and his son in Mussorgsky's opera version of Pushkin's play: contrasting Marlowe's Tamburlaine's frustration, after killing thousands of innocents, over what he had not achieved:

> "And shall I die, and this unconquered?",

with Mussorgsky's Boris's despair over the hollowness of what he had, after killing one:

> "Nothing attracts me more!
> Nor glory nor applause...
> Like beasts, the famished multiply,
> And the whole realm weeps and suffers!
> These awful ills that Heaven,
> For my crime, sends down on me...".

139 Of this we can be certain: the greatest product of the Marlowe industry is a *Concordance* (R.J.Fehrenbach et al; Ithaca NY 1982) which lists every use of every word in all Marlowe's works – 1,681 pages, with 92 lines to the page, listing lines of verse containing "of" (3,022), "my" (2,506), "that" (1,892), etc, etc, etc, as well as "Tamburlaine", "blood", and so on. There is no reference in *Tamburlaine* connected with China, and only one anywhere else: in one of the poems, to "Seres" silk, from the conventional Latin term for the otherwise unknown Eastern country where silk originated.

"Since he was enough protected from the cold without, he wished something to be made for him, which would drive the cold from him and so he ordered to be distilled for him arrack blended with hot drugs and several health–giving spices which were not harmful...Therefore Timur took of that arrack and drank it again and again without pause, not asking about affairs and news of his army or caring concerning them or hearing their petitions, until the hand of death gave him the cup to drink...

But that arrack, as though making footprints, injured his bowels and heart, whereby the structure of his body tottered and his supports grew weak. Then he summoned doctors and expounded his sickness to them, who in that cold treated him by putting ice on his belly and chest...And his liver was crushed and neither his wealth nor children availed him aught and he began to vomit blood and bite his hands with grief and penitence...if one saw him, he coughed like a camel which is strangled, his colour was nigh quenched and his cheeks foamed like a camel dragged backwards with the rein; and if one saw the angels that tormented him, they showed the joy with which they threaten the wicked, to lay waste their houses and utterly destroy the whole memory of them...

Then [the angels] brought garments of hair from Hell and drew forth his soul like a spit from a soaked fleece and he was carried to the cursing and punishment of God, remaining in torment and God's infernal punishment".

Ibn Arabshah's avenging angels notwithstanding, on his deathbed Tamburlaine appointed his grandson Pir Muhammed as his heir, and made all his family and emirs and commanders swear to follow him. He died on 18 February 1405. But, as Grousset put it, "on the very morrow of Tamerlane's death, the quarrels, coups and palace revolutions began". The invasion of China was cancelled forthwith. Tamburlaine's body was carried back to Samarkand – some said, in a wedding palanquin, to prevent news of his death becoming known – and in due course it was buried – embalmed with musk and rose–water and wrapped in linen, according to Curzon – in the Gur Emir next to his beloved grandson Muhammed Sultan.

According to Shterenshis, the Russian scholar Barthold, "using primary sources", analyzed the burial and mourning procedures; and on the basis of "specific nomadic rituals such as, for example, scratching faces until they bled", and the placing of "dress, weapons and other belongings" at the tomb, he concluded that Tamburlaine was initially buried according to Mongol custom, not Islamic ritual. Ibn Arabshah had observed that Tamburlaine

> "clung to the laws of Jenghizkhan...and he observed them in preference to the laws of Islam",

but this had been regarded as another piece of the old orthodox Moslem's bigotry. But...perhaps not. It was only four years later that Tamburlaine's son Shahrukh changed the tomb's decoration to be in accord with Moslem piety. When the tomb was opened by Soviet archeologists in 1941, it contained the remains of a well-built man, lame in the right leg – and just 165cms tall.

But the tomb was not the end, according to Schiltberger:

> "After he was buried, the priests that belong to the temple, heard him howl every night during a whole year. His friends gave large alms, that he should cease his howlings. But this was of no use. They asked advice of their priests, and went to his son and begged that he would set free the prisoners taken by his father in other countries, and especially those that were in his capital, who were all craftsmen he had brought to his capital, where they had to work. He let them go, and as soon as they were free, Tämerlin did not howl any more".

Tamburlaine's soul had reason to howl as his two surviving sons – he had only had four (and three known daughters) despite at least twelve wives – and grandsons set about fighting each other for the inheritance. But, given his failure to establish an imperial administration, it is not surprising that his empire did not survive him. Shahrukh, the younger surviving son, who was left with Herat, gradually wrested control over the rest of Tamburlaine's legacy from his older brother and nephews, and ruled for forty years. Shahrukh married a Chagatei princess, Gohar (or Gawhar) Shad, who was one of those practical Mongol women who had been disposed to give parties in the gardens around Samarkand, though she also did good works, most notably building a huge mosque in the holy city of Mashhad (now in northwest Iran).[140]

Shahrukh re–established relations with China; and there is a delightful report by an overwhelmed Ghaiassudin Nakkash, whom he sent as head of an embassy to Beijing in 1419–1422, of the "New Palace" – the original Forbidden City – that Tamburlaine's old opponent the Emperor Yongle was just then finishing laying out:

> "It would be impossible to give a just description of this edifice. From the gate of the hall of audience to the outer gate there is a distance of 1985 paces...To the right and left there is an uninterrupted succession of buildings, pavilions, and gardens. All the buildings are constructed of polished stone and glazed bricks of porcelain clay, which in lustre are quite like white marble...In the arts of stone–polishing, cabinet–making, pottery, brick–making, there is nobody with us who can compare with the Chinese".

Not since Tamburlaine had captured the best craftsmen of all western and south Asia, and brought them back to beautify Samarkand.

Nevertheless his grandson Ulugh Beg presided over a new golden age in Samarkand, particularly in astronomy, literature and miniature–painting, partly as governor of Transoxiana during his father's reign, then in succession to him.[141] Then after two years he was killed by one

---

140   In *The Road to Oxiana* the English writer Robert Byron recounted a wonderful story about Gohar Shad, taken from a 19th century Indian antiquarian called Mohun Lal. She also built a large *medresseh* adjacent to the mosque; and when she came to inspect it with a train of two hundred young ladies, the young scholars were sent on leave – all but one, who had fallen asleep, and woke to catch the eye, and more, of "a ruby–lipped lady". When this irregularity was discovered Gohar Shad promptly married all her ladies to the students, providing each also with clothes, salary and bed on condition the couple met only once a week, so as not to interfere with studies. "She did all this", Byron said Mohun Lal added piously, "to arrest the progress of adultery".

141   The first British Astronomer Royal, John Flamsteed, drew on some of the corrections made by "Ulugh Beigh" to the work of the 2nd century Ptolemy of Alexandria, his major predecessor, in his 1725 *Historia Coelestis Britannica* recounting astronomical observation.

of his sons in 1449, and the divided Timurids were gradually driven back to Herat and then into oblivion by the Uzbeks, a Mongol–Turkic people named after Uzbeg, great–great-grandson of Batu Khan. In 1500 the second last of Tamburlaine's descendants to rule Samarkand was naïve enough to come out of the city to try to negotiate at the invitation of the beseiging Uzbek Khan, Muhammed Shaybani; he was promptly executed and the city taken. Later, the Sunni Shaybani, confident in the support of his fellow Sunni Ottoman Sultan Bajazeth II (great–great-grandson of Tamburlaine's victim), was himself foolish enough to command the Shiite Shah Ismail of Persia to abjure his "heresy" or be converted by the sword; Ismail won the challenge, made Shaybani's head into a drinking cup (as one did), but to cap things off sent the skin, stuffed with straw, to Bajazeth for his contemplation.

Tamburlaine's real successor was to be the last, brief, Timurid ruler of Samarkand, his great–great–great-grandson, Zahir al–Din Muhammed Babur, Khan of Ferghana, who as a young man sought to emulate his famous ancestor and twice captured Samarkand, though only for a year or so each time, and only to lose it twice as well. According to his delightful memoirs, it was only after his second failure, while he was in hiding in 1498, that he heard of India from an old crone of 111 years, who told him stories she had heard from men who had accompanied Tamburlaine to rape the fabled riches of Delhi exactly one hundred years before. It was to take Babur another twenty–seven years until, on his fifth campaign into India, he finally achieved, at Panipat, the very same battlefield where Tamburlaine had triumphed over the Sultan of Delhi, the victory that led to the establishment of the great and glorious Indian Empire of the Moghuls (a corruption of "Mongols"). It lasted for more than three hundred years, until other conquerors passed that way for a time; and its achievements, especially in art and architecture, were beyond the gold of Samarkand – though Babur himself said he could never forget "the flavour of melons and grapes". But that is another story.

Notwithstanding Shaybani's ignominious end, and Babur's post–filial efforts, Samarkand finished under the control of the Uzbeks. They were descendants of Kipchaks of the Golden Horde, against whom Tamburlaine had struggled for so long a century before. For posterity, Toqtamysh was thus the ultimate victor, the ruins of Samarkand Tamburlaine's only monument. But what a monument!

The divisions in the heart of Central Asia disrupted the fabled Silk Road, just as the Ottoman Turks' ultimate triumph against Byzantium four years after Ulugh Beg's murder sealed off China and Europe from contact for a century – until Portuguese merchants gained a foothold in China itself, at Macau, and a new and very different relationship began. But, even without the Westerners' markets, the Silk Road still did not disappear (nor even British merchandise), as an Englishman, Lieutenant Alexander Burnes of the East India Company – known as "Bokhara" Burnes for having ridden there from Delhi – noted while he was in this city in 1832. With about a hundred and fifty thousand people it was much bigger then than Samarkand, which he was not permitted to visit, but which he was told had

> "at most 10,000 inhabitants, and gardens and fields occupy the place of its streets and mosques".

In Bokhara there were twenty caravanserais for merchants from different countries; and Burnes wrote that in the Registan, the central square dominated by the huge walls and soaring central portal of the 16th century citadel, known as the Ark,

> "A stranger has only to seat himself on a bench...[to] converse with the natives of Persia, Turkey, Russia, Tartary, China, India and Cabool".

Burnes reported a 1300–camel annual caravan from Russia bringing all sorts of cloth (including English broad–cloth and "chintses"), furs, cochineal (for dying silk), metal–wares of all kinds, furs, paper, honey (just as to Byzantium eight centuries before – see 1000 chapter); from Persia shawls, but mostly opium; from India and "Cabool" 500 camel-loads of indigo, as well as sugar and muslins; from China, "a coarse kind of China ware", musk and bullion, but mainly 950 horse–loads of tea; and Bokhara itself exporting (as Uzbekistan does still) silks and the celebrated Karakool lambskins now known as "Astrakhan". The volumes were no doubt less, but the trade still covered the same sort of wide range as had existed in Tamburlaine's own time.

As we saw earlier in this chapter, the separate Emirates established in Central Asia by the Uzbeks – of Samarkand, Khiva, Bokhara, Tashkent – were eventually subjugated by Russia late in the 19th century. Following the Revolution the Bolsheviks promised independence, but after forming them in 1924 into the "Uzbekistan Soviet Socialist Republic", maintained an iron grip on it (and all of neighbouring Central Asia) as a constituent part of the USSR, ruled by Russians. Then in 1991, with the collapse of the USSR, it became the independent Republic of Uzbekistan. And the new Republic's Uzbek leaders proclaimed the Mongol Tamburlaine "Father of the Nation". It had a certain geographical, if not historical, logic.

Tamburlaine, the musical

Tamburlaine's real place was in history – and in literature, and, especially, in what might seem the unlikely sphere of music. Between Marlowe's plays and the early 18th century there were at least a dozen more plays published (and perhaps produced) in Europe: in Valladolid (1642), Paris (1647, 1672, 1675, 1681), Amsterdam (1657, 1710) and London (1653, 1681, 1686, 1702).[142] The first of these London versions was by Samuel Clarke, who, perhaps trying to outdo Marlowe himself, managed to convey almost the entire action in the title alone:

> "The life of Tamerlane the Great, with his wars against the great Duke of Mosco, the King of China, Bajazet the Great Turk, the Sultan of Egypt, the King of Persia, and some others, carried on with a continued series of success from the first to the last. Wherein are rare examples of heathenish piety, prudence, magnanimity, mercy, liberality, humility, justice, temperance, and valour".

One cannot help wondering whether Mr Clarke was writing about the same Tamburlaine – but at least he included the "King of China".[143]

---

142   And in addition, in 1667, in *Paradise Lost*, Milton's Archangel Michael showed Adam, from the Hill of Paradise, amongst

> "all Earths Kingdomes and thir Glory...
> City of old or modern Fame, the Seat
> Of mightiest Empire,...
> *Samarchand* by *Oxus*, *Temirs* Throne".

143   The 1702 London version, by Nicholas Rowe, also presented Tamburlaine in a favourable light: indeed, it was an allegory representing King William III as the great conqueror, and Louis XIV of France, with whom England was then at war, as the execrated Bajazeth. According to *The Oxford Companion to English Literature*, the play was revived annually for more than a century on 5 November, the anniversary of Protestant William's landing in England in 1688 to displace Catholic King James II.

However, after the Renaissance, the second period of fascination with Tamburlaine really came with the great flowering of Italian opera in the 18th century. It is not clear whether the Italians wrote any stage plays on the subject, but the greatest spread of his story in the whole of Europe stemmed from prolific opera composition based on three librettos by Italians: one by Giulio Cesare Corradi of Parma (1689), used in probably the first Tamburlaine opera the same year by the Venetian Marc'Antonio Ziani; another by the Florentine Antonio Salvi (1706), used in two operas, in 1706 (by Alessandro Scarlatti, one of his sixty–seven), and 1717; and, above all, a third by the Venetian patrician Agostino Piovene (1711), whose libretto was used by *twenty–three* Italian composers (by my best count in *Grove Opera*, but there could well be more) during the course of the century – in 1711 (in Rome, one of fifty–two operas by Francessco Gasparini, revised in 1719 and again in 1723), 1720, 1722, 1727, 1730 (two), 1732, 1735 (by Vivaldi in Venice, one of his forty–seven), 1742, 1743, 1746 (two), 1753, 1754 (two), 1763, 1764, 1765 (three), 1771, 1773, 1783, and (as interest ran out) 1799. For his text Piovene (and Salvi) drew on the 1675 Paris play *Tamerlan* by Nicolas Pradon, itself based on the 1672 *Bajazet* by his rival and superior, Racine. The operas tended to have either Tamburlaine as the dramatic hero or Bajazeth as the tragic one, and to be named accordingly (with the former winning seventeen to eight). But it is said that somewhere, in all versions, there lurks an echo, however faint, of the *Narrative of the Embassy of Ruy Gonzales de Clavijo to the Court of Timour, at Samarkand, AD 1403–6*.

The only version based on Marlowe that I have discovered, and the only one whose title gave the two protagonists equal billing, was *Bajazeth und Tamerlan* by the Hamburg composer Johann Förtsch, in 1690. Another German, George Frederick Handel, also wrote a *Tamerlano*. He had gone to Florence in 1706, at the age of twenty–one, at the invitation of Prince Ferdinando de' Medici, whom he had met in Hamburg where his first two operas had been performed; and he probably saw Alessandro Scarlatti's *Il gran Tamerlano* (with libretto by Salvi) when it was first performed there that year at the Court of the Prince's father, the Grand Duke Cosimo III of Tuscany. The Prince was not altogether satisfied, and wrote to Scarlatti:

"I shall be very pleased if you make the music rather more easy, and noble in style; and if, in such places as is permissible, you will make it rather more cheerful".

(Handel himself was more successful: his third opera, *Rodrigo*, was performed in Florence the following year – and handsomely rewarded by the Grand Duke with "a service of gold plate".)

When he came in 1724 to write his own *Tamerlano*, his seventeenth opera, Handel turned to the Piovene libretto, which was adapted by the Roman musician Nicola Haym, then revised by Handel himself under the influence of Gasparini's 1719 version. Haym, who adapted others' librettos for seven of Handel's operas between 1713 and 1728, had begun his own musical career in 1694 as a sixteen–year–old cellist in the orchestra directed by the great Arcangelo Corelli for Cardinal Ottoboni in Rome (see 1700 chapter). Written in less than three weeks, *Tamerlano* is one of the masterpieces among Handel's forty–six operas. By the time of its composition he had been resident in London for twelve years, but it owed nothing to Marlowe. The prophet who had led the way for Shakespeare was without musical honour in his own country.

In the 19th century Tamburlaine became a chapter in books about other things, as opera composers moved away from the previous century's obsession with ancient and medieval history and mythology (often confounded) and sought the more soulful heroes and heroines of Romanticism or heeded the siren call of Nationalism (Mussorgsky, Wagner, Verdi – Gilbert and Sullivan). Genghis Khan continued to be a household name in the 20th century, for obvious reasons, but not Tamburlaine.

Still, in 1913, in a poem called *The Golden Journey to Samarkand*, a young Englishman, James Elroy Flecker, posted as a consul in Beirut near Tamburlaine's rampaging route through Syria in 1400, recalled, without naming him, the passage of the great conqueror, a premonition only a year before the world began a convulsion on a scale even Tamburlaine would have found difficult to recognize. And the second part of the Prologue seems a fitting conclusion to our journey with him:

> "And how beguile you? Death has no repose
> Warmer and deeper than that Orient sand
> Which hides the beauty and bright faith of those
> Who made the Golden Journey to Samarkand.
>
> And now they wait and whiten peaceably,
> Those conquerors, those poets, those so fair:
> They know time comes, not only you and I,
> But the whole world shall whiten, here or there;

When those long caravans that cross the plain
With dauntless feet and sound of silver bells
Put forth no more for glory or for gain,
Take no more solace from the palm–girt wells.

When the great markets by the sea shut fast
All that calm Sunday that goes on and on:
When even lovers find their peace at last,
And Earth is but a star, that once had shone."

The Angel appearing to Saint Joachim, Marcantonio Raimondi,
engraving after woodcut by Albrecht Durer. Author's own engraving.
Photo courtesy Tim MacDonald.

ITALY

MARCANTONIO RAIMONDI: SELLING THE RENAISSANCE

"I now have goods in Rome to the value of three thousand golden ducats, and an income of fifty gold crowns, because, since I am to be overseer of the building of St Peter's, His Holiness the Pope has granted me a provision of three hundred gold ducats, to be paid to me so long as I live, and I am certain to receive more in future, and then I am paid for my work whatever sum I deem fitting, and have now begun [frescoing] another room for His Holiness which will amount to one thousand two hundred ducats...and I dwell in Rome in a House worth more than a hundred ducats..."

Raphael: letter to his uncle, 1 July 1514

My interest in "the Great Masters" of painting began – along with an interest in the wider world in general – at about eight years old when my grandfather gave me a set of Arthur Mee's 10-volume *Children's Encyclopedia*. For a long time I was more interested in history pictures – knights, battles, explorers – than in the portraits, landscapes and altar-pieces of the greatest Great Masters. But something of the latter seeped into my awareness as well, though not in the proportions Arthur Mee presented them. I have just looked again at his coverage (in the 1930s) of the great names, and the statistics are an interesting indication of fashions in artistic taste. Being English, his countrymen are well represented with reproductions: Gainsborough had 11, Burne-Jones 10, Constable 6, though Turner, the greatest, only 3; across the vast divide of the narrow Channel Velasquez had 22, far and away the individual leader, Rembrandt and David 15 each, Dürer 8; from Italy a wide range of Renaissance artists is included, and of the three usually regarded as constituting its apogee, Raphael had 15, Michael Angelo (as Mee wrote) 6, but also 9 sculptures, Leonardo da Vinci 5 – the same number as the no-longer-household-name Paul Delaroche, a painstaking and painful French Romantic painter of...English history. The French moderns hardly made it: Cézanne, Manet, Monet, Renoir 2 each; Matisse and Picasso merely a single unillustrated reference. Our own passions, the great pre-First World War German Expressionists – Kirchner, Marc, Macke, Schmidt-Rotluff and the rest – and their great Russian *avant-garde* contemporaries – Kandinsky, Goncharova, Lentulov, Malevich, Popova and the rest – had still not registered in England. As a national group, the artists of the Italian Renaissance were the winners.

My first chance to see the real thing came when I went to England in 1956 for post-graduate study: the National and Tate Galleries in London, then Paris and Amsterdam at Easter 1957, and Vienna, Venice, Florence and Rome in the summer, in a beat-up Bedford mini-van with a bunch of Australian friends also studying in England. It was on that trip that we decided five minutes in the Uffizi are better than none at all. However longer is best; and during later postings with my wife (who also grew up with Arthur Mee) and children in Asia and Europe we were able to indulge a passion for art and architecture which seemed to be forever expanding in time, style and geography. But at the centre of my recollection of a good deal of looking I can still feel the impact of seeing for the first time in that summer of 1957 Raphael's great frescoes in the Vatican *Stanze*.

During our Brussels years, while accompanying the annual Australian Parliamentary Delegation to meetings with the European Parliament in Strasbourg, we discovered during a weekend excursion with them the glory of nearby Colmar: the works of Martin Schongauer, and particularly his exquisite engravings. "*Le beau Martin*" was one of the first masters of works on paper, along with Lucas Cranach, an exhibition of whose works we happened upon in Bamberg, and Albrecht Dürer, selections from whose considerable output were often on display. And it was while looking for Dürers in pursuit of this new passion that we found, in a Belgian antiquarian's, a superb print from his *Life of the Virgin* series.

Well that is what it looked like: but it was in fact by an Italian contemporary of Dürer's, one Marcantonio Raimondi. Fortunately for us – there is no way we could afford a Dürer. But the Raimondi hangs on our wall, in a beautiful Renaissance frame my wife spotted in the *Marché aux puces* in Paris; and Raimondi himself led us on a merry dance through Bologna, Venice, where he became entangled with Dürer (in what came to be seen as a very early intellectual property case over the above copy of his work...but maybe wasn't), then Florence, where he overlapped with Raphael and possibly Leonardo da Vinci and Michelangelo as well, and finally on to Rome, where he worked for... Raphael. But that was still not the end of Raimondi – his influence carried on for several centuries, through the unlikely list of Rembrandt, Sir Joshua Reynolds, Manet and Picasso. This chapter is mostly about the relations between and influence of artists, in Renaissance Italy and more widely across European cultural viewpoints then and later, some much later.

> ## The principal people in this chapter are as follows:
>
> - **Marcantonio Raimondi** (c.1480-c.1534) – Italian Renaissance engraver. Worked in collaboration with or produced prints based on work by Raphael and Albrecht Durer.
>
> - **Albrecht Durer** (1471-1528) – German Renaissance artist. Talented painter, draftsman and writer, but noted particularly for revolutionising printmaking as an art form.
>
> - **Raphael** – or Raffaello Sanzio da Urbino (1483-1520) – Italian Renaissance painter and architect known for his Madonnas and his large figure compositions in the Vatican.
>
> - **Giorgio Vasari** (1511-1575) – Italian Renaissance painter, architect and writer known primarily for his book Lives of the Most Eminent Painters, Sculptors, and Architects – biographies of mostly Italian Renaissance artists, some of whom he knew personally.

And it turns out that Raimondi is the first of our ten characters of whom we have an authentic portrait: not just a drawing or even an easel head-and-shoulders, but standing, life-size, also painted by Raphael...and *in* the *Stanze*.

Prints on paper, drawings, woodcuts, engravings, etchings, began to be regarded as works of art during the fifteenth century, and towards its end already had the three practioners (who were also great painters) who were recognized then, and still are, as among – if not *the* -greatest masters of the art: in Mantua, the Italian Andrea Mantegna, about 70 years old in 1500; and three Germans: Martin Schongauer, *le beau*

Martin, who had died in Colmar in 1491; in Vienna, Lucas Cranach the Elder, who in 1500 was 28; and Albrecht Dürer, 29, in Nuremberg.

The "Dürer" my wife and I thought we had found is a superb print of an Annunciation, though not the usual one: an absolutely splendid angel telling the aged St Joachim that his equally aged wife St Anna would give birth to the Virgin Mary.[144] They are set against towering trees and cliffs on the left; on the right, shepherds look after a large herd of sheep straggling down a slope, beyond which is a distant view of a small town and ships across a bay. At the bottom right of the sheet, the initials "AD" in a small tablet, Dürer's familiar signature. Lower left, a small Roman "2"; and that, we learned, was the give–away: it was an engraving by Marcantonio Raimondi – a good, indeed an exact, contemporary copy of a Dürer. At the very beginning of his career, Raimondi had discovered there was money to be made in art.

Who was this Raimondi, so skilfully impersonating the great Albrecht Dürer? As it transpired – allowing for the stylised sculptured busts of 1200's Jayavarman VII – he is the first of the leading characters whom we have met in this scurry through the Millennium of whom we have a fully authentic, naturalistic portrait – painted by none other than Raphael. Life-size, in one of his great frescoes in the Popes' apartments in the Vatican. (And looking curiously *like* Dürer, but we shall come to that.) A counterfeiter, immortalised by the great Raphael? Then, as our search continued, we discovered that, three and a half centuries later, Manet, the father of modern art, as some say, had turned to this Raimondi for the form of one of his most famous paintings. Which, a century later, Picasso – who, admittedly, sooner or later did just about everything – worked over and "repainted", dozens of times. Dürer? Raphael? Manet? Picasso? *Raimondi* ?

Beginnings

Most of what we know about Marcantonio Raimondi comes from the first dictionary of biography after Plutarch wrote his *Lives* about the end of the first century: the *Lives of the Most Eminent Painters, Sculptors and Architects*, published by the Florentine painter and architect Giorgio

---

144   The New Testament makes no reference to either of Mary's parents, who only appear in the apocryphal "Gospel of St James"; but they gave rise to prodigious theologising and wonderful paintings, from the Middle Ages until the Renaissance.

Vasari, first in 1550, then in a greatly expanded version in 1568.[145] With about a hundred and fifty biographies and descriptions and critiques of the work of (mostly) Italian artists, it covers almost three centuries from the beginnings of the Renaissance in the late 13th century until the death of Michelangelo four years before the second edition. A hundred and forty-four of the biographies were accompanied by a portrait, of which about two-thirds are considered true likenesses. Raimondi's is from the Raphael fresco.

Though criticised by modern art historians as "notoriously unreliable", Vasari's work has nevertheless remained an indispensable source of information on one of the greatest periods of human creativity – even if information to be sifted, corrected by other sources where they exist, or sometimes taken with a pinch of salt. Vasari did often try to see the best in everyone – not a fashion in contemporary art criticism – and tended to record anything and everything; but with his concurrent work as Court painter and architect to Cosimo I de' Medici, Duke of Florence, which Vasari considered, wrongly as it turned out, to be his greatest achievement, he probably had little enough time to check all his sources.

Marcantonio Raimondi appeared in Part III of the second edition of the inestimable *Lives*, included in a chapter entitled "The Lives of Marc' Antonio Bolognese and of Other Engravers of Prints" – the "others" being all those engravers of whom Vasari knew, or thought he knew, starting with Schongauer and Dürer (both of whom he mis-placed in Flanders) and continuing with Raimondi and the other Italians in the school which developed in Rome under Raphael's aegis between his arrival there in 1508 and his death in 1520.

What there is of Raimondi is only a bare outline, to which historians of Italian Renaissance art have added the occasional reference in a few

---

145   The title of the 1550 edition was *The Lives of the Most Eminent Italian Architects, Painters and Sculptors, from Cimabue down to our own Time*. In the initial "Preface to the Whole Work" he described architecture as

"the most universal and the most necessary and useful to men, and as that for the service and adornment of which the two others exist",

but did not explain why, in the second edition, he moved architecture to third place. All quotations here are from the handsome version of the 1568 edition, translated by Gaston du C. de Vere, published by Harry N. Abrams, New York, in 1979.

documents by or about someone else.[146] But Renaissance art history has been such an industry of expertise that the artistic life of the main centres, and the remarkable movement of people and of influences between them, have been extraordinarily well identified. And by exploring where he might have fitted into these movements and contexts, who he knew or could have met, a picture of Marcantonio Raimondi can be discerned against a vivid and frequently turbulent background.

Raimondi was born near Bologna about 1480, a date based on the impression that he looks about thirty in the portrait Raphael painted in the Vatican apartments in 1511. Earlier in the 15th century there had been two Raimondi Bishops of Bologna (uncle and nephew, a common pattern in the contemporary Papacy also), but no firm connection with Marcantonio has been established. Instead, his name became connected with someone else entirely – the Bolognese painter and goldsmith with whom he served his apprenticeship, Francesco Raibolini, known as Francia. According to Vasari,

"While Francesco Francia was working at his paintings in Bologna, there was among his many disciples a young man called Marc' Antonio, who, being more gifted than the others, was much brought forward by him, and, from having been many years with Francia and greatly beloved by him, acquired the surname of De' Franci".

Vasari usually referred to Raimondi as Marc' Antonio Bolognese; but when Raimondi signed his engravings he always used the letters "MAF" – Marc' Antonio de' Franci – a striking acknowledgement of the debt he owed to his teacher.

Many of the early engravers – including both Schongauer and Dürer – learned their art as goldsmiths' apprentices. In Italy, since the early Renaissance, many others had also begun their careers in goldsmiths' workshops: the painters Andrea Pisano, Paolo Uccello, Andrea del Verrocchio, Leonardo da Vinci, Benozzo Gozzoli, the sculptors Orcagna, Ghiberti, Luca della Robbia, Donatello, the architect Brunelleschi; and Vasari himself, who was to chronicle them all, also began as a goldsmith's as well as a painter's apprentice. Why this should have been so is not altogether clear. Perhaps, apart from those like

---

146 A summary of all the references is in *The Engravings of Marcantonio Raimondi* by Shoemaker and Broun

Schongauer and Dürer who followed their fathers, the others were placed by parents in a profession regarded as being at the upper end of the tradesman's social scale, and one which, unlike others, would be safer against the economic downturns associated with the incessant outbreaks of plague, civil unrest and foreign invasion in renaissance Italy – the more elaborate commissions may dry up, but even today troubled times see a move of assets into gold.

There was also an interesting variety in the goldsmiths' work, which might have attracted the parents of a lad not sure of what he could do. There was apparently no goldsmiths' guild in Bologna, but in due course Francia was admitted to its *Società delle Quattro Arti* – painters, saddlers, sheath-makers and swordsmiths. In Venice, the painters' guild, the *Arte dei Pintori*, also included craftsmen who painted curtains, chests and playing cards, and who gilded leather: both Giovanni Bellini and Giorgione painted furniture. The arts were broader then.

Like many goldsmiths, Francia made not only jewellery, but gold and silver objects – bowls, platters, chalices; some, like Benvenuto Cellini, made table centrepieces closer to sculpture. Francia also designed and manufactured the coinage, and carved and cast portrait medals, including, of course, of Bologna's ruler:

> "He made medals", Vasari wrote, "of Signor Bentivogli, in which he appears alive, and of an infinite number of princes, who would stop in Bologna on their way through the city...; for which, besides immortal fame, he also received very rich presents".

Giovanni Bentivoglio also commissioned frescoes in his palace and chapel by Francia, who had taken up painting, very successfully, when he was about thirty-five, a very late start in those days. The work was shared with his workshop colleague Lorenzo Costa, who would later succeed Mantegna as court painter in Mantua, and the younger painter Amico Aspertini, who had rather adventurously spent the three years 1500-1503 in Rome drawing classical remains, one of the earliest examples of a study that was soon to be of enormous significance to the artists and architects of the high Renaissance. When Aspertini brought them back to Bologna, those sketch-books were probably Raimondi's introduction to classical design, the influence of which would be evident right from his earliest known works; in due course more than a dozen of his engravings would be based directly on classical Roman bas-reliefs and sculptures.

We do not know when exactly Francia took on the young Marcantonio Raimondi. But it was a time when apprentices began work very young: Mantegna had been apprenticed (to Squarcione) at 12; Dürer (as noted, to his father) at about the same age; Giulio Romano, with whom Raimondi would later be closely associated in Rome, was described by Vasari as beginning as "a boy"; Raimondi would in due course copy a sophisticated engraving made by the Antwerper Lucas van Leyden when the latter was perhaps as young as 11, and appropriate for one of his own more notable prints an elaborate background from another that Lucas made at 14. Presumably Raimondi also began with Francia in his early teens; but his earliest dated engraving is only from 1505, a dozen or so years later.

What was he doing during that interval? It is unlikely, however much of a favourite he was, that Francia supported him for such a long time merely as an apprentice engraver; he was surely expected to learn and pull his weight in the whole range of activities of the workshop: regular goldsmithing, the various processes of jewel-making, contributing in some way to the master's medal-making. Did Raimondi also learn painting from his master? We do not know: no paintings remain that are attributable to him. Italian Renaissance paintings have been examined by the Renaissance industry with the most unbelievably fine eyes, and there is no way, no way at all, that a Raimondi painting could have escaped their scrutiny. But it would have been logical for Raimondi to at least try his hand at it, to learn drawing and the elements of design and colour: an additional attribute for a young tyro. At the minimum he appreciated his master's artistic skills: 32 of his engravings would be based on works by Francia, the third largest group following those after Raphael (110) and Dürer (74); the largest group was of more than 130 engravings based on his own designs.

In addition to painting and doing all these things that goldsmiths did, Francia himself also worked in niello, a process in which plates of silver or gold are engraved with a design which is then filled with *niello*, a metallic alloy like a black enamel. It is a process dating back to antiquity, and had been used for such disparate items as reliquaries, candlesticks, buckles and sword scabbards. But it had had an unexpected offshoot some fifty years before Francia's time when someone – the Florencentric Vasari claimed it was the Florentine Maso Fininguerra – first smoothed a piece of paper over a still-wet niello design to make a print. Perhaps so, or perhaps it was somewhere on the Rhine. But the making of engravings was born. Some of Francia's old–style niello prints have survived; and it was probably with this process that Marcantonio began his career in print-making. Soon, however, he was working with the much more versatile process of using more controllable ink with more economical copper plates. The elements of Raimondi's talents and interests were all coming together.

Upheavals

It is not long after we first know of Raimondi engraving that we find him moving. The extent of movement by artists in Italy during the decades either side of the turn of this century was quite astonishing: journeying to study under this or that master; fleeing from the wrath of this or that patron or falling for the lure of this or that new prince or prelate; and, above all, flooding to Rome to benefit from the extravagant patronage of the Popes who created the Renaissance city. This spectacular project had been launched a short time before by Pope Sixtus IV della Rovere (1471-1484); it culminated in the reigns of his nephew – one of the six he created cardinals – Julius II (1503-1513), followed by Leo X de' Medici (1513-1521), and then the latter's (illegitimate) cousin Clement VII (1523-1534). These were the three Popes who were the chief patrons of Michelangelo and Raphael, and thus, indirectly, of Raimondi.

There are blanks in our knowledge about Raimondi's own movements in the new century – what induced him to go first to Venice in 1506, then to Florence, or then to Rome via Florence within the next two years. Given the thrusting nature of the times, and what we see later of that aspect in Raimondi himself, the main reason was probably, after such a long period in Francia's workshop, simply to make a name on his own account. His moves, and the possible associations involved – with Dürer and Raphael in particular – form the basis of much of this chapter.

During the previous quarter-century Florence, where the Medici court of the humanist Lorenzo the Magnificent had blazed, would have been seen as the greatest draw in Italy. But the Magnificent's successor had been driven out of Florence; his nemesis, the militant puritan Savonarola, had been martyred; and for three years a weak Florentine Republic faced the threat of the blood-drenched ambition of Cesare Borgia, son of the venal and nepotistic Pope Alexander VI, a Spaniard, nephew of an earlier Pope, and noted for having purchased the papal throne by bribery in 1492, and for dividing the world, newly expanded by the discovery of the Americas, between Portugal and Spain in 1493.

Rome was not yet the artistic magnet it would soon become. In any case, from Bologna it may not have appeared all that welcoming at that particular time. Bologna, technically part of the States of the Church, had been in practice virtually independent under its local Bentivogli rulers; but it was about about to be descended upon by a militant – military – new Pope, bent on recovering his Papal patrimony by force of arms. By comparison, Venice must have seemed stable and prosperous, though it would in fact be hit commercially before long by the newly discovered trade route to the East Indies around the south of Africa.

In the autumn of 1506 Julius II, wearing full armour, led his troops out of Rome on the way to recover the Holy See's errant cities. After taking Perugia and crossing the Appenines, Julius paused during October at Cesena, south of Ravenna, where he issued a Bull excommunicating Giovanni Bentivoglio as an enemy of the Church and delivering his possessions to pillage. And it seems that Francesco Francia was also in Cesena at exactly the same time, working on his painting *Presentation in the Temple* in the Benedictine Abbey of Madonna del Monte (where it is still). Perhaps he had no choice, perhaps he sought employment from the man who was about to conquer Bologna. In any event, Francia, who had lovingly painted Giovanni Bentivoglio's chapel and palace, and had made medals in which he appeared alive, now accepted Julius's commission to strike a medal with *his* portrait on the one side, and on the other the words

BONONIA . PER . JULIUM . A . TYRANNO . LIBERATA

- "Bologna freed from tyranny by Julius". Giovanni and his family fled Bologna on 2 November 1506, and, without a fight, Julius triumphantly entered the city at the head of his army on the 11th, mounted, a record said, on "a great white horse", and distributing "with his own hands" Francia's medallions.

Many of Bologna's artists, including Francia's partner Lorenzo Costa, fled with the Bentivogli's overthrow, perhaps fearing punishment for having been identified with them. Francia, on the other hand, returned with the Pope, who in the same month appointed him as the city's Master of the Mint; and he would remain in favour, going on to make five more portrait medals of his Pontifical patron. Then, in May 1507, expectations of a move by the Bentivogli to recover the city led a mob, egged on by the Papal Legate, Cardinal Francesco Alidosi, to decide that "to prevent the vulture's return, we must destroy his nest" (as one account had it); and it burned Giovanni Bentivoglio's great palace to the ground – all 244 rooms, all their treasures, and Francesco Francia's frescoes included.

Another artistic loss was to follow, in the reverse sense, as it were. Julius had summoned Michelangelo to join him when he conquered Bologna, with a commission (apparently to placate him after a blazing row in Rome) to make a larger than life-size bronze statue of the Pope enthroned, to be placed above the main entrance to the Cathedral of San Petronio. Michelangelo had Julius holding St Peter's keys in his left hand, but with his right arm raised in such a violent gesture that the Bolgnese wondered whether he was supposed to be blessing or threatening them. Within two years they decided it was the latter: fed up with Cardinal Alidosi's oppressive rule, they rose again, this time to support the return of the Bentivogli (now under French sponsorship) and to destroy in turn the castle that Pope Julius had built. And, to underline their point, they hauled down Michelangelo's statue from the cathedral and sold it as scrap to the Duke of Ferrara, who melted it down and had it cast as a cannon, which he named "La Giulia", after the Pope.[147]

The lure of Venice

Somehow, Francia juggled his allegiances through all these upheavals. But Raimondi had already left for Venice. There was a combination of allurements there at the beginning of the 16th century. There was of course – and still is – Venice itself: on a diplomatic mission there in 1494 for France's King Charles VIII (currently invading Italy) the chronicler Philippe de Commynes was conveyed, on his arrival, by boat

> "a long through the great Streat called the great *Chanell*, which is so large that the Gallies passed to and fro through it...Sure in mine opinion it is the goodliest Streat in the world, and the best built, and reacheth in length from the one end of Town to the other...To be short, it is the most triumphant City, that ever I saw, and where Ambassadors and Strangers are most honourably entertained, the Common–wealth best governed, and God most devoutly served" (from the first English translation, by Thomas Danett 1596).

---

147   Cardinal Alidosi, who had been less than vigorous against the French invaders, was stabbed to death in the streets of Ravenna by Francesco della Rovere, the Pope's nephew.

A decade later, when Raimondi arrived, probably by foot, the arts were flourishing in the Queen of the Adriatic: the painters Gentile and Giovanni Bellini were at the height of their fame, and had large and flourishing schools, in which the young Titian, five or so years younger than Raimondi, was a participant.[148] Vittore Carpaccio had finished his great cycle of *The Legend of St Ursula* (now in the Accademia) and was still working on his cycle of *Scenes from the Lives of Sts George and Jerome,* which is still in the little Scuola di San Giorgio for which it was painted. Carpaccio was also working on his huge painting (almost four metres square) for the cycle *Miracles of the True Cross* in the Scuola Grande di San Giovanni Evangelista (now also in the Accademia); Perugino, who was to become Raphael's teacher at the beginning of the new century, was also painting a work (now lost) for the same cycle. Perugino had undoubtedly met Francia on his way through Bologna. We have no indication that Francia personally knew the other Venetian painters, to be able to introduce Raimondi; but he undoubtedly knew of them, and certainly of his counterpart goldsmiths and medal–makers.

The most notable of the latter at that time was Alessandro Leopardi, already famous for having cast the Florentine Andrea del Verrocchio's superb bronze equestrian statue of the *condottiere* Bartolommeo Colleoni, which still stands in Venice's Campo SS Giovanni e Paolo. It was only the second life-size bronze equestrian statue to have been made since Roman times, the first being that of another *condottiere,* Gattamelata, by the Florentine Donatello, erected in Padua half a century earlier. (Envy of the Gattamelata statue was at the root of the invitation in the early 1480s to Leonardo da Vinci by Lodovico il Moro, who had usurped his nephew's Dukedom of Milan, to cast a bronze equestrian statue of his father, Francesco Sforza, another *condottiere,* who had gained his dukedom by sensibly marrying his predecessor's daughter. But Leonardo kept getting involved in other projects, in Milan – including on the fore-doomed *Last Supper* – and elsewhere, and it was only in the late 1490s that he finally got round to making a model of what by then everyone had long been calling "the horse". Whether it was through Lodovico's or Leonardo's *chutzpah,* or both, it was a gigantic 7.6 metres high – more than twice the size of Donatello's "horse".

---

148 Titian went on to become so famous that of all the Italian Renaissance painters only he, together with Raphael and at one time Michael Angelo, had their names anglicized; the French, claiming a pseudo-ownership or showing less discrimination, gallicized just about everyone.

But alas, like Lodovico himself, it was also doomed: when the new French King Louis XII invaded Milan in 1499, il Moro himself was carted away to France, to die in prison, and Leonardo's "horse", after all those delays, was used by Louis' troops for archery practice.)

The other prominent Venetian goldsmith was Vittore Gambello, employed, like Leopardi, at the Venetian Mint as an engraver of dies and medal-maker; he had already made portrait medals of both Gentile and Giovanni Bellini, so was equally well-connected. These two could have provided a natural focus for a skilled young Bolognese medal-maker wanting to move into the art world of Venice. There was probably another channel. A prominent Bolognese lawyer, theologian, musician and litterateur, Giovanni Achillini, known as Philotheo, wrote a poem in 1504 on various local luminaries, in which he included a verse along the following lines:

> "I also laud Marcantonio Raimondi,
> Who grasps the ancients' sacred shapes
> In drawing and graving profoundly,
> As you see in his beautiful plates,
> Like (as I write) my portrait engraving,
> So I doubt which of us is more living".

Raimondi showed Achillini playing a guitar, and the print is perversely known as *The Guitar Player* even though it includes a small tablet hanging from a tree, labelled, on three lines, PHILO/THE/O.

Raimondi was clearly well acquainted with the humanist circle in Bologna, centred on its ancient university, the oldest in Europe (though the city's intellectual reputation was not quite grasped by Byron, who wrote three centuries later that it was "celebrated for the production of Popes – Cardinals – painters – sausages"). Achillini was the founder of a famous humanist academy which met in the Palazzina della Viola, the only Bentivogli building, in the Palace grounds, that survived the latter's destruction.[149] He and his circle would have been well placed to introduce a promising young artist – and portrait-maker – to their equally self-regarding Venetian counterparts. These were not large groups in those (or any) days, and they travelled and mixed as did the artists.

---

149 Now the Istituto di Meccanica Agraria, sadly looking more like its present name than its original one.

But perhaps, by the middle of the first decade of the 16th century, Raimondi had already decided that he wanted, above all, to be an engraver. And perhaps it was primarily this ambition that took him north to Venice: because Venice had overtaken the German cities to become the greatest centre of publishing in Europe. Between 1480 and 1500 Venice printed "twenty times more books than it had inhabitants", according to Wills. The output of the great book publisher Aldus Manutius alone, between 1491 and 1515, was some 120,000 volumes. Venice also had the great advantage, through its far–flung trade, of an intelligence system which told the climates of opinion, the markets of patronage and scholarship, and the costs of competition.

The publishing industry had developed extraordinarily quickly right from its beginning.[150] It has been estimated that by 1500, less than fifty years after the introduction of printing, between eight and ten *million* books had been produced in Europe – and that was before the propaganda war that accompanied the Reformation, which began seventeen years later. Quite a few early books were copies, and copies of copies. Publishers pirated one another's editions, sometimes with the connivance of authors – including even the highly respected Erasmus of Rotterdam – who wanted their works to penetrate more and more markets.

On a smaller scale, much the same kind of expansion had been happening with the printed image. Although woodcuts were used by the ancient Babylonians and Egyptians, and to some extent by the Romans, it is not until 1423 that the first one is known of in Europe. Just over thirty years later, as publishers began using the new movable type carved in wood, they realised almost immediately that woodcuts could also be produced on their new printing presses, as illustrations for their books or as separate prints. Information on the size of print editions in these early days seems to be sparse; but given the huge numbers of books already published, and the widespread use of woodcuts of the Virgin and the Saints through this period for popular devotional purposes – known in Italy as *santini*, and produced, in the term used in Germany, by "Jesus-makers" – there must have been hundreds of thousands.

Engravings, which began to be made later in the second half of the 15th century, were mostly not suitable for book illustration because they were too labour intensive to produce. Those printed individually

---

150   The following section draws on Landau Parshall: *The Renaissance Print 1470–1550* (cited as Landau) and Jardine: *Worldly Goods*

were made in far fewer numbers, because the fine lines on the plates began (depending on the quality of the metal) to wear out after fifty to a couple of hundred good copies, with anything between 500 and 3000 additional "usable" versions. Only a handful of sheets would be produced for a commission by a prince of Church or State; although, even in that context, Dürer made 700 impressions of two portraits he made (in 1519 and 1523) of Cardinal Albrecht of Brandenburg, presumably for His Eminence to hand out or send to fans. And the 1513 inventory of a Florentine printer listed twenty-six lots of prints in his workshop, one of them being of about 26,000 sheets, half woodcuts and half engravings, "of good and bad quality".

In Venice, the production of prints as independent objects had its greatest boost in the year 1500 itself when the hitherto unremarked Jacopo de' Barbari produced, out of the blue, one of the most accomplished and stunning prints of all time: a bird's-eye *View of Venice*, every building and waterway faithfully reproduced, down to the tiniest, in perfect perspective, and printed in six sheets measuring overall an extraordinary 2.82 metres wide by 1.39 high.[151] The *View of Venice* was commissioned by Anton Kolb, a merchant from Nuremberg, Dürer's home town, now resident in Venice: we shall meet him again before long. This triumph was followed by another: in 1504 an illuminator and woodcut illustrator of books, Benedetto Bordon, produced in Venice a *Triumph of Caesar* in multiple sheets measuring more than 4.5 metres in length.

The scale of these works obviously meant they were intended for institutions or very large private mansions. However the market for smaller works, both woodcuts and engravings, was also being developed as prints became more acceptable as collectors' items – and by those who could afford paintings, as well as by those who could not. By 1512 Venetian painters complained to the Signoria that prints were even being hand-coloured, pasted on board, and sold as paintings. Given what we know of his future career, it would be reasonable to suppose that Raimondi saw the Venice of burgeoning print publishing and collecting as a promising market for his own talents.

Until about the time of his move, Venice was better known for woodcutters than engravers. But some time around 1506 the Paduan Giulio Campagnola, who was about the same age as Raimondi, moved

---

151 Twelve copies still exist in European museums; the original woodblocks are preserved in the Museo Correr in Venice.

to Venice from Ferrara, where he had already produced engravings influenced by both Mantegna (with whom he may have previously worked in Mantua) and Dürer. Raimondi's own earliest engravings also, according to the experts, were influenced by both Mantegna's and, especially, Dürer's, as well as by the classicism he had discovered from Aspertini's drawings. Campagnola, with skills in Latin, Greek and Hebrew, and a singer and lute–player, appears to have had ready access to the humanist circles that Raimondi would also want to be known by in Venice, and would have been an obvious point of contact. It is possible that what precipitated both young men's move to Venice in 1506 was the presence there of – Albrecht Dürer. In Raimondi's case there is, however, a quite different possibility as well. The truth is probably lost forever; but his encounter with the thirty-five-year-old German master was to be of such significance that it is worth pursuing down some intriguing speculative routes – geographical as well as metaphorical.

Dürer and Italy

Dürer had in fact visited Italy before, from late 1494 into early 1495, passing through and sketching Trento and other landscapes in the Dolomites on his journey. It has been said he was really fleeing an outbreak of the plague, the fact that he left his wife behind being accounted for by his notorious lack of affection for her. An alternative theory is that he was intending to visit his bosom Nuremberg buddy Willibald Pirckheimer, who was then studying law in Pavia, south of Milan, though we only know for certain of Dürer's having got as far as Venice. (There is one theory that Dürer accompanied Pirckheimer to Rome, but there is no surviving evidence of such a trip.) Pirckheimer, from a patrician family of the Bavarian town of Eichstätt, was a family friend from childhood; during his three years studying law in Padua and then four in Pavia he became interested in the whole range of humanist pursuits – philosophy, theology, history, poetry, geography, mathematics, astronomy, medicine[152] – and although he went on to a distinguished

---

152 How much he dabbled in medicine is unclear, but it perhaps lies behind one curious story. In *The Borgias*, Marion Johnson says that when the notorious Cesare Borgia, the illegitimate son of Pope Alexander VI, was beginning his military conquests in 1499 he addressed a list of ninety scientific questions to Lorenz Behaim, a Nuremburg scientist attached to the Papal court, thirteen about how to poison cups, perfumes, flowers, saddles, stirrups; and Behaim, a

career as a Nuremburg city official, military commander, diplomat and counsellor to the Emperors Maximilian I and Charles V, it was as a humanist that he was best known: translator of the Greek clasics, bibliomaniac (particularly of Aldus Manutius's publications), friend of Erasmus and Melanchthon (both of whom Dürer was to portray) and Luther, as well as of Dürer himself right up to his funeral oration in 1528, two years before his own death.

Dürer was presumably anxious to see the new art for which Italy was becoming known, though, given what seems to have been the limited travel of artists across the Alps, he may have known very little about it before he went. But perhaps there had been reports from Rome of the frescoes in Sixtus IV's rebuilt Sistine Chapel, painted in the previous decade by the mostly Florentine galaxy of Ghirlandaio, Perugino, Pinturicchio, Botticellio, Signorelli, Cosimo Rosselli and others; accounts, as well, of earlier Florentine masters, Masaccio, Fra Angelico, Andrea del Castagno, Uccello, and the brilliance of Lorenzo the Magnificent's humanist court; but also, and perhaps more vividly, descriptions from his fellow Nuremberger Anton Kolb of the flourishing Venetian school of painters, led by the Vivarinis and the Bellinis. Kolb could well have helped persuade Dürer to visit the city.

Whatever Italian works Dürer may have heard of, he would not have seen copies of them: reproductions were still in the future, for Raphael and Raimondi to launch. But he had seen and admired engravings, some based on antique motifs, made by Mantegna – the Bellinis' brother-in-law – in the 1460s and 70s; indeed, in 1494, just before he set out for Italy, he had made drawings of at least three of them. The strong possibility thus exists that he crossed the Alps to see the master himself. There is no record of their having met; but while before this first Italian visit Dürer had made no engravings, he began to do so almost as soon as he returned to Nuremberg, and the influence of Mantegna on both them and his ensuing woodcuts was immediately apparent. For that matter, there is no record of anyone else he met, in Venice, or wherever else he may have gone; but there is a belief that he did get to know, and esteem, Jacopo de' Barbari (who had trained in the Vivarini school), from whom he got hints on the theory of human proportion, "when I was still young and had never heard of these things", he wrote

---

friend of both Dürer and Pirckheimer, forwarded them to the latter - but perhaps as an example of Vatican morals, rather than because Pirckheimer (who at that time was involved in a military campaign) was "a foremost European authority".

later. This and the theory of perspective were to be constant concerns throughout his career.

There is no record either of what art Dürer saw in Venice. There was plenty to see, the greatest work of art being the serene beauty of the city itself: but although some charming sketches made on his travel through the Alps still exist, there is unfortunately nothing at all of Venice. There was the publishing industry, of course, in which Dürer had already become engaged during his visit to Rhineland cities earlier in the nineties (originally with the intention of meeting Martin Schongauer, but he had died just before Dürer reached Colmar). Giovanni Bellini's altarpieces were spread through Venice's innumerable churches; and Vittore Carpaccio was nearing the end of his extraordinary narrative cycle of the St Ursula legend.

The same years in which the New World was being discovered seem an unlikely time for the extravagant and retrospective piety of the Life of St Ursula: but it was being painted twice virtually simultaneously, at opposite ends of Europe, in extraordinarily contrasting styles and scales: in Venice, by Vittorio Carpaccio; in Bruges, by Hans Memling. The unlikely story, which was embroidered from the fifth century on, begins with the agreement of Ursula, a Christian Princess of Brittany, to marry a pagan Prince of Britain – on condition that he became a Christian himself, allowed her three years to make a pilgrimage to visit the Pope and the holy places in Rome, and provided her with an escort of eleven thousand virgins. Even that did not faze him. Ursula's voyage with her eleven thousand escorts proceeded through Cologne, went up the Rhine, over the Alps to Rome, and back again to Cologne, where Ursula and every last virgin was massacred by Attila and his Huns. When a horde of bones was uncovered there in 1106, and immediately presumed, without close counting, to be saintly, Ursula's legend and Cologne's coffers were alike boosted by widespread sales of virginal relics and expensive reliquaries.

Carpaccio's cycle was inspired by the story of the departure in 1472 of the Venetian aristocrat Caterina Cornaro to marry James of Lusignan, King of Cyprus, the last Crusader state, and her return after reigning as Queen of Cyprus from 1473 until 1489, when Venice decided to transform its indirect rule to annexation of the island. Both her going and her coming were attended by "a riot of pageantry", on which Carpaccio – already in his early twenties when she left – is believed to have drawn for his cycle, painted for the centuries-old Scuola di Sant' Orsola, one of the ancient Venetian confraternities, and which had close connections with Cyprus. Napoleon abolished all these *scuole* in 1806, presumably because they were "undemocratic" and, more to the point, potential centres of resistance to Venice's French "liberators". Surprisingly, Napoleon did not loot Carpaccio's paintings; they were transferred in 1810 to the Accademia Galleries – where they were cut to size to fit the room. They are still there, eight canvases, four of them almost three metres high by six long, an almost overwhelming panorama of great pageants in sumptuous and marvellous Renaissance settings.[153]

Memling's St Ursula cycle, however, is a series of six exquisite small panels, 37cms high and 25cms wide, painted in 1489, closer in feeling to illuminated manuscripts than to great wall paintings; they are set three each into the longer sides of a gilded Gothic shrine, also designed by Memling; and this is still in its original home in Bruges, the late 12th century Hospital of St John. At one end of the shrine are the Virgin and Child and the two Hospital nuns who commissioned the reliquary; at the other, St Ursula and little virgins within her miraculous protective cloak, which made her the patron saint of drapers as well as young girls. Memling succeeds in making the saga of the Saint and her eleven thousand virgins wonderfully intimate, the scenes (with the exception of course of the audience with the Pope in Rome) set, both for the voyages and their grisly culmination, against real architectural backgrounds, on a Rhine which, unlike Carpaccio, Memling knew personally.[154]

And yet, despite the contrast between the Latinate sweep of Carpaccio's aristocratic pageantry, and the Netherlandish realism of Memling's miniaturist approach, there is the same feeling in both cycles of great deeds nobly done, of the intense spiritual passion of Ursula and her companions, of the awe that the great legend held for the members of the Scuola and the Hospital who simultaneously commissioned them. In 1828, in an early outburst of ecological concern, the English poet Coleridge, the apostrophiser of Kublai Khan, less reverentially recalled

---

153 The Scuola di Sant' Orsola itself disappeared: in the middle of last century its site was identified behind the apse of the great Dominican Church of SS Giovanni e Paolo.

154 Their accuracy is evident from the elegant topographical drawings made a century and a half later, in 1635, by the twenty-eight year old Bohemian artist Wenceslaus Hollar, in Cologne to join, and then record, the voyage of the art-collecting Thomas Earl of Arundel up the Rhine and down the Danube, on the way to his appointment as English Ambassador to the Holy Roman Emperor Ferdinand II.

the remains of the eleven thousand Virgin Martyrs and their resting place, in his poem *Cologne*:

> "In Kohln, a town of monks and bones,
> And pavements fang'd with murderous stones
> And rags, and hags, and hideous wenches;
> I counted two and seventy stenches,
> All well defined, and several stinks!
> Ye Nymphs that reign o'er sewers and sinks,
> The river Rhine, it is well known,
> Doth wash your city of Cologne;
> But tell me, Nymphs, what power divine
> Shall henceforth wash the river Rhine?"

But the bones represented a spirituality to which Dürer responded: in an entry in his diary for early November 1520, during his visit to the Low Countries, he noted that

> "At Köln I went to St Ursula's church and to her grave, and saw the great relics of the holy maid and the others".

Yet there is no mention of seeing Memling's reliquary when he gets to Bruges five months later; and as we noted there is no record of anything he saw on his first visit to Venice. However during his second visit, in one of his letters to his old mate Willibald Pirckheimer, by then back making a name for himself in Nuremberg, he wrote, on 7 February 1506, that

> "[Giovanni Bellini] is very old, but is still the best painter of them all. And that which so well pleased me eleven years ago pleases me no longer; if I had not seen it for myself I should not have believed any one who told me".[155]

Eleven years before, the most important paintings in Venice – apart from Bellini's – were Carpaccio's great new St Ursula cycle. Is *that* what Dürer found had lost its charm? – the young man's delight in the meticulously executed pageantry lost to the older man's increasing preoccupation with psychological exactness?

---

155   All quotations from Dürer's letters are from the translation by Conway

It is startling to find that Dürer's 1494-1495 expedition to Italy, to see at firsthand the fruits of the Renaissance there, was the first known by a German artist. Dürer came to believe that all his fellow German artists needed to benefit from what he called the "regrowth" of the arts that their Italian counterparts had achieved "in the last one hundred and fifty years after they had been in hiding for a millennium". It would soon become the norm: German – and for that matter Dutch, French, English – painters, sculptors and architects would make the pilgrimage, though more to Florence and Rome than to Venice, to learn what the rediscovery – and reinvention – of the classical canon had been capable of achieving. Following Bismarck's reunification of Germany in 1871, nationalist zealotry would produce the idea of un–German "degenerate art"; twenty years before Hitler, who was to apply the term in trying to abolish modern art, a prominent German art historian saw Dürer's embrace of the Italian Renaissance as "the catastrophe from which German art and architecture never completely recovered".

The lure of Dürer and the beginnings of intellectual property rights
During the heady times of the peak of the Italian Renaissance, making your name was something that the mutually reinforcing interests of artists and patrons esteemed as an essential attribute of talent. Raimondi's ladder to success began with Dürer. But whether the method he chose to make money – and a name for himself – was ethical, to Dürer's as well as our way of thinking, has been obscured by Vasari, the only person whose account has survived.

As we have noted, Raimondi's engravings before he even left Bologna had shown the influence of Dürer's work. He was soon to carry that influence to the ultimate, but exactly how, where and when is an intriguing puzzle. "With the gracious leave of Francia", says Vasari, Raimondi moved some time in the second half of 1506 to Venice, "where he was well received by the craftsmen of that city"; and he goes on:

> "About the same time there arrived in Venice some Flemings with many copper-plate engravings and woodcuts by Albrecht Dürer, which were seen by Marc' Antonio on the Piazza di S. Marco; and he was so amazed at the manner and the method of the work of Albrecht, that he spent on those sheets almost all the money he had brought from Bologna. Among other things, he bought the Passion of Jesus Christ, which had been engraved on thirty-six

wood-blocks and printed not long before on sheets of quarter-folio by the same Albrecht".

With Dürer's fame already well established, and a whole new series of prints available on the Piazza, young Raimondi, new in town from little Bologna, nearly broke, dazzled by the wealth of Venice and its citizens, felt, according to Vasari, that he was onto a sure thing:

> "Marc' Antonio, having considered what honour and profit might be acquired by one who should apply himself to that art in Italy, formed the determination to give his attention to it with all possible assiduity and diligence. He thus began to copy those engravings by Albrecht Dürer, studying the manner of each stroke and every other detail of the prints that he had bought, which were held in such estimation on account of their novelty and their beauty, that everyone sought to have some. [He]... then counterfeited on copper, with engraving as strong as that of the woodcuts that Albrecht had executed, the whole of the said Life and Passion of Christ in thirty-six parts...".

However the key to Vasari's account comes next: Raimondi, having so excellently "counterfeited...the whole of the said Life and Passion in thirty-six plates",

> "added to these the signature that Albrecht used for all his works, which was 'A.D.', and they proved to be so similar in manner, that, no one knowing that they had been executed by Marc' Antonio, they were ascribed to Albrecht, and were bought and sold as works by his hand".

And allegedly the sequel was an unhappy one:

> "News of this [counterfeiting] was sent in writing to Albrecht, who was in Flanders [i.e. Germany]...; at which he flew into such a rage that he left Flanders and went to Venice, where he appeared before the Signoria [the Doge's six virtual co-rulers in the *Minor Consiglio*] and laid a complaint against Marc' Antonio. But he could obtain no other satisfaction but this, that Marc' Antonio should no longer use the name or the above-mentioned signature of Albrecht on his works".

And thus, according to Vasari, the artist's intellectual property rights were given formal – if qualified – recognition.

Vasari was mistaken in thinking that Raimondi had copied the thirty-six woodcuts in Dürer's series *The Life and Passion of Christ*. This series (eventually of thirty-seven sheets, including the title page), known as the *Little Passion* because of its size (12.6 x 9.7 cms), was made only in 1509-1511. What Raimondi actually copied was the larger seventeen *Life of the Virgin* woodcuts (29.5 x 21.3 cms) which had been executed by Dürer between 1502 (or perhaps as early as 1500 in one case) and 1505.[156]

Altogether, according to the monumental study of European print-making by the early 19th century German scholar Adam Bartsch,[157] Raimondi made copies of seventy–four of Dürer's prints. Seventeen, as we know, were the *Life of the Virgin*, with Dürer's signature. He had previously made copies between 1495 and 1505 of five engravings and five woodcuts by Dürer, also complete with the AD. Thereafter, Raimondi's practice raises the possibility that he was obeying new rules: after he went to Rome he copied a 1511 woodcut without the initials, and, later, as we shall see, the *Little Passion* series, with Dürer's little tablet in the right place, but not a single AD.

However Raimondi also copied Dürer's 1511 woodcut of the *Mass of St Gregory* with the AD most definitely there at the base of the altar – though without the date which Dürer's original had included just above it. There is no telling why this reversion occurred, but the subject itself was a real money-spinner. The legend of Christ's appearance while Pope Gregory the Great (reg. 590-604 CE) was saying mass developed a natural popularity when extravagant indulgences began to be attached to it: the contemporary German goldsmith and engraver Israhel van Meckenem had already produced an engraving of the subject with an inscription guaranteeing 20,000 years relief from purgatory for saying the *Credo*, *Ave Maria* and *Lord's Prayer* in front of it – then produced a second version, perhaps when sales began flagging, amended to write

---

156   He made two other *Passions* as well: a *Great Passion* of twelve woodcuts, seven published in 1497-1500, the remaining five in 1510-1511; and a different *Little Passion* of sixteen engravings, in 1507-1513.

157   *Le Peintre Graveur*, 21 Vols (Leipzig 1803-1821); Raimondi is in Vol 14 (Parts 1 2, 1813). This has now been supplemented by *The Illustrated Bartsch*, Vols 26 27: *The Works of Marcantonio Raimondi and of His School*, edited by Oberhuber.

off 45,000 years. While not authorised by the Church, these pseudo-ecclesiastical extravaganzas fitted in with the rapid expansion of official indulgences issued by Popes Julius II and Leo X to cover their lavish spending on the Vatican, and which contributed significantly to the reaction which Martin Luther was to launch six years after Dürer made his print.

If Vasari sounds somewhat more impressed by Raimondi's skill than shocked by his apparently dodgy scheme he is showing a viewpoint that was still common at the turn of the 16th century: "counterfeiting" meant copying, not forging in the modern sense. It had long been acceptable practice for artists to learn and hone their skills by drawing or making copies of works by earlier masters. The idea of copyright – of a writer's or artist's ownership of his work as his intellectual property – had not existed in western Europe before the development of publishing. But the introduction of printing from movable type in Germany in the 1450s, and then the printing of woodcuts and engravings as independent items around the end of the century began to change the scene dramatically. No longer were artists confined to learning only from their teacher and the altar-pieces in their local churches: the widespread circulation of prints meant that they could draw on a rapidly burgeoning range of sources. As we saw, Dürer copied Mantegna before his first visit to Venice; five years earlier, Michelangelo copied a Schongauer while he was apprenticed to Ghirlandaio. Over the next couple of decades, a quite extraordinary number of artists used elements taken from Dürer's prints in shaping their own works, not merely on paper but in paintings as well. The use of someone else's grouping of figures, or a pose, or a gesture, is generally accepted as a legitimate reflection of "influence" – and this was to be a crucial aspect of the future Raphael–Raimondi partnership, and of other works much much later, as we shall see. But reproduction for commercial purposes also was initially pretty much open slather: it has been estimated, for example, that *ninety* percent of Israhel van Meckenem's output of several hundred prints were copies or reworked versions of someone else's. Raimondi was small fry.

But there were already objections. Mantegna is said to have tried what might be called a personal approach to protect his work: in 1475 a Mantuan engraver named Simone Ardizoni da Reggio complained to the Marquis Ludovico Gonzaga that he and another engraver named Zoan Andrea had been brutally assaulted on Mantegna's orders because he claimed they had re-engraved some of his original plates. It is unclear whether they had or not, but in any case it was obviously not a long-term solution to the problem – not least because we next hear of Zoan Andrea copying Dürer in 1505, a year before the Raimondi episode. Venice had in fact already granted "privileges" (in effect copyright) to publishers: the first as early as 1484 for a book, the first for a print in 1500 – Jacopo de' Barbari's *View of Venice*. But these privileges had no effect outside the city.

Which is one of the problems of the Vasari story: without a specific grant of a privilege by the *Signoria*, any claim by Dürer would have had no standing in the city, whatever protection his work may have been given by the authorities in Nuremburg (or anywhere else, for that matter). It is certainly true that Dürer was concerned about copyright. When he published the *Life of the Virgin* as a book in 1511 – the original seventeen woodcuts plus an extra three made after his return from Venice – he prefaced it with a very blunt message:

> Beware you envious thieves of the work and invention
> of others; keep your thoughtless hands from these
> works of ours. Know that we have received
> a privilege from the famous Roman
> Emperor Maximilian, that none
> of these images shall
> be dared to be
> printed
> in spurious
> forms, nor shall
> such prints be dared to be
> sold anywhere within the boundaries
> of the Empire; for if such a greedy crime is
> committed, understand that you will be pursued at law
> for the confiscation of your goods.[158]

---

158 The Latin preface, set out as above, is reproduced in Lisa Pon: *Raphael, Dürer, and Marcantonio Raimondi*, together with the first half of the translation, in paragraph form; but the above layout does not precisely reproduce Dürer's lines. Pon's study, published in 2004, and which I therefore saw only after this chapter had been written, is an interesting academic analysis of "practical collaboration and possessive authorship" by printmakers and artists in the early 16th century, a quite different approach from mine. I have however drawn on it in the present context, and in relation to Raimondi's publisher in Venice (see below).

This thundering might even have carried (some) moral force in Venice, or elsewhere outside the Empire: but it was only within the Empire that it had any legal force. The very next year Dürer was involved in another case: the Nuremberg City Council, presumably in response to his action again, ordered sellers of counterfeit prints of the *Mass of St Gregory*, bearing his signature, to desist – though it still did not prosecute them. In Rome by then, safe from the Council's and the Emperor's reach, Raimondi could still put AD on his own copy of that same print; but it was the last time he did so.

Intellectual property law had a long way to go from these beginnings. In 1515 Pope Leo X tried to expand protection by threatening illicit copiers with excommunication – after he discovered that a Milanese publisher was pirating a book for whose manuscript he himself had paid the huge sum of 500 ducats! Before Vasari wrote, a first, limited, copyright provision was enacted in France, in 1537, but implementation was slow. Elsewhere was slower: the first copyright law in England did not come until 1710. And our courts are still having to be asked to renew the *Signoria*'s ban on the misappropriation of someone else's signature – or these days, usually, trademark, as third, second and first world entrepreneurs churn out Raimondi Reeboks and Rolexes.

The Bologna connection

But was there really a ban in the first place? After being taken as gospel for centuries, in our more sceptical times Vasari's story of *Dürer v. Raimondi* has been undermined, even scoffed at. Such a case has not been found in the Venetian official records (though admittedly they are apparently not complete); and the story has been held, at best, to be a mis-location of that very similar episode that did occur in Nuremburg in 1512. Nor is there any mention of the case in Dürer's series of letters to Pirckheimer during this visit to Venice. But then there is no mention of a lot of other things either, not least because eight of the nine letters that have survived are mostly full of details about how tied up Dürer was buying things on behalf of friend Willibald: pearls, precious stones, books, olive wood, burnt glass, crane feathers for hats, paper, oil, jewellery (including a sapphire ring for which he searched "all the goldsmiths in Venice, German and Italian"), Greek books, and finally two carpets for which he searches "every day...and so does Anton Kolb".

It all seems both comical and an appalling waste of Dürer's time. But as Pirckheimer had lent him a substantial sum of money for the visit,

Dürer acknowledged – not least because he kept putting off repaying him – that he was honour bound to meet his friend's wishes. Though not without affectionate exasperation:

> "Your servant and slave Albrecht Dürer [he wrote on 18 August] sends salutation to his magnificent master Willibald Pirckheimer...I wonder how it is possible for a man like you to stand against so many wisest princes, swaggerers and soldiers...You want to become a real silk-tail and you think that, if only you manage to please the girls, the thing is done. If you were only as fetching a fellow as I am, it would not provoke me so... I know that there is no lack of wisdom in you. If only you had my meekness you would have all the virtues. Thank you also for all the good you have done me, if only you would not bother me about the rings! If they don't please you break their heads off and pitch them out on the dunghill...What do you mean by setting me to such dirty work? I have become a *gentleman* at Venice".[159]

Could mention of the Raimondi affair have been in a letter that got lost? Dürer did write, after only four or so months in Venice, that

> "The painters here, let me tell you, are very unfriendly to me. They have summoned me three times before the magistrates and I had to pay four florins to their school".

It gives the impression of a litigious society, in which Dürer had somehow very rapidly become involved; it would not in fact be surprising if a counter-claim by him, even though well–known in artistic circles, against a Raimondi showing the true spirit of Venetian-style enterprise, had failed to fully convince a *Signoria* concerned essentially only with the publication rights of Venetians to whom it had granted such a privilege.

---

159   Dürer had made a great drawing of Pirckheimer in 1503, just a couple of years before this second Venice trip (now in the Kupferstichkabinett, Berlin). It shows Willibald in profile, with a magnificent boxer's busted nose. He looks very much the high-liver conveyed by Dürer's letters. Two decades later, in 1524, Dürer made a copperplate engraving of Pirckheimer at the mature age of fifty-three. The busted nose is still there, and now also eyes and a face showing the wear and tear of all that good living. "The flabby epicure", Waetzoldt says, making the best of it, "is endowed with the autocratic head of a lion".

But the over-riding fact remains: there is no surviving corroboration for Vasari's case of *Dürer v. Raimondi*.

However, the focus on Dürer's alleged assertion of his intellectual property rights (which he did without question a few years later) or, alternatively, on the apparently bogus nature of Vasari's story, has obscured an entirely different and fascinatingly extraordinary aspect of Vasari's references to the relationship between Dürer and Raimondi. It occurs in the very last sentence of his account of Dürer's work, *before* the story we have just been examining:

> "[It] would take too long if I were to try to enumerate all the works that issued from Albrecht's hand; let it be enough for the present to tell that, having drawn a Passion of Christ in thirty-six parts, and having engraved these [in fact they were woodcuts], he made an agreement with Marc' Antonio Bolognese that they should publish the sheets in company; and thus, arriving in Venice, this work was the reason that marvellous prints of the same kind were afterwards executed in Italy".

This seems a remarkably casual reference to what would have been a startling collaboration between a virtually unknown young Italian printmaker and an already famous and established German artist, of whom even Vasari had shortly before condescended to allow that

> "Of a truth, if this man, so able, so diligent, and so versatile, had had Tuscany instead of Flanders for his country [Flanders being Vasari's insouciant term for most places north of the Alps]...he would have been the best painter of our land, even as he was the rarest and most celebrated that has ever appeared among the Flemings".

Yet after making this statement about an "agreement" between Dürer and the ambitious Bolognan, Vasari completely drops that story in favour of what he must have judged – and what turned out – to be the more sensational version of Raimondi's "counterfeiting" and Dürer's complaint. But the possibility of an actual collaboration seems just as intriguing. It seems astonishing of course that, as Vasari at first glance seems to imply here, Dürer could have known of Raimondi and reached an agreement with the latter *before* his second visit to Venice in 1505. But the sentence does not have to be read this way: it does not say that

Raimondi's "work" actually arrived in Venice before Dürer did; and that opens up a quite new perspective.

In Dürer's last surviving letter of the series to Pirckheimer, dated 13 October 1506, after he had been in Venice for about a year, he said

> "I shall have finished here in ten days; after that I should like to ride to Bologna to learn the secrets of the art of perspective, which a man is willing to teach me. I should stay there eight or ten days and then return to Venice. After that I shall come with the next messenger";

and he added ruefully,

> "How I shall freeze after this sun! here I am a gentleman, at home only a parasite".

In 1499, Leonardo da Vinci, leaving his still unfinished "horse", left Milan for Venice just after Duke Lodovico il Moro's fall, some think on a diplomatic mission from Milan's new master, the French King Louis XII. He was accompanied by a monk called Fra Luca Pacioli, a noted mathematician and teacher, who had been a pupil in Urbino of Piero della Francesca, the wonderful 15th century Tuscan fresco painter. In 1493, after teaching in various italian universities, Pacioli had been threatened by his Franciscan Order with excommunication as a free–thinker; though he somehow ducked the charge and spent the next three years back in Urbino, where the painter Giovanni Santi, father of the teenage Raphael, was prominent at the glittering Montefeltro court. In 1490 Piero had published a ground-breaking work *On Perspective in Painting*, and in 1494 Pacioli followed up with his own first major work, the *Compendium of Arithmetic, Geometry, Proportions and Proportionality* (1494). When he subsequently moved to Milan, Pacioli's portrait was painted by another of Piero's former pupils, Bramante, whom Raphael would succeed as architect of the new St Peter's Basilica in Rome; and he came to know Leonardo, who later collaborated with him with the illustrations for Pacioli's *On Divine Proportion* (1509).

We do not know whether Dürer was already aware of Piero's and Pacioli's works before he left Nuremburg, though given his closeness there to the book trade it seems quite possible. At all events, because of common approaches between Pacioli's writings and Dürer's subsequent work on perspective, it has been thought that it was the mathematician, who had continued to teach in various northern Italian cities, whom Dürer went to Bologna to study with. In fact Pacioli may not have been in Bologna then; but on arrival in the city Dürer was given a formal welcome, according to a contemporary source, with a poetic encomium by one Riccardo Sbrullino, another of the city's humanist poets; and it is likely that Dürer would have found others in that lively intellectual centre who were familiar with the mathematician's work.

In October 1506 Bologna was, as we saw earlier, on the brink of being taken over by Pope Julius II and his Papal forces. As Dürer must have arrived there between late October and mid–November he would have found more excitement than just perspective: one wonders if he could even have seen the Pope there – and if so, how he thought his recent portrait of Julius in the *Feast of the Rose Garlands* (which we will come to shortly) compared with the real thing. He would have found a range of artists who had accompanied Julius in the expectation of new commissions, the most significant being Michelangelo. When exactly Michelangelo actually arrived, to make his statue of the Pope seated, is not known, though probably it was by December. He already knew the city: between autumn 1494 and late 1495 the nineteen-year-old Michelangelo, who had fled the unfriendly Florentine court of Lorenzo the Magnificent's son, Pietro II di Medici, was hosted in Bologna by Giovanni Francesco Aldrovandi, a fellow humanist of the litterateur Giovanni Achillini who in 1504 had versified his praise of Raimondi's "drawing and graving" and "beautiful plates".

It was during this stay that Michelangelo carved three small statues for the tomb, in the church of St Dominic, the Spanish founder of the Dominican Order, who had died in Bologna in 1221. It would be nice to think that, even though Michelangelo was completely focussed on sculpture at that time, he had visited Francia's workshop, where Raimondi had already started his apprenticeship, and then renewed his acquaintance again during this second visit in 1506. (It has also been suggested that Leonardo may have been passing through Bologna at the same time, on his way from Florence back to Milan in obedience to the summons of the French King – perhaps on a diplomatic side-trip to meet the Pope: it was only two years until the victorious Julius would join Louis to fight, and defeat, Venice; and only four until he would join Venice to fight Louis, and barely escape from Bologna when the latter restored the Bentivogli.)

Bologna's painters shared their humanists' high opinion of Dürer: they are reported to have said, with a certain flourish, that "they were now the more ready to die that their longstanding desire to meet Albrecht Dürer had been fulfilled". Surely, in their company, Dürer must have met Raimondi's old master, Francesco Francia, the Pope's new Master of the Mint. And thus also Marcantonio Raimondi? It is certainly possible that Raimondi had not yet actually left for Venice. Lisa Pon cites an Italian study suggesting just that: and that Raimondi may even have begun his copies of the *Life of the Virgin* in Bologna after he met Dürer there.

But what of an "agreement"? Dürer had left Nuremburg for his second visit to Venice late in 1505 – perhaps having waited to complete the *Life of the Virgin* series before setting out so he would have something brand new to offer the Italians, as his two great series of the late 1490s, the *Apocalypse* and the *Great Passion*, would have been on the market there, and probably sold out, long since. As we know, he had had to borrow from Pirckheimer to finance the trip, so he must have been more than usually anxious – he was always anxious – to make money. But while he had this new work ready for marketing, he could not of course carry with him large quantities of prints of the *Life of the Virgin*, let alone the seventeen large original woodblocks; and the prints may well have run out by the time of his visit to Bologna.

The idea of engraving them may well have occurred to Dürer earlier; but the commission for a large painting (the *Feast of the Rose Garlands*) that he had received just after his arrival in Venice, not to mention the endless demands for gew-gaws from Pirckheimer, meant that he could not undertake such an onerous task himself, and if he had thought to have them engraved by someone else he may not have been able to find anyone in Venice sufficiently competent to do so, or been hampered by his obviously prickly relations with the artistic community there. If Raimondi was still in Bologna when Dürer visited there, there would have been an obvious connection through the humanist-artistic circle there, not least through Raimondi's leading admirer, Giovanni Accillini. And Dürer would have seen immediately the quality of Raimondi's work – not least in the copies Raimondi had already made of ten of Dürer's own woodcuts and engravings. So they agreed (as the first scenario stated) to "publish the sheets in company".

If so, the modern sceptics may be right: there was no such event as Dürer's outraged complaint to the *Signoria*. But in one sense it doesn't really matter whether Vasari's story of *Dürer v. Raimondi* was true or not: its real significance was that it spread the idea of an artist's intellectually property rights across Italy and Europe in a hugely successful and widely read publication.

A Venetian publisher

It is not known how a publisher was found (or by whom): but who it was, is. It was, Lisa Pon confirms in her study, the firm of Niccolò and Domenico Sandri dal Jesus, one of a number of printers and booksellers in the Merceria, then as now Venice's main shopping street that meanders from the Piazza San Marco to the Rialto, their premises being "alongside San Zulian" (the church of San Giuliano), about a third of the way along. As there could already have been up to two hundred printers in Venice by that time – there were more than that a few decades later – the choice must have been ample , but perhaps difficult. There were some twenty on the Merceria, though a fashionable address did not necessarily guarantee quality: the workshop of Aldus Manutius, the most famous printer and publisher of all, was across the Grand Canal, down a little alleyway behind the Campo San Polo.

So why the brothers Sandri dal Jesus? The clue lies in the printing. The seventeenth plate in Raimondi's copies of the *Life of the Virgin*, "The Virgin worshipped by Angels and Saints", is different in a crucial respect from the previous sixteen. Like all of them, it has Dürer's initials at the bottom, though, unlike all but one other, not in his usual tablet but (as in the original) between the legs of a cherub in the middle foreground. Unlike all the other plates, it also has Raimondi's own initials, the run-together MAF version, fairly prominently displayed on the globular base of a candlestick looming above the Virgin's head on the left side of the print. And also uniquely, there are the two devices used by the brothers Sandri: the personal one of two small triangles, "vertex to vertex", surmounted by a cross, on a small plaque near the bottom left corner, with the letters 'ND' in the top triangle, 'SF', entwined, in the lower one, standing (as Pon notes) for "Niccolò et Domenico Sandri Fratelli" [brothers]; and also their religious colophon-equivalent, the monogram 'yhs' (the top of the 'h' in the form of a cross) in large letters in a squared quatrefoil on the very prominent door of a cabinet above the Virgin's head on the right side of the print.

This originally Greek monogram for the name of Jesus (the 'y' representing 'i' or 'j') was first recorded in a 5th century codex of the Gospels, and subsequently became associated with the Dominicans and then the Jesuits – who with their usual aplomb sometimes claimed it stood for "*Jesum Habemus Sociam*" ("We have Jesus as our companion"). But it was also used by the Gesuati (as distinct from the Jesuit Gesuiti), the mid-14the century lay order of Apostolic Clerics of St Jerome, dedicated to charitable works, who frequently proclaimed the name of Jesus in their preaching: most conspicuously, in Venice, the monogram features on the pediment of the church of Santa Maria della Visitazione, which was still being built on the Zattere at the time Dürer and Raimondi were there.[160] It was their close association with the Gesuati resulted in Niccolò and Domenico being known as Sandri dal Jesus.

And in 1505 the Sandri brothers had published what Pon describes as an "especially sumptuous" book of Saints' lives, "copiously illustrated with some one hundred and eighty woodcuts", copies of which must presumably have still been well known in Venice over the next few years. But they were also well known for *santini*, printed images of the Virgin and Saints produced in large numbers for private devotion; and (Pon says) their surviving account books show they were made in small medium and large sizes, and "priced by the hundred".

Raimondi himself also made *santini*, at least sixty-three small ones approximately 8 x 5 cms, as well as a number in medium and large sizes; unfortunately I have not discovered whether he had already started by this time or was inspired by the Sandri. Dürer would certainly not have wanted his *Life of the Virgin* to be taken for humble *santini*; but its plates were nevertheless certainly intended as a devotional series, not merely as works of art. The Sandri's sumptuous book would have been testament enough to their artistic competence as well as their standing in the market for religious works; and to them the *Life of the Virgin* plates were taken, and were printed.

And by them they would also have been sold. As usual, we do not know what sort of arrangement was made about the number of copies they were required to print, or about the division of the profits – or whether they printed more copies than they were supposed to, as often happened, and didn't divide the profits. As publishers, the Sandri would have been operating under a privilege granted by the *Signoria*: in Venice they were thus in the box seat. Did Raimondi, who still had another couple of years in Venice, perhaps make some dodgy arrangement with the Sandri after Dürer had left the city, for his (and their) profit and at Dürer's expense? It is obvious that Dürer could have been upset by any of these aspects, particularly given his intense interest in income.

---

160 Confusingly, it is right next door to the church of Santa Maria del Rosario, which is usually known as the Gesuati, though it was only built in the 17th century on a former Gesuati site after the Order itself had been suppressed.

But perhaps, giving some foundation to Vasari's law-suit scenario, he really "flew into a rage" not simply, as Vasari stated, over the presence of his own signature on all the plates – which he could well have wanted included for publicity purposes, particularly if he had had an "agreement" with Raimondi – but over the incorporation on the colophon-sheet, more prominently than his own signature, of Raimondi's own initials, and above all, even more prominently, the two devices of Messrs Sandri Fratelli. This was perhaps the last straw: just whose work was this? As Pon points out, Dürer's thunderous warning (imitated above), in the published version of these same plates, to would-be "thieves of the work and invention of others", is oviously in the same shape of two triangles, vertex to vertex, as in the Sandri's personal colophon; and the single word at the very centre of the composition, *imprimere*, refers to their role in the Raimondi copies: printing.

It will be nearly ten years later when Vasari's report of a development in the context of Dürer's realtions with Raphael, which we shall come to in due course, may clear things up a bit. But Vasari has already got us ahead of what Dürer was doing in Venice before that fateful encounter with Raimondi.

Artistic connections

Among the Fratelli Sandri's principal clients for *santini* was the Scuola di Sant'Orsola, which of course housed Carpaccio's great cycle on Queen Caterina Cornaro as the martyred Saint. It is tempting to think that the Sandri might have taken Dürer and Raimondi on a guided tour of the Scuola to see the paintings, which had been completed after the end of the former's first visit to the city. But in the midst of all Dürer's shopping reports to Pirckheimer during this Venice visit there was no mention of Carpaccio, or Raimondi. There was also no mention of Gentile Bellini, Giovanni's slightly older brother and still-active member of the most prominent artistic family in Venice, who by now had completed his three great contributions to the *Miracles of the True Cross*, the vast cycle that Carpaccio and Perugino had been working on at the time of the 1494-95 visit.

It is worth mentioning that the period of Dürer's visits coincided with a Venetian fascination with their fearsome new Ottoman Turk neighbours, who only fifty years before had finally destroyed Byzantium and captured Constantinople. Gentile Bellini had been sent by the Signoria twenty years before, in the usual Venetian interests of protecting and promoting its trade, to flatter Byzantium's conqueror the Sultan

Mahomet II with an exquisite portrait,[161] notwithstanding Islamic prohibitions of representational images; and he was just then, when Dürer was again in Venice, including realistic Oriental figures and wonderfully imaginative Veneto-Saracenic architecture in the spectacular and gigantic (7.7 x 4.5 *metres) St Mark Preaching at Alexandria*,[162] which he would leave to Giovanni to finish following his death in early 1507 just about the time Dürer was leaving Venice to return to Nuremburg. While not mentioning him, Dürer was not above copying one of Gentile's Turks in one of his own etchings.

There is no mention of Titian or Giorgione ither, who must both have already been part of the Venetian art world. There are hints of other painters; early in this second visit, in the 7 February 1506 letter in which he described Giovanni Bellini as "the best painter of all", Dürer wrote boisterously to Pirckheimer:

"How I wish you were here at Venice! There are so many nice men among the Italians who seek my company more and more every day – which is very pleasing to one – men of sense and knowledge, good lute-players and pipers, judges of painting, men of much noble sentiment and honest virtue, and they show me much honour and friendship. On the other hand there are also amongst them some of the most false, lying, thievish rascals; I should never have believed that such were living in the world...".

Could the engraver Giulio Campagnola have been one of the lute-players? At some point Campagnola included a portrait of Dürer in his frescos in the Scuola del Carmine at nearby Padua.

Indeed, if there had not in fact been any Bologna connection, Dürer and Raimondi could have met through Campagnola. About this time, using a stippling technique newly developed by Campagnola, Raimondi made an engraving – subsequently known by the cryptic title *The Dream of Raphael*, though it had nothing to do with him – based on a lost and obscurely allegorical Giorgione painting, with two naked women sleeping, brooding urban background half on fire, and a collection of little Hieronymous Bosch monsters. About a year later, Campagnola, who, as we know, had previously made prints inspired by Mantegna and

---

161   Now in the National Gallery, London - and also in Arthur Mee.
162   Now in the Pinacoteca di Brera, Milan

Dürer, made a *Venus* with one of these same naked women. (It would be fascinating to know who she was, and whom *she* knew!). And not long after, Titian would also borrow a Raimondi figure, less than two years after it was made, for his *Triumph of Christ* engraving. The hints of connections are tantalising.

Dürer's letter continued:

> Amongst the Italians I have many good friends who warn me not to eat and drink with their painters. Many of them are my enemies and they copy my work in the churches and wherever they can find it; and then they revile it and say that the style is not *antique* and so not good. But Giovanni Bellini has highly praised me before many nobles. He wanted to have something of mine, and himself came to me and asked me to paint something and he would pay me well for it. And all men tell me what an upright man he is, so that I am really friendly with him…You must know too that there are many better painters than Master Jacob [Jacopo de' Barbari]".

There is a smugness about Dürer's view of his special relationship with Giovanni Bellini; it is not surprising that his success with the reigning master of Venetian painting produced a jealous reaction amongst some other painters who may have been vying for such accolades for a much longer period than two to three months.

There is probably also a hidden agenda in the snitchy remark about Barabari: after the famous 1500 *Venice*, Barbari had been appointed, probably (Waetzoldt believed) thanks to the German colony in Venice, as "Counterfeiter and Illuminist" to the Emperor Maximilian, in which capacity he spent the next seven years in Germany, including in Nuremburg. Dürer almost certainly met him again there, not simply because they had probably met during his first visit to Venice, but also because he was keen to get more detail from Barbari of his theory of measurement and numbers in the human body. But without success: it was still on Dürer's agenda many years later.

But were Titian and Giorgione, some of whose works the experts often find hard to distinguish, among those "better painters"? The year after Dürer's departure, these two, by then about 20 and 30 respectively, completed frescoing the façade of the huge Fondaco dei Tedeschi, next to the Rialto Bridge (now the General Post and Telegraph Office), the lodgings and warehouse of the German merchants resident in Venice.

The Fondaco was run by guilds of merchants from Nuremberg and Augsburg, and of course among the most prominent of the former, after such a long time in Venice, was – Anton Kolb.

Kolb must have been involved in commissioning Titian and Giorgione to paint the frescoes (now reduced to fragments in the Ca' d'Oro); did he introduce his friend Dürer to these rising stars? Dürer's subsequent portrait-paintings are said to show that he "learned much" from Giorgione's; Giorgione's late paintings are said to be "responses" to Dürer's art. Given Kolb's long residence in the city, and his civic prominence with the commissioning of Jacopo de' Barbari's *View of Venice*, he must have been in a position to make numerous introductions. But he is only mentioned in Dürer's letters in the hunt for Pirckheimer's damned rings and carpets.

Dürer was himself also employed by the Fondaco dei Tedeschi, presumably at Kolb's suggestion. Already, in his very first letter of 6 January 1506, he wrote:

"I have a panel to paint for the Germans for which they are to pay me a hundred and ten Rhenish florins – it will not cost me as much as five…if God will, it shall be in its place above the altar [of the Fondaco's chapel in the nearby Church of San Bartolomeo] a month after Easter".

The painting, *The Feast of the Rose Garlands*,[163] was apparently finished about the end of May; but the next mention of it is only in Dürer's letter of 8 September, with a mixed verdict. As usual, money was the problem – Dürer had totally miscalculated his expectations – but the work itself was a success:

"My picture if you must know, says it would give a ducat for you to see it; it is well–painted and beautifully coloured. I have earned much praise but little profit by it. In the time it took to paint I could easily have earned 220 ducats…I have stopped the mouths of all the painters who used to say I was good at engraving but, as to painting, I did not know how to handle colours. Now everyone says that better colouring they have never seen".

---

163   Now in the National Gallery, Prague

And the letter continued:

"Item: my French mantle greets you, and my Italian overcoat too.

Item: you stink so much of whores that it seems to me I can smell it from here! When you go courting, they tell me here, you pretend to be no more than 25 years old. Ocha! Double that and I'll believe it [Pirckheimer was actually thirty–six]. God's body! There are so many Italians here who look exactly like you; I don't know how that happens!

Item: the Doge and the Patriarch have also seen my picture...I have to hurry over this letter; read it according to the sense. You would doubtless do better if you were writing to a lot of princes".

The painting's subject, laid down by the Fondaco merchants, was to portray the unity of Church and (their) state. Dürer presented the theme in a manner that paid tribute to Giovanni Bellini's style: the Virgin and Child respectively crowning with rose garlands the Holy Roman [German] Emperor Maximilian I and Pope Julius II, surrounded by a pressing crowd of worshippers, some also being garlanded. A number of these onlookers are members of the great Augsburg Fugger banking family; one is the Augsburger Hieronymus, architect of the Fondaco, set-square in hand. And above and beyond the bankers, the scene is surveyed by Dürer himself, and a companion – some say Willibald Pirckheimer, in gratitude for his loans; alternatively, that it is another Augsburger, the merchant and humanist Konrad Peutinger, best known for supplying the Emperor with a list – the product of his vast learning – of a hundred famous women, whose names Maximilian could give to his favourite cannon. Is Anton Kolb among the garlanded? Disappointingly, he has not been identified.

Even Dürer's recalcitrant Venetian competitors came round: a fortnight later he was writing to Pirckheimer again with his usual heavy-handed humour:

"Your letter telling me of the praise that you get to overflowing from Princes and nobles gave me great delight. You must be altogether altered to have become so gentle; I shall hardly know you when I meet you again...And as you are so pleased with yourself, let me tell you that there is no better Madonna picture in the land than mine; for all the painters praise it, as the nobles do. They say that they have never seen a nobler, more charming painting, and so forth...In order to come home as soon as possible, I have, since my picture was finished, refused work that would have yielded me more than two thousand ducats...".

There was a follow-up to Dürer's search for knowledge of perspective before he finally left Venice, delayed perhaps by spending longer than he originally intended in Bologna: a copy of Euclid's geometry, which still exists, with the inscription "This book have I bought at Venice for a ducat in the year 1507. Albrecht Dürer". It was a new passion, and in due course he would write on the mathematics of perspective himself; but he was conscious, as always, of the expenditure of every single coin.

The height of the High Renaissance

Apart from the huge amount of sometimes arguable information he passed down, Vasari's greatest legacy was the enshrining in the Western European consciousness, for the following three hundred years until the late 19th century, of the view that all art had been a progression up to the Italian High Renaissance, which he regarded as the greatest artistic period ever.

It certainly had a lot going for it. Lists as a rule do not convey a great deal; but there is unmistakable dazzlement as the eye slips along the names of the major artists – whose works may be seen in Washington, London, Paris, Berlin, as well as in Florence, Milan, Rome, Venice – who were working in Italy in the year 1500 itself: Gentile and Giovanni Bellini, Mantegna, the della Robbias, Signorelli, Botticelli, Perugino, Leonardo, Pintoricchio, Carpaccio, Filippino Lippi, Fra Bartolommeo, Michelangelo, Giorgione, Lorenzo Lotto. Within the previous ten years Italy had lost Piero della Francesca, Ghirlandaio, Melozzo da Forli, Benozzo Gozzoli and Carlo Crivelli. Still in their teens, but probably already studying with a master or apprenticed, were Raphael, Sebastiano del Piombo, Titian and Andrea del Sarto. Correggio, Giulio Romano, Pontormo and Rosso Fiorentino were still small boys, Benvenuto Cellini a baby. Amongst this galaxy, Vasari, writing in the 1550s and 1560s, especially extolled Leonardo (who in 1500 was 48), Michelangelo (25) and Raphael (17) as the three peaks of this summit of all artistic endeavour.

Vasari had not been born when Leonardo went in 1506 to work for Louis XII's son Francis I in France, from which he never returned. He tended to treat the unconventional Leonardo a little warily – and in only 17 pages – and with a splendidly backhanded compliment:

"It is clear that Leonardo, through his comprehension of art, began many things and never finished one of them, since it seemed to him that the hand was not able to attain the perfection of art in carrying out the things which he imagined; for the reason that he conceived in idea difficulties so subtle and so marvellous, that they could never be expressed by the hands, be they ever so excellent".

Leonardo's prodigious explorations in the functioning of the physical world – anatomy, mathematics, engineering, optics, astronomy, physics, warfare, flight, botany, geology, hydraulics, mechanics – were beyond Vasari's interests, and, probably, comprehension. At the same time he recognised Leonardo's genius as a painter:

"Wherever he turned his thought, brain and mind, he displayed such divine power in his works, that, in giving them their perfection, no one was ever his peer in readiness, vivacity, excellence, beauty, and grace".

Vasari's approach to Michelangelo was quite different. He had known him since 1524, when he was taken to Florence, where Michelangelo was working on the tomb of Pope Leo X de' Medici, to be educated – as Michelangelo himself had been three decades earlier – with the Medici children. Vasari's companions, both his own age, were illegitimate offspring: Alessandro, half-brother of the future Queen of France, Catherine de' Medici, later installed as Duke of Florence by Leo's nephew Pope Clement VII; and Ippolito, his second cousin, whom Clement made a Cardinal at twenty. (Ippolito, who was said to keep a court of "three hundred poets, musicians and wits" and an international human menagerie of twenty strapping "barbarians", in due course rescued his former school-mate Vasari after the invasion of the Emperor Charles V, and set him on his career as artist and historian.) Later, Vasari learned about painting from Michelangelo, and on occasion received his approval; he cultivated the friendship of this man who did not make friends easily, and received it – "Messer Giorgio, dear friend", Michelangelo wrote in 1556. Vasari gave Michelangelo his unstinting admiration until he died in 1564, fourteen years after the first edition of the *Lives* and four before the second.

Michelangelo rated 122 pages, partly reflecting his enormously long life, partly the abundance of Vasari's first-hand knowledge – some of which he still managed to get wrong – and partly the sheer prodigiousness of the man himself. But it also reflected Vasari's view of Michelangelo's work as the apogee of human creativity, the very peak of the summit of the High Renaissance. This Vasari makes clear in his opening peroration – which can truly be described as Florentine:

"The most benign Ruler of Heaven in His clemency...became minded to send down to earth a spirit with universal ability in every art and every profession, who might be able, working by himself alone, to show what manner of thing is the perfection of the art of design in executing the lines, contours, shadows, and high lights, so as to give relief to works of painting, and what it is to work with correct judgement in sculpture, and how in architecture it is possible to render habitations secure and commodious, healthy and cheerful, well-proportioned, and rich with varied ornaments. He was pleased, in addition, to endow him with the true moral philosophy and with the ornament of sweet poesy, to the end that the world might choose him and admire him as its highest exemplar in the life, works, saintliness of character, and every action of human creatures, and that he might be acclaimed by us as a being rather divine than human.

And since he saw that in the practice of these rare exercises and arts – namely, in painting, in sculpture, and in architecture – the Tuscan intellects have always been exalted and raised high above all others...He chose to give him Florence, as worthy beyond all other cities, for his country, in order to bring all the talents to their highest perfection in her, as was her due, in the person of one of her citizens".

The adulation has continued ever since, though Vasari's view was not shared by Mark Twain. Writing in *Innocents Abroad* exactly three hundred years later, he complained of his visit to Italy:

"I used to worship the mighty genius of Michael Angelo...But I do not want Michael Angelo for breakfast – for dinner – for tea – for supper – for between meals...In Genoa, he designed everything: in Milan he or his pupils designed everything; he designed the Lake of Como; in Padua, Verona, Venice, Bologna, who did we ever hear of, from guides, but Michael Angelo? In Florence he painted everything, designed everything...He designed the piers of Leghorn and the customs–house regulations of Civita Vecchia. But, here [in

Rome] – here it is frightful. He designed St Peter's; he designed the Pope; he designed the Pantheon, the uniform of the Pope's soldiers, the Tiber, the Vatican, the Coliseum... I never felt so fervently thankful, so soothed, so tranquil, so filled with a blessed peace, as I did yesterday when I learned that Michael Angelo was dead".

Raphael, who died when Vasari was only nine, comes in, at 37 pages, way behind Michelangelo, and not quite divine – after all, he wasn't a Tuscan. But Vasari has a warm feeling for his lovability as a painter and a person:

"How bountiful and benign Heaven sometimes shows itself in showering upon one single person the infinite riches of its treasures, and all those graces and rarest gifts that it is wont to distribute among many individuals, over a long space of time, could be clearly seen in the no less excellent than gracious Raffaello Sanzio da Urbino...

For in truth we have from him art, colouring, and invention harmonized and brought to such a pitch of perfection as could scarcely be hoped for; nor may any intellect ever think to surpass him...[Other artists] were overcome both by his courtesy and by his art, and even more by the good disposition of his nature, which was so full of gentleness and so overflowing with loving-kindness".

The monumental, driven, Michelangelo could never have been accused of such sweetness, even by Vasari; and Leonardo was too various, too... undisciplined, to encompass with comfort. But in this encomium of Raphael, of the sheer lovingness which shows in the perfection of his painted form, Vasari zeroes in on the aspect of his work that pushed him to the heights of both critical and popular esteem. And Marcantonio Raimondi, not one of the celebrities in our 1500 list, helped keep Raphael there for three hundred years.

Raimondi and the road to Rome

From the autumn of 1504, until March 1505, Leonardo, Michelangelo and Raphael were all in Florence at the same time. It was the only period when the three peaks of the High Renaissance were together on the same terrain, and the first period when Leonardo and Michelangelo were thrown into direct competition. The cause was the decision of the then ruler, the Gonfalionier Piero Soderini, and his republican government of the city to commemorate itself by paintings, on the two huge walls of the Sala Grande del Consiglio of the Palazzo Vecchio, of two earlier republican victories against Florence's traditional enemies: the 1364 Battle of Cascina against Pisa (in which the victorious Florentine army was commanded by the English *condottiere* Sir John Hawkwood, whose stunning equestrian memorial fresco by Paolo Uccello is on the north wall of the Duomo), and the 1440 victory over Milan at Anghiari.

In April 1503 the Signoria had commissioned Leonardo to do the Battle of Anghiari, and a few months later apparently considered giving him the other Battle as well. But mid-1504, possibly because his work was proceeding so slowly, or perhaps just wanting to keep both of Italy's greatest artists in Florence, they commissioned Michelangelo to do the Battle of Cascina. The two great projects were the talk of the town from the outset, and Raphael's decision to move to Florence in the autumn of 1504 presumably reflected his interest in seeing them as well as earlier works by both his elders: Leonardo's *Adoration of the Magi*, *Virgin and Child with St Anne* and the *Mona Lisa*; Michelangelo's sculpture, The *Centaurs*, *Bacchus* and *David*, and his first great painting, the so-called *Doni Tondo* of the Holy Family – with a frieze of naked athletes in the background.

Raphael came to Florence, at the age of 19, under the best possible auspices. He had left his native Urbino about five years earlier to study with Perugino in Perugia; but in 1504 the Duke of Urbino's sister-in-law, Giovanna Feltria da Montefeltro, wife of Giovanni della Rovere, the Prefect of Rome and brother of the new Pope, Julius II, recommended him to the patronage of Gonfalionier Soderini:

"This comes by the hand of Raphael, painter of Urbino, who is clever at his art and wishes to stay for some time in Florence to learn. As his father, a good friend of mine, was a virtuous man, and his son is a discreet, gentle youth, I am very fond of him, and desire that he perfect his art. I therefore recommend him to Your Honour as warmly as I may, and beg you for my sake to lend him your aid and favour in his every need...".

We do not know whether the busy Gonfalonier had time for the young artist; but Raphael had the talent – and the personality – to be able to make his own way. Over the course of the next four years he produced a series of luminous devotional paintings of the Madonna and Child or the Holy Family for wealthy Florentines.

But – and more importantly for the future – he also spent a great deal of time on an intense study of, and making drawings from, the sculptures of Michelangelo and the paintings of Leonardo, the latter's influence quickly showing in his own work. Included in his study were both the great Palazzo Vecchio battle scenes: the life-size cartoon of Leonardo's *Battle of Anghiari* was complete by March 1505, when he began transferring it to the wall in fresco; Michelangelo seems to have finished his cartoon about the same time, having worked much more quickly. It was from the cartoons, with their vigorous athletic, mostly nude, figures, that Raphael got his introduction to the study of the human form. But, drawn to other commissions that were more interesting or more pressing, Leonardo never finished his fresco, Michelangelo never began transferring his cartoon to the wall. Within a few decades the immense cartoons were gone, Michelangelo's allegedly destroyed by his rival Florentine sculptor Baccio Bandinelli in a jealous rage. What there was of Leonardo's fresco deteriorated and disintegrated until, in 1557, in the conversion of the Sala del Consiglio into the present–day Salone dei Cinquecento, the remains were cleared away by…Vasari, whose vast frescos now fill the hall.

Various preparatory sketches by both Leonardo and Michelangelo survive, more of the former's than the latter's, but Michelangelo's overall scheme has been the better preserved, in a copy made by Aristotile (Bastiano) da Sangallo, cousin of the Antonio da Sangallo who was to briefly be Raphael's co-architect of St Peter's in Rome and then his successor. Some of Raphael's own sketches deriving from aspects of both *Battles* survive; in addition, Raimondi's *Standard Bearer*, whose figure Titian borrowed for his *Triumph of Christ*, is believed to have been based on a Raphael drawing inspired by Michelangelo's *Battle of Cascina*. And two other engravings by Raimondi, the *Climber* and the *Climbers*, are of figures from the lower left corner of Michelangelo's cartoon.

We do not know exactly when Raimondi left Venice after the heady year there when he overlapped with Dürer. Nor why. But by 1510 at the latest, and perhaps as much as two years earlier, he was working for Raphael in Rome. How on earth did he get to the very centre of the Renaissance within a couple of years of leaving Bologna? Vasari's explanation was this:

"Having arrived in Rome, [Marc' Antonio] engraved on copper a lovely drawing by Raffaello da Urbino, wherein was the Roman

Lucretia killing herself, which he executed with such diligence and in so beautiful a manner, that Raffaello, to whom it was straightway carried by some friends, began to think of publishing in engravings some designs of works by his hand, and then a drawing that he had formerly made of the Judgment of Paris...[was] engraved by Marc' Antonio in such a manner as amazed all Rome".

An engaging story, but not borne out by the current dating of Raimondi's engravings: *Lucretia* to 1511-12, the *Judgement of Paris* not until 1517.

It seems reasonable to ask whether Raphael could have known of Raimondi *before* Rome. It has often been suggested that the connection may have come through Francia. An exchange of correspondence between the elderly Francia and the young Raphael that has survived from 1508 suggests that they had in fact actually met before that date, presumably in Bologna. Francia sent a sonnet to Raphael in admiration; the last stanza read:

> "O happy Boy, who at such tender age
> Excels so many, what shall be thy fame
> When ripening years have lengthen'd out the story,
> And Nature, caught on each enchanted page,
> Shall speak with tongue of silver to proclaim
> Thee prince of painters, as thy meed of glory!"

On 5 September 1508 Raphael replied:

> "My dear Master Francesco: I have just received your portrait... and I thank you most warmly for it. It is of a rare beauty, and so lively that at moments I am verily misled, thinking I behold you in your own person and hear you speak. I beg you be indulgent and pardon the delay of my own picture...Meanwhile I send you by the same messenger...another drawing, of that adoration of the Child in the cradle, albeit, as you will perceive from the work, a great deal altered. You were once so good to give it high praise...Monsignore the Chancellor most anxiously awaits his small painting of the Madonna, and Cardinal Riario his large one...I shall see them as I look upon all your works, praise and esteem them. For I have not seen any, by whatsoever hand, of greater beauty, deeper feeling or finer workmanship...Continue to love me as I do you with my whole heart...Your most dutiful Raffael Sanzio".

These messages were discovered and published in 1678 by a Bolognese art historian, Carlo Cesare Malvasia, in his *Felsina Pittrice* ["Bolognese Painters", Felsina being the city's Latin name], the first book of artists' lives since Vasari's. Then, from the beginning of the twentieth century, some non-Bolognese art historians decided that the letters were Malvasia's own forgeries, largely, it seems to me, because they could not imagine the divine Raphael praising the provincial Francia in such a lavish manner. Admittedly, Malvasia had probably had it coming to him, for a long time, after what he had said about Raphael. Three years before Malvasia's book was published, Florence's Grand Duke Leopoldo de' Medici died, and the inventory of his possessions recorded, amongst the vast Medici treasures, over eight hundred pieces of porcelain, and more than five hundred of majolica, "painted, they say, by Raphael of Urbino". Raphael himself was never a potter; but, as we shall see later, his designs were indeed often used on ceramics, especially large bowls and salvers, and from his day to this. Malvasia, however, outraged by a critic's unfavourable comparison of a Bolognese painting with Raphael's, spat back with Bolognese venom:

> "I will never believe that such elevated and assured inspiration [of the former] could have chanced to enter into the petty not to say humble imagination of an Urbino mug maker!"

It may well not be the last word on the matter, but the latest word seems to be that of Charles Dempsey, an American historian neutral between Bologna and Rome, who, in 1983, went back to Malvasia's manuscript notes for his book, and came away convinced not only that the letters are authentic, but also that Francia and Raphael had known each other for several years *before* the Pope's overthrow of the Bentivogli – and thus, we can add, since before Raimondi's departure for Venice. There are others who also, largely from tracing stylistic influences, believe Raphael visited Francia in Bologna – and at the same time went on to Venice to see Giovanni Bellini's work, and first came across the Dürer prints that were already well known there and which influenced some of his own earliest works.

Vasari has a sad story of the end of the friendship between Francia and Raphael. In 1514 Raphael painted a panel of *The Ecstasy of St Cecilia*[164] for a chapel of the Convent of S. Giovanni in Monte in

---

164 Now in the Pinacoteca Nazionale, Bologna; it was one of the innumerable artworks looted by Napoleon, "re-painted" (sic) in Paris, and returned after his fall

Bologna (a commission in itself suggesting some kind of continuing close connection there):

> "This he packed up and addressed to Francia, who, as his friend, was to have it placed on the altar of that chapel...Right readily did Francia accept this charge, which gave him a chance of seeing a work by Raffaello...And having opened the letter that Raffaello had written to him, in which he besought Francia, if there were any scratch in the work, to put it right, and likewise, as a friend, to correct any error that he might notice, with the greatest joy he had the said panel taken from its case into a good light. But such was the amazement that it caused him, and so great was his marvel, that, recognising his own error and the foolish presumption of his own rash confidence, he took it greatly to heart, and in a very short time died of grief".

Alternatively, says Vasari cheerfully,

> "certain others say that his death was so sudden, that from many symptoms it appeared to be due rather to poison or apoplexy than to anything else".

Dempsey also believed Raphael might have been among the artists who, like Michelangelo, went with or were summoned by Julius to Bologna in 1506-1507 to mark his recovery of this state of the Church. The Pope had already seen his first Raphael painting, and we happen to know exactly when: on 20 September 1506, on his way to Bologna, Julius celebrated Mass in the Church of San Francesco al Prato in Perugia, for which a *Coronation of the Virgin*[165] had been painted three years before by the then twenty-one year old Raphael. Perhaps, indeed, this accomplished if ungainly painting caused him to summon Raphael to Bologna. Did Raimondi, too, go back to Bologna while the Pope was there, rejoicing in Francia's success with Papal commissions and appointments, and on the lookout for something for himself? Could he have met Raphael there – again? Raphael was back in Florence in 1507-1508, the period when Raimondi would have arrived from Venice. It is

---

165 Known as the Oddi Altarpiece, after the family which commissioned it, and now in the Vatican Picture Gallery; it too was swiped by Napoleon and transferred from panel to canvas in Paris

pleasant to fantasise that, having met in Bologna before and perhaps during the Pope's incursion, Raimondi and Raphael (now about twenty-seven and twenty-four) bumped into each other again in Florence – in the same room, perhaps, both making drawings (as they did) from Michelangelo's *Battle of Cascina*. And Raphael saying: "Come to Rome, mate – I've got a great idea!"

There was another link between Raimondi and Raphael as well. One of Francia's prized pupils, from 1490 to 1495 – originally as a goldsmith – was Timoteo Viti from Urbino[166]: "my dear Timoteo", Francia recorded when he left to return to Urbino, "may God give him every good and fortune". Viti arrived home to find the town's leading painter, old Giovanni Santi, had died the previous year, and his twelve year old son Raphael had inherited the studio, which Viti then joined. Furious debate has raged in the industry about whether the divine Raphael could ever – even at twelve – have been taught anything by the likes of Timoteo Viti. The interesting facts from our viewpoint are that Viti and Raimondi were apprentices together in Francia's workshop for two or three years, and Viti subsequently worked with, taught, or learned from (according to taste) the young Raphael. It also seems entirely likely that the origin of the connection and friendship between Raphael and Francia would have been through Timoteo Viti. Indeed, one or two modern critics have discerned a direct influence by Francia on Raphael's early development as a colourist, before he went to study with Perugino; so it does not stretch the imagination too far to envisage Timoteo taking Raphael back to Bologna to meet his revered teacher. And of course his ex-colleague Raimondi.

Raimondi and Raphael
Raphael left Florence for Rome in the autumn of 1508, summoned by Pope Julius II – another reason for suspecting they may have met in Bologna – to decorate the Papal apartments in the Vatican Palace. It is not known (as usual) exactly when or how Raimondi began working with him. Dates from 1508 to 1510 have been guessed at, and it is hard to find any way of pinning it down closer than that.

However, the dating of the two engravings Raimondi made from Michelangelo's *Battle of Cascina* cartoon suggests that he also moved to Rome in 1508. The second, known as *The Climbers*, is dated 1510 on

---

166   Referred to by Vasari as Timoteo da Urbino or Timoteo della Vita

the sheet, and is accepted as having been made in Rome; it shows three of Michelangelo's naked, muscular figures on the edge of a grassy bank, as in the original; and it is this print which incorporates the background Raimondi took from a very sophisticated engraving made by the fourteen year old Lucas van Leyden two years earlier. But the first of Raimondi's two engravings from the *Battle of Cascina*, showing only one climber, with a rather cursory background, is usually dated back to 1508. The question is whether, when simply passing through Florence on his way to Rome, Raimondi would have had access to a workshop in 1508 and 1509 where he could have made this and several other prints (including the copy of the earlier van Leyden mentioned long ago). It is probably more likely that, after making his drawings of Michelangelo in Florence in 1507 or 1508, Raimondi went on to Rome to start working there.

There were in fact two significant Bolognese connections with Rome at this time which could have played a significant role for Raimondi's move, quite apart from any connection with Raphael. One was Jacopo Ripanda, a Bolognese painter and engraver who had gone to Rome about the turn of the century, perhaps with Francia's partner Amico Aspertini, to study classical antiquities. Unlike Aspertini, Ripanda stayed on in Rome, becoming instantly famous when he designed an apparatus enabling him to make accurate drawings of the two hundred metres of spiral frieze that winds its way around Trajan's thirty metre high Column, earning him both Papal painting commissions and the patronage of the powerful Cardinal Raffaele Riario (he who was awaiting his "large" painting from Francia) and his circle of antiquarians and humanists. Raimondi's very first known Roman engraving was of a *Triumph* drawn by Ripanda, a crowded scene based on figures from the latter's classical studies; this suggests that the two had already known each other in Bologna, most likely in Francia's capacious workshop. A dozen years later, Raimondi would engrave a section of the Trajan Column frieze itself, again no doubt from Ripanda's drawing, rather than from the top of a ladder.

As time went on it was clear that Raimondi and Raphael shared an intense interest in Rome's classical past. Raphael was in due course to have a major responsibility for those remains: in 1515 Pope Leo X appointed him "Superintendent of all pieces of marble and all stones which from this time forth may be brought to light in Rome or within a distance of ten miles from that city", and "to make ancient Rome visible in drawings". Although Leo probably mainly had his eye on securing building materials for St Peter's, he nevertheless instructed that all inscriptions be preserved, "to the advantage of learning and the preservation of the Latin tongue". But Raphael's inventory of Rome's ancient monuments began with a pointed lament:

"How many Popes have busied themselves in destroying ancient temples, statues, triumphal arches and other structures deserving of fame! How many have suffered foundations to be undermined, only in order to obtain sand for cement, so that within a short time the buildings collapsed! How great quantities of lime have been burnt from statues and other ancient decorative works! I would venture to assert that this new Rome, great as it is, beautiful as it appears to us with its palaces, churches and other buildings, has been built entirely with the lime obtained from ancient marble".

It is interesting that our search for Raimondi has found him at the beginnings of intellectual property law, and now close to the beginnings of heritage protection.

Through Ripanda, Raimondi would have had access, right from the start of his time in Rome, to the circles around Cardinal Riario's Accademia Romana. The second of the Bolognese in Rome was even more well-placed: Paride de Grassis, Pope Julius II's Master of Ceremonies, who had succeeded to the position in 1506, just before the expedition to conquer his home town. Paride (i.e. Paris, his classicist parents having named his brothers Agamemnon and Achilles) made clear his distaste for charging around the country in battle order by telling the Pope he kept his boots on so long that "no one can kiss your feet". But he had to accompany Julius everywhere he went, and it might well have been he who was responsible for engaging Francesco Francia, whom he would have known long since, to produce the medals for Julius to distribute during his triumphal entry into conquered Bologna, and perhaps for his subsequent appointment to the Papal Mint there. Grassi, who greatly admired Raphael, would no doubt have found satisfaction in seeing his young compatriot Raimondi, Francia's favourite pupil, teaming up with Julius's chief painter to spread the genius of Raphael's art.

Did Raimondi work with Raphael from the beginning of his time in Rome? The answer depends on a judgement as to when Raphael decided he was interested in making money as well as a name for himself; and to go by Vasari, that was probably as soon as possible:

"Raffaello had kept an assistant called Baviera for many years to grind his colours; and since this Baviera had a certain ability, Raffaello ordained that he should attend to the printing of the engravings executed by Marc' Antonio, to the end that all his compositions might thus be finished, and then sold in gross and in detail to all who desired them. And so, having set to work, they printed a vast number, which brought very great profit to Raffaello"

– and, no doubt, some to Raimondi and Baviera, in addition to the other advantages that would have accrued to them in that society from their close association with one of its greatest stars. There is very little else known about this Baviera – sometimes called Baviero de Carocci – other than that he was from northern Italy, and apparently of German extraction (so who did *he* train with?); he enters the world right there in the Raphael workshop.

Raphael must have been well aware of the extent to which Dürer's prints – and hence his fame – had spread in Italy, and influenced a whole range of his own young contemporaries; his contacts with Francia and perhaps with Raimondi himself in Bologna would have revealed the money-making possibilities which had been demonstrated, impudently or by agreement, with his Dürer-copying in Venice. As we saw earlier, even Vasari, in his version as to how the Raphael/Raimondi enterprise was established, gave the initiative to Raphael. One can easily imagine that, when the Pope's summons came, Raphael put the proposition to Raimondi – perhaps while still in Florence, perhaps not till they were both in Rome – for going together into a business that would effectively be underwritten by Julius himself.

The extent to which artists moved around during these decades has been apparent throughout our survey. The Raphael workshop in Rome, however, was to become a drawcard – and obviously a honeypot – like no other. But it is hard to judge which was the greater attraction: the apparently endless cascade of money dispensed by the Popes, or the generosity with which Raphael – in marked contrast to Michelangelo – shared his designs and his genius in a large workshop and a larger acquaintance. Raphael's reputation for consideration and generosity towards his fellow artists seems to have been accurate: there was never any detectable hint or gossipy shadow of disagreement or discontent in the studio as long as he lived.

Several dozen painters were associated with Raphael in Rome during the twelve-year period he worked there: some over short periods, famous names like Fra Bartolommeo, Correggio, Sodoma; others for years in his workshop, Giulio Romano and less well known names like Giovanni da Udine (who had studied with Giorgione), Polidoro da Caravaggio, Giovanni Francesco Penni, Perino del Vaga, Raffaello dal Colle, all of whom painted Raphael's designs in the Vatican stanze and loggias. Sebastiano del Piombo, a former student of Giovanni Bellini and Giorgione, was transplanted to Rome by the fabulously wealthy Sienese banker Agostino Chigi, to work, as Raphael would also, on his Villa Farnesina. But he aligned himself with Michelangelo against Raphael in the competition that still existed between them in Rome; and in obvious reference to Raphael Inc. he was moved, when accused of laziness, to remark (says Vasari) that

> "there are now in the world men of genius who do in two months what I used to do in two years...And since these stalwarts can do so much, it is well that there should also be one who does nothing, to the end that they may have the more to do".

Others kept coming after Raphael's death, when the workshop continued under his chief pupil Giulio Romano. Raimondi's own workshop, which likewise continued, equally became the place to go for engravers, who came from the main artistic centres of the north and subsequently spread Raimondi's style of engraving throughout Italy.

In those days there was a less clear distinction between the Artist and the artisan – Vasari calls them all craftsmen (*artefici*). Raphael however rapidly achieved and kept an unparalleled stature in Rome as a Papal favourite. He was offered in marriage (but declined) the niece of Cardinal Bernado Bibbiena, such a close adviser to Pope Leo X as to be known as the "Other Pope"; the Cardinal inherited his mansion, designed by Bramante. And it was said Raphael was about to be made a Cardinal himself at the time of his unexpectedly early death – from what Vasari describes as "more than his usual excess" of the "pleasures of love". He had lived for only thirty-six years, one more than Mozart would.

That the Raphael/Raimondi partnership went well, and from a very early stage, is testified to by Raphael's life-size portrait of Raimondi as the foremost bearer of Pope Julius II's gestatorial chair in the great fresco *The Expulsion of Heliodorus*, in the room in the Papal apartments in the Vatican known as the *Stanza di Eliodoro*. This is next to Raphael's even more famous *Stanza della Segnatura*, the first of the series for which Pope Julius II summoned him to Rome. It is one of the most visually stunning and intellectually sophisticated series of paintings in the entire history of art, especially the *School of Athens*, dominated by Plato (a portrait of Leonardo) and Aristotle (curiously, unidentified); Michelangelo, added like an after-thought after the other fifty-five figures had been finished, is isolated in the foreground as Heraclitus, the misanthropic Greek philosopher known for his theory on the dynamic tension between competing opposites – perhaps an acknowledgement by Raphael on the one hand of the harmonious beauty of Michelangelo's just-unveiled Sistine Chapel ceiling, and on the other a sly dig at his cantankerously stormy relationship with their mutual patron Pope Julius II and just about everyone else.[167]

The mere fact that Raphael put Raimondi in such a major work as *The Expulsion of Heliodorus*, and in such a prominent position – actually in front of the Pope – looks very much like a statement of esteem that went beyond an ordinary working relationship, and of a friendship that went back beyond the relatively recent establishment of their commercial collaboration.

The *Expulsion of Heliodorus* fresco, which gave its name to the *Stanza* as a whole, was intended to represent the Pope himself presiding triumphantly over the expulsion of the Borgias from the Church, or, but only in the nick of time before the completion of the painting, the expulsion of the French from Italy, or, happily, both – omitting of course the minor detail that Julius had himself not long since encouraged French intervention in Italy to further his own military ambitions against Venice. And according to Ludwig Pastor's monumental *History of the Popes*, the theme had a somewhat less sophisticated origin:

> "We gather", he wrote, "that the subject was chosen by Julius himself from the fact that while he was still a Cardinal, he had bought a piece of tapestry representing the history of Heliodorus".

Such are the well-springs of art – and theology.

The complete *Stanza di Eliodoro* was painted between 1512 and 1514, with the wall of *The Expulsion* being the first completed of the four, a remarkably short time after the beginning of Raphael's and

---

167   An aside: in the *Stanza dell'Incendio di Borgo*, the third of Raphael's Vatican rooms, on the opposite side of the *Segnatura* stanza from that of *Eliodoro*, Giulio Romano painted, among other historic figures, Godfrey of Bouillon (see 1200 chapter).

Raimondi's collaboration. The figure of Raimondi (and to a slightly less extent that of Giovan Pietro de Foliari, a Secretary of the Petitions, next to him, in the corner) almost dominates the seated figure of the Pope himself, immediately behind and above, just emerging from under the huge trompe-l'oeil arch that embraces the entire huge fresco, eight metres wide and five high at the top of the arch. Raimondi, who holds the front end of the right carrying-pole of the litter-like chair, is standing stock still, feet planted firmly apart; curiously, his colleague carrying the front end of the left pole appears to be still walking – which might seem a slip, except that it is most likely Raphael himself, a mirror-self-portrait, looking straight at the viewer, with the same cock of the head as in the more famous self portrait next door in the *School of Athens*. Raphael and Raimondi together carrying the Pope – the Pope whose patronage was carrying their joint business partnership. It looks like a great in-joke, right under the Pope's nose.

Raimondi's portrait shows him dressed in what has been described as "German style", with a short dark beard and shoulder-length hair, staring calmly directly at the viewer – and looking, as has been long since remarked, extraordinarily like...Dürer.

Raphael, Raimondi and Dürer: portraits
There are suggestive but, as so often, tantalisingly inconsistent references in Vasari to this new Dürer connexion, with Raphael. After describing, in his chapter on Raimondi, a number of the portraits the latter had engraved, spread over his entire time in Rome, Vasari says, as usual without indicating any dates:

> "Of these sheets Raffaello sent some into Flanders to Albrecht Dürer [whom,
> it will be recalled, he almost always described as a 'Fleming'], who praised Marc' Antonio highly, and sent in return to Raffaello, in addition to many other sheets,
> his own portrait, which was held to be a miracle of beauty".

However a section in Vasari's chapter on Raphael gives a different version:

> "Now, the fame of this most noble craftsman...having passed into France and Flanders, Albrecht Dürer, a most marvellous German painter, and an engraver of very beautiful copperplates,

rendered tribute to Raffaello out of his own works, and sent to him a portrait of himself, a head, executed by him in gouache on a cloth of fine linen, which showed the same on either side, the lights being transparent and obtained without lead–white, while the only grounding and colouring was done with watercolours, the white of the cloth serving for the ground of the bright parts. This work seemed to Rafaello to be marvellous, and he sent him, therefore, many drawings executed by his own hand, which were received very gladly by Albrecht"

It is thus not clear whether it was Dürer or Raphael who initiated this exchange. And the question is not resolved by an annotation that Dürer himself made on a drawing:

"1515 – Raffahell di Urbin, who is held in such esteem by the Pope, he made these naked figures and sent them to Albrecht Dürer at Nürnberg to show him his hand".

Dürer was famous for his self-portraits. He drew himself often, starting at the precocious age of thirteen, once, just after his return from Venice, full-length and stark naked. He was the first artist outside Italy to make his self-portrait as an independent painting, and by 1500 he had done three in oils. It is fascinating that in Raphael's *Eliodoro* Raimondi shows a striking resemblance to Dürer in the second,[168] painted in 1498 in his late twenties, about the same age as Raimondi – the lean face, bearded and with shoulder-length hair, the head slightly turned but looking directly at the viewer. Raimondi is also dressed like Dürer, in "German style". There is a similar uprightness in the figures, and even a similar reserve in the expression, not unexpected in the young Dürer but surprising in the bouncy young Raimondi – perhaps still a bit startled to find himself here in the centre of things.

Raphael is unlikely to have seen the Dürer painting. But it had long been common for artists to include their self-portrait in a commissioned work, either in the guise of some long dead worthy whose features were no longer known, or simply as a bystander in a crowd scene; and as we saw earlier, Dürer had included himself in the latter way in his Venice *Feast of the Rose Garland*, his appearance remarkably like that in the

---

168   Now in the Prado, Madrid

1498 oil self–portrait. The painting had caused such a stir in Venice that Raimondi had surely seen it in San Bartolomeo; and even if he had not actually met Dürer, he must have been struck by the resemblance of the self–portrait to himself. Raphael and Raimondi had both long been admirers of Dürer; it was said that some of Dürer's prints were pinned up on the wall of Raphael's studio. The Raimondi/Dürer look-alike portrait in the foreground of the *Expulsion of Heliodorus* must have pleased, and perhaps amused, them both.

Did Raimondi return the compliment? There is one of his engravings, of around 1518, which has long been said to be a portrait of Raphael – sprawled on a low step, wrapped, arms and all, in a heavy cloak, and looking like thunder. Some Raphael admirers have claimed it was made when he was sick with a fever, to explain the usually charming master's cranky look; others have said it is not Raphael at all, to explain that away completely. The fact that by the 19th century there were only two known copies has been attributed to Raphael's having been displeased with the portrait and demanding that prints of it be destroyed. Vasari does not mention it: his confirmation might have solved the argument (except for those whom it suited to say he was wrong again), but his silence proves nothing. So is the engraving of Raphael or not? All we can say is that it could be. And that black look? – well, even those overflowing with loving-kindness can have their off days.

Raphael, Dürer and Raimondi: exchanges

Some believe Raphael's admiration for Dürer was of long standing, dating back to quotations of the latter's prints in the paintings of about 1505 of *St Michael* and *St George*. But their eventual mutual recognition of the other's talents did not lead to much more influence on their actual works. There seems in fact to be only one instance: in 1517 Raphael borrowed directly from Dürer the figure of Christ from the woodcut "Christ bearing the Cross" in the *Little Passion* series for his own painting on the same theme, known as *Lo spasimo di Sicilia*.[169] Raphael's model on this occasion may have come to Rome in the 1515 exchange of works – but it might equally have been a Raimondi version: in concluding his description of Dürer's work, Vasari says

"...it would take too long to enumerate all the works that issued from Albrecht's hand; let it be enough for the present to tell

---

169   Also in the Prado

that, having drawn a Passion of Christ, in thirty-six parts, and having engraved these [they were actually woodcuts] he made an agreement with Marc' Antonio Bolognese that they should publish the sheets in company".

It is hard to tell whether this is simply a repetition of what we earlier called Vasari's "first scenario" or something new: because while that scenario had mistakenly called Raimondi's copies of the *Life of the Virgin* copies of the [Little] "*Passion* in thirty-six scenes", around 1515 Raimondi finally *did* engrave Dürer's *Little Passion* – with the latter's signature tablet, but this time without, as was mentioned earlier, the initials AD.

Perhaps this could be taken to resolve the puzzle Vasari created about Raimondi's relations with Dürer: while Raimondi's copying of the *Life of the Virgin* series was the result of an agreement with Dürer, the story of the subsequent intellectual property case could have reflected some sort of falling out (though not one that went as far as to appear in the *Consiglio*'s records) over Raimondi's inclusion on those reproductions of his own signature or particularly the colophons of the publisher (as we speculated earlier), as well as the AD; but a decade later, if Raphael's exchange with Dürer had included some of Raimondi's finer work, as seems highly likely, Dürer was sufficiently impressed by its quality – as well as still looking for ways to make money – to now ask Raimondi to publicise the *Little Passion* in Italy, the new agreement being that neither of their signatures, nor any publisher's colophon, should be included. And for Raimondi to take time out from the lucrative trade in engraved Raphael drawings would confirm Dürer's judgement that there was still money to be made in Italy out of reproduction Dürers.

Vasari clearly believed there were limits to what a Raphael would be able to borrow from a Dürer: noting that in Italy his and other northerners' works "are commended only for the diligent execution of the engraving", he goes on:

> "I am willing, indeed, to believe that Albrecht was perhaps not able to do better because, not having any better models, he drew, when he had to make nudes, from one or other of his assistants, who must have had bad figures, as Germans generally have when naked...".

Dürer's earliest known drawings of a nude woman are of a somewhat lumpish Nuremberg bath–house attendant, in 1493, and a considerably more sensuous courtesan drawn two years later in Venice. Dürerites have come to regard the difference as indicating the progress he made in interpreting the female figure under the influence of Venetian painting. But perhaps Vasari was right?

There was to be one more, last, contact involving Raphael, Raimondi and Dürer, but not until 1520, when Raphael was dead and Dürer was in Antwerp. The latter's diary of his twelve month visit to the Low Countries is as obsessive about money, acquisitions and free meals as his Venice letters were about Pirckheimer's trinkets. Early in September 1520 he was recording that, at the beginning of the second month in Antwerp,

> "I dined early with the Portuguese [Francisco Brandan, Portugal's trade representative]. He gave me three pieces of porcelain and Rodrigo [his assistant] gave me some Calicut feathers. I have spent 1 fl. And paid the messenger 3 st[170]...My wife paid 4 fl. Rhenish for a wash-tub, a bellows, a bowl, her slippers, fire-wood, knee-hose, a parrot-cage, two jugs, and tips. She has spent besides for eating, drinking and other necessaries 21 st...I gave Niklas, Tomasin's man [Tomaso Bombelli, a rich merchant from Lucca], 1 st. I paid 5 st. for the little frame, and 1 st. more. My host gave me an Indian cocoa-nut and an old Turkish whip. Thus often have I dined with Tomasin".

And there are many more fls and sts throughout the diary.

There are also scattered though fewer references at various times to paintings he saw by the great Flemish masters, Jan van Eyck, Hugo van der Goes, Rogier van der Weyden (but not, as we saw, Memling); later, in Mechelen, he admired a collection of paintings by Jacopo de' Barbari, who had died there five years before, and met and greatly impressed Barend van Orley, the Regent's court artist; and in Bruges there was Michelangelo's small marble *Madonna and Child*, part of whose composition had been borrowed by Raphael, before it had left Florence, for his *Madonna of the Goldfinch*. In Antwerp he met and drew a portrait of Lucas van Leyden, and they exchanged prints. Did they talk about the young Italian scamp who had copied both their works? Within a few years of their meeting, which increased Dürer's influence

---

170   fl. = florin, a small gold coin; st. = stiver, a cent or penny

on van Leyden's style, that style would change again under the influence of Raimondi's engravings of Raphael which were then reaching northern Europe.

Then, at the end of September 1520, in Antwerp, Dürer recorded:

> "The studio of Raphael of Urbino has quite broken up since his death [on 6 April 1520], but one of his scholars, Tommaso Vincidor of Bologna by name, a good painter, desired to see me. So he came to me and has given me an antique gold ring with a very well cut stone. It is worth 5 fl. but already I have been offered the double for it".

Trust Dürer to check the price even of a gift! Tommaso di Andrea Vincidor, quite possibly a friend of Raimondi from Francia's studio, had just arrived in Flanders, on instructions from Pope Leo X, to oversee the conclusion of the weaving by Pieter van Aelst of Brussels of a set of ten great tapestries of scenes from the Acts of the Apostles, designed by Raphael to hang on the lower walls of the Sistine Chapel Raphael.[171] Leo wanted them as his counterpart to Julius II's Sistine ceiling by Michelangelo: now, after Michelangelo's contest of the *Battles* with Leonardo in Florence, Raphael was to contest directly with Michelangelo in Rome. He succeeded magnificently, and within twenty-odd years sets of his tapestries had been made not only for the Pope but also for Francis I of France, Henry VIII of England and the Emperor Charles V.

Some time later, Dürer saw Vincidor again:

> "On Monday after Michaelmas 1520, I gave Thomas of Bologna a whole set of prints to send for me to Rome to another painter who should send me Raphael's work in return. I dined once with my wife"

- short shrift for poor Agnes Dürer. We do not know who the painter in Rome was; but as "Raphael's work" had to be that on paper, it would have been a whole set of Raimondi's engravings of Raphael drawings that was sent off to Dürer.

---

171   Leo X's tapestries are now in the Raphael Room of the Vatican Picture Gallery; seven of Raphael's cartoons (three have been lost) are in the Victoria and Albert Museum, London. The cartoons are mostly about 4.5m wide and 3.5 high

Dürer was not quite finished with connections from the time of his Venetian visits. In 1521, after he had heard in Mechelen of the death of Jacopo de' Barbari, he asked Charles V's Regent, his aunt the Archduchess Margaret of Austria, to present him with "Master Jacob's little book" containing the secret of his theory of proportion, which he was still chasing after all those years. But the Archduchess had already promised the little sketchbook to Barend van Orley.

The selling of Raphael and the conquest of the Academy
Exactly how many of Raphael's works Raimondi did engrave is a debated question. Vasari describes a number of them, some of which still exist among the one hundred and four listed by Bartsch; but he goes on to claim that Raimondi and his assistant, Agostino Veneziano, "in the end...between them engraved almost all the works that Raffaello ever drew or painted". This claim has not been able to be documented; among Raimondi's surviving engravings there are no copies of Raphael's oil paintings, and almost nothing of his major works: one of the Sistine Chapel tapestry cartoons, and one of the great frescoes Raphael painted in the Papal apartments in the Vatican, the *Parnassus* in the *Stanza della Segnatura* – but it is based on a preparatory study, not the work as actually painted. (Interestingly, Vasari's description of *Parnassus* was based on the Raimondi version, not the finished work.) Nevertheless the belief of more persisted: the four volumes of engravings after Raphael – "very valuable...very fine impressions", almost certainly most by Raimondi – listed in a 1656 inventory of Rembrandt's huge collection of prints, are said to have included the frescoes. But almost certainly not by Raimondi.

What then did Raimondi do for Raphael and his reputation? With an echo of Vasari, Sir Ernest Gombrich, in the 16th edition (and 44th printing!) of his *The Story of Art*, notes that the achievement for which Raphael has remained famous throughout the centuries is "the sheer beauty of his figures". And it was his figures that, largely, Raimondi transmitted to future generations – what Elizabeth Broun called "the portable Raphael".

Ms Broun was writing for an exhibition of Raimondi's engravings in the United States in 1982, the first – anywhere – since one in New York in 1909, which was in turn the first since one in London in 1868. Raimondi has certainly not been overexposed of late. But for three centuries he was the medium through which artists themselves received the message of the High Renaissance. Nearly three hundred years after the time we have been looking at, in the late eighteenth century, when he was the arbiter of art in Britain, Sir Joshua Reynolds wrote:

> "It is by being conversant with the inventions of others, that we learn to invent. For over three centuries, most artists relied on reproductive engravings for information about inventions they could not know firsthand, and the inventions they studied most closely were the expressive ideal forms of the Renaissance created by Michelangelo and Raphael. Marcantonio Raimondi played a crucial role in transmitting these forms to later generations. His prints were the established conduit for classical style…".

Reynolds laid down a hierarchy for painting: he believed it should appeal to the imagination, not just the eye, and therefore the most important was "history" painting (from actual historical events, Christian tradition, or classical mythology), followed by landscape, (individual) portraits, and finally "genre" scenes (in other words, scenes of real life). The "classical style" being purveyed by Raimondi was thus essentially the style for the human figure in "history" paintings, where both the educative function and the imaginative stimulus were integral to the actual art.

Basing himself on drawings specially prepared by Raphael, or sketches in which Raphael had explored images for his paintings, but sometimes also on figures from finished works, Raimondi engraved powerfully-moulded men and women, singly and in groups, crystallized like antique statues, or fleetingly captured full–flood in delightful dalliance, pompous processions, brutal battles and miraculous martyrdoms, with the finest gradations and contrasts of light and dark. These figures were presented with a technique whose strength and clarity has been compared to Dürer's own, and with a grandeur which matched Raphael's models. They were then drawn upon by generations of artists, as Broun says, as "a dictionary of the new visual language of the High Renaissance in Rome" – gestures, the angle of a wrist or a neck, the interplay between a young man and an old. Dürer's request to Tommaso Vincidor for a complete set of Raimondi's engravings was a recognition of the importance he attached to Raphael's models, even though he did not specifically draw on them himself.

Raimondi was also important for his expertise as an engraver; and precisely because he was selling Raphael and the High Renaissance down the years, he passed on that too. Vasari himself noted the point:

"Our arts are much indebted to Marc' Antonio, in that he made a beginning with engraving in Italy, to the advantage and profit of art and to the convenience of her followers".

And not one to leave a chauvinistic stone unturned, Vasari later comes back to the issue:

"For all the assistance that the ultramontanes [i.e. the Germans and the Flemish] have received from seeing the various Italian manners by means of engravings, and that the Italians have received from having seen those of the ultramontanes and foreigners, thanks should be rendered, for the most part, to Marc' Antonio Bolgnese, in that, besides the circumstance that he played a great part in the beginning of this profession,...there has not as yet been one who has much surpassed him".

Looking back four centuries later, Ms Broun's co–author, Innis Shoemaker, notes this point of
Raimondi's technique and its subsequent influence:

"Marcantonio's prints not only spread the images of Raphael and other artists throughout Europe in the succeeding centuries, but also gave wide currency to a new engraving technique which, as so many scholars have written, was imitated by generations of reproductive engravers".

Raimondi's "highly systematized" technique had, in Ms Shoemaker's summing–up, "discipline, logic, and clarity"; and this is what made it easy for later artists to copy – even much lesser ones.

Starting with the next generation of engravers after Raimondi, printed reproductions of all Raphael's works *were* made – along with everyone else's: Vatican frescos, the Sistine ceiling, Last Judgements, Annunciations, Crucifixions, Saints, Madonnas. But also Venuses, Aphrodites, Apollos. And portraits: Popes, Cardinals, nobles, and women – demure, enticing, challenging. These reproductions showed *what* Raphael and others had painted, and they had an enormous influence, especially on public taste. Raimondi's "style dictionary" showed later artists *how* they had painted, and with the aid of the Academies which taught and policed the style, the consequent pervasiveness of Renaissance idiom reinforced that taste even until after the revolt against it by the artists who became known as Impressionists had begun.

It is interesting to see the change in that taste after those three centuries. It shows in the short interval between Renoir, already well-established in the post-Classical Impressionist canon, and the British curator and critic Roger Fry, one of the early champions of Cézanne and the Post-Impressionists. In about 1881 Renoir – who tended to the over-luscious – saw Raphael's *Madonna of the Chair* at the Pitti Palace in Florence, and wrote of finding it "of such freedom and stability, of such marvellous simplicity and life as one could ever imagine". Less than fifty years later, in 1926, Fry saw Raphael as "frankly and vulgarly sentimental", tending to appear "superficial and – without exaggerating – at times even silly"; and the "loveliness" of Raphael's Madonnas has continued to put off some cultivated twentieth century taste as too saccharine. But Raimondi and the Academies did their work well: there is still a taste for Raphael. As there is for Renoir: Impressionism became the new High Art, at least to judge from the galleries and the auction rooms. But taste is now far more diversified than it ever has been, and our access to high quality reproductions, including increasingly on the Internet, will make the efforts of Artistic Correctness more and more difficult.

In the Academies, Elizabeth Broun noted, Raimondi's prints began to be replaced as teaching aids about the same time as the English-born American photographer Eadweard Muybridge began making his studies of the movements of horses and men. Delacroix worked with Raimondi's engravings until he became fascinated by the new unstudied photographs. Within a generation, the advent of Cubism resulted in the depiction of deconstructed human forms (especially by Picasso) that turned their backs (and faces) on Renaissance idealism; and then along came other isms which repudiated the idea of the human form – and sometimes of form itself – altogether.

Raimondi and posterity: Manet's scandal
An assiduous German scholar, Albert Oberheide, in a doctoral thesis prepared for Hamburg University in 1933, reported, Ms Broun says, having found over five hundred probable references to Raimondi by later sixteenth century painters in Germany, the Netherlands and France alone. The most famous addition to his list, if he had included Italy, would have been Titian; in the next century, Rembrandt and Poussin.

The most extraordinary quotation of Raimondi, however, was by Manet. Although not one of the Impressionists (though he influenced them considerably), Manet came right at the changeover from the Academic to the Impressionist style, and the poor man was consistently abused as one of the latter by the adherents of the former, and claimed by the avantgarde against his will. In fact all he said he wanted to do was to paint the world as it was – but this was highly heretical to an esthetic which held that only the historical in subject, and only the classical in style, was suitable for Art.

The quotation came in Manet's second major work, *Déjeuner sur l'herbe*[*],[172] exhibited at the Salon des Refusés in 1863, an organisation itself established in that year as the first breakaway from the increasingly conservative Salon of the official Academy, for which Manet's work had proved too much. Manet's famous painting of two well-dressed gentlemen in discussion in a shaded dell, in company with a naked woman who looks directly at the viewer, was taken straight from the three figures in the front right of an engraving of *The Judgement of Paris* made by Raimondi in about 1517, based on a now lost drawing by Raphael. Raphael himself had taken the three figures from an ancient Roman sarcophagus in the Villa Medici in Rome – the same sarcophagus that had provided the basis for one of Mantegna's most important prints.

Manet was by no means the first to use the *Judgement of Paris*: Oberheid's researches found thirty-eight borrowings during the sixteenth century, on reliefs in stone, alabaster and silver, on enamel, glass, medallions and carved gems, and – shades of Malvasia! – on a large majolica plate[173] made in Raphael's Urbino. In due course it spread to France, where at the end of the 17th century it added a Gobelins tapestry to its conquests.

While it is possible that Raphael drew the design for a painting, it is generally believed that the *Judgement of Paris*, like the designs of some of Raimondi's other major prints, were drawn specifically for engraving – not just to advertise Raphael's style, but to make money. It is interesting to note that Vasari divided the contemporary accolade for the *Judgement of Paris* fairly evenly between Raimondi and Raphael. The latter, he says,

---

[*] Musée d'Orsay, Paris
172 Musée d'Orsay, Paris
173 In the Metropolitan Museum of Art, New York

"...began to think of publishing in engraving...a drawing that he had formerly made of the Judgement of Paris, wherein, to please himself, he had drawn the Chariot of the Sun, the nymphs of the woods, those of the fountains, and those of the rivers, with vases, the helms of ships, and other beautiful things of fancy all around; and when he had made up his mind, these were engraved by Marc' Antonio in such a way as amazed all Rome".

But the over-elaborate composition – with its three groups of figures across the print and two more in the sky above, not to mention the odd tree, bullrush, cows and dog – does not have great appeal for modern taste. Kenneth Clark expressed that view in *The Nude*:

"In spite of the classical ampleness of each group the engraving has an air of frigid and fanciful pedantry, as of some old-fashioned cabinet of antiquities".

Clark also noted that the *Judgement of Paris* was the first example of the predominance of the female nude over the male. Raphael was one of the first artists to use female nude models, in the loggia of Agostino Chigi's Villa Farnesina; previously he had employed comely boys. In his preparatory drawings for paintings and frescoes Raphael frequently drew the male figures nude, from live models, to be sure of getting physiques, movements, gestures to be absolutely accurate representations of the human body; and it is somewhat startling to see, for example, in a preparatory study for the figures of Pope Julius II as Pope Gregory the Great, and all his attendant bearded bishops and theologians to the left of the altar in the *Disputà*, the *Stanza della Segnatura*'s first fresco, the identical line-up...of athletic young men wearing nothing but tight-fitting caps to hide their hair.

Vasari, after referring to other Raimondi versions of Raphael drawings (including "*The death of S. Felicita, who is being boiled in oil while her sons are beheaded*"), goes on to say that

"These works acquired such fame for Marc' Antonio, that his engravings were held in much higher estimation, on account of their good design, than those of the Flemings",

by whom of course he meant Lucas van Leyden and, especially, the mis–placed Durer; and, he concludes, "the merchants made very large profits out of them". Which is exactly what Raphael and Raimondi had in mind.

Vasari's description of *The Judgement of Paris* is a bit vague, not to mention inaccurate: in referring to the three groups of "nymphs" he omits to mention that the most prominent group, the focus of the picture, is of the three nude goddesses Juno (with her peacock), Minerva (with her helmet), and Venus (with Cupid), to whom Paris is awarding the golden apple. This myth, the origin of Homer's Trojan War, had of course been represented innumerable times before, from Greek pottery to medieval illuminated manuscripts and early Renaissance *cassoni* (marriage chests); though one of the most successful versions must have been the relatively recent one on the occasion of the Triumphal Entry of Duke Philip the Fair of Burgundy into Antwerp in 1494:

"The stand at which people looked with the greatest pleasure", a contemporary recorded, "was the history of the three goddesses represented nude by living women".

The "nymphs" whom Manet chose for his ground-breaking painting, and all the other extra terrestrial and celestial groupings, were an addition by Raphael to the classic version, to provide a more complex composition, and no doubt to provide further opportunity to portray the naked human figure. Manet's nymphs were "those of the rivers", though they do not have the usual classical iconographic clues of wreaths of leaves and an overturned urn pouring out the symbolic river of water. Not the least of the iconographic twists is the fact that while nymphs are supposed to be female, Raphael/Raimondi's are males, the one on the left a slightly ambiguous-looking youth though based, it has been suggested, on the totally unambiguously Roman male *Belvedere Torso* in the Vatican (on which Raimondi also based a standing Apollo in a separate engraving). Manet resolved any ambiguity in no uncertain manner, transcribing the figure as a highly sculptural woman, completely naked, staring straight out of the painting with a look of challenging amusement.

Manet, who had had a traditional academic training, had presumably come across Raimondi's "portable Raphael" in his studies. But the irony of using a High Renaissance Raphael as a model for Second Empire "life as it is" seems to have escaped those who were scandalised by the painting when it was exhibited. Of course as it was only known in the version of Raimondi's engraving it would not have had wide public recognition – in fact it took a while for even the art experts to twig. But Manet gave the irony a double twist by using a second, and perfectly public, inspiration: the painting called *Le concert champêtre*, then hanging in the Louvre as a Giorgione but now attributed to Titian, though, covering all bets, "perhaps with Giorgione's collaboration". This painting also has two well-dressed young men, seated, though in a different arrangement, in a rustic landscape in the company of a nude young woman – with another at a nearby well, whom Manet dressed, more or less, and put in a pond in the background.

Manet's inspiration was far from revolutionary. He told a friend:

"When we were in [Couture's – his teacher's] studio, I copied Giorgione's women, the women with the musicians. It's a really dark picture in which the ground has come through. I want to make a new version, with a transparent atmosphere, with figures like those you can see over there. They'll tear me apart. They'll say I'm being influenced by the Italians after being influenced by the Spanish masters".

"The figures…over there" were in fact women emerging from bathing in the Seine at Gennevilliers, opposite Argenteuil, a short distance to the northwest of Paris. These rustic maidens gave Manet the idea for that look, perhaps. But the model was no innocent river nymph; she was Manet's favoured model, Victorine Meurent, who was to reappear two years later, even more challengingly naked, as *Olympia*.[174]

It is difficult at this distance to grasp all the undertones of the uproar that were caused by Manet's play with these two Renaissance "inventions" (as Sir Joshua Reynolds called them). There was the change from "classical" themes: it was all right to portray nudes in religious contexts, Lot and his daughters for example; and even more so in mythological scenes, where Jupiter's coupling with a whole raft of naked goddesses could be represented almost explicitly. But nudes were not acceptable if they were real people, revealed by tearing aside the veil of hypocrisy that passed for contemporary morals. Even worse, Manet had shown "respectable" men – they were in fact Manet's brother and future brother-in-law – in the company of a woman who, by the very fact of being naked, was "obviously" a prostitute. This was indeed "life as it is"

---

174   Also in the Musée d'Orsay

for a lot of the Second Empire bourgeoisie; but it was highly unacceptable and uncouth to say so in public.

Over forty years before his famous defence of Alfred Dreyfus, the twenty-six year old Émile Zola, already with a name after a collection of short stories and his first novel, sprang to Manet's defence. After ridiculing the Salon jury who had rejected the painting, and the critics who had lambasted it, he wrote,

"The *Déjeuner sur l'herbe* is Édouard Manet's largest canvas, that where he has achieved the dream that all painters have: to put life-size figures in a landscape. We know how powerfully he has overcome this difficulty...".

Then, after describing the group of figures, he goes on:

"This naked woman has scandalised the public, which has seen nothing but her in the painting. Good God! What obscenity: a woman without the least covering between two clothed men! That has never been seen before. And this belief was a stupid error, because in the Louvre museum there are more than fifty paintings in which there are clothed and naked figures mixed together... Painters, above all Édouard Manet, who is an analytical painter, do not have this preoccupation with the subject that above all torments the crowd; the subject for them is the pretext for painting, while for the crowd only the subject exists. Thus, most certainly, the naked woman in the *Déjeuner sur l'herbe* is there only to provide the artist with the opportunity to paint a bit of flesh. What should be seen in the painting is not a luncheon on the grass, it is...this huge ensemble, full of atmosphere, this corner of nature depicted with such an accurate simplicity, all this admirable picture in which the artist has put the particular and rare elements that were within him".

He was undoubtedly right, and posterity supported him. But there is a bit too much high-mindedness here: Manet had originally called the painting *The Bathe* (*Le Bain*) – he was, notwithstanding his particular and rare elements, thinking of that "bit of flesh". And indeed rather more: speaking to his life-long friend Antonin Proust he called the painting *La partie carrée* – a slang term for a two-couple exchange of partners.

There is a nice story that that epitome of French bourgeois respectability, the Emperor Napoleon III, was titillated by all the fuss caused by *Déjeuner sur l'herbe*, and went for a walk himself at Gennevilliers – though, discreetly, not until six years later – to see the river nymphs with their swains. But in the meantime the Emperor's town-planner Baron Haussmann had diverted Paris's sewage through a great system of pipes he called the Cloaca Maxima, which emptied into the Seine at Asnières not far upriver from Manet's spot. And alas! the nymphs had gone.

In the event, Manet's daring – not with a couple of nudes, but with his new approach to light and brushwork – gave him elder statesman status in what was soon a race for novelty. But it did nothing for sales in his lifetime. In 1882, after the (next) revolution in France, the Third Republic – or rather, Antonin Proust, who had become Minister of Fine Arts – honoured him with the *Légion d'honneur*, but the sale of his estate after his death two years later was not a great success; in particular, it was reported at the time, "the Louvre, which establishes reputations and is a sort of Temple to Glory for artists…gave no sign of life". A century later Manet had the better of Raphael: the highest price ever paid for a Raphael was £233,000 in 1931, when Andrew Mellon bought the *Alba Madonna* from the Soviet Government; in 1989 Christie's sold Manet's *La rue Mosnier aux drapeaux* for $26.4 million, getting on for double the price of the Raphael in current terms.

Raimondi and Picasso – via Manet

Raimondi's direct influence can hardly be stretched any further, but Manet's was. Within a short time there were two other *Déjeuners* inspired by his: by Monet(1865) and Cézanne (1870), both with everyone fully clothed; then two more variations on the theme, Gaugin's *Where do we come from? Who are we? Where are we going?* (1897), with some of the figures half–dressed in a Tahitian grove, and Matisse's *Luxe, Calme, et Volupté* (two almost identical versions, both 1904), with all but one figure stark naked on a beach. It is interesting that these other artists were happy to pick up the characters from where Manet left off, and amusing to note that in his immediate aftermath propriety took over, then was progressively undressed as the 20th century began undressing everyone and dismantling everything else.

That was still not the end. Half a century after Matisse's paintings there came another progeny of Manet, a "grandson of Raimondi", as it were: Picasso, who, in the course of his extraordinarily prolific career, did almost everything, and in every conceivable way – including, *pace* Malvasia, ceramics.

In addition to his prodigious output of paintings, the catalogue in the Glimchers' *Je suis le cahier: The Sketchbooks of Picasso* shows an astonishing range of private work in the 175 surviving sketchbooks, in which Picasso tested ideas, over and over, worked and reworked them, developed some of them for paintings and discarded some, from 1894 when he was thirteen until 1967, his eighty-seventh year. And the sketchbooks show that, starting early in his life, increasingly in his later years, Picasso reworked specific paintings by a remarkable range of earlier artists (as distinct from those of his paintings that were generally influenced by an earlier painter, as were, most notably, the cubist works by Cézanne).

Amongst those with which he played were works by Ingres, Cranach, Altdorfer, Delacroix, Rembrandt, Holbein, Vermeer, Poussin and David, Renoir, Le Nain, Grünewald, Courbet, El Greco and Velasquez – and there are bound to be some names missing from this formidable list. From this art historical profusion Picasso produced three major series of paintings between 1955 and 1962: some fifteen canvasses based on Delacroix' *Women of Algiers*; more than forty variations inspired by Velazquez' *Las Meninas*; and then twenty-seven paintings from Manet's *Déjeuner sur l'herbe*[175] – plus one hundred and forty drawings, three linocuts, eighteen cardboard maquettes for sculptures, five concrete sculptures, three linoleum cuts and "several" ceramic plates.

Picasso's interest in Manet was much the longest. Indeed, one of his earliest sketches from a painting was an amusing parody made in 1901 of Manet's scandalous nude *Olympia*, with an equally nude Picasso beside the divan, along with one of his mates from Barcelona's (still-existing) "Els 4 Gats" bar. But his longest love affair was with *Déjeuner sur l'herbe*: he began making drawings of the Manet in 1954; there were over a hundred more between 1959 and 1962, together with the small cardboard cutout models, as well as the twenty-seven paintings; then even another drawing as late as 1970, eight years after the series of oils and only three before his death – a fascination, even an obsession, that went on for at least twenty-six years.

---

175   Three of the paintings are in the Musée Picasso, Paris; all twenty-seven were reproduced in the catalogue for their exhibition at the Galerie Louise Leiris in Paris in 1962; some of the models have been made in concrete, on a monumental scale, for the Moderna Museet, Stockholm

Two decades earlier, in 1951, Picasso had used another Manet, the *Execution of the Emperor Maximilian* – itself a second generation work based on Goya's *May 3rd, 1808* – as the basis for a rather cartoon-like *Massacre in Korea*. Picasso, having joined the French Communist Party in October 1944 – a month after the liberation of Paris from the Nazis – had been awarded a Lenin Peace Prize by the USSR in 1950; however genuine his stated outrage at "American aggression" in Korea, the *Massacre,* and the following year's murals *War* and *Peace* – understandably rarely reproduced in the glossy volumes – have the air of favours returned. A second Lenin Peace Prize followed in 1962.

One wonders at the possible connexion with the *Rape of the Sabines*, painted later in 1962: was it inspired by Picasso's outrage at the developing American intervention in Vietnam, or the line adopted by the Moscow-obedient French Communist party? At all events, the outcome was stronger than the Korean War efforts. And there are interesting cross-references to where we have already been. The Glimchers' catalogue indicates that Picasso made at least fifty-two preparatory studies for his series of *Rape* paintings, based on the paintings on the same subject by Poussin (*L'enlèvement des Sabines*) and Jacques-Louis David (*L'intervention des Sabines*).[176]

Poussin, who evolved the archetypical History Painting against which Manet was to begin the revolution, borrowed "inventions" not simply from Raphael, but from, in particular, three Raphaels that were known only through their engravings by Raimondi. For one of these Raimondis, *The Massacre of the Innocents* (made about 1511, early in the Raphael/Raimondi association, and generally accepted as one of the finest), six of Raphael's preparatory studies still exist; and they show, in turn, in the moulding and posing of the nude figures, the influence of Michelangelo's cartoon for the *Battle of Cascina* – from which, as we have noted, Raphael made drawings between 1505 and 1508, and from which Raimondi engraved figures, with the background of one taken from the real Fleming, Lucas van Leyden. In addition, one pair of figures in Raphael's drawing for Raimondi's *Massacre of the Innocents* appears to have been taken from the fresco of the same subject painted in the late 1480s by Ghirlandaio, Michelangelo's teacher, in the Tornabuoni Chapel of Florence's Santa Maria Novella. Poussin's *L'enlèvement des Sabines* (about 1650) relates in a general way to the Raphael/Raimondi *Massacre*;

---

176   Both in the Louvre

David's *L'intervention des Sabines* (1799) does so even more clearly, in its overall composition, its Raphaelesque figures and use of gestures, even aspects of the architectural background (though rather smartened up for the elegant viewers of the late Directoire).

Here are Sir Joshua's inventions piled on inventions – Ghirlandaio, Michelangelo, Raphael, Raimondi, Poussin/David, Picasso! But by the time we get to Picasso's works, the references have moved far from those of classical perfection to the shock of twentieth century reality – the deformed and smashed elements of broken bodies directly descended from Picasso's most famous statement against violence and war, *Guernica* (1937). And a final footnote: the Poussin and the David paintings are of course both in rich colours, as is the first of Picasso's *Rape of the Sabines*; but *Guernica* is in grisaille, black and white and tones of gray – like an engraving.

There has of course been much speculation about why, as he got older, Picasso did so much reworking of the Old Masters. The least likely explanation, though it has been put forward, is that he had run out of subjects. More convincing, and that given, for example, by the Musée Picasso in Paris, is that he developed the feeling as he neared the end of his life that he should – and could – measure himself directly against his great predecessors. As we have glimpsed, the Old Masters swapped and borrowed enough between themselves; but Picasso's repeated reworkings of individual paintings was, like so much else he did, a new development, a "window opening", as he himself put it. Perhaps that is explanation enough, for Picasso. Plus a sense of sheer playfulness – and chutzpah: look what I've done with the twentieth century – now look what I can do with the centuries before!

But this does not explain the almost obsessive fascination with Manet, and with *Déjeuner sur l'herbe* in particular. Perhaps the answer lies in the fact that Manet had been the first modern painter, the first to overturn classicism, just as Picasso had overturned – sometimes after inventing – most of the isms since. It was a fellow-feeling, as well as a homage. And *Dejeuner*? The answer must lie in part in the nude Victorine shocking public and critics alike in the company of her menfolk. Picasso also liked to cock snooks. But above all, for Picasso the explanation must lie in a fascination with Manet's handling of the figure itself. For all of Picasso's dazzling inventions (even in Sir Joshua Reynolds' sense), his real fascination, his real obsession, throughout his life, was with the female figure. Manet painted the first woman in modern art; Picasso would too. Yet when all those drawn and painted variations are considered, one is left with the feeling that, somewhere along the line, Manet got lost: Picasso's pursuit of *Déjeuner sur l'herbe* became an end in itself.

What would Raimondi have made of the paintings and drawings based on the river "nymphs" in his *Judgement of Paris*? Or of the other nymphs whom Picasso painted in such huge and rambunctious variety over his seventy active years? I suspect he would have been shocked at first, as have many on seeing Picasso, almost every time he adopted a new style of expression. But, eventually, he might have been intrigued, just as many in the twentieth century have come to be, by some of the alternatives to classical beauty with which Picasso jolted viewers.

And Raphael? At the very least, he would have appreciated Picasso's success: All that fame! All those ducats!

The Age of Reconnaissance and the Renaissance

It is curious that the great European voyages that were going on during these years, and their discoveries of people and products, had so little impact on the Italian Renaissance painters. The Classical world which they exploited so brilliantly also confined their terms of reference. Renaissance humanism was inventing the individual, but the individual was a *European*. The debate, still in the future, over whether South American "Indians" had souls, and if so how they should be treated, indicates that assimilating the new worlds took time. The exotic images coming back to Europe, from Panama in the west as far as Malacca in the east, did not tempt Raimondi in the way that Dürer's Virgins and Lucas van Leyden's landscapes had. As far as I have been able to discover, there is not a single reference to the New World or to Asia by Michelangelo, who lived for sixty years beyond the great rush of discoveries, or in any of the prodigious quantity of drawings done by Leonardo, who died in 1519; as far as I have found, only Raphael, who died the following year, seems to have registered, briefly, what was going on in the wider world, with a passing reference to the Americas and only a little more to the East – the latter because, as we shall see, he was in Rome when the exotic East turned up there.

In the museums-full of Italian Renaissance pictures that the engravers made known to all Europe, seascapes are something of a rarity, even in Venice, Queen of the Seas. Before long, Venice's own economic strength and political power, based on its control of the spice trade with Asia, were undermined with the direct access to the East Indies spice islands by Portuguese sailing around the Cape of Good Hope and Spaniards sailing around Cape Horn. The Italians Christopher Columbus and Amerigo Vespucci who were discovering new worlds across the Atlantic were not, of course, sailing for Italian sponsors: they did not sail out of Italy, the loot did not come back there.

And this was set in concrete by Rome itself: with a breathtaking presumption typical of Papacy and Europe alike, the Spanish Borgia Pope Alexander VI in 1493, as soon as Columbus returned from his first voyage to "the Indies", divided all new lands discovered – already or in future – down a line near the Azores, the Portuguese to have all those east, the Spanish all those west. The following year the Treaty of Tordesillas gave a bit more of the east to Brazil by moving Alexander's line a bit further west. Until challenged by Protestant England and Holland after the Reformation, this invisible Roman line established the way the world was. Nevertheless, Alexander VI – "the most notorious Pope in all of history" in the view of McBrien in his *Lives of the Popes* – issued a Bull in 1501 ordering that these new possessions were to be used for the propagation of the faith, not for military conquest or commercial exploitation; one particular "grant" he expressly made conditional on the free consent of the inhabitants. But the Catholic kings and conquistadors paid no more attention to the Pope in America than they did in Europe.

Tradition holds that the first gold brought back from the Americas by Columbus was presented by his patrons Ferdinand of Aragon and Isabella of Castile to Pope Alexander, and that it was used to gild the spectacular coffered ceiling of Rome's Santa Maria Maggiore, said to have been designed by Giuliano da Sangallo, uncle of Raphael's collaborator on St Peter's. Thus Spain's triumph began to be spread abroad. And the inordinate number of Spaniards at the Papal Court during that decade of Columbus's four voyages must have meant his discoveries in the New World were well known not only in Rome but beyond. One might wonder whether the hated Borgia Papacy was the reason Italians declined to be more celebratory of Columbus's achievement.

The Florentine Vespucci, a friend of Leonardo da Vinci and Botticelli, provides one of the rare visible links with the new age from this early period: his portrait was painted by Ghirlandaio, in the early 1470s, in the fresco of *The Madonna of Mercy protecting the Vespucci Family*, in the Vespucci Chapel of Florence's Ognissanti Church – but he was then only in his early twenties, nearly thirty years before his first voyage. Immortalisation by Ghirlandaio was the first of Amerigo Vespucci's happy accidents: for it was he for whom, in one of history's great ironies, the German geographer Martin Waldseemüller – acknowledging Vespucci's judgement that the explorers had reached an entirely new continent rather than Columbus's persistence in believing they were in Asia – in 1507 named the new discoveries *Terra America* (from the explorer's name in Latin, Americus). The name stuck, for the whole continent, though Vespucci probably never got further north than the Guyana coast.

Visible Italian links to the Americas contemporary with the thirty years between Columbus's first voyage and Raimondi's death are very rare. Houghton, in *The New Golden Land – European Images of America from the Discoveries to the Present Time*, found what seems to be the earliest: a woodcut frontispiece to an Italian translation – in verse! – by one Giuliano Dati of Columbus's first letter from the New World, published in Florence as early as before the end of 1493 – though, as Houghton pointed out, the ships and naked figures dancing on an island could equally well have appeared on a contemporary Florentine *cassone* (wedding chest). And he notes that the Ferrarese ambassador in Lisbon, Alberto Cantino, had a map made there in 1502 showing the new discoveries in a map of the world, together with the Tordesillas line dividing Portuguese from Spanish "possessions" and three brilliant red and green parrots in Brazil.

But this was not for the public domain: the first printed map showing the New World was made from an engraving in 1506, the year before Waldseemüller's map – and published in Florence. It was a *Map of the World*, drawn by Giovanni Matteo Contarini and engraved by Francesco Rosselli, brother of the painter Cosimo Rosselli, who had contributed to the first Sistine Chapel campaign.[177] Published at almost exactly the time Columbus died in Spain, it was the first map to record the transplanted Genoan's discoveries on his four transatlantic voyages. Most of the images purporting to be of the New World over the next couple of decades were also prints, appearing in German editions of Vespucci's reports to Florence of his own discoveries – which, some say, were either

---

177 The only surviving copy is in the British Museum. It is interesting to note that it was only six years before, in 1500, that the Nuremburg map-maker Erhard Etzlaub first suggested something we now take for granted: using different colours on maps to indicate different countries - or rather, in his original proposal, where different languages were spoken.

due to his commander, Alonso de Ojeda, or were fanciful.[178] But Italian painters – even those of Spain and Portugal themselves – continued mute on the new discoveries, though Carpaccio included a large West Indian parrot (probably copied from a stuffed bird) in his *St George Baptizing the Gentiles* (1507), one of the St George and St Jerome series on which he was working for the Scuola di San Girgio degli Schiavone in Venice when Marcantonio Raimondi first arrived there.

Asia also began to be opened up to Europe by sea, around southern Africa, by Portuguese explorers and traders who reached India in 1498, Malaya in 1511 and China in 1516, and it finally registered in Rome two years before this last step – or second last: the Portuguese stumbled on Japan in 1542 (see 1600 chapter: Hideyoshi Toyotomi). It came in the form of an Indian elephant from the Portuguese colony at Cochin (now Kochi), in Kerala in the south of India's Arabian Sea coast, a gift to the Pope from King Manuel I of Portugal. When the elephant reached Italy from Lisbon it was landed, for unknown reasons, but with great difficulty, at the tiny port of Porto Ercole on the Monte Argentariao peninsula, 160 kms up the coast from Rome. It then took weeks and weeks to get the elephant, causing a sensation as it went, through bad weather and across bad roads to Rome, where it arrived in March 1514. There it was met and escorted into the city by its governor, members of the Pope's family, a bunch of cardinals, the Portuguese ambassadors, courtiers, clergy, trumpets and bands. In front of Castel Sant'Angelo the poor beast knelt in homage to Pope Leo – and sprayed him and bystanders with water from a nearby trough, to the Pope's great amusement we are told.

The Romans nick-named the elephant Hanno, a name thought to come from a somewhat irrelevant Greek legend about an ancient voyage down the coast of Morocco, but more probably a close version of the Keralan word for elephant. It featured in numerous papal and civic festivities, notably the state entry into Rome in March 1515 of Leo's brother, Giuliano de'Medici, restored ruler of Florence after the suppression of Savonarola's republic (and, incidentally, Leonardo da Vinci's current patron); but on this auspicious occasion its silver howdah fell off after Hanno was frightened by a welcoming cannon salute. Giulio

---

178   One wonders how much impact Vespucci's fame had in his native city. Four and a half centuries later the massive *History of Florence* by the great University of Chicago historian Ferdinand Schevill makes no mention of him - or of the New World either.

Romano must have been there, as he made a sketch of the incident, which Raphael later used in a drawing for a tapestry (not made in his life-time) of the "Triumph of Scipio". The mishap was taken as a bad omen (especially in hindsight): Giuliano died in March 1516, still only thirty-seven, Hanno three months later.

While Hanno was already entertaining the Romans, Lisbon was amazed by the arrival of a rhinoceros, another gift to the King of Portugal, some said from "King Muzafar of Cambodia", but in fact from King Muzafar of Cambay, as Gujerat in western India was then called by Moslems and the Portuguese.[179] It was the first rhinoceros to be seen anywhere in Europe since Rome itself had had one in the menagerie of the Emperor Heliogabalus, early in the 3rd century CE, though the Portuguese did not bestow a nickname on it as the Romans had on Hanno. By now King Manuel had more elephants in his own menagerie, and a month later the youngest was pitted against the rhinoceros in a re-creation of contests in ancient Rome; but the royal and other spectators were deprived of a bloody battle when the elephant panicked at first sight of the rhino and charged straight through the brick wall and out into the streets. Whether because of the rhinoceros's triumph, or because it made blood-sport bloodless, it too was then shipped off as a present to Pope Leo. On the way to Rome it was unloaded onto an island in the bay of Marseilles for inspection by King Francis I of France, who was so delighted as to send someone to Lisbon forthwith to buy elephants. But on the next stage the ship was wrecked in a storm on the Italian coast near La Spezia, and the rhinoceros drowned. However in 1515 it finally made it to Rome – stuffed, probably back in Lisbon.

Both Michelangelo and Leonardo were in Rome during these years of the exotic beasts, though neither seems to have noticed them. Marcantonio Raimondi was also there, but left no hint of New World or Asia. But in 1516 Raphael incorporated both the rhinoceros and the elephant – as well as some West Indies parrots – in the Pompeiian-style decorations on the walls of the Vatican loggia that now bears his own name, just outside the *Stanze* – Asia's only appearance in the Italian Renaissance.[180]

---

179 The stories of both beasts are told in the delightful book *The Pope's Elephant* by an American historian, Silvio Bedini.

180 I thought - briefly - that I had found another Italian reference to the New World in these years: a turkey, big and fat, front and almost centre in Andrea del Sarto's fresco "representing [in Vasari's words] Caesar being presented with tribute of all kinds of animals", commissioned by Pope Leo X for

It was Dürer, with his endless curiosity for the new, who delighted in the wonders that were coming to Europe from the East and the new transatlantic West. The first was his famous 1515 woodcut of the King of Portugal's Indian rhinoceros, drawn partly from a sketch and partly from its description in a letter from a Nuremberg merchant in Lisbon: in the course of a century it ran into nine editions, and made the rhinoceros more recognisable than the Pope.[181] Five years later, during his visit to the Low Countries, he found revelations from the Americas: only a year after Hernando Cortés had begun his conquest of Mexico, he saw, in Brussels, the first of the looted treasures of Montezuma:

"I saw the things that have been brought to the King [the Emperor Charles V] from the new land of gold, a sun all of gold a whole fathom broad, and a moon all of silver of the same size, also two rooms full of the armour of the people there, and all manner of wondrous weapons of theirs, harness and darts, very strange clothing, beds, and all kinds of wonderful objects of human use, much better worth seeing than prodigies [freaks]. These things were all so precious that they are valued at 100,000 florins. All the days of my life I have seen nothing that rejoiced my heart so much as these things, for I saw amongst them wonderful works of art,

---

the Villa Medici Poggio a Caiano, near Florence, which had been built by his father Lorenzo the Magnificent. Now known as the *Tribute presented to Julius Caesar in Egypt* or just *Tribute to Caesar*, and dated 1521, the fresco is a flattering allegory of the 1487 presentation to Lorenzo by the Sultan of Egypt of a menagerie of exotic animals – including a giraffe, the first ever seen in Florence, eighty years after Tamburlaine was presented with one, and seventy after China's Emperor Yongle was (see 1400 chapter). The turkey came to Europe from Montezuma's Mexico, not from Egypt - or New England - so what was one doing in the Sultan's gift? - only four years after the Spaniard Francisco Fernandez de Cordoba made the first visit by a European to Mexico, and about the same time as Cortes and his Spanish troops were capturing Montezuma's capital, massacring perhaps a hundred thousand of its inhabitants, and looting what was left of the city. But it turns out that only the left half of the fresco was completed by Andrea del Sarto in 1521, without the giraffe (though it had appeared, rather wispily, in a preliminary study): the right half was added in 1582 by his fellow Florentine Alessandro Allori, with the 1521 date - and the Mexican turkey.

181 The Augsburg engraver and painter Hans Burgkmair the Elder, who also had merchant contacts in Lisbon, likewise made a woodcut of the rhinoceros in 1515, but as only one copy survives it is believed not to have been widely circulated.

and I marvelled at the subtle inborn talent [Latin *ingenia*] of men in foreign lands. Indeed I cannot express all that I thought there".

It is a touching testament of cross-cultural understanding and sympathy. And then, in the next sentence, more all-encompassing curiosity:

"At Brussels I saw many other beautiful things besides, and especially a fish bone there, as vast as if it had been built up of squared stones. It was a fathom long, and very thick...".

From the New World there also came to Europe – most from Columbus's four expeditions, all in Raimondi's lifetime – potatoes, chilis, tomatoes, pineapples, sweet potatoes, corn, haricot beans, avocados, peanuts and turkeys, which were to change the world's eating habits, and chocolate and tobacco which were to change its recreational behaviour. And then there was syphilis. The British historian John Hale neatly described it as "an aspect of America's revenge on its conquerors"; Byron had wanted to send it back, as he wrote in a nasty little piece of early anti-Americanism in *Don Juan* (Canto I, cxxx–cxxxi):

"I said the small–pox has gone out of late;
Perhaps it may be followed by the great.

'Tis said the great came from America;
Perhaps it may be set out on its return, –
The population there so spreads, they say
'Tis grown high time to thin it in its turn,
With war, or plague, or famine, any way,
So that civilisation they may learn;
And which in ravage the more loathsome evil is –
Their real lues or our pseudo-syphilis?"

There is still argument as to whether syphilis existed in Europe in pre-Columbian times, or whether it was at least a new and extremely virulent form that Columbus's men brought back in 1493 from their first visit to the New World. The first scientific "thesis" on syphilis was written – in verse! – in 1521 by the Veronese philosopher, medic and logician, Girolamo Fracastoro, who had studied anatomy under Alessandro Achillini, older brother of the Achillini who had sung Raimondi's praises – and he was unsure of its origin even then. However almost instantaneously-established tradition had it that the ferocious new epidemic came from America: it was first noticed in Naples in 1494, amongst French soldiers who had caught it, so it was claimed, from prostitutes infected by some of Columbus's sailors; from which it was somewhat unfairly called "the French sickness" – except of course in France, where it was "Naples disease".

Syphilis spread faster than either chocolate or smoking. The armies that were then fighting back and forth across Europe carried it everywhere: in 1495 it reached France, 1496 Switzerland, Germany and Holland, 1497 England and Scotland, 1499 Prague, 1500 Moscow. European sailors took it to the East: 1498 Azerbaijan and India, 1505 Japan. The following year Dürer wrote, from Venice, to Pirckheimer:

> "Give my willing service to our Prior for me; tell him to pray God for me that I may be protected, and especially from the French sickness; I know of nothing that I now dread more than that, for well nigh everyone has got it. Many men are quite eaten up and die of it".

Life in Venice was obviously not all work – or life elsewhere. Leaving Rome in 1515, at the height of the Hanno the elephant hullabaloo, the German humanist Ulrich von Hutten wrote

> "Farewell, Rome, I have seen you,
> And I am ashamed of having seen you.
> Farewell, buffoons, elephants, prostitutes,
> Procurers, male prostitutes,
> Heralds, odious ones, rapists, perjurers, thieves,
> The sacrilegious, the incestuous,
> Godless Rome, farewell."

By 1518 he was writing to Pirckheimer, by then Secretary to the Emperor Maximilian I:

> "Oh century! Oh letters! It is a joy to be alive."

But Rome caught up: five years later he was dead – of syphilis.

Dürer knew what he was talking about: he had made one of the earliest depictions of the disease, a woodcut which he dated 1 August 1496, of a soldier perhaps, hideously covered with syphilitic sores. But syphilis was not confined to the ranks. A victim in 1513 was Pope

Julius II – the Pope being carried, in the Vatican's *Stanza di Eliodoro*, by Raphael and Marcantonio Raimondi.

Raimondi after Raphael : pornography

After Raphael's early death in 1520 Raimondi continued working with the master's most celebrated pupil and assistant, Giulio Romano, who left Rome in 1524 to become court architect and painter to Federigo Gonzaga, Duke of Mantua, where he designed and decorated the celebrated Palazzo del Te. His fame was such that he was mentioned by Shakespeare, in *The Winter's Tale*, the only Renaissance artist to be referred to in the plays. But fame is fickle – Shakespeare thought he was a sculptor. Benevenuto Cellini, son of the Florentine carpenter who built the scaffolding in the Palazzo Vecchio for Leonardo da Vinci to paint his *Battle of Anghiari*, was a brilliant goldsmith and sculptor, but probably almost as famous eventually for his *Autobiography*. In it he tells of his membership in the early 1520s of a "club of painters, sculptors and goldsmiths, the best that were in Rome", given more to carousing and womanising than artistic pursuits. Cellini named Giulio Romano as another member, so it is very likely that Raimondi was also associated with this ribald crowd.

Certainly, before Giulio Romano left Rome, he and Raimondi had a fling for which Cellini's club would have been the obvious immediate audience – a fling which has its echoes in some of Picasso's sketchbooks. As Vasari tells the story:

> "Giulio Romano caused Marc' Antonio to engrave twenty plates [of his drawings] showing all the various ways, attitudes, and positions in which licentious men have intercourse with women; and, what was worse, for each plate Messer Pietro Aretino wrote a most indecent sonnet, insomuch that I know not which was the greater, the offence to the eye from the drawings of Giulio, or the outrage to the ear from the words of Aretino. This work [known as *I Modi* – "The Positions"] was much censured by Pope Clement; and if, when it was published, Giulio had not already left for Mantua, he would have been sharply punished for it by the anger of the Pope".

Whether Vasari was wrong or some have been lost, only sixteen of the sonnets and engravings are now known; but he did in fact conflate the chronology – and omitted an important contextual point. When Pope

Leo X died in 1521 he was replaced by a Dutchman, Pope Adrian VI, the last non-Italian Pope until John Paul II's election in 1978; and following the lavish living and spending of Julius II and Leo, artistic commissions came to a halt under the puritanical Adrian. When he in turn died in 1523 it was "the Divine Aretino", as famous for making powerful enemies as friends with his mordant wit, who pronounced his epitaph:

"Here lies poor Adrian, made by wine divine.
He was a Dutchman, a shipbuilder's son.
To be a cardinal he surely won
By teaching [the Emperor] Charles the alphabet to whine.
He was a pedant and he used to hold
A school for janitors. This makes me weep.
He was named shepherd, though himself a sheep...".

Adrian was replaced by Leo's equally spendthrift nephew, Clement VII. The relief in Rome's high-living artistic circles was immediate; and it was in this atmosphere that *I Modi* emerged.[182] It is said that Giulio Romano originally sketched the sixteen positions, in 1523 – on the walls of the *Sala di Costantino*, the fourth of Raphael's Vatican apartments, which Giulio was finishing after Raphael's death, in a moment of anger at Clement for a delay in payment for the work. Perhaps the Pope did not get to hear of this; but when Raimondi's engravings of the series appeared in print the next year, and no doubt started to spread, Clement decided they had gone too far. However as Giulio had already taken up employment in Mantua (as Vasari reported), Raimondi was left holding the short end of the stick:

"And since some of these sheets were found in places where they were least expected, not only were they prohibited, but Marc' Antonio was taken and thrown into prison; and he would have fared very badly if Cardinal de' Medici [Ippolito, the other of Vasari's two school-mates, Clement's distant cousin, at that time only thirteen years old and not yet a Cardinal] and Baccio Bandinelli, who was then at Rome in the service of the Pope, had not obtained his release".

---

182   A full account is in Lynne Lawner, ed.: *I Modi - The Sixteen Pleasures*, in which the whole series of sonnets (with somewhat fudged translations) and engravings is reproduced.

The scandal was no doubt all the greater if (as Ms Lawner believes) *I Modi* was in effect a guidebook to high-class contemporary Roman courtesans as well as to gymnastic couplings, with recognisable portraits – and also, one wonders, of their aristocratic and probably in some cases ecclesiastical patrons?

Years later, when Raimondi was already dead, Aretino claimed to have secured his release through his own efforts. At some stage Raimondi did an extraordinarily fine engraved portrait of Aretino, with the inscription "Sharp-tongued exposer of virtues and vices" which he is known to have cherished. Some have said Raimondi made the portrait in gratitude for Aretino's help; but Ms Broun believes, from the workmanship, that it was the other way round: Raimondi made the portrait before the *I Modi* affair, and by interceding with the Pope Aretino was repaying Raimondi for it and for his friendship when he had first come to Rome. Aretino's closest friend in this earlier *belle époque* before the world collapsed was Giovanni de' Medici delle Bande Nere, a brilliant soldier who would go hell-raising with him when not in the field at the head of his feared cavalry; and one of Giovanni's staff was Celllini's younger brother. One can imagine them all, artists, poets, soldiers, carousing together from time to time – but Cellini's autobiography does not mention Aretino, though he mentions everybody else who was anybody.

Bandinelli's interest in getting Raimondi released was undoubtedly in re–acquiring his services, for Vasari continues:

> "Released from prison, Marc' Antonio finished engraving for Baccio Bandinelli a large plate that he had previously begun, with a great number of nude figures engaged in roasting S. Laurence on the gridiron, which was held to be truly beautiful…".

Such is art. Titian subsequently used the Raimondi engraving for both of his versions of the *Martyrdom of St Lawrence*.

However, as Vasari noted, it was also Aretino who in 1525 had added fuel to the fire by composing the fifteen sonnets to go with the *I Modi* plates. In a letter to a friend he explained that he had been spurred to do so out of disgust with hypocrisy – as well as hostility to the Pope's secretary and Papal Censor, Monsignor Gianmatteo Giberti, with whom he had already clashed and who would later try to have Giulio murdered, though probably for being personally insulting rather than for publicising intercourse:

"After I arranged for Pope Clement to release Marcantonio of Bologna, who was in prison for having engraved on copper the 'Sixteen Positions', I desired to see those figures which had driven Giberti and his followers to cry out that the virtuosic artist who had conceived them should be crucified. As soon as I gazed at them I was filled with the same spirit that had moved Giulio Romano to draw them...What harm is there in seeing a man mount a woman? Should beasts, then, be freer than we are? We should wear *that thing* nature gave us for the preservation of the species on a chain around our necks or as a medal on our hats; for that is the fountain rivers of human beings come forth from...It created me, and I am better than bread. It produced...the Titians and the Michelangelos, and after them the popes, emperors and kings...We should celebrate all this by establishing special holy days and festivities in its honour, rather than confining it in a small piece of cloth or silk".

And he apparently appended to the letter a "Hymn to the Penis". It is not surprising that his sonnets for *I Modi* are even more explicit than the classically-inspired engravings.

Aretino was writing much later, in 1537 – about the time he was being immortalised by Michelangelo in *The Last Judgement* in the Sistine Chapel, though with a bald head, as St Bartholomew, seated just below Christ and to the right, holding, aptly, considering his reputation, the Saint's flaying knife and an empty skin: Michelangelo's, ready to be dropped into the Inferno below. Aretino admired the great painting but, somewhat inconsistently, was one of those scandalised at all those "things" in such a sacred place; he suggested they be painted over, as was done by Daniele da Volterra – nicknamed *Il Braghettone*, "the Britches-maker" as a result – on the orders of Pope Paul IV, who also instituted the infamous Index of Forbidden Books about the same time. Only thirty years after *I Modi*, the Counter-Reformation was in full flood.

Even in those looser earlier days, while Pope Clement could cheerfully put up with Aretino's lampooning of his dour Dutch predecessor, when the sonnets appeared he sided with his secretary, and pounced on the verses as peremptorily as he had on the engravings, though Aretino like Giulio Romano kept out of the Pope's reach. Although *I Modi* had become the rage of Rome, Clement and Giberti seem to have practically succeeded in wiping them out, at least in the Eternal City – though one wonders if Ippolito de' Medici was old enough to have kept a set in an undiscovered "least expected" place. One complete set is known to have reached Venice, perhaps even with Aretino himself, who moved there permanently in 1527; and a second edition was printed there, of engravings plus sonnets. Two were passed by Aretino to friends, others may have gone elsewhere; but for a long time they all disappeared from view. Rembrandt is believed to have had a set with his Raimondis, and a large collection besides of other erotic prints, including his own.

But it is startling to find *I Modi* in Oxford, at All Souls College no less, in 1675 (six years after Rembrandt's death), when a gentleman named Humphrey Prideaux wrote that the University Press

"hath been imployed about printeing Aretin's *Postures*. The gentlemen of All Souls had got them engraved, and had imployed our presse to print them off. The time that was chosen for the worke was the eveneing after 4, Mr. Dean after that time never using to come to the theator; but last night, beeing imployed the other part of the day, he went not thither till the work was begun. How he tooke to find his presse workeing at such an imployment I leave you to immagin. The prints and the plates he hath seased, and threatens the owners of them with expulsion; and I thinke they would deserve it were they of any other colledge than All Souls, but there I will allow them to be vertuous that are bawdy only in pictures. That colledge in my esteem is a scandalous place".

The next recorded appearance was in the mid–1850s, when a French traveller and amateur archeologist, Baron Jean-Frédéric-Maximilien de Waldeck, produced ink and wash reconstructions based on original prints he claimed to have seen in a Mexican convent. Then, in 1928, Walter Toscanini, the son of the famous conductor, came upon an early 16th century copy of *I Modi* in Italy, with woodcuts of just fourteen of the positions and their matching sonnets; it now belongs to another private collector in the United States. Lawner's 1984 edition includes both the Waldeck and the Toscanini plates. The only known prints presumed to be original Raimondis are of Posture 1, in Vienna and London, and nine fragments in the British Museum – but only the most innocuous heads, busts, arms and legs, all without their original contexts. Pope Clement, and no doubt others scandalised later, did a thorough job.

Raimondi after Raphael: posterity
By the time of Raphael's death in 1520 Raimondi had trained a school of his own, which worked with Giulio Romano during his last four years

in Rome but then continued of itself. Some of its engravers would become independently known for their skills: Marco Dente da Ravenna, Raimondi's first pupil and principal assistant; Agostini dei Musi, better known as Agostino Veneziano, who had begun in Venice around the time Raimondi himself was there, copying and perhaps studying with Campagnola; Ugo da Carpi; Giovanni Antonio da Brescia, who had probably begun as a student of Mantegna and continued as a copier of Dürer before joining Raimondi; Giovanni Jacopo Caraglio, one of his last apprentices.

There was also the very good engraver known only as "the Master of the Die". Some have identified him as Tommaso Vincidor, with whom Dürer arranged exchanges of his and Raphael/Raimondi prints in Antwerp. Others believe he could have been one Giorgio Benedetto Verini, said to have been Raimondi's own son, presumed illegitimate; that would not be surprising given Raimondi's heady days in the company of the likes of Cellini and Aretino – or the womanising Raphael himself for that matter. Another 17th century report said Raimondi had married "a woman of quality" in Rome; that too would not have been surprising given the standing his association with Raphael would have conferred, but there is nothing else about any wife. The same report also said she was an engraver herself; in that male-dominated world, that *would* be surprising.

Taking time off from his sculptural battles with Michelangelo, Baccio Bandinelli became associated with the workshop for a time. He enhanced his artistic reputation with a large two–sheet *Massacre of the Innocents*, engraved by Marco Dente, which was inspired by Raimondi's earlier version; Raimondi himself, taking time off from Raphael, made three more modest engravings from other Bandinelli drawings. Bandinelli was obsessed by scale: at about the same time, England's King Henry VIII commissioned him to make his tomb, for which Bandinelli constructed a model in wood and wax which included 142 figures, *life-size*. It would have cost more than Henry was prepared to pay.

Three of Dürer's own pupils are said to have come to Rome to learn from Raimondi. And even before the term "degenerate art" had appeared in Germany, J.D.Passavant, who in 1860–64 published a supplement to Bartsch's catalogue of works on paper up to the end of the 16th century, blamed Raimondi for "harming the development of German art" by making them lose "much of the style of composition peculiar to Germany". One can imagine how idiotic Raimondi would have found this.

After about 1510, Vasari said, "printmaking had become praised and well thought of"; and Raphael's – and Raimondi's – perception of their market value was perfectly timed to help create the collecting of prints as a reputable artistic activity. The evidence lay in the increasing production of prints, after Raimondi's school was dispersed by the Sack of Rome in 1527, by publishers running a print-making industry. By mid-century it was possible – and clearly thought desirable – for a collector to have a huge range of prints. Landau reports a Venetian, Gabriele Vendramin, of the family which provided Venice with a Doge and a Patriarch, with a collection of more than a thousand prints, including a number by Dürer (including his rhinoceros) and others by "Raphael d'Urbin" – Raimondis.

By then, the price of a Raimondi print was said to equal a manual worker's wages for seven days. They kept being sold – for a long time. Raphael had bequeathed all the plates of his engraved drawings to Baviera, the Raphael/Raimondi workshop's printer, publisher and marketer, because, Vasari says, he "had charge of a mistress whom Raffaello loved to the day he died". But Baviera apparently now kept the profits from new editions for himself; as a result Raimondi and his two closest associates, Marco Dente and Agostino Veneziano, made "forgeries" of some of the plates to try to keep up their income. Marco Dente in fact made an exact copy of *The Judgement of Paris* – ironically, right down to Raimondi's initials – presumably for just this purpose.

After Baviera's death the Raphael/Raimondi plates became the property of the Roman publisher Antonio Salamanca, in the Campo de' Fiori, and then passed on from publisher to publisher until, in 1738, they were sold to Pope Clement XII, the builder of Rome's Trevi Fountain, who established the Calcografia (now the Istituto Nazionale per la Grafica) in Rome to house them and other copperplate engravings. And the Calcografia continued printing and selling Marcantonio Raimondis until 1934.

Reformation and riot

It seems incredible that throughout the entire period of this chapter, when some of the greatest art of the Renaissance was being created, Italy was in a state of constant political, military and often civil uproar and chaos, thanks to the ambitions of Princes of Church and State. We saw a little of this in the contestation of Bologna, but confusion, double-dealings and betrayals were almost continuous everywhere throughout the thirty or so years from 1494: France invading Milan and Naples; alliance between Pope, Holy Roman Empire, Venice, Milan against France; France, Spain, Empire against Milan and Naples; Empire,

France, Spain, Pope against Venice; Pope, Spain, Venice against France; Empire, Milan against France; France, Florence, Venice, Milan, Pope against Empire; in Florence, Savonarola's republic, the Medici restored, expelled again; everywhere, Italians against Italians. Twice, French troops penetrated as far as Rome, first in 1494, again in 1501. It is perhaps not surprising that the artists' vision did not extend to new worlds when their own was in such persistent chaos. And, during all this, in 1517 Martin Luther posted his Ninety-five Theses to the door of Wittenberg Cathedral and the Reformation was on. And as if all this were not enough, there were severe outbreaks of the plague, especially throughout the 1520s, accompanied often by famine when the weather failed even if the workforce managed not to.

One of the earliest disasters caused by the new fanaticism which arose when religious differences were grafted on to dynastic ambitions was to prove the greatest disaster for Raimondi, and for many others: the Sack of Rome by the Imperial forces after the Empire's invasion and devastation of Italy in 1527. Sometimes called "the end of the Renaissance", it was the worst disaster to hit Rome since its devastation by Alaric and his Visigoths over a thousand years before in 410 CE. This second sacking was reminiscent on a smaller scale of the Crusaders' treatment of Jerusalem in 1099; though this time both invaders and inhabitants were nominally of the same faith, the capacity for faith to become fanaticism was manifested once again.

The victorious mob, half German, half Spanish, was leaderless and unpaid; and many of the former, influenced by the gathering momentum of Luther's movement at home, were already persuaded that the Roman Church was the Antichrist. Pope Clement VII and most of the Cardinals escaped into the Castel Sant' Angelo, where Cellini became an instant and, in his view, outstanding artilleryman – "every day performed some outstanding feat", he claimed in his Autobiography, including personally blowing up the Prince of Orange. Sebastiano del Piombo, the Venetian painter who had started as a pupil of Giovanni Bellini before switching to Giorgione, and who had become – apart from his friend Michelangelo – the leading painter in Rome after Raphael's death, also stayed with the Pope in Castel Sant' Angelo.

But the rampage outside made no distinction between the remaining Cardinals and the Roman people. The murder, rape and pillage went on for eight days. Twelve thousand or more were massacred (which was still less than half the number of Moslems and Jews slaughtered by the Crusaders in three); total social breakdown renewed the plague even more virulently, though at least it also killed half the invading army. Churches and monasteries were ransacked, works of art and libraries destroyed, from religious fervour or just rampant vandalism. The Vatican was occupied, graffiti were scribbled over Raphael's *Stanze;* but miraculously the Library was saved by the Prince of Orange, the most senior officer left, who made it his headquarters until Cellini got him. The Emperor Charles V, absent in Spain, expressed his horror at the sack, and promptly took whatever advantage he could of the Pope's helplessness.

Thousands were held for ransom, and were tortured until they died if they could not raise it. The great Florentine historian of the period, Francesco Guicciardini, who was governor of the Papal state of the Romagna but was in Rome at the time, later wrote:

"Many were suspended for hours by the arms, many were cruelly bound by the private parts; many were suspended by the feet high above the road, or over water, while their tormentors threatened to cut the cord upholding them; others were nailed up in casks while many were villainously beaten and wounded; not a few were burnt all over their persons with red hot irons. Some were tortured by extreme thirst, others by insupportable noise and many were cruelly tortured by having their good teeth brutally drawn. Others again were forced to eat their own ears, or nose, or their roasted testicles and yet more were subjected to strange, unheard of martyrdoms that move me too much even to think of, much less describe".

Puritans, it seems, were just as capable of atrocities as any other religious persuasion we have come across.

Raimondi was lucky enough to avoid being massacred, and well enough off to be worth ransoming. But it was the end of his known career, and Vasari takes abrupt leave of him:

"Marc' Antonio became little less than a beggar, seeing that, beside losing all his property, he was forced to disburse a good ransom in order to escape from the hands of the Spaniards. Which done, he departed from Rome, never to return".

Included in that property were all the plates of his work (other than those Baviera had inherited from Raphael), "carried away by the

Germans and others" and never seen again. Baviera himself, presumably because of his German origins, together with his Raimondi/Raphael plates, survived the sack. He was soon providing work for the Florentine Perino del Vaga, a member of Raphael's workshop, who as a boy had studied with Ghirlandaio's son and drawn from Michelangelo's *Battle of Cascina*, and who had also, Vasari said, been caught in the Sack,

> "and having a wife and a baby girl, ran from place to place in Rome with the child in his arms, seeking to save her, and finally, poor wretch, was taken prisoner and reduced to paying a ransom, which hit him so hard he was like to go out of his mind".

Many others were also ill-treated by the invaders: scholars lost manuscripts and libraries; painters seem to have been targeted as much as prelates, perhaps because they so often made images that the largely illiterate German puritan soldiery had been told were abominations in the sight of their reformed God. The horrors everyone experienced were obviously engraved in people's minds, such that Vasari (who was in Florence in 1527) could obtain, as he put his *Lives* together over the next quarter of a century and more, vivid details of their sufferings. One of these was the Florentine Rosso Fiorentino, who as a nineteen year old had also drawn from Michelangelo's *Cascina*, who subsequently, in Rome, succeeded in antagonising both Michelangelo and Raphael, and who, just before the Sack, was commissioned by Baviera to contribute to a series on *The Loves of the Gods* which was intended to be a more respectable version of the Romano/Raimondi love-makings of the Gods. Rosso was captured by the German rabble of the turncoat French Duke of Bourbon, who had been killed in the first attack on the city walls; he was

> "used very ill, for, besides stripping him of his clothes, they made him carry weights on his back barefooted and with nothing on his head, and remove almost the whole stock from a cheesemonger's shop";

but he managed to escape.

Another who escaped after capture, Vasari relates, was Baldassare Peruzzi, the architect who designed the Villa Farnesina, where Raphael had used female models for the loggia decorations:

> "Our poor Baldassare was taken prisoner by the Spaniards, and not only lost all his possessions, but was also much maltreated

and outraged, because he was grave, noble and gracious of aspect, and they believed him to be some great prelate in disguise, or some other man able to pay a fat ransom. Finally, however, these impious barbarians having found that he was a painter, one of them, who had borne a great affection to Bourbon, caused him to make a portrait of that most rascally captain, the enemy of God and man, either letting Baldassare see him as he lay dead, or giving him his likeness in some other way, with drawings or with words. After this, having slipped from their hands...on the way [to Siena] he was robbed of everything and stripped to such purpose, that he went to Siena in his shirt".

The young Parmigianino[183] was more fortunate. Author at twenty-one of a virtuoso *Self-Portrait in a Convex Mirror*, he had been attracted to Rome by the revival of the arts after the election of Clement VII, and was commissioned by the latter to fresco the Vatican's Sala dei Pontefici. (In the event he did not do so, which was to be a constant in this strange man's working life: he did a portrait of the Emperor Charles V at his coronation in Bologna in 1530, but did not deliver it; a commission from the Emperor to decorate a chapel of Bologna's St Petronio was not carried out; and when he returned to his native Parma his work on the vault of the Madonna della Steccata was so slow he was arrested and imprisoned later in the decade, just before he died.) Vasari says that during the Sack of Rome, when German soldiers burst into Parmigianino's house,

"he did not move from his painting for all the uproar they were making; but...they were so struck with astonishment at the work, that, like the gentlemen that they must have been, they let him go on...All the hardship that he suffered at that time was this, that he was forced, one of them being a great lover of painting, to make a vast number of drawings in watercolours and with pen, which formed the payment of his ransom".

He was later robbed anyway, in the street, though only of "some few crowns".

But poor Marco Dente, Raimondi's first apprentice and copier, was among the least lucky: he was killed.

---

183 Referred to by Vasari by his birth name, Francesco Mazzuoli. The *Self-Portrait* is in the Kunsthistorisches Museum, Vienna

End in Bologna

The rest that Vasari knew about Raimondi he was able to say briefly:

"This Marc' Antonio died at Bologna, not long after his departure from Rome".

Was there more? The Sack of Rome scattered its art community all over Italy: Agostino Veneziano to Venice; Polidoro da Caravaggio to Naples; Rosso Fiorentino to Florence and Perugia; Giovanni da Udine, who had worked on Raphaels's decorative schemes in both the Villa Farnesina and Vatican Loggias, back to Udine (where he married and in due course had twelve sons). It is to be expected that Raimondi would return to Bologna. When he died, though, is not known. The only documentation is a reference to him, in the past tense, in Aretino's play *La Cortigiana* of 1534: one of the protagonists describes to another the great men of contemporary Italy – the rulers, the ecclesiastics, the humanists, artists such as Michelangelo and Titian – and adds, in that company, "and I cannot deny that Marcantonio was unique with the burin (engraving)".

Perhaps Raimondi died soon after the Sack of Rome, as the result of his mis–treatment by the Emperor Charles's German rabble. He would have been about 47 at that time, not a great age even in those shorter-lived days: Michelangelo, who died at 89, and Giovanni Bellini at 86, were long–lived by any standard, but Leonardo da Vinci, Francia, Bandinelli all lived to about 67, Dürer to 57. A century and a half later, in *Felsina Pittrice*, Malvasia, who patriotically regarded Raimondi as the father of Italian print-making, recounted what must have been an old Bologna story that he had been murdered there, by the patron who had ordered the *Massacre of the Innocents*, because Raimondi had made a second plate of the engraving for his own profit. It would have irritated Vasari if he had known he missed this juicy bit of gossip, though such violence would not in the least have surprised him.

But it does not hold water – as far as that particular engraving is concerned. Raimondi *did* make a second version of it, but both were based on the Raphael drawing, so not commissioned by a patron, and they were made in about 1511 and 1514 respectively. Nevertheless, we saw earlier that Raimondi and his associates did make "forged" copies of some Raphael plates after they had passed to Baviera. After losing all his plates in the Sack of Rome, and destitute after paying his ransom, Raimondi would certainly have been in need of money by the time he got back to Bologna. Even though there are now no known Raimondi prints from these last years, could Malvasia's story simply have become confused over the years about which engraving Raimondi perhaps illicitly replicated, to the ultimate ire of some Bolognese patron?

The implication is also, of course, that Raimondi did not die immediately after he fled from Rome. But there is another reason to believe that he was active following his return to Bologna. After he was robbed in the street, Parmigianino escaped from Rome and in due course also made his way to Bologna; and it was there, the experts agree, that he first took up etching – almost certainly taught by Marcantonio Raimondi.

Raimondi had been the first engraver in Italy to take up this brand new art of print-making: the first known etchings were only made early in the 16th century, in Augsburg; the earliest surviving etching is Swiss, dated 1513; Dürer's six between 1515 and 1518 – the last, a landscape including the figure of a Turk from Gentile Bellini's *Procession of the Holy Cross in St Mark's Piazza*, which Dürer had copied in watercolour during his first visit to Venice in 1495. Raimondi's forty etchings, most believed to have been done from his own designs, and some combined with engraving, were made at about the same time as Dürer's brief excursion into the new medium, allowing one to wonder whether there was an element of interchange here also.

Parmigianino, who had undoubtedly known Raimondi in Rome, would undoubtedly have found it useful to be able to learn the new art when he arrived in a strange city, just as Raimondi would have welcomed being able to help make ends meet by taking on such a talented student. Nevertheless Parmigianino, like Dürer and Raimondi, made etchings for only a limited time, producing only seventeen in all. And he had more trouble with his printer, Antonio da Trento, than he had had with the Germans: Antonio, Vasari says,

"opened a strong-box and robbed him of all the copper-plate engravings, woodcuts, and drawings that he possessed; and he must have gone off to the Devil, for all the news that was ever heard of him. The engravings and woodcuts, indeed, Francesco recovered...; but the drawings he was never able to get back".

Before the theft, Ugo da Carpi, one of Raimondi's main assistants in the Rome workshop, who had also returned to Bologna after the Sack of Rome, made a number of prints from Parmigianino's drawings; it is said he was involved in a workshop. Were they all working together for a time – Raimondi, Ugo da Carpi, Parmigianino? From what we have seen of Raimondi – highly talented, ambitious, a co-operative and congenial partner, and a risk-taker – he does not seem to be one who would just give up.

If he was indeed still living, Raimondi would surely have been involved also in Bologna's next starring event on the European scene. In 1528 Clement VII accepted that the Emperor had the better of him; in return for his freedom from the Castel Sant' Angelo and the restoration of his family in Florence (though it would be another three years before Vasari's schoolmate Alessandro de' Medici could be installed there), he agreed to meet Charles in Bologna the following year to consecrate him as Holy Roman Emperor.

By the time they reached Bologna in 1529 their attention would have been seized by events 600 kilometres to their north: the still expanding Ottoman Turks, who had finally destroyed Byzantium seventy-five years before – about the time of Francia's birth – had invaded southeast Europe and were besieging Vienna, though this time it was to be only briefly. It was the beginning of a reverse Crusade, by Moslems against Europe, which lasted another century and a half until after the failure of the next Ottoman siege of Vienna in 1683; its legacy is still capable of ripping the Balkan peninsula apart. But as the glittering cavalcades were leaving Bologna in 1530 they were still blissfully ignorant of another development that, like the Renaissance and Reformation, would also prove to be revolutionary: 350 kilometres further north from Venice, in Breslau [Wroclaw] in Poland, Nicolas Copernicus was finishing writing his *De revolutionibus orbis coelestium* proving that the Earth revolved around the Sun. It was banned by an outraged Church for two and a quarter centuries, and the relationship between Faith and Science has never recovered.

The Bologna meeting of Pope and Emperor was another occasion like that in 1506 when the artists congregated in hope of commissions, all the more now that the great Roman honey–pot had been destroyed by the Emperor's army. We know that Baccio Bandinelli was there, picking for himself an aristocratic family name to become eligible for a Papal knighthood; Sebastiano del Piombo, still accompanying the Pope, and making a drawing for a double portrait of the Pope and Emperor; Titian may have come down from Venice. Amico Aspertini, who had worked with Francesco Francia all those years before on the Bentivoglio Chapel, and who had spent all but a couple of the intervening years in Bologna, now had the standing to be selected, "with another artist", to design a triumphal arch for the entry into Bologna of the Pope and the Emperor.

Was Raimondi there? Could he, as an old colleague of Aspertini, have been that other artist?

One wonders if their model was the vast *Triumphal Arch* that the Emperor Charles's grandfather, Maximilian I, had commissioned in 1512 from Dürer,

> "after the manner of the '*arcus triumphales*' of the Roman Emperors in the City of Rome, of which some have been destroyed and some can still be seen".

It could well have been, because Maximilian's Arch was on *paper*, intended for wide circulation to spread his fame. Dürer was involved for three years in producing (with others) the 92 woodcut sheets of amazing architectural, symbolical and Imperial detail – and a reduced version of the King of Portugal's rhinoceros; when fitted together the sheets made an "Arch" over three metres high and almost as wide. Just afterwards Dürer also made an equally ornate two-sheet drawing, of Maximilian and his wife, Mary of Burgundy, on a carriage, as his contribution to an accompanying *Triumphal Procession*; when finally printed, but only in 1528, the year Dürer died, the whole 138 half-metre-high joined woodcut sheets stretched for *54 metres*. That commission, too, would have reached Bologna before his grandson's investiture. Dürer's admirers have had difficulty forgiving him for wasting his time on such frivolous undertakings, unworthy of the name of High Art.

Perhaps Charles, fighting the ambitious French, the aggressive Turks and the apostate Protestants, had less money for such things: his entry into Bologna with Clement only got a nine–metre–long commemoration. It was in a woodcut by Robert Péril, "a playing–card maker" from Liège, who was an eyewitness of the procession from San Petronio to San Domenico on 24 February 1530, the day after Charles' investiture by the Pope. (The only known copy, on parchment, is in Antwerp's Plantin-Moretus Museum).

Did Raimondi live until the Imperial investiture? Did he, too, witness that procession? Could he – at the end of thirty extraordinary years that had taken him from obscurity in Bologna, to fame at the very heart of the Vatican, and back again – have been invited to the feast given to celebrate the coronation?

If so, he would have found turkeys on the menu.

Portrait of Toyotomi Hideyoshi. Wikimedia

Japan

Toyotomi Hideyoshi:
Tea for one

A Japanese verse, known to every schoolchild, asks:

What if the bird will not sing?

Nobunaga answers,	"Kill it!"
Hideyoshi answers,	"Make it *want* to sing."
Ieyasu answers,	"Wait."

Eiji Yoshikawa: *Taiko*

Anyone with even the slightest acquaintance with Korea knows of the difficulties in its relations with one of its two great neighbours, the one it has become most like, Japan. This is not just the reflection of intense commercial competition. During our posting in Seoul between 1980 and 1984 it was abundantly apparent that the visceral current reality of Koreans' distrust and at times downright hostility was still securely anchored in experience of the brutal Japanese occupation of their country between 1905 and the end of World War II in 1945. Fortunately we were nowhere near the firing line in the latter, but many Australians were certainly in the fire. I could well understand Korean feelings: I was from just one Australian family that eventually suffered from Japanese brutality during that War.

But closer acquaintance revealed that Korean attitudes dated back even further, derived from the record and the folk history of attempts, in 1592 and again in 1597, by the unifier and first military dictator of Japan, Toyotomi Hideyoshi, to invade China...via Korea. How much Hideyoshi knew about China before embarking on this vainglorious and costly adventure is not clear: there had long been a strong religious and cultural flow from China to Japan; Hideyoshi might well have seen at the

Todai Temple in Nara the vast Shoso-in collection of artifacts from across the Silk Road and Tang China that had been collected by Japan's 8th century Emperor Shomu, objects from China's golden age which had had a strong influence on many of the Japanese decorative arts in which Hideyoshi himself had a keen interest. But contemporary political and military intelligence seem to have been altogether another story, and Hideyoshi's invasion armies did not get near to setting foot in China, stopped in their tracks in Korea. That the Koreans beat the Japanese on both land and sea, though at huge cost, forcing Hideyoshi to abandon his plans, was a succour to the unquenchable Korean spirit through the four 20th century decades which had turned out so disastrously differently.

We were surprised to learn that a relic of Hideyoshi's invasion still existed at the end of the 20th century. A close friend, the wife of a distinguished Japanese diplomat, introduced us, through her translation of and notes on a charming book, *The Heart Remembers Home*, to the other side of Hideyoshi: the dictatorial patron of the arts, who forcibly abducted Korean potters to Kyushu, Japan's southern-most island, to bring their sense of refinement to bowls for the increasingly fashionable tea ceremony, which he patronized. And Eileen Kato also introduced us to the delightful village of Naeshirogawa, not far from the volcano-shadowed city of Kagoshima, where, to our astonishment, we met working potters descended in fourteen generations from those shanghaied by Hideyoshi. This was another tale in which the brutality of the protagonist contrasted with his aesthetics; and in modern times there are eerie echoes of actions and attitudes that Hideyoshi adopted and provoked.

That earlier time of Japan's first foreign ambitions was also when, first, Hideyoshi's predecessor, then Hideyoshi himself cautiously began opening Japan to European ideas and technology, both brought by a series of remarkable Portuguese Jesuits vigorously following up their compatriots' opening of the Indian Ocean sea-route. The Portuguese fortunately recorded their intercourse with Hideyoshi until, first he, then subsequently, even more firmly, his successor slammed shut those gates to the outside world – gates that would remain shut until a century and a half ago when Japanese receptivity to some Western ideas and most technology was resumed with a vengeance. The Portuguese accounts, quite apart from the information they give about Hideyoshi himself, are a fascinating record of acute anxiety to learn about another people but incomprehension at some of the resultant knowledge, and of a sincere empathy with an absolute ruler (no doubt being a Jesuit helped) of a country for which the Jesuit Fathers in many ways evinced a profound distaste.

The principal people in this chapter are as follows:

- Oda Nobunaga (1534-1582) – Japanese warrior responsible for unifying half of Japan after a long period of feudal wars.

- **Toyotomi Hideyoshi** (c.1536-1598) – Feudal lord who completed the unification of Japan begun by Nobunaga. Chief Imperial minister from 1585-1598.

- Tokugawa Ieyasu (1543-1616) – Successor to Hideyoshi and founder of the Edo shogunate.

- Father Francis Xavier (1506-1552) – One of the founding members of the Jesuits. Spanish Jesuit missionary instrumental in the establishment of Christianity in India, the Malay archipelago and Japan. First Christian missionary in Japan from 1549-1551.

- Father Gaspar Coelho (unknown-1590) – Portuguese Jesuit, Superior and Vice-Provincial of the Jesuit mission to Japan from the 1560s until his death.

- Father Luiz Frois (1532-1597) – Portuguese Jesuit missionary to Japan, accompanying Father Coelho. Japanese speaker and author of History of Japan.

- Father Alessandro Valignano (1539-1606) – Italian Jesuit Visitor to the Portuguese missions in Asia, strongly supportive of adapting religious practices to local customs.

- Father Matteo Ricci (1552-1610) – Italian Jesuit missionary to the Imperial Court in Beijing from 1601-1610. Supported the adaptation of religious rites to to local languages and customs in China in what became known as the controversial issue of Chinese Rites.

Before the Portuguese Jesuits' fifty-year cross-cultural experience in Japan came to its abrupt and bloody end, Italian Jesuits began an equally extraordinary relationship with the Imperial court in Beijing that lasted nearly two centuries. Their knowledge of Western technology and willingness to reconcile Catholic theology with Confucian practices, together with a succession of Emperors' curiosity about Western science, marked the different approaches on both sides from those of their counterparts in Japan; at its best, John E. Wills Jr has observed, in China "neither side of this great encounter feared ambiguity or complexity".

We shall meet all three of the men in the Japanese children's verse, successive rulers of Japan: Oda Nobunaga (1534-1582), Hideyoshi's predecessor, whose military unification Hideyoshi completed; then Toyotomi Hideyoshi himself (c.1536-1598), in all his complexity; then, briefly, his successor, Tokugawa Ieyasu, in many ways a much more recognisable figure from the perspective of our time. And we shall see all three of the verse's answers as the answerers created a Japanese nation. But in truth the answers overlapped the answerers, and not least with Hideyoshi.

We meet Hideyoshi on 4 May 1586, in his fiftieth year, and hear him saying

> "...that he had reached the point of subjugating all Japan; whence his mind was...solely upon immortalising himself with the name and fame of his power; in order to do which he was resolved to reduce the affairs of Japan to order, and to place them on a stable basis; and, this done, to entrust them to his brother...while he himself should pass to the conquest of Korea and China, for which enterprise he was issuing orders for the sawing of planks to make two thousand vessels in which to transport his army. And for himself, he wished nothing from the [Jesuit] Fathers, except that through them he should get two great and well-equipped ships from the Portuguese, whom he would pay liberally for everything, giving the very best wages to their officers; and if he met his death in that undertaking he did not mind, inasmuch as it would be said that he was the first Lord of Japan who had ventured on such an enterprise; and if he succeeded, and the Chinese rendered obedience to him, he would not deprive them of their country, or remain in it himself; and because he only wished them to recognise him for their Lord, and that then he would build churches in all parts, commanding all to become Christians, and to embrace our Holy Law".

This is not an extract from a best-seller or a movie script about early modern Japan: it comes from a more-or-less verbatim report by the Portuguese Jesuit missionary Father Luiz Frois, who had accompanied the new Vice-Provincial of the Jesuit Mission to Japan, Father Gaspar Coelho, for his courtesy call on Toyotomi Hideyoshi, the *Kwampaku*, Regent for the figure–head Emperor at Kyoto, military dictator of Japan.[184]

The audience took place in Hideyoshi's great new castle stronghold in Osaka. Coelho, no doubt trying to impress Hideyoshi with something of the majesty of the Catholic Church, arrived at the Castle with a train of more than thirty people, with four other priests besides the interpreter Frois, three Japanese postulants and a gaggle of students from the seminary that had been founded several years earlier in Kyoto. The Jesuits were left in no doubt as to Hideyoshi's own majesty: at the end of the audience he personally conducted them on a tour of the castle-palace, guiding them from floor to floor, opening doors and windows "as if he were an ordinary householder", and giving a running commentary –

"Here you see this room full of gold, this of silver, that of silk and damask, that of clothing, that of swords and rich weapons".

And Frois added an intimate detail:

"Along all these floors and stairways, the *Kwampaku* was preceded by a richly dressed young girl who carried his sword on her shoulder, and with whom he joked from time to time".

Only a few weeks before, at Easter, Hideyoshi had turned up unannounced at the Jesuit Mission house in Osaka, poked his nose into everything as usual, and then made an expansive little speech:

"Well do I know that the Fathers are better than the Bonze [Buddhist abbot] of Osaka; for you maintain a different purity of life, and the filth in which he is so absorbed, and all the other Bonzes, is not your practice...I am pleased by everything this law of yours preaches..."

---

184 The Jesuits' reports are taken primarily from C.R.Boxer: *The Christian Century in Japan 1549–1650* and M.Cooper S.J.: *The Southern Barbarians*

- and then the twist in the tail:

> "...and I feel no other obstacle to becoming Christian than its
> prohibition against keeping many wives. If you stretched a point
> for me there, I would turn Christian myself".

A joke, no doubt, though the Jesuits must have thought: How near! Yet
how far! And they were never to give up hope, right to his deathbed.

Coelho was certainly justified in expecting a friendly reception at the
Castle on that 4th of May. But to have the Japanese military dictator pour
out his plans to a Portuguese Christian priest! Can you imagine Philip II
of Spain revealing his plans for the Armada to a visiting Japanese
Buddhist monk whom he had never set eyes on before? His military,
political and personal ambitions? Hideyoshi's were all there: the
immediate intention to reduce Kyushu, the southernmost of Japan's main
islands, essential for his control of Honshu as well as for a springboard
to the mainland; reduction of "the affairs of Japan to order", which he
was to achieve through the domination and strict stratification of the
feudal lords, the *daimyo*, the warrior *samurai* class and the peasantry
alike; the grandiose intention to launch an invasion of China, which
followed in six years' time, at the end of which he did indeed meet his
death – at home, in bed; and, not least, the intention to immortalise his
name and fame, which he sought not only in the pursuit of military and
political power but also increasingly in the display of his artistic
cultivation and cultural patronage.[185]

Then there was the spread of Christianity. The Jesuits must have
noticed that Hideyoshi spoke of the conversion of China, not of Japan.
And Vice-Provincial Coelho put his foot into this gap in a way which
assuredly led on to the abyss that was to follow.

The rise and rise of a nobody

Hideyoshi's origins were the most obscure of anyone who has ever
governed Japan during its millennium and a half of recorded history.
He began life, in 1536 or perhaps 1537, in the province of Mikawa
(southeast of Nagoya), and he may or may not have been called
Hiyoshimaru, possibly the son of a peasant, Kinoshita, who, like all the

---

185   The only two full non-Japanese biographies of Hideyoshi of which I am
aware are Elisseef and Berry, but this chapter also draws on other works listed
in the Bibliography.

Japanese peasantry, had only the one name; but, it was later reported, "he so resembled a monkey that everyone called him *Sarunosuke*".[186] The Japanese practice of adopting different names at different times of their lives, for social or other purposes (and which in some forms still continues), led in Hideyoshi's case to a bewildering array which was eventually overtaken by his titles. While still a child, Hiyoshimaru became Tokichiro, shortened to Tokichi about 1551 when he first became a humble soldier in the employ of a minor warlord. Around 1558 he entered the service (some say as sandal-bearer) of a more ambitious and, as it turned out, spectacularly more successful warlord, one Oda Nobunaga, with whom his name was to be forever linked – and changed his name again, or had it changed, to Kochiku. Some time in the early sixties "Hideyoshi" appeared as his given name, and it was to stay with him until the end.

By about 1565 he had adopted his father's "Kinoshita" as his family name, but in 1573 changed *that* to Hashiba, apparently a pure invention. In 1585, after he had succeeded Nobunaga as dictator and just after he had risen to the Regency, he changed his surname again, and for the last time, adopting "Toyotomi", composed of an auspicious combination of characters meaning "bountiful minister". It manifested not only the exalted status to which he had risen but also suggested his devotion to the Throne, an attitude he adopted and maintained to help overcome the stigma of his excessively humble origins in a highly stratified society.

The Emperors, though descended from the Sun Goddess, had long since been deprived of all power, not to mention revenue: at the beginning of the century a deceased emperor went unburied for six weeks for lack of funds. Unaccustomed even to the degree of purely formal respect displayed by Hideyoshi, the reigning Son of Heaven responded by endowing him with ever more honorific titles. First came *Kwampaku*, Regent, in 1585, the first Regent in Japan's history not related to the aristocratic Fujiwara family which had dominated Japan's golden age, the Heiean era, at the end of the first millennium CE. Hideyoshi, trying

---

186   It is at this point that Eiji Yoshikawa's wonderful novel *Taiko* (1967; tr. W.S.Wilson, Tokyo 1992), quoted at the head of this chapter, begins its account of Hideyoshi's rise; it concludes at the point where, three years after the assassination of Nobunaga, he reached supreme power following his accommodation with Ieyasu. This epic novel splendidly conveys the atmosphere surrounding Hideyoshi's ambitions and times, but, apart from the epigraph, I have not drawn on it for this chapter.

to cook up a fanciful connection, sat through interminable genealogical arguments between Fujiwara branches; at last, says the Japanese historian Yosoburo Takekoshi,

> "he got bored and told them that their discussions did not touch the point after all, and that he would rather have a new family name and become its founder than be a branch of such a confused house as the Fujiwara family".

So he became Toyotomi; but his own house lasted only twenty-nine years. Hideyoshi's next title, in 1586, was *Daijo-daijin*, Great Minister of State, the very top Court rank outside the imperial family. Finally, from 1591, when he ceded the Regency to his nephew in order to concentrate on his mainland invasion plans, he was entitled the *Taiko*, Retired Regent. This also remained with him for the rest of his life – as did his all-controlling power – and it how he is usually still known in Japan.

Despite this unprecedented rise in power and status, Hideyoshi remained acutely conscious of the obscurity of his origins. On 27 December 1593 he thus aimed for the ultimate ancestry, placing his golden seal on this document:

> "When I was about to enter my dear mother's womb, she had an auspicious dream. That night, the sunlight filled her room so that it was like noontime inside it. All were overwhelmed with astonishment. The attendants gathered, and the diviner proclaimed: 'This is a wondrous sign that when the child reaches his prime, his virtue will shine over the Four Seas, and he will radiate his glory to the Ten Thousand Directions' ".

Sun Goddess and Virgin Birth! But Hideyoshi continued to be called *Saru*, "Monkey", by Oda Nobunaga, his commander and mentor, until the latter's murder in 1582.

The cake
Only two (or three) years older than Hideyoshi, Nobunaga had begun the unification of Japan towards the end of a century of incessant civil war amongst endlessly changing combinations of local warlords, *daimyo*, some two hundred and sixty of them, who, as one of the Jesuit onlookers put it,

"promiscuously defraud and deceive each other in turn, with artifice, fraud and stratagem everywhere dominant".

Nobunaga had the advantage of being one of those petty lords to start with, albeit a minor one; and through a combination of skill and ruthlessness he had eliminated local rivals – including family members – and become master of his strategically-placed home province of Owari (around Nagoya) by 1559. He was then all of twenty-two, and the sandal-bearer Hideyoshi seems to have already become a trusted soldier. Two years later Nobunaga was joined by another young warrior, seven years Hideyoshi's junior, Tokugawa Ieyasu, who switched sides as his former lord was swept into oblivion by Nobunaga's seemingly inexorable progress.

These three, in succession, were to personally dominate Japanese history for the next fifty–five years. In addition to the verse quoted earlier about their characters, there was another old saying about their achievements: Oda Nobunaga prepared the dough; Toyotomi Hideyoshi baked the cake; and Tokugawa Ieyasu enjoyed eating it. There are others who say this seriously under-rated Ieyasu's achievement in establishing a regime which was to endure for two hundred and fifty years until the political and economic earthquake unleashed after Commodore Perry's visit in 1854. But it seems a fair enough summation of Nobunaga's and Hideyoshi's roles.

Nobunaga's military successes continued, helped increasingly by the tactical brilliance of the other two as they rose steadily through the ranks of junior commanders, and in 1568 he captured the imperial capital of Kyoto. Never a dissimulator, there he adopted, on his seal, the motto "Rule the Empire by Force". He did not yet by any means have the whole Empire: more than fifty of Japan's provinces, in Kyushu and both western and eastern Honshu, remained under the control of greater or lesser but mostly hostile warlords. Even within the swath of a dozen or so central provinces now controlled by Nobunaga there were powerful centres of resistance in the major Buddhist monasteries, especially at the important temple complex of Hieizan, just northeast of Kyoto, and the great castle-monastery of Honganji at Osaka. These religious establishments were military powers in their own right, their votaries more like the orders of Christian Crusader knights than the "gentle Buddhists" so often envisioned by Westerners; and they engaged to the full in the cabals and treacheries confronting Nobunaga's drive for unification.

For reasons that are not entirely clear, Nobunaga had a greater hatred for his Buddhist than for most of his other opponents; perhaps it was simply that he found the gap between their beliefs and their actions unacceptably hypocritical. In any event it led him to detest their religion also, and the Portuguese Fathers were to benefit from this through his tolerance of their activities, if not the conversion for which they so ardently longed: the Nobunaga who rejected all forms of Eastern religion was not about to adopt a Western one.

In 1571 he gathered his forces and alliances to make his first strike against the warrior-bonzes, at Hieizan, the fountain–head of Japanese Buddhism. Frois himself reported from first-hand accounts, with cool detachment, that as Nobunaga approached with an army of thirty thousand men the bonzes sought to buy him off; but he declared that "he had not come there to enrich himself with gold but to punish their crimes with all severity and rigour". When the bonzes heard this reply, Frois says,

"although they knew that Nobunaga had but scant respect for the [gods], they still did not believe that he would destroy the idol of Sanno, for it is greatly venerated and its punishments were no less feared. And so for this reason they all decided to gather in the temple (which is on the top of the mountain) and to abandon all the other monasteries and their treasures. At the same time the bonzes persuaded the people of the [dependent] town of Sakamoto to go up as well with their womenfolk and children.

Knowing that he had them all on the top of the mountain, Nobunaga immediately gave orders to set fire to Sakamoto... And in order to show the bonzes who were up the mountain the little regard he paid to the chimeras (which they had described to him) of the punishments of Sanno, the second thing he did was to burn all the temples of this idol which were below the foot of this mountain...Then deploying his army of 30,000 men in the form of a ring around the mountain, he gave the order to advance to the top. The bonzes began to resist with their weapons and wounded about 150 soldiers. But they were unable to withstand such a furious assault and were all put to the sword, together with the men, women and children of Sakomoto...

The next day, the last in September and the Feast of the glorious St Jerome, they burnt down the large temple of Sanno, which, as I have said, was on the top of the mountain. Then Nobunaga ordered a large number of musketeers to go out into the hills and woods as if on a hunt; should they find any bonzes hiding there, they were not to spare the life of a single one of them. And this they duly did."

A Japanese contemporary wrote: "The whole mountainside was a great slaughterhouse, and the sight was one of unbearable horror". At Hieizan Nobunaga showed no mercy to his opponents; and Father Frois showed no compassion to his.

The decade of the seventies went on with seemingly endless battles, endless manoeuvrings, endless massacres. Nobunaga's reputation for ruthlessness increased with his successes. It was reported that, at the 1574 New Year celebration he received a lacquer box containing the severed heads of three of his enemies, and that he was delighted with the gift. This is a startling perspective on another time; but although the method of presentation might differ, it is an atrocity we have seen before in this book, and will see again. We change little, it seems.

The only surprise throughout those years was the fate of the Honganji fortress-monastery, besieged for some six years and increasingly isolated from the support of others resisting Nobunaga: in mid-1580 an Advice from the Throne, conveyed by Imperial Messenger, resulted in its surrender, without bloodshed, and without loss of face for either besieged or besiegers. It is not surprising that the Emperor acted on the advice of Nobunaga; but it is surprising that Nobunaga was prepared to allow a peaceful outcome at a point where the warrior-bonzes were close to being starved into submission. He showed no such moderation in his last great battle, in 1581, against the Takeda *daimyo* of Suruga, Kai and Shinano provinces west-northwest of Edo (now Tokyo), whom he overwhelmed with massive and violent force, eliminating them and their followers with an insane hatred: even the bonzes of the temple housing the remains of his principal Takeda opponent were roasted to death over a huge bonfire.

By the beginning of 1582 Nobunaga was master of twenty-nine of the sixty-six provinces that made up Japan at that time. Throughout central Honshu there was finally peace, after a century of anarchy, under his military dictatorship. Although he took no special titles – unlike Hideyoshi, who couldn't seem to get enough – he nevertheless took a step that really scandalised Father Frois:

"Thus he finally decided to imitate the temerity and insolence of Nabuchodonosor, demanding that everyone should worship him not as a human and mortal man but as if he were divine and the lord of immortality. In order to carry out his wicked and abominable desire, he commanded a temple to be built next to his palace near the mountain fortress [of Azuchi, on Lake Biwa, to the east of Kyoto] and there he wrote out the aim of his poisonous ambition. Translated from Japanese...it ran as follows:

In this great kingdom of Japan, Nobunaga, Lord of All Japan, has erected this temple called Sochenji at Azuchiyama Castle on this mountain, which, even when seen from afar, causes joy and happiness to all those who behold it. The rewards and benefits which are to be gained by those who worship him with awe and devotion are as follows:

1. *Rich people who come here to worship will acquire even greater wealth; poor and wretched people who come here to worship will also become rich as a reward for visiting this temple. Those who have no children or heirs to carry on their line will soon have descendants and will enjoy a long life with much peace and rest.*
2. *Their lives will be lengthened to 80 years of age, they will be cured of their ailments, their desires and longings will be realised, they will have peace.*

The day on which I was born will be observed every month [Frois says later that it was once a year] *as a solemn and regular festival on which to visit this temple. All who have faith need have no doubt that these promises will be fulfilled; the wicked and unbelievers will be condemned to hell both in this life and the next. I therefore repeat that it is essential that everybody should show the deepest reverence and veneration.*

As I have already mentioned," Frois continued, "Nobunaga always made little account of the cult and worship of [Shinto and Buddhism] during his reign. But now it seems that he reached the limit of his blindness, for the devil persuaded him to issue orders that the statues which were most venerated and visited by pilgrims throughout Japan should be brought to this temple; he did this, not that the statues might be worshipped, but that with this pretext he might increase his own cult."

This was not at all what the Jesuit Fathers had had in mind in seeking to get closer to Nobunaga and his leading vassals; but one might wonder whether the annual celebration of his birth was an idea he might have picked up from their teaching. Hideyoshi never went this far – notwithstanding the sun's annunciation to his mother.

But Nobunaga's divinity was insufficient to the temper of the time. On 20 June 1582, in a demonstration of the cultural sophistication that was expected of all true *samurai*, he hosted a large gathering of his leading nobles and warriors at the Honnoji, his fortified monastery-residence in Kyoto; the occasion was a tea ceremony, but the purpose was as much to display a selection of the rare and prestigious tea implements he had been collecting – or extorting from other collectors – since before his capture of Kyoto fourteen years ago. Neither Hideyoshi nor Ieyasu was in Kyoto at the time. Before dawn the following day, Akechi Mitsuhide, a general of the same level and background as Hideyoshi, turned on his leader, for reasons that are unknown if they went beyond simple brute ambition. As it happens, Father Frois was nearby:

"As our church in [Kyoto] is situated only a street away from the place where Nobunaga was staying, some Christians came just as I was vesting to say an early Mass, and told me to wait because there was a commotion in front of the palace and that it seemed to be something serious as fighting had broken out there. We at once began to hear musket shots and see flames. After this another report came, and we learned that it had not been a brawl but that Akechi had turned traitor and enemy of Nobunaga and had him surrounded. When Akechi's men reached the palace gates, they at once entered as nobody was there to resist them because there had been no suspicion of treachery. Nobunaga had just washed his hands and face and was drying himself with a towel when they found him and forthwith shot him with an arrow. Pulling the arrow out, he came out carrying a *naginata*, a weapon with a long blade made after the fashion of a scythe. He fought for some time, but after receiving a shot in the arm he retreated into his chamber and shut the doors.

Some say that he cut his belly, while others believe that he set fire to the palace and perished in the flames. What we do know, however, is that of this man, who made everyone tremble not only at the sound of his voice but even at the mention of his name, there did not remain even a small hair which was not reduced to dust and ashes".

And also, Japanese historians sadly recorded, the precious tea implements, the tea caddy called *Tsukumogami*, the water jar known as *Matsushima*...

There is something chilling in Frois's cold account: this was a man he knew personally, the most powerful man amongst these people whose lives he and his fellow Jesuits were trying to radically change, a man who had been interested in them and even shown them a degree of support. Was this man, in the end, like the people at Hieizan, just another dead pagan?

The cook

In 1573, after a series of victories, Nobunaga had rewarded Hideyoshi with lands in Omi province, just east of Kyoto, a singular mark of confidence and a major promotion for the young general; with the building of his first castle, Hideyoshi was clearly now *samurai* and at the forefront of Nobunaga's armies. During the remainder of the decade his military skills were increasingly in evidence, along with those of Tokugawa Ieyasu, and both were rewarded as time went on with further promotions and appanages. At the time of Nobunaga's assassination, Ieyasu was on leave somewhere south of Osaka; Hideyoshi was invading Bitchu province (between Fukuyama and Okayama in the latter present-day prefecture), pushing Nobunaga's power further west than it had ever been, though at the moment facing a more powerful force of the Mori clan than his own army could comfortably cope with.

Hideyoshi was considerably further from Kyoto than Ieyasu, but his intelligence system was better and his instincts sharper. By the night of 22 June, the day after Nobunaga's death, he had received the news. Keeping it secret, he immediately arranged a truce with the Mori, and by the night of the 24th was back at the great Castle of Himeji, a distance of 110 kilometres. From there, and raising what forces he could as he went, he pushed on towards the capital, near which, on 30 June, he overwhelmed Akechi, who was killed as he fled. The would-be ruler had lasted ten days. Hideyoshi displayed his head in the ruins of Honnoji to assuage Nobunaga's spirit.

On hearing the news of the assassination, Ieyasu had made a dangerous journey through the bandit-infested Kii Peninsula and across Ise Bay to his home province of Mikawa, where he could raise troops; but his continued absence from Kyoto meant that he played no part in the early succession to Nobunaga – Hideyoshi had a clear field. Hideyoshi was certainly now in a strong position, but he proceeded with great care and adroitness: finessing Nobunaga's family while confirming Nobunaga's laws; sharing with other leading generals castles and provinces that had been under Nobunaga's direct rule, while making sure that they moved to areas where they had no traditional authority; ensuring that Ieyasu, his only possible rival in the inner circle, was kept informed of the end of Akechi and the aftermath, while assuring him that his military assistance was not required. But many must have held their breath – and withheld their loyalties – as both sides maintained the stand-off for the remainder of 1582, through the whole of 1583 and into 1584. Then Ieyasu's dissatisfaction with his situation resulted in his patience cracking: under pressure from Nobunaga's remaining son making his last fling, his forces participated in two small engagements against Hideyoshi's – both indecisive, but in which Hideyoshi had the advantage.

It was then that Hideyoshi showed how different he was from Nobunaga. Whereas the latter would undoubtedly have sought to eliminate Ieyasu and his followers as completely as possible, Hideyoshi was not too proud to seek an arrangement with his opponent. Ieyasu, suspicious at first, in due course also decided to avoid bloodshed, and came to terms early in 1585. With Hideyoshi treating Ieyasu with special consideration, and Ieyasu exercising remarkable patience, the alliance between the two remained firm until Hideyoshi's death thirteen years later.

Although it was only now that Hideyoshi became Nobunaga's clear successor, he had already continued the latter's drive for unification on both the military and civil fronts. Administratively he launched a series of programs (in some cases broadening earlier Nobunaga initiatives) designed to strengthen central control – *his* control – over Japan in a way that had never previously existed, and scarcely been thought possible. They continued throughout his rule, gradually strengthening central power at the expense of all levels of society, and implemented simultaneously with military campaigns designed to bring more and more of the country within the scope of that power.

Hideyoshi's moves started with the construction of a great castle at Osaka (predecessor of the present one) for his headquarters, powerfully fortified and well-placed to control the approaches to the capital, and luxuriously fitted out with great artworks no doubt intended to excel those of Nobunaga's Azuchi. At the same time he ordered the dismantling of all other castles but those of his chief supporters, to undermine the subversive capacities of the turbulent petty warlords who had contributed so much to the anarchy of the past century.

Also starting in the first couple of years, he instituted a national land survey – only finally completed the year of his death – designed to impose a unified system of land tenure and taxation, to reach "to the recesses of the mountains and by sea as far as can be reached by oars" throughout the entire country; thus would he bring the farm population, eighty percent of the whole, under his discipline and, with a produce tax of "two [measures] to the prince and one to the people" (as he laid down), tie them to the soil to give the ruler control of the food supply.

A further tightening in the same direction, but with a sharper military purpose, was the "Sword Hunt", a compulsory weapons amnesty he ordered in 1588. Hideyoshi's edict stated:

"1. Farmers of all provinces are strictly forbidden to have in their possession any swords, short swords, bows, spears, firearms, or other types of weapons. If unnecessary implements of war are kept, the collection of annual rent may become more difficult, and without provocation uprisings can be fomented...

2. The swords and short swords collected in the above manner will not be wasted. They will be used as nails and bolts in the construction of the Great Image of Buddha [in Kyoto]. In this way, farmers will benefit not only in this life but also in the lives to come.

3. If farmers possess only agricultural implements and devote themselves exclusively to cultivating the fields, they and their descendants will prosper. This compassionate concern for the well-being of the farmers is the reason for the issuance of this edict, and such a concern is the foundation for the peace and security of the country and the joy and happiness of all the people...".

The sword lobby of the day had to content themselves with the prospect of benefit in lives to come; but the promise did not pay off: both the *Daibutsuden*, the Great Buddha Hall of *Hoko-ji* temple, and its huge lacquered wooden image of the *Vairochana* Buddha, some forty metres high, were both destroyed by earthquake shortly after completion in 1595.[187] Others may well have found that the measure's contribution to stability was worth the restriction on the age-old habit of peasant uprisings. Hideyoshi would also seem to have been preventing the emergence of another Hideyoshi from the peasantry. Surely he did not fear such a threat to himself; but did his sense of his "name and fame" induce him to try to ensure his own uniqueness?

And, finally, he dealt with the *daimyo*: in 1595 he ordered

> "1. The *daimyo*, when contracting marriage among their houses, must first receive the approval [of Hideyoshi himself], and then proceed to complete the arrangement.
> 2. The *daimyo* and *shomyo* [lesser lords] are gravely warned that it is strictly forbidden to enter into contract or swear an oath among themselves..."

...and there were rules about who may use a palanquin. There were few details he did not oversee.

By now his control of the country and of all classes in it was such that it scarcely required edicts to maintain it: he was, in effect, legislating the future structure of Japan, and his successors of the Tokugawa Shogunate did indeed adopt and develop Hideyoshi's design. In parallel, he had been waging relentless campaigns against those *daimyo* who were still outside central control at the death of Nobunaga. His moves were carefully planned and meticulously executed, ensuring that his rivals did not coalesce so as to pick them off one by one. Within a year of Nobunaga's assassination he had increased the number of provinces under his control from the twenty his predecessor had taken twenty years to subdue by another twenty adjoining central Honshu. An early

---

187 The *Vairochana* Buddha is known in Japan as the Cosmic Buddha, with the title Great Sun - not, one imagines, an accidental choice by Hideyoshi among Buddha's many manifestations. The *Daibutsuden* (reproduced from a screen in Hickman: *Japan's Golden Age*, p.18) measured 81 x 50 metres and 45 metres high; 62,000 workmen were involved in the construction. Apart from the enormous stone foundations, according to Kinoshita and Palevsky, all else that remains is the huge bell (4.4m high, 2.8m in diameter) cast by Hideyoshi's son and successor Hideyori, with an inscription insulting the Tokugawa by comparison with the Toyotomi; Tokugawa Ieyasu used it as an excuse to attack Osaka Castle in 1615 and destroy Hideyori and the Toyotomi line (see below).

campaign was against the warrior-Buddhist holdouts left over from Nobunaga's ruthless suppressions: Negoro was reduced to ashes but without a massacre; Koyasan was addressed thus:

> "The monks have neglected their religious studies. It is treason and wicked to make and accumulate insane arms as they have done, muskets and the rest...After having seen with your own eyes that Hieizan and Negoro temple were eventually destroyed for having set themselves against the Crown, you will readily understand".

The bonzes readily understood – they surrendered immediately, and kept their heads. Shikoku, the smallest of Japan's four main islands, quickly followed. The Mori, dominant in most of the rest of western Honshu, stuck to the agreement reached with Hideyoshi the day after Nobunaga's murder, and gradually became firm and acquiescent allies, though it was a Mori's treason after Hideyoshi's death that doomed his heir.

As Hideyoshi told Father Coelho on 4 May 1586, the way was now open to Kyushu. But northern Kyushu was the stronghold of the Portuguese missionaries in Japan; and Father Coelho's use of that fact on that day, in what he thought would be helpful to the Church, turned out to be a blunder that undermined the whole Portuguese and Christian position in Japan.

The arrival of the Europeans

The Portuguese had discovered Japan in 1543; blown off course by a storm, three of its merchants trading the China coast were the first Europeans known to have ever to set foot in the country – actually, the small island of Tanegashima, off the southern tip of Kyushu. These accidental Europeans there and then introduced the first Western custom to influence the island nation: the use of firearms – arquebuses at the time. For the next sixty years firearms would be known in Japan as "Tanegashima guns", not just because that was where they first appeared, but because that was where Japanese immediately began copying and manufacturing them on their own.

Europeans had scarcely known that the country even existed: there had only been two previous references to it in European literature. The first was in Marco Polo's sometimes suspected *Travels*, which first became public about 1320:

"Chipangu is an Island towards the east [from China] in the high seas, 1500 miles distant from the Continent; and a very great Island it is.

The people are white, civilised, and well-favoured. They are Idolators, and are dependent on nobody. And I can tell you the quantity of gold they have is endless...few merchants visit the country because it is so far from the main land, and thus it comes to pass that their gold is abundant beyond all measure";

And Marco goes on (as usual) about the Palace of the Lord of that Island, all made of solid gold – the roof, the windows (!), the floors "like slabs of stone, a good two fingers thick". Then silence for a century and a half until the Florentine astronomer, Paolo Toscanelli, suggested to the King of Portugal and Christopher Columbus, in about 1480, that golden Chipangu could be reached by sailing west across the Atlantic. Then "Cipango" appeared as a large island, in the west of an Atlantic Ocean bounded in the east by Europe and Africa and in the west by Cathay and India, on a map produced by the German cartographer Martin Behaim in 1490. It is not known whether Columbus saw this; but his list of destinations already included Chipangu, along with Cathay and the Spice Islands; and in 1492 he was convinced he had found it, duly naming the island of Hispaniola (Haiti) "Chipangu".

The other reference was less well known than Marco Polo's: to the island of "Jampon" in a book about the Orient written about 1515 by a Portuguese official, Tomé Pires, apparently the first European use of this name, which he picked up from Malay traders in Southeast Asia. And after Tomé Pires, further silence. Both *Chipangu* and *Jampon* (soon to become Japan) derived from the Chinese *Jih–pen–kuo*, "Land of the Rising Sun", itself from the Japanese *Nihon-koku* or *Nippon-koku*. (This is all quite straightforward by comparison with some of Japan's ancient names for itself, such as *Toyo-ashi-wara-no-chi-aki-no-naga-I-ho-aki-no-mizu-ho-no-kuni*, "Luxuriant-Reed-Plains-the-Land-of-Fresh-Rice-Ears-of-a-Thousand-Autumns-of-Long-Five-Hundred-Autumns".) The Chinese had of course known about Japan for centuries, traded with it, twice tried to invade it (under Marco Polo's supposed patron, the Mongol Kublai Khan, in 1274 and again in 1281), suffered from its pirates. But, as with Cathay and China, it was to be a long time before any European realized that Chipangu and Jampon referred to the same place.

Although it has been claimed that Columbus sailed west to find Marco Polo's Chipangu, it says something about how Marco's story was regarded that on the other hand not even the Portuguese went chasing after his land of gold: after all, in a succession of extraordinary explorations in search of trade and treasure, they had pushed further and further east after rounding the Cape of Good Hope for the first time in 1498, capturing Goa in India in 1510, Malacca on the west coast of the Malay peninsula in 1511, reaching the Moluccas and China in 1513, and sending an embassy to Peking in 1519 – though diplomatic efforts were somewhat discouraged when the ambassador, poor Tomé Pires, and his retinue were thrown into jail at Canton on their way back, for the rest of their lives. Despite this prodigious effort, and continuing exploration up the coast of China by intrepid and skilful Portuguese navigators, it was still another quarter of a century before someone was accidentally blown into Tanegashima by a storm. It was rather like the equally intrepid and skilful north Atlantic Vikings' discovery half a millennium earlier of both Greenland and the North American continent only when blown off-course in storms.

The clerics

But unlike the Vikings, who were uncharacteristically dilatory in following up their accidental discoveries, the news of the Tanegashima landing set off a flurry of expeditions by merchants from the Portuguese possessions in Asia: they sailed, one of them remarked, "against the wind, against the monsoon, against the tide, and against reason". By 1544 they reached Kyushu itself; and one merchant brought back to Malacca a *samurai* called Yajiro, who in 1547 was by chance introduced to the Spanish missionary working under Portuguese auspices, Father Francis Xavier, one of the co-founders in 1540 of the Jesuit Order, the future "Apostle of the Indies" and Catholic Saint.[188] Thus began, again by accident, the second European export to Japan: Christianity. Like the manufacture of firearms, it soon became something of an industry.

It was part of the extraordinary spread of the Jesuits as missionaries and educators not only throughout Catholic Europe and America but everywhere else where they could establish themselves through their carefully-honed combination of an intellectual as well as theological knowledge, a surprising degree of responsiveness to new cultural

---

188 "Clerks Regular of the Society of Jesus" were not called "Jesuits" until 1544 - and then mostly satirically by Jean Calvin, the intolerant French non-conformist theologian and briefly dictator of a theocratic city of Geneva. Before long, however, it became a badge of honour.

backgrounds, and an adamantine certainty in the correctness of all they thought, said and did. Some of Hideyoshi's greatest contemporaries were among their targets, though two in Asia sought them out. In India, the second and perhaps greatest Moghul Emperor, Akbar, forever intellectually curious, seems to have taken the initiative by making contact in 1573 with Jesuits working in Bengal; and, certainly, in 1580 he invited Jesuits to join the extraordinary Thursday evening debates he had initiated between Moslem theologians and subsequently expanded to include Hindus and Parsis (Zoroastrians). In Persia, the great Safavid Shah Abbas I sent an emissary to the Pope in 1601 seeking an alliance against the Ottoman Turks and requesting priests for his Catholic subjects; but a first Jesuit mission was undermined for some reason by the Portuguese Viceroy at Goa, leaving it to the Carmelites to establish a mission in Isfahan in1607. In China, meanwhile, the remarkable Father Matteo Ricci had established himself, as we shall see later, at the Imperial Court in Beijing by 1601.

Japan was the earliest: Father Francis Xavier visited there between 1549 and 1551, landing at Kagoshima, capital of the Satsuma *daimyo* in the south of Kyushu, and travelling as far as Kyoto in the hope of Christianizing the entire country through the conversion of the Emperor. But he found Kyoto a wasteland from the *daimyo's* internecine wars and the depredations of the monks of Hieizan; the Emperor was powerless and penniless, reduced to occasionally selling autographed verses or precious tea ceremony utensils; and consequently Xavier re-focused, accurately, on the *daimyo*, the territorial warlords, as the main objectives of Christian missionary work. Xavier liked what he found right from the beginning:

"The people whom we have met so far," he wrote, "are the best who have as yet been discovered, and it seems to me that we shall never find among heathens another race to equal the Japanese...

They are people of very good will, very sociable, and very desirous of knowledge; they are very fond of hearing about things of God, chiefly when they understand them".

That last little caveat was of some importance: Xavier spoke not a word of Japanese, though it was said that his dignity and manifest honesty contributed to his achievement. So did the help of the now-converted Yajiro, and together they secured the conversion of some thousand people, principally in the southern and northeastern Kyushu provinces of

Satsuma and Bungo, and in Yamaguchi in the extreme west of Honshu. The problem was to remain: many a later foreign visitor would share a subsequent Jesuit's disappointed hope that "Our Lord would help us, as he did the primitive Church, by granting the gift of tongues and miracles".

However Portuguese interest in Japan was as much in commerce as in conversion, and right from the beginning the Japanese evinced a sharp appreciation of the connection: missionary activity by the Portuguese Jesuits would be allowed because Portuguese traders could ensure the regular provision of high-quality Chinese silks and other valued imports – including the new-fangled firearms, though within a few years the Japanese were themselves manufacturing sufficient to meet their considerable needs. Xavier's most important successor, Father Alessandro Valignano,[189] the Italian Jesuit Visitor to the Portuguese missions in Asia, was to write in 1580 on his first visit:

"For as the lords of Japan [the *daimyo*] are very poor...and the benefits they derive when the ships come to their ports are very great, they try hard to entice them to their fiefs. And since they have convinced themselves that they will come to where there are Christians and churches, and whither the padres wish them to come, it therefore follows that many of them, even though they are heathen, seek to get the padres to come thither and to secure churches and converts, thinking that by this means the ships will secure other favours they wish to obtain from the padres".

Following Xavier's visit, missionary activity was put on an increasingly organised basis, focused primarily in Kyushu and western Honshu; it was only in 1560 that permission was given to establish a church in Kyoto itself. With the conversion of *daimyo* in western Japan, the

---

189   Valignano (1539-1606) was ordained priest in Rome in 1570, and only three years later was appointed Visitor to the Jesuit missions in the Indies, which included Japan and China (Macao only at that time) as well as India. The appointment to India ended in 1595, but he remained in charge of Japan (which he visited three times) and China (where Father Matteo Ricci established missions in the south from 1582 and in Beijing in 1601) until his death in Macao in 1606. He was instrumental in keeping the Japan and China missions supplied with new priests, to the extent the local authorities permitted - and, if possible, beyond - and strongly supportive, as we shall see, of adapting as much as possible to local customs.

number of those who were claimed to be Christian increased markedly, though Valignano himself conceded (in the same letter) that

> "...since the Japanese are so much at the disposal of their lords, they readily become converted when told to do so by their lords and they think it is their wish. This is the door by which entered most of those who were baptised in the beginning...;
>
> ...and since they are white and of good understanding and behaviour, and greatly given to outward show, they readily frequent the churches and sermons, and when they are instructed they become very good Christians, albeit the lords who have an eye on the main chance and are so preoccupied with warfare are usually the worst".

Three years later his perspective had changed:

> "If the Portuguese would pay more consideration to the service of Our Lord and less to their own purely selfish interests, and would go one year to one port and the next year to another, in conformity with the decision of the local Jesuit superior, the whole of that Christianity [in Kyushu] could be controlled very easily and smoothly...
>
> Since we cannot now force the captain-majors [the officials in command of what after 1550 was the government-regulated annual great trading vessel, the Black Ship] to go into the ports that we wish, it seems both necessary and expedient that we should obtain a brief from His Holiness [the Pope], forbidding the Portuguese, on pain of excommunication, to enter the ports of lords who persecute Christianity or who are reluctant to allow their vassals to be converted. For the Portuguese would lose none of their profits thereby, whereas we could raise up or pull down the *daimyo*".

Valignano's impractical effort failed: economic rationalism won. He had in fact already been undermined by the first Christian *daimyo*, Omura Sumitada, a minor Kyushu warlord who in 1567 had offered the Portuguese the use of his little fishing port of Nagasaki. Its advantages for shipping were such that three years later it had become the official port for all the Black Ships from Macao, as well as the Jesuits' base and the major centre of Christianity in Japan, though the fact that it was not a territorial concession caused Valignano to point out that the Japanese could not be treated like the Indians:

> "For we have no jurisdiction whatsoever in Japan, nor can we compel them to do anything which they do not wish to do, other than by pure persuasion and force of argument; they will not suffer being slapped or beaten, nor imprisonment, nor any similar methods commonly used with other Asiatic Christians, for they are so punctilious that they will not brook even a single harsh or impolite word...".

Valignano was the apostle of trying to get his missionaries to succeed by adapting wherever possible to Japanese ways. But pure persuasion and force of argument turning out to be so manifestly inadequate to achieve his objectives, and his frustration at having to remain subject to a Japanese overlord so great, that he added:

> "If we could govern these places [such as Nagasaki] with true Japanese severity, killing whenever necessary, they would be much more useful to us than they are now".

If these views indicate a brutal, and for Valignano, uncharacteristic, colonialism, it must be remembered that they amounted to no more than Church practice in Europe itself, particularly following the schism that Martin Luther had precipitated six decades earlier. But even without the leverage of any temporal power of their own, the very prospect of the Jesuits "raising up or pulling down" the *daimyo* was eventually to prove their Achilles' heel.

Jesuit perceptions of the Japanese

The Christian, mostly Portuguese Jesuit, mission in Japan over the century following St Francis Xavier's pioneering visit was little more than a minor episode in Japanese historical development: the great unification campaigns and administrative reforms undertaken by Oda Nobunaga, Toyotomi Hideyoshi and Tokugawa Ieyasu, which were virtually coterminous with the mission's active life, were of vastly greater significance in determining the nature of the Japanese state and the direction of its policies. What gave the Jesuit mission its unique historical value are the observations made by the Fathers on many aspects of Japan and the Japanese during that time, as well as some of their reports about the three great players on the contemporary stage of Japanese history – the public acts and the revealing intimacies.

Some of their comments on the Japanese character suggest interesting comparisons with images of Japan at various times during the past century since its final emergence onto the world stage. These early European visitors were struck in particular by three aspects of the Japanese people: their extraordinary politeness, to one another as well as to foreigners; their lively curiosity about the Europeans and their homelands and "ingenuity in learning new ways"; and their ruthlessness and bellicosity. These sound surprisingly like some modern stereotypes; but they were written by men who were seeing the Japanese during the second half of the sixteenth century with few preconceptions about what characteristics they would find – other than, of course, the spiritual ignorance common to all those who had not yet received the Church's teaching.

A Portuguese ship's captain, Jorge Alvarez, visiting southernmost Kyushu only two years after the Tanegashima landing, commented on politeness: the Japanese were extremely formal, punctiliously observed every detail of propriety and the strict rules governing relations between superiors and inferiors, esteemed self–abnegation and self–control, always spoke deferentially in a near whisper. Valignano, making implicit comparisons in his 1580 report with non-Europeans who were the focus of missionary zeal elsewhere – Central and South America, India, the Southeast Asian "Spice Islands" – commented likewise:

> "The people are all white [Valignano was transfixed by the prevalent European notion that white skin conferred its own virtue], courteous and highly civilised, so much so that they surpass all the other known races of the world...they are the most affable people and a race more given to outward marks of affection than any yet known".

Frois, making for a European a more significant comparison, had previously gone even further, writing to his superiors in Rome and Portugal of the Japanese that

> "In their culture, deportment and manners, they excel the Spaniards in so many ways that one is ashamed to tell about it"

- though not entirely, if one were Portuguese.

On one thing, however, the Jesuits were unbendingly censorious: homosexual behaviour. In 1549, in one of his first letters from Japan, Francis Xavier had expressed his shock at the bonzes' casual use of boys for sexual pleasure:

> "The evil is simply become a habit, the [Buddhist] priests are drawn to sins against nature and don't deny it, they acknowledge it openly. This evil, furthermore, is so public, so clear to all, men and women, young and old, and they are so used to it that they are neither depressed nor horrified".

Thirty years later, Father Valignano, admitting that young Japanese studying in Jesuit houses "lived such unhappy lives", and concerned still about what he called "the corrupt character of the people (beyond that corruption to which we are all naturally prone)", prescribed that the students should have their tatamis separated by wooden benches, and that a light should be kept burning all night.

The number of willing students no doubt contributed to the Portuguese being particularly impressed by Japanese curiosity about themselves and all things European – including their religion. The Buddhist monks, with whom the missionaries shared an attitude of active mutual hostility, tried to discourage the latter; and conversions in the *samurai* class were not always helped by what was regarded as unseemly missionary concern for the outcasts of society. In addition, from the time of Francis Xavier himself, questioning by curious laymen was not necessarily to the Jesuits' advantage: like many Europeans before and since, there were those who had trouble with the existence of evil in a world created by God's goodness, and above all, in Japan, with the eternal condemnation to Hell of revered ancestors who had never had the opportunity to know about this new Christian God – let alone why such a supposedly good and all-merciful one would have concealed himself from those ancestors in the first place. But of course pagan ignorance was still of a different order from Protestant apostasy.

For their part, the Jesuits themselves – with the exception of a few chauvinists like Father Francisco Cabral, Provincial of the Order in Japan between 1570 and 1580 – made a remarkable effort to adapt to Japanese ways, in dress and manners, and to learn as much as possible of Japanese life, customs and of course language, in the justifiable belief that such accommodation would facilitate the entry of their faith into

Japanese hearts and minds.[190] It was a practice to be adopted with even greater success in China, at least as far as access right up to the level of the Emperor was concerned; but the Church and Jesuit authorities in Rome maintained the uneasy suspicion that, in both countries, "going native" was more conducive to worldly comfort than religious zeal.

The most famous instance of Japanese curiosity experienced by the missionaries was Hideyoshi's visit to the Jesuits' house in Osaka that Easter of 1586 which opened this chapter. Father Coelho, somewhere between impressed and amused, said

> "he doubtless wished to take them by surprise so that he could inspect the cleanliness and neatness of our houses, because he is a great enemy of dirt and disorder..." [as were the Japanese generally, at a time when Europeans scarcely noticed, and still thought regular bathing injurious to the health]. "He went along to look at the clock, and he also saw a harpsichord and viol which we have in the house. He had them both played and took great delight in listening to their music...After that he went to see the bell and other curious things which the Fathers keep in that house".

The Jesuits' possessions were not there by accident, Coelho noted:

> "Such things are very necessary to attract the pagans who flock to see them out of curiosity; we have learnt from our daily experience that these things act as a bait, because they help the people to get to know us and to listen to our sermons. Of all the things introduced into Japan so far, the playing of organs, harpsichords and viols pleases the Japanese most".

And guns. This was not exactly the same quality bait as Father Verbiest's Copernican astronomical calculations for the Emperor of China; but it served the same purpose.

In contrast to these virtues of politeness and curiosity, the third aspect of prominent Japanese characteristics remarked upon by the Europeans in these early contacts was the most problematic: on the one hand,

---

190   It was in marked contrast to practice in the Portuguese colonies in India, where priests were still being discouraged from learning the native language because this was regarded as a weakness, an admission of equality, a view shared by Cabral. There were no doubt some linguists among the chauvinists, as later in British India.

extraordinary self-control, respect and loyalty; on the other dissimulation and ruthless self-interest. Each trait was attested to, yet confuted by observation of contrary behaviour. These contrasts baffled the missionaries then as they have other observers since.

Valignano observed of their self-control and pacific nature that

> "the Japanese are slow and deliberate in their dealings, and similarly they never display outward resentment or impatience, even when they are inwardly much upset. They do not lightly murmur or complain, nor do they speak evil of one another. They are very secretive in their hearts. They are greatly addicted to formal manners and empty compliments, but know how to bide their time in silence very patiently... They have such control over their anger and impatience that it is almost a miracle to witness any quarrel or insulting words in Japan".

On the other hand St Francis Xavier had remarked, at the beginning of European contact, that the Japanese

> "think themselves superior to all nations in military glory and valour...[They prize arms] more than any people I have ever seen";

and Valignano later agreed that while

> "they are naturally very intelligent...they have no knowledge of sciences, because they are the most warlike and bellicose race yet discovered on the earth. From the age of fifteen onwards, all youths and men, rich and poor, in all walks of life, wear a sword and dagger at their side. Moreover, every man, whether a gentleman or a common fellow, has such complete control over his sons, servants, and others of his household, that he can kill any of them on the smallest pretext at any time he likes...They will think nothing more of killing a man than they do an animal; so that they will kill a man not only on the smallest excuse but merely to try the edge of their swords".

Probably the most generous summation was made by Xavier's immediate and longest–serving successor (1551–1570) as head of the Jesuit mission, Father Cosme de Torres. The Japanese reminded him, he said, of the ancient Romans: sensitive, proud and warlike by disposition, impatient, resolute, and courageous in their actions – but quickly resorting to arms to avenge the honour of their gods, family or good name, reprisals against perceived offences being violent and swift.

Perhaps the chief puzzle, against this background of obsession with personal honour, was the Japanese attitude to loyalty observed by the missionaries. Xavier had written that

> "they are men of honour to a marvel, and prize honour above all else in the world...They have one quality which I cannot recall in any people of Christendom; this is that their gentry however so poor they be, and the commoners however so rich they be, render as much honour to a poor gentleman as if he were passing rich...
>
> Those who are not of gentle birth give much honour to the gentry, who in their turn pride themselves on faithfully serving their feudal lord to whom they are very obedient. It seems to me that they act thus more because they think that they would lose their honour if they acted contrarily, rather than for fear of the punishment they would receive if disobedient".

But Xavier was virtually alone in this view. Valignano, who had considerably longer experience in Japan, and a much broader range of contacts both socially and geographically, was to write thirty years later:

> "They are the most false and treacherous people of any known in the world; for from childhood they are taught never to reveal their hearts, and they regard this as prudence and the contrary as folly...Even fathers and sons never reveal their true thoughts to each other, because there can be no mutual confidence between them in word or deed...Every individual acts in such wise that he will take any chance of increasing his income or rank by deserting his natural lord and taking service with another or betraying him, even their own fathers on occasion".

There is a different concept of behaviour involved here: "honour" lies in being on the winning side.

There is a further dimension in Valignano's observation of Japanese conduct:

> "When they are most determined to do evil to someone, the more outward compliments they pay him. Thus when they wish to kill

somebody, just when they are about to do so, they show him more politeness and kind words, in order the better to effect their intention...".

And so he concludes:

"For this reason, and because Japan is divided between so many lords and fiefs, it is continually torn by civil wars and treasons, nor is there any lord who is secure in his domain...[These lords] promiscuously defraud and deceive each other in turn, with artifice, fraud, and stratagem everywhere dominant".

This is a pitiless critique of a people whom the Jesuit Visitor professed to admire more, even, in some respects, than Europeans; but there are those who recalled his words when Japan attacked Pearl Harbour in 1941, without a declaration of war.[191] Father Valignano would not have been surprised.

The cook and the clerics
There has of course been a considerable commentary on the attitudes of Oda Nobunaga and Toyotomi Hideyoshi towards the Europeans – traders as well as missionaries. That both saw tolerance of the latter as essential to continued benefits from the former seems clear. It is also clear that it was only the latter whom either of the two dictators ever got to know: men in their position did not mix with merchants, who, in accordance with the Confucian ranking adopted from China, came at the very bottom of the Japanese social scale, behind the nobles/*daimyo*,

---

191   A friend in Japan has commented: "It is well maybe to remember that the successful surprise attack has been from time immemorial a most recommendable strategy in all the Far East", and often lauded in the west too. When Japan made such an attack [in 1904, on Port Arthur, then Imperial Russia's Pacific naval base on China' Liadong Peninsula] setting off the Russo-Japanese war, British papers wrote enthusiastically about gallant little Japan successfully waking the Russian bear" [see 1900 chapter: Yuan Shikai]. Following Nazi Germany's as well as Japan's practice of making such attacks in launching and spreading the Second World War, the Charter of the United Nations was designed to prevent them - and indeed war in general; but its provisions have been gravely undermined by the United States government's adoption, since the terrorist attacks of 9 September 2001, of the doctrine of unilaterally-determined "pre-emptive strikes".

military/*samurai*, and the peasantry. Not that they would eschew commercial profit if they could get it: in 1581 and again in 1582 Hideyoshi had his agents buy up the bulk of the hugely profitable Portuguese cargoes of Chinese silk. In any case the Portuguese traders were for the most part operating in the ports of Kyushu, and indeed increasingly confined to the single location of Nagasaki, not merely through Japanese effort to minimise social or political contamination but as much through Portuguese determination to preserve the Black Ship's monopoly – a position strongly supported by the Church as we saw: illegal trade incurred excommunication.

What is more problematical is why Nobunaga so consistently displayed not simply an acceptance of the importance of the missionary presence for the continuance of profitable trade relations with Portugal, but a positive liking, even admiration, for the Jesuit Fathers. Their common detestation of the Buddhists, as previously noted, was undoubtedly a significant element; Nobunaga never seems to have experienced any disquiet, as Hideyoshi was subsequently to do, about such acts of fanaticism as the destruction of Buddhist temples and persecution of their bonzes by *daimyo* who converted to Christianity, without doubt encouraged by their Jesuit mentors. Nobunaga hated the Buddhists as political – and, as at Hieizan and Honganji, military – opponents; the Jesuits' animosity was of course for religious reasons, but the militantly irreligious Nobunaga was still not perturbed by their determination to supplant one theology by another. By the time of his assassination in 1582 the Jesuits put the total number of their converts at 150,000, mostly in Kyushu and mostly consequent on being obliged to adopt Christianity by their *daimyo* (just as the Jesuits hoped would happen). Nobunaga perhaps had a more realistic apprehension of the likely extent of the missionaries' appeal to the Japanese population as a whole than did Hideyoshi, who came to be extremely sensitive to the implications of *daimyo* conversions for his own ambitions.

The great British historian of Japan, Sir George Sansom, thought there was also a strong personal factor involved: Nobunaga was

> "an autocrat who could afford no intimacy with his vassals and probably welcomed intercourse with men of strong character and high attainments from whom he had nothing to fear. There is ample proof that he admired their courage. Cruelly intolerant these Jesuits may have been, but they kept a severe rule, they had

breeding and learning and a touch of haughtiness – all qualities that were admired in feudal Japan".

There is of course the direct parallel, as we saw, with the similar familiar treatment accorded to other Jesuit priests by the Moghul and Persian Emperors and the Court in Peking (with the Emperor's encouragement at one remove).

The similarities between the strict training of the Jesuits and the spartan demands on *samurai* have of course been suggested as an element also in the appeal of the Jesuits in less exalted circles. There were other factors, not all without ambiguity: right at the beginning, the fact that Francis Xavier came from Goa created an impression that his preaching – to the extent it could be understood at all through the language barrier – was in some way a new form of Buddhism. This impression was not disabused by the missionaries' early use – or rather misuse – of Buddhist terms for the un-Japanese concepts of "God", "Mother of God", "Holy Trinity", and so on. The missionaries also benefited to some extent from the natural respect for the Buddhist priesthood that (aside from Nobunaga) was prevalent in Japan, in contrast to China. But there is no doubt that as time went on the Jesuits also benefited from Nobunaga's positively friendly attitude, not simply by the discouragement of *daimyo* persecution in the provinces but by the acceptance of conversion by many influential civil and military officials in Kyoto itself as the result of Christianity's high-level protection. That it even became fashionable in some quarters to carry a rosary or affect Portuguese dress comes as no surprise following the crazes for things foreign of the past half-century.[192]

Crazes were not only one way. Valignano thought things were going so well that in 1581 he came up with the idea of sending four fourteen-to-fifteen-year-old sons of Kyushu Christian *daimyo* on an "embassy" to Europe.[193] They were received with great ceremony by Ferdinand II of Spain in Madrid, by the Grand Duke Francesco de'Medici of Tuscany in Florence, and by Pope Gregory XIII (he of the reformed calendar) in Rome, who presented them with three outfits of European clothing because their "native costumes" were causing too much public hilarity;

---

192 My friend in Tokyo has reported that at the beginning of the 21st century a revival there of the craze for all things foreign included, at one point, crosses and full rosary beads.

193 It is described in Lach: *Asia in the Making of Europe*

in return they gave the Pope two six-fold screens of Nobunaga's Azuchi fortress-palace – which he had given to Valignano. Gregory died while they were in Rome, and the young Japanese were portrayed among the honoured guests in the fresco of one of his successor Sixtus V's installation ceremonies, in the Vatican's Sistine Hall (not the Sistine Chapel, built a century before by Sixtus IV, but the Vatican Library built by Sixtus V, connecting the centre of what are now the two long Vatican Museum galleries). The "embassy" went on to Venice to be entertained by the Doge Nicoló da Ponte and have their portraits painted by Tintoretto, though he only finished one. The visit was a huge propaganda success for the Jesuits and the Catholic Church – to the extent that a German Protestant complained that the Japanese had not been permitted to visit "Germany and Saxony" where they could have learned "the true light of Christ...[from] the followers of that dear man of God, Martin Luther". In Europe, Japan was finally on the map thanks to four schoolboys.

Nobunaga's Christian contacts were only with the missionaries; but the succession saw a real change, as some of Hideyoshi's principal military and civil advisers were practising Christians or at least sympathizers. The conversion of his immensely learned personal physician caused a popular sensation; Hideyoshi must surely have known of the move beforehand, but he neither tried to prevent it nor reacted afterwards. At the same time Hideyoshi was not as fiercely anti-Buddhist as his predecessor; perhaps this simply reflected the fact that, by the time he had finished off at Negoro the purge Nobunaga had unleashed at Hieizan and Honganji, the bonzes no longer represented a significant target. But, despite his apparent irreligiosity, Hideyoshi was to come back to the monks in due course – on their side.

However, to begin with, Hideyoshi continued his predecessor's policy of friendliness towards the missionaries, as we saw earlier, culminating in his visit to the Jesuit House in Osaka at Easter 1586 and then his reception at Osaka Castle of Vice-Provincial Coelho and Father Frois on 4 May. And it was here, as Hideyoshi laid out his grand plans for the future of Japan and the whole of East Asia, that Coelho, presumably thinking to cement Hideyoshi's relations with the Jesuits, committed his irrecoverable blunder – in fact two.

The first was in relation to Hideyoshi's imminent campaign to reduce the *daimyo* of Kyushu who were opposing his authority, and to bring the whole of that island under his central control: Coelho offered his best efforts to put all the Christian *daimyo* of Kyushu on Hideyoshi's side.

Hideyoshi remained affable, but he must instantly have thought: if these foreigners can meddle in Japanese politics on my side, they can just as easily do the opposite. But there was more to come: when Hideyoshi announced his plans for the invasion of China and Korea, Coelho's second blunder was not only to promise to provide the two Portuguese carracks Hideyoshi had requested, which implied Jesuit control over Portuguese warships, but also to volunteer other (unspecified) help from Portuguese India, which Hideyoshi had not asked for, and which implied even greater Jesuit military authority. And Hideyoshi must have thought: if these foreigners can intervene militarily on my side to invade China, they can just as easily invade Japan. Hideyoshi's Christian secretary, Kiroda Josui (known by the Christians as Ai Simão), who was present, told the Jesuits immediately after the interview that he feared the results would be unfortunate. He was right, though not immediately.

There was no sign at this stage that Hideyoshi doubted the loyalty of any of his Christian vassals, but Coelho's offer to influence them undoubtedly put the thought irrevocably into his mind. As for the possible external threat: beginning in 1584, Coelho had already sought from the Spanish in Manila the despatch of

"four ships laden with men, artillery, and food...to succour the Christians of Japan that are pressed by the heathen"

- specifically to support one of those Christian *daimyo* of Kyushu. Cooler heads prevailed, but one wonders whether Hideyoshi's ubiquitous spies informed him of Coelho's military adventurism after the spectre of Portuguese intervention had been let loose by the imprudent Jesuit Vice-Provincial.

The Kyushu expedition went ahead in 1587 to complete success, not surprisingly inasmuch as Hideyoshi raised and deployed no fewer than three hundred thousand troops, among them those of his Christian vassals:

"Here in Osaka", wrote the Jesuit Father Antonio Prenestino, "I saw the departure of the *Kwampaku*, and although there was much to see I nonetheless found the greatest comfort at the Christians, who marched in the most beautiful order among the companies of unbelievers, some with the cross in their armorial bearings and on the helmet, others on the flag, and others again on the tunic".

The Satsuma forces put up a hopeless resistance, falling back almost to Kagoshima. Hideyoshi then displayed his capacity for restraint that made him so unlike Nobunaga: in reply to a request for a truce he persuaded the Satsuma *daimyo* to submit in return for confirmation of his overlordship of his traditional provinces in the south of the island, while satisfying his own more belligerent colleagues – including two Christian *daimyo* – with new fiefdoms in the north.

Hideyoshi then withdrew to Hakata Bay (near Fukuoka), where, we are told, "the [most famous tea ceremony] master Sen no Rikyu prepared fragrant tea in a pine grove near the shore". And he wrote to his wife about his plans...and about himself:

> "I have sent word by fast ship to Korea ordering them to appear and submit to the Emperor. I told them if they do not appear I will punish them next year. And I will also get China in my grasp...

Since the last battle I am feeling old; my grey hairs are becoming so numerous that I can no longer pluck them out. I am ashamed to be seen like this; only you could put up with it, but I am ashamed all the same".

Mastering the missionaries

Following Hideyoshi's arrival at Hakata Bay, Father Vice-Provincial Coelho came to visit him from Nagasaki to convey the Jesuits' congratulations on his victory in Kyushu. Coelho arrived by sea in a small Portuguese vessel; he was cordially received, and his request for a plot of land to build a church in Hakata was granted. Hideyoshi asked to visit Coelho's ship, and admired its equipment; though when he asked for the Portuguese Black Ship lying at nearby Hirado to be brought round for him to see as well, Captain-General Monteiro came to explain that Hakata was not a suitable harbour for the great carrack. Hideyoshi appeared to accept this explanation, and Coelho and Monteiro were dismissed with presents, which apparently confirmed the friendship he had been displaying to the Jesuits since his accession to power.

But all was far from well that night of 24 July 1587. Amongst all the efforts to reconstruct the sequence of events, two strands stand out. One is that Hideyoshi's first visit to Kyushu brought him to a direct realisation of the inroads Christianity had made into Japan. It was not the Christian *daimyo* of Kyushu whom he had cause to distrust – they had loyally supported his recent campaign – but the Jesuit Fathers nevertheless clearly had a powerful influence over them, as was attested by the disturbances caused in their domains by violent measures against the Buddhists and their temples. Equally seriously, the Jesuits had a base at Nagasaki which was to all intents and purposes independent of his control – and which, some Christians subsequently opined, was depriving him of concubines from the area, celebrated for the beauty of its women. There, and elsewhere, the Fathers were deeply involved in the Portuguese trade, seemed even to control it given the deference they received from the Portuguese merchants; they also acted as brokers in gold and silver for the Kyushu *daimyo* and generals. And here was the ever-insensitive Father Coelho, the man who had the year before offered to manipulate his *daimyo* and help him invade China, arriving to visit him, in his own headquarters, in a foreign ship armed with cannon – a gunship!

The other major strand has often been attributed to a bout of heavy drinking by Hideyoshi that night – ironically, Portuguese wine supplied by Coelho. That seems too simple; but among his companions that evening was Seiyakuin Hoin, another physician but a bitter opponent of Christianity, who sharply criticised the destruction of Buddhist and Shinto temples and shrines, and the forced conversion of the Christian *daimyo*'s subjects; and in this context Hoin attacked in particular one of Hideyoshi's chief lieutenants, the Christian Takayama Ukon, *daimyo* of the strategic province of Harima, just to the west of Osaka. Hideyoshi was obviously susceptible – whether through the Portuguese wine or his Kyushu conclusions – and eventually sent a messenger to demand that Ukon either give up his Christianity or surrender his fief and go immediately into exile. Ukon responded at once choosing exile; and perhaps it was this evidence of the Jesuits' hold over such a close companion that led Hideyoshi to act. Coelho was woken at once by a courier with four questions:

1 "Why are the Fathers so desirous of making converts, and why do they even use force on occasion?
2 Why do they destroy Shinto and Buddhist temples, and persecute the bonzes, instead of compromising with them?
3 Why do they eat useful and valuable animals like horses and cows?
4 Why do the Portuguese buy many Japanese [people] and export them from their native land as slaves?"

The bewildered Coelho cobbled together a reply as best he could: he denied the first and second charges; denied the eating of horseflesh and promised the Fathers would refrain from beef; and deprecated the slave trade but, asserting that the Jesuits could not prevent it because the sellers were Japanese in Japan, tartly suggested to Hideyoshi that he himself end it by forbidding it. This response, and no doubt its tone, was not what Hideyoshi required, though it is no doubt a question whether even complete submissiveness would have turned his purpose. Interestingly, his first edict was directed at his own subjects – and, surprisingly, took Coelho's advice: "Whether one desires to become a follower of the Fathers is up to that person's own conscience"; any forcing of followers to convert to Christianity was a crime "worse than the followers of Honganji" (the rebel Buddhist temple that he had put down many years before); anyone with land above a low limit needed permission to become a convert, but below that anyone could "select for himself from between eight or nine religions"; and, finally,

> "It is illegal to sell Japanese people to China, to the South Seas, or to Korea. Henceforth sale of persons in Japan is forbidden".

The following morning Hideyoshi exclaimed bitterly to his entourage that the Jesuits were deceitful propagators of a devilish and subversive creed; their smooth and specious arguments had deceived many *daimyo* and *samurai*, and might even have deceived him had he not been clever enough to see through them. They were even more dangerous than the Honganji monks as the latter's devotees were the rabble, whereas the Fathers had concentrated on the Japanese elite, who were so submissive to the Jesuits that the state was endangered.

Father Coelho's victory on slavery was then followed by Hideyoshi's second edict:

> "1. Japan is the country of gods, but has been receiving false teachings from Christian countries. This cannot be tolerated any further.
> 2. The missionaries approach people in provinces and districts to make them their followers, and let them destroy shrines and temples. This is an unheard of outrage. When a vassal receives a province, a district, a village, or another form of fief, he must consider it as a property entrusted to him on a temporary basis. He must follow the laws of this country, and abide by their intent. However, some vassals illegally [ceded part of their fiefs to the church]. This is a culpable offence.

3. The Fathers, by their special knowledge, feel that they can at will entice people to become their believers. In so doing they commit the illegal act of destroying the teachings of Buddha prevailing in Japan. These Fathers cannot be permitted to remain in Japan. They must prepare to leave the country within twenty days of the issuance of this notice...

4. The Black Ships come to Japan to engage in trade. Thus the matter is a separate one. They can continue to engage in trade.

5. Hereafter, anyone who does not hinder the teachings of Buddha, whether he be a merchant or not, may come and go freely from Christian countries to Japan".

Further proclamations specified that all Japanese as well as European Jesuits must leave the country, on pain of death; all crosses, rosaries and other signs of Christianity should be removed from the army; all Jesuit properties were confiscated and their churches closed; all Japanese Christians were ordered to recant or take the alternatives of exile or death; and Hideyoshi assumed direct control of Nagasaki, whose inhabitants got a large fine for good measure.

The Portuguese Fathers, thunderstruck by this drastic and totally unforeseen change in their fortunes after their warm reception by Hideyoshi at Hakata Bay, must have recalled Father Valignano's words:

"When they are most determined to do evil to someone, the more outward compliments they pay him. Thus when they wish to kill somebody, just when they are about to do so, they show him more politeness and kind words, in order the better to effect their intention...".

But after the edicts...nothing. Or at least nothing much, on either side. Coelho said the Jesuits could not leave until the Black Ship sailed in six months; Hideyoshi meekly accepted. By then, well over a hundred Jesuits had assembled at Hirado, but only three sailed on the Black Ship; Hideyoshi said nothing. Meanwhile, Coelho took further leave of his senses: he made (unsuccessful) efforts to persuade the Christian Kyushu *daimyo* to launch armed resistance to the expulsion edict; he sent (unsuccessful) pleas to Manila, Macao and Goa for three hundred fully armed men to stiffen the *daimyo*; and he (successfully) imported firearms from Macao. Valignano, furious when he learned of Coelho's "ravings of an afflicted mind", said later that only the Vice-Provincial's death, early in 1590, had saved him from severe punishment, and sent the compromising weapons back to Macao. It seems unlikely that Hideyoshi's spies did not tell him what was going on; but, whatever he learned, he did nothing.

None of the Christian *daimyo*, other than the already exiled Takayama Ukon, was acted against either. Indeed, Omura Sumitada, the Christian *daimyo* who had ceded Nagasaki to the Jesuits, claimed it back as part of his fiefdom; Hideyoshi agreed, perhaps an indication that he knew Omura had refused Coelho's call to arms. Christian generals were soon to be promoted. The Jesuits proceeded to drastically lower their public profile – but not their proselytising. They estimated that there were about 200,000 Christians in Japan at the time of the edicts; none was exiled, let alone executed, as had been proclaimed. Only sixty of their two hundred and fifty establishments in the country were actually destroyed, and they brought the others back into use during the coming years. In 1590 Valignano nervously asked permission to return to Japan; Hideyoshi promptly agreed, provided he came in his capacity as diplomatic, not ecclesiastical, representative of the Vatican. The next year Hideyoshi was seen strolling through his Kyoto palace in Portuguese dress, and wearing a...rosary.

What on earth was he up to? It would seem that while he was prepared to tolerate the existence, even the quiet expansion of Christianity amongst the Japanese people, the *samurai* and even some of his senior officials, he was anxious to make abundantly clear to the Portuguese Jesuits that he would not tolerate direct interference in Japan's – in *his* – affairs. But he was also anxious to maintain and even expand foreign trade; and he and his chief supporters, even those hostile to Christianity, were, as Father Valignano noted during his visit,

> "convinced that there was no trading with the Portuguese in Japan unless the Fathers acted as intermediaries"; "which opinion", he added, "is of no small help to us at this juncture".

Indeed, in one of his private chats with Rodrigues the Interpreter[194] towards the end of Valignano's mission, Hideyoshi explicitly confirmed

---

194   The Portuguese Jesuit Novice João Rodrigues (c.1561-1633) had sailed to Japan as an orphan in his mid-teens, possibly as a deck-hand, and possibly in 1574 in the same fleet that carried Valignano and forty-one other Jesuits to Goa that year, five of whom were among the fourteen Jesuits who reached Japan in 1577, most likely with the young Rodrigues as a protégé. In 1580 he entered the Jesuit novitiate at Usuki, in Kyushu's Bungo province, and began formal Japanese

his interest in increasing Portuguese trade, and said that neither the missionaries nor their religion was the cause of the four-year-old expulsion edict; but, somewhat contradictorily, he added (Cooper relates) that the simple fact of the matter was that Japan was "the land of the *kami* [local deities]" and Christianity was not a suitable religion for the Japanese.

But, despite the periodical soothing words, the necessary edicts were there on the statute books as a continual reminder to the Jesuits that their status in Japan had irrevocably changed.

The Emperor pays a visit

There is perhaps another explanation for Hideyoshi's lack of focus on the Jesuits once the expulsion edicts were in place: his attention was on more important things – not least, himself. At the beginning of 1588 he very deliberately arranged for the seal to be set on his arrival at the summit of power, political legitimacy and aristocratic acceptability: the newly enthroned Emperor Go-Yozei accepted an invitation to visit his extravagant new fortress-palace in Kyoto, the *Jurakutei*, the "Mansion of Assembled Pleasures". Built with audacious symbolism on the site of the Heian-period Imperial compound, and occupying an area almost equal to the contemporary Imperial Palace, Hideyoshi's *Jurakutei* was built in about eighteen months by over a hundred thousand workers and artisans, craftsmen and artists; the moats and stone fortifications surrounded several luxurious residential complexes, decorated by the finest painters of the *Momoyama* period;[195] and there were gardens,

---

studies as well. Father Valignano, at the beginning of his second visit in 1590, appointed Rodrigues, then almost thirty and pretty much bi-lingual, as his interpreter, which is how he came to meet, and impress, Hideyoshi. After a brief visit to Macao to be ordained in 1596, he worked continuously in Japan as a priest, as well as as interpreter again for Valignano's third visit in 1598, as a confidant for Hideyoshi up to his death, and finally, from 1601, as Ieyasu's personal commercial agent in Nagasaki, a heady but unwise conflict of interest that led to his expulsion from Japan in 1610. He died in Macao in 1633. The main source for his life is Cooper: *Rodrigues the Interpreter*, from which his remarks on the Japanese invasion fleet are taken.

195 *Momoyama*, a term mostly met as descriptive of artistic style during the period of Nobunaga's and particularly Hideyoshi's ascendancy, is also used in a political sense, which, like the style, spills over to some extent in both directions. The *Encyclopædia Britannica* notes that it is sometimes dated from 1568, when Nobunaga took Kyoto, or 1573, when he expelled the last Ashikaga Shogun from the city; and it ends variously in 1600, with Tokugawa Ieyasu's victory at

pavilions for tea ceremonies and a stage for traditional *Noh* theatre, plus all the other buildings necessary for guards, servants and storage.

Hideyoshi was keenly aware of the only two precedents for a reigning Emperor to so honour a Commoner by a visit to his residence, in 1408 and 1427, when the hosts were members of the vastly aristocratic Ashikaga family which ruled Japan, in the Emperor's name, for the two hundred years preceding Nobunaga's rise to power. Hideyoshi's extravaganza, which lasted a week, was to outdo them. It began with his personally escorting the Imperial family from the Imperial Palace to the *Jurakutei*, a mile-long processional way lined by six thousand ceremonial guards: the Emperor, riding in his court vehicle, then Hideyoshi, his generals and their aides-de-camp, the ex-Emperor, the Empress and the Dowager-Empress, the great Court nobles, their wives and attendants, hosts of guards of honour, mounted warriors, companies of men-at-arms. The Emperor's state carriage was, in fact, according to an observer, a bullock cart, but cart and bullocks richly decorated with Chinese silks of five colours, and even the bullocks' hooves gilded; the other great personages were carried in similarly decorated palanquins. By the time the Emperor arrived at the *Jurakutei* the tail of the procession had still not emerged from the Palace. There followed days and days of banquets, musical entertainments and dance, daily gift-giving of robes, coins, incense, precious paper, *Noh* performances – perhaps including that shown in the eight-panel folding screen in the Kobe City Museum[196] – and poetry competitions in which both the Emperor and Hideyoshi participated. The official record saw no irony in the farmer's son reading his poetry to the one hundred and fourth Emperor of Japan.

The two most significant events took place on the second day, and they surely demonstrated to the Emperor and every one of his subjects that the farmer's son was no more. In the morning Hideyoshi, the newly "Bountiful Minister", in the reverse of the usual relationship between

---

Sekigahara, or in 1603 with his elevation to the Shogunate, or in 1615 with his defeat of Hideyoshi's son and the end of the Toyotomi. The term itself derives from a hill south of Kyoto called Momoyama, Peach Blossom Hill, where Hideyoshi built his fortress-palace Fushimi Castle; the period is less frequently referred to as *Azuchi-Momoyama* to include Nobunaga's own fortress east of the city, where Japan's "Golden Age" of the arts is regarded as having begun. There is nothing left of either castle, but some of the artworks are now in various Japanese museums.

196 Reproduced in Hickman: *Japan's Golden Age*, pp.112–3, still the outstanding work in English on the *Momoyama* period.

monarch and subject, magnanimously bestowed various sources of revenue on the cash-strapped Emperor and some of his Court. Then in the afternoon Hideyoshi's vassals – including Tokugawa Ieyasu – set their names to the following before the Emperor:

"We solemnly swear:

Item 1. The measures ordained by the Kwampaku on the occasion of this Imperial visit to the *Jurakutei* move us to tears of gratitude.

Item 2. If any impious person should dare to interfere with the ground rents and other Income appertaining to the Imperial Estate or with the several holdings of the court nobles and imperial abbacies, we shall admonish him severely.

We commit not only ourselves but also our children and children's children, who shall be instructed not to contravene this pledge.

Item 3. *We shall obey the Lord Kwampaku in everything and shall not violate his orders even in the slightest"*.

And that, of course, was the icing on the cake.

The last domestic campaign

Contrary to his promise to his wife from Hakata Bay, Hideyoashi was not to punish the Koreans the next year: first, he had to complete the unification of Japan by subduing the Kanto, the group of eight provinces around Edo, the future Tokyo. The north of Honshu would then also submit. But in the event he was not ready to act until 1590, the interval being taken up with the delicate manoeuvring, on the one hand, of the Hojo *daimyo* of the Kanto into a position of apparent disobedience to the Emperor; and, on the other, of Tokugawa Ieyasu, who held the provinces between central Honshu and the Kanto, into accepting Hideyoshi's leadership of a military campaign through and beyond his own territories. There was also the matter of raising a new army of two hundred thousand men. Another touching letter from Hideyoshi to his wife has survived, written on his way to besiege Odawara, the Hojo capital:

"You have not written to me and I am very worried. Is the young prince [his son Tsurumatsu, born in 1589 to his favourite concubine, Yodo-gimi[197]] growing bigger and bigger? It is very important that strict orders are given to your guards so that your house is protected from fire and that they don't allow disorder to develop amongst themselves and their subordinates. About the 20th [of May] I will definitely see you and will embrace the young prince, and, that night, you will sleep beside me: wait for me.

I repeat: you must tell them to prevent the young prince from catching a cold; you must not be careless about anything at all".

And shortly after:

"We have surrounded Odawara with two or three lines, have dug moats and built walls and we will not let a single enemy get out...I repeat: I have caught the enemy in a cage, and therefore there is no danger; don't be afraid! I long for the young prince, but, as I am looking to the future and above all because I want to have my men pacify the whole country, I have put aside my personal sentiments".

In three months Odawara surrendered unconditionally; Northern Honshu duly submitted as anticipated. The Kanto was conferred on Ieyasu in exchange for his old provinces; these were then divided amongst other of Hideyoshi's trusted vassals, so that his central authority was bolstered by the balancing of power among his subordinates.

By the end of 1590 Hideyoshi was thus master of all sixty-six provinces of Japan. Vaingloriously, but accurately, he told a Spanish visitor three years later:

"During the one hundred and four reigns that have passed, there has never yet been an Emperor who has ruled and governed the whole of Japan – and I have subdued all of it!"

Since then, apart from the two-year split amongst Hideyoshi's successors that Tokugawa Ieyasu ended at the battle of Sekigahara in 1600, Japan has remained unified.

---

197 It is an indication of the success of the Jesuit missionaries that, despite Yodo-gimi's being Hideyoshi's consort and mother of his heir, her sister was a Christian, married to a prominent *daimyo*.

Hideyoshi was right to worry about the young prince: Tsurumatsu died the following year, leaving him without an heir. There is a touching small memorial portrait statue of the little boy at the Rinka-in Temple in Kyoto,[198] solemn-faced, seated cross-legged and wrapped in a plain kimono like a swaddling-cloth, but with the long lower sleeves sticking out sideways like little aeroplane wings. Another son, Hideyori, was born to Yodo-gimi in 1593; by then Hideyoshi had already cleared the way to undertake his Korean campaign by ceding, reluctantly, the Regency to his twenty-three year old nephew Hidetsugu, becoming himself at this point the *Taiko*, Retired Regent.

Hidetsugu's behaviour was dissolute and bloodthirsty, though Hideyoshi's decision in 1595 to exile him and command him to commit suicide, *seppuku*, could well have been prompted by the desire to eliminate any possible challenge to Hideyori's succession. Hideyoshi adored his baby heir: he wrote to Yodo-gimi that

"I cannot begin to express how much I feel alone away from Hideyori and to what extent I cannot overcome my sadness. I repeat once again: give strict orders to your servants to take precautions against fire. Every night, send them to inspect the rooms two or three times. You must be vigilant"

Yodo-gimi obviously responded, because Hideyoshi wrote back playfully and passionately to the child – in one such letter he said

"I am very happy that you wrote to me. Because of work here, as I told you in my letter yesterday, I had not sent you a single word although I greatly wanted to. I shall return very soon at the end of the year, and I will kiss your lips...I imagine you are becoming more and more handsome".

While Hideyoshi's love for the boy clearly transcended the issue of the succession, the succession was undoubtedly a crucial preoccupation. Nevertheless his behaviour following the purging of Hidetsugu went completely haywire, exhibiting the first sign of the obsessiveness which marred his later years: not only were Hidetsugu's main vassals and followers put to death, but his wife, his two children, and more than

---

198   Reproduced in Hickman: *Japan's Golden Age*, p.37

thirty of their women companions and servants were paraded through the streets of Kyoto and brutally decapitated in front of a stake displaying Hidetsugu's head, their bodies then thrown into a common criminals' grave. And his insane vengeance was carried to a further extreme: as *Kwampaku*, Hidetsugu and his family had been living in the *Jurakutei*, the luxurious scene of the triumphant visit by the Emperor; but Hideyoshi now had it pulled down, every last stone and structure, completely dismantled and demolished. All that remained were the picture of pavilions seeming to float amongst the golden clouds of the six-panel folding screen now in the Mitsui Bunko collection in Tokyo.[199] The Japanese, reluctant to part forever with such a treasured place, subsequently maintained that fine structures at various places had their origins in the fabled compound. But, alas, this has never been able to be proved.

Korea: the first invasion 1592–1593

Korea, the Land of the Morning Calm, has more accurately been the land caught in the middle, permanently stranded between China and Japan, its would-be and often actual masters. At the end of the 19th century and again after World War II Russia also became deeply involved in Korea's affairs. It has been the perfect spot to invade, not so much buffer state as doormat, the result not least of Koreans' inability to get along with one another. The first Chinese invasion was in 109 BCE; from then until 1894 Chinese influence in Korea, from political, religious and cultural configuration to outright suzerainty, was virtually continuous; and these influences – theories of government, Buddhism, the art of writing, cultural values – flowed on to similarly make Japan an off-shore projection of China, notwithstanding its image as a self-contained island.

During these two millennia there were two serious mainland attempts by China to invade Japan through Korea, both by the Mongols, who at the first attempt in 1271 were just about to become the rulers of China, and at the second in 1281 had just done so, as the Yuan Dynasty. Both attempts were supported by the Koryo Dynasty which gave Korea its name, both were unsuccessful, largely due to ferocious storms (*kamikaze*) which wrecked the invasion fleets both times; and both attempts appeared in Marco Polo's *Travels*. The remains of the huge fosse dug in

---

199   Reproduced in part in Hickman: *Japan's Golden Age*, pp.110-111

northern Kyushu to halt the second invasion can still be seen around Hakata Bay near Fukuoka. The Manchus also invaded Korea, in 1627, shortly before they became rulers of China as the Qing Dynasty; for reasons that are unclear, they never made an effort against Japan, by then tightly closed off from the world under the Tokugawa Shogunate, Hideyoshi's successors. Korea, however, was to remain a Qing tributary until Japan's invasion in 1894.

Hideyoshi was the first to reverse the flow.[200] In 1577, well before his revelation to Father Coelho, quoted at the beginning of this chapter, of his intention to invade Korea and China, and when he had not long risen to be one of Nobunaga's generals, he is said to have told the latter that

"When I have conquered the Chugoku [western Honshu], I will go on to Kyushu and take the whole of it. When Kyushu is ours, if you will grant me the revenue of that island for one year, I will prepare ships of war and supplies and go over and take Korea. Korea I shall ask you to bestow on me as a reward for my services, and to enable me to make still further conquests; for with Korean troops, aided by your illustrious influence, I intend to bring the whole of China under my sway. When that is effected, the three countries – China, Korea, Japan – will be one. I shall do it all as easily as a man rolls up a piece of matting and carries it under his arm".

There seems to be no record as to whether Nobunaga was amused or alarmed by his thirty-year-old subordinate's bragadoccio.

We hear no more of the idea until 1586, when Hideyoshi ordered the *daimyo* of western Honshu and the island of Tsushima, midway between Japan and Korea, to prepare for the invasion, and made his startlingly frank remarks to the Jesuits. As he told the latter, his objective was to "immortalise himself with the name and fame of his power". This was undoubtedly true; but, by the end of the 1580s his broader experience and understanding had added the motive of access to Chinese and

---

200   Hideyoshi's Korean campaigns are dealt with in W.G.Aston's articles: *Hideyoshi's Invasion of Korea* and (a century later) in Park Yune-hee: *Admiral Yi Sun-shin and his Turtleboat Armada*, as well as, of course in his biographies. Detailed information on Admiral Yi's view of the war is contained in *Nanjung Ilgi: War Diary of Admiral Yi Sun-shin* (cited as *War Diary*), and *Imjin Changch'o: Admiral Yi Sun-shin's Memorials to Court*.

Korean resources and the development of trade, which China had banned but which the Portuguese had demonstrated as so profitable. But, as far as can be seen, this was all there was to Hideyoshi's intentions: there is no sign that he knew anything much else about either Korea, the pathway to, or China, the goal, of his ambition, no sign of the accumulation of political-military intelligence about them of the kind that Tamburlaine so patiently collected over so many years before he ventured – too late for his own body – to move against the vast Chinese Empire.[201]

Then in 1587, at the end of the Kyushu campaign, came his peremptory message to Korea itself, which not surprisingly failed to elicit the requisite humble response. In any case, with the Kanto still in hostile hands, there was no way Hideyoshi could yet launch into foreign adventurism. A series of semi-comic exchanges then ensued, with the Tsushimans, nominally Japanese but with ties to the Koreans, trying to negotiate a peaceful understanding by deceiving both about the intentions of the other. It thus came as a shock when Hideyoshi discovered the Koreans had not agreed to submit and join his campaign against China; meanwhile the Koreans discovered he did intend to invade (yet) anyway; and when the Chinese discovered this also, they became convinced that they had been deceived by the Koreans who had never even mentioned the possibility.

It was during these shenanigans that we find a rare description of Hideyoshi, in a Korean report. In 1590, when the King of Korea sent his personal envoys to Kyoto, the Imperial Court refused to allow "Koreans and such people" into the Imperial Palace, so their reception fell to Hideyoshi – after making them wait five months while he "repaired the Hall of Audience". Finally, when they were received:

> "They ascended into the Hall, where they performed their obeisances. Hideyoshi is a mean and ignoble-looking man, his complexion is dark, and his features are wanting in distinction. But his eyeballs send out fire in flashes – enough to pierce one through. He sat upon a three-fold cushion, with his face to the south [an assumption of Imperial style]. He wore a gauze hat and a dark-coloured robe of state. His officers were ranged about him, each in his proper place... The refreshments offered were of the

---

201   See 1400 chapter: Tamburlaine of Samarkand

most frugal description. A tray was set before each [ambassador], on which was one dish containing steamed *mochi* [rice cake], and saké of an inferior quality was handed round a few times in earthenware cups and in a very unceremonious way. The civility of drinking to one another was not observed. After a short interval, Hideyoshi retired behind a curtain, but all his officers remained in their places. Soon after a man came out dressed in ordinary clothes, with a baby in his arms, and strolled about the Hall. This was none other than Hideyoshi himself, and every one present bowed down his head to the ground...He was suddenly reminded that babies could despise ceremony as much as princes, and laughingly called for one of his attendants to take the child and to bring him a change of clothing...This audience was the only occasion on which [the ambassadors] were admitted to Hideyoshi's presence".

The description of Hideyoshi strikingly matches the scroll portrait, painted shortly after his death, in the Saikyo-ji Temple at Otsu, on Lake Biwa[202] – the worn, scrawny features and the staring eyes vividly recall Nobunaga's young monkey-face *Saru*. The contemptuously insulting treatment of the Koreans, whom he was supposedly wooing as allies, was an antic contribution to the mutual incomprehension that surrounded preparations for the expedition. The Korean King's subsequent jibe that Hideyoshi's China scheme was like "a bee trying to sting a tortoise through its armour" put paid to any more talk of alliance – which is probably all that it had ever been.

When unification of Japan had been completed with the subjection of the Kanto, preparations for the invasion got underway; Father Valignano recorded that there was no great enthusiasm for Hideyoshi's plan:

"All the nobles are dismayed about Korea, but they all say *Euge, Euge* [Hooray, Hooray], for Hideyoshi has said that he will kill any dissenters".

The Jesuits themselves do not seem to have had any qualms on moral grounds: they were accustomed, in contemporary Europe, to wars of ambition or supposed defence on dynastic or economic or, within

---

202   Reproduced in Hickman: *Japan's Golden Age*, p.72

their own compass, religious grounds. To the extent that they benefited from Hideyoshi's tolerance, and hoped for more, they were probably dazzled by the prospect of his conquering two more lands which could then welcome Christianity also – *cuius regio, eius religio* [the nation's religion is that of its ruler]: not so much a doctrine as an automatic assumption by Europeans when all Europe was Catholic, and from which their cause had benefitted in Japan when they managed to convert a *daimyo*.[203]

On 13 April 1592 Japanese forces landed in Pusan, virtually unopposed – the Korean naval officer (later Admiral) Yi Sun-shin said his counterpart on the southeast coast had assumed they were Japanese trading boats, until there were four hundred of them in Pusan harbour! Japanese troop numbers were substantial – 130,000 in the first wave, 50,000 reinforcements a few months later – but the fact that they were not even as big as those he had mustered to overwhelm Kyushu and the Kanto suggests that he had an unrealistic conception of what invading China would mean. The main commanders were the Christian General Konishi Yukinaga, with 18,700 of his own troops, mostly Christian like him, and his rival, the bitterly anti-Christian General Kato Kiyomasa, with 22,800 of his: a neat balancing act that insured against Japanese forces in Korea developing any idea of independence of Hideyoshi's authority. (Konishi's father, also a Christian, had been Hideyoshi's trading agent, and the brilliant commissary of the huge forces used in the Kyushu campaign. It was perhaps Hideyoshi's loyalty to this connection, apart from Konishi's own military ability, that was to save the latter's head on a number of occasions when it might well have rolled.[204])

---

203   The principle was about to be adopted, within half a century, at the end of the bitter and bloody Thirty Years War, for the quite different purpose of resolving post-Reformation hostilities between Catholic and Protestant rulers.

204   In his book *The Memory Palace of Matteo Ricci*, Jonathan Spence describes the intense suspicion he and other Catholics in China came under because of the Christian Konishi's prominent role in Hideyoshi's invasions of Korea on the way to crush China - though, ironically, in 1595 Ricci managed to hitch a ride from southern China as far as Nanjing on the barge of the Vice-President of the Ministry of War, summoned by the Emperor to command a new army against the Japanese, still occupying southern Korea. A bizarre footnote is that that same prominence of Konishi's Christians, against the background of Hideyoshi's turbulent relations with the Christian missionaries and their converts, gave rise to an odd Korean theory that the young American diplomat

Hideyoshi himself established headquarters at Nagoya-jo – not the central-Honshu city midway between Osaka and Tokyo, but a great castle (*jo*) he had had built in the usual rush at the tip of Kyushu's Higashi-Matsu'ura Peninsula overlooking the Tsushima Straits, sixty-odd kilometres west of Hakata/Fukuoka. His intention was to follow his victorious troops; as it turned out, he never set foot in Korea. Neither did Tokugawa Ieyasu, nor any of his men: did Hideyoshi fear that Ieyasu also could develop independent ideas if he got to Korea? or did Ieyasu choose to guard the home front so he would be ready if Hideyoshi's enterprise stumbled?

Initially, Hideyoshi's invasion was triumphantly successful. In less than three weeks the Japanese forces overran south Korea and occupied Seoul, as they were to do again in 1894, Konishi and Kato competing to take the capital first. Konishi then pushed on two hundred kilometres to Pyongyang in the north, while by 22 July Kato had amazingly raced a further six hundred to the Tuman River in the farthest northeast of the country, not far from the Pacific coast and what is now the Russian border. Korean resistance was nugatory, and desperate pleas to Peking for assistance went unanswered: the Chinese would not believe that Japanese forces could have advanced so rapidly without the active support of the Korean authorities themselves.

However by this stage the Japanese were already stretched rather thin, and Hideyoshi despatched the first of his reinforcements. It was now that a major gap in his preparations and strategy was brutally exposed by the Koreans: he had not ensured command of the Straits of Tsushima between Japan and Korea. And he had certainly not been prepared for the naval skills and ingenuity of Korea's naval hero, Admiral-to-be Yi Sun-shin. As noted earlier, the Korean navy at Pusan had made no effort to oppose the Japanese landing, even though the Japanese naval forces had still not left Nagoya; and it was another three weeks before Yi received orders to move east from his base in Korea's southwest Cholla province.

After a series of victories in minor skirmishes, on 8 July, in the beautiful Hansan Bay between Chungmu and Okpo, Yi Sun-shin, with

---

William Sands (see Bibliography: 1900) found still current in Seoul at the end of the 19th century: that to rid Japan of Christians, Hideyoshi had sent Konishi's army first, Kato's behind, in the expectation that China would send an army in response and Konishi would be crushed between the Chinese and Kato. It is not clear how this idea could have survived the actual result, in which the Koreans themselves, not Konishi, turned out to be the meat in the sandwich.

forty-eight ships, finally came upon the second Japanese invasion fleet of almost ninety. Sending a few fast ships to lure the Japanese into open sea, the rest of Yi's fleet then fell on the invaders, spear-headed by his famous "turtle-ships" – wooden oared vessels as in the Japanese fleet, but with steel plates on their sides and forming a canopy over the rowers, the tops covered with long sharp iron spikes to impale boarders, a dragon's-head at the prow through whose mouth cannon could fire, another cannon at the stern, and six gun-ports each side. The Koreans claim they were the world's first ironclads, but perhaps the first ironclads that worked might be more accurate. During the preparations for war the Portuguese Jesuit João Rodrigues had several times visited the Japanese invasion fleet at Nagoya, and noted that

> "the newly built vessels were protected by iron plates from the water line upward; the decks and gangways were also plated so that no wood at all was visible".

He added that the ships themselves, many more troop-carriers than battleships, were apparently not strong enough for the armour, and the heavy superstructure frequently upset their stability;[205] how many actually got to come to grips with Yi's fleet is thus unclear, but those that did were in any case outmanoeuvred by a master tactician. It is curious that Hideyoshi did not have Yi's almost invincible turtle-ships copied for his own naval forces: perhaps his humiliated naval officers concealed the extent of the Koreans' successes; perhaps it was felt to be culturally inappropriate to copy the works, however effective, of what he considered an inferior race.

The Koreans proudly accept an American historian's description of the battle of Hansando as "the Salamis of Korea": their forebears sank seventy-three of the Japanese ships and, Yi wrote in his subsequent *Memorial to the Court*, they then – as the rest tried to flee –

> "darted at flying speed, vying with one another, as they hailed down arrows and bullets like a thunder storm, burning the enemy vessels and slaughtering his warriors completely".

After describing mopping up operations against Japanese sailors who had managed to make the shore, Yi Sun-shin somewhat defensively

---

205   Rodrigues' remarks are cited in Cooper: *Rodrigues the Interpreter*

recorded his handling of another aspect of Korean post-battle military orders:

"As for the ninety enemy heads which my officers and men had cut off, I had their left ears cut off and preserved with salt in a box to be sent up to the Royal Headquarters. Ninety is rather a small number, but that is because from the beginning I warned my officers and men that if they should compete in cutting off enemy heads for battle recognition they would be likely to suffer more casualties on their own side, and I promised to reward the valour of those who kill the most living enemy even though not cutting off their heads".

From then on the Korean fleet, while not totally cutting off the Japanese invasion army's supply route, nevertheless dominated the seas to an extent that undermined Hideyoshi's strategy. In particular it ruled out the proposed despatch of reinforcements by sea up the west coast to enable Konishi to launch his attack into China itself from north-west Korea – which would have been a sort of preview of General MacArthur's landing at Inchon in September 1950 during the Korean War. Instead Konishi and Kato went unreinforced, and increasingly confronted by guerrilla activities as Korean farmers showed a fighting spirit that continued to be almost totally lacking in their civil and military leaders.

When the Chinese were finally persuaded to help they at first misjudged the enemy with a small force which Konishi easily defeated; but when they intervened effectively, crossing the Yalu in January 1593 – the Japanese said with 200,000 troops, the Koreans 50,000, a neat example of subjective intelligence – the Japanese began the long retreat. Kato especially had the difficult task of fighting his way down through northwest Hamyung province – rather like the bloody retreat of American UN forces from the Chosin Reservoir before the Chinese in December 1950. The Chinese reached Seoul in February 1593; the Japanese held it successfully until May, but were then obliged to retreat southwards to Kyongsang Namdo province in the southeast corner of the peninsula (as South Korean and Americans did in the face of the North Korean invasion in mid-1950, in the much shorter period of thirty-six days), and over the next three months dug in sixteen "fortresses" in this first "Pusan perimeter". It was during the retreat that Yi Sun-shin bluntly and bitterly reminded the Royal Headquarters of his repeated unrequited calls for access to men and provisions under army control:

"I, as a common sailor, have fought many sea battles, so I take the liberty of comparing the easy and hard points in land and sea battles. Among our Korean people, out of every ten there are eight or nine faint-hearted persons as against one or two lion hearts...Had they entrusted many choice recruits to the valiant and intelligent commanders to train and lead to war, today's emergency should not have come to this tragic end. In sea battle, all the sailors take one boat, and they cannot run away at the sight of enemy vessels even though they wish to do so...because the supervising officers will kill them outright if they disobey the order. There is no alternative. The sailors must fight with their whole might...pouring down fire-balls and mortal arrows like rain and hailstones until the enemy loses his morale and his bleeding warriors drop into the water like falling leaves in the autumn wind".

Negotiations then began for a resolution of the conflict: they would drag on for three and a half years, even longer than the two year armistice negotiations to bring last century's Korean War to an end (though not a conclusion: the armistice has still not been converted into a peace agreement). Yi Sun-shin maintained a blockade of the coast as much as he was able, but was further frustrated by the ceasefire negotiations until the Chinese general sent to negotiate with the Japanese sent him this peremptory order:

"Many Japanese generals take off their helmets and armour, and swear not to fight: you are expected to return to your home station and not to approach the Japanese war camp lest you should create confusion and disturbance".

Then he was outraged:

"The seacoast of Kyong-sang Province is a part of my country. What can you mean by saying that I am approaching the Japanese camp on it? You tell me to return to my home station. Which home station do you mean? The Japanese have no sense of keeping faith, so what they talk for peace is a trick and a lie. I am a subject of

Korea, and for justice's sake I cannot live with these robbers under the same heaven".

But he had no more say then than his South Koreans did three hundred and fifty years later – for all practical purposes the negotiations were between the big boys: China and the Japanese invaders then, the United States and the Chinese invaders last century.

At the end of 1593, as the negotiations passed their first half-year mark, General Konishi Yukinaga invited a Spanish Jesuit priest, Father Gregorio de Cespedes,[206] to come across from Japan to bring spiritual support to his mostly Christian troops, especially his aristocratic commanders, frustrated and dispirited like Yi Sun-shin – and perhaps himself. In a letter de Cespedes reported that

"These Christians are very poor and suffer from hunger, cold, illness and other inconveniences...Although Hideyoshi sends food, so little reaches here that it is impossible to sustain all with it, and moreover the help that comes from Japan is insufficient and comes late. It is now months since ships have come and many craft were lost...The cold is very severe...All day long my limbs are half numbed, and in the morning I can hardly raise my hands to say Mass".

Which suggests Yi Sun-shin's blockade was having some effect. But some things went on as usual:

'I was astonished to see the beautiful things [one of the commanders] has...as if he intended to stay here all his life...many war objects and gilded screens".

And we shall see more of Japanese looting – at the highest level.

The race north towards the Yalu and Tuman, the rapid reversal with Chinese intervention, Seoul changing hands, stalemate and armistice, several years' negotiations for a settlement which was never reached – the course of Hideyoshi's first Korean campaign uncannily prefigured many aspects of the Korean War of 1950-1953.

---

206 Some say de Cespedes actually accompanied Konishi in the original invasion. He is the first known Christian cleric to have landed in Korea; it is not known how long he stayed, but the exigencies of the times resulted in his never meeting a Korean.

The second Korean campaign 1597–1598

Notwithstanding the Japanese retreat right down the Korean peninsula, Hideyoshi, with remarkable assurance, demanded at the beginning of the negotiations in 1593 that a daughter of the Ming Emperor be sent as a consort for the Japanese Emperor, and that trade be resumed by both private and government vessels, a clear indication of this major war aim; as for Korea, its King would get back the northern provinces and the capital, Seoul, but had to undertake that Korea would never rebel against Japan. It was unstated that Japan would exercise suzerainty over it – and take the southern provinces. Hideyoshi's demands finally brought the split between Konishi and Kato into the open, the latter supporting the demands, Konishi opposing them because he had already inexplicably told the Chinese army commander that Hideyoshi would settle for being named King of Japan by the Ming Emperor.

When the Chinese Ambassadors finally came to Kyoto in December 1596 it was not to acknowledge or even discuss Hideyoshi's unrealistic demands, but to invest him with crown and royal robes as King of Japan. Hideyoshi's lack of intelligence on China was more than matched by the Emperor Wanli's lack of intelligence on Japan. The degree of the Chinese Court's delusion about Hideyoshi's nature was especially apparent in the Emperor's Patent of Investiture, the essence of which read:

"You, Toyotomi Taira Hideyoshi, having established an Island Kingdom, and knowing the reverence due to the Central Land, sent to the west an envoy, and with gladness and affection offered your allegiance. On the north you knocked on the barrier of ten thousand *li* [the frontier], and earnestly requested to be admitted within our dominions. Your mind is already confirmed in reverent submissiveness. How can we grudge our favour to so great meekness?

We do therefore specially invest you with the dignity of King of Japan...Faithfully defend the frontier of the Empire; let it be your study to act worthily of your position as our minister; practice moderation and self-restraint; cherish gratitude for the Imperial favour so bountifully bestowed upon you; change not your fidelity; be humbly guided by our admonitions; continue always to follow our instructions.

Respect this!"

Hideyoshi was taken completely by surprise by this patronizing condescension, as of course were the astounded Chinese ambassadors when he flew into a fury because the message was precisely the opposite of what he was expecting: an early English translation of a Portuguese report said

> "He flew into such a Passion and Rage, that he was perfectly out of himself. He froth'd and foam'd at the Mouth, he ranted and tore till his Head smoak'd like Fire, and his Body was all over in a dripping Sweat".

The Patent was accompanied by a Letter of Instruction, which made abundantly clear that Peking's position was also based on Konishi's quite different assurances to it, which caused further astonishment:

> "What Konishi led me to believe was that the chief of the Mings was to acknowledge *me* Ming Emperor!"

Konishi's head must now have been in considerable jeopardy, but for a while nothing happened. Then in March 1597 Hideyoshi decided, with the support of Kato and the "war party", and still with Konishi opposing him, to take out his anger with China on hapless Korea, proclaiming he would never make peace with that country. A further 100,000 troops, this time with stronger naval support, were ordered to join the 50,000 who had been left in the Pusan perimeter after the first invasion. It might have been expected, after Konishi's apparent role in the China debacle, and with his continuing as leader of the "peace party", that now Hideyoshi, having spared his life, might at least have replaced him in the second invasion; but Konishi as well as Kato went back to Korea. At a minimum, it was a striking confirmation of Hideyoshi's continued tolerance of Christians if they were of value to him.

The new Japanese invasion force had not advanced far when it was confronted by a new Chinese army, which had begun to incorporate recovering Korean units as it advanced rapidly south from the Yalu. The Chinese established their headquarters in the fortress at Namwon, in the southeast corner of present–day North Cholla Province; and in the first major battle of this second campaign Kato Kiyomasa's army, 100,000 men it is said, breached the defences after a thirteen-day siege, only to find the Chinese had fled (according to the small Korean garrison abandoned there) or withdrawn to fight another day (according to the Chinese). 3,726 heads were reported to have been taken from the Koreans, the officers' heads and the privates' noses being pickled in salt and lime and sent to Hideyoshi. This seems to have been the first atrocity recorded during Hideyoshi's Korean war; unfortunately it was not to be the last.

The Chinese recovered, and the battle swayed to and fro across the south of the peninsula; and as it turned against the defenders, Konishi, advising withdrawal back to Pusan itself, provoked another of Hideyoshi's increasingly frequent rages, leading to the irrational withdrawal of all but 60,000 Japanese troops, about the same number as had been in Korea before this second campaign had begun. Extraordinarily, this beleaguered garrison, mostly tough Satsuma warriors, turned the tables on the Chinese and began rolling them back up the peninsula. The greatest massacre of the war occurred on 30 October 1598 at Sochon, west of Pusan, where the victorious Japanese defeated and cut off the heads of (they claimed) 38,700 Chinese and Koreans. The ears and noses were once again cut off, packed in barrels of salt, and sent to Japan, where they were buried under the *Mimi-dzuka*, the "Ear–mound", in the grounds of the *Hoko-ji*, Hideyoshi's Great Buddha Hall in Kyoto.

The advance rolled on apparently unstoppably; but by the time it had reached within eighty kilometres of Seoul news came that Hideyoshi had died on 18 September, his last will ordering withdrawal from Korea. In fact peace moves were already underway again: Konishi had (again) welcomed Chinese overtures for a ceasefire; and Hideyoshi himself, weary of the see-saw conflict, had already asked Ieyasu and another *daimyo* to try to end hostilities. It is reported that agents were sent secretly to the Koreans offering peace if a Korean Prince were sent to Japan, and the withdrawal of all Japanese forces in return for gifts of tiger-skins and ginseng to Kyoto.

The Japanese generals, now anxious to return their armies to Japan, once again failed to reckon on Admiral Yi Sun-shin: on 15 September, some Japanese having already been observed slipping away, he called his commanders together and told them:

> "The Japanese are an irreconcilable enemy who have inflicted much damage and harm upon us. Therefore, you should not let even a single enemy ship leave this country before being made to pay for their unforgivable crime".

After numerous small engagements, on 18 November Yi launched a surprise attack on a large Japanese armada withdrawing forces, presumably, in accordance with Hideyoshi's last orders. While half the Japanese fleet was destroyed the remainder rallied and turned to attack. Towards dawn the next day, as the Japanese began to disengage, Yi ordered the pursuit – and a stray bullet hit him, fatally. His eldest son, who was with him, reported with appropriate filial pride – and perhaps even accurately, so single-minded had Yi Sun-shin been in opposing the Japanese – that his last words were

> "Don't let anyone know of my death now that the fight is at its peak".

Later Korean historians have of course observed the parallel with Nelson's death during his victory at Trafalgar.

The Japanese withdrawal went on; in December 1598 the last forces left Pusan. Japanese troops would return, almost four hundred years later, en route to defeating China in 1894; again in 1905 to make Korea a Japanese protectorate, and in 1910 to annex it, finally meeting one of Hideyoshi's aims.[207] And his main objective, when he had set out in 1592 with such ebullient hopes, was then met with Japan's invasion, in 1931, of Manchuria, and progressively from 1937 to 1945, of northeast China and the Yangtze River basin almost as far west as Chongqing (Chungking).

So ended Hideyoshi's Korean adventure: thousands killed, the Japanese economy drained, many *daimyo* disaffected, the generals frustrated by inconclusive campaigns, his "name and fame" inescapably sullied. He was not of course concerned with the impact on Korea, whose population suffered, far more than its army, from the brutality of the Japanese forces, the commandeering of foodstuffs, the ruin of crops – though the resulting famine also caused acute difficulties for the Japanese and Chinese armies alike. The devastation, the brutality, the atrocities, the abductions all engendered a lasting bitterness that was inevitably rekindled by the equally brutal Japanese re-occupation of Korea between 1905 and 1945; and neither act of aggression has yet been fully acknowledged by the Japanese, or been forgotten or forgiven by the Koreans.

Immediately after the capture of Seoul in April 1592, in the third week of the first invasion, Hideyoshi told his mother that he would be in Peking by September; but by their final withdrawal at the end of the six years' war not a single Japanese soldier had set foot in China. But the

---

207   See 1900 chapter: Yuan Shikai of China

Ming Empire did not long outlast their penultimate enemy: China's two interventions in Korea, although limited in numbers and in time, seriously weakened its forces guarding the north-east frontier facing Manchuria, and within forty years Manchu forces would drive across this border, sweep the Ming Dynasty into oblivion, and establish China's last imperial dynasty, the Qing. They were the only winners from Hideyoshi's vainglorious gamble.

Portuguese Jesuits vs Spanish Franciscans...and others

In 1591, the year before the Korean adventure began, Hideyoshi had ordered a Portuguese vessel at Nagasaki to hand over its cargo of gold at a discounted price; the merchant involved said he could not do so without the approval of the Jesuits. Unless the gold was Jesuit property – which is quite possible: notwithstanding Rome's disapproval, the Fathers, starting with Visitor Valignano himself, had financed their missionary work by trading – the merchant was just being cunning; but of course his reaction reinforced the Japanese conviction that they could not have the Portuguese trade without the Portuguese missionaries. Hideyoshi's realisation that, despite his overwhelming success in unifying the sixty-six provinces, he was still not completely master in his own country must have added to the distrust of the foreigners, lay and clerical alike, that he had developed at the time of the Kyushu campaign.

It is therefore somewhat surprising to find him, the same year, allowing the Father Valignano back into the country, though he told the clerical ambassador that the Hakata Bay expulsion order would not be rescinded. And it is very surprising to find him, two years later, granting Spanish Franciscans – who had come from Manila with a deputation of merchants – a site for a church in Kyoto, and allowing them to preach in open defiance of the Hakata Bay edict against proselytizing. The explanation seems to lie in Hideyoshi's conviction that foreign trade was essential to Japan's well-being: it was about the same time, at the end of the first year of the Korean campaign, as he was specifying the resumption of open trade relations as his major demand for peace with China. Spanish merchants would be able to break the Portuguese monopoly on trade with China, and he no doubt assumed that they would be as dependent on their Franciscan priests as the Portuguese merchants appeared to be on their Jesuits.[208]

The arrival of the Spanish Franciscans caused the Portuguese Jesuits far more anguish and anger than they did Hideyoshi. Since 1587 the Jesuits had been operating very much underground, though with considerable success: converts were estimated to have increased to some 300,000 by 1592. They were therefore aghast when the Franciscans recklessly displayed great public fervour but no political sense. But the heart of the Jesuits' objections lay elsewhere than in fear.

China's view that, as the Middle Kingdom, the only relations other states could have with it were as tributaries, has often struck Westerners as an amusing or appalling misjudgement of its place in the world. The Papal division of the entire globe between Portugal and Spain was equally deluded. It began in 1494 when the most notorious Pope of all time, Alexander VI Borgia, drew a line between Spanish and Portuguese zones of exploration in the New World; and his successors went further and awarded colonial, commercial and ecclesiastical monopolies everywhere west of it to Spain and everywhere east to Portugal. But it was no laughing matter to the recipients of this Papal bounty: where the zones met up again around the globe in Asia these monopolies became highly nationalistic rivalries. This division of the spoils was taken particularly seriously by the Portuguese in Asia, where they operated alone until Spain seized the Philippines in 1564, and especially in Japan, where they were unchallenged until this commercial-clerical incursion from Manila in 1593.

Father Valignano had in fact foreseen the danger, to the Jesuits, of Spain's wanting to compete in Japan; in his 1583 letter he had lectured Rome on "Why it is not convenient that other religious orders should come to Japan". One of his reasons for maintaining a Jesuit monopoly over Japanese souls was blatantly partisan: "whether it be through pure zeal or whether through something else", the Mendicant Orders always ganged up against the Jesuits; this could lead to doctrinal disputes,

> "...and if suchlike controversies occurred among those of the primitive Church, where there was such holiness and doctrine,

---

Spaniard Francis Xavier, and Alessandro Valignano was of course Italian. It is nevertheless true overall to say that while the major rivalry was between Jesuits and Franciscans for doctrinal reasons, nationalism also played a significant role because of the missions' close ties with, respectively, Portuguese and Spanish traders.

being so close to the Supreme Pontiff...it can easily be imagined what will happen here in Japan which is so distant and isolated".

However Valignano had a much broader perspective of the Church's relations with the Japanese:

"On no single point", he wrote, "will they adjust themselves to our usages, but on the contrary, we have to accommodate ourselves to their ways in everything. This is very difficult for us, but if we did not do so, we would lose face, and do no good at all".

His other reasons manifested this unusually acute sensitivity to the Japanese. One was perhaps fairly obvious: the tightly disciplined Jesuits' success reflected Japanese disillusionment with Buddhist "splinter sects". His intuition about the Japanese put him far in advance of Church thinking then about the role of non-European converts:

"Japan is not a place which can be controlled by foreigners, for the Japanese are neither so weak nor so stupid a race as to permit this...Therefore there is no alternative to relying on training natives in the way they should go and subsequently leaving them to manage their church themselves. For this, a single religious order will suffice".

But Valignano's final reason, while making abundantly clear his fundamental distrust of the Spanish, was the sharpest assessment of the Japanese:

"Hitherto many of the Japanese lords had a great fear that we were concocting some evil in Japan, and that if they allowed the conversion of Christians in their fiefs, we could afterwards use them to raise rebellion on behalf of the King who supports us; for they could not understand why these monarchs should spend such vast sums on the mission, if it was not with the ultimate intention of seizing their lands...And now that they know that the kingdoms of Spain and Portugal are united, this existing suspicion would be vastly strengthened by the arrival of new foreign religious".

It was exactly what Hideyoshi would soon come to fear.

Somewhat surprisingly, Rome bought all Father Valignano's arguments; and influenced in large degree also by the huge success of the four young Japanese nobles' "embassy", in 1585 Pope Gregory XIII promulgated the Bull *Ex Pastoralis Officio* confirming Japan as a Jesuit monopoly. At the same time, Phillip II, King of the recently united but still distinct kingdoms of Spain and Portugal, confirmed Japan as a Portuguese commercial monopoly. It would not be surprising if Hideyoshi's learning of these unilateral dispositions of Japanese interests contributed significantly to his developing suspicions of the foreigners. The Jesuits saw to it that they were brought to the fore again after the arrival of the Spanish in 1593, but their efforts to have the Papal Bull enforced met no success; and the Franciscans, boasting of Hideyoshi's favourable reception, accused the Jesuits of cowardice for operating in disguise "as we do in England".[209]

Father Valignano was again perturbed by the next decision from Rome, to appoint a Bishop in Japan, which would inevitably further complicate – the Jesuits', his – lines of command and coordination of the Christian mission there. He lost this argument, and was not much assuaged that the new Bishop, the Portuguese Father Pedro Martins, was a Jesuit, the Order's former Provincial in India: Martins was pompous, pretentious, and told Valigano that he would keep his distance from the Jesuits now he was directly responsible to the Pope. Martins arrived in Nagasaki in August 1596 – and immediately found that there was one Jesuit he could not hold at arm's length: the new Father Rodrigues. The latter, with the assistance of the Christian General Konishi, still between campaigns in Korea, then secured permission for the Bishop, with himself as interpreter, to visit Hideyoshi at his not-long-completed Fushimi Castle, southeast of Kyoto.

But by the time they arrived in mid-November the Castle had been destroyed in a great earthquake that also destroyed much of Osaka Castle, and, in Kyoto itself, collapsed the Imperial Palace, and wrecked the *Daibutsuden*, Hideyoshi's Great Buddha Hall, and the mansions of a number of great nobles, including Ieyasu's. Hideyoshi was said to have only escaped from Fushimi Castle with difficulty, carrying three-year-old Hideyori in his arms. Nevertheless he received Martins amicably, perhaps in the open, as he expressed his shame at not having a house to receive him in; but it was Rodrigues whom he asked separately about a Spanish

---

209 There was an interesting and grisly parallel less than seventy years later in the Congo: newly-arrived intransigent Italian Capuchin missionaries actually fomented a war against a neighbouring territory where Portuguese Jesuit missionaries had been willing to compromise with local custom (Wills: *1688*).

ship that had recently been driven ashore on the coast of Shikoku: and in particular, whether (as was indeed the case) the King of Mexico and the Philippines was the same as the King of Portugal and India. Hideyoshi was clearly aware of what lay behind these missionaries.

And despite the long eerie calm since the 1587 expulsion order, despite the earlier welcome to the Spanish Franciscans and now the Portuguese Bishop, with the Spanish shipwreck it was all to come grievously unstuck, exactly as Valignano had foreseen thirteen years before. It was Spain's great Manila galleon, the *San Felipe*, bound for Acapulco with a fabulously rich cargo, that had been driven onto the shore of Shikoku, the day before Hideyoshi had been enraged by the Ming Emperor's attempt to create him King of Japan in return for his "reverent submission". The Shikoku *daimyo* promptly appropriated the cargo, as would have happened anywhere in Europe also; and the Franciscans, cocky as ever about their favoured status, rejected the Jesuits' offer to act as intermediaries (or so the Jesuit Fathers claimed), and confidently employed Masuda Nagamori, Hideyoshi's Commissioner of Investigations, to secure the recovery of the Spanish cargo. Bad mistake: when the ever-helpful Konishi suggested that Masuda take a good interpreter, the latter responded that

> "if I was going with the intention of reaching an agreement, I would need a good tongue; but as I am only going to collect the swag, hands are all that I need".

Perhaps Hideyoshi thought the Spanish treasure would be a welcome injection into his already depleted coffers for a renewal of the war in Korea to avenge China's insult; on the other hand, he still did not wish to jeopardise trade with the Philippines with its promise of breaking the Portuguese monopoly.

The *San Felipe*'s Pilot-Major (captain) resolved any such dilemma: in order to impress the Japanese with Spain's power, he showed Masuda a map of the extent of the Spanish Empire and told him its conquest had been greatly facilitated by the Church acting as what we would call – since the Spanish Civil War – a "fifth column". It confirmed Hideyoshi's worst fears, and he reacted at once: all six of the Franciscans in Japan and seventeen of their local followers were crucified (a Japanese form of execution, only incidentally a mockery of Christianity) at Nagasaki in February 1597. Hideyoshi threatened to include all the Jesuits as well, then decided their role in the China trade was too valuable, though three

Jesuit laymen were included in the crucifixion by mistake. In Japan, outside the limits of the Christian community itself, the crucifixions were barely noticed. The Spanish, on the other hand, were probably more outraged at the Portuguese than at the Japanese: they accused the Jesuits of denouncing the Franciscans as conquistadors, and claimed that the Portuguese Fathers had not only refused to intervene on behalf of the Spanish priests but had even entertained their executioner. The bitterness fostered Spanish-Portuguese antagonism throughout the remaining forty years of their united kingdom.

Despite, or perhaps because of his long efforts to make the Jesuits acceptable to Japanese leaders, Father Valignano now turned tough himself, urging Philip II to cancel the annual Black Ship from Macao in order to cause an economic crisis in Japan which could bring about Hideyoshi's official recognition of Christianity or his overthrow. His advice was not taken. Hideyoshi himself, replying to the Governor of the Philippines' protest at the confiscation and crucifixions, was the more measured. Pointing out the threat to Japan's social structure by Christian propagandising, he went on:

> "If perchance, either religious or secular Japanese proceeded to your kingdoms and preached the law of Shinto therein [interestingly, he did not refer to Buddhism], disquieting and disturbing the public peace and tranquility thereby, would you, as lord of the soil, be pleased thereat? Certainly not; and therefore you can judge what I have done".

Outside the bias of religious dogmatism, this was unanswerable.

It seems all the more extraordinary that Hideyoshi nevertheless still allowed the Jesuits to continue their "underground" activities: he must have known of all of them, all the "secret" churches, all the continuing conversions, including more at high level. But in ordering the crucifixions then leaving the missionaries be, as had happened with the expulsion edict, Hideyoshi was not being inconsistent or exhibiting a flash of madness – as he had in slaughtering Hidetsugu's family in 1595 – but was issuing a warning, creating an atmosphere of uncertainty that he hoped would keep the Christians within bounds, *his* bounds, while not interfering with trade. So the (discreet) proselytising continued. The Fathers estimated their flock at around 500,000 by 1600, a considerable growth despite the uncertainty many must have felt about the potentially conflicting claims of religion and county. But by then Hideyoshi was dead.

Hideyoshi: last rites

As Konishi and Ieyasu were already exploring the possibilities for the settlement of the war in Korea, Hideyoshi was dying, and his major concern was to secure the succession for five-year-old Hideyori. As much as the failure of his plans to conquer the Asian mainland, he probably regretted the loss of some of the greatest architectural and artistic creations on which he had lavished so much more than the mere passing fancy of the parvenu: the *Jurakutei* palace where he had entertained the Emperor, sacrificed in 1595 to his rage at Hidetsugu's failure to measure up as his heir; the *Daibutsuden* Great Buddha Hall destroyed in the great earthquake of 1596, along with his newest castle-palace at Fushimi, on the hill called Momoyama. Fushimi Castle was so badly damaged it could not be rebuilt, and its remains were dismantled twenty years later as the Tokugawa finished obliterating the Toyotomi; gilded roof tiles excavated in modern times are the last gleaming hint of its splendour.

His fame nevertheless secure, Hideyoshi was now obsessed with perpetuating his name. Some time earlier, he had expressed the wish to be given the posthumous title of *Shin-Hachiman*, the "New God of War". *Hachiman* had been the title appropriated by the semi-legendary 4th-5th century fifteenth Emperor, Ojin, supposedly claiming the credit for his mother's conquest of Korea while she was pregnant with him. People would have recognized the connection, even though Hideyoshi's ambition had been to go further, to conquer China. Whether Hideyori, his son and successor, bestowed the title I have not discovered; but it may have been in Hideyoshi's mind in the period leading up to his death as he focused increasingly on trying to ensure Hideyori's succession. In July 1598 he had senior *daimyo* swear an oath of loyalty to Hideyori; in August he established a Regency Council of five of them, including Ieyasu, and (according the Jesuits) had the latter, his son Hidetada, and four colleagues then repeat their oath, and do so again, separately or together, on 5 and 8 September, and yet again "a few days later" – appealing

> "to you addressed here to establish Hideyori. Nothing weighs on my mind other than this. Again and again I appeal to you over Hideyori...I grieve at this parting".

In August, Father Valignano, accompanying the new (and last) Bishop replacing Martins, had arrived in Nagasaki, without prior notice or permission, for his third visit to Japan; by the first week in September, accompanied of course by his interpreter, the Jesuit Father João Rodrigues, they arrived at Fushimi to pay respects to the *Taiko*. But while Hideyoshi ordered their gifts to be brought for him to see, it was Rodrigues alone whom he invited, on 6 September, to visit him in the dazzlingly restored splendour of Fushimi Castle. Rodrigues found him looking grotesquely emaciated, but still mentally active, appreciative of the Jesuit's frequent visits and regretful there would soon be no more; and he urged that the Portuguese delegation visit Hideyori. On 7 September Hideyoshi summoned Rodrigues again, to invite him to attend betrothal ceremonies he had previously arranged for that day for the offspring of various *daimyo*, to try to tie them together and help protect his life's work. But when Rodrigues, inevitably, made a last attempt to raise the salvation of his soul, Hideyoshi "kindly but firmly" changed the subject.

Outside his immediate family and the Regency Council, and perpetuating ambiguity to the end, Rodrigues, himself sorrowing that "a man of such undoubted genius is destined for hell-fire", was one of the last people to see the dying dictator, an extraordinarily touching end to an extraordinarily complex relationship between Hideyoshi and the Christian Westerners who had been fascinating, worrying and outraging him for almost thirty years, since the days when he no doubt observed and wondered at Nobunaga's friendship with Father Frois.

Shortly before his death, in keeping with aristocratic cultural tradition, Hideyoshi composed his last poem:

> "Coming like the dew
> Going like the dew
> My life
> Osaka
> The dream of a dream".

And so he died, before mid-September, aged sixty-three, after a life, between the dews, lived at full flood. At his deathbed he was surrounded by his innermost circle, no doubt already calculating their future chances: his treasured little only surviving son and heir Hideyori, Kita-no-Mandokoro, his still-loved wife of thirty-eight years, his beloved consort Yodo-gimi, mother of both his sons, the five great *daimyo* of the Regency Council. Not long afterwards the Emperor Go-Yozei, who ten years before had bestowed on Hideyoshi the enormous honour of visiting his private mansion in Kyoto, now declared him a divinity of the first rank, with the title *Hokoku Daimyojin*, Most Bright God of Our Bountiful Country. Little Monkey had come a long way to this.

But his succession indeed turned out to be only a dream. Almost at once the innermost circle split, with Tokugawa Ieyasu, backed by two more members of the Regency Council, setting himself in opposition to little Toyotomi Hideyori, who was supported by the other two; and in 1600 Ieyasu pushed the split to open warfare, culminating in his crushing victory at the battle of Sekigahara. In 1603, when he secured from the Emperor appointment to the traditional role of Shogun, or commander-in-chief of the army, Ieyasu effectively became ruler of Japan; and, despite formally ceding the title to his son Hidetada three years later, he maintained his grip on the country and his hostility to Hideyori, holed up in the great fortress of Osaka Castle but still regarded by many as the legitimate ruler to whom Ieyasu had himself repeatedly sworn allegiance.

Initially Ieyasu continued Hideyoshi's ambiguous policy towards the Christians – and also took on Rodrigues as his interpreter. By this time the Portuguese commercial monopoly was under challenge from total newcomers, the Dutch and the English, without priests but seeking nevertheless to use their Protestantism to undermine their Catholic rivals – a doctrinal confusion that Valignano had not foreseen in his worst imaginings. But Ieyasu's extreme conservatism led to his suppression of Christianity in 1614; and with many Christian samurai and their followers then joining Hideyori's forces, the stand-off with the latter could not continue. In 1615 Ieyasu attacked Osaka Castle. It was reported that the Christians, probably by now a majority of the defenders, openly displayed their faith: an observer wrote that

> "there were so many crosses, *Jesus* and *Santiagos* on the flags, tents and other martial insignia...that this must needs have made Ieyasu sick to his stomach".

But a traitor – said to be a Mori, one of Hideyoshi's oldest allies – set fire to the Castle, and Ieyasu's forces triumphed. Hideyori's supporters were all killed, some say 100,000. Hideyori himself and his mother are presumed to have committed *seppuku*. Hideyoshi's line was finished.

In Europe there were two contemporary examples of usurpers vilifying their predecessors in order to shore up their own claims to rule. One usurpation had in fact occurred in the late 15th century when Richard III of England was overthrown by the remotely-related Henry Tudor, who became Henry VII; based on the researches, now challenged as a Tudor hatchet job, of Henry VIII's loyal (up to a point) and otherwise admirable servant Sir Thomas More, Richard was eventually very publicly demonised in Shakespeare's *Richard III* in 1592 (the year of Hideyoshi's first invasion of Korea). The other usurpation, in Russia in 1606 (the year Ieyasu passed on the title of Shogun), was the overthrow of Boris Godunov's infant son, the year after his own death, by disloyal nobles in connivance with the Poles (supported, incidentally, by the Jesuits); the noble family which came out on top from the ensuing troubles, the Romanovs who would rule Russia for the next 304 years, then vilified Boris, who would eventually be likewise very publicly demonised in Pushkin's drama and Mussorgsky's subsequent great opera. I wondered if Hideyoshi was ever subjected to such infamy from the Tokugawa who overthrew him: but a shrewd and knowledgeable friend in Japan suggested that Tokugawa writers (one would assume reflecting their rulers, as had happened in England and Russia) "in their prudence and 'wisdom' treated Hideyoshi with benign neglect". A hero is not readily disparaged in Japan.

Christianity in Japan: last rights
Tokugawa Ieyasu only lived another year to enjoy his victory. While he had begun the persecution of Japanese Christians, and disposed of many more in the battle of Osaka, it was his son and grandson who were more ruthless, the thousands executed over the next two decades culminating in the deaths of 37,000 men, women and children, mostly Christians, in the suppression of the peasant rebellion in the Shimabara Peninsula of Kyushu, in 1637-1638.

Atrocities were not confined to foreigners.

As the Jesuits' fifty-year penetration of Japan was being forcibly closed down, they were beginning an extraordinary, almost two-centuries' long, advance into China. It is interesting to compare these first examples of direct cross-cultural contact between the West and the East, without the intermediary roles previously played by the various ethnic and religious groups across the Silk Road. Japan was previously completely unknown in the West, China only through Marco Polo's Cathay; the three letters from Franciscan Giovanni da Montecorvino, the "Archbishop of Cathay" in Yuan Dynasty Beijing three centuries before, were lying buried in the Vatican archives, unknown to his Jesuit successors.[210]

---

210   See 1300 chapter: Devorguilla of Galloway

The first and perhaps the greatest of these, the Italian Father Matteo Ricci, arrived by sea in 1582 at the Portuguese colony of Macau; but, after a difficult translation to the mainland against strong Chinese resistance, in 1601, the year after Sekigahara, he too succeeded in establishing himself in Beijing,[211] where his deep personal understanding both of the Chinese and of their philosophical beliefs made him far more successful than Giovanni in developing access to the Imperial Court – though he never did succeed in gaining direct access to the Emperor himself, something that would have to await another dynasty and another seventy years. Nevertheless the relationship Ricci and his China Jesuit successors established with some Court mandarins and some Emperors enabled their mission to survive the Ming's fall forty years later and endure (with hiccups) for almost another century and a half, through the greatest years of the successor Qing dynasty.

Like the (mostly) Portuguese Jesuits in Japan, the (mostly) Italian Jesuits in China, like Giovanni before them, believed that if the ruler could be converted to Christianity, the multitudes would necessarily follow, or be made to follow, a view Europe was moving towards sanctifying in the post-Reformation practice of *Cuius regio, eius religio* [the nation's religion is that of its king]. But in China the Jesuits brought to their efforts two approaches not shared by their counterparts in Japan, and based them on a social standing not available to the latter which they secured by their own skilful contrivance.

After ten years Ricci realised that equating his priestly role with that of the Buddhist and Taoist clergy, which initially seemed the natural course, was a serious mistake: the bonzes were mostly ignorant, idle and corrupt, and, worse from the viewpoint of his objectives, despised by the Confucian mandarins who governed China for the Emperor. His real breakthrough thus came when he succeeded in assimilating himself to the mandarinate, giving him access to those whom he really wished to

---

211 Two years later, in 1603, a Portuguese Jesuit, Bento de Goes, set out for Beijing by the old Silk Road spur from India, through Afghanistan and over the Hindu Kush and Pamir ranges to the northern route around the Taklamakan Desert; and though he died near Jiayuguan at the extreme western end of the Great Wall after a gruelling three-year journey, through his last letter he was instrumental in confirming Ricci's belief that China was, in fact, one and the same as Marco Polo's Cathay, not a separate country - Ricci being unaware that the identification had previously made by an Augustinian friar, Martín de Rada, in a book probably published in 1577, the year he had left Europe.

influence – and of course convert. This was largely achieved, and his and his successors' subsequent influence enhanced, by their knowledge of the latest Western mathematics and technology which evoked the serious interest of some of the most important Emperors.

This process began with the clocks Ricci gave the Ming Emperor Wanli, and developed with his skills in map-making, and in theoretical astronomy, especially for establishing the correct days for sacred Imperial rites: Ricci's teacher was a friend of Galileo. These and related attributes were shared by many of his successors, and they included, in due course, the manufacture of guns: Father Adam Schall established a cannon foundry by the 1630s. In addition to these intellectual advantages, and the assistance of converts in the mandarinate, imperial acceptance of the China Jesuits' presence at Court, as well as tolerance of their sometimes not very vigorous proselytising efforts, was considerably eased by the ingenious philosophical and theological efforts they made to reconcile Christian doctrine and liturgy with Chinese Confucian practices (until these "Chinese Rites" were prohibited by a closed-minded Pope in 1704).[212]

In Japan, on the other hand, things were rather different: bonzes were on the whole equally despised but there was no mandarinate to provide a channel for acceptability; Hideyoshi was essentially intellectually uncurious; astronomical calculations did not figure significantly in the maintenance of his authority; and the missionaries there could hardly arouse in him a scientific interest in their unsophisticated collection of a clock, a bell, "organs, harpsichords

and viols", even though he "took great delight in listening to their music".[213] Hideyoshi also wanted cannon, but there were no foundrymen among the Japan Jesuits. Amongst the Jesuits that were there, the closest

---

212   See 1700 chapter: Sophie Charlotte of Prussia

213   Something very close to the sound of the Jesuits' music-making - but in China - has been reconstructed on the CD *Messe des Jésuites de Pékin* (AUVIDIS/ ASTRÉE E8642; Paris 1998), which includes settings from a book of music brought to Beijing a decade after Ricci's death. The program notes mention that the astronomer Father Ferdinand Verbiest was appointed "Master of Music" in 1666 by the Emperor Kangxi, and that by the middle of the following century, at the court of the Emperor Qianlong, there were eighteen choirboys [cf. Giovanni da Montecorvino's forty choirboys in Beijing in 1305 - 1300 chapter], ten violins, 2 cellos, a double bass, eight wind instruments, four ivory flutes, seven lutes, a harpsichord, a bagpipe, and a "set of bamboo plates". One of the Fathers wrote about this time:

in attitude to Matteo Ricci was, not surprisingly, his own former mentor, the Italian Father Valignano, who had received Ricci into the Jesuit novitiate, shared his Japanese experiences with him when they overlapped in Macao while Ricci awaited permission to enter China, and subsequently resolutely supported Ricci's skilful and subtle handling of the issues associated with the "Chinese Rites" (as well as his adoption of mandarin dress, just as his disciple in Japan, João Rodrigues, adopted Japanese dress); but he was only ever an infrequent visitor in Japan, and with less tractable clay – Jesuit and local – to deal with. More significantly, while the Japan Jesuits were tolerated because the Portuguese commercial operations were thought to be dependent on them, they were severely compromised through being associated with the Christian *daimyo* whose loyalty Hideyoshi suspected – and Ieyasu was only too anxious to do away with all three.

This was the main difference: the Portuguese Jesuits in Japan were at a distance from the capital, and had to cope with the very present Portuguese merchants; the Jesuits in China were at the Imperial Court, and merchants were securely sequestered far away in Macao. Perhaps there was also another reason for the different experiences: Italian Jesuits were more subtle than Portuguese in imparting their evangelical message, Chinese rulers were more subtle than Japanese in deflecting it. The mutual attractions and repulsions in the brief Western-Japanese encounter still ring familiar bells of good and ill; the longer mutually-rewarding interplay in China has little echo in the pattern of recent and contemporary Western-Chinese relations. The ambiguity and complexity are still with us. But greatness?

By the time of the Shimabara massacre, the English had already stopped coming to Japan, their trading post having collapsed through mismanagement in 1623, and the East India Company, chartered in 1600, focusing increasingly on India proper; the Spanish had been evicted in 1624; and the Portuguese were finally sent packing in 1639, immediately after the Shimabara revolt in which they were suspected of being involved. When fourteen courageous – or naïve – Portuguese arrived at Nagasaki the following year, to petition the Shogun for

---

"Mass began to the sound of musical instruments and vocal music, which is very much to the liking of the Chinese and sometimes also quite pleasing to Europeans"

- a viewpoint the CD might possibly still evoke.

549

renewed access, most were executed and their ship burnt. From then on only the Dutch remained, confined to the tiny island of Deshima in Nagasaki harbour, and solely for trade.[214] Apart from that small window, every shutter around the whole of Japan was slammed shut, and stayed shut for two hundred and fourteen years: not only were no foreigners allowed anywhere else in the country, but Japanese were forbidden to go abroad under pain of death. Then, after the importunings of Commodore Perry, Japan was again confronted with the schizophrenic problem, which still endures, of dealing with the West – how to remain Japanese while beating the West at its own game.

In 1864, soon after Japan was "opened", it was discovered that there were Christians still living in the village of Urakimi, south of Nagasaki; for two hundred years they had been practising their religion in great secrecy, as best they could, including with female officiants. As Christianity was still outlawed they were promptly rounded up by the authorities and exiled to remote parts of Japan, until the law's repeal in 1872 allowed the few survivors to return. At 11.02am on 9 August 1945 the plutonium bomb intended for Nagasaki's Mitsubishi shipyards exploded over Urakimi.

In all of Japan's "Christian century", those six Spanish Franciscans crucified after the *San Felipe* disaster were the only Christian missionaries executed by the Japanese authorities. For most of the sixty-five years up to the 1614 suppression order the missionaries were received courteously by the rulers and permitted great freedom to preach their alien gospel through many parts of Japan. Those were the years of the wars and religious purges of the Reformation and Counter-Reformation in Europe, the executions of Catholic and Protestant statesmen and clerics in Tudor England, the depredations of the Spanish Inquisition, the Huguenot wars in France, all Europe divided by religious fanaticisms that were about to devastate the entire continent in the Thirty Years War. What, one wonders, would have been the fate of a hypothetical reciprocal group if, as Hideyoshi asked the Governor of the Philippines, a Japanese group had proceeded to those kingdoms and preached the law of Shinto therein.

---

214   There is an interesting ancient parallel: in the 8th century BCE the Etruscans are said to have isolated Greek traders on the island of Pithecusae (modern Ischia) in the Bay of Naples, their first base in the western Mediterranean, in order to keep foreign influence out of the mainland. As in Japan, the policy eventually failed.

Tea and treason

When Hideyoshi installed his ill-fated and ill-treated nephew Hidetsugu as *Kwampaku* in 1592, he had had the young man swear an oath which included:

> "Item. I will follow Hideyoshi's example, except in three things –
> in the tea ceremony, in hawking, and in the courtship of women".

Tea, only introduced commercially into Europe from China, by the Dutch, in 1610, had long been universal in Japan, regardless of class. But Hideyoshi would have been referring to his addiction to the lengthy and elaborate tea ceremony, to the creation of the most un-Zen-like ostentation of golden tea chambers, to the search for rare and fabulously expensive tea utensils, to the excessive pride in displaying these treasures, and perhaps particularly to the indulgence of famous but ultimately politically unreliable tea masters – all that, notwithstanding the twinkle clearly in his admonition (in all three, for that matter).

The traditional Japanese tea ceremony was of course noted by the Jesuits. In a wonderfully lucid passage, Father Luis de Almeida reported, about the time of Hideyoshi's assumption of power, that

> "There is a custom among the noble and wealthy Japanese to show their treasures to an honoured guest at his departure as a token of their esteem. These treasures are made up of the utensils with which they drink a powdered herb, called *cha*, which is a delicious drink once one becomes used to it. To make this drink, they pour half a nutshell of this powdered herb into a porcelain bowl, and then adding very hot water they drink the brew. All the utensils used for this purpose are very old – the iron kettles, the porcelain bowl, the vessel containing the water to rinse the porcelain bowl, the tripod on which they place the lid of the iron kettle so as not to lay it on the mats. The vessel containing the *cha* powder, the spoon used to scoop it out, the ladle to draw the hot water from the kettle, the hearth – all these make up the treasures of Japan, just as rings, gems and necklaces of precious rubies and diamonds do with us. There are experts who evaluate such utensils and act as brokers when they are bought. Best quality *cha* costs about nine or ten ducats a pound and is drunk at gatherings at which the host, according

to his means, shows off his treasures, These gatherings are held in special houses, which are used only on such occasion and are kept wonderfully clean".

The value and consequent display of tea utensils was clearly as striking to Father Almeida as the ceremony itself.

But it is precisely the ceremony that has long bemused Western observers: epitomizing in some ways a society that to most of them has long been and still remains an enigma. The greatest tea master in Japan's history, Sen no Rikyu, who served both Nobunaga and Hideyoshi, laid down his *Seven Secrets*:

"Make a delicious bowl of tea; lay the charcoal so that it heats the water; arrange the flowers as they are in the field; in summer suggest coolness, in winter, warmth; do everything ahead of time; prepare for rain; and give those with whom you find yourself every consideration".

The rules sound straightforward enough when expressed so simply and elegantly; but they require the seamless performance of a prescribed ritual to reach their objective.

Perhaps it was this ritualistic aspect that initially attracted Father Rodrigues to the tea ceremony, though as in the Church liturgy he saw the focus of the ritual itself as something higher – and not a little Christian:

"The aim of this art of tea is to produce courtesy, politeness, modesty, exterior moderation, calmness, peace of body and soul without any pride or arrogance, fleeing from all ostentation, pomp, external grandeur and magnificence".

Tea itself however is attributed with entirely practical qualities – by the Chinese and Japanese, he says:

"It aids digestion, expels drowsiness, and relieves headaches; it brings down fever, eases the heart, and relieves melancholy; it is conducive to chastity, because it cools the kidneys, and it flushes out excess body fluid, thus bringing relief to pain caused by the stone";

but he adds his own deduction:

"As a result of these healthy properties, plague and pestilence are seldom experienced in China and Japan, despite the densely populated nature of these two countries".[215]

These and highly detailed observations about the tea ceremony, its appropriate setting and its purposes were included in a long exposition which he wrote to back up his instruction that all Jesuit residences in Japan should have a tearoom to facilitate their assimilation to the Japanese and their customs. He himself had one: in 1612, two years after Rodriguez had been expelled from Japan, Father Francisco Pires wrote that he had closed off a part of his lodgings, and

"made an entrance, with a door and steps, to the outside, whereby lay people could enter. He set up for himself a *chanoyu*, which is an iron kettle in which water is kept boiling the whole day and a charcoal fire. This", Pires added, and it was not with approval, "is a Japanese custom in the houses of the nobles".

To a Westerner, the way from the rules to the achievement of the objective Rodrigues described seems less a "dewy path", as it was described, than a minefield of potential shades of incorrectness. And I will step on one of the bigger mines: the proposition that "acting in full consideration of others" in the tea ceremony has a wider social value is difficult to reconcile with the ruthlessness and aggressive militarism of Hideyoshi and his contemporaries. And if it be argued that tea is for friends, ruthlessness for others, let us not forget his nephew Hidetsugu's poor wife and children.

Hideyoshi's practice certainly did not meet Father Rodrigues' understanding of the purpose of tea ceremonies: rather, it justifies

---

215 In his essay "The Historical Significance of the Way of Tea", in Varley and Isao: *Tea in Japan*. McNeill endorses Rodrigues' view of tea-drinking as contributing to the control of diseases, and hence population growth, in early modern Japan and China because it involved nearly everyone boiling otherwise-contaminated water.

evaluating them in political rather than in purely cultural terms. The great American historian William McNeill has observed that Sen no Rikyu's popularisation of the tea ceremony for *daimyo*, samurai and citizens enabled them to preserve

> "fellowship and freedom in the limited environs of the teahouse at a time when those values were fading before the advancing power of bureaucrats and armed hosts obedient to a single commander".

For all the self-abnegation that may have been involved in the actual conduct of the ceremony, there was still a clearly competitive edge to the entertainment, to demonstrate an aspect of an individual's worth.

> "Conspicuous restraint," McNeill remarked, "pressed to its limit, becomes flamboyant virtuosity; simplicity, valued highly enough, becomes luxury".

And for Hideyoshi it was a good deal more: the cultivation of the tea ceremony, and all that – and who – accompanied it, was a very deliberate cultural measure designed to demonstrate the completeness of his supremacy over other *daimyo*, to reinforce the legitimisation of his rule.

Over his declining years, when he might have been expected to be totally concentrated on the highly uncertain fortunes of the Korean campaigns, he displayed an increasing tendency to demonstrate this superiority through the cultivation of a whole range of the traditional arts. Apart from the construction and decoration of the castle-palaces, and the increasing employment of Sen no Rikyu, there were a huge falconry hunt in the provinces of Owari and Mikawa in 1591, and two famous cherry blossom-viewing excursions: in 1594, a huge expedition to the hills of Yoshino, south of Nara, commemorated in two richly elegant six-fold screens showing the aged Hideyoshi and a European (Jesuit?) onlooker; and, only a few months before his death, an even more extravagant excursion to view the cherry blossoms at the Daigo-ji, south of Kyoto, for which he had constructed a series of residences, tea houses and viewing platforms, all gone, as well as the elaborate garden still in the temple grounds.[216]

And then there was his running infatuation with *Noh* drama. He began sponsoring performances when he was created *Kwampaku* in 1585, though his personal participation began only in 1593: from his Korean war headquarters in Nagoya-jo he wrote to his wife that he had learned parts in fifteen or sixteen plays over two months. Later that year he acted before the Emperor in Kyoto in eleven plays over three days; the following year he commissioned a cycle of plays on his own life, and acted the lead in five at Osaka Castle; and his stage career continued to the end of his life. The great *daimyo*, Ieyasu included, had to act too, just as Louis XIV's nobles would a century later: as Richard Cocks, the last manager of the English godown at Nagasaki, was to report at the time Fushimi Castle was being finally dismantled, the *daimyo*,

> "now on a suddaine, are all sent for againe to come to the Court, which angereth them not a little, but they must, will they nill they; in paine of belly-cutting".

For Hideyoshi, the apogee of professional critical acclaim, for the Kyoto series, was that "the *Taiko*'s performance conveys the impression of enormous development"; but undoubtedly his audiences responded less scrupulously, as did those of the Sun King at Versailles.

However one of the most famous of Hideyoshi's cultural events, and certainly the most public, was the great tea gathering he held in 1587, just after his victory in Kyushu, in the spacious grounds of the *Kitano Tenman-gu* (shrine) in Kyoto. This was tea and circuses aimed at impressing everyone, not just the *daimyo*: the announcement, posted throughout the city, proclaimed:

> "Item. We order that a grand tea party be held in the woods of Kitano from the first to the tenth of the tenth month, depending upon the weather; in conjunction with this party, the famous tea vessels, without exception, will be assembled.

---

216 A detail of the Yoshino screens is reproduced in Hickman: *Japan's Golden Age*, p.41, and of a screen of the Daigo-ji viewing in Yamane: *Momoyama Genre Painting*, plate 32.

This event is being held so that the vessels can be displayed to serious persons.

Item. Persons serious about the tea ceremony, whether they are military, townsmen, or farmers, should bring along one kettle, one ladle, one drinking vessel, and either tea or barley...

Item. The Japanese, needless to say, even the Chinese, anyone with a connoisseur's interest, should join us...".

Fifteen hundred small enclosures, spread through the Kitano's plum trees, filled with people. On the first morning Hideyoshi himself and three tea masters, including Sen no Rikyu, served eight hundred of the guests; in the afternoon Hideyoshi wandered the grounds, seeing and being seen. There were also performances of music, dancing and plays. But the most important viewing was of the treasured tea utensils, displayed in a special enclosure within the shrine itself, together with his extraordinary portable "Golden Tea Chamber", which always accompanied him on his travels. But although the festival was scheduled to last ten days, it lasted only that first day, for reasons now unknown.[217]

The largest, the Kitano tea gathering, was still only one of Hideyoshi's many tea meetings where displays of his rare tea utensils were held to impress connoisseurs and collaborators – and even foreign clerics. For the latter, though, they were not always conducted with the solemnity usually associated with the taking of tea: in 1593 Father Pedro Bautista Blanquez, and two other Spanish Franciscans also crucified at Nagasaki four years later, had an audience with Hideyoshi at his Nagoya-jo field headquarters, and reported that, afterwards, the attendants

"took us to a chamber completely lined with gold plates [the portable Golden Tea Chamber] and on [Hideyoshi's] orders we were given food to eat with gold utensils – even the chopsticks were of gold. And at the end of the repast they gave us a delicate drink which they call *cha*. Then [Hideyoshi] came in and sat next to me, and taking hold of the girdle which I wore around my waist he flipped himself over the shoulders with it. Then he spoke for

---

217 According to Kinoshita and Palevsky, the event is still re-enacted every 1 December in the *Kitano Tenman-gu* park.

a short while with Father Gonçalo about the state of our holy religion".

It redounded to Hideyoshi's credit that since Nobunaga's death his tea ceremonies had been under the elevated guidance of Sen no Rikyu – supported in due course by seven other tea masters besides. As time went on Rikyu came more and more into Hideyoshi's confidence in administrative and political matters as well, even as his own way of tea became increasingly introverted while Hideyoshi's was manifested in outward display designed to impress, the Golden Chamber and its accoutrements the very opposite of rustic restraint, like *Le Hameau* of Marie Antoinette at Versailles. But it seems more likely that it was Rikyu's involvement in some inopportune political activity – not to mention his installation of a portrait bust of himself in a prominent Zen temple, or (as it was rumoured) his daughter's refusal to become one of his master's concubines – that led Hideyoshi, in 1591, to suddenly order him, now seventy-nine, to take his own life. Three thousand troops surrounded the tea master's house to ensure he did so; and the statue was displayed in public, hanging from a crucifix. For a master of an ascetic aesthetic, a highly ceremonial worldly renunciation, Rikyu's death poem contrasted sharply with Hideyoshi's elegiac resignation:

> "Seventy years of life –
> Ha ha! And what a fuss!
> With this sacred sword of mine,
> Both Buddhas and Patriarchs I kill!"

But then, look who actually killed whom.

In the shocked aftermath, there were those who thought tea was behind the tragedy after all – not the philosophical differences over the tea ceremony ethic, but something much grubbier:

> "In new vessels [Rikyu] has wilfully declared good points bad and bought them for mean prices. In rough vessels he has declared bad points good and bought them at high prices. He has called new pieces old and old pieces new. Bad he has called good, false he has called genuine".

The truth will never be known; could Hideyoshi, obsessed by his precious utensils, have killed because of "treasures of Japan"...tea bowls, for example?

Naeshirogawa

Tea bowls had even been part of his Korean war strategy.

The modern visitor to Japan, hurrying, mostly, between Osaka and Tokyo in central Honshu, has a tendency to think all Japan must be like that: buildings and people, people and buildings, with scarcely a gap between them the entire way. Already in 1609, when Don Rodrigo de Vivero y Velasco, Governor of the Spanish Philippines, was shipwrecked there, he said

> "you will not find even a quarter of a league unpopulated. Whenever the traveller raises his eyes, he will always see people coming and going".

But the Satsuma Peninsula, at the southern tip of Kyushu, is quite, quite different: a beautifully bucolic area, with rolling hills and patches of thick forest, an area dotted with tiny rustic villages. Memory plays false, I know; but I recall a green countryside, neatly-tended fields of tea bushes, a few people quietly going about their business, an atmosphere of intense calm.

The area is best known, nowadays, for the eighteenth century *samurai* village of Chiran, only an hour or so's drive from central Kagoshima, the capital of the ancient Satsuma province, whose people Father Francis Xavier found "the best who have yet been discovered" when he stepped ashore there in 1549, and whose next *daimyo* was so overwhelmingly put in his place by Hideyoshi in his Kyushu campaign thirty-eight years later. Implementing the obverse of Hideyoshi's ban on farmers from carrying weapons, the Tokugawa prohibited *samurai* from farming; but Chiran's *samurai* were so far from Edo/Tokyo that (as Kinoshita and Palevsky say) they "took up tea cultivation as a profitable yet suitably genteel occupation". Both the gentility and the profits are evident in the sturdy stone walls, the elaborately landscaped gardens and the comfortable-looking thatched and tiled houses. The nearby "Peace Hall" Museum commemorating Chiran's World War II air-base for *kamikaze* operations is a chill reminder of the *samurai*'s more usual role in Japanese history.

About another hour northwards, up the peaceful coastal road skirting Satsuma's west coast, is the even smaller village of Naeshirogawa, straggling along a tiny street that really doesn't lead from anywhere

much to anywhere else. There are no stately *samurai* residences here: this
is a village of potters. But they are no ordinary potters.

A number of the Japanese commanders in the Korean campaigns,
and notably Kato Kiyamasa, forcibly took hundreds of Korean potters
back to Japan at various times during the hostilities, and had them set
up kilns in their fiefdoms: so many, that the campaigns were even
referred to in later times as "the Pottery Wars". This ceramics campaign
against Korean potters was not the result of the accidental discovery
of their wares: Korean pottery, and the attractions of the simple Korean
rice bowl for use as a Japanese tea bowl, were well known before the
invasion. Korean potters were targeted.[218] Some of the captives established
kilns in western Honshu; but more of the Japanese officers involved seem
to have been from Kyushu, so the potteries were strewn across that
island, many going on to produce still-famous wares: Imari, Satsuma,
Takatori, Karatsu...

There were already potteries in Japan, and while their surviving
output is important historically, it was clearly inferior to Korean work.
It is curious, to those who are smitten by the sophistication and elegance
of Ming porcelain, that the Japanese did not seek to emulate its
perfection, but were attracted by the much simpler Korean wares. One
reason may be that Ming porcelain was less well known in Japan at the
time, given the Chinese ban on direct trade between the two countries,
though some must have filtered through in the voyages of the Portuguese
Black Ships during the second half of the sixteenth century. (*Kraak
Porselein* exportware, named after the Portuguese carracks by the Dutch,
does not seem to have entered Japan until the latter's trading began there
at the beginning of the 17th century.) Given the undeveloped state of
Japanese pottery, another reason may have been that Korean techniques
appeared far more accessible than Chinese. But the main reason was
undoubtedly aesthetic.

Korean ceramics, long influenced by the Chinese, took a different
turn during the 14th century, the first century of Korea's last reigning
dynasty, the Yi, who were to be deposed by the Japanese in 1910. The
new style was less refined in both shapes and finish: unstudied "peasant"
wares, with a whitish slip coating under a *punch'ong* glaze (celadon
glaze, called *Mishima* in Japan) producing a stoneware varying through
a range of understated colours from off-white to "mouse-grey" to a

---

218   In much the same way that Tamburlaine targeted artists and craftsmen.
See 1400 chapter: Tamburlaine

creamy-buff or a pinkish-beige. Curiously, although the style emerged after the suppression of Buddhism in Korea in 1392, its spirit became closely associated with Buddhist sensibility in Japan.

The tea masters, seeking with great art to create the appearance of unaffected simplicity, induced the cult of peasant rice bowls in this style, variously described as "unpretentious and spontaneous", or "rustic and dynamic", and they came to be regarded as ideal for the "refined pottery aesthetic" of the tea ceremony. As a consequence the intrinsically unfashionable became the "treasures of Japan" that were so fiercely sought after and treasured by Hideyoshi and the great collectors ever since. One of the most famous and rare Korean tea bowls, which still survives, was given its name *Tsutsuizutsu*, "well curb", at the time it was owned by Hideyoshi. All the great tea bowls were given such individual names, their provenance and history carefully recorded, changing hands at huge prices (which amazed the Jesuit Fathers even then), bequeathed to descendants, church or state – all exactly as the Old Masters in Europe.

The concept of artlessness was sometimes pushed to extremes, drawing sharp attention to the fine line between appreciation of what *is*, however imperfect, and the creation of imperfection for its own sake. There is a certain cultural gap between admiration for simple unpretentious bowls made by simple unpretentious Korean craftsmen, and adulation of objects that have been made "rustic" through maladroitness or artifice – so redolent of the technically-limited pots produced by Japanese kilns before Korean expertise was introduced by Hideyoshi's army's prisoners-of-war, as to risk giving the impression of being products of an atavistic chauvinism. It will be obvious that it is not a gap I have learned to cross.

The ancestors of the potters of Naeshirogawa were also Korean, among the defeated at the battle for Namwon Fortress in September 1597, and kidnapped by Hideyoshi's cohorts after the battle. But unlike other hi-jacked potters, captured at various times and places, who were brought back to Japan with the withdrawing Japanese forces, these were separated from their captors somewhere and somehow between Korea and Japan. From then on, on their own, their experience was different from the others'; and their story is beautifully told in the little volume *The Heart Remembers Home*, written by Shiba Ryotaro during the 1960s and '70s, elegantly translated and with a valuable background essay by our friend of many decades, Eileen Kato, the Irish wife of the distinguished late Japanese diplomat Yoshiya Kato.

Family history related to Shiba Ryotaro by Chin Jukan, the fourteenth generation descendant of these potters, said they had drifted ashore on Shimabara beach on the west coast of Satsuma province, just south of the little fishing port of Kushikino, a short distance from Naeshirogawa, and just after Tokugawa's victory at Sekigahara in October 1600, almost exactly three years after their seizure at Namwon. But it had not preserved how they lost their Japanese captors, how they found their way to the southwestern-most coast of Kyushu, whose ships they came in, why it took them so long. Chin Jukan relates their confusion at finding themselves in an uninhabited country:

> "Every house [in Naeshirogawa]", Shiba Ryotaro wrote, "hands down the traditional telling of the terrible sadness and homesickness suffered at this time; the memory of it was something that lived among them like a house spirit".

It clearly still does.

The survivors eventually moved a little way inland, built huts – and a kiln. Still there was no sign of any officialdom, Satsuma being preoccupied with the problems of having been on the wrong side at Sekigahara, but locals began to show up; amazed by the pottery, they barged in, caused damage, a blow was struck in the mutual incomprehension, and the local bully-boys came and bashed and destroyed. The Koreans moved further inland, and came to a place with gentle hills, trees in abundance, and "a wide sky" (always important to Koreans), that reminded them of the countryside around Namwon. It was Naeshirogawa. Nearby villagers treated them better than the coast people, but it was another three years before the authorities caught up with them. Their condition was so pitiful that the Satsuma *daimyo*, Shimazu Yoshihiro, offered them accommodation in Kagoshima; but they refused to move:

> "'Look at yonder hill', they said" [Chin Jukan told Shiba Ryotaro], "'When we climb that hill called Sanburaka, we can see beyond it to the East China Sea by which we came. Far, far away beyond the sea route, on the other side, lie the beloved hills and rivers of Korea. We in our misfortune have had to abandon the tombs of our ancestors and have been carried off and brought here to this alien place, but if we stand upon that hill and build an altar and perform the rites for our ancestors, the good effect will reach out to the far-off hills and rivers of the homeland and

console the spirits of our ancestors where they lie sleeping in that distant land' ".

So the Koreans stayed at Naeshirogawa. The hill is now called Gyokuzan-gu, but the shrine is still there.

Shimazu Yoshihiro also decreed non-combatant *samurai* status for the potters, for protection from any more importunate neighbours, and they settled down to serious potting. But they never forgot their origins, and neither did their neighbours: when the Meiji Government abolished social classes late in the nineteenth century, they were exposed to serious abuse, even though they had long since been full Japanese citizens.

Apart from securing acceptance from the local inhabitants, the main problem the first potters had was finding good quality kaolin, the white clay they needed to make their Korean-style white pots and bowls; but when some was found, the resulting "White Satsuma" ware delighted the *daimyo*, who presented a great quantity to the Tokugawa Shogun, and it rapidly achieved great fame:

"Although it lacked the charming simplicity of Yi ware," Shiba Ryotaro wrote, "never before had people seen ceramics of such refined elegance and grace. It was even said, 'Satsuma was once renowned for the valour of its fighting men; now it is known for the beauty of its ceramics' ".

In gratitude – and exclusiveness – Yoshihiro elevated Naeshirogawa into a domain manufactory, exclusively for the Shimazu clan,

"and so it came about that the richest merchants of the realm, even if they put up ten thousand gold pieces, could not purchase a single tea bowl of White Satsuma".

Naeshirogawa's other main ware, the gleaming Black Satsuma, *Gozenguro*, "the Lord's black", was allowed "as general necessity demanded it". The highly decorated "brocade" ware more generally associated with the name Satsuma was not a specialty here.

And so Naeshirogawa has continued for three hundred years, though of course it lost its *daimyo* privileges when the Meiji era replaced the long Tokugawa Shogunate. It is twenty years now since my wife and I visited the house and kiln of the fourteenth generation Chin Jukan, on the long straggling street of Naeshirogawa, not long after Eileen Kato published Shiba Ryotaro's book. Chin Jukan himself was away on one of his many trips for business and cultural education, but Mrs Chin kindly received us, and showed us his traditional Korean-style "climbing kiln" up the hill-slope at the back of the garden, and then, in the elegantly simple house, their stunning collection of treasured White Satsuma and *Gozenguro*, at least one piece from the hand of every one of the fourteen Chin Jukans until now.

So, in a unified Japan, in Naeshirogawa, in this peaceful and beautiful backwater, the story of the potters' brutal uprooting and the long celebration of their artistic genius seems to be a metaphor for the two natures of Toyotomi Hideyoshi himself, and the periodic revival of this duality among his countrymen.

Portrait of Sophie Charlotte. Wikimedia

GERMANY

SOPHIE CHARLOTTE OF PRUSSIA: *KULTUR* VERSUS *KAMPF* IN BERLIN

"Germany is warlike out of morality – not out of vanity or glory-seeking imperialism... Germany's whole virtue and beauty...first flowers in war. Peace does not always suit it."

Thomas Mann: *Thoughts in Wartime*

Thomas Mann's encomium to war was not the braying of a member of the Kaiser's Imperial General Staff, or the twittering of some addle-pated pensioned cavalryman: it was written in 1914, when he was thirty-nine, a year after *Death in Venice*, fifteen years before his Nobel Prize for Literature. Mann's super-patriotism lasted throughout the First World War, though he was to become an early and outspoken critic of the Nazis before Hitler's rise to power. But how could he have ever thought this way? And he was surely not alone, not in the First World War, not in the Second. What have we here?

We have travelled quite a bit, though not lived, in Germany; but everyone in the 20th century lived, to a greater or lesser extent, *with* Germany. I first experienced it personally only in 1957, when, on the way to a student holiday in Italy, I stopped off in Munich to go to the jolly Hofbräuhaus beer-hall and the Dachau concentration camp 16 kms to the northeast. Germany appears here because of the persistence of that contrast – and Sophie Charlotte, the attractive and intelligent first Queen of Prussia, appealed to me not only for herself but also for the contrast between her Berlin and the Prussian Berlin that lasted until just over half a century ago.

She was the daughter of the formidable Sophie, Electress of Hanover, grand-daughter of King James I of England and Scotland, and the sister of the rather boorish King George I of England. As Sophie Charlotte was a woman, less is known of her than of her husband, Frederick of Brandenburg, the first King of Prussia: an Irish visitor wrote a brief but engaging account of his meetings with her in 1701, and some of the letters she exchanged with her mother have survived. It was the age of the Baroque that swept Europe – and not least Frederick's and Sophie Charlotte's Berlin – in the wake of Louis XIV, whose sister-in-law was Sophie Charlotte's favourite cousin, the source of a few more epistolary references.

Sophie Charlotte played a large role in developing a somewhat frontier-Berlin's cultural life. But what was particularly striking was the regard held for her intellectual interests and her open-mindedness by her friend and mentor, Gottfried Wilhelm Leibniz, the great polymath, the other important witness. Leibniz himself was an historian, philosopher and mathematician; he had one of science's most celebrated feuds, with Isaac Newton, on the latter; and in a political-religious-diplomatic role was consulted by – or at least offered his advice to – not only the Court of Hanover, by whom he was employed, but also those of Prussia, Saxony, England, France, Austria and Russia, not to mention the Vatican. He tried particularly hard to interest them in intellectual and commercial exchanges with China, no longer possible through Moslem-controlled Central Asia, though his efforts foundered against Peter the Great's resolute determination to keep the trade route to China all Russia's own, a policy followed by most of his successors. And Leibniz vigorously supported the China Jesuits' accommodation with Confucian practice that Matteo Ricci had begun, when it came under Vatican condemnation.

Most of this was beyond Frederick's field of interest, or perhaps grasp, though he did appoint Leibniz to found a Prussian Academy of Science in imitation of Newton's Royal Society. On his death his son and successor could only think of calling him, insincerely, Frederick the Magnanimous – what he really meant was Frederick the Profligate – though that perhaps reflected more on junior's judgement than on his filial piety. Frederick I of Prussia was a monarch who preferred to impress his neighbours with his style rather than his soldiers, an obviously painful misfit in a line of Prussian militarists who stretched from his father to Hermann Goering; and he has still not been quite forgiven by even the most liberal German historians for his failure to recognise the importance of being *ernst*. Sophie Charlotte was more cultivated and more intelligent, both more serious and more interesting; but together they stand out against the Prussianism that ensnared Germans and embroiled Europe for two centuries.

The principal people in this chapter are as follows:

- Electress Sophie of Hanover (1630-1714) – Granddaughter of King James I of England. Mother of George (later King George I of Great Britain) and Sophie Charlotte.

- **Sophie Charlotte** (1668-1705) – Married Frederick III of Brandenburg. Electress, and later Queen of Prussia.

- Liselotte (1652-1722) – Beloved niece of Electress Sophie of Hanover. Married to Philippe, Duc d'Orléans, "Monsieur".

- Frederick (1657-1713) – Husband of Sophie Charlotte. Elector Frederick III of Brandenburg, later King Frederick I in/of Prussia.

- Frederick William (1688-1740) – Son of Sophie Charlotte and Frederick. King Frederick William I of Prussia – the Soldier King.

- Gottfried Wilhelm Liebniz (1646-1716) – German philosopher, mathematician, scientist and political adviser. Associate of Sophie Charlotte.

- John Toland (1670-1722454) – Irish theologist and writer, pioneer of free thought. Attendee at Sophie Charlotte's philosophical salons in Berlin.

I first visited Berlin in 1958, before the Wall, flying into Tempelhof Airport in West Berlin, the anchor of the airlift that had broken the Soviet blockade a decade before. I crossed into East Berlin on the S-Bahn, without authorization: Allied nationals were legally entitled to move anywhere within the double city, but I felt daring, foolhardy and somewhat nervous the whole time. I don't remember the already flourishing Western Zone of Occupation that much: Berlin had not yet had the burst of striking architecture that would accompany its return as the capital of Germany four decades later; but I have a vivid memory of block after block of mountains of concrete rubble in the Eastern Zone, behind the single rows of Soviet apartment buildings either side of a great avenue stretching away from Karl Marx Platz, with gangs of elderly women pecking at the debris and moving it somewhere else in straw baskets. The *Museum Insel*, before World War II and now again a treasure house of looted Near Eastern monuments, had still not re-opened – the Pergamon Altar was not returned by the Soviet Union until 1959. But in due course, a quarter of a century later, we got there to see it, and a good deal else, in an East Berlin which, to us, coming then from Moscow, seemed amazingly Western. We explored again post-Wall, then amongst the forests of construction cranes in Berlin-again-the-capital.

On my first visit to Germany and for a long time after I found myself, like many a visitor, looking at the burghers going about their business and asking myself "And what did *you* do during the War, Papa?". With determined and unforgiving self-analysis, Germans – unlike the Japanese, the Russians and the Chinese – have faced up to the horrors of their recent past in an extraordinary re-creation of their nation; but there is, still, the wonder that the people who could produce Charlottenburg and Ottobüren, Bach and *Faust*, Dürer and Käthe Kollwitz, could go on to produce Hitler and the Holocaust. The question is trite, profound, and still unanswered, and I am far from alone in asking it: a German journalist, Thomas Kielinger, wrote just before the sixtieth anniversary of D-Day:

> "As a German I have learnt to live with the unease that comes with so much shame for ever held aloft in its immediacy. Between Goethe's Weimar and next-door Buchenwald there is a truce that defies all peace-making" (*The Observer*, London; 30 May 2004).

The answer to the question certainly does not lie in Sophie Charlotte or Frederick the Magnanimous; but they provide an unexpectedly temperate footnote in the whole haunting and haunted German story.

In 1700 Leopold I, the Hapsburg Holy Roman Emperor, authorized Frederick III of Hohenzollern, Elector of Brandenburg, to make himself King in Prussia. Seeking Leopold's permission was a tactical rather than a necessary move, because the Prussian part of Frederick's domains, as a result of those quirky historical accidents that have blighted or blessed the course of history in dense and disputatious Europe, did not come within the bounds of the Empire. Two and a third centuries later, after the Hohenzollerns had soundly defeated the Hapsburgs at their own empire-building game, and both had disappeared from the face of Europe, Prussia's last ruler was to be Hermann Goering, in Hitler's Third Reich.

Just because, in history, something happens after something else, we can not claim it was inevitable: as Ben Franklin said, things might, but for want of a horseshoe nail, have turned out otherwise. But there is nevertheless, in the quickening reach of Prussia and Prussianism, a chilling sense of the inexorable. It could be said that when Frederick was crowned in Königsberg – then capital of Prussia, now in Russia – he got Prussia on the march. And, from 1698, literally, in his army, to the goose-step.

But in fact Frederick is regarded by most historians, as well as by his son, as completely out of step, a frivolous, spendthrift buffoon: this inexorable march, they say, was really initiated by his father, Frederick William of Brandenburg, known as the Great Elector for the same military reasons as Frederick's son was called the Soldier King and his grandson, Frederick II, was also called the Great. It was the son who began the denigration, and it was set in concrete by Frederick the Great's remark that his grandfather "was great in small things, small in great".

It is instructive that, in the histories of Prussia's rise to greatness, the frivolous Frederick is lucky to get a passing, and then usually disparaging, mention. Even though he increased his father's standing army from 29,154 to 39,963 troops (note the German precision), about the same as the population of Berlin at the time. What *did* you have to do to satisfy historians? Germans wrote off frivolous Frederick for interrupting "Germany's whole virtue and beauty" of going to war, to push out, first, Brandenburg-Prussia's boundaries, and then to consolidate an ever more cohesive and powerful German state. From outside, everyone else, seeing the same unbelligerent Frederick, wrote him off because he did not form part of the terrifying Prussian push to dominate, first, Germany, then Europe, then the world.

The back of German history is broken by Hitler. Ben Franklin notwithstanding, it is difficult, if not impossible, not to see that history as an inevitable sequence – precisely because, in trying to explain Hitler and his conversion of the German people into Nazi Germany, you have to keep going back somewhere to explain the origins of such evil in all that went before. Every step taken by the Great Elector, by the Soldier King, by Friedrich der Grosse and by their successors – every step *not* taken by frivolous Frederick – contributes to that explanation. Which of course always ends up inadequate to the evil anyway.

Poor Frederick. All he ever did – apart from increasing the army by only a third – was patronize architecture, jewellers and learning, in about that order. Admittedly he bankrupted the Treasury in doing so; but it would have been to the advantage of us all – Germans and the rest of us alike – if nationalist Prussian historians had focussed rather more on Frederick and less on his father and his descendants: on his interest in creating not only a beautiful capital in the somewhat grubby little Berlin he inherited, but also in establishing teaching and learning in the hitherto somewhat unlettered Brandenburg. But fixation on the "progress" of Prussia resulted in derision for Frederick's "aping" of Louis XIV: as if the grandeur of Versailles was justified by its scale and the belligerence of its creator, while the lesser splendour of Berlin was an unwarranted interference in Prussia's true destiny. We could have all done with a lot more Prussian frivolity and a lot less of Thomas Mann's "German morality".

Because of the disdain with which the historians of all stripes have treated Frederick, it is somewhat difficult to discern his real character. But they have almost all attributed his interests – whether grudgingly acknowledging his promotion of learning, or dismissing his encouragement of culture – to the influence of his second wife, Sophie Charlotte of Hanover, great-grand-daughter of the Stuart King James I of England, grand-daughter of Frederick the Winter King of Bohemia, daughter of the formidable Electress Sophie of Hanover, sister of the man who became King George I of England, and like her mother, a friend, socially and intellectually, of the mathematician, philosopher and all-round Enlightenment polymath Gottfried Wilhelm Leibniz. To his critics, poor Frederick had no character: not only did he not have the strengths of his family of soldier-kings, even his weaknesses were his wife's idea.

The making of a royal bluestocking

Sophie Charlotte – known to her Hanoverian family by the nickname "Figuelotte" – was, in her own right, very much an individual and an intellectual, both uncommon characteristics of royal wives who for centuries were required only to produce an heir suitable to ensure their husband's inheritance would be maintained.

The only biography of Sophie Charlotte I have been able to find is *Mémoires pour servir à l'Histoire de Sophie Charlotte, Reine de Prusse*, originally read – in French – during ten public sessions of the Prussian Royal Academy of Sciences and Literature in Berlin, between September 1790 and January 1800, by Monsieur Erman, Historiographer of Brandenburg, and published in Berlin in 1801 "at the expense of the author".[219] Erman's lectures were based partly on letters made available to him by the then King, Frederick William II, Sophie Charlotte's great-grandson, the nephew and successor of the childless Frederick the Great, and partly on the recollections of

> "those contemporaries of all levels of the state whom we were able to know during our youth";

they still convey a wonderfully musty whiff of 18th century elegance – and correctness.

Other aspects of Sophie Charlotte's life and character appear from the letters of her own contemporaries – her mother, Leibniz, John Toland, in particular – but she seems to have left little in writing herself outside a small number of letters: her passion was for the lively exchange of opinion, for conversation and debate on held beliefs and the consideration of alternatives, rather than on trying to record fixed conclusions, perhaps because she suspected they might prove intellectually limiting.

Sophie Charlotte's native intelligence was carefully fostered by the attention her remarkable mother paid to her upbringing and education. Sophie herself had had a most unhappy childhood: born in exile ten years after her father had been driven from the throne of Bohemia at the outset of the Thirty Years War, still only nineteen when her mother's brother Charles I of Great Britain lost not only his throne but his head. It was a dour start for someone who would die, at eighty-four, only two months short of becoming Queen of Great Britain herself.

It was not just that as the wife of Ernst August, youngest son of the modest North German House of Brunswick-Lüneburg, Sophie had limited social obligations. Her own experiences had made her positively interested in her children, and she gave them her love, personal attention and care: at one point, her husband accused her of loving them more than she loved him. She required their nannies and tutors to be loving and cheerful, and refused to have any who were "excessively religious" as she regarded them as too inflexible. Extraordinarily for those days, all seven children grew to healthy adulthood, which says a good deal for their genes and upbringing. They all began under the care of the remarkable Katherine von Harling, wife of Ernst August's

---

219 Microfilm from the British Library Reprographic Section. I have also drawn on Kroll's *Sophie: Electress of Hanover*, itself based on family letters in German collections, and *Letters from Liselotte* (see below).

chamberlain, a born educator whose cheerful but careful discipline was repaid with their affection. She was to stay with Sophie Charlotte when she went to Berlin, and in due course tried, unsuccessfully, to exercise a similar influence on the next generation, the intractable young Frederick William.

All her life Sophie maintained both her love and support for them all, in some cases through difficult times when sons rebelled against their father. However, as the only daughter in the middle of six sons, it is perhaps not surprising that Sophie Charlotte was Sophie's darling. What is surprising, for that time and many since, is that she was carefully educated, at least in her mother's interests: German, French, Latin, English, some Italian (the Electress herself was said to speak five languages, each of them without a pause), music, philosophical debate. They were to maintain an affectionate and intellectual closeness until Sophie Charlotte's death.

In 1679 the good Protestant Sophie took the eleven-year-old Sophie Charlotte to France, to visit her own older sister, Louise Hollandine, and a favourite niece, Elisabeth Charlotte, daughter of her older brother the Elector Charles Louis of the Palatinate.[220] However she made the voyage supposedly incognito, as Madame d'Osnabrück, to avoid having to submit to "humiliating" French rules of precedence. Probably it was also to play down any religious aspect to such a venture into Catholic France. But it was no great disguise: Ernst August was at that time Prince-Bishop of Osnabrück, the apanage of the youngest son of the House of Brunswick-Lüneburg.

Princess Louise Hollandine had herself in fact become Catholic and was now Abbess of Maubuisson;[221] but that she had converted was no impediment to Sophie's affection and intellectual companionship. Despite Louise's new piety, some old princely habits had died hard:

---

220 The Palatinate (Pfalz in German), with its capital at Heidelberg, was one of the secular electorates of the Holy Roman Empire. It is now part of the *Land* Rhineland-Pfalz. Charles Ernst, Louise Hollandine and Sophie were three of the thirteen children of Frederick of Bohemia, the "Winter King" (because his reign only lasted that one season), and Elizabeth of England, sister of Charles I.

221 At Saint-Ouen-l'Aumône, about 30kms northwest of Paris near Pontoise. This Cistercian convent was founded in 1236 by Blanche of Castile, daughter of Eleanor the sister of Richard the Lionheart and King John of England, wife of Louis VIII of France, and mother of the Crusader St Louis (see 1300 chapter: Devorguilla of Galloway). The Abbey was destroyed during the French Revolution; only a few (unvisitable) ruins remain.

it was only when the French church authorities raised their eyebrows at her worldliness that Louise Hollandine had been obliged to cease giving elegant parties and keeping thoroughbreds. During the Hanoverian princesses' stay at the Abbey there was only a donkey for Sophie Charlotte to ride.

Elizabeth Charlotte was the wife (as well as second cousin) of Philippe, Duke of Orleans, who as King Louis XIV's (only) brother was known with splendid inverted snobbery simply as Monsieur. Known as Madame in France – but in her German family as Liselotte – she was thus at the very centre of the greatest court in Europe. Liselotte played her role impeccably; but she was considerably less impressed by her exalted surroundings than she might have been, never lost her robust good sense or a rollicking sense of humour amongst all the grandeur, and in letters to her aunt Sophie only really pined for her native cuisine:

> "I am amazed that people here are so fond of coffee, tea, and chocolate. To my way of thinking sauerkraut and smoked sausages make a meal fit for a king";

and she missed good old German soups:

> "I like cabbage-soup with bacon in it better than all the dainties people prize so much in Paris"; and again, "Give me a beer-soup; that is what I should like best. But you can't get it here, for French beer is no good".

Despite all the nonsense about being incognito, when Sophie and Sophie Charlotte first arrived at Maubuisson they were met not only by Louise Hollandine but also by Elisabeth Charlotte and Monsieur as well, the latter rigged out (in Kroll's words) "in his great lion-wig, satin bows and high-heeled little shoes, looking much like a performing poodle". Sophie wrote to Liselotte's father that his daughter

> "looked happy and fat...[being] the most fortunate woman in the world...[and Monsieur was] the best prince in the world and looks exactly what he is"

- which was possibly a reference to the fact that (as Durant delicately put it) he "loved feminine adornments and masculine forms".

However Monsieur was enormously hospitable to his wife's aunt throughout her visit – in fact he was glad to have the company of someone who, somewhat unexpectedly for Sophie, was prepared to share his passionate interest in fashions and jewellery, unlike Liselotte, who usually wore her riding habit from morning to night. And he readily solved the major problem of Sophie's status: she could go anywhere, including at his and brother Louis' courts, provided she wore a black sash indicating she was "incognito". Sophie solved some protocol problems in her own typical manner: when Louis' Spanish-born Queen Maria Teresa gave her the hem of her robe to be kissed, Sophie pretended not to see it. The King himself found her "a truly intelligent woman".

A Paris education

Mother and daughter stayed in Paris for almost two years. Sophie clearly enjoyed it enormously, and it was a marvellous time for the intelligent and impressionable girl to be at the French court. The King was still based at the Château of St Germain-en-Laye (the remains of which now house the Museum of National Antiquities), twenty or so kilometres west of Paris, but the central core of the Château of Versailles, around the great entrance courtyards, was virtually complete – Louis would move the court there permanently within three years. André Le Nôtre's hundred-hectare gardens had already been laid out for ten years, with their artificial ponds, lakes and canals, formally laid-out terraces, pleasant alleyways with distant vistas through well-grown trees, to be joined eventually by the stillness of hundreds of sculptures and the splashing of dozens of fountains.

Versailles was intended as, and of course became, *the* symbol of the Sun King's glory; in its Baroque splendour it was the decorative arts – elaborate plasterwork and woodcarving, extravagant gilding, vast Gobelin and Aubusson wall tapestries and Savonnerie carpets, exuberant but exquisitely detailed furniture, chandeliers, mirrors, porcelains, gold and silver plate – that set the fashion for every court in Europe. It was not a setting for easel painting: great expanses of ceilings and untapestried walls required frescoes by square metres, and Charles Le Brun supplied them – and at Fontainebleau and the Louvre – with blatant allegorical or straightforwardly sycophantic celebrations of Louis' sanguinary victories abroad and supposed virtues at home.

The residence of Monsieur and Madame was the Château of St Cloud, above the Seine just southwest of Paris. Philippe had the original castle rebuilt on a sumptuous scale by Jules Hardouin-Mansart, who followed Louis Le Vau as the architect of Versailles; and Le Nôtre, again, extended the gardens from twelve to six hundred hectares, along the lines already such a triumphant success at Versailles. It was here that the first Madame, Philippe's first wife, Princess Henrietta of England – as the daughter of Charles I both Philippe's and Sophie's first cousin – had died suddenly amidst (misplaced) suspicions of poisoning, leaving Louis more distressed than Philippe; her successor Liselotte, introduced into the Bourbons to meet Louis' requirement at the time for German alliances, outlived her husband by over two decades.

Sophie reported to Liselotte's father that when Monsieur gave her a guided tour he pointedly emphasized the splendour in which he maintained Liselotte's apartments, though he had not received a cent of her dowry; that the hint did not have any effect eventually proved rather costly to the Palatinate. As Sophie Charlotte would later arrange for herself at Charlottenburg in Berlin, Liselotte's rooms led straight out into the gardens, which she thought better than Versailles, where, she said, "money rather than nature had produced the greatest marvels". The Château itself was destroyed by the Germans in the occupation following France's defeat in the Franco-Prussian War in 1870, but two-thirds of the park, with Le Nôtre's famous Grand Cascade and their view over Paris, still delight visitors – just as they did Sophie Charlotte.

It was also a stimulating time for the German visitors to be in Paris. Louis was not currently fighting any of the German states, and had just finished the Second Dutch War against William of Orange, at whose grandparents' court Sophie's parents had been given a penurious refuge when they had been driven out of Bohemia by the Hapsburgs, and where she herself had been born. And it was still five years before Louis, under the fiercely Catholic influence of his newly-married mistress, Madame de Maintenon, grand-daughter of a Huguenot, revoked the Edict of Nantes, resulting in the mass murder of French Protestants and the mass emigration of those who could escape.

During this interlude Court life was brilliant. Jean-Baptiste Lully (originally Giovanni Battista Lulli of Florence) was at his height as the director of the Académie Royale de Musique and dictator over the whole of French musical life – the King had become godfather to his eldest son two years before. Before he began writing operas a good deal of Lully's musical output had been in the form of ballets or *comédies-ballets* for performances at the various royal palaces – Compiègne, Louvre, Tuileries, Fontainebleau, Palais Royal, Vincennes, Saint-Germain,

Versailles, Chambord – some of which the Hanoverian princesses presumably attended with Liselotte when they were performed again; and it is unlikely that their Protestantism prevented their hearing some of the series of church motets Lully wrote, designed (as *Grove Music* puts it) "to glorify the King of France as much as the King of Heaven". Lully was also wildly popular with the public: just before the princesses arrived in Paris his opera *Bellérophon* had opened at the ten-year-old Opera (then on the Left Bank, off the Rue de Seine behind the Institut de France, and directed by Lully himself), and it ran for nine months during this first season.[222]

Some of Lully's musical entertainments were collaborations with two of France's most famous dramatists: the ballets for Molière's *Le Bourgeois Gentilhomme* and a number of others, and for Corneille's *Oedipe*. Molière had died in 1673, and Corneille had stopped writing by the time of the Hanoverian visit; but both were very much in the theatrical repertoire (as they are still). La Fontaine, whose *Fables* were the most widely read works in the country, had lost his patron with the death of the Dowager Duchess of Orleans, the aunt of Louis XIV and Monsieur, but was being looked after – for twenty years! – by the saintly Madame de la Sablière. Racine, the third of the great French classical dramatists, had just written *Phèdre*, and been appointed Royal Historian along with Nicolas Boileau. The latter, who had an enormous influence on the age of classical French literature, as on England's "Augustan Age", was noted for introducing restraint and Cartesian reason into the principles of his poetry:

> "Aimez donc la raison; que toujours vos écrits
> Empruntent d'elle seule et leur lustre et leur prix".
> (Love reason then; let your writings always
> Take from it both their brilliance and their worth.)

This was precisely the attitude that would have appealed to Sophie, and which she passed on to Sophie Charlotte. Indeed, Cartesianism was already in the family: Elizabeth, Sophie's eldest sister, also converted to Catholicism and Abbess of Herford (near Bielefeld in northwest

---

222 *Kobbé's Complete Opera Book*, the most famous opera guide in English, contains none of Lully's sixteen operas. The *Phaidon Book of the Opera*, with 750 "rarely performed [and] ever-popular" operas, includes ten - but not *Bellérephon*. The transience of "popular"!

Germany), was a convert to Descartes as well. Monsieur Erman wrote of the "brilliant role" that Elizabeth had played

> "in the great revolution which towards the end of the past [17th] century had given Philosophy a new form. 'In her childhood [he quoted from a work by a French Academician, Antoine-Léonard Thomas] her mother had her learn six languages. She had perfect knowledge of *Belles Lettres*. Her genius took her to the serious sciences. She studied Philosophy and Mathematics. But from the moment Descartes' first works fell into her hands, she considered she had learned nothing' ".

Elizabeth developed a "strong passion" for Descartes' philosophy: one wonders whether for his careful distinction between faith and science, which he thought avoided contradicting the Church, or for his system of sceptical reasoning, which proved in due course so incompatible with the Church's dogma. Descartes himself was clearly pleased by Elizabeth's interest, both royal and ecclesiastical, at a time when he had reason to be wary of both. He found in her, Thomas continued,

> "a spirit as open as it was deep. In a short time she found herself up to the level of his Geometry and his Metaphysics. Soon afterwards, Descartes dedicated to her his *Principles of Philosophy* [the third of his three major philosophical works, published in Latin in 1644]. He congratulated her on having been able to accumulate so much learning, at a time when the majority of women thought only of pleasure. This dedication...is not a monument of flattery:.. 'How', [Descartes] said, 'at the front of a work where I set out the foundations of truth, would I dare to betray it?' ".

She continued in correspondence with the philosopher until his death in 1650, and subsequently introduced his work in the philosophical academy she founded at her Abbey, where, Monsieur Erman says,

> "without distinction as to sex or Religion, were admitted all those drawn to it by a passion for the sciences and Letters".

Before setting out for Paris Sophie had written to Liselotte's father that

> "I am no longer of an age to go and see the *faschions*",

but after arriving in Paris she added:

"Another historian might describe the journey, but I am quite overwhelmed by the here and now, and all that has gone before went clean out of my head".

We know that the Hanoverian princesses saw and were influenced by the splendid new architecture, interior design and landscaping of the French royal palaces, but not of course what, precisely, of all the equally spectacular flowering of music, drama, literature and philosophy Sophie ensured that her almost teen-age daughter was exposed to during their two years in Paris. Overshadowed as she was at that age by her mother, she nevertheless left one mark on the French court: "her brilliant technique on the cembalo" [the Baers say], "acquired under the tutorship of Anton Coberg, earned her much admiration". We shall find that when, within a decade, Sophie Charlotte had her own court in Berlin, her interests closely reflected these very same entertainments and intellectual pursuits.

Dynastic pursuits

However the visit to Paris was not just a family reunion or educational expedition: Sophie's intention, it would seem, was to trail the girl before the marriage strategies of the French King. Monsieur Erman, on the other hand, believed that it was Louis (no doubt encouraged by his sister-in-law Liselotte) who had the idea of a marriage between his son the Dauphin and Sophie Charlotte in order to detach the Brunswick-Lüneburg-Hanover Dukes from their alliance with his enemy Austria – and (though not to their knowledge at this stage) the Palatinate from the Dukes themselves. But this seems unlikely.

In his *Memoirs of Brandenburg* Sophie Charlotte's grandson Frederick the Great wrote that

"Sophie Charlotte was intended for the throne of France. Louis XIV was impressed by her beauty"

(though Frederick mistakenly had her as intended for the Dauphin's son, by his future Bavarian wife). Adolphus Ward's book on Sophie reproduces a charming painting of "Electress Sophia and her daughter Sophia Charlotte" by Louise Hollandine,[223] presumably painted at

---

223 At Combe Abbey, collection of the Earl of Craven.

Maubuisson on their way to Paris, showing a pretty enough eleven-year-old girl, her face already showing the fullness of features that was to become much more pronounced by the end of her short life. Louis' impression was no doubt enhanced by the lively intelligence the child already displayed; but the painting in fact shows her looking a trifle apprehensively at her famously accomplished and self-confident mother, perhaps wondering how she could ever match her mother's achievements – or current expectations. But the latter came to nothing: the Dauphin was already eighteen, "fair, fat and dull" according to contemporaries, and Louis wanted him married as soon as possible to ensure the succession.

It seems surprising that Sophie herself would not have realised this, but there is one thing of which we can be certain as having played no role in the failure of her plans: the difference in religion between Catholic France and Protestant Hanover (of which she became Duchess at the end of 1679 when her husband Ernst August unexpectedly succeeded to the Dukedom). Two years afterwards, the Sieur de Gourville, Louis' very capable envoy to Hanover, having noted that the Duke was Lutheran and the Duchess Calvinist, asked Sophie what religion her daughter was; and Sophie told the obviously scandalised Ambassador that the Princess

"had none as yet; they were waiting to know what religion the prince who would marry her would be, in order to instruct her in the religion of her husband, whether he be Protestant or Catholic".[224]

Three years later, shortly before her marriage to Calvinist Frederick of Brandenburg, Sophie Charlotte herself duly made public profession as a Calvinist. In due course she would emulate and even surpass in Berlin the unusual tolerance of her parents' court.

On their departure from Paris, they stayed again at Maubuisson with Louise Hollandine; then back to Hanover where Sophie was now its new Duchess following the death of Ernst August's brother. Ernst August's

---

224 *Mémoires de J.H. de Gourville, Conseiller d'État*, in *Collection des Mémoires relatifs à l'histoire de France, depuis l'avénement de Henri IV jusqu'à la Paix de Paris conclue en 1763* (Paris, 1826). De Gourville recorded that on his departure from Hanover he declined the gift of a valuable diamond from Sophie, but accepted the Duke's present of eight superb horses (which he passed on to King Louis). His mission had failed in its objective.

first words, when he too arrived home a few days later, were "I'm glad it's not me that's dead". Apart from the Dukedom, Ernst August also inherited his brother's librarian – Gottfried Wilhelm Leibniz. It was the beginning of a long and close association between the polymath and both Sophie and Sophie Charlotte. He preferred princesses to princes, as Kroll notes, because they had more time for his interests, and could persuade their husbands to enhance their magnificence by instituting intellectual projects – run by Leibniz. For a quarter of a century he would stimulate mother's and daughter's courts at Hanover and Berlin.

Courtships and marriages

It would not be long before the matter of Sophie Charlotte's marriage prospects had to be pursued again, but first there was her older brother George. He had already demonstrated his capacity to ensure the succession to the House of Hanover, in 1676 at the age of sixteen, by "putting in the family way" Sophie Charlotte's under-governess. Ernst August, when he calmed down, ruled that George could bed whom he wished

> "as long as he remained circumspect enough not to have his name bawled from the housetops as the progenitor of bastards".

George obliged, on both fronts: he promptly took the sister of his father's mistress as his own, and never acknowledged any bastard offspring, not the under-governess's nor the rest that came later. Early in 1680, before Sophie's return from Paris, he was sent off to England in response to hints of an alliance with Princess Anne, the younger daughter of the Duke of York (later King James II) and, against all the odds, future Queen between 1702 and 1714, the last monarch of the House of Stuart. But nothing came of the visit; some contemporaries believed Anne's subsequent loathing of Sophie – her father's cousin, and her designated successor after the death in 1700 of the last of her seventeen children – dated from young George's lack of interest.[225]

Instead, in order to consolidate the wider family holdings, a marriage was laboriously negotiated to unite the two main branches of the House of Brunswick-Lüneburg in 1682 through the marriage of George to his

---

225 References to George are derived in the main from R.Hatton: *George I* (1978), only the third biography in English, all in the 20th century; there has apparently never been one in German.

first cousin Sophia Dorothea, the sixteen-year-old daughter of Ernst August's older brother Georg Wilhelm, Duke of Celle. She had only been legitimised seven years earlier when Georg Wilhelm had received ecclesiastical and imperial approval to legally marry her French Huguenot mother, his long-time mistress. Sophie was a bit sniffy about an alliance with the offspring of such a marriage – Liselotte said unequal marriages into the nobility were "like mouse-droppings in the pepper" – but in the end, as usual, practical: she explained to a Hanoverian diplomat, the Abbé Ballati, that

> "It is highly advantageous for *la maison*, as long as one can overcome the scruples of the Germans, who desire their genealogies to be equally illustrious on both sides".

To her brother, Prince Rupert, the former dashing cavalry and naval officer under Charles I during the English civil war and a co-founder of the Hudson's Bay Company, she was more blunt: the marriage, she wrote, was

> "a bitter pill, but so well gilded that one must shut one's eyes and swallow it down".

Which was ironic: Rupert was by then living in Windsor with his English actress mistress and their daughter...Ruperta.

The union between George and Sophie Dorothea was to last twelve years, produced a King of England and a Queen of Prussia, and ended in a spectacular scandal when her indiscreet affair with a Swedish officer, Count Phillipp von Königsmarck, became known; though George himself kept numerous mistresses, this was totally unacceptable: he had Königsmarck killed, divorced Sophie Dorothea, and kept her imprisoned for the remaining *thirty-two* years of her life. He never remarried.

The same Ballati was commissioned around the time of George's marriage to make the next sounding, after Paris, on behalf of Sophie Charlotte, now fourteen: she was to be offered to the heir to the Elector of Bavaria, Prince Maximilian Emanuel. But she was turned down, not because of her age, but, to Sophie's fury, because the young man thought she was not sufficiently beautiful. Two decades later, according to Monsieur Erman, when they met in Brussels, Sophie Charlotte got her own back on Maximilian, by then Elector and married to a much less agreeable wife:

"Without wishing to flatter myself", she said to him with startling candour, " I think I would have better suited you as wife than the one you have: you like pleasures, and I don't hate them; you are a flirt, I am never jealous; you would never see me sulk; I think we would have made a good couple together".

More ambitiously, the following year when Louis XIV's Queen Maria Teresa suddenly died, "murdered by her doctors" according to Sophie, the peripatetic Abbé Ballati was again commissioned to put forward Sophie Charlotte, who had been rejected for the French Dauphin, to marry...his father, the Sun King himself. Sophie of course already knew that Louis, unlike the untutored Bavarians, was impressed by Sophie Charlotte's beauty; but this scheme, too, failed: no-one knew at that stage that almost immediately after Maria Teresa's funeral Louis had secretly married his long-time mistress, fateful Madame de Maintenon.

While the Abbé was still negotiating in Versailles fate intervened elsewhere: the sudden death mid-1683, from smallpox, of Elizabeth Henriette, the first wife of Frederick, the heir to the Great Elector Frederick William of Brandenburg, whose only child had been a daughter – with Louis XIV as one of her god-fathers. The whole Hanoverian family had visited Berlin the year before to see if Princess Maria Amalia, one of Frederick William's daughters by his second wife, would be suitable for George (she wasn't: too unhealthy), and whether one of her brothers might do for Sophie Charlotte (apparently not, but the reason was not specified). It is hard to tell, when the vastly more valuable Brandenburg heir himself suddenly became available, whether it was Ernst August or Sophie who moved first.

Ernst August saw political advantage. The House of Brunswick-Lüneburg had not managed to reach the top rank of German princes: Elector of the Holy Roman Empire. These had been set at seven by the Holy Roman Emperor Charles IV of Luxemburg as long before as 1356: the three Prince-Bishops of Mainz, Trier and Cologne, reflecting the temporal power of the territories rather than the spiritual power of the incumbents; the King of Bohemia, the Count Palatine of the Rhine, the Duke of Saxony and the Margrave of Brandenburg. It is ironical that political manoeuvring at the time caused the omission of the Hapsburg Duke of Austria: but after the seven elected Duke Albert V of Hapsburg as Emperor Albert II in 1438 they never elected – or "elected" – another non-Hapsburg again, until the end of the Empire in 1806.

The first change in the Empire's constitution was only made in 1623: the Emperor Ferdinand II, responsible more than any other single person for precipitating the Thirty Years War between Catholic and Protestant Europe, transferred to the Catholic Duke of Bavaria the Electoral vote of the then Count Palatine – Frederick V, Sophie's father – for having accepted the throne of Bohemia. This was Ferdinand's second blow against him: in a single military campaign he had already deprived Frederick of the throne, earning him his nickname, half-mocking, half-tragic, as the Winter King. With the Peace of Westphalia, which effectively ended Europe-wide wars of religion – leaving the way open for the next two centuries' wars of nationalism – the Electorate of the Palatinate was restored to Frederick's eldest son, Sophie's brother and Liselotte's father, Charles Louis (Karl Ludwig). But it had to be an eighth electorate, given that there could be no question of destituting the Bavarian ruler.

And it was this expansion which gave the House of Brunswick-Lüneburg the opening to push for an electoral seat for itself. Ernst August recognised that to persuade the Catholic Hapsburgs he would need the strong support of the Protestant Great Elector of Brandenburg; and the marriage of his daughter to the Electoral Prince would be a significant first step for which he was prepared to make suitable concessions in the never-ending game of border-readjustments that kept the German princes bemused or belligerent until Bismarck straightened them out in a Prussian straightjacket.

Sophie, for her part, ever the practical one, had a Venetian artist, currently working on her ceilings in the ducal palace at Hanover, paint Sophie Charlotte's portrait, and promptly despatched it to Berlin. It was well received, though Sophie had seen insurance in its quality, observing that

"it was always a good thing for the original to have the edge over her portrait".

A Brandenburg representative came to inspect the original, and was pleased by her viewpoint, though, Sophie remarked, it "didn't commit her to anything" – apparently negotiations were continuing with the duplicitous now-married Louis. Sophie Charlotte, perhaps with clear memories of the French court's dynamism, was still keeping open her options, like her religious profession: when someone remarked on the constraints on a Queen of France, she said she would have to deal with those anywhere, and Louis "would be more worth the effort". But by mid-1684 Louis was clearly no longer a prospect, and a further visit from

Berlin conveyed the widowed Frederick's clear impatience to proceed with the match.

Frederick had not found it all plain sailing: Louis XIV was not pleased at the prospect of a union between Hanover and Brandenburg, and the Great Elector did not want to turn off his support for Brandenburg against the constant pressure of Hapsburg Austria. But Frederick prevailed, a significant achievement against such a formidable father, and he duly married, at twenty-seven, the sixteen-year-old Sophie Charlotte in Hanover in October 1684. For some reason, not Liselotte but the Abbé Ballati, still in Paris but now supposed to be discussing religious reunification, was turned by Sophie into a purchasing agent for the finery required by Sophie Charlotte and both her parents – as well as a doll, "dressed and coiffed like a little girl of quality aged four", for Figuelotte to give to her new step-daughter. No wonder, then, at the lack of religious unity.

There was a week of ballets, plays, operas and fireworks, which Sophie excused as "prepared as best we could in the short space of time" and the French ambassador described as *fort, fort mal*. Then Frederick returned to Berlin, and Sophie Charlotte followed three weeks later.

Frederick, Electoral heir of Brandenburg

Frederick counted it lucky that he was still around, not only to be able to marry a second time, but at all.[226] To begin with, he was dropped by an inattentive nurse at the age of six months, injuring his back so badly that he grew misshapen, something like a hunchback. He remained acutely self-conscious at a time when such things were still regarded as signs of divine disfavour (though sensitivity to such suffering is still not guaranteed: a distinguished modern historian calls him "The Deformed Dandy"). The result was an emphasis on elaborate costume, unfortunately drawing attention to his small, irregular stature rather than, as he vainly

---

226 Frederick's life and character are to some extent based, carefully, on the only biography that has been published in English, as far as I am aware - L.M. Frey: *Frederick I: The Man and his Times* (1984); it contains the results of a lot of research in German archives, but is inconsistent and on occasion even inaccurate. But they are also covered in many other dynastic and national histories.

imagined, disguising it. Sophie Charlotte knew what to expect, having met him on that earlier family fishing expedition to Berlin; in any case, the practical-minded Sophie remarked, "It is fortunate that she does not care for externals".

As a consequence of his physical misfortune Frederick's mother, the gentle and loving Louise Henriette of Orange, William of Orange's aunt and Sophie's second cousin, protected and pampered the little boy, whom she called Fritsie; she encouraged him to study, including music and drawing as well as more traditional subjects; and the Great Elector went along with it, presumably because he assumed young Frederick was unfit for anything more martial – and was only his second son anyway. But when Frederick was seventeen his older brother died; he became heir to the Electorate, and loyally – and competently – joined his father campaigning, as was expected of heirs. By then his mother had died and the Great Elector had remarried, to Dorothea, a Princess of Holstein-Glücksberg with attitude – and also four sons of her own, for whom she was scheming for the succession.

What followed was farce or tragedy, depending on whether the rumours were true or manipulations: Frederick at least acted as though he believed his wicked step-mother wanted to poison him, and after one bitter quarrel fled from the Court to an aunt at Hesse-Kassel whose daughter Elizabeth Henrietta he wanted to marry anyway, and, a year later, did. Briefly reconciled to Berlin, Frederick was then taken violently ill after drinking coffee with his step-mother; this time he was convinced she had poisoned him, and equally convinced he was saved by an emetic administered by his tutor, Eberhard von Danckelmann, who in consequence became his Prime Minister for the first nine years of his reign.

Frederick believed he had had a second lucky escape; others, like Thomas Carlyle in his *History of Friedrich II of Prussia*, said Dorothea, though a hard lady, was above such things: much devoted to

> "practical economics, dairy-farming, market-gardening, and industrial and commercial opportunities such as offered;...was thought even to have, underhand, a commercial interest in the principal Beerhouse of the city";

and, about the time of the coffee party, had planted the first of Berlin's subsequently famous Linden trees on the edge of her dairy-farm. Though when was silviculture, or publicanism, incompatible with dirty tricks?

Rumours of poisoning came up again when Frederick's first wife, Elizabeth Henriette, suddenly died, and again, less surprisingly, when Sophie Charlotte's first-born son died less explicably at five months. Whether Sophie Charlotte believed all this talk of poisoning is unknown; but the loss of his heir, who of course would have taken precedence over Sophie Dorothea's sons, undoubtedly reinforced Frederick's strong suspicions of his stepmother; so when Sophie Charlotte became pregnant again the couple fled from Berlin. But this baby, another son, was stillborn at Magdeburg on their way to Hanover. Then, not long after they had obeyed the Great Elector's command to return to Berlin, Frederick's younger brother Ludwig also suddenly died after eating an orange at a ball given by their stepmother. An investigation eventually decided he had died of scarlet fever, but when Frederick himself became ill shortly afterwards he and Sophie Charlotte promptly fled yet again to Hanover.

The young couple themselves were still at this stage completely devoted to each other, and one wonders whether other factors besides rumours of poison played a role in their readiness to fly to Hanover. Sophie Charlotte was of course – and always remained – extremely close to her mother, but she had also apparently not been entirely happy in Berlin. She had got off to a bad start with the court women because she would not adopt the local custom of kissing all and sundry – prompting Sophie to say succinctly that she hoped her daughter would cure them of

"taking every fart for a thunderclap, and get them used to the ways
of Hanover where intrigues are unknown".

But there was more to it than that. Frederick's biographers the Freys, who display a consistently strong, unexplained, and it must be added unique hostility to Sophie Charlotte, profess that Frederick William "could not tolerate" her, apparently because he had long detested her mother. But the dramatic escapes in particular did nothing to help relations between the two royal governments, and Frederick William is said to have now feared Hanover would seek to take political advantage of the split with his son. Curiously, if so, he does not seem to have focussed on Ernst August's hope for his support for a Hanoverian Electorate.

When in due course the young couple were again winkled back to Berlin by the ever-resourceful Danckelmann it was to find the Great

Elector in seriously declining health, and living largely as a recluse at Potsdam, where their grandson Frederick the Great would design and build Sanssouci ("without a care"), one of the most ravishing palaces in the country. Reconciliation with Frederick William resulted in Frederick's becoming more and more involved with his father's council – which is probably why he became determined to get rid of the "thieves and untrue people" who had latched on to the Great Elector. But there was one area from which, to his increasing alarm, he was resolutely excluded: the contents of Frederick William's will. He learned of them only on his accession to the Electorate on his father's death in May 1688, and found his concern fully justified.

Frederick's Hohenzollern inheritance had in any case some very peculiar features, which we need to skim through to have an idea of the limits, and the possibilities, of what Frederick – and Sophie Charlotte – now had to deal with. There were in fact two inheritances, a Brandenburg one and a Prussian one; and though they had converged they were still being stitched together.

Prussia begins – in Palestine

Prussia had begun as an offshoot – appositely enough, as things turned out – of the Crusades, and with the extermination of the original eponymous inhabitants, the Baltic Borussi, who gave it their name. In its origins it was largely the creation of the Order of the Knights of the Hospital of St Mary of the Teutons in Jerusalem. Better known as the Teutonic Knights, the Order was founded by Germans in Acre in 1191, a century after the capture of Jerusalem and the massacre there, and eleven years after the Holy City had fallen to Saladin. The founders of the Order were not content merely to try to recover Jerusalem or hang on to the remains of *Outremer*: they wanted to expand, but the much older Knights Templar and Knights Hospitaller of St John were already so well entrenched in what was left of the Crusaders' Middle East that the German Knights turned their ambitions nearer home.

Around 1200 they established a fortified base and chapel – a "temple", after the Templars – at what was to become Tempelhof, close to what had originally been a Slav settlement known to the Germans as "Brennaburg" (Brandenburg). Berlin was under way. In 1226 the Knights secured from the Holy Roman Emperor, Frederick II, *Stupor Mundi*, the right to retain the lands they conquered, ostensibly on behalf of Poland, in a fully sanctioned – indeed sanctified – Crusade against the pagan Borussi in north-eastern Europe.

587

So began the first *Drang nach Osten* ["drive to the east"], and Prussia was under way. In 1240 the Knights were bypassed by the extreme western thrust of the Mongols' Golden Horde, following its sweep through Kievan Rus and the utter destruction of its capital, when Western Europe was saved by the Horde's sudden departure back into Asia on the death of the Great Khan, Genghis Khan's son Ogadei.[227] Only two year later, the Knights' attempt to expand into the northern rump of Russia that had escaped Mongol domination was soundly repulsed at the River Neva by Alexander of Novgorod, "Alexander Nevsky", the monk-warrior greatly admired by Peter the Great and Stalin. The heavily armoured Teutonic Knights sinking into the frozen Peipus Marsh – vividly portrayed in Sergei Eisenstein's 1938 film *Alexander Nevsky* – prefigured the foundering of the frozen Nazi German armies in the Russian winters of 1941-42 and 42-43.

But within fifty years of the Battle on the Ice, with the chilling war-cry *Tod oder Taufe* – "Death or baptism", an invitation one might have expected to have at least been in reverse order – the Teutonic Order had not only largely wiped out the Borussi but also finessed the Poles, creating a separate Prussia stretching across northern Poland and most of the Baltic States. The Order placed their new state under Papal suzerainty in order to establish its independence from the Holy Roman Empire, and colonised their vast *Junker* estates with German settlers. The Teutonic Knights' main activities were thus in eastern Europe, although their headquarters and some knights remained in Acre until the latter's fall in 1291 and then moved briefly to Venice; but finally in 1309 they settled in the great fortress of Marienburg in the new Prussian state (back in Poland since World War II and called Malbork, to the south of Gdansk).

The last expansion of the Knights' Prussia was the purchase of Estonia from Denmark in 1302. But its strength was drained by interminable war with an expanding Lithuania throughout much of the succeeding century; and the Knights were heavily defeated by the Poles in the battle of Tannenburg in 1410, five centuries before their German descendants defeated – and thereby terminally undermined – the Russian Empire on the same battlefield in the first month of the First World War. Nevertheless Prussian independence was maintained under the Teutonic Knights until long after the suppression of their

---

227   See 1000 Chapter: Vladimir of Kiev

former rivals the Templars between 1307 and 1314, even until after the capture, by the Ottomans' Suleiman the Magnificent in 1522, of the last base in the eastern Mediterranean of their other erstwhile rival, the Knights Hospitaller.

The rise of Brandenburg

As so often in Europe, dynastic politics then produced, over the following century, the next fateful steps in the sequence, the main dynasty concerned being the Hohenzollern, which would extend its reach until its last grasp came crashing down in 1918. The frontier region (*Mark*, or March) around Brandenburg had been established in 1134 as a part of the Holy Roman Empire. The first recorded mention of the little twin villages of Berlin and Cölln, either side of the River Spree, is claimed to date from 1237;[228] a document of 1295 notes already the presence of Jewish residents in Berlin – and forbids their burial within the town walls. As we saw earlier, in 1356 the Emperor Charles IV created the Margrave of Brandenburg one of the four secular Electors of the head of the Empire; and in 1411, after both the first and second ruling dynasties had died out, the Emperor Sigismund established his closest political ally, Frederick of Hohenzollern, in Brandenburg as the new Margrave.

It was a branch member of the Hohenzollerns, Albert of Brandenburg, who, as Grand Master of the Teutonic Order, was responsible for the next step, in 1525. There was a certain family irony involved. Eleven years earlier yet another Albert of Brandenburg had become Cardinal-Archbishop of Mainz, one of the three ecclesiastical Electors; and it was he who authorised the Dominican Johann Tetzel to preach the indulgences for the construction of the new St Peter's in Rome that precipitated Martin Luther into nailing his momentous Ninety-five Theses to the door of the cathedral at Wittenburg in 1517. The Reformation was under way. Eight years later, his relation, the Teutonic Grand Master Albert proceeded to become one of the new Protestants; and the same year, acting on Luther's advice, he abolished the Catholic Teutonic Order for

---

228 Berlin was on the north side of the river, where the St Nicholas Quarter (*Nikolaiviertel*) is now; Cölln was on the opposite southern bank, the area now known as Fisherman's Island (*Fischerinsel*), in the southeast corner of Museum Island (*Museuminsel*) between the Spree and the Spree Canal (built by the Great Elector).

his people's salvation, and converted Prussia into a personal hereditary Dukedom for his own.[229]

Brandenburg and Prussia, now both ruled by Hohenzollerns, continued side by side for almost another century; but it was not until 1618, when the Hohenzollern Dukes of Prussia died out, that the Hohenzollern Electors of Brandenburg got their hands on both. Germany was under way.

Brandenburg-Prussia, in the middle of a lot of dynastic and military power grabs, now stretched discontinuously across the north German plain from the Rhine to Russia, with the still-insignificant little town of Berlin in the middle. Brandenburg was also in the middle of the 1618-1648 Thirty Years War. Being Protestant did nothing to save it from the depredations of Protestant Sweden chasing out the Catholic Imperial army after its depredations. Nor did it stop the Great Elector Frederick William, our Frederick's father, from fighting Sweden afterwards while playing along with Louis XIV's Catholic France; or, afterwards again, from reversing both postures. Clearly, religion no longer mattered: nationalism was on the upswing. But Brandenburg was a wreck: half the population (it is estimated) killed, in Berlin two-thirds, with only about 6,000 left, agriculture destroyed, cities and towns ruined.[230]

The Great Elector, who had inherited Brandenburg-Prussia in 1640, earned his sobriquet from his measures designed to secure undisputed Hohenzollern control internally, and security against predatory neighbours externally. But he was slow to reconstruct an economy which could provide the necessary basis, relying for the most part on establishing a central tax regime on just about everything, falling on the poor and the rich alike. The latter's bitter opposition came to an end when the leader of the resistance, Albert von Kalckstein, who had eventually fled to Poland, was kidnapped on Frederick William's orders,

---

229 It was the next year again, 1526, as Western Europe continued to line up into opposing religious camps, that Suleiman the Magnificent's huge Turkish army, still on the march after the fall of Byzantine Constantinople seventy years before, conquered Hungary, then moved on to besiege Vienna - while, in 1527, the Emperor Charles V's troops, heedless of the Ottoman Moslem threat to Christian Europe, preferred to sack...Rome (see 1500 chapter: Marcantonio Raimondi).

230 One of the rare benefits bestowed on northern Europe by the Thirty Years War was the potato, introduced by the Emperor's Castilian mercenaries, who of course had them from the Spanish New World. They were eaten raw; it was a long time before anyone peeled them, longer still before they were cooked.

smuggled back across the border wrapped in a rug, tried, tortured, condemned and executed.

But the most important measure he took, which set the state on the road to economic growth, was to invite French Huguenot refugees to come and settle in Brandenburg. On 17 October 1685 Louis XIV, under pressure from the Catholic Church and egged on by his wife, Madame de Maintenon, revoked the Edict of Nantes which had been issued in 1598 by his grandfather King Henry IV, the first of the Bourbon dynasty: he was a Calvinist who, deciding that "Paris is worth a Mass" and defeating his remaining Valois rivals, had brought an end to France's religious wars by the Edict's guarantee of religious freedom for the Protestant Huguenots.

Louis' Revocation was as brutal as anything the Spanish Inquisition is criticised for: all Protestant churches and schools were abolished, ministers were given two weeks to leave France, but all others were forbidden to do so and condemned to the galleys if caught. All children were to be immediately baptised as Catholics, and although it was not specified, several hundred thousand adults were subjected to forcible conversion also, and countless more hunted down, tortured and massacred by soldiers and zealots. Louis proclaimed France purified of heretics; leading lights – including La Fontaine – proclaimed it his greatest act of statesmanship.

In fact it was an act of economic stupidity, and Louis' Protestant neighbours were quick to capitalise on it. On 8 November, only twenty-two days after Louis' Revocation, Frederick William issued the Edict of Potsdam, but it was not just an offer of "safe and free asylum" to his co-religionists: it was also a deliberate scheme to develop Brandenburg's economy. The Great Elector promised Huguenot noblemen commissions in the army; agriculturalists were promised farming land; merchants and entrepreneurs, craftsmen, artisans and industrial workers were promised housing and working quarters; all were promised equipment, tools and interest-free loans to establish themselves and new businesses. Some Huguenots, aristocrats and intellectuals, quickly found themselves welcome at Court. Monsieur Erman tells the story of one brave soul who was asked by the Great Elector what he thought of a wine he had had made at Potsdam;

"In all honesty", the Frenchman replied, "I think, Your Highness, that all the thrushes who ate the grapes from which it was made, died of colic".

Whatever else the Huguenots introduced into Brandenburg-Prussia, levity was not to be one that took on.

Frederick William kept his promises: commissioners were stationed at frontier entrance points to help the refugees choose places to settle and work to take on; relief programs were instituted, special courts established, a clergyman financed in each settlement towns; state commissions were given to new enterprises. Some twenty thousand French Huguenots came to Brandenburg and another ten were absorbed from other territories subject to Louis' military ambitions. Five thousand settled in Berlin, whose population had previously been about fourteen thousand. The impact on the Brandenburg economy was enormous, contrary to the later assertion by Mirabeau, the French historian and revolutionary, who said the Huguenots only introduced sugar and vegetables; together with the much greater numbers of Huguenots who managed to escape to the Dutch United Provinces and England, the economies – even the army commands – of Louis' enemies were greatly strengthened, and Prussia began on the road to industrialisation.

The revived economy of course provided in the first place the basis for an expanded army. Given Brandenburg-Prussia's experiences during the Thirty Years War there was some force in Frederick William's observation to his son that

"Alliances to be sure are good, but forces of one's own are still better. Upon these one can rely with more security";

but that was also because he was no better than his allies:

"No alliance needs to be kept", he said, "once it has served its purpose, and no treaty is binding forever".

So he developed the Prussian Army: from only about 2,500 men at the end of the War to those 29,154 so carefully counted for Frederick's inheritance, strictly subordinated to his own command, well provisioned, and with iron discipline.[231]

---

231 More quixotic was Prussia's first navy-cum-colonial adventure. Portugal, Spain, England and Holland had begun colonies and trade - especially in slaves - in Africa from the middle of the previous century; and the English and Dutch had established their East India Companies at the beginning of the century to found colonies and trade with - or exploit - the markets of Asia in competition

Together with recovery and economic growth, and a credible standing army, Frederick William's other aim was, as Reddaway succinctly expressed it, "to beat down all competing authority", and he largely succeeded in bringing the constituent statelets and the Prussian *Junkers* into line in an armed autocracy. Brandenburg-Prussia thus joined the ranks of absolutist states of Europe. When the Great Elector's reign began Charles I was still on the throne of England; nine years later he would be beheaded by his outraged subjects. It has been said that "absolutism might never have left its stamp on Germany had someone, somewhere, sometime, executed a Hohenzollern". But no-one ever did.

The Elector Frederick III of Brandenburg

Although, as the result of the Great Elector's measures, the country was strong both institutionally and economically, and was ruled as one, the state which Frederick inherited in 1688 was still divided constitutionally: within the Holy Roman Empire was Brandenburg, with a population of some 276,000; outside was the marginally smaller Prussia, with the more significant population of about 385,000. Berlin, with over 21,000, was considerably smaller at that time than the 70,000-strong Prussian capital Königsberg [now Kaliningrad, the ice-free port in the little pocket of Russia tucked between Poland and Lithuania on the eastern Baltic], but under Frederick Berlin more than doubled.

He has been given little credit by the champions of Prussia for his very first act: the preservation of the country's integrity. He did so by repudiating the will his father had kept from him, which, very curiously,

---

with their Portuguese and Spanish predecessors. Frederick William does not seem himself to have been seized, as was his descendant the Kaiser William II, with a burning desire to establish colonies in emulation of his European neighbours, but he was interested in competing with them in trade to avoid having to pay others for increasingly fashionable eastern spices. But he never got to the spice islands. A small navy established for him by a Dutchman during the Thirty Years War seems to have been made available much later to a Brandenburg-Africa Trading Company, which eventually, in 1683, established a trading post, naturally called Gross-Friedrichsburg, on what is now the coast of Ghana, and a bit later one in Senegal, to trade in gold, ivory and of course slaves. But it could not compete with the well-established Dutch in West Africa; after struggling through the whole reign of son Frederick, who does not seem to have been interested, the enterprise was sold to them in 1721, "for a ridiculously small sum", by grandson Frederick William, who said he regarded the whole exercise as "a chimera". I have been unable to discover whether anything remains in Ghana or Senegal of Germany's first colonial ventures.

would have undermined the unity Frederick William had so long struggled to achieve, by dividing the state between Frederick and his four surviving step-brothers, the sons of his scheming step-mother Dorothea. Frederick argued, successfully, that the will was contrary to Brandenburg inheritance law; and when Dorothea died the following year he bought off, with surprisingly little difficulty, each of her sons. Thus, while he made no effort to aggrandise the state he inherited, this establishment of the rule of primogeniture was crucial in the maintenance of the territorial integrity of Brandenburg-Prussia. And three months after Frederick's accession Sophie Charlotte gave birth to a healthy son, named Frederick William... to add to the difficulty of keeping track of all these Hohenzollerns.

As it was, the state taken over by Frederick was secure and rich enough to allow the new ruler to indulge his taste for artifice and architecture – and if this, as his critics complain, ruined the budget, there was nevertheless enough revenue left over to increase the standing army to those 39,963 troops. In fact half the budget went on the army, and additional sums were raised by renting it out to Brandenburg's more belligerent and not always reliable allies.

The line-up in western Europe had evolved during the course of the decade of the 1680s, as Louis XIV's ambitions gradually forced more and more of his neighbours into combinations to withstand them, although their own differing ambitions were to result in a certain fluidity. 1686 saw the birth of the League of Augsburg: the Empire, Spain, Sweden and the United Provinces, combined against France. The Germans were not far behind: when the Elector Charles of the Palatine, Liselotte's brother, died childless in 1685, Louis had claimed the Palatine, allegedly for Liselotte in lieu of her still-unpaid dowry; in 1688 he invaded. By early 1689 the new Elector Frederick of Brandenburg personally led his troops in action near Bonn, to cover, against the possibility of a French attack, William of Orange's passage to England to become King William III. Sophie Charlotte accompanied him, and waited, apparently confidently, in nearby Cologne during the action.

But battle was not to Frederick's taste. In the War of the Spanish Succession, the great struggle that succeeded the War of the League of Augsburg, dominating the opening of the eighteenth century until 1714, England, Holland and the Empire resumed resistance to Louis XIV, and gradually Brandenburg-Prussia, like other German states, was again drawn in. Frederick did not himself take the field again, but he ensured his army played an active role when the occasion appeared to offer a suitable opportunity to advance his interests – and held back if not. His troops in fact fought with distinction in the Duke of Marlborough's campaigns at Blenheim, Oudenarde and Malplaquet: the Duke himself called them "the first and best in Europe", though possibly only because he wanted more. Frederick's manoeuvring amongst his allies – and when he thought it desirable, between them and France – inevitably undermined his international reputation. There was advantage, though, at least for the people, in keeping almost all the scattered territory of Brandenburg-Prussia out of the ruins of a quarter-century of wars.

It was the use of *condottiere*-Brandenburg's troops in support of the Emperor in particular that clinched for Frederick the crown of Prussia. This was his prime objective, and for him his greatest success. Later nationalists ridiculed it as a poor substitute for territorial expansion at the expense of someone else; his grandson Frederick the Great patronisingly observed in his *Memoirs*:

> "The ambition of Frederick III was confined, as well by his station, as by his dominions. He was too weak to raise himself above the heads of his neighbours, who were as strong and as powerful as himself; therefore he had no other expedient left but the pomp of titles, to supply this intrinsic defect of power".

Grandson Frederick had no inhibitions about using jackboots to overcome this defect.

Frederick the Frivolous

Poor Frederick. He reigned at a time when the Sun King was setting the pace for all Europe's great and small Courts. All of them, from London to St Petersburg, Stockholm to Naples, spent fortunes that often they did not have in building various-sized reproductions of the vast extravaganza of Versailles, and on filling the results with national or provincial versions of Louis' glittering and suffocating Court, their captive nobilities entertained – and constrained – like his by an endless round of masques, musical performances, operas, plays, portraits, furniture, fireworks, walks, hunts, gossip, mistresses, marriages, intrigues and, where desirable, assassinations.

It is instructive that Frederick was, and still is, so often singled out for puritanical disapproval of his efforts to keep up with the Bourbons and all the other players of the European princely competition, because he sought to match Louis XIV in glory but did not compete in militarism.

His notoriously belligerent grandson scoffed of Europe's rulers during Frederick's day,

> "There is not one of them, down to the youngest son of a youngest son of an appanaged line, who does not preen himself on some resemblance to Louis XIV. He builds his Versailles; he has his mistresses; he maintains his standing armies"

- and so did he himself, but his brutal use of his armies made him Great. Even though the Brandenburg armies were not simply maintained but increased during grandfather Frederick's reign by those 10,809 troops, and were used, to political effect, during the wars Louis unleashed on most of his princely imitators, grandfather Frederick was indeed guilty of failing to wage any war of aggression for the purpose of increasing Brandenburg-Prussia's acreage and power.

But luxury did not begin with Frederick: at his father's court twenty-four trumpeters announced that dinner was served, consisting usually of twenty courses, on great occasions as many as a hundred; the furnishings and dress were equally lavish. Nor did Francophilia begin with Frederick: already, by the end of his father's reign, an anonymous writer was complaining about the Francophile invasion –

> "French language, French clothes, French food, French furniture, French dances, French music, the French pox".

Of course what the German Francophiles most admired about France was Louis XIV's absolute power. Just so, the extravagances of which Frederick has been accused were very much tied up with increasing his own domination of the *Junkers* and burghers of Brandenburg and Prussia; with cementing these two main parts of his realm into a unified state; and with amplifying Brandenburg-Prussia's standing in Europe. At a time when the King was – as Louis himself famously noted – the State, the standing of the ruler contributed significantly to the standing of the country; and Frederick's advances in this respect were a good deal cheaper than those of his more admired Prussian successors, though of course only in human life.

But first he had to be a King; and the money went, at least to begin with, on showing himself worthy of being elevated from an Elector of the Holy Roman Empire to a King in his own right – and then, when that succeeded, on showing himself worthy of being the King he had now become. Alas, he got carried away on the latter aspect. The most brutal critique of Frederick was again made by his aggressive grandson, who was to say of his grandfather:

> "He was small and deformed; his expression was haughty, his physiognomy was vulgar. His mind was like a mirror, which reflects each object. So those who had obtained a certain influence on him could excite or subdue his spirit at their pleasure. The praise given so copiously to Louis XIV impressed him, and he came to believe that if he elected himself King, he too would receive unfailing praise. In short, the Berlin Court would ape the Court of Versailles; everything was imitated: the ceremonials, the fine speeches, the measured steps, the precise words, the '*Grand Mousquetaires*', and so on. The generosity which he loved was wastefulness".

Never mind that Frederick the Great himself preferred, like the whole of Europe, to use French to speak and write, in his case every line of thirty-one volumes; and that he built, at Potsdam, starting thirty years after Louis XIV's death, one of the largest and most elegant French-style palace complexes in Europe.

There was in reality some pretty twisted Hohenzollern family history involved in his vitriol about his grandfather: each generation from the Great Elector on had the heir at loggerheads with the father. First Frederick himself fled the Great Elector's court, though, as we saw, he largely blamed his step-mother. His son, the next Frederick William, indulged by Sophie Charlotte, reacted violently against the frivolities of his father and pursued policies of rigorous austerity and military discipline. And Frederick William atrociously mistreated his son, the future Frederick the Great, physically and psychologically, and publicly: on one occasion when young Fritz was almost twenty his father, irrationally dissatisfied over something or nothing at all, seized him by the throat, threw him to the ground, forced him to kiss his boots and beg forgiveness, then taunted:

> "If my father had treated me like this, I would have put an end to my life long ago. But you, you have no courage".

It is not surprising that this tough Frederick should blame his weak grandfather for the brutalities of his own father – even though, as a typical Hohenzollern, he came to admire his father's military achievements.

In any case, Frederick's drive to become King was more than – as one historian summarised Frederick the Great's view – "overcompensation for the hump on his back". As the Lord's anointed he would have a new claim on the devotion of his subjects; and it *was* a step that could be taken to enhance the status of Brandenburg on the European scene without going unnecessarily to war. There was obviously also personal vanity involved in keeping up with the neighbours: Frederick's cousin Prince William of Orange became King of England in 1689; the Elector of Saxony became King of Poland as well in 1697, at the mere price of converting to Catholicism; in Hanover Sophie Charlotte's father achieved promotion to an Electorate just before he died in 1698; even the Grand Duke of Tuscany, whose Medici family only went back 250 years, became a Royal Highness the following year. But it was also a matter of ensuring that *Protestant* Brandenburg, the leader of the German Protestant states, could hold its own with the Catholic Empire and the challenge of Catholic France. The great nineteenth century German historian Leopold von Ranke was in no doubt:

> "The elevation of the Elector to a royal title was an important, nay even a necessary, impulse to the progress of Prussia".

The quest was a bit complicated: as an Elector of the Holy Roman Empire Frederick required the approval of the Catholic Emperor to become a Protestant King; on the other hand, he could not be King of any territory within the Empire as that would conflict with the Emperor's exclusive sovereignty. Frederick resolved the issues with an ease that has been somewhat overshadowed by the ridicule his pretensions elicited. In the first place he purchased the Emperor's agreement by the loan of eight thousand of his Protestant troops to assist Catholic Leopold I's campaigns against the Catholic Louis XIV, and by agreeing to support Leopold's son for the Imperial succession. That hurdle cleared, he cleared the second by accepting the curious title of "King *in* Prussia", referring only to that Protestant part of Prussia lying outside the Empire and omitting the Catholic part belonging to Poland within it – at least which did so until grandson Frederick the Great grabbed all of it by leading the (first) carve-up of Poland in 1772.

Leopold gave his blessing on 16 November 1700, egged on by a Jesuit advisor who, some said, thought the new Protestant King would thereby be more susceptible to Jesuit missions, but who others said had been handsomely subsidised by him. And thus Protestant Frederick made his own addition to the anachronisms of what Voltaire would soon describe as "a Holy Roman Empire in no way holy, nor Roman, nor an empire".

King Frederick at last

The next step, which Frederick obviously enjoyed a good deal more than either war or diplomacy, was the coronation of the new Majesties. This had to be held in the capital of Frederick's piece of Prussia, Königsberg; it was also his birthplace. It was immediately clear that Frederick had everything planned and ready long since for a ceremony only eight weeks after his elevation. Beginning in mid-December, the entire Court was translated, in the depths of winter, eight hundred kilometres to the east through forests and bogs, often over corduroy roads, requiring, it was reported, eighteen hundred carriages with relays totalling thirty thousand horses, more than one for every inhabitant of Berlin as it then was. The strains of the voyage were relieved by banquets and balls in the afternoons. Even so, the whole vast excursion was completed in twelve days.

First Königsberg for the Elector's arrival, subsequently Berlin for the new King's return, were decorated extravagantly: triumphal arches; "no end of draperies and cloth", Carlyle complained, "cloth enough, of scarlet and other bright colours, to thatch the Arctic Zone";

the King in scarlet robes for the ceremony, the diamond buttons of his coat costing a thousand five hundred thalers each, at a time when Leibniz was promised (though not paid) five hundred by Peter the Great to design a modern Russian Government. The whole thing was said to have cost more than a year's revenue in Brandenburg, though as a cynic might have noted, it undoubtedly gave a short term boost to the Königsberg economy.

This extravaganza, on 18 January 1701, nevertheless had a minor longer term interest: to underline that Prussia was all his own, Frederick crowned himself, and Sophia Charlotte, with his own hands – only the second European ruler not to be crowned by a cleric in the nine hundred years since Charlemagne created the Holy Roman Empire, the first having been the fifteen-year-old Charles XII of Sweden in 1697.[232] A century later, Napoleon copied them and crowned himself Emperor of the French and Josephine Empress; though he, being more or less

---

232 The mounts of the crowns - without jewels and velvet linings - are still in the Crown Treasure at Scloss Charlottenburg. Frederick's will listed 153 faceted diamonds and brilliants, and 8 drop-pearls, on his crown, 147 faceted diamonds, 25 brilliants, 8 drop-pearls and 48 round pearls on Sophie Charlotte's.

Catholic and the master of rather more than half Europe at the time, had the Pope on hand.

There had been no question of the Emperor's conferring the new crown; now, by crowning himself in his own castle, Frederick made sure that the Church did not confer it either. A blessing there had to be of course, but it was in a separate ceremony, by one Lutheran clergyman and one Calvinist, to please both brands of his subjects, and both created Bishops by Frederick himself especially for the occasion. Frederick set more store by symbols than by slaughter, but he was a true Hohenzollern in making sure the symbols were of his own creating. Prussia would be independent of any other power, secular or religious; and mostly of any other rules. One hundred and seventy years later to the day, on 18 January 1871, Frederick's great-great-great-great-grandson would be crowned Emperor of Germany in Louis XIV's palace Chateau of Versailles in a defeated and humiliated France.

At the coronation it was Sophie Charlotte who struck the only note discordant with Frederick's lengthy and grandiloquent pomposity:

"she cared not much about crowns," [Carlyle again], "or upholstery magnificences of any kind...[and] was distinctly seen to smuggle out her snuff-box, being addicted to that rakish practice, and fairly solace herself with a delicate little pinch of snuff...[An] inexorable, quiet protest against cant, done with such simplicity".

She wrote to Leibniz:

"Do not imagine that I prefer these grandeurs and these crowns, to which people attach such importance, to the delights of the philosophical discussions we have had at Charlottenburg".

She said herself that she was "the first Prussian Republican". Her grandson Frederick the Great wrote that she (less kindly) referred to Frederick as "King Aesop"- the author of the ancient Greek fables was said to have been deformed – when despairing of her own role as "Player-Queen" that she was obliged to perform in Prussia.

Frederick, on the other hand, now called himself King in Prussia, Margrave of Brandenburg, Lord Chamberlain and Elector of the Holy Roman Empire, Sovereign Prince of Orange, Magdeburg, Cleve, Jülich, Berg, Stettin, Pommern, Cassuben and Wenden, also in Silesia, Duke of Crossen, Baron of Nuremberg, Prince of Halberstadt, Minden and

Camin, Count of Hohenzollern, March, Ravensberg, Lingen, Moerss, Bühren, and Lehrdam, Marquis of Vehre and Blisslingen, Lord of Ravenstein, as also of Launberg and Bütow, Arlay and Breda…the very plethora of old titles rolling out underlining the incredibly patchwork nature of his dominions, as of Germany as a whole.

But those dominions were already on the way to change. King *in* Prussia Frederick might officially be, but he ignored the limitation: in no time at all we have the Royal Prussian Army of the whole state, the Royal Prussian Administration, the Royal Prussian Academies, the Royal Prussian Everything. In any case, in the French that was the common language of the whole of royal, official and intellectual Europe, the German (and English) distinction did not exist: Frederick was simply *Roi de Prusse*. In no time at all he regarded himself and was seen as King of a whole new Prussia, united under a new sovereign and on the way to being unified under his son and aggrandised by his grandson. Though only then, on the latter's death in 1786, would Catholic France and Catholic Spain recognise its ruler as anything more than Margrave of Brandenburg. At the time Frederick became king, the Pope, Clement XI, had lamented that the Emperor had

"sanctioned an act so detrimental to the Church, without reflecting that the Holy Chair alone has the power of appointing kings".

But even at the time Frederick elevated himself and his new Prussia to the top rank of Europe, and the continent sniggered at his pretensions, there was a more prescient voice: the great Hapsburg Field Marshal, Prince Eugene of Savoy, liberator of Hungary and Serbia from the Turks and co-victor with Marlborough at Oudenarde and Malplaquet – and a friend of Leibniz – remarked that

"The Imperial Ministers who advised the Emperor to recognise the King of Prussia deserve hanging".

He could hardly have been imagining that the upstart Hohenzollerns could ever displace the great Hapsburgs as the leaders of Germany. But in due course, a hundred and sixty -five years later, they did.

Queen Sophie Charlotte
The pursuit of Frederick's ambitions have obscured Sophie Charlotte for the past decade, and indeed she seems somewhat lost during that period

in the sources themselves. Most of the references involve travels: after she accompanied Frederick to Westphalia in 1689, on his one and only military campaign, she also went with him the following year on his first visit as Elector to Königsberg in Hohenzollern Prussia. Frederick ensured it was a triumphal progress,

and a comfortable one. Monsieur Erman quotes, with uncharacteristic disrespect for his royal house's ancestor, a diary entry by Frederick's contemporary, Karl Ludwig von Pöllnitz, the son of the Great Elector's Governor of Berlin, who related that timber rest-houses had been especially constructed all the way across the eight hundred kilometres of the journey, and commented caustically that

"Frederick found everywhere his furnished apartments, his guards, his officers, so he couldn't tell he had left his capital".

And von Pöllnitz added that Sophie Charlotte hated it all.

In 1693 she accompanied her husband to two family occasions, a wedding in Leipzig, and the Venetian-style Carnival in Hanover, which her father Ernst August had initiated, this one particularly joyful as the first after the success of his campaign to be created the ninth Elector. But whether to avoid Frederick's obsession with protocol even on tour, or whether because of a growing distance between them – perhaps over Frederick's domination by his old saviour Danckelmann, of whose influence Sophie Charlotte was resentful – there seems to have been only one minor official joint trip until the coronation at the beginning of 1701. Despite her interest in intellectual pursuits, she did not go to Halle in 1694 for Frederick's dedication of his new "modern" university there (designed to reinvigorate university teaching at a time when Heidelberg, for example, averaged only eighty students a year); nor again in 1696 when Frederick visited The Hague to secure, successfully, William III's support for Brandenburg-Prussia's elevation to a kingdom, an occasion where one might have expected Sophie Charlotte's Stuart family connections to have been useful.

There were however regular visits to Hanover to be with her mother: for Carnival again in 1695; for Peter the Great's visit in 1697, as we shall see later; and again in 1700, when mother and daughter travelled on to Brussels, where she taunted Maximilian of Bavaria over his choice of wife. On this last excursion the two women went on to Rotterdam with the express purpose of meeting the French philosopher Pierre Bayle, whose works they admired – Sophie Charlotte, Monsieur Erman said, "always carrying them with her". Bayle, originally Protestant, then temporarily Catholic, had been forced to flee France in 1681 for his defence of religious toleration, and had now been persecuted in Holland, for contending that morality was independent of religion in his 1696 work *Dictionnaire historique et critique*. The visit was brief – Bayle was ill, and it is not clear how much time they had with him – but their interest in someone of such unorthodox views speaks for itself. Sophie Charlotte was later to take up his views with one of Bayle's own philosophical sparring partners: Leibniz.

It was during the visits to Hanover that Sophie Charlotte came to know Leibniz so well, and to appreciate him so much; and it was perhaps his inability to visit Berlin that leaves her life there during the last decade of the 17th century so curiously out of focus by comparison with the succeeding years. But there were preoccupations, some delightful, some more arduous. Increasingly there was the establishment of her separate court in the country to the west of Berlin at Lützenburg (also spelled Lietzenburg), where the palace was begun in 1695 in the gardens begun several years earlier. (After Sophie Charlotte's death Frederick renamed the palace Charlottenburg, and for topograhical clarity it will be referred to by that name here.)

More arduous was the requirement to give attention, at least to some extent, to the supervision of the early years of the increasingly refractory Frederick William, in which she cannot be accounted a success, as we shall see later, though much of his upbringing was in the hands of a governor whom she distrusted. But one of her greatest delights came when she also took on, from 1696, the thirteen-year-old orphaned daughter of the Margrave of Brandenburg-Ansbach, a distant relation of Frederick. Caroline, although Frederick's ward, was largely brought up by Sophie Charlotte at Charlottenburg, and educated with the same loving care as she had experienced herself. The attachment between the two became very close: one of Caroline's biographers remarked on the "remarkable likeness between the two in speech and gesture...[as well as in] views, not only in ethics and philosophy, but in conduct and morals", to which a delighted Leibniz contributed. Sophie Charlotte said she found Charlottenburg "a desert" when Caroline was away.

Sophie Charlotte's distance from Frederick seemed to contemporaries to have been growing as his attention focussed increasingly on manoeuvring towards a crown. Danckelmann continued as a major barrier between them, Sophie Charlotte convinced, apparently correctly, that to cover his own ambitions he was persuading Frederick that she was more concerned for Hanover's interests than Brandenburg's. She was particularly hurt that he had made Frederick

reject her own choice of a governor for Frederick William and had installed his own. Danckelmann finally over-reached himself; his sudden fall, arrest and exile at the end of 1697 gave renewed hope to both husband and wife. Sophie Charlotte wrote to her mother that now she could have a happier "second" marriage; Frederick told Sophie that he could "not thank God enough" for such a wife, and that they "now lived entirely well together". Sophie happily wrote her daughter that in Berlin "they will see that you can do more than play the clavichord".

But hope was short-lived and Sophie was wrong, or at least premature: the drift during thirteen years of Danckelmann had gone on for too long, the gap between Sophie Charlotte's real interests and the formalities and petty intrigues of Fredrick's court had become too great.

Sophie Charlotte preferred books and music at Charlottenburg. "I console myself in solitude", she wrote; "Let others play the comedy". Curiously enough, towards the end of his life, Frederick himself made the observation that "the world is comedy enough, one needs no other". One wonders whether things might have been different had he seen that sooner.

For the present, though, there was little comedy. But it was at this point that Leibniz intervened. As far as Sophie Charlotte was concerned, it proved to be the start of a new life.

Leibniz

Leibniz has been described as "the last universal genius"; Sophie Charlotte's grandson Frederick the Great called him "a whole academy in himself". He was one of the greatest intellectuals of his time: metaphysician, theologian, philologist, historian, genealogist, poet, inventor, scientist, mathematician, logician, lawyer, diplomat, Europeanist – and would-be Sinologist. Liselotte typically had a blunter perspective, writing to Sophie, from the Paris perspective, that

> "From all I hear of Leibniz he must be very intelligent, and pleasant company in consequence. It is rare to find learned men who are clean, do not stink and have a sense of humour".

His papers and letters survived in prodigious quantity: since 1923 some twenty volumes have been published in Berlin, and at the present rate of work the project is expected to take two more *centuries*! He entered into learned discourse and sometimes disputation with a galaxy of correspondents -Bayle, Hobbes, Spinoza, Newton, Addison, the Duke of Marlborough, rafts of Frenchmen and Jesuits, heads of states and churches – but one of his favourite sayings was "*Je ne méprise presque rien*": I have contempt for virtually nothing. This universalism, of interest and sentiment, shines through all his efforts, however incomplete some were, or ham-fisted.

Some twenty years older than the young woman who was to become his pupil and admirer, his position as Brunswick family historian-librarian had been transferred, as we saw, to her father, Ernst August, when he became Duke of Brunswick while she was with her mother still visiting Louis XIV's Paris. But Leibniz was no mere book-worm: he longed to play a part in the big wide world – in particular, having experienced as a boy in Leipzig the ravaged aftermath of the Thirty Years War, to encourage schemes for the preservation of peace in Europe.

Ten years before his move to Hanover, in his first employment under the Electoral Prince-Bishop of Mainz, he had already, at twenty-four, persuaded his master to propose to Louis XIV that, instead of seeking to grab the Spanish Netherlands, France should invade Egypt instead, primarily to preserve harmony in Europe, but with the possible side-advantages of weakening the Ottoman Empire (Egypt's overlord), converting the Moslem people to Christianity, and re-opening the land route across Asia that had been closed since the Ottoman conquest of Constantinople in 1453. In 1672 the Elector sent Leibniz to Paris to argue his *Consilium Ægyptiacum* directly with Louis' ministers, but they scornfully responded that "Crusades had gone out of fashion since the days of St Louis". Louis' ambitions were closer to home, so he duly invaded the Netherlands the same year.[233] In 1798 Napoleon Bonaparte

---

233 It was this war which lay at the root of one of the most courageous criticisms ever levelled at Louis by a subject: the churchman and writer François de Salignac de la Mothe-Fénélon. In 1699, when he was Archbishop of Cambrai, he published a treatise, known as *Télémaque*, written previously when he had been governor to Louis' grandson and heir, in which he had advised his young charge that

"War is sometimes necessary, but it is the shame of the human race...Do not tell me, O kings, that one should desire war to acquire glory...Whoever prefers his own glory to sentiments of humanity is a monster of pride and not a man; he will gain only false glory...Absolute power degrades every subject to the condition of a slave...",

finally followed Leibniz's advice, all the way to the Pyramids, though he only learned of it when he captured Hanover in 1803 – *Consilium Ægyptiacum* was in the library there.

Although he had been educated in philosophy and law, Leibniz's four-year stay in Paris resulted in his development of a lively interest in mathematical and scientific topics. By the time of his Hanoverian employment he was still working on the development of the calculus, a crucial mathematical tool which both he and Isaac Newton published in circumstances which allowed their supporters to accuse – though less, perhaps, lately – the other of having plagiarised. It is now generally agreed that they each achieved their result independently: Newton earlier in time, but without making it public; and (the experts say) Newton's version more profound, but Leibniz's notation clearer and simpler – it is Leibniz's that is still used. Newton pursued the feud ferociously and unattractively until his opponent's death, when he was reported by a colleague to have said "pleasantly" that he "had broke Leibniz's heart with his [final] Reply to him".

Like just about every Enlightenment thinker – and a good (and bad) many since – Leibniz hoped to develop a Theory of Everything. It is as a philosopher that he is now chiefly known; there, too, while he was a would-be rationalist, he sought to produce a comprehensive metaphysics, deriving everything up to God from an infinitesimally small and irreducible foundation of the physical world. Scholars have said that, as far as philosophy was concerned, "he never developed an ample and systematic expression of his position", perhaps because he was too busy with other things.

One that he himself regarded as equally important was his pursuit of religious unity to secure the peace of Europe – which lapped over into his continued yearning for a personal role in diplomacy and politics. What he searched for – in decades of visits to and correspondence with Berlin, Dresden, Vienna, Paris, London and Rome, often at the highest levels of church and state – was the idea not so much of a united church or a universal religion as such, but a more practical religious alliance based on "diplomatic combinations and theological concessions" by all the "*esprits éclairés et bien intentionnés*" (the enlightened and well-intentioned minds) in the different Christian confessions.[234]

---

and so on. Fénélon claimed he did not have Louis in mind in this broadside, but was not believed. Surprisingly, he kept his head, and his archdiocese.

234   Leibniz underlined the collegial nature of his proposal in a very personal way. During his long stay in Rome in 1689 he was offered the post of Vatican

Side by side with the growing rationalist questioning of religion, it was a quest that was in the air – as we saw earlier with the Abbé Ballati, Sophie's enforced marriage-broker and purchasing-agent for dresses and dolls. Sophie nevertheless encouraged these irenic researches herself – in her own fashion:

> "As Christianity came into the world through a woman", she wrote to Leibniz at one stage, "I should be proud if its unification were due to me".

But Leibniz failed her: his idea met with an almost universal approbation... on condition that it was based on the particular respondent's own theological requirements.

And there were to be other schemes as well, as we shall see, all of which extraneous pursuits sat ill with the rulers of Hanover, who were paying him to write a history of their House of Brunswick from its putative origins in the very far distant past, not just out of vainglory (though that too) but for the very practical purpose of establishing certain ancient and still desirable rights and claims. The Duke who became Elector, and his son who became King George I of England, both tried to keep poor Leibniz – even though he played a helpful if small role in securing both promotions – to this genealogical contract; and from Leibniz's own viewpoint, his researches, like his pursuit of Christian reunification, at least gave him the excuse for enjoyable travels and contacts throughout Europe with the great and the clever. Because of his habitual thoroughness, and the more delectable distractions of philosophy and politics, by the time of his death in 1716 he was up to AD 1005. However it is a matter for conjecture whether George's rejection of Leibniz's pressing pleas to accompany him to the new fields of England resulted from the new King's concern for the family history, or from his unwillingness to cross his new country's unchallenged (otherwise than by Leibniz's mathematical genius) intellectual icon – Sir Isaac Newton.

Leibniz comes to Berlin
The fall of Danckelmann in Berlin opened up a new field. Leibniz promptly wrote confidentially to Sophie and Sophie Charlotte that since the latter

---

Librarian - with a cardinal's hat - provided he became Catholic. But he declined, saying that while he would continue to work for Christian unity, he could not see errors in his own Lutheranism that would require his conversion.

"had now secured the entire confidence of the Elector her husband, she would recognize the necessity of taking advantage of the situation [to] *ménager la conjoncture*...It is only fitting that the mother should assist the daughter with good advice on how to repair the damage done by Danckelmann and his government... [provided] all was done discreetly without causing suspicion or, God forbid, offence";

and, to avoid such dangers, Leibniz offered himself, as one who "knew his way about affairs of state", as the most appropriate person to carry out the role of confidential intermediary. What of course he really wanted Sophie Charlotte to *ménager* was himself into a more active role in improving the prickly relations between her Elector husband in Berlin and her Elector brother in Hanover. And for this purpose he suggested that he

"be appointed to some supervising post connected with Science and Art at Berlin",

so he would have an unarguable reason for making visits there despite his genealogical duties in Hanover.

In 1696 Frederick had founded, one suspects with Sophie Charlotte's encouragement, an Academy of Arts (*Kunsthochschule*), in imitation of Paris's Académie Royale des Beaux Arts (founded 1664) and Vienna's Reichsakademie (1692). It may have been on her own initiative that next, in 1699, Sophie Charlotte also proposed to her husband, with the support of the still-in-office Danckelmann, that he could embellish his reign by establishing a Royal Observatory in Berlin: though the capital was the meeting place of so many scholars, she observed, no calendar was produced and there was no astronomer as well as no observatory. Leibniz now broadened this scheme by proposing that, by emulating Paris's Académie Française (founded 1635, of which he had been made a a foreign associate in 1669) and London's Royal Society (1662, of which he had been a member since 1673), Frederick's glory could be even further extended by establishing a similar full Academy of Sciences in Berlin – with Observatory and Leibniz attached.

He enlisted Sophie Charlotte's support, including with a fossilised mammoth's tooth found near Hanover, and an accompanying dissertation, to stimulate her scientific curiosity. He succeeded, but repeated invitations to Leibniz from Sophie Charlotte to come to Berlin to further his proposals were turned down by an increasingly hostile Elector George, who complained that he never knew the whereabouts of Leibniz, who, whenever asked why he was so elusive, "always had the excuse that he was working at his invisible books". But an invitation from the Elector Frederick himself saw Leibniz in Berlin in mid-1700, the first of a number of extensive visits over the next five years. And negotiations, which proceeded rapidly on the basis of the previous correspondence between Leibniz and Sophie Charlotte, and on flattering comparisons between Frederick and Louis XIV, resulted in Frederick's proclamation of the *Societas Regia Scientarum*, the Royal Society of Sciences, in July that year, with Leibniz as perpetual President.

Like the other scientific academies of the time, the Society was not to be a research institution but an intellectual clearing house, in which individual scientists could benefit from exchanging with others the results of their research and their theories about them; and there were four sections:

- Physics, chemistry and medicine
- Mathematics and astronomy
- German language and history
- *Belles-lettres* and Oriental languages.

In fact Leibniz saw his Society as not simply devoted to scientific curiosity but as benefitting the country also through the application of scientific knowledge to the promotion of manufacturing and commerce. And it was with a realistic eye to the endurance of his academy – and perhaps to his own remuneration, a constant preoccupation – that he sought over a period of time, though in vain, to have it endowed with the revenues of the Harz silver mines, lotteries, and the checking of standards of weights and measures. Eventually it was granted a monopoly on the printing and sale of calendars, and – for the somewhat longer term – on the plantation of mulberry trees and the introduction of silk-culture. Alas, the mulberry trees never prospered, though Leibniz pursued the project to the end of his life.

The visiting Irishman John Toland, whom we shall meet very soon, recorded the Berlin of the new academies: King Frederick had built new Royal Stables, he wrote,

> "which may be properly call'd magnificent, and are often mistaken by Strangers for som great Minister's Palace...Over head is the

Academy of the Painters, of the Learned, and of all the gentile Arts which are much incourag'd here; and there is likewise rais'd a conspicuous Observatory for Astronomers. This gave occasion to a Person, who had no great opinion of the Men of Letters in this Academy, to tell the King that he did very well to lodge his Horses and his Asses together".

Sophie Charlotte's philosophical salon

All in all, the Society of Sciences did not meet Leibniz's ambitions during his lifetime; and his proposals for similar societies in Dresden and Vienna came to nothing. Likewise the two Electors never saw any diplomatic role for Leibniz to play, and to the extent that he tried one between the two of them they each came to suspect him of sinister manoeuvring on behalf of the other. It was the beginning, however, of a close and deepening association with Sophie Charlotte. She regarded him as her intellectual mentor, but he also sensed the sharpness of her mind: "she wants", he informed a correspondent with what may have been exasperation as well as pride, "to know the why even of the why".

Sophie Charlotte did not suffer fools, and was more suspicious of the great than of those they held to be less worthy. She wrote on one occasion to a confidante, the wife of a senior court official:

> "I understand that aspects of the great can be intimidating, and take away from others the ability to shine and be noticed, and then I am reassuring. But when conceit is involved, and presumption and stupidity destroy the esteem owed to genuine merit, I am pitiless and have no mercy at all".

But there was more than just hostility to pretension and cant: she was positively and intelligently interested in serious opinions, especially on the religious and philosophical issues of the day.

Here of course her mother's influence had been crucial even before the development of her association with Leibniz. She was extraordinarily open-minded for the times, though admittedly, for all the formal requirement that, on her marriage, Sophie Charlotte had finally had to declare for the royal family's Calvinism, the Berlin Court was unusually tolerant: in the first place, of course, of the Lutherans, who were the majority of the population, despite their frequent spats with the Calvinists. Toland, no friend of the Established Church at home, made a sharp little observation on the matter:

"In most places the Calvinists have better Livings than the Lutherans; and since the Distinction is solely confin'd to the Clergy, without a Layman's getting or losing any thing in his Honor or Profit by professing either Religion, 'tis very probable that they have fewer Hypocrites than where it is beneficial or detrimental to be of a certain Sect".

But tolerance was much wider: of Catholics – after all, Sophie Charlotte had been expectantly to Paris; and to some extent of Jews, the Great Elector having invited a (limited) number of Jewish bankers expelled from Vienna to settle there, and Sophie Charlotte was herself present at the consecration of the first private synagogue in the city.

In addition, Leibniz's pursuit of a universal – or at least European – religious harmony was itself an idea which encouraged unorthodox debate; and as Thomas Carlyle said in his vast biography of her grandson, Frederick the Great, Sophie Charlotte herself liked nothing better than unorthodox debate. At her intellectual gatherings she frequently had, on the one side,

"Reverend Edict-of-Nantes gentlemen [Huguenot refugees], famed Berlin divines; whom, if any Papist notability, Jesuit Ambassador or the like, happened to be there, she would set disputing with him, in the Soiree at Charlottenburg. She could right well preside over such a battle of the Cloud-Titans, and conduct the lightnings softly, without explosions".

Carlyle went on to give an example of Sophie Charlotte's "dextrous conducting" – she wrote placatingly, in March 1703, to soothe the Polish King's Jesuit confessor, Father Charles Maurice Vota, who had apologised for his sharp reactions, during one of her evening debates, to Protestant criticisms of the Church Fathers and Church Councils. But she nevertheless herself neatly skewered both of these by mischievously citing one of the former, St Gregory Nazianzen, on the latter:

"No Council ever was successful; so many mean human passions getting into conflagration there; with noise, with violence and uproar, more like those of a tavern or still worse place"

- "with more of the like sort", Carlyle says, noting further citations, "all delicate, as invisible needle-points, in her Majesty's hand". Maybe not so invisible, though, in Warsaw.

John Toland gives us a contemporary glimpse of Sophie Charlotte in action in her salon in 1701. Oxford-educated, he was a controversial free-thinker – characterised by the British *Dictionary of National Biography* with sniffy abruptness as, simply, "deist", as though his unorthodox theology were some sort of unsuitable trade. Toland was in the embassy of Lord Macclesfield, who had just presented the English Parliament's Act of Succession to her mother, the Electress Sophie, making her heir to the English throne after Anne, following the death of the latter's last surviving child.[235] Having created an uproar with the publication in 1696 of his *Christianity Not Mysterious*, and being chased out of both England and Ireland for arguing that Christian morality could be deduced by reason without divine revelation, one must wonder how such a dangerous character came to be in the noble Earl's train on such a critical state occasion. For Sophie Charlotte the spice of such unorthodoxy was irresistible.

In a letter written to a Dutch "Minister of State" in 1702, which he had published in London in 1714, Toland described Sophie Charlotte as "the most beautiful Princess of her Time", a conventional enough encomium for a commoner to make of the sister of the, by then, heir to the English crown. A few added details were a shade more precise:

---

235   As it turned out, Sophie was to die in 1714 just two months before Anne, so the United Kingdom succession went from the last Protestant Stuart to Sophie's son the Elector of Hanover, Sophie Charlotte's older brother, who became King George I. The choice of Sophie, retrospectively through her grandmother Elizabeth of Bohemia, eldest daughter of James I, was to ensure the exclusion of Anne's Catholic brother, the deposed King James II - and his son, the Old Pretender (who was recognised by a trouble-making Louis XIV as James III on his father's death in September 1701, just six months after Parliament's passage of the Act of Succession). While they were the most obvious pretenders to succeed Anne, they were not the only ones with a claim. An 18th century Hanoverian historian counted,

"between Sophie and the throne to which Parliament called her, fifty-four Princes or Princesses, who, by the proximity of blood and marriages, had rights prior to those which circumstances caused to prevail".

It is not often noted that the Hanoverian Succession excluded not only all these Catholics with a possible claim, but also William III's Protestant first cousin Frederick of Brandenburg-Prussia - though Frederick, who tried (unsuccessfully) to grab William's Netherlands possessions as his heir to the House of Orange-Nassau, in fact made no bid to succeed him as heir to England. But it is a might-have-been to give pause: the Hohenzollerns in Buckingham Palace.

"as for her Person, she's not very tall, but somewhat too plump: all her Features are extremely regular" – an attribute Toland admired equally in physiognomy and architecture – "her Complection fair and lively, her eyes Blue, and her Hair Cole-black".

One suspects this was entirely frank: in Hanover he found her mother Sophie extraordinarily youthful for her age – "not one tooth missing". A portrait of Sophie Charlotte made the same year by F. W. Weidemann[236] shows an ample enough woman in a reasonable décolletage, with slightly mischievous, smiling eyes, no sign of haughtiness about her – but with an even greater fullness of face than that promised by the earlier childhood portrait by Aunt Louise Hollandine, and a substantial double chin.

Having made obeisance to "the most beautiful Princess of her Time", Toland went straight on – in the same sentence – to what he and a good many others regarded as her real attractions:

"...second to no Person in the Justness of her Thoughts, the Delicacy of Expressions, or the Graces of Conversation".

And lest it be thought he is still speaking in expected formulas, Toland continued:

"Her Reading is infinit, and she is conversant in all manner of Subjects; nor is She more admir'd for her inimitable Wit, than for her exact Knowledg of the more abstruse parts of Philosophy: and (without flattering her high Dignity in the least) I must freely own that I never heard Objections more pertinently made, the Sophistry of an Argument quicker detected, nor either the difficulty or weakness of any Opinion more easily penetrated by any other in my whole Life".

Toland knew what he was talking about. During his stay in Berlin he had been admitted by Sophie Charlotte into the regular conversations and debates which she held with philosophers and theologians. Toland himself, with his unorthodox theology, knew well enough about Argument and the difficulty and weakness of Opinion – even the *Dictionary of National*

---

236   Now in the Schloss Charlottenburg, Berlin

Biography concedes that he "deserves real credit as a pioneer of free thought", though this broadmindedness breaks down in Anglican condescension:

> "Allowance must be made for the unfortunate circumstances which compelled him to make a living in the ambiguous position of a half-recognised political agent and a hack author dependent upon the patronage of men in power".

In brief, he was constantly hounded for his heretical free thinking. And herein lies the clue to the genuineness of his admiration for Sophie Charlotte: he was not merely flattered by being welcomed into her philosophical *soirées*, he genuinely appreciated and enjoyed the fact that she was open, original, and none too orthodox a believer. Her mother, and Leibniz, had done their work well.

Sophie Charlotte's earnestly Calvinist biographer Monsieur Erman was less than happy about her meetings with Toland. Even a century later, he could still rail:

> "Toland..showed himself in Berlin just as he had been seen in his own country. With his ideas and his writings, he brought there, at a time when the liberty, or I should say, the licence of the press had not spread them as in our century, these bold and dangerous works which aim at overturning the principles most essential to the peace of nations and the welfare of humanity".

The most outrageous of these tomes was by Giordano Bruno, the ex-Dominican burned by Rome for heresy, and published in...1584! The worst outrage however was that

> "during his stay in Berlin [Toland] had worked to bring Sophie Charlotte around to his beliefs".

Oddly, but perhaps significantly, he does not entirely absolve her: notwithstanding the intellectual and debating skills with which she was so well endowed, to deal with Toland she produced, apparently on only one occasion, one of her Reverend Edict-of-Nantes gentlemen, and the two debated for two hours; when "the conversation began to get *piquante*", Her Majesty, without having intervened, and without comment, simply ended it – and invited Toland back. One has the clear impression that, as far as religion was concerned, it was the arguing, not the outcome, that engaged her: as Leibniz said, "the why of the why".

Passion for China

One of Leibniz's life-long passions was China, and he eventually sought, with indifferent success, to have Sophie Charlotte share it. There had been a fascination with fabled Cathay ever since Marco Polo's *Travels* came out in 1298; the second half of the 17th century had seen something of an explosion in awareness of a more real China: reports from the (mostly) Jesuit missionaries installed in Beijing, some at the Emperor's Court, since 1601; exquisite porcelains, silks, lacquers, shipped as part of their expanding commerce by the great European trading companies. In 1664 John Evelyn, the noted English diarist, recorded that

> "One Tomson, a Jesuit, showed me such a collection of rarities,... brought to London by the East India ships,...as in my life I had not seen. The chief things were, rhinoceros's horns; glorious vests, wrought and embroidered on cloth of gold, but with such lively colours, that for splendour and vividness we have nothing in Europe that approaches it;"

and a long list more – knives, papers, pictures, silks, medicines.[237] Later, Liselotte created a sensation in Hanover when she sent Sophie a pair of fat jewelled Buddhas with heads that nodded. She was the same shape, she noted, "only with clothes on".

By early the next century things Chinese had become the rage; in 1725 Evelyn's younger contemporary John Gay wrote in delicious celebration:

> "What ecstasies her bosom fire!
> How her eyes languish with desire!
> How blest, how happy should I be,
> Were that fond glance bestowed on me!
> New doubts and fears within me war:
> What rival's near? A *China* jar.

---

237 Evelyn's wonderment at China's treasures exactly parallels Dürer's, a century and a half before, on seeing Montezuma's treasures in Brussels (1500 chapter). Evelyn, a Balliol (see 1300 chapter), was also a well-known author, and became an active member of the Royal Society.

China's the passion of her soul;
A cup, a plate, a dish, a bowl
Can kindle wishes in her breast,
Inflame her joy, or break her rest."[238]

The first sign of Leibniz's interest in things Chinese came four years after Evelyn's, when he was still a twenty-two-year-old student in Leipzig; on the basis of reports he had found in the library there, he concluded that Chinese medicine was superior to European. And a French scholar believes that during Leibniz's time in Paris in the early 1670s he was already urging Colbert, Louis XIV's chief minister since 1661 and founder of the Académie des Sciences, to send an information-gathering mission to China.[239] Later he became infected by more philosophical considerations, but that interest in what China could offer always remained alongside – and at times in front of – the variety of benefits he thought at different times the West could bestow on a more or less receptive China. Before its establishment, he was concerned that one of the chief aims of a Society of Scientists in Berlin should be the organisation of a scientific expedition to both Russia and China, for "the propagation of light and wisdom".

But it was also his intention from the beginning that the Society should be a vehicle for establishing practical, as well as scientific and

---

238   There are connections to both Hanover and Berlin. In 1714 Gay was secretary to Lord Clarendon when he led an embassy to the Electress Sophie in Hanover; he told his friend Jonathan Swift that he spent his time perfecting himself in "the diplomatic arts of bowing profoundly [and] speaking deliberately". They would have escorted her to London as Queen of England following the death of the seriously ailing Queen Anne had not Sophie died unexpectedly two months before. Gay went on to become most famous for *The Beggar's Opera*, which was (in part) set to music by the ex-German composer Johann Christoph Pepusch. Pepusch had been employed at Frederick's court at the time of the latter's marriage to Sophie Charlotte, but had moved from Berlin to London after witnessing the execution without trial of a Prussian officer, "to put himself under the protection of a government founded on better principles". Late in life he was elected to the Royal Society. His oboist brother Gottfried remained in Frederick's employ.

239   Colbert later made plans to send a group of Jesuits to establish a mission in Beijing; but they went only in 1685, two years after his death. The five included Father Jean François Gerbillon, who was to play an important part in Sino-Russian relations, as we shall see below. Leibniz developed an active correspondence with the French as well as other Jesuits in the China mission.

cultural, relations between Prussia and China. An important aspect would be the development of commercial exchanges: not merely, he wrote to a Jesuit missionary, Father Philippe-Marie Grimaldi, whom he got to know in Rome in 1689, for

> "getting things European to the Chinese, but rather about getting remarkable Chinese inventions to us; otherwise little profit will be derived".

And he went on to ask Grimaldi for further information, when he returned to China, on just about everything you could think of: plants and drugs that could be introduced into Europe; the manufacture of metals, tea, paper, silk, "true" porcelain, dyes, glass, Japanese sword blades; geographical details on North Asian islands; Chinese agricultural, military and naval machines that could help improve European ones; books on history and natural history; a key to the Chinese language; living comforts that might be useful for Europeans. It was an indication of his curiosity about and desire to understand others, even a culture as different as China's.

It was also the template for his approach to Chinese philosophy. The more he learned of China – as much as anyone in Europe who had not been there, the result of his active correspondence with (mostly) missionaries over the three decades from the 1680s to the end of his life – the more he came to the view that a junction between European and Chinese learning could lead to a universal civilisation. He also came to view the then ruler of China, Kangxi (K'ang-hsi), the greatest of the Ching Emperors, as

> "a god-like mortal, ruling all by a nod of his head, who, however, is educated to virtue and wisdom...thereby earning the right to rule",

the epitome of the enlightened despot, in short, a figure (in Europe) about to become the cynosure of the Enlightenment philosophers.[240]

---

240 One famous such attachment was between the initially-admiring and initially-admired Voltaire and the benevolent despot Frederick the Great, who made him his Chamberlain for the three years between the Frenchman's offending Louis XV's Queen and offending Frederick himself. Despite the

To help spread knowledge of China Leibniz published in 1697 *Novissima Sinica* ("Latest News of China") based on missionary reports. It included the account by the Portuguese Father Joseph Suarez of the edict issued in 1692 by granting toleration for Christianity – provided they followed the Chinese Rites, the observance accommodating Chinese custom – tolerance of Confucian writings, ancestor worship, traditional rites. This had originally been devised by Father Mateo Ricci, the first and one of the greatest of the Jesuit missionaries, who had secured permission to live in Beijing nearly a century before, in 1601.

Ricci's argument, that these customs were purely civic in nature, and that Western theology had to be placed in the context of this Chinese intellectual tradition, had made a decisive contribution to the acceptability of Christianity by many Chinese, including even members of the Imperial family. Much of the Jesuit missionaries' credit derived also from the important contribution they had made to successive Emperors' concerns with astronomy, time-pieces, military and civil technology; but the edict was a tremendous breakthrough for the wider dissemination of Western (Christian) ideas. It was also a tremendous contrast with Louis XIV's brutally reactionary revocation of the Edict of Nantes just seven years before.

However, with exquisite timing, in 1704 Leibniz's Vatican correspondent and King Frederick's opponent, Pope Clement XI, prohibited outright the use of the Chinese Rites. It was a fatal blow to the so-recently successful missionary effort in China. Although Kangxi came to be concerned also about Portuguese, Spanish, Dutch and English merchants sniffing around China's coast, Clement's ban undoubtedly contributed to his observing:

"I fear that some time in the future China is going to get into difficulties with these various Western countries. That is my prediction".

---

bruising Voltaire gave Leibniz in Candide (see below), he shared the latter's admiration for Chinese philosophy -

"[Confucius] appeals only to virtue, he preaches no miracles, there is nothing...of religious allegory"

- but he was unable to interest Frederick:

"I leave the Chinese to you", he wrote to Voltaire, "along with the Indians and Tartars. The European nations keep my mind sufficiently occupied".

And he expelled any missionary who would not adhere to the terms of his toleration edict.[241]

While Leibniz was concerned that the dispute could lead to contact between China and the West being broken, it was characteristic of his capacity for cross-cultural understanding that he strenuously argued in favour of the Jesuits' "accomodationist" position, including, in 1716, the last year of his life, in one of his very last works, the *Discours sur la Théologie naturelle des Chinois* (often referred to as "Letter on Chinese Philosophy").[242] The *Discours* was essentially a summary of what he understood of Chinese thought and what it could contribute to universal knowledge and understanding. He had come to the view, after three decades of study and debate, that the Chinese classical texts were

"quite excellent, and quite in accord with natural theology...It is pure Christianity, insofar as it renews the natural law inscribed on our hearts"

- though he never went to the extreme of the philosopher François de La Mothe le Vayer, who, in his younger, wilder days before he developed orthodoxy and was appointed by Louis XIV as tutor to the Dauphin and Royal Historiographer (like Erman), was claimed to say "*Sancte Confucii, ora pro nobis*": Saint Confucius, pray for us. Leibniz was particularly struck, also, by parallels between Chinese mathematics and the binary system he had himself invented, which he regarded as the "basis of natural science". His conclusion, as summarised by Rosemont and Cook, was, thus, that there was a

"proper method for engaging the Chinese in ecumenical dialogue: show them the truth, but not simply by quoting from the Bible and giving them telescopes; show them also how both theological and scientific truth could be read in their most ancient writings".

Leibniz's acceptance that morality could exist without being based on a revealed religion had led him to assert earlier, in *Novissima Sinica,* that

---

241 He was of course right - see 1900 chapter: Yuan Shikai. The ban was only revoked by Pope Pius XII in 1939.
242 It was first published, in the original French, in 1735. It was not translated into German until 1966, or English until 1977.

"the condition of our affairs, slipping as we are into ever greater corruption, seems to me such that we need missionaries from the Chinese who might teach us the use and practice of natural religion, just as we have sent them teachers of revealed theology".

Perhaps to placate disturbed ecclesiastical correspondents, he came up with the bizarre expectation that China would eventually yield even further untold knowledge and wisdom preserved since the most ancient Chinese emperors, because they had been close to the Biblical Flood... and therefore among the first descendants of Noah. And he did not entirely surrender to Confucius: with his experience of the settlement of the Thirty Years War on the basis of *cuius regio, eius religio* (subjects to adopt the religion of their ruler) he told one correspondent that

"to win the conversion of a single man, such as the Tsar or the monarch of China, and to turn it to good ends; by inspiring in him a zeal for the glory of God and for the perfection of mankind, this is more than winning a hundred battles, because on the will of such men several million others will depend".

This was of course precisely the objective the Jesuits had had firmly in mind, from the very beginning of their mission, as the best route to success.

As his interest in China, and the list of his correspondents, grew, Leibniz told Sophie Charlotte that

"I shall have to hang a sign on my door with the words: *bureau d'adresse pour la Chine* [forwarding office for China]".

He repeatedly sought to interest her in his China schemes, and in 1697 offered to teach her Confucianism, Chinese history, the Chinese idea of immortality, and "matters which are a trifle more certain". But he was still in Hanover when he wrote this and Sophie Charlotte was not yet able to engineer an invitation to Berlin. We do not know what Sophie Charlotte thought of his China passion, for all her admiration of Leibniz: was Monsieur Erman silent because he was not interested in such esoteric pursuits? or because they were so dangerously unorthodox? Perhaps she focussed on the proposal to convert the Chinese from the Emperor down, and shared the down-to-earth scepticism of Leibniz's other great admirer, her mother:

"To me it seems", the Electress Sophie told him, "that the first thing ought to be to make good Christians at home in Germany, without going to so great a distance for the purpose of manufacturing them".

Russian aspirations

At the opening of his preface to *Novissima Sinica* Leibniz spelled out another aspect of his China passion: it was not only Cathay that interested him, but also, of necessity, the way thither:

"I consider it a singular plan of the fates", he wrote, "that human cultivation and refinement should today be concentrated, as it were, in the two extremes of our continent, in Europe and in Tschina (as they call it)...Perhaps Supreme Providence has ordained such an arrangement, so that, as the most cultivated and distant peoples stretch out their arms to each other, those in between may gradually be brought to a better way of life. I do not think it an accident that the Muscovites, whose vast realm connects Europe with China...should be led to the emulation of our ways through the strenuous efforts of their present ruler".

Leibniz regarded Russia "as the *tabula rasa* of the east", and this attempt to flatter Tsar Peter already had a long history.

A quarter century earlier Leibniz had been interested, as we saw, in opening communication eastward across Asia, as one element in his *Consilium Ægyptiacum* case for Louis XIV to invade Egypt. It had only been at the beginning of the 17th century that Father Matteo Ricci had identified China as the same country as Marco Polo's Cathay; but it is strange to realize now that in Leibniz's day, four centuries after the Polos, Westerners still had no more recent idea of the course or condition of the route through Siberia between Moscow and Beijing.

It was not for want of trying: beginning in the 1620s appeals had been being made to the first of the Romanovs and to all his successors for the opening of the Siberian route to China. Most were made by or on behalf of the Jesuits, to facilitate communications with their increasingly important mission in Beijing, not least because the sea-route was under increasing threat from the Dutch and English; in due course trading interests in Western Europe added to the pressure on the Tsars. But as the century passed they refused everyone: Popes, Hapsburg Emperors, Polish Kings and Louis XIV, Dutch and Brandenburg ambassadors,

Polish, Swedish and French merchants, and of course the Jesuits themselves. By the 1680s some of the latter even tried being helpful to Russian interests: Father Ferdinand Verbiest, head of the Jesuit mission in Beijing and Director of the Emperor Chenlung's Bureau of Astronomy; and a short-lived Jesuit mission in Moscow itself, under Father Vota, who had participated in Sophie Charlotte's philosophical debates. All to no avail.

By the end of the decade what none of them knew was that Moscow, determined to retain a monopoly on commercial relations between Russia and China, and to gain an opening for the Orthodox Church there, was preparing to pursue these objectives, and settle impeding border disputes, by negotiating with China directly. The negotiations in 1689 resulted in the Treaty of Nerchinsk, named after the small town then between the two countries, now well inside Russia, on the Trans-Siberian Railway some thousand kilometres east of Baikal.

It was China's very first treaty with anyone; and the irony of it, in the light of the long campaign by successive Chinese governments in the 20th century to overturn the "unequal" treaties forced on China by European powers in the 19th, is that it too was unequal – in China's favour. The Russians were obliged by superior Chinese military presence in the area, which they had not been expecting, to cede the large triangle north of the great loop in the Amur River, between Nerchinsk and the Pacific, which they had themselves held since the

1650s.[243] However Russia's other objectives were achieved: an Orthodox mission was established in Beijing; great camel caravans began

---

243 In our time in Moscow, the Soviet Union was still outraged at the unfairness of it all. A prominent Soviet historian, Vladimir Miasnikov, wrote in 1980:

" There were no objective reasons for Ch'ing expansion in Northern Manchuria and Amuria...It was planned and carried out to indulge the personal ambitions of the man occupying the Dragon Throne...[T]he Treaty [was] unequal, that is, concluded under duress...It is hard to estimate the damage done to the Russian state by the territorial articles of the Treaty of Nerchinsk...Capture of part of Russian Amuria was a blow at...development of Russia's Far Eastern outlands..."

- for which there were presumably "objective" reasons. And so things stayed for a century and a half. Then in 1858-1860, after Admiral Count Euphemius Putiatin had given notice of Russian intentions by forcing his way down the Amur in a little 6-gun paddle-steamer exotically called the *Amerika*, Moscow seized back the Amur triangle from a China prostrated by the Second Opium

crossing Siberia, part government, part private until 1706, when Peter made the trade a state monopoly.

For the negotiations, as neither side could converse directly with the other, Kangxi included in his delegation two trusted Jesuits as interpreters: Father Verbiest's successor, the Portuguese Father Thomas Pereira (who amongst other things taught Kangxi the rudiments of playing the harpsichord), and one of the five French Fathers, Jean-François Gerbillon (some of whose letters from Nerchinsk were reprinted by Leibniz in *Novissima Sinica*); the negotiations, and the Treaty itself, were accordingly in Latin and Manchu. The Jesuits were convinced a successful outcome would open the trans-Siberian route; and to help get one, as well as Moscow's permission to use it, Pereira and Gerbillon (like Father Verbiest before them) passed helpful hints to the Russian delegation on how to deal with the Chinese, assuring it that, while they would serve the Emperor as long as he allowed them to preach the Gospels, they would not "go against Christian law" to help "the heathens". This did not go far enough for the Russians; and when Pereira and Gerbillon refused to be bribed by the promise of stipends and "the favour of the Tsar", they accused the Jesuits of perfidy. And the trans-Siberian route remained firmly shut.

It was also in 1689 that the Beijing Jesuit Father Philippe Grimaldi approached Leibniz, when they were both in Rome, to seek his assistance in changing Peter's mind. The numerous conversations with Grimaldi over a period of six months contributed significantly to Leibniz's knowledge of China, and led to his support of the Jesuits' position on both Siberia and the Chinese Rites. The Jesuits for their part recognised the value of Leibniz's connections and influence in many of the German states and elsewhere in Europe.

For most of the next decade Moscow remained obdurate against all entreaties on access to Siberia. Then: the possibility of a breakthrough! An astonished Europe learned that the mysterious Tsar of all the Russias, Peter Romanov, was embarking on a journey to the West in the guise of "Peter Mikhailov", a shipwright in a "Grand Embassy" led by his ex-Genevan adviser General Franz Lefort (father of another Leibniz correspondent). The incognito was about as effective as Sophie's had

---

War, and for good measure the coastal province of Ussuri, which it had never held. After China's next defeat, following the Boxer Rebellion in 1900, Russia seized the whole of Manchuria as well - only to lose it when it in turn went down to defeat by Japan in 1905 (see the 1900 chapter: Yuan Shikai).

been in Paris; and its transparency mattered as little to Peter in the West European shipyards, where he spent most of his time, as it did in the courts where he reluctantly revealed himself to his boggle-eyed fellow monarchs. Right at the beginning of the tour the Elector of Brandenburg staged an enthusiastic and extravagant welcome in Königsberg. In appreciation, Peter played a drum, his favourite instrument, for his bemused host. Frederick observed that the Prussian penal system had particularly fascinated the Tsar, who had offered one of his own servants to be broken on the wheel to see how it worked, and had become bad-tempered when the offer was declined.

Surprisingly, Frederick also had a crack at the overland route to China. Although not interested in Africa, he had apparently come to recognise the importance to the Dutch and English of their trade with Asia. Accordingly he too wanted the Siberian route opened so that Brandenburg trade could compete, and he put this to Peter when the latter sought his support against Sweden. Frederick and Peter reached a purely oral agreement that they would render mutual assistance in case of a Swedish attack on either; and then they signed a treaty of friendship, trade and defence which, for the first time for any non-Russians, gave Brandenburgers

"who wish to traverse the Muscovite lands on their way to Persia or China shall, after payment of the requisite transit tax, be accorded free passage both going and returning and without suffering indignities or offence".

But there was a catch: what Peter really wanted was to drive the Swedes out of the coastal regions which were barring Moscow from the Baltic; so when he himself attacked Sweden, he demanded Brandenburg's support. And when Frederick, already involved with the wars against Louis XIV in the west, refused to become involved in a new northern war, Peter promptly rescinded free passage across Siberia.

Leibniz seems to have been slow in keeping up with the state of Brandenburg-Russian relations: still in 1700 he was writing to Frederick:

"[W]ith the help of the special dispensation of Providence, the uncommonly good personal relations with the Tsar opens a wide gate to Great Tartary and to magnificent China. Through this gate not only goods and other wares but also light and knowledge may find an entrance into this other civilised world and 'Anti-Europe', and many would therefore be attracted to seek the protection of Your Electoral Highness, especially since it is also known that of all European natural products almost nothing is more sought after and prized in China than amber [which was plentiful in Prussia]. It is just as if God willed that Your Electoral Highness should also have this natural advantage".

Leibniz might have had more success if God had willed that China would provide a supply of diamonds and pearls to Frederick.

Leibniz himself sought an audience with the Tsar during the latter's passage through Germany, to support the Jesuits. The same purpose was intended to be served by the publication during the tour of *Novissima Sinica*, which included, as well as Jesuit letters, an account of a Prussian mission to Beijing during 1693-1695 by the Lübecker Adam Brand, who planned a second expedition to China but became Frederick's commercial adviser instead. It should be noted, though, that *Novissima Sinica* was also intended to encourage Protestant missionary activity in China, certainly not for any sectarian attempt to supplant the Jesuits there, but to share what Leibniz saw as their advantage. In the same 1700 letter he tried Frederick on this front also:

"On several occasions I have deplored among other matters in published writings that only the Roman missionaries have a chance to turn to use the incomparable inclination and desire for learning of the Chinese monarch and his subjects...It seems as if God has in this case also elected and especially prepared Your Electoral Highness to act as a great instrument. Particularly since nowhere among the Protestants has such a foundation been laid as in Berlin for Chinese *Literatura et propaganda fide*".

Alas! the none too subtle reminder to Frederick of the contribution Leibniz could make to his glory was no more successful than his flattery of the Tsar.

It seems highly unlikely, given his persistent fierce determination to keep the Siberian route solely in Russian hands, that Peter ever seriously intended to honour his undertaking to Frederick. As time went on nothing, and nobody, succeeded in persuading Peter or his 18th century successors to share the route with any Westerners, diplomats, missionaries, traders, or travellers. The "American Marco Polo", John Ledyard (1800 chapter) was one of the few foreigners who much later in the century managed to get across Siberia, at least as far as Yakutsk, but not to Beijing – and not with permission. Westerners had to remain dependent on the sea route to Cathay until well into the 19th century; and early in the 20th the Bolsheviks slammed Siberia shut again.

After Peter had managed to pass through Berlin unseen he was ambushed in Hanover: the Electress Sophie and the visiting Sophie Charlotte (who had not been in Königsberg) were not about to let him slip through, and headed him off in the small town of Koppenbrügge. Over a dinner, where he sat between them, initially rather stiffly, they plied him with questions; then during dancing, which lasted till four the next morning, Peter unwound, and ended up planting exuberant kisses on his dwarf and Sophie's two grandchildren, the future King George II of England and Queen Sophie Dorothea of Prussia. Both Sophie and Sophie Charlotte wrote their impressions of this strange new bear of an autocrat from the east – both letters quoted by Monsieur Erman. Sophie Charlotte:

> "…he seemed shy, hid his face in his hands, and said: "*Ich kann nicht sprechen*"[I don't know what to say]. But we tamed him a little, and he sat down at the table between my mother and myself, and each of us talked to him in turn, and it was a strife who should have it…[A]ssuredly he said nothing that was not to the point on all subjects that were suggested…As to his grimaces [he had a facial tic], I imagined them worse than I found them, and some are not in his power to correct. One can see also that he has had no one to teach him how to eat properly, but he has a natural unconstrained air which pleases me, because from the beginning he behaved just as if he were at home".

Her mother's impressions were characteristically similar:

> "The Tsar…has great vivacity of mind, and a ready and just repartee. But, with all the advantages with which nature has endowed him, it could be wished that his manners were a little less rustic…[He said] from his earliest youth, [he] had had a real passion for navigation and fireworks. He told us that he worked himself in building ships, showed us his hands, and made us touch the callous places that had been caused by work…He is a very extraordinary man…He has a very good heart, and remarkably noble sentiments. I must tell you, also, that he did not get drunk

in our presence, but we had hardly left when the people of his suite made ample amends...[T]he three Muscovite Ambassadors absolutely drowned their senses in wine".

Just so. In later comments she added that

"in dancing, [the Russians] took the whalebones of our corsets for our bones, and the Tsar showed his astonishment by saying that the German ladies had devilish hard bones...He has quite the manners of his country. If he had received a better education, he would be an accomplished man, for he has many good qualities, and an infinite amount of natural wit".

But his presents to Sophie did not live up to expectations: four sable skins, which were full of moths, and three pieces of damask, only big enough for chair-covers. Sophie Charlotte scored better: the Tsar presented her with a crested silver snuffbox which he had made himself.[244]

---

244   In her letters in response to Sophie's reports Liselotte was agog at the Tsar's visit - though in relative terms:

"I've been told that the Muscovite envoys won't come to France, as those who were here ten or twelve years ago behaved in such an extraordinary fashion that the King had them thrown out. This gentleman [Peter], however, seems so good-humoured that I'm sure he can't be as bad as the others, who did nothing but steal, drink, fight and misbehave themselves with animals. Still, this Tsar can't be so very noble after all, if he is so familiar with the tradespeople";

and later:

"Blowing one's nose with one's hand must be the height of fashion in Moscow if the Tsar himself goes in for it. It must save handkerchiefs".

Peter's manners were also the subject of comment, years later, when he visited Frederick and his third wife, Queen Sophie Louise, Sophia Charlotte's successor, in Berlin in 1712, and was in their company on a number of occasions. Parts of his reputation survived from his earlier visit: one of Frederick's principal aides reported that

"The Tsar surpassed himself during all this time. He neither belched, nor farted, nor picked his teeth at least, I neither saw nor heard him do so - and he conversed with the Queen and with the Princesses without showing any embarrassment".

The only surprising thing about this is that Peter was not embarrassed by the mad Sophie Louise; but more of that later.

Having failed to secure an audience with the Tsar, Leibniz pursued him by correspondence in Holland and all the way to his last stop in Vienna about the Siberian route.[245] He also never gave up on the proposal he had been making since the mid-1690s for the establishment in St Petersburg of yet another academy along the lines of the Berlin Society of Sciences – with himself, again, as president; and, notwithstanding his schemes for Christian proselytising in China, violently opposed a proposal in the Berlin Society of Sciences to propagandise the Orthodox Russians on behalf of Lutheranism, as likely to interfere with his scientific proposal.

Then Leibniz's judgement slipped badly: in 1700, after Russia's crushing defeat by the Swedes at Narva, near the Baltic (now in northern Estonia), he expressed the wish that the victorious Charles XII would "reign in Moscow and as far as the River Amur". Perhaps it was frustration with Peter's unresponsiveness – or perhaps it was an unattractive Vicar-of-Bray switch to a potential new sponsor for his designs on using Russia as a mine of information and a laboratory for ideas. Matters seem to have gone silent for the rest of the decade; then in 1709, after Peter's decisive defeat of Charles at Poltava, in southern Russia (now in Ukraine), Leibniz proclaimed it a glorious turning point in history:

"I am very glad that so great an empire is putting itself in the ways of reason and order, and I consider the Tsar in that respect as a person whom God has destined to great works...I shall be charmed if I can help him make science flourish in his country"

- and offered to design not only a Russian academy but also medals to commemorate Poltava.

It was at any rate a turning point – of a sort – for Leibniz's long campaign. In 1711 he finally met the Tsar, on the occasion of the

---

245 After his long stay in Amsterdam Peter also spent three months in London, renting (with William III paying) John Evelyn's house at Deptford, on the Thames near Greenwich, near the naval dockyard (founded two centuries before by Henry VIII), "having a mind to see the building of ships", as Evelyn put it. His servant told him the Russians were "right nasty", and the damage they caused cost William an extra £150. Even Evelyn's celebrated holly-hedges were ruined: Peter's favourite recreation was being driven through them in a wheelbarrow.

wedding in Torgau (a 100-odd kms south of Berlin) of Charlotte Christina Sophie, the granddaughter of Duke Anton Ulrich of Brunswick-Wolfenbüttel (a distant cousin of the Hanoverian Electoral family in a collateral line), to Peter's heir, the Tsarevich Alexei Petrovich.[246] The Tsar found Leibniz a *"forte honnête homme"* – a good honest man – and awarded him a stipend to draw up a reform of Russian laws and administration of justice. After he met Peter again the the following year in the Bohemian spa town Carlsbad (now Karlovy Vary in the Czech Republic), the year Peter moved the capital of Russia to the nine-year-old St Petersburg and married his Lithuanian mistress (the future Empress Catherine I), Leibniz was still whistling with exuberant optimism, telling correspondents that

> "I am to be in a sense the Solon of Russia, although at a distance";
> "Peter the Great is someone who will make a great noise in the world...He will be a sort of Grand Turk of the North...He means to be Alexander the Great at the very least".

But he was whistling in the wind: there was no sequel, worse, no stipend.

In 1716 Leibniz met the Tsar for the third and last time in another spa town, Bad Pyrmont in the Electorate of Hanover. Peter had rheumatism in the right hand, so Leibniz invented an instrument to enable him to hold a knife. It probably earned him extra time to badger the Tsar again about the Russian Academy, and though disappointed again he was still much impressed:

> "I cannot enough admire the vivacity and judgment of this great Prince", he wrote to one correspondent. "He inquires about all the mechanical arts, but his great curiosity is for everything that

---

246 Alexei was another un-military son of a militaristic father. Originally deeply religious, he took to drinking and whoring when Charlotte refused to convert to Orthodoxy from Lutheranism. In 1715 she died in childbirth. Given an ultimatum by his father to become his "worthy successor" - in the army - or become a monk, Alexei fled in disguise from Russia to Vienna, then again to Naples as Peter's agents tracked him down. Promised a pardon by Peter, his son returned to St Petersburg; but under torture his mistress accused him of plotting against the Tsar. Alexei was also repeatedly tortured, brutally, on one occasion with Peter reportedly striking the first blows, found guilty of treason, condemned to death - then found dead in his cell. His mistress married a Guards officer and lived comfortably for another thirty years.

relates to navigation, and consequently he always likes astronomy and geography. I hope we shall learn through his aid if Asia is joined to America".

We did, in the sense that it was Peter – perhaps remembering Leibniz's curiosity – who sent his outstanding Danish sailor Vitus Bering off on the first of the expeditions that led eventually to the discovery of the dividing Strait named after him. And Peter did eventually establish a Russian Academy, but only at the end of his reign, a decade after Leibniz's death.

This final meeting was also another chance for Leibniz to try to convert the Tsar to his views about China: if understanding, exchange and communication with the Chinese were not actively promoted, he told him,

"It will follow that when the Chinese will have learnt from us what they wish to know they will then close their doors to us".

And he suggested that his own "arithmetic machine" (a calculating machine, whose mechanism was later the first to be produced commercially), might "serve as a present to the emperor of China". But Peter had no time to learn from the Chinese: he was more concerned with trying to teach Russians to become Europeans.

Baroque Berlin in a Baroque Europe

Once he became King, Frederick re-doubled his efforts to create a Berlin worthy of his status: sycophants were quick with an anagram turning the Latin *Berolinum* into *Lumen Orbi* (Light of the World). He was in no way constrained – on the contrary, aided and abetted – by Danckelmann's replacement, Count Kolbe von Wartenberg, his new first minister, who was to personally profit very substantially before famine and plague exposed his corruption and the state's bankruptcy at the end of the decade, and whose domestic arrangements were to prove such a great disturbance to Sophie Charlotte's own. Much of the money went on architecture, in the first substantial campaign to produce what was to become modern Berlin.

In the early 1700s Frederick of Prussia was not the only one building palaces in the Baroque style made all the rage from the mid-17th century by Bernini's work in Rome. It was the fashion throughout Europe, as everyone tried to imitate or at least to simulate – but never to outdo –

Louis XIV's Versailles, building since 1668 and still being extended a century later: the Emperor Leopold I's Schönbrunn (begun in 1696) and Belvedere Palaces (Lower 1697, Upper 1714) in Vienna; the Elector of Saxony's Zwinger (1709) in Dresden; Petrodvorets (Peterhof, also 1709), begun by Peter the Great outside St Petersburg only six years after he began building the city itself; not to mention non-royal Blenheim (1705), the gift of a grateful nation to the victor of the eponymous and other battles in which the Duke of Marlborough had the valued support of Frederick's troops; and the extraordinary Residenz of the Prince-Bishops of Würzburg (1720), with its huge staircase ceiling vault – six hundred square metres – stunningly frescoed thirty years later by Giovanni Battista Tiepolo with *The Four Continents*.

It was also the time of some of the great Baroque churches of Western Europe: St Louis-des-Invalides (begun in 1671) in Paris, by Hardouin-Mansart, who was simultaneously trebling the size of Versailles; in London, St Paul's Cathedral (1675), by Christopher Wren, a co-founder of the Royal Society. And, not least, it was the beginning of the incomparable series of great Baroque monasteries of the Benedictine Order in the Catholic German-speaking south: in Austria, Melk (1702), high on a cliff overlooking the Rhine and across it to Bavaria; Ottobeuren (1711) in Bavaria itself; and Einsiedeln (1719), just to the south of Lucerne in Switzerland (to name only my own favourites), fabulous abbeys which offer a unified vision of both the sacred and secular aspects of the Baroque – their churches on the scale of cathedrals, the monastery buildings, with their princely apartments and libraries, on that of palaces, all covered within an ace of excess in gloriously extravagant stucco, sculpture and fresco.

Only a little of Frederick's Berlin still exists, in some cases reconstructed or restored after war damage. The most important loss is the Royal Palace on Unter den Linden, whose bombed-out ruins the German Democratic Republic blew up in 1950, thirty-two years after the last Hohenzollern had been removed, because it symbolized Germany's "feudalist and imperialist past". On the other hand, a little further along the Unter den Linden, the *Zeughaus*, the great Arsenal of the militaristic Hohenzollerns, was rebuilt. So was Sophie Charlotte's Palace at Charlottenburg. But apart from the dummy Berlin Royal Palace of painted canvas that was erected in 1993 to see if anyone wanted to rebuild the real one (they didn't, at least not at that price), the only images of Frederick's main construction available since 1950 have been the model in the Charlottenburg Palace, and photographs.

While the rest of the Kings, Princes, Cardinals, Archbishops, Abbots, Dukes, Margraves and other rulers of large and small slices of Europe were hiring French architects and decorators to create their mini-or not-so-mini-Versailles, Frederick, in 1696, engaged a Pole, or to be precise, a Danziger, Andreas Schlüter.[247] Schlüter, who had been working for the King of Poland, was originally to become co-director of Frederick's new Academy of Arts and to execute sculptures; but Frederick also used him as an architect. In particular, he had him extend and transform the old *Schloss*, which the never-frivolous Great Elector had nevertheless begun to reconstruct in 1660; and it was this architectural work that was regarded as Schlüter's masterpiece. Toland, who saw the Palace before its completion, was as usual particularly impressed by its symmetry: in his 1702 letter to an un-named Dutch Minister he wrote that

"notwithstanding you have travel'd very far, yet you never saw anything more exact, commodious, or stately; tho I confess you have bin in one or two that might be more Capacious, but they were less regular".

Capacious it became: larger (though more compact) than Versailles. Photographs show aspects of the huge building, a rectangular figure-eight with two enormous enclosed courtyards, their wings dominated, like the exterior façades, by gigantic orders, all in a heavy style that came to be called Prussian Baroque.

Experts have noted Schlüter's use of elements from Rome – the Forum of Nerva, Michelangelo's Palazzo dei Conservatori and, in the sumptuous interior, Pietro da Cortona and, again, Michelangelo, in the form of sculptured versions of the famous *ignudi* on the Sistine Chapel ceiling. Schlüter had never visited Italy, and the source of his influences was no doubt engravings of Rome and perhaps architectural pattern-books of the type Marcantonio Raimondi had produced for painting.[248] Interestingly, the most important stateroom, the Knights' Hall, prefigured Tiepolo's theme at Würzburg with figures, by Schlüter, over the main entrances representing the Four Continents. Both from the city streets and within the courtyards the Palace of the Hohenzollerns had a dour northern Protestant solemnity, the extravagant interiors a heaviness that could not match the elegant lightness favoured by the straying southern

---

247 The basic source on Schlüter is *Grove Art*
248 See 1500 chapter

Benedictines. The *Stadtschloss* ended up looking overwhelming. Which was no doubt exactly what Frederick intended.

It outlasted the Hohenzollerns themselves by thirty-two years. Sixty years before its demise, Schlüter's fine Old Post Office – Leibniz's academy-financing Post Office – had already been demolished in the interests of Wilhelmine progress. Schlüter's surviving masterpieces are thus all sculptural. The earliest are in the *Zeughaus*, and are the most surprising: twenty-two heads, in the courtyard, of Dying Warriors – not as triumphs of Prussian arms, but in various conditions of agony or distress. These suffering men convey nowadays an unexpected awareness of the price of war in what was a military arsenal; but at the time they may have been recognised simply as defeated foreigners, testimony to the victory of Frederick's armies on the Rhine.

Schlüter's other two great works were family affairs: the more conventional but splendid equestrian statue of Frederick's father, the Great Elector, made for the Langebrücke (now the Rathausbrücke) near the city Palace but moved since the Second World War to the courtyard in front of the Charlottenburg Palace; and the last, Frederick's and Sophie Charlotte's own funerary monuments, in the Berliner Dom opposite where the Royal Palace used to stand; we shall come to them in due course.

There was, in addition, something else: a proposal for the reconstruction of the centre of Berlin. In about 1702 the Frenchman Jean-Baptiste Boebes, Frederick's chief engineer since 1692 and a member of the Royal Academy of Arts, engraved an *Idealised View of Royal Berlin* showing how Schlüter "might have transformed the architectural setting of the Hohenzollern court".[249] The bird's-eye view, from above the north end of the present Rathausbrücke over the River Spree, shows the bridge leading to a large plaza; on the right is Frederick's *Stadtschloss*, as rebuilt by Schlüter during the 1690s; on the left the *Marstall*, the vast Royal Stables (not by Schlüter as subsequently built); and in the distance, set back on the right on Unter den Linden, the *Zeughaus*, at that time still under construction. Also included, beyond the *Stadtschloss*, is the enormously tall and slender *Münzturm* (the Mint Tower), the demolition of which in 1706 for fear it would collapse, effectively terminated Schlüter's employment by Frederick.

---

249   Boebes later published the engraving in a book, in 1733, long after he had left the Prussian capital. It is reproduced in J.Adamson, ed.: *The Princely Courts of Europe*, p.223. It is not mentioned in Schlüter's entry in *Grove Art*.

There end the similarities to what was actually built. In the engraving, behind each of the two river-front giants, further similar huge buildings stretch southwards into old Cölln; and across the end of the foreground plaza is an enormous domed cathedral, in style very similar to the present Berliner Dom across the road from where the old Palace stood, but in that position an announcement of the integration of spiritual with temporal power in the person and role of the King of Prussia. The whole design, with the vast scale of the buildings and the huge area over which they march, the regularity of their placement, the rigid conformity of their classical elements, the vista towards the huge domed cathedral, carries an eerie Baroque-scale premonition of Albert Speer's megalomaniac scheme for Hitler's Berlin.

In addition to recreating the *Stadtschloss*, and building Charlottenburg, Frederick also built or extended larger or smaller country houses at Oranienburg, Niederschönhausen, Tegel, Hermsdorf, Rosenthal, Blankenfelde, Altlandsberg, Ruhleben, Friedrichsfelde, all with splendid gardens, a ring of Baroque pleasure palaces around Berlin, most long since swallowed up by urban sprawl or war. Toland found excuse for this extravagance, but slyly injected criticism of Frederick that he never allowed himself of Hanoverian Sophie Charlotte: he drew attention to

"the great number of Houses which his Majesty builds in several Places for his own Use, but especially in the Neighborhood of Berlin...I know very well from Men of no contemtible Judgment are of Opinion, that it were more advisable not to build so many Houses, and confine the Expence of them all to two or three... [But] his Subjects do likewise receive therby considerable Profits, both by their Labor, and by the Materials they Furnish...They are most neatly kept, as becomes a Prince; and so completely provided according to their various Bulk or Uses, that nothing is ever remov'd from one House to another, each having whatever is fit for it self, without excepting even the Services of Gold and Silver Plate, which I am inform'd is a thing that cannot be said of any other Prince in Europe".

Frederick's Court in Berlin

This architectural splendour was the setting for a Court whose elaborateness was also modelled on Versailles. Toland, still needling Frederick, wrote that

" 'Tis at Berlin that his Prussian Majesty dos commonly keep his Court, especially in Winter. It is very numerous and magnificent. Every thing shines with Gold, Silver, and Jewels. The Equipages are sumptuous, the Courtiers well bred, and obliging to Strangers... Som of the foren Ministers [amassadors] pretend that they overdo in the finery of their Habits and in the expensiveness of public Festivals; but whether they have Reason or Envy of their side, I shall not take upon me to judg".

Toland also commented tartly on Frederick's Crown Jewels, observing that

"his very Crown and Scepter, by the Number, Splendor, and Value of their precious Stones, have already eclips'd [those of all other European rulers]. There are those who blame this Profusion of Diamonds, and think they might be better improv'd than thus to ly in dead stock: but tho the differences between Princes and private Men be a sufficient Answer, yet 'tis not my business to enter into the Reasons of such things, but to give you, SIR, a true Relation of Fact".

There was of course a counterpart to all these bedizened personages and architectural masterpieces: a degree and extent of poverty at least as bad as that now known as "Third World". The aristocratic English eloper, society hostess, writer, traveller and sponsor of vaccination against smallpox, Lady Mary Wortley Montagu, toured through Germany in 1716 and compared free towns like Nuremberg with those "under the government of absolute Princes":

"In the first there appears an air of Commerce and Plenty. The streets are well built and full of people neatly and plainly dress'd, the shops loaded with Merchandize, and the commonalty clean and cheerfull. In the other, a sort of shabby finery, a Number of dirty people of Quality tawder'd out, Narrow nasty streets out of repair, wretchedly thin of Inhabitants, and above halfe of the common sort asking alms. I can't help fancying one under the figure of a handsome clean Dutch Citizen's wife and the other like a poor Town Lady of Pleasure, painted and riban'd out in her Head dress, tarnish'd silver lac'd shoes, and a ragged under petticoat, a miserable mixture of Vice and poverty".

At this stage Berlin certainly still shared the poverty of the absolutist princedoms; but the impetus given to its economic development as the result of the Great Elector's invitation, fifteen years before, to the French Huguenots had already become evident. Toland was expansive on the country –

"The Highways are here kept in better Order than elsewhere, the Posts are more regular, public Carriages more expeditious" –

but more grudging on the capital – Berlin was

"indifferently spacious, but extremely fine...The Streets are very large and noble, much better pav'd than is usual in Germany...The new Houses are mostly built after the better Tast of Architecture, being generally beautify'd on the outside, and not always ill-furnish'd within".

For some reason Toland did not elaborate on his remark that the Court was "very numerous", or observe that, as a result, the city must have thereby achieved "considerable Profits", as from Frederick's building program. In his history of *The Four Georges* Thackeray has however given us what must be close to an accurate picture of the Court of Berlin in the register of Sophie Charlotte's brother's contemporary Electoral Court of Hanover, all in order of precedence: the Princes of the Blood; the Field Marshal of the Army; the working Privy Councillors; the Generals of Cavalry and Infantry; the High Chamberlain; High Marshals of the Court; High Masters of the Horse; the Major-Generals of Cavalry and Infantry; the Majors; the Court Pages; the Secretaries and Assessors (all nobles); two Chamberlains for the Elector and one for the Electress; five Gentlemen of the Chamber; five Gentlemen Ushers; eleven personal Pages, and "personages to educate these young noblemen – such as a governor, a preceptor, a fencing master, and a dancing ditto"; three Body and Court physicians; a Court barber; a Court organist; two music masters; four French fiddlers; twelve trumpeters and a bugler; ten Chamber waiters; twenty-four lackeys in livery; a maître-d'hôtel; attendants of the kitchen; a French cook; eleven other cooks; six cooks' assistants; two roast-masters; a pastry baker; a pie baker; three scullions; four "sugar-chamber" [dessert] cooks; seven officers in the wine and beer cellars; four bread bakers; five men in the plate-room; for the twenty teams of princely carriage horses, eight to a team, there were sixteen coachmen, fourteen postilions, nineteen ostlers, thirteen help, smiths, carriage-makers, horse-doctors, stable hands; a dozen female attendants "about the Electoral premises" – and only two washerwomen for the entire Court!

Frederick spent much of his time in regulating Berlin's no less numerous or elaborate Court, and in devising ways of entertaining it and himself. A Court Ordinance spelled out no fewer than one hundred and forty-one degrees of hierarchy in which the Court and, in effect, the entire Prussian population was ranged, with precedence, speaking, moving, seating, standing, bowing, curtsying and other etiquette to match. Apart from being aimed at securing social stability, there was no doubt an expectation that a nobleman trying to secure his rise from the twenty-second rang to the twenty-first would not have much time for causing other sorts of mischief; but the result was endless factions.

Occasionally questions of protocol were even referred to higher intellectual authority: there is record of Leibniz laying down the number of horses to be harnessed to a carriage, the number of pages to attend a prince, the seating of guests at a sovereign's table. (Laughable as it is, where you sit is still rigorously laid down at the tables of sovereigns, their governments, and their ambassadors.) The ways of God could be questioned, but not the rules of etiquette.

Frederick also supervised the details of the liveries of the Court officials: it was remarked that some were so covered with gold lace that it was difficult to determine the colour of the uniform itself. At least he made use of the result: Toland reported – his capitals getting out of hand at the Honour of the Occasion – having been at Oranienburg for

> "[the arrival of] the presumtive Successor of our English Crown, her Royal Highness SOPHIA, the Electress Dowager of Hanover, who coms generally every Summer to pass som Time with the Queen her Daughter...His Majesty receiv'd the Electress coming out of her Coach, under the Discharge of thirty six Pieces of Cannon, four and twenty Trumpets sounding, two Pairs of Kettle-Drums, and I know not how many Hautboys. There were three Companys drawn up before the Gate, of which two belong'd to this new Militia, having grey Coats lin'd with Orange".

All this for his mother-in-law.

The foundations of bureaucracy
In addition to the Academy of Arts and the Society of Scientists, Frederick also established at the turn of the century the *Ritterakademie,*

the Academy for Noblemen, a Berlin version of France's post-World War II ENA (*Ecole Nationale d'Administration*, the *sine qua non* education ever since for anyone aspiring to run France or a French company). John Toland published in London in 1714 in an English translation the "Ordinances, Statutes, and Privileges" of the *Ritterakademie*, which he saw as

> "further Confirmation...concerning the King of Prussia's exalted genius for Roman Antiquitys, Medals, Inscriptions, Architecture, Statuary, Painting, or, to say it in fewer words, the Incouragement and Protection he gives to Arts and Learning. But his Majesty being further inflam'd with the Godlike Passion of dispensing the Influence of his Goodness to the most universal purposes, and justly considering the Education of Youth, as the only proper means of begetting the same laudable Disposition and Habit in his Subjects, has lately made known his Intentions of erecting an Academy of a new Model in his Capital City of Berlin, supported by two firm and unshaken Pillars, I mean most ample Salarys for the Teachers, and most easy Expenses for the Learners; which will infallibly attract the best of the first, as well as the most of the last.
>
> I cannot but here observe, what a sure Foundation is thus laid to supply his Majesty with an inexhaustible stock of able Ministers and Officers, as well as all Europe with polite Gentlemen!...And what a mighty Increase of Trade and Wealth will this Institution bring to the City of Berlin! So real a Benefit will it prove, if duly executed, that supposing the King's Expences shou'd not be made good by the Entrance-mony and Pensions of the Academists, yet in the public his Majesty will be a mighty Gainer, considering the accidental Expences, which in Persons of that Age and Quality are unavoidable; joining to this the Curiosity of Travellers, with the Visits and Correspondence of their Friends, Relations and Acquaintance, which will quickly appear in the Post-Office, and in all the several Excises".

Toland was clearly no economist. The Statutes of the Noblemen's Academy, Toland reported, provided that there would be taught

> "all the ordinary Exercises, such as Riding, Fencing, Vaulting, and Dancing; but his Majesty has further ordain'd, out of his high Grace, that it be furnish't with most celebrated Professors,

to teach those Noblemen and Gentlemen the Sciences which are convenient and necessary to their Quality: such as are Morals, Politics, the Laws of Nature and Nations, the Principles of the civil and municipal Law, Blazoning or the Art of Heraldry, the Genealogy and Interests of Princes, Philosophy, and especially Experiments in Physical Matters. Likewise the Mathematics, and all parts of the same, as Arithmetic, Geometry, Mechanics, Optics, Dyalling, Architecture Civil and Military; and even Designing or Drawing, Perspective, the Exercise of the Pike and Musquet, and all military Evolutions...There will also be taught in the same all the Languages which are at present the most in use; as Latin, French, Italian, Spanish, English, and" – a radical innovation at a time when universities and courts used only, respectively, the first two – "even the German shall be taught there in all its Purity".

In an age when established universities like Oxford were still largely teaching only theology and law, this was a remarkable project to develop the well-rounded aristocrat, bureaucrat and officer. They were guaranteed freedom of religion, at least among the three

"tolerated in the Empire...the Reform'd, the Evangelic, and the Roman Catholic:...Provided that among themselves they avoid impertinent Controversys and useless Disputes".

But, Toland observed, theology itself was not taught, nor medicine.

Some of the injunctions were more pious: on the one hand, the Professors

"shall not be tedious or obscure in their Lectures, but they are to deliver themselves in the most intelligible manner that's possible for them", and,
"above all things, the Professors and Masters of Exercises must pay due Honour and Respect...to one another";

on the other hand, the Academists (students)

"shall not neglect the public Lectures, during which they are to suppose that they must not sleep, be trifling, whispering, or disputing together".

But there was no sense of fantasy in the final injunction of the Statutes, addressed to the Director himself:

"[He] shall from time to time assemble the Professors and Masters of Exercises to hear their Sentiments; ever concerning himself for the Profit, Good, and Advantage of the Academists. But he shall have regard in a particular manner to the Glory and Intentions of his Majesty".

The Academy was one of the building-blocks in the growing edifice of Prussian absolutism. I have not found any indications that Leibniz was involved in the project, though its remarkably broad and liberal curriculum match very well with his own approach to learning – and interest in everything. It is also interesting that at about this time competitive examinations for public office were introduced in Prussia, the first in Europe. Leibniz, and the Jesuits, had been greatly impressed by the Chinese system of examinations, and the consequent bureaucracy based on merit; but again, a connection has so far apparently not been made between the Prussian experiment and the Chinese system, or any specific influence by Leibniz.

Toland understood the Statutes of the *Ritterakademie* to have been drawn up, under His Majesty's direction, principally by Count von Wartenberg, the new chief minister. The latter, Toland said in his breathless introduction,

"advised his Royal Master to lay out those immense Sums for the Public Good, which Ministers of baser Spirits wou'd have expended in effeminat Luxury, and rather have profusely bestow'd on the corrupt Instruments of their Vices, on flattering Poetasters, and obscene Stage-players, than to confer such Favors (no, not for their own Credit) on such as were able and ready to assist Nature in her Pangs, and to help into the World those heroic Births and surprizing Discoverys, which would bring Mankind to a clearer knowledg of themselves and other things, doing Honor at once to their Country, and enrolling at the same time their own Names in the eternal Monuments of History, by their transcendent Performances in all the Arts and Sciences".

Notwithstanding Wartenberg's own eventual corruptness, and Toland's earlier raptures on Frederick's inflam'd Godlike Passion, there is mischief in his pointed distinction between Royal Master and Minister: most of the characteristics of "baser Spirits" were attributed by his subjects to Frederick himself.

Festivities in Berlin

Frederick himself directed the expensive public festivals, already noted by Toland, that marked birthdays and marriages. On his first visit to Sophie Charlotte in May 1700, and before Frederick's birthday party, Leibniz was present for one of these festivities, on the occasion of the marriage of her stepdaughter to a Prince of Hesse-Kassel. He described the first day to the Electress Sophie as the day of gold, marked by the bridegroom's arrival with a splendid retinue, followed the next day by the day of diamonds, with the wedding ceremony. The celebrations then continued for a further *twelve* days, with ballet, opera, masquerade, a bear hunt, a firework display, and a fête with a flotilla of gondolas on a nearby canal.

This was in fact the occasion of the first performance in Berlin of an opera in the modern sense of the term, and the "opera house" was specially built over the Elector's stables for the occasion (and subsequently turned by his son, the Soldier King Frederick William, into an army supply depot). The opera, *La Festa del Hymeneo*, was by Attilio Ariosti, *Kapellmeister* to the Electress, written with the collaboration of Karl Friedrick Rieck, a Court musician since 1683. In addition to the musicians and singers, it required a dancing company of forty – mostly Court personnel, including the unwilling and highly resentful Frederick William – as well as enough machinery to make haloed angels fly around. Clearly, opera producers have been the way they are since the beginning.

Before the end of the wedding festivities there was another opera at Oranienburg Palace and a third, also by busy Ariosti, at Charlottenburg, with the entire Court and all the guests, but without the angels, moving from one to the other in vast retinues of carriages and escorts. Long before this, Leibniz, to whom Sophie Charlotte had assigned a room in the Charlottenburg Palace, confided to her that he was "rather deranged", because the social life left him with only four hours sleep a night. By the end of the celebrations he was feverish and required a rest cure.

He had to recover quickly. Only a month later Charlottenburg was the scene of another extravagance, a *Wirtschaft* in honour of the Elector's forty-third birthday. In this peculiarly German form of entertainment the members of the Court drew lots and then had to dress as the character they had chosen, an opportunity for a variety of ambiguities.

This occasion, to follow Leibniz's description, was decorous enough, a village fair, with a variety of stalls selling hams, smoked sausage, ox-tongues, wine, lemonade, tea, coffee and chocolate. The entertainment began with a procession in which a quack doctor arrived on "a kind of elephant", followed by his wife – acted by Sophie Charlotte – in a sedan chair carried by Turks (possibly real ones: Ranke said Frederick liked to have "a few blackamoors and a baptized Turk or two in his service"), then a clown (not necessarily Frederick's full-time Court Fool), dancers and ...a dentist. There was a variety of performances, including "comic teeth extractions" and a ballet, and finally Frederick himself, "disguised" as a Dutch sailor, who made unspecified purchases at some of the stalls. The ambassadors of Denmark and Holland were peasants – probably preferable to having to participate in karaoke.

Leibniz was detailed to be an astrologer carrying a telescope (most astronomers, like the great Sir Isaac Newton himself, still being astrologers in those days); but the Perpetual President of the Society of Sciences and Astronomer Royal was aghast, and was relieved of the effort by no less a personage than the Duke of Wittgenstein, illustrating the respect Leibniz commanded. Leibniz told the Electress Sophie that this home-made entertainment "gave as much pleasure as a costly grand opera would have done" – which suggests that Leibniz was not an opera buff.

The following year, for Frederick's forty-fourth birthday, Rieck, by now *Oberkapellmeister* of the Royal Chapel, composed a cantata on a poem called *The Quarrel Between the Old and New Centuries*, written by Benjamin Neukirch. Neukirch was one of the earliest members of the Society of Sciences, but what he wanted to be was Poet Laureate at the Court. Instead, he was appointed Professor of Poetry and Rhetoric at the *Ritterakademie*, which, he recognized,

"did not represent a favourable reaction to [my] poems from the King...They tell me that my poems are not in courtly style".

Frederick may well have been as alarmed at the poems' content as at their style, as may be judged by the appositeness of a poem Neukirch wrote for the wedding of an academic colleague:

"His life did lack one thing
That could have been his ruin:
I mean a wife. For nothing is as common
As being married for one night and already in torment.

This sickness can infect the very fairest form;
And Socrates said well, that no more days than two
Are good with a woman: the first when she is wed,
The second when her husband buries her."

Not calculated to appeal to Sophie Charlotte either.

Frederick's Berlin was no sillier and possibly less tasteless than the future King George I's Hanover: Leibniz recorded the carnival of 1702 there as

"a Roman feast representing that given by Trimalchio in the *Satyricon*...When nature called, the person who played Trimalchio did not put himself out; if the call was urgent, he left the stage and returned without ceremony. Incidentally a chamber-pot of enormous size, in which he could have drowned at night, followed him everywhere".

The person who played Trimalchio was in fact Charles Louis, Liselotte's illegitimate half-brother, surrounded by empty bottles (an unfortunately apposite stage-prop: within a few months he would finish drinking himself to death), and reclining on a Roman bed along with Sophie Charlotte and George himself, amongst others. The absent Frederick was shocked at Sophie Charlotte's participation in such un-Berlin goings-on.

The silliness and expense of Frederick's own entertainments has frequently been contrasted with the sobriety of his son Frederick William's devotion to the restoration of the state's finances and the expansion of the army from Frederick's thirty thousand to eighty. It is not often noted that Frederick William also had his entertainments: wild animal fights. On one occasion, after six bears had fought six bison in the arena, Frederick William sportingly killed the surviving bison with his arquebus, to clear the way for new bears to be brought in and dogs unleashed against them.

Charlottenburg

Toland again:

"The Queen spends much of her Time in a Palace which is not yet finish'd on the Banks of the Spré, near the Village of Lutzelburg, whence it takes its Name, and within a little League of Berlin, from which you go to it all the way thro a Park and in a Treckschuit or

Draw-boat by Water. Altho I speak of it after all the rest, yet it is far from being the least either in Capaciousness, or Regularity, or Magnificence... But as nothing is yet brought to Perfection here, I shall not at present send you a more particular Description; tho there is no room to doubt but in a little time it will be a charming Place, under the direction of SOPHIA CHARLOTTE".

Boat trips still go along the River Spree, from the old *Schlossplatz*, along the edge of the Tiergarten, and on to Charlottenburg, though Toland would be lost in the urban and industrial sprawl that has long since covered the open country between the two.

The original Palace, built for Sophie Charlotte in 1695-96, consisted of only the eleven central bays that you see now; at the time Toland was there in 1702 Frederick was having the two wings forming the Court of Honour built, to make the palace more suitable for a Queen...and King. It was not until the end of the decade that Frederick added the commanding tower and cupola over the centre of the original building, and the Orangery on the west side,

"to make Charlottenburg, as an eternal memorial to Her Majesty the Queen, of most blessed memory, into a place of incomparable beauty".[250]

The architectural style of the day dictated that the staterooms and the private apartments of the princely occupants went on the main floor, the *piano nobile*, one storey up from ground level. This was not for Sophie Charlotte: she had Schlüter install her apartment, with its lovely oval central room, on the unfashionable ground floor, at the rear, so she overlooked and had ready access to the gardens on that (the north) side, just like Liselotte's at St Cloud. After Sophie Charlotte's death Frederick

---

250 Their Francophobe grandson Frederick the Great added, in the style of Versailles, the long gallery of splendid Rococo rooms on the east, with their collection of his favourite - French - paintings; Frederick William II then added the Opera (now a museum) on the extreme west. The palace has been almost totally reconstructed, following Allied bomb damage on 23 November 1943, and refurnished to some extent with original pieces of furniture, paintings and other objects; the re-creation of Frederick's *Porzellankammer*, with Chinese porcelains, was only completed in 1993. Unfortunately it has apparently not been possible to find sufficiently detailed pictures to enable the repainting of some ceiling frescoes.

blamed a fire in the palace on "that rogue Schlüter" for being careless about chimneys; Leibniz wrote a paper on how to make more effective pressurised hoses, and had it published by the Society of Sciences.

The garden, over five hundred metres wide across the end of the *parterre* next to the original palace, stretches for more than a thousand metres along the Spree, widening as it goes but now cut off from the river by railway lines in the extreme north. It is not surprising that, recalling the gardens of Versailles and St Cloud from her late childhood visit with her mother, Sophie Charlotte turned immediately to their designer, André Le Nôtre to design her own. Still busy for Louis XIV, Le Nôtre sent an assistant to make the design; Sophie Charlotte cautiously sent his plan back to Le Nôtre for approval. And so it survived until 1945, with differently laid-out and planted sections, sight-lines through rows of linden trees to the garden fountain and the artificial lake, and high hedges cut like walls, affording "shade from the summer heat for those wanting a quiet *tête-à- tête*".[251]

However much – or little – Sophie Charlotte shared Leibniz's passion for China, she certainly became enamoured of the taste for decoration in the usually-imaginary-Chinese style which came to be called *chinoiserie*, and which was to sweep royal Europe throughout the 18th century, from the short-lived *Trianon de Porcelaine* of Louis XIV (of course) in the 1670s to George I's great-great-grandson's Brighton Pavilion in the 1820s (pseudo-Moghul on the outside but pure chinoiserie within). The style was the direct offshoot of acquaintance with the real treasures of China which, as we noted earlier, had been coming into Europe in increasing quantities in the second half of the 17th century, and which fitted readily into already-burgeoning baroque fashion.

Along the way furniture, wallpaper and porcelain were produced in the style: in 1689 John Evelyn describe a neighbour's house as

"a cabinet of elegancies, especially Indian; in the hall are contrivances of japan [in the context 'japanned', i.e. lacquered] screens, instead of wainscot...the landscape of the screens depicts the manner of living and country of the Chinese".

The confusion about what the Orient was composed of, and how the parts related to one another, was still widespread: at one point in what

---

251 The description is a summary of that in Baer.

was apparently the first chinoiserie stage performance, in Paris in 1692, appropriately called *Les Chinois*, an actor disguised as a more-or-less Chinese pagoda appeared and sang:

"I come straight from the Congo, ho, ho, ho".

Sophie Charlotte's preference was for pieces of furniture in the chinoiserie style. They were made for her in Berlin by Gerard Dagly, from Spa in present-day Belgium, who had been appointed *Directeur des Ornements* of the Court by the Great Elector, and later confirmed by Frederick. He specialized in pieces japanned and decorated with a variety of Chinese-style motifs, some copied from objects in the royal collection, some entirely imaginary, and became well known for the quality of his work. On one occasion Sophie sent Frederick a clock-case, remarking

"It comes from England, but Dagly makes much better ones";

and Liselotte, still muddled, wrote her that

"Perhaps it is an Indian who makes the lovely Berlin cupboards".

When he came to the throne in 1713 Frederick William sacked the "Indian" together with all his father's other appointees. Poor Dagly then disappeared from history, apart from a cry the following year that

"the future is so uncertain that I don't know how to give you any positive news"

- in a letter to Leibniz, who had probably been interested in his work, along with everything else anyone did well. Amongst the chinoiserie – and some real Chinese pieces – still at Charlottenburg some of Dagly's work has survived, including especially, in the Tapestry Room to the west of the Oval Hall, Sophie Charlotte's cembalo [harpsichord], exquisitely decorated with small Chinese figures and landscape on white lacquer.

Frederick also developed a taste for chinoiserie: in a further expansion of Charlottenburg in 1706, after Sophie Charlotte's death, he included, on the garden side at the western corner of the extended central range of rooms, a splendid *Porzellankammer* (Porcelain Chamber), one of the earliest of a whole series in palaces all over Europe. It was originally furnished with more than *three thousand* pieces of late-16th century Chinese and Japanese porcelain, ranged in rows and elaborate patterns on whole walls of baroque shelves and brackets. The idea, the Baers write, was to

> "overawe the visitor with a feeling both of lavishness – heightened by the multiplicatory effect of the mirrored walls – and of wide-ranging international connections".

One imagines that Leibniz must have been enchanted, and probably encouraged, mistakenly, into believing it foreshadowed an interest by Frederick in other things Chinese. When Augustus the Strong, Elector of Saxony and King of Poland, saw the Chamber in 1709 he was not so much overawed as over-stimulated: he reportedly swapped a whole regiment of Saxon Dragoon Guards for forty-eight of Frederick's porcelain vases.

Quiet at Charlottenburg

Here, in this pleasant and in her day unpretentious place – where simplicity, typified by black dress, was said to be the rule – Sophie Charlotte created a circle of her own to escape from the ceremonial vapidity of her husband's court. She could do so, Monsieur Erman stated, with something less than candour,

> "the more easily, because as a result of the extraordinary favour which he enjoyed from Frederick I, the Grand Chamberlain the Comte de Wartemburg with his wife did the honours at Berlin, where Sophie Charlotte only appeared on grand occasions".

Sophie Charlotte only appeared on grand occasions because the rest of the time Madame de Wartenberg enjoyed the extraordinary favour of being Frederick's mistress at the *Stadtschloss*.

To Charlottenburg came Berlin intellectuals and clergymen, including Calvinists, Lutherans, Catholics, Reverend Edict-of-Nantes gentlemen and other Huguenot refugees, visitors of all sorts and stations – including the young Princess Caroline from an early age – if she thought they could contribute to intelligent conversation. Ranke, the historian, offered the splendidly inegalitarian encomium that indeed Sophie Charlotte's

> "peculiar talent – perhaps the one most suited to the mature female intellect – was conversation".

Toland said

> "She loves to see Strangers, and to inform her self of all that's
> worthy or remarkable in their several Countrys; and she has so
> just an Idea of Government, that in all Germany they call her the
> Republican Queen. All that's gay and polite resort to her Court,
> where you may see a complete Harmony between what most of
> the World believe to be contrary if not extremes, I mean Learning
> and Mirth".

It was here that she held the night-sessions of debate with and between
philosophers and theologians that so marked her off from virtually all
her contemporary sovereigns other than her own mother. Everything was
debatable: there is one report of a "long and animated" discussion of the
question whether marriage was, or was not, ordained for the procreation
of children.

Her tone comes out clearly in the previously-quoted letter, reproduced by Monsieur Erman, in which she could not resist good-
humouredly tweaking Father Vota's earnestness. Vota had written, after
the mauling he felt he had received during his first visit to her philosophical salon, that

> "A similar encounter has never been my experience in forty
> years of controversy with the finest brains, in Rome, in Paris and
> elsewhere, where civility and courtesy have always been matched
> with doctrine".

Sophie Charlotte matched solicitude with bluntness in her response:

> "I recognise [in your letter] the character of an honest man and a
> Christian, which clearly evokes the rare qualities of your mind...
> What is said a little strongly on one side or the other on these
> occasions, is only meant to make the conversation more lively, and
> can in no way alter the esteem that is mutually expected and that
> no-one would deny to your great talents. On the other hand, I am
> not surprised that in a very short space of time you have heard said
> in a country of freedom, a number of things one would not hear
> in forty years in countries of authority, for these are two countries
> where people speak very different languages...I more or less
> understand what unconsciously caused these gentlemen [Vota's

Protestant opponents] to depart a little from *decorum* in their remarks...you spoke so disobligingly of reason, whose authority alone should prevail in this world and to which even you have so much responsibility".

Here at Charlottenburg she tried to make reason prevail. And in the house and in long walks in the garden, she had her long discussions with Leibniz on faith and reason, God and man, good and evil, the rational and irrational, the material and the immaterial.

"Leibniz today talked to me of the infinitely little", she wrote her mother at one point, exhausted by Frederick's ceremonials: "As if I did not know enough of that here".

Sophie Charlotte's Italians

There was also music.[252] "It is a loyal friend", Sophie Charlotte wrote in 1702 to Agostino Steffani, a composer, Catholic churchman, diplomat and long-time friend of Leibniz. He had met her at the beginning of the 1680s when involved with the Abbé Ballati in a possible Bavarian marriage for her, before he became director of court music and opera composer, then diplomat, for her father in Hanover.

"It does not let you down or deceive you" she went on; "it is not a traitor and is never cruel. No: it gives you all the charms and delights of heaven, whereas friends are indifferent or deceitful, and loved ones ungrateful".

Three years before, Steffani had written for her four in the long series of chamber duets (for two voices and harpsichord) which became the cornerstone of his reputation. One was to a text of Sophie Charlotte's own: *Crudo Amor, morir mi sento* – "Cruel Love, I feel I am dying". It undoubtedly fitted the baroque fashion for sighing over unrequited love; but it could also have been a metaphor for the sadness expressed in her letter.[253]

---

252 Much of the information on music and musicians is based on *Grove Music*

253 After working for Ernst August's promotion to Elector of Hanover Steffani became in the new century head of government of Liselotte's nephew the Elector Palatine, wrote an opera for him also, and was promoted titular bishop

But music was indeed her solace, and all was by no means always sad at Charlottenburg.

> "No Body better understands the Art of giving an improving Relish to all Entertainments", the admiring Toland wrote; "but her favorit Diversion is Music, and one must judg as well of it as her Majesty (which is not easily don) to love it with a Passion equal to her's. She plays to Perfection on the Harpsichord, which she practises every day: she sings finely; and the famous BONONCINI, one of the greatest Masters alive, told me, that her Compositions are most exact".

Toland, as we noted earlier, was always susceptible to "exactness" – regular architecture, regular physiognomies, regular Compositions. Unfortunately none of those Compositions has survived.

Johann Anton Coberg, the musician who had taught her the harpsichord technique so much admired in Paris, followed her from Hanover, where he was Ernst August's court organist, to Berlin, where he perhaps helped Sophie Charlotte maintain her proficiency: in her small theatre she sometimes conducted opera performances from the harpsichord. It seems to have taken her a long time after her arrival in Berlin in 1684 to develop a musical establishment. It really had to await the independence that came with Charlottenburg: Frederick preferred the more ceremonial tones of drums and trumpets, which Sophie Charlotte detested. Even then, she grumbled, Frederick gave her insufficient allowance to maintain her own orchestra, so she had to make do with "borrowed musicians". But in the last decade of her life she managed to borrow a steady stream of highly competent ones.

While many were German, Sophie Charlotte preferred the Italian composers, fashionable at the time throughout Europe. And she preferred to have them right there in Charlottenburg when she could: that they were Catholic, even in holy orders, was no inhibition – indeed, added spice. The two chief musical adornments of her court, Ariosti and Bononcini, we have already met in passing. The first, Attilio Ariosti – the composer of the extravaganzas for Frederick's daughter's wedding in 1700 – was a Servite

---

by the China missionaries' nemesis Pope Clement XI. He spent most of the rest of his life back in Hanover as Apostolic Vicar for northern Germany. *Grove Music* notes that Handel borrowed from his operas and duets, and that some of his works were turned into anthems in England, with sacred words substituted.

monk whom Sophie Charlotte got from the Duke of Mantua in 1697, and then had a constant battle to keep. She enlisted the support of Italian dukes and cardinals against the demands of his Order to get him back, and succeeded for six years. Leibniz supported the campaign: knowing Sophie Charlotte's cash-strapped situation, he recognised that Ariosti could not easily be replaced, as he could sing, perform on a variety of instruments and write librettos, as well as compose.

As well as directing and conducting the court's music, he wrote altogether five stage works in Berlin, two to librettos by the Catholic priest Ortensio Mauro, secretary for over fifty years to Duke then Elector Ernst August in Hanover, much regarded by him, Sophie, and Leibniz. Sophie Charlotte's attachment to Ariosti is evident from the fact that she had a portrait made of him, still at Charlottenburg. He went on, two decades later, to compose, harmoniously, for Handel's opera in London. But, in the end, success gave way to poverty: he died in London in 1729, and a fellow-Italian, the librettist Paolo Rolli, wrote an epitaph suggesting personal experience:

> "Here lies Attilio Ariosti,
> He'd borrow still, could he accost ye.
> Monk to the last, whate'er betide,
> At other's cost he lived – and died."[254]

---

254 After leaving Sophie Charlotte's service, and spending most of the next two decades on diplomatic missions for Austrian, Italian and French courts - musicians in those days seem to have been dab hands at diplomacy! - Ariosti moved to London instead of settling back in his exasperated Order. His music was already known there: in 1710 the score of one of his Viennese operas, brought there by the Imperial Ambassador, became the first opera sung in London entirely in Italian - well, part thereof: the producer replaced all but 11 of the 43 arias with pieces written for other Vienna operas by...Bononcini. Ariosti's first actual performance in London, in 1716, was of a "New Symphony...on a New Instrument call'd Viola D'Amour", between the acts of a Handel opera. Eight of his own thirteen operas followed for Handel's Royal Academy of Music during its nine years of existence (to Handel's own fourteen out of an eventual forty-six, Bononcini's seven of thirty-one); it is sometimes claimed that his friendship with Handel dated back to having met the latter as an eleven-year-old on his only visit to Berlin. For a while Ariosti became fashionable in London as well as successful: a published collection of cantatas and lessons for the new viola d'amore sold to 764 subscribers, including 42 Dukes and Duchesses, 105 Earls and Countesses, and 146 Lords and Ladies. But fashions changed.

Giovanni Battista Bononcini overlapped with the end of Ariosti's time in Berlin. He arrived in 1702, with "a group of musicians", including his composer-cellist brother Antonio, from Vienna, where he was court musician to the Emperor but where musical life was stalled with the outbreak of the War of the Spanish Succession. He was more famous than his countryman, having made his name initially in Rome as well as Vienna; this time Sophie Charlotte could only hang on to him for less than two years, during which he composed two operas, the second to a libretto by...the verstile Ariosti.

Sir John Hawkins, the mid-18th century musicologist (and Samuel Johnson's literary executor), was to write that Bononcini's recitatives were "marked with great exactness and propriety". Toland would have liked that. Sophie Charlotte told Steffani of her delight at having "il grande Bononcini" at Charlottenburg; and his portrait is also still there. He too went on eventually to work for Handel's opera in London, anything but harmoniously – John Byrom (author of "Christians awake! Salute the happy morn!") introduced two new words into the English language to commemorate their relationship:

> "Some say, that Signor Bononcini,
> Compared to Handel's a mere ninny;
> Others aver, that to him Handel
> Is scarcely fit to hold a candle.
> Strange! That such high dispute should be
> 'Twixt Tweedledum and Tweedledee."[255]

---

255   After Berlin Bononcini returned to Vienna and again to Rome. It was there that the gilded 3rd Earl of Burlington (Privy Councillor at nineteen, and architect: of the House in Piccadilly, not the Arcade) enticed him away to the Royal Academy of Music in 1720. Although commissioned to write the anthem for the Duke of Marlborough's funeral, anti-Catholic prejudice drove him out of the Academy in 1723; but the new Duchess then employed him for the next seven years to direct his music at her private concerts, after which he eventually ended up in Vienna, with a pension from the Empress Maria Theresa. The only public performance of his work during those last years in England was of the opera *Astianatte*, in 1727, which became notorious when the two rival leading ladies, the reigning star Francesca Cuzzoni (whom Handel had once threatened to throw out the window when she threw a tantrum at a rehearsal) and the newly arrived diva Faustina Bordoni, tried to rip each other's hair out on stage. John Gay later satirized them as Polly and Lucy in *The Beggar's Opera*.

The most famous composer with whom Sophie Charlotte's name is associated never even visited Berlin: Corelli, appositely named Arcangelo by his parents but popularly promoted to *Il Divino*, described in *Grove Music* as having "exercised an unparalleled influence during his lifetime and for a long time afterwards...[becoming] a European phenomenon". And a long-lasting one: his works have remained in print ever since his own day, and have never passed out of the repertory. As a girl she may possibly have met him in Hanover not long after returning from Paris, but that is not certain; and a supposed visit later to Berlin was a confusion with another contemporary composer, Giuseppe Torelli, who performed for her in 1697, and dedicated a set of concertos to her.

Nevertheless, Corelli also dedicated a set of pieces to Sophie Charlotte, in 1700: his Opus 5, twelve sonatas *a violino e violone o cembalo* – for violin and violone (a bass viol, even a cello) or harpsichord. It became his most famous and most influential composition. It was also his most popular work: by the end of the 18th century more than fifty editions had appeared, in ten different cities. It is often played as *concerti grossi* in the transcription by his celebrated pupil Francesco Geminiani; other transcriptions followed; the final sonata, known as *La Folia* (or *Follia*), a vigorous Spanish dance in origin, was used by Liszt in his *Rhapsodie espagnole* and by Rachmaninov in *Variations on a Theme by Corelli*.

But why did Corelli, who spent his entire career in Rome, dedicate Opus 5 to Sophie Charlotte? Any personal connection was remote, even if it had existed at all. One suggestion is that, having admired his earlier works, she had sent him some sort of honorarium, and the dedication was thus in appreciation. It is not documented, but it would be no surprise if we were to learn somehow that Leibniz played a role in some such scenario: Corelli's first two collections had been published in 1681 and 1685, the third in 1689, possibly while Leibniz was himself in Rome cultivating and being cultivated by the China mission Jesuits. The idea that the composer was grateful because he was poverty-stricken seems highly unlikely: he had been music master since 1689 to two of the richest men in Rome, first, Cardinal Camillo Pamphili (a relation of Pope Innocent X), then Cardinal Pietro Ottoboni (made Cardinal at twenty-two by his uncle Pope Alexander VIII), to whom Corelli dedicated his Opus 3.[256] Another theory, that somehow Corelli's gesture was intended

---

256   Samuel Pepys' nephew attended midnight mass at San Lorenzo in Rome, at Christmas 1699: "Paluccio, an admired young performer, singing, and Corelli,

to encourage the Protestant House of Brandenburg to enter into the bosom of the Catholic Church, seems wholly fanciful.

Monsieur Erman is of no assistance whatever: his only remark is that

> "One sees in the Memoirs of the time, that the Queen made a valuable collection of works of Music of the most skilled artists of France and Italy, of which she played the themes, above all those of the celebrated Corelli, with a superior talent";

as though he had no knowledge at all of the dedication. He did note that Frederick II had removed the collection from the Royal Library to give to one of his nieces, after which it disappeared. Perhaps, he added regretfully,

> "it might have offered some proof of the talent that was attributed to the Queen for musical composition"

- and posterity a priceless Corelli manuscript score.

Making music in baroque Germany

It was ironic, this preference of Sophie Charlotte's for Italian music, because it was in the German states that European music was on the brink of reaching a new height. But she was just a fraction too early. In the eighteen pages of the *Grove Music* listing the works of Johann Sebastian Mighty Bach (as Dylan Thomas called him), the earliest dated is an organ chorale of 1700. He was fifteen. His prodigious life's work, the backbone of Western classical music, was still ahead. His great contemporary, George Frederick Handel, was actually born, the same year as Bach, in the Electorate of Brandenburg, at Halle, where Frederick was to establish the University and its famous law faculty in 1694. We have noted that he was sometimes supposed to have visited Berlin as a youth, already passionate about music, but until 1702 his father was intent on having him go into law studies at Halle. And he never went back to Berlin, if he ever had gone.

After he lost Sophie Charlotte, Frederick showed little interest in music – there were two more operas performed in 1708, none in the last five years before his death in 1713. When their son Frederick William

---

the famous violin, playing in concert with above thirty more, all at the expense of Cardinal Ottoboni".

then became the Soldier King he banned all musical performances. It is not surprising that the focus of the new wave of German composers was not on Berlin. Late in 1705 – Sophie Charlotte dead almost a year – Bach *walked* well over three hundred kilometres from Arnstadt to Lübeck, then one of the last free Hanseatic cities that had dominated trade in the Baltic for five centuries, to hear the organist Buxtehude, his great Danish forerunner. Handel had also gone to hear him, two years earlier, but only the sixty-six kilometres from Hamburg – and by coach. Handel traveled with their other great contemporary, Georg Philipp Telemann (subsequently godfather to Bach's composer son C.P.E.); and all three young musicians went not only to hear the old master but to see if one of them could succeed him at Lübeck's Marienkirche. However as it turned out that one of the conditions of that appointment was to marry Buxtehude's daughter – "not", in the delicate words of *Grove Music*, "in her first youth" – they all decided not to pursue that particular career.

Handel was to become Court musician to Sophie Charlotte's brother, the Elector of Hanover. The Dowager Electress Sophie was enchanted:

> "He plays the clavichord more perfectly than anyone else, and composes too. Such a good-looking man".

But, neglecting his duties while trying the London theatrical market, he then had to overcome the Elector's displeasure when the latter also arrived in London as King George I. His career in opera, in the prevailing Italian style, which never interested Bach, had its ups and downs, even after surviving the concurrence of Ariosti and the competition of Bononcini: still, in 1733, after Handel had conducted a performance of *Athalia* in Wren's Sheldonian Theatre at Oxford, the noted antiquary Thomas Hearne could complain of

> "Handel and his lowsy Crew, a great number of forreyn fidlers",

and a learned Don could protest after the same performance that

> "the Theater was erected for other-guise Purposes, than to be prostituted to a Company of squeeking, bawling, out-landish Singsters".

But after Handel developed the oratorio, for which he was long known best, he was established indelibly as an Englishman, almost an Anglican, rewarded eventually, nine years after Bach's death, with a tomb in Westminster Abbey. But fame and fate are still fickle: from the late 20th century it was Handel's Italian operas that were increasingly performed, the English oratorios less so.

It was Bach, however, who was to exercise the greater influence. His first connection with the Hohenzollerns came when he met, in 1719 in Berlin, where he was negotiating for a new harpsichord, the Margrave Christian Ludwig of Brandenburg-Anhalt, the youngest of Frederick I's half-brothers, who invited him to send "some compositions". Bach said he took "a couple of years" over the commission, and his celebrated *Brandenburg Concertos* were then dedicated to Christian Ludwig in 1721. The Margrave did not thank Bach, or send a fee, or use the score.

While it was as a keyboard virtuoso that Bach achieved in his lifetime what *Grove Music* describes as "an almost legendary fame", it was the mastery and "encyclopedic nature" of his composing that gave him "a unique historical position" in Western music – though only after a century of considerable neglect. The vast range and sheer quantity of Bach's (surviving) compositions is breathtaking: the great organ chorales and preludes and fugues; the harpsichord suites; the vocal and choral masterpieces – the motets, cantatas, Passions, B minor Mass, Christmas Oratorio; the concertos for orchestra and instruments; the monumental *Goldberg Variations*, supposedly written to be played by one of his pupils, Johann Gottlieb Goldberg, to help put the insomniac Russian Ambassador to Saxony to sleep; the last, extraordinary, work, *The Art of the Fugue*, a "how to" work for great virtuosos, with its single, double, triple, quadruple fugues, culminating in a mirror fugue – a summation of Bach's entire life and work. It is the ultimate testament to musical exactness and order.

This northern musical flowering heralded a German domination of classical music that was to last throughout the eighteenth, nineteenth and very early twentieth centuries, when the Russians took over. Hitherto, as indicated by Sophie Charlotte's tastes, European music had been largely in the highly capable hands of the Italians. As the young Germans began to make their marks it was their older Italian contemporaries who still led the way: Bach and Telemann were both much influenced by Corelli, and Bach eventually transcribed for the organ or harpsichord many of Vivaldi's concertos. Handel developed a good deal of his polish from his mixing with every composer who was anybody during his stay in Italy between 1706 and 1709 – Corelli, Alessandro Scarlatti, Vivaldi, Albinoni; and he had a famous harpsichord contest (which he lost) with

Scarlatti's son Domenico, the same age as himself, who in due course composed over *six hundred* sonatas for that instrument.

Handel must have also met Bartolomeo Cristofori – they were both at the Medici Court in Florence at the same time – who was then in the process of inventing the pianoforte, which he apparently succeeded in doing by 1709.[257] Handel does not seem to have used the new instrument, but Bach did, on a famous occasion. In 1747 he was invited to the new palace at Potsdam by Frederick the Great, our Frederick's martial and musical grandson, to try his new German-made version of Cristofori's pianoforte. Bach had to improvise on the spot on a fugue theme given to him by the accomplished King himself, which, later, feeling he had performed inadequately, he developed as the *Musical Offering* to the Prussian monarch. Still, although a keen and talented musician, Frederick the Great was nevertheless the son of his father – he was later to write:

"To convince you of the lack of taste which still reigns in Germany, you have only to visit a public performance. You will see abominable plays by Shakespeare translated into our language, and the whole audience swooning as they listen to these ridiculous farces, worthy only of savages in Canada. I describe them in this way because they violate every rule of the theatre".[258]

Last view of Sophie Charlotte

There are glimpses which indicate that all was not always solemn at Sophie Charlotte's Court – that coronation pinch of snuff is suggestive of

257 There is a 1720 Cristofori piano (which has been recorded) in the Metropolitan Museum of Art in New York; the only two others remaining are in Leipzig and Rome.

258 The really fortunate Hohenzollern, musically speaking, was Frederick's successor, his nephew Frederick William II - fat, dull, and a mystical Freemason, given to spending evenings communicating with Marcus Aurelius and Leibniz, among others, "to learn greatness". But he also loved music, and was a competent cellist. In 1789 he invited Mozart to Berlin to play at Court; the visit prompted the last three string quartets, the "Prussian Quartets". In 1796 Beethoven followed in Mozart's footsteps to Berlin, playing for the same Frederick William II. The often unbending Beethoven outdid himself, composing for the occasion a set of variations for the King's cello and his own piano on the theme, from Handel's oratorio *Judas Maccabeus*, "See the conqu'ring hero comes". Frederick William took the point, and presented Beethoven with a gold snuffbox filled with gold pieces - "such a one", Beethoven later said, "as it might have been customary to give to an Ambassador". If only.

other forms of cocking snooks. Leibniz admired the erotic poetry of the Master of Ceremonies, Johann von Besser, for "presenting the indecent with such decency". It was said that Besser well understood the taste of his age:

> "a lewd poem should be lewd but not coarse; only the rhymes need be pure".

Harold Nicolson, in *The Age of Reason*, saw the principal virtues of that time as the ideas of sincerity, good sense, balance, moderation, order, taste, intellectual truthfulness, tolerance, political and intellectual cosmopolitanism. Sophie Charlotte could be attributed all these characteristics, but the 19th-20th century evangelicals' sense of purity was not included or expected. Irreverent Berliners punned on Schloss Lützenburg to make it *Lottchens Lustenburg* – "Little Lottie's Pleasure Palace" – but there is no surviving evidence that she lived a profligate life. Ward, her mother's biographer at the beginning of last century, noted that Sophie Charlotte was

> "beyond a doubt, very much [unconstrained] in her relations with persons whom she liked; but, though scandal was busy with these freedoms, she never compromised herself by indulging in them too far".

There is encouragement to believe that she was better than she might have been.

Frederick, on the other hand, was no better than he ought to be. As we have seen, unfortunately for Sophie Charlotte, following the fall of Danckelmann her husband not only installed the Count von Wartenberg as his new chief minister but also the Countess – "apparently", Ward excuses, "only for the completeness of the thing" – as his Mistress *en titre*. It is hard to tell whether Sophie Charlotte found the situation harder to bear because the Countess was of rather humble origins or because of her "undistinguished manners"; or whether, with her awareness of political niceties, she deprecated the implication of conflict of interest in the King's involvement with his chief advisor's wife – being the king's favourite was not merely a source of honour for the lady but a source of substantial profit for her husband.

But Sophie Charlotte recognised that, as Versailles had dictated in this as in everything else, princes (and prelates) did have mistresses in those times; indeed, the Elector of Saxony met *five* of his mistresses at a supper offered a few years afterwards by her own successor as Queen of Prussia. So, with a steely will, Sophie Charlotte resolved not to let the wretched Wartenberg woman "interfere with the maintenance of a good understanding between her consort and herself". What it cost her to receive the woman at Charlottenburg she partially recompensed by welcoming her there in French – "oblivious", Ward said, "of her guest's imperfections of education". One doubts very much that Sophie Charlotte ever suffered from obliviousness.

The situation was to worsen, however, as the King's infatuation deepened: at the end of 1704 he would only permit Sophie Charlotte to make her annual visit to Hanover to see her mother on condition that La Wartenberg was also invited. Frederick would never see Sophie Charlotte again. On the way to Hanover she caught a chill; once there it worsened into pneumonia, though she still danced at the Carnival ball given in her honour. On 1 February 1705 Sophie – herself ill and unable to visit her daughter – wrote to Frederick that Sophie Charlotte had been "bled to ease her breathing", and was now out of danger. But she died that night. She was not yet thirty-seven.

As she lay dying, Sophie Charlotte had what can only be described as an entertaining encounter with the French Chaplain at Hanover, the respectable Edict-of-Nantes Pastor de la Bergerie, who offered his services. There is dispute amongst the sources about what Sophie Charlotte said to him; but the version rejected by those for whom the consolations of religion were regarded as essential sounds more in keeping with the Sophie Charlotte whom we have come to know. According to this version, on the last day of her life she is supposed to have said politely, when the Pastor asked if she wished him to speak with her, that she had devoted twenty years of study to religious questions, and he could tell her nothing that she did not already know. She was dying in peace.

> "Do not torment me now, for I now go to satisfy my curiosity on the principle of things that Leibniz has never been able to explain to me; on space, infinity, being and nothingness. And I prepare for my husband the King the spectacle of a funeral, where he will have a new opportunity to display his grandeur".

She deserves to have gone with such a perspicuous summation of her life.

Afterwards, as if in echo of the long-ago scares, at the start of her marriage, which Frederick thought he got from his nasty step-mother

Sophie Dorothea, there was to be another bizarre story of poisoning. It was recounted in England by Lady Cowper, a lady-in-waiting to Princess Caroline of Ansbach, by then Princess of Wales, wife of the future King George II. Waiting one day, she said, while the Princess was visiting King George I, she and

> "the attendant courtiers, obliged to cool their heels outside, were entertained by Mahomed, the King's Turkish servant, who described in macabre detail the death of his master's sister, the late Queen of Prussia. This unfortunate lady was thought to have been poisoned by diamond-powder mixed in her food, 'for when she was opened her Stomach was so worn, that you could put your Fingers through at any Place', as did Mahomed. Her brother the King, said Mahomed, was so affected by his loss that he went five days without eating, drinking or sleeping, but continued to pace up and down his chamber, banging his toes against the wainscot ('which he ever does when he walks') till he had worn out his shoes and his 'Toes came out two Inches at the Foot' ".[259]

But there was never any other suggestion, outside Mahomed, of any sort of foul play.

Frederick himself, for all his infatuation with La Wartenberg, seems to have been genuinely grief-stricken, and duly used Sophie Charlotte's funeral to display his grandeur. A huge cavalcade escorted her body from Hanover back to Berlin; a vastly expensive catafalque bore her to the Berlin Cathedral opposite the *Stadtschloss*; and as if in belated homage to his wife's musical passions, he commissioned the funeral music – Ariosti and Bononcini having both long gone – from another Italian, Ruggiero Fedeli, who had been composer at the Berlin court chapel from 1691 to 1695, then gone on to Hanover and several other courts before being brought back by Frederick at the time of Sophie Charlotte's funeral. This music, like so much of the other music associated with her, has also been lost.

Leibniz also was stricken, and composed an enormously long elegy – in German, surprizingly – in which he concluded that to have had such qualities she must have been more angelic than human. He wrote sadly to an old correspondent, the Reverend William Wotton, a Cambridge

---

259   From Peter Quennell: *Caroline of England*

scholar who had been able to translate the Bible from Latin, Greek and Hebrew before he was six:

"What has interrupted my correspondence with you and my other friends this year, is the turmoil into which the death of the Queen of Prussia has thrown me...She wanted me to be with her often, and I frequently enjoyed conversation with this great Princess, whose genius and humanity nobody equalled. Our discussions focussed on topics, on which, in seeking to satisfy her curiosity and her anxiety to learn, she revealed to me points of view and ideas, which, if her death had not intervened, could have contributed to the public good".

He would soon find that when Sophie Charlotte died so, too, did all his influence in Berlin.

Sophie Charlotte's memorials today, now that she has been largely forgotten as a person except in the old books, are the pretty butter-yellow Charlottenburg Palace, of which only half was hers, and, much less visited, Schlüter's tomb in the Berlin Cathedral. Like the old *Stadtschloss* that used to be across the Unter den Linden, from which Sophie Charlotte escaped to Charlottenburg, the tomb is in the rather heavy Berlin Baroque manner, but with a symbolism neatly in keeping with Sophie Charlotte's own vision of herself – one wonders if, in some premonition of her fate, she had discussed it with the sculptor before that last journey to Hanover.

At the head of the casket is a medallion with her portrait, in profile. It looks an honest one: the double chin and the fullness of face that was already implicit in the small girl are in no way disguised; it is a face that looks comfortable, but a good deal older than Sophie Charlotte's thirty-six years. Supporting the medallion are two very attractive young women, both beautifully modelled, in elegant contrast to the heavy Prussian formality of the casket and its aquiline supports. The two women on Frederick's tomb (also by Schlüter), supporting his portrait medallion, are crowned, to represent the Electorate and the Kingdom. It is less clear what those on Sophie Charlotte's tomb were intended to represent; even the little guide to the Hohenzollern tombs in the Cathedral is not sure: *Leben und Vergehen*, Life and Passing on, it suggests, or else Day and Night.

Life and Passing on is not a common symbolic pairing, even, I am told, in German. But you can see that perhaps this was exactly what

Schlüter had in mind, the quite specific personification of two of the most distinctive aspects of the late Queen's character: the young woman on the right paying alert attention to Sophie Charlotte's face – as she herself must have paid attention to the stream of interlocutors she encouraged in her philosophical discussions; the other stretched out in totally languid repose (she owes something to Michelangelo, this young lady), left arm thrown up casually over her head – as if to suggest the serenity with which Sophie Charlotte took her leave of her mortal coil.

However the element which is the crowning touch of the whole work is the figure of Death seated at the foot of the casket, inscribing Sophie Charlotte's name in the Book of Eternity – the existence of which, as posited by Leibniz, she had been curious to discover on her real death-bed. The ancient skull, with its taut skin, is in masterly contrast to the two young women with their pretty faces, an allegory of the distinction between the apparent and the real. But Death's figure as a whole is stunningly *beautiful*: it is clothed in a superb flowing robe, a completely elegant masterpiece of swirling Baroque folds. Could Death *be* beautiful? Perhaps if it were to satisfy your "curiosity on the principle of things".

Afterward: Leibniz

Sophie Charlotte's other memorial was the book written by Leibniz called *Essais de Théodicée*, written in French, of course, for the educated public; it is known in English as *Theodicy*. It appeared in 1710, the same year as the first volume of *Miscellanea Berolinensia*, the first published fruit of the Berlin Society of Sciences. While *Theodicy* was still in the press Leibniz described its origin in a letter to the English clergyman Thomas Burnet, who had been obliged ten years before to resign his position at the court of William III for publishing a work which treated the Fall of Adam and Eve as an allegory.[260]

---

260   A contemporary wit summarised Burnet as contending

> "That as for Father Adam
> And Mrs. Eve, his Madame,
> And what the devil spoke, Sir,
> 'Twas nothing but a joke, Sir,
> And well-invented flam";

and, for good measure,

> "That all the books of Moses
> Were nothing but supposes".

The greatest part of his new book, Leibniz said, had been written piecemeal during the time of his discussions on philosophy with Sophie Charlotte while walking in the garden at Charlottenburg. The Queen had often encouraged him to set out in writing his arguments against the view of the French Protestant philosopher Pierre Bayle (which had greatly attracted Sophie Charlotte) that morality was independent of religion; and after her death he had collected these writings together into a large work on Divine Providence, the freedom of Man, and the origin of Evil. There were those who took "Theodicy" to be the name of an otherwise unknown author, and others, recognising some of the argument, as Leibniz's pseudonym. The word was Leibniz's own invention, from the Greek words for God and justice, to signify the vindication of God for the existence of evil; or, as the *Oxford English Dictionary* also defines it, quoting from the opening of Milton's *Paradise Lost*, "a writing, doctrine, or theory intended to 'justify the ways of God to men' ".

It was really "the trial of God for the creation of evil", and Leibniz issued a triumphant verdict of "Not guilty". God did not create evil: he had no choice but to permit it. As I understand it, his reasoning went something like this. First, metaphysical evil is simply imperfection; if humans did not have imperfections they would themselves be the same as God, which is logically impossible. Second, physical and moral evil are not necessary in this sense, but are consequent on God's allowing humans free will. So none of these kinds of evil is the result of an actual *choice* by God. But Leibniz went further, and his reputation has never quite lived it down: the world as it actually exists is only one of an infinity of possible worlds; and because, by definition, God has perfect wisdom and goodness, this world must therefore be "the most perfect actual world which is possible". It seems unlikely that Sophie Charlotte would have been convinced to forsake Bayle.

Leibniz had hesitated to publish *Theodicy* because Bayle was not still alive to defend himslf against its critiques. Nearly half a century later Voltaire had no such qualms when he publicly demolished Leibniz's optimism with his bitingly funny satire *Candide*, in which Dr Pangloss-Leibniz sees the innocent young Candide through disasters natural, man-made and self-inflicted, in four continents, until he decides to stay at home and "cultivate his garden" – proving, as his sufferings had brought him to this happy conclusion, the correctness of Dr Pangloss's philosophy that this *must* be the best of all possible worlds. It was brilliantly clever; but it was Voltaire, not Leibniz, who finally submitted to the orthodoxy of the Church – and, after building himself a chapel dedicated to God but not the Saints, asked the Pope to send him sacred relics for it.

Voltaire is best known for *Candide*; but he is also remembered for what he had been at the height of the Enlightenment, excoriating the bigotry of the church and the tyranny of the monarchy, fostering the ferment leading up to the fall of the Bastille a decade after his death. Leibniz, living in the quite different circumstances of almost a century earlier, less directly influential politically, is now scarcely known at all; but, despite the anti-rationalism of the *Theodicy*, he played a significant role in developing the ideas that the Enlightenment came to embody with his conviction that only through using reason would man be able to "strive towards the development, improvement, complete understanding and correct application of ideas".

His longer term reputation rested on the whole range of contributions he made to intellectual enquiry and learned debate on just about everything, at that time when the old certainties were beginning to be subjected to scientific and rational scrutiny. And, the experts say, even in more recent times some of his ideas in mathematics and physics have influenced Bertrand Russell's symbolic logic, and Einstein's approach to relativity – in which regard it is a curious coincidence that, in a letter to Sophie Charlotte, John Toland also argued that motion is "essential to matter".

Even before Sophie Charlotte's death, when she could still play a mediating role, Leibniz got caught in the middle of a squabble between her husband in Berlin and her brother in Hanover. It is not clear what it was about – if it was indeed about anything more than petty pride – but it did not help the coalition against Louis XIV: exasperated, Leibniz wrote that

"The German nation appears to have a death-wish, and will be entirely to blame for a disastrous outcome of the war".

He eventually realised that, on the one hand, Frederick suspected he was a Hanoverian spy; on the other, he exasperated George by the length of time he spent in Berlin. His excuse that it was caused by ulceration of a leg did not wash: Sophie wrote from Hanover that

"My son says it is your head for which you are valued, not your feet", and warned him that his ailment was undoubtedly caused by drinking coffee, which caused anything "from consumption to brain tumors" – he should stick to chocolate.[261]

---

261   Coffee was widely drunk but also widely distrusted from its introduction mid-to-late 17th century through much of the 18th. England had been more receptive to it than anywhere in Europe north of Italy. It was first recorded being drunk there in 1637 in Balliol College, Oxford, by a Cretan student, Nathaniel Conopios, afterwards Bishop of Smyrna. The first English coffee-house was also opened in Oxford, in 1650. The habit was encouraged nine years later when the University's famous Orientalist Edward Pococke, Professor of Hebrew (formerly of Arabic), translated and published *The Nature of the Drink Kauhi, or Coffee, and the Berry of Which it is Made, Described by an Arabian Phisitian*; it proclaimed coffee was

> "by experience found to conduce to the drying of rheumes, and flegmatick coughes and distillations, and the opening of obstructions, and the provocation of urin...it allayes the ebullition of the blood, is good against the small poxe and measles, the bloudy pimples";

but there were costs: it also

> "causeth vertiginous headheach, and maketh lean walking, and the Emrods, and aswageth lust, and sometimes breeds melancholy...Some drink it with milk, but it is an error, and such as may bring danger of the leprosy".

But enthusiasm was much greater than any concern: within one year the government taxed coffee-drinking; within two an Oxford Don was fuming at the decline of "solid and serious learning" because

> "nothing but news and the affaires of Christendome is discoursed off and that also generally at coffee houses".

In Germany, the first coffee was introduced by the Great Elector of Brandenburg to his court in the 1670s; but Berlin did not get its first coffee-house ("The English") until 1721, under Frederick William I; and in 1734 Bach was writing his *Coffee Cantata* (BWV 211) to poke fun at coffee sceptics:

> "Dear father, do not be so strict", a daughter sings; "If I can't have my little demi-tasse of coffee three times a day, I'm just like a dried up piece of roast goat!"

However by 1777 Frederick the Great was thundering that

> "It is disgusting to notice the increase in the quantity of coffee used by my subjects, and the like amount of money that goes out of the country in consequence. Everyone is using coffee. If possible this must be prevented. My people must drink beer. His Majesty was brought up on beer, and so were

The last ten years of Leibniz's life seems to have been considerably less happy than it was when he had the sparkling Queen to enliven it. There were gratifying honours: he was a Privy Councillor to the King of Prussia, the Elector of Hanover, the Tsar of Russia and the Holy Roman Emperor, who also created him a noble (*Reichsfreiherr*) of the Empire. But there was also a whole string of disappointments: fewer visits to Berlin in the face of Frederick's hostility, none after 1711; the unfairness and humiliation of Newton's underhanded campaign against him; the failure of the Berlin Society of Sciences to register any practical – or money-making – achievements; Peter the Great's repeated postponement of a Russian Academy; the increasingly bad-tempered demands by the Elector of Hanover for the history of Brunswick; and his refusal when he became King of England to let Leibniz come to London too. He continued producing papers – including the *Discours sur la Théologie naturelle des Chinois* – but his body was seriously failing him.

When he died at the end of 1716 few even noticed the departure of one of the period's most brilliant minds. His secretary, Eckhart, was the only person who followed his body to the grave: no clergyman, not a single member of the Hanoverian court, for which he had worked, on and, it must be said, off, for thirty-seven years. A visiting Scotsman wrote that he

"was buried more like a robber than what he really was, the ornament of his country".

The Berlin Society was silent on the death of its perpetual president. The only organisation of all those which he had created or belonged or contributed to that marked his passing was the Académie Française, where a eulogy was read by Bernard le Bovier de Fontenelle, author and president of the Académie des Sciences, and a nephew of Corneille. This gesture had at least one significant resonance: Leibniz, in contemplating his life and work, had written:

"Provided that something of importance is achieved, I am indifferent whether it is done in Germany or in France, for I seek the good of mankind".

---

his ancestors, and his officers. Many battles have been fought and won by soldiers nourished on beer; and the King does not believe that coffee-drinking soldiers can be depended upon".

Afterward: Frederick

King Frederick lived another eight years after he lost Sophie Charlotte, still concerned for his magnificence, still sending his soldiers to fight on the Po, the Rhine and the Meuse in the endless war against Louis, still keeping in touch with him as he backed and filled and weaved to keep Brandenburg-Prussian territory out of the battle zones. He is said to have negotiated with Louis via the Genevan representative in Paris, the Bavarian agent in Berlin, the French ministers in Danzig and Copenhagen, and a Swedish merchant in Berlin who was really a general in French employ, and leaked news of his transactions to encourage his exasperated British, Dutch and Hanoverian allies to pay his subsidies and meet his territorial claims. At the same time he backed and filled and weaved between Russia, Sweden and Poland to continue to keep out of Tsar Peter's Northern War. If it shredded his reputation in the east as in the west, too bad: it worked.

There are first-hand glimpses of him at home during this period, in letters to an Oxford mentor from another Briton, the Reverend William Ayerst, from 1705 to 1711 chaplain to Queen Anne's Ambassador to Prussia, Thomas, Lord Raby (later Earl of Strafford). Ayerst was also active in discussions, in which Frederick himself showed a lively interest, on a union, or at least doctrinal and liturgical conformity, between the Church of England and the Lutheran Church in Prussia, to try to establish what his court preacher described as a

"middle way between the superstition of the Catholics and the frigidity of the Calvinists".

It was a mini-version of Leibniz's dream of Christian unity; in fact Leibniz had himself thought that Anglican theology might provide a middle way between Protestant and Catholic orthodoxies.

But the scheme Frederick fostered faced the same fundamental flaw as did Leibniz's much wider one. Ayerst reported:

"Especially ye Lutherans seem to be very positive th't they cannot make one step towards ye other, nor yeild ye least point or Ceremony without offending God ye memory of y'r B. Luther, as one of th'm affirmed in a scandalous Pamphlet w'ch ye K. order'd to be burnt by ye Com. Hangman".

In addition to working for the Anglican viewpoint, Ayerst found other work to do as well: Toland was back in Berlin in 1707, a "Serpent" still "very Jesuitically" espousing unacceptable positions, but obviously still getting some sort of hearing somewhere, even without Sophie Charlotte. The outraged Ayerst

> "made it my business to attaque [them – or him]...in 2 Sermons w'th w'ch his Lords'p told me he was not dissatisfied".

If the project could not succeed under Fredrick it was certainly not likely to under his heir, Frederick William, who, Ayerst observed,

> "one may without Prophecy assure will never do it, his mind being wholly given to thick scull'd Heroes ye war, and looking down w'th ye greatest Contempt on any thing th't looks like learning".

Although the eager Frederick laid the foundation stone for a *Unionskirche* in Charlottenburg in 1712, the scheme foundered – to re-emerge, over a century later, in the establishment in 1841 of an Anglo-Prussian Bishopric of...Jerusalem.[262]

It is not clear how much effort Ayerst's "Lords'p" put into Church unity: he was more preoccupied with Prussia's uncertain role in the alliance against Louis XIV, somewhat hampered by personal rivalry between himself and the Duke of Marlborough, who thought Raby "impertinent and insignificant". In fact both helped keep Frederick in the alliance, Marlborough, enormously famous after Blenheim, by periodical doses of charm – Sophie Charlotte thought him "the most polished Englishman I have ever seen" – Raby by establishing a close relationship with Frederick, all the more remarkable in that he established an even closer relationship with Madame von Wartenberg, still the King's mistress *en titre*, who became Raby's mistress *en lit*. It puts a new perspective on a Prussian official's complaint that "nothing can be hidden" from Raby, who could repeat "syllable by syllable" what was

---

262   The Bishop was to be from Prussia and England alternately. The first was Michael Solomon Alexander, born in 1799 in Posen (then in Prussia following the second partition of Poland under Frederick William II, now, after changing hands five times since then, Poznan in western Poland). He was raised in Orthodox Judaism to become a Rabbi, moved to England in 1820, converted and was ordained as an Anglican in 1827, and appointed to the Jerusalem Bishopric in 1841. Once again the scheme foundered, the Lutherans disliking the British episcopalianism, the Anglicans the German nonconformism, and came to an end in 1886.

said in the King's chamber. He was accused by London of being too favourable to his host (indeed an all too frequent diplomatic failing), but shrugged off the charge:

> "I must vindicate my little king as you call him – tho he thinks himself great enough".

That sounds to me like someone who had not lost his bearings. Ayerst's descriptions of Frederick's world echo Toland's,

> "finery Splendour being ye whole Delight of this King Court indeed of ye whole Town, where a man is amaz'd to see in a poor barren country as this is ye riches of ye Indies in appearance".

Wartenberg, who contributed so much to the extravagance, finally fell in 1711:

> "his Maj'ty finding his Purse exhausted by his great Magnificence, Rary-shews, Jewels, Presents to his Favorites, buildings c, is now willing to throw ye fault upon his Ministers squeese it out of them".

For all that, half the state's income was still available to be spent on the army – though this was an inadequate proportion for Frederick's later more militaristic detractors. On his deathbed the Great Elector had abjured his son to treat the Huguenots "as a father does his children"; and Frederick did. When he died in 1713 he left Frederick William no debt, and an income more than double that which his father had left him, thanks not least to his father's Huguenots.

After mourning Sophie Charlotte for three years, Frederick married, in 1708, his third wife and second Sophie, the twenty-four-year-old excessively religious Sophie Louise of Mecklenburg-Schwerin, who was to be the death of him. It was another – the last – occasion for Frederick to "display his grandeur". Ayerst was there. First there was the ceremonial entry into Berlin,

> "with all ye gaudy Coaches Liverys fine Embroideries c w'ch a Prussian Court was capable of. There were at least an hundred magnificent Coaches 4 or 5 Regim'ts of Guards Dragoons, all ye Gentry both of Town Court Country on horse back...I can not pretend to reckon up all ye show. I can only say 'twas th' K. of

Prussia's th't for 2 hours it was passing I cou'd but admire at ye Extravigance Splendour where they find ye Mony for so vast an expence".

But that was merely the preliminary: the next scene was

"ye Ceremony of confirming ye Marriage in ye Dome or great Church as they call it, w'ch was if possible still more splendid, ye Church was nobly adorned ye Procession glorious. Ye K. Q. went under different Canopys supported by their Nobles a Mob of German Princes. One cou'd see nothing of ye Little Man but a Cap of Feathers a great many Diamonds on a short Spanish mantle w'ch made him look so much like a Poppet th't I wonder those about him cou'd hold their Countenance, but ye Queen taller by ye Head shoulders".

And, finally, the celebrations:

Ye rest of this week has past in Balls and Feasts w'th a continual noise of Cannon every health. The Rejoycings are to last 40 Days within w'ch we are to have ye Combat of wild Beasts in ye Amphitheatre, Operas, Comedys Masquerades Balls in abundance as soon as ye malicious Moon will hide her Horns ye Fire works Illuminations w'th mottos Painted Devices as is ye way of this Country. In short I think we shall loath despise Pageantry fine Coats ever after".

The marriage was prompted by Frederick's desire to produce another male heir to the Hohenzollern dynasty following the failure up to that point of his and Sophie Charlotte's only son, Frederick William, and his wife, his first cousin Sophie Dorothea, daughter of Sophie Charlotte's brother King George I, to produce a survivable heir. Initially, the newly-weds were said to have "caressed each other furiously in public"; but bliss did not last in private. Sophie Louise also failed to produce an heir, though after the birth of the future Frederick the Great to Frederick William and Sophie Dorothea in 1712 that did not matter any more. By then it was in any case far too late – retreating into religious obsession under the ministrations of a puritanical pastor, Queen Sophie Louise had become increasingly deranged, and had eventually to be safely confined in an apartment in the Palace.

But one day early in 1713 she evaded her attendants, and clad only in her nightgown, walked right through a glass door leading into her husband's bedroom. Poor Frederick, violently woken to the sight of an apparition in white, spattered with blood from broken shards of glass, thought she was the legendary White Lady of the Hohenzollerns, the ghost of the medieval Agnes von Orlamünde which was reputed to appear when a Hohenzollern was about to die. Frederick had a heart attack and died several days afterwards, still only fifty-six. And a German historian said,

> "with him all courtly pomp was consigned to the grave, to make way for bourgeois simplicity and military austerity."

From Prussia to Germany

But not quite yet: the new King Frederick William I gave his father the sort of magnificent funeral the old King would have regarded as appropriate to a King of Prussia – "no cost was spared, no pretentiousness avoided": and he personally drilled the guard of honour, and gave the order for the last artillery salute. But that was the end of it. Most of the palaces were closed down at once, apart from five rooms in the *Stadtschloss* for the new royal family. Schlüter was dismissed, and took himself off to St Petersburg to work for Peter the Great on sculpture for the exquisite little Summer Palace in the Summer Garden on the Neva: the bas relief panels outside, and, within, the staircase balustrade and the playful boy on a dolphin in Peter's Dutch-style study. One hundred and twenty-nine of the *Stadtschloss*'s one hundred and forty-one courtiers were sacked; court dress was replaced by the Prussian army uniform. The diamonds, the wines, the coaches, the animals in the Royal Zoo were sold off.

All theologians but the official ones, all the philosophers and savants – all the *Schwarzscheisser*, the "shitters of black ink", as Frederick William called them – were sent packing; and first of all the opera-singers and musicians, though his taste in music unexpectedly ran to Bach: a military band playing his setting of *A Mighty Fortress is Our God*, "God Almighty's grenadier-march". When he was not playing soldiers, or hunting – his best: 3,602 wild boar in one season – Frederick William walked the streets, breaking noses and teeth as he beat idlers with his stick, requiring market women to knit stockings between sales, ordering terrified citizens that they must not fear him – "You must *love* me, scum!".

Sophie Charlotte, the indulgent mother, must bear some of the blame. Frederick William himself later accused his mother of having spoiled him: "My mother was a good woman", he said, "but she was a sad Christian" – leaving open in fact whether he was criticising her mothering or her open-mindedness. Having got used as a child to having entirely his own way, he was incapable of exercising restraint as an adult, still less as an absolute monarch. He was sent as a child of five to Hanover to school and to play with his cousin, the future English King George II; little Frederick William hated and fought him, and went on hating him all his life, though he married his sister.

Back home, he resisted learning – then and all his life – though the way he was taught by the tutor Danckelmann foisted on him against his mother' wishes obviously played a part. Monsieur Erman told his Academy colleagues that he had seen

"a big volume written in the young Prince's hand, which contains his first exercises…: in it, set out in five columns, are passages from all the books of the Old Testament from Genesis to Malachi",

with, in succession, the main words, their translation into German, into French, "a Latin version", and the actual texts, "undoubtedly not the best model of Latinity". Learning was stifling. So too were the elaboratenesses of the Court, but the boy showed precocious and what became permanent interest in all the various elaboratenesses of soldiering, starting by spending his pocket-money to set up a company of noble cadets, precursors of those "thick scull'd Heroes", which of course he commanded.

Into his teens, we find Sophie Charlotte, in a handwritten note that somehow survived the destruction of her papers after she died, telling his tutor that he

"should not prohibit the Crown Prince's love affairs, love brightens the spirit and softens the manners. But he should direct his taste, so it is directed at nothing base",

a further piece of indulgence that earned Sophie Charlotte the reproof of "innate grossness of thought and obliquity of vision" from pure-minded and Stuart partisans in Britain, still unreconciled two hundred years later to the Hanoverian Succession. Just before she died she sent her son off, at sixteen, to try to broaden his interests and his outlook in Holland and

England; the depth of her attachment to him was observed on a paper she left on her desk the day he departed, a heart with around it the words "*Il est parti*", He has gone – always in French. She never saw him again: before he got to either country he had to return to Berlin for her funeral, and he only ever went abroad afterwards on military campaigns.

Frederick himself also indulged the boy, if differently. When Sophie Charlotte died his father gave him a real infantry regiment, and before his marriage in 1706 he went off to campaign with the Duke of Marlborough on the Rhine. Frederick outdid even his usual extravagance for the wedding feast when Frederick William and cousin Sophie Dorothea of Hanover were married later that year: 640 calves, 100 fat oxen, 1102 turkeys, 650 ducks, 1000 doves and 7200 eggs. And, after all these years, the indomitable Liselotte supplied the Crown Princess's wedding finery from Paris. A few weeks later the old Electress Sophie wrote to Frederick saying she hoped

"God will soon make you a grandfather...to which end, as I hear, they are working night and day in Berlin".

But Frederick William went back to war, including the bloody battle of Malplaquet, where 36,000 men died.

After he became King he never went to war again; but expanding the army, and strictly controlling state finances to be able to keep expanding the army, became his obsessions. It is instructive how often those who condemned the father for wasting state revenues on architecture and entertainments admired the son for making strict economies so he could spend by the end of his reign *eighty* percent of the increased revenues on the army, up from Frederick's fifty.[263]

Frederick William loved soldiers:

"The most beautiful girl or woman in the world would be a matter of indifference to me, but soldiers: they are my weakness."

Not as a substitute – he fathered fourteen children – but as trophies. And his obsession with soldiers encompassed an even greater obsession: very

---

263   By comparison, in the United States in FY 2003, the year following the attack on the World Trade Centre, expenditure on defence (including homeland security) increased to approximately eighteen percent of the budget.

tall soldiers. He filled a special regiment with them, called the Giants' Guard, the Great Grenadiers, the Big Prussian Blues, the Potsdam Giants. Four thousand men over two metres tall, the front row those nearer three metres. As well as Germans of all persuasions, French, Italians, Spaniards, Portuguese, Hungarians, Serbs, Croats, Poles, Bohemians, English, Irish, Russians, Turks, Swedes, Danes, Ethiopians, "and other foreigners from Asia, Africa and America". They were of all classes, all religions (though about half Catholics, whom Frederick William singled out as trouble-makers), and all professions and none. Those from his own dominions were simply press-ganged; others came at a price: his son Frederick the Great said he could have sixteen infantry battalions for the cost of his father's Guards.

Some were bought in other countries – his ambassador in London paid the record price of a thousand pounds for an Irishman called James Kirkland; or were deployed by neighbouring monarchs in place of threats or diplomacy – England on one occasion sent a bribe of fifteen tall Irishmen, also press-ganged no doubt. Some were traded – for a hundred a year from Russia, Frederick William sent Peter the Great the famous Amber Room (still missing today since being stolen from the Catherine Palace outside St Petersburg by the Prussian Army's military descendants during World War II), plus Prussian drill-sergeants, probably the originators of the Russian army's continued disconcerting use of the goose step. When his father's foundation the University of Halle bravely protested against the abduction of a law student, the King curtly justified himself by citing the first Biblical Book of Samuel, chapter eight, on "the manner of the king that shall reign over you":

"And he will take…your goodliest young men, and your asses, and put them to his work".

He saw little difference.

Frederick has been regarded as responsible for Frederick William's obsession with the army, a reaction – a reasonable reaction, indeed a necessary reaction, depending on the standpoint – to his father's disgraceful, un-Prussian, frivolity. But his obsessive ruthlessness and outbursts of uncontrollable rage, his increasing derangement as he got older, were, it now seems, attributable to the genes he inherited from Sophie Charlotte. The Soldier King suffered from porphyria, the same disease descended from the Stuart line through the Electress Sophie that caused the "madness" of Frederick Williams' third cousin, King George III.

Perhaps it, as well as his gargantuan appetite – a hundred oysters at a sitting, for example – contributed to the grotesque bloated mass he became: by his death, at fifty-two, this stumpy man weighed a hundred and twenty-four kilograms; his waistline measured over two and a half *metres*.

He liked to be known as the Soldier King; Berliners called him the Drill Sergeant, or even Fatso, as they did the last boss of Prussia, Hermann Goering, two hundred years later. Frederick William was frequently incapacitated, and then liked to have the Potsdam Giants march through his sickroom for distraction. His eccentric behaviour affected his role as King, for all his increase of the Prussian army from thirty to eighty thousand men: late in his reign the French ambassador observed that

> "Thanks to his instability, the King of Prussia is neither useful to
> his friends nor dangerous to his enemies";

in England someone sneered that "he only acted the wolf in his own fold" – he was widely thought a coward because he never used that enormous army.

His successor, his son, did. As we saw earlier, the butt of his outbursts was frequently the boy and young man who was to become Frederick the Great, born, to his grandfather Frederick's great delight, in 1712, a year before his own death from the Ghost of the Hohenzollerns. The dynasty would continue; it was a bitter irony that he had not needed to marry the mad Sophie Louise after all. The baby was christened Charles Frederick – the first name perhaps for one of this good little Calvinist's godfathers, the Holy Roman Emperor Charles VI (another was Peter the Great) – but when he became King this savage critic of his grandfather Frederick and his French ways elected to be the second Frederick, and always referred to himself, in the French way, as *Frédéric*. German, he said, "compared unfavourably to the neighing of a horse".

Frederick II was to pick and choose amongst Frederick William's "Instructions for his Successor", laid down when he was still only ten. Not surprisingly, Frederick William had ruled out his own father's favourite pursuits, "operas, comedies, ballets, masquerades, mistresses, drinking and feasting [don't do as I do, do as I say], and other scandalous pursuits of the devil". But son Frederick's very first building as King was the wildly extravagant Opera House, the *Deutsche Staatsoper*, still on Unter Den Linden after being rebuilt in 1843, 1941 and again in 1955.

It opened in 1742 with a performance of *Cesare e Cleopatra*, an opera in the still-fashionable Italian style by Carl Heinrich Graum, with whom Frederick had been surreptitiously studying music behind Frederick William's back. Telemann's godson, Carl Philip Emannuel Bach, played harpsichord. Frederick was later to become infatuated by the house's star Italian dancer Barberina (sic), paying her three times as much as he paid his Ministers; the portrait of her that he had painted now hangs in his extension to Charlottenburg Palace.

But the part of Frederick William's "Instructions" that Fredrick II followed to the letter was what resulted in his being called Great:

> "Stamp into my son a true love for the profession of soldier; and impress upon him that as there is nothing in the world which can bring a prince renown and honour like the sword, so he would be a despised creature before all men if he did not love it and seek his sole glory therein".

Frederick did love it. He raised the army to 200,000 men; by the end of his reign it was remarked that "Prussia was not a country with an army, but an army with a country", and he had doubled the size of the country.

Prussia was well and truly on the march, the only set-back being Napoleon's invasion early in the new century, initially welcomed by the Berliners, who changed their minds when – as everywhere – he stole the city's treasures. Under Frederick the Great's impetus the city had become more consistently elegant – with "long stretches of uniform houses, the long wide streets", the revolutionary intellectual and poet Heinrich Heine noted, adding: "but with no care given to the opinion of the masses". The European-wide revolution against autocracy in 1848 lasted only twenty-four hours in Berlin, although more than two hundred and thirty of the masses were killed in one night's insurrection. Alexis de Tocqueville remarked that "There are no revolutions in Germany, because the police would not allow it". In 1866, under the ultra-royalist and ultra-nationalist Prince Otto von Bismarck, Prussia fulfilled Prince Eugene of Savoy's hundred and fifty year old premonition and decisively defeated Hapsburg Austria-Hungary: he would never, Bismarck said, allow Prussia to be destroyed "in a stinking brew of cosy southern German sentimentality". Using this clear lead and trumped up pretexts, Prussia went straight on to decisively defeat the French Second Empire, Bismarck then, in 1871, creating the German Empire...at Versailles.

From then on it was all downhill: the Reich's increasing belligerence under Kaiser William II – whose braying militarism, echoing Frederick William's mania, recalled Sophie Stuart's porphyrian genes – led, with the assistance of the stiff-necked and shortsighted leaders of the rest of Europe, to the bloodbath of the First World War. Then post-Hohenzollern Germany succumbed to Hitler and National Socialism, which led as soon as they could to the horrors of the Second World War and the Holocaust.

Was this the inevitable consequence of Prussia? In his thoughtful book on *Pietism and the Making of Eighteenth Century Prussia* the American historian Richard Gawthrop argues that

> "what galvanised Prussian society in the early eighteenth century..." – under Frederick William – "was an essentially cultural phenomenon: the propagation and pervasive acceptance of an ideology of unconditional service to the state. This Prussian ideology came, of course, to exercise a fateful fascination for the modern German intelligentsia and, to a considerable extent, the German people as a whole".

To the extent that his parents were responsible for Frederick William's character, Frederick, the least Prussian of the Hohenzollern rulers, and Sophie Charlotte, the most cultivated, have a lot to answer for.

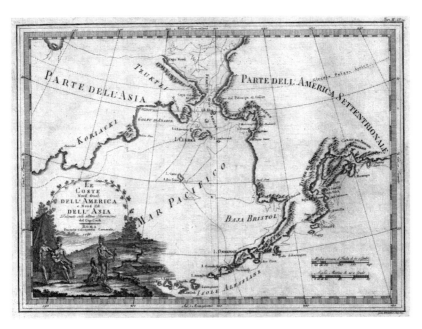

Le Coste Nord Ovest Dell' America e Nord Est Dell' Asia Delineate sulle
ultime Osservazioni del Cp. Cook (The North West Coast of America and
the North East of Asia according to the latest observations of Captain Cook),
Giovanni Maria Cassini. Wikimedia/http://www.geographicus.com/mm5/
cartographers/cassinigm.txt

AMERICA

JOHN LEDYARD:
TOO MUCH IMAGINATION

"The history of every country begins in
the heart of a man or woman."

Willa Cather: *O Pioneers!*

Over five and a half years in the United States, in the late 1950s and mid
1960s, I studied, at Princeton and Berkeley, worked, in New York, in
the Australian Mission to the United Nations, and travelled, almost
all over. Like everyone else alive at the time, I remember exactly where
I was when President Kennedy was shot early in my second American
stay. I remember the reports, also, when he told a gathering of Nobel
Prize-winners that they were the

> "most extraordinary collection of talent, of human knowledge,
> that has ever been gathered together at the White House, with the
> possible exception of when Thomas Jefferson dined alone".

And, like many, I made pilgrimages to Monticello, the elegant home in
Virginia that Jefferson designed, with its un-European charm, its clever
gadgets and conveniences, and its Indian (Native American) treasures
collected by the Lewis and Clark expedition he sent to explore the Pacific
Northwest.

I began this chapter by looking into the origins of the intensely
European-oriented Jefferson's interest in America's West. Then I
discovered John Ledyard, the first American to envisage trans-Pacific
trade from the fur-rich Northwest territory to the fabulous markets of
China. He had actually *been* to the Pacific Northwest – with the well
known navigator Captain James Cook. Later, after the failure of a joint
fur-trade venture with John Paul Jones, the naval hero of the new United

States' War of Independence, Ledyard turned to urging Jefferson, years before the Lewis and Clark expedition, to do something about securing the wealth of the Pacific Northwest territory, to compete with the British both in Canada and in China – and, two centuries before the Cold War, to beat the Russians at their own game. Jefferson was captivated, and, with total irresponsibility, sent Ledyard off ("with two shirts, and yet more shirts than shillings") to explore the Northwest – via Siberia! Poor Ledyard: this, like everything else he turned his hand to, turned out disastrously, usually through no fault of his own – he was a fore-doomed figure, who moved among and impressed and failed some of the leading lights of his time. Most often, himself.

Jefferson went on to buy Louisiana and send Lewis and Clark on their brilliant exploration. His actions inaugurated America's Pacific destiny, which would turn out to be of world-wide significance in relations between the West and Asia, if, at times, a poisoned chalice. That role was part of my studies at university in Adelaide at the time American diplomats were being persecuted by Senator Joseph McCarthy for having "lost" to the Communists a China America had never had in the first place, studies I resumed later at Princeton and Berkeley. Subsequently my diplomatic life included work in Phnom Penh and Saigon relating to the United States' involvement in Cambodia and Vietnam during the second Indochina War, and in the 1980s in Seoul, on a divided Korean peninsula whose southern half was still supported by the United States after three decades of shaky "armistice". And of course, even after the wars, after Mao Zedong, twenty years on, an isolationist, unpredictable and potentially nuclear North Korea, as well as the unresolved relationship between China and Taiwan, keep America involved in East Asian uncertainties, though in a role whose focus is now itself uncertain, diffused by greater attention to problems elsewhere.

Ledyard just wanted to be a trader: he could never have conceived of such imperial reach. But if you look at the map of the continental United States today, you might find it interesting to know how young John Ledyard of Connecticut was more than just present at the creation of that stretch from sea to shining sea.

21 February 1827. Johann Wolfgang Goethe was speaking to his faithful amanuensis, Eckermann, about Alexander von Humboldt's recent proposal for a canal between the Atlantic and the Pacific:

The principal people in this chapter are as follows:

- John Ledyard (1751-1789) – American adventurer and explorer with a fascination for the Pacific Northwest of America.

- Thomas Jefferson (1743-1826) – American statesman and architect. Draftsman of the US Declaration of Independence and third US President.

- Captain James Cook (1728-1779) – British naval captain, navigator and explorer.

- Joseph Billings (1758-1806) – British sailor and later officer and explorer with the Russian navy.

- Sir Joseph Banks (1743-1820) – British explorer, naturalist and president of the Royal Society.

"All this is reserved for the future and for an enterprising spirit. So much, however, is certain that, if they succeed in cutting such a canal that ships of any burden and size can be navigated through from the Mexican Gulf to the Pacific Ocean, innumerable benefits would result to the human race. But I should wonder if the United States were to let an opportunity of getting such a work into their own hands escape. It may be foreseen that this young state, with its decided predilection to the west, will in thirty or forty years have occupied and peopled the large tract of land beyond the Rocky Mountains. It may furthermore be foreseen that along the whole coast of the Pacific Ocean, where nature has already formed the most capacious and secure harbours, important commercial towns will gradually arise for the furtherance of a great intercourse between China and the East Indies and the United States...Would that I might live to see it! – but I shall not."

Goethe was right: he died five years later. But how could this German literary giant have made such an accurate forecast of the United States' Pacific destiny? The first overland trek by Americans to California had only taken place the year before his remarks; California only became part of the United States sixteen years later; the Panama Canal did not open to shipping until 1914. Of course, as Goethe said, he had the idea of the Canal from von Humboldt, whose warm admiration, when he became aware of it, he warmly reciprocated. But I suspect his view of the United States' Pacific future also came from von Humboldt, and that von Humboldt got it from Thomas Jefferson. And Jefferson got it from John Ledyard, an extraordinary ordinary seaman turned failed trade promoter.

Von Humboldt had made a remarkable voyage of exploration and scientific observation in Central and South America between 1799 and 1804; but although the idea of a sea route through the narrowest part of Central America was first raised early in Spanish colonial times, its reiteration was not one that von Humboldt put forward straight after his journey. However on his way back to Europe through the United States, von Humboldt, who was to become the most famous man in Germany in his time, asked to be presented to Thomas Jefferson, then President and the most famous man in America, as much for his learning as for his position. The introduction was made by Jefferson's friend Charles Willson Peale, the young country's most famous (if not best) portraitist and painter of the Revolution, and a distinguished naturalist and inventor, at both of which pursuits Jefferson on occasion collaborated. Von Humboldt and Jefferson instantly formed a close friendship based on mutual intellectual stimulation, a friendship which was maintained by letter – they never met again – for the remaining twenty–one years of Jefferson's life.

The new American empire

The President was fascinated and impressed by von Humboldt's Central and South American scientific explorations, and he had relevant news of his own to convey: as a vicarious explorer himself, he had just despatched, on 4 July 1804, an American expedition, led by his own former personal secretary, Meriwether Lewis, with William Clark, to

> "explore the Missouri river, such principal stream of it, as, by its course and communication with the waters of the Pacific ocean, whether the Columbia, Oregon, Colorado or any other river may offer the most direct practicable water communication across this continent for the purposes of commerce".

Jefferson's other piece of news, of which von Humboldt may or may not have heard in the depths of South America, was that the year before he had bought from Napoleon the whole of French (lately Spanish) Louisiana, the entire territory from the Mississippi to the Rocky Mountains.

That the native American inhabitants might see this overland imperialism on a continental scale as of a piece with the colonial subjection the new Republic had just overthrown seems not to have entered anyone's mind: the Indians would be blessed by United States citizenship and the benefits of civilisation. But the Louisiana Purchase was mainly part of Jefferson's vision of a nation not only secure from the Atlantic to the Pacific, but also with direct access from the latter to the still fabled East, with its great markets for selling the new republic's furs and for buying silks and spices, which would then no longer be prey to British malice on the seas. It was a remarkable vision for a man who never travelled westwards more than 60 kms from Monticello, his home in Virginia.

Before Jefferson went to Paris in 1784, where he succeeded Benjamin Franklin as Minister to crumbling Bourbon France, there seems little evidence that he had had any interest in China – other than the idea of a Chinese roof (if it were not to be a Grecian one) on a temple in a romantic family burial ground about which he had fantasised many years before, following the death of his favourite sister. Jefferson had been occupied with founding the United States of America; but he had also begun what was to be his remarkable involvement with the American West.

Franklin, active in Philadelphia and national liberation politics for thirty years, and also a founder of the United States, had been sent by Pennsylvania to London in 1764 to protest against the British Parliament's decision, that same year, to tax the American colonies without their being consulted. This was not the beginning of the deterioration of relations with George III's England: it was the beginning of the end. Receiving no satisfaction to their arguments, His Majesty's increasingly disloyal subjects in the thirteen colonies in due course plunged into armed revolution, in 1775; adopted the Declaration of Independence, initially drafted by Jefferson, in 1776; were recognised in 1778 as an independent country by France, which was England's opponent, and Holland, which was sometimes not; finally forced the British forces to surrender in 1781; and secured British recognition of their independence in 1783. Jefferson was prominently involved in aspects of these developments, which seem to make an inevitable progression when viewed in retrospective summary, but which were anything but at the time. Franklin was one of the principal peacemakers on the American side; shortly after the Treaty of Peace was signed he expressed, to his friend Sir Joseph

Banks in ex–enemy England, one of the most notable of his innumerable aphorisms:

"In my opinion, there never was a good war or a bad peace".

Ironically, twenty years earlier when Franklin had had an interest in companies seeking land grants along the Ohio River, he had apostrophised the role the expansion westwards of the North American colonies could play in developing…British power. Henry Nash Smith quotes one of Franklin's "rare moments of enthusiasm":

"What an Accession of Power to the *British* Empire by Sea as well as Land! What Increase of Trade and Navigation! What Numbers of Ships and Seamen!"

Five years before the Declaration of Independence, two members of the graduating class of the College of New Jersey (Princeton), Philip Freneau and Hugh Brackenridge, wrote *The Rising Glory of America* to expand the vision well beyond the Ohio:[264]

> "Say, shall we ask what empires yet must rise,
> What kingdoms, pow'rs and states where now are seen
> But dreary wastes and awful solitude,
> Where melancholy sits with eye forlorn
> And hopes the day when Britain's sons shall spread,
> Dominion to the north and south and west
> Far from th' Atlantic to Pacific shores?"

But, Smith wryly notes,

"In 1771 the vision was ambiguous: the question of whether Britain's sons on the Pacific shore would be loyal subjects of the crown was left tactfully vague".

---

264 Freneau's passion for westward expansion led him subsequently to celebrate the Mississippi, "this prince of rivers, in comparison of whom the Nile is but a Rivulet and the Danube a mere ditch". At Princeton, Freneau, later known as "the Poet of the Revolution", was the room–mate of James Madison, who became Jefferson's closest political ally, his Secretary of State and then his successor as fourth President of the United States.

However the idea of a *new* empire in America was already half a century old: George Berkeley, Irish, Anglican and philosopher, had spent the years 1728 to 1731 in Rhode Island, waiting for funds, which never eventuated, to found a college in Bermuda – for some reason – to promote "the propagation of the Gospel among the American savages"; and while there he had penned *Verses on the Prospect of Planting Arts and Learning in America* –

> "The Muse, disgusted in an age and clime,
> Barren of every glorious theme,
> In distant lands now waits a better time,
> Producing subjects worthy fame...
>
> There shall be sung another golden age,
> The rise of empire and of arts,
> The good and great inspiring epic rage,
> The wisest heads and noblest hearts...
>
> Westward the course of empire takes its way;
> The first four acts already past,
> A fifth shall close the drama with the day;
> Time's noblest offspring is the last."

The four previous empires were Greece, Rome, France and Spain; the fifth would be for him, as for the early Franklin, *Britain–in–America*. As it turned out, of course, Britain's empire still had quite a course to run even *minus* America; but it too would eventually fall, though it would indeed be replaced by its American offspring, in a way that the Bishop could not have conceived of. For a long time many people would agree with the Founding Fathers of the United States of America that this new republic was "Time's noblest offspring", not least for the ideas, put forward by Thomas Jefferson, which *The Declaration of Independence* rang around the world:

> "We hold these truths to be self–evident, that all men are created equal, that they are endowed by their Creator with certain inalienable rights, that among these are life, liberty and the pursuit of happiness".

But would Time's noblest offspring be the last? In October 1755 John Adams, who would become Jefferson's great friend, rival and predecessor as President, had been even more sanguine than Franklin about the transfer from Britain of "the great seat of Empire into America". But Adams, with his typical cold–eyed view of history, would apply to the United States as well his conviction that when great nations reached

> "the summit of Grandeur, some minute and unsuspected Cause commonly effects their Ruin, and the Empire of the world is transferr'd to some other place":

towards the end of his days, seventy years later, he would give the new American republic's cycle as between (at his most gloomy) twenty years and (on what Ellis calls "a more buoyant occasion") a hundred and fifty. Adams' hundred and fifty years from the Declaration of American Independence were up just before World War II brought on the greatest extension of American power; within the next fifty years it had outlasted its greatest rival, the Soviet Union. How long would Adams have given now?

Thomas Jefferson looks West

Notwithstanding his cyclical view of history, throughout his political career John Adams fought to ensure that the executive branch of the new federal government would have sufficient power not merely to hold the republic together against the fissiparous tendencies of the states, reflected in Congress, but also to be able to pursue desirable national objectives. The great irony is that it was Thomas Jefferson, consistently opposing to Adams's vision the desirability of a federal executive with minimal authority – preferably confined exclusively to external affairs – who was responsible, without bothering to consult Congress, for the greatest increase in the nation's territory in its history, over which the federal government held complete power.

The first sign of Jefferson's interest in the West came very soon after the end of the Revolutionary War in 1783. He had been excited by the first news of the success in June that year of the Montgolfier brothers' manned hot–air balloon flight in France, though not as excitable as the French poet who wrote:

> "Cook marche aux fonds des mers. Montgolfier vole aux Cieux;
> Ouvrez–moi les Enfers, j'éteindrai les feux!"
> (Cook goes to the ends of the seas. Montgolfier soars to the Heavens.
> Open up Hell for me, I will put out its fires!)

Fascinated as usual by scientific advances, Jefferson immediately speculated, rather, on the balloon's possible practical uses:

> "Traversing deserts, countries possessed by an enemy, or ravaged by infectious disorders, pathless and inaccessible mountains; the discovery of the Pole which is but one day's journey in a balloon, from where the ice has hitherto stopped adventurers".

Captain Cook would have appreciated that day's journey to the Pole, as we shall see.

In December Jefferson for the first time raised the future of the West, almost as a throwaway in a letter to his friend George Rogers Clark, who had ousted the British from the area of Ohio early in the Revolution and then been made a general in Virginia:

> "I find they have subscribed a very large sum of money in England for exploring the country from the Mississippi to California. They pretend it is only to promote knowledge. I am afraid they have thoughts of colonising into that quarter. Some of us have been talking here in a feeble way of making the attempt to search that country, but I doubt whether we have enough of that kind of spirit to raise the money. How would you like to lead such a party? "Though I am afraid our prospect is not worth asking the question."

No suggestion of a balloon. And although Clark responded positively and constructively:

> "It is what I think we ought to do...[But] large parties will never answer the purpose. They will allarm the Indian Nations they pass through. Three or four young Men well qualified for the Task might perhaps compleat your wishes at a very Trifling Expence,"

no more is heard: for once suspicion of the British was unfounded, and Jefferson had more pressing things to do. But Jefferson's concern with Western exploration would revive within two years, in Paris of all places; and, with nice symmetry, when President Jefferson two decades later decide to send the first overland American expedition to the Pacific Northwest, Meriwether Lewis, its leader, would invite Clark's younger brother William to be his co–commander.

Within two months of his letter to General Clark, Jefferson was already taking his first practical step for the future of the West. He had returned to the Continental Congress, after being Governor of Virginia through some of the most difficult years of the War of Independence – much of which was fought in his own state – to join the great sequel to the War, the establishment of a functioning democratic federation. It was in the Congress, early in 1784, that Jefferson drafted an ordinance for the government of what was then called the Northwest Territory, between the Ohio and Mississippi Rivers; and the draft became the basis for the Ordinance of 1787 which set the terms for the creation of new Western Territories and for their subsequent admission into the Union as states, with the remarkable requirements that they should be self-governing throughout the process, which was observed, and that they should not permit slavery, which was not. At the time, the American frontier was still not much further west than the Appalachian Mountains. In due course, the very idea of the Frontier would be the motor for the expansion of the United States the entire way to the Pacific Ocean; Jefferson's ideas underlying the Ordinance would be the mechanism and the democratic underpinning.

John Ledyard, "America's Marco Polo"

General Clark had suggested that "three or four young Men well qualified for the Task" might explore beyond the Mississippi. But just one? It was in 1786, during Jefferson's service as American representative in Paris during the last five years of France's *ancien régime,* that he met the man who projected his thoughts about the American West well beyond the Mississippi – in fact all the way to the Pacific, and beyond, to the markets of China. This was John Ledyard. The man called by his contemporaries "America's Marco Polo" and "the Great American Traveler" was also the Great American Talker; but events, and perhaps his own immoderate imagination, kept conspiring against his becoming the Great American Achiever.

It is a pity Ledyard appears so rarely and even then so little in the history books, presumably because the historians have tended to focus on those who succeeded rather than on those whose failures became tragicomical. But, between the disasters, a picture emerges – from Ledyard's own writings,[265] from the biography published in Boston

---

265 These are *John Ledyard's Journal of Captain Cook's Last Voyage* (first published 1783; ed. JK Munford 1963) and *John Ledyard's Journey Through*

in 1828 by the Reverend Jared Sparks, based on material from and interviews with Ledyard's family and acquaintances (including Thomas Jefferson, whom Sparks travelled to Monticello to see not long before his death), as well as from Jefferson's letters to, from and about Ledyard – of a man with a remarkable vision and a remarkable influence on Jefferson himself. He came to it by luck – inasmuch as becoming possessed by an obsession can be considered luck.

Ledyard, who was born in 1751 at Groton, Connecticut, began this precarious progress at Dartmouth College, in New Hampshire. Jared Sparks, who talked with members of Ledyard's family when compiling his biography, said that his mother had

> "felt a strong compassion for the deplorable state of the Indians, and it was among her earliest and fondest hopes of this her favourite son, that he would be educated as a missionary, and become an approved instrument in the hands of Providence to bring these degraded and suffering heathen to a knowledge of pure religion, and the blessings of civilised life".

But while the 21–year–old Ledyard was enrolled for this purpose in the new college in 1772, his focus was not entirely in the right direction: he submitted a petition for

> "having Liberty allowed us by our Worthy and ever dear President to spend certain leisure hours allotted to us for the relaxation of our minds, in such sort as stepping the Minuet and learning to use the Sword".

Helen Augur found among the Ledyard papers descriptions recorded years later by some of his college contemporaries, and notes that "they all used the same word: singular":

Russia and Siberia 1787–1788 (first published 1966, ed. SD Watrous); the latter also contains previously unpublished letters, and others are cited in Helen Augur's *Passage to Glory*. I have retained Ledyard's orthography as it appeared in his journals and letters, as it gives a wonderfully colourful impression of the reach of his intellect, despite a nugatory formal education. And I have done likewise for others: even Jefferson had not fixed on a consistent system of spelling, capitalisation or punctuation.

"As a scholar he was respectable", said one, "though he did not excel. He was gentlemanly, and showed an independence and singularity in his manners, his dress and appearance". And another: "He was of middling stature, rather thickset. His hair was white, not of the silvery cast as it commonly is when the effect of age, but of a slight yellow tinge. His manners were singular".

Augur commented that the

"really singular thing about Ledyard is his modernity. He wore his clothes and his manners in the same way, easily".

But perhaps another Dartmouth friend put his finger on the essence of Ledyard:

"He was a Locomotive Machine".

In fact it rapidly became clear that it was the life of the Indians – as Native Americans were of course then called, the result of Columbus's mistake about where he had arrived in 1492 – that was much more attractive to him than the life of a missionary. Hating the discipline of the college, he frequently disappeared to live with neighbouring Iroquois Indians, part of the confederacy across the northern parts of the the American colonies which had been allied with the British against French pressure southwards from Canada during the French and Indian Wars, in which France had finally lost Canada only nine years before, in 1763. His uncle, Thomas Seymour, later observed that in the times spent with the Indians Ledyard

"acquired a tincture of the language manners of the Natives of the forrest".

In fact he acquired a good deal more. The experience gave him a sympathetic and uncondescending interest in all native peoples, wherever he found them in his extraordinary travels, in sharp contrast with the accepted contemporary attitudes reflected by his mother. And it resulted in his eventual conviction – as he wrote to Jefferson in 1788, the last year of his life – that

"the great general analogy in the customs of Men can only be accounted for but by supposing them all to compose one family".

More immediately, his escapades with the Iroquois surely must also have contributed to his ability to convert a seventeen metre tree, in the neighbouring woods, into a canoe. In 1773 he used it to escape from academia, forever, down the Connecticut River; he told Jefferson fourteen years later, in Paris, that he had taken two of his school–books with him, a Greek New Testament and Ovid, and had narrowly avoided catastrophe in Below's Falls rapids because he was reading one of them.

He next made desultory attempts to become a clergyman, with no study and not much more faith; but his potential sponsors required "a regular dismission" from the President of Dartmouth, and Ledyard wrote:

> "The clergy are very exact in these things, and I have sometimes thought that they meant to keep me humming around them till I was tired, and so get clear of an absolute refusal, or, as Dr Young expresses it, to –
>
> > 'Fright me, with terrors of a world unknown,
> > From joys of this, to keep them all their own' ".

Within the year, the improbable life of an ecclesiastic forever behind him, he had entered on his true career as a rolling stone: he decided to sail even further than Connecticut, as an ordinary seaman on a New London ship captained by a friend of his father. It was going to the Barbary Coast, as North Africa was then known, still sixty years before the French began their conquests there, to pick up a cargo of mules. In Gibraltar, on the way, and on the spur of the moment, he joined the British Army, with what intentions or blandishments is now unknown; but he was rescued by his captain. It was only another two years until the British Army would be fighting his fellow Americans yearning to be free. While in Gibraltar he wrote his family that

> "I allot to myself a seven years' ramble more, although the past has long since wasted the means I possessed".

In truth, he had never possessed any means, and his "rambling" over the next fourteen years would also mostly be undertaken without means either. But somehow he always managed to make do.

To the Pacific with Captain Cook

Ledyard's luck turned for the first time two years later, in England. Almost immediately after his return from Gibraltar he had re–crossed the Atlantic to Bristol to seek his fortunes with – or at least support from – supposedly wealthy Ledyard relatives in England. They knew nothing of him, but offered to look into his claim; but, Sparkes says, "his own haughty spirit seems to have been the chief enemy to his success". Back in Bristol, no doubt flat broke, he had his next encounter with the British Army, described in 1783 in his "Memorial to the Connecticut Assembly" (written in the third person):

> "he was however so unfortunate then as to be apprehended by a kind of police in that city who obliged him either to ship himself for the coast of Guinea or to enter the British Army. Your memorialist, young, inexperienced destitute of friends, chose the latter as the least of two evils".

This is all rather mysterious. These were the times of the infamous naval press–gangs, but they would not have given Ledyard a choice, much less one of entry into the Army. The Guinea coast suggests slave-trading, in which Bristol was still deeply involved; but what slaver able to hijack a fit, destitute, unconnected young man would have offered him an alternative career?

Was, rather, Ledyard memorialising something else entirely? He went on:

> "He continued in the Army until early in the year 1775 when he was ordered to Boston in New England: to this your memorialist objected being himself a native of that country desired he might be appointed to some other duty, which ultimately was granted: matters continued thus until July 1776 when the equipment for discovery [the ships for Cook's third voyage] came round from London to Plymouth your memorialist esteeming this a favourable conjuncture to free himself forever from coming to America as her enemy prompted also by curiosity disinterested enterprise embarked in that expedition".

There we have it: service in the British armed forces during the War of Independence had to be explained away somehow; and, back in America in 1783, seeking support for the publication of his account of Cook's voyage, Ledyard was doing it by a mixture of obfuscation and lies. He even managed, posthumously, to confuse Jared Sparks, who thought he joined the Marines "as a first step towards becoming connected with [Cook's] expedition". But Sinclair Hitchings (who wrote the introduction to Munford's edition of Ledyard's journal of Cook's voyage) discovered in the Royal Marine archives that Ledyard was enlisted as a corporal in the 24th Company of Marines, Plymouth Division, on 15 July *1775*. Cook only returned from his second voyage fifteen days *after* that, on 30 July. A third voyage was being mooted in the Admiralty, but no decision had yet been taken; Cook would only be appointed to command the following January. John Ledyard was a Royal Marine long before his "curiosity and disinterested enterprise" drew him to the more neutral expedition of the great Captain Cook.

Various parts of Ledyard's account remain unravelable. What did he do between his rejection by – or rejection of – the English relatives in the second half of 1774 and joining the Marines in July 1775? Perhaps he was indeed in the British Army, but was he really press–ganged into it? – he had already tried once, in Gibraltar, to join up, presumably because it appealed to his sense of adventure. On what grounds he would have persuaded the Army to release him to the Navy is unknown, though possibly such prior experience would account for his enrolment in the Marines as a corporal. Perhaps another example of the Great Talker; but in any event the move still left him in the way of "coming to America as her enemy".

And did he, as he claimed, seek out Cook to persuade him to take him on the third expedition? If so it is unlikely to have been in Plymouth: Cook's ship, the *Resolution*, on which Ledyard sailed, only reached Plymouth on 30 June 1776, for a twelve–day layover, during which the Marine contingent, already including Ledyard, was taken on board. It was a family tradition that Ledyard had in fact gone up to London not long after the announcement of Cook's appointment, and sought him out in his lodgings to persuade him of his, Ledyard's, potential value to the expedition. Ledyard was certainly never backwards about making such approaches. It is generally said that Cook was impressed by Ledyard's handsome, vigorous appearance and his keen adventurousness; but, while those attributes would no doubt have helped Ledyard's cause, it seems likely, if the meeting did indeed take place, that it would have been something else entirely which persuaded the great explorer of his possible usefulness.

As noted earlier, even before Cook's return in July 1775 from his second voyage – in the South Pacific, like the first – the British authorities were deciding to send a further expedition, but this time to the North Pacific. The intention would be to search for "a Communication between the Atlantic and Pacific Oceans", the legendary Northwest Passage which was believed to link the two oceans and provide a more direct route from Europe to China and the East Indies than those around the Cape of Good Hope at the bottom of Africa, then in sometimes hostile Dutch hands, or Cape Horn at the bottom of South America, a continent, apart from Portugal's Brazil, controlled in its entirety by almost always hostile Spain.

The search for a Northwest Passage starting from the North Atlantic Ocean was already almost three hundred years old, having begun within a decade of Columbus's discovery of the West Indies, which he was convinced were the East, and had been searched for, always unsuccessfully, ever since. In January 1776 the Government made the decision to try again to find the Northwest Passage, this time starting from the North Pacific and going eastwards; failing that, the expedition was to try to sail westwards around the top of Siberia. To the Admiralty's surprise, but probably relief, Cook volunteered to set sail again, only seven months after his return from his second voyage.

It is likely that Ledyard would have joined an expedition to anywhere, but the prospect of visiting the Pacific Northwest of North America, which Cook was instructed to explore, was undoubtedly a special lure. Ledyard, better than the Admiralty, could have envisioned the likelihood of finding there Indians such as those he had come to know so well in Vermont. For his part, Cook would have surely welcomed this young American frontiersman's knowledge of the Indians, part of his instructions for the voyage being explicitly to cultivate friendship with whatever "natives" the expedition might encounter. That the Indians of Vermont in the American northeast and those on the Pacific coast in the northwest were 4,000 kms apart would not have daunted Ledyard, as we shall see; but in any case, it would not necessarily have been daunting to Cook either, at a time when the possibility was still imagined of a short route connecting Canada's Baffin Bay, which was known but not yet fully explored, to the Pacific coast, which was still scarcely known to the British, though grandly called "New Albion" on their maps.

In addition, Cook's voyage was to be not only imperial, to take "possession of any uninhabited places in the name of His Majesty", but also intended to increase English commerce, through the invaluable Northwest Passage that it was hoped his explorations would finally reveal. As proof, the Government offered £20,000 to the ship's company which found it (an added inducement to the ever financially strapped Cook to volunteer), and a further £5,000 for the sheer British vainglory of getting to within 1° of the North Pole. In these circumstances, Cook, who had never met an American Indian, may well have asked the young New Englander whether the "natives" had anything to trade; and Ledyard's answer would almost certainly have been, even if he had never considered the question before: furs and skins. Perhaps it was then, at that interview with the great Englishman who had to imagine possible sea routes and landfalls before he set out to explore them, that Ledyard first imagined a fur trade from Northwest America to China. It was an idea that was to obsess him all his life.

Cook's *Resolution* and the companion ship *Discovery* got away from England on 13 July 1776. It was already fifteen months since the outbreak of the American colonies' hostilities with Britain with "the shot heard round the world" at Lexington/Concord, Massachusetts, on 19 April 1775, at the beginning of the American Revolution, but only nine days since the adoption of Jefferson's Declaration of Independence. This decisive development was of course still unknown in England, but as the expedition was leaving Plymouth Sound they passed a convoy of ships carrying troops to fight in what was to be a long and bitter war. The editor of Cook's published Journal added a sombre reflection on this coincidence:

> "It could not but occur to us as a singular and affecting circumstance that at the very instant of our departure upon a voyage, the object of which was to benefit Europe by making fresh discoveries in North America, there should be the unhappy necessity of employing others of his Majesty's ships, and of conveying numerous bodies of land forces, to secure the obedience of those parts of that continent which had been discovered and settled by our countrymen in the last century".

We do not know what Ledyard was thinking.

Fellow travellers

Ledyard was in fact one of seven Americans on the voyage; none seems to have experienced any difficulties for being so, despite the outbreak of war. The most prominent was Cook's second–in–command on the *Resolution*, the enormously experienced New York–born Lieutenant John Gore, brought to England at the age of three, and in the Royal

Navy since before the Seven Years War. He had circumnavigated the world no fewer than three times, first with John ("Foulweather Jack") Byron, the poet's grandfather, in 1764–66; then with Samuel Wallis in 1766–68, when they were the first Europeans to find Tahiti; and then in 1768–71 on Cook's first voyage, in the *Endeavour*, during which Eastern Australia was first discovered by a European. Through the successive deaths of Cook and Clerke, the captain of the *Discovery*, this third expedition to the Pacific would return home under Gore's command.

Before that return over four years later, in October 1780, the fortunes of the Americans' nine–day–old country would have fluctuated violently, the outcome still far from certain. While the *Resolution* was still in the Atlantic, in the second half of 1776, Long Island was lost to the British, then, three months later, Manhattan; but over Christmas and New Year, while the expedition was at the bleak Sub–Antarctic island of Kerguelen, Washington made his famous crossing of the Delaware and restored American hopes with victories in the battles of Trenton and Princeton. In the meantime the Continental Congress, seeking legitimacy and support for the independent colonies, had appointed Benjamin Franklin, Thomas Jefferson (later replaced) and Silas Deane to negotiate treaties of friendship and commerce with European states, starting with France. And a month later, in October 1776, in the area towards which Cook was eventually heading, the Spanish had founded on the California coast a little settlement which was to become San Francisco.

The twenty–five–year–old Ledyard had other interesting shipmates, many also still young: the *Resolution*'s sailing master, the not yet notorious William Bligh, who was twenty–two and already a ten–year veteran of three navy ships; and Midshipman George Vancouver, nineteen, who often teamed up with Ledyard for shoreside adventuring – he had already sailed on Cook's second voyage at the age of fifteen, and would go on in his own great voyage in 1792–4 to thoroughly explore Canada's Pacific coastline. There was also James (Jem) Burney, twenty–five, the future novelist Fanny's brother, and the only one of the group to reach the rank of admiral; he had also been on the second voyage, and was now second–in–command of the *Discovery*; his father, a distinguished musician and musicologist, would have dealings with Thomas Jefferson – and Joseph Haydn – in years to come.

And there were the sixteen–year–old Midshipman James Trevenen, just graduated from the naval academy at Portsmouth, and Able Seaman Joseph Billings, about two years older, who shipped on the *Discovery* but was transferred after Cook's death to the *Resolution*: both, like Ledyard, would eventually make their way to Russia; and Billings would play a role, and perhaps a sinister one, in Ledyard's greatest (and penultimate) adventure, in the depths of Siberia. Unfortunately the voyage missed out on one notable: James Boswell, Dr Johnson's biographer, who was tempted by the position of official expedition historian, but decided to stay in Edinburgh lawyering, politicking, drinking, writing and womanising.

Not the least interesting of Ledyard's sailing companions was Omai, a Tahitian who had been taken by Tobias Furneaux, the unsatisfactory commander of the second ship on Cook's second voyage, to England, where for two years he had become a celebrity as "The Noble Savage". He impressed Dr Johnson, so James Boswell recorded, with "the elegance of his behaviour", and provided the great man with the opportunity he could never resist of scoring a point off the aristocracy:

"Lord Mulgrave and [Omai] dined one day at Streathem; they sat with their backs to the light fronting me, so that I could not see distinctly; and there was so little of the savage in Omai, that I was afraid to speak to either, lest I should mistake one for the other".

Omai succeeded in London society despite the fact, or perhaps because, he addressed George III as "King Tosh".

But he had, not surprisingly, become "spoiled"; perhaps, more accurately, he was confused by his role as a cultural amusement. His wearied guardian, Sir Joseph Banks, arranged for Cook to take him back to Tahiti, armed with the gift of a sword from Banks himself, a suit of armour from Banks's friend and Cook's political master, the Earl of Sandwich,[266] First Lord of the Admiralty, and what Ledyard, who must have seen a lot of him shipboard, described as a "proud, empty, ambitious heart". The editor of *The Gentleman's Magazine*, an influential London journal of opinion with which Samuel Johnson had earlier been associated, summarised the whole episode:

"I might add to all the cruelties of discovery that of transporting a simple barbarian to a christian and civilised country, to debase him into a spectacle and a maccaroni, and to invigorate the seeds of corrupted nature by a course of improved debauchery, and then

---

266   i.e. Navy Minister. It was he who was said to have invented the snack that bears his name, to eat at the gaming table.

to send him back, if he survives the contagion of English vices, to revenge himself on his enemies, and to die".

During his stay in England, Omai's involuntary role as a Noble Savage had also been seized on by critics of the standards and behaviour of the day, a clear echo of the view which Jean–Jacques Rousseau had been propounding so forcefully. The most scathing example, Bernard Smith recounts, was an anonymous poem, published in 1775, entitled *An Historic Epistle, from Omiah to the Queen of Otaheite; being his Remarks on the English Nation*, in which the rich and fashionable are denounced:

> "Can *Europe* boast, with all her pilfer'd wealth,
> A larger store of happiness, or health?";

and the Church, both Established and Evangelical:

> "Here bloated bishops loll in purple coach,
> On turtle dine and luxuries reproach...
> Whilst hackney curates starving on the town,
> *Retail* divinity for half a crown...
> Heav'n has no room, but merely to contain
> A cassockt, canting, methodistic train";

and, finally, the imperialist designs of Britain and its European contemporaries, which

> "...in cold blood premeditately go
> To murder wretches whom they cannot know.
> Urg'd by no inj'ry, prompted by no ill,
> In forms they butcher, and by systems kill;
> Cross o'er the seas, to ravage distant realms,
> And ruin thousands worthier than themselves".

Omai had in fact hugely enjoyed the attentions of the cream of Church and Society; and would undoubtedly have been far too polite to have denounced the British Government's ambitions in terms such as these even had he thought that way, of which there is no evidence. But it was a cry which was well–founded, and resolutely not heard either in the colonies Britain was just about to lose in America or in the Empire it was about to create in Canada, India, Australia, New Zealand, South Africa and in due course, with other Europeans, other empires around the entire globe.

Just over two centuries later Omai came back into the limelight when his portrait was sold. It is by Sir Joshua Reynolds, who was then painting everyone who was anyone: Omai stands in a noble pose, strikingly handsome, looking, in white robes and flowing turban, something like a cross between a Roman and a Turk. First exhibited at the Royal Academy in 1776, the painting was kept by Reynolds until his death in 1792; at the subsequent sale of his effects in 1796 it was sold to a dealer for 100 guineas, then to Byron's second cousin the 5th Earl of Carlisle [267] (whom Reynolds painted three times) of Castle Howard, where it hung until sold by the estate at Sothebys in November 2001 for more than £10 million.[268]

---

267 Carlisle had been one of the British Peace Commissioners sent by Lord North in 1778 to negotiate with the American revolutionaries, but the gap was too wide, and they left after six months; Carlisle meanwhile had managed to provoke Lafayette, who had arrived in America the previous year, into challenging him to a duel. There was no love lost between Carlisle and his cousin either: Carlisle dabbled in poetry, and Byron commented, in *English Bards and Scotch Reviewers,*

> "No muse will cheer, with renovating smile,
> The paralytic puling of Carlisle.
> The puny schoolboy and his early lay
> Men pardon, if his follies pass away;
> But who forgives the senior's ceaseless verse,
> Whose hairs grow hoary as his rhymes grow worse?"
> Byron later apologised: not personally – in verse.

268 £10,343,500, to be precise. The British Government subsequently put a stop on its export, pending efforts by the Tate Gallery to purchase it, aided in March 2003 by the anonymous donation of £12.5 million. As of late 2005 the matter had apparently still not been resolved. Another portrait of Omai, by William Parry, showing him standing with Sir Joseph Banks and Daniel Solander, the Swedish naturalist and pupil of the great Linnaeus, who had accompanied Banks on Cook's first voyage, came on to the market just after the Reynolds, and was sold to an "overseas gallery" for £1.8 million. It too was barred from export, and in 2003 was secured jointly by the British National Portrait Gallery, the Captain Cook Memorial Museum at Whitby, and "another institution".

To complete the two ships' complement there was a whole menagerie:

> "four horses, six horned cattle, a number of sheep and goats, hogs,
> dogs and cats, besides, hares, rabbits and monkeys, ducks, geese,
> turkies and peacocks; thus", Ledyard wrote, "did we resemble the
> Ark, and appear as though we were going as well to stock, as to
> discover a new world".

The whole lot was presented by George III, for the purpose of
providing his anticipated new subjects in Tahiti with a better diet,
an improved landscape, and an alternative occupation to fighting
bloody civil wars. Despite his little overcrowded ship – a mere 340
tons – Cook could scarcely refuse this misguided philanthropy from
"Farmer George".

Cook and Ledyard in the Pacific

Cook's third voyage was not, of course, successful in achieving its main
objective, and it ended in disaster. He himself had neglected to oversee
the *Resolution*'s fitting out; he was fitful in pursuing the expedition's
timetable; and he seems at times to have had strange, savage mood
swings. He flew into periodic rages with members of his crews; and to
the natives with whom he was supposed to cultivate friendship he was
bafflingly inconsistent, taking their leaders hostage to recover stolen
property, then offering gifts and musical entertainments. And he ordered
frequent and at times horrifying beatings and reprisals, in Tonga, Tahiti
– where the now thoroughly deracinated and disoriented Omai was
returned to live, for a short unhappy time, among his baffled countrymen
– and Hawaii, where they were the first Europeans ever to visit, and
where Cook's intemperate moods eventually contributed to his doom.
Ledyard remarked in his account of the voyage:

> "It must be remembered that the ability of performing the important
> errand before us, depended very much, if not entirely, upon the
> precarious supplies we might procure from these and other such
> islands, and he [Cook] must of consequence be very anxious and
> solicitous in this concernment; but perhaps no consideration will
> excuse the severity which he sometime used towards the natives
> on these occasions; and he would probably have done better to
> consider, that the full exertion of extreme power is an argument
> of extreme weakness; and nature seemed to inform the insulted

natives of the truth of this maxim by the manifestation of their subsequent resentments...".

Ledyard was subsequently attacked for criticising the great explorer, but in fact his remarks were quite circumspect: Midshipman George Gilbert, who greatly admired Cook, wrote in his diary at Tongatapu (the main island of the Friendly Islands, the Tonga group):

> "This [thieving] which is very prevalent here, Captain Cook punished in a manner rather unbecoming of a European, viz by cutting off their ears, firing at them with small shot, or ball, as they were swimming or paddling to the shore; and suffering the people as he rowed after them to beat them with the oars, and stick the boat hook into them".

But Gilbert did not publish.

Ledyard was consistently understanding of the Pacific islanders, or "Indians" as he sometimes referred to them. (He was later to refer equally impartially to the very mixed inhabitants of Siberia and Alaska as "Tartars". These terms represented in a way a shorthand version of his belief in the unity of the human race.) The only exception to his warmly responsive approach to the local inhabitants occurred in Van Dieman's Land (now Tasmania):

> "I cannot but remark the disparity which is so obvious, between a noble country and its ignoble inhabitants...[The Van Dieman's Land native] is a mere savage, nay more he possesses the lowest rank even in this class of beings – at least those I saw to the southward were such. They are the only people who are known to go with their persons entirely naked that have even yet been discovered. Amidst the most stately groves of wood they have neither weapons of defence, or any other instruments applicable to any other of the various purposes of life; contageous to sea they have no canoes and exposed from the nature of the climate to the natural inclemencies of the seasons as well as from the annoyances of the beasts of the forest they have no houses to retire to, but the temporary shelter of a few pieces of old bark laid transversely over some small poles: They appear also to be inactive, indolent and unaffected with the least appearance of curiosity, they are of a middling stature, but indifferent in their persons, of a dark

complexion bordering on black, their hair a little wooly, their features discordant and without any kind of ornament or dress".

The *Resolution* was only in Tasmania for the last six days of January 1777, the first watering stop after Capetown; but where others merely remarked on the Aborigines' listlessness and passivity, and diet apparently solely of crustaceans, Ledyard's reaction was uncharacteristically harsh. The thought did not occur to him that these Tasmanians did not have clothing or shelter as they did not need them, or that they could obtain enough to eat without having to put to sea. Ledyard was undoubtedly comparing them with New England Indians who had developed quite differently over the millennia. In Tasmania he was disappointed of his usual image of the "noble savage".

His response shortly afterwards to the people of Tongatapu was strikingly different:

> "The inhabitants like those of the other inhabited islands we visited in its neighbourhood are a very fine people, exceeding in beauty, in stature, strength, and the improvements of their mental capacities any of the great variety of people among the islands scattered throughout this ocean...The pains they have taken to clear up the woods when we consider the disadvantages they must have labored under for want of husbandry implements, is astonishing, and as strong a proof of their unlimited industry, as the elegance in which they have laid it out and otherwise improved it, is of their rural taste and good judgment".

It was in Tongatapu also that Ledyard's instinctive sympathy for the "native" shone through in an extraordinarily modern way. The "pilfering disposition of the inhabitants" had caused the usual difficulties; two "noble Indians" had rendered "particular assistance" in resolving them; but

> "notwithstanding this general attachment to our interest and friendship, which did them so much honour, and us so much essential service, they sometimes fell into temptation themselves and did as the others did".

Ledyard went immediately on, in relation to one of the two chiefs:

> "How often, Phenow, have I felt for thee, the embarrassments of these involuntary offences against a people thou didst as well love

and wouldst as soon have befriended when thou wast accused and stood condemned as when not, and at that instant would most willingly have shared with thee those distresses which resulted only from imputed guilt and a theory of moral virtue thou couldst no farther be acquainted with, than from the dictates of uncultivated nature or imagine from the countenances of strangers – more savage themselves with all their improvements than thou wert without a single one of them".

This acute understanding is as distinctively Ledyard as is his style of 18th century prose.

Cook had previously visited the Friendly Islands on his second voyage, but for some reason he now lingered there for ten weeks, a month at Tongatapu alone; there was no prospect of reaching the North American coast during that summer of 1777. The long stay no doubt contributed to enabling some crew members to take a souvenir with them: Hitchings found that the Pay Book of the *Resolution* listed sixty–six men with venereal disease after leaving Tongatapu. Ledyard was among them.

While the expedition was proceeding across the South Pacific to Tahiti a Frenchman arrived in Philadelphia, on 27 July: Marie–Joseph–Paul–Yves–Roch Gilbert du Motier, Marquis de La Fayette – better known to posterity simply as Lafayette. After only two years garrison duty as a captain of dragoons, and notwithstanding his wealth and place in the high aristocracy, Lafayette had secretly contracted with Silas Deane, one of the American Commissioners in Paris, to serve in the American Continental Army as a

"defender of that liberty which I idolize…The welfare of America", he wrote to his wife of three years, "is intimately connected with the happiness of all mankind; she will become the respectable and safe asylum of virtue, integrity, tolerance, equality, and a peaceful liberty".

He bought the ship that took him across the Atlantic, then offered to serve on Washington's staff as an unpaid volunteer. Washington found him a keen disciple, Lafayette found Washington his ideal mentor; with no experience whatsoever, Lafayette was made a major–general by the Continental Congress. He was nineteen. It was the beginning of a mutual admiration that was to stand Ledyard himself in good stead, in Paris, a decade later.

Cook had previously visited Tahiti on both his first and second voyages, and Ledyard recorded the people dancing and running "frantic with joy" at the return, in mid August 1777, of Cook and "some of their old acquaintance". Ledyard found the "natives" attractive enough, though there is no indication of his having ever seen languidly sensual beauties like those painted a hundred years later by Gauguin. He simply recorded that

"The inhabitants are of the largest size of Europeans, the men are tall, strong well limed and fairly shaped. The women of superior rank among them are also in general above our middle size...Their complexion is a clear olive or brunette and the whole contour of the face quite handsome, except the nose, which is generally a little inclined to be flat. Their hair is black and course...they are vigorous, easy, graceful and liberal in their deportment, and of a courteous hospitable disposition, but shrewd and artful".

Later, somewhat contradicting their vigour, he added that they are

"extremely indolent, and sleeping and eating is almost all they do".

It was in Tahiti that Ledyard's fascination with the connections between, and the origins of, various peoples began. He subsequently wrote:

"The language at Otaheitee is the same as that spoken throughout all the south–sea islands...; but how it should equally correspond with that of New–Zealand is still more remarkable...That the inhabitants of the south sea islands are the same people with each other and all derived from the same common source is beyond doubt, but from what source is yet difficult to determine. If we endeavour to determine the question by reasons founded on the analogy of language, as well as manners we shall most certainly conclude that they all originally came from the westward, that is, from Assia; but...consideration of the situation of those isles, particularly respecting the winds, as well as a variety of other causes, it is as probable and perhaps more so they came from the eastward, which is America".

The debate was to continue into the second half of the 20th century. Ledyard was by no means the last to underestimate the incredible navigational skills of the Austronesian Polynesians from South China and Taiwan who, over the course of 3,500 years, island hopped not only as far as Tahiti and New Zealand, but to Hawaii in the North Pacific, Easter Island in the Southeast Pacific, and also as far west as Madagascar in the western Indian Ocean. It was in fact the very end of the human race's migration from central Africa to all the ends of the earth – except Antarctica. This had been missed by Cook, by 120 kms – blocked by ice, as he would be in the Arctic – on 18 January 1773, during the circumnavigation of the last continent on his first voyage; it was not even seen by humans until 1820.[269]

While in Tahiti Ledyard adopted a native custom. In the *Journal* he described how the people

> "have a custom of staining their bodies in a manner that is universal among all those islands, and is called by them tatowing; in doing this they prick the skin with an instrument of small sharp bones which they dip as occasion requires in a black composition of coal–dust and water, which leaves an indelible stain. The operation is painful, and it is some days before the wound is well".

Nothing about himself; but Munford found among his papers a letter written from France in August 1786 in which he confessed to his cousin Isaac that the mistress and maids in a country tavern in Normandy had discovered "the Otaheite marks on my hands". Jefferson, with his endless curiosity about everything, probably remarked on them also: writing from Siberia in July 1787, Ledyard told him that

> "Unfortunately, the marks on my hands procure me my Countrymen the appelation of wild–men".

Cook again dallied in the Society Islands [Tahiti], until December 1777. During that time there had been dramatic developments in America itself. The war still see–sawed. In September the British captured Philadelphia, the independent states' capital, forcing the Continental

---

269   This was by the Russian expedition of Thaddeus von Bellingshausen, sponsored by Tsar Alexander I. Bellingshausen hero–worshipped Cook, and asked Sir Joseph Banks, Cook's naturalist on the first voyage, to find some naturalists to accompany his own expedition; Banks was unable to find anyone willing to go, but provided charts and other information.

Congress to flee to central Pennsylvania, for ten months; two weeks later the Americans trounced General Burgoyne at Saratoga in New York. Just after Cook left Tahiti, in December, General Washington moved his army to winter quarters at Valley Forge, just northwest of Philadelphia, where, desperately short of food, clothing and equipment, they hunkered down through a terrible winter, until June 1778. It was a low point for American spirits. But on the political front the Americans had made a significant step towards establishing a national government when, on 15 November, the Continental Congress endorsed the Articles of Confederation; the revolutionary States were now on the way to a firmer compact, though the Articles were not finally ratified until March 1781 (and the States were not United, under the subsequent and still current Constitution, until June 1788).

On leaving Tahiti Cook headed slightly west of due north, across the Equator straight in the direction of Bering Strait still over nine thousand kilometres away. On 18 January 1778, almost 4,000 kms from Tahiti, the expedition came across a group of islands unknown to Europeans. Cook named them the Sandwich Islands after the First Lord of the Admiralty (now the Hawaiian Islands), though on this first visit they saw only the western group of Kauai, Oahu (site of present–day Honolulu) and Niihau. John Ledyard was thus one of the first seven Americans to see the future fiftieth State of the Union. During their week–long stay at Kauai, where they traded with the people in canoes and finally themselves went ashore, Ledyard was once again delighted to find the oceanic connection:

"We had exchanged but few words with them before we found to our joy and surprize that with little variation their language was the same as that of our acquaintances at the southern islands".

They traded again at Niihau, and left the Sandwich Islands after only twelve days, without sighting Molokai, Maui or the main island, Hawaii itself.

The North Pacific: Indians and furs
Before the expedition reached the North American coast, at the beginning of March 1778, the American ex–colonies had achieved a major international breakthrough: on 6 February the American Commissioners in Paris, Benjamin Franklin, Silas Deane and Arthur Lee (another Virginia planter who had replaced Jefferson), reached a double

agreement[270] with France. First was a treaty of friendship and commerce; second, a treaty of alliance against Britain, if/when war broke out between it and France (which was four months later), aimed to "maintain effectually the liberty, sovereignty, and independence" of the American States. Less elevatedly, but in keeping with the times, the latter were given a free hand to conquer Canada and Bermuda, France a free hand to grab the British possessions in the West Indies.

Cook's North American landfall was just north of Cape Blanco, 185 kms southwest of present–day Eugene, Oregon. It was 600 kms above eighteen–month–old San Francisco, and 500 kms below the northernmost point last reached by an Englishman, exactly two hundred years before: by Sir Francis Drake, who was the one responsible for naming the area New Albion and "taking possession" of it in the name of Queen Elizabeth I, en route to his own failure to find a shortcut to Cathay. However it was not known to Cook at the time that only three years before a Spaniard, Juan Bodega y Quadra, had sailed another 1,000 kms north of Drake, near to present–day Juneau, Alaska. It would be another ten weeks before Cook himself reached that far north, as he followed the great arc up the coast of Oregon and Washington State (missing as he did so the mouth of the Columbia River, which Bodega had seen), then British Columbia, round Alaska, and down the Alaska Peninsula; then cut through the Aleutians almost straight north through the Bering Strait and the Bering Sea; and so to the Polar ice.

But alas! near Icy Cape, on the American side, the ice blocked a Northwest Passage to the Atlantic going eastwards around the top of Canada; and then, near Cape Schmidt on the Russian side, it blocked a Northeast Passage going westwards back to the North Sea around the top of Siberia. Cook's efforts were extraordinary for the time, and the double defeat was not quickly reversed. The Northeast Passage was first traversed in 1878–79 by the Swede Nils Adolf Nordenskjold, in a steamer exactly the same size as the *Resolution*; the Northwest Passage not until 1903–06, in a tiny single–masted sailing smack, by the

---

270 Agreement among the Commissioners themselves was another matter. Shortly afterwards Lee accused Deane, accurately as it turned out, of having leaked news of the impending treaties to some business associates, enabling them all to "promote their speculations" on the London Stock Exchange. Lee's own hands not being entirely clean, Congress in due course dismissed them both, leaving Franklin as the sole American representative to France until Jefferson replaced him in 1785.

Norwegian who was to conquer the South Pole, Roald Amundsen. And these heroic ventures still did not open up practical routes, which had to await vastly improved technology, achieved in 1932, by a Soviet icebreaker, through the Northeast Passage around Siberia, but only in 1969, by a US icebreaking oil tanker, through the Northwest around Canada.

As they approached their first American landing, at Nootka Sound (on Vancouver Island),

> "It was a matter of doubt with many of us", Ledyard wrote with a blast of his open–mindedness, "whether we should find any inhabitants here, but we had scarcely entered the inlet before we saw that hardy, that intrepid, that glorious creature man approaching us from the shore".

He already felt curiously at home:

> "Though more than two thousand miles distant from the nearest part of New England", he wrote in his account of the voyage, "I felt myself plainly affected...It soothed a homesick heart, and rendered me very tolerably happy".

Helen Augur, in a happy phrase, describes "Ledyard's flash of recognition as the first thin cable thrown across the gulf between colonial America and continental America". It is not surprising that Jefferson, who was himself soon to be casting his thoughts across that gulf, would be quick to recognise in Ledyard a kindredness of spirit.

A large part of Ledyard's satisfaction with the expedition's first landfall in the Pacific Northwest lay precisely in his ready sympathy for Indians: whereas the first focus of several of the journal–keepers on the expedition was, like Cook's, that they were "slovenly and dirty to the last degree", Ledyard's was more understanding and more interested in people he perceived as fellow countrymen:

> "I had no sooner beheld these Americans, than I set them down for the same kind of people that inhabit the opposite side of the continent".

His admiration of their workmanship suggests that they had developed some items which he had not observed among the New Hampshire Iroquois:

"These people are possessed of a variety of impliments calculated for war, hunting, fishing and other purposes, some of which are remarkably analogous to ancient models, particularly the lance... They have also a kind of armour that covers the body from the breast downward to the knees...Their fishing geer is highly curious. I can give no adequate description of the variety and singularity of these matters: They have near a dozen different kinds of fish–hooks...They have a harpoon, made from a mushel shell only, and yet thay have so diposed of it as to subdue the great leviathan [whale], and tow the unwieldy monster to their shores".

The recital moved him to another of the philosophical encomiums to which native peoples' innate character and skills could move him:

"If Descartes and Newton from the improvements of ages could produce at last the magnificent system of Philosophy that hath immortalized them; why should not these glorious savages, who, without any of those great collateral assistances, without which THEY [Descartes and Newton]could have done nothing, have discovered such astonishing sagacity, be intitled to equal veneration, and the name of Ben Uncus be as great as that of Isaac Newton".

It is interesting that, though prompted to this outburst by the Nootka Sound Indians, he chose as Newton's Indian counterpart Ben Uncus of Connecticut, the first of the Mohicans, the tribe which Uncus formed and led brilliantly in the mid–17th century English–Indian wars in New England.

Ledyard's keen eye missed little:

"[The Indians'] richest skins, when converted to garments, are edged with a great curiosity. This is nothing less, than the very species of *wampum* [threaded cylindrical beads, made from polished shells], so well known on the opposite side of the continent. It is identically the same...".

But he went further: though Cook believed, probably correctly, that they were the first Europeans to have visited the area, Ledyard, on the basis of some copper bracelets and rough knives amongst the Nootka Indians, concluded from these items, "not unlikely from Hudson's Bay", that the

Indians had contacts extending far eastwards, and that "no part of America is without some sort of commercial intercourse, immediate or remote"; as Helen Augur commented, "a chain of Indians across America".

It is also interesting to note that, despite Cook's frequently explosive temper towards the native inhabitants of virtually all the Pacific islands visited on this voyage, especially in response to pilfering, there was none of this with the American Indians, even though some petty theft did occur during shore expeditions to Indian settlements. It would be going too far to see Corporal Ledyard as playing some moderating role in this singular exception, and he never claimed it. But on that voyage he must have been close to unique in his responses to all the native peoples (excepting the Tasmanians) whom they encountered, and rare for any time. He had no fear whatever of the strange or the unknown – "All uncivilised men are hospitable". And his enthusiasm for understanding the Indians, which he had first developed at Dartmouth, must have contributed to his eventual conception of doing business with them.

> "In their manners", he wrote of these Northwest Indians in the *Journal*, "they resemble the other aborigines of North America. They are bold and ferocious, sly and reserved, not easily provoked but revengeful; we saw no signs of religion or worship among them, and if they sacrifice, it is to the god of liberty".

For all his open–mindedness, Ledyard felt more comfortable if the Americans of Nootka Sound worshipped the same god as the disaffected Americans of the Thirteen States.

However, as far as John Ledyard's own life was concerned, the greatest value in being on the voyage was in what the expedition found almost whenever they went ashore: furs. In his book, five years later, he rhapsodised:

> "The light in which this country will appear most to advantage respects the variety of its animals, and the richness of their furs. They have foxes, sables, hares, marmosets, ermines, weazles, bears, wolves, deer, moose, dogs, otters beavers, and a species of weazle called the glutton [the wolverine]. The skin of this animal was sold at Kamtschatka, a Russian factory on the Asian coast, for sixty rubles, which is near twelve guineas, and had it been sold in China, it would have been worth thirty guineas...[Other] skins,

which did not cost the purchaser sixpence sterling, sold in China for one hundred dollars".

By the time he wrote this Ledyard had already done his homework, at Macao, where the expedition had put in at the end of 1789 on its way back to England, and his life–long obsession had firmly taken root.

After Nootka Sound Cook's ships sailed, as mentioned earlier, around the Canadian–Alaskan–Aleutian arc, meticulously charting all the way, as far as the island of Unalaska. The seven Americans were thus also the first to see the future forty–ninth State of the union; and in fact a fortnight after their arrival in Unalaska the first step towards that end condition took place in Philadelphia when the delegates to the Continental Congress from Massachusetts, Rhode Island, Connecticut, New York, Pennsylvania, Virginia and South Carolina signed the Articles of Confederation (the remaining colonies signing over the succeeding eleven months).

En route to Unalaska the ships put in to what Cook named Prince William Sound, after the future William IV, known as the "Sailor King", for his service as a regular officer in the Royal Navy, and as the father of the actress Mrs Jordan's ten children. Here Cook, Ledyard and most of the crew met their first Aleuts, identified as native North Americans by those sailors who had earlier met other Eskimos in Northeast Canada. They had piles of furs to trade, and something else entirely: a box with a letter in an unknown script, with the date 1778. Further, on Unalaska itself, there were more Aleuts, this time with a worn pair of breeches and a black waistcoat. They were obviously no longer in territory unknown to Europeans; but again Cook decided against an exploration on land, wanting to press on to the expedition's goal.

So from Unalaska Cook sailed north through the Bering Strait. On the day he began the traverse, 11 August 1778, the weather was brilliantly clear, with the Siberian and Alaskan coastlines both perfectly visible. Cook's second lieutenant, the young James King, recorded everyone's "high spirits" in seeing the open sea widening out before them, "free of land and, we hope, of ice". It prompted in him the inevitable optimism about the longed–for shortcut back to the Atlantic:

"All our sanguine hopes begin to revive, and we already begin to compute our situation from known parts of Baffin Bay".

But, as we know, there was ice, and six days later they recognised that they could not get through the barrier: four metres high, unbroken to both east and west, and, Cook said, "as compact as a wall".

The first détente

Cook turned back to Unalaska, which they reached early in October 1778. Ledyard continued to exhibit his fascination with the native peoples. Earlier, on the voyage northwards, he had noticed at Prince William Sound (southeast of present–day Anchorage) that

> "The inhabitants seem to be a distinct tribe from those at [Nootka Sound, 2,500 kms to the south], and bear a very striking resemblance if not an exact one to the Esquimaux...Their skin–canoes, their double bladed paddles, their dress and other appearances of less note are the same as on the coast of Labrador and in Hudson's–Bay. We found...the wampum among them, which proves the commercial intercourse as universal as I before observed it to be".

Now, back at Unalaska,

> "We found among the inhabitants of this island two different kinds of people, the one we knew to be the aborigines of America [the Aleuts], while we supposed the others to have come from the opposite coasts of Asia".

Again, he was correct: they were Kamchadales, closely–related to the Aleuts, but from Kamchatka. A decade later, not far from those opposite coasts, in the depths of Siberia, he would speculate on the origins of and connections between all these peoples, in terms which were well ahead of his contemporaries.

This time in Unalaska Cook decided to try to establish contact with the source of the European items they had observed on their previous visit, not least because, on the fifth day there, Ledyard said,

> "the most remarkable circumstance was a cake of rye–meal newly baked with a piece of salmon in it seasoned with pepper and salt, which was presented to Cook by a comely young (Aleut) chief", who managed to convey that "there were some strangers in the country, who were white, and had come over the great waters in a vessel somewhat like ours".

Cook felt uncertain of the temper of the native inhabitants, did not want to risk losing a party of men, and did not want to order anyone to put himself at risk. So he called for a volunteer; and Ledyard, through his friendship with his fellow American Lieutenant Gore, successfully wangled Cook's agreement. Cook was to lose his uncertainty: in due course he was to note in his journal, in a tribute all the more impressive for being so uncharacteristic of his attitude to "natives", that the Unalaskan Aleuts

"...(to all appearances) are the most peacable inoffensive people I ever met with, and as to honisty they might serve as a pattern to the most civilized nation upon earth".

He added, however, that "they are not so dirty in their persons as Indians...but they are full as lousy and filthy in their houses". If Ledyard even noticed these shortcomings he did not comment on them.

By now the voyagers must have been fairly certain that the various European items were Russian. Vitus Bering's 1727 voyage, on behalf of the Russians, through the Strait that bears his name was well known in Europe, but he did not then see any land on the east side. His 1741 discovery of the coast of Alaska, just to the east of Prince William Sound, only thirty–seven years before Cook's visit, was of less value: it was far from clear exactly where that one landing and the few sightings of unknown islands on Bering's heroic but appallingly unfortunate second voyage fitted in with Cook's punctilious charts. The chief scientist on Bering's elaborately planned expedition, the German Georg Wilhelm Steller, later lamented:

"For ten years Bering had equipped himself for the great enterprise; the exploration lasted ten hours!"

Ledyard allowed himself a more sympathetic view of Bering's failure – at Cook's expense:

"Bheering's discoveries", he wrote in the published *Journal*, "were antecedent to Cooks, and they not only much facilitated his own navigation, but deprived him of the honor of being the sole discoverer of the N. W. continent of America, though it must be acknowledged that Bheering's knowledge of such parts as he did explore were incorrect, imperfect and infinitely below the consummate accuracy. Bheering's discoveries were those of an obscure unassisted genius who has every difficulty to surmount that can be thought incident to a man illiberally educated, and to such a vast undertaking; Cook's those of a person whose fame had already been established, whose genius had all the assistance of art, and whose equipments in other respects were the studied accommodations of the greatest nautical kingdom on earth".

Allowing for a personal animus against Cook – the origin for which is unknown – this sympathy for the underdog is of a piece with Ledyard's understanding of the Pacific islander's situation in the face of European expectations and his direct criticism of Cook in that regard. Together, these aspersions on Cook would cause reactions against Ledyard over an extraordinary period of time.

Siberian fur traders, following in Bering's path and going beyond it, soon learned of Alaska's coastal riches, but had managed to keep them secret. On 8 September 1778 their secret was out. Ledyard had set out two days before, escorted by Aleut guides, to walk halfway across Unalaska Island:

"I took with me some presents adapted to the taste of the Indians, brandy in bottles, and bread, but no other provisions. I went entirely unarmed, by the advise of Captain Cook".

The first night was spent at a village in the interior – agreeably, it would appear:

"The women...were much more tolerable than I had expected to find them; one, in particular, seemed very busy to please me; to her, therefore, I made several small presents, with which she was extremely well pleased...Our entertainment, the subsequent part of the evening, did not consist of delicacies or much variety; they had dried fish. And I had bread and spirits, of which we all participated. Ceremony was not invited to the feast, and nature presided over the entertainment".

The next night, after a rather scary final passage across a lake stretched out on his back in the bottom of a covered canoe, not knowing where or what his destination, John Ledyard did indeed find Russians: fur traders, who welcomed him warmly – perhaps not surprisingly, as he still had some brandy.

As far as is known, it was the very first encounter between a citizen of the new United States and a citizen of Russia: a contact half way between their two countries in about as remote a place as possible. Alaska itself was about to be occupied by the Russians, to pre–empt any more British following Cook, before being sold to the Americans seventy–eight years later for two cents an acre. Catherine II, aghast from the beginning of the American colonies' revolt and its unsavoury implications for Royal prerogative, refused to recognise the new country for seven years, as we shall have occasion to note later. (After the Bolshevik Revolution in 1917, the United States, aghast at the implications for traditional political and economic systems, refused to recognise the USSR for sixteen.) The amiable beginning of the relationship, between a Connecticut Yankee and a bunch of Russian fur–traders, was unfortunately rarely symbolic of its future course. In fact the very first setback came the next morning: Ledyard was introduced to the sauna, which caused him to faint, to his embarrassment, followed by breakfast,

> "mostly of whale, sea–horse and bear, [which] though smoaked, dried and boiled, produced a composition of smells very offensive at nine or ten in the morning";

risking offence, he ate none of it.[271]

The fur–traders had a semi–permanent settlement at Iliuliuk (now Dutch Harbour): there were, Ledyard recorded, about thirty wood and earth huts, housing about thirty Russians and seventy "Kamtschadales", Kamchadals, close kin, as Ledyard noted, to the Alaskan Aleuts, accompanying the Russians from their trading base at Petropavlovsk on the Kamchatka coast, established in 1740 as the base for Bering's expedition. They were all based at the settlement for about five years at a time, a small number going to Petropavlovsk once a year to deliver their accumulation of furs and to stock up on supplies. Cook deduced that this group had already been at Unalaska for about four years. Ledyard, for his part, undoubtedly frustrated, as Cook was to be, by the inability to communicate, nevertheless had his interest further focussed

---

271 Having been prepared to do many things (all legal) for my country, except eat, there were occasions in a number of places where I too ate none of favoured cuisine. And offended.

by his discovery of the Russians' occupation and what he called their "pelt and fur factory". Cook also showed an interest in the fur trade, noting that the Russians were on the island

> "for the sole purpose of furing, and the first and great object is the Sea Beaver or Otter; I never heard them inquire after any other Animal, not that they let any other furs slip through their fingers whin they can get them".

Ledyard took three of the Russians back to the *Resolution* to meet Cook; and these were eventually joined by the leader of the current team, Gerassim Grigorovich Ismailov, sometimes exaggeratedly referred to as the Governor, the orthography of whose name, transliterated from Cyrillic to English, almost beat Cook. Indeed, the absence of any common language and of any interpreter limited the value of the attempted exchanges about the accuracy of charts and the direction and distance of Bering's Strait and Sea, though the Englishmen thought they understood one of the Russians to claim he had actually been a member of Bering's second expedition. Mutual comprehension would not have helped much even if so: weather and other conditions were so bad during Bering's own voyage that he saw little and understood not much more, finishing by making a fateful, and as it turned out for him, fatal turn northwards into his own empty Sea when he tragically mistook Attu Island, at the extreme south end of the Aleutians, for the Kuriles island chain south of his home base on Kamchatka. Language difficulties notwithstanding, the broader meetings between traders and explorers over the ensuing seven weeks that Cook stayed at Unalaska were equally as convivial as the initial one with Ledyard, who observed that the Russians

> "were very fond of the rum, which they drank without any mixture or measure".

Cook himself noted that all but one of the Russians who visited the *Resolution* were "immoderately fond" of strong liquor. He was neither the first nor the last to so comment on Russians; but the exception he recorded is a puzzle.

Ismailov did not need a common language to realise that the presence of these well-equipped and obviously well-financed English voyagers meant that the monopoly he and his Russian colleagues had hitherto enjoyed over the Alaskan fur trade was at risk. His report had to get back to Petropavlovsk, across the Kamchatka peninsula, over the Sea of Okhotsk to Okhotsk, at that time Russia's only Government base on the Pacific coast, almost 1,000 kms overland on the terrible Yakutsk–to–Okhotsk Track to Yakutsk, and finally some 2,000 kms up to the headwaters of the Lena River and thence to Irkutsk, the Imperial administrative capital for Eastern Siberia. And there was still a further 5,500 kms of unmade roads to St Petersburg.

Catherine II recognised the danger immediately, not only to Russian trade but also to Russian sovereignty. As we shall see, her alarm turned out to be very much to the disadvantage of John Ledyard ten years after his happy encounter on Unalaska. Before then, within only six years of Cook's visit, the Russians had established their first American base, on Kodiak Island (off the northern end of the Alaskan Peninsula), to be followed, until the sale of Alaska in 1867, by a string of other military–cum–fur–trading posts right around the coast as far as Fort Ross (originally Fort Russ), only 80–odd kms north of San Francisco, and, for a time, as far as the Farallon Islands, 50 kms out in the Pacific, due west of it.

Death in Hawaii

For Cook's expedition, the end of any idyll was approaching. Wanting to have another crack at finding the elusive Northwest/Northeast Passages the following summer, he decided to winter back in the newly–discovered Sandwich Islands. He had his fiftieth birthday on their second day at sea. This time, at the end of November 1778, they made landfall further east at Maui, then discovered the group's main island, Hawaii itself. They anchored in Kealakekua Bay on the west side of the latter, and were met to their astonishment by

> "so great a number of canoes that Cook ordered two officers into each top to number them with as much exactness as they could, and as they both exceeded 3000 in their amounts I shall with safety say there was 2500 and as there were upon an avarage 6 persons at least in each canoe it will follow that there was at least 15000 men, women and children in the canoes, besides those that were on floats, swiming without floats, and actually on board and hanging round the outside of the ships. The crouds on shore were still more numerous. The beach, the surrounding rocks, the tops of houses, the branches of trees and the adjacent

hills were all covered, and the shouts of joy, and admiration proceeding from the sonorous voices of the men confused with the shriller exclamations of the women dancing and clapping their hands, the overseting of canoes, cries of the children, goods on float, and hogs that were brought to market squealing formed one of the most tumultuous and the most curious prospects that can be imagined".

And, just as in Nootka Sound, Ledyard followed this vivid picture with an exclamation of his affinity:

"God of creation these are thy doings, these are our brethren and our sisters".

A week after their arrival Ledyard sought Cook's permission to explore inland and "if practicable to reach the famous peak that terminated the height of the island" – 4,170 metre Mauna Loa. Cook agreed, but sent a small party, including Midshipman Vancouver, Cook's follower in the North Pacific, and David Nelson, described by Midshipman Trevenen as "the Botanist, or rather, gardener, sent out by Sir Joseph Banks, to make a botanical collection". Ledyard was impressed by the fertility of the country:

"Here is neither toil or care, man stretcheth forth his hand and eateth without parsimony or anticipated want".

However three days out, still at least 16 kms from the mountain, and finding no way through the woods – "very thick and luxuriant, the largest trees are nearly thirty feet in the girt, and these with the shrubbery underneath and the whole intersected with vines renders it very umbrageous" – they were obliged to turn back.

Before they had set out relations with the islanders were going, as Ledyard put it, "in the old Otaheite style"; on their return they found the joy of the welcome was dissipating. One aspect of the relationship – perhaps that very "Otaheite style" – was clearly two–edged. Cook said that

"Women were also forbidden to be admitted into the ships, except under certain circumstances. But the evil I meant to prevent, by this regulation, I soon found, had already got amongst them"

– though he did not specifically blame the expedition's first visit, perhaps because he had been assured by David Samwell, the surgeon's mate in the *Resolution*, that (as he later wrote)

> "There is every reason to believe, that they were afflicted with [venereal disease] before we discovered these islands".

A certain scepticism might be permitted: Captain Clerke described the women as

> "rather masculine and by no means to be compared with the Otaheite damsels";

but it is instructive that Samwell saw things somewhat differently:

> "They seem to have no more sense of modesty than the Otaheitian women, and in general they were as fine girls as any we had seen in the South Sea islands".

Certainly Ledyard was not persuaded of Samwell's official view. He had not commented on the subject in either Tongatapu or Tahiti; but when on their way back north again they put briefly into Kauai, their short-stay base during their time in the Sandwich Islands the year before, he wrote – sounding in fact, uncharacteristically, somewhat rattled – that

> "we had not only more wild uncivilized men to deal with, but an injured and exasperated people; nay more, a people who had heard of our transactions at Owhyee [which had led to Cook's death], and knew us to be no more than men like themselves, and therefore no longer in dread of us: we had also at our first visit here spread the venereal disease among them, which had since made the most shocking ravages".

He gave Cook credit for having tried to ban sexual relations during that first visit, but on the second he found Cook's ban against women being allowed on board the ships or to enter the shore encampments completely useless. As he said of the latter,

> "There was in short no alternative but for our people" – "our enamouratoes" as he splendidly called them – "to go without the

lines and meet their mistresses upon neutral ground. This was at first done by the officers with the utmost secrecy – but what can be hid from jealous love, and the sleepless eyes of enxiety – our soldiers and sailors saw it and practised it. It was impossible for a number of men upon half an acre of ground to go out and return all upon the same business and not have some rencounter that would lead to a discovery, which was soon the case both between officers and men, and then the covenant was no more...it was taken no other notice of by people in general: but the chiefs thought differently, they knew it was a breach of covenant. This might be esteemed trivial on our part and indeed it was, but it was the beginning of our subsequent misfortunes".

It is not known why, but Cook suddenly reversed his prohibition against fine girls on board. Perhaps he recognised the futility of trying to stymie human ingenuity. Perhaps, in the face of all the other difficulties, he no longer cared.

Ledyard made a whole series of observations on the Sandwich Islanders: their burial customs ("an example that will put seven eights of Christendom to blush"), housing, governmental organisation, appearances, customs. Here, the delicacy of one aspect, which flabbergasted, embarrassed and intrigued him simultaneously, caused him to produce one of his most wonderfully convoluted paragraphs ever:

"It is however very manifest among the chiefs, that not only marriage, but a commerce with the women in any other respect is in very indifferent estimation, and it is a disagreeable circumstance to the historian that truth obliges him to inform the world of a custom among them contrary to nature, and odious to a delicate mind, yet as such a remarkable incident in the history of a new discovered, a remote and a numerous people, will tend to illucidate the enquiries of the ingenious in such subjects as may transpire from the various accounts of men and manners here or elsewhere given, it would be to omit the most material and useful part of historical narration to omit it; the custom alluded to is that of sodomy, which is very prevalent if not universal among the chiefs".

No wonder that, recalling Ledyard forty years later, James Burney said that at the time "his ideas were thought too sentimental, and his language too florid".

But, after all this constricted prose, Ledyard went on in typical fashion to remark that

"We did not fully discover this circumstance until near our departure, and indeed lamented we ever had, for though we had no right to attack or ever disapprove of customs in general that differed from our own, yet this one so apparently infringed and insulted the first and strongest dictate of nature, and we had from education and a diffusive observation of the world, so strong a prejudice against it, that the first instance we saw of it we condemned a man fully reprobated".

And, once again, Ledyard speculated percipiently on the origins of these people, and thought

"this reduces the enquiry to two questions: From which of the continents America or Asia did the inhabitants of these islands immediately emigrate, and what island or islands did they first emigrate to?"

By the time the little group returned from their inland excursion other troubles had already begun: some seemingly just mischievous, but also the usual petty thieving, and in due course a growing resistance to the expedition's continuing demands for food for the personnel and materials for the ships. All those years later James Burney would admit that, contrary to Ledyard's – and assuredly others' – impression of a land where man simply "stretcheth forth his hand and eateth without parsimony or anticipated want", the situation was otherwise: the people

"had parted with as much as they could afford, or were willing to spare;...the whole mass of the people, would have to fare slenderly for no short time, to recover from so great an expense".

This is not the place to recount the mutual incomprehension between the Polynesians and the Europeans, and the tragic sequence of rapidly escalating aggressiveness on both sides, which Cook, who was more irascible than usual, unfortunately exacerbated rather than allayed.

These elements together led to his being killed among the foreshore rocks of Kealakekua Bay on 14 February 1779. Ledyard was in one of the groups on the beach at the time, but not in the party of marines with Cook, four of whom were also cut down.[272]

There was of course retribution from the ships, led initially by hot-headed Bligh; it got worse, and more general, destroying the entire Polynesian village, when the following day a friendly Polynesian priest brought a parcel with (in Hough's description) "a slab of partly burned flesh from one of Cook's hips". Cook's bones had been distributed amongst all the main chiefs, but on 19 February some of them were returned too, along with peace offerings; and on the 22nd Captain James Cook's available mortal remains – the scalped skull (with "all the brains taken out" Ledyard noted), lower jaw, leg bones, feet, the hands alone with the flesh still on them (but "scored and salted") – were committed to the deep as the *Resolution* and *Discovery* made way in a state of shock back to the frozen north.

The horror of Cook's death and the subsequent bloodletting turned out to be sufficient for everyone: in the ships' remaining days in Hawaii there were no more threats by the Polynesians, no more retribution against them. Then again, there are those who feel that Cook's opening of the Pacific to the Europeans – their colonisers, their fishing fleets, their missionaries, their whalers – turned out, in the long run, to be retribution enough.

Adventures in the fur trade

The *Resolution* and *Discovery*, both now under the dying Charles Clerke, still had their mission to fulfil; so again they headed northwards through Bering Strait, and again they came up against the Polar ice and had to turn back to Petropavlovsk, in Kamchatka. There, in August 1779, they buried Clerke, and Gore took over, presumably the only American in command of one of His Majesty's Ships in this fifth year of the War of Independence. The War still dragged on indecisively. The same day, 10 July 1778, that France declared war on Britain, a small French fleet, obviously despatched long before, arrived on the east coast to support the Americans; it was the first significant foreign assistance, but proved to be of little effect. Much of the fighting was a debilitating and, for the Americans, deteriorating see-sawing in the South, leading to

---

272 Jared Sparks mistakenly placed Ledyard with Cook's group, an error which was often repeated by others.

British capture and burning of Portsmouth and Norfolk, Virginia, in May 1779. In August the British were finally cleared out of New Jersey; but in October Washington would take his suffering and at times near–mutinous army into winter quarters there, in Morristown, through even severer weather than at Valley Forge two years before.

On the way northward through Petropavlovsk Ledyard had noted the presence of "several Russian and Polish fur traders" buying furs from Kamchatka. As he had been in Van Dieman's Land, he was again harshly judgemental of "Kamchatkadales" who had not had the at least marginal benefit of direct Russian supervision:

"They are of a diminutive size, narrow foreheads, high cheek–bones, small eyes sunk into their heads and guamy: Almost no nose, a monstrous mouth and thick lips; their hair is black and strait: They are indolent, ignorant, superstitious, jealous, cowardly, and more filthy and dirty than the imagination can conceive in persons dress and manner of living".

John Ledyard clearly had a preference for the Noble Savage. Nearly ten years later, back in Siberia but coming overland from the opposite direction, Ledyard would write to Thomas Jefferson with the conclusion to his observations either side of Bering Strait, decades ahead of anyone else:

"America was peopled from Asia".

Ledyard's aspersions on the Kamchadales were almost the last of his own record of the expedition; the remainder was taken, probably by Ledyard's publisher, from the anonymous account published in London in 1781 and attributed to John Rickman, Second Lieutenant on, first, the *Discovery* and then on the *Resolution.* From Petropavlovsk the expedition sailed for home at the beginning of October 1779, passing but not stopping at Honshu, Japan's main island, and Iwo Jima, which was erupting, before putting in to Macao in December.

At Macao they got magazines and newspapers for 1776, 1777 and 1778, and learned for the first time that Britain – and thus they themselves – had been at war with France for the previous eighteen months; but fortunately they encountered no French men–of–war. And it was at Macao that Ledyard's vision of an America–China fur trade was consolidated into an obsession. At that time, and until China's defeat by

British gunboats in the first Opium War which began fifty years later, Canton was the only port it allowed foreigners to visit, in limited numbers and under strict controls. Because of these restrictions, and within them the jealousy with which the British, French and Dutch trading companies established in Canton guarded their own monopolies, only three officers and ten men (not including Ledyard) were permitted to go on up to the East India Company's factory, or trading base, at the port. They reported, Ledyard said,

> "that the skins we had brought with us from the N.W. continent of America, were of nearly double the value at Canton, as at Kamchatka".

James King, now in command of the *Discovery*, who led the party to Canton, recounted in Volume III of the official account of the voyage, that

> "a few prime skins, which were clean, and had been well preserved, were sold for one hundred and twenty [dollars] each"

– even more than those which Ledyard reported could be bought for "six pence sterling". Ledyard himself lamented,

> "Neither did we purchase a quarter part of the beaver and other fur skins we might have done, and most certainly should have done, had we known of meeting the opportunity of disposing of them to such an astonishing prifit".

And King's account continued:

> "The rage with which our seamen were possessed to return to Cook's River [now Cook Inlet, the great bay near Anchorage], and, by another cargo of skins, to make their fortunes, at one time, was not far short of mutiny".

Strong language for an official report.

Thus, from the Canton party, and from the "many visitors" who came on board at Macao, Ledyard was able to discover enough of market values to persuade him to his lifelong quest. It must have been about now that he developed the great China illusion that has mesmerised

– and still does – so many would–be traders with that country: the delusion of an almost infinite number of Chinese buyers anxious for an almost endless amount of whatever they have to sell.

Awkward explanations

By the time the two ships arrived back at the naval base at Deptford, on the Thames, in October 1780, having sailed via Capetown and Stromness in the Orkneys en route, the military situation of the Confederal American States had deteriorated further in the South: Charleston, South Carolina, had fallen the previous May to the British, who in September then begun the invasion of North Carolina. Six months later, in April 1781, General Cornwallis began to invade Virginia, and on 4 June Jefferson himself had to flee from a British raid on Monticello. It was only at the end of August, with the arrival of a French fleet and army under Admiral François de Grasse, that the tide turned, quickly and definitively: in October Cornwallis was forced to surrender at Yorktown, Virginia, to the combined forces of Washington and de Grasse. In February 1782 the House of Commons voted against further war, leading a new British Government to seek peace negotiations.

It took until November to agree on a preliminary peace treaty between Britain and America, the last battle of the war, now in its eighth year, having been fought in the Ohio Territory – by George Rogers Clark – only three weeks before, but against American Loyalists and Indians, not the British themselves.[273] It then took another nine months again before the definitive Treaty of Paris was signed, in September 1783, between the Confederated American States and Britain, held up by France's insistence on a simultaneous peace treaty between itself and Britain.

For two years after the *Resolution*'s return to London Ledyard continued in the British armed forces. He was now a Sergeant, having

---

273 Mozart, in a letter to his father in October 1782, just before the Clark engagement, exclaimed with spectacular mis–timing how he was "greatly delighted" by news of England's victories in America, "for you know that I am an out–and–out Englishman". He had just written *The Abduction from the Seraglio*, in which one of the two heroines, the English maid Blonde, brow–beat the villain Osmin on her rights as a subject of King George III to choose whom she would be agreeable to *and* to choose to drink tea. Goodness knows what "news" Mozart had heard: by then it was a whole year since Cornwallis's surrender, and most of the other British troops had been withdrawn from America.

been promoted on 23 September 1780 when the original sergeant on the ship died just after they had left Stromness on the way back to Deptford. In October he was paid off for the voyage, with the amount of £27–16–2½, and in November he was assigned to the 27th Company, Plymouth Division, Royal Marines. What his activities were during those next two years is not entirely clear. In his January 1783 Memorial to the Connecticut Assembly, which we noticed earlier in relation to his entry into the British army, Ledyard said of this period:

> "After having solicited the Earl of Sandwich in vain for his discharge from the service [your Memorialist] was obliged in October 1781 to take his tour of duty which was to America where he remained on board a British Frigate many months before he could meet with an opportunity to renounce the service return to his country".

Sparks, writing from family accounts, says of this period that

> "It is only known, that he refused to be attached to any of the squadrons, which came out to America, giving as a reason, that he would not appear in arms against his native country. Growing weary, however, of a mode of life little suited to his disposition, unless on some adventurous enterprise…his thoughts began to wander homeward. Apparently conquering his scruples, which he had hitherto urged as the motives of his reluctance, he sought the first opportunity to be transferred to the American station, and in December, 1782, we find him on board a British man–of–war in Huntington Bay, Long Island Sound" [opposite Stamford, Connecticut].

There he jumped ship when he was given a seven days' leave of absence,

> "being persuaded", Sparks reminds us again, "that no principles of justice or honour could make it his duty to act with the enemies of his country".

But, as with his joining the British army, amid all these protestations there is something odd about the timing of his leaving. When he returned to London in October 1780 he would of course have found out that the Revolutionary War was still going, and the precarious situation the Confederated States were still in. It seems unlikely, from everything else we know about Ledyard, that he would have been afraid of fighting –

though, curiously for those war–sodden times, he never did participate in any hostilities other than against islanders on the beach in Hawaii. Perhaps it was the obvious fact that he bore no animus against the British, with whom he had been happily working throughout the War, that resulted in his apparently making no attempt to rush back to his hard–pressed country's support. Or perhaps it was that, having travelled to the far corners of the world and seen the similarities between men, he saw the futility of war between peoples and wanted nothing to do with it. But that would be pure conjecture. Whatever the reason, by 1783 when he did get home, his failure to participate in the Revolutionary War patently required some explanation.

If not by the time he made his escape from British service, certainly by three months later in January 1783 when he was seeking the Connecticut Assembly's support for the publication of his Cook journal, Ledyard must have been aware of the pain and suffering of his countrymen through the eight long years of fighting for their independence from the hated King George he had been happily serving, and the legacy of bitterness this had left perhaps even in his own family – his mother, whom he went to see as soon as he jumped ship, was running a boarding house for British officers, who no doubt treated their colonial landlady the way British officers usually did treat colonials. Thus, both the confusion about just when and how he had been "forced" into British service, and now that relating to his departure from it, suggests that John Ledyard was embarrassed by his lack of service to America, and perhaps felt a sense of guilt about it. Certainly he would have needed all the obfuscation and patriotic protestations possible in the circumstances to overcome his compatriots' doubts about his course of action – or inaction.

In the summer of 1783 Nathaniel Patten, a bookseller in Hartford, Connecticut, published a small volume of 208 pages, in elongated format, 19 cms high by 11.5 wide, dedicated

"To his Excellency Jonathan Trumbull, Esq; Governor and Commander in chief of the Militia of the State of Connecticut, and Admiral of the same".

In the dedication Ledyard was at his floweriest:

"The affability and generosity I was honored with by you at my first arrival in my native country, after a long absence, was truly worthy the distinguished character you always have had, and I sincerely hope ever will sustain in this country; I have received it as a testimony of that original urbanity and dignified familiarity which distinguishes the magistrate from the tyrant——the people from slaves, and is still the boon of which every son of this country participates. Such virtues, like the rose in bud, are lovely in ordinary life; but when transferred to the bosoms of the fair and great, become by the contrasting change more perfectly beautiful: This amiable character alone naturally aspires an attachment and a wish to participate of its favors".

The book's title was a good deal crisper:

A

JOURNAL

OF

CAPTAIN COOK's

LAST

VOYAGE

TO THE

Pacific Ocean,

AND IN QUEST OF A

North-West Passage,

BETWEEN

ASIA AMERICA;

Performed in the Years 1776, 1777, 1778, and

1779.

Illustrated with a C H A R T, shewing the Tracts of

the Ships employed in this Expedition.

Faithfully narrated from the original MS. of

Mr. *JOHN LEDYARD.*

As we saw earlier, it was not all narrated from Ledyard: in addition to the last thirty–eight pages from Rickman's account, perhaps added by Patten when Ledyard failed to complete his manuscript, Munford noted that some of the description of Tahiti was taken, by Ledyard, from a compilation of accounts of Cook's first voyage in *An Account of the Voyages Undertaken by the Order of His Present Majesty for making Discoveries in the Southern Hemisphere*, edited by John Hawkesworth and published in 1773. Ledyard had sold his manuscript to Patten for 20 guineas; Sparks was told that

> "the work was very popular at the time, that Mr. P. made no inconsiderable sum from the Publication".

Rickman's narrative recorded that as soon as the expedition came back into contact with Europeans, in Macao,

> "the Commodore called all hands aft, and ordered them to deliver up their journals, and every writing, remark, or memorandum that any of them made of any particular respecting the voyage, on pain of the severest punishment in case of any concealment, in order that all …might be sealed up, and directed to the Lords of the Admiralty".

No notes by Ledyard were found amongst the other papers that came into his family's possession. But, curiously, no notes by Ledyard have ever been found in British archives either. Yet on occasion it is hard not to feel, from the immediacy of his descriptions and remarks from time to time, that Ledyard was in fact working from at least some notes made during the voyage, which he had somehow managed to conceal from the great paper round–up, and which perhaps he destroyed as of no further use after writing his manuscript.

The British Admiralty's publication of Cook's far more detailed, and more accurate, journal would not appear for another year, so Ledyard found himself suddenly a celebrity in the United States, "the Great American Traveler". In Paris he gave Jefferson a copy; in a letter to him in July 1786 Jefferson said

> "I am sorry it is not in my power to send you your book. Very soon after I received it from you I lent it to Madame de la fayette, who has been obliged to lend it from hand to hand has never returned it".

Ledyard must have been considerably flattered.

Contrary to his American successes, in England Ledyard was regarded as a blackguard for his critical remarks about Cook. Extraordinarily, the bitterness this caused amongst the more uncritical of Cook's worshippers has lasted well into the twentieth century: as recently as 1930 a former Premier of Australia's state of New South Wales, Sir Joseph Carruthers, fulminated, with comical indignation on behalf of the British class system, that the views of "a man like Ledyard, who held no commissioned rank", had exacerbated Americans' natural prejudices against a great Englishman for a hundred and forty years.

Endless frustrations

On his return to the United States Ledyard claimed to be worn out by his exertions and experiences over the previous several years: his person, he wrote at that time, made so

> "perfect a contrast to beauty or elegance, that Hogarth himself could not deform it",

an allusion that suggests he had not spent all the last two years in the stews of Plymouth. Almost immediately he was to put his life's objective squarely up front: in the Memorial he submitted to the Connecticut Assembly in January 1783, seeking support for the book which at that stage can have scarcely been much more than just started, he said it

> "may be essentially useful to America in general but particularly to the Northern states by opening a most valuable trade across the north pacific Ocean the east Indies".

This was, to say the least, visionary at a time when the northern states stretched no further west than the Mississippi; it was a year before Jefferson wrote wistfully to George Rogers Clark about exploring the country from the Mississippi to California.

Throughout his life Ledyard's focus maintained the duality of his initial approach: he certainly saw his proposal for a Pacific Northwest fur trade with China as a way of becoming rich; but he also thought it would be for his country's good. And he was virtually uniquely qualified to pursue it. But, alas, despite Ledyard's repeated efforts, it was not to be, at least for himself; and for his remaining six years his life became a roller-coaster of over-confident promise and unforeseeable, sometimes bizarre, disappointment – mostly financed by friends or mere acquaintances whom he assumed would share his enthusiasm for the riches and/or the glory of his quest. Sparks, years later, absolved him of sponging:

> "He suffered under the pressure of want, and a corroding sense of dependence; and occasionally his finances were at so low an ebb, that he was compelled, however reluctantly, to be a pensioner on the bounty of his friends. So disinterested were his aims, however, and so entirely did he sacrifice every selfish consideration in prosecuting them; so benevolent was his disposition, and so enlarged his views of serving mankind, that no one considered favours of this sort in the light of obligations conferred, nor so much acts of charity, as a just tribute to the singleness of his heart, the generosity of his purposes, and the effective warmth of his zeal".

Admittedly, no–one ever lent him much, which was why he had to call on so many tributes; but of course Sparks himself was never called upon to make one.

The book done (more or less), never shy, Ledyard began his commercial quest in 1783 at the top, with Robert Morris of Philadelphia. It was about the time the Treaty of Paris, formally ending the Revolutionary War and recognising American independence, was signed, on 3 September, with Britain by John Adams, Benjamin Franklin and John Jay (in that order). Morris was probably the richest man in America; a signer of the Declaration of Independence, he had become known as "the financier of the Revolution". While other shipping firms in Philadelphia turned him down, Ledyard obtained Morris's support for a voyage around Cape Horn to Nootka Sound and thence with furs to China, and went off to look into the cost of purchasing and outfitting a suitable ship. He immediately wrote to his cousin and closest confidant throughout his life, Isaac Ledyard:

> "What a noble hold he [Morris] instantly took of the enterprise!...I take the lead of the greatest commercial enterprise that has ever been embarked on in this country, and one of the first moment, as it respects the trade of America".

He found a ship in Boston, then one in New London, then another there, but each was diverted to another purpose in turn; then on to New York, where yet another ship was offered, but it turned out to be unseaworthy. By then the season was too late for sailing; but yet another ship was procured, to be made ready for the next summer, but again there were delays, and that deal too fizzled out. After a year's futile efforts Morris's financial caution prevailed over enthusiasm: he had, Ledyard said later, "shrunk behind a trifling obstruction" – possibly, Augur thought, qualms about the passage around Cape Horn.

Instead, undoubtedly influenced by Ledyard's reports of the riches to be had at Canton, Morris financed in January 1784 the first American voyage to the Orient, by a New York ship, the *Empress of China*, direct to Canton via the Cape of Good Hope (still avoiding Cape Horn), loaded with furs and ginseng, a plant root long regarded in East Asia as a benefit to masculine virility. Philip Freneau, our Princeton prophet of American dominion, now famous as "the poet of the Revolution",[274] celebrated the ship's departure and the new country's challenge to the restrictions imposed on its commerce by its former masters:

> "To that old trade no more confined
> By Britain's jealous court assigned,
> She round the Stormy Cape shall sail
> And, eastward, catch the odorous gale.
>
> Thus commerce to our world conveys
> All that varying taste can please;
> For us, the Indian looms are free
> And Java strips her spicy tree".

The *Empress of China* was greeted on its return, in May 1785, with what a New York newspaper termed the "very prosperous achievement" of a cargo of chinaware, tea, cinnamon, silk, and cotton nankeen cloth, and to the proclamation, by a sister journal, that Providence itself was "countenancing our navigation to this new world". The assurance that

---

274 At some stage in his younger years Ledyard had spent holidays with the Forman family at Middletown Point, Long Island; their daughter Eleanor was his favourite, "Good Nel of the Point". In 1790 Eleanor married Philip Freneau. It is not even known whether he and John Ledyard ever met – it was possible, at Middletown Point, during that year when Ledyard was searching for a ship. Later Freneau began collaborating with Isaac Ledyard on a biography of John, but it came to nothing.

becoming rich was a sign of God's approval was a powerful motivation for private enterprise.

If John Ledyard ever thought he must have lacked Divine approbation he never showed it. After his failure with Morris he tried every ship again in New London, all without success. He came closest to persuading Captain Deshon, whose uncle had rescued the young Ledyard from his first attempt to join the British army in Gibraltar; Deshon later admitted Ledyard had been right about the prospects of the Pacific fur trade, and lamented his own lack of enterprise. In June 1784 Ledyard gave up on his fellow Americans and sailed for Cadiz, on his way to France. He had wasted eighteen months.

Why he spent a month in Cadiz is not known, though even there he did not give up on his objective: in mid–August he told Isaac that

"I yesterday conversed with an Englishman, who is commissioned to treat privately with our States in behalf of the Emperor of Morocco; but if I can persuade him to send his Arabic commission back, and join me with his cash and importance at Bordeaux, or Nantz. The preliminary step is accomplished, and he is now somewhere in the town, as busy in the affair as a dozen such heads as mine could be".

Optimistic as ever, but nothing more is heard of the Cadiz caper.

He sailed on to Brest, in Brittany, where he wrote that

"I saw an English gentleman at Cadiz, who assured me, that about six months past, a ship of seven hundred tons, commissioned by the Empress of Russia, was fitted out in the English Thames on a voyage to the back parts of America; that she was armed, and commanded by a Russian, and that some of her officers were those who had been with Cook".

It is extraordinary that the Empress Catherine II did indeed decide to send an expedition to explore the extreme northeast coast of Siberia, and with one of Cook's men in charge; but that was not decided until 1787, as we shall see later. What was behind this earlier story of an English–built vessel is a complete mystery. Now, still without prospect of a voyage of his own to the Pacific Northwest, Ledyard cried:

"You see the business deserves the attention I have endeavoured, and am still striving to give it; and had Morris not shrunk behind a trifling obstruction, I should have been happy, and America would this moment be triumphantly displaying her flag in the remote and beneficial regions of commerce. I am tired of my vexations".

But his vexations were still far from over as he moved philosophically on:

"Tomorrow, if my horses please, I will be in L'Orient. 'What will you do there?' The best I can".

Robert Morris had at least armed him with letters of introduction to "gentlemen of the first character" there; and, Sparks related,

"within twelve days he completed a negociation with a company of merchants, and a ship was selected for the intended voyage".

For once Ledyard did not go overboard:

"I have been so much the sport of accident", he wrote, "that I am exceedingly suspicious…here comes a *but*, – ah, these *buts*; pray Heaven they may not *but* the modicum of brains out of my head, which Morris has left there."

The *but* was – as had happened the preceding year – the lateness of the season; but Ledyard agreed to wait the ten months his fine merchant friends said they would need to equip the voyage. In February 1785 he was ebullient again:

"My affairs in France are likely to prove of the greatest honour and advantage to me".

By July, however, it was all over, and he was in Paris, where he "had the pleasure of being at the Doctor's [Benjamin Franklin's] house but once only before his departure" – on the 12th, just before the latter left for home at the end of his nine–year assignment in Paris, the last two as the Americans' first Minister to France. Like Ledyard, he had missed the whole Revolutionary War.

There is no record of what happened about the promising Lorient scheme; but there is a strong suspicion that it was cancelled by royal command – or by pre–emptive mercantile prudence – so as not to compete with the La Pérouse expedition, which was to sail for the northern Pacific that August as a result of the Louis XVI's concern at Cook's successes there. However it must have been in Lorient that Ledyard first met the great American naval hero John Paul Jones, who was there over the winter of 1784–1785 trying to obtain his prize money for ships he had captured during the Revolutionary War and harboured in France. That meeting would lead to the next scheme.

Ledyard and Jefferson

It may well have been Jones who introduced Ledyard to the new American diplomatic representative in Paris, Thomas Jefferson, who took over from Franklin as Minister to France.[275] Whereas he had failed with the financiers and merchants of the United States, once again he impressed a great man – though admittedly there was no question of Jefferson's becoming an investor in Ledyard's plans. But there is no doubt that Jefferson gave a close and understanding hearing to Ledyard in the course of a number of meetings and dinners at the American Legation. In 1821 he recalled in his *Autobiography*:

> "While at Paris I became acquainted with John Ledyard of Connecticut, a man of genius, of some science, and of fearless courage and enterprise. He had accompanied Captain Cook in his voyage to the Pacific, had distinguished himself on several occasions by an unrivalled intrepidity, and published an account of that voyage, with details unfavorable to Cook's deportment towards the savages, and lessening our regrets at his fate. Ledyard had come to Paris, in the hope of forming a company to engage in the fur trade of the Western coast of America."

Jefferson must have found in Ledyard's reports on his voyage with Cook and his consequent trade proposal a stirring echo of his own nascent interest in the American West; and it is not going too far to suggest that both these aspects of what Ledyard had to tell him were what provided Jefferson with the clinching focus for the great designs he was to carry out in his first term as President: the Louisiana Purchase and the Lewis and Clark expedition. There were four aspects of Ledyard's account that

---

275   In fact Jefferson had been in Paris since July 1784, having been sent by the Continental Congress to join Franklin and John Adams in the negotiation of commercial treaties with the Europeans. In February 1785 Congress had appointed Adams as the first American diplomatic representative to Britain.

would have resonated with the direction that Jefferson's own thinking was already taking.

First, there was the question of the territorial integrity of the American continent. Not long before Jefferson had left the Continental Congress for Paris he was the author, as was noted above, of a draft ordinance for the government of the Northwest Territory, running from the Thirteen States to the Mississippi; and he had raised with George Rogers Clark the exploration of the West from that boundary to California. Ledyard could now give him a first–hand account of the northern part of that Pacific coast, recalling the similarities between its forests and those of the East in a way which would have made the more vivid the visualisation of a single country united from east to west.

Second, there was a further link spanning the continent that Ledyard's reports would have brought home to Jefferson: the trans–continental occupation of the land by the Indians. Jefferson had a naïve sympathy for the Indians: he had first learned about them as a child from his father's stories of his own activities in the wilderness, and he had met Indian chiefs as his father's guests in his own home. Unlike the blacks, who were slaves, the Indians were, in the thinking of the times, like Omai, "noble savages". In fact in that same year, 1785, Jefferson wrote

"I believe the Indian then to be in body and mind equal to the whiteman".

Ledyard's own sympathy for the Indians, his knowledge of them in both the Northeast and the Northwest, his views about their relationship to the Eskimos, Aleuts and Kamchadales, all this would have fascinated Jefferson, who had an extraordinary interest in new ideas. The link between Ledyard's vision of the Indians, connected by nature and by commerce from coast to coast, must have reinforced the continental strand in Jefferson's thinking about the future of the country.

Third, Jefferson was well aware that the California to which he had thought of sending Clark was in the hands of the Spanish, along with the whole south of the continent from Louisiana westwards. He was also suspicious of French intentions, and one wonders whether Ledyard's enthusiasms had already reinforced his interest in them. In any event, on 3 August, two days after la Pérouse sailed from Brest, Jefferson asked John Paul Jones to "be so good as to make an enquiry into all the circumstances relative to Peyrouse's expedition which seem to ascertain his destination. Particularly the number of men and of what conditions and vocations had he on board? What animals, their species and number? What trees, plants, or seeds? What utensils? What merchandize or other necessaries? This enquiry should be made with as little appearance of interest in it as possible...Commit all the circumstances to writing, and bring them when you come yourself, or send them by a safe hand".

He was clearly concerned at the possibility of an attempt at colonisation somewhere on the coast that Cook had explored; and presumably after hearing back from Jones he wrote to his friend and colleague John Jay, back in Washington as Secretary of Foreign Affairs after having been one of the negotiators of the peace settlement with England, that the French

"give out that the object is merely for improvement of our knowledge of that part of the globe. Their loading [of men and supplies]...and some other circumstances appear to me some other design; perhaps that of colonising the West coast of America".[276]

Ledyard could now inform Jefferson also of the Russian movement that had already begun eastwards to the Alaskan coast, including the stories he had heard since his arrival in Europe of new Russian voyages. Not least, he could underline the new British interest represented by Cook's explorations. Although these had not found the Northwest Passage, which looked more and more mythical, they represented, with continued British activity west of the Great Lakes, a revival of the British claim to the long dormant New Albion. Jefferson had already reacted once, though desultorily, to a rumour of a British attempt to colonise the West; he would have seen all these developments as threats to his new country's

---

276 As it happened, that was not in fact La Pérouse's design. After exploring parts of both the American and Asian sides of the North Pacific he arrived in Botany Bay, just south of Sydney Harbour, on 26 January 1788, only a few hours after Captain Arthur Phillip and his First Fleet of convicts had begun establishing the new British penal colony of New South Wales; and when he sailed on his two ships disappeared completely, until found forty years later at the bottom of the sea in the New Hebrides.

sovereignty, British expansion in North America, indeed, as a threat to its hard won independence.

Finally, there was Ledyard's vision of a lucrative trade from this Pacific Northwest to China and the East Indies. Here again he could speak as an expert: his experiences at Nootka Sound, as well as further round the coast to Unalaska, confirmed the ready availability of superb furs, and, of course, the capacity of the Indians to assist in securing them. His observations of the Russian fur trade, and of market values in Canton, would obviously also have carried conviction with Jefferson. Jefferson had earlier seen commerce as one of the main causes of conflict between nations; if his broader exposure to the world from Paris was now bringing him to recognise its inevitability, he nevertheless saw international trade being, for America (as W.H.Adams noted) the export of surplus agricultural products by a nation whose backbone was composed of smallholders. Ledyard's plans for the fur trade slotted neatly into this conception, as well as offering a method of contributing to a unified, sovereign commonwealth.

Further adventures in the fur trade

Jefferson recognised Ledyard as a visionary, certainly; but he also treated his trade proposals seriously and as entirely feasible. So, it is clear, did John Paul Jones, who now proceeded to work with Ledyard on a proposal for a voyage by two ships to the Pacific Northwest, Ledyard to remain at Nootka Sound with one ship as a trading–post, Jones to sail on to Canton with a cargo of furs. Jones "intimated", Ledyard claimed, that if the King of France declined to finance the expedition, they would

"reduce the outfits within the limits of his own private fortune and make the whole independently".

But after all this enthusiasm Jones, always much more careful with his considerably more money than Ledyard ever was with his considerably less, got cold feet: the huge amount of the possible profit became less real than the unexpectedly large cost of the preparations; not surprisingly, Robert Morris was discouraging when consulted; and when he even asked about Spain's attitude, the American Chargé d'affaires in Madrid of course advised that "Spain is too jealous to permit any commercial speculation in the neighbourhood of California", which it then claimed.

That did it. Jones was less brave in commerce than in combat: Bourbon Spain was a close ally of Bourbon France, and he had no intention of offending the *régime*, though he was neither the first nor the last to be seduced by insincere French flattery. Now yet another enterprise was wrecked, but Ledyard would not give up to mere European pretensions:

"I die with anxiety to be on the back of the American States, after having either come from or penetrated to the Pacific Ocean", he wrote to Isaac; "A blush of generous regret sits on my Cheek, when I hear of any discovery there, which I have had no part in, and particularly at this auspicious period. The American Revolution invites to a thorough discovery of the Continent...It was necessary that an European should discover the Existence of that Continent, but in the name of *Amor Patriae*. Let a Native of it Explore its Boundary. It is my wish to be the Man I will not yet resign that wish nor my pretension to that distinction".

Offsetting yet another disappointment, the nobility of patriotic endeavour was displacing the thoughts of making a fortune in the fur trade.

Though not just yet. Ledyard's next effort turned out pure farce, through even less fault of his own than was customary. Out of the blue, one Sir James Hall[277] turned up, a British visitor to the right circles in Paris – British circles, Ledyard wrote: "two Members of the house of Commons, two Lords, Beaumarchais, and several Members of the Royal Academy at Paris at his table". How they met is unknown, but Hall became enthusiastic about Ledyard's ideas, and secured him a passage on a British ship intending to trade in the Pacific Northwest. From there, he told Colonel William Stephen Smith,[278] Secretary of the American Legation in London, he would attempt

---

277 Hall was twenty–five at the time, a student geologist on his way home from researches in the Alps and Italy. He went on to achieve some eminence in his field through initiating experimental geology, and to become President of the Royal Society of Edinburgh.

278 Smith (1735–1816), another Princetonian, had served on the staffs of both Lafayette and Washington during the Revolutionary War, and at the end of 1783 had supervised the British evacuation of New York City. When Ledyard met him he had just married John Adams's daughter. "In later life", the *American National Biography* observes, "he had a reputation for being weak–minded, greedy, vain, and pompous", and Adams considered him "a disappointment and an embarrassment".

"a march thro' the Indian nations, to the back parts of the Atlantic States, for the purpose of examining the Country and its Inhabitants".

Keeping Thomas Jefferson in the picture, he wrote that

"Sir J. Hall presented me with twenty Guineas Pro Bono Publico – I bought two great Dogs, an Indian pipe and a hatchet. My want of time as well as more money, will prevent my going other than indifferently equipped for such an Enterprise: but it is certain I shall be more in want before I see Virginia: why should I repine?".

He was not soliciting funds: he was always much more direct about that. He was content to live off the land – and off the Indians whom he would undoubtedly befriend on the way across the continent. He has been accused of fecklessness for what he did equip himself with; but there was method in Ledyard's wildest schemes: the dogs were for protection as well as company, the pipe as evidence to the Indians of his peaceful intentions, the hatchet for chopping logs for cooking and shelter, and, if pressed, defence. It was minimal, but Ledyard could manage with the minimum.

But, as it turned out, he did not sail with Sir James Hall: patriotism got in the way. What happened was explained in a letter to Secretary of Foreign Affairs John Jay from Colonel Smith, who said he had "formed an acquaintance" with Ledyard in Paris in 1785:

"In consequence of some allurements from an English nobleman at Paris, [Ledyard] came here with an intention of entering into the service of this Country for the purpose of visiting exploring [the western coast of America] –

Upon being acquainted with his pursuits, I endeavour'd to convince him that it was his duty as an American Citizen, to exercise his talents and Industry for the immediate service of his own Country – and if the Project he was upon, could be beneficial to any, his Country upon every Principle was entitled to those services. After a few conversations on the subject, he consented to move independent of this Court – and a vessel being on the point of sailing for that Coast,...he secured a passage".

Smith's concern was solely for American glory, not a whit for Ledyard himself: he added, to Jay:

"It is a daring, wild attempt – and I have my doubts of his success – but finding him determined to pursue the subject, I thought he had better do it in the way he now is, than bind himself in any manner to this people [i.e. the British]…If he fails, and is never heard of – which I think most probable, there is no harm done".

However, even as Smith was writing, this scheme, too, came to grief. British trade in the Pacific was riven by commercial and territorial jealousies between the great East India Company and the new South Seas Company; in September 1786, just out of London, one of them caused Ledyard's ship to be seized by Customs, falsely, as it turned out, and with it, he told his cousin,

"everything, all my little baggage, shield, buckler, lance, dogs, squire – all gone. I only am left – left to what?"

This was, by my count, at least the ninth time he had been defeated. Characteristically, the dogs were given back to him by the English; he told Jefferson he thought them "haughty turbulent and very insolent people". Jefferson shared his view: the following year he wrote to a friend that the English "deserve to be kicked into common good manners".

The great Russian caper
The next wild scheme was Thomas Jefferson's; in fact it dated back to the beginning of 1786, long before Sir James Hall appeared on Ledyard's doorstep. There are unfortunately no letters recording the conversations that Jefferson had with Ledyard in Paris in the period between the latter's arrival in July 1785 and his departure for London on Hall's scheme a little over a year later. It is clear that there was a series of conversations, and that Ledyard focussed on his passionate convictions about the Pacific Northwest's economic prospects; but while sympathising with his spirit of enterprise, Jefferson also drew Ledyard more and more to the exploration of the area in the interests of newly independent America. Jefferson wrote in his *Autobiography* that

"I suggested to him the enterprise of exploring the Western part of our continent, by passing through St. Petersburg to Kamschatka, and procuring a passage thence in some of the Russian vessels to Nootka Sound, whence he might make his way across the continent to the United States; and I undertook to have the permission of the Empress of Russia solicited. He eagerly embraced the proposition".

The Lorient scheme had failed by the time of Ledyard's arrival in Paris; we do not know when exactly the John Paul Jones scheme had followed it onto the rocks; but Jefferson must have put his own proposition to Ledyard right afterwards. The latter then wanted to head off immediately, but Jefferson, perhaps unwisely as it turned out, obviously felt it was wiser to go through channels. On 9 February 1786 Jefferson personally introduced the proposed voyage to Lafayette, the Americans' hero and friend, who would ask the French ambassador in St Petersburg, the Comte de Ségur, to approach the Empress Catherine II for a visa for Ledyard.[279]

Lafayette seems to have known of the plan beforehand, presumably from Ledyard himself whom he had met through John Paul Jones or perhaps Jefferson. Jefferson now wrote to him that Ledyard

"has genius, an eduction better than the common, and a talent for useful interesting observation. I believe him to be an honest man,

---

279 In those more relaxed days, and until the First World War, visas were required only by Russia and Turkey. Ségur, born in 1753, son of a Marshal of France and a friend of Queen Marie Antoinette and Diderot, was a childhood friend of Lafayette and later, by a quirk of relationships in the tight–knit French high aristocracy, his uncle by marriage. They both started military careers, and together offered their services to Benjamin Franklin when he and his fellow American Commissioners (Silas Deane and Arthur Lee) arrived in Paris to seek French military assistance against the British; when the Court, still trying to avoid war with Britain, forbade them to go, Ségur obeyed, Lafayette, immensely wealthy, slipped across the Pyrenees and sailed to America on a ship he purchased in Spain. When Ségur finally got to take his regiment to America in 1782, Cornwallis had already surrendered; so instead of fighting he dined with everyone who was anyone, and, a committed liberal, left eight months later impressed that "people here think, say, and do what they like; nothing compels them to submit to the caprices of fortune or of power". He was appointed Minister to the court of Catherine II in 1784 (at thirty–one!), and returned to Paris in 1789 to – somewhat like a more choosy Talleyrand – support the Revolution, hide from the Terror, become Grand Master of Ceremonies under Napoleon, vote for Louis XVI's restoration, join the Bonapartist opposition, switch again to welcome Louis–Philippe's overthrow of Charles X in 1830 – then die later the same year.

and a man of truth. To all this he adds just as much singularity of character, and of that particular kind too, as was necessary to make him undertake the journey he proposes".

A few days later Lafayette, knowing the way to get direct to Catherine, passed Jefferson's letter "and the proposals of Mr. Ledyard" to Baron Friedrich von Grimm, Minister to the French Court of the small German principality of Saxe–Gotha, and Catherine's favourite intellectual confidant and agent for a quarter of a century.[280] Lafayette recommended Ledyard warmly in the sort of terms calculated to appeal to Catherine's well–publicised vanities:

> "With his personality I would believe him to be made expressly for that which he proposes;...I think that Mr. Ledyard's person should rather encourage you than hinder you in communicating his plan to the Empress of Russia, who is Empress of the universe in all that pertains to sciences, discoveries, literature, philosophy, and glory".

Already at this very preliminary stage Ledyard himself was up to his old trick: over–confidence. Although, he told Isaac, he had been

> "the verry football of chance and I have continued so untill within a verry few days of the date of this Letter...without any thing but a clean shirt was I invited from a Gloomy garret to the splendid Tables of the first characters in this Kingdom...In about fourteen days I leave Paris for Brussells, Cologne, Vienne, Dresdon, Berlin, Varsovie, Petersburg, Moscow, Kamchatka Sea of Anadivy [the Gulf of Anadyr in the Bering Sea], Coast of America, from whence if I find any moe cities to New York, when I get there I will name them to you in *propria persona*".

---

280 Catherine was of course herself the daughter of the minor German princely house of Zerbst–Anhalt. Von Grimm was introduced to the Empress by his friend Denis Diderot, the French Enlightenment man of letters who had produced the celebrated thirty–five volume *Encyclopédie* between 1751 and 1776, and who spent five months at Catherine's court in 1773, at a time before the American and then the French Revolutions shocked Catherine out of her flirtation with the liberal theories of the *philosophes*.

But two months later he had to tell Isaac he was still in Paris:

"I would freely have relinquished the pleasure I have in writing this Letter, to have been where I supposed I should have been when I wrote you last: but soon after...our minister [Jefferson], the Russian Minister [Ivan Matveevich Simolin] and the American Broker (I mean the marquiss La Fayette) took it into their heads that I should not go directly to St Petersburgh, but wait untill I was sent for...You see I have so many friends that I cannot do just as I please...I am not certain about the result of this Business, and shall not be perfectly at ease, untill I have been introduced to the Empress".

However the Empress, it turned out, was not having it, either his making a lone excursion or, as von Grimm had apparently suggested, joining up with a Russian expedition already underway to the Pacific northwest. By an extraordinary coincidence this was being led by Ledyard's former and unremarked *Resolution* shipmate Able Seaman Joseph Billings. Billings had subsequently entered the Russian Navy as a Lieutenant, it would seem on the basis of self–promotion as "Cook's companion"; then, on the apparently casual recommendation of Sir Joseph Banks to Professor Pallas, and with Billings himself claiming to have been "Astronomer's assistant" on the *Resolution*, he was appointed by Catherine in August 1785 to command the expedition as "Captain–Lieutenant of the Fleet", in charge of thirty–six officers and seventy men. In the course of twenty pages of instructions the Empress had ordered the Captain–Lieutenant to explore "the sea between Kamtschatka and America" and to take possession of "such coasts and islands as you shall be the first to discover". Catherine was generous: she decreed

"double pay for the different ranks obtained during the Expedition; and, as a gratuity, a year's double pay according to the rank they return in; over and above which you and your subalterns, returning safe, will receive for life the single pay received during the Expedition".

Billings had left St Petersburg in October 1785; he was by now already past Yakutsk in eastern Siberia, and on 3 July would reach Okhotsk on the Pacific coast. Catherine accordingly replied to von Grimm's suggestion about Ledyard, on 17 June 1786 ("at 4 o'clock after dinner"), that

"M. Ledyard would do well to take another route than that of Kamtchatka, because, as far as this [Billings] expedition is concerned, there is no longer a way to reach it. Besides, everything that has been written about this expedition is perfectly false and an empty dream: there never has been a party on foot, it all amounts to the expedition of Captain Billings and a team chosen by him and Pallas.[281] Let the American have the money you have given or promised him [Ledyard]; but do not in future throw my money out the window: I do no[t] know these people at all and have had nothing to do with them up to now".[282]

Before Catherine's message reached Paris, Ledyard, desperate to be on the move, appealed directly to von Grimm to talk to Jefferson about his proposed excursion; but the German told Jefferson that (as the latter then told Ledyard)

"he had informed the Empress from the beginning that it was with the M. de la fayette he was negotiating the matter that therefore he should not be justified in treating it with any other person".

This may not have been just a diplomatic minuet: Russia had recognised America's independence as long ago as July 1783, but perhaps there was still a problem about dealing with the arch–anti–royalist Jefferson, even vicariously through von Grimm. This may well, in hindsight, have been a premonition of the difficulty Ledyard was to get into in Siberia eighteen months later.

Still stuck in Paris, Ledyard lamented to cousin Isaac:

"You wonder by what means I exist having brought with me to Paris this time only three Louis d'ors. Ask vice consuls, consuls,

---

281   Peter Pallas (1741–1811), a brilliant German naturalist, had been invited by Catherine II to be Professor at St Petersburg's Academy of Sciences, in order to survey the newer parts of the Russian Empire, and to observe in 1769 the same transit of Venus Captain Cook was sent by the Royal Society to observe in Tahiti, during the first of his three Pacific voyages. Pallas, who was himself already a member of the Royal Society, spent 1768–1774 surveying across the south Russian and southwest Siberian steppes from the Volga to the Altai range.

282   The original was in French, as was customary at the Russian Court. I have modified Watrous's translation: in writing that everything written about "this expedition" was false, Catherine was obviously referring to misinformation about the *Billings* expedition, not Ledyard's proposed one.

plenipotentiaries, ministers and whores of fortune all of whom have had the honour to be tributary to me".

Despite his bitterness at his dependence, there were, amazingly, all sorts of people willing to keep him – and his project – alive. Here indeed was the "just tribute to the singleness of his heart". He told Isaac in rather more insouciant – not to mention democratic – terms of the two chief ones:

> "He is a good fellow this...Marquiss [de Lafayette]: I esteem him and even love him, and so we all do except some few who worship him. I make these trips to Paris [from St Germain on the western outskirts, where he was now living] often sometimes to dine with this aimiable Frenchman, sometimes with our minister who is a Brother to me, sometimes I go buy a fine pair of pumps to walk in. I am too much alive to care and Ambitiou[s] to sit still".

On 16 August, eight days after the letter to Isaac, Jefferson wrote to Ledyard to pass on the bad news from Catherine:

> "I saw Baron de Grimm yesterday at Versailles, and he told me he had received an answer from the Empress, who declines the proposition made on your account. She thinks it chimaerical".

But, Jefferson added, making clear he had not given up on Ledyard,

> "I am in hopes your execution of it from our side of the continent will prove the contrary".

The implication is that Jefferson knew of the Hall scheme.

What he did not know was that Ledyard was already in London: the very same day Ledyard himself was writing from there to tell Jefferson that he had bought the two great dogs, the Indian pipe and the hatchet for his exploration of the American Northwest under Hall's aegis. As we know already, Colonel Smith's intervention followed, then that of His Majesty's Customs, and Ledyard was back in London, re-equipped with the two dogs, but without pipe or hatchet.

So what does Ledyard do? – go to the top again. This time the man who would undoubtedly wish to be his tributary was Sir Joseph Banks, Cook's botanist on his first voyage, now in the eighth of his forty–one years as President of the Royal Society, and the leading figure in encouraging British exploration (and the colonisation, only two years later, of New South Wales on the east coast of Australia). Ledyard undoubtedly presumed on the Cook connection; Banks encouraged his audacious new scheme. On 25 November 1786 Ledyard, writing to Jefferson – "My friend, my brother, my Father, – I know not by what title to address you – you are very dear to me" – informed him that

"If a small subscription now begun in London by Sr Joseph Banks Doct^r Hunter[283] will enable me to proceed you will probably hear from me at Hamburgh: if I arrive at Petersbourg you certainly will. You see the course I was pursing to fame reverted I am now going across Siberia as I had once before intended from Paris this time twelvemonth – what a twelve months! I do defy fortune to be more malicious during another".

Ledyard should never, never have defied fortune.

The announcement of the Subscription in November was in terms that might have surprised Jefferson:

"The Enterprize is to cross the continent of north America from Nootka to New York, to be done either by sailing from London to Nootka or by passing east from London to Petersbourg Moscow Kamchatka thence across the northern pacific ocean to Nootka from New York *to London*" [emphasis added].

The document was published with contributions by Banks of five guineas and two others of a guinea each, and not surprisingly they apparently expected Ledyard to report back to them. However the copy in the New York Historical Society (published by Watrous) has a handwritten addendum by Leyard's American mentor in London:

"W.. S.. *Smith* wishing Mr Ledyard not to confine himself to the particular views of any Gentlemen in England and that he should not be under the necessity of reporting to them the discoveries

---

283   John Hunter (1728–1793) was the most prominent surgeon and anatomist in Britain, and taught Edward Jenner, the discoverer of vaccination. Since 1776 he had been Surgeon–General to George III. His wife wrote a number of songs that were set to music by Haydn.

he may make in America will make such advances of Cash as will enable him to move upon principles of economy free from those shackles which they appear disposd to confine him with – £ .. – .. – .. –".

Ledyard's patriotic duty is again drummed into him by Colonel Smith; but the figures are blank. How much Ledyard got from his British patrons and how much from Smith is unknown. But on 20 December 1786 he is writing to the Colonel from Hamburg:

"I am here with ten guineas exactly I am in perfect health, one of my Dogs is no more. I lost him in my passage up the River Elbe in a Snow storm".

At long last he was actually off on the great Russian caper.

Stalled in St Petersburg

Snow storms were of course to be expected: it was mid–winter. Three months later, in March 1787, he wrote to Jefferson from St Petersburg:

"I cannot tell you by what means I came to Peterbourg, hardly know by what means I shall quit it in the further prossecution of my tour round the world by Land:…how the matter will terminate I know not: the most probable Cojecture is that I shall succeed, be kicked round the world as I have hitherto been from England thro Denmark, thro Sweden, thro Sweedish lapland, Sweedish finland the most unfrequented parts of Russian finland to this Aurura Borealis of a City".

He had in fact been unable to make the usual winter crossing by ice directly across the Baltic Sea from Stockholm through the Åland islands to Turku, west of Helsinki in Finland: the sea had not frozen solid that winter. Instead he had had to go overland, often on foot, 1,000 kms northwards up the Swedish coast of the Gulf of Bothnia to Tornio at the top – as far north as Bering Strait – then almost the same distance again southwards, probably mostly alone, across the little–populated centre of Finland to the Russian capital. It would have been an extraordinary journey if he had gone no further.

Ever on the lookout for news related to his obsession, he told Jefferson, in the same letter,

"There was a report a few days ago of which I have heard nothing since, that the french ships under the command Capt Lapereux [La Pérouse] had arrived at Kamchatka. There is an equipment [expedition] now on foot here for that ocean it is first to *visit* the NW Coast of America: it is to consist of four ships. This the equipment that went from here 12 months since by land to Kamchatka are to cooperate in a design of some sort in the northern pacific Ocean – the lord knows what".

The proposed four-ship expedition was in fact to be of Russian Navy vessels being sent by Catherine to link up with the Billings overland expedition. In an agonisingly close missed opportunity, Ledyard as a newly arrived foreigner apparently did not know who was to be in command of this new expedition: by another extraordinary coincidence it was yet another of his *Resolution* shipmates, the former young Midshipman James Trevenen. He saw further active service for Britain in the West Indies; his subsequent idea of a commercial venture to Nootka Sound, the *Resolution*'s first American landing – no doubt like Ledyard's, to ship furs to China – fell through; and the Admiralty turned down his request for an appointment to the new settlement at Botany Bay, on the east coast of Australia. So the dissatisfied Trevenen had then offered his services only the month before, in February 1787, to the Russian Minister in London, to take a Russian expedition to the North Pacific. The proposal, coinciding with views already current in the Russian Government, was approved by St Petersburg, where Ledyard must have heard about it perhaps even before Trevenen did; but it had the revised objective of having the naval expedition join up with the Billings expedition to counter the effects of Cook's activities in the North Pacific.

If Ledyard had known of Trevenen's command he would surely have clamoured to join him – and maybe he could have been successful. But in the ten or so weeks he spent in the Russian capital he obviously heard nothing further to induce him to wait. It is harder to guess how Ledyard would have fared if he had still been in St Petersburg a year later, when his former business partner John Paul Jones, recruited by Caherine and her co-ruler and secret husband Prince Grigory Potemkin, arrived to fight Russia's enemies: "I think he'll do marvellous things for us", Catherine wrote somewhat breathlessly to von Grimm. When the British officers in the Baltic fleet fighting Sweden refused to serve under the "infamous corsair", Potemkin gave Rear-Admiral Pavel Dzhones command of the battleships fighting the Turks in the

Black Sea, where, amongst others, Jeremy Bentham's young brother Samuel happily served under him. It came to a disastrous end: the following year the prickly Jones quarrelled extremely imprudently with the all–powerful Potemkin, was recalled by Catherine, and a few months later accused in St Petersburg of the rape of a nine–year–old girl. Only the Comte de Ségur, with his admiration for Americans, believed that Jones had been set up, perhaps by a rival officer; but even he, despite his own friendship with Potemkin, could not get Jones cleared or reinstated. However he was not charged, and returned to Paris, where he spent his last two years, sick and writing angry self–vindications.

Trevenen's expedition would have amounted to a much sharper military focus of Catherine's earlier instructions to Billings to take possession of "such coasts and islands as as you shall be the first to discover". The new policy it was to carry out had already been under consideration before Trevenen's approach: Catherine had endorsed in December 1786 the necessity of undoing the threat to Russian interests represented by Cook's exploration, because of "encroachments on the part of English traders on trade and hunting in the eastern sea". And the policy asserted that

"To Russia must indisputably belong:

1) the American coast from 55° 21′ extending northward...; [i.e. the entire coast of the State of Alaska north of the Canadian border]
2) all the islands situated near the mainland and the peninsula Alaska that were discovered by Bering and Cook...;
3) all the islands called the Fox Islands and the Aleutians...".

One can see why the Russians must have been delighted to obtain the services for this purpose of someone who had actually been with Cook in Alaska and the Aleutians; though Trevenen may not have known of this focus before he set out from London.

In any case the naval expedition was not to be: it had to be cancelled as relations with Turkey deteriorated, with war breaking out in August 1787 before Trevenen had even arrived in St Petersburg. The Russians nevertheless expected him to serve in their navy; he agreed subject to the British Admiralty's approving; and did so anyway when it didn't. Then in mid–1788 King Gustavus III of Sweden also declared war on Russia, setting up the pretext by using his own troops in Russian uniforms to "attack" his own frontier (like Hitler in Eastern Europe); and Trevenen was killed in a naval engagement without having left the Baltic.

The other news Ledyard picked up, of La Pérouse's expedition, was of a piece with this heightened sense of vulnerability in St Petersburg in relation to its eastern seaboard, though it was in fact incorrect: La Pérouse did not reach Petropavlovsk (where Captain Clerke had been buried on the *Resolution*'s return visit to Bering Strait after Cook's death) until six months later. He had spent the second half of 1786 exploring the coast of North America from Mt St Elias (near the western edge of the Canadian Yukon) south to Monterey (in California). It is possible that Ledyard's intelligence reflected a misunderstanding of a report by Russian traders (perhaps despatched *through* Petropavlovsk) of La Pérouse's presence on what was regarded as Russia's Alaskan coast.

It does not seem to have crossed Ledyard's mind that Russian sensitivities might be the reason for his continuing troubles in getting permission to cross the country to the North Pacific coast. He was still optimistic in his March letter to Jefferson:

"I dined today with Doc^t Pallas Professor of Natural history c c – an accomplished Sweed: my friend: has been all thro European Asiatic Russia...We had a Scythian at table that belongs to the royal society of Physicians here: the moment the savage [sic!] knew me my designs he became my friend it will be by his generous assistance joined with that of Doct^r Pallas that I shall be able to procure a *royal passport* without which I cannot stir: but this must be done th[r]o the application of the *french* Minister (there being no American one here)... beg liberty to make use of your name the Marquis la fayettes as to my character...I first applied to the English Embassy: but with^t success: the ostensible apology was that the present political moment between England Russia would make it disagreeable for the English minister to ask my favour: but I saw the reason — the true reason in the specula of the secretarys eye — so damn his eyes— which in this case particularly I conceive to be polite language".

Almost every one of the many aspects of Ledyard's list of efforts to obtain permission for his voyage was to be involved in its disastrous end.

He must have known that delay was inevitable. Catherine had left Moscow on 7 January (with fourteen carriages and a hundred and twenty–four sledges) to make an Imperial Progress through the new territories in southern Russia conquered by her legal husband and permanent favourite, Prince Grigory Alexandrovich Potemkin:

> "...a great thing" [as Byron said] "in days
> When homicide and harlotry made great;
> If stars and titles could entail long praise,
> His glory might half equal his estate.
> This fellow, being six foot high, could raise
> A kind of fantasy proportionate
> In the then sovereign of the Russian people,
> Who measured men as you would do a steeple."[284]

But not only was Catherine absent, so was Ledyard's chief channel of approach as previously laid down by Lafayette: the French Minister, the Comte de Ségur, a close friend of Potemkin's, was travelling with him and Catherine in the Crimea.

What Ledyard saw in the English secretary's eyes he did not say; but in his letter to Colonel Smith the previous December he had burst out

> "I cannot submit to a haughty eccentricity of manners so prevalent among the English. They have millions of Virtues but damn their vices, they are enormous".

However on this occasion the British diplomat was telling the truth: Catherine was not at all pleased with the way Britain was playing its balance–of–power policy at that stage, egging on Prussia against her ally the Emperor Joseph II of Austria, encouraging France and a miscellany of European states to support Turkey against her designs on the Crimea and the Black Sea.

That there was no American diplomatic mission in St Petersburg is a fascinating story in itself. In July 1781 the Americans had in fact sent Francis Dana, a member of the Continental Congress during the Revolution, to obtain from Russia recognition of American independence, a commercial treaty and a commitment to defending the freedom of the seas; with him Dana took as his secretary John Adams's thirteen–year–old son John Quincy Adams, the future sixth President of the United

---

284 *Don Juan*, Canto the Seventh, XXXVIII; it and the following Cantos relate to the Russo–Turkish War.

States – because the boy had learned French during his father's posting in Paris. But at that stage Catherine was still so horrified at the revolutionaries' repudiation of her brother monarch King George III that she would not even receive Dana; and everyone else gave him the run-around for two years. Even after the signature (including by John Quincy's father) of the British–American preliminary peace treaty in November 1782 Catherine would not budge.

She was probably encouraged in this intransigence by the French, hostile to a commercial treaty and irritated that the Americans had not first consulted them about their peace treaty with Britain; the then British Minister, James Harris (later first Earl of Malmesbury), only half-jokingly suggested that Catherine was "afraid of incurring the censure of a nation who write memoirs and epigrams". In August 1783, disgusted, Dana took himself back to Washington. On 9 June, however, he had been able to tell a correspondent

> "The flagg of the United States is now displayed at Riga upon a ship of about 500 Tons…This is the first and only arrival of an American Vessel in any port of Russia".

But there would be no American diplomatic representative in St Petersburg for another quarter of a century, until the appointment in 1809 of…John Quincy Adams.

All that was left was Professor Pallas, a German, not a "Sweed", and of immense scientific distinction. As usual, Ledyard's natural optimism – or perhaps desperate need to find grounds for optimism – led him to immediate judgement: after one meeting Pallas was "my friend". It is thought that Sir Joseph Banks probably sent Ledyard to Pallas with a letter of introduction, as he apparently had Joseph Billings. If so it did not work for the former as it did for the latter, and one may wonder why: perhaps it was that Billings joined the Russian navy and was assumed therefore to be working for Russia; no–one was sure whom Ledyard was working for. Perhaps more important, however, was the fact that Billings had been one of George III's subjects: Ledyard was a fellow–countryman of American revolutionaries. At all events he was still hanging round St Petersburg two months later; how he was surviving, who was paying for him, we do not know. He wrote on 15 May to Colonel Smith that

> "You I had both conceived wrong notions about traveling in this country…: there is no country in Europe or Asia (leaving out of

consideration the extent of a tour) so difficult to pass through as this the difficulty arises from the manners dispositions of the inhabitants".

How many subsequent travellers have echoed Ledyard's cry of pain! He went on:

"The Comte de Ségur has not yet sent my passport: but this shall not stop me...I had however a visit this afternoon from a Russian officer a great favourite in the family of the Grand Duke: a friend of mine...he is more, he is a *thinking* Russian. The best of all is that I am likely to obtain a passport by his means of the Chancellor: if so I set out immediately".

Optimistic again, he also reported – as Francis Dana had four years earlier – that

"There are 4 American Ships here 4 more expected: you see by this I am not the only American of enterprize".

And as he did set out, sixteen days later, on 1 June 1787, it is assumed that this new channel worked. But it could well have been fatal to his purpose: the Grand Duke was Catherine's son Paul by the Emperor Peter III, grandson of Peter the Great, whom she had deposed and murdered after only six months on the throne which she then seized. Paul hated his mother; Catherine constantly feared he could become the focal point of a conspiracy against her, and, intensely suspicious of all his contacts, isolated him from any form of official activity. He was the worst possible sponsor Ledyard could have found in Catherine's Russia.

Across Russia and Siberia

However Ledyard now did have one stroke of good fortune: he was able to travel as far as Barnaul, south of Novosibirsk in central Siberia, with a Scottish physician, William Brown, who was in Russian employ; he had (relative) comfort and company roughly half–way to his destination on the Pacific coast. One assumes that Dr Brown (or his employers) paid Ledyard's way.

Three weeks after they had set out Jefferson recounted to a fellow Virginia landowner:

"I had a letter from Lediard lately dated at St Petersburg. He had but two shirts, and yet more shirts than shillings. Still he as determined to obtain the palm of being the first circumambulator of the earth. He sais that having no money they kick him from place to place and thus he expects to be kicked around the globe".

One might have expected Ledyard's great friend to have been a little more concerned about his circumstances on this madcap scheme of which Jefferson himself claimed to be the author. Perhaps he considered himself absolved by Catherine's veto. Or perhaps he felt he had done enough in providing Ledyard with some useful but unencumbering tools: a Captain Nathaniel Cutting said that Jefferson taught Ledyard

"a method of recording certain important observations which he might make, which to prick certain Characters into his own skin with the juice of some herbs which had a knowledge of. These remarks are indelible...Mr. J. also instructed him in a very simple, and tollerably accurate method of measuring the breadth of a River [using a combination of sticks]".

Ledyard had to survive on an endless succession of little "tributes"; this was one of the more skin–flint.[285] Later in the year Jefferson wrote to another colleague of Ledyard and his intention to cross Siberia and America:

"He is a person of ingenuity and information. Unfortunately he has too much imagination. However, if he escapes safely, he will give us new, various, and useful information. I had a letter from him dated last March, when he was about to leave St. Petersburg on his way to Kamschatka"

– as though he were going from Monticello to Washington. Jefferson's insouciance towards his own scheme comes as a surprise, towards the man as a shock.

---

285 Cutting also told this to the ever–earnest John Quincy Adams, who wrote in his diary that if Ledyard had

"pursued his north–west road, whatever benefit his success might have procured to mankind, his journal upon his skin would not, I think, have been worth much".

However from "Barnowl", at the end of July, Ledyard was in fine form, writing to Jefferson of his old anthropological interest from the Cook voyage,

> "to inform you how universaly circumstantialy the Tartars resmble the aborigines of America: they are the same people—the most antient, most numerous of any other, had not a small sea divided them, they would all have been known by the *same name* [Ledyard in any case had a tendency to call all the Siberian peoples "Tartars", just as he had to call the Pacific islanders "Indians"]. The cloak of civilisation sits as ill upon them as our American tartars—they have been a long time tartars it will be a long time before they are any other kind of people".

The attempt to impose European civilisation on native peoples continued to disturb him. En route he had commented in his journal on the "Tartars" he saw, beginning near Kazan, before reaching the Urals:

> "They deviate less from the pursuit enjoyment of real sensual pleasure, than any other people...Would a Tartar...spend ten years in constructing a Watch? or twenty in forming a Telescope? In the United States of America as in Russia we have made our efforts to convert our Tartars to think and act like us, but to what effect?"

And colour reared its head, as it never had in the Pacific:

> "The nice Gradation by which I pass from Civilization to Incivilization appears in everything: their manners, their dress, their Language, and particularly that remarkable important circumstance of Colour which I am now fully convinced originates from natural Causes; and is the effect of external and local circumstances".

Later, in Yakutsk, after pages and pages of comments in the journal on the Tartars' origins, appearances and customs, he continued the thought:

> "General Remark is that far the greatest part of mankind compared with European Civilization are uncultivated that this part of Mankind are darker Coloured than the other part *viz* European. There are no white Savages few uncivilized people that are not black".

It is natural, from the perspective of present day convictions on the unacceptability of racism, to condemn such sweeping characterisations as indeed racist. But the intellectual climate of Ledyard's time was different: even those, like John Adams, who advocated the abolition of slavery, rarely accepted that blacks were the equals of whites; Adams himself did not believe that whites themselves could ever all be equal. Jefferson, who had written "all men are created equal" into the Declaration of Independence, also condemned slavery in his *Notes on the State of Virginia* (1782); but he still thought blacks were by nature inferior to whites – and kept his own slaves until he died, condemning him forever as hypocritical. One wonders if he and Ledyard ever discussed the question in the context of Ledyard's accounts of his experiences and observations in the Pacific and Alaska.

Ledyard regarded himself as an objective observer of human life in all its aspects, and, as we saw, his sympathetic understanding of the Pacific islanders, and of their difficulties in the face of European expectations of them, was remarkable, especially for that time. His observations on the Siberians were made in the same vein; and though he obviously found them personally less attractive than the Pacific's "Noble Savages", he still did not regard them as people you could not mix with. In fact, four journal pages after the last of the above entries, he made his celebrated remarks about women in the context of his commentary on the Tartars:

"I observe too that the Woman wherever found is the same kind, civil, obliging, humane, tender, being; that she is ever inclined to be gay cheerful; timorous modest; that she does not hesitate like Man to do a generous action of any kind. (And yet nature has bestowed more beauty on the Male of every Species of Animal)— The Woman is never haughty, arrogant or supercilious; full of courtesy fond of Society; economic, ingenious; more liable, in general, to err than man, in general have more virtue perform more good actions than him: they have not so great a variety of character as Man few are above or below this Description. I do not think the Character of Woman so well ascertained in that Society which is highly civilized and polished as in the obscure plain walks of Life; it assumes an importance here unknown to higher Life. My general Remark is that Climate Education makes a great difference in the Character of Men than Women. That I never addressed myself in the Language of Decency Friendship to a Woman whether civilized or savage without receiving a decent friendly answer—even in english Billinsgate. With Man it has often been otherwise. In wandering over the barren plains of inhospitable Denmark; thro' honest Sweden frozen Lapland; rude churlish Finland, unprincipled Russia with the Wandering tartar, If hungry, dry cold, wet, or sick Woman has ever been friendly to me and uniformly so"

– and he goes right on, with typical Ledyard omnivorousness: "Every body at Yakutsk has two sorts of Windows; the one for Summer the other for Winter…". Accompanying the splendidly sweeping generalisations there is of course a very traditional view of the status and role of women; but there is no racism.

It was in Barnaul that Ledyard told Jefferson of being called a wild man because of his tattoos; but, he said,

"Among the better sort we [Americans] are somewhat more known…We have however two Stars that shine even in the Galaxy of Barnowl, the healths of Dr Franklin of Genl Washington have been drank in compliment to me at the Governor's table: I am treated with great hospitality here…: hospitality however I have found as universal as the face of man".

In the apparently unlikely event that Jefferson had any pangs of guilt about his young explorer, his own absence from this list of distinguished Americans may have assuaged them.

Ledyard pressed on to Irkutsk, where he arrived on 15 August and stayed for ten days. This time he wrote to Colonel Smith that

"At this place I am in a circle as gay, rich, polite, and as scientific, as if at Petersburg I drink my French and Spanish wines[which, in his journal, he said were "so adulterated, that I was told of it before I knew it was wine"]: and I have Majors Colonels, and Brigadiers, by Brigades, to wait on me in the town, and disciples of Linnaeus to accompany in my philosophic walks".

Ledyard was thoroughly enjoying himself, apart from being uncomfortable about being "so poorly and oddly attired", which on one occasion kept him from dining with the Governor–General, I.V.Jacobi (who had a private band). But somehow he made it; and once again he noted that Franklin and Washington had been toasted – again in that order – and that, in addition, "the name of Adams has [also] found its way". Jefferson, if ever he knew this, might have felt his young protégé might have talked him up a little in Siberian society.

The Governor–General's mansion where Ledyard dined still hides behind its 19th century classical entrance portico. As recently as the late 20th century sections of Irkutsk were not much changed from the time of Ledyard's visit: some of the 18th century churches and a few other mansions still stood, though at the time of my own visits most of the churches had been closed, and converted to, for example, "a school of cine–mechanics". But it was nearby, still in the old central section, that the small wooden houses, some made of planks but some of logs, and often trimmed round doors and windows with surprising Baroque arabesques, still stood on their uncertainly–settled foundations in patches of grass, beside dirt streets ankle–deep in dust or mud depending on the season. It must have been in one of these that Ledyard found lodging during this first stay.

On the face of it, all went well in Irkutsk: the Governor–General, whose authority extended as far as the Pacific coast,

"wished me a successful voyage, and that my travels might be productive of information to mankind";

and the director of the bank, Aleksander Matveevich Karamyshev, who, surprisingly, had done his dissertation under the great Swedish naturalist Linnaeus (Professor Pallas's mentor), was "very assiduous to oblige me in everything".[286]

---

286   There is an amusing footnote to his acquaintance with "Karamyscheff". Karamyshev believed the movement of the earliest peoples had been from North America to Siberia rather than, as Ledyard correctly believed, vice–versa, because in the latter's view he had been "bedevil'd with the wild system of the french naturalist [Georges de] Buffon". This view of Buffon, the brilliant author of a thirty–six volume *Natural History* (1749–1789) foreshadowing the theory of evolution, must have come from Jefferson, who regarded Buffon as "the best informed of any naturalist who has ever written", but had been outraged by the Frenchman's assertion that the warmer New World was inferior to the colder Old World, and the animals there, both native and introduced, smaller than those in Europe. Regarding patriotism as supported by science, Catherine the Great loaded rich presents on Buffon, delighted at the kudos for Russia in his theory that new species originated in the colder latitudes and migrated towards the tropics. A grateful Buffon told Catherine, who was embarked on the Turkish wars, he hoped to see

Perhaps as important as anything else he did, he mentioned, casually, that he went

"to see a Merchant owner of a Vessel that had passed from Kamschatka to different parts of the Coast of America".

This is believed to have been Grigory Shelikov, who had established a fur–trading company on Kodiak Island off the Anchorage coast of Alaska in 1783. No doubt, in his open friendly way, Ledyard told him about his own experiences a decade earlier on the coast of Alaska with Cook, explained his present intention to pass over from Okhotsk to explore the American northwest, probably spilled out his long–term obsession with getting the United States into the Northwest Pacific fur trade with China, and then pumped Shelikov for information that could be useful to both his own plans. And Shelikov may have become very uneasy about just who and what was behind them.

Ledyard, always anxious to identify everyone as "my friend", detected no sign of any cloud on this rosy horizon; but in four months' time, when he would be arrested here in Irkutsk, none of his "friends" lifted a finger to help him – indeed, were possibly involved in the disaster. It was not in his nature to dwell in retrospect on who the villains might have been; but he did subsequently refer to "Karamyscheff" as that "Scoundrel".

"beautiful nature and the arts descend a second time from the North to the South under the standard of [Her Majesty's] powerful genius".

Regarding such science as incompatible with patriotism, the outraged Jefferson not only refuted Buffon in principle, as well as animal by animal, in *Notes on the State of Virginia*, but took a smelly hair–shedding moose carcass to Paris to show Buffon, and extended the argument to humans – inviting for good measure tall Americans and short Frenchmen to dinner in Paris in case the question arose. He had a standing order with George Rogers Clark, Mapp says, to send him any large–size mammal skeletons he came across in the Ohio; twenty years later, perhaps still smarting, he instructed Lewis and Clark to watch out, as they made their way across America, for – among a thousand and one other things "worthy of notice" – for dinosaur bones and *living* mammoths (mastodons), to disprove Buffon's theory that species could die out. Karamyshev told Ledyard that "extraordinary large bones" found near Irkutsk, which really were from Eurasian mammoths, "they suppose here were the Behemoth"; and Ledyard frequently mentioned other fossil discoveries in various places as he made his way across Siberia, probably intending to please Jefferson - and because he was himself also interested in everything.

On 25 August he set out for Yakutsk. Travelling with a Swedish Lieutenant in Russian employ, Adam Laxmann,[287] oblivious of any difficulty other than the cold and "these cursed unbroke tartar horses" conveying them northwards for 250 kms, then a further 2,000 by canoe down the River Lena, they arrived at Yakutsk on 18 September. There, he wrote in his journal, he delivered his

> "letters to the Commandant of the town, who very politely procured me quarters and waited on me there: but in our first conversation received the dejecting intelligence that it is impossible to proceed to Ohotsk in the winter".

Ledyard was devastated:

> "What alas! shall I do for I am miserably provided for this unlooked for delay…My funds! I have but two long frozen Stages more and I shall be beyond the want of aid or money, until emerging from her deep deserts I gain the American Atlantic States and then the glow[i]ng Climates. Africa explored, I lay me down and claim a little portion of the Globe I've viewed—may it not be before…"This is the third time I have been overtaken and arrested by winter and in both the others by giving time for my *evil genius* to rally her hosts about me have defeated the Enterprise. Fortune thou has humbled me at length, for I am at this moment the slave of cowardly solicitude, least in the womb of this dread winter, there lurks the seeds of disappointment to my ardent desire of gaining the opposite Continent".

"I submit", he went on, "and proceed with my remarks": and launched into a disquisition on the climate of Yakutsk, the salary of the Viceroy, the cost of furnishing a house, and a comparison of the manner in which the Swedish Finlander and northern Tartar, and the Otaheitan, Italian peasant and Spanish fisherman eat…cake. His curiosity was truly insatiable.

But Ledyard did not in fact submit that easily: in a letter to Smith a month later, on 22 October, he admitted that

---

287   Laxmann was subsequently sent to Japan, in 1792, where he gained approval for Russian ships to enter Nagasaki harbour – sixty years before Commodore Perry.

"I almost rudely insisted [to the Commandant] on being permitted to depart immediately was surprized that a Yakutee Indian a tartar horse should be thot incapable to follow Man educated in the Lat^d of 40: he declared upon his honour that the journey was impracticable; the contest lasted 2 or 3 days…The Commandant at length waited on me brot with him a Trader…who had for 9 or 12 years uniformly passed from to Ohotsk here as a witness of the truth propriety of his advice to me: I was obliged however severely I lamented the misfortune to surrender to two such advocates for my happiness".

But he burst out in more Ledyardish style:

"The difficulty of ye journey I was aware of: when I consented to the impracticability of it, it was a compliment for I do not believe it is so to a European hardly any thing else—it is certainly bad in theory to suppose that the seasons can triumph over the efforts of an honest man".

For someone who had walked around the Gulf of Bothnia from Stockholm to St Petersburg in the depths of winter Ledyard clearly had a point. But picking himself up, he told Smith that

"The only consolation I have of the argumentative kind is to reflect that him who travels for information must be supposed to want it…I shall be able by being here 8 months to make my observations much more extensive with respect to the Country its inhabitants than if I had passed immediately thro that also is a satisfaction"

– and off he went again on the Siberian tribes and "great quantities of elephant bones" – in fact, Jefferson would have been delighted to hear, mammoths. Jefferson himself, however, was focussed at this stage on matters domestic: the previous month, on 28 September 1787, the Constitutional Convention in Philadelphia had adopted the Constitution and submitted it to the States themselves for ratification. Ledyard was missing the last great stage in the foundation of the United States of America, just as he had missed most of the rest.

Shortly after Ledyard's eventual departure, a Russian naval Lieutenant, Gavriil Andreevich Sarychev, on his way to join Billings's expedition, arrived to considerable gossip in Yakutsk about Ledyard, who, he reported, "is said to have been a colonel in the army of the United States during the war", though where that came from goodness knows: it would have been totally out of character for Ledyard to have claimed to have been anything he was not. Sarychev said Ledyard's "eccentric conduct [had] excited considerable attention": he was destitute and on an "absurd" enterprise, but in return for "extraordinary hospitality" from the Commandant and others all he did was

> "calumniate and abuse every one; and finally, after a reminder of decency to him, he dared to challenge the commandant to a duel".

Ledyard's actions may well have ben embroidered in the telling: But it is also possible that his own account to Smith of "almost rudely insisting" to the Commandant about his wishes was not entirely frank – he must assuredly have been greatly stressed as well as intensely frustrated by his situation. Martin Sauer, an Englishman who was secretary to the Billings expedition and therefore knew Ledyard from Yakutsk (and subsequently the journey back to Irkutsk), was clearly sympathetic to him; but he later commented in his *Account of a Geographical and Astronomical Expedition to the Northern Parts of Russia* that

> "Ledyard's behaviour had been Haughty, and not at all condescending, which certainly made him enemies".

Sarychev added to his account, no doubt accurately, that "the commander wrote a letter of accusation against him to the governor–general" in Irkutsk.

Whatever his conduct, it does not seem to have occurred to Ledyard that any other considerations than concern for his own "happiness" were involved in his being stopped in Yakutsk. Equally blithely, he recorded in his journal absolutely deadpan that

> "Captain Billings's Command from the River Kolyma arrived here the beginning of this month (Novr 1787) I went to live with him a few days after at his lodgings as one of his Family and his Friend" – of course.

On the 24th he elaborated on this development in his journal:

> "The arrival of Captain Billings at Yakutsk is a circumstance that gives a turn to my affairs. I have before had no occasion to write

Journialment.[288] I now commence. Captain Billings is last from the Kolyma River where he has some small Cutter built vessels in which he last Summer made an attempt to [explore the Arctic Coast eastwards]. The Event of this Undertaking other circumstances relative to the Tour both by Land Water I am yet uninformed of, perhaps some accounts will be kept secret from me, but as others will naturally transpire in the course of my acquaintance with him I shall write them as they occur".

This last sentence makes it obvious that it had never crossed Ledyard's mind that his diary (and correspondence) could be – and probably was – read by Catherine's spies: keeping tabs on foreigners did not begin with the Soviets, though they were probably better at it. Billings was also probably reading the journal. Nor does Ledyard seem to have noticed that no pieces of information "naturally transpired" over the course of the ensuing month they were together in Yakutsk: the journal records only a few observations by Billings on the customs of "Tartar" groups Ledyard had not come in contact with, but in whom he was of course fascinated as always.

Finally, at the end of December 1787, Billings announced that he had decided to return to Irkutsk to check on supplies he had been expecting, and get them forwarded as soon as the Lena unfroze in spring; and he invited Ledyard to go with him. But why would Billings want to make a 2,500 kilometre trip overland in the middle of winter, to arrange a movement of supplies that would only be possible the following May? And admittedly Ledyard would have had nothing to keep him in Yakutsk until May, but why did Billings invite him? Was it just for the company? – or something else? Was the "invitation" related to the Commandant's letter about Ledyard to the Governor–General in Irkutsk? Sarychev, in his account, said specifically that

"The arrival of Mr Billings...prevented any farther serious consequences from [Ledyard's behaviour towards the Commandant], by
his taking this man with him to Irkutsk".

All the elements were now in place for Ledyard's doom. But Ledyard himself seems to have had no inkling of any of them. He had however

---

288 A stab at *journellement*, a French word for "daily"; the English equivalent is the obsolete "journally", with the same meaning.

– despite many people's kindnesses in keeping him alive and moving eastwards – already developed a sweepingly jaundiced view of the Russians. Before he left Yakutsk he expostulated to his journal in terms marvellously reminiscent of those used almost exactly a century earlier in the Englishman John Speed's *Prospect of the Most Famous Parts of the World*:

> "I have observed", Ledyard wrote, "from Petersburg to this place here more than any where that the Russians in general have very few moral Virtues, the body of the people are almost without. the Laws of the Country are mostly penal Laws; but all civil Laws are but negative instructors; they inform people what they must not do, and affix the penalty to the transgression. but they do not inform people what they should do and affix the reward to Virtue, Untaught in the sublime of morality the Russian has not that glorious basis on which to exalt his nature. This in some countries is made the business of Religion and in a few instances of the civil Law. In this unfortunate Country it is a business of neither civil nor ecclesiastical Concernment... They have never heard the sweet Truth that virtue is its own Reward...It is for this Reason that their Peasantry, in particular are indubitably the most unprincipled in Christendom. I look for certain Virtues of the heart that are called natural. I find them not in the most remote obscure Villages in the Empire but on the contrary I find the rankest vices to abound as much as in their Capital".

There are curious parallels to much later American views of this evil empire.

The empire strikes back

Having been arrested by winter in Yakutsk, Ledyard was now arrested in Irkutsk by the police. On the Empress's orders. On 18 December 1787, before he and Billings had left Yakutsk, the following entry was made by Catherine's personal secretary, Alexander Khrapovitsky, in his official diary:

> "It is ordered to send back the American John Ledyard, making his way from Okhotsk to America, from that place; he was a naval cadet with the famous Cook".

Sentence was executed on Ledyard in Irkutsk on 24 February 1788.[289]
How was recounted by Martin Sauer:

"In the evening of 24th February", he wrote in his *Account of
a Geographical and Astronomical Expedition to the Northern
Parts of Russia*, "while I was playing at cards with the Brigadier
and some company of his, a secretary belonging to one of the
courts of justice came in, and told us, with great concern, that the
Governor–General had received positive orders from the Empress,
immediately to send one of the Expedition, an Englishman, under
guard to the private inquisition at Mosco; but that he did not
know the name of the person, and that Captain Billings was with
a private party at the Governor–General's. Now, as Ledyard and
I were the only Englishmen here, I could not help smiling at the
news, when two hussars came into the room, and told me that the
Commandant wished to see me immediately. The consternation
into which the visitors were thrown is not to be described. I assured
them that it must be a mistake, and went with the guards to the
Commandant. Here I found Mr. Ledyard under arrest. He told me,
that he had sent for Captain Billings, but he would not come to
him. He then began to explain his situation, and said that he was
taken up as a French spy, whereas Captain Billings could prove
the contrary; but he supposed that he knew nothing of the matter,
and requested that I would inform him. I did so; but the Captain
assured me that it was an absolute order from the Empress, and he
could not help him".

It was all over very quickly:

"Ledyard took a friendly leave of me, desired his remembrance
to his friends, and with astonishing composure leaped into the
kibitka [post–carriage], and drove off, with two guards, one on
each side".

Sauer described it all with exemplary clarity. What is not clear is how
this sudden turn of events came about; and it is worth looking again at

---

289 It was twenty–nine days after Governor Arthur Phillip arrived at Port
Jackson (Sydney Harbour) to establish the first British penal colony in Australia,
promoted by Joseph Banks.

the attitudes and actions that were possible reasons for this ultimate Russian distrust and displeasure.

Subsequently Ledyard himself simply wrote, when he next had the opportunity to do so in June, that

> "The motives of the Empress in arresting me are found upon examination to have been a mixture of jealousy envy malice".

He never explained his "examination" any further. But he was, of course, right: at the centre was Catherine herself – the decision was hers, whatever the elements that went into her making it.[290] She had refused Ledyard permission to make his "chimaerical' voyage across Siberia to North America; but behind her back Ledyard had come to St Petersburg anyway, and there had somehow managed to get her detested son, the Grand Duke Paul, to authorise the excursion after all. Catherine had returned to St Petersburg from her progress through southern Russia with Potemkin and the Austrian Emperor towards the end of July of 1787. When did she find out that, contrary to her command, Ledyard had in fact set out for Siberia at the beginning of June? It is possible, perhaps likely, that she did not discover the truth until a report reached her from her Governor–General in Irkutsk, with Ledyard already well over half–way to the Pacific.

But what could the Governor–General have reported in any case that would have prompted such a severe reaction by the Empress? Later, in his journal, Ledyard referred to "the Scoundrel Chevalier Karamyschew", suggesting that he at least believed his "obliging" banker acquaintance in Irkutsk was involved in the arrest. Jared Sparks began speculation on the subject in 1828 in his biography of Ledyard, and firmly fixed on Shelikov, the Alaskan fur trader, as the villain:

> "Now the head–quarters of this company were at Irkutsk, and it could not have escaped the sagacity of its conductors, that a foreigner, visiting their islands, would make discoveries which might be published to their disadvantage, both in regard to the resources of traffic, and to the cruel manner in which the traders habitually treat the natives, in extorting from them the fruits of

---

290   We can dispose first up of Sauer's furphy of Ledyard's being a "French spy". There was no such reference in Catherine's command as recorded by Khrapovitsky; and it makes no sense on any consideration. It must have been a slip of confusion on Ledyard's or Sauer's part.

their severe and incessant labours. To obviate such a consequence, it was necessary to cut short the traveller's career, before he had penetrated to the eastern shores of Asia".

Concern about the fur trade, including on the part of the Governor–General, who was responsible for its oversight, could indeed have been involved in Catherine's decision. But if the Governor–General had sent a report soon after Ledyard's departure from Irkutsk for Yakutsk, on 25 August, it should have reached St Petersburg by the end of October (as we saw, her *ukase* of 18 December reached Irkutsk by 24 February, a lapse of seven weeks). Why would it have taken almost two more months for it to be considered and acted on? It could have taken time for Court officials to decide when would be a propitious occasion – or the least inauspicious occasion – to inform the Empress that, in her absence, not only had her direct command about Ledyard been ignored but so had her instructions on the exclusion of the Grand Duke from government. Catherine's wrath was not to be provoked lightly. But two months' delay?

And why, if the Governor–General's concern was so great, and his report so crucial, had he allowed Ledyard to go cheerily off to Yakutsk, armed, to boot, with his own letter of introduction to the Commandant of the latter, Grigory Alekseevich Marklovsky? –

"With this letter the American 'gentleman' John Ledyard comes to you travelling from St Petersburg through this country to America for the acquisition of knowledge and information about natural history in all its departments. He is a pretty good man and his intention inclines toward joining up with a secret naval expedition [presumably Billings's]; and for this reason I request you humbly to receive Mr Ledyard with as much favour as possible, and in all his desires uniformly to render him assistance in every possible way and to deliver him to the above–mentioned Expedition without the slightest delay".

Was this just for Ledyard's consumption? Was there a secret message telling the Commandant to hold Ledyard – for his "safety" during the winter – and send him back to Irkutsk? Why not hold him in Irkutsk in the first place?

Does whatever went on in Yakutsk fit into the equation? It seems highly improbable that Ledyard's alleged or real bad behaviour would have been reported to the Empress. But Joseph Billings could have played a sinister role. When Sauer published his account of the Billings expedition it became apparent to everyone that the "Captain–Lieutenant" had been incompetent and, not to put too fine a point upon it, less than bold. In fact in 1800 the English traveller Dr Edward Clarke met Professor Pallas in St Petersburg, and later wrote in his *Travels in Russia, Tartary and Turkey*:

> "That the expedition might have been confined to better hands, the public have been since informed by the secretary Sauer. This, Professor Pallas lamented to have discovered when it was too late...[T]he sudden recall of the unfortunate Ledyard...it is said, would never have happened, but through the jealousy of his own countrymen, whom he chanced to encounter as he was upon the point of quitting the eastern continent for America, and who caused the information to be sent to Petersburg, which occasioned the order for his arrest".

Many years after that, in 1819, Rear–Admiral James Burney FRS – Jem Burney, Ledyard's and Billings's midshipman colleague on the *Resolution* – in his compendium *A Chronological History of North–Eastern Voyages of Discovery*, sarcastically remarked that

> "If the Empress had understood the characters of the two men, the commander of the expedition would probably have been ordered to *Moscow*, and Ledyard instead of being denied entertainment in her service, have been appointed to supply his place".[291]

Clarke does not exactly say that Pallas himself gave him the explanation for Ledyard's arrest, and there is no other indication as to where he picked it up. Sparks dismissed it on the spurious ground that Billings, as an Englishman, was not Ledyard's "countryman", and that there was no

---

291   It is rather startling to discover that by this time James Burney had been the author of a considerable scandal: in 1798 he had left his wife and children and eloped with his...half–sister, Sarah Burney; after living with her for five years he returned home to his extraordinarily understanding wife. It is little wonder that his sister, the novelist and diarist Fanny Burney, commented that James "had the eccentric idea he might hold himself above the controul of opinion, or custom".

proof of Billings's hostility to him, or that he "could have any reasons for thwarting [Ledyard's] designs". Perhaps Billings did recognise that Ledyard, even alone, was a living reproach to his own conduct, that if Ledyard succeeded he would completely overshadow his own fumbling efforts and reap who knows what rewards. Billings may have *behaved* in a friendly way towards Ledyard – inviting him to share digs, inviting him to come back to Irkutsk with him (which also suited the Commandant at Yakutsk, as Sarychev said). What better way to keep an eye on Ledyard, to find out more about his plans – just as (somewhat comically) Ledyard thought he was doing about Billings's! – than to turn him back from Yakutsk? And then there was Billings's disgraceful and cowardly behaviour *after* Ledyard's arrest at Irkutsk: admittedly, Sauer curtly says, Billings "sent him a few roubles, and gave him a pelisse"; but he steadfastly refused even to see Ledyard, much less to intercede on his behalf. Was this just cowardice? Or shame? Yet whatever role Billings may have played in getting Ledyard out of his and the Commandant's hair in Yakutsk, it could not have contributed to Catherine's decision to arrest Ledyard: as Billings only arrived in Yakutsk at the beginning of November there was no way any message could have reached St Petersburg before 18 December. It is a pity the theory was wrong: it is easy to dislike Billings.[292]

We will not be able to fathom why Catherine did not make her decision until mid–December. Why she made it at all we probably can, and there were probably three aspects to it. One was that, despite her having forbidden Ledyard's voyage across Siberia, he had turned up in St Petersburg anyway, still determined to make it; the fact that Grand Duke Paul, who must have been apprised of her earlier position, had nevertheless authorised Ledyard's travel would no doubt have angered her further, and hardened her determination to remove the American.

Ledyard's origins were a further factor: he was a foreigner. On the other hand the Court, the army, the navy, other branches of the administration were in fact all stuffed with foreigners, at all levels.

---

292   Although Sauer found Billings "greedy, selfish, ignorant, and tyrannical", the *DNB* says he "successfully commanded the expedition during the whole time [nine years], and that by it were made many large additions to our knowledge of the geography of those inclement regions". Billings then disappears from view; perhaps he saw out his days in St Petersburg on Catherine's gratuity and life pension. That nothing more is heard of him puts a question mark, however, over the "success" of his apparently one and only command.

The Empress herself was a foreigner, come to that: little Princess Sophia of Zerbst–Anhalt, become Catherine the Great through her own efforts. Catherine admired enterprise and achievement, whoever provided it – provided it was for the greatness of Catherine. But Ledyard was an American foreigner. The most striking contrast with his treatment was the experience of Jeremy Bentham's young brother. When the twenty–year–old Samuel Bentham just turned up in St Petersburg in 1780 to make his fortune, he had been taken up by Potemkin, who sent him the following year to Irkutsk and other parts of Siberia...to analyse its industries; though he was given a small military escort "for his safety", a young Englishman could clearly be trusted. But even Ledyard's nationality was obviously not of itself decisive: after all, Catherine's characterisation of his old business partner Captain John Paul Jones' plans as "marvellous" came only one year later. Of course Jones was going to the Black Sea, under the command of her Potemkin, not roaming around alone.

However Ledyard was not just another American. Admittedly John Paul Jones had fought for the American rebels against her brother monarch King George III. But Ledyard (who had not) was sponsored by Thomas Jefferson, the man who, even before his Declaration of Independence, had written a pamphlet in July 1774, *A Summary View of the Rights of British America*, in which he not only asserted "The British parliament has no right to exercise authority over us", but, as Joseph Ellis has pointed out, used a "tone towards George III [which] ranges between the disrespectful and the accusatory" – the King was

"not some specially endowed ruler but merely 'the chief officer of the people, appointed by the laws, and circumscribed with definite powers, to assist in working the great machine of government erected for their use, and consequently subject to their superintendence' ".

Catherine did not give support to George during the Revolutionary War, despite his asking – that was a matter of power politics – but she would have been outraged by Jefferson's disrespect for the ordained order of things. At the least Jefferson's sponsorship, even with the endorsement of von Grimm and Lafayette, would not have helped Ledyard's position when Catherine came to focus on it.

But the key to his doom was not his disobedience to her ruling, nor the added insult of Grand Duke Paul's assistance, nor Thomas Jefferson's sponsorship, but Ledyard's own background. Catherine said so in her order of 18 December 1787:

"he was a naval cadet with the famous Cook".

As we know, Cook's third voyage had already prompted Catherine's interest and concern. Was there a curious symmetry of concern going on? On the face of it, Jefferson's sole interest, as it appeared in his letter to Lafayette asking him to get the Comte de Ségur in St Petersburg to approach Catherine on behalf of Ledyard, was in the discovery of the American West. If so, why this madcap excursion across 12,000 mostly appallingly difficult kilometres of Europe and Asia? Could not Ledyard have awaited another ship, English or French, no–one seemed to mind which, to get to the Pacific Northwest? Or go back across the Atlantic and try "from our side of the continent". What exactly *did* Jefferson have in mind? That he wanted Ledyard, as the next cab off the rank after his flyer with George Rogers Clark in 1783, to explore the West was apparent; was he, however, also concerned about Ledyard's report of Russian activities on the American coast?

Thirty–five years later the Comte de Ségur wrote to Lafayette (in response to an enquiry prompted by Jared Sparks) recalling Jefferson's approach at the beginning of 1786:

"I remember only, that, in compliance with your request, I furnished [Ledyard] with the best recommendations at the court of Russia. He was at first very well received; but the Empress, who spoke to me on the subject herself, observed, that she would not render herself guilty of the death of this courageous American, by furthering a journey so fraught with danger, as that he proposed to undertake alone, across the unknown and savage regions of North–western America".

This we knew. But Ségur now added:

"Possibly this pretext of humanity, advanced by Catherine, only disguised her unwillingness to have the new possessions of Russia, on the western coast of America, seen by an enlightened citizen of the United States".

Russian–American suspicions did not begin with the Bolsheviks.

And so Ledyard was transported by Catherine's guards back across Siberia and European Russia, and, only about four weeks and 6,000 kms later, tipped over the border into Poland as it was then at the village of Tolochin.[293] The stages of his ordeal are hard to reconstruct from the now fragmentary journal. At Nizhni Novgorod, almost as far as Moscow, he struck a philosophical note:

"There are two kinds of People I could anathematize...; those who dare deprive others of their Liberty, those who could suffer others to do it",

but then cried out in anguished bewilderment:

"It is more than 20 days since I have eat in that time have been dragged in some miserable open Kabitka 5,000 Versts [approx.= kms]. Thus am I treated in all respects (except that I am obliged to support myself with my own Money) like a vile Convict. Was I guilty of any the least thing against the Country or any thing in it, or was there even a Crime alledged against me, I could suffer with some patience or at least resignation".

Nevertheless he still included further speculation on "the cause of the difference of Colour in the human Species"; unsavoury though conventional (for the time) anti–Semitic comments, especially in Poland where he was at liberty to mix with the population; a long disquisition on rivers; and observations on everything under the sun, encompassing reports on tattooing in Moldavia and Turkey, and (if you please) on wampum again – "or if you will, Beads, Tassels, Rings, Fringes, easter Gewgaws, are as much here [near the Volga] as in Siberia".

Ledyard crossed Poland through Vilnius (now the capital of Lithuania) to Konigsberg in East Prussia (now Kaliningrad, in the Russian Baltic Sea enclave), thence to London, possibly by sea. However the journal (as it has survived anyway) ended just after Vilnius, and there is an amusingly suggestive entry on the very last page. At some point along the road Ledyard had "taken under my protection" a "distressed Girl of Dantsic [Danzig]"; now he says that as they were leaving Vilnius

---

293   This is now in Byelorussia, 400 kms east of the present Polish border, and about half–way between Minsk and Smolensk (in Russia).

"the Postillion begged I would not.......the young Woman I had with me in the Kabitka for if I did the Horses would certainly be taken with Sickness".

The text is a transcript of his original manuscript: we do not know who censored it.

But, even while tending to the distress of a Girl from Dantsic, his anger at his experience in Russia breaks through again: in the very last sentence he recorded in the journal he exclaimed emphatically:

"Let no European put entire Confidence in a Russian of whatever Condition...".

Again John Ledyard presaged the view of many future sojourners in that extraordinary and extraordinarily difficult country.

Africa – the last great caper

Ledyard was back in London by the beginning of May 1788, "disappointed, ragged, penniless", as he wrote cousin Isaac. It was the first Isaac had heard of him for two years; and in addition to a miscellaneous collection of Ledyard's observations on the climate at Yakutsk, the origins of racial colours and such like, he was sent a miscellaneous collection of Russian and "Tartar" fur garments, together with

"the cloak...which they are wrapt up in [which] was made in London. I traveled on foot with it in Danemarc Sweeden Lapland Finland the Lord knows where: in opulence in poverty I have kept it slept in it, eat in it, drank in it, fought in it, negociated in it: it has been thro every scene my constant faithfull servant from my departure to my return to London to give it an asylum for I have none here I send it to you".

This little passage conveys more of the loneliness and disappointment of his great quest than any of the more passionate outbursts, eloquent though some are, condemning Catherine or lauding liberty.

But Ledyard also told Isaac that he was now going "to travel through the continent of Africa". Without wasting any time, he had turned again to Sir Joseph Banks: perhaps to thank him for honouring the drafts he had drawn against the great botanist's bankers during his eastern travels, perhaps because his antennae had quickly detected something in the wind. Banks had previously been impressed by – as Jefferson put it – Ledyard's "ingenuity and information". Jefferson had added, in an uncharitable reproof by the man who had conceived of the Russian caper on which Ledyard was at the time still stranded, that "unfortunately he has too much imagination." Now, for the next venture he was sponsoring, Banks was looking for a good dose of imagination. The Association for Promoting the Discovery of the Interior Regions of Africa was only founded on 9 June 1788, but it had already been in the minds of its promoters: Banks, principally, but also a distinguished supporting cast: Henry Addington, a Member of Parliament and future Prime Minister; the Earl of Bute and the Duke of Grafton, both former Prime Ministers; General Henry Conway, Walpole's nephew, a veteran of Dettingen and Culloden, and a former MP; Edward Gibbon, the historian; the Duke of Northumberland; and William Wilberforce, the great slavery abolitionist.

The step from there to Ledyard is told by Henry Beaufoy, another MP and Secretary to the Association, in his first report to it. Ledyard, he said, on arriving in London

"Immediately waited on Sir Joseph Banks, who told him, knowing his temper, that he believed he could recommend him to an adventure almost as perilous as the one from which he had returned...LEDYARD replied, that he had always determined to traverse the Continent of Africa as soon as he had explored the Interior of North America; and as Sir Joseph had offered him a Letter of Introduction, he came directly to the Writer of these Memoirs. Before I had learnt from the note the name and business of my Visitor, I was struck with the manliness of his person, the breadth of his chest, the openness of his countenance, and the inquietude of his eye. I spread the map of Africa before him, and tracing a line from Cairo to Sennar [in Sudan, on the Blue Nile south of Khartoum], and from thence Westward in the latitude and supposed direction of the Niger [River], I told him that was the route, by which I was anxious that Africa might, if possible, be explored. He said, he should think himself singularly fortunate to be entrusted with the Adventure. I asked him when he would set out? 'Tomorrow morning,' was his answer".

Too soon for Beaufoy: but Ledyard did leave as early as 30 June, only three weeks after the Association's inauguration.

It would be the first known European exploration through these parts of what was then still a huge blank space on the map of the "Dark Continent". Certainly nothing much had changed in Europe's knowledge since Jonathon Swift's delightful verse that Sparks quoted:

> "Geographers, in Afric maps,
> With savage pictures fill their gaps,
> And o'er uninhabitable downs
> Place elephants for want of towns".

Writing to tell cousin Isaac that he had once again fallen on his feet, Ledyard indicated that his own grasp of African geography was still a little uncertain:

> "My route lays from here to Paris, to Marseilles, across the Mediterranean to Alexandria, to Grand Cairo in Egypt to Mecca on the Red Sea" – in the opposite direction to the Niger.

He is initially more sober than he used to be:

> "Beyond is unknown my discoveries begin; where they will terminate or how you shall know if I survive";

but soon the old optimism oozes through:

> "The Society consists at present of 200 Members. It is a growing thing, the King privately promoting encouraging it will make its objects more extensive than at first thought of. The king has told them no expence should be spared".

But, as usual, there was already disappointment in store: George III welched on the financing. So the only funds available were small contributions from the core members of the Association who – for the highest of reasons – had no intention of being improvident: they were

> "persuaded that in such an Undertaking Poverty is a better protection than Wealth, and that Mr Ledyard's address will be much more effectual than money, to open him a passage to the Interior of Africa".

To his friend Thomas Jefferson, still in Paris, Ledyard sent only an hilariously lapidary note on 4 July after arriving there:

> "Mr Ledyard presents his compliments to Mr Jefferson—he has been imprisoned and banished by the Empress of Russia from her dominions after having almost gained the pacific ocean. He is now on his way to Africa to see what he can do with that continent".

It was of course the twelfth anniversary of the adoption of the Declaration of Independence, and just two days after Cyrus Griffin of Virginia, President of Congress under the Articles of Confederation, had formally announced that, with Virginia's ratification, the new Constitution of the United States of America was now formally in effect. Though of course this would not be known in Paris for weeks yet, the American Revolution was finally complete – apart from the abolition of slavery, which the Founding Fathers, fierce opponents like John Adams and of course slave–holders like Thomas Jefferson alike, had avoided for fear of preventing the establishment of the Union.

Jefferson, who had not heard from Ledyard since he was at Barnaul in central Siberia two years before, must have been rather startled at his change of direction, though gratified to hear from Thomas Paine that Banks

> "has a high opinion of Ledyard, and thinks him the only man fitted for such an expedition".

There is no specific record of any meetings between the diplomat and the adventurer during his week in Paris, but Ledyard seems to have called on Jefferson, and was perhaps specifically asked by him to do a note on his conclusions about his Siberian expedition. In any event, later on the 4th or the next day, while still in Paris, Ledyard sent Jefferson another letter, no longer about about the fur trade, but, after some philosophising, about the anthropological conclusions he had arrived at in Siberia:

> "S^r I am certain (the negroes excepted because I have not yet personally visited them) that the difference in the colour of Men is the effect of natural causes".
>
> S^r I am certain that all the people you call red people on the continent of America on the continents of Europe Asia as far south

as the southern parts of China are all one people by whatever names distinguished...

...I am satisfied myself that America was peopled from Asia".

He reached a bit far into China; but he finished with the most impressive conclusion, for his time, that he ever came to:

"I am satisfied myself that the great general analogy in the customs of men can only be accounted for by supposing them all to compose one family".

The fact that the letter made no mention of anything else suggests that Ledyard must have given an oral account of his Russian experiences. This shows, too, in a letter written just afterwards by Jefferson himself: writing on 19 July to the Reverend James Madison (not the Revolutionary statesman but the president of Jefferson's alma mater, William and Mary College in Williamsburg, Virginia), Jefferson indicated he knew more about the Russian trip than was in Ledyard's brief first note, and went on to say more specifically that

"Mr Lediard...passed by this place, which he left a few days ago... [to] explore the Nile to its source, cross to the head of the Niger, and descend that to its mouth. He promises me, if he escapes through this journey, he will go to Kentucky and endeavour to penetrate Westwardly from thence to the South sea"

by which he presumably meant the Pacific Ocean. He had presumably pressed Ledyard yet again to carry out his own dream of having the Pacific Northwest explored by an American. It would be fascinating to know Jefferson's reactions to Ledyard's earnest anthropologising as well, but sadly there is no record of his views.

However, like Colonel Smith all those years back, Jefferson was apparently not too pleased about Ledyard's new exercise in Africa, for the latter was to write later from Egypt that

"I shall never think my letter an indifferent one, when it contains the declaration of my gratitude and my affection for you; and this, notwithstanding you thought hard of me for being employed by an English Association, which hurt me much while I was in Paris".

It was not just the auspices, it was also the irrelevant destination: Jefferson was obviously determined not to give up on his desire for Ledyard to explore the American West; indeed he came back to it in another letter the following year, in March 1789, though this time with a repeat of the casual carelessness for Ledyard that he had displayed early in the Russian voyage. Jefferson, noting that he had just heard from "Admiral Paul–Jones" back in St Petersburg "on the call of the Empress" (after falling out with Potemkin), this time wrote that

> "My last accounts from Lediard (another bold countryman of ours) were from Grand Cairo. He was just plunging into the unknown regions of Africa, probably never to emerge again. If he returns, he has promised me to go to America and penetrate from Kentucke to the Western side of the Continent".

One can not help wondering why on earth Jefferson had not sent Ledyard westwards from "Kentucke" in the first place, in 1785, instead of heading him off on the hare–brained trans–Siberian crossing. But by the time Jefferson wrote this letter poor Ledyard was long dead.

All we know of Ledyard in Africa is from his last three letters to Jefferson. He found terminally sick Ottoman Egypt even more dislikable than Russia: whatever he thought of the condition of the people, at least Russia had the kind of wilderness that he had loved so much in the Northeast and Northwest of his native America. Egypt was, initially, *just* people, and the country man found Alexandria, where he arrived in August 1788, overwhelming and appalling:

> "poverty, rapine, murder, tumult, blind bigotry, cruel persecution, pestilence".

In Cairo, which he reached mid–August, he met "the Aga Mahommed, the confidential minister of Ismael, the most powerful of the four ruling Beys", who told him he would "see in his travels a people, who had power to transmute themselves into the forms of different animals"; and later, in his "ignorance, simplicity, and credulity" told more "fables". Ledyard exclaimed

> "Is it not curious, that the Egyptians...are still such dupes to the arts of sorcery? Was it the same people who built the pyramids?"

He was clearly becoming impatient and irritable. The Aga Mahommed also asked him – not unreasonably –

"how he could travel, without the language of the people where I should pass?"; and he remarked waspishly: "I told him, with vocabularies. I might as well have read him a page of Newton's Principia".

People kept getting in the way of his observation of the country, but he did not think much of that either:

"Sweet are the songs of Egypt on paper. Who is not ravished with gums, balms, dates, figs, pomegranates, circassia, and sycamores, without recollecting that amidst these are dust, hot and fainting winds, bugs, musquitoes, spiders, flies, leprosy, fevers, and almost universal blindness".

Ledyard had found what would come to be called "the Third World", and he was not ready for it.

Nevertheless, a whole new continent revived his endless observations designed to determine the origins of and connections between races; inevitably, he found wampum – on "a small mummy". But there was also some very down–to–earth work:

"I wonder why travellers to Cairo have not visited these slave markets, and conversed with the Jelabs, or travelling merchants of these caravans; both are certainly sources of great information... For my part, I have not expended a crown, and I have a better idea of the people of Africa, of its trade, of the position of places, the nature of the country, and manner of travelling, than ever I had by any other means".

However the wait for the caravan to Sennar, with which he was to travel up the Nile, dragged on from August into September, then October, finally into November; and the waiting, the climate, the conditions, the people, all took their toll.

Here he was among the stupendous relics of Egypt's great past, or, more accurately, layer upon layer of the past: the Pharaonic treasures of Giza and Memphis, the Islamic jewels of the Ayyubids and Mamluks; but he had nothing to say about all those treasures. Even history had let him down: in his last letter, to Thomas Jefferson, written from Cairo on 15 November 1788, Ledyard wrote:

"I think I know your taste for ancient history; it does not comport with what experience teaches me...[M]ost historians have written more to satisfy themselves than to benefit others. I am certainly very angry with those, who have written of the countries where I have travelled...They have all more or less deceived me";

his final reflection, encompassing Russia as much as Egypt:

"Religion does more mischief than all other things".

It was not quite his final word: he concluded the letter, no doubt thinking of the risks of the move into the unknown that he was about to make, with a touching personal message to Jefferson:

"Do not forget me. I shall not forget you. Indeed, it would be a consolation to think of you in my last moments. Be happy".

If he was envisaging a heroic end, somewhere in the darkest depths of Africa, he was to be disappointed yet again, for the last time: he died, still in Cairo, on 10 January 1789, of a burst blood vessel caused by a violent rage at still more delays in the departure of the Sennar caravan.

Beaufoy summed up Ledyard's character in a way which seems a fair match to the man we have come to know a little:

"[H]is manners, though unpolished, were neither uncivil nor unpleasing. Little attentive to difference of rank, he seemed to consider all men as his equals, and as such he respected them. His genius, though uncultivated and irregular, was original and comprehensive. Ardent in his wishes, yet calm in his deliberations; daring in his purposes, but guarded in his measures; impatient of controul, yet capable of strong endurance; adventurous beyond the conception of ordinary men, yet wary and considerate, and attentive to all precautions, he appeared to be formed by Nature for achievements of hardihood and peril".

Jefferson responded to the news with anxiety for more precise details; but there were none. Sir Joseph Banks, no doubt disappointed at the loss of the expedition (six years later he was to send Mungo Park in search of the Niger, but from the west), was no less distressed at the loss of the man. Writing to Jefferson, back in the United States, in June, Thomas Paine quoted Banks as saying

> "We sincerely lament [Ledyard's] loss, as the papers we have received from him are full of those emanations of Spirit which taught you to construct a Bridge without any reference to the means used by your predecessors in that Art".

Notwithstanding Beaufoy's fine and just tribute, Paine noted that

> "[Ledyard's] manner of writing had surprised them [the members of the Association for Promoting the Discovery of the Internal Regions of Africa] as they at first conceived him a bold but illiterate adventurer. That man said Sir Joseph one day to me 'was all Mind' ".

Those class–ridden English assumptions, the "insolence" Ledyard himself had found objectionable, were also noted by his French admirer, Lafayette. Writing in 1823 to Jared Sparks, he referred to the entry on him in the extant edition of the *Encyclopedia Britannica*, which, Lafayette said,

> "does not appear to me so correct...[for example] the surprise expressed by the English author to find a man of no disagreeable manners who despises the accidental distinctions of Society and seems to regard no man as his superior".

An American patriot could have had no finer epitaph. But Ledyard probably would have preferred "America's Marco Polo".

President Jefferson: gaining a continent

In April 1789, before Jefferson left Paris, George Washington was elected first President under the new Constitution of the United States of America. It took eight years to secure independence, less than one to reach agreement on the constitution which still governs the United States two hundred years later. The American Revolution was over, just before the French Revolution began a process which has produced thirteen constitutions, so far.

On arriving back in America from Paris in November 1789, Jefferson discovered that Washington had appointed him the first Secretary of

State. Ironically, his first responsibility, in 1790, was to deal with a crisis at Nootka Sound where the Spanish had captured a colony of British fur traders, and both countries appealed for American support. Steering warily between the two to see what concessions the United States might obtain in return, Jefferson must have reflected on Ledyard's accounts of the growing competition for the Pacific Northwest. But the crisis fizzled out, and Jefferson's preoccupations became mostly his political struggles with his close friend John Adams and their mutual bitter political enemy Alexander Hamilton.

Perhaps, though, he might have learned of the return to Boston on 10 August of two ships, outfitted three years before by Boston merchants, while Ledyard was on Jefferson's wild goose chase across Siberia, to round Cape Horn and collect at Nootka Sound, for sale in Canton, a cargo of sea otter skins – which Cook had noted as the Russian fur traders' chief objective in Alaska. Commanded by Captain Robert Gray, they were the first American ships to circumnavigate the globe, and the first to engage in Ledyard's desperately desired Pacific Northwest fur trade. And surely Jefferson would have heard of Gray's discovery, two years later, on his second circumnavigation in the fur trade, of the Columbia River, which he named after his ship. In ten years it would figure very prominently in Jefferson's own plans for the future of the United States.

After four years (1796–1800) with the consolation prize of the Vice-Presidency under John Adams, who succeeded Washington, Jefferson was elected third President of the United States in 1800, on the thirty-sixth ballot in the House of Representatives, the members voting by states. It is extraordinary how rapidly Jefferson moved in this first term – for he was to be re–elected in 1804 – to extend the United States' control over the North American continent south of Canada. He went about this in two ways, as we saw when he talked with von Humboldt just as his second term was getting under way: the first was a matter of skilfully seizing an extraordinary opportunity; the second was the bringing to fruition of his twenty–year–old musings with General George Rogers Clark and scheming with John Ledyard.

The Louisiana Purchase

New Orleans had originally been colonised by the French at the end of the seventeenth century, but, as the French and Indian Wars were ending disastrously, in 1762 the French secretly ceded it and the Louisiana Territory to the west to Spain. Forty years later, with dreams of an

American as well as a European empire, Napoleon thought otherwise, and forced Spain to retrocede it, also secretly, in 1800; though for the present the Spanish would remain in control. The United States had had increasing problems with Spain over the vital right to share navigation of the Mississippi. Jefferson, already distrustful of Napoleon's ambitions, was even more perturbed when word of this new move reached Washington the next year. With great foresight Jefferson soon began making clear that he was determined to prevent the French from re–occupying New Orleans and threatening Mississippi navigation. He certainly did not want war, but if France would not cede New Orleans in turn to the United States, the latter would place self–preservation above old enmities; and he went to the extraordinary but unmistakably clear length of letting Napoleon know that

> "The day that France takes possession of New Orleans...we must marry ourselves to the British fleet and nation".

It did not quite come to that, but it was Napoleon who blinked first.

He did so partly because France was already bogged down in a losing campaign in Hispaniola (present–day Haiti and Dominican Republic), where the former slave Toussaint L'Ouverture, once made commander–in–chief in the colony, was now leading a black revolution against Napoleon's attempt to re–establish slavery. His struggle was to result, in 1804, after his death by French trickery, in the second independent state in the Americas. With the death in January 1803 of the commander of his expeditionary force, which was being ravaged by black guerrillas and yellow fever, Napoleon realised that he could not hold this base, and that without it France could not hold New Orleans against British seapower:

> "Damn sugar! Damn coffee! Damn colonies".

Negotiations for New Orleans began in Paris in March. On 11 April Talleyrand, currently Napoleon's Foreign Minister, shocked the American negotiator, Richard Livingston, a co–author with Jefferson of the Declaration of Independence and now in the latter's old job as American envoy to France, by asking, "What will you give for the whole of Louisiana?". Talleyrand meant, of course, "What will you give *me?*" Talleyrand's ability to survive fixed his reputation: as a Paris newspaper would later say, he was "laden with the ignominy of nine governments that have rolled over France for half a century, traitor to God and Man, who has wasted a lifetime bartering morality, selling consciences...";

but he wasted no time and no conscience on behalf of Louisiana. Though Napoleon's brothers, Joseph and Lucien, tried to stop the sale, not out of patriotism but because they had been bribed by the British, it only remained for the price – including Talleyrand's – to be agreed. It was the biggest real estate deal in history: over two million square kilometres, at 6 cents a hectare. The treaty of purchase was signed on 30 April 1803, and Napoleon resumed the war with England on 16 May; it would continue until Waterloo, twelve years later.

In a breathtaking two months Jefferson had doubled the size of the United States, and permanently ensured there would be no more Manon Lescauts in North America.[294] Not everyone rejoiced: some in the Northeast feared an expanded agrarian South and West would tilt the balance of the Union against their industrial and commercial interests; and Massachusetts Senator Timothy Pickering, who had been Washington's Secretary of State two after Jefferson, tried to organise the secession of a Northern Confederacy. But the move fizzled in 1804 when their expected champion, Vice–President Aaron Burr, was defeated for Governor of New York and then killed Alexander Hamilton in a duel. The Northeasterners turned out to be not entirely wrong, at least in the medium term: of the three states that had been carved out of the Louisiana Purchase by the time of the Civil War, two joined the seceding Southern Confederacy, and although the third did not, it was also a slave–holding state.

An interlude: coincidences and connections
Napoleon was lucky to still be around to sell the Louisiana territory. At the end of 1800 he had survived the most serious of the several attempts on his life, and one chillingly familiar in our own day: on his route from the Tuileries Palace to the Opera a cart packed with two

---

294   Manon Lescaut, the heroine of Puccini's eponymous 1894 opera, based on the Abbé Prévost's 1731 novel; her confused love–life leads to her arrest and exile to the French colony of New Orleans, from which she and her first and final lover escape, to die in the boondocks searching for an English (of course) colony. On the other hand, in Massenet's 1884 opera *Manon*, also based on Prévost, she gets no further than Paris. However it was the Italian composer who got it right.

barrels of gunpowder was blown up, but just after Napoleon's carriage had passed. Miraculously his famous luck held, and he was uninjured. The following carriages however were obliterated; nearby buildings were so severely damaged that some had to be demolished; several dozen among Napoleon's suite and the bystanders were killed, and many injured. He was on his way to the first performance in Paris of Josef Haydn's new oratorio *The Creation*. Perhaps he did not know that the text of the work was written in enemy England (it is not sure by whom), and had perhaps been originally intended for George Frederick Handel, favourite composer of the grandfather of Napoleon's current opponent, King George III. Though considerably shaken, he stayed for the entire performance, which showed even greater sang–froid in the circumstances – *The Creation* runs for close on two hours.

The Creation and Haydn's other oratorio, *The Seasons*, were inspired by his experience in 1791 of Handel's oratorios *The Messiah* and *Israel in Egypt* on the first of his two visits to London, during which he wrote the last twelve of his hundred and eight symphonies and still had time to be lionised by everyone, including King George. *The Creation* was an instant success: first performed in Vienna March 1799; the score published February 1800; first performance in London March 1800. On 2 April 1800, in Vienna, not yet under Napoleon's guns, the thirty–year–old Beethoven gave his first concert for his own benefit, and the program included a Mozart symphony, excerpts from Haydn's *Creation*, and two new works of his own, the Septet and the First Symphony, in one evening summing up Vienna's musical pinnacle at that time. Napoleon's (eventual) presence at the first performance in Paris on Christmas Eve 1800 underlined the international dimension of Haydn's triumph.

Whatever Napoleon made of the music – it seems to be one of the rare occasions on which his views do not seem to have been recorded – Haydn did not think much of Napoleon. At this time, interspersed with the Handel–inspired oratorios, Haydn was in the midst of producing his most triumphant and inspired music of all: six masses written for the Name Day of Princess Maria Hermenegild, wife of Prince Nikolaus II Esterházy, the fourth member of that family for whom he had worked since 1761. The series began in 1796 with the *Paukenmesse*, the Kettle Drum Mass, also known as the "Mass in Time of War", Haydn's first reaction against Napoleon as his armies were advancing on Austria. In 1798 came the Nelson Mass, originally the *Missa in angustiis*, "Mass in a Time of Anguish", alluding to continued French successes against Austria in northern Italy and Napoleon's invasion of Egypt that year.

It was re–named in 1800 when Haydn conducted it before Lord Nelson himself, accompanied by the scandalous Lady Hamilton, when they visited Prince Esterházy. Nelson had in fact defeated the French fleet in the Battle of the Nile in August 1798, unknown to Haydn, at the same time as he was writing the mass.[295]

It is a pity that Jefferson and Haydn never met, were never in the same city, though in due course they were to be linked together – thanks to the French. Jefferson himself was interested in music throughout his life, sometimes from unlikely sources. In 1762, the year Jefferson graduated from the College of William and Mary at Williamsburg, Virginia, Mozart, six years old and already composing for a year, made his first concert tour from Salzburg, finishing up in Vienna with two harpsichord concerts before the Empress Maria Theresa; it was the year that Haydn began his employment with the second of his four rich Esterházy patrons; and it was the year that the ever–busy Benjamin Franklin turned the armonica – " a sophisticated form of musical glasses", according to *Grove*, not the harmonica/mouth organ – into "a practical musical instrument".[296]

Jefferson was described in 1765, by a perhaps not unqualifiedly admiring contemporary, as

"A gentleman of thirty–two who could calculate an eclipse, survey an estate, tie an artery, plan an edifice, try a cause, break a horse, dance a minuet, and play the violin".

---

295 The Battle of the Nile, which undermined and soon led to the end of Napoleon's conquest of Egypt, was not surprisingly also commemorated in London, where J.M.W. Turner, one of the greatest painters of landscapes, seascapes and especially watercolours, exhibited at the Royal Academy in 1799 a painting (now lost) of Nelson's victory; it was one of five versions of *Battle of the Nile* at the Academy that year, two others being by the former Bristol sea–captain Nicholas Pocock (now at the National Maritime Museum, Greenwich).

296 The armonica, first referred to in a Milanese book of 1492, and also known as musical glasses, glass harmonica (hence nominal confusion), or "glassy–chord", was tuned – as in many a school project – by varied amounts of water in the glasses, and could be struck, like a xylophone, or rubbed, to give an effect "like the strings of a bowed instrument". The ever–tinkering Franklin sought to improve the rubbing method of playing by fitting increasing–sized glass bowls into one another, and mounting them concentrically on a horizontal central spindle rotated by a pedal–activated crank. According to *Grove*, "The proximity of the rims... enabled the player to produce chords and runs with far greater ease than had been possible when each glass stood separate on its base". It apparently still did not produce harmonious sounds – see *Grove*'s judgement below.

Mapp notes that during his travels he used a "tiny" instrument on which "he could practice in public inns and welcoming homes without disturbing other people". This is more than could be said of the armonica, which, *Grove* says, had a "distinctive tone of vibrant, piercing sweetness", but was "apt to have a deranging effect on the nerves of the player". In due course, however, the Franklin version of the instrument became popular on both sides of the Atlantic, though *Grove* says that "in some German towns the armonica was banned by the police". Trust Germany to have music–critic police.

Franklin's armonica was to enrapture both Jefferson and Goethe, the latter, out of step with the police, finding in its sustained chords "the heart–blood of the World". Jefferson was induced by the instrument into comparably wild prediction, greeting news of its even further improvement by his friend and co–signer of the Declaration of Independence, the writer and musician Francis Hopkinson:

> "I am very much pleased with your project on the Harmonica and the prospect of your succeeding in the application of keys to it. It will be the greatest present which has been made to the musical world this century, not excepting the Piano forte".

There is perhaps a study to be made of the mesmerising effect of this piercing, deranging instrument on the Founding Fathers of the United States of America.

Jefferson's interest in music, "the favorite passion of my soul", fortunately developed beyond the tiny violin and the armonica. Just after his marriage in 1772 he engaged a Venetian musician, one Francesco Alberti, to improve his violin playing and help his new wife with the harpsichord. Whether Alberti achieved any advance in the Jeffersons' music–making may be problematical; years later a friend in Richmond wrote to Jefferson in Paris:

> "Bye the bye old Alberti died and was interrd last night here. He was one of a Band of musick to whom I have subscribed tho never heard them, at all; they surpass in execution, hardly the Jews Harp and Banjer performers".

By 1778 Jefferson's musical interest had become more expansive, but characteristically economical: he wrote to an Italian friend of Filippo Mazzei, the Tuscan whom Benjamin Franklin had encouraged to bring labourers and grapevines to Virginia to establish a wine industry, with a new scheme presented in terms at once crafty and wistful:

"The bounds of an American fortune will not admit the indulgence of a domestic band of musicians. Yet I have thought that a passion for music might be reconciled with that oeconomy which we are obliged to observe. I retain for instance among my domestic servants a gardener (Ortolano), weaver (Tessitore di lino e lan,) a cabinet maker (Stipettaio) and a stone–cutter (Scalpellino lavorante in piano) to which I would add a Vigneron. In a country where, like yours, music is cultivated and practised by every class of men I suppose there might be found persons of those trades who could perform on the French horn, clarinet or hautboy and bassoon, so that one might have a band of two French horns, two clarinets and hautboys and a bassoon, without enlarging their domestic expences. A certainty of employment for a half dozen years, and at end of that time to find them if they chose it a conveyance to their own country might induce [them] to come here on reasonable wages".

But the project came to nothing: Italian cabinet makers were either insufficiently versatile or insufficiently adventurous. Jefferson would have been envious of Haydn: the orchestra at Esterháza which he was engaged to compose for and direct comprised between ten and fifteen musicians; by the time of Jefferson's letter to Mazzei it had grown to close to twenty–five.

Jefferson maintained his interest in music during his time in Paris, both as a player and a concert– and opera–goer. While he was still Governor of Virginia a visitor to Monticello had remarked on seeing there "an Elegant harpsichord piano forte and some Violins". In his first year in Paris he rented a piano, and bought a music stand and music – and, in due course, a debt–ful of new clothes, silver, wine, sixty–three paintings, hundreds of books, the model of a hydraulic engine, and a house full of fine furniture. There were also terra–cotta busts by Houdon of his revolutionary heroes: Voltaire, Turgot, Washington, Franklin, Lafayette and John Paul Jones – very satisfactory, though not quite the fourteen antique sculptures he had planned thirty years before to acquire, for an art gallery at Monticello, from...the Uffizi.

Within a month of his arrival in Paris he attended his first concert, in the inappositely named Salle des Machines (after its elaborate stage–

machinery) in the Château des Tuileries, the palace on the Place de la Concorde which was destroyed during the Commune in 1871. He went a dozen or so times during his stay, and, according to Howard Rice, the programs, which followed a standard pattern, usually included one or sometimes two Haydn symphonies – by the end of Jefferson's posting Haydn had written ninety–two – followed by a miscellany of shorter pieces. During Jefferson's only visit to London, in 1785, where a biographer said he "thought only the shops worthy of attention", he met Dr Charles Burney, Jem Burney's father, a well–known composer, organist, music historian and amateur astronomer, who had played violin or viola in Handel's orchestra. The senior Burney had been for a long time a friend and correspondent of Haydn; it was he who facilitated Haydn's visits to London in 1791–92 and 1794–95, and they spent a good deal of time together. Dr Johnson said of him

> "I much question if there is in the world such another man for mind, intelligence, and manners".

Jefferson himself came to develop a genuine admiration for Burney. During 1786 they engaged in an extensive correspondence over the precise specifications of a Jacob Kirckman harpsichord that Burney helped Jefferson purchase in London for his daughter Martha. When the instrument finally reached him in Paris, Jefferson wrote conveying

> "my sincere thanks for your very kind attention to the instrument I had desired... Besides the value of the thing therefore, it will have an additional one with me, of the nature of that which a good catholic affixes to the relick of a saint".

For Jefferson the piano would never displace the harpsichord; and he bought a second Kirckman instrument in 1798 for his other daughter, Maria.[297]

It is amusing that, to the famous musicologist, Jefferson was vastly more circumspect about Francis Hopkinson's new and improved armonica:

---

297 The instrument now at Monticello is also a Kirckman, but Maria's has disappeared, and, says Susan Stein in *The Worlds of Thomas Jefferson at Monticello*, Martha's was long ago made into furniture.

"However imperfect this instrument is for the general mass of musical compositions", he went on in the above letter to Burney, " yet for those of a certain character it is delicious".

The armonica was no longer the world–beater. But in between Jefferson's two harpsichord purchases the armonica received its highest accolade ever: Mozart had been introduced to the instrument in 1773 by Marianne Davies,[298] a protégé of Benjamin Franklin's, and in 1791, the last year of his life, he wrote an Adagio and Rondo (K.617) for a quintet of armonica, flute, oboe, viola and cello. And Marianne introduced the instrument to Anton Mesmer, who used it to "induce a receptive state in his hypnotic subjects". Rather like the effect on the Founding Fathers.

After Jefferson had become President the link with Haydn finally came about, when he received a significant recognition of his intellectual – as distinct from political – status (though it is not unknown for intellectual contributions to be enhanced by the contributor's status). In 1802 Jefferson was elected a Foreign Associate of one of Europe's most prestigious societies for the arts and sciences, the French *Institut national*, created in 1795 to supersede the more ancient *Académie française* and its four sister academies (which, re–established after Napoleon, remain within it still as constituents of the *Institut de France*). It is interesting that this honour was bestowed at a time of considerable political strain between France and the United States, with Jefferson seriously concerned about Napoleon's intentions in the Louisiana Territory he had then just extorted from a defeated Spain.

Jefferson was amongst a distinguished company. By coincidence two others of the Foreign Associates elected by the *Institut* that year were connected to John Leydard: Professor Peter Pallas, whose lukewarm attitude towards him by comparison with his enthusiastic promotion of the incompetent Billings is something of an enigma; and his last patron, Sir Joseph Banks. Then there was another Englishman, Henry Cavendish, the chemist whose discovery of hydrogen had contributed to the development of Montgolfier's hot air balloons; the German William Herschel, a former oboist in the band of George III's Hanoverian Guards,

---

298 Marianne's sister Cecilia, a singer, had become a favourite of the Empress Maria Theresa, and had taught singing and acting to her daughters, including the future Queen Marie Antoinette of France. She also impressed Dr Burney with her voice – and the year of Mozart's quintet she sang in the Handel oratorio season in London attended by Haydn.

then the astronomer who discovered the planet Uranus; and the Italian Alessandro Volta, who had developed the theory of electric current, and whose name was given to the "volt". But Jefferson's most famous fellow laureate was Joseph Haydn.

In 1797, at twenty–eight, Napoleon himself had been elected a member of the Institut's section on mathematics and physics. While no doubt honouring the geometrical accuracy of the "whiff of grapeshot" with which he had already disposed of Parisian counter–revolutionaries and Austrian overlords of northern Italy, the honour carried a whiff of political calculation on the part of the *Institut*. By 1802 it would have been even less likely to flout the wishes of the First Consul for Life. Yet, in addition to France's difficulties with President Jefferson's United States at the time, it had been involved in war for many years with almost all the other countries whose citizens were being honoured that year. The 1802 elections were indeed a recognition of the broader, higher, international republic of letters that the egregious nationalist and ideological passions of the two succeeding centuries has frequently jeopardised.

It is well known that after Napoleon's assumption of the Imperial purple two years later, in 1804, Beethoven changed the dedication of his Third Symphony from "Bonaparte" to the disillusioned "To celebrate the memory of a great man". It is less well known that to rub it in further, Beethoven went on, in 1813, to the musically unheroic and infrequently played but politically unambiguous *Battle Symphony*, to celebrate "Wellington's Victory in the Battle of Vittoria", the turning point in the Peninsular War against Napoleon's forces – and, to rub it in further still, dedicated it to the otherwise not particularly worthy Prince Regent of England. Musically, however, Wellington lost hands down to Napoleon in this exchange.[299]

---

299 Beethoven was not alone in apostrophising Wellington: it was the latter's victory at Waterloo in 1815, with the aid of the Prussians under Blücher, that prompted Beethoven's younger contemporary Carl Maria von Weber (who had gone to Vienna when he was nineteen to study under Haydn, but somehow didn't) to write his cantata *Battle and Victory*. Its resounding success, reflecting relief at the outcome of the Battle of Waterloo as well as contemporary taste, was an interesting example of a composer's achieving fame for a composition for which he is no longer even remembered. I happen to have a *Battle and Victory* recorded during the Cold War in East Germany, with the comically unfaithful correctness required by its late and unlamented regime: in the original text, says the sleeve note,

That same year, as Napoleon reeled back from Moscow, defeated by General Kutuzov and "General Winter", Jefferson fired off his own salvo at the Louisiana salesman: like any reasonable person, he described the Emperor of the French as

"a cold–blooded, calculating unprincipled Usurper, without a virtue, no statesman, knowing nothing of commerce, political economy, or civil government, and supplying ignorance to bold presumption".

The Pacific at last: the Lewis and Clark expedition

Jefferson would have felt, rightly, that Napoleon's agreement to sell Louisiana had reflected desperation rather than design. But we have to go back a little to the other strand in Jefferson's approach to extending United States control across the North American continent. After Ledyard broke his promise to Jefferson to "penetrate from Kentucky to the western side of the Continent" by dying in Cairo, there was a gap of four years until Jefferson tried in 1793 to have the French botanist André Michaux

"pursue such of the largest streams of [the Missouri River] as shall lead by the shortest way and the lowest latitudes to the Pacific ocean";

but how hard Jefferson pressed Michaux (who was, after all, in French employ) and how hard the latter tried, is unclear – the episode largely disappeared from memory.

However Jefferson had certainly not given up. Bernard De Voto suggests that on becoming President he may well have chosen Meriwether Lewis, an Army Captain and a family friend, as his secretary precisely for the purpose of planning the Western expedition. They certainly began

---

"the frequent alternation of war glorification and 'gods of vengeance' with appeals to a Christian God and the Holy Fatherland retains certain characteristics which are not reassuring. For the present performance, however, the text has been largely 'internationalised', by omitting direct references to the Germans, to Prussia, and to the Rhine; to avert confusion, the triumphal appearance of the melody 'God Save the King'..., symbolising Wellington's part in the battle, has also been left out".

Poor Blücher, poor Wellington. Poor Weber.

serious planning after the publication in London in 1801 of the account by a young Scots–Canadian fur trader, Alexander Mackenzie, of his two explorations in the northwest of the continent: first following to the Arctic Sea, while looking for the Pacific, the Canadian river named after him; then, in 1793, becoming the first recorded European to cross the Rocky Mountains to the Pacific coast, reaching it at the mouth of the Bella Coola River just north of Vancouver Island.

Following the Nootka Sound crisis, with its evidence of increasing international competition for the fur trade, and the explorations of the Canadian Pacific coast by Ledyard's *Resolution* shipmate, George Vancouver, Mackenzie's accomplishment added to Jefferson's concerns about the activities of British Canadian fur traders to the northwest of the United States and, the flag so often following trade, about British territorial intentions in what was now coming to be known as Oregon Country. In addition, the huge Louisiana Purchase, stretching westwards from the Mississippi to the Stony Mountains (the Rockies, whose whereabouts were still not precisely known) and from about the Red River northwards to British Canada, vastly increased the United States' need to know about the West, much of it still as blank on the map as the interior of Africa.

For the expedition he now firmly decided on, and proposed secretly to Congress on 18 January 1803, Jefferson's prime concern was the old one he had raised with George Rogers Clark: to find a water route from the Mississippi river system to the Pacific coast (whose distance from the east coast was still known only from Captain Cook's meticulously accurate charts). In this respect the expedition was to be a variation on the search for a Northwest Passage which had persisted from the Cabots, while Columbus was still sailing to the Caribbean, until Cook's last voyage. But now, reflecting the extent to which trade had already borne out John Ledyard's reports and interests, the purpose of finding this route was to be explicitly for the facilitation of America's fur trade with China, already running, according to O'Connor, at about half a million dollars a year, far and away the United States' most valuable export. Congress authorised an expedition the same day Jefferson proposed it.

Jefferson, with his wide scientific interests, and an eye to the future, considered it would also be important to gather information on flora, fauna (and fossils, especially large ones), soils, crops and minerals, and on the native inhabitants. To the latter, he instructed Lewis to be as friendly as "their own conduct will admit", and "to acquire what knolege you can of the state of morality, religion information among them, as it may better enable those who endeavor to civilize instruct them, to adapt their measures to the existing notions practises of those on whom they operate".

In a different category from Blacks, whose enslavement Jefferson could neither excuse nor repudiate, the Indians were to be treated as people. Jefferson, like his more enlightened contemporaries undertaking European colonial ventures at the same time, saw them as Noble Savages. They should be treated well, but in due course turned, if possible, into honorary Whites, who should nevertheless not be allowed to stand in the way of White ambition. The unenlightened tended to shoot first.

All the public requirements of the expedition were issued to Lewis in writing on 20 June 1803 – thirteen days before Jefferson heard of the successful purchase of Louisiana. That crucial development meant that the expedition would now be passing through American territory, at least as far as the Rockies; and clearly Jefferson already had in mind that it would necessarily strengthen the United States' claim to sovereignty over the Pacific Northwest.

Lewis, now 29, took all this on board over three years of discussions with his boss; recruited, entirely on his own initiative, another Army Captain, William Clark, 33, youngest brother of George Rogers Clark, as his co–leader; and recruited as well, mostly from the Army, the personnel for the "Corps of Discovery". The expedition finally set off in May 1804 from St Louis, on the lower Missouri, the farthest west settlement of any significance. This was a military exercise, outfitted by the Army on the President's instructions and with Congress's approval, adequately manned without being unwieldy, carefully instructed and correctly disciplined. It was about as far removed as possible from Jefferson's despatch of poor Ledyard, with two shirts and fewer shillings, across the length and breadth of Europe and Siberia.

Lewis and Clark followed the Missouri northwards to Fort Mandan (across the river from Bismarck, North Dakota, almost up to the Canadian border), from where they packed up "Sundery articles to be sent to the President of the U.S." – we shall come across them again at Monticello; then westwards to the end of the Missouri system; crossed the Continental Divide (in mid–Idaho) in August 1805; and reached the mouth of the Columbia River on the Pacific Ocean on 7 November. "*Ocian in view!* O! the joy", Clark wrote in his notebook, though the joy did not last: after twenty-four days he called it "the Great Western Ocian, I cant say Pasific as since I have seen it, it has been the reverse".

They were almost without supplies, the country was poor and perpetually sodden, no trading ships appeared to provision them or convey them home. So they set out back overland in March 1806, and were in St Louis again in six months. In 10,000 kms and almost two and a half years they had lost only one man – probably to a ruptured appendix.

It was one of the world's great explorations: thoroughly planned; meticulously organised, though it is a great pity that it did not include an artist; brilliantly led, and sensitively, in its contacts with the Indian nations – Clark especially, like Ledyard, genuinely liked Indians. On the level of contributing to knowledge of the West, it was outstandingly successful. Curiously, though, despite intense interest both in America and Europe in the expedition's discoveries, Lewis did not get round to editing the journals before he committed suicide in 1809; and although a narrative account was published that year by a Philadelphia journalist, the complete journals did not see print for another century, in 1904.

On top of the implications for American sovereignty, the scientist in Jefferson must have found Lewis and Clark's conscientious reports on all they had seen enormously satisfying. There is an engaging image, recounted by Ambrose from a letter Jefferson wrote years later, of the President and Meriwether Lewis, when the latter finally reached Washington in December 1806, spreading Clark's map on the floor of the White House, and getting down on their hands and knees to examine it.

America's Pacific destiny

But the expedition did not find a water route to the great South Sea and Cathay. The "single portage" that Jefferson had imagined linking the voyages up the Missouri and down the Columbia turned out to be a gruelling land passage of 250 kms through the Rockies. Finally, after three hundred years of theorising and questing, there was no such thing as a Northwest Passage, either by sea or by river.

However the Louisiana Purchase and the Lewis and Clark expedition opened the way for vast new territories to be settled. With the Purchase, settlers could cross the Mississippi, and, as De Voto said, "American sovereignty was manifestly certain to follow them". So were land–steals from the Indians, who, notwithstanding treaties and promises, were gradually forced westwards, or into areas considered unproductive by white men, or decimated. Jefferson, unlike Cook, did not like conquest by armed force; but, like Cook, he unbottled the genie, unleashing westwards across the North American continent, as Russia did eastwards across Siberia, a land–borne colonialism as remorseless as – and ultimately far more permanent than – the sea–borne colonialisms of the European powers, against which he and the other American Founding Fathers had so nobly and valiantly struggled.

The next step after Lewis and Clark was the establishment in 1811, not far from the camp at the mouth of the Columbia River where they had spent the wet winter of 1805–06, of John Jacob Astor's fur trading post at Fort Astoria. In 1819 the United States bought Florida from Spain, completing the eastern seaboard; Texas, independent under Americans for ten years, was annexed in 1845; the following year the northwestern Oregon Country border with Canada was fixed; in 1848 California was added following war with Mexico; and in 1867 Alaska was bought from Russia, completing a United States (apart from Hawaii, annexed in 1898) more extensive in the West and Northwest than Jefferson had ever conceived in his most expansionist moments. Two years later, despite the disruptions the Civil War had caused, the first transcontinental railroad was completed, and the way was open beyond the New Frontier to America's Pacific Destiny. It gave way to the lure of imperialism, with the coerced opening of Japan, trade and missionary pressures on China, the seizure of the Philippines as a European–style colony; and three major wars, Pearl Harbour to Tokyo, Korea, Vietnam.

In his first inaugural address, in 1801, Jefferson proclaimed his four objectives for the foreign relations of the United States:

"Peace, commerce, and honest friendship with all nations – entangling alliances with none".

Noble objectives, however, his very creation of a continental United States, through his purchase of Louisiana and direction of national interest, beginning with Lewis and Clark, across the Mississippi, westwards and northwest, eventually, inexorably and inevitably, undermined each one.

American century
Although Germany set a good deal of the dreadful agenda of the first half of the twentieth century, it was in fact the American century: its weight finally swung the balance against Germany over the last year of the First

World War; its military weight, and above all its prodigious economic capacity, prevented the defeat of Britain during the first two years of the Second World War, when Hitler had the benefit of an alliance with the Soviet Union, then assisted the latter, substantially carried through the Western front, and simultaneously, apart from the aid of small allies in Australia and New Zealand, single-handedly pushed Japan's conquests almost back to its home islands – the atomic bombing of Hiroshima and Nagasaki obviating the need for an invasion of Japan proper. Following this war, in Europe the United States carried the extraordinarily imaginative but huge burden of the Marshall Plan for the reconstruction of Europe, and a disproportionate part of the burden, as it continually reminded its NATO allies, of the defence against the Soviet threat during the ensuing forty years of Cold War. In Asia it contributed significantly to the reconstruction of Japan, and to defence against the USSR's and Communist China's real and suspected anti-Western activities in Asia, not always happily.

Thomas Jefferson was opposed to entanglements with the Old World, but was clearly tempted by the promise of East Asia. It is ironic that American entanglements with Europe – at least after the absurd episode of the War of 1812 – could mostly be counted as successes: it secured European neutrality during the Civil War, and played the crucial role just noted in the twentieth century's great wars and their aftermath during the ensuing fifty years. But entanglements with Asia were mostly either a disappointment or a disaster: seizing control of the Philippines (and Cuba) from Spain in dirty little wars at the turn of the twentieth century forever destroyed America's moral high ground vis-à-vis the European imperialists. The enormously strong missionary involvement in China resulted in an excessive entanglement with the incompetent but intransigent Chiang Kai-shek, which led to McCarthyism in the recriminations following his defeat by Mao Tse-tung. In Korea the United States led a successful resistance to the North's aggression and Communist China's invasion in support, but half a century later the situation on the Korean peninsula remains unresolved, the last leftover of both the Second World War and the Cold War. And then there was Vietnam, an intrusion made with honourable intentions into a war of national liberation (partly provoked by French colonial stupidity), misjudged, by analogy with Korea, as an invasion of the South by the North, and in which, with unreliable local allies, American forces were continually sucked in to a conflict they could neither win nor easily extricate themselves from.

There were other mistaken and downright harmful American involvements abroad during the last half of the 20th century, but in the great causes of the First World War, the Second World War and the Cold War the role of the United States was crucial to the maintenance of the freedoms for which Thomas Jefferson and his colleagues had so resolutely fought in the creation of the country. What might have been averted if the United States had not turned its back on the world in its inter–war isolationism is one of the great what-ifs of the 20th century. We now have to contemplate what price might have to be paid for the opposite policy that accompanied the beginning of this new century: of unilateral pre–emptive intervention, the curtailment of civil liberties for which the American revolutionaries fought, and the under–mining of the forms of international cooperation that have been developed since their founding by those who fought the last World War. It is hard to avoid the suspicion that Thomas Jefferson would have been appalled at all three.

President Yuan Shih-kai of China, 1915. Wikimedia/The World's Work, 1915:
https://archive.org/stream/worldswork30gard page/378/mode/2up

CHINA

YUAN SHIKAI:
THE END OF EMPIRE

"The good subject is the obedient subject."

Confucius

Yuan Shikai became, in succession, and then failed as: the last Imperial Chinese viceroy in Korea, as a commanding general during the Boxer Rebellion, as the first President of the Chinese Republic, and finally as the last Chinese Emperor – for three months. His life, encompassing the last appalling decades of the Qing Dynasty, came to interweave with its collapse the heyday of European and the beginning of Japanese imperialism in China and East Asia. Not only China but the whole of East Asia changed in Yuan's six decades, but his abilities did not match up to his larger-than-life career, let alone the demands of those overwhelming changes in which he was intimately involved. While in most ways at the opposite end of the spectrum of influence from John Ledyard,[300] Yuan Shikai was in many ways a Ledyard sort of character: often at the centre of things, usually a failure, but continually bobbing up in pursuit of something else.

Other countries' relations with or attitudes towards China have been touched on in many of the previous chapters, in the context of relations across the Silk Road and otherwise. By the end of the 19th century China had had an appalling sixty years, first and foremost through the increasing inflexibility, incompetence and corruption of the decaying three-hundred-year-old Qing Dynasty [then known in English as the Ch'ing];[301] and taking advantage of this, the Western colonial powers

300 See 1800 chapter
301 Note: This chapter raises the horrible problem of the romanisation of Chinese. At the time this chapter covers, and until 1979, writers mostly used the

had added a significant degree of territorial and administrative dismemberment. The two Opium Wars, to force China to import more opium from British India and open more ports to do so, had culminated in a British-French attack in 1860 on Beijing itself, in the course of which they deliberately destroyed Yuan Ming Yuan, one of the most fascinating cross-cultural monuments of all time, built by one of the missionary Matteo Ricci's Jesuit successors. By century's end an even wider range of imperialist powers – West Europeans, Russians, Americans and Japanese – was hacking away at China with gunboats, commerce and missionaries, threatening its total dismemberment, when they suffered an unexpected and unprecedented counter-blow – not from the feeble Imperial Army, but from a rag-tag bunch of rebels known as Boxers, who besieged the foreign diplomatic legations in Beijing. After which the imperial powers exacted enormous "reparations", and the British and French again sacked the Imperial palaces. The thread between West and East was no longer silk: it had become guncotton.

Nevertheless, the Boxers' humiliation of the Westerners began to undermine the European position in Asia, though it had nothing like the impact caused four years later when the quaint little Mikado's Japan inflicted a crushing defeat on white, European, Imperial Russia, ruled by the cousin of the King of England and the German Kaiser. Japan exploded out of its two-and-a-half centuries of self-imposed isolation after Hideyoshi,[302] and began the series of military assaults that would seize Korea from China's suzerainty and brutally subjugate it for forty

---

Wade-Giles system, established by British diplomat-academics in the 19th century (though Americans sometimes used a variation). Old Wade-Giles Mao Tse-tung not surprisingly introduced a Chinese system, Pinyin, in the People's Republic of China, becoming Mao Zedong; most (though not all) more recent studies, as well as modern maps, now use this system, though Taiwan and many American writers continue to use Wade-Giles. There is no elegant solution that I am aware of that overcomes the need to use both. Some place names which have since been changed for non-romanisation reasons have been retained so they are more easily recognisable historically, if not on current maps - e.g. Canton (now Guangzhou), Mukden (Shenyang), Port Arthur (Lüshun). Pinyin is otherwise used throughout the text, both in this chapter and elsewhere in the book where China is referred to, with the Wade-Giles equivalent used at the time concerned indicated in square brackets on first usage; on the other hand, Wade-Giles is retained in all quotations where it was used by their authors or translators, followed by the Pinyin version where necessary. A memory better than mine would be of some assistance in this briar-patch.

302   See 1600 chapter

years, decisively humiliate Imperial Russia, ruthlessly invade China itself through the 1930s, until, widening its attacks following Pearl Harbour, it would conquer, as Nazi Germany's ally during the Second World War, most of the Western colonial dependencies in Southeast Asia and the South Pacific.

The principal people in this chapter are as follows:

- **Yuan Shikai** (1859-1915) – Imperial Chinese viceroy in Korea, commanding general during the Boxer Rebellion, first President of the Chinese Republic, and last Chinese Emperor.

- **Guangxu** [Kuang–hsü] (1871-1908) – Chinese Emperor, reigned from 1875-1908. Nephew of Cixi.

- **Cixi** [Tzu–h'si] (1835-1908) – China's Dowager Empress of China, and Regent from 1862-1889 and 1898-1908.

- **Li Hongzhang** [Li Hung–chang] (1823-1901) – Cixi's chief statesman in diplomatic, political and military affairs.

- **Ito Hirobumi** (1838-1909) – Japanese statesman, counterpart of Li Hongzhang, Prime Minister of Japan and "Protector" of Korea (1905-1909).

- **George Nathaniel Curzon** (1859-1925) – British aristocrat and statesman, traveller, author, and Viceroy of India from 1899-1905.

The humiliation inflicted by Japan contributed to the fall twelve years later of Russia's own decrepit Imperial autocracy; and in Asia the anti-colonial genie was out. The world would never be the same again, but it would still take half a century and two World Wars before China and India, and then other colonies in Asia and elsewhere, could become independent of imperialist occupations. A century and a half's mistreatment of China left a bitter legacy of anti-Western feeling that was still evident at the time of the return of Hong Kong to Chinese sovereignty in 1997. That legacy remains part of the ambiguous and complex relations between Westerners and Chinese, now centred on mutual suspicions about intentions towards Taiwan, one of the most dangerous and difficult situations in the world in the early 21st century.

Before the decisive fall of empire in China, Yuan Shikai's brief grab at the Mandate of Heaven was time enough for him to order from the renowned kilns at Jingdezhen [Ching-tê Chên], in northern Jiangxi province, the last pieces of still-exquisite Imperial reign-marked porcelain – and many years ago my wife was lucky enough to find a lovely piece in an antiques shop in Taipei. It is not very widely known, or, at least, written about; in any case, beautiful porcelain was not enough for Yuan Shikai to be remembered kindly. This chapter nevertheless begins in 1860 – as it, and Yuan Shikai, will end six decades later – with ceramics, for centuries the quintessential manifestation of China's artistic genius.

Breaking China

The ceramics concerned in 1860 were roof tiles. Not your ordinary roof tiles, or an ordinary amount, but a huge number: thousands upon thousands of tiles glazed in deep blue, dark green and Imperial yellow, exploding in intense heat, crashing to the ground, shattering as the myriad palaces and pavilions of the Qing Emperors' great Summer Palace, the Yuan Ming Yuan, "the Garden of Perfect Clarity" – just to the northwest of the four cities of Beijing[303] – were destroyed by British soldiers. On orders. One of them wrote:

> "We accordingly went out, and after pillaging it, burned the whole place, destroying it, in a Vandal–like manner, most valuable property, which could not be replaced for four millions...You would scarcely imagine the beauty and magnificence of the places we burnt. It made one's heart sore to burn them; in fact, these palaces were so large, and we were so pressed for time, that we could not plunder them carefully...It was a scene of utter destruction which passes my description".

This was Captain Charles Gordon, to be known soon as the stirring Victorian hero "Chinese" Gordon, after overcoming in central China the Taiping rebels against the declining Qing Empire, and later as the sentimental Victorian martyr "Gordon of Khartoum", after under–estimating in the Sudan the Mahdist opponents of the expanding British Empire.

---

303 These were the Forbidden City, enclosed by the Imperial City, which was enclosed by the Tartar (Manchu) City, with the Chinese City adjacent on the south side. They were all within the area now enclosed by the Second Ring Road.

In his letters home Gordon slithered between high moral tone and Victorian practicality:

"It was wretchedly demoralising work for an army. Everybody was wild for plunder…The French have smashed everything in the most wanton way".

On the other hand:

"We got upwards of £48 a–piece prize money before we went out here; and although I have not as much as many, I have done well" –

a throne (which ended up in the Royal Engineers Museum at Chatham), and divers objects, sables, porcelain, jade, cloisonné, which he instructed be divided up

"A to my father, B, C and D for general and fair distribution amongst the 'tribe' of Gordons, E and F to my father, G to Aunt Amy…P, Q and R to my mother…".

By far the largest portion of the loot went eventually to Queen Victoria (some of which is now in the Victoria Albert Museum, London) and Emperor Napoleon III (some now in the Musée Chinois, Château de Fontainebleau).

The man who had given the orders was James Bruce, 8th Earl of Elgin, responsible for the British contingent in the joint British–French forces which had just defeated the Chinese Emperor's army outside Beijing. He was the son of the 7th Earl who had appropriated the celebrated Parthenon marbles from Athens half a century before. James had grown up in France, to which father had fled to escape the consequences of his artistic profligacies; and this no doubt eased his relationship with his counterpart responsible for the French contingent in the forces in China, Baron Jean–Baptiste Louis Gros, also a diplomat. The Baron did not agree with the Earl's decision to destroy the Summer Palace: such an act, he said,

"against an undefended site in the country would appear a useless sort of vengeance";

he urged Elgin, in preference, that

> "the complete destruction of the Palace in Pe–kin [the Forbidden City]...seat of the sovereign power, would be a more striking expiatory act than the burning of a country cottage".

Perhaps Gros had not actually seen the Emperor's "cottage". In any event, Elgin went ahead and burned it.

This was Britain's third diplomatic effort to engage the attention of the Son of Heaven. The first had been in 1793 when Lord Macartney, an Irish peer who had previously been sent to beguile (apparently successfully) Catherine the Great of Russia, was given four audiences by the 82–year–old Emperor Qianlong[304] but famously refused to perform the ritual of kowtowing to him – kneeling with head touching the ground nine times – in order to present his credentials. The Emperor, making the best of this unprecedented behaviour by a barbarian emissary, equally famously responded to King George III that

> "I have perused your memorial. The humble terms in which it is couched reveal a humility on your part, which is highly praiseworthy... Strange and costly objects [King George's gifts] do not interest me. As your Ambassador can see for himself, we possess all things. I set no value on objects strange and ingenious, and have no use for your country's manufactures...It behoves you, O King, to respect my sentiments and to display even greater devotion and loyalty in future...[and] perpetual submission to our Throne".

The expedition – unlike modern ambassadors, Macartney had a retinue of ninety–five, including five German musicians – achieved nothing more than the acquisition from the unwilling Chinese of silkworms and tea specimens for commercial development in the botanic gardens established in Calcutta by direction of Sir Joseph Banks.

Before trying diplomacy with Beijing again London waited until the twentieth year of the reign of Qianlong's successor, his fifteenth son, Jiaqing [Chia-ch'ing] – 1816. This time it was a farce: the envoy, Lord

---

304 This was not his personal name but his reign name: to be correct, he was the Qianlong Emperor. But the Chinese Emperors are commonly and certainly more conveniently referred to by their reign name.

Amherst, arrived late at the Summer Palace for his audience, exhausted from travelling all night, which he believed his escorts, fearful at telling the Emperor of another obstinate barbarian, had arranged so that somehow, in his weakened state, he could be persuaded to make the dreaded kowtow, or perhaps be knocked flat if ultimately necessary. Having got as far as the ante–chamber to the Throne Room without changing his mind, Amherst was hurried by his escorts to a rest–house while a high Manchu dignitary told the impatiently waiting Emperor that the Ambassador had a severe stomach–ache. When Jiaqing then courteously called in members of Amherst's suite they, too, had diplomatic – and, from experience, by then probably very real – stomach–aches. So the enraged Emperor expelled the entire British mission from China forthwith. The second British effort to establish diplomatic relations with China lasted a whole ten hours, but Amherst was consoled with the Governor–Generalship of India. Before the third attempt – Elgin's – Britain fought two wars against China: the Opium Wars.

Foreign Devils

Europe's two earlier involvements with China had both been theological: the long lonely preaching mission of Giovanni da Montecorvino, the Archbishop of Cathay, at the end of the 13th century, and the extraordinary long campaign of the Jesuit astronomer–priests, between 1600 and 1784, to convert the Emperors through applied science. Both these efforts were based in, and largely confined to, Beijing. Guangzhou [Canton] however had long been China's door for foreign traders, originally Arabs trading from the Gulf and South Asia, then Westerners as they established bases in Southeast Asia and penetrated the China seas; it had been controlled by Imperial officials and opened as little as possible, as John Ledyard found. By the end of the 18th century economic and technological advances had made European traders anxious to push the door open wider, and European governments were soon eager to back them with gunboats. The Middle Kingdom was no longer able to resist Western power: initially, ostrich–like, it was blissfully unaware of it, then incapable of dealing with it as pressure grew throughout the 19th century, and eventually came to harbour a bitter resentment that the 20th century has not yet cured.

The British took the lead in the trade push, shipping into the Guangzhou trading warehouses in particular, but also anywhere else they could smuggle it, increasing volumes of Indian opium, access to which had been inherited by their East India Company from the Moghul

Emperors with Clive's victory in the Battle of Plassey in Bengal in 1757. The Dutch had already been using opium to weaken resistance to their colonisation of Java; disapproving, Warren Hastings, the Governor of Bengal, thought opium

> "not a necessary of life but a pernicious article of luxury, which ought not be permitted, but for the purposes of foreign commerce only".

Opium had in fact previously reached western China overland through Tibet and Burma, and repeated Imperial Edicts tried to stop its use other than for medicinal purposes. But the interests of foreign commerce were too strong: a substantial part of the British Government's revenues came from the import duty on Chinese tea; tea could no longer be paid for in Spanish silver because Spain had allied itself with the rebelling American colonies; so the solution hit upon was to sell the Chinese opium – which of course had the added advantage of creating its own demand. Hastings himself sent the first consignment to China in 1781 – and made a loss. But both supply and demand soon grew: by the 1820s a tenth of London's entire revenues resulted from the wild British demand for tea from China; so increased opium production, which lowered the price, demanded – and enabled the creation of – increasing numbers of Chinese opium addicts.

When the Chinese tried to resist, outraged British traders, already trying to force open the wider Chinese market, persuaded an outraged British Government, led by the new Queen Victoria's dear Lord Melbourne, to prosecute a war unleashed by the cynical Foreign Secretary, Palmerston, whose support for European independence movements did not extend to the East. In the Parliamentary debate on the war in 1840, Gladstone made his first foreign policy inter-vention, denouncing it. China, its military power dissipated in the reveries of the declining Manchu Middle Kingdom, lost the war, and Hong Kong, in 1842. Within two years the United States, which had remained aloof from its own traders' heavy engagement in the opium trade, negotiated a treaty giving it the same trading privileges that Britain had extracted by force. The absence of any territorial demands became the foundation of the United States' long–held moral superiority over European imperialists; but the Americans' suc-cessful insistence on extraterritorial rights for its citizens – so they could be tried *only* in their own national courts, a privilege that then extended of course to all foreign powers – became a serious affront to Chinese sovereignty.

Six years later the great Taiping Rebellion broke out against the incompetent Qing, still alien despite two centuries of rule. It spread rapidly northwards from west of Guangzhou up to the Yangzi [Yangtse] Valley and Nanjing, the ancient southern capital which became their headquarters for eleven years; and it caused upwards of twenty million deaths before it was overcome in 1864. The Taiping Heavenly Army were basically peasants with nothing to lose, but the conviction of its leader, Hong Xiuquan, that he was the son of the Christian God, introduced Biblical elements that the ever–hopeful Europeans and, increasingly, Americans, wondered might be a conduit to the long–awaited Christianisation of China. It was not, of course; and the increasing depredations of the rebels against the so–called Treaty Ports where the Westerners had installed themselves since the First Opium War led to the revised view that the Qing might remain the better bet.

It is curious, in our age of instant, global, real–time news coverage, to note that six years after the Taiping Rebellion had begun, the Indian Mutiny, the first great Asian anti–colonial war, had broken out against the British in India, but, as far as I can make out, there was never any linkage between the two.[305] It is not surprising that neither group of plebeian revolutionaries was aware of the other; but it is a measure of the distance of the Qing Court from the wider world that China made no effort to fend off the increasingly threatening British menace by trying to take advantage of Britain's severe difficulties in India. Somewhat later, according to Beeching, Russian diplomats in Beijing urged the Chinese to "stir up trouble in India", something which could have benefitted Russia in its "great game" of seeking to destabilise the British Raj. While the Chinese had reason enough to be sceptical of Russian solicitude, the response was typically elevated:

"The Heavenly Dynasty, in dealing with the outer barbarians, has always emphasised truthfulness. It never resorts to plots leading to war".

---

305   One parallel with events three years later in Beijing might be noted here: when Delhi was captured from the rebellious Indians, in September 1857, the victorious British soldiers went on a riot of revenge, looting the city's mosques, bazaars and thousands of private houses – and also murdering hundreds, perhaps thousands, of sepoys and civilians.

Not so its opponents. The Chinese, as if they did not have enough on their hands trying to contain the Taipings, dared to resist Western demands for the broadening of the extraterritorial privileges extracted in 1842. Lord Palmerston, now Prime Minister, thought that

> "The Time is fast coming when we shall be obliged to strike another blow for China...These half–civilised governments such as those in China...all require a Dressing every eight to ten years to keep them in order. Their minds are too shallow to receive an Impression that will last longer than some such Period, and warning is of little use. They care little for words and they must not only see the stick but actually feel it on their shoulders before they yield".

Britain attacked again in 1859, this time with France, and secured in the ensuing Treaties of Tientsin the ability to do pretty much what they wanted: wider trading access, including up the Yangzi River, though little effort was made to abide by the limitations they accepted; the opening of resident Legations in Beijing; and they also succeeded in getting the Chinese to agree to their long–standing demand for the trade in opium to be legalised.

Never far behind, missionary activity was opened up throughout the country. The dream of a Christian China would not go away; nor, over the succeeding decades, would the competitive squabbling of the missionaries themselves, now with national pride added to doctrinal differences. This is not to question the sincerity of their devotion, the value of their medical treatments, or their usefulness to the development of their countrymen's commerce; but the willingness of some of them to call for the backing of their country's military force had the effect of undermining the better efforts of all of them.

But the Treaties were not to be the end of the Second Opium War: despite its agreement to their provisions, the Manchu Court was still appalled above all at the implications of conceding residence in the Imperial City to barbarian representatives. Accordingly, when the British and French arrived to open their Legations in Beijing in 1859 Chinese forces blocked their passage at the Taku Forts (near present–day Dagu) at the mouth of the Baihe River linking Beijing to the sea, and sank four British gunboats when they tried to force their way through. In what turned out to be a rehearsal for the next war, forty years on, the two European powers returned in force the next year, captured the Chinese forts and marched on the capital. In a last effort to avoid further conflict Elgin made a belated effort to negotiate the way forward; but in their last stab, the Chinese took hostage the chief British negotiator and his retinue, including *The Times*'s correspondent, and incarcerated them in the Yuan Ming Yuan. And it was specifically the mis–treatment of this group, resulting in the death of several (including the unfortunate journalist), that led Elgin to order the destruction of the Summer Palace. Elgin justified his action as "the least objectionable of the several courses open to me", as the punishment, he said,

> "was one which would fall, not on the people, who may be com-
> paratively innocent, but exclusively on the Emperor, whose direct
> personal responsibility for the crime committed is established not
> only by the treatment of the prisoners at Yuen Ming Yuen [sic],
> but also by the edict in which he offers a pecuniary reward for the
> heads of the foreigners, adding that he is ready to expend all his
> treasure in these wages of assassination".

Elgin was subsequently made Governor–General of India.

East meets West

Preferable as it was for the noble Lord to vent his outrage on "the Yuen Ming Yuen", on an object rather than a populace, it was unfortunate that Elgin ordered the indiscriminate destruction of a unique one. In the first place it was far from being one object. The old "Summer Palace" consisted of some two hundred pavilions and palaces scattered through a series of three major gardens of artificial hills, lakes and tree plantings, covering an area of 350 hectares – more than three times the area of Versailles – to the east of the present (new) Summer Palace. The first palace–garden was the Chang Chun Yuan, "the Garden of Eternal Spring", laid out by the Emperor Kangxi at the end of the 17th century. The second, on its west side and about double its size, bore the name Yuan Ming Yuan, "the Garden of Perfect Clarity", which was eventually applied to the entire complex; it was originally laid out by Kangxi's son Yongzheng while still a prince, then expanded into his principal residence after he became Emperor in 1723. The third palace–garden, on the south side of the Chang Chun Yuan, was the Yi Chun Yuan, "the Garden of Luxuriant Spring", originally established by a half–brother of Yongzheng; it went on being developed almost until the end of the reign of Yongzheng's grandson, the Emperor Jiaqing, in 1820.

This vast complex of garden and architecture, developed over a century and a half, decorated by the cream of the country's craftsmen, was the culmination of centuries–old Chinese tradition associating nature and art in perspectives of delight and contemplation, a philosophical as much as a physical statement of deeply–held values. Virtually everything was destroyed by Elgin's troops. We have, however, some conception of the variety and elegance of at least the second of the gardens, the original Garden of Perfect Clarity, from a two–volume album containing forty views painted on silk for the Emperor Qianlong, Yongzheng's son, in 1747. It was fortunately preserved in 1860 because, just before the destruction of the Summer Palace, Lieutenant–Colonel Charles Louis Désiré Dupin, the French president of the joint commission for dividing war spoils, looted it for himself from one of the Emperor's private apartments.[306]

The only significant remains are those nowadays known as "the Great Fountain Ruins", or simply as Yuan Ming Yuan. Unlike the wooden palaces elsewhere in the gardens, these had been constructed of stone and marble, and they were built at the direction of Qianlong himself by the Milanese Jesuit priest and painter Brother Giuseppe Castiglione – known in Beijing as Lang Shining, "Lang Calm Life". Although Castiglione had arrived in Beijing in 1715 as a missionary, five years before the Emperor Kangxi's death, he came to be employed full–time as a painter by his grandson Qianlong. Castiglione's work, like that of his more scientific and technological predecessors, all the way back to 1601 when Father Matteo Ricci had founded the Jesuit mission in Beijing, was seen by his Order as a means of promoting the missionaries' theological objectives through their continuing closeness to the Dragon Throne itself and its highest scholar–officials. Rome at times wondered how effective this policy was, with reason: Qianlong, for example, although raising Castiglione to the third rank of the mandarinate, nevertheless periodically resorted to brutal efforts to prevent the conversion of his subjects.

---

306 In 1862 when Dupin tried to sell the album at auction in Paris it failed to meet his reserve price of thirty thousand francs, and was knocked down at the next auction for a mere four thousand – and was promptly preempted by the Bibliothèque Nationale. Dupin was censured, but eventually made "Commander of the Counter–Guerrilla Forces" in Mexico during the French campaign that led to Napoleon III's short–lived installation of the Archduke Maximilian of Austria as Emperor of Mexico. The paintings have now been reproduced in the splendid volume *Yuanming Yuan* by Che Bing Chiu (Paris, 2000).

Some of Castiglione's prodigious output still exists, particularly from the thirty years he worked for Qianlong; it was all of subjects nominated personally by the Emperor, who liked to watch Castiglione at work. There are vivid portraits of the Emperor, exquisite flower studies, superb paintings of animals, especially of the Imperial stable's elegant Ferghana horses, spectacular scrolls depicting in the minutest detail various activities of the Emperor, his Court and his armies – four, each 27 metres long, showing him hunting.[307] Castiglione's paintings show a rare talent for combining fine European realism with sensitive Chinese visualisation, the result not being kitsch but utterly charming.

A decade into his reign a picture of a European–style fountain led the Emperor to commission Castiglione also to design the "Great Fountain" garden complex: a series of European–style palaces, aviary and follies, with fountains, canals, reflecting pools and Qianlong's own favourite, a water–clock made of the twelve animals of the Chinese zodiac, in bronze, spouting water on the hour. Father Michel Benoist provided the expertise for the hydraulics.[308] Between 1747 and 1768 the new palaces were constructed in an elongated T–shape across the extreme northern edge of the Chang Chun Yuan. The cross–bar contained (from south to north) the Palace of the Delights of Harmony, and the Labyrinth; the longer (west–east) axis consisted of the Belvedere, the Palace of the Calm Sea (with the water–clock), the Observatory of Distant Oceans and the Great Fountains, the Hill of Perspective with triumphal gates to either side, and finally the Water Theatre lake. The succession of buildings was designed not for living in but for the entertainment and repose of the Emperor, his consorts and immediate entourage, and for the display of the European treasures he had come by in various ways. None of the

---

307 Most of Castiglione's surviving works are now in the National Palace Museum, Taipei, and the Forbidden City Palace Museum, Beijing; the hunting scrolls are in the Musée Guimet, Paris.

308 There is an interesting contemporary footnote on the fate of the bronze animals: in April–May 2000 the heads of the monkey, the ox and the tiger were sold at auction in Hong Kong, although a Chinese official stated that "it was an insult to the Chinese government and people" for these "looted" antiques to be auctioned there. All three were purchased by the China Poly Corporation, for US$1.05 million, $990 thousand and $1.98 million, respectively, for the Poly Art Museum in Beijing, the first private museum in China, directed by the son–in-law of the former Chinese leader Deng Xiaoping. Further details are in *Arts of Asia* Vol.30 No.4 July – August 2000, pp 5–6.

palaces was allowed to be of more than one storey, as Qianlong said he would not "live in the air" like Europeans:

"One would have to be very poverty–stricken and lack land like the Europeans, to live like that".[309]

The architecture, known to us only through a series of engravings made in 1786 by Castiglione's pupils,[310] was a unique combination of a wild version of the Baroque style currently fashionable in Italy and France with the sensibilities of Chinese construction and placement in the landscaping. Elgin succeeded in destroying it all. The main ruins left to us to admire today, the only ensemble giving even a whiff of what was originally here, are parts of the two ranges which surrounded the Great Fountains. The most dazzling, on a little hillock in a field of weeds, consist of an elegant, extravagantly voluted white marble arch, perhaps eight metres high, its columns themselves voluted outwards at the bottom to form inverse arches with the remains of the pillars to either side, they in turn flanked by more fallen volutes resting on huge rococo shells. The reverse of the arch is a fantasy of ferns and shells, surmounting two huge fat pods of peas in sinuous framing. Opposite, a finely carved low wall is surmounted by five marble panels of European–style heraldic panels of arms and armour. Scattered elsewhere are the remains of elaborately carved columns, a water basin, bits of capitals and pedestals, all identifiable by geography if not necessarily, any longer, by function. It is all rather sad, but beautiful in its way, and great fun to explore. One of Castiglione's fellow Jesuits remarked that it was impossible not to "admire the art with which this irregularity was carried out".

In 1861, the year after the devastation of the Yuan Ming Yuan, Elgin was the guest of honour at a Royal Academy dinner in London. He

---

309 In the 1860s a British Peer said to Wade (of Wade–Giles):

"Peking's a gigantic failure, isn't it? not a two–storied house in the whole place, eh?"

310 The engravings have been reproduced in a slim volume, *Le Yuanmingyuan*, published in Paris by Éditions Recherches sur les Civilisations in 1987 for the projected French participation in "studies preliminary to the conservation, presentation and eventual restoration of the 'European Palaces' ". The publication includes several tantalisingly small photographs of a model of the original palaces based on the suite of engravings.

repeated the justification he had already given for his action, but clearly felt that his cultivated audience, not to mention his own damaged reputation, required something more:

> "I am not so incorrigibly barbarous as to be incapable of feeling the humanising influences which fall upon us from the noble works of art by which we are surrounded. No one regretted more sincerely than I did the destruction of that collection of summer houses and kiosks, already, and previously to any act of mine, rifled of their contents, which was dignified by the title of Summer Palace of the Chinese Emperor... I felt the time had come when I must choose between the indulgence of a not unnatural sensibility, and the performance of a painful duty".

But how painful? In case any of his auditors might think his reference to the Yuan Ming Yuan as a "collection of summer houses and kiosks" was mere pomposity, he went on to deliver himself of his considered opinion as to what had really been involved:

> "I do not think in matters of art we have much to learn from that country...The most cynical representations of the grotesque have been the principal products of Chinese conceptions of the sublime and beautiful. Nevertheless I am disposed to believe that under this mass of abortions and rubbish there lie hidden some sparks of a divine fire, which the genius of my countrymen may gather and nurse into a flame".

One imagines there was sustained applause by fellow countrymen. This was the spirit behind the British belief that they not only could but were entitled to do whatever they thought best with whomever they thought merited their attention – if British interests would profit thereby.

British imperialism was not even at its peak yet; France and the other European powers were beginning to emulate it; Japan, which, after the Tokugawa's two-and-a-half centuries of self-imposed isolation since Hideyoshi's fall, had only begun to rejoin the world since the 1853 visit of Commodore Perry of the United States, a new player in Asia, and had still not begun to learn all that Europeans could teach it – including their aggressive imperialism. This was what China was facing at the time of Yuan Shikai's birth.

Soldier

At the time of Elgin's speech Yuan Shikai was only two. Through chance and ambition his life became inextricably involved in the naked imperialism, political and military manoeuvring, and emperors' dooms, which established the outlines of developments in East Asia throughout the 20th century.

Yuan Shikai was one of China's millions of usually unknown rural babies.[311] He was born on 16 September 1859, the day before the British Cabinet of Prime Minister Palmerston supported the Earl of Elgin's wish to fight on to Beijing, despite the Navy's recent losses at the Taku Forts, and despite the opposition of W.E.Gladstone, who again objected to war in China, this time (as Chancellor of the Exchequer) because of the expense. It is questionable how much Yuan's parents are likely to have known about these new British attacks on the Middle Kingdom; although the wider family have been described as significant landowners in the middle of Henan Province in central China, his father seems to have been a fairly ordinary farmer near Hiangzheng, around halfway between Wuhan and the Huang He [Yellow River].

But Yuan was lucky in starting with connections. The first was his father's uncle, a middle–level official who had been co–opted into the military to fight the Taiping rebels as they pushed north of the Yangzi River, and whose adopted son adopted Yuan. The boy was taken to Shandong Province to be educated, but was an unwilling student, preferring what Ch'en describes as "riding, boxing and debauchery".

At the age of twenty–one, after an unlikely start and an unpromising education, Yuan Shikai had found his métier as aide–de–camp to General Wu, in charge of his brigade's training and discipline. He had been fortunate to be related to a successful official who adopted him and who had had an influential general as a friend. Yuan was now in the right place to make the most of the latter advantage: Shandong Province was not only close to the capital but also to China's most active neighbours, Russia, Japan, and, in the middle, sleepy little Korea. He was also there

---

311   The two main English versions of Yuan Shikai's early life, the entry in AW Hummel's *Eminent Chinese of the Ch'ing Period* and J Ch'en's *Yuan Shih-k'ai*, do not agree in all respects. What follows is an attempt to select what seem to be the essentials. Subsequently Ch'en is the main, more detailed, source, though for the years after 1900 I have also drawn on SR MacKinnon's *Power and Politics in Late Imperial China*. From the 1880s there is an increasing number of contemporary references.

at the right time: sleepy little Korea was about to become the cockpit of a contest between Russia and Japan for supremacy in East Asia.

The contrast between the leadership of the two countries could not have been more striking. In 1880 the Emperor Meiji had already been on the throne, now moved from Kyoto to Tokyo, for thirteen years, and the Meiji Restoration, as the modernisation of Japan was known, was in full swing. The feudal *daimyo* domains had been abolished – or crushed – and replaced by a national administration and a national army; and both were in the early stages of adopting Western techniques and technology to develop national industrial and military power. Japan Inc., strongly supported by the twenty–eight–year–old Emperor, had well and truly begun. Ito Hirobumi, born to an even poorer peasant family than Yuan Shikai's, had been adopted like Yuan by better–placed connections and sent to Nagasaki to learn how to manufacture firearms. Like the other early leaders of the Restoration, as a youth he was violently opposed to the "opening" of Japan: he and associates tried to burn down the newly established British Legation, and he then smuggled himself aboard a British ship to go off to learn how to build a navy to defeat the foreigners.[312] By 1880 he was a convinced Westerniser, and about to become the dominant political figure of the new Japan.

The year before, in Russia, the fourth attempt to assassinate Tsar Alexander II had failed, but the emancipator of the serfs had long since recoiled from the other reforms he had originally favoured; with the success of the fifth attempt the following year his son Alexander III launched a policy of unrelieved oppression. He had been strongly influenced by his tutor, Konstantin Petrovich Pobedonostzev, the Curator of the Holy Synod, an uncompromising proponent of tsarist autocracy based on pervasive police controls, of religious conformity based on the Orthodox Church and the persecution of religious minorities, especially the Jews, and of an expansionist nationalism based on a xenophobic Pan–Slavism. In 1880 Pobedonostzev was tutoring the twelve–year–old Nicholas, about to become Tsarevich; he would remain the most powerful Russian minister for a quarter of a century.

During this coming period Russian intentions would become a major concern of Yuan Shikai, of the Emperor Meiji and Ito Hirobumi, and, unlikely as it would have seemed in 1880, of the Englishman George Nathaniel Curzon. Curzon, born eight months before Yuan and then

---

312   A fictionalised version of Ito Hirobumi's early life is in James Clavell's novel *Gai–jin* (1993)

also twenty–one, had been born into a family at the opposite end of the social scale, though one more distinguished for having held the same estates for eight hundred years than for any particular contribution to state, church or the armed services. By 1880, after schooling at Eton, Curzon was mid–way through a classics degree at Devorguilla of Galloway's Balliol College,[313] then at its peak in producing the rulers of Britain and its far–flung Empire. The man responsible was the Master, Benjamin Jowett; his raw material was inevitably, at the time, mostly the well–born, like Curzon; but their achievements were attributable in great measure not simply to social status as to Jowett's unremitting emphasis on the necessity of dedicated, intellectually honest application to their studies and to their chosen careers. At the same time, he once admitted, he had "a general prejudice against all persons who do not succeed in the world". Curzon already had every intention of succeeding.

The mentor

For China, the twenty years between the destruction of the Summer Palace and the beginning of Yuan Shikai's army career had been divided almost equally into a decade of promise and a decade of missed opportunity. The first became known as the Tongzhi Restoration, after the new Emperor who had ascended the throne in 1861 at Jehol, the Court's summer capital in southern Manchuria where it had fled to escape the Earl of Elgin. New ministers, led by Prince Gong [Kung], half–brother of the late Emperor Xianfeng, began a policy of "self–strengthening": seeking to maintain traditional Confucian systems and values, while at the same time adopting Western methods to train and re–equip the army, build naval vessels and munitions factories, re–organise the Customs Service (under an Englishman!) to put state finances on a more secure basis, even seeking more productive relations with the foreign powers, all aimed at underpinning a Dynasty severely shaken by the Taiping Rebellion and the Anglo–French seizure of Beijing.

The problem was that Tongzhhi had become Emperor at the age of five, and the real ruler was the Regent, his father's chief concubine, the twenty–six–year–old Manchu Yehanola, now to be known as the Dowager Empress Cixi. Extremely strong–willed, cunning, duplicitous, and determined, Cixi was also uneducated, avaricious and – unsurprisingly, having barely escaped the sack of the Summer Palace – fundamentally

---

313   See 1300 Chapter

anti–foreign. She established her dominating position with extraordinary skill and speed, using then dumping Prince Gong by the end of the decade, manipulating and outwitting everyone else. No–one proved strong enough, not only to stand up to her, but, more seriously, to persuade her to consistently support the self–strengthening program. When her son unexpectedly died in 1875 the Dowager Empress was powerful enough to install his cousin, against all the dynastic and Confucian rules of strict generational succession, as the next Emperor, Guangxu. He was only four, so her imperious and reactionary Regency could continue unthreatened.

By the decade of the 1870s there was no further talk of reform, and officials were cowed in the face of her capriciousness:

> "The Court listens eagerly to the opinions of all", she said at this stage, "and seeks the truth about conditions...You officials should each purify your hearts and trembling obey the repeated Imperial commands to reveal your loyal counsels. But you must not irresponsibly offer personal opinions".

There was of course only one counsel that was loyal, that was not personal opinion. But there was one innovative figure, Li Hongzhang, perhaps because he was able to establish a career away from the Dowager Empress's repressive hand in Beijing, which also helped him, as a Chinese, avoid the direct jealousies of the privileged Manchu princes. He was of the previous generation, born in 1823 into a rich Anhui family, and had begun, like Yuan Shikai, the traditional career path into the civil service through the state examinations. Unlike Yuan he was successful; but again like him, he moved into the army, rising during the Taiping Rebellion to command of the Anhui Army. It was during this period that he encouraged the creation by Westerners of the "Ever Victorious Army", commanded first by the extraordinary but almost unknown Frederick Townsend Ward[314] and then by the future "Chinese" Gordon. Li wrote of the latter:

> "What a sight for sore eyes and elixir for a heavy heart is to see this splendid Englishman fight!..."He is a glorious fellow";

---

314 There is a splendid biography of Ward by Caleb Carr: *The Devil Soldier* (New York 1992)

and Gordon tried to persuade the profoundly Confucian Li of the "moral superiority" of Christianity.

Even before the end of the Rebellion Li Hongzhang was made Governor of Jiangsu Province, and in 1867 became Viceroy of Henan and Hubei. In 1871 Cixi called on him to take over as Viceroy of Chihli,[315] the all–important metropolitan province surrounding Beijing itself. Her move was prompted by the murder of a number of French Catholic missionaries in Tianjin [Tientsin], the capital's seaport, just upstream from the Taku Forts of fateful memory. The tragedy was typical of the misunderstandings inevitable in the conjunction of such mutual incomprehensions: out of kindness, nuns had paid people to bring in orphaned babies, to save their lives and of course their souls; but the death of large numbers of them in an epidemic was interpreted locally as ritual murder for arcane Christian purposes. An angry mob descended on the cathedral and nunnery; magistrates came to investigate; the French Consul lost his temper, abused them, fired his pistol at one, missed; but then he shot an official who tried to help him through the angry crowd. It went berserk, tore the Consul limb from limb, murdered and mutilated ten nuns, and killed two priests and six other French.

The Dowager Empress was still treading warily with foreigners after the 1860 disaster, and Li Hongzhang was appointed to resolve the issue with the Western powers in as conciliatory manner as possible. Although their gunboats had immediately begun to gather off the coast, the Westerners also behaved reasonably (in their terms), largely because on this occasion France was in no position to attack China again – it had just been defeated by Bismarck's Prussia, and Napoleon III had been captured and then overthrown. In Tianjin Li executed eighteen (ringleaders or not was probably irrelevant: it was the same number as the French killed), imprisoned others, and agreed that China would pay a large indemnity. But not a square metre of territory had to be ceded. Li was well on his way to being China's leading statesman. As the century wore on to its end Cixi loaded Li with increasing honours and responsibilities, but she never really accorded him her complete confidence, let alone her unqualified support.

---

315 Chihli [Pinyin Zhili] no longer exists: it corresponded approximately with present–day Hebei Province plus Tianjin special municipality and the area of Beijing Municipality outside the old city centre. It will thus continue to be referred to as Chihli.

One of Li's two main roles in the last quarter of the century was as a leader of economic development, inspired as much by Restoration Japan's model as by his knowledge of and brief visits to Europe. Using state funds he established a series of manufacturing enterprises, opened a variety of mines, and began the construction of railway and telegraph lines; the risks were the state's, the profits Li Hongzhang's, and he became immensely rich. Princely amounts of his gains were prudently and successfully deployed in buttering up the rapacious Dowager Empress; in thereon leaving Li to his numerous devices Cixi made one of her few contributions to the modernisation of China. But Li's sphere of action was limited; unfortunately for China, after the fitful start of the Tongzhi Restoration there was no central direction of national economic development during the remainder of the century.

Li Hongzhang's other major role was that of virtual foreign minister over the same period. It was in this capacity that George Curzon, a Member of Parliament since 1886 and Under–Secretary for India in 1891, called on him in Tianjin in 1892, in the course of a study–tour of Japan, Korea and China. In his subsequent book *Problems of the Far East* Curzon described the man he met:

"The Viceroy entered, a tall and commanding figure, considerably over six feet in height, dressed in a long grey silk robe, with a black silk cape over his shoulders...He continually put the most searching and ingenious questions; being renowned, indeed, for his faculty of 'pumping' others about what he desires to ascertain, without emitting the least corresponding drop of moisture himself. While speaking or listening his small, black, restless eyes follow keenly every movement of the features".

Li's role as chief interlocutor with foreign countries was in part consequent on his front–line position as Viceroy of Chihli and simultaneously Commissioner of Trade for the Northern Ports; but it also reflected his ability, repeatedly demonstrated, to deal with the importunate Foreign Devils, whom everyone else in the Manchu Court found not only incomprehensible but utterly intolerable. Unfortunately Confucian contempt did not provide protection against gunboats. Li was not always successful in heading off the foreigners' demands, but on a number of significant occasions he clearly prevented a good deal worse, largely because he recognised China's inability to match their power. It was for this reason, as well as the profits, that he encouraged industrial and military modernisation where he could; in the meantime he believed that China's only choice frequently needed to be acquiescence in the foreign powers' demands, while seeking to use their mutual jealousies to try to limit their rapacity.

Trouble in the Land of Morning Calm

It was in this respect in particular that Li Hongzhang came to know Yuan Shikai. The latter had only been on General Wu Changqing's staff for two years when his whole army division was despatched by Li to put down a rebellion in Korea, in 1882. It has to be said that Korea was not, on the whole, one of Li's success stories; it was, rather, a perfect demonstration of China's lack of power to match rapacious foreigners – in Korea's case, repeatedly and, ultimately, permanently, Japan. The "opening" by Westerners of Korea, the Hermit Kingdom, left alone even by Japan during the two and a half centuries since Hideyoshi's invasions, had been more brutal than Commodore Perry's "opening" of Japan. Foreigners were forbidden to live in the country, but from early in the 19th century French Catholic priests began smuggling themselves in, until in 1866 they and their converts were wiped out by the xenophobic Tai Won Kun, the Regent for his young son King Kojong. A French military retaliation was driven off, as were two bizarre raids by private American ships, the second guided by a French priest, apparently seeking to rob the royal tombs; to avenge the crew of the first, two American warships destroyed the forts guarding the sea approach to Seoul, but then retired.

Japan was less reticent: in less than a decade since the Meiji Restoration it had learned Western lessons too well. It also now pressed for access to Korea, which resisted – in 1868, 1869, and again in 1872 – just as Japan itself had resisted foreigners only twenty years before; and like them it was not disposed to take no for an answer. When a Japanese ship was fired on in 1876 pressure mounted in Tokyo for revenge, but Ito Hirobumi, Li Hongzhang's counterpart at the head of Japanese diplomacy, was able to have Japan's demands satisfied by the Kangwha Treaty, opening several Korean ports to Japanese merchants, and authorising a resident diplomatic representative in Seoul.

Korea had acknowledged China's suzerainty for centuries: its second dynasty, the Koryo, had accepted Kublai Khan's rule in the 13th; its successor, the Yi dynasty, had seized power with Ming support at the end of the 14th, and was still ruling, subject to the traditional annual tribute to the Dragon Throne. In 1885, Yuan was appointed

Chinese Resident in Seoul. Curzon described the situation in the following terms:

"in Söul itself every one of the Foreign Diplomatic Corps, though he gaily proclaimed himself the representative of his sovereign at an allied and equal Court, knew perfectly well who was the real master. The Chinese Resident, who was a man of great energy and ability, named Yuan Shih Kai, was in the position of a Mayor of the Palace, without whose knowledge nothing, and without whose consent little was done. Alone among the foreign representatives, he was entitled to sit when received by the King" – a vital distinction for those who declined to kowtow to a far grander monarch – "...The various champions of the academic theory of Korean independence have one by one disappeared from the stage, but the Chinese Resident remained. Time after time he had been reappointed...He is one of the few Chinese I have met who impressed me with frankness as well as with power".[316]

But tension was rising between Korea's traditional masters and the increasingly aggressive and expansionist Japanese. After one set of negotiations with Japan over Korea, Yuan's superior, Li Hongzhang, wrote secretly to the Zongli [Tsungli] Yamen – the Foreign Ministry – about his Japanese counterpart, Ito Hirobumi. Ito, he wrote, had:

"travelled long on the continents of Europe and America and is strongly imitating them. He really has the ability to govern his country. He pays particular attention to these policies: to encourage trade and to be harmonious with neighbouring nations, to enrich the people and strengthen the troops...In about ten years Japan's

---

316 Curzon had another, amusing, encounter, with the head of Korea's self–styled Foreign Office. As he related it in *Problems of the Far East*:

"Conscious that in his own country it is not easy for any one to become a member of the Government, unless he is related to the family of the King or Queen, he said to me, 'I presume you are a near relative of Her Majesty the Queen of England'. 'No', I replied, 'I am not.' But, observing the look of disgust that passed over his countenance, I was fain to add, 'I am, however, as yet an unmarried man,' with which unscrupulous suggestion I completely regained the old gentleman's favour".

wealth and power will be considerable. She is China's future disaster, not our present anxiety".

Li's prediction proved chillingly accurate.

Internal dissension, on both domestic and foreign affairs, left both the Korean court and its opponents weak and ineffective, though both at various times tried to undermine Yuan. The divisions undoubtedly helped Yuan succeed, at least for the time being, in undermining any pro–Russian ventures, even though concern about Japan's intentions remained strong. The deliberate build–up of Japanese settlement in Korea continued; and it is notable that, on his 1892 visit, Curzon, who saw Japan as a potential barrier to the further Russian encroachment in East Asia which he feared, observed:

> "The race hatred between Koreans and Japanese is the most striking phenomenon in contemporary Chosen. Civil and obliging in their own country, the Japanese develop in Korea a faculty for bullying and bluster...The lower orders ill–treat the Koreans on every possible opportunity, and are cordially detested by them in return".[317]

Yuan himself was active in challenging Japan's economic predominance, and towards the end of the decade China had come close to matching Japanese exports to Korea. For most of the period Yuan appeared to be shoring up China's position, though at the cost of making more enemies than he probably needed to, a problem that was to come back with a vengeance at the peak of his career.

Then, in 1894, Yuan Shikai's tenth year as Resident, disaster came. And when it came it was total. The trigger was a rebellion of peasants and the poor. It was led by the Tong Hak – "Eastern Learning" – Society,

---

317 A conviction of racial superiority on the part of many Japanese was not confined to the Koreans, or to the 19th century: in a television interview in 2002 a former Japanese soldier who had been in Japanese–occupied Manchuria during the 1930s–1940s said, in confessing to participating in war crimes against the Chinese,

"We didn't think of the Chinks as human. They were sub–human".

Not the first time this sentiment has appeared in our meanderings through history, and certainly not the last. We shall find the precise reverse view later in this chapter.

a semi–religious and anti–foreign (especially anti–missionary) sect, which at the same time protested its loyalty to the Korean King. Troubles spread as famine added to resistance to government oppression. The indefatigable traveller Isabella Bird Bishop,[318] who was spending an extended period in Korea at this time, wrote of

"Yuan, the Minister Resident and representative of Korea's Suzerain, by many people regarded as 'the power behind the throne', who is reported to have gone more than once unbidden into the King's presence, and to have reproached him with his conduct of affairs...so far as I could learn his chief fault was that he let things alone, and neglected to use his unquestionably great power in favour of reform and common honesty – but he was a Chinese mandarin!"

She found one thing in Yuan's favour, if somewhat back–handedly:

"He possessed the power of life and death over Chinamen, and his punishments were often to our thinking barbarous, but the Chinese feared him so much they treated the Koreans fairly well, which is more than can be said of the Japanese".

Apart from Yuan's failure to press reforms or assistance to the starving peasantry, the inability of Korea's new army to curb the revolt, which seems to have been the government's only response to the disturbances, certainly reflected on his role in its training. At the same time, the Reverend James Gale, an American missionary who had been in Korea since 1890, noted that

---

318   Born Isabella Bird, in England, in 1831, she had become a semi–invalid after a brief visit to the United States in 1854. However in 1872 she followed the recommendation of her physician to resume travelling for her health. The doctor may have had in mind a trip to Brighton, or perhaps Biarritz; over the course of the next thirty years, however, Isabella spent a total of fifty months travelling – the hard way, by horse, donkey, camel, canoe and, when there was no alternative, on foot – and writing about the Sandwich Islands (Hawaii), the Rocky Mountains, Japan, the Malay peninsula, Tibet, Persia, Kurdistan, Korea, China and North Africa. Her book *Korea and its Neighbours*, published in 1897 following three extensive periods in the country between 1894 and 1897, was one of the earliest foreign accounts of the Hermit Kingdom.

"It is generally admitted that the rising of the Tonghaks was instigated by outside parties".

And now Japan, Li Hongzhang's "permanent and great anxiety", waiting and watching for ten years, did seize the opportunity to "pry into China's emptiness", this time with full force – not just against Korea, but, indeed, against China itself. Japan's excuse was – as so often with all the foreign states pressing on China from most sides – the need to "protect" its nationals. And it was now that the provisions of the Treaty of Tientsin turned the tables not only on Yuan Shikai but on Li as well. Yuan, either in panic at the Tong Haks' progress or because he thought he saw a chance to strengthen China's position, persuaded the King, at the end of May 1894, to call for the assistance of Chinese troops against the rebels. The Japanese Legation, hearing of this almost immediately, also asked Yuan to bring in Chinese forces. Li Hongzhang despatched 1,500 soldiers and, as the Treaty required, notified Japan.

But Japan was no longer interested in equal standing. Its "request" to Yuan soon proved to be totally disingenuous, presumably designed to give a fig–leaf of legitimacy to decisions already taken in Tokyo: in less than three weeks of the King's request to China Japan had landed fifteen thousand troops, with three months' provisions, and they had taken up positions at Pusan on the south coast, at Seoul, and at Chemulpo (present–day Inchon), the capital's port, where General Douglas MacArthur would land United Nations forces against North Korean and Chinese forces in late 1950, two Korean Wars later. Isabella Bird Bishop, landing at Chemulpo at the time after a brief absence from Korea, noted that the Japanese movements

"were carried out with a suddenness, celerity, and freedom from hitch...To any student of Far Eastern politics it must have been apparent that this skilful and extraordinary move on the part of Japan was not made for the protection of her colonies in Chemulpo and Seoul...There can be no question that Japan had been planning such a movement for years. She had made accurate maps of Korea, and had secured reports of forage and provisions, measurements of the width of rivers and the depth of fords, and had been buying up rice in Korea for three months previously, while even as far as the Tibetan frontier, Japanese officers in disguise had gauged the strength and weakness of China, reporting on her armies on paper and, in fact, on her dummy guns,...and knew better than the

Chinese themselves how many men each province could put into the field, how drilled and how armed, and they were acquainted with the infinite corruption and dishonesty, combined with a total lack of patriotism, which nullified such commisariat arrangements as existed on paper, and rendered it absolutely impossible for China to send an army efficiently into the field, far less sustain it during a campaign".

Harsh words, but all too soon to be abundantly confirmed.

In the face of Japan's pre–emptive strike Li Hongzhang, anxious to avoid war, ordered China's troops to halt south of Pyongyang (now the North Korean capital). The Japanese side was now being led by Otori, the Japanese Minister to China, who "happened" to be in Seoul at this crucial stage. Isabella Bird Bishop said she had frequently seen "Otori San",

> "a Japanese of average height, speaking English well, wearing European dress as though born to it, and sporting white 'shoulder–of–mutton' whiskers...He lounged in drawing–rooms, making trivial remarks to ladies, and was remarkable only for his insignificance...[Now] he showed himself rough, vigorous, capable, a man of action, unscrupulous, and not only clever enough to outwit Yuan in a difficult and hazardous game, but everybody else".

With the Chinese forces still well to the north of the capital, Yuan now agreed to Otori's proposal that neither country would send more soldiers – leaving Japan at an even greater advantage. Li next asked Britain, France, Russia and the United States to mediate; their proposal for simultaneous troop withdrawals from Korea was accepted by China.

The same day on which Japan rejected it Otori demanded that King Kojong declare Korea's independence from China. This fig–leaf failed: so within a month Japanese troops forced their way into the palace and hauled King, Queen and Crown Prince off to the Japanese Legation, and reinstated the discredited Tai Won Kun, whom the Chinese had allowed back into Korea many years earlier as a possible counter to pro–Russian ideas. Now, both Li's colleagues in Beijing and Yuan himself pressed for a firm stand against Japan. Li was still vividly aware of China's relative weakness, but agreed to reinforce Chinese forces in Korea. One of the first wave, a private British ship with twelve hundred Chinese troops on board, was sunk by a Japanese naval vessel. In an eerie phrase, the Reverend Gale (writing forty–three years before Pearl Harbour) said

"The transport ship was as helpless as Honolulu would be in case of an attack by sea".

As for those who did not go down with the ship, Gale wrote that

"It is said on good authority that Japan turned her machine guns on these poor wretches".

Before there could be any response, the captive King was forced by the Japanese to have Korea declare war on China – which was patently too absurd even to serve as a fig–leaf. It was only two months since he had asked for the Dragon Throne's help. Li Hongzhang had no further room to manoeuvre: war with Japan followed.

The war itself was an unmitigated disaster for China – and of course for Korea. The opening battles were around Pyongyang, which was devastated. Isabella Bird Bishop visited the area three months later, to find, for a distance of seventy kilometres,

"partially destroyed villages, relapsing plains, and slopes denuded of every stick which could be burned. There were no wayfarers on the roads, no movement of any kind"

– a spectral landscape that would unfortunately be familiar from our first chapter until the present century. The land war moved on across the Yalu River into Manchuria, where the Chinese armies were annihilated.

Disaster on land was accompanied by disaster at sea. But that had been in preparation for some time. In the mid–1870s the Dowager Empress Cixi made her first effort to have the Yuan Ming Yuan restored; but the ruins had deteriorated further since Elgin turned his back on them, and she uncharacteristically had to give way in the face of criticism of the expense at a time when the country had not recovered from the Taiping Rebellion and was still facing a Moslem revolt on the Russian frontier in Xinjiang. But she was not one to give up permanently. In the later 1880s she went ahead with the construction of the I Ho Yuan, the cutely but in Cixi's case inaccurately–named "Garden for the Cultivation of Harmonious Old Age" – the new (present) Summer Palace, on the site of a long–abandoned palace–park to the west of the Yuan Ming Yuan. To head off criticism this time Cixi announced that she was

> "aware that the Emperor's desire to restore the Palace in the west springs from his laudable concern for my welfare, and for that reason I can not bear to meet his well–meaning petition with a blunt refusal. Moreover the costs of the construction have all been provided for out of the surplus funds accumulated as a result of rigid economies in the past…no harm will be done to the national finances".

The Dowager Empress's modesty was matched only by her mendacity: the new Summer Palace was built from the funds intended to build a new navy after France's destruction of the first fleet during the Tonkin war in 1884. What navy there was in 1894–1895 was then sunk by the Japanese in the Yellow Sea. A palace eunuch was philosophical on Cixi's misappropriation of funds:

> "What does it matter?" he is reported as saying; "The Japanese would have beaten us all the same. As it is, at least we have the Summer Palace".

Though, as it would turn out, not for long.

Twilight of the Hermit Kingdom

There was one more act before this second Korean crisis was concluded. Japan now dominated the whole of Korea. A young diplomat in the American Legation, William Franklin Sands, who arrived in Seoul in 1898, recorded that

> "The Japanese minister…generally took on the air of a resident, above and apart from the general ruck of diplomatic representatives…Other legations had marine guards, from a sergeant's squad to a company. He had a miniature army, with artillery, cavalry and infantry, engineers and field telegraph corps. A considerable body of army officers was attached to him, moving through the country, sometimes openly and in uniform, sometimes as private travellers *en civile*, sometimes even disguised…The Chinese resident [Yuan Shikai] had exercised the function of a moderator in the affairs of the Korean king. The Japanese minister

grew to act habitually as if he had succeeded to that office, or rather, as if he had expelled from it a usurper".[319]

Succeed he had indeed: Japanese control in the south had already been so complete that Yuan, with no role left, had returned to China even before the outbreak of the war.

After it there was however one small fly left in Japan's ointment: Queen Min, who continued to try to manoeuvre, through her feeble husband or others, for some degree of Korean independence. The end of the crisis came in October 1895. A few months before, Isabella Bird Bishop was summoned to an audience with the King and Queen; in a sad little episode the latter spoke of Queen Victoria:

"She has everything that she can wish – greatness, wealth, and power. Her sons and grandsons are kings and emperors, and her daughters empresses. Does she ever in her glory think of poor Korea".

She probably did not; nor, following the ousting of China, did anyone much else apart from Japan. And Japan's patience ran out. At 3am on 8 October, using the disgruntled Tai Won Kun, his allies and Japanese dressed in Korean police uniforms as a front, some four hundred Japanese troops overwhelmed the Palace guard, broke into the royal apartments, roughed up the King and Crown Prince, but cut down the Queen as she fled down a corridor and immediately incinerated her body in the garden with kerosene. "The whole affair", Isabella Bird Bishop noted, "did not occupy much more than an hour".

In the morning, with the new Japanese Minister, General Viscount Miura, present, the treacherous Tai Won Kun announced that he himself,

---

319 Sands, who was born in 1874, has left an engaging record, *Undiplomatic Memories*, of his time in Korea as one of the new trainee American career diplomats:

"There was no particular reason why I should be appointed to be the first of these", he begins disarmingly, "except that both the President and the Secretary of State were friends of my father".

After two years in the Legation he became personal adviser to the Emperor of Korea (as King Kojong had become), between 1900 and 1904; subsequently he went on to diplomatic posts in Latin America, then careers in business and finally academia.

the National Grand Duke, had

> "entered the Palace to aid His Majesty...[and] is returned to power to inaugurate changes, expel the base fellows [who had invaded the Palace], restore former laws, and vindicate the dignity of His Majesty".

Even all this was not enough for Miura and the Tai Won Kun. Three days later a fraudulent edict was issued in the King's name, and counter-signed by the entire new puppet cabinet, stating, after a lengthy denunciation of Queen Min's political and moral turpitude, that

> "We have endeavoured to discover her whereabouts, but as she does not come forth and appear We are convinced that she is not only unfitted and unworthy of the Queen's rank, but also that her guilt is excessive and brimful...So We hereby depose her from the rank of Queen and reduce her to the level of the lowest class".

Her death was not announced for another six weeks.

In the meantime the other foreign Ministers in Seoul were so much in the dark as to what had happened that they actually asked the Japanese Minister to use his troops to disarm the Tai Won Kun's rabble and take over "protecting" the King and Crown Prince. Miura ducked this; but the King and his son remained prisoners until February 1896, when they were smuggled out of the Palace, sitting in sedan chairs behind two (presumably bulkier) housemaids, who had established a pattern of daily movement that aroused no suspicion. And they were smuggled right into...the Russian Legation. A new and fateful player was suddenly on the scene in East Asia. Isabella Bird Bishop wrote just afterwards:

> "Forecasts are dangerous things, but it is safe to say that if Russia, not content with such quiet, military developments as may be in prospect, were to manifest any aggressive designs on Korea, Japan is powerful enough to put a brake on the wheel!"

Before she died, in 1904, she knew how right she had been.

The aftermath of defeat
While Li Hongzhang was blamed for the loss of the war, and lost his Viceroyalty of Chihli, the Dragon Throne had no–one else to turn to

when it came to the treaty negotiations that as usual followed the end of hostilities early in 1895. Curzon astutely commented that

"though he emerges from the terrible ordeal of the war, to use a colloquial phrase, as only 'the best of a bad lot', he...continues to offer to the foreigner the interesting spectacle of the only Chinaman who with the ingrained characteristics of his countrymen combines a diplomatic astuteness, and a respect for the externals of reform that are variously described as admirable and deceiving".

In 1885, to settle the first Korean crisis, Ito Hirobumi had come to Tianjin to negotiate the settlement with Li; this time Li had to go to Shimonoseki in western Honshu to negotiate with Ito. Now, at their second meeting, an extraordinary exchange took place. Li began by saying

"In Asia, our two countries, China and Japan, are the closest neighbours, and moreover have the same language...Now for the time being we are fighting each other, but eventually we should work for permanent friendship. If we are enemies endlessly, then what is harmful to China will not necessarily be beneficial to Japan...We ought vigorously to maintain the general stability of Asia, and establish perpetual peace and harmony between ourselves, so that our Asiatic yellow race will not be encroached upon by the white race of Europe".

Ito responded that he was "very much pleased with the idea of the Grand Secretary [Li[320]]", but he was not really listening: Japanese nationalism did not have much room for perpetual peace. Instead, with extraordinary bluntness, he went on:

"Ten years ago when I was in Tientsin, I talked about reform with the Grand Secretary. Why is it that up to now not a single thing has been changed or reformed?"

---

320 Li Hongzhang was the first person of Chinese race to be appointed to the Grand Secretariat of State, the Emperor's highest advisory body, since the foundation of the Qing Dynasty in 1644.

Li must have been considerably taken aback by such uncharacteristic frankness; his controlled and courteous response nevertheless could not conceal his chagrin at the truth in Ito's accusation:

"At that time when I heard you, Sir, talking about that, I was overcome with admiration, and furthermore I deeply admired, Sir, your having vigorously changed your customs in Japan so as to reach the present stage. Affairs in my country have been so confined by tradition that I could not accomplish what I desired...I am ashamed of having excessive wishes and lacking the power to fulfil them".

Talk on this tricky topic then faded away.

The Treaty of Shimonseki, on the other hand, raised a storm. Its terms would probably have been worse had not an attempt by a Japanese to assassinate Li not embarrassed Japan, but they were bad enough: Chinese recognition of "the full and complete independence and autonomy of Korea"; the cession to Japan "in perpetuity and full sovereignty" of the Liadong Peninsula in southern Manchuria, including Lüshun/Port Arthur,[321] Formosa [Taiwan] and the Pescadores Islands off the latter's southwest coast; a huge indemnity, with Japan occupying Weihai [Weihaiwei] on the Shandong peninsula until it was paid; and the opening of four new treaty ports, including Chongqing [Chungking] way up the Yangzi River. A well-known thirty-seven-year-old intellectual, Kang Youwei [K'ang Yu-wei], organised a petition signed by twelve hundred other scholar-bureaucrats, from eighteen provinces, calling for the Treaty to be repudiated and, more positively, for reform of the education system and for Westernisation of the army. Candidates in Beijing for the civil service examinations demonstrated against the Treaty, unheard of behaviour at that time, but the Court was too paralysed even to respond to that.

The major uproar, however, was foreign: immediately, Russia, aghast that the territorial advantages Japan had forced China to concede would

---

321 Lüshun is now the southernmost part of the city of Dalian [also known at various times as Dalny or Dairen]. Although established as a Chinese naval base by Li Hongzhang, it was the Russians who developed it into an "impregnable" fortress – like 1930s Singapore – known as Port Arthur. As this was the name by which it subsequently became famous, at least for a time, I have continued to use it.

stand in the way of its own ideas of further advance in the region, secured the support of France and Germany to demand the restoration of the Liadong Peninsula to China, and Japan had to give way, in return for increased reparations. Kaiser Wilhelm II wrote to his cousin Tsar Nicholas II celebrating their victory:

"I was glad to be able to show how our interests were entwined in the Far East, that my ships had been ordered to second yours in case of need when things looked doubtful, that Europe had to be thankful to you that you so quickly had perceived the great future for Russia in the cultivation of Asia and in the defence of the Cross and the old Christian European culture against the inroads of the Mongols and Buddhism".

Japan's humiliation of China began what was to be a seismic change in the political geography of East Asia: its effects are still clearly visible today, and not just in the still hot "cold war" across the Strait of Formosa [Taiwan Haixia] between mainland China and Taiwan. In the first instance it unleashed a new wave of European pressure on China, begun by Germany. Already expecting recompense for its support of the restitution of the Liadong Peninsula, it seized on the providential murder of two German Jesuit missionaries in Shandong Province. Although the Jesuits were banned in Germany itself, the Kaiser saw the murders as a "splendid opportunity" to demand in recompense a lease on Qingdao [Tsingtao] and its neighbouring bay on the province's southern coast – plus, as was the usual European pattern, an indemnity to cover the cost of its naval expedition to occupy Qingdao before China accepted its demands. Wilhelm was "firmly determined", he said, to

"demonstrate through our use of sternness and, if necessary, of the most brutal ruthlessness towards the Chinese, that the German Emperor cannot be trifled with...Hundreds of thousands of Chinese will quiver when they feel the iron fist of Germany heavy on their necks".

When China gave way the immediate effect was Russia's seizure of Port Arthur and the lower Liadong Peninsula, that it had just forced Japan to disgorge, in order to "redress the balance of power".

Britain had already sorely tried the Imperial Government: in 1896, when the Chinese Legation in London had entrapped China's most prominent young revolutionary, Sun Yatsen, a Christian who had launched an abortive uprising in Guangzhou the previous year, with the intention of smuggling him out of the country, the British government had increased pressure on the Legation until it was forced to release him. Now, to balance Russia's move in Manchuria, Curzon persuaded the British Cabinet to demand the lease of Weihai for an equivalent period, as otherwise Germany would take it: to doubtful colleagues he argued

"If we mean no–one else to swallow the cherry, why not take it ourselves, instead of having a bite at it, and still leaving it on the plate to excite the appetite of others?".

They took it, and the additional cherry of Hong Kong's New Territories behind Kowloon.

In addition, demands were made that China not "alienate" to any other power a whole series of regions where the various foreigners wanted an exclusive "sphere of interest": Britain in all the provinces along the Yangzi, France in the southern provinces of Yunnan, Guangxi and Guangdong; Japan in Fujian, opposite Taiwan. All of them demanded concessions to build – and control – railways; Britain insisted that one of its citizens should continue to head the Imperial Maritime Customs Service, France that China should "take account of its recommendations" on staffing a postal service.

As its practitioners were about to discover, right here in China, it was the absolute pinnacle of European imperialism. Britain was at the top of the league, and intensely irritated everyone else by coating its strategic and commercial interests and greed with an air of moral superiority. And George Nathaniel Curzon, the quintessential representative of that "effortless superiority" for which his generation of Balliol–educated British empire–builders was known – and who at one time or another managed to irritate many of his own countrymen as well – had just dedicated his *Problems of the Far East*

TO THOSE

WHO BELIEVE THAT THE BRITISH EMPIRE

IS, UNDER PROVIDENCE, THE GREATEST INSTRUMENT FOR GOOD

THAT THE WORLD HAS SEEN

AND WHO HOLD, WITH THE WRITER, THAT

ITS WORK IN THE FAR EAST IS NOT YET ACCOMPLISHED

At this point the "Chinese melon" was in greater danger of being divided up than it had ever been, and the seeds of the next war were sown. Japan, already bruised by Russia's lead in forcing the retrocession of the Liadong Peninsula to China following the Treaty of Shimonoseki, was now particularly outraged at its cynical grab of what Tokyo wanted itself. And thus were sown the seeds of the war after that.

Reformer

Since the Treaty of Shimonoseki, Li Hongzhang had been deprived of any active role in official life, a huge crash for someone whose seventieth birthday three years before had been celebrated by the Empress Dowager and the Emperor themselves. As one of Li's most prominent protégés, Yuan Shikai might have been expected to suffer a similar fate. Indeed, he might also have been expected to bear a good deal of the blame for the state of affairs in Korea leading up to Japan's initial military incursion, if not for the conduct of the war, in which he – perhaps cunningly – played no part. But he appears to have escaped completely. By mid–1895 he was even being consulted on the future of the army, on the basis of proposals he had submitted to a member of the Grand Council:

> "The weakness of our troops does not lie so much in quantity as in quality, not so much in their physical strength as in their lack of training. Worst of all, they lack uniform organisation, a unified command, and stern discipline...We ought to employ foreign instructors to assist in the work of reorganisation. Both our own traditional methods and European methods should be adapted, after careful deliberation, to create a new system...At the same time, military academies to train selected cadets must be set up and staffed with foreign experts; later these cadets should be sent abroad for further study"

– all ideas which of course the Japanese had put into effect within a couple of years of the Meiji Restoration thirty years before, and without such concern with their "own traditional methods".

There was some opposition to Yuan, but it was mostly personal:

> "I have had several talks with him", another of Li Hongzhang's protégés wrote to the same Grand Councillor, "and found him boastful and utterly unreliable. His past history shows that he is conceited, extravagant, lecherous, ruthless, and treacherous...

having misled Li Hongzhang, he may now attempt to mislead you and indeed our country".

There was certainly something in the criticism, and a good deal more such behaviour would be seen in the future. But at this stage Yuan had the advantage of being one of the few army officers with any practical ideas about rescuing the army from its current degradation; he also worked on getting the support of Prince Qing, a member of the Imperial clan, and of Ronglu [Jung–lu], a Manchu noble, favourite – some said more – of the Empress Dowager. At the end of 1895, at thirty–six, Yuan Shikai was made commander of the Newly Created Army, based at Beiyang, between Beijing and Tianjin. The Beiyang Army, as it became known, was to become a powerful force in Yuan's political armoury.

Although plans for an army of fifty to a hundred thousand had been discussed, and one proposal insisted three hundred thousand were required, the decision came out that Yuan was to train three thousand infantry, one thousand cavalry, five hundred engineers and half that number of artillery. As his chief–of–staff he appointed Xu Shizhang, the first of his teenage scholar friends, who had no military experience whatsoever. While this was not the most promising omen for the Newly Created Army, Yuan did in fact succeed in creating a professional force, and within a year he had expanded it to a full–size division of twelve thousand, described by a visiting British admiral as, "by Western standards...the only completely equipped force in the Empire". It was – and remained – Yuan's personal power base. Perhaps of even more significance, Yuan created an officer corps who gave him unstinting loyalty. This was to prove a vital asset during the extraordinary roller-coaster of the ensuing twenty years.

More remarkable, for a man who had mostly benefited to date by being in the right place at the right time, Yuan now also ventured into the highly contentious and highly dangerous area of political reform. While the defeat by Japan had abundantly demonstrated the need for reforming more than just the armed forces, it had also totally paralysed a Manchu Court that had already been stagnating under Cixi's reactionary control since the failure of the fitful Tongzhi Restoration three decades before. There was one new factor in the equation: when Guangxu had reached eighteen years of age in 1889 the Empress Dowager had had no alternative but to give up her regency. But there was no way she was going to adopt a completely hands–off policy towards her nephew; and to make sure he remained enmeshed in the coils of her lust for power she obliged him to marry his cousin, the Lustrous Concubine, her sister's daughter.

However an unforeseeable outside influence entered the young Emperor's life after the war. Kang Youwei, the organiser of the intellectuals' protest against the Treaty of Shimonoseki, submitted to the Emperor, as the latter became more and more interested, literally dozens and dozens of memorials on reform, as well as his books on the reforms of Peter the Great of Russia and the Emperor Meiji of Japan as examples of what could be done, and on the partition of Poland as an object lesson on what to avoid. Kang's disciples were also active more widely: between 1895 and 1898 reform groups were organised in many parts of the Empire – at the same time as Sun Yatsen was trying to organise revolutionary groups abroad. An American missionary, the Reverend Timothy Richard, is also credited with playing an important role in influencing intellectual opinion through his pro–reform publication, *Tracts for the Times*, and in engendering the support of senior officials whom he had come to know well during his forty–five years in Hebei, encouraged by his Viceroy for the last twenty, the now out–of–office Li Hongzhang.[322]

In mid–June 1898 there took place a crucial nine–hour meeting between ruler and reformer, with no officials present, no eunuchs, none of the Dowager Empress's spies. The Emperor, still nervous, lamented that

> "The four barbarians are all invading us, and their attempted partition is gradually being carried out: China will soon perish...
> All that is being caused by the conservatives";

and Kang responded with a winning image:

> "If Your Majesty wishes to rely on them for reform, it will be like climbing a tree to seek for fish".

---

322 In his autobiography, *Forty–five Years in China*, Richard ruefully noted that

> "Notwithstanding that [Li] had shown his appreciation of the value of some of (our) publications, he would not contribute any donation to our Society. After my twenty years' work within his Viceroyaltyship of relief distribution, press work, and Reform work, he would not own that Christian Missions were doing any good to China".

It was one of the issues on which Li Hongzhang had differed with "Chinese" Gordon nearly forty years before when fighting the Taiping rebels.

Guangxu was a weak character, but he was now sufficiently impressed by Kang's arguments, and sufficiently persuaded by his pro–reform advisers, to take the unprecedented step of acting for himself, without reference to Cixi – though taking the precaution of proclaiming that the Empress Dowager's "wisdom and goodness" were behind the new edicts. Over the next three months he issued a cascade of unprecedented edicts: abolishing the five–hundred–year–old state examination system, establishing schools, a university and a translation system to promote Western studies, especially in science, requiring young Manchus to study foreign languages and travel abroad, and establishing a patent office "for the encouragement of everything new and useful". Kang was appointed head of the Office of the Constitution. But when the Emperor began abolishing "useless offices" Cixi and the conservatives began marshalling their forces.

One of the remarkable differences between the xenophobic Dowager Empress and her circle and the reformers was the latter's anxiety to obtain the advice of foreigners across virtually the whole range of government: constitution building, administrative reform, revamping the education system, modernising the armed services and their equipment. Some time during that feverish summer Kang Youwei asked the Reverend Richard to be one of the Emperor's foreign advisers. Shortly before, when Richard had been consulted by Kang on what he called the "measures of Reform", he had suggested that the Chinese Government invite (now Marquis) Ito Hirobumi to Beijing as an adviser, because he had been "so successful in converting Japan into a strong Power". After Japan's recent humiliation of China and Ito's role in the Treaty of Shimonoseki it might have been seen as an outrageously foolhardy proposal; but Richard saw Ito in Beijing in September; and a foreign journalist who had a meeting with him then wrote afterwards that Ito

"despairs of reform in China...There is no statesman, no man willing to take responsibility, no man standing out boldly and conspicuously before his fellows. Edicts decreeing reforms are being issued by the Emperor in profusion, but they are never acted upon".

On 20 September Ito actually had an audience with Guangxu. But by then it was far too late to give advice to the poor Emperor: it was the last day of his rule.

Traitor or loyalist?

It turned out that Yuan Shikai would now play the crucial role for the future of China. In 1895 he had contributed funds to one of the Reform Movement's groups, but he does not seem to have participated actively in the political ferment of the ensuing year. It may not have been a merely opportunistic move: given his commitment to applying Western methods in his army, he probably did agree with the reformers' call for the more general spread of Western knowledge and technology, but it may be questioned that he ever supported the more radical constitutional changes that some were proposing. At the same time, the reformers themselves were keen to have the support of Yuan's highly efficient army, located so close to the capital; and the fact that he was Li Hongzhang's protégé, may well have encouraged them to be more trusting than was warranted. For a while, each party was prepared, perhaps anxious, to look for what it wanted to find.

It was certainly in Yuan's character to watch carefully for which way the wind was blowing, and to trim his sails accordingly. The crucial date on which the wind changed was 20 September, and there were two versions of what happened. Both more or less agreed that on the night of 19 September Yuan had been approached by the reformers, on behalf of the Emperor, to move his army to Beijing to support Guangxu. Then they differ. Yuan's own version was given years afterwards to an Australian, George Ernest Morrison, two-and-a-half years younger than Yuan, and Beijing correspondent for *The Times* of London between 1897 until 1912 when he became personal adviser to Yuan Shikai, by then President of a republican China.[323] Yuan said the message

---

323 Morrison was the journalist who talked to Ito in Beijing. He was born in Geelong, Victoria, in 1862. After odd–jobbing in tropical Australia and the South Pacific islands, and two extraordinarily long walks across Australia – 1250 kms from Melbourne to Adelaide; over 3000 kms north to south across the continent, from Normanton on the Gulf of Carpentaria, to Melbourne – he qualified as a medical doctor at Edinburgh University, then odd–jobbed again until he decided in 1894 to cross China from east to west, alone and with no knowledge of the language – 2500 kms up the Yangzi to Chongqing, then another 2500 kms by pony and foot via Yunnan to Bhamo on the Irrawaddy River in British Burma. This feat led to the achievement of a long–held ambition to become a journalist. Though born in Australia, throughout his time in Beijing Morrison saw himself as a – at times *the* – representative of the British Empire. The main source for his career and observations is Cyril Pearl: *Morrison of Peking*. A fascinating account of a modern journey retracing Morrison's footsteps across China can be found in "The Five Foot Road" by Angus MacDonald.

supposedly from the Emperor required him to seize the Dowager Empress and execute Ronglu, her chief support and, as Viceroy of Chihli and commander of the Central Division of the Imperial Guard Army, Yuan's own direct superior; but he did not believe it was genuine, and when he was received by the Emperor in a formal audience the next morning nothing was said. Accordingly, believing the Emperor himself was in danger from "dangerous elements", he went back to Tianjin and the *following* morning reported the plot to Ronglu. The reformers, on the other hand, claimed that when, on the morning of the 20th, Yuan Shikai had pledged his allegiance to the Emperor, he already had or then received proof that the latter wished him to use his troops to dispose of Ronglu and isolate the Dowager Empress at the Summer Palace. But, they claimed, when he saw Ronglu that *same* night Yuan had deliberately betrayed Emperor, reformers and China itself.

Which was it? Many years later the Emperor himself made the somewhat ambiguous remark that

> "I had never even suggested that Yuan Shikai, or anyone else, raise a hand against Her Majesty".

Did "raise a hand" just imply harm – and exclude incarcerate? If so, did the reformers, in their zeal, mislead Yuan, or did he, in his anxiety, misunderstand them? Even if not, had he imagined before the night of 19 September that the Emperor might not only seek to eliminate Ronglu but also imprison the Dowager Empress? – after all, Guangxu's edicts had been accompanied by the assurance that in her wisdom and goodness she supported them. Did this lead Yuan to doubt that they were really the Emperor's own wishes, and to believe that the reformers were trying to manipulate him in the Emperor's name? The reformers assumed he decided to betray the Emperor because his ambition led him to believe he could do better with the Empress Dowager. But this would not follow if he had believed the Emperor would prevail: as more or less king-maker he would have been in an equally strong position.

This is not to accept Yuan's somewhat convoluted and certainly self-serving version of events. But there is a more serious puzzle: there does not seem to be any evidence that he acted the way he did because he had come to doubt the desirability of reform, let alone suddenly – in one night – had decided to undermine it.

Other coups have gone awry because the conspirators failed to keep a key participant fully in the picture as their plans evolved. Yuan wanted reform on the practical level of new military techniques and equipment, new communications, new technology, new mining and manufacturing. This obviously required administrative reform; but how much interest had he taken in more fundamental constitutional reform, how much had the reformers engaged him in that side of their ambitions? It seems possible that the Emperor's (and his new advisers') projected coup caught Yuan by such surprise that he could not imagine China being able to function without the guiding hand that the Empress Dowager had exercised for almost forty years – during half of which he had loyally served her, with, since Korea, her obvious if indirect support. He wanted reform, but could not envisage it at that cost.

But the balance of later opinion, particularly in the light of his role during the first five years of the Republic, has sided with the reformers, and has denounced Yuan as a venal, ambitious and traitorous black-guard whose betrayal cost China the chance of a peaceful constitutional evolution.

Governor

The Empress Dowager certainly rewarded Yuan Shikai. On 21 September, as soon as Ronglu informed her of the plot, she raced from the Summer Palace to the Forbidden City, incarcerated the Emperor himself, and issued a laconic proclamation:

> "The Emperor being ill, the Empress–Dowager has resumed the regency".

There would be no more nonsense about being the power behind the throne: henceforth she ruled in her own name, though to begin with she deliberately humiliated the Emperor by repealing in his name every one of the reform edicts. Dismissed officials were reinstated and reformers punished, though the Emperor managed to forewarn Kang Youwei, who escaped to Hong Kong on a British freighter. Guangxu's reform movement had lasted just one hundred and three days. And the Emperor would remain "ill" – imprisoned – for ten years, until he died, the day before his aunt–nemesis, in November 1908.

Yuan was made Governor of Shandong Province. It was a plum appointment, but it turned out to put him at the centre of a problem which over the course of the next two years blew up in the face of Yuan himself, of the Dowager Empress, and of the foreign powers and their representatives in Beijing. The cause of the problem was the "Boxers

United in Righteousness". They were members and followers of a semi-religious–mystical–political sect, which, beginning in Shandong before mid–1898, and without any central leadership, spread across northern China throughout that and the following two years. As its central slogan was "Support the Qing, destroy the foreigners", the authorities did not see it as subversive, like the reformers; and its attacks on Christians were not unwelcome to them.

However the possible reactions of the Europeans ought to have suggested more caution, particularly as the attacks on Christian missionaries – called by the Boxers, along with other Westerners, "Old Hairy Ones" – and their converts – "Secondary Hairy Ones" – grew and grew as the movement spread. There had been a lull in such attacks after the Tianjin massacre in 1870; and when they resumed after 1886, up to 1895 they were mostly spread around southern China and the Yangzi region where missionaries had been longer, were more numerous and more widespread. At about this time, Curzon, that arch–pillar of the British Anglican establishment, expressed serious reservations about the missionary effort after his visit to China earlier in the decade; he wrote in *Problems of the Far East* that

> "The presence of the missionaries is a testimony to the continued ascendancy of an alien Power, still maintained, as it was originally introduced, by force. As such, the Chinese, who dislike all foreigners, regard the missionaries in particular with an intense aversion, considering them the agents of a policy which has been and is forced upon them in opposition both to the interests of the Government, the sentiments of the *literati*, and the convictions of the people".[324]

He went on with the sharp observation:

> "Nor is this impression diminished by the attitude of the missionaries themselves, many of whom, though they buckle on their armour as the soldiers of Christ, remember only in times of

---

324   Curzon went on to say that

"A converse illustration, minus the stimulus of the *odium theologicum*, is supplied by the detestation with which the Chinese immigrant is himself elsewhere regarded by the white man, by the Australian in Sydney, or the American in San Francisco".

It was – and unfortunately often still is – a justified comment.

peril that they are the subject of this or that empire or republic, and clamour for a gunboat with which to insure respect for the Gospel".

As for popular Chinese fears that missionaries were engaging in witchcraft and ritual murder of children and the sick – such as had sparked the 1870 Tianjin massacre – Curzon bluntly said he was

> "compelled to remind my readers that to this day there are many parts of Europe where precisely analogous superstitions prevail among the ignorant peasantry, against the Jews in particular; and that the last decade alone has witnessed a longer list of murders and outrages in Christian Europe, due to an almost identical cause, than has been contributed in the same period by the whole of pagan China".

And Curzon drew up a damning list of specific missionary attitudes and practices that justifiably raised problems for the Chinese: hostility to Chinese ethics, doctrinal insensitivity to Chinese custom (notably ancestor "worship"), confessional competitiveness, claims made for special legal privileges for converts.[325]

But his final conclusion was that

> "to the thoughtful Chinaman's eye...the real political danger is more deeply rooted than any such superficial symptoms might appear to suggest. He sees in missionary enterprise the existence of an insidious *Imperium in imperio*, of a secret society hostile to the commonwealth, of damage and detriment to the State";

and while most of his remarks related to Protestant missionaries in China, he noted also that, although the Jesuits had been expelled from France in 1879,

---

325 Provocatively, Curzon also noted that

"There seems, at least to my mind, to be small doubt that the cause of Christianity is not advancing in China with a rapidity in the least commensurate to the prodigious outlay of money, self–sacrifice and human power":

with (in 1890) 1,300 Protestant missionaries and only 37,300 native converts,

"or a fold of less than 30 to each shepherd...it must be admitted that the surviving harvest after half a century's labour is not large".

"the Chinese see that the French Government is here engaged in forcing upon them the very men and the selfsame religion whom it has sought to expel from its own land – an act of duplicity which in their minds can only mask some dark political cabal".

It was this sentiment of Christianity as not only ethically and socially but also politically subversive that resulted in attacks on Christians not being vigorously repudiated – where they were not actually encouraged – by officialdom, from the highest level down.

At the time of Curzon's writing the situation was about to get considerably worse. In 1895, to celebrate the centenary of their work in China, Protestant missionaries began pouring into the hitherto scarcely proselytised north of China, in a "Great Forward Movement" designed to bring Christianity to everyone in the Empire. And unlike the majority of their Catholic counterparts, who since the time of Brother Matteo Ricci three centuries before had seen integration with the Chinese mandarinate as their best way forward, the Protestants included large numbers dedicated to the encouragement of social, economic and political reform, or even, like their convert Sun Yatsen, revolution. From the perspective of concerned Chinese, the Reverend Timothy Richard combined both threats: like the Jesuits he consciously sought to influence the top of the power structure, and in so doing played a significant role in the Emperor's unprecedented reform bid. Coinciding with the renewed territorial inroads of the foreign powers, much of it concentrated in Shandong itself, and their extraterritorial citizens' racing ahead to construct railways and put up telegraph lines, without consideration of the local impact, again much of it in the same area, the missionary move to a higher profile could not but be provocative. The Boxers played on all these elements, and the uprising continued to intensify.

There were, in addition, severe drought conditions in north China in 1898–1899, which pushed increasing numbers of out-of-work and starving peasants into the arms of the Boxers. One of their widely-disseminated jingles pointed the finger:

> "No rain comes from heaven,
> The earth is parched and dry.
> And all because the churches
> Have bottled up the sky."

As late as mid–May 1900 the British Minister in Beijing, Sir Claude McDonald,[326] was telling London that

"a few days' heavy rainfall...would do more to restore tranquility than any measures which either the Chinese Government or foreign Governments could take".

But it did not rain, and the Chinese Government was not prepared to take measures.

In Shandong, Yuan Shikai received the ambiguous instruction from Beijing – reflecting the Dowager Empress's hope of using the Boxers to strengthen the Dynasty against foreign pressures – not to wield a heavy hand "lest the people be frightened into revolt", but he was firmly on the side of restoring law and order. To Cixi's prevaricating justification that

"When peaceful and law–abiding people practise themselves in the mechanical arts for the preservation of themselves and their families, or when they combine in village fraternities for mutual protection, this is in accordance with the public spirited principle enjoined by Mencius[327] of keeping 'mutual watch and giving mutual aid' ",

Yuan bluntly responded:

"These Boxers, gathering people to roam on the streets and plundering over distances of several hundred miles, cannot be said to be defending themselves and their families; setting fire to houses, kidnapping people, and offering resistance to government troops, they cannot be said to have no criminal activities; plundering and killing the common people, and stirring up disturbances, they cannot be said to be merely anti–Christian".

---

326 Morrison recorded that when McDonald, not a career diplomat but a former soldier, was appointed to Beijing he was criticised in England as

"imperfectly educated...weak, flippant and garrulous...the type of military officer rolled out a mile at a time and then lopped off in six foot lengths".

His seriousness was not enhanced by preposterous long, waxed, upturned moustaches.

327 The 3rd century BCE follower and populariser of Confucius

His most celebrated measure was to test by firing squad the Boxers' mystical claim to invulnerability to bullets; and he firmly opposed the government's idea of converting the Boxers into armed militia units. Regarding them as no better than bandits, he eliminated their leaders whenever he could find them, and generally forcefully suppressed them throughout his province. There was a popular jingle in Shandong:

> "After we've killed the bastard Yuan
> It'll be easier for us to get on".

The Russian Minister claimed Yuan

> "assured me many times – and I had no grounds to doubt his word
> – that he had had forty thousand Boxers put to death".

The ironical and disastrous result was that thousands more fled before his campaign into neighbouring Chihli Province surrounding the capital. Shandong was to remain calm throughout the crisis that was about to burst on Beijing.

The siege of the Peking Legations[328]: I – Encirclement

Tension had been mounting in Chihli throughout early 1900; the foreign Ministers made a series of representations to the Zongli Yamen demanding firmer action against the spreading uprising; but the authorities were not disposed to act while the Dowager Empress dallied with the idea the Boxers could be useful to her. Then, in mid–May, about seventy Christian converts were massacred at Baoding [Pao Ting Fu], about a hundred and thirty kilometres southwest of Beijing. This time the provincial army did react, successfully it seemed; but a week later the Boxers rallied, and routed and killed their first Government military commander.

This action immediately galvanised Boxer activity throughout the province, not only against scattered Christian missions but now also against other aspects of what was regarded as foreign penetration:

---

328 There is an extensive literature on the fifty–five day "siege of Peking" – as it was known at the time, though it was only the foreign Legations that were besieged – including some fifty–odd personal accounts by foreigners involved. The following brief account is based on the sources referred to and others listed in the bibliography.

stretches of the Beijing–Baoding and the Beijing–Tianjin railway lines were ripped up, bridges and telegraph lines were destroyed; two British missionaries and four French and Belgian railway engineers were murdered. The government still did not know how to react; but the foreign diplomats, who spent much of their time talking to each other, were now sufficiently alarmed to call in – without Chinese approval – extra guards for their Legations, a move which itself added to anti–foreign fury in the capital. At the same time their naval vessels assembled again off the Taku Forts where the 1860 troubles had begun. As late as 3 June Sir Claude McDonald, head of the "stoical, sceptical, ill–informed British legation" (as an American diplomat put it), referred to the "wholesome calm" in the city, though in fact Boxers were now infiltrating Beijing in large numbers with the refugees pouring in from the disturbances in the surrounding areas.

With their extra guards against such a rabble the Legations "felt quite safe", Lancelot Giles, a twenty–two–year–old British Consular Service student interpreter in the British Legation, recorded on 4 June in his engaging diary,[329] "particularly as the ministers had all telegraphed for reinforcements". Even Morrison, who usually knew more about what was going on because, unlike the diplomats, he had such extensive local contacts, did not pick up the seriousness of the mounting threat in the city, perhaps because he was more focussed on Russian machinations in the Far East: young Giles recalled that the *The Times's* correspondent had been

> "laying heavy odds on war between Russia and Japan being declared before July 31st. He was also betting on the Japanese occupying Port Arthur before December 31st".

Morrison turned out be right on both counts, though four years too early.

After his earlier travels throughout East, South and West Asia Curzon had quipped in a speech that

> "From my own experience, I would say that the first thing an Englishman does in the outlying portions of the Empire is to make a racecourse".

---

329 Printed for the first time in 1970 in *The Siege of the Peking Legations*, edited by L.R. Marchant

On 9 June the Boxers burned down the foreigners' Peking Racecourse just to the west of the city. At last there was really cause for alarm; Sir Claude McDonald, declaiming that this more than anything else had "more vividly" brought home "to the minds of all Europeans in Peking, a sense of the perilous position in which they stood", telegraphed to the offshore navy for help. The next morning a multinational relief force of about two thousand men, under the command of the British Admiral Sir Edward Seymour, left Tianjin for Beijing – in trains. It was another intelligence failure: with the tracks wrecked the trains could not get through, Boxer resistance was far tougher than anticipated, and Sir Edward soon ended up cut off and stranded only a quarter of the way up the track. In Beijing, the diplomats confidently went to the station to meet the relief trains, but had to give up. Going alone again later, Sugiyama Akira, the Chancellor of the Japanese Legation was hacked to pieces.

From then on events seemed to develop a momentum beyond anyone's capacity to control. By 13 June the Legation quarter south of the Imperial City, where the foreigners were virtually all located in a fairly compact grouping, had been surrounded by Boxers and often hostile Imperial troops, and the Legations had adopted defensive measures; that day they were completely isolated when their last telegraph link to the outside world was cut; the next night open hostilities commenced when Germans on the adjacent city wall (now demolished) killed a group of Boxers, followed later that night by the first Boxer attack, against the British Legation; and the same night Boxers destroyed foreign churches throughout the capital and killed every Christian convert they could find:

> "Many were found roasted alive", Giles recorded, "and so massacred and cut up as to be unrecognisable...It is a noteworthy point that all over the city the Boxers knew which of the Chinese were Christians and where they lived. This points to the Chinese government having a finger in the pie".

Two days later a largely British patrol, though with some Americans and Japanese, massacred in cold blood forty–six Boxers found with Chinese Christian prisoners in a nearby temple.

With atrocities thus readily commenced on both sides the prospects for a resolution were already grim. Then a rumour on 14 June from a news agency that the German Minister had been killed galvanised the assembled admirals at the coast more than Sugiyama's real death had: they decided, on the 16th, to occupy the Taku Forts during that same night, as a first step to re–establishing contact with Seymour's force and the Legations. It has often been argued that the Imperial Government would have acted no differently even had this attack not taken place; after it did the position of the foreigners in Beijing was undeniably worse. In the first instance, however, the Zongli Yamen, on 19 June, issued an ultimatum for the Legations' 473 civilians (including women and children) and 409 guards to leave Beijing within twenty–four hours, under "safe escort" to Tianjin. Not surprisingly, given the previous inability of the Government to restrain the Boxers, and indeed clear complicity with them, the Ministers had no faith in these assurances, especially with such large numbers; and they were also concerned about the fate of the 2,750 Chinese "Secondary Hairy Ones" who had been given refuge in the Legation quarter.

The next day the German Minister, Baron von Ketteler, was really killed, shot by a Manchu soldier on his way to the Zongli Yamen to discuss the ultimatum before it expired. There was no question of any evacuation now, and the total siege of the Legations began that same afternoon, followed by China's formal declaration of war on 21 June. In it the Dowager Empress nailed her colours to the Boxers' mast:

> "The foreigners have been aggressive towards us, infringed upon our territorial integrity, trampled our people under their feet...They oppress our people and blaspheme our gods. The common people suffer greatly at their hands, and each one of them is vengeful. Thus it is that the brave followers of the Boxers have been burning churches and killing Christians".

At least for a time her position was clear. Generalised attacks continued with greater or lesser ferocity until 14 July, by which time the Belgian, Austrian and Dutch Legations and part of the French had had to be abandoned as the besieged diplomats pulled back on the British, Russian, Spanish, Japanese, United States, German and the rest of the French compound. On 20 July Giles recorded that the French and Russian Ministers had burned their Legation files:

> "Dr. Morrison, of *The Times*, offered Captain Strout, who was in charge of the burning, $5,000 if he could have a look at the French papers, but $50,000 for a sight of the Russian ones".

Morrison was joking, but sticking to his suspicions of Russian objectives.

The foreigners, undermanned and underarmed, still had a long perimeter to have to defend, and subsequent opinion was that a concerted Chinese attack would have overwhelmed them without undue difficulty. But it did not come. Boxer firing dwindled and became more sporadic, though there were still days and nights which strained the Legations' defenders and dwindling military supplies; and an increasing problem was the shortage of food, especially for all the Chinese converts. Still, morale held up remarkably, prompting an ever–hopeful American missionary participant, the Reverend W.A.P. Martin, to write on 16 July:

> "The perils of the siege have obliterated the lines of creed and nation, making a unity, not merely of Christians, but bringing the Japanese into brotherhood with us. To them the siege is a step toward Christianity".

During the worst days the Empress Dowager sent unconciliatory telegrams to the Emperor Meiji, Tsar Nicholas and Queen Victoria insisting on *their* need to maintain good relations with China, and saying to the latter – in a macabre echo of the wistful remarks of Korea's poor Queen Min a long five years before – that "as two old women they should understand each other's difficulties".

The Dowager Empress's loyal opposition

It was a measure of the incipient warlordism prevalent in late Qing China, of the divisions at the Manchu Court between the more moderate but out–of office Prince Qing and his successor the reactionary pro–Boxer Prince Duan [Tuan], husband of Cixi's niece, and the indecisiveness of the Dowager Empress herself, that some of the major Viceroys outside Chihli failed to give her clear support before and during the siege. It was a reflection to some extent of her ambivalence as to whether or not she could control the Boxers for her own ends; and it reflected the Viceroys' uncertainty not only about what she really wanted of them, but also about whether the Court, in its ignorance of the outside world, knew that the foreign "Old Hairy Ones" were not just annoying barbarians to be swatted down, but potentially overpowering military threats. Thus, despite the Dynasty's worst crisis since the Taiping Rebellion, the Empire's principal provincial governors were able to deflect or dodge what few instructions Cixi did give, or if necessary disguise disobedience behind feeble displays of dutifulness.

Li Hongzhang however refused outright the Dowager Empress's command to come to Beijing in June, early in the siege. The period of his total disgrace following the war with Japan had ended after a year, when he went to St Petersburg to represent China at Tsar Nicholas II's coronation at the end of 1896 – because the Russians, according to the Chinese, insisted he was "the most suitable person" to do so, an extraordinary but characteristic intrusion into Chinese sovereignty if so; or because the Chinese, according to the Russian most directly involved,

"wished to express their gratitude to our youthful Emperor for all his benefactions to the Chinese Empire"

– these benefactions of course not yet including the seizure of Port Arthur and the Liadong Peninsula. The writer was Count Sergei Witte. Witte who, was born in 1843 in a non–aristocratic official family in the Caucasus, had been Minister of Finances since his appointment by Alexander III in 1892, and was perhaps better known amongst Russians for having made vodka sales a state monopoly, a sure money–spinner for the Tsarist as later for the Soviet state. Nicholas however detested the powerful Minister for being politically liberal and theologically unsound, unmannerly and unkempt, and married to a Jew.

However Witte had a vision of the economic development of the Russian Far East for which he gained Nicholas's support, for the wrong reasons as he subsequently found out; and he saw Li Hongzhang's visit as the opportunity to obtain Chinese agreement to his major instrument to that end: the extension of the Trans–Siberian Railway, still under construction, straight across Chinese Manchuria from Lake Baikal to Vladivostok. Witte was therefore, as he said in his memoirs,

"empowered by His Majesty to conduct the negotiations with our Chinese guest" because "our Minister of Foreign Affairs was entirely ignorant of our Far–Eastern policy".[330]

---

330 It is amusing – but instructive of contemporary European political perspectives – that just three years later Curzon wrote of Britain:

"We never had and we have not any policy towards China...But of course, the supreme lesson of the F(oreign) O(ffice) is that there is no determined policy about anything".

It would also, Witte argued, raise the productivity of the Chinese territories it would cross; but the real sweetener was to be an undertaking to "render China armed assistance" to uphold "the principle of China's territorial integrity" – obviously aimed against Japan, though with a straight face Witte claimed to have assured Li that

"Japan was likely to assume a favourable attitude towards the [rail] road, for it would link her with Western Europe, whose civilisation she had lately adopted".

It must be assumed that the reason Li was sent to Russia in the aftermath of its humiliating defeat was to explore the possibility of some sort of guarantee against further Japanese designs on China, and Li must have expected to have to pay some price for it; and though he initially balked, he soon agreed to a secret treaty – it was strongly rumoured for the additional, personal, sweetener of five hundred thousand roubles. Witte of course denied it; but it was probably true. The treaty began with the key provision:

"In the event of a Japanese invasion of the territory of Russia in Eastern Asia, or the territory of China, or the territory of Korea,... both contracting powers promise to dispatch all the military and naval forces that can be mobilized for mutual assistance; they shall also supply each other with munitions and provisions as far as possible".

After the Tsar's coronation[331] Li Hongzhang signed the treaty as

"Imperial Commissioner and Plenipotentiary of the first class, Grand Tutor of the Heir Apparent, Grand Secretary of the

---

331   After the coronation, which was at the Kremlin in Moscow, there was a large people's celebration in a field outside the city; but in a stampede to receive coronation souvenirs – enamel mugs with the Imperial cypher and coat–of–arms in a then–fashionable Arts–and–Crafts tracery: there is one on my desk as I write – some three thousand people were killed. Li Hongzhang asked Witte if the Tsar knew, and on being told that Nicholas knew everything, he said

"Well, I don't see the wisdom of that. I remember when I was Governor-General, ten million people died from the bubonic plague in the provinces confined to my charge, yet our Emperor knew nothing about it. Why disturb him uselessly?"

Wen–hua Palace, Stern–and–resolute Earl of the first rank, and Superintendent of Trade for the Northern Ports"

– Beijing had agreed to his deal. It is interesting that another negotiation was attempted during Nicholas's coronation celebrations: Japan's representative, Field Marshal Yamagata Aritomo, the moderniser of Japan's army, proposed the division of Korea at the 38th parallel, with Russia controlling the north and Japan the south. But on this there was no deal: the Tsar still had hopes of an ice–free port in the south. Yamagata's plan would not be adopted until 1945, when, over a prostrated Japan, the Soviet Union occupied Korea north of the parallel and the United States occupied the south; and of course the peninsula remains divided between their Korean successors.

Extraordinarily, the terms of the Li–Witte treaty remained secret until briefly summarised by China at the 1922 Washington Conference, well after the new Soviet regime had released the texts of other Tsarist treaties. In his memoirs, written in France years later to avoid confiscation by the Tsar's secret police, Witte acknowledged that "the terms of the railroad concession were very favourable to Russia". He recalled that in informal talks Li had emphasised that

"as Russia's friend, he advised us not to go south of the line along which the Trans–Siberian Railroad was to run. Any movement southward on our part, he assured me, might result in vast and unexpected perturbations which would be disastrous both for China and Russia";

and Witte commented on this prophetic warning:

"I mention this to show what an eminently sane statesman was Li Hung–chang, this representative of what to the Europeans appeared to be a semi–civilised people".

But Witte savagely criticised his own Tsar:

"The agreement was an act of the highest importance. Had we faithfully observed it, we would have been spared the disgrace of the [1904–1905] Japanese war and we would have secured a firm foothold in the Far East. Anticipating on the course of events, I may say here that we ourselves broke the agreement…It was an act in which treachery and giddy–headedness were curiously mingled".

From Russia Li Hongzhang travelled across Germany, the Low Countries, France, Britain and the United States, calling on the Kaiser, Queen Victoria and President Theodore Roosevelt among others. In England, at the beginning of August, Curzon, now Under–Secretary for Foreign Affairs, was careful to renew the acquaintance he had made with Li in Tianjin in 1892.[332] However Li was not yet to return to China's diplomatic helm: in fact, after his triumphal world progress, he arrived home to what Hummel called

> "a very cool welcome…"it was owing to the Empress Dowager alone that his enemies did not reach him; and Chinese writers hint that her protection at this juncture was secured at a very high price".

Li remained at the Zongli Yamen, but, in early September 1898, he fell victim to the Emperor Guangxu's Hundred Days Reform.

It was just three weeks after Curzon's appointment as Viceroy of India had been announced. Four years before, in his introduction to the first edition of *Problems of the Far East*, Curzon had grandiloquently written that

> "The true fulcrum of Asiatic dominion seems to me increasingly to lie in the Empire of Hindustan. The secret of the mastery of the world, is, if only they knew it, in the possession of the British people".

At the beginning of 1899, when Li Hongzhang was employed as supervisor of conservancy work on the Yellow River, Curzon (now Lord

---

332 Curzon's biographer Kenneth Rose records another occasion on which Curzon came up against the frequent Asian fascination with one's age. This time, at a garden party given by the British Prime Minister, Lord Salisbury, Li Hongzhang asked Curzon how old he was. On Curzon's saying thirty–six, Li remarked, "Dear me, exactly the same age as the German Emperor. The German Emperor, however, has six sons. How many have you?" Curzon: "I have only recently been married, and I regret that so far I have none". Li Hongzhang: "Then what have you been doing all this time?"

Curzon) became master of "Hindustan". But the world – not to mention London – was to be another matter.

The Manchu Court, for its part, was not so rich in competent servants as to be able to leave Li running water–works forever – quite apart from Li's own assiduity in gratifying the restored Dowager Empress's inexhaustible cupidity. Thus, a year later, at the end of 1899, she appointed him, at the age of seventy–six, as Viceroy of Guangdong and Guangxi in south China; and it was from here that he refused the Imperial command to return to Beijing the following June, early in the siege of the Legations. In July 1900 Cixi again ordered him to Beijing. This time he made the obedient gesture of travelling north, but at Shanghai he firmly declined to go further because of…"illness".

There was in fact little Boxer activity in south China or the Yangzi provinces during this critical period. The Viceroys maintained order, and ensured the protection of foreigners whose compatriots were under a threat that was tolerated, at the least, by the Empress Dowager, and actively encouraged by the Manchu Princes who were her principal advisers. Yuan Shikai, situated more vulnerably in Shandong near the capital, never wavered from his policy of forceful suppression of all Boxer activity in the province. When, in mid–June, he was commanded by Cixi to send troops to Tianjin, he dissembled obedience with a farcical display of sending a small force, stopping it part way, sending replacements, then recalling them too; asked to reconsider he cryptically replied:

"The critical illness is undergoing a change. Better not hurry with medicine".

Was the "illness" the Boxers? Up to now he had had his troops fighting the Boxers; why, then, delay using "medicine" against them at Tianjin. Did he therefore mean the "illness" was Cixi's intention to fight the foreigners at Tianjin? – Yuan himself reached an accomodation to avoid unpleasantness with the British at their concessions in Shandong – Chefoo [now Yantai] and Weihaiwei. But if he was not prepared to support the Empress Dowager's reckless intention to set China against the foreign powers, he was also not prepared to undertake any reckless opposition to her: early in July, when Li Hongzhang pressed him to move his troops into Chihli against the Boxers, he responded:

"If I lead my troops to save the foreign ministers at Peking without Imperial sanction, I am afraid I shall be defeated on the way".

With such trimming by an ostensible ally, no wonder Li stayed in Shanghai. And no wonder Yuan managed to prevaricate his way through the minefield of the Boxers' siege of the Legations.

The siege of the Peking Legations: II – Relief

The siege itself dragged on:

> "August 1st, Wednesday
> Another month begun!", Giles wrote. "Where can the relief force be? We are, however, all very well here, and can hold out another month at this rate".

Well might Giles ask about the relief force. Since the last week of June foreign military contingents for a relief force had begun arriving at Tianjin, coming from their concessions in China, Russians from the Liadong Peninsula, British from Hong Kong and India, Americans from the newly–occupied Philippines, and the largest of all, nine thousand troops from Japan. Before any move could be made towards Beijing, however, Tianjin itself, where the foreign quarter had also come under siege right after the attack on the Taku Forts, had of course to be taken, a chaotic operation with no overall command and a lot of jockeying and ill–feeling amongst the individual national commanders. Still, Tianjin fell to them on 15 July, thanks largely to the Japanese heroically storming the strongly–held Chinese defences, but followed by the massacre of many Chinese and widespread looting and rape by most of the contingents.

The following day, driving the dismal news of Britain's war against the South African Boers off the front page, the London *Daily Mail* published, with the headline screaming THE PEKIN MASSACRE, a report from a "Special Correspondent" on the Legations' last stand on the morning of 7 July:

> "...the walls of the Legation had been battered down...the remaining small band who were still alive took refuge in the wrecked buildings...Thus standing together as the sun rose fully, the little remaining band, all Europeans, met death stubbornly. There was a desperate hand–to–hand encounter...finally, overcome by overwhelming odds, every one of the Europeans remaining was put to the sword in the most atrocious manner".

The Times intoned

"of the ladies, it is enough to say that in this awful hour they showed themselves worthy of their husbands. Their agony was long and cruel, but they bore it nobly, and it is done",

and published obituaries of Sir Claude McDonald and G.E.Morrison, its own correspondent. Lancelot Giles more reliably recorded on 7 July that

"During the morning a big round shot passed through the roof of Sir Claude's dining–room. It caused some alarm in the heart of that worthy",

and, on the day of the *Daily Mail*'s "Death not Dishonour", that Morrison was "slightly wounded in the leg".

But if the voice of Britain was still the pompous heroics of a fading age, the Kaiser, addressing the advance German contingent embarking for China on 27 July, foreshadowed darker times still to come:

"You are about to meet a crafty, well–armed foe! Meet him and beat him! Give no quarter! Take no prisoners! Kill him when he falls into your hands! Just as the Huns a thousand years ago, under the leadership of Attila, gained a reputation by virtue of which they still live in historical tradition, so may Germany become known in such a manner in China, that no Chinese will ever again dare to look askance at a German!"

It was an historical tradition that the next two generations of Europeans would also come to know in such a manner.

Although the allies' capture of Tianjin was a serious blow to the Manchu Court, militarily as well as psychologically, rather than following up this advantage it still took another three weeks to organise the force to relieve Beijing. This was partly because more reinforcements were felt to be needed after Admiral Seymour's experience, partly because, as the generals started to arrive, there were further national jealousies to be overcome in organisation and command. Eventually the Kaiser's pressure on Russia and France resulted in agreement on the appointment of his Field Marshal Count von Waldersee as supreme commander – though he was not due to leave Germany until...18 August! However, after numerous attempts, at the beginning of the last week of July a message was got through from Beijing to Tianjin confirming that the Legations were still holding, though were becoming desperate for help. Despite the absence of the Commander–in–Chief, and of expected reinforcements hitherto held to be essential, this managed to galvanise the other commanders into launching the relief expedition...eleven days later, on 5 August. And, even then, only because the new British commander, Lieutenant–General Sir Alfred Gaselee, threatened to go it alone.

This time, sustained allied pressure steadily overcame Chinese resistance, and by 12 August the last Chinese force in their way was routed. As the generals halted while the strength of Beijing's defences were scouted, the night of the 13th saw what Giles described as "our heaviest attack of all during the siege". But it was a last gasp: on 14 August the relief column reached the capital, different contingents entering by different gates. Giles told his father:

> "At 2.30 a.m. we heard distant firing and the rattle of Maxims in the distance. Grand indeed!!!!!...
>
> At 3 p.m., amidst shouts and howls, a few of the 7th Rajputs [a British Indian regiment] entered the Legation, quickly followed by Gaselee and his staff, and we were actually at last relieved!!!!!!!!!!...
>
> That afternoon I went with a party who cleared the wall, to the Ch'ien Men [Qian Men, the southern gate in the city wall]. Some Chinese soldiers ran out in the yard below the gate and started firing up at us. They were all shot.
>
> Two Maxims were fixed up on Ch'ien Men and turned on a stream of people who were hurrying across the inner Palace yard. About fifty to seventy rifles were turned on them too. Any amount slaughtered.
>
> Every day looting parties go out and get what they can. I have done some splendid looting already. You wait and trust to me, before you speak".

There is no record of what the resourceful young man laid his hands on as he followed his elders and betters out into Beijing's palaces.[333]

---

333 Young Lancelot Giles's diary–letter ended with an extraordinary P.S. for his professor father:

> "I hope you did not have to pay too much for this letter, but there are no stamps in Peking, so you will excuse it this once".

This once!

Private and official reprisals

With deplorable repetitiveness, the victors again sacked the Imperial Palaces, the new Summer Palace – Cixi's navy – as their predecessors had sacked the Yuan Ming Yuan forty years before, and the Forbidden City itself as well. This time there was no high moral dissembling about justifiable reprisals: troops, officers and diplomats simply looted everything they could lay their hands on.[334] Finger–pointing and recriminations – not to mention competition – went on between the various contingents, but when Field Marshal von Waldersee finally arrived he recorded that

> "Every nationality accords the palm to some other in respect to the act of plundering, but it remains the fact that each and all of them went in hot and strong for plunder".

Von Waldersee himself, however, approved the removal by the German and French generals of astronomical instruments from the Imperial Observatory on the city wall, which had been presented to the Emperor Kangxi by Louis XIV and installed by the Jesuit missionaries then at the Court.

Only three days after the relief of the Legations General Gaselee announced to the British contingent that he was

> "aware of the difficulty in restraining the unmilitary practice of looting in a force composed of mixed nationalities. He has now felt obliged to countenance the systematic collection of articles which may be found in unoccupied houses [for auction] for the benefit of the whole force".

---

334   There is an amusing footnote to this outrage related by Count Witte:

"The pillaging of the Imperial palaces was accompanied by the seizure of Chinese State documents of the highest importance. Among the papers taken there was, curiously enough, the original agreement signed in 1896 by... myself, on one side, and Li Hongzhang, on the other. It appears that the Empress Dowager attributed such a high importance to this document that she kept it in her bedroom in a special safe. When Peking was besieged, the Empress was forced to flee from the palace in such great haste that she left the precious document behind".

And Witte added:

"At my recommendation, this agreement, which we had so treacherously violated, was returned to the Chinese Government".

The following day Lt Richard Steel, who had been aide–de–camp to Lord Curzon, the Viceroy of British India, and was now Gaselee's, wrote that he

> "Heard a looting party of marines was going to Prince Kung's [Gong's] house and went with them along a road *horrible* with Chinese corpses in all stages of decomposition and was nearly sick. Kung's palace is a perfect wonder of wealth, and we carried away any amount of treasure for the common fund".

From Calcutta, then the capital of India, Curzon himself telegraphed £1000 to the Beijing manager of the Hong Kong and Shanghai Bank "to invest in curios" – but with what success is not known. Morrison was told by British officers, but did not report, that Sir Claude and Lady McDonald had "185 boxes at least" of loot. It was not included in the auction.

The Reverend Martin wrote that

> "Of the public treasures, the Japanese, knowing the exact points to seize on, succeeded in getting the lion's share",

and Morrison commented on the "continuous chain of mules" carrying bullion into their Legation. He did report that the Japanese had seized a hoard of silver bullion in the Forbidden City, and that

> "the systematic denudation of the (new) Summer Palace by the Russians has been completed",

though the Russians had at least previously persuaded its allies to stop shelling the Forbidden City. In Morrison's view, however, the French were the worst offenders, as

> "Not content with looting, they commandeer the despoiled Chinese to carry the spoils down to the French camp".

Two months later the French writer and naval officer, Pierre Loti, part of the French naval contingent before going on later to Saigon and Angkor,[335] rummaging around in the Forbidden City, found what he

---

335   There is a description of Loti by William Franklin Sands, who met him on Korea's Cheju Island during a visit by the French Pacific fleet after the Boxer

called, in *Les Derniers Jours de Pékin*, the Dowager Empress's "curio storeroom":

> "First the Japanese had rummaged around there; then the Cossacks came, and finally the Germans, who have turned the place over to us. Now, there is...an indescribable disarray; boxes opened or smashed; their precious contents tipped out, in heaps of fragments, in streams of remnants, in torrents of enamel, ivory and porcelain".

He stole nothing, but helped himself to a miraculously untouched billet where only the highest members of the Manchu Court and their concubines and their eunuchs had ever been before:

> "In the middle of a grey wall, an opening where an African *chasseur* stands guard; on one side, there is a dead dog, on the other a heap of rags and rubbish smelling of corpse...At the end of [the] courtyard, however, the first appearance of magnificence... We are seated, my comrade and I, at an ebony table, wrapped up in our greatcoats with collars turned up, shivering with cold...A little Chinese candle of red wax, stuck in a bottle – a candle picked up over there, in the remains of some ancestral altar – barely gives us light, blown by the wind. Our plates, our dishes are priceless porcelain, Imperial yellow, with the reign–mark of a luxury–loving

---

Rebellion:

> "On [the Admiral's] staff was a Commander Vignaud, better known as Pierre Loti, a short little man, with high heels to give him stature, corseted tightly as a belle of former days, cheeks and lips rouged like a modern flapper. It was incredible that any man could live under such studied rudeness and contempt as that of the sturdy Breton officers of the flagship. They disliked his effeminacy as only a blue-water sailor can detest such things; they studied the insults in which they expressed their feelings as only a french courtier could - to remain well within bounds of civilised intercourse while making life unbearable for one whom they quite plainly believed to be unfit for the company of men...The Admiral did not even trouble to be civil. His language about Pierre Loti and to him was unstudied and without reserve".

Sands was obviously unfamiliar with the imperturbable self-confidence of the French intellectual. Loti's subsequent visit to Angkor appears in the 1200 Chapter: Jayavarman VII of Angkor

Emperor, a contemporary of Louis XV…Our frozen feet rest on Imperial carpets, yellow, of deep wool, where dragons with five claws are coiled…".

During his stay in Beijing Loti, already a well–known author, was invited to meet Li Hongzhang, still enormously tall, a head above his attendants. Recalling Curzon's description, Loti wrote of Li's

"prominent cheekbones under little eyes, quick and searching little eyes; an exaggerated version of the Mongol type, with a certain handsomeness nonetheless and the manner of a great lord, even though his fur–lined robe, when moved carelessly, showed stains and wearing";

but Loti said

"I was warned about this in advance: His Highness, in these days of desolation, is believed to have to affect being poor".

Li began by asking Loti – as he had asked Curzon – his age and income. At the end of their meeting Li

"expressed pity for China, for the ruins of Peking. 'Having visited the whole of Europe, he said, I have seen the museums in all your capitals. Peking had its own as well, because the entire 'Yellow City' was a museum, begun centuries ago, that one could compare with the most beautiful amongst yours…And now, it is destroyed…' He then asks me what we are doing in our Northern Palace, finds out, with amiable consideration, whether we are causing damage there. What we are doing, he knows as well as I, having spies everywhere, even among our porters".

Loti concludes:

"Despite the perfect graciousness of my welcome, due above all to my title of 'mandarin of literature', this elderly Prince of the Chinese 'Thousand and One Nights', in threadbare clothes, in a setting of destitution, did not at any stage stop seeming to me disquieting, veiled, elusive and perhaps silently disdainful and ironic".

By this stage, disdain and irony were all that the old fox had left.

Far worse than the sack of the palaces were the reprisal raids undertaken by military expeditions in the surrounding countryside, particularly by Germans making sure no Chinese would look askance at them, but also by the British, against Boxers, Chinese troops and, if they felt like it, villagers. Using the Boxers as a pretext, the Russians had already cold–bloodedly massacred in July perhaps as many as twenty thousand Chinese civilians in what would now be called the ethnic cleansing of two areas on the Russian side of the Amur River, in the far north of Manchuria; but the world did not notice. Witte related that when his colleague the new Foreign Minister, Count Nicholas Lamsdorf, protested to the Tsar about these episodes, Nicholas simply said that

> "after all, the Asiatics deserved the lesson which they had been taught".

Two hundred foreigners, missionaries and soldiers, had been killed during the Boxer disturbances, and thirty thousand Chinese Christian converts; it has been estimated that now, again with minimal attention, many times more Chinese were slaughtered in the revenge killings which went on during and even after the ensuing peace negotiations. Von Waldersee conceded that "our policy, apart from the punishment of the Chinese, followed no definite purpose". But Germany was outraged when Morrison, accusing von Waldersee's troops of the indiscriminate killing of fighters and civilians, recommended the removal of British forces from his overall command.

Panic and peace

The Dowager Empress and the captive Emperor had fled from Beijing twelve or so hours after the arrival of the relief force, northwards through the Great Wall. Early in her flight Cixi was helped by a district magistrate called Wu Yung, whose record of accompanying her onwards[336] contains her wonderful account to him of her precipitate departure from the Forbidden City:

> "The foreign soldiers had already come into the city and no one in the palace knew about it. We heard bullets flying, making noises like the cries of cats." [Wu Yung said "She imitated the cry of a

---

336   Edited and transcribed by Ida Pruitt: *The Flight of an Empress*

cat at this point".] "I wondered how there could be so many cats. I was dressing my hair at that moment. Another 'miaow' was heard and a bullet flew in through the window. It dropped to the floor and bounced and rolled. We examined it closely. Just when I had decided to inquire into the matter, Tsai–lan [a eunuch] was seen outside the curtain at the door. He said with a shaking voice, 'The foreign soldiers have entered the city. Go quickly, Old Buddha!' I stood up with surprise and asked where the Emperor was...Learning that I wanted him, he came in great haste, wearing his red tasselled official hat and a gown with official squares. I said, 'Foreign soldiers have arrived and we must go immediately'. The Emperor was more frightened than I, and wanted to run away with me at once. I said, 'Look at your dress; how could you go out this way?' Then with frantic haste we threw away his dress of pearls and his red tasselled hat and pulled off his official gown. He put on another long coat. I disguised myself as a maidservant. We escaped immediately."

Cixi fled on, complaining bitterly of the treachery of the Boxers, of senior officials, of the army, of junior officials, not further north to the Qing summer capital–cum–Imperial hunting reserve at Jehol in southern Manchuria, as she had done as a twenty–six–year–old concubine in 1860, but westwards then south for twelve hundred kilometres to Xi'an [Sian] in Shaanxi Province, the bedraggled procession of disguised "peasants" in carts gradually turning into an Imperial "tour of inspection" as it got further from the capital and the foreigners. She would not return to Beijing until January 1902.

Notwithstanding her panic, the Dowager Empress saw to the appointment of – who else? – Li Hongzhang to negotiate (together with Prince Qing) the inevitable peace treaty with the victorious and vengeful foreign powers. Li was (as Hummel put it) "the only acceptable spokesman for the scattered and discredited" Manchu Court. It was his fourth major international negotiation, his second on behalf of a defeated China. At the same time he was again appointed Viceroy of Chihli. Despite all his experience and all his efforts, the situation was such that the foreigners would prevail in forcing on China whatever punishments they wished.

The negotiations dragged on for months, not because of the need to achieve agreement with China, but because of the difficulties in reaching agreement among the victorious allies as to who should get how much of what after they had initially decided that the ruling Qing Dynasty should remain.[337] There were then two major issues in contention: punishment of the guilty, and indemnities. There was no question in those days of an international tribunal to try war crimes or crimes against humanity: the victors demanded death sentences for twelve major military and Court supporters of the Boxers, and death sentences for another hundred lesser officials for the murder of foreign and Chinese Christians. Despite resistance, the Empress Dowager ended up having to sacrifice some of her lieutenants, but the allies allowed her – no doubt because of the divinity that doth hedge a monarchy – to save two of the most noxious, her nephew–in–law Prince Duan and his brother Prince Dai Lan, by exiling them to Chinese Turkestan.

Money was more divisive. Squabbling went on over the absolute value of damages to the Legations, over the relative value of contributions to the war effort, over the expectation of occupation costs, over the requirement for financial punishment of the regime for not stopping or for encouraging the Boxers. Even Morrison, who had lost his twenty–six–room house, furniture and books, put in a claim for £5,804 10s. 3d; and as the wrangling went on he reported that John Hay, the American Secretary of State, had cabled the American Minister "For God's sake, finish it, settle it, we are tired of it". But it was not until the middle of 1901 that the powers agreed amongst themselves that China should pay £67 million /$335 million – about $4.5 *billion* in current values – over the thirty–nine years up to 1940. But, contrary to all previous treaties forced on China by foreign countries, on this occasion, saved by the United States' Open Door Policy, guaranteeing all countries equal commercial rights, China did not have to concede a single square metre of its territory.

The Germans thought Li Hongzhang was pro–British; the British had always suspected him of being pro–Russian; Li himself described the Germans and Russians as "equally pernicious and brutal". This time, though, the game of playing one imperialist off against the others did not work. Having done what he could with the hand that he held to minimise China's bill and humiliation, Li signed the treaty in September. Russia, already in possession of most of Manchuria, was still hounding him for a permanent free hand there when he died, in November. Wu Yung recorded that when news of Li's final illness had reached the Dowager

---

337 At the end of the Pacific War in 1945 the Allies did the same in Japan, though the constitution they imposed stripped the Emperor of all political power.

Empress, in Henan province as she was on the way back to Beijing, she wept to him

"The country is not in good order. If he dies, who will shoulder the heavy burden?"

The next day, when news of Li's death arrived, Wu Yung said he

"was told that the Two Palaces [as he reverentially referred to Cixi] were deeply afflicted and had lost their usual manner. All the Court officials, eunuchs, and guards, looked at each other as if the beams and posts of the house had fallen and they had nobody to depend upon...I think that everyone, foreigners and Chinese alike, must have been thinking the same".

Yuan Shikai was made Viceroy of Chihli the same day.

Viceroy

Wu Yung, who had been a younger protégé of Li Hongzhang, claimed that the latter had burst out after a visit by Yuan several years before,

"Don't you know Shih–k'ai? He is a small minded man! He flattered Weng Shu–p'ing [a would–be political rival of Li's] and came to speak for him. He talked shrewdly...Face to face, I exhorted him and reviled him so that he will not come and trouble me a second time. I have worked many decades and experienced everything. How could his generation deceive me?"

There is a clear enough implication here that Li Hongzhang was not only repeatedly called back to office because he had no equal in the Qing bureaucracy, but also that he was not happy about ever having to give office up. Despite his outburst, in his last memorial to the Empress Dowager he wrote:

"I have looked for men of ability all over the Empire. I can find no one better than Yuan".

It was perhaps not an unqualified endorsement, but it was sufficient for a generational change. First however, tradition required a show of humility, so Yuan immediately declined the appointment in a cunning telegram to the Empress Dowager:

"My waning health and confused mind do not permit me to do as I am commanded. If I go, Shandong will certainly fall into chaos like Mukden.[338] How can Chihli look after itself, if both Shandong and Mukden are in turmoil?...Please think it over and drop this matter altogether".

So Yuan got control of Shandong as well. Now the only remaining member of the old guard was the Old Buddha herself, the Empress Dowager, sixty–six.

Yuan was to be Viceroy of Chihli from the end of 1901 until 1907, and, also like Li, in charge of foreign affairs in northern China. He was also in charge of military affairs, and the efficiency of his Beiyang Army probably counted as much as anything else in his appointment by Cixi – in addition to his continued careful cultivation of her support: he had been the first to send money, silks and even food to her on her destitute "tour of inspection" flight, and he had continued this support with huge financial contributions from Shandong, both to the Dowager Empress herself and to payment of the foreign indemnity, thereby bolstering her credibility with the Powers at a time when the Imperial coffers were as empty as they had ever been. Yuan also gave her first new–fangled horseless carriage. Paul Reinsch, who was American Minister in Beijing a decade later, related that

"The Empress Dowager before her death had acquired a large collection of these foreign vehicles, which interested her greatly; but up to the time of her death the Board of Ceremonies had not succeeded in solving the problem how she might ride in an automobile in which there would also be, in sitting posture, one of her servants, the chauffeur...the poor empress Dowager never had the pleasure of the swift ride she so much coveted".

As Cixi was returning to Beijing in 1902 Yuan was responsible for preparing the first stretch of her roadway through Chihli, up to the rail–head at Zhengding; Morrison cabled *The Times*:

---

338 Now called Shenyang. It was known as Mukden, its Manchu name, throughout the period of this chapter

"Throughout its entire distance the road over which the Imperial palanquins were borne had been covered into a smooth, even surface of shining clay, soft and noiseless under foot; not only had every stone been removed, but as the procession approached gangs of men were employed in brushing the surface with feather brooms. At intervals of about ten miles well appointed rest-houses had been built, where all manner of food was prepared...This King's highway [was] quite useless, of course, for ordinary traffic of the country";

and it was 250 kilometres long. Despite the astronomical cost per kilometre, Yuan knew what he needed to do.

In his appointment to Chihli Yuan's standing with the foreigners was undoubtedly also a significant factor: they had strongly approved of his vigorous anti–Boxer policies in Shandong, and when the foreign negotiators were trying to decide what punishments should be inflicted on China for the siege of the Legations, Yuan intervened to oppose any suggestion of removing the Dowager Empress from the Regency. His relationship with the British soon became particularly close as a result of his negotiations on the restoration of Chinese control over Tianjin and the railway north from Beijing to Mukden, in both of which he was successful; when his handling of the latter aroused criticism at Court, Sir Ernest Satow, the new British Minister, told Prince Qing that any attack on Yuan Shikai was an attack on him also.

But his real power base was the army – his Beiyang Army. And he worked assiduously on training and expanding it throughout his Viceroyalty. To his original force of twenty thousand, an additional division was added in 1902, another in 1903, two in 1904 and two more in 1905, bringing the entire Army to something close to a hundred thousand men. The division commanders, the heads of planning, training and supplies, numerous other officers throughout the Army and down the chain of command were trained, encouraged, promoted and cultivated by Yuan Shikai. But he frequently moved military commanders round so they could not develop personal loyalties of their own: all loyalty was to be to Yuan.

Although squarely focussed on his military power base, Yuan had also undertaken some educational reform and economic development in Shandong, especially in Tianjin, which, with its new municipal transport, electricity, water supply and sewerage, came to be regarded by foreigners at least as China's model city. He now carried some of these measures further into the Viceroyalty, and made an attempt – unsuccessful, as it turned out – to introduce a modest degree of local government in Tianjin. As with his Army, he also cultivated senior bureaucrats in the civil administration, not only in Shandong and now Chihli, but particularly in the broader national railways and telegraph commissions, both of which he was appointed to head, which gave him a powerful political base in Beijing itself. Together, his protégés became a significant support network for his future ambitions, and then an extended structure of military and civil command, control and influence as he worked on bringing those ambitions to fruition. There were naturally some defections, but there were many in key military and civil positions right to the end. With this power structure Yuan became immensely powerful – at least in the north. The south was to be a different matter. So, in the short term, was the north itself, under a Manchu backlash, the last gasp of the dying dynasty.

The Russo–Japanese War[339]

But before this happened, Yuan Shikai had his first experience of international affairs since his Korean days. Unlike then, it was now as a cautious – though not exactly uninvolved – spectator. On 8 February 1904 George Morrison's pre–Boxer prophecy of war in the Far East came true, four years late: Japan launched a sneak attack on the Russian fleet at Port Arthur, just as it would on the American fleet at Pearl Harbour thirty–seven years later. (Japan was very much aware of the continuity: the battle–flag flown by its flagship in 1905 was flown again by the flagship in 1941.) The ensuing war after the attack on Port Arthur was ostensibly fought over which of the two countries was to be predominant in Korea (which was not of course asked), but in fact it was over which was to dominate the entire East Asian region in the new century. The young American diplomat William Sands, now the Korean ruler's adviser, summed up the view from Seoul before the war broke out:

"Russia was penetrating everywhere upon the eastern and northern Asiatic continent and seemed in a fair way to become the greatest of Asiatic powers as well as a power in Europe. Whatever Russia's

---

339 My main source on the war is *The Tide at Sunrise*, a magisterial comprehensive study by Denis and Peggy Warner, friends from Indochina days, but there are interesting contemporary viewpoints in *Cassell's History of the Russo–Japanese War*.

dark intentions might be it seemed fairly certain that ice–free ports in the Pacific must be part of their preparation. Korea was in direct line in that advance, and Korea's land's end was quite too close to the very heart of Japan, only a few hours' full steam. That much was perfectly clear of what Japan's situation must be. Nobody believed that Japan could stand alone against the enormous weight of Russia...Anyone could know that the Japanese were alarmed and angry. Anyone could know that they would not tolerate a Russian advance into Korea, but nobody in our part of the world knew whether Russia was in the hands of irresponsible people (we now know that she was)...Every move anybody made began to wear the meaning of a manoeuvre on the chessboard of war".

Count Witte himself sought to counter the policies of Russia's "irresponsible people": as early as November 1901, three months after the conclusion of the difficult inter–allied post–Boxer negotiations, and three weeks after the death of Li Hongzhang, he wrote to his colleague the Foreign Minister with a prophecy remarkably akin to Morrison's the year before:

"It is my profound conviction that unless we remove our misunderstandings with Japan in a peaceful fashion and by making mutual concessions, we shall not only be under the constant menace of an armed clash with that Power, but we shall also be unable to stabilise our relations with China...*An armed clash with Japan in the near future would be a great disaster for us.* I do not doubt that Russia will emerge victorious from the struggle, but the victory will cost too much and will badly injure the country economically. Furthermore, and that is most important, *in the eyes of the Russian people a war with Japan for the possession of distant Korea will not be justified, and the latent dissatisfaction may render more acute the alarming phenomena of our domestic life, which make themselves felt even in peace time...".* [340]

Witte was right on every count – except Russia's victory.

Although Russian forces which had entered Manchuria during the Boxer crisis were due to be withdrawn by 1903 under the subsequent

---

340 Witte's italics

settlement, Russia refused more than partial withdrawal when China rejected its demand for further "guarantees" for its "interests" there. Japan, still angry at Russia's seizure of the Liadong Peninsula after forcing Japan itself to surrender it after the Sino–Japanese war, had strengthened its position in 1902 in an alliance with Britain to maintain the status quo in East Asia – clearly a marker put down in front of Russia. Witte noted that

> "the attitude of the court clique and of the Emperor himself towards England was one of strong hostility. This was due to England's agreement with Japan and also to the fact that she furnished refuge to the Russian revolutionists. To the Japanese His Majesty was in the habit of referring as macacoes (monkeys), using the term even in official documents. The English he called Jews. 'An Englishman,' he liked to repeat, 'is a *zhid* (Jew)".

As Witte feared, the Tsar, anxious for a military victory, somewhere, convinced of his destiny to push Russian power further into Asia, and egged on by his cousin the Kaiser who was looking for a freer hand in Europe, played an increasingly irresponsible role: encouraging dubious business projects by one Captain Alexander Bezobrasov, a malign pre–Rasputin adventurer, encroaching on Japanese–dominated Korea in the Yalu River region; supporting the more belligerent generals and ministers in St Petersburg;[341] appointing a hawk as a new Viceroy of the Far East, a position which Cabinet Ministers learned of from the press. Bezobrasov's influence at Court increased to the point where Witte could write:

> "In those days two currents became clearly distinguishable in our Far-Eastern policy: one, official, represented by the Ministers and moderate in character, the other, secret, inspired by Bezobrasov and led by the Emperor himself".

In both St Petersburg and Tokyo the war parties were inexorably gaining in power. Two weeks after announcing the new Viceroyalty the Tsar dismissed Witte from the Finance Ministry. Nicholas wrote in his diary: "Now I rule".

---

341   It was in relation to this time that someone in St Petersburg translated "le bien–être général en Russie" as "It's good to be a general in Russia".

"We were headed straight for a war", Witte wrote, "and at the same time we did nothing to prepare ourselves for that eventuality. We acted as if we were certain that the Japanese would endure everything without daring to attack us".

There was indeed a widespread assumption not only in Russia but also in Western military and political circles elsewhere that there would be no contest between the huge army of the mighty Russian Empire and the Oriental Mikado's "dwarf soldiers" (as they were often called). A Paris newspaper, *La Vérité Française*, expressed a similar conclusion from another viewpoint:

"God cannot do otherwise than give victory to the Russians, for they are only schismatics, whilst the Japanese are terrible pagans".

A Moscow newspaper wanted to be sure:

"In this war with a half–savage and barbarous nation...we are like a man attacked by a viper. It is not enough to frighten it and leave it to hide in a bush; it must be destroyed; and we must do this without considering whether England and the cosmopolitan plutocracy [code for 'Jews'] object or not...No quarter and no prisoners should be our motto". [342]

Russian confidence was based not only on Divine providence and racial superiority, but on ignorance. Nicholas was the outstanding example of combining conviction about the first two with the third; both the army and the navy were the same: there was only one officer working on Japanese intelligence on the Russian General Staff – perhaps it was he who estimated Japan's total army and reserve forces at a *sixth* of the actual figure.

It was very different in Japan. William Sands, still in Korea at this stage, remarked later that

---

342 On the other hand, national interest overcame Britain's usual racial prejudices: its ally Japan's crippling sneak attack against its own opponent Russia's fleet at Port Arthur was hailed for the "splendid audacity" of the "gallant Japanese" - "The admiration of a people so keenly appreciative of courage and *élan* could hardly be withheld from a deed so stimulating in its conception and execution alike" (*Cassell's History of the Russo–Japanese War*). This was not the case after Pearl Harbour.

"whether in consular courts, diplomacy or business policy, everything Japan did in China, Manchuria or Korea shaped toward one end. It is impossible to separate their activities. They were the only ones who, having a definite national policy, carried it out to the last detail".

Sands observed in Korea, as Isabella Bird Bishop had noted earlier in relation to China, that the very considerable Japanese military intelligence organisation had long had attachés and spies reporting in detail on Russian military dispositions, communications and the terrain throughout the area where any war would be fought. Unknown to anyone else – above all in St Petersburg – they also had an active presence in European Russia itself, including the extraordinary Colonel Akashi Motojiro who contributed to Japan's war effort by spending vast sums of money funding revolutionary movements in Finland and Poland, then part of Russia, as well as some in Russia itself (though not, as was widely believed at one stage, Lenin's Bolsheviks).

Russian over–confidence also gave Japan some advantages that must have amazed it: Sands said

"Russia's [Far Eastern] fleet wintered habitually in Japan's southern island, in the harbour of Nagasaki, and those of us who knew Japan knew also that this custom was an unfortunate one for Russia. Little by little astute Japanese observers must become aware of weak spots where strength was essential...All supply or construction and repair accounts were padded to sums made possible only by connivance of the ministry of marine at St. Petersburg, and everybody knew it...It was in the harbour of Nagasaki that Russia lost the war of 1904; it was there that the Japanese learned that no matter how fine and gallant the Russian might be personally, no efficient fighting machine that is based upon official corruption can endure long".

Sands was right: there was immense incompetence and corruption prevalent throughout the Russian army as well as the navy, and it did indeed contribute a great deal – along with incompetent commanders – to the ensuing disaster. On the eve of war Sands' viewpoint was very different from that in virtually all the Western capitals:

"The Russians themselves seemed so different from the rest of mankind...One felt oppressed by their colossal weight and could understand what must be the Japanese state of mind confronted by it, menaced by it, without knowing exactly in what the menace might consist. Even those Westerners who did not like or trust Japan thrilled in admiration when Japan determined to see what this ogre was made of".

Sir Claude McDonald, now British Minister in Tokyo, had yet another viewpoint: on 4 February 1905, four days before the Japanese attack on Port Arthur, he told *The Times* correspondent there that war would never occur.

Witte wrote, with bitterly laconic resignation, of the relentless Japanese advance:

"The course of the war presents itself as follows (the dates are according to the Russian calendar[343]): On March 31, our flagship *Petropavlovsk* was sunk, and [Pacific Squadron Commander] Admiral Makarov and a part of the crew went down with the ship. That catastrophe condemned our entire Far–Eastern fleet to complete inaction. In the middle of April we lost the battle of Turenchen [Chiu–lien–cheng: the battle for the Yalu River crossing]. At the end of May we were defeated in an engagement off Port Arthur. In August we lost an important battle near Liao–Yang [cutting off Port Arthur] and began our retreat towards Mukden. When we reached that city, [Commander–in–Chief General Alexei] Kuropatkin declared in his order of the day that we would not retreat another step. On December 20, Port Arthur fell. Then we were defeated near Mukden and were forced to retreat in the direction of Kharbin [Harbin]".

But it was still not the end of Russia's bitter road: after the defeat at Mukden the high command decided that the war could still be saved by the despatch of the Baltic Fleet, with many unoperational ships and no bunkering facilities en route for a belligerent, two–thirds of the way around the world: through the Baltic and the North Sea, where it managed to sink a British fishing trawler which it mistook for an advance Japanese destroyer, down the Atlantic and around South Africa, across

---

343   Thirteen days behind the Western calendar

the Indian Ocean and through the China Sea to Vladivostok. Again, Witte was scathing:

"They believed that...our Baltic fleet would defeat the Japanese. Of course, it was a wild fantasy. It was a thoughtless plan, dictated by hope rather than by cold reason. It was clear to every sane observer that the fleet was doomed...On May 14, 1905, there occurred the disastrous [Strait of] Tsushima battle and our entire fleet was buried in the Japanese waters. It was the death blow to our ambitions in the Far East".

And Witte added sarcastically:

"After this crushing defeat His Majesty became inclined toward the idea of peace".

Witte's conclusion was succinct:

"[Tsar Nicholas] alone is to be blamed for that most unhappy war...At heart His Majesty was for an aggressive policy, but as usual his mind was a house divided against itself. He kept on changing his policy from day to day. He tried to deceive both the Viceroy of the East and the Commander–in–Chief of the army, but, of course, most of the time he deceived nobody but himself".

Witte reported with relish that the presentation of icons by the Emperor and Empress to troops departing for the front had led General Mikhail Dragomirov, the army's leading strategist, to make the widely–known comment that

"We are attacking the Japanese with icons, while they use bullets against us".

In the shocked aftermath of the loss of the Baltic Fleet a St Petersburg newspaper got away with a daring explanation for this state of affairs:

"The Japanese prepared for the campaign by sending troops; and we answered by opening our folding icons and raising aloft our religious banners and crosses...At last, with a wagon–load of holy images our Commander–in–Chief set out hopefully...The religious among the masses explain our reverses by saying that on the journey to the Far East two different consignments of holy images got mixed; and those which were to have helped the Admiral at sea, were exchanged for the icons meant for the General of the land troops".

To those involved the war had been no joke. Russia's dead and wounded amounted to 320,000; Japan's superior preparations, equipment, supply, strategy, tactics and command still cost it 170,000.

By now His Majesty had the other problem that Witte had foreseen in 1901: serious popular discontent. The dismal news from the battle-fronts had played into the hands of the revolutionary groups active in Russia – even without the assistance of Colonel Akashi. But the turning point came with Bloody Sunday in St Petersburg: 22 January 1905, when huge numbers of unarmed workers were fired on by troops as they tried to converge on the Winter Palace to present a petition to the Tsar (though he was not in residence). The number killed varied reportedly from ninety–two to around two thousand; the number outraged was in the hundreds of thousands. Strikes eventually culminated in a two–week general strike declared by a workers' Soviet in St Petersburg on 18 October, there were risings also in Moscow, Odessa and, notably, Warsaw, and turmoil throughout Russia, the Caucasus and Siberia; but the 1905 Revolution, as it became known, was forcibly suppressed before the end of the year.

However on 17 October Nicholas had given way to more moderate pressures for change: he granted the country a limited constitution, with a restrictively–elected parliament (*Duma*) with carefully circumscribed powers. On 18 October Witte was recalled to office as President of the Council of Ministers (Prime Minister). He only lasted as Prime Minister for six months: partly because Nicholas could not stand him, partly because he had no support from the moderates who felt he could not control the reactionaries' measures, partly because the latter thought he was too soft:

"One of the faults with which I have been charged", he wrote in his *Memoirs*, "is that during my premiership I did not shoot enough people and kept others from indulging in that sport".

His successor, Pyotr Stolypin, was responsible for the summary trial and execution of thousands of those involved in the strikes and uprisings – the gallows was known in those days as "Stolypin's necktie".

The Tsar's reforms were too much and too little and too late. Too much for Nicholas, who dismissed the first Duma in 1906, the second in 1907; and the third was engineered by the Court and the conservatives to underwrite the careful program of educational, economic and land reform of Witte's successor, Pyotr Stolypin. Too little and too late not only for the moderates pushing for genuine constitutional change, but above all for the totally disillusioned and increasingly revolutionary workers. With Witte gone there was no longer anyone standing between Tsar Nicholas II and Lenin's basement room in Ekaterinburg ten years later. Witte felt that

> "[the Tsar's] character is the source of all our misfortunes. A ruler who cannot be trusted, who approves today what he will reject tomorrow, is incapable of steering the Ship of State into a quiet harbour. His outstanding failing is his lamentable lack of will power. Though benevolent and not unintelligent, this shortcoming disqualifies him totally as the unlimited autocratic ruler of the Russian people...He is incapable of playing fair and he always seeks underhand means and underground ways. He has a veritable mania for secret notes and methods...But inasmuch as he does not possess the talents of either Metternich or Talleyrand, he usually lands in a mud puddle or in a pool of blood".

In that basement room the blood would be Nicholas's own.

China sits out a war...in China

After the battle of Chiu–lien–cheng, when Japanese troops crossed the Yalu from Korea into Manchuria, the entire land war was fought over the next twelve months on Chinese territory – though at the outset of the war China had declared its neutrality. Outside Manchuria both Russia and Japan mostly respected that neutrality; in that northeastern region itself they behaved as though it belonged to whichever of them could capture it. Yuan Shikai, as Viceroy of Chihli, was also responsible for the security of the whole of northern China, but there was no way in which his army, even expanded as it had been by 1904, could counter both the Russians and the Japanese in Manchuria. As the war developed across the province Yuan reacted in the only way he could: by carefully keeping his own forces disengaged, to protect the northern and seaward approaches to the Chinese capital, and in so doing to preserve the formal neutrality of China.[344]

But behind the appearance he played a rather different game. Despite the difficulties he had had twenty years before with Japan's first push into Korea, after the Russian counter–push into Manchuria following the Boxer settlement he decided there was a greater danger from St Petersburg than from Tokyo. By now he had made considerable use of Japanese army officers in training his own new divisions, and had encouraged young Chinese officers to continue their studies in Japan itself; and the British, under their 1902 treaty with Japan, actively encouraged him to oppose Russia and to provide various forms of discreet support to Japanese forces. The provision of supplies to the Japanese army became routine: transport horses and foodstuffs flowed continuously; two hundred thousand sets of winter clothing were supplied before winter, presumably from factories that had been established for Yuan's own armies. As the war developed, other aspects of Yuan's assistance were closer to active participation in hostilities: the provision of intelligence from his agents in Russian–occupied towns, cooperation with bands of Chinese guerrillas that Japan was using against Russian lines of communication as far north as the Amur River border:

"Some of the Japanese squad members spoke Chinese and wore Chinese clothing, including pigtails", the Warners wrote, "but for more effective operations Yuan Shih–k'ai agreed to assign selected Chinese non–commissioned officers to the squads and to provide Chinese cavalry for operations around Liaoyang and elsewhere".

High–ranking Chinese officials in the main Manchurian centres were instructed to cooperate with the Japanese.

Russia became concerned quite early in the war about China's intentions. The contemporary *Cassell's History of the Russo–Japanese War* reported that

---

344 Of Yuan's role during the war, his main English–language biographer, Ch'en, simply says that "When the war erupted, his [Yuan's] main task was to preserve China's neutrality" – nothing else. My account is based on the Warners' considerable information from Japanese sources.

"Accordingly Russia, through her diplomatic representatives, urges most strongly a stricter preservation of Chinese neutrality, and complains that she is waging war in a hostile country – a complaint which, taking into consideration all the circumstances of her presence in Manchuria, is, perhaps, a little thin".

Later, as the Russians became convinced that Yuan saw their defeat as the only way for China to recover Manchuria, they sponsored an attempt to assassinate him; but it was foiled by Japanese intelligence. It was a foolish ploy, not least because it contributed to Yuan's letting down his guard against Japanese intentions.

Although George Curzon was not directly involved in this encouragement of Sino–Japanese resistance to Russia, his influence had been strong in the development of the British policy of containment of Russia in Asia, from Turkey to the Pacific. It is curious, however, and no doubt a sign of his other intense preoccupations at this time, that although he must have taken a close interest in the course of the war, he does not seem to have made any of his usual crisp pronouncements on Japan's resounding successes or Russia's discomfiture – indeed, Lord Ronaldshay, author of the three–volume "authorised biography" of Curzon, makes no mention of the Russo–Japanese War. The main concern of the policy with which Curzon had been so closely associated for so long was of course the protection of Britain's Indian Empire, with the focus on Russian expansion in the Persian Gulf and Central Asia, of which Curzon had made careful studies during visits to Russian Turkestan in 1888, to Persia in 1889, and to Afghanistan in 1894.[345] While some of the alarm was fanciful there were real grounds for concern: Russia had been taking over one Khanate after another since the annexation of Tamburlaine's Samarkand in 1868, revenging the great conqueror's attack on Moscow half a millennium before,[346] and foreshadowing Russia's apparently inexorable expansion across Central Asia, to Bokhara (also in 1868), Khiva (1873), Khokand (1876), Merv

---

345 These visits resulted in an influential series of books – influential not merely because of who Curzon was, but because they were among, if not the first, political analyses of these places rather than just accounts of exploration and travels, adventurous though they were at the time: *Russia in Central Asia* (1889), *Persia and the Persian Question* (1892), and *The Pamirs and the Source of the Oxus* (1896).

346 See 1400 Chapter

(1884) and Pendjeh in Afghanistan (1885), with the closely following construction of the Transcaspian Railway to Tashkent for the forward movement of troops. After his 1888 visit Curzon wrote

"This railway makes them prodigiously strong. And they mean business".

Curzon did not believe Russia would try to conquer India, but he was firmly convinced that it could try to invade,

"To keep England quiet in Europe by keeping her employed in Asia. That, briefly put, is the sum and substance of Russian policy".

And in fact in 1885 General Alexei Kuropatkin, now Russia's Commander-in-Chief in Manchuria against the Japanese, had come up with just such a plan for an invasion of India, via both the Persian Gulf and Afghanistan.

Now also, as Viceroy of India, countering that policy by protecting the northwest frontiers of the subcontinent was in the forefront of Curzon's responsibilities – somewhat too much so, as his views aroused increasing concern in London about the military implications of a "forward policy" against Russia. Years before, in fact, Lord Salisbury, under whose Prime Ministership Curzon had first held office, had complained that his young protégé "always wants me to negotiate with Russia as if I had 200,000 men at my back, and I have not". The last straw for London was Curzon's despatch of an expedition to Tibet in 1904, while the Russo–Japanese War was at its height; his decision was prompted by persistent rumours of Russian penetration of Tibet and of preparations there of a base for intrigue and disturbance in Nepal, Bhutan and Sikkim on India's northern frontier. The expedition was led by Colonel Francis Younghusband, an adventurous army officer who, after exploring Manchuria, had crossed China in 1887 from east to west – like Morrison, but further north – and found the Himalayan pass from Kashgar in Chinese Turkestan into northern India. Younghusband succeeded in overcoming a sprightly Tibetan resistance, and the Dalai Lama fled northwards before the British force entered Lhasa – to find no sign of Russians, Russian arms or Russian plots.

Younghusband nevertheless forced the remaining Tibetan authorities to accept a treaty requiring Tibet "to have no dealings of any kind with any Foreign Power without Britain's consent", thus taking care of the

Russians should they ever try to pursue the involvement they had turned out not to have had before, and to pay an indemnity – as was usual for the losers in these colonial wars – not excessive in itself, but in seventy-five *annual* instalments. On two counts however Younghusband went beyond his instructions: his treaty also required the stationing of a British Agent in the country, and British occupation of a stretch of southern Tibet "until the indemnity had been paid (i.e. for seventy–five years)", as he spelled it out. London was appalled, publicly repudiated the agreement, and recalled Younghusband in disgrace (though an admiring King Edward VII insisted on giving him a knighthood). It was partly a matter of timing: just at this stage Britain was becoming concerned that the disasters Russia was suffering in the Far East were beginning to undermine its position as a counterweight in Europe to an increasingly assertive Germany. The balance of power was already swinging into the configuration that would launch the First World War.

Curzon also suffered in the fallout: he was suspected by the British Government of having encouraged Younghusband behind its back; in fact he had not – he had been on leave in England during the expedition itself – though he did believe it was essential for Britain to have a resident Political Agent in Tibet to oversee regular contacts. But, together with the insidious personal treachery of his military Commander–in–Chief, the odious Lord Kitchener, and the political hostility of the Secretary of State for India, St John Brodrick, a former Balliol friend, Curzon's position in Calcutta was definitively undermined. He resigned as Viceroy in August 1905, and returned to London and the political wilderness.

Since the eighteenth century China had exercised suzerainty over Tibet; Britain, as ruler of India, Tibet's only other neighbour, recognised China's position. Despite preoccupations with the war on its own territory, Beijing had accordingly protested at the despatch of Younghusband's expedition, though its representative in Lhasa had slightly confused things by participating in the negotiations with the British in an attempt to reinforce Chinese interests there. After London's repudiation of Younghusband's treaty Beijing again tried to shore up its interests by sending an envoy to Calcutta to negotiate a settlement with the Government of British India. The envoy was Dang Shaoyi [Tang Shao–i], a protégé of Yuan Shikai. Dang, from a rich Cantonese merchant family – his father had been comprador for the prominent British trading firm Jardine, Matheson – had been one of the first Chinese to study in the United States (at Columbia University), following which he became, in 1882, Yuan's assistant in Korea, a position he held until

Yuan's departure in 1894. After experience liaising with the British on the Beijing–Mukden railway, Dang rejoined Yuan in Shandong as head of his Bureau of Foreign Affairs. During his liaison role Dang became a friend and confidant of Morrison, to whom he confessed his former addiction to opium – twenty-four pipes of Indian opium a day; now clean, he strongly pushed Yuan's anti–opium campaign in Shandong.

Yuan took Dang with him to Chihli, as head of Customs, and protested against his despatch to Calcutta. In the event, the negotiations there with the British stalled. Two years later, when Dang had become Vice–President of the Ministry of Foreign Affairs, he successfully negotiated a settlement of Tibet with the British, who evolved a splendid formula – worthy of Li Hongzhang – recognising China's suzerainty but not sovereignty. Dang's work did not last: China's position in Lhasa had effectively been undermined by Younghusband's invasion, and despite this and subsequent attempts by Beijing to reassert its authority, Tibet came to be regarded by the world community as virtually independent; up to the Second World War, whenever that autonomy was threatened by the Chinese, the Tibetans themselves sought support from...the British. Here were the roots of current difficulties over Tibet.

Post–war "settlements"

In March 1905 United States President Theodore Roosevelt had begun putting out peace feelers to the belligerents and other powers, but was knocked back all round, not least by the British. In June however, within a week of the Battle of Tsushima, Japan asked him to propose peace to Russia; and he promptly cabled an offer to arrange a meeting between the Russian and Japanese Governments, without any intermediary, to bring an end to the hostilities. Publicly the United States had been neutral throughout the war. But Roosevelt was concerned about Russia's "grossly overbearing" attitude in the Far East towards other nations, including the United States, particularly by excluding others from trade with Manchuria; and when the war began he warned France and Germany, Russia's allies, not to even think about joining it against Japan. While he had told a visitor, nine months into the war, that "we don't want the Japanese to come trailing their men–of–war across *our* ocean", privately he was more than satisfied with the outcome: he wrote to his son

> "Between ourselves – for you must not breathe it to anybody –
> I was thoroughly pleased with the Japanese victory, for Japan is
> playing our game".

Roosevelt nevertheless remained wary: as Japanese successes had accumulated he had said to a confidant:

> "I am not inclined to think that Tokyo will show itself a particle more altruistic than St Petersburg, or for the matter of that, Berlin. I believe that the Japanese rulers recognise Russia as their most dangerous permanent enemy, but I am not at all sure that the Japanese people draw any distinctions between the Russians and other foreigners, including ourselves. I have no doubt that they include all white men as being people who, as a whole, they dislike, and whose past arrogance they resent; and doubtless they believe their own yellow civilisation is better".

Japan's proposal to Roosevelt is at first sight surprising. But in fact, although the Japanese had won all the battles, some – especially those at Port Arthur and Mukden – had been at such a cost that the Japanese army was seriously stretched; and even Mukden had still not been decisive. For Russia to have accepted seems obvious: but Tsar Nicholas was being pressed by the Empress Alexandra to fight on, and some of the generals were claiming that previous problems of training and supply across the Trans–Siberian Railway had been overcome. However the unrest in Russia itself was compelling, and St Petersburg also accepted Roosevelt's offer. But before the negotiators met in Portsmouth Navy Yard, New Hampshire, in August, Japan increased the pressure on Russia: in July it invaded Sakhalin to its north, its first strike against Russian territory; in four weeks it had captured this island strategically located off the coast of Siberia's Maritime Province, thereby further enclosing Russia's great eastern stronghold at Vladivostok.

Both sides had trouble appointing their chief negotiator. "Anyone but Witte", the Tsar said; but there was no–one else able to do the job. Equally obvious, in Japan, was Ito Hirobumi. Ito had visited St Petersburg in 1902 to explore with Witte an alliance with Russia because he feared the Anglo–Japanese Alliance pending at that time would inevitably lead to a war between Japan and Russia which would be disastrous to his country. Witte was impressed by him, though St Petersburg did not respond quickly enough to head off the Japanese agreement with Britain; but now Witte had a message passed to Japan with the highly unusual suggestion that a negotiation between himself and Ito would offer the best prospects for both sides. Witte underestimated the extent to which he would be on the end of the Tsar's puppet–strings;

and Ito refused to serve as he doubted that peace could be secured at that stage. The representation of Japan accordingly went to the Foreign Minister, Komura Jutaro, a graduate of Harvard Law School; he had been Japanese Minister in St Petersburg, then in Beijing immediately after the siege of the Legations; and there, during the negotiations for the post–Boxer settlement, he had led the opposition to Russia's abortive attempt to secure its position in Manchuria by separate treaty with China. In his *Memoirs* Witte slightingly dismissed him:

> "I had met him in St Petersburg while he was Japanese ambassador…Komura is, no doubt, a man of prominence, but his appearance and manners are rather unattractive".

At Portsmouth Witte and Komura reached agreement fairly soon on the recognition of Japan's "paramount political, military, and economic interests" in Korea, on Russian withdrawal from Manchuria south of Harbin (the existing military line of demarcation), and on the transfer to Japan of Port Arthur and the Liadong Peninsula, which Russia had lost. But deadlock ensued when the Russians absolutely refused Japan's demands for the cession of Sakhalin and the usual victor's indemnity. At this point Roosevelt intervened personally to propose a compromise based on a Russian payment for "the cost of transferring" the southern half only of Sakhalin to Japan. The Tsar however declared his preparedness to take the field himself rather than pay even a disguised indemnity, not because he really wanted to fight on – though some of the generals still did – but because of fear that giving in would encourage the revolutionary movement in Russia. Roosevelt was furious:

> "Bad as the Chinese are, no human beings, black, yellow or white, could be quite as untruthful, as insincere, as arrogant – in short as untrustworthy in every way – as the Russians under their present system. I was pro–Japanese before, but after my experience with the peace commissioners, I am far stronger pro–Japanese than ever".

Witte, Roosevelt thought, was "totally without ideals".

It was of course unfair to put all the blame on Witte, who personally favoured a compromise – and, after all, it was not American territory that Roosevelt was proposing be handed over to Japan. But it was Japan that blinked. Tokyo had recognised that it simply did not have the additional troops needed to continue the war, or the finances to raise and equip them. Komura was therefore instructed to give way, when there was no other prospect of securing an agreement, on both the indemnity and Sakhalin – amended to the northern half of the island when the British told Tokyo they understood the Tsar would accept that. There is an amusing divergence over who gave in to whom at the final tense session. Komura reiterated the Roosevelt proposal; Witte rejected it. A Russian delegation member subsequently claimed that Komura then said:

"We make you another offer. To withdraw the money payment and give you half of Sakhalin";

and that Witte immediately replied

"I accept your offer".

But the British author of *Cassell's History of the Russo–Japanese War*, presumably informed by the Japanese, claimed it was the other way around: that Witte, after reiterating the Tsar's refusal to pay any form of indemnity,

"then intimated that he was prepared to offer the cession of the southern part of Sakhalin Island. Baron Komura is reported to have replied: 'I accept that' ".

Either way, the war was over.

The repercussions were not. Outside the conference room, a reporter asked Witte "What about the indemnity?", and his crisp reply, "Not a sou", revealing the stunning reversal of the loser–pays principle, was the beginning of his proclamation of "complete victory". But for him this propaganda success, beyond most Russians' expectations, was temporary: it led to his brief appointment as Prime Minister to deal with domestic discontent and resurrect the economy, but (as we have seen) Nicholas could not stomach him for more than six months. He never held office again. Komura, on the other hand, had to creep back into Japan in secret, reviled for having had to renounce an indemnity on behalf of the Japanese Government. Roosevelt commented with exasperation:

"It does not seem to me that the Japanese are wise in letting everybody talk as if they got the worst of it. They have won an astonishing triumph and have received a remarkable reward. They have secured control of Manchuria and Korea. They have Port Arthur and Dalny, and the south half of Sakhalin. In destroying the Russian navy they have made themselves a formidable sea power – one which, in the Pacific, is doubtless a match for any nation save England. Under such circumstances, it seems to me that they are very unwise, because they could not get an indemnity to which they had no real title whatever, to make it appear as if the terms of peace were utterly unsatisfactory".

But the Government had allowed the population to expect a huge windfall from the Russians: the propaganda war was already lost in Japan. Popular outrage against both the Government and President Roosevelt spilled over into the streets, with mob attacks on the American Legation, police, public transport and Christian churches; a newly-erected statue of Ito Hirobumi, who had opposed the war and declined to be involved in the peace, was pulled down and dragged through the streets. Roosevelt's role in securing the peace settlement soon resulted in the vetoing of American joint–investment proposals in Manchuria, and in anti–Americanism becoming a permanent factor in Japanese foreign policy debate.

China was of course not present in Portsmouth, nor did anyone bother to ask it if it was acceptable to transfer its territory in Manchuria from Russian to Japanese occupation. Morrison's attitude had been as bad as anyone's: having propagandised strongly in favour of Japan's going to war with Russia, he now campaigned for Japan to continue it:

"Why should there be peace?" he asked his editors in London; he could "find no interest whatever in China in favour of peace except among the Chinese themselves".

It was only at the end of 1905 that Komura travelled to Beijing to secure China's "agreement" to Japan's new "rights" in Manchuria. "If Yuan Shih–k'ai expected", the Warners wrote, "that his wartime collaboration would be rewarded with the coming of peace, however, he was gravely mistaken". Yuan surely did not expect Japan would concede anything in relation to its territorial gains; but Komura made no offer of any other sweeteners. China – not for the last time – had no alternative but to accept a decision reached without its involvement. From having been seen as a valuable counterweight against Russian expansionism after the

Boxer uprising, Chinese perceptions moved Japan back to the distrusted position it had held before then. Now however, securely based in Manchuria, Japan presented an altogether more menacing image than when it had merely been claiming a special position in Korea.

And Korea? The war had supposedly been fought because Japan had wanted to protect that special position against Russian designs. Clearly things had gone a great deal further than that, and Korea had been forgotten in the process – except by Japan. When, four days after the start of the Portsmouth Conference, the Anglo–Japanese Alliance of 1902 was renewed for ten years, to the satisfaction of both powers – "intolerable arrogance and insolence", Nicholas fumed – Japan secured in addition Britain's agreement to recognise its special interests in Korea. This was a euphemism for giving it a free hand there; and in return Japan recognised Britain's own special interests in "all that concerns the security of the Indian Frontier" – clear confirmation that Curzon's anxieties continued to occupy minds in London. Both agreements were made public three days after the Witte–Komura settlement at Portsmouth. And to cap off this achievement, General Katsura Taro, Prime Minister of Japan since 1901, reached a secret agreement with Roosevelt's Secretary of War (and eventual successor as President), William Howard Taft, recognising Japan's suzerainty over Korea "to the extent of controlling her foreign relations and thus obviating future trouble", in return for an assurance that it had no designs on the United States' new colony of the Philippines. The young Korean nationalist Syngman Rhee – president of South Korea during the Korean War fifty years later – was actually in Washington trying to plead Korea's cause with President Roosevelt when this insouciant disposition of his country occurred. No–one would see him.

Korea was now securely Japanese, with everyone's blessing but the Koreans'. Before the war, the young American diplomat William Sands, who had been adviser to the Korean ruler – grandly though ineffectually styled Emperor since 1897 to claim equality with his Chinese and Japanese counterparts – had tried to have a series of modernising reforms introduced: abolition of official bribery, establishment of an effective rural bureaucracy, and most ambitious of all, a scheme for international recognition of Korean independence and neutrality. Sands admitted frankly that he had trouble getting anyone, Korean or foreign, even to listen to him. Apart from his boss:

> "Of course I had urged my simple plan upon the emperor frequently
> and at length. He always listened courteously and trustingly, but

the poor man never had the first glimmering of what it was all about. The sum of his philosophy was that he was the master of his people and what was theirs was his".

When Ito was visiting Korea late in 1903, Sands, with that admirable American sense of can–do, determined to put his ideas to him directly, in the hope, not entirely naïve given Ito's role in the modernisation of Japan and introduction of a constitution there, that "we might be able to work together":

> "I found him in a tea house, alone except for a group of the best geisha the Japanese town could produce, in most jovial mood and flushed with sake. To my astonishment, I interrupted the great statesman in a song, a frivolous song, and to his astonishment I told him that I had heard the substance of his very secret interview with the emperor and wanted to be quite sure of what he had actually said, or, as in the simplicity of my heart I told him, I would not know how to advise...I waited for the inevitable stroke of apoplexy, but it did not come. Instead he asked me to sit down, offered me a cup of native wine and suggested that we talk it out".

Sands commented afterwards, still with a sense of wonder in his voice, that

> "I never got a full and intelligent hearing anywhere but in the quarter where I had the least right to expect it...I can only say that Prince Ito was serious and receptive, as he sat there on the floor of the tea house, a little elderly man, stoking his thin grey beard as he listened, kindly and attentive, or talked with excellent knowledge of Korean conditions, as if I were really a power there and not the adventurer in diplomacy the local [Japanese–controlled] press considered me to be, whom the Japanese government would sweep away or crush when its patience was exhausted. I left him with the deep satisfaction of having been heard by an intelligent man with sympathy, and of having put Korea's case and my own before the leading statesman of Japan".

And he added laconically:

> "Nothing tangible came of it".

It was of course far too late: Japan had determined on war for the control of Korea. As the Japanese main fleet attacked Port Arthur on 8 February 1904, another fleet attacked Russian ships in the harbour at Chemulpo, the port of Seoul – the Russians fought back, but "incommoded nobody but the fish", a Japanese officer said – and began landing the army of occupation. In a few days the Secretary of the Japanese Legation approached Sands with a message:

> " 'I am instructed,' he said, 'to invite you to join Prince Ito in the temporary administration which is to be established here'...I was enormously flattered and appreciated what was a real compliment, but I had been opposing their policies for four years".

Sands was promptly escorted onto a transport leaving for Japan. In addition to the army, Japanese financial and diplomatic "advisers" arrived in Korea in 1904; at the end of 1905, Ito Hirobumi obliged the Emperor to accept the establishment in Seoul of a Resident–General to control Korean foreign affairs, and was then appointed to the position. He was ruler in all but name.

Ito's rule was relatively liberal in the circumstances, especially as the resentful Koreans withheld cooperation with their Japanese advisers when they could, and the Japanese military leadership, both in Korea itself and particularly in Tokyo, was constantly pressing for more direct control. To try to head this off Ito in 1907 presented new demands to the Emperor for an expanded Japanese role in the civil administration; rather than accept these humiliating new conditions Kojong abdicated, but his feeble–minded son Sunjong was more malleable. In 1909, with the return to power of General Katsura, Ito resigned. Shortly afterwards he set off overland for St Petersburg, still with the idea of trying to arrange the kind of Russo–Japanese cooperation that he had put to Witte seven years before. But as he reviewed a Russian guard of honour at Harbin he was assassinated. As he lay dying, he was told his assassin was a young Korean nationalist. Ito reportedly said "He is a fool!". Korea had lost the last Japanese willing to try to work with it: within a year Japan annexed it outright. And so began thirty–five years of brutality and humiliation in which every effort was made to annihilate the very identity of Korea and Koreans.

Wider repercussions
Scarcely noticed at the time, as other nations took stock of Russian defeat, and began the readjustment of the European balance of power that

became the preoccupation of the last decade before the far greater "war to end all wars", was the reaction elsewhere in Asia to the defeat of a European great power by a small Asian country newly emerged from two centuries of obscurantist isolation. In China it underpinned the belief of the modernisers that technological and industrial progress was essential to successfully resisting foreign intrusions; and for those demanding political reform it demonstrated the victory of "constitutionalism" over "autocracy" – even though this was a superficial judgement given the authoritarian nature of the Japanese system.

Nationalist sentiment had scarcely stirred as yet in Southeast Asia, but in West Asia young constitutionalists seized on Japan's example. In Persia it inspired a movement which successfully forced the Shah to grant a new constitution in 1906; similarly, two years later in Turkey, where two army officers had written a *five–volume* history of the Russo–Japanese War, revolutionary Young Turk army officers secured from the Ottoman Sultan the reactivation of an earlier parliamentary constitution that had been suppressed. Commenting at the time on the Young Turk revolt and associated disturbances in Russian Azerbaijan, Lenin wrote that

"the awakening of the Asiatic peoples received special impetus from the Russo–Japanese War and the [1905] Russian Revolution";

but his ideological evolution subsequently suppressed all reference to Japan's victory: only the 1905 Revolution was allowed to inspire Asiatic peoples.

These movements in West Asia were of course focussed on internal domestic reform. It was in subject India that the impact of Japan's victory had a nationalist as well as a modernising dimension. In his *Autobiography* Jawaharlal Nehru, the future architect of Indian independence, recalled that in 1905

"Japanese victories stirred up my enthusiasm and I waited eagerly for the papers for fresh news daily. I invested in a large number of books on Japan and tried to read some of them. I felt rather lost in Japanese history, but I liked the knightly tales of old Japan... Nationalistic ideas filled my mind. I mused of Indian freedom and Asiatic freedom from the thraldom of Europe. I dreamt of brave deeds, of how, sword in hand, I would fight for India and help in freeing her. I was fourteen".

In a letter to his daughter Indira (later Mrs Gandhi, also to be Prime Minister of India), when she was about the same age, he wrote further of the impact of the war's outcome:

"The victory of Japan, an Asiatic country, had a far–reaching effect on all the countries of Asia...A great European power had been defeated; therefore Asia could still defeat Europe as it had done so often in the past. Nationalism spread more rapidly over the eastern countries and the cry of 'Asia for the Asiatics' was heard. But this nationalism was not a mere return to the past, a clinging on to old customs and beliefs. Japan's victory was seen to be due to her adoption of the new industrial methods of the West, and these ideas and methods became more popular all over the East".

No mention of Korea here.[347]

Unlike most of his Western contemporaries, a long–time British missionary in India, the Reverend C.F.Andrews, observed the reaction, and was as stirred as any Asian:

"A stir of excitement passed over the North of India. Even the remote villagers talked over the victories of Japan as they sat in their circles and passed around the *huqqa* [pipe] at night. One of the older men told me, 'There has been nothing like it since the Mutiny'...The old–time glory and greatness of Asia seemed destined to return. The material aggrandisement of the European races at the expense of the East seemed at last to be checked... Behind these dreams and visions was the one exulting hope – that the days of servitude to the West were over and the day of independence had dawned. Much had gone before to prepare the way for such a dawn of hope: the Japanese victories made it, for the first time, shining and radiant".

Part of the reason for Indian rejoicing lay in reaction to two blunders which had just been made by Curzon as Viceroy in the first months of 1905. The first was entirely avoidable: in a speech as Chancellor of Calcutta University he spoke in what Rose smoothly called "silkily offensive terms" –

---

347 To be fair, in a later letter Nehru told his young daughter that Japan's suppression of the Koreans was a "sad and dark chapter in history".

"I hope I am making no false or arrogant claim when I say that the highest ideal of truth is to a large extent a Western conception. I do not thereby mean to claim that Europeans are universally or even generally truthful, still less do I mean that Asiatics deliberately or habitually deviate from the truth. The one proposition would be absurd, and the other insulting, but undoubtedly truth took a high place in the moral codes of the West before it had been similarly honoured in the east, where craftiness and diplomatic wile have always been held in much repute. We may prove it by the common innuendo that lurks in the words 'Oriental diplomacy', by which is meant something rather tortuous and hypersubtle".

The contrast with Roosevelt's perceptions of the two participants at Portsmouth is interesting – but then Curzon would not have regarded Russians as exactly European.

His words, which exacerbated Indian intellectuals' anger at university reforms Curzon was imposing at the time, have long since merged into the legacy of British imperialist arrogance. Shortly afterwards however Curzon pushed through a policy measure which is still held responsible for having irrevocably damaged the Subcontinent. It was summarised by Nehru in 1932 in another of his letters to his daughter, where he wrote in simple but stark terms of Curzon's autocratic decision: to divide

"the great province of Bengal...into two parts, one of these being East Bengal. The growing nationalism of the *bourgeoisie* in Bengal resented it. It suspected that the British wanted to weaken them by thus dividing them. Eastern Bengal had a majority of Muslims, so by this division a Hindu–Muslim question was also raised. A great anti–British movement rose in Bengal...The movement even spread to the masses to some extent, and partly it drew its inspiration from Hinduism. Side by side with it there arose a Bengal school of revolutionary violence, and the bomb first made its appearance in Indian politics".

Lady Minto, the wife of Curzon's successor as Viceroy, wrote sharply but perceptively of

"Lord Curzon's marvellous ability and undefeated power of working beyond the endurance of any other man have dissected and laid bare the innermost workings of every department throughout India. But he has treated the 300,000,000 people as puppets".

The still–fledgling Indian National Congress had been established in 1885 to represent all Indians in the struggle for independence from Britain. Now a separate Moslem independence movement, established in 1906, grew out of the division of Bengal;[348] and in due course it produced the Islamic state of Pakistan, separated from India in a bloody forced exchange of populations at the time of independence, the end of Britain's Indian Empire, in 1947.

Eminence and exile
In China even the Dowager Empress recognised the strength of feeling among intellectuals and many officials on the superiority of a constitutional form of government, but she was not about to rush into one. At the end of 1905 she sent a small group of officials abroad to study foreign constitutions; late in 1906 it recommended a programme for the establishment of a constitutional monarchy – and Cixi then submitted it to an advisory institute for "study". Yuan Shikai was among those who felt there was a need for speedier constitutional reform, and he memorialised the throne to that effect in August 1907, calling also for compulsory education – even some education for girls, a thorough investigation and reform of China's finances, and the end of discrimination between Manchus and Chinese. But he was also one of those who questioned whether the Chinese people were "ready" for elective government at a national level, particularly after the dismal results of his experiment with local government elections in Tianjin, and felt that was the level at which political reform should start.

While nothing happened on the constitutional front, Yuan's position underwent a significant change in September 1907 when the Dowager

---

348   In July 2002, as the two countries exchanged threats of nuclear war, an Indian author, Pankaj Mishra, still recalled, in *The New York Review of Books*:

"Such classic British colonialist strategies of divide and rule as the partition of Bengal in 1905 and the decision to have separate elections for Muslims further reinforced the sense among many upwardly mobile Hindus and Muslims that they belonged to irreconcilable religious communities".

The present situation is not all of course just Curzon's fault: Mishra's concern was with both Hindu and Moslem politicians who have staked – and are still staking – their ambitions on perpetuating and exacerbating the religious divide.

Empress transferred him from the Viceroyalty of Chihli to Beijing as President of the Ministry of Foreign Affairs – Foreign Minister – and a member of the Grand Council, the highest level to which an ethnic Chinese was permitted to rise in the Qing Empire. Having just survived a hostile political manoeuvre against him by a reactionary Manchu faction at Court, he was apparently unsure that this was a real promotion: in the first place it meant losing direct control over the Beiyang Army, in the second that in Beijing his power might more easily be circumscribed by his enemies at Court. But it became apparent that the reason for his transfer was a genuine desire by the Empress Dowager to have strong and stable leadership in the capital to deal with the vexed question of constitutional reform and the continuing difficulties with the foreign powers over Manchuria.

With her firm support Yuan's power and influence increased over the course of the next year. His own carefully cultivated network under-pinned it: MacKinnon has identified supporters who either ran or were prominent in the Ministries of Civil Affairs, Finance, Education, War, Justice, Posts and Communications, and Agriculture, Industry and Commerce – virtually the entire gamut of government – and his influence in the army actually increased as he was able to place his protégés in additional units. The strength of his position was dramatically demon-strated on his fiftieth birthday in September 1908, when all Beijing pre-sented congratulations and gifts – none more spectacular than those of the Empress Dowager, carried by Court servants in a long procession of yellow sedan chairs and placed on tables covered with yellow cloth. Fully sensible of the honour being done him, Yuan bowed to Cixi's gifts twenty–seven times.

One person was absent and sent no present: Prince Chun, younger brother of the Emperor Guangxu and father of Puyi [P'u I], the heir apparent.[349] The reason was Chun's hatred of Yuan for having betrayed his brother and the Hundred Days Reform in 1898; he also knew that, in discussions on the succession to the childless Guangxu, Yuan had supported the Dowager Empress's original choice, not the infant Puyi whom she now favoured in the expectation of being able to continue her Regency during his childhood. But for now Chun waited.

---

349 In 1900, at the age of eighteen, Prince Chun had been sent by the Dowager Empress, in accordance with the terms demanded in the Boxer settlement, to apologise personally to the Kaiser for the murder of Baron von Ketteler, the German Minister, during the siege of the Legations.

Yuan was active in his new Ministry, which he quickly staffed with men trained in Japan and the West, and where he demonstrated an ability to work with but hold off the insistent foreigners to an extent not previously seen: recovering railways, securing loans, and continuing an anti–opium campaign he had begun in Shandong a decade before. An Imperial edict in 1905 had made the campaign national; considerable progress was made in converting Chinese opium land to food crops – perhaps eighty percent by 1911, it was estimated – but ultimate success was undermined by British legalism as much as by domestic corruption: the Foreign Office argued that opium could be imported under the Opium War treaty rights until one hundred percent of Chinese production had been stopped, and British gunboats continued to force the sale of British opium.

Right from the beginning – indeed, as we saw, even during the Boxer period – Yuan carefully cultivated a close relationship with the British; this was helped by the constant support of Morrison, and through him of *The Times* in London, and became strongly personal after the transfer in 1906 of the career diplomat Sir John Jordan from Seoul to Beijing as British Minister, for which Morrison had actively lobbied the British Government.

But there was a catch: developing good relations with the foreign powers was essential to China's recovery from the disasters of the new century; but the consequent concessions undermined the success of the policy domestically. And Yuan's diplomacy experienced a major failure in Manchuria, where he tried to encourage American investment as a means of countering the strong Japanese influence that existed there following its victory in the war with Russia. But the Americans did not understand his purpose; when Morrison had met Theodore Roosevelt after the Portsmouth Conference the President said dismissively that he doubted China would ever recover Manchuria. In a repeat of Syngman Rhee's experience, Yuan's envoy Dang Shaoyi was actually in Washington when the United States signed, in Tokyo, an agreement in effect recognising Manchuria as in Japan's sphere of influence. This was enormously damaging to Yuan: not only had he more or less "lost" Manchuria, but his efforts to pre–empt Japan there earned him the active enmity of Tokyo.

In 1908 – three years after Tsar Nicholas had yielded – the Empress Dowager likewise announced "Principles" for a constitutional process, leading to the election of a national parliament...in 1917. Provincial assemblies were to be established in 1909, followed by graduated steps covering feasible goals such as local self–government, law reform, and a census, and sweepingly ambitious intentions to reduce illiteracy. Yuan was directly involved in the formulation of this program: he saw reform as necessary for the re–establishment of the central Government's authority, but its time–frame fitted with his belief that China required a long lead–time to a new constitutional system. To what extent the details reflected his views, however is less clear, and Cixi's hand can certainly be seen in the sweeping powers reserved to the Throne: the Emperor's right to summon and dismiss parliament, his continued power over the executive, and, not least, command of the armed forces. Ominously, the edict announcing the "Principles" asserted that

> "The government of China is to be constitutional by Imperial decree" to ensure that "the [Qing] Dynasty shall rule over the [Qing] Empire for ever and ever, and be honoured through all ages".

As it turned out, the gradualist scheme promoted revolutionary activity: the promise of reform raised expectations, including in army circles, that soon could not be confined to the long drawn–out timetable envisaged by the Government; and that timetable, together with the reserved powers and other exemptions from democratic processes, raised the anger of those who saw the demise of the Manchu dynasty as essential to genuine progress. These views were soon to be crystallised by Sun Yatsen. After spending the intervening years since his failed Canton uprising in Europe and America, drumming up support among overseas Chinese and especially the students Yuan and others were encouraging to train abroad, in 1905 Sun had founded the revolutionary organisation that was to evolve into the Guomindang [Kuomintang] Party of Nationalist China. He had four objectives: to restore China to the Chinese, establish a republic, equalise land ownership, and

> "drive out the Tartars, [for] the extreme cruelties and tyrannies of the Manchu government have now reached their limit".

Totally unexpectedly, fate now intervened in the progress of both dilatory reform and accelerated revolution: two months after Yuan Shikai's birthday celebrations Emperor Guangxu died suddenly – some said suspiciously – at the age of thirty–three, followed by the Dowager Empress herself the very next day, at seventy–three. The twenty–six–year–old Prince

Chun became Regent, which undermined the theory that Yuan himself had had Guangzu murdered: Yuan realised of course that he was now in serious trouble. The only question was how definitive it would be. After Yuan had organised the two lavish funerals Chun made his move. At the beginning of January 1909 an Imperial edict announced:

> "The Grand Councillor and President of the Ministry of Foreign Affairs, Yuan Shikai, in times past has received repeated promotions at the hands of their departed Majesties. Again on Our accession, We honoured him by further rewards as an incentive to him to display his energy, for his ability was worth using. Unexpectedly, Yuan Shikai is now suffering from an infection of the foot; he has difficulty in walking, and it is hardly possible for him to discharge his duties adequately. We command Yuan Shikai to resign his offices at once, returning to his native place to treat, and to convalesce from, the ailment. It is Our resolution to show Our consideration and compassion".

It was all very decorous, and totally disingenuous. But it was compassionate: it was a miracle that Yuan did not lose his head. Instead he was able to extract himself safely from the capital and establish his exile on an estate in northern Henan which he slyly named *Yuan Shou Yuan*, the Garden for Cultivating Longevity – near an important railway junction, where friends and allies could easily visit despite the surveillance of the new Regent's spies. His close friendship with Sir John Jordan and the British may have played a role in his survival: in a return to old habits Sir John had no compunction about intervening in China's affairs by promptly protesting Yuan's dismissal, and making clear that he enjoyed British "protection". It did not save Yuan's job, but may well have saved his life.

Fall of the Dynasty

Yuan did not have long to wait before it became clear that the new dispensation in Beijing was in trouble. The Englishman R.F. (later Sir Reginald) Johnston, who became tutor to Puyi, described Prince Chun:

> "He is well–intentioned, tries in his languid and ineffectual way to please everyone, succeeds in pleasing no one, shrinks from responsibility, is thoroughly unbusinesslike, is disastrously deficient in energy, will–power and grit, and there is reason to believe that

he lacks both physical and moral courage. He is helpless in an emergency, has no original ideas, and is liable to be swayed by any smooth talker. After he became regent, however, the flattery of sycophants tended to make him obstinately tenacious of his own opinions, which almost invariably turned out to be wrong. During several years of fairly intimate contact with prince Ch'un I came to be so deeply impressed by his fatal tendency to do the wrong thing...that I once made the suggestion to my colleagues in the Forbidden City that we might actually turn that tendency to good account by adopting the following general principle: If two possible courses of action present themselves, ask prince Ch'un which in his opinion should be followed – then follow the other".

Johnston conceded, however, that

"he must be given credit for being one of the two Manchu princes... who has a respectable knowledge of the Manchu language".

The absence of any effective leadership in Beijing inevitably amplified the impact of even the meagre constitutional reformed that Cixi had just announced. When the provincial assemblies gathered in 1909, supposedly to examine and prepare for the future path towards constitutional government, there were instead demands for full political reform, by 1911 at the latest. Zhang Jian, the scholar who had given the young Yuan Shikai poetry lessons when he first joined the army, now a prominent industrialist and supporter of the monarchy, was active in these moves; his pressure, supported by several provincial governors, persuaded the Regent at the end of 1910 to move the establishment of a national parliament back from 1917 to 1913. But the process was still demonstrably too slow. And the Regent behaved exactly as Johnston described: in what was supposed to be another concession to the constitutionalists, in April 1911 he appointed China's first supposedly Western–style Cabinet of thirteen Ministers – nine of them Manchus, five from the Imperial clan itself. Zhang commented despairingly:

"It is contrary to the tradition of the dynasty to entrust the army, the navy, and all other important ministries to members of the imperial clan. This move has altered nothing and has only made the situation more untenable. The country is rapidly disintegrating".

Zhang was right: events were spinning out of hand. The bumbling Government's attempt to nationalise the railways was the final straw: there was a revolt in September in Sichuan [Szechwan], where the Viceroy was beheaded by the rioters; and on 10 October anti–Manchu revolution began in Wuchang, now part of the city of Wuhan on the Yangzi River – the date, "the Double Tenth", still celebrated as China's National Day. At this point Beijing sent a panic–stricken message to the Garden for Cultivating Longevity asking Yuan Shikai to return to office. Yuan, fully briefed by his succession of visitors, was able to match the solicitude with which he had been bundled off into exile:

> "My weakening body is constantly troubled by illness", he replied; "The coming of autumn does it no good...I beseech you to recommend someone else".

Five days later, as the revolution spread through other southern centres, Beijing was begging him:

> "Please think of your important duties. How can you possibly be happy in the wilderness? It is better for you to come too soon than too late".

Yuan still held out:

> "All the troops in Hubei have mutinied, and there is no money left in the provincial treasury. What can I do with my bare hands?"

So the Regent appointed him Viceroy of Hubei and Hunan. And Yuan responded:

> "My foot is not yet healed".

At this stage the revolutionaries in Hubei asked Yuan to join them, promising him the presidency if a republic could be established. But power in Beijing was more promising than a gamble in Wuchang: he obviously believed that the Government had no choice but to give in to his conditions, which included parliamentary government in 1912, legalisation of political parties, a pardon for the Wuchang revolutionaries – and his own appointment as commander–in–chief of all the armed forces. By now three provinces had declared their independence from the

Government. The dithering Regent stalled as long as he could, but on 7 November surrendered completely and appointed Yuan Prime Minister. Six days later Yuan, with a bodyguard described by Morrison as "wild–looking halberdiers carrying long two–handled swords", entered Beijing at the head of two thousand of his old troops, and swore his loyalty to the Throne.

That was then. By the end of November fifteen of China's eighteen provinces had declared independence. Fighting had been going on in some between government forces and the revolutionaries, largely dependent on the inclination of the commanding generals concerned, but efforts began for a cease–fire. On 6 December the Regent stepped down and Yuan was given full authority by the current Empress Dowager, Guangxu's widow, to achieve a settlement with the revolutionaries. Negotiations began in Shanghai on 18 December, with the revolutionaries demanding in the first session the abolition of the Qing Dynasty. On 28 December, the Dowager Empress agreed to a proposal by Yuan and Prince Qing for a national convention to meet in Shanghai on 8 January to decide between a monarchy and a republic. The Manchus, bitterly divided amongst themselves, had given up.

Meanwhile, in late December Sun Yatsen – who was later to be canonised by both Chiang Kai-shek's Nationalists[350] and Mao Zedong's Communists as *the* revolutionary leader – had arrived in Shanghai from the United States, and been elected by the revolutionaries' provisional legislature to be president, as from 1 January 1912, of a provisional republican government based in Nanjing [Nanking]. Well–known abroad, Sun was less so in China: one of the revolution's leaders, General Li Yuanhong, later said

"The world has a false idea about Sun Yatsen. He had nothing to do with the actual work of overthrowing the monarchy. The Revolution was finished when he reached China...None of the real leaders of the Revolution, for various reasons, desired to take the position of Provisional President, which we felt would be of short duration. Sun Yatsen, from being out of the country for so long, was not associated with any faction here; his name was known abroad, and he seemed to suit the occasion".

---

350 The Pinyin version of Chiang Kai-shek is Jiang Jieshi; it is thus commonly left in its more familiar Wade–Giles version.

After his election, and again after his swearing–in, Sun undertook to relinquish his position if Yuan Shikai would give a republic his full support. This was not just the implementation of Li Yuanhong's short-term view: the southerners were simply being realistic. With the loyalty Yuan still enjoyed from the powerful army he no longer commanded he was the only leader who could offer the possibility of securing stability in the north, and of holding the country as a whole together if he and the revolutionary south could work together. This was of course the key question.

Yuan responded at this stage by stalling the peace negotiations. Perhaps he was still not decided as to which system was preferable, republic or monarchy – in other words, which he could more easily control; perhaps he wanted a more concrete guarantee from the republicans that Sun Yatsen would step down specifically in his favour. Probably both. But there may have been another factor. His biographers have felt that his primary loyalty had always been to the Empress Dowager as a person rather than simply to the Manchu Dynasty – hence his betrayal of the Hundred Days Reform when he thought Guangxu would strike against her. Perhaps though, while recognising that preservation of the Dynasty was no longer a realistic alternative, he was still sensitive to the accusations that had followed his actions in 1898 and now wanted an outcome that would avoid another accusation of betrayal.

On 31 December Morrison told Yuan's confidant Zai Dinggan of an idea he had been "developing", which he had in fact put in a letter to a friend two days before: he noted that Yuan had told Sir John Jordan that

"he and his ancestors have served the Manchu dynasty faithfully, and he could not go down to the future as a usurper. But suppose the Manchus themselves should desire his appointment? Their interest would be better safeguarded with him in the Presidency than with other Chinese in the Empire...I do not see why it cannot be arranged that the Manchus themselves shall support his appointment".

Zai passed the idea on to Yuan, and later told Morrison:

"Yuan was tickled to death at your suggestion for the establishment of a Constitutional Republic by the Throne in an Imperial edict... [A]s the foreign legations are now accredited to the Court, they cannot refuse recognition of a Government delegated by the Court. The Republic will then be legally, legitimately and constitutionally established".

The situation however now began turning ugly. A small group of revolutionaries in Beijing, convinced Yuan was opposed to a republic, and acting independently of Nanjing, tried to assassinate him on 16 January as he was on the way to present a Cabinet petition to the Dowager Empress. Twelve of his guard were killed, as well as one of the horses pulling his carriage, which overturned; but Yuan was unhurt and rode off on horseback. Not surprisingly he accused Nanjing of bad faith, began arresting revolutionaries in Beijing – and asked the Dowager Empress for a month's leave! This was ludicrously unrealistic, but it carried a threat, reinforcing the memorial he was carrying: the Cabinet petition urged the Dynasty's early abdication.

The Imperial Princes were divided, the Empress Dowager reportedly hugged Puyi, the three–year–old Emperor Xuantong, and wept. Then on 26 January the chief–of–staff of the army, a Manchu opposed to Yuan, was assassinated, some thought with Yuan's connivance. The Imperial family now feared for their personal safety. The next step was a telegram to the Throne from forty–four commanders of Yuan's troops urging abdication. It was a decisive blow. On 30 January the Dowager Empress decided to abdicate on behalf of little Xuantong and – reflecting Morrison's idea – at the same time proclaim a republic by Imperial edict. But before she did so she tried to compromise Yuan by creating him a marquis of the dying Empire; it took him four refusals to escape this poisoned chalice, the final one with the splendid formula that

> "the uneasiness of his conscience did not enhance the reverent reflection that the Divine Will is irrevocable".

The peace negotiations in Shanghai promptly resumed. Yuan insisted on guarantees for the Manchus' safety and livelihood; it was agreed that, as ex–Emperor, little Puyi, his family and a limited retinue could retain the Great Within in the Forbidden City, though not the three great ceremonial halls immediately inside the Wumen, the Meridian Gate. Fifty years later, as a gardener in the People's Republic of China, Puyi would write of his Imperial prison in terms that recalled Pierre Loti's discovery in the wake of the relief of the Legations in 1900:

"Whenever I think of my childhood my head fills with a yellow mist. The glazed tiles were yellow, my sedan–chair was yellow, my chair cushions were yellow, the linings of my hats and clothes were yellow, the girdle around my waist was yellow, the dishes and bowls from which I ate and drank, the padded cover of the rice–gruel saucepan, the material in which my books were wrapped, the window curtains, the bridle of my horse…everything was yellow".

Zhang Jian was deputed to draft the Emperor's last edict. The looming civil war was averted, though centuries of domination by the Manchus were repaid in outbreaks of violence against them – mostly ordinary ones, of course, who had no special protection. On 12 February 1912 the abdication was read out to the Court and the Cabinet by the copiously-weeping Dowager Empress. Yuan Shikai was duly appointed to organise a provisional republican government. Thus the 267–year–old Qing Dynasty and the 2,000–year–old Chinese Empire were no more.

President

The accommodation between Yuan Shikai and Sun Yatsen went smoothly: on 15 February the republican provisional legislature – in Nanjing – accepted Sun's resignation and elected Yuan – in Beijing – provisional president of the Republic.[351] Yuan appointed Sun to direct the national railway system. But that was all. Argument immediately ensued on the location of the capital: Yuan insisted on staying in the north because his military power base was there, the revolution's base was in the south. Yuan won that round, and was inaugurated Provisional President on 10 March. Morrison, who was there, jotted down that

"Yuan came in wobbling like a duck looking fat and unhealthy, in Marshall's uniform loose flesh of his neck hanging down over his collar, hat too large for him, nervous and uncomfortable".

---

351 Pearl pointed out that, by a curious coincidence, another Australian newspaperman, W.H. Donald, Shanghai correspondent of the *New York Herald*, had hammered out Sun Yatsen's first Republican Manifesto "on a battered typewriter with the aid of a bottle of bourbon". Donald was close to the Guomindang, but scathing about Sun as "absolutely unpractical, without common sense" – not least in regard to his scheme for covering China, Tibet and Mongolia with a dense spiderweb of railway tracks.

To mark China's new modernity everyone else was in the Western–style frock–coats then fashionable.

Despite Yuan's reported confidence that Morrison's abdication idea would ensure the support of the foreign legations, the Powers were in fact highly sceptical of the new experiment. Morrison, writing to the just–departed American Minister, W.W. Rockhill, observed that

> "It is a curious feature of the present trouble that the great majority of Englishmen in China are in favour of the revolutionaries, whereas the great majority of the Americans are in favour of a continuance of monarchical government – of course, a reformed government".

Rockhill replied:

> "You say most Americans are in favour of the monarchical principle. I thoroughly concur in this opinion for I cannot see how China can stand without it, it is the keystone to the whole fabric ethically and politically...I cannot believe that a republican form of government will endure. It will be a provisional one leading to the founding of a new dynasty. Will it be Y.S.K. who will found it or will he simply be a king–maker?"

Reginald Johnston quoted an earlier authority:

> "As Jowett, the Master of Balliol, is reported to have said – 'You cannot have a republic without republicans' ".

It is interesting to note that, not long before, Jowett's pupil Curzon had expressed similar doubts about Indians' capacity to deal with the gradual introduction of political reform:

> "Remember that to these people...representative government and electoral institutions are nothing whatsoever...I am under the strong opinion that as government in India becomes more and more Parliamentary...so it will become less paternal and less beneficent to the poorer classes of the population".

It seems that every Westerner knew what was best for Asians.

The difficulties the provisional Chinese Republic had to overcome were enormous: the treasury was empty, government was divided between conservatives in Beijing and revolutionaries in Nanjing, there was every reason to be concerned that foreign powers would seek to take advantage of China's weakness and divisions. To add to the difficulty of dealing with these problems, the constitution proclaimed by Sun Yatsen failed to specify whether the Cabinet was responsible to the President or the National Assembly. Yuan himself had no doubt, and from then on began tightening his own grip on executive power and subverting every elected body that China's supposedly "constitutional" system tried to establish. A series of assassinations of revolutionaries culminated in March 1913 in that of – clearly by Yuan's own henchmen – Song Jiaoren, briefly one of Yuan's first ministers, a founder of the new Guomindang Party and leader of the majority in the newly elected National Assembly. This was followed soon after by the raising of a huge foreign loan without reference to the Assembly, as the constitution required, giving Yuan an entirely new independence of the south. Together these actions precipitated the so–called "Second Revolution" in July, an uncoordinated rising by a number of southern leaders. It was crushed by Yuan's troops; Nanjing was captured and sacked, Sun Yatsen fled to Japan.

The ineffectual Assembly then elected Yuan Shikai formally as President of the Republic under the new constitution – though not by a large margin, and only after three ballots, ahead of the southern republican General Li Yuanhong, who became Vice–President. The newly–arrived American Minister, P.S. Reinsch, met Yuan for the first time at this stage; more respectful than Morrison, he wrote that

"His expressive face, his quick gestures, his powerful neck and bullet head gave him the appearance of great energy. His eyes, which were fine and clear, alive with interest and mobile, were always brightly alert. They fixed themselves on the visitor with keen penetration, yet never seemed hostile; they were full always of keen interest. These eyes of his revealed how readily he followed – or usually anticipated – the trend of conversation...".

On the Double Tenth of 1913 Morrison was present for Yuan Shikai's formal inauguration, this time in the first and largest of the great pavilions that march through the centre of the Forbidden City, the *Taiheidian*, the Hall of Supreme Harmony, where both Ming and Qing Emperors had been enthroned. From then on his steps towards absolutism became more and more naked: in November the Guomindang was declared illegal, and all its members were expelled from the National Assembly. Several days later he cheerfully told Morrison that

> "Parliament was an unworkable body. 800 men! 200 were good, 200 were passive, 400 were useless. What had they done? They had not even agreed on procedure".

A week later the Assembly was "adjourned", and a puppet group was appointed to revise the constitution. In February 1914 the old Assembly was finally dissolved, and in May the new constitution sanctioned Yuan's dictatorship: complete control over internal and external affairs, power to appoint and dismiss ministers, power to rule by decree – and it provided for a new Legislative Assembly which was never convoked.

The foreign powers went smoothly along with this progression of misrepresentation, manipulation, assassination and intimidation: their concern was the protection of their concessions and investments. They had been unsure about Yuan's survivability to begin with: although Yuan became provisional president in March 1912, it was not until May 1913 that the first formal diplomatic recognition was extended to the Republic by the newly elected President Woodrow Wilson of the United States – influenced, perhaps, by Yuan's clever request to American Protestants to pray for China when the first National Assembly was to convene that April. Wilson declared that he did not know when he had been "so stirred and cheered". Britain's Sir John Jordan, however, was "outraged" at America's unilateral action in the absence of guarantees of foreign rights and investments by Yuan, a major aspect of which, in London's view, would have to be his recognition of Tibetan autonomy, though Yuan – like the Qing – had asserted that Tibet was a Chinese dependency. For six months both sides dug their heels in, until in October Yuan conceded, and Britain then also recognised the Republic of China. Japan followed, after securing agreement to further extensive Japanese railway deals, then Russia, once Yuan acknowledged the autonomy of Outer (i.e. present–day) Mongolia. Bit by bit the foreigners' acceptance of the new Republic was undermining Yuan Shikai as they undermined China's integrity.

Not long before, in August 1912, Morrison had been appointed by Yuan to be his political and foreign policy adviser. He was joined by a small united nations: a Japanese railway expert (not surprisingly, but he turned out a loyal employee), a French military adviser, a Belgian jurist.

Among the congratulations Reginald Johnston, then Commissioner in Britain's Weihaiwei concession, wrote that

> "*The Times*'s loss is China's gain. I am glad you are not going to throw yourself away on Australian politics".

J.O.P. Bland, a powerful business figure in Shanghai, where he had been *The Times*'s stringer until Morrison forced his dismissal in 1911 out of sheer jealousy, was understandably less laudable, but, as it turned out, more accurate:

> "I trust the good Yüan may find his newest adviser useful...All the same, for a man who does not speak Chinese to be adviser to a Chinese who does not understand English is a position unique in its way. Yüan will soon either be a corpse or a dictator...".[352]

Morrison, who had been intending to leave *The Times* because of a variety of dissatisfactions, was delighted to move to the centre of power, and proved – because of his enormous reputation as a brilliant correspondent – a very effective and influential apologist for the increasingly unappealing Yuan regime. Starting during a visit to England in the summer of 1914, he stretched the truth to the limit in his new role:

> "The prevalent view here", he said to the London Chamber of Commerce, "seems to be that China...is at present in a state of anarchy, the country fast drifting to perdition under the regime of an autocratic dictator of unbridled ambition. Such a view seems to me to be in direct conflict with all the evidence available to me".

Together with Sir John Jordan's parallel stance, Morrison's "evidence" on Yuan Shikai continued to prevail in London virtually to the end.

---

352 Bland had been co–author with the sinologue Sir Edmund Backhouse of a highly successful book *China Under the Empress Dowager*, based on a diary supposedly by a Manchu scholar related to Cixi herself. From the beginning Morrison had doubts as to the diary's authenticity; and it was in fact a complete forgery by Backhouse himself. This, and Backhouse's breathtaking list of other scams, have been uncovered in a marvellous investigation by Hugh Trevor-Roper: *Hermit of Peking* (London 1978).

Privately, he was a good deal less enchanted. A year earlier, after less than a year in his new position, Morrison had been decorated with the "Second Class Order of the Excellent Crop" by Yuan Shikai; what he really wanted was something else:

"What I want is work and no work is being given to me, that is to say no work is being entrusted to me. These suspicious Orientals suspicious of each other especially suspicious of the foreigner are impossible people to understand. Unwilling to learn the truth they have confidence only in those base and servile foreigners who tell them what they want to hear...No post is worth holding under the Chinese that does not carry with it authority and executive power. And I have neither the one nor the other...You cannot bustle the East. You cannot advise an Oriental like Yuan Shih–k'ai surrounded as he is by a cohort of unscrupulous Chinese jealous of the foreigner".

The following January he again confided:

"On no financial matter have I been consulted...nor are any enquiries addressed to me as to the standing of foreign concession hunters. My opinion in fact is not asked about anything more important than the shape of the President's hat".

His ignorance of Chinese – still, after sixteen years in Beijing! – does not ever seem to have struck him as an impediment to his usefulness. Nor, blinkered by his self–appointed mission as a strong advocate for Britain's imperial role – the Curzon–style role of bringing good government to those judged to need it, not merely commercial exploitation – did it seem to occur to Morrison that his lack of "authority and executive power" may have reflected a Chinese wish to govern themselves – however badly. Yuan's foreign advisers, the vastly knowledgeable Morrison included, were window–dressing to help keep the foreign powers from even more forceful "advice". In August Yuan awarded him the "*First* Class Order of the Excellent Crop", the highest honour authorised for a foreigner. It was followed by even greater exclusion.

Japan resumes expansion
China was soon to feel the impact of the armageddon beginning right then in Europe. On 23 June the heir to the Austrian throne had been

assassinated by a Serbian nationalist on a street–corner in Sarajevo. On 28 July Austria declared war on Serbia. Serbia's ally Russia began mobilisation, and on 1 August Austria's ally Germany declared war on Russia, two days later on Russia's ally France, and on the same day invaded neutral Belgium. On 4 August Britain, allied to both Russia and France, despite having been their opponent for most of the previous century, declared war on Germany over Belgium. The First World War had begun.

The first thing Morrison knew about it was an offer by Yuan Shikai, only days after the war began, to Britain's Sir John Jordan (as Dean of the Diplomatic Corps) for China to provide fifty thousand troops to assist in the capture of Germany's concession at Qingdao in Shandong province. The ineffable Sir John refused the offer on the spot without consulting his Allied colleagues or London; angry at the unexpected rebuff Yuan took some time before being prepared to offer any further assistance to the Allies.

In any case, one of them, Japan, was on an entirely different track. As early as 8 August Japanese warships arrived off Qingdao; on 15 August Japan sent Germany an ultimatum to hand over the concession by 15 September; on 20 August it informed the Foreign Ministry in Beijing that the situation no longer concerned the Chinese Government; on 23 August Japan declared war on Germany and besieged Qingdao. Helping its ally Britain was not its first concern: Japan wanted to grab German possessions in Asia and the Pacific before anyone else could get to them, at a time when the European powers were totally preoccupied with the unfolding horror in Europe. On 29 September, with Qingdao still under siege, Japan informed the Chinese that "military necessity" required it to take over the entire railway system in Shandong. Obviously smarting at Jordan's reaction, Yuan turned not to Japan's ally Britain but to the United States, telling Minister Reinsch

"From information in my possession, I am convinced that the Japanese have a definite and far–reaching plan for using the European crisis to further an attempt to lay the foundations of control over China. In this, the control of Shantung through the possession of the port and the railway is to be the foundation stone...it will bring the Japanese military forces to the very heart of China";

and Yuan asked that President Wilson approach the British to restrain their ally. As far as Shandong was concerned, it was too late to even try.

Reinsch recorded a perceptive remark by his colleague the Russian Minister about continuing political and social unrest in China:

"The situation itself does not impress me as serious", he said; "the only serious thing about it is that the Japanese say it is serious".

How serious became clear to Yuan Shikai on the night of 18 January 1915, when, having sought a private meeting, the Japanese Minister, Hioki Eki, presented what became known as the infamous "Twenty–one Demands". In doing so Hioki made a series of scarcely veiled threats: that there be absolute secrecy on pain of serious consequences; that "it may not be possible for the Japanese Government to restrain" Chinese revolutionaries, who had "very close relations with many Japanese outside of the Government,...from stirring up trouble in China unless the Chinese Government shall give some positive proof of friendship"; and that if Yuan Shikai himself, whom the Japanese people believed was strongly anti–Japanese, would grant these demands, "the Japanese people will be convinced that his feeling is friendly, and it will then be possible for the Japanese Government to give assistance to President Yuan". As if that were not clear enough, Reinsch noted, "the Chinese considered it an ominous fact that the paper on which the demands were written was watermarked with dreadnoughts and machine guns". It was assuredly not a coincidence.

Short of an outright threat to attack, the Twenty–one Demands were one of the most brutal ultimatums ever issued by a supposedly friendly country. The shock was the greater in that the Demands came from a government headed by one of Japan's oldest, most distinguished and most liberal politicians, Okuma Shigenobu. Born in 1838, three years before Ito Hirobumi, Okuma was one of the original Meiji Restoration oligarchy that had promoted and controlled Japan's development ever since; but he had been an early promoter of radical constitutional change and at seventy–six still had a reputation as a champion of popular rights. The liberalism for which he was known obviously did not extend to his foreign policy: as Prime Minister he saw rather to the interests of the industrialists who supported him, which in relation to China coincided with the ambitions of the expansionists in the Army.

These mutually reinforcing designs were evident in the overall thrust of the Twenty–one Demands: a strengthening of the controls Japan already exercised over Manchuria directly and through railway concessions, and their extension to Shandong and Fujian Provinces, giving it three centres from which Japanese military, administrative and economic influence could be extended over most of China. There were additional specifics, to extend Japanese influence over Inner Mongolia to strengthen its hold in the north, and restrictions on foreign economic activities in favour of Japan in the middle Yangzi valley. All this was bad enough, but finally came the notorious Group V demands: the employment of Japanese political, financial and military "advisers" throughout the Chinese Government, joint Japanese–Chinese control of major police forces, and the obligatory purchase of armaments from Japan or joint Japanese–Chinese arsenals. Japan, protesting that it wished to avoid any interference with the "integrity, sovereignty and independence" of China, was threatening to destroy all three. Hioki then demanded China's acceptance in principle of all Twenty–one Demands.

A stunned Yuan subsequently told Reinsch that all he could say to Hioki was "You cannot expect me to say anything tonight". In fact the Government as a whole was so stunned that they missed what Reinsch called its first opportunity: to immediately inform all the other foreign powers whose existing treaty rights in China would inevitably also be affected by such sweeping Japanese gains. But the threat to keep the Demands secret worked: when Morrison reported to Yuan two days later on the investigation he had just made into Japanese commercial activities in Manchuria – mainly opium, gambling, pseudo-aphrodisiacs and prostitution – the President, who was "extraordinarily cheerful", asked him how England viewed the extension of Japanese influence in the Yangzi region, and said the Japanese had swelled heads and caused him endless trouble. Yuan did not so much as hint at the Twenty–one Demands, which in due course Morrison described as "worse than many presented by a victor to his vanquished enemy". His former newspaper no longer shared his view; *The Times* blithely commented:

> "We are told that [the Demands] have caused a great commotion in Peking. There is nothing unusual about that. Commotion, genuine or feigned, is the ordinary result of all applications to Chinese authorities...These terms do not look harmful or unreasonable in principle".

As word – inevitably – leaked out about the Demands Tokyo simply flatly denied that there were any. Under pressure however from the other powers it finally, a month later, released the text of...eleven, omitting some of the Twenty–one and watering–down others. Later again it admitted to Group V, but insisted to third parties that these demands had been "mere suggestions" for China's consideration. Morrison discussed the Japanese move with a "doddering" Sir John Jordan, who said China had "brought it on herself"; he had told the Chinese Government "to be conciliatory and run no risks". Japan was, after all, an ally; but Washington was no more robust. President Wilson told Reinsch:

"I have had the feeling that any direct advice to China, or direct intervention on her behalf in the present negotiations, would really do her more harm than good, inasmuch as it would very likely provoke the jealousy and hostility of Japan, which would first be manifested against China"

– as distinct from Japan's current friendly "negotiations"?

As the Chinese tried wriggling out of the tight corner in which they had been abandoned the Japanese began making threats of military action to back the Demands: in mid–March China was informed a Japanese fleet had sailed for Chinese ports; this was followed by an increase in Japanese military forces in both Shandong and Manchuria. The Chinese kept the Americans fully informed as they continued to stall the negotiations, still hoping for support from Washington. Yuan told Reinsch:

"Against any action taken by Japan, America will not protest, so the Japanese officials tell us".

The Japanese were basically right. Morrison, who had commented scathingly of Jordan that

"The Japanese have kept him in entire ignorance of the demands have said nothing to him at all...and he knows nothing more than the man in the street",

was treated likewise by his employer, and had to find out what he could from the American Legation; as he fumed on 7 May, he was

" '*the political adviser*' who not once since the crisis arose has been asked a single question by any Chinese official. So entirely am I kept in the dark that correspondents...don't waste time to come and see me".

That very day Tokyo issued an ultimatum threatening military action if China did not accept its demands within two days. In delivering it Hioki bluntly stated, with diplomatically unprecedented candour, that

> "The present crisis throughout the world virtually forces my Government to take far–reaching action. When there is a fire in a jeweller's shop, the neighbours cannot be expected to refrain from helping themselves".

Britain, as China's neighbour's friend, had managed to persuade Japan not to press for acceptance of the Group V Demands; equally it and its allies advised China not to attempt armed resistance against Japan. The State Department cabled Reinsch, helpfully "counselling patience and mutual forbearance to both governments". Sir John Jordan now advised Yuan Shikai to accept the modified Demands.

Yuan had no alternative to doing so – and due to lack of coordination, the Chinese also unfortunately agreed to last minute Japanese insistence that they "postpone [the Group V Demands] for later discussion". Not that anything China agreed to or didn't agree to mattered to Japan: the dominant military and political war party in Tokyo determined to continue expanding Japanese power over those areas of its mainland neighbour that suited its interests. In 1931 this would result in the outright annexation of Manchuria – with the installation of the Manchu Puyi, deposed by Yuan, as the puppet emperor – and in 1937 in the beginning of an eight–year–long attempt to invade the whole of the rest of China. And Japan might very well have achieved Toyotomi Hideyoshi's ambition of three centuries before if it had not allowed its bitterness at American opposition to its aims there and in the Pacific to lead it to Pearl Harbour.

Emperor

The Chinese President had accepted Japan's demands; not so the Chinese people: widespread demonstrations, strikes and an extensive boycott of Japanese goods followed Yuan's surrender. They of course achieved no practical result, other than to become part of the political mythology of "National Disgrace Day". When Morrison saw Yuan two weeks later he found him uninterested in various business deals he (Morrison) wanted to talk about:

> "Japan is his obsession. Japan intriguing. Japan working against England, suffering from swelled head, trying to stir up strife in India

etc...The President had no continuity of policy, no constructive statecraft, his whole talk was...the need of endeavouring to wean the powers from the Alliance or understanding or agreement with Japan...[and guarantee] the integrity of China for a period of 10 or 20 years during which China could devote itself to the development of her resources...He is hypnotised and paralysed by fear of Japan like a frog in the presence of a snake. He is doing no constructive work, not a single industrial enterprise is being carried out in the whole country".

While Morrison was right about the stalling of development efforts, he might have been expected to be more aware of the seriousness of the Japanese threat to China. Perhaps the strong encouragement he had given as a journalist to Japan to go to war against Russia, in the years following the Boxer war, unconsciously continued to lead him to underestimate Japan's designs on China. It is curious at the very least that his anger at being excluded from the negotiations on the Twenty-one Demands should lead him to this petulant irritation at Yuan's preoccupation with the implications of having had to give in to them – with Group V still on the table.

But it was also of course a measure of Morrison's disillusionment with Yuan Shikai, with his own position as Yuan's adviser with no role, with the prospects for China. A couple of weeks later he wrote in his diary:

"How can a country become great and powerful ruled by Ministers of such matchless ignorance and corruption? How can a country become strong that has no Navy or Army, no strategic railways, whose territory is traversed by railways policed by the military of powerful neighbours, a country without industries, without...a currency, without a police service, without a single public work, whose cities have the most primitive form of government and taxation known, whose government enjoys so little confidence that no domestic loan is possible except by compulsory levy, who has no education system, who has no mining laws, whose Minister of Education is innocent of all knowledge either of administration or Western Education, whose Minister of Finance is ignorant of the rudiments of arithmetic, whose Minister of Communications is lethargic from much opium!"

It was all true, including the fact that the President, who had gathered all the power to himself by fair means and foul, was not focussing on it. Morrison set out his views in a message to one of Yuan's oldest and closest allies; but it was as much for himself as for China:

> "I prepare these papers so that I can subsequently defend myself", he wrote to Sir John Jordan, "so that it cannot be said of me what it may be said of others in similar position, that an adviser is one who tells you what you are doing is the proper thing to do".

Why did he not resign? Did he still believe, after three years of frustration and increasing isolation from Yuan himself, that he might still be able to play a useful role? Morrison was neither the first nor the last adviser who has found just closeness to power impossible to resist – like a frog in the presence of a snake.

Nevertheless, Morrison was right in saying Yuan Shikai was not focussing on the economy. What he was focussing on was the Dragon Throne. The former American Minister, Rockhill, had not been the only observer to wonder about Yuan's eventual ambition, and rumours surfaced from time to time during the first three years of his presidency that he had further ambitions. A change in the constitution in December 1914 confirmed the direction of Yuan's thinking: the Presidential term was extended from five to ten years, with no limit on the number of terms; a new term could be decided by the Council of State which the President appointed; and a successor could be nominated secretly by the President, allowing one of Yuan's sons to succeed should he so wish it.

This was as close to an hereditary monarchy as could be got without a crown. Why would Yuan want to press for more? There has naturally been much speculation about this. Some believed he saw himself as like one of the "deliverers" of China's earlier history, who, by overthrowing a declining dynasty, had claimed the Mandate of Heaven and founded a new one. Some thought it was Yuan's supporters who were responsible for the whole campaign, for the status and (additional) riches they thought they would be able to get out of a new dynasty, the leading candidate for this role being Yuan's eldest son, Yuan Keding, who stood to become Heir Apparent. Amongst all the cynicism, some, then and later, thought that while it was certainly Yuan himself pushing for a monarchy, it was not for personal aggrandisement but as a step that could help unify a nation which many – and not only Westerners – were still claiming was essentially monarchical at heart; it would be easier, on this view, for people to be loyal to the familiar emperor than to an alien constitutional principal. A strong element of this argument was that a restoration of Confucian tradition could strengthen resistance to Japanese depredations; the obverse was that Yuan had surrendered to the Twenty–one Demands in return for the promise of Japanese support for his ascent of the Dragon Throne. Apart from this last, which was comprehensively given the lie by the actual Japanese reaction, the various theories were not of course mutually exclusive.

Yuan himself made no public comment on the early speculation, and in 1915 the drama of the Twenty–one Demands silenced rumours for a time. By mid–year however it was clear that the attempt to restore the monarchy was no mere rumour. From here on the movement was never far from farce. While Yuan disclaimed any interest in the Throne – though reviving traditional rites and ranks of nobility – two groups of his supporters began competing with each other to create a "popular" monarchical movement. The faction which eventually seized the leading role created, in August, the "Society for Planning Peace and Stability". Four of the six founders had been active southern revolutionaries before 1911, opposed to Yuan, but obviously now with new ambitions; only one was a reluctant participant: the scholar Yen Fu, who had translated Adam Smith and John Stuart Mill into Chinese, and who joined up after receiving a message from the principal organiser saying

"Let me tell you candidly that I am acting on instructions of the highest authority, who insists that your name be included on the list of sponsors. It would be inconvenient for you to refuse, and it would be unwise to lose this opportunity".

The Society's first announcement caused something of a stir by citing a distinguished American academic, Professor F.J. Goodnow, the United States' "great expert in political theory", as declaring that

"as a political system, monarchism is actually better than republicanism, and that China should choose monarchism".

In 1913 Goodnow, Professor of Political Science at Columbia University, had been selected by the Carnegie Endowment for Peace to fill Yuan Shikai's request for an adviser on the drafting of a constitution; he found his position as unused and frustrating as Morrison found his, perhaps because, on the usual Western view that the Chinese people were too politically immature, he advocated the need to concentrate executive and legislative power in the hands of the President, at a time, ironically, when Yuan was still favouring a cabinet system of government; unlike Morrison, Goodnow left after a year, and went off to become President of Johns Hopkins University.

When Yuan invited him back in mid–1915 Goodnow took his old view further, producing a paper which spoke of a country's constitution as the product of history, tradition, and social and economic conditions, but adding that

> "almost all monarchies owe their origin in the last analysis to the exertions of some one man who has been able to organise the material power of the country in such a way as to overcome all competitors";

and on this basis he indeed concluded

> "It is not susceptible of doubt that a monarchy is better suited than a republic to China".

Goodnow appended the condition that the monarchy should be constitutional so that it would be supported by the people, but he was naïve, and he had not done his homework: too late he found out that his invitation had been organised by the Society for Planning Peace and Stability, which was not of course interested in conditionality. His endorsement embarrassed the American Legation, confounded the few senior officials and generals who were trying to persuade Yuan not to try to become emperor, and encouraged the sycophants to press full steam ahead on the advice of a leading constitutional expert from the foremost republic in the world. In September it was announced that a "National Congress of Representatives" – hand–chosen by "election" – would decide the issue. At the beginning of October, in an interview with Reinsch, Yuan, maintaining the fiction of being drafted,

> "assumed complete indifference as to the popular vote soon to be taken. 'If the vote is favourable to the existing system,' he said, 'matters will simply remain as they are; a vote for the monarchy would, on the contrary, bring up many questions of organisation. I favour a representative parliament, with full liberty of discussion but with limited powers over finance' ".

Apart from Goodnow, Yuan had no foreign support for his plan, constitutional or not. In October the Japanese objected, perhaps giving the idea that a monarchy would promote national unity more credit than anyone else did, but also fearing disturbances that could endanger its "interests"; it was the latter concern that led Britain, France, Russia and the United States to join Japan at the end of the month in publicly urging postponement of any move to a monarchy. Even Morrison urged Yuan to defer:

"I told him that I was opposed to the change at the present time, thinking the time most ill–chosen and unsettling to men's minds that energies ought to be devoted to work not to futile changes in the title of the ruler";

and to his diary he raged again self–pityingly:

"Here am I political adviser kept in entire ignorance until the campaign has started of the intentions of the President to break all his promises and cast to the winds all his declarations, and engineer himself to the throne. Never would he accept the Imperial Yellow and yet under the influence of his son" – "half–paralysed...half–witted", he noted elsewhere – and his discarded first wife, he is manoeuvring himself to the throne. This is in accordance with the prophecy of the Japanese and Sun Yat–sen. He makes himself, his country, and his advisers a byword and a derision".

Yuan paid no attention. Over the ensuing month an avalanche of carefully orchestrated messages was sent to Beijing from all over the country imploring him to ascend the Dragon Throne. A confidential official telegram was sent to provincial governors and commanding generals"

"The following words must be included in your messages exhorting the president to accept the throne: 'We, the representatives of the people, represent the true wishes of the whole nation in urging the present president, Yuan Shikai, to assume the title of emperor and in giving him all the powers of an emperor. May Heaven save him. May his sons and grandsons inherit this position for a myriad of generations to come".

Everyone was instructed to supervise the destruction of this and two further similar messages in person.

On 21 November all 1,993 members of the National Congress voted in favour of Yuan's ascension to the throne. Zhou Ziqi, one of Yuan's closest supporters, told Reinsch:

"We tried to get some people to vote in the negative just for appearance's sake, but they would not do it".

Sensible people. On this basis, on 12 December, the Council of State adopted a memorial proposed by the Manchu and ex–heir to the Throne Prince Pulun urging "Your Holy Majesty" to accept the Mandate of Heaven. According to tradition, Yuan twice rejected the proposal, then accepted it the same day. Three days later Yuan began handing out titles of nobility, the same day that the Ministers of Britain, France, Russia, Italy and Japan delivered a statement, orchestrated by the Japanese, frankly doubting Yuan's ability to maintain order during the change–over and stating with fine diplomatic ambagiousness that they would "reserve their rights, maintaining the attitude of vigilance as to the further development of the situation" – in other words, withhold recognition if he went ahead. Sir John Jordan was not happy about Britain's participation in this démarche: he complained to the Foreign Office that the Japanese

"have been making themselves and us ridiculous by all these representations which have produced no effect except antagonising the Chinese...We all feel that we are so many puppets pulled by Japanese strings".

Japan was well aware that the European powers were preoccupied with the war in Europe.

Yuan himself was unfazed. It was announced that his new dynasty would be called Hung–hsien,[353] "Grand Constitutional Era", which fooled no–one, and an avalanche of decisions and decrees followed on preparations for Yuan's enthronement: a new great seal in jade, new imperial robes for the Emperor and high officials, new gilding and new carpets for the Hall of Supreme Harmony, and (Reinsch recorded with

---

353 Hongxian in Pinyin; but in its abbreviated circumstances I have retained Hung–hsien throughout.

amusement) "a nicely upholstered throne" from Beijing's Western–style department store. On 23 December Yuan, still President of the Republic, performed the most sacred rite of the Emperors of China: making the offerings to Heaven on the day of the winter solstice, at the Temple of Heaven, to pray for bountiful harvests in the coming season. The Manchus' faithful Reginald Johnston was appalled:

"When Yüan stood in all the splendour of his imperial sacrificial robes on the central square of the great marble altar, with only the stars above him, he was as near to being emperor of China as any man below the throne could be. It would seem, however, that the divine being whom he thus solemnly invoked at dawn on that winter morning was not deceived by the outward display of glittering regalia but looked straight into the soul of the man who wore them, spurned his sacrilegious sacrifice and rejected his presumptuous claim to be the Son of Heaven".

With republican cynicism the Minister of the Interior cheerfully told Reinsch:

"Of course the worship will not guarantee good crops, but at any rate it will relieve the government of responsibility".

On the last day of 1915 it was announced that the Hung–hsien reign would commence on 1 January 1916; the enthronement was to follow in a few weeks.

Lame duck
In fact the new reign commenced a week after the beginning of its end:

"Suddenly, on Christmas Day", Reinsch recalled, "came the report that an opposition movement had been started in Yunnan Province. A young general, Tsai Ao [Zai Ao], who had for a time lived in Peking where he held an administrative post, had left the capital during the summer and had coöperated with Liang Chi–chao [Liang Jizhao, Kang Youwei's chief lieutenant during the Hundred Days reform in 1898, subsequently Yuan Shikai's Minister of Justice]...Liang Chi–chao attacked the monarchical movement in the press, writing from the foreign concession at Tientsin. General Tsai Ao returned to his native Yunnan, and from that mountain fastness launched a military expedition which was opposed to the Emperor–elect. So the dead unanimity was suddenly disrupted. Now voices of opposition came from all sides".

Yunnan declared its independence. Zai Ao turned out to be a brilliant commander, and rapidly carried the revolt into Sichuan province, and subsequently Hunan and Guangdong.

Some in Beijing were not impressed. On 14 January Sir John Jordan wrote that

> "the Yunnan movement is one of those things which have marked the beginning of all dynasties in China and is accepted as an ordinary incident in Chinese history";

on the 19th Reinsch himself recommended to Washington immediate United States' recognition of the new monarchy. Yuan himself affected to be similarly sanguine: he had immediately begun reinforcing Sichuan at the beginning of January, and by the middle of the month he told Morrison the revolt would be quelled in twenty days. Ominously, however, he could not find a general willing to take command, and ended up directing the campaign himself from a supreme headquarters set up in the palace he had had built in the Nantai park on the west of the Forbidden City. In contrast to what has been called Zai Ao's ability "to achieve superb coordination among the different segments of his expeditionary force",[354] Yuan's troops were receiving commands simultaneously from Beijing, Chongqing and Chengdu.

Yuan himself was not entirely focussed on the challenge to his Empire: he was practising for it. During January Morrison made notes on a dress rehearsal in the Hall of Supreme Harmony:

> "Yuan Shih–k'ai sitting with his Crown; 3 thrones at his side for the 1st 2nd and 3rd wives on descending levels. First wife came in arrayed; kowtowed; took her proper seat. Long delay and 2nd wife the Korean wife, failed to come. Sent for peremptorily. She came in but refused to take her seat, saying Yuan had promised her a throne on the same level as the No.1. Hearing this, No.1 jumped down from the Throne and went for No.2 with her fingers.

---

354   E.P.Young: *The Presidency of Yuan Shih-k'ai*

The Master of the Ceremonies…was supervising the Enthronement, but he could not lay impious hands on the struggling Empresses, where upon Yuan waddled down from the throne and tried to separate the two combatants. Order was finally restored but the rehearsal was postponed".

No–one, perhaps including Yuan himself, ever knew exactly how many wives and concubines he had; his eldest son said there were sixteen sons and fourteen daughters.

It was not just military confusion that was revealing the Emperor's clothes. Reinsch wrote later:

"The Chinese are fatalists. The movement to carry Yuan into imperial power had seemed to them irresistible; many had therefore suppressed their doubts and fears. But when an open opposition was started they flocked to the new standard and everywhere there appeared dissenters…hesitation and delay strengthened the opposition".

It was not quite as inevitable as that; though unfortunately for Reinsch's judgement at the time, the situation was such that on 21 January, two days after his recommendation to Washington, Yuan decided to postpone the still–unannounced date of his enthronement, presumably not solely because the rehearsal had gone badly. Then at the end of the month Guizhou [Kweichow] Province declared its independence. But it was still only the second province to do so; elsewhere there was still apathy, indifference, uncertainty – and caution:

"The prevailing fear of Japanese intervention on behalf of the secessionists", a Chinese subsequently observed, "made many staunch advocates of republicanism hesitate to oppose the coming of the change in government".

Such a perception might have suggested to Tokyo that continued diplomatic representations were not having the desired effect. And, if so, this might have contributed to a shift to far more active Japanese intervention in support of the anti–monarchists.[355] The Japanese Government

---

355 Japanese policy decisions are from Kwanha Yim's research in the Japanese Foreign Ministry Archives for *Yüan Shih–k'ai and the Japanese*

had been debating, since before the formal decision to restore a monarchy, whether to press for its cancellation, watch developments, or accept and recognise it. The 15 December note delivered by the Allied powers – pulled by Japan's "puppet strings" – had reflected the second alternative. Japan was also able to put economic pressure on Yuan by opposing foreign loans, on which he was dependent, at a time when very little money was available from Europe in any case because of the situation there, and the United States was not prepared to fill the gap.

But there were forces in Tokyo who were determined to move policy up to the first alternative, and at the end of December the Army, with Gaimusho complicity, moved General Aoki Nobuzumi – "known and admired", Yim says, "for his outspoken enmity towards Yüan and his advocacy of continental expansion" – to Shanghai to support "anti-Yüan movements throughout the southern part of China". Aoki reached China shortly after Zai Ao's revolt in Yunnan; but there may have been Japanese input through General Li Liezhun [Li Lieh–chun], who had led the "Second Revolution" against Yuan in 1913; he had travelled to Yunnan via Japan where he had close connections, and it was his army as well as Zai Ao which led the revolt. Japanese agents were supplying arms to Yunnan; General Aoki would supply more elsewhere in southern China.

Yuan thought he still had a Japanese card of his own to play: he had earlier nominated the ineffable Zhou Ziqi as his personal representative at the coronation of the new Emperor Taisho of Japan, as a gesture of friendship towards his brother monarch which he clearly hoped would be reciprocated; but after a lavish farewell banquet for Zhou on 17 January Minister Hioki "suggested" that he not go as Japan's allies were "doubting its sincerity" in opposing the monarchy. This embarrassing public rebuff was just the beginning. Two days later the Japanese Cabinet, under further pressure from the Army, took the decision not to recognise the Chinese monarchy, even if the Yunnan uprising did not stop it. It was the day of Reinsch's call for recognition, and, more significantly, two days before Yuan's postponement of his move – though whether he already had a whiff of Japan's new policy is not known. When Reinsch saw the Emperor–elect in mid–February he was still calmly playing the role of draftee:

> "I have not sought the new honours and responsibilities, but now that a course of action has been formally decided upon, it is my duty to carry it out".

Six days later, on 22 February, Yuan announced the second postponement of his enthronement.

As February went on, the revolt began to stall and even be reversed in the face of the large reinforcements Yuan had sent south, to the extent that the Japanese Army reached the conclusion that it would be defeated unless Japan intervened decisively. As a consequence, on 7 March the Cabinet adopted a seven–point program for immediate implementation:

"(1) *Establishment of Japanese hegemony in China*...Japan was to secure this on Chinese soil and make the Chinese people accept it. This was considered to be an essential condition for promoting friendly relations between the two countries.

(2) *Elimination of Yüan Shih–k'ai*. Yüan was held to be a chief obstacle in attaining the first objective. The text of the decision emphatically stated 'whoever may come after him, the new one will serve Japan's interests better than did Yüan'.

(3) *Let the Chinese themselves get rid of Yüan*. This was a better method; but Japan should be prepared to take steps in order to benefit by the change.

(4) *Avoid open intervention*. Related to the third item; this would save Japan from embarrassing criticism abroad.

(5) *Recognition of southern belligerency.*

(6) *Aid to the anti–Yüan forces through civilians*. The government should do nothing to discourage civilians from extending assistance to the dissident elements.

(7) *Unity of action*. All governmental activities should be coordinated by the Gaimusho".

Yim added that

"Paragraph 6 was phrased carefully so that assistance could be given to the Manchu royalists in southern Manchuria as well as to the Yünnan rebels".

In reality, the seven–point program was just a further extension of the Okuma Government's Twenty–one Demands: it did not really involve any new departure in the way Japan construed "friendly relations" with China. The same day it was adopted in Tokyo General Aoki gave Morrison the fanciful persiflage that Japan was opposed to Yuan "because he violates the teachings of Confucius. He was not faithful to his Empress, he is not faithful to his people".

What is again not clear is the extent to which the programme became known to Yuan; but the contending sides in China were so porous that it would be hard to believe he did not come to have some knowledge of Japan's intention to ratchet up the pressure begun with the Twenty–one Demands and now directed against him personally as well. After his forces' recent successes there was also a setback: on 15 March Guangxi changed sides, but this was still only the third province against him after nearly three months of hostilities. It therefore seems more likely that it was the Japanese threat that led Yuan on 22 March to decree that the Hung–hsien Empire was abolished, and that he would remain as President of the Chinese Republic. The Empire lasted eighty–three days, seventeen shorter than the Hundred Days Reform.

"How could I dare to aspire to the throne from simple ambition?", Yuan's proclamation stated; "But the national representatives did not understand how sincerely I longed to decline the honour. Since then some people suspect that I have been moved by dreams of power. Truly, my lack of virtue is to be blamed for the compliance with the wishes of others which has brought discord on the country".

The Empire went out with the same fictions as it had come in.

Reinsch commented on the suddenness of the decision – and on the fact that such a unilateral concession,

"without a guaranteed *quid pro quo* by way of submission to the Central Government by the revolting forces, came as a surprise".

This was certainly the reaction amongst some of his main supporters, while for their part the revolutionaries had gone too far to be able to return to Yuan's fold whatever it was called. Or wish to – they still wanted him out.

"Thus", Reinsch commented, "the President had lost his friends and failed to placate his enemies".

Not least, the Japanese. And it soon became abundantly clear in China. On 6 April Guangdong declared independence, followed by Zhejiang

[Chekiang], just south of Shanghai, on 21 April. The revolution had broken out of the southwest. It was no longer just a question of losing the Empire; the question now was whether Yuan would be able to keep the Presidency.

In between the two provincial moves, the Chinese Minister in Tokyo had appealed to Foreign Minister Ishii Kikujiro, undoubtedly on Yuan's instructions, for the Japanese Government to ease pressure on the President because there was no–one else in China who could replace him. Ishii, according to Yim,

> "replied coldly that President Yuan would be welcome to bring his family to Japan and spend the rest of his life there".

When Morrison saw Yuan at the end of April – having just been "ashamed to admit" that he had not seen him for nearly three months – he received the same refrain: a "podgy" Yuan returned to it again and again –

> "The South say, if Yuan retires order will be restored. The North declares, if Yuan retires, China will be broken up. If he retires, who will maintain order? I [Morrison] said to him, if order were not maintained in Peking...immediate Japanese armed intervention would be invited...Japan was all ready to send troops to Peking... He knew this".

As the conversation went on, Morrison on this occasion seemed to show a less realistic view of the rebellion than Yuan did:

> "I said surely the Southern leaders realise that continuation or extension of the present turmoil means Japanese intervention. He said they seemed rather to desire such intervention...He asked me did I think the Japs would use military force to remove him from his post? I said no. Yet they were determined he should retire? I said they were but they would use other means...He said their policy was to starve him in finances...Japan was furnishing munitions also to the rebels".

Yuan still clung to office, but he now agreed to turn over full governmental powers to a newly–installed cabinet: according to Reinsch, he "ceased his personal control over all important branches of the

Administration". Authority over the Army, with the exception of Yuan's twenty–thousand–strong "bodyguard", was transferred to the Minister and Board of War. Although he still had the loyalty of many military commanders, Yuan was no more than a figurehead. And even those loyalties increasingly slipped away: Shaanxi [Shensi] Province declared independence on 9 May, Sichuan on 22 May, Hunan on 25 May.

"All reports of local troubles", Reinsch wrote, "coming from reliable sources in various parts of China spoke of the participation of Japanese in revolutionary activities...It is not clear whether the Japanese were systematically working for the establishment of an independent government in the south, or whether they were merely covertly encouraging opposition to the Central Government, to foment division and unrest".

Yuan's own thoughts now turned away from saving his Presidency to saving himself: Ishii's sarcastic offer of exile in Japan being spurned, Reinsch "was sounded as to giving him safe conduct and asylum" in the United States. But he could no longer move, confined to his room during the latter half of May as his health gave way. Not that Yuan had been visible before: Reinsch noted that since his arrival at the end of 1913 Yuan had left his palace compound only twice. His contact Zhow Zuqi told him that now

"The President's power of quick decision has left him; he is helpless in the troublesome alternatives that confront him. Formerly it was 'yes' or 'no' in an instant...Now he ruminates, and wavers, and changes a decision many times".

It was not for much longer. By the last days of May Yuan's health was clearly deteriorating rapidly, despite – or possibly because of – the ministrations of several Chinese and three French doctors. On the morning of 6 June he died, of uremia and nervous exhaustion. He was still only fifty–six.

Despite the utter collapse of the Imperial scheme, Yuan's funeral procession on 28 June, judging by Reinsch's description, sounded extraordinarily like that for the Empress Dowager as described by Morrison eight years earlier, though on this occasion there was more of a mixture of resurrected Qing ceremony and modern accoutrements: traditionally–attired heralds, infantry and cavalry, musicians playing "weirdly plaintive" dirges, Buddhist monks beating drums and cymbals, a "soul tablet" in a sedan chair, lines of officials bearing food offerings and attributes of Yuan's personal life, family mourners in white; and interspersed, Western–style military bands playing funeral marches, senior generals in full–dress uniforms of Prussian influence, Chinese and foreign Ministers in frock coats and top hats. Most spectacular of all was the catafalque bearing Yuan's body, covered in crimson silk embroidered in gold, and carried by a hundred men "by means of a complicated arrangement of poles". The Empress Dowager's catafalque had been borne by eighty men inside the city walls – but by a hundred and twenty outside.

Yuan's body was then carried by train to a traditional tomb which had already been constructed near Anyang in Henan Province, not far from the Garden for Cultivating Longevity where he had waited to be called back to supreme power in Beijing four tumultuous years before. It is still there,[356] crowded–in now by post–Cultural Revolution offices; but the long traditional "spirit path" of gateway, columns, statues of animals and men, stele pavilion, incense burner, sacrificial hall and five sacred vessels leading to the tumulus at the far end have all been preserved. The paired statues of men are an unusual feature for a supposedly Imperial tomb: two civil officials in traditional full–length court robes, and two soldiers – in the tasselled cap and uniform with epaulettes and sash of a German officer, standing at parade rest with their hands on their swords. And the military figures have the short, stocky build, the drooping moustache, and features very much like those of Yuan Shikai.

Legacy

Before Yuan died there had been an unseemly squabble in Beijing as to whether the Vice–President could succeed a President who had torn up the constitution under which his deputy had also been elected; it was only partly over principle. In the event the succession went unnervingly smoothly: on 7 June Vice–President Li Yuanhong became President in a simple ceremony. All the provinces, including those that had declared their independence from Yuan Shikai, telegraphed their support for the new President. It did not last: Li was merely the first of six presidents, assisted or thwarted by twenty–five cabinets, that contested for power

---

356 I regret I have not seen it. The following description is based on the fully–illustrated article by Barry Till in *Arts of Asia*, Vol.19 No.6, November–December 1989

during the next twelve–year "warlord period". Yuan is usually blamed for this chaos, as many of the warlords were his old commanders; but there was a cruel irony in this outcome: Yuan had developed a large and disciplined army, beginning under the Manchus, precisely to restore a strong central government that could prevent the disintegration of China.

Within a decade almost all of those in this century's–end cavalcade were gone. Witte had died, full of bitterness and apprehension, three months before Yuan. Typically, the Tsar greeted his greatest servant's demise with frivolous venom: leaving for the battlefront he wrote to the Empress –

> "I am going with such a calm in my soul that I am myself surprised. Whether it is because I had a talk with our Friend" – the evil Rasputin – "or because of the newspaper telling of the death of Witte I don't know".

Theodore Roosevelt, having been defeated in 1912 in his bid to be elected President again, died early in 1919, shortly before his vanquisher, Woodrow Wilson, in the context of the Versailles settlement, betrayed China by supporting all Japan's claims to a special position there. China's friends in Congress repaid him by defeating American membership of his League of Nations.

In 1920 Morrison followed. Staying on with President Li Yuanhong, he was now increasingly hostile to Japanese expansion in China and the South Pacific, and working particularly to persuade China to join the Allies in the war against Germany (which it did in 1917), not least because – ever supportive of the British Empire – he believed that, with its twenty million Moslems, China's participation would have "a material effect upon Mohammedan feeling in India, Persia, and Mesopotamia". Britain's last great imperialist, George Curzon, now Marquis Curzon of Kedleston, died on 20 March 1925. He had joined the British War Cabinet in 1915, and from 1919 to 1924 had been Foreign Secretary through the Versailles and other post–war conferences. But he too died disappointed: expecting to succeed as Prime Minister in 1923, he had been ruled out because he was no longer a member of the House of Commons. He had never visited Asia again.

Eight days before Curzon's death Yuan's first republican challenger, Sun Yatsen, had also died. From his exile after his defeat by Yuan in the "Second Revolution" he had returned as generalissimo of a separatist regime in Guangdong in 1916; he was forced out after sixteen months, made a comeback, was forced out again after another sixteen months, but finally became in 1917 head of a southern republic based on Canton. After his death his body remained unburied until his Guomindang successor, Chiang Kai-shek, had it interred in 1929. The year before, thieves had broken into the tombs of three of the Manchu Emperors in the Eastern hills and of Cixi herself – her body, stripped of its funeral robes and regalia, was thrown to the dogs. 1928 was also the year in which Chiang Kai-shek turned on the Communist Party of his former ally, Mao Zedong, and established a Nationalist Chinese Government in Nanjing.[357] In 1931 Japan, pursuing unfinished business, would begin to implement, by military force, the first in its 1916 seven–point programme: hegemony over China.

Yuan Shikai's failure, as much as anything, lay in not recognising that, while many Chinese still wanted an effective central government – not least to be able to stand up to the increasing Japanese threat – key figures in the political–intellectual class and among the generals them-selves were no longer prepared to accept a personal authoritarianism which toyed with, ignored, and then overturned constitutional ideas they saw as being able to secure a wider power base and a more stable system of government. He had never really moved on from the political model of the Imperial dynasties: even where he had instituted reforms they were designed to re–energise or reconstruct it. Was he doing it for China, as he and his defenders claimed? – or purely for personal ambition, as his detractors, then and since, have insisted? Are not political leaders ambitious because they believe they know what is in the best interests of their country?

Sir John Jordan was almost alone in speaking well of Yuan when he died. He wrote to the Foreign Office:

"I have a great personal liking of the man and feel both his loss and the manner of it acutely...During his early life in Korea he

---

357 In considering the end of empires, it is interesting to note that when President Richard Nixon was preparing for his visit to China in 1972, the French literateur–politician (and sometime thief of antiquities from Angkor) André Malraux told him he had once asked Mao, ruler of the People's Republic of China since 1949,

"if he did not think of himself as the heir of the last great Chinese emperors of the sixteenth century. Mao said, 'But of course I am their heir' ".

formed friendships with a number of Englishmen...and to his last day he remained a firm friend of Great Britain...Almost the last time I saw him, he said that he had been on very friendly terms with Englishmen since his early manhood and that he had learned to trust and like them. Of this he gave innumerable proofs by appointment of British advisers...by sending three of his sons to school in England...and in general by his admiration for British ideals...I could go on indefinitely reciting acts to the credit of my dead friend – for simply as a friend I shall always remember him... He fell in an unequal struggle and to me he was greater in adversity than he had been even at the height of his power".

Sir John was probably not the first and was certainly not the last ambassador to believe he had a unique relationship with the head of the state to which he was accredited, and that this confirmed said head's admiration for the ideals the ambassador was supposed to represent.

Morrison, as one of those British advisers, did not see his appointment in such rosy terms. He wrote later that he recalled

"vividly many of the endearing qualities of the famous ruler, his generosity, his kindness, his loyalty to his friends, his consideration for others, his invincible good humour and courage under difficulties";

but Morrison inevitably came back to the issue on which he had always been so frustrated and which gave the lie to Jordan's breezy encomium:

"The most striking characteristics, as I observed them, of [Yuan's] relations with the foreigners was his caution, his unwillingness ever to give full confidence".

And his summary of his time with Yuan crystallised the complaint he had made so often over the previous four years:

"I honestly believed in the greatness of China's future, and I was anxious to be associated with her rise to power...taking part, perhaps a leading part, in the *guidance of a semi–civilized country along the paths which alone can lead to success and honour*".[358]

---

358   Emphasis added

The Earl of Elgin would have been proud of him.

Which brings us back to ceramics, where Elgin's actions in 1860 started this chapter – though not, this time, to breakages. In late 1915, at the same time as Yuan was ordering the new trappings for his new Empire, he sent one Guo Baochang, with enamels that had been held in the Forbidden City, to order the re-opening of the former Imperial porcelain manufactory at Jingdezhen [Ching–te–chen], east of Boyang Lake in northern Jiangxi Province, and to supervise the manufacture of 40,000 pieces of Hung–hsien Imperial porcelain. As the former workshops and kilns had decayed since the fall of the Qing in 1912, Guo contacted some of the most skilful potters and painters who were still in the area to carry out the commission.

The first idea, in accordance with Yuan's interest in the archaic as distinct from the merely traditional, had been to copy "Ru" style, the imperial pottery of the Song dynasty of 960 to 1279 CE; but after investigations for materials had begun in the original manufacturing areas it was recalled that the Song had succumbed to a series of foreign invasions – notably that of Kublai Khan. So it was decided to imitate instead the delicate "Gu yue xuan" style of famille–rose porcelains made during the long peaceful reign in the 18th century of the Emperor Qianlong – builder of the Yuan Ming Yuan and Giuseppe Castiglione's patron. How much was actually able to be made between the order and the cancellation of the new Empire in March 1916 is not known.

In fact it is typical of so much of Yuan's career that when experts came to examine surviving pieces of this porcelain in the 1970s a polite controversy erupted in the leading Asian art journal *Arts of Asia* over how much had been made, when, and with what identifying marks on their base.[359] The balance of opinion was that some porcelain had been made for Yuan before the declaration of the Empire, and probably continued to be made afterwards until late 1916, with marks indicating they were intended for use in his principal palace, or that they were made "in the first year of Hung Hsien". But the final word in the debate came in a letter from someone who knew one of Yuan's daughters–in–law, who had been living in Hong Kong for many years; and the presumably, by then, venerable lady recalled from her days in Beijing that

---

359 The relevant articles and letters are in *Arts of Asia* Vol.7 No.2 March – April 1977, Vol.7 No.5 September-October 1977 and Vol.8 No.2 March – April 1978. The following descriptive terms are from Rose Kerr: *Chinese Ceramics* (London 1968), as is the concluding quotation.

"Among the pieces ordered were ordinary dinner and tea services for the family's use and those to be bestowed on his followers as commemorative gifts. All these bore the mark of Hung Hsien Nien Chih in iron red"

– made, specifically, "in the reign of Hung Hsien", during those first eighty–three days of 1916. These translucent eggshell porcelains, glazed with a warm tone and decorated in delicate enamels (to use Rose Kerr's words) are Yuan Shikai's finest legacy.

Forty years later, in a different era of Chinese history, a contributor to a history of Jingdezhen wrote:

"With the failure of Yuan Shikai's imperial reign, the department set up to supervise the making of official ware was also closed down. Now this group of ancient buildings is used as an army barracks. Their broken roof tiles and damaged walls can be seen, between the long grass, in the light of the setting sun. These ruined old halls are the remnants of the history of the factory and are going to crumble away unregarded".

Just like Yuan Shikai.

Broken Connections:
A Sort of Summing Up

Silence is the real crime against humanity.

Nadezhda Mandelstam

Some of the tensions, conflicts, misunderstandings and obsessions that occupied our ten characters are still evident today. In their chapters we were mostly looking at personal connections between people and places. This summing up looks more at the connections between states and societies now: not at each of the societies we have been concerned with, rather at some of the historical developments in which the ten characters were involved – as players or as others' playthings – which form the background, and in some respects the foreground, of connections that still exercise a significant influence on our own world.[360]

Heritage
At the price of gross oversimplification, two broad phases can be identified over the Millennium that brought us up to the 20th century, and with the speeding up of everything in the latter, two more are apparent. The first phase, the growth of ethnically-based nationalism, is still around in some respects, though this understandable but highly dangerous development was largely established by around the middle of the Millennium by the Europeans who had begun moving in that direction two centuries or so before. The second, the growth of imperialism, the conquest, rule and exploitation of others, was also developed to a wide extent by Europeans in their overseas empires in the second half of the Millennium; but the establishment of empires by overland conquest, practised from ancient times and still going, has not always been recognised as having the same essential characteristics.

---

360 For brevity, themes are cross-referenced to individual chapters in the book simply by their century.

The first of the two 20th century phases was one of human and physical destruction and devastation: the two World Wars begun by Germany but eventually extended far wider than Europe, especially the Second when Germany was joined by Japan, and the appalling human costs of the totalitarian dictatorships of Lenin and Stalin, Hitler, and Mao Zedong. The second phase, heavily influenced by the first, involved implementing widely-accepted objectives that turned out to embody inherent contradictions: the establishment of the United Nations to prevent wars, and the dismantling of the European overseas colonial empires (but not others), this proliferation of independent countries adding to the institutional difficulties of an international organisation based on, in some cases, highly antagonistic nation states.

Nationalism and imperialism

Humanity, unfortunately, seems to be more marked by intolerance than by any other characteristic: religious, racial, national, political, geographic, ideological, ethnic, social, philosophical, economic, cultural – just about any form of intolerance you can think of. People define themselves mostly by membership of one or more groups; and these groups tend to define themselves by contrast with other groups. These others may or may not be actually competing; but this sense of the otherness of others slithers all too readily and all too often between smugness, envy and rage.

The worst crimes of which we know come within these categories. No religions can claim their hands have never been bloodstained; some of their practitioners' hands still are. Few races can claim never to have exploited, misused, enslaved or killed those on the far side of the river, the mountains or the ocean – those whose main culpability has been their different ethnicity. At an extremely early time tribe began fighting tribe, but this custom became increasingly deadly as tribes coalesced – or were bulldozed – into larger and larger groupings, the culmination of which was the nation state – widely regarded in the 19th century as the epitome of human social and intellectual progress. But then we had the 20th century.

In the earlier centuries of this last Millennium the development of a sense of independent national identity ran directly counter in Europe to the Catholic Church's claim to universal dominion, itself based on the universality of ancient Rome. But although wars during this period were usually contests between competing royal dynasties, the ethnicity of their main support bases proved more cohesive than did creed, as we saw in the Scottish resistance to the territorial ambitions of England's King Edward [1300]. From this time on powerful monarchies consolidated their hold over areas formerly independent or belonging to other dynasties, until by around mid-Millennium present-day Britain, France and Spain became geographically recognisable. Germany's diffuseness fluctuated with the authority exercised by the reigning Holy Roman Emperor; Italy's was united by the cultural vigour and splendour of the Renaissance. And with territorial influence and power at stake, the leadership of the Church divided on parallel lines throughout Western Europe, until the more drastic split precipitated by the Reformation created a new alignment of creed and nation. But even then, for the next few centuries alliances still frequently fluctuated more on the basis of nation than confession [1700].

Nationalism was not of course a purely Western development. Indeed, one of the most significant, in the longer term, was Vladimir of Kiev's establishment of Russia's identity as a separate nation by his own and his people's conversion to Orthodox Christianity [1000]. That the Russian Chronicles claimed this conversion was based on a careful evaluation of all the neighbouring religions and the explicit rejection of the others – Catholicism, Islam and Judaism – served to underline the exclusive nature of Russia's relationship with the Orthodox Byzantine Empire and Church which it copied; and this translated into Russia's uniqueness when it claimed to be the Third Rome after the Ottoman Turks' final destruction of Byzantium. Russia's Orthodox Church, with its doctrine of serving God through serving the State, created as much as it endorsed the pretensions of the Tsars; and this sense of Holy Russia being not only set apart from everyone else, but set apart on a higher plane, has been a defining theme in its attitude to its neighbours and the rest of the world right through Tsarist Russia, into the Soviet Communist Party's claim to be "the Vanguard of the Proletariat" and can still be seen in Vladimir Putin's Russia.

But the sense of national identity was never solely European: the Cambodians of Angkor clearly saw themselves as different from the Cham on the east, the Burmese and, later, the Thai on the west, even though they all shared the same devotion to Buddhism [1200]. Jayavarman VII had no more inhibitions about wiping out the ruling Cham dynasty than the English and French did in fighting a Hundred Years War. And as we saw in the commentary by the Chinese traveller Zhou Daguan on Angkor just after its heyday, there could be no mistaking the sense of ethnic separateness, and superiority, of the Han

Chinese. Chinese separateness and superiority was not the result of a turning-in of the Middle Kingdom: it was "middle" precisely because it had such a long and extensive, if not in all cases intensive, relationship with its neighbours in all directions, and superior because at most times and in most respects it found, like Zhou Daguan, the neighbours wanting. The fact that this attitude could survive right through the rule of conquerors, like Zhou's Yuan (Mongol) Dynasty employers and the Qing (Manchu) Dynasty over almost the whole of the last third of the Millennium, reflected the extent to which these usurpers adopted Chinese customs and attitudes, and succeeded in persuading themselves and foreigners alike that they were the genuine article. When Mao Zedong repudiated Moscow's claim to be the unique interpreter of the new orthodoxy of Marxism-Leninism (which of course reflected Russia's historical tradition), he was reasserting that traditional sense of China's own uniqueness and centrality. Mao, mercifully, has gone: but China's sense of itself is growing with its economy.

Imperialism, too, goes back a long way before this last Millennium, but we first came across it in Tamburlaine's conquest of the whole of the centre of Eurasia, from southern Russia to the Persian Gulf and from Damascus to Delhi [1400]. We saw parts of its later development in the wake of the great European sea voyages [1500], especially in 16th century Japan, with the competitive probing of European priests and merchants [1600] and in China right up to the beginning of the 20th century [1900]. European imperialism manifested itself in three main ways: in the conquest of native populations, and rule over them which might range between brutal and benign but which always involved economic exploitation; in the forceful displacement of native populations from their ancestral lands, rarely with any kind of compensation, to enable the establishment of permanent European settlements; and in the tragic and horrific African slave trade, in which, over three and a half centuries, some thirteen million slaves were shipped from Africa to the Americas.

By 1800 Europeans had appropriated all of the Americas, North and South, and made a good start on South and Southeast Asia and Australia. The United States, having thrown off British rule, then spread its own rule westwards over Native Americans, and picked up pieces of territory from France by purchase[1800], and Spain and Mexico by conquest. By around 1900, although Latin American countries had wrested their independence from their Iberian masters, the other European imperialists between them had spread their tentacles even further, over all of Africa and the rest of Southeast Asia, where they were joined by the United

States; and Britain had consolidated its hold over India despite a serious semi-nationalist uprising against it mid-century. The Russian Empire, avoiding, like the United States, the opprobrium of colonialism by grabbing extra territory overland rather than by sea, had pushed aggressively eastwards to incorporate all the Central Asian khanates from the Caspian Sea to the border of Mongolia, and the huge eastern Maritime Province down the Pacific coast as far as Vladivostok – 142 square kilometres *per day* for a hundred and fifty years.

The unstable areas between the Russian and British Indian Empires, rent by warring tribes and dynasties, became in the 19th century the scene of the so-called Great Game, espionage, counter-espionage, missions of "protection" and campaigns of annexation as the Russian Empire pressed south to hedge British influence and expand its own, and British officials in London and India acted to counter real and imaginary Russian designs on Afghanistan, Xinjiang, Tibet, and the Subcontinent, with China largely an ineffectual onlooker in its own former spheres of influence. The "Game" was anything but for the populations involved: it ranged from the brutality of the Russians in Transcaspia, to the repeated incompetence of British invasions of Afghanistan and an unauthorised invasion of Tibet, and to pure farce when the lone Russian and British foreign Consuls isolated in Kashgar in far west Xinjiang did not speak to each other for two years [1900].

Not much of the world was left to its own devices. There was the Ottoman Empire, which had by now lost its Balkan provinces to Russian and West European sponsors, but which still maintained its tottering authority over all the Middle East except for Egypt; Persia, under the undistinguished and almost finished rule of the Qajars, successors to the Safavids; Thailand; Japan, "opened" by the United States in the 1850s after two and a half centuries of closure to the outside world by the victors over Toyotomi Hideyoshi [1600]; and, increasingly precariously, China. The Qing Dynasty now ruled a Chinese Empire no larger than that held by the Ming, having lost its earlier gains in Xinjiang and Tibet, and the imperial powers were pressing their economic and political interests increasingly aggressively on its coastal and riverine provinces. The first Chinese revolt against these foreign pressures, the Boxer Rebellion, preceded by only five years Japan's devastating defeat of Imperial Russia and the destruction of its navy; Japan's turning the tables on Europe paved the way for its own conquest of China [1900], but the idea of Asians – and others – freeing themselves from European domination became a realistic prospect.

By the 19th century the European empires were regarded by their rulers as great national achievements, especially the British, over which "the sun never sets". Britain completed its dominion over the Subcontinent and Malaysia, the Netherlands over Indonesia, France over North Africa and Indochina, both Britain and France over great swathes of Sub-Saharan Africa, with Italy and Germany carving out small portions like those the Portuguese had held long since. Everyone picked up everywhere enclaves and islands, "unclaimed" bits and pieces. The European powers' claim to be bringing enlightenment to "the natives" was based on racism but it was also fostered or at least condoned by a muscular Christianity which saw the profits of global economic exploitation as a sign of Divine favour, a viewpoint that has not disappeared with the empires.

During the 20th century, these assumptions began to be questioned, albeit in a very selective manner. America's President Woodrow Wilson gave powerful impetus to the idea of national self-determination at the end of the First World War, but at the Versailles conference it came to be applied only to the losers, resulting in the dismantling of the Austro-Hungarian Empire as well as of Germany's overseas empire. At this stage the victorious West Europeans' collections of overseas dominions and colonies were not regarded as fit for independence. Bolshevik Russia also excused itself from the growing opprobrium of imperialism. Lenin and Stalin speciously equated it with capitalism when it suited them: Nazi Germany was imperialist before the Ribbentrop-Molotov Pact, and again afterwards, but not during, and the United States and its West European allies continued to be "imperialists" even when their colonies had become independent; the Soviet Union itself, of course, was not, even though it had forcibly incorporated the Ukraine and the Caucasian and Central Asian states.

An important factor in the end of empires was the enormous encouragement to ideas of nationalism and freedom from European domination given by Japan's spectacular victory in the Russo-Japanese War in 1904-1905, when it demonstrated that a small Asian country could defeat a major European power. During the century, with a strong lead from the Indian Congress Party of Gandhi and Nehru, the demand for national self-determination spread to all the West European Empires. Nehru himself was inspired by Japan's victory; but unfortunately it was at the expense of the enslavement of Korea for half a century and the military conquest of a large part of China; Japanese imperialism was also overtly racist, and in a shorter time-span managed to be just as brutal as Western [1900].

Calls for self-determination were reinforced by a contradiction in European imperialism itself: while philosophical objection to colonialism as such grew very slowly, progessive thinkers and forward-looking governments in the home countries, wanting to make the colonies more efficient administratively and more profitable economically, began introducing native education, not only locally on a more or less broad basis but also in the metropole for the élites. The irony was that in the latter they learned doctrines of Westminster democracy and *Liberté, Égalité, Fraternité* which sat very ill with imperial rule based on racial superiority and guns. And, in due course, they undermined it.

War and ideology

Nationalism and imperialism are still with us, sometimes in transmuted forms, but still as capable of evil as ever. As we have seen, it has not been only Western states that have inflicted their damage on other states or societies; but Western ideas and Western technology were responsible for their transformation into the ideologically-based totalitarian dictatorships that blighted the 20th century. The extent of the control that (listing them chronologically) Lenin and Stalin, Hitler, and Mao Zedong established over their populations would have astounded their predecessors; the sharpness of their hostility to unbelievers and other non-members shocked the rest of the world. Both the Soviet Union and Nazi Germany were fortunately extinguished again during the century. China, on the other hand, was re-established by Mao Zedong to a greater level of cohesion and international influence than under any of the old Dynasties; but fortunately for the people he dominated and experimented with, he too eventually went, allowing his system to begin to mutate, at least economically.

For much of its existence between 1917 and 1991 Bolshevik Russia and later the Soviet Union was regarded as a successful democratic socialist experiment by an extraordinary number of foreigners fed propaganda propounded by beneficiaries of the system. These were the progeny of Karl Marx's dialectical analysis of history that predicted the dictatorship of the proletariat as the inevitable solution to the poverty and inequality in 19th century Europe. But those foreigners were not listening carefully: the USSR proclaimed itself to be based on Marxism-*Leninism*; and Lenin, like Stalin, believed in the dictatorship of the dictators, the Communist Party that they successively controlled with iron fists and that in turn similarly controlled a proletariat that was as powerless as everyone else in the country.

The relationship between state and party was closer in practice to that which had existed virtually since the time of Vladimir of Kiev between the imperial autocracy and the Orthodox Church than it was to any genuine democratic or socialist tradition [1000]; the only contrast was between the Church's long-standing aversion to doctrinal change and Stalin's nightmarish arbitrary changes of the Party line, in the service of autocracy in the one case and totalitarianism in the other. Stalin, who had four times as long in power as Lenin and more than twice as long as Hitler, also ranged more broadly across the domestic political, economic and racial spectrum for the targets of his paranoia: opponents, presumed opponents, and possible opponents in the Communist Party; with exquisite timing on the brink of the Second World War, the military High Command; a good part of the Ukrainian peasantry and, everywhere, the so-called kulaks, anyone who owned so much as a horse and who might therefore oppose what turned out to be the disastrously unproductive collectivisation of agriculture; whole populations – Crimean Tartars, Volga Germans, peoples of the northern Caucasus, suddenly deemed to be potentially traitorous in the face of the Nazi advance – cattle-trucked to Central Asia, their lands given to Russian settlers; after the war, all the German soldiers who had been prisoners-of-war, sent to the Gulag; and in due course, the Jews, the old Russian habit, a new pogrom cut off by Stalin's timely death.

Although the facts were known pretty much all along, there were far too many people who regarded them simply as anti-communist propaganda until Khrushchev, who had emerged as Stalin's successor, shocked the Party and its domestic and foreign faithful in 1964 by admitting some of them. The numbers who died in this staggering series of purges were enormous: around twenty million before the war (as calculated by the dogged research of Westerners like Robert Conquest), and several millions more in the vast concentration camps of the Gulag afterwards. Unlike Hitler's victims indiscriminately spread across almost every country in Europe from Coventry to the Caucasus, Stalin's victims were mainly his own citizens. Some Soviet de-Stalinisation and still inadequate post-Communist revelations have confirmed a good deal of the crimes committed by Lenin, Stalin and their comrades; but there have been no trials, no full-scale official enquiries, no proper recognition of the vast murderous wastefulness of forcing an entire people into a megalomanic strait-jacket, no monument to its victims. And the embalmed Lenin still lies in state in Red Square.

Hitler's "Thousand Year Reich" began in 1933 thanks to other German political parties' divisions, pusillanimity, and underestimation of his ruthlessness. His opponents, on the left and the right, both inside Germany and in the Western democracies, made serious misjudgements in the years before and after his rise to power; Stalin, for his own devious reasons, supported Germany's rearmament in the early 1930s, then maintained a non-aggression pact with the Nazis (after splitting Poland with them) from 1939 to 1941 while they conquered Western Europe and North Africa. Nazism was a descendant of the old-fashioned Prussian militarism that we saw when it was first being instituted on a national scale by Sophie Charlotte's son, Frederick William I, with his "thick scull'd Heroes...and Contempt for any thing th't looks like learning" [1700]; but, drawing on the useful precedent of Stalin's ruthlessness, Hitler transformed it, along with his "willing executioners", into a machine designed not merely to achieve military domination of Europe but to eliminate the continent's entire Jewish population and permanently enslave the peoples of Eastern Europe.

These were unprecedented dimensions even for a Europe whose ambitious nationalisms had sparked the continent-wide wars of Louis XIV, Napoleon and Kaiser William II. In the Holocaust, the culmination of the Europe-wide anti-Semitism that has been noted in these pages since the First Crusade [1100], Hitler came close to completing his purpose, with six million Jews killed; his second objective resulted in perhaps an even greater number of deaths in Russia and the Ukraine as resistance to enslavement there prompted the extensive massacre of Soviet military personnel as well as civilians. Perhaps fifty million people died in the conflict in Europe, ten million of them civilians, twenty million in the Soviet Union. But no-one really knows.

The war which Hitler had begun became truly global at the end of 1941 with Japan's simultaneous surprise attacks on Pearl Harbour and the Southeast Asian colonies of the United States and Hitler's European opponents; the defeat of Germany and Japan then took until 1945 and required the combined and total effort of almost all the rest of the world. Japan, under an imperially-sanctioned military dictatorship, had been invading northern and central China for ten years by 1941, but as we have seen, Japan's efforts to dominate Asia began in the period from its surprise attack on China in 1894 to its surprise attack on Russia in 1905, the defeat of both, and the annexation of Korea [1900]. Japan's rule of Korea was overtly racist, designed to stamp out not only any Korean sense of independence but also any sense of identity: the Korean people as a whole were reduced to something close to slavery. Later, amidst other racist atrocities during its invasion of China, the Japanese Army in 1937 massacred three hundred thousand people in Nanking over the course of a few days, more than the casualties of Hiroshima and Nagasaki combined. Total numbers of Chinese killed by Japan's war against them between 1931 and 1945 have been more difficult to estimate than most: the Chinese were too disorganised politically and geographically to keep any sort of a count, the Japanese saw no point in recording the fate of people it regarded and treated as vermin. The best estimates think a figure of around twenty million is likely; and to that must be added deaths caused by Japan's invasions of Southeast Asia and the Pacific islands and the campaigns to push them back.

The horrors inflicted by the two atomic bombings have rightly caused much soul-searching about the reasons and justifications for them, in both the United States and Japan; but in the latter its military aggression and often brutal occupation policies, in Korea and China especially, have largely been avoided, even where they have not actually been denied. Indeed, Japan's neighbours are regularly enraged by new governmental school text-books justifying or ignoring the brutal policies of 1905-1945. And Japanese leaders still pray at the *Yasukuni Jinja*, the shrine where Japan's war criminals are commemorated along with its war dead.

Mao Zedong restored the territorial integrity of China that we saw being carved up during and especially at the end of the 19th century [1900]. Internally his victory ended the incessant and destructive jockeying of the warlords who had inflicted misery and ruin on most of China since the death of Yuan Shikai; but his dictatorship went on to exercise a level of all-pervasive control that the country had not even experienced during the reigns of the most powerful Ching emperors in the 17th-18th centuries. When that central power was used in the 1950s and 1960s to implement brutal policies designed primarily to prove Mao's Marxist-Leninist supremacy over the ideologically-deviant Soviet communist leaders, the people, as usual, paid. The total numbers killed as the result are even less known than those in the Soviet Union: something like 30 million died in the famine the "Great Leap Forward" caused between 1958 and 1961; unknown further millions died in the ensuing violence of the "Great Proletarian Cultural Revolution" between 1966 and Mao's death in 1976 – along with the deliberate destruction of a great deal of China's cultural heritage.

Communist China's extraordinarily secretive leadership and extraordinarily efficient control of information about everything have meant that much of the history of Mao's rule is still not known; despite economic de-Maoisation since his death, the tightly held Chinese leadership of his collaborators and their protégés had no interest in revealing crimes in which many had themselves been implicated or done nothing about. The successors to the original court have enthusiastically embraced a vast economic transformation, but have equally fiercely continued to resist political change; there have been no public enquiries, no proper recognition of the vast wastefulness of forcing another people into a variant murderous megalomanic strait-jacket. And the embalmed Mao Zedong still lies in state in Tiananmen Square.

Stalin's Russia, Hitler's Germany, Mao's China, Imperial Japan: 120,000,000 killed, a chilling monument to what ideas and technology of European origin allowed these murderers to achieve in the ruthless pursuit of their misbegotten utopias. These monstrous systems dominated the three-quarters of a century during which I have lived to such an extent that I find it hard to believe we have seen the last of their kind. Germany alone, of all these dictatorships that made such a wreckage of the 20th century, has made serious and sustained efforts to investigate how such an appalling period in its history came to pass, to hold some of its perpetrators and accomplices accountable, and to make some but obviously inadequate amends to its victims. No-one else has tried, leaving the seeds for hankerings after the restoration of national "glory" or ideological "purity", and preserving the same old idea that these systems can not have been as bad as their critics and opponents have claimed. Their disastrous failure, in a summation from the British historian Alan Bullock's great study *Hitler and Stalin: Parallel Lives*,

> "does not mean the end of ideology. Continuing inequalities and injustices can be expected to keep alive the search for a just and more equitable society and for myths [or, I would add, visions] to sustain the hope of creating it. In the same way hatred of foreigners, fears of a flood of refugees and increasing tensions in multi-racial societies can be expected to keep alive ethnic antagonisms and the racist fantasies that sustain them. It remains an open question whether these will produce new versions of millenarianism, based on class, race or religious fundamentalism".

The deconstruction of empires

Within the first quarter of the 20th century, the empires of the authoritarian states were gone, with varying degrees of outside pressure but basically because they were all discredited, their internal support collapsed: in 1911 the Chinese Empire, corrupt, derelict, oppressed by foreigners; in 1917 the Russian Empire, vainglorious, morally bankrupt, militarily and politically incompetent; in 1918 the German and Austro-Hungarian Empires, bombastically over-ambitious, militarily and economically defeated by the First World War that Germany itself had precipitated; and in 1922 the Ottoman Empire, the dismembered husk of its former empty shell. Of the western European empires that still survived, the British and French actually grew with the redistribution of the German Empire's colonies and the carving up of the Ottoman Middle East, though in all cases as "mandates" (i.e. not outright colonies) under the League of Nations, President Woodrow Wilson's effort to end all wars, doomed from the start by his failure to persuade his own country to participate.

The huge human and economic costs of the Second World War completely undermined the authority of and the capacity to maintain the remaining European Empires. Japan again contributed to their downfall in Asia when it expelled France, Britain and the Netherlands – as well as the United States – from their colonies in Southeast Asia; and United States President Franklin Roosevelt, leader of the overwhelmingly dominant post-war Western power, was determined that his wartime allies would not resume their old possessions on any sort of permanent basis; and the Soviet Union, which had used the war to swallow the Baltic states, and indirectly (and sometimes directly) the whole of Eastern Europe, avidly supported national liberation movements with propaganda and, where it could, money and arms.

The game was certainly up. The British began the dismantling, in India in 1947, incapable of continuing economically, but by now also unwilling to do so philosophically or politically. In futile battles, costly in human, economic and political terms, France, the Netherlands and Portugal all tried to resist what in the aftermath of the War seemed inevitable, and in due course they all lost to economic weakness, domestic hostility and international opprobrium. These once-great imperiums were lamented only by the old guard aristocracies and the civil and military placemen who had still enjoyed the privileges of rule during their twilights.

The outcome of the disappearance of the old European Empires, and the bit-by-bit dismantling of the colonial system that had dominated recent centuries, was the explosion in the number of nation states. At the beginning of the 20th century there were only about 40 independent states in the world, and the achievement of national independence for everyone was a major goal in the establishment of the United Nations.

In 1945, 51 nations founded the Organisation; there were 82 at the first General Assembly I attended fourteen years later, and membership increased by a further 40 over the next seven years up to my fifth and last in 1966. In 2011 there were 193 members, including Russia's former colonial possessions – the Ukrainian, Baltic, Caucasian, and Central Asian so-called "Republics" of the USSR – that it lost (though some not yet entirely) in 1991.

The dismantling of the old empires was followed, not surprisingly, by recriminations about the state of the political institutions, economies and societies that they left behind. One significant legacy was the national borders the colonial powers had created, often artificial, dictated by military-administrative reach or deals with other European empires with little regard to ethnic or other pre-colonial coherence. Nevertheless those existing frontiers for the most part had to stay, for want of any practicable, let alone peaceable, means of rearranging or reversing political and social structures, economies and languages; the major exception, the division of the Subcontinent into India and Pakistan, was a major tragedy. Perhaps more important than legacies of the old colonial systems were the bi-polar pressures of the Cold War. Some leading newly independent countries sought to establish a "non-aligned" grouping, but as the United States was commonly seen as the successor to Anglo-French hegemony an even-handed position was rarely sustained.

Another legacy has been "neo-colonialism", described in various ways but essentially referring to what is regarded by some as the inability of almost anyone in the former colonial powers, Britain and France in particular, and now the United States, to regard or interact with the former colonies and their peoples as equals, with a concomitant aura in the latter of victim-hood and sometimes self-exculpation for ongoing problems. There is of course no question that various aspects of the experience of imperialism have influenced the present, some damagingly; but there are as well other pasts, internal to different states' traditional political, religious and social values, that have also affected their present situation.

Some countries, while not forgetting their interrupted pasts, have nevertheless been successful in focussing on opportunity rather than blame, to produce varying degrees of economic and social advancement, by a variety of paths not always internally consistent, immediately effective politically and economically, or in all cases acceptable to Western democratic opinion: witness the remarkable achievements we see now in India, most of Southeast Asia, South Korea and China.

These states have shown that the creation of a new present and a more hopeful future derives from the conscious and deliberate evaluation of the past as well as of the present, for the contribution they can both make or the constraints they can both impose. Westerners sometimes still regard non-Western societies as unchanging. That is their mistake and will be their loss: non-Western societies will increasingly prove such views irrelevant.

But there are still many former colonial territories where political stability and economic development have remained elusive if not absent. The colonial experience, though progressively more distant, is still often blamed for this, and there is no doubt that the traumas of racial, political and economic subjection are not easily overcome, just as their ancestors' experience of slavery is still traumatic for African Americans, and of dispossession of their lands is still traumatic for Native Americans, Australian Aborigines, and other native peoples elsewhere. But there is no single reason for post-colonial state failure: problems of ethnic rivalry, poor climatic conditions, bad agricultural practices, lack of administrative and technological infrastructure, education and leadership, venal political ambitions and practices, all come into it, sometimes all in the same place at the same time.

On the other hand, more than by colonial policies or neo-colonial attitudes, the rich countries have disadvantaged many of the poor by a range of protectionist trade practices, excessively demanding investment arrangements, and punitive intellectual property regimes, especially in pharmaceuticals. Foreign aid is often uncertain, insufficient, unsustained, sometimes based more on donor policies than recipients' needs, stadiums for demonstration effect rather than long-term basic health programmes – but unfortunately too often misappropriated by venal leaderships anyway. In various places around the world we can see political and military ambitions and rivalries which result in domestic or cross-border conflicts, often with ethnic components; and they are then often compounded by consequent refugee flows, some of them huge. Notwithstanding critiques of colonial borders, nationalism within them remains more powerful than cooperation across them.

The absent Middle East

The Middle East largely fits into this category of states which have failed their peoples, despite the vast oil resources possessed by some of them. After appearing several times in chapters in first part of the Millennium, the region has been notably absent from the West-East contacts we have looked at since the sea routes were begun by Western navigators and traders mid-Millennium.

This lacuna of course mostly reflects my choice of people and places. But it also reflects the reality: not only the precipitous decline in the overland trade and social exchanges across the Silk Road, but also Islamic withdrawal from intellectual and social interaction with a Europe undergoing rapid scientific and industrial modernisation and consequent social change, and Europe for its part leaving engagement with the Moslem world largely in the hands of travellers, archeologists, novelists and painters. I have neither the knowledge nor the temerity to attempt to evaluate the variety of reasons scholars and protagonists have given for this situation; but the continuities and contrasts with earlier times become apparent when noting the disparate pattern of nationalist, doctrinal and ideological differences that now characterise the Middle East.

For the first millennium and a half of our era the Silk Road between the Mediterranean and China was the primary means for the wide range of exchanges from which virtually all its participants benefitted – commercially, spiritually, intellectually, technologically, culturally, culinarily. Within this great Eurasian web the Islamic societies at its centre came to play an often brilliant role, inventive and imaginative in their own right as well as preservers and transmitters of classical Greek medicine, astronomy and philosophy, of Indian mathematics and science, of Chinese technology. But then Western maritime innovation, enterprise, and aggressiveness displaced these vibrant threads – and the Islamic states and societies not only all but disappeared from European view, but also lost a great deal of the vitality they had previously displayed while at the centre of the known world.

Islam's triumphant expulsion of Christian Crusaders in the 12th-13th centuries did not lead on to a revival of the brilliant Abbassid Caliphate: the Mongols saw to that; but the following centuries saw elsewhere in Islam new peaks of military, political, intellectual and cultural achievement. First came Tamburlaine's brutally successful but short-lived domination of the whole of central Eurasia, though the artistic and intellectual flowering which was nourished for a while longer under his Timurid offspring in eastern Persia did not long survive the murder of his grandson Ulugh Beg in 1449 [1400].

The Ottoman Turks next seized the flame: already masters of Bulgaria and Serbia in Europe as well as of Anatolia, in 1453, only forty-five years before Vasco da Gama's epic first European voyage to India, they swept the sad remains of Byzantium into oblivion; they went on to add Greece, Syria, Egypt and Arabia to their empire, and to reach the peak of their glory a century later under Sultan Suleiman the Magnificent (1520-1566). This was just before Persia's last great flowering, under the Safavid Shah Abbas the Great (1586-1628); successful militarily, he also unleashed Persians' creative genius, as well as, interestingly, being in active contact and exchange with Europe, India and China. Contemporaneously with Suleiman, Tamburlaine's great-great-great-grandson Babur was founding the great Moslem Moghul Empire in India, which reached its peak under his grandson, Shah Abbas's contemporary Akbar the Great (1556-1605); he also encouraged active exchange with the outside world, and within his own with people of other religions, Hindus, Jains, Christians. This brilliant society outlasted Ottoman and Safavid greatness alike; but it faltered under the military obsessions of Akbar's great-grandson Aurangzeb, was fatally weakened by Persian invasion, and was finally terminated by longer-term British depredations.

The problem, for the future of the Middle East, about these Islamic military triumphs – symbolised by Tamburlaine's Samarkand, Suleiman the Magnificent's Constantinople, Abbas the Great's Isfahan, Akbar the Great's Agra – was, and is, that none of them was *Arab*. These great cultural flowerings were all based on military success; but there has been no Arab triumph of a comparable nature since the victory of Saladin (though, ironically, he was one of the subsequently reviled Kurds) over the Crusaders at the end of the 12th century – and no brilliant Arab intellectual or cultural renaissance since the last great flowering under the Abbassid Caliphs Harun al-Rashid and his son Ma'mun at the turn of the 8th-9th centuries.

After Suleiman, the Ottoman Empire began its long decline; but the Arab Middle East remained firmly under its control, and its deadening hand stifled enquiry and innovation in administration, the arts, and the sciences just as the Enlightenment in Europe was beginning the transformation of political and scientific thinking that led in due course to the American, French and industrial revolutions and the modern world. Moslem sovereigns and their followers, like their Christian counterparts in Western Europe, fought each other century after century to expand, preserve or recover their dynastic, territorial or economic power; after extremist Shi'ites took control of Persia, in 1500, they and Sunni Moslems were able to share with their European contemporaries the experience of fighting to the death to protect and, whenever possible, impose alternative versions of the One True Faith, a phenomenon repeated, with the Ayatollahs' recovery of Iran in 1979, down to our own time.

The question of balance between zeal and tolerance has long been argued in, and about, Islam, in relation both to these divisions between the faithful themselves, and to confrontation with the infidel, especially the other Peoples of the Book, the Jews and the Christians. For both the latter, the issue became inextricably mixed up in the 19th and 20th centuries with Arab resistance to European colonialism, and to European Zionism.

The Western colonial interlude inserted into a faltering Moslem world was longer in North Africa than in the Arab Middle East: France annexed Algeria from 1830 until, after a bloody war of independence, it was forced to cede it independence in 1962; it established "protectorates" over Tunisia from 1882 and Morocco from 1912, both until 1956; Egypt was ruled in practice (but not annexed) by Britain from 1882 until 1954; and Libya was annexed by Italy between 1912 until the latter's defeat in 1943 in the Second World War, following which it was ruled by an Allied Military Government until the United Nations took over between 1949 and its independence in 1951.

Western colonialism in the Arab Middle East, on the other hand, was a relatively short period by comparison with most imperiums: outside Egypt, it only began following Turkey's involvement on the losing side in the First World War, with the victors' allocation, under the 1920 Treaty of Sèvres, of League of Nations "mandates" over the former Ottoman provinces of Lebanon and Syria to France and Iraq, Palestine and Transjordan (now Jordan) to Britain; and these were terminated by the independence of Iraq in 1932 and of Lebanon, Syria and Jordan in 1946. These states' accession to independence varied from the peaceful transfer of power to violent revolution, but usually did not result in a democratic system of government, not altogether surprising in societies where often tribal, ethnic and religious origin dictated allegiances.

Colonialism in the Arab Middle East, with its European domination and economic exploitation, had not been ameliorated in the eyes of Arab nationalists by fitful efforts to introduce education, industry and public works. In addition, the large gap in Islamic experience resulting from the relative isolation of the Ottoman Empire from movements transforming the West was compounded in the 20th century when some Moslem leaders came to repudiate modern scientific and intellectual developments and even secular education as manifestations of the strongly-resented colonial presence; some religious leaders have opposed the very idea of innovation, as undermining Mahomet's perfect revelation of the ideal society. Arab marginalisation thus also owed more than a little to the legacy of its own nationalist, religious and social rigidities and antagonisms. The Cold War added new dimensions to Arab disorientation: the USSR had supported the foundation of Israel, but cynically shifted to the Arab side to undermine Western interests in the region; the United States too readily supported dictators so long as they were anti-communist. From the viewpoint of the Arabs, the Cold War resulted in a continuity from European colonialism to American heavy-handedness.

While Iraq, Lebanon, Syria and Jordan all gained independence peacefully, Palestine was another matter entirely. Britain was unable to resolve Jewish demands for an independent state and Arab refusal to countenance it, with the result that in 1947 the United Nations, including the USA and the USSR, voted to partition Palestine between the already-warring Jews and Arabs. The latter vowed to resist partition in 1948, when the British finally withdrew and the Jews proclaimed the State of Israel, and again in wars in 1967 and 1973. The failure to provide for the Palestinian Arab population, by both the departing colonial power and the new state of Israel, and the Arab states' long refusal to accept the internationally incontrovertible existence of Israel, created a bitterness that has been exacerbated by fanaticism and terrorism whose roots are partly religious, partly political, partly simply – or rather extremely complicatedly – territorial. Too many Israelis and Palestinians, including among those in political and religious authority, pursue the ideological chimera of their respective visions of victory; whereas their accumulated history leaves them with having to face the excruciating but inexorable choice between the compromise of peace but not justice for all, and what ought to be the appalling prospect of no peace or justice at all for anyone.

In the wider Arab Middle East the marginalisation which began under the Ottomans, and largely continued under the colonial/Cold War experience, goes on. It seems foolish, and dangerous, not to recognise how this impacts on Arab and indeed other Moslem countries where poverty, frustration, ignorance, intolerance, and repression provide a galling contrast with Islam's long-ago glorious central role in Eurasian exchanges of the arts, scholarship and commerce and a ripe field for ideologues and extremists.

In 2001 the marginalised reinserted themselves into the centre of everything, not with goods and ideas, but with a terrible bang. At the beginning of a new Millennium, extremist Islamic fundamentalists add another layer to the already troubled relationship between the Middle East and the rest of the world. Now, when considering relations between the West and the Moslem world, there is argument as to whether and what extent the present situation reflects these external factors or nationalist, religious and social rigidities and antagonisms within the region and its societies themselves, and over the respective influence of traditional Islam repudiating the West and the West not engaging seriously and respectfully with the Arab world. I am not qualified to make judgements on which factors have been or are still responsible for the very considerable gaps that have become so obvious in Western-Islamic intercourse and understanding.

Nations united?

By mid-century the multi-nation age of imperialism had evolved into a world dominated by two super-powers: the Soviet Union and the United States, each with its allies, and most of the growing number of newly independent countries in the middle. During the forty-year Cold War there was frequently a tendency in the latter, for various reasons, and in too many Westerners concerned by the dangerous standoff, to make a false equation between the two sides, a refusal to recognise that the Soviet Union was a brutal dictatorship behind its sham democratic façade and its Warsaw Pact allies totally subject to Moscow's direction, or to recognise that the United States for all its faults was a functioning democracy, its NATO allies also democracies which were at times a pain in its neck.

By the end of the Millennium the world-equation had changed again: the collapse of the Soviet system in the USSR and its East European sphere left the United States as the sole, initially somewhat uncertain, super-power. But, early in the third Millennium, this position tempted a right-wing American government to seek to exercise a dominating and increasingly ideological role everywhere, including over its European allies, whose European Union has not proved sufficiently coherent as yet to produce a persuasive alternative pole. The simultaneous rise of China, however, still politically authoritarian but increasingly economically powerful, and increasingly willing and able to project itself internationally, is reopening the future shape of the world equation.

The dramatic changes in balance of power have led to a crisis of confidence in the patiently constructed post-Second World War multilateral system. While the United Nations has the scope to – and has had some success with – dealing with political and social conflicts and crises, blaming it for failure to act in this or that situation is as completely misplaced as it is widespread. It is no more than a voluntary association of nation states, and it thus does not have the power to enforce political outcomes or arbitrate solutions that are not acceptable to significant parts of the membership, or the ability to provide disaster relief that is not adequately financed by the membership. The even more misguided paranoia in the United States in particular about the United Nations being a sinister "World Government" would be laughable if it did not contribute so apparently strongly to American rejection of cooperative solution-seeking to international problems. Unfortunately the eight years of aggressive unilateralism exercised by the United States at the start of the 21st century seriously set back international cooperation, just at a time when the challenge of terrorism makes such cooperation even more essential, including for the United States' own security.

Working through the United Nations to try to secure action or solutions that will be workable because they are acceptable is an extremely complex task requiring great patience; overall solutions are rarely instantly achievable, and most efforts can be furthered only in incremental stages; all can be undermined by the excessively narrow nationalist objectives of major member states or significant groups of members. The multilateral system is certainly far from perfect; but it is better than any alternative so far attempted, and almost always certainly better than war except in the most dire circumstances.

In some ways the most striking achievement of the post-War world has been by the long-warring states of Europe – leaving aside the recent wars of religion and ethnic cleansing in former-Yugoslavia and the war of religion in Northern Ireland: unwarranted, unspeakable, the participants only degraded by their blindness and brutality. But that the most difficult and tragic past can be consciously put behind – though still certainly not forgotten – has been demonstrated by the enormously encouraging creation of the European Union, even though it has obviously not yet resolved, and may never completely resolve, the tangled legacy of nationalisms of which Europeans have made such a disastrous world-shattering speciality. This has been the result of a long, often tedious, sometimes acrimonious, not always successful but almost universally patient exercise of determination, restraint and vision.

If anyone could visit us from the last turn of a millennium they would undoubtedly observe that we have failed to make much progress with human nature; but we have succeeded beyond anyone's wildest imagination with human cleverness, so that we now have the capacity, if we have the will, to better the lives of most of the planet's population. Unfortunately, they would also notice that we have the capacity, *unless* we have the will, of destroying the planet. Perhaps an optimist might hope human beings will not behave any worse in the future than we have done thus far.

BIBLIOGRAPHY

The following is not a complete list of everything consulted in the preparation of this book, but it includes general sources, and, for each chapter, the principal sources of information, with the authors in **bold**, together with other sources I have found useful for particular reasons of fact or interpretation. Footnotes to the text indicate major sources for particular aspects, and for quotations. Much of the material is in our own library; for the rest I am indebted to the State Library of New South Wales and the staff of its Inter–Library Loans service.

My love of history began when my grandfather gave me when I was seven an old *Children's Encyclopedia*, edited by Arthur Mee. It was first published, in England, in 1910; my revised edition, undated, had been published, judging by the text, at the end of 1936, when I was two. (A decade later my wife was also given a copy, by her father; it is still on our bookshelves.) In my childhood I found its wonderful mixture of history, geography, science, pictures, paintings, maps, games, crafts and poems an endless source of fascination and delight. The history sections were my favourites, with their stirring emphasis on illustrated pageantry and derring–do; as I look at them again now I am pleasantly surprised to see – allowing for their pro–British bias – their general accuracy, and their criticism of political, religious and racial intolerance and brutality. There were not many publications criticizing Hitler's persecution of the Jews in 1936.

Three authors in particular contributed to my comprehension, such as it is, of where all the parts fit together. The wonderful histories of the world written by Professors W. H. McNeill and J. M. Roberts were what set me to looking at broad sweeps of history; though I could in no way emulate either their comprehensiveness or their keenness of insight. But I must also pay tribute to Will Durant's monumental *The Story of Civilization* (the later volumes in collaboration with his wife Ariel): while I have not drawn on it specifically to any extent, I have lived for a long time now with its comprehensiveness, erudition, beautiful prose, sly humour and sustained open–minded honesty. Ever minuter detail has become a strong and in many cases important focus of historians over the past half century, but an encyclopedic survey such as the Durants' can still be valued for its encompassing elegance and excellence. A number of the other older books in the

Bibliography are included precisely because I have lived with them also over a long time.

Unlisted – unless directly quoted – because there are too many, are the guidebooks that accompanied us on our travels, and, from museums, art galleries and exhibitions, the many catalogues that accompanied us home.

Note: quotations from books marked * are in my translation.

GENERAL
American National Biography (24 vols; New York 1999)

Barzun, J: *From Dawn to Decadence* (New York 2000)
Billington, J.H: *The Icon and the Axe* (London 1966)
Boulnois, L: *Silk Road*, tr. H.Loveday (Hong Kong 2004)
Brent, P: *The Mongol Empire* (London 1976)
Buchanan, K, C.P.Fitzgerald C.A.Ronan: *China* (New York 1981)
Bullock, A: *Hitler and Stalin: Parallel Lives* (London 1998)

The Cambridge Encyclopedia of India, Pakistan, etc, ed. F.Robinson (Cambridge UK 1989)
The Cambridge Encyclopedia of Russia and the Soviet Union (Cambridge UK 1982)
Cantor, N.F: *The Civilization of the Middle Ages* (New York 1993)
Chambers Biographical Dictionary (Edinburgh 1995)
The Columbia History of the World, ed. J.A.Garraty P.Gay (New York 1981)

Davies, N: *Europe* (London 1997)
Davis, P.K: *Encyclopedia of Invasions and Conquests* (New York 1996)
DNB: (British) *Dictionary of National Biography* (Oxford 1917–)
Durant, W: *The Story of Civilization* (11 vols; New York 1954 – 1975)

Ebrey, P.B: *The Cambridge Illustrated History of China* (Cambridge UK 1996)
Edwardes, M: *East–West Passage* (New York 1971)
Encyclopædia Britannica *CD 98 Multimedia Edition* (Chicago 1997)
Encyclopædia of Religion and Ethics, J.Hastings (13 vols; Edinburgh 1908–1926)
Encyclopædia Universalis (Paris 1990)
Encyclopedia of Islam (Leiden 1986 –)

Fairbank, J.K, E.O.Reischauer A.M.Craig: *East Asia* (Boston 1973)
Fernandez–Armesto, F: *Millennium* (London 1995)
Foltz, R.C: *Religions of the Silk Road* (London 1999)

Gascoigne, B: *The Great Moghuls* (London 1973)
Gibbon, E: *The History of the Decline and Fall of the Roman Empire* (Halifax UK 1854)
Grun, B: *The Timetables of History* (New York 1991)
Grousset, R: *The Empire of the Steppes* (New Brunswick NJ 1997)
Grove Art – The [Grove] *Dictionary of Art* (34 vols; New York 1996)
Grove Music – The New *Grove Dictionary of Music and Musicians* (20 vols; London 1980)
Grove Opera –The New *Grove Dictionary of Opera* (4 vols; London 1992)

Hale, J: *The Civilisation of Europe in the Renaissance* (London 1994)
Hall, D.G.E: *A History of South–East Asia* (London 1966)
Heer, F: *The Holy Roman Empire* (tr. J.Sondheimer 1968; London 1995)

Johnson, P: *A History of the Jews* (London 1997)

Lapidus, I.M: *A History of Islamic Societies* (Cambridge UK 1990)
Lattimore, O: *Studies in Frontier History* (London 1962)
Lerner, M: *America as a Civilization* (London 1958)
Lewis, B: *The Middle East* (London 1995)

McBrien, R.P: *Lives of the Popes* (San Francisco 1997)
McEvedy, C. R.Jones: *Atlas of World Population History* (London 1978)
McNeill, W.H: *The Rise of the West* (Chicago 1965)
Massie, S: *Land of the Firebird* (New York 1980)
Medley, M: *The Chinese Potter* (Oxford 1980)
Morison, S.E: *The Oxford History of the American People* (New York 1965)

The New Columbia Encyclopedia, ed. W.H.Harris J.S.Levy (New York 1975)
The New Jewish Encyclopedia, ed. D.Bridger (New York 1976)
The New York Review of Books

The Oxford Dictionary of the Christian Church, ed. F.L.Cross (London 1958)

Roberts, J.M: *History of the World* (New York 1976; rev. as *The Penguin History of the World*, London 1995)

Schlesinger, A.M. Jr, ed: *The Almanac of American History* (New York 1986)
Shorter Encyclopedia of Islam, ed. H.A.R.Gibb J.H.Kramers (Karachi 1981)

Terras, V ed: *Handbook of Russian Literature* (Yale 1985)
Thomas, H: *An Unfinished History of the World* (London 1981)
Toussaint–Samat, M.: *History of Food* (Oxford 1998)
The Times Atlas of European History (London 1994)
The Times Comprehensive Atlas of the World (11th ed.: London 2003)
The Times History of the World, ed. G Barraclough (London 1999)

Vernadsky, G: *A History of Russia* (New Haven 1969)
Vinacke, H.M: *A History of the Far East in Modern Times* (New York 1950)

Wills, J.E.Jr: *1688 A Global History* (New York 2001)
Wood, F: *The Silk Road* (Berkeley CA 2002)

Younger, W: *Gods, Men and Wine* (London 1966)

1000 : VLADIMIR OF KIEV

Ascherson, N: *Black Sea* (London 1996)
Auty, R. D.Obolensky eds: *Russian Language and Literature* (Cambridge UK 1980)
Baedeker, K: *Russia* (facsimile of 1914 edition; New York 1971)
Brumfield, W.C: *Gold in Azure* (Boston 1983)
Chadwick, N.K: *The Beginnings of Russian History* (Cambridge UK 1946)
Dunlop, D.M: *The History of the Jewish Khazars* (Princeton 1954)
Franklin, S. J.Shepard: *The Emergence of Rus 750–1200* (London 1996)
Gurok, S. B. Lobanovsky: *Kiev* (Leningrad 1987)
Jones, G: *The Vikings* (London 1997)
Louis, V. J: *The Complete Guide to the Soviet Union* (New York 1976)
Maclean, F: *Holy Russia* (London 1982)
Norwich, J.J: *Byzantium* (3 vols; London 1990–1996)

Norwich, J.J: *The Normans in Sicily* (London 1992)

Pitirim, Archbishop of Volokolamsk: *L'Eglise Orthodoxe Russe** (Paris 1982)

The Russian Primary Chronicle, tr. ed. S.H.Cross O.P.Sherbowitz–Wetzor (1930; Cambridge MA 1973)

Vernadsky, G: *Kievan Russia* (New Haven 1948)

Volkoff, V: *Vladimir the Rusian Viking* (Woodstock NY 1985)

1100 : GODFREY OF BOUILLON

Andressohn, J.B: *The Ancestry and Life of Godfrey of Bouillon* (Bloomington IND 1947)

Aubé, P: *Godefroy de Bouillon** (Paris 1985)

Boulger, D.C: *The History of Belgium* (London 1902 1909)

Burns, R: *Monuments of Syria: An Historical Guide* (London 1999)

Chazan, R: *European Jewry and the First Crusade* (Berkeley CA 1987)

Cowdrey, H.E.J: *Pope Urban's Preaching of the First Crusade*, in *History* Vol 55 (London, June 1970)

Eidelberg, S. tr.: *The Jews and the Crusaders* (The Hebrew Chronicles; Madison WIS 1977)

Erdmann, C: *The Origin of the Idea of Crusade* [1935], tr. M.W.Baldwin W.Goffart (Princeton 1977)

Foss, M: *People of the First Crusade* (London 1997)

France, J: *Victory in the East* (Cambridge 1994)

Hillenbrand, C: *The Crusades: Islamic Perspectives* (Edinburgh 1999)

Krey, A.C. trans: *The First Crusade – The Accounts of Eye–witnesses and Participants* (Princeton 1921)

Lawrence, T.E: *Crusader Castles* (London 1986)

Maalouf, A: *The Crusades Through Arab Eyes* (New York 1984)

Parkes, J: *The Jew in the Medieval Community* (London 1938)

Raymond d'Aguilers: *Historia Francorum Qui Ceperunt Iherusalem*, tr. J.H. L.L.Hill (Philadelphia 1968)

Riley–Smith, J: *The Oxford Illustrated History of the Crusades* (Oxford 1997)

1200 : JAYAVARMAN OF ANGKOR

Boxer, C.R. ed: *South China in the Sixteenth Century* (Hakluyt Society, London 1953)

Briggs, L.P: *The Ancient Khmer Empire* (Bangkok 1999)

Chandler, D.P: *A History of Cambodia* (Boulder CO 1992)

Chou Ta–Kuan [Zhou Daguan]: *Notes on the Customs of Cambodia*, tr. J.G.D'Arcy Paul (Bangkok 1967)

Coedès, G: *Angkor*, tr. E.F.Gardiner (Hong Kong 1963)

Coedès, G: *The Indianized States of Southeast Asia*, tr. S.B.Cowing (Canberra 1968)

Da Cruz, G: see Boxer

Dagens, B: *Angkor*, tr. R.Sharman (London 1995)

Freeman, M. C. Jacques: *Ancient Angkor* (Bangkok 1999)

Groslier, B.–P: *Angkor et le Cambodge au XVIe Siècle d'après les Sources Portugaises et Espagnoles** (Paris 1958)

Groslier, B.–P: *Angkor, Hommes et Pierres** (Paris 1965)

Groslier, B.–P: *Inscriptions du Bayon**, with J.Dumarçay: *Histoire Architecturale du Temple** (Paris 1973)

Higham, C: *The Archeology of Mainland Southeast Asia* (Cambridge 1989)

Higham, C: *The Civilization of Angkor* (London 2001)

Jacques, C: *Angkor* (Cologne 1999)

James, J: *Chartres: the Masons Who Built a Legend* (London 1982)

Jessup, H.I. T.Zephir eds: *Sculpture of Angkor and Ancient Cambodia* (Washington 1997)

Loti, P: *Un Pèlerin d'Angkor** (Paris 1925)

Ma Tuan–lin: *Ethnographie des Peuples Étrangers à la Chine**, tr. Marquis d'Hervey de Saint–Denys (1876; repr. Farnborough UK 1972)

Mannikka, E: *Angkor Wat* (Honolulu 1996)

Mannikka, E., writing as E. Morón: *Configurations of Time and Space at Angkor Wat* (Studies in Indo–Asian Art and Culture, Vol 5; New Delhi Dec. 1977)

McArthur, M: *Reading Buddhist Art* (London 2004)

Mouhot, H: *Travels in the Central Parts of Indochina (Siam), Cambodia and Laos, during the years 1858, 1859, and 1860* (2 vols; London 1864)

Osborne, M: *Southeast Asia* (Sydney 2000)

Rooney, D.F: *Angkor* (Hong Kong 1999)

Stern, P: *Les Monuments Khmers du Style du Bayon et Jayavarman VII** (Paris 1965)

Zhou Daguan: see Chou Ta–Kuan

1300 : DEVORGUILLA OF GALLOWAY

Cameron, N: *Barbarians and Mandarins* (New York 1970)
Dawson, C: *Mission to Asia* (Toronto 1980)
Huyshe, W: *Devorgilla, Lady of Galloway* (Edinburgh 1913)
Jones, J: *Balliol College – A History 1263–1939* (Oxford 1989)
Keay, J. J: *Collins Encyclopedia of Scotland* (London 1994)
Macquarie, A: *Scotland and the Crusades* (Edinburgh 1997)
Marco Polo: *The Travels of Marco Polo*, tr. H.Yule H.Cordier (1903 1920; 2 vols, New York 1992)
Prestwich, M: *Edward I* (London 1988)
Richardson, J.S: *Sweetheart Abbey* (Edinburgh 1995)
Reese, P: *Wallace* (Edinburgh 1996)
Traquair, P: *Freedom's Sword* (London 1998)
Wood, F: *Did Marco Polo go to China?* (London 1995)
Ziegler, P: *The Black Death* (London 1984)

1400 : TAMBURLAINE OF SAMARKAND

Barthold, V.V: *Four Studies on the History of Central Asia*, Vol. II, tr. V.T. Minorsky (Leiden 1958)
Bentley, J.H: *Old World Encounters* (New York 1993)
Blunt, W: *The Golden Road to Samarkand* (New York 1973)
Burnes, A: *Travels into Bokhara* (London 1834)
Clavijo, Ruy Gonzales de: *Narrative of the Embassy of Ruy Gonzales de Clavijo to the Court of Timour, at Samarcand, AD 1403–6* (1582); tr. introd. by C.R.Markham (1859; repr. New Delhi 2001)
Curtin, P.D: *Cross–Cultural Trade in World History* (Cambridge UK 1984)
Curzon, G.N: *Russia in Central Asia in 1889* (New York 1889, repr. 1996)
Fischel, W.J: *Ibn Khaldun in Egypt* (Berkeley 1967)
Flecker, J.E: *Collected Poems* (London 1947)
Foltz, R.C: *Religions of the Silk Road* (New York 1999)
Hookham, H: *Tamburlaine the Conqueror* (London 1962)
Ibn Arabshah (Ahmed Ibn Muhammed): *Timur, the Great Amir*, tr. J.H.Sanders (London 1936)
Levathes, L: *When China Ruled the Seas* (New York 1994)
Lo, Jung–Pang: *Policy Formulation and Decision–Making on Issues Respecting Peace and War*, in C.O. Hucker ed.: *Chinese Government in Ming Times* (New York 1969)

Manz, B.F: *The Rise and Rule of Tamerlane* (Cambridge UK 1999)

Maclean, F: *To the Back of Beyond* (Boston 1975)

Marlowe, Christopher: Plays (Everyman's Library 1906; repr. London 1947)

Moranvillé, H: *Mémoire sur Tamerlan et sa Cour par un Dominicain, en 1403** (*Bibliothèque de l'École des chartes*, Vol. 55; Paris 1896)

Pelliot, P. trans.: *Histoire secrète des Mongols** (Paris 1949)

Rossabi, M: *Cheng Ho and Timur: Any Relation?* (*Oriens Extremus*, Vol. 20; Wiesbaden 1973)

Schiltberger, Johann: *The Bondage and Travels of Johann Schiltberger, a Native of Bavaria, in Europe, Asia, and Africa, 1396–1427*, tr. J. Buchan Telfer (London 1879)

Schuyler, E: *Turkistan* (London 1876)

Shterensis, M: *Tamerlane and the Jews* (London 2002)

Sykes, P: The Quest for Cathay (London 1936)

The Cambridge History of Iran, Vol.6: *The Timurid and Safavid Periods*, ed. P.Jackson L.Lockhart (Cambridge UK 1986)

Yule, H: *Cathay and the Way Thither* (Hakluyt Society Series 2; London 1915–1916)

1500 : MARCANTONIO RAIMONDI OF BOLOGNA

Bartsch, A: *Le Peintre–graveur*, Vol.14 (Vienna 1813)

Beck, J: *Raphael Before Rome* (National Gallery Studies in the History of Art, Vol.17; Washington 1986)

Cellini, B: *The Life of Benvenuto Cellini*, trans. J.A.Symonds (London 1995)

Cleugh, J: *The Divine Aretino* (New York 1966)

Conway, W.M. trans.ed: *The Writings of Albrecht Dürer* (London 1958)

Delaborde, H: *Marc–Antoine Raimondi* (Paris 1888)

Del Priore, B. F.Rossi: *Michelangelo and Raphael in the Vatican* (Vatican City 1978)

Dempsey, C: *Malvasia and the Problem of the Early Raphael and Bologna* (National Gallery Studies in the History of Art, Vol.17; Washington 1986)

Dürer, A: *Albrecht Dürer – œuvre gravé**, ed. S.Renouard de Bussierre (Paris 1996)

Dürer, A: *The Complete Engravings, Etchings Drypoints of Albrecht Dürer*, ed. W.L.Strauss (New York 1973)

Dürer, A: *The Complete Woodcuts of Albrecht Dürer*, ed. W.Kurth (New York 1963)

Dürer, A: *Drawings of Albrecht Dürer*, ed. H.Wölfflin (New York 1970)

Dürer, A: *L'opera completa di Dürer*, ed. G.Zampa (Milan 1968)

Dürer, A: *The Writings of Albrecht Dürer*, trans. W.M.Conway (London 1958)

Glimcher, A. M: *Je Suis le Cahier – The Sketchbooks of Picasso* (New York 1986)

Landau, D. P.Parshall: *The Renaissance Print* (New Haven 1994)

Lawner, L: *I Modi – The Sixteen Pleasures* (London 1988)

Meyer zur Capellen, J: *Raphael in Florence* (London 1996)

Oberhuber, K: *The Illustrated Bartsch* Vols. 26 27 (New York 1978)

Panofsky, E: *Albrecht Dürer* (London 1945)

Passavant, J.D: *Le Peintre–graveur*, Vol.1 1860, Vol.5 1864 (New York)

Picasso, P: *Le Déjeuner sur l'herbe* – exhibition catalogue, Galerie Louise Leuris, Paris (Paris 1962)

Pon, L: *Raphael, Dürer, and Marcantonio Raimondi* (New Haven 2004)

Raphael: *The Complete Paintings of Raphael*, ed. P. de Vecchi (London 1969)

Raphael: *The Complete Work of Raphael*, ed. M.Salmi (New York 1969)

Rubin, W: *Pablo Picasso – A Retrospective* (Museum of Modern Art, New York 1980)

Shoemaker, I.N. E.Broun: *The Engravings of Marcantonio Raimondi* (Lawrence KA 1984)

Tucker, P.H.ed: *Manet's Le Dejeuner sur l'herbe* (Cambridge 1998)

Vasari, G: *Lives of the Most Eminent Painters, Sculptors and Architects*, tr. G du C de Vere (New York 1979)

Waetzoldt, W: *Dürer and His Times* (London 1955)

Williamson, G.C: *Francesco Raibolini called Francia* (London 1901)

Wills, G: *Venice: Lion City* (New York 2001)

Zola, É: *Mes Haines* (1866; Paris 1907)

1600 : TOYOTOMI HIDEYOSHI OF JAPAN

Aston, W.G: *Hideyoshi's Invasion of Korea* (Transactions of the Asiatic Society of Japan; Yokohama 1878, 1881, 1883)

Berry, M.E: *Hideyoshi* (Cambridge MA 1982)

Boxer, C.R: *The Christian Century in Japan 1549–1650* (Berkeley 1967)

Cooper SJ, M: *Rodrigues the Interpreter* (New York 1974)

Cooper SJ, M: *The Southern Barbarians* (Tokyo 1971)

Cooper SJ, M: *They Came to Japan* (London 1965)

Cronin, V: *The Wise Man from the West* (London 1955)

Elison, G. B.L.Smith: *Warlords, Artists Commoners* (Honolulu 1981)

Elisseeff, D: *Hideyoshi – Batisseur du Japon moderne** (Paris 1986)

Henthorn, W.E: *A History of Korea* (New York 1974)

Hickman, M.L. ed.: *Japan's Golden Age: Momoyama* (Catalogue of an Exhibition at the Dallas Museum of Art (New Haven 1996)

Kato, E: see Ryotaro

Kinoshita, J. N.Palevsky: *Gateway to Japan* (Tokyo 1998)

Lach, D.F: *Asia in the Making of Europe* (Chicago Vol I 1965, Vol II 1970)

Lu, D.J: *Japan – A Documentary History* (Armonk NY 1997)

Murdoch, J. I.Yamagata: *A History of Japan 1542–1651* (Kobe 1903)

Park Yune–hee: *Admiral Yi Sun–shin and his Turtleboat Armada* (Seoul 1978)

Ryotaro, S: *The Heart Remembers Home*, tr., with a background essay, by E.Kato (Tokyo 1979)

Sansom, G.B: *A History of Japan 1334–1615* (London 1961)

Sansom, G.B: *The Western World and Japan* (New York 1950)

Spence, J: *The Memory Palace of Matteo Ricci* (New York 1984)

Storry, R: *A History of Modern Japan* (London 1990)

Tagai, H: *Japanese Ceramics*, tr. J.Clark (Tokyo 1981)

Takakoshi, Y: *The Economic Aspects of the History of the Civilization of Japan* (London 1930)

Varley, P. and K. Isao, eds: *Tea in Japan: Essays on the History of Chanoyu* (Honolulu 1989)

Yamane, Y: *Momoyama Genre Painting* (Tokyo 1973)

Yi Sun-shin: *Nanjung Ilgi: War Diary of Admiral Yi Sun-shin*, tr. Ha Tae-hung (Seoul 1977)

Yi Sun-shin: *Imjin Changch'o: Admiral Yi Sun-shin's Memorials to Court*, tr. Ha Tae-hung (Seoul 1981).

1700 : SOPHIE CHARLOTTE OF PRUSSIA

Aiton, E.J: *Leibniz* (Bristol 1985)

Ayerst, W: *Letters 1706–1721*, ed.C.E.Doble (*The English Historical Review*, Vol. III: London 1888)

Baer, W.I, eds: *Charlottenburg Palace, Berlin* (Berlin 1995)

Erman: *Mémoires pour servir à l'Histoire de Sophie Charlotte Reine de Prusse** (Berlin 1801)

Frederick the Great: *Memoirs of the House of Brandenburg,* tr.? (London 1758)

Frey, LM: *Frederick I: The Man and his Times* (Boulder CO 1984)

Gawthrop, R.L: *Pietism and the Making of Eighteenth Century Prussia* (Cambridge UK 1993)

Hatton, R: *George I* (1978; New Haven CT 2001)

Hellman, H: *Great Feuds in Science* (New York 1998)

Holborn, H: *A History of Modern Germany 1648–1840* (London 1965)

Kroll, M: Sophie *Electress of Hanover* (London 1973)

Kroll, M. tr.ed: *Letters from Liselotte* (London 1970)

Lach, D.F: *The Preface to Leibniz'* Novissima Sinica (Honolulu 1957)

Lach, D.F: *Leibniz and China* (Journal of the History of Ideas Vol VI; Baltimore MD 1945)

Leibniz, G.W: *Discourse on the Natural Theology of the Chinese,* tr. introd. H.Rosemont D.J.Cook (Honolulu 1977)

Massie, R.K: *Peter the Great* (New York 1981)

Miasnikov, V.S: *The Ch'ing Empire and the Russian State in the 17th Century,* tr. V.Schneierson (Moscow 1985)

Nelson, W.H: *The Soldier Kings* (New York 1970)

Ranke, L: Memoirs of the House of Brandenburg and History of Prussia, Vol.1 1849 (New York 1968) Richie, A: Faust's Metropolis (London 1999)

Rosemont Cook: see Leibniz

Schevill, F: *The Great Elector* (Chicago 1947)

Schuyler, E: *Peter the Great* (London 1884)

Streidt, G. P.Feierabend eds: *Prussia Art and Architecture* (Cologne 1999)

Toland, J: *An Account of the Courts of Prussia and Hanover* (London 1714)

Volkel, M: *The Hohenzollern Court,* in *The Princely Courts of Europe 1500–1750,* ed. J.Adamson (London 2000)

Ward, A.W: *The Electress Sophia and the Hanoverian Succession* (London 1903)

1800 : JOHN LEDYARD OF CONNECTICUT

Adams, W.H: *The Paris Years of Thomas Jefferson* (New Haven 1997)

Ambrose, S.E: *Undaunted Courage* (New York 1997)

Augur, H: *Passage to Glory – John Ledyard's America* (Garden City NJ 1988)

Australian Dictionary of Biography 1788–1850 (2 vols, Melbourne 1966–67)

Beaglehole, J.C: *The Life of Captain James Cook* (London 1974)

Burney, J: *A Chronological History of North-Eastern Voyages of Discovery; and of the Early Eastern Navigations of the Russians* (1819; repr. Amsterdam 1969)

Carter, H.B: *Sir Joseph Banks 1743–1820* (London 1988)

Cook, James: *The Journals*, Vol III, ed. J.C.Beaglehole (Cambridge UK 1967)

De Voto, B. ed: *The Journals of Lewis and Clark* (Boston 1997)

Ellis, J.J: *American Sphinx* (New York 1998)

Gould, S.J: "The Man Who Invented Natural History" (review of Jacques Rogers: *Buffon*), New York Review of Books (Vol. XXXXV No. 16, 22 October 1998)

Hough, R: *Captain James Cook* (London 1995)

Hough, R: *The Murder of Captain James Cook* (London 1979)

Jefferson, Thomas: *Papers*, ed. J.P.Boyd (vols 2, 8–14, Princeton 1950, 1953–58)

Ledyard, J: *John Ledyard's Journey through Russia and Siberia 1787–1788*; ed. Introd. S.D.Watrous (Madison WIS 1966)

Ledyard, J: *A Journal of Captain Cook's Last Voyage to the Pacific Ocean* (Hartford CN 1783)

Mapp, A.J. Jr: *Thomas Jefferson* (2 vols, Lanham MD 1987 1991)

Mumford, J.K. ed: *John Ledyard's Journal of Captain Cook's Last Voyage* (Corvallis OR 1963)

O'Connor, R: *Pacific Destiny* (Boston 1969)

Sauer, M: *An Account of a Geographical and Astronomical Expedition to the Northern Parts of Russia* (1802; repr. Richmond UK 1972)

Smith, B: *European Vision and the South Pacific* (Oxford 1960)

Smith, H.N: *Virgin Land: The American West as Symbol and Myth* (Cambridge MA 1950)

Sparks, J: *Life of John Ledyard, the American Traveller* (Cambridge MA 1828)

The Oxford History of the American West, ed. C.A.Milner, C.A.O'Connor M.A.Sandweiss (New York 1994)

1900 : YUAN SHIKAI OF CHINA

Beeching, J: *The Chinese Opium Wars* (New York 1975)

Beurdeley, C. M: *Giuseppe Castiglione*, trans. M.Bullock (Rutland VT 1971)

Bishop, I.B: *Korea and Her Neighbours* (1897; repr. Seoul 1970)

Ch'en, J: *Yuan Shih–k'ai* (Stanford 1972)

Cohen, P.A: *History in Three Keys* (New York 1997)

Curzon, G.N: *Problems of the Far East* (rev.ed. London 1895)

Dennett, T: *Roosevelt and the Russo–Japanese War* (1925; repr. Gloucester Mass. 1959)

Dua, R.P: *The Impact of the Russo–Japanese (1905) War on Indian Politics* (Delhi 1966)

French, P: *Younghusband* (London 1994)

Giles, L: *The Siege of the Peking Legations*, ed. L.R.Marchant (Perth 1970)

Hummel, A.W. ed.: *Eminent Chinese of the Ch'ing Period* (Washington DC 1943–1944)

Johnston, Sir R.F: *Twilight in the Forbidden City* (London 1934)

Loti, P: *Les Derniers Jours de Pékin** (Paris 1925)

MacKinnon, S.R: *Power and Politics in Late Imperial China* (Berkeley 1980)

McKenzie, F.A: *Korea's Fight for Freedom* (1920; repr. Seoul 1969)

Pearl, C: *Morrison of Peking* (Sydney 1967)

Reinsch, P.S: *An American Diplomat in China* (London 1922)

Rose, K: *Superior Person* (London 1969)

Sands, W.F: *Undiplomatic Memories* (n.d., 1906?; repr. Seoul 1975)

Spence, J.D: *The Search for Modern China* (New York 1990)

Warner, D. P: *The Tide at Sunrise* (New York 1974)

Warner, M: *The Dragon Empress* (London 1972)

Witte, S.Y: *The Memoirs of Count Witte* (London 1921)

Wright, M.C: *China in Revolution: The First Phase 1900–1913*, Introd. (New Haven CN 1968)

Wu Yung: *The Flight of an Empress*, ed. I.Pruitt (London 1937)

Yim, Kwanha: *Yüan Shih–k'ai and the Japanese* (The Journal of Asian Studies Vol.XXIV No. 1; New York Nov. 1964)

Young, E.P: *The Presidency of Yuan Shih–k'ai* (Ann Arbour MI 1977)

Lightning Source UK Ltd.
Milton Keynes UK
UKOW04n0424180615

253696UK00002B/18/P

9 781781 484555